Volume 1 • 2015

WHAT DO
I READ
NEXT?

A Reader's Guide
to Current
Genre Fiction

- Fantasy
- Popular Fiction
- Popular Romances
- Horror
- Mystery
- Science Fiction
- Historical
- Inspirational

ISSN 1052-2212

Volume 1 • 2015

WHAT DO I READ NEXT?

A Reader's Guide
to Current
Genre Fiction

- Fantasy
- Popular Fiction
- Popular Romances
- Horror
- Mystery
- Science Fiction
- Historical
- Inspirational

DANIEL S. BURT

DON D'AMMASSA

HOLLY HIBNER

MARY KELLY

CLAIR LAMB

KRISTIN RAMSDELL

LYNDA LEE SCHAB

GALE
CENGAGE Learning·

Farmington Hills, Mich • San Francisco • New York • Waterville, Maine
Meriden, Conn • Mason, Ohio • Chicago

What Do I Read Next 2015, Volume 1

Project Editors: Sara Constantakis, Michelle Kazensky

Composition and Electronic Prepress: Gary Leach, Evi Seoud

Manufacturing: Rita Wimberley

For product information and technology assistance, contact us at **Gale Customer Support, 1-800-877-4253.**
For permission to use material from this text or product, submit all requests online at **www.cengage.com/permissions.**
Further permissions questions can be emailed to **permissionrequest@cengage.com**

Gale
27500 Drake Rd.
Farmington Hills, MI, 48331-3535

LIBRARY OF CONGRESS CONTROL NUMBER 91656062

ISBN-13: 978-1-5730-2318-4

ISSN: 1052-2212

Printed in Mexico
1 2 3 4 5 6 7 19 18 17 16 15

Contents

Introduction

Thousands of books are published each year intended for devoted fans of genre fiction. Dragons, outlaws, lovers, murderers, monsters, and aliens abound on our own world or on other worlds, throughout time—all featured in the pages of fantasy, romance, mystery, horror, science fiction, historical, inspirational, and popular fiction. Given the huge variety of titles available each year, added to the numbers from previous years, readers can be forgiven if they're stumped by the question "What do I read next?" And that's where this book comes in.

Designed as a tool to assist in the exploration of genre fiction, *What Do I Read Next?* guides the reader to both current and classic recommendations in eight widely read genres: Mystery, Romance, Fantasy, Horror, Science Fiction, Historical, Inspirational, and Popular Fiction. *What Do I Read Next?* allows readers quick and easy access to specific data on recent titles in these popular genres. Plus, each entry provides alternate reading selections, thus coming to the rescue of librarians and booksellers, who are often unfamiliar with a genre, yet must answer the question frequently posed by their patrons and customers, "What do I read next?"

Details on Titles

Volume 1 of this year's edition of *What Do I Read Next?* contains entries for titles published primarily in the first half of 2015. These entries are divided into sections for Mystery, Popular Romances, Fantasy, Horror, Science Fiction, Historical, Inspirational, and Popular Fiction. Experts in each field compile the entries for their respective genres. The experts also discuss topics relevant to their genres in essays that appear at the beginning of each section.

The criteria for inclusion of specific titles vary somewhat from genre to genre. In genres such as Romance and Mystery, where large numbers of titles are published each year, the inclusion criteria are more selective, with the experts attempting to select the recently published books that they consider best. In genres such as Horror, where the amount of new material is relatively small, a broader range of titles is represented, including many titles published by small or independent houses and some young adult books.

The review citations included in many entries have been removed. Most entries will now have a larger number of recommended similar titles represented to ensure the reader has a wider variety of options to explore similar to each main title.

The entries are listed alphabetically by main author in each genre section. Most provide the following information:

- **Author or editor's** name and real name if a pseudonym is used. Co-authors, co-editors, and illustrators are also listed where applicable.

- **Book title.**

- **Date and place of publication; name of publisher.**

- **Series name.**

- **Story type:** Specific categories within each genre, identified by the compiling expert. Definitions of these types are listed in the "Key to Genre Terms" section.

- **Subject(s):** Gives the subject matter covered by the title.

- **Major character(s):** Names and brief descriptions of up to three characters featured in the title.

- **Time period(s):** Tells when the story takes place.

- **Locale(s):** Tells where the story takes place.

- **What the book is about:** A brief plot summary.

- **Other books by the author:** Titles and publication dates of other books the author has written, useful for those wanting to read more by a particular author.

- **Other books you might like:** Titles by other authors written on a similar theme or in a similar style. These titles further the reader's exploration of the genre.

Indexes Answer Readers' Questions

The nine indexes in *What Do I Read Next?* used separately or in conjunction with each other, create many pathways to the featured titles, answering general questions or locating specific titles. For example:

"Are there any new Stephanie Plum books?"

The SERIES INDEX lists entries by the name of the series of which they are a part.

"I like Regency Romances. Can you recommend any new ones?"

The GENRE INDEX breaks each genre into story types or more specialized areas. In the Romance genre for example, there is a story type heading "Regency." For the definitions of story types, see the "Key to Genre Terms."

"I'm looking for a story set in Paris."

The GEOGRAPHIC INDEX lists titles by their locale. This can help readers pinpoint an area in which they may have a particular interest, such as their home town, another country, or even Cyberspace.

"Do you know of any science fiction stories set during the 22nd century?"

The TIME PERIOD INDEX is a chronological listing of the time settings in which the main entry titles take place.

"What books are available that feature teachers?"

The CHARACTER DESCRIPTION INDEX identifies the major characters by occupation (e.g. Accountant, Editor, Librarian) or persona (e.g. Cyborg, Noble woman, Stowaway).

"Has anyone written any new books with Sherlock Holmes in them?"

The CHARACTER NAME INDEX lists the major characters named in the entries. This can help readers who remember some information about a book, but not an author or title.

"What has Laurell K. Hamilton written recently?"

The AUTHOR INDEX contains the names of all authors featured in the entries and those listed under "Other books you might like."

The TITLE INDEX includes all main entry titles and all titles recommended under "Other books by the author" and "Other books you might like" in one alphabetical listing. Thus a reader can find a specific title, new or old, then go to that entry to find out what new titles are similar.

"I'm interested in books that depict military life."

The SUBJECT INDEX is an alphabetical listing of all the subjects covered by the main entry titles.

The indexes can also be used together to narrow down or broaden choices. A reader interested in Mysteries set in New York during the 19th century would consult the TIME PERIOD INDEX and GEOGRAPHIC INDEX to see which titles appear in both. Time Travel is a common theme in Science Fiction but occasionally appears in other genres such as Fantasy and Romance. Searching for this theme in other genres would enable a reader to cross over into previously unknown realms of reading experiences. And with the AUTHOR and TITLE indexes, which include all books listed under "Other books by the author" and "Other books you might like," it is easy to compile an extensive list of recommended reading, beginning with a recently published title or a classic from the past.

Also Available Online

The entries in this book can also be found online in Gale's *Books & Authors* database. This electronic product encompasses over 196,000 books, including genre fiction, mainstream fiction, children and young adult fictioin, and nonfiction. All the books included in the online version are recommended by librarians or other experts, award winners, or appear on bestseller lists. The user-friendly functionality allows users to refine their searching by using several criteria, while making it easy to identify similar titles for further research and reading. *Books & Authors* is updated with new information weekly. For more information about *Books & Authors*, please visit Gale online at gale.cengage.com.

Suggestions Are Welcome

The editors welcome any comments and suggestions for enhancing and improving *What Do I Read Next?* Please address correspondence to the Editor, *What Do I Read Next?*, at the following address:

Gale, Cengage Learning

27500 Drake Rd.

Farmington Hills, MI 48331-3535

Phone: 248-699-GALE

Toll-free: 800-877-GALE

Fax: 248-699-8884

About the Genre Experts

Daniel S. Burt (Historical Fiction) Burt is a writer and college professor who has taught undergraduate literature and writing courses at New York University, Trinity College, and Northeastern and graduate literature courses at Wesleyan University, where he was a dean for nine years. He is the author of *The Chronology of American Literature* (Houghton Mifflin, 2004), *What Historical Novel Do I Read Next?* Volumes 1-3 (Gale, 1997-2003), *The Novel 100*, revised edition (Facts on File, 2010), *The Literary 100*, revised edition (Facts on File, 2008), *The Biography Book* (Greenwood/Oryx, 2001), and *Drama 100* (Facts on File, 2007). He lives with his wife on Cape Cod, Massachusetts.

Don D'Ammassa (Science Fiction, Horror, and Fantasy) D'Ammassa was the book reviewer for *Science Fiction Chronicle* for almost thirty years. He has had fiction published in fantastic magazines and anthologies and has contributed essays to a variety of reference books dealing with fantastic literature. D'Ammassa is the author of the novels *Blood Beast* (Windsor, 1988), *Servants of Chaos* (Leisure, 2002), *Scarab* (Five Star, 2004), *Haven* (Five Star, 2004), and *Narcissus* (Five Star, 2007) and the nonfiction works *Encyclopedia of Science Fiction* (Facts on File, 2005), the *Encyclopedia of Fantasy and Horror* (Facts on File, 2006), and the *Encyclopedia of Adventure Fiction* (Facts on File, 2008).

Holly Hibner (Popular Fiction) Hibner manages the Adult Services department at a public library in Michigan. She received an MLIS degree from Wayne State University in 1999. Since that time, she has published and spoken on a variety of topics, and received the 2007 Loleta Fyan award from the Michigan Library Association for innovation in library service. She loves all things techie and the challenge of a good reference question. Together with Mary Kelly, Hibner created the popular blog "Awful Library Books," which led to an appearance on *Jimmy Kimmel Live,* and has also co-authored the book *Making a Collection Count: A Holistic Approach to Library Collection Management.*

Mary Kelly (Popular Fiction) Kelly is a Youth Services Librarian at the Lyon Township Public Library in Michigan. She has worked in a variety of library jobs for more than ten years. Kelly has published and presented on topics such as computer instruction, reader's advisory, and providing tech support. She received both an MBA and an MLIS from Wayne State University. Kelly is passionate about collection quality and technology. Together with Holly Hibner, Kelly created the popular blog "Awful Library Books," which led to an appearance on Jimmy Kimmel Live, and has also co-authored the book *Making a Collection Count: A Holistic Approach to Library Collection Management.*

Lynda Lee Schab (Inspirational Fiction) Schab got her writing start in greeting cards and from there went on to write articles and short stories for national print magazines and many online publications. She works full-time as a freelance writer and editor, and is the Grand Rapids Christian Fiction Examiner and the National Christian Writing Examiner for Examiner.com. Her passion has always been fiction, and in 2011 Lynda achieved her dream of becoming a published novelist with *Mind over Madi* and *Madily in Love*, the first two books in the Madi Series, and *Sylvie & Gold*. Schab lives with her husband and two teenagers in Michigan.

Clair Lamb (Mystery) Lamb is a writer, editor, and researcher whose clients include award-winning, bestselling authors and first-time novelists. She is a regular contributor to *Crimespree* magazine, has written The Mystery Bookstore's (www.mystery-bookstore.com) weekly and monthly newsletters since 2000, and maintains a personal blog at www.answergirlnet.blogspot.com.

Kristin Ramsdell (Romance Fiction) Ramsdell is the romance columnist for *Library Journal*; the author of the first and scond editions of *Romance Fiction: A Guide to the Genre* (Libraries Unlimited, 1999 and 2012) and its predecessor, *Happily Ever After* (Libraries Unlimited, 1987); a frequent speaker and panelist on the romance genre; and a Librarian Emerita at California State University, East Bay. She received the Romance Writers of America Librarian of the Year Award in 1996 and the Melinda Gelfer Fairy Godmother Award from *Romantic Times* in 2007.

John Charles (Romance Fiction) Charles, a reference librarian and retrospective fiction selector for the Scottsdale

Public Library, was named 2002 Librarian of the Year by the Romance Writers of America. Charles reviews books for *Library Journal, Booklist*, the *Chicago Tribune*, and *VOYA (Voice of Youth Advocates)* and co-authors *VOYA*'s annual "Clueless: Adult Mysteries with Young Adult Appeal" column. John Charles is co-author of *The Mystery Readers' Advisory: The Librarian's Clues to Murder and Mayhem* (ALA, 2001). Along with co-author Shelley Mosley, Charles has twice been the recipient of the Romance Writers of America's Veritas Award.

Shelley Mosley (Romance Fiction) A retired library manager, Mosley has co-authored several non-fiction books: *The Suffragists in Literature for Youth, Romance Today: An A-to-Z Guide to Contemporary American Romance Writers, The Complete Idiot's Guide to the Ultimate Reading List*, and *Crash Course in Library Super-*

vision. With John Charles, she has won two Romance Writers of America's Veritas awards. Mosley, Romance Writers of America's 2001 Librarian of the Year, reviews books for *Booklist* and writes essays and articles for *Novelist*. She has written five romantic comedies with Deborah Mazoyer under the pen name Deborah Shelley. Their novels have been translated into Dutch, Danish, French, Russian, Norwegian, and Portuguese.

Sandra Van Winkle (Romance Fiction) Van Winkle is co-author of *Romance Today: An A-Z Guide to Contemporary American Romance Writers, The Complete Idiot's Guide to the Ultimate Reading List*, and *Crash Course in Dealing with Difficlt Library Customers*. She is an avid Romance reader, reviewer, and editor who has contributed to WDIRN since 2009. Van Winkle holds a Bachelor of Arts degree in Public Administration from Ottawa University.

Key to Genre Terms

The following is a list of terms used to classify the story type of each novel included in What Do I Read Next? along with brief definitions of the terms. To find books that fall under a particular story type heading, see the Genre Index.

Action/Adventure ▌ Minimal detection; not usually espionage, but can contain rogue police or out of control spies.

Adult ▌ Fiction dealing with adult characters and mature, developed ideas.

Adventure ▌ The character(s) must face a series of obstacles, which may include monsters, conflict with other travelers, war, interference by supernatural elements, interference by nature, and so on.

Alternate History ▌ A story dealing with how society might have evolved if a specific historical event had happened differently, e.g., if the South had won the American Civil War.

Alternate Intelligence ▌ Story featuring an entity with a sense of identity and able to self-determine goals and actions. The natural or manufactured entity results from a synergy, generally unpredictable, of individual elements. This subgenre frequently involves a computer-type intelligence.

Alternate Universe ▌ More accurately, in most cases, alternate history, in which the South won the Civil War, the Nazis triumphed, etc. The idea is a venerable one in SF.

Alternate World ▌ The story starts out in the everyday world, but the main character is transported to an alternate/parallel world by supernatural means.

Amateur Detective ▌ Detective work is performed by a non-professional rather than by police or a private detective.

Americana ▌ A romance set in the present that features themes that are particularly American; often focuses on small-town life.

Ancient Evil Unleashed ▌ The evils may take familiar forms, like vampires undead for centuries, or malevolent ancient gods released from bondage by careless humans, or ancient prophecies wreaking havoc on today's world. The so-called *Cthulhu Mythos* originated by H.P. Lovecraft, in which *Cthulhu* is prominent among a pantheon of ancient evil gods, is a specific variation of this.

Anthology ▌ A collection of short stories by different authors, usually sharing a common theme.

Apocalyptic Horror ▌ Traditionally, horrors that signal or presage the end of the world, or the world of the characters, and the establishment of a new, possibly very sinister order.

Arts ▌ Fiction that incorporates some aspect of the arts, whether it be music, painting, drama, etc.

Biblical Fiction ▌ Novels that take their plots or characters from the Bible.

Black Magic ▌ Magic directed toward malevolent ends, as distinct from white magic, which is directed toward benevolent ends. Witchcraft is commonly thought of as a black art. Voodoo consists of mysterious rites and practices, including sorcery, magic and conjuration, and often has evil goals.

Carnival-Circus Horror ▌ Derived from its setting, especially the freakish world of the sideshow, in which the distorted or horrific is the norm and is sometimes used as a distorting mirror to reveal hidden selves.

Chase ▌ A traditional Western in which the action of the plot is based on some form of pursuit.

Child-in-Peril ▌ The innocence of childhood is often used to heighten the intensity and unpredictability of evil.

Collection ▌ A book of short stories by a single author.

Coming-of-Age ▌ A story in which the primary character is a young person, usually a teenager. The growth of maturity is chronicled.

Contemporary ▌ A story set in the present.

Contemporary/Exotic ▌ Set in the present but with an especially unusual or exotic setting, e.g., the tent of a desert sheik or a boat on the Amazon.

Contemporary/Fantasy ▌ A contemporary story that makes use of fantasy or supernatural elements.

Contemporary/Innocent ▌ Story set in the present that contains little or no sex.

Contemporary/Mainstream ▌ A story set in the present that would be more properly categorized as general fiction rather than a work in a specific genre.

Contemporary Realism ▌ An accurate representation of characters, settings, ideas, themes in the present day. Not idealistic in nature.

Cozy Mystery ▌ Most often "gentle" reads that frequently downplay graphic violence, profanity, and sex.

Curse ▌ Words said when someone wishes evil or harm on someone or something, such as a witch's or prophet's curse.

Cyberpunk ❚ Usually applied to the stories by a group of writers who became prominent in the mid-1980s, such as William Gibson and his *Necromancer* (1984). The "cyber" is derived from cybernetics, nominally the study of control and communications in machines. These books also feature a downbeat, punk sensibility reminiscent of the hardboiled school of detective fiction writers.

Disaster ❚ A tale recounting some event or events seriously disruptive of the social fabric but not as serious as a holocaust.

Domestic ❚ Fiction relating to household and family matters. Concerned with psychological and emotional needs of family members.

Doppelganger ❚ A double or alter ego, popularized in the works of E.T.A. Hoffmann, Edgar Allan Poe, and Robert Louis Stevenson.

Dystopian ❚ The antonym of utopian, sometimes called anti-utopian, in which traditionally positive utopian themes are treated satirically or ironically and the mood is downbeat or satiric.

End of the World ❚ A story that concerns the last events following some sort of disaster.

Erotic Horror ❚ Sexuality and horror are often argued to be inextricably linked, as in Bram Stoker's *Dracula* and Sheridan Le Fanu's "Carmilla," although others have argued that they are antithetical. Sexuality became increasingly explicit in the 1980s, sometimes verging on the pornographic, as in Brett Easton Ellis' *American Psycho*.

Espionage ❚ Involving the CIA, KGB, or other organizations whose main focus is the collection of information from the other side. Can be either violent or quiet.

Espionage Thriller ❚ Plot contains a high level of action and suspense relating to espionage.

Ethnic ❚ A work in which the ethnic background of the characters is integral to the story. Usually the focus is on an American ethnic minority group (e.g., African American, Asian American, Native American, Latino) and the two main characters are members of this group.

Evil Children ❚ The presumed innocence of a child is replaced with adult-like malevolence and cunning, contradicting the reader's usual expectations.

Family Saga ❚ Stories focusing on the problems or concerns of a family; estrangement and reunion are common themes.

Fantasy ❚ A story that contains some fantasy or supernatural elements.

Femme Fatale ❚ A seductress for whom men abandon careers, families, and responsibilities and who feels no pity or compunction in return; a common figure in history and literature.

First Contact ❚ Any story about the initial meeting or communication of humans with extraterrestrials or aliens. The term may take its name from the eponymous 1945 story by Murray Leinster.

Future Shock ❚ A journalistic term derived from Alvin Toffler's 1970 book and which refers to the alleged disorientation resulting from rapid technological change.

Futuristic ❚ A story with a science fiction setting. Often these stories are set on other planets, aboard spaceships or space stations, or on Earth in an imaginary future or, in some cases, past.

Gay/Lesbian Fiction ❚ Stories portraying homosexual characters or themes.

Generation Starship ❚ If pseudoscientific explanations involving faster-than-light drives are rejected, then the time required for interstellar travel will encompass many human generations.

Genetic Manipulation ❚ Sometimes called genetic engineering, this assumes that the knowledge exists to shape creatures, human or otherwise, using genetic means, as in *Brave New World* (1932).

Ghost Story ❚ The spirits of the dead, who can be benevolent, as in Charles Dickens, or malevolent, as in the tales of M.R. James.

Gothic ❚ A story with a strong mystery suspense plot that emphasizes mood, atmosphere, and/or supernatural or paranormal elements. Unexplained events, ancient family secrets, and a general feeling of impending doom often characterize these tales. These stories are most often set in the past.

Gothic Family Chronicle ❚ A story often covering several generations of a family, many of whose members are typically evil, perverted, or loathsome, and in which family violence is common. The family may live in a decaying mansion suggestive of those in 18th century Gothic novels.

Hard Science Fiction ❚ Stories in which the author adheres with varying degrees of rigor to scientific principles believed to be true at the time of writing, principles derived from hard (physical, biological) rather than soft (social) sciences.

Haunted House ❚ Literally, a house visited by ghosts, usually with evil intentions in horror fiction, but sometimes the subject of comedy.

Historical ❚ Set in an earlier time frame than the present.

Historical/American Civil War ❚ Set during the American Civil War, 1861-1865.

Historical/American Revolution ❚ Set during the American Revolutionary period.

Historical/American West ❚ Set in the Western portion of the United States, usually during the second half of the 19th century. Stories often involve the hardships of pioneer life (Indian raids, range wars, climatic disasters, etc.) and the main characters (most often the hero) can be of Native American extraction.

Historical/American West Coast ❚ Set in the American Far West (California, Oregon, Washington, or Alaska). Stories often focus on the Gold Rush and the tension between Spanish Land Grant families and immigrants from the Pacific Rim, usually China.

Historical/Americana ❚ A story dealing with themes unique to the American experience.

Historical/Ancient Egypt ❚ A novel set during the time of the pharaohs from the fourth century B.C. to the first century A.D. and the absorption of Egypt into the Roman Empire.

Historical/Ancient Greece ▌ Set during the flowering of the ancient Greek civilization, particularly during the age of Pericles in the 5th century B.C.

Historical/Ancient Rome ▌ Covering the history of Rome from its founding and the Roman Republic before Augustus through the decline and fall of the Roman Empire in the fifth century.

Historical/Antebellum American South ▌ Set in the American Old South (prior to the Civil War).

Historical/Canadian West ▌ Set in the western or frontier portions of Canada, usually during the 19th century. Stories most often revolve around the hardships of frontier life.

Historical/Colonial America ▌ Set in America before the American Revolution, 1620-1775. Stories featuring the Jamestown Colony, the Salem Witch Trials, and the French and Indian Wars are especially popular.

Historical/Depression Era ▌ Set mainly in America during the period of economic hardship brought on by the 1929 Stock Market Crash that continued throughout the 1930s.

Historical/Edwardian ▌ Set during the reign of Edward VII of England, 1901-1910.

Historical/Eighteenth Century ▌ A work of fiction set during the eighteenth century.

Historical/Elizabethan ▌ A novel set during the reign of Elizabeth I of England (1558-1603). There is some overlap with the last part of the Historical Renaissance category but the emphasis is British.

Historical/Exotic ▌ Setting is an unusual or exotic place.

Historical/Fantasy ▌ A historical work that makes use of fantasy or supernatural elements.

Historical/French Revolution ▌ Set during the French Revolution, 1789-1795.

Historical/Georgian ▌ Set during the reigns of the first three "Georges" of England. Roughly corresponds to the 18th century. Stories often focus on the Jacobite Rebellions and the escapades of Bonnie Prince Charlie.

Historical/Mainstream ▌ Historical fiction that would be more properly categorized as fiction rather than a specific genre.

Historical/Medieval ▌ Set during the Middle Ages, approximately the fifth through the fifteenth centuries. Stories feature battles, raids, crusades, and court intrigues; plotlines associated with the Battle of Hastings (1066) are especially popular.

Historical/Napoleonic Wars ▌ Set between 1803-1815 during the wars waged by and against France under Napoleon Bonaparte.

Historical/Post-American Civil War ▌ Set in the years following the Civil War/War Between the States, generally from 1865 into the 1870s.

Historical/Post-American Revolution ▌ Set in the years immediately following the Civil War, 1865-1870s.

Historical/Post-French Revolution ▌ Set during the years immediately following the French Revolution; stories usually take place in France or England.

Historical/Pre-History ▌ Set in the years before the Middle Ages.

Historical/Regency ▌ A novel that is set during the Regency period (1811-1820).

Historical/Renaissance ▌ Novel set in the years of the Renaissance in Europe, generally lasting from the 14th through the 17th centuries.

Historical/Roaring Twenties ▌ Usually has an American setting and takes place in the 1920s.

Historical/Russian Revolution ▌ These stories are set around and during the 1917 Russian Revolution.

Historical/Seventeenth Century ▌ A work of fiction set during the 17th century. Stories of this type often center around the clashes between the Royalists and the Cromwellians and the Restoration.

Historical/Tudor Period ▌ A novel set during the Tudor dynasty in England (1485-1603). Roughly corresponds to the Renaissance, but the emphasis is British. Overlaps with the Elizabethan period, which is marked by the reign of Elizabeth Tudor.

Historical/Victorian ▌ Set during the reign of Queen Victoria, 1837-1901. This designation does not include works with a predominately American setting.

Historical/Victorian America ▌ Set in America, usually the Eastern part, during the Victorian Period, 1837-1901.

Historical/War of 1812 ▌ Set during the British-U.S. conflict which lasted from 1812 to 1814.

Historical/World War I ▌ Set during the First World War, 1914-1918.

Historical/World War II ▌ Set in the years of the Second World War, 1939-1945.

Holiday Themes ▌ Fiction that focuses on or is set during a particular holiday or holiday season (e.g., Christmas, Valentine's Day, Mardi Gras).

Horror ▌ Refers to stories in which interest in the events, the intellectual puzzle characteristic of much of SF, is subordinated to a feeling of terror or horror by the reader, which could result from a variety of causes, including a disaster or an invasion of earth.

Humor ▌ Story with an amusing story line.

Immortality ▌ Usually includes extreme longevity, resulting from fountains of youth, elixirs, or something with a pseudoscientific basis.

Indian Culture ▌ These novels center on the lives, customs, and cultures of characters who are American Indians or who lived among the Indians.

Indian Wars ▌ Often traditional Westerns, these stories are set during the period of the Indian wars and rely on this warfare for plots, characters, and themes.

Inspirational ▌ A novel with an uplifting, often Christian theme, and usually considered "innocent."

Invasion of Earth ▌ An extremely common theme, often paralleling historical events and reflecting fears of the time. Most invasions are depicted as malign, only occasionally benign.

Legal ▌ Main focus is on a lawyer, though it does not always involve courtroom action.

Legend ▌ A story based on a legend, myth, or fairy tale that has been rewritten.

Lesbian/Contemporary ▌ A story with lesbian protagonists set in the present.

Lesbian/Historical ▌ Historical fiction with lesbian protagonists.

Light Fantasy ▌ There is a great deal of humor throughout the story and it is almost guaranteed to have a happy ending.

Literary ▌ Relates to the nature and knowledge of literature; can be applied to setting or characters.

Lost Colony ▌ Stories centering around a colony on another world that loses contact with or is abandoned by its parent civilization and the type of society that evolves under those conditions. Conflict usually arises when contact is re-established between the colony and its home world.

Magic Conflict ▌ The main conflict of the story stems from magical interference. Protagonists may be caught in the middle of a conflict between sorcerers or may themselves be engaged in conflict with other sorcerers.

Magic Realism ▌ A style of prose fiction writing in which the author blends the realism of describing ordinary places and incidents with fantastic, dreamlike, or mythical events and does not differentiate between the real and the magical.

Man Alone ▌ A lone man, alienated from the society that would normally support him, faces overwhelming dangers.

Medical ▌ Stories in which medical themes are dominant.

Military ▌ Stories have a military theme; may deal with life in the armed forces or military battles.

Modern ▌ Reflection of the present time period.

Mountain Man ▌ Any story in which the principal characters are mountain men and women, living in mountain areas remote from civilization and depending upon their own resourcefulness for survival.

Multicultural ▌ A romance in which the ethnic background of the characters is integral to the story.

Mystery ▌ Usually a story where a crime occurs or a puzzle must be solved.

Mystical ▌ Fiction dealing with spiritual elements. Miraculous or supernatural characteristics of events, characters, settings, and themes.

Nature in Revolt ▌ Tales in which normally docile plants or animals suddenly turn against humankind, sometimes transformed (giant crabs resulting from radioactivity, predatory rats, plagues, blobs that threaten London or Miami, etc.).

Occult ▌ An adjective suggesting fiction based on a mystical or secret doctrine, but sometimes referring to supernatural fiction generally. Implies that there is a reality beyond the perceived world that only adepts can penetrate.

Paranormal ▌ Novel contains supernatural elements. Story may include ghosts, UFOs, aliens, demons, and haunted houses among other unexplained phenomenon.

Parody ▌ A narrative that follows the form of the original but usually changes its sense to nonsense, thus making fun of the original or its ideas.

Police Procedural ▌ A story in which the action is centered around a police officer.

Political ▌ The novel deals with political issues that are skewed by the use and presence of fantastic elements.

Possession ▌ Domination, usually of humans, by evil spirits, demons, aliens, or other agencies in which one's own volition is replaced by an outside force.

Post-Disaster ▌ Story set in a much degraded environment, frequently involving a reduction in population and the resulting loss of access to processes, resources, technology, etc.

Post-Holocaust ▌ The events following a world-wide disaster, often the result of human folly rather than natural events (collision with a meteor, etc.).

Post-Nuclear Holocaust ▌ The events following a world-wide nuclear disaster.

Private Detective ▌ Usually detection, involving a professional for hire.

Psychic Powers ▌ Parapsychological or paranormal powers.

Psychological ▌ Fiction dealing with mental or emotional responses.

Psychological Suspense ▌ Tales in which the psychological exploration and quirks of characters generate suspense and plot.

Quest ▌ The central characters are on a journey filled with dangers to reach some worthwhile goal.

Ranch Life ▌ The basic cowboy story, in which the plot and characters are inextricably bound up in the workings of a ranch.

Regency ▌ A light romance involving the British upper classes, set during the Regency Period, 1811-1820. During this time, the Prince of Wales acted as Prince Regent because of the incapacity of his father, George III. In 1820, "Prinny" became George IV. These stories, in the style of Jane Austen, are essentially comedies of manners and the emphasis is on language, wit, and style. Georgette Heyer set the standard for the modern version of this genre. This designation is also given to stories of similar type that may not fit precisely within the Regency time period.

Reincarnation ▌ A tale in which the horror arises in connection with the reincarnation of one of the characters.

Religious ▌ Religion of any sort plays a primary role in the plot.

Revenge ▌ A character who has suffered an unjust loss returns to take vengeance. This is one of the most common traditional themes.

Robot Fiction ▌ From the Jewish Golem to the traditional clanking bucket of bolts to the human-like android, robots in various guises have been among us for centuries. The term comes from Karl Capek's play, *R.U.R.*, which stands for Rossum's Universal Robots. Robots are often surrogates for humans and may be treated seriously or comically.

Romance ▌ Stories involving love affairs and love stories; deals with the emotional attachments of the characters.

Romantic Suspense ❚ Romance with a strong mystery suspense plot. This is a broad category including works in the tradition of Mary Stewart, as well as the newer women-in-jeopardy tales by writers such as Mary Higgins Clark. These stories usually have contemporary settings but some are also set in the past.

Saga ❚ A multi-generational story that usually centers around one particular family and its trials, tribulations, successes, and loves.

Satanism ❚ Suggests worship of evil rather than benevolent gods, the antithesis of conventional theism, whether Christianity or other religions. Evil demons are Satan writ small and usually lack the awful majesty of their parent.

Satire ❚ Fiction written in a sarcastic and ironic way to ridicule human vices or follies; usually using an exaggeration of characteristics to stress a point.

Science Fantasy ❚ A somewhat vague term in which there are "rational" elements from SF and "magical" or "fanciful" elements from fantasy, which hopefully cohere in a plausible story.

Science Fiction ❚ Although the story has been classified in another genre, there are strong elements of science fiction.

Serial Killer ❚ A multiple murderer, going back to Bluebeard and up to Ed Gein, who inspired Robert Bloch's *Psycho*.

Series ❚ A number of books united either by continuing characters and situations or by a common theme. Series books may appear under a single author's name or each book in the series may be by a different author.

Small Town Horror ❚ The coziness and intimacy of a small community is disrupted by some sort of horrific happening, suggesting an unjustified placidity and complacency on the part of the citizens.

Space Colony ❚ A permanent space station, usually orbiting Earth but in principal located in deep space or near other planets or stars.

Space Opera ❚ Intergalactic adventures; westerns in space; a specialized form of the genre type Adventure.

Steampunk ❚ Genre fiction typically set in Britain in the 1900s when steam power was prevalent and prior to the broad use of electricity. The location can be anywhere, however, including North America. Steampunk usually encompasses alternate history elements and fantastical inventions powered by steam or other more anachronistic energy sources for the time period.

Supernatural Vengeance ❚ Punishment inflicted by God or a godlike creature, whether justly or capriciously.

Sword and Sorcery ❚ Often a muscle-bound swordsman, who is innocent of thought and common sense, up against evil sorcerers and sorceresses, who naturally lose in the end because they are evil.

Techno-Horror ❚ Suggests a catastrophe with horrific elements resulting from a scientific miscalculation or technological hubris; Victor Frankenstein's unnamed monster or a plague resulting from a laboratory mishap.

Techno-Thriller ❚ Stories in which a technological development, such as an invention, is linked to a series of suspenseful (thrilling) events.

Theological ❚ Stories in which religion or religious belief plays an important role.

Time Travel ❚ A story in which characters from one time are transported either literally or in spirit to another time period. The time shifts are usually between the present and another historical period.

Traditional ❚ Traditional stories may deal with virtually any time period or situation, but they are related by shared conventions of setting and characterization.

Trail Drive ❚ Any story in which a cattle drive (or, more rarely, a drive of sheep or horses) is a major plot component.

UFO ❚ Unidentified Flying Objects, literally, although sometimes used more generally to refer to any object of mysterious origin or intent.

Urban ❚ Stories set in large cities; usually the tone of the novel is gritty and realistic and may involve issues such as drugs and gangs.

Utopia ❚ A large, often influential, story type that takes its name from Thomas More's 1516 book. Usually refers to a society considered better by the author, even if not perfect. Aldous Huxley's *Island* (1962) is a utopia, whereas his more famous *Brave New World* (1932) is a dark twin, a dystopia.

Vampire Story ❚ Based on mythical bloodsucking creatures possessing supernatural powers and various forms, both animal and human. The concept can be traced far back in history, long before Bram Stoker's famous novel, *Dracula*.

Wagon Train ❚ A book that deals with wagon trains traveling across the American West.

Werewolf Story ❚ Were is Old English for man, suggesting the ancient lineage of a creature that once dominated a world in which witches and sorcerers were equally feared. Sometimes used to refer to any shape shifter, whether wolves or other animals.

Wild Talents ❚ The phrase comes from Charles Fort's writings and usually refers to parapsychological powers such a telepathy, psychokinesis, and precognition, collectively called psychic or psi phenomena.

Witchcraft ❚ Characters either profess to be or are stigmatized as witches or warlocks, and practitioners of magic associated with witchcraft. This can include black magic or white magic (e.g., Wicca).

Young Adult ❚ A marketing term for publishers; one or more of the central characters is a teenager often testing his or her skills against adversity to achieve a greater degree of maturity and self-awareness. A category used by librarians to shelve books of likely appeal to teenage readers.

Young Readers ❚ A novel with characters, plot, and vocabulary primarily aimed at juveniles.

Zombie ❚ A creature that is typically a reanimated corpse or a human being who is being controlled by someone else by use of magic or voodoo.

Award Winners

Since these awards are all presented retroactively, the individual titles below may have been covered in earlier editions of *What Do I Read Next?*.

Fantastic Fiction Awards by Don D'Ammassa

Various awards for science fiction, fantasy, and horror fiction are presented by several professional and fan organizations, primarily on an annual basis, sometimes with open balloting, sometimes confining the final decision to a group of judges, or a combination of methods. These awards typically cover short fiction of varying lengths, dramatic presentations, and other categories in addition to those involving a specific book.

Hugo Awards: The Hugo Awards are named in honor of Hugo Gernsback for his pioneering work in creating science fiction magazines. This is fantastic fiction's oldest continuing award, originating in 1953 and awarded every year since with one lapse. Anyone who purchases membership is entitled to nominate and vote in all categories. They are presented at the World Science Fiction Convention, which took place August 14-18, 2014, in London, England. The 2014 winners (awards given to 2013 titles) in selected categories are as follows:

Best Novel: *Ancillary Justice* by Ann Leckie

Nebula Awards: The Nebula Awards were presented by the Science Fiction and Fantasy Writers of America on May 17, 2014 at the Nebula Awards Weekend. Only full members are entitled to vote for the final selection. The award has been presented annually since 1965. The 2013 winners in selected categories are as follows:

Best Novel: *Ancillary Justice* by Ann Leckie

Andre Norton Award for Young Adult Science Fiction and Fantasy: *Sister Mine* by Nalo Hopkinson

Bram Stoker Awards: These awards were presented by the Horror Writers Association at the World Horror Convention, which took place May 7-10, 2015, in Atlanta, Georgia. All members can nominate but only full members can vote on the final ballot. The award is named after the author of *Dracula* and has been presented since 1987. The 2014 winners for superior achievement in selected categories are as follows:

Novel: *Blood Kin* by Steve Rasnic Tem

First Novel: *Mr. Wicker* by Maria Alexander

Young Adult Novel: *Phoenix Island* by John Dixon

Graphic Novel: *Bad Blood* by Jonathan Maberry

Fiction Collection: *Soft Apocalypses* by Lucy A. Snyder

Anthology: *Fearful Symmetries* edited by Ellen Datlow

Nonfiction: *Shooting Yourself in the Head For Fun and Profit: A Writer's Survival Guide* by Lucy A. Snyder

Poetry Collection: *Forgiving Judas* by Tom Piccirilli

The Shirley Jackson Awards: These awards are selected by a panel of editors and writers to reward outstanding achievement in psychological suspense and horror. The awards were given on July 13, 2014, at Readercon 25, Conference on Imaginative Literature, in Burlington, Massachusetts. The 2013 winners in selected categories are as follows:

Best Novel: *American Elsewhere* by Robert Jackson Bennett

Best Single-Author Collection (tie): *Before and Afterlives* by Christopher Barzak and *North American Lake Monsters* by Nathan Ballingrud

Best Edited Anthology: *Grimscribe's Puppets* edited by Joseph S. Pulver, Sr.

Mystery Awards by Clair Lamb

The Anthony Awards: The Anthony Awards are presented annually at Bouchercon, the World Mystery Convention. They are named after Anthony Boucher, a founder of Mystery Writers of America and the first mainstream literary critic to consider mysteries as serious literature. Books are nominated and voted on by conference participants. The awards were presented at Bouchercon 2014 in Long Beach, California on November 13-16, 2014. The 2014 winners in selected categories are as follows:

Best Novel: *Ordinary Grace* by William Kent Krueger

Best First Novel: *Yesterday's Echo* by Matt Coyle

Best Paperback Original: *As She Left It* by Catriona McPherson

Best Critical or Non-Fiction Work: *The Hour of Peril: The Secret Plot To Murder Lincoln Before the Civil War* by Daniel Stashower

The Macavity Awards: The Macavity Awards are presented annually at Bouchercon, the World Mystery Convention, by the members of Mystery Readers International. The Macavity Award is named for the "mystery cat" of T.S. Eliot's *Old Possum's Book of Practical Cats*. The 2014 awards were presented at Bouchercon 2014 in Long Beach, California on November 13-16, 2014. The 2014 winners in selected categories are as follows:

Best Mystery Novel: *Ordinary Grace* by William Kent Krueger

Best First Mystery: *A Killing at Cotton Hill* by Terry Shames

Best Nonfiction: *The Hour of Peril: The Secret Plot to Murder Lincoln Before the Civil War* by Daniel Stashower

Sue Feder Memorial Historical Mystery: *Murder As a Fine Art* by David Morrell

The Hammett Prize: The Hammett Prize is awarded by the North American Branch of the International Association of Crime Writers (IACW) for literary excellence in the field of crime-writing. Only U.S. and Canadian citizens or permanent residents are eligible. Nominations are solicited from the membership, and winners are chosen by a panel of outside (i.e., non-member) judges.

2013 Winner: *Angel Baby: A Novel* by Richard Lange

The Nero Award: The Nero Award is an annual award presented to an author for literary excellence in the mystery genre by The Wolfe Pack, an organization devoted to the study of Rex Stout's Nero Wolfe mysteries. The Nero is presented at the Black Orchid Banquet, which was held on December 6, 2014, in New York City.

2014 Winner: *Murder as a Fine Art* by David Morrell

The Shamus Awards: The Shamus Awards are presented annually by the Private Eye Writers of America (PWA) for excellence in writing about private eyes. The PWA defines a "private eye" as any mystery protagonist who is a professional investigator, but not a police officer or government agent. The 2014 awards were presented at Bouchercon 2014 in Long Beach, California on November 13-16, 2014. The 2014 winners in selected categories are as follows:

Best Hardcover: *The Good Cop* by Brad Parks

Best First P.I. Novel: *Bear is Broken* by Lachlan Smith

Best Paperback Original: *Heart of Ice* by P.J. Parrish

Popular Fiction Awards by Holly Hibner and Mary Kelly

Man Booker Prize: The Man Booker Prize promotes the finest in fiction by rewarding the very best book of the year. The prize is the world's most important literary award and has the power to transform the fortunes of authors and even publishers.

2014 Winner: *The Narrow Road to the Deep North* by Richard Flanagan

Nobel Prize in Literature: Awarded by the Swedish Academy, the Nobel Prize in Literature is given to an author from any country whose work has lasting literary merit and which is idealistic in nature.

2014 Winner: Patrick Modiano

National Book Award: The National Book Award is given to writers by writers. The award is given in four categories: Fiction, Nonfiction, Poetry, and Young People's Literature and were awarded at a ceremony in New York City on November 19, 2014. The 2014 winners are as follows:

Fiction: *Redeployment* by Phil Klay

Non-fiction: *Age of Ambition: Chasing Fortune, Truth, and Faith in the New China* by Evan Osnos

Poetry: *Faithful and Virtuous Night* by Louise Glück

Young People's Literature: *Brown Girl Dreaming* by Jacqueline Woodson

National Book Critics Circle Awards: The National Book Critics Circle Awards honor the best literature published in English. The awards were given at a ceremony in New York City on March 12, 2015. The 2014 winners in selected categories are as follows:

Fiction: *Lila* by Marilynne Robinson

Nonfiction: *The Problem of Slavery in the Age of Emancipation* by David Brion Davis

Biography: *Tennessee Williams: Mad Pilgrimage of the Flesh* by John Lahr

Poetry: *Citizen: An American Lyric* by Claudia Rankine

Autobiography: *Can't We Talk About Something More Pleasant?* by Roz Chast

Pen Faulkner Awards: The PEN/Faulkner Award for Fiction was founded in 1980 by National Book Award winner Mary Lee Settle. Her goal was to establish a national prize that would recognize literary fiction of excellence, an award juried by writers for writers, free of commercial concerns. The prize was named for William Faulkner, who used his Nobel Prize funds to establish an award for younger writers, and PEN, the international writers' organization. The award was given in a ceremony at the Folger Shakespeare Library in Washington, D.C., May 2, 2015.

2014 Winner: *Preparation for the Next Life* by Atticus Lish

Next Generation Indie Book Awards: The Next Generation Indie Book Awards is the largest Not-for-Profit book awards program for indie authors and independent publishers. The 2014 winners are as follows:

Fiction: *A True Novel* by Minae Mizumura

Nonfiction: *The Boy Who Lived With Ghosts: A Memoir* by John Mitchell

The 2015 winners are as follows:

Fiction: *Topeka, ma'shuge* by Raymond Hutson

Nonfiction: *Thrown* by Kerry Howley

Historical Awards by Dana Ferguson

Walter Scott Prize: The Walter Scott Prize is a British literary award for historical fiction founded in 2010. The award was created by the Duke and Duchess of Buccleuch, whose ancestors were closely linked to Scottish author Sir Walter Scott, who is generally considered the originator of historical fiction with the novel *Waverly* in 1814. The award was given at the Brewin Dolphin Borders Book Festival in Melrose, Scotland on June 13, 2015.

2014 Winner: *The Ten Thousand Things* by John Spurling

James Fenimore Cooper Prize: The James Fenimore Cooper Prize is a biannual award given for the Best Historical American fiction by The Society of American Historians and is named for nineteenth-century American historical novelist James Fenimore Cooper. The prize has been awarded since 1993, in odd-numbered years, to "honor works of literary fiction that significantly advance the historical imagination" to a novel about American history. The 2015 award was given on May 11, 2015, in New York.

2015 Winner: *Saint Monkey* by Jacinda Townsend

The Michael Shaara Award for Excellence in Civil War Fiction: This literary award is given annually to the writer of a work of fiction related to the American Civil War. The award was started by Jeffrey Shaara and named for his father, the writer of historical fiction Michael Shaara. It is given at the Civil War Institute at Gettysburg College in Pennsylvania.

2014 Winner: *Nostalgia* by Dennis McFarland

Romance Awards by Kristin Ramsdell

As romance fiction has attained increased recognition as a legitimate literary genre, various publications, organizations, and groups have developed to support the interests of its writers and readers. As part of this mission, a number of these offer awards to recognize the accomplishments of the practitioners. Some awards are juried and are presented for excellence in quality and style of writing; others are based on popularity; some are based on sales. Usually awards are given for a particular work by a particular writer; however, some awards are presented for a body of work produced over a number of years (a type of career award) and others are given for various types of contributions to romance fiction in general. The included categories may change over time to reflect the changing nature of the genre. The Romance Writers of America and the *RT Book Reviews* (formerly called *Romantic Times*) are the sponsors of most of the awards listed below. Awards information courtesy of the Romance Writers of America, RomCon, and the Romantic Times Publishing Group.

RITA Awards for Published Novels: These awards were presented by the Romance Writers of America at their annual conference, July 23-26, 2014, in San Antonio, Texas. Named for Rita Clay Estrada, RWA's first president, RITAs for published works are given in a number of categories, some of which have changed over the years. The 2014 winners (awards given to 2013 titles) are as follows:

First Book: *The Sweet Spot* by Laura Drake

Contemporary Romance: *Crazy Thing Called Love* by Molly O'Keefe

Historical Romance: *No Good Duke Goes Unpunished* by Sarah MacLean

Paranormal Romance: *The Firebird* by Susanna Kearsley

Romantic Suspense: *Off the Edge* by Carolyn Crane

Inspirational Romance: *Five Days in Skye* by Carla Laureano

Golden Heart Awards: These awards were presented by the Romance Writers of America at their annual conference, July 23-26, 2014, in San Antonio, Texas. Awarded for the best romance novel manuscript by an unpublished writer, Golden Hearts are given in a number of categories, some of which have changed over the years. The 2014 winners (awards given to 2013 titles) are as follows:

Contemporary Romance: *Too Good to Be True* by Suzanne Kaufman Kalb

Historical Romance: *Charlene and the Duchess Factory* by Lenora Bell

Paranormal Romance: *Beyond the Fire* by Marni Folsom

Romantic Suspense: *Chasing Damn* by Denny S. Bryce

Young Adult Romance: *The Thing with Feathers* by McCall Hoyle

Readers' Crown Awards: These awards are chosen by romance readers and presented at the annual RomCon, a reader/author event in Denver, Colorado. The 2015 winners are as follows:

Best First Book: *Slim to None* by Freya Barker

Best Series/Category Romance: *Tell Me Something Good* by Jamie Wesley

Best Inspirational Romance: *A Thousand Little Blessings* by Claire Sanders

Best Romantic Suspense: *Saving Sophie* by Cate Beauman

Best Erotic Romance: *All Hat No Cattle* by Randi Alexander

Best Paranormal Romance: *Outfoxed by Love* by Eve Langlais

Best Science Fiction/Fantasy/Time Travel Romance: *Mystic's Touch* by Dena Garson

Best Historical Romance: *Invitation to Passion* by Bronwen Evans

Best Urban Fantasy Romance: *Anointed The Cantati Chronicle* by Maggie Mae Gallagher

Best Mystery Romance: *Guidebook To Murder* by Lynn Cahoon

Best Mainstream Romance: *Drown* by Jennifer Rae Gravely

Inspirational Awards by Lynda Lee Schab

The Christy Awards: The 15th annual Christy Awards were held in Atlanta, Georgia, on June 23, 2014. The Christy Awards were named in honor of *Christy*, a 1967 novel by Catherine Marshall that marked a turning point in religious fiction and served as the inspiration for a television series that ran from 1994-1995. The Christy Awards are presented to honor the inspirational novels released by Christian publishing houses. The entries are submitted by publishers, and a panel of independent judges narrows the field to the top three nominees in nine genres. The 2014 (awards given to 2013 titles) winners in each category are as follows:

Contemporary Romance/Suspense: *Dangerous Passage* by Lisa Harris

Contemporary Series: *Take a Chance on Me* by Susan May Warren

Contemporary Standalone: *Stones for Bread* by Christa Parrish

First Novel and Historical: *Burning Sky* by Lori Bento

Historical Romance: *Harvest of Gold* by Tessa Afshar

Visionary: *Dragonwitch* by Anne Elisabeth Stengl

The Carol Awards: The Carol Awards are the American Christian Fiction Writers recognition for the best Christian fiction published by traditional publishing houses in the previous calendar year. Named after Carol Johnson of Bethany House, who years ago took a step of faith and signed Janette Oke to write her prairie romance stories, introducing us to a new world of Christian fiction, Carol Awards are presented to authors in 15 Inspirational Fiction categories. In addition, ACFW hands out Genesis Awards to authors still unpublished in fiction. The awards were presented in September, 2014 at the ACFW Awards Gala in St. Louis, Missouri. The 2014 winners are as follows:

Contemporary: *Dear Mr. Knightley* by Katherine Reay

Debut Novel: *Dear Mr. Knightley* by Katherine Reay

Historical: *When Mountains Move* by Julie Cantrell

Historical Romance: *A Noble Groom* by Jody Hedlund

Mystery/Suspense/Thriller: *Truth Stained Lies* by Terri Blackstock

Romance: *Undeniably Yours* by Becky Wade

Romantic Suspense: *Jungle Fire* by Dana Mentink

Speculative: *A Cast of Stones* by Patrick W. Carr

Young Adult: *A Simple Song* by Melody Carlson

Classic Fantasy Writers
by
Don D'Ammassa

For most of the last century, fantasy fiction was considered a subcategory of science fiction even though tales of magic have been around for much longer than those of science. Although at one time considered appropriate for adult reader—the fairy tales of Hans Christian Andersen and the Brothers Grimm were not intended specifically for children—fantasy was relegated largely to a predominantly juvenile audience by the twentieth century even though it was written by brilliant and serious-minded adults. J.R.R.Tolkien's Lord of the Rings trilogy had been published in the 1950s, but fantasy as a whole languished unappreciated until the mass market paperback editions of Tolkien's work in the 1960s generated widespread interest. Fantasy soon would supplant science fiction as the predominant form of fantastic literature. Initially there were not enough new writers working in that tradition, so publishers began looking at work that previously had been unavailable, sometimes for generations. The most notable of these efforts was the Ballantine Adult Fantasy series edited by Lin Carter. Now that there are scores of writers producing new fantasy, most of this classic fiction has lapsed once more into undeserved obscurity, with the obvious exceptions of L. Frank Baum and Lewis Carroll, both of whom wrote for children.

One of the earliest of these was George MacDonald (1824–1905), a Scottish author who also wrote some children's fantasies—*At the Back of the North Wind* (1870), *The Princess and the Goblin* (1871), and *The Princess and the Curdie* (1882). But MacDonald also wrote fantasy for adults. The most significant of the latter was *Phantastes* (1858), in which a young man from our world is transported into a mysterious fantasy realm where he searches for the ultimate in female beauty. He has a series of adventures including a battle with giants before returning as a sadder but wiser man. *Lilith* (1895) is superficially very similar: The protagonist crosses through a mirror for a somewhat darker series of encounters, heavily embroidered with Christian symbolism. MacDonald also wrote a number of shorter fantasies that were collected as *The Complete Fairy Tales of George MacDonald* (1961), and smaller collections have appeared periodically in subsequent years.

English writer William Morris (1834–1896) led a crowded life as a designer, inventor, and prolific author. Morris is credited with being the first writer to set his fantasy in entirely imaginary, invented worlds. Although most of his fantasy was written quite late in his life, there are hints of his interest in magic and legends in his Viking adventure novel, *The Roots of the Mountains* (1889). His first overtly fantastic novel was *The Glittering Plain* (1891), in which the protagonist sets out to rescue the woman he loves—who has been kidnapped by pirates—and finds a mythical land where immortals live in a kind of Utopian society. This novel followed his futuristic Utopian and best known novel, *News from Nowhere* (1890).

The Wood beyond the World (1894) is probably the best of Morris's fantasy novels. Once again the protagonist is on a perilous journey and eventually arrives in an undiscovered country where he attempts to rescue a captive woman, who turns out to be more competent at derring-do than he is, and the two have more adventures before arriving in a distant kingdom where they become the rulers. *The Well at World's End* (1896), his longest fantasy novel, is another quest story. A young knight sets out to find the well of the title, which bestows near immortality and other benefits to those who drink from it. After a rather long string of adventures, our hero achieves his goal but other characters with similar intentions endure different fates. *The Water of the Wondrous Isles* (1897) is somewhat more polemic: A witch's involuntary servant escapes and visits various other realms, some of which are meant as satires of rampant capitalism. The major protagonists are all women, which was rather unusual in Victorian fantasy. His final fantasy novel, published posthumously, was *The Sundering Flood* (1897). The plot is closer to contemporary high fantasy in that the hero uses a magic sword to help unseat a tyrannical ruler and restore freedom. The best of Morris's short fantasy has been collected as *Golden Wings and Other Stories* (1976) and *Early Romances* (2004).

Ernest Bramah (1868–1942) wrote in various genres and is noted for his Max Carrados mystery stories. He also wrote a series of episodic Oriental books featuring Kai Lung, a professional storyteller. The individual stories often are humorous as well as fantastic and Bramah created an artificial prose style to add an exotic air to these books, which are filled with amusing aphorisms. The first three in the series are the best and they have remained popular ever since they were first published. These are *The Wallet of Kai Lung* (1900), *Kai Lung's Golden HoursWit* (1922), and *Kai Lung Unrolls His Mat* (1928).

The most important American fantasy novelist of this era was James Branch Cabell (1879–1958), whose novel *Jurgen* (1919) was banned in some places as obscene, although it is extremely tame by contemporary standards and the objectionable material was almost certainly Cabell's criticism of established religion rather than the occasional double entendre. Most of his fantasy fiction was included in the loosely organized 25-volume Biography of the Life of Manuel, which includes essays and poetry as well as prose fiction. Most of these are set in the fictional European country Poictesme. Cabell was fond of anagrams and a large number of proper names from the books can be rearranged into other and sometimes amusing words.

The Manuel books vary considerably in quality and subject matter. The most famous is, of course, *Jurgen*, an episodic adventure in which young Jurgen visits a variety of different worlds including Heaven and Hell, frequently becoming involved in sexual escapades. It was a satire on what Cabell saw as hypocritical and illogical aspects of contemporary American life. Several other books in the series are of exceptional quality. *Figures of Earth* (1921) is the story of Manuel himself, a swineherd who through extraordinary means become a count. *The Silver Stallion* (1926) describes the gradual embellishment of his career following his death. *Domnei* (1913 but revised as *The Soul of Melicent* in 1920) involves courtly intrigues and the rescue of a fair maiden in a parody of medieval fantasy tales. *The High Place* (1923) takes aim at the story of sleeping beauty and similar romantic fairy tales. The hero has married the fair lady, but marriage proves to be more of a challenge than expected. *Something about Eve* (1921) is an anecdotal quest story featuring one of Manuel's descendants, and *The Cream of the Jest* (1917) features a hero who discovers he has godlike powers and decides to make use of them.

Lord Dunsany (1878–1957) was actually Edward John Moreton Drax Plunkett, a prolific English writer who dabbled in multiple genres. Dunsany's short fantasy fiction is generally better than his novels and many of his short tales such as "The Fortress Unvanquishable Save for Sacnoth" and "The Distressing Tale of Thangobrind the Jeweler" are acknowledged classics. Most of his best short fantasy can be found in *At the Edge of the World* (1970) and *Beyond the Fields We Know* (1972). His most famous fantasy novel is *The King of Elfland's Daughter* (1924), in which a mortal man marries the daughter of the king of the elves, with amusing consequences for the village in which they live. Other titles worth noting include *The Charwoman's Shadow* (1926), in which a working woman puzzles her neighbor because she casts no shadow, and *The Curse of the Wise Woman* (1933), in which developers unwisely begin draining a mysterious bog, releasing an ancient force that can be countered only by means of magic.

E.R. Eddison (1882–1945) was a colleague of C.S. Lewis and J.R.R. Tolkien. His first and most famous fantasy novel is *The Worm Ouroboros* (1922), set supposedly on the planet Mercury although after the first chapter that conceit is never mentioned again. The plot involves a multi-sided war among the various nations of that world—dubbed goblins and elves and so forth although all of the characters are entirely human. The story ends with the villains vanquished but the heroes, bored by the aftermath, discover that time is a circle and they can look forward to the conflict all over again. The novel is related to the Zimiamvian trilogy, consisting of *Mistress of Mistresses* (1935), *A Fish Dinner in Memison* (1941), and the unfinished *The Mezentian Gate* (1958). The novels chronicle the adventures of a man from our world who is transported to the magical world of Zimiamvia where he rises and falls in influence.

Mervyn Peake (1911–1968) is remembered almost exclusively for the Gormenghast trilogy—*Titus Groan* (1946), *Gormenghast* (1950), and *Titus Alone* (1959)—although he wrote some other fantasy, notably *Mr. Pye* (1953). All three books are set in Gormenghast castle, a vast, sprawling environment that is almost a world in itself, although the main character, Titu, leaves home in the third to explore a world dominated by industrialism, though clearly it is not our world. Although Titus is central to the plot, many of the subsidiary characters provide intricate and fascinating sideplots.

These were the major writers of fantasy fiction until the second half of the twentieth century, but there are also several isolated works that deserve to be remembered. Victorian novelist George Meredith ventured into Oriental fantasy for his episodic 1856 novel, *The Shaving of Shagpat* (also published as *The Story of Bhanavar the Beautiful*), in which an itinerant barber has a series of adventures in a fictional version of China. *Lud-in-the-Mist* by Hope Mirrlees (1926) is a frequently overlooked fantasy in which the inhabitants of a small English town encounter some enchanted food and are forced to reconsider their refusal to recognize that they live close to the land of fairies. William Beckford's *Vathek* (1792) is arguably not in the same fantastic tradition but it was an interesting combination of Oriental fantasy elements with the popular gothic themes of the time and it was undoubtedly an influence on some of the better known fantasists. F. Marion Crawford was best known for his short tales of horror and his contemporary novels set in India, but he also wrote *Khaled* (1891), one of the best Arabian Nights style fantasies. Arthur Machen is also better known for his horror fiction but his novel *The Three Impostors* (1895) follows the quest to find a magical coin in modern London.

Finally we should mention Robert E. Howard (1906–1936), creator of Conan the Barbarian, Kull the Conqueror, and Solomon Kane, among others. Howard was not, however, writing in the same tradition as the other authors mentioned. He was writing for the pulp magazines where fantasy was almost always in the style we now refer to as sword and sorcery. His characters were indigenous to the magical realms rather than visitors from our world, the emphasis was on action rather than reflection, and the settings were more likely to be primitive and unpleasant than whimsical or inspirational. He was undoubtedly enormously influential despite his short career, but his fiction bore little resemblance to that of Morris, Cabell, or Eddison.

Today there are literally scores of fantasy novelists, all of whom were influenced to at least some degree by those who went before. It remains to be seen which of the newcomers will have similar effects on writers to come.

Recommended Titles

The first half of 2015 has not revealed any surprising changes in the fantasy genre. Urban fantasy, steampunk, and high fantasy were all well represented. The first new fantasy novel by Michael Moorcock in many years has been highly anticipated but George R.R. Martin has not yet finished the long awaited new installment of A Song of Ice and Fire, the series upon which *Game of Thrones* is based. The best from this period include the following:

Foxglove Summer by Ben Aaronovitch

Half the World by Joe Abercrombie

The Diamond Conspiracy by Philippa Ballantine and Tee Morris

Voyage of the Basilisk by Marie Brennan

Dead Heat by Patricia Briggs

The Fall of Fair Isle by Rowena Cory Daniells

The Very Best of Kate Elliott by Kate Elliott

Fall of Light by Steven Erikson

First and Last Sorcerer by Barb Hendee and JC Hendee

The Whispering Swarm by Michael Moorcock

Uprooted by Naomi Novik

The Book of Phoenix by Nnedi Okorafor

Fields of Wrath by Mickey Zucker Reichert

Fantasy Fiction

BEN AARONOVITCH

Foxglove Summer
(London: Gollancz, 2014)

Series: Peter Grant Series. Book 5
Series: Rivers of London Series. Book 5
Story type: Child-in-Peril; Contemporary - Fantasy
Subject(s): Magic; Detective fiction; Missing persons
Major character(s): Peter Grant, Police Officer (constable), Wizard (in-training)
Time period(s): 21st century; 2010s
Locale(s): England

Summary: Peter Grant is a talented police constable and wizard in training. Normally his beat keeps him in London, but a strange case of disappearing girls in rural Herefordshire requires his attention in the country. Two young girls are missing, and his superiors think the case should be checked out. Grant can't find anything magical or paranormal about the case, but feels as though he should offer his assistance to the local police anyway. Out of nowhere, however, the boundaries between the mortal plane and that of the fairy realm open up and he realizes that the small village harbors deadly and terrible secrets. Grant feels out of place in the country and in such a tight-knit village. He wasn't prepared for the angry fae and monsters that want him dead, but he's determined to help. Using science and empirical knowledge combined with his police experience and magical talents, Grant faces down carnivorous unicorns and other beasts as he fights for answers. This is the fifth Rivers of London novel.

Other books by the same author:
Broken Homes, 2014
Rivers of London, 2012
Whispers Under Ground, 2012
Midnight Riot, 2011
Moon Over Soho, 2011

Other books you might like:
Stephen Blackmoore, *Hungry Ghosts*, 2015
Jim Butcher, *Small Favor*, 2008
Simon R. Green, *A Hard Day's Knight*, 2011
Laurell K. Hamilton, *Hit List*, 2011

Richard Kadrey, *The Getaway God: A Sandman Slim Novel*, 2014
Lisa Shearin, *The Dragon Conspiracy*, 2015

2

JOE ABERCROMBIE

Half the World
(New York: Del Rey, 2015)

Series: Shattered Sea Series. Book 2
Story type: Adventure; Series
Subject(s): Fantasy; Adventure; Epics
Major character(s): Thorn Bathu, Crime Suspect, Companion (of Brand), Young Woman; Brand, Young Man, Warrior, Orphan, Companion (of Thorn); Father Yarvi, Leader (minister of Gettland)
Time period(s): Indeterminate
Locale(s): Gettland, Fictional Location

Summary: In the second novel in the Shattered Sea series, Thorn Bathu makes her next move after being accused as a murderer. She had been training as a warrior when the questionable incident took place. Now she must set aside her plan to take revenge for her father's death and embark on a new quest. Her territory, Gettland, is facing the threat of invasion, and Gettland's minster, Father Yarvi, has sent Thorn on a sea voyage to round up allies for the coming battle. Thorn is in the company of a young man named Brand, a warrior doomed to fail because he detests the act of killing. Thorn and Brand's journey is dangerous, and their mission is not as clear as it first seemed. Father Yarvi has his own agenda, and he has drawn the unwitting Thorn and Brand into his scheme.

Other books by the same author:
Half a King, 2014
The Heroes, 2011
Best Served Cold, 2009
Before They Are Hanged, 2008
Last Argument of Kings, 2008

Other books you might like:
Lynn Abbey, *Rifkind's Challenge*, 2006
Gail Dayton, *The Barbed Rose*, 2006
Lynn Flewelling, *Hidden Warrior*, 2003
Barb Hendee, *Witches with the Enemy*, 2015
Joel Shepherd, *Sasha*, 2009
Jo Walton, *The King's Name*, 2001

3

C.T. ADAMS

The Exile

(New York: Tom Doherty Associates, 2015)

Series: Book of the Fae Series. Book 1
Story type: Alternate World; Contemporary - Fantasy
Subject(s): Fairies; Magic; Alternative worlds
Major character(s): Brianna Hui, Supernatural Being (fairy), Daughter (of High King Hui), Friend (of Pug and David), Royalty (princess), Businesswoman (owner of occult shop); Leu Hui, Supernatural Being (fairy), Royalty (King of the Fae), Father (of Brianna); Pug, Mythical Creature (Gargoyle), Friend (of Brianna); David, Friend (of Brianna), Worker (on occult shop), Homosexual, Young Man; Angelo, Detective—Police; Mei, Dragon, Friend (of Brianna)
Time period(s): 21st century; 2010s
Locale(s): Faerie, Fictional Location; United States

Summary: Brianna Hui straddles the line between the magical world and the human world. A painting in her home hides the doorway to Faerie, where her father, High King Leu, rules. The store she runs sells souvenir trinkets, but primarily supplies witches and other magical purveyors with the tools of their trade. Someone must be aware of Brianna's double life, because her home is broken into in a way that only someone with magical powers could have accomplished. What's more, Brianna learns her father is in trouble. With the help of her friend David, a gargoyle named Pug, and a police detective and skeptic named Angelo, Brianna returns to the Fae world from which she escaped and fights to protect her friends and her father. This is the first novel of the Book of the Fae series by C.T. Adams.

Other books by the same author:
Serpent Moon, 2010
Cold Moon Rising, 2009
Howling Moon, 2007
Moon's Fury, 2007
Captive Moon, 2006

Other books you might like:
Patricia Briggs, *Masques*, 1993
Diane Duane, *Stealing the Elf-King's Roses*, 2002
Laurell K. Hamilton, *A Caress of Twilight*, 2002
Karen Marie Moning, *Faefever*, 2008
Kristine Kathryn Rusch, *The Resistance*, 1998

4

JOHN JOSEPH ADAMS

Operation Arcana

(Riverdale, New York: Baen, 2015)

Story type: Collection; Military
Subject(s): Fantasy; Short stories; Military life

Summary: In this anthology editor John Joseph Adams presents a collection of 16 short fantasy stories that share the common theme of war and military life. The stories, which are all published here for the first time, concern conflicts from human history as well as wars created in the authors' fictional worlds. In a World War I story, dark magic blends with the human atrocities of the conflict. In a story set in modern times, zombies test the skills of the military's most skilled warriors. The collection includes "The Damned One Hundred" by Jonathan Maberry, "Sealskin" by Carrie Vaughn, "Bomber's Moon" by Simon R. Green, and "In Skeleton Leaves" by Seanan McGuire. Myke Cole's "Weapons in the Earth" complements the novels in his Shadow Ops series.

Other books by the same author:
Wastelands 2, 2015
Armored, 2012
Brave New Worlds, 2011
Lightspeed Year One, 2011
Federations, 2009

Other books you might like:
Myke Cole, *Shadow Ops: Control Point*, 2012
Glen Cook, *A Path to Coldness of Heart*, 2012
Simon R. Green, *Tales from the Nightside*, 2015
Tanya Huff, *The Enchantment Emporium*, 2009
Carrie Vaughn, *Kitty's Greatest Hits*, 2011

5

ALEX ARCHER

Death Mask

(Don Mills, Ontario, Canada: Gold Eagle, 2015)

Series: Rogue Angel Series. Book 52
Story type: Adventure; Series
Subject(s): Fantasy; Adventure; Mystery
Major character(s): Annja Creed, Archaeologist, Television Personality, Friend (of Garin), Colleague (of Roux); Garin Braden, Captive, Friend (of Annja); Roux, Colleague (mentor of Annja)
Time period(s): 21st century; 2010s
Locale(s): Spain

Summary: Archaeologist Annja Creed, host of the television program *Chasing History's Monsters*, is taking some time off in Madrid after filming a segment about gargoyles in Valencia. She is awakened early by a cell phone call that directs her to an Internet link. Annja is shocked to see a live video of her friend, Garin Braden, who has a countdown clock bound to his chest. The mysterious caller tells Annja that she must find and deliver the mask of Torquemada in 24 hours, or Garin will die. Annja knows that locating the mask, which belonged to a key figure in the Spanish Inquisition and has been missing for centuries, is next to impossible. But with Garin's life at stake, Annja embarks on the most important—and most dangerous—archaeological quest of her career. This novel is the 52nd in the Rogue Angel series.

Other books by the same author:
The Pretender's Gambit, 2014
River of Nightmares, 2014
Fury's Goddess, 2012
False Horizon, 2011
The God Catcher, 2010

Fantasy

Other books you might like:
James Alan Gardner, *Lara Croft Tomb Raider: The Man of Bronze*, 2005
E.E. Knight, *Lara Croft Tomb Raider: The Lost Cult*, 2004
Andy McDermott, *Return to Atlantis*, 2012
Mike Resnick, *The Amulet of Power*, 2003
James Rollins, *The Eye of God*, 2013

6

ALEX ARCHER

Bathed in Blood

(New York: Harlequin, 2015)

Series: Rogue Angel Series. Book 53
Story type: Alternate World; Amateur Detective
Subject(s): Fantasy; Serial murders; Murder
Major character(s): Annja Creed, Archaeologist, Television Personality, Detective—Amateur; Elizabeth Bathory, Serial Killer (aka the Blood Countess), Noblewoman
Time period(s): Multiple Time Periods; 17th century; 21st century
Locale(s): Slovakia

Summary: Annja Creed, an archaeologist with her own television show, has always been intrigued by the story of one of the most infamous female serial killers of all time. Elizabeth Bathory, otherwise known as the Blood Countess, thought bathing in blood would keep her eternally young and beautiful, and 650 young women were reported to have lost their lives in her quest. Annja thought it was nothing more than an intriguing story, until young women drained of their blood began showing up in her small town in Slovakia. Annja learns that more than 20 beautiful young women have been killed, and the murderer is still at large. The people of the town are tight-lipped, as are the police. Annja decides to lure the killer out—using herself as the bait. This is the fifty-third book in the Rogue Angel series.

Other books by the same author:
Celtic Fire, 2014
Staff of Judea, 2013
Sunken Pyramid, 2013
The Matador's Crown, 2012
The Oracle's Message, 2011

Other books you might like:
Ilona Andrews, *Magic Bites*, 2007
Elaine Bergstrom, *Baroness of Blood*, 1995
Jasper Kent, *Thirteen Years Later*, 2010
Richard A. Knaak, *Ruby Flames*, 1999
Andy Remic, *Kell's Legend*, 2009

7

JENNIFER ASHLEY

Shifter Mates

(New York: Penguin Group, 2015)

Series: Shifters Unbound Series
Story type: Romance; Series

Subject(s): Romances (Fiction); Fantasy; Parapsychology
Time period(s): 21st century; 2010s
Locale(s): United States

Summary: This volume collects two novellas from Jennifer Ashley's Shifters Unbound series, which concerns the adventures and romances of modern-day shapeshifters. Ellison Rowe, the main character in *Lone Wolf*, values his independence, but he still longs for companionship. Although he is a wolf Shifter, Ellison finds himself attracted to a human woman, Maria, who has made a home among the Shifters. In *Feral Heat*, an attraction develops between Jace Warden and Deni Rowe as they work to free Shifters who have been forced to wear collars. Jace and Deni want to release the Shifters from their bond, but they may not be able to escape the mate bond that is growing between them.

Other books by the same author:
Mate Bond, 2015
Primal Bonds, 2011
Pride Mates, 2010
The Calling, 2007
The Gathering, 2007

Other books you might like:
Clare Bell, *Clan Ground*, 1984
Elizabeth H. Boyer, *Keeper of Cats*, 1995
Christine Feehan, *Viper Game*, 2015
Esther M. Friesner, *Majyk by Accident*, 1993
Mercedes Lackey, *Reserved for the Cat*, 2007
Michael Peak, *Catamount*, 1992

8

JENNIFER ASHLEY

Mate Bond

(New York: Penguin Group, 2015)

Series: Shifters Unbound Series. Book 7
Story type: Paranormal; Romance
Subject(s): Fantasy; Romances (Fiction); Parapsychology
Major character(s): Bowman O'Donnell, Shape-Shifter (wolf), Leader (of Shiftertown); Kenzie, Woman, Shape-Shifter (wolf)
Time period(s): 21st century; 2010s
Locale(s): North Carolina, United States

Summary: Wolf shifters Bowman O'Donnell and Kenzie should be the perfect mates. Strong and respected, they serve as the leaders of their Shiftertown in North Carolina. Although they are mates, Bowman and Kenzie have not achieved the mate bond—a powerful bond that would strengthen their union. When the town is threatened by a dangerous creature, the community's trust in Bowman and Kenzie's leadership begins to falter. If they don't share a mate bond, will Bowman and Kenzie be able to protect the other Shifters during the crisis? The mates have no choice but to confront the danger and trust that the bond they have—though imperfect—will give them the strength they need.

Other books by the same author:
Wild Cat, 2012
Primal Bonds, 2011
Pride Mates, 2010

The Calling, 2007
The Gathering, 2007

Other books you might like:
Clare Bell, *The Jaguar Princess*, 1993
Christina Dodd, *Wilder*, 2012
Diane Duane, *The Book of Night with Moon*, 1997
Christine Feehan, *Savage Nature*, 2011
Thea Harrison, *Dragon Bound*, 2011
Marjorie M. Liu, *The Wild Road*, 2008
Pamela Palmer, *Hunger Untamed*, 2011
Jennifer Roberson, *The Lion Throne*, 2001
Christopher Stasheff, *The Feline Wizard*, 2000
Tad Williams, *Tailchaser's Song*, 1986

9

VICTORIA AVEYARD

Red Queen
(New York: HarperTeen, 2015)

Series: Red Queen Series. Book 1
Story type: Dystopian; Series
Subject(s): Fantasy; Dystopias; Social class
Major character(s): Mare Barrow, 17-Year-Old, Young
    Woman (peasant); Maven, Young Man, Royalty
    (prince)
Time period(s): Indeterminate
Locale(s): Norta, Fictional Location

Summary: The first novel in the Red Queen series
introduces a dystopian world in which social standing is
determined by blood color. The commoners bleed red
blood, while silver blood courses through the veins of
the royal family and other members of the elite class.
The Silvers have paranormal powers that further set them
apart from the Reds. Seventeen-year-old Mare Barrow is
a Red. She knows that she has little hope of escaping her
destiny, so she makes her way in the world by thieving
and trying to avoid being forced into military service.
But after an unexpected series of events, Mare makes
her way to the palace. It is there that she discovers that
her ancestry is both Red and Silver—and that she possesses her own magical talents. The royal family tries to
pass Mare off as a relative and marry her to Prince
Maven. However, Mare may want to use her magic to
help the Red rebellion that's rising against the Silvers.
First novel.

Other books you might like:
Karen Bao, *Dove Arising*, 2015
Holly Black, *The Darkest Part of the Forest*, 2015
Pierce Brown, *Red Rising*, 2014
Cassandra Clare, *City of Ashes: The Mortal Instruments*,
    2009
Suzanne Collins, *Hunger Games Trilogy*, 2008
Bruce Coville, *The Last Hunt*, 2010
Galaxy Craze, *The Last Princess*, 2012
Sarah J. Maas, *A Court of Thorns and Roses*, 2015
Dianne Salerni, *The Inquisitor's Mark*, 2015
Diane Stanley, *The Chosen Prince*, 2015
Sabaa Tahir, *An Ember in the Ashes*, 2015
J.D. Vaughn, *The Second Guard*, 2015

10

PHILIPPA BALLANTINE
TEE MORRIS, Co-Author

The Diamond Conspiracy
(New York: Ace Books, 2015)

Series: Ministry of Peculiar Occurrences Series. Book 4
Story type: Series; Steampunk
Subject(s): Steampunk; Fantasy; Mystery
Major character(s): Eliza Braun, Agent (Ministry of
    Peculiar Occurrences); Wellington Brooks, Agent
    (Ministry of Peculiar Occurrences)
Time period(s): 19th century
Locale(s): London, England

Summary: Ministry of Peculiar Occurrences agents Eliza
Braun and Wellington Brooks are on their way home following an assignment. When they receive word that other
Ministry agents are in danger, however, they rush back
to London to learn that the Ministry has been disavowed
by the monarchy. Without any legitimacy, the agents are
soon being tracked by the Department of Imperial
Inconveniences, which intends to find and kill them to
wipe out any trace of the Ministry's existence. Brooks
and Braun won't stand for that, however—they know
who is behind this, and they know that to save themselves
and their fellow agents, they need to somehow reach the
Queen. This steampunk fantasy is the fourth novel in the
Ministry of Peculiar Occurrences series by Tee Morris
and Philippa Ballantine.

Other books by the same author:
Dawn's Early Light, 2014
Kindred and Wings, 2013
The Janus Affair, 2012
Phoenix Rising, 2011
Spectyr, 2011

Other books you might like:
David G. Barnett, *Gideon Smith and the Mechanical
    Girl*, 2013
Gail Carriger, *Waistcoats and Weaponry*, 2014
Steven Harper, *The Impossible Cube*, 2012
Tim Powers, *The Anubis Gates*, 1983
Cherie Priest, *Ganymede*, 2011

11

STEVE BEIN

Disciple of the Wind
(London: Penguin Group, 2015)

Series: Fated Blades Series. Book 3
Story type: Contemporary; Occult
Subject(s): Japanese (Asian people); Terrorism; Occultism
Major character(s): Mariko Oshiro, Rogue, Detective—
    Police
Time period(s): 21st century; 2010s
Locale(s): Tokyo, Japan

Summary: When a terrorist attack hits Tokyo, police detective Mariko Oshiro wants justice. She knows who the
perpetrator is, but she just doesn't have the evidence to

prove it. Her superiors, however, do not share her convictions. When she pushes her argument too far and loses her temper, she finds herself off the force and out of a job. To hunt down the terrorist mastermind, Mariko must go it alone, relying only on her investigative skills and her cursed Inazuma sword. But her efforts have also attracted the attention of Japanese crime syndicate, the Wind, a group with its own powerful, mystical relics. Mariko has to make a choice: join forces with evil to capture evil or remain loyal to the law that abandoned her. This is the third book in Steve Bein's Fated Blades series.

Other books by the same author:
Daughter of the Sword, 2013
Year of the Demon, 2013

Other books you might like:
Elizabeth Bear, *Shattered Pillars*, 2013
Laurell K. Hamilton, *Blood Noir*, 2008
Richard A. Lupoff, *Sword of the Demon*, 1976
Lindsey Piper, *Hunted Warrior*, 2015
James Rollins, *Innocent Blood*, 2013
Diana Rowland, *Mark of the Demon*, 2009

`12`

JOHN BIRMINGHAM

Resistance: Dave vs. the Monsters

(New York: Del Rey, 2015)

Series: David Hooper Trilogy. Book 2
Story type: Series; Urban
Subject(s): Fantasy; Violence; Sexuality
Major character(s): Dave Hooper, Vigilante (monster slayer)
Time period(s): 21st century; 2010s
Locale(s): Las Vegas, Nevada

Summary: In this second novel in the David Hooper Trilogy by John Birmingham, champion monster slayer Dave has decided to head to Las Vegas after his success—and his newfound wealth—in New Orleans. He's ready to party, and he doesn't hold back, enjoying the taste of fame and fortune that his skills have finally brought him. He's living it up, at least until the monsters from the UnderRealms make their next move. Dave avoids the amateurish trap they set for him, but he knows another battle is just around the corner. And when a beautiful Russian spy suddenly appears in Dave's life, he thinks he knows what the next move is going to be—but that doesn't mean he can't have a little fun first.

Other books by the same author:
Ascendance: Dave vs. the Monsters, 2015
Emergence: Dave vs. the Monsters, 2015
After America, 2010
Without Warning, 2009
Final Impact, 2007

Other books you might like:
Jim Butcher, *Blood Rites*, 2004
Larry Correia, *Monster Hunter Nemesis*, 2014
Simon R. Green, *Something from the Nightside*, 2003

Kat Richardson, *Greywalker*, 2006
Anton Strout, *Stonecast*, 2013

`13`

JOHN BIRMINGHAM

Ascendance: Dave vs. the Monsters

(New York: Del Rey, 2015)

Series: David Hooper Trilogy. Book 3
Story type: Series; Urban
Subject(s): Monsters; Fantasy; Violence
Major character(s): Dave Hooper, Vigilante (monster slayer); Karin Varatschevsky, Spy, Vigilante (monster slayer), Assassin
Time period(s): 21st century; 2010s
Locale(s): Los Angeles, California

Summary: In this third and final novel in the David Hooper Trilogy by John Birmingham, champion monster slayer Dave and his partner, beautiful Russian spy and assassin Karin Varatschevsky, are kept busy by the Horde that has been relentlessly attacking cities across the United States. But when the small town where his family lives is attacked, Dave's ex-wife demands his help. This puts Dave in a spot, because giving in to her demands might mean failing in his duties to protect the world. And to be honest, he's not exactly thrilled about saving the woman who made his life miserable, and now refuses to believe that Karin is his partner, not his girlfriend. But a monster slayer's work is never done, and Dave knows he owes this to his family, no matter the consequences.

Other books by the same author:
Emergence: Dave vs. the Monsters, 2015
Resistance: Dave vs. the Monsters, 2015
After America, 2010
Without Warning, 2009
Final Impact, 2007

Other books you might like:
Jim Butcher, *Fool Moon*, 2001
Harry Connolly, *Game of Cages*, 2010
Seanan McGuire, *Pocket Apocalypse*, 2015
Dean Wesley Smith, *The Green Saliva Blues*, 1999
Rob Thurman, *All Seeing Eye*, 2012

`14`

JOHN BIRMINGHAM

Emergence: Dave vs. the Monsters

(New York: Del Rey, 2015)

Series: David Hooper Trilogy. Book 1
Story type: Series; Urban
Subject(s): Fantasy; Monsters; Demons
Major character(s): Dave Hooper, Worker, Vigilante (monster slayer)
Time period(s): 21st century; 2010s
Locale(s): United States

Summary: In this first novel in the David Hooper Trilogy by John Birmingham, Dave is just an ordinary guy who works on an oil rig. Dave has a fondness for hookers and booze. All he really wants in life is to avoid the IRS and his miserable ex-wife. But when an explosion and attack on the rig occurs one night, Dave suddenly finds himself face-to-face with a seven-foot-tall demon. Dave kills the thing, and the next thing he knows, he wakes up in a hospital bed, surrounded by Navy SEALs. Though the news is calling it a terrorist attack, everyone knows better—and suddenly, Dave finds himself thrust into a most unlikely new role. Dave is now a monster slayer responsible for saving all of humanity.

Other books by the same author:
Ascendance, 2015
Resistance, 2015
After America, 2010
Without Warning, 2009
Final Impact, 2007

Other books you might like:
Jaci Burton, *Hunting the Demon*, 2007
Larry Correia, *Monster Hunter Alpha*, 2011
Casey Daniels, *Don of the Dead*, 2006
Simon R. Green, *The Good, the Bad, and the Uncanny*, 2010
Seanan McGuire, *Half-Off Ragnarok*, 2014

15

ANNE BISHOP

Vision in Silver

(New York: Roc, 2015)

Series: Others Series. Book 3
Story type: Contemporary; Series
Subject(s): Fantasy; Prophecy; Magic
Major character(s): Meg Corbyn, Prophet (blood prophet); Simon Wolfgard, Shape-Shifter
Time period(s): 21st century; 2010s
Locale(s): United States

Summary: Meg Corbyn is a *cassandra sangue*, a blood prophet who can foretell the future by reading the blood that spills from her self-inflicted wounds. Her gift has made her the target of dark forces in the past, and now Meg is being called on once again to use her powers. This time Simon Wolfgard, a shape-shifter who serves as the leader of the Others, seeks Meg's help. Simon knows he is asking a lot of Meg, but the Others have no other way of getting the information they need. In addition to the threats imposed upon Meg by enemies who want to control her, Meg is also dealing with an internal struggle. She knows how dangerous her cutting is, but she can't seem to resist the urge to bleed and prophesy. This novel is the third in the Others series by Anne Bishop.

Other books by the same author:
Murder of Crows, 2014
Written in Red, 2013
Bridge of Dreams, 2012
Belladonna, 2007
Dreams Made Flesh, 2005

Other books you might like:
Patricia Briggs, *Dead Heat*, 2015
Kim Harrison, *A Perfect Blood*, 2012

Katharine Kerr, *Love on the Run*, 2012
Laura Resnick, *Vamparazzi*, 2011
Tad Williams, *Happy Hour in Hell*, 2013

16

MARIE BRENNAN

Voyage of the Basilisk: A Memoir by Lady Trent

(New York: Tom Doherty Associates, 2015)

Series: Natural History of Dragons Series. Book 3
Story type: Adventure; Alternate World
Subject(s): Dragons; Adventure; Interpersonal relations
Major character(s): Lady Isabella Camherst, Noblewoman (the Lady Trent), Naturalist (expert in dragons), Mother (of Jake); Jacob "Jake" Camherst, Son (of Isabella); Tom, Archaeologist, Traveler
Locale(s): the *Basilisk*, At Sea

Summary: Isabella Camherst, the Lady Trent, is a much admired Victorian lady who just happens to also be an expert in dragons. In this third in a series of memoirs of her adventures in search of the creatures, Isabella and her son, Jake, are setting off on a ship called the *Basilisk* on a two-year dragon study trip. Their around-the-world adventures will take them to exotic places as they discover several different types of dragons. The voyage will also be complicated by the presence of a foreign gentleman, Tom. This archaeologist shares Isabella's fascination with dragons, and interests the widowed Lady Trent in other ways as well. Isabella triumphs scientifically when she makes a remarkable discovery, but a shipwreck tests her mettle on this adventure.

Other books by the same author:
The Tropic of Serpents, 2014
A Natural History of Dragons: A Memoir by Lady Trent, 2013
A Star Shall Fall, 2010
Midnight Never Comes, 2008
Witch, 2006

Other books you might like:
Pip Ballantine, *Dawn's Early Light*, 2014
Susanna Clarke, *Jonathan Strange & Mr. Norrell*, 2004
Esther M. Friesner, *Druid's Blood*, 1988
Mercedes Lackey, *Phoenix and Ashes*, 2004
Robert V.S. Redick, *River of Shadows*, 2011

17

PETER V. BRETT

The Skull Throne

(New York: Del Rey, 2015)

Series: Demon Cycle Series. Book 4
Story type: Ancient Evil Unleashed; Series
Subject(s): Fantasy; Demons; Adventure
Major character(s): Ahmann Jardir, Ruler (former, of Krasia), Spouse (former, of Inevera); Arlen Bales,

Enemy (deceased, of Ahmann Jardir), Spouse (former, of Renna Bales); Inevera, Spouse (former, of Ahmann Jardir); Renna Bales, Spouse (former, of Arlen Bales)
Time period(s): Indeterminate
Locale(s): Krasia, Fictional Location

Summary: Krasia is a changed place since the realm's ruler, Ahmann Jardir, and Jardir's challenger, Arlen Bales, fell from a cliff. The men have not been seen since. Without a king to sit on the Skull Throne, Krasia is more susceptible than ever to the demons that hunt at night. The corelings have already culled the human population drastically, and the demon forces are now gaining strength. The territory is also fraught with personal and political problems. An alliance is in the works in the north that is designed to protect duchies that are threatened by the Krasians. Jardidr's former wife is trying to control her sons, whose ongoing feud will have far-reaching repercussions. Meanwhile, Renna Bales—who was married to Arlen—has important information, but she has gone missing.

Other books by the same author:
The Daylight War, 2013
The Desert Spear, 2010
The Warded Man, 2009

Other books you might like:
Joe Abercrombie, *Last Argument of Kings: The First Law*, 2008
Dave Duncan, *The Jaguar Knights*, 2004
David Gemmell, *Hero in the Shadows: Waylander the Slayer Stalks an Ancient Evil*, 2000
Ari Marmell, *The Warlord's Legacy*, 2011
L.E. Modesitt Jr., *Lady-Protector*, 2011

18

PATRICIA BRIGGS

Dead Heat

(New York: Ace, 2015)

Series: Alpha and Omega Series. Book 4
Story type: Alternate World; Contemporary
Subject(s): Fantasy; Werewolves; Adventure
Major character(s): Charles Cornick, Werewolf, Worker (enforcer for his father), Lover (of Anna Latham); Anna Latham, Werewolf, Lover (of Charles)
Time period(s): 21st century; 2010s
Locale(s): Arizona, United States

Summary: In the fourth novel in the Alpha and Omega series, werewolf shape-shifters Charles Cornick and Anna Latham travel to Arizona for a romantic getaway. Charles is planning to surprise Anna with an extravagant birthday gift—a horse—and Anna is hoping that for once Charles is beyond the reach of his demanding father. But Charles and Anna's itinerary changes when they learn that dark forces are at work in Arizona. Evil Fae are stealing human children and leaving impostors in their places. The human-Fae conflict that's been simmering below the surface is about to erupt, and Charles and Anna find themselves in the wrong place at the wrong time.

Other books by the same author:
Night Broken, 2014
Frost Burned, 2013
River Marked, 2011
Hunting Ground, 2009
Dragon Blood, 2003

Other books you might like:
Cat Adams, *Blood Song*, 2010
Kelley Armstrong, *Broken*, 2006
Anne Bishop, *Murder of Crows*, 2014
Anne Bishop, *Vision in Silver*, 2015
Laurell K. Hamilton, *Dead Ice*, 2015
Laurell K. Hamilton, *Jason*, 2014
Laurell K. Hamilton, *A Kiss of Shadows*, 2000
Carrie Vaughn, *Kitty Goes to War*, 2010

19

KRISTEN CALLIHAN

Soulbound

(New York: Forever Books, 2015)

Series: Darkest London Series. Book 6
Story type: Paranormal; Romance
Subject(s): Steampunk; Demons; Fairies
Major character(s): Adam, Royalty (King of GIM), Demon (soul mate of Eliza), Prisoner (of Mab); Mab, Royalty (Queen of Fae), Aunt (of Eliza); Eliza May, Woman (soul mate of Adam), Niece (of Mab)
Locale(s): London, England

Summary: Eliza May owed the demon Adam her life after she was murdered on the smoky streets of Victorian London. However, she did not realize that accepting his offer of salvation would chain her to him as a slave. Adam recognizes Eliza for what she truly is—his soul mate—and only through her presence can he truly be free. When Eliza escapes she lands in the house of her aunt, Mab. Mab is the Queen of the Fae and sets about grooming Eliza as a member of the court. At first Eliza relishes her freedom and the luxurious lifestyle of Mab's household, but soon the underlying cruelty and lascivi- ousness begins to grate upon her. When Mab captures Adam, Eliza realizes that she doesn't hate him. She frees him and flees Mab's house with Adam. Adam is deter- mined to make her understand that only by staying together can they both find true freedom. This is the sixth book in the Darkest London series.

Other books by the same author:
Evernight, 2014
Winterblaze, 2013
Ember, 2012
Firelight, 2012
Moonglow, 2012

Other books you might like:
Kresley Cole, *A Hunger Like No Other*, 2006
Larissa Ione, *Rogue Rider*, 2012
Katie MacAlister, *Holy Smokes*, 2007
Katie MacAlister, *Playing With Fire*, 2008
Nalini Singh, *Blaze of Memory*, 2009

20

JANET LEE CAREY

In the Time of the Dragon Moon
(New York: Penguin Young Readers, 2015)

Series: Dragon's Keep Series. Book 3
Story type: Mystical; Young Adult
Subject(s): Father-daughter relations; Dragons; Kidnapping
Major character(s): Uma Quarteney, Young Woman, Daughter (of Euit healer), Hostage, Friend (of Jackrun), Healer; Jackrun Pendragon, Young Man (dragonrider), Royalty (prince), Friend (of Uma), Supernatural Being (human, dragon, and fairy), Cousin (of Desmond), Nephew (of Adela); Adela Pendragon, Mother (of Desmond), Aunt (of Jackrun), Royalty (queen); Desmond Pendragon, Royalty (prince), Son (of Adela), Cousin (of Jackrun)
Time period(s): Indeterminate Past
Locale(s): Wilde Island, Fictional Location

Summary: Young Uma, born of an Euit father and English mother, has dreams of becoming the next healer of her father's tribe. But those dreams are torn away when the English queen Adela Pendragon, desperate to conceive an heir to the throne, hears of a fertility treatment developed by Uma's father. Adela kidnaps the pair and demands they help her. When Uma's father dies, the unstable queen demands the girl complete the task by the time of the Dragon Moon, or she will be executed. Uma's only hope is a member of the royal family, Jackrun, a dragonrider in whose veins runs fairy, dragon, and human blood. Together, they must solve a murder, skirt deadly intrigue, and uncover the dark secrets of royalty to survive. This is the third book in Janet Lee Carey's Dragon's Keep series.

Other books by the same author:
Dragonswood, 2012
Stealing Death, 2009
Dragon's Keep, 2007
Talon, 2007
The Beast of Noor, 2006

Other books you might like:
Kate Elliott, *The Gathering Storm*, 2003
Alan Dean Foster, *Kingdoms of Light*, 2001
Simon R. Green, *Blue Moon Rising*, 1991
Michael Moorcock, *Elric in the Dream Realms*, 2009
Michelle Paver, *The Eye of the Falcon*, 2015

21

VIOLA CARR

The Diabolical Miss Hyde
(New York: Harper Voyager, 2015)

Series: Electric Empire Series. Book 1
Story type: Historical - Victorian; Series
Subject(s): Fantasy; History; Steampunk
Major character(s): Dr. Eliza Jekyll, Doctor, Investigator, Daughter (of Dr. Henry Jekyll), Woman (also known as Lizzie Hyde); Remy Lafeyette, Agent (Royal Society); Slicer, Serial Killer
Locale(s): London, England

Summary: Dr. Eliza Jekyll is a gifted scientist, as was her father Dr. Henry Jekyll. Like her father, Eliza is susceptible to the effects of a certain potion that transforms her into the wild woman Lizzie Hyde. She must resist her craving for the potion, however, or she could jeopardize her standing in society and her position as a crime scene investigator. Eliza is currently working on an especially gruesome case that involves a serial killer known as the Slicer. After subduing his female victims with drugs, the Slicer dismembers them and takes their limbs. As Eliza searches for a madman in Victorian London, the Royal Society dispatches one of its members, Remy Lafayette, to investigate Eliza. The society suspects that Eliza has magic powers, which they want to expose. Eliza must keep Lizzie Hyde hidden if she wants to keep Lafayette from discovering her secret. First novel.

Other books you might like:
Tim Akers, *Dead of Veridon*, 2011
Kristen Callihan, *Moonglow*, 2012
Gordon Dahlquist, *The Dark Volume*, 2009
Delilah Dawson, *Wicked After Midnight*, 2014
Tracy Fobes, *Forbidden Garden*, 2000
Ari Marmell, *In Thunder Forged*, 2013
Bec McMaster, *Kiss of Steel*, 2012
Devon Monk, *Dead Iron*, 2011
S.M. Peters, *Whitechapel Gods*, 2008
Amanda Quick, *Crystal Gardens*, 2012

22

GAIL CARRIGER

Prudence
(London: Orbit, 2015)

Series: Custard Protocol Series. Book 1
Story type: Series; Steampunk
Subject(s): Fantasy; Steampunk; Adventure
Major character(s): Prudence "Rue" Alessandra Maccon Akeldama, Daughter (of Lord Akeldama and Alexia), 20-Year-Old, Friend (of Primrose Tunstell), Psychic (borrows powers of werewolves and vampires); Lord Akeldama, Vampire, Spouse (of Alexia), Father (of Prudence), Wealthy; Alexia, Spouse (of Lord Akeldama), Mother (of Prudence); Primrose Tunstell, Young Woman, Friend (of Prudence)
Locale(s): London, England; Bombay, India

Summary: The first novel in the Custard Protocol series, a follow-up to the Parasol Protectorate series, introduces 20-year-old Prudence "Rue" Alessandra Maccon Akeldama. The daughter of a vampire father, Lord Akeldama, and a paranormally gifted mother, Alexia, Rue is able to assume the powers of werewolves and other supernatural creatures with which she comes into contact. And in the Victorian steampunk London Rue inhabits, there are many such creatures. When Lord Akeldama sends Rue and her friend Primrose Tunstell to India in search of a special tea, Rue encounters some of Bombay's more unusual residents. Rue and Primrose fly east in a zeppelin dubbed the *Spotted Custard*. In the bustling exotic city, the young women are drawn into an adventure that includes politics, kidnapping, and werewolves. Rue does her best to play the role of lady as she tries to untangle a complex scheme.

Other books by the same author:
Waistcoats and Weaponry, 2014
Etiquette and Espionage, 2013
Timeless, 2012
Heartless, 2011
Blameless, 2010

Other books you might like:
James P. Blaylock, *The Aylesford Skull*, 2013
Thomas Brennan, *Doktor Glass*, 2012
Mark Hodder, *The Strange Affair of Spring Heeled Jack*, 2010
Andrew Mayer, *The Falling Machine*, 2011
Devon Monk, *Cold Copper*, 2013
Cherie Priest, *Jacaranda*, 2015

23

BETH CATO

The Clockwork Crown
(New York: Harper Voyager, 2015)

Story type: Romance; Steampunk
Subject(s): Magic; Healing; Questing
Major character(s): Octavia Leander, Healer, Lover (of Alonzo); Alonzo Garrett, Assassin, Lover (of Octavia)
Time period(s): Indeterminate
Locale(s): Caskentia, Fictional Location

Summary: The sequel to *The Clockwork Dagger* continues the story of magical healer Octavia Leander and her lover, Alonzo Garrett. Octavia is still struggling to understand and control her expanded abilities. Together Octavia and Alonzo seek information about the Lady, whose tree may be the source of Octavia's abilities. Alonzo and Octavia must journey into the desolation of the Wastes to find the Lady's Tree. War between Caskentia and the Dallows is consuming the lands as the bitterness between the rival territories increases. The rebels in the Wastes are determined to break free from Caskentia, and they believe that they need Octavia's powers to succeed. Caskentian forces are equally determined not to allow Octavia or her healing gifts into the hands of their enemies. Octavia and Alonzo find themselves in danger of death and betrayal at every turn.

Other books by the same author:
The Deepest Poison, 2015
The Clockwork Dagger, 2014

Other books you might like:
David G. Barnett, *Gideon Smith and the Mechanical Girl*, 2013
Thomas Brennan, *Doktor Glass*, 2012
Gail Carriger, *Blameless*, 2010
Andrew Mayer, *The Falling Machine*, 2011
Devon Monk, *Cold Copper*, 2013
Ian Tregillis, *The Mechanical*, 2015

24

ANDY CHAMBERS

Path of the Dark Eldar
(Nottingham, United Kingdom: Black Library, 2015)

Series: Warhammer 40,000: Dark Eldar Path Series
Story type: Anthology; Collection
Subject(s): Elves; Wars; Civil war
Major character(s): Asdrubael Vect, Leader (of the Dark Eldar)
Time period(s): Indeterminate
Locale(s): Commorragh, Fictional Location

Summary: This is an omnibus edition collecting the novels of the Path of the Dark Eldar series: *Path of the Renegade*, *Path of the Archon*, and *Path of the Incubus*. The dark eldar are humanoids who often live as pirates and mercenaries. Enslavement and torture are common enough in their society, much of which resides in the city of Commorragh. The supreme leader of the dark eldar is Asdrubael Vect, a one-time slave and founder of the Kabal of the Black Heart. The series traces Vect's battles to retain his power and control over the dark eldar against his enemies and the Dysjunction. Those who stand against him lead the city of Commorragh into horrors and open war. Vect must be absolutely ruthless even against his own people if he is to retain both his life and his grip on power.

Other books by the same author:
Path of the Archon, 2014
Path of the Incubus, 2013
Path of the Renegade, 2012
Survival Instinct, 2005

Other books you might like:
John French, *Ahriman: Exile*, 2013
Nick Kyme, *Tome of Fire*, 2012
Steven Savile, *Curse of the Necrarch*, 2008
Mitchel Scanlon, *Call to Arms*, 2010
C.L. Werner, *Deathblade: A Tale of Malus Darkblade*, 2015

25

DAVID B. COE

Spell Blind
(Riverdale, New York: Baen, 2015)

Series: Justis Fearsson Series. Book 1
Story type: Contemporary; Mystery
Subject(s): Fantasy; Urban life; Mystery
Major character(s): Justis Fearsson, Detective—Private, Supernatural Being (weremystes); Blind Angel, Serial Killer
Time period(s): 21st century; 2010s
Locale(s): Phoenix, Arizona

Summary: A serial killer is at work in Phoenix, Arizona, who mutilates the bodies of his victims in a unique way: He burns their eyeballs out of their sockets. Private detective Justis Fearsson knows that the Blind Angel—as the serial murderer has been called—accomplishes his gruesome task through magic. Justis is a weremyste, a magically gifted human who has ties to the supernatural realm. Like others of his kind, Justis has adverse reactions to a full moon. For Justis, the Blind Angel case brings back memories of the time he spent on the police force. The same murderer went on a previous spree that was never solved. Now it looks as though Justis is getting a second chance to stop him. The Blind Angel is cunning, however. He has already claimed several victims, and he may make Justis one of his targets. This is the first novel in the Justis Fearsson series.

Other books by the same author:
The Dark-Eyes' War, 2010
The Horseman's Gambit, 2008
The Sorcerers' Plague, 2007
Shapers of Darkness, 2005
Rules of Ascension, 2002

Other books you might like:
Jim Butcher, *Cold Days*, 2012
Harry Connolly, *Child of Fire*, 2009
Simon R. Green, *The Man with the Golden Torc*, 2007
Simon Hawke, *The Wizard of Santa Fe*, 1991
Ben Macallan, *Pandaemonium*, 2012

26

MYKE COLE

Gemini Cell
(New York: Penguin Publishing Group, 2015)

Series: Shadow Ops Series
Story type: Adventure; Military
Subject(s): Fantasy; Science fiction; Military life
Major character(s): Jim Schweitzer, Military Personnel (Navy SEAL), Reanimated Dead
Time period(s): Indeterminate Future
Locale(s): United States

Summary: As a Navy SEAL, Myke Cole is bound by a sense of duty to his country and loyalty to his family. When he witnesses suspicious activity, he questions it instead of keeping quiet. He realizes that his actions have put his wife and child in danger, but he is determined to protect them from harm. When payback time arrives, Jim is killed. He dies without knowing what happened to his family. Jim's death is only temporary, however. He is resurrected and trained to be part of a new breed of fighter. His reanimation comes at a cost. Jim must struggle against his sinister commanders and the darkness that has taken hold inside him as searches for answers about the strange world he has awakened in and the whereabouts of his family. This events in this novel precede the story line of Myke Cole's *Control Point*, which is the first entry in the Shadow Ops series.

Other books by the same author:
Breach Zone, 2014
Fortress Frontier, 2013
Control Point, 2012

Other books you might like:
Glen Cook, *Soldiers Live*, 2000
Stan Nicholls, *Orcs*, 2004

Weston Ochse, *Seal Team 666*, 2012
Joel Shepherd, *Tracato*, 2010
David Sherman, *Gulf Run*, 2004

27

ROWENA CORY DANIELLS

The Fall of Fair Isle
(Oxford, United Kingdom: Solaris, 2015)

Story type: Adventure; Collection
Subject(s): Fantasy; Wars; Loyalty
Major character(s): Imoshen, Mythical Creature (a throwback, last pureblood female T'En); Reothe, Mythical Creature (a throwback, last pureblood male T'En), Rebel (Leader of rebellion against Ghebite); Tulkhan, Military Personnel (General of Ghebite, invader of Fair Isle)
Time period(s): Indeterminate
Locale(s): Fair Isle, Fictional Location

Summary: It has been 600 years since the T'En were banished in the Outcast Chronicles, by author Rowena Daniells. Imoshen the First is long gone, and much of the wisdom and lore of her people has been lost or set aside. This is the world of another Imoshen, a descendant of the First, and the last pure-blooded woman of her kind. True T'En like Imoshen are called throwbacks. Direct descendants of those who founded Fair Isle, throwbacks have special responsibility to their people. Reothe, the last male throwback, is fulfilling that requirement by leading a rebellion against General Tulkhan, an invader from Ghebite, who has taken over Fair Isle. Both throwbacks know their duty, but their willingness to fulfill their roles will be challenged when they meet and fall in love. This omnibus contains *Broken Vows*, *Dark Dreams*, and *Desperate Alliances*.

Other books by the same author:
Besieged, 2012
Exile, 2012
Sanctuary, 2012
The King's Bastard, 2010
The Uncrowned King, 2010

Other books you might like:
Sara Douglass, *Beyond the Hanging Wall*, 2003
Kate Elliott, *Cold Fire*, 2011
Jennifer Fallon, *The Immortal Prince*, 2008
Katharine Kerr, *The Shadow Isle*, 2008
Tad Williams, *Caliban's Hour*, 1994

28

JENNIFER DONNELLY

Rogue Wave
(New York: Disney-Hyperion, 2015)

Series: Waterfire Saga. Book 2
Story type: Series; Young Adult
Subject(s): Fantasy; Adventure; Mermaids
Major character(s): Serafina, Teenager, Mythical Creature

Fantasy

(mermaid); Neela, Teenager, Mythical Creature (mermaid); Ling, Teenager, Mythical Creature (mermaid); Ava, Mythical Creature (mermaid), Teenager; Becca, Teenager, Mythical Creature (mermaid); Astrid, Teenager, Mythical Creature (mermaid)

Time period(s): Indeterminate

Locale(s): At Sea

Summary: In the first book in the Waterfire Saga, teenage mermaid Serafina and her friends learned that their ancestors were the rulers of Atlantis. The continent was destroyed by sinister magic, and that dark force is on the verge of returning. Now the mermaids must locate the artifacts that the Six Who Ruled once possessed. This second series entry follows Serafina and her friend Neela as they search for their talismans. Serafina hones in on a sunken ship, believing that the relic she needs is buried with it. She narrowly escapes being caught by a death rider patrol and is shocked when she realizes that the patrol leader is someone who broke her heart in the past. Neela visits her family to tell them about the rising threat, but she flees when her parents refuse to believe her. When Neela tries to retrieve her artifact, she finds herself face-to-face with the razormouth dragons who possess it.

Other books by the same author:
Deep Blue, 2014

Other books you might like:
Charles de Lint, *Our Lady of the Harbor*, 1991
Esther M. Friesner, *Yesterday We Saw Mermaids*, 1992
Vonda N. McIntyre, *The Moon and the Sun*, 1997
Alida Van Gores, *Mermaid's Song*, 1989
Jane Yolen, *Neptune Rising: Songs and Tales of the Undersea Folk*, 1982

29

KATE ELLIOTT

The Very Best of Kate Elliott

(San Francisco: Tachyon Publications, 2015)

Story type: Collection

Subject(s): Fantasy; Imagination; Short stories

Summary: This short fiction collection includes work from fantasy writer Kate Elliott encompassing more than 20 years of her career. It includes many of her earlier out of print titles along with four unpublished essays and a new release, "On the Dying Winds of the Old Year and the Birthing Winds of the New," from her Crossroads Story series. Kate Elliot has published more than 30 novels in her writing career. Such titles as "The Memory of Peace," "The Queen's Garden," and "Riding the Shore of the River of Death" are included in this collection.

Other books by the same author:
Traitor's Gate, 2099
Cold Fire, 2011
Cold Magic, 2010
Shadow Gate, 2008
In the Ruins, 2005

Other books you might like:
Barbara Hambly, *Circle of the Moon*, 2005

Nina Kiriki Hoffman, *Permeable Borders*, 2012
Katharine Kerr, *The Red Wyvern*, 1997
Dennis L. McKiernan, *Red Slippers*, 2004
Diana L. Paxson, *The Golden Hills of Westria*, 2006

30

STEVEN ERIKSON

Fall of Light

(New York: Tor Books, 2015)

Series: Kharkanas Trilogy. Book 2

Story type: Adventure; Magic Conflict

Subject(s): Adventure; Deception; Demons

Major character(s): Mother Darkness, Deity (goddess), Mother (of Anomander, Andarist and Sichas Ruin), Ruler (of Kurald Galain, the realm of darkness); Vatha Urusander, Leader (in Urursander Legion), Man; Lord Draconus, Deity (Elder God), Lover (of Mother Darkness), Demon (winged darkness); Anomander Rake, Brother (of Andarist and Silchas Ruin), Shape-Shifter (dragon), Son (of Mother Darkness), Supernatural Being; Andarist, Brother (ofAndomander and Silchas Ruin), Son (of Mother Darkness), Shape-Shifter, Supernatural Being; Silchas Ruin, Brother (of Anomander and Andarist), Shape-Shifter (albino dragon), Son (of Mother Darkness), Supernatural Being

Time period(s): Indeterminate

Locale(s): Kurald Galain, Realm of Darkness, Fictional Location

Summary: Kurald Galan is devastated by civil war. Amidst the cold winter, Ursurander's Legion plans to attack the city of Kharkanas. The enemy is without its rightful leader now that Anomander has abandoned his throne and has embarked on a mission to locate his estranged brother, Andarist. Anomander has left their other brother, Silchas Ruin, to protect and lead Kharkanas. The ruling members of Urursander's Legion are playing politics by pushing for Vatha Ursurander to marry the Mother of Darkness, but Lord Draconus stands in the way of the suggested union. To the west, an army is rising. Tensions are growing and magic is bleeding into the world, causing ancient and new evils to arise. This is the second novel in the Kharkanas Trilogy by Steven Erikson, which predates events of his Malazan novels.

Other books by the same author:
Forge of Darkness, 2012
The Wurms of Blearmouth, 2012
Dust of Dreams, 2009
House of Chains, 2002
Deadhouse Gates, 2000

Other books you might like:
Steven Brust, *Iorich*, 2010
Ian C. Esslemont, *Blood and Bone*, 2012
L.E. Modesitt Jr., *Princeps*, 2012
Patrick Rothfuss, *The Name of the Wind*, 2007
Brandon Sanderson, *Firefight*, 2015

31

STEVEN ERIKSON

Forge of Darkness
(New York: Tor, 2012)

Series: Kharkanas Trilogy. Book 1
Story type: Magic Conflict; Series
Subject(s): Magic; Fantasy; Wars
Major character(s): Mother Dark, Ruler; Vatha Urusander, Hero; Lord Draconus, Nobleman, Lover (of Mother Dark)
Time period(s): Indeterminate
Locale(s): Kurald Galain, Fictional Location

Summary: In the first novel in Steven Erikson's Kharkanas Trilogy, the realm of Kurald Galain faces the prospect of civil war. Mother Dark is the ruler of the realm, but she is only the latest figure in the long history of the land to assert her power there. The subjects of Kurald Galain want their champion Vatha Urusander to marry Mother Dark. Lord Draconus, Mother Dark's lover, is opposed to the move. The dispute unsettles the region, and war seems inevitable. Meanwhile, the realm's lifeless waters reveal a long-hidden force. This trilogy is a prequel to Erikson's Malazan Book of the Fallen series.

Other books by the same author:
Crack'd Pot Trail, 2011
The Crippled God, 2011
Dust of Dreams, 2010
Bauchelain and Korbal Broach, 2009
The Bonehunters, 2007

Other books you might like:
Kate Elliott, *Cold Magic*, 2010
Ian C. Esslemont, *Blood and Bone*, 2012
Raymond E. Feist, *A Kingdom Besieged*, 2011
David Gemmell, *The Hawk Eternal*, 1996
Robert Jordan, *The Eye of the World*, 1990
Brandon Sanderson, *Elantris*, 2005

32

CATHERINE FISHER

The Door in the Moon
(New York: Dial Books, 2015)

Series: Chronoptika Series. Book 3
Story type: Series; Time Travel
Subject(s): Time travel; Friendship; History
Major character(s): Jake, Time Traveler, Friend (of Sarah); Sarah, Time Traveler, Friend (of Jake); Janus, Ruler (tyrant)
Time period(s): Multiple Time Periods
Locale(s): France

Summary: In this third novel in the Chronoptika fantasy series for young adults by Catherine Fisher, the obsidian mirror has brought a great deal of unwanted attention to Wintercombe Abbey and time travelers Jake and Sarah. While the Abbey is under attack by the fairy queen and her Shee, Jake and Sarah are kidnapped and taken back in time to the Reign of Terror, the French Revolution.

Meanwhile, Janus, a future ruler, is reaching back through the mirror to try to secure his power by any means necessary. Jake and Sarah will have to fight their way back to their own time and stop Janus before he brings destruction to the present and the future. At the same time, Jake still hopes to find and rescue his father, and their friends are searching for clues as to where and when Jake and Sarah have been taken.

Other books by the same author:
The Slanted Worlds, 2014
Sapphique, 2010
Incarceron, 2007
Day of the Scarab, 2006
Darkhenge, 2005

Other books you might like:
Maggie Furey, *Echo of Eternity*, 2003
Elizabeth Haydon, *The Merchant Emperor*, 2014
Mary Robinette Kowal, *Glamour in Glass*, 2012
Sarah Monette, *The Mirador*, 2007
Tad Williams, *Shadowheart*, 2010

33

SHARON LYNN FISHER

Echo 8
(New York: Tor Books, 2015)

Story type: Alternate World; Doppelganger
Subject(s): Alternative worlds; Deception; Romances (Fiction)
Major character(s): Tess, Woman, Paranormal Investigator (parapsychologist); Jake, Alien (aka Echo 8), Prisoner; Ross, Man, FBI Agent
Time period(s): Indeterminate Future
Locale(s): Alternative Earth; Earth

Summary: When doppelgangers or eEchoes start appearing on Earth, Tess, a parapsychologist who studies paranormal psychic phenomenon, is called in to investigate. These Echoes are from a parallel Earth that has been struck by an asteroid. The Echoes need to feed off human energy to survive, though this vampiric element is unexpected. To feed means to kill the human source. Tess is assigned to study a prisoner, Echo 8, named Jake. When Jake touches Tess and steals her energy, Tess survives and causes a ripple effect across both Earths. FBI agent Ross is assigned to protect Tess. Tess has feelings for her protector, and Jake becomes attracted to Tess. Eventually, Tess must choose, and Ross must weigh his feelings for Tess against his duty as an agent.

Other books by the same author:
The Ophelia Prophecy, 2014
Ghost Planet, 2012

Other books you might like:
Ben Aaronovitch, *Midnight Riot*, 2011
Marie Brennan, *Doppelganger*, 2006
Greg Cox, *A Touch of Fever*, 2011
Katharine Kerr, *Apocalypse to Go*, 2012
Devon Monk, *Magic in the Shadows*, 2009

34

CHARLIE FLETCHER

The London Pride

(New York: Hachette Children's, 2015)

Series: Dragon Shield Series. Book 2
Story type: Adventure; Contemporary - Fantasy
Subject(s): Adolescent interpersonal relations; Adventure; Supernatural
Major character(s): Jo Carter, Sister (of Will), Detective—Amateur; Will Carter, Brother (of Jo), Detective—Amateur
Time period(s): 21st century; 2010s
Locale(s): London, England

Summary: Sister and brother Jo and Will face even more trouble in this continuation of the Dragon Shield series. Something went very wrong in the British Museum, causing all the people to turn to statues and all the statues to come alive. The people all seem to still be alive, they just can't move, as if they are simply frozen in time. Somehow, Will and Jo are the only two humans not affected by this time freeze, and they have been trying to solve the mystery and reverse whatever dark and mysterious power has caused this to happen. The statues had been helping them dodge the dragons that are trying to stop them, but now the statues are frozen, too. Jo and Will must fight on alone—and they'd better hurry, because the frozen-in-place humans are getting colder and time seems to be running out for all of London.

Other books by the same author:
The Oversight, 2014
Silvertongue, 2009
Ironhand, 2008
Stoneheart, 2007

Other books you might like:
Dave Barry, *Peter and the Starcatchers*, 2004
Eoin Colfer, *Artemis Fowl*, 2001
Peter Dickinson, *The Weathermonger*, 1968
China Mieville, *Kraken*, 2010
Rick Riordan, *The Lost Hero*, 2010
Dianne Salerni, *The Inquisitor's Mark*, 2015

35

JACQUELYN FRANK

Cursed by Ice

(New York: Ballantine Books, 2015)

Series: Immortal Brothers Series. Book 2
Story type: Paranormal; Romance
Subject(s): Fantasy; Romances (Fiction); Mythology
Major character(s): Garreth, Man, Warrior, Captive, Immortal; Weysa, Deity (goddess of conflict); Sarielle, Woman, Warrior
Time period(s): Indeterminate
Locale(s): Fictional Location

Summary: In the second novel in the Immortal Brothers series, Garreth endures a chilling punishment for offending the gods. He and his brothers gained immortality when they found the fountain of eternal life, and now Garreth is sentenced to be repeatedly frozen and thawed for the rest of time. When Weysa, the goddess of conflict, needs Garreth's help in a battle among the gods, she offers him a reprieve from his punishment. If he agrees to fight for her, he will only be frozen for a portion of each day. Back in the mortal world, Garreth prepares for battle in Kith. But when he arrives in the city, he finds a warrior woman named Sarielle who has been imprisoned there. Kith's leader fears Sarielle because she controls a powerful dragon. Garreth is smitten with Sarielle and frees her, even though he is unsure of the repercussions his actions will have.

Other books by the same author:
Cursed by Fire, 2015
Forged, 2014
Forever, 2013
Ecstasy, 2009
Damien, 2008

Other books you might like:
Yasmine Galenorn, *Night Myst*, 2010
Faith Hunter, *Black Arts*, 2014
Larissa Ione, *Ecstasy Unveiled*, 2010
Marjorie M. Liu, *The Wild Road*, 2008
Nalini Singh, *Bonds of Justice*, 2010

36

JACQUELYN FRANK

Cursed by Fire

(New York: Ballantine Books, 2015)

Series: Immortal Brothers Series. Book 1
Story type: Paranormal; Romance
Subject(s): Fantasy; Romances (Fiction); Mythology
Major character(s): Dethan, Warrior, Captive, Immortal; Weysa, Deity (goddess of conflict); Selinda, Young Woman, Fiance(e) (of abusive man)
Time period(s): Indeterminate
Locale(s): Fictional Location

Summary: The first novel in the Immortal Brothers series introduces Dethan, a young man who is serving an eternal sentence for his transgression. Dethan and his brother discovered a fountain that granted them immortality, but in doing so, they attracted the ire of the gods. Now Dethan is imprisoned in a never-ending inferno that will burn his flesh forever. The pain is unbearable but inescapable, so when Weysa, the goddess of conflict, offers Dethan a bargain, he takes it. His suffering will be greatly diminished if he helps Weysa battle a band of enemy deities. When Dethan is released back into the mortal world, he is distracted from his duty by a beautiful young woman named Selinda. Dethan strikes an agreement with Selinda, even though he hasn't yet fulfilled his promise to Weysa.

Other books by the same author:
Forsaken, 2014
Forever, 2013
Adam, 2011
Ecstasy, 2009
Damien, 2008

Other books you might like:
Jennifer Ashley, *Immortals: The Calling*, 2007
Alexandra Ivy, *Darkness Revealed*, 2009
Marjorie M. Liu, *The Red Heart of Jade*, 2006
Nalini Singh, *Angels' Flight*, 2012
Eileen Wilks, *Blood Magic*, 2010

37

C.S. FRIEDMAN

Dreamseeker

(New York: DAW, 2015)

Series: Dreamwalker Chronicles. Book 2
Story type: Contemporary; Series
Subject(s): Fantasy; Dreams; Adventure
Major character(s): Jessica Drake, Supernatural Being (Dreamwalker), Enemy (of Isaac and Morgana); Isaac, Apprentice (Shadow), Enemy (of Jessica); Morgana, Psychic, Enemy (of Jessica)
Time period(s): Indeterminate
Locale(s): Fictional Location

Summary: C.S. Friedman returns with the second book in the Dreamwalker Chronicles. Teenager Jessica Drake is a Dreamwalker. She has the ability not only to influence others' dreams, but also to travel across worlds and dimensions. Jessica's adventures continue as she escapes from the Shadows, only to learn that she's far from safe. She is tormented by the presence of a stranger in her dreams—a figure that's causing uncontrollable nightmares that expose her to hunters who are not confined to the dreaming world. Jessica knows that only two people can save her: the Shadow apprentice Isaac and the Seer Morgana. Only they have the ancient knowledge to break the power of the nightmares and hunters. Jessica must return to their world to request their assistance, even though doing so could put her life in even greater danger. And when she arrives, what will Isaac and Morgana demand in return?

Other books by the same author:
Dreamwalker, 2014
Legacy of Kings, 2011
Wings of Wrath, 2009
Feast of Souls, 2007
Crown of Shadows, 1995

Other books you might like:
James P. Blaylock, *Land of Dreams*, 1987
Stephen Bowkett, *Dreamcatcher*, 2000
Charles de Lint, *Yarrow*, 1989
Andre Norton, *Deadly Dreams*, 2011
Eric S. Nylund, *Pawn's Dream*, 1995

38

CLAUDIA GRAY

Sorceress

(New York: HarperTeen, 2015)

Series: Spellcaster Series. Book 3
Story type: Magic Conflict

Subject(s): Magic; Witchcraft; Good and evil
Major character(s): Nadia Caldani, Witch, Girlfriend (of Mateo); Elizabeth Pike, Sorceress; Mateo Perez, Boyfriend (of Nadia); One Beneath, Supernatural Being
Time period(s): 21st century; 2010s
Locale(s): Captive's Sound, Rhode Island

Summary: In the third and final installment of the Spellcaster Series, Nadia has agreed to learn black magic and serve the One Beneath so she can save the people in Captive's Sound. She plans to learn just enough black magic to protect the town from the darkness that's invading, but her plan places her in danger. Nadia is separated from the ones she loves, including Mateo, and she becomes more susceptible to dark forces. As she tries to fight of the darkness, Nadia's time begins to run out as the sorceress Elizabeth closes in on Captive's Sound. The townspeople work together to fight off Elizabeth as she attacks the town with one disaster after another. Can Nadia save the town before the One Beneath reaches the mortal world?

Other books by the same author:
Steadfast, 2014
A Thousand Pieces of You, 2014
Spellcaster, 2013

Other books you might like:
Rachel Caine, *Firestorm*, 2006
P.C. Cast, *Hidden*, 2012
Casey Daniels, *The Chick and the Dead*, 2007
Melissa de la Cruz, *Lost in Time*, 2011
Seanan McGuire, *One Salt Sea*, 2011

39

CHRIS MARIE GREEN

Every Breath You Take

(London: Penguin Group, 2015)

Series: Jensen Murphy Series. Book 3
Story type: Ghost Story; Mystery
Subject(s): Ghosts; Crime; Murder
Major character(s): Jensen Murphy, Detective—Private, Spirit, Crime Victim
Time period(s): 21st century; 2010s
Locale(s): California, United States

Summary: Jensen Murphy's life really began when it ended. Jensen was a typical, beach-loving, 1980s California girl, right up to the day she was murdered. For 30 years she relived the moment of her death, until her spirit was brought back into the real world by a psychic. These days she spends her afterlife as a ghostly private detective, seeking justice for the dead and scaring the truth out of the living. Her latest case is a very personal one. She's going to try and solve her own murder. But it won't be easy. A paranormal reality show is dredging up secrets she would rather keep buried, and an evil spirit entity is targeting the people and ghosts for whom she cares. This is the third book in Chris Marie Green's Jensen Murphy series.

Other books by the same author:
Deep in the Woods, 2010

A Drop of Red, 2009
Break of Dawn, 2008
Midnight Rising, 2007
Night Rising, 2007

Other books you might like:
Juliet Blackwell, *If Walls Could Talk*, 2010
E.J. Copperman, *An Uninvited Ghost*, 2011
Casey Daniels, *Wild Wild Death*, 2012
Rick Hautala, *Beyond the Shroud*, 1995
James Herbert, *Fluke*, 1977

40

SALLY GREEN

Half Wild

(New York: Penguin Young Readers Group, 2015)

Series: Half Bad Trilogy. Book 2
Story type: Coming-of-Age; Contemporary - Fantasy
Subject(s): Witches; Witchcraft; Alternative worlds
Major character(s): Nathan, 17-Year-Old, Witch (half witch)
Time period(s): 21st century; 2010s
Locale(s): London, England

Summary: Humans and witches live side by side in twenty-first century England. However, two opposing groups of witches are anything but peaceful. But both groups agree on one thing: the half-breed son of the most powerful of all the witches and her lover is a danger and must be contained or eliminated. Seventeen-year-old Nathan, the object of their fear and enmity, was kept caged and chained for a long time. One day, his special Gift was revealed and he was able to escape. Since then the witches have been hunting him, but Nathan is growing more confident. He is learning to use his Gift even though he is on the run. He must now decide if he will use his talent for good or evil. This is the second title of the Half Bad Trilogy by Sally Green.

Other books by the same author:
Half Bad, 2014
Half Lies, 2014

Other books you might like:
Amber Benson, *The Witches of Echo Park*, 2015
Yasmine Galenorn, *Harvest Hunting*, 2010
Brenda Jordan, *The Brentwood Witches*, 1987
Melinda Metz, *Payback*, 2009
Samantha Shannon, *The Mime Order*, 2014
Vivian Vande Velde, *Magic Can Be Murder*, 2000

41

SIMON R. GREEN

From a Drood to a Kill

(London: Penguin Group, 2015)

Series: Secret Histories Series. Book 9
Story type: Adventure; Series
Subject(s): Magic; Family; Contests

Major character(s): Eddie Drood, Magician (aka Shaman Bond), Supernatural Being, Boyfriend (of Molly); Molly Metcalf, Girlfriend (of Eddie)
Locale(s): Indeterminate

Summary: His name is Drood, Eddie Drood. Eddie is a member of a group charged with protecting humanity from monsters, demons, and other assorted evil beasties throughout history. He's following in the footsteps of his parents, who have sold their very souls to get their job done. But now Eddie has a new problem. His parents and his girlfriend have been kidnapped, and if they don't pay a ransom, they'll be forced to play the Big Game—a race to the death across another dimension where the winner goes free and the loser gives up everything, including his or her soul. To save those he loves, Eddie is going to have to win the Big Game, which is undoubtedly rigged against him. This is the ninth book in Simon R. Green's Secret Histories series.

Other books by the same author:
Once in a Blue Moon, 2014
Live and Let Drood, 2012
A Hard Day's Knight, 2011
Hell to Pay, 2007
Hex and the City, 2005

Other books you might like:
Kelley Armstrong, *Dime Store Magic*, 2004
Jim Butcher, *White Night*, 2007
Charlaine Harris, *Dead and Gone*, 2009
Lindsey Piper, *Hunted Warrior*, 2015
Irene Radford, *Guardian of the Freedom*, 2005
Anton Strout, *Dead Matter*, 2010

42

SIMON R. GREEN

Tales from the Nightside

(New York: Penguin Publishing Group, 2015)

Series: Nightside Series
Story type: Collection
Subject(s): Fantasy; Short stories; Urban life

Summary: When author Simon R. Green released the twelfth novel in his Nightside series, *The Bride Wore Black Leather*, in 2012, he indicated that it would be the last novel in the series "for the time being." With this collection of short stories, Green revisits the secret London locale known as Nightside and follows some of its mysterious residents on their otherworldly adventures. There are shady human figures, such as Dead Boy and Razor Eddie, and sinister supernatural characters that include a vampire king. The collection includes "Lucy, at Christmastime," "Appetite for Murder," "The Difference a Day Makes," and "Some of These Cons Go Way Back." The book's final story, "The Big Game," is a novella whose cast of characters includes private detective and Nightside protagonist John Taylor.

Other books by the same author:
Voices from Beyond, 2014
Spirits from Beyond, 2013
Live and Let Drood, 2012
Just Another Judgment Day, 2009

Hex and the City, 2005

Other books you might like:
John Joseph Adams, *Operation Arcana*, 2015
Kelley Armstrong, *Personal Demon*, 2008
Mercedes Lackey, *The Wizard of London*, 2005
Graham Masterton, *The Doorkeepers*, 2001
Michael Moorcock, *The Whispering Swarm*, 2015
Lisa Shearin, *All Spell Breaks Loose*, 2012

43

PAULA GURAN

Mermaids and Other Mysteries of the Deep

(Gaithersburg, Maryland: Prime Books, 2015)

Story type: Collection
Subject(s): Mermaids; Fantasy; Greek history, to 330
(Ancient period)

Summary: Born from the myths of the ancient Assyrians and given life in in the perilous sirens of classical Greece, or the whimsical tales of Hans Christian Andersen, mermaids have part of human legend for thousands of years. In this collection of 22 short stories, some of today's best fantasy and science fiction writers put their spin on the mermaid myth. Stories include "The Sea Change," by Neil Gaiman; "The Nebraskan and the Nereid," by Gene Wolfe; "Magritte's Secret Agent," by Tanith Lee; "Salt Wine," by Peter S. Beagle; "Driftglass," by Samuel R. Delany; "Each to Each," by Seanan McGuire; and "The Mermaid of the Concrete Ocean," by Caitlin R. Kiernan.

Other books by the same author:
New Cthulhu 2: More Recent Weird, 2015
Zombies: More Recent Dead, 2014
Zombies: Recent Dead, 2013
Witches: Wicked, Wild, and Wonderful, 2012
Embraces: Dark Erotica, 2000

Other books you might like:
Neil Gaiman, *Fragile Things: Short Fictions and Wonders*, 2006
Caitlin R. Kiernan, *Alabaster*, 2006
Margo Lanagan, *Tender Morsels*, 2008
Tanith Lee, *Forests of the Night*, 1989
Jane Yolen, *Neptune Rising: Songs and Tales of the Undersea Folk*, 1982

44

DAVID GUYMER

Gotrek and Felix: Slayer

(Nottingham, United Kingdom: Black Library, 2015)

Series: Warhammer 40,000: Gotrek and Felix Series. Book
Story type: Quest; Series
Subject(s): Fantasy; Friendship; Wars
Major character(s): Gotrek Gurnisson, Warrior, Dwarf,

Friend (of Felix); Felix Jaeger, Human, Writer (scribe), Friend (of Gotrek)
Time period(s): Indeterminate
Locale(s): Kislev, Fictional Location

Summary: Long-time friends and travel companions Felix Jaeger and Gotrek Gurnisson say good-bye in the final installment of the Gotrek and Felix series, set in the Warhammer universe. Their enemies have fallen, but Gotrek cannot escape his final fate. Felix must choose whether to accompany Gotrek into doom or flee to preserve his own life. Their sworn oath is at a turning point. It is the End Times, the world is coming to pieces, and battles are everywhere. The friends ruminate on their adventures together and their other comrades over the years. Traveling to the Empire to reunite Felix with his wife, the friends encounter enemies and develop an even deeper understanding of the depth of their friendship.

Other books by the same author:
Kinslayer, 2014
City of the Damned, 2013
Headtaker, 2013

Other books you might like:
Andy Chambers, *Path of the Incubus*, 2013
Ben Counter, *Van Horstmann*, 2013
Graham McNeill, *Sons of Ellyrion*, 2011
Josh Reynolds, *The Serpent Queen*, 2014
Gav Thorpe, *Malekith*, 2009
C.L. Werner, *Deathblade: A Tale of Malus Darkblade*, 2015

45

JOHN GWYNNE

Ruin

(New York: Hatchette USA, 2015)

Series: Faithful and the Fallen Series. Book 2
Story type: Adventure; Alternate World
Subject(s): Adventure; Rebellion; Fantasy
Major character(s): Corban, Hero, Resistance Fighter; Nathair, Royalty (High King); Queen Edana, Royalty, Leader (of resistence)
Time period(s): Indeterminate
Locale(s): Banished Lands, Fictional Location

Summary: Rebellion, deceit, treachery, war, and potential disaster threaten to engulf the Banished Lands. High King Nathair pursues cauldron, one of the seven treasures, and is bent on strengthening his grip on the land. Resistance leader Queen Edana continues to draw help for her fight against him. Corban is caught up in it all. He has tired of all the loss and suffering swirling around him and wants to put an end to it all. Corban gathers an unlikely group of allies—mythical beings, a talking crow, and a handful of family and friends—and sets off on a quest to take possession of another of the seven treasures, the spear of Skaid. Corban heads for Dassil, where rumors say the spear can be found. Ancient prophecies have foretold that a Bright Star will challenge the Black Sun in Dassil. This is the second novel in the Faithful and the Fallen series.

Other books by the same author:
Valor, 2014
Malice, 2012

Other books you might like:
Raymond E. Feist, *Into a Dark Realm*, 2007
C.S. Friedman, *Crown of Shadows*, 1995
Maggie Furey, *Heritage of the Xandim*, 2006
Mickey Zucker Reichert, *The Return of Nightfall*, 2004
Janny Wurts, *Initiate's Trial*, 2012

46

STEVEN HARPER

Iron Axe

(London: Penguin Group, 2015)

Series: Books of Blood and Iron Series. Book 1
Story type: Adventure; Quest
Subject(s): Monsters; Slavery; Elves
Major character(s): Danr, Friend (of Aisa), Slave, Mythical Creature (half troll); Aisa, Human, Slave, Friend (of Danr); Talfi, Friend (of Danr)
Locale(s): Fictional Location

Summary: Danr is a half-human, half-troll bound to a life of ridicule and miserable servitude to humans. While working on a farm, he befriends the human slave Aisa and violently defends her from an attack by a nobleman's son. For his transgression, Danr and Aisa are banished from the human lands and must fend for themselves in a world overrun with dangerous spirits, vicious beasts, and slave-trading elves. Along the way, they meet up with Death herself, who sends them on a quest. They are tasked with retrieving the fabled Iron Axe, an ancient weapon that split open the very land a thousand years ago and still holds the power to destroy the world. This is the first book in Steven Harper's Books of Blood and Iron series.

Other books by the same author:
The Havoc Machine, 2013
The Dragon Men, 2012
The Doomsday Vault, 2011
Unity, 2007
Trickster, 2003

Other books you might like:
Troy Denning, *Beyond the High Road*, 1999
Ed Greenwood, *The Vacant Throne*, 2001
Paul Kearney, *The Ten Thousand*, 2008
Stan Nicholls, *Orcs*, 2004
R.A. Salvatore, *The Orc King*, 2007

47

AIDAN HARTE

The Warring States

(London: Jo Fletcher Books, 2015)

Series: Wave Trilogy. Book 2
Story type: Alternate History; Political

Subject(s): Fantasy; Engineering; Politics
Major character(s): Torbidda, Apprentice (engineers), Boy; Sofia Scaligeri, Noblewoman, Mother (expecting)
Time period(s): 14th century; 1340s
Locale(s): Concord, Italy; Rasenna, Italy

Summary: The second volume of the Wave Trilogy, an alternative fantasy history, narrates events both prior to and after the events of the first installment. Torbidda is a young boy who is apprenticed to the engineer's guild two years before the events of *Irenicon*. As he learns his craft and realizes the extensive and daunting frameworks of the guild, Torbidda is determined to succeed where others have failed. Gifted at his work, Torbidda is soon to discover that his destiny is more than he can even fathom. Another narrator, Sofia Scaligeri, a noblewoman of Rasenna, is coping with an unexpected and seemingly miraculous pregnancy. With the political scene shifting dangerously in Rasenna, Sofia realizes that both her life and the life of her child are in danger. She takes to heart the prophecy that will send her to the Kingdom of Oltremare. In this alternative history of Europa, Herod killed Christ in infancy, and the Kingdom of Concord has seized control over the lands.

48

RACHEL HAWKINS

Miss Mayhem

(New York: Penguin Young Readers Group, 2015)

Series: Rebel Belle Series. Book 2
Story type: Romance; Series
Subject(s): Magic; Romances (Fiction); Mysticism
Major character(s): Harper Price, Teenager, Warrior (paladin), Girlfriend (of David), Magician, Student (high school); David Stark, Magician, Student (high school), Boyfriend (of Harper), Teenager; Bee, Teenager, Kidnap Victim, Student (high school), Friend (of Harper); Ryan, Teenager, Magician, Boyfriend (ex, of Harper)
Time period(s): 21st century; 2010s
Locale(s): United States

Summary: Harper Price is a typical teenage girl, dealing with high school, best friends, and boyfriends. Or rather, she would be a typical teenager if she wasn't also a paladin. She is tasked with protecting the oracle—who just so happens to be her boyfriend, David—from an ancient Greek society known as the Ephors. Harper's job is made tougher when the Ephors decide to use David's abilities for their own treacherous needs and test her by forcing her to undergo three trials. If she passes, she will become a full-fledged paladin and David's protector. The problem is that success also means David would lose his humanity and become a tool of the Ephors. If Harper fails, she dies, and her best friend, Bee, would inherit her duties. This is the second book in Rachel Hawkins's Rebel Belle series.

Other books by the same author:
Rebel Belle, 2014
School Spirits, 2013
Spell Bound, 2012
Demonglass, 2011

Hex Hall, 2010

Other books you might like:
Mindee Arnett, *The Nightmare Charade*, 2015
Rachel Caine, *Heat Stroke*, 2004
Steven Charles, *Academy of Terror*, 1986
Elizabeth Massie, *Southern Discomfort: Selected Works of Elizabeth Massie*, 1993
Cherie Priest, *Not Flesh nor Feathers*, 2007

49

MARKUS HEITZ

Righteous Fury

(London: Jo Fletcher Books, 2014)

Series: Legends of the Alfar Series. Book 1
Story type: Adventure; Series
Subject(s): Fantasy; Elves; Dwarfs
Major character(s): Caphalor, Warrior (of Alfar race), Immortal; Sinthoras, Warrior (of Alfar race), Immortal, Artist; Raleeha, Woman, Human, Slave (of Sinthoras)
Time period(s): Indeterminate
Locale(s): Dson Faimon, Fictional Location

Summary: The Alfar are a race of immortals who are skilled artists and architects. But the Alfar, who live in Dson Faimon, are also fierce warriors who enjoy the acts of violence they commit against the human and elven inhabitants of their realm. The race is ruled by two terrifying siblings, who have decided that the elves should be exterminated. Two Alfar warriors, Sinthoras and Caphalor, are sent to form an alliance with a mist-demon. Sinthoras is the owner of a human slave, whom he blinded for committing a small transgression. Caphalor has also demonstrated his capacity for cruelty, but his military philosophy is somewhat tamer than that of Sinthoras. Caphalor is a proponent only of defensive action; Sinthoras wants to launch a full-scale attack. As the two warriors make their way to the mist-demon, they encounter a number of obstacles and sinister characters. This novel is the first in the Legends of the Alfar series, which is a companion to Markus Heitz's Dwarves series.

Other books by the same author:
The Fate of the Dwarves, 2012
The War of the Dwarves, 2010
The Dwarves, 2009

Other books you might like:
Terry Brooks, *Straken*, 2005
Elaine Cunningham, *The Dream Spheres*, 1999
Ed Greenwood, *Dark Lord*, 2007
Paul S. Kemp, *The Godborn*, 2013
R.A. Salvatore, *The Ancient*, 2008

50

ALYC HELMS

The Dragons of Heaven

(Nottingham, United Kingdom: Angry Robot, 2015)

Story type: Contemporary; Urban
Subject(s): Fantasy; Magic; China

Major character(s): Missy Masters, Magician (also known as Mr. Mystic); Lung Huang, Magician, Brother (of Lung Di), Enemy (of Lung Di); Lung Di, Brother (of Lung Huang), Enemy (of Lung Huang), Magician
Time period(s): 21st century; 2010s
Locale(s): China

Summary: Missy Masters isn't your ordinary street performer. The magic she demonstrates for her audiences is only a small sampling of her talents. Missy has real supernatural powers that were handed down to her from her grandfather. She also is heir to her grandfather's alter ego, Mr. Mystic, a rogue hero persona. Missy attempts to assume the Mr. Mystic role, but realizes she needs guidance. She travels to China and seeks out Lung Huang, the man who helped Missy's grandfather hone his skills. Missy is surprised by what she discovers in China. Lung Huang is not the only magician in his family. His brother and rival, Lung Di, also has powers, which he uses to create an enclosure around China. If Missy can successfully embody the hero Mr. Mystic, she may be able save the country from annihilation. She must first consider the repercussions the dismantling of the wall will have.

Other books you might like:
Leah R. Cutter, *Paper Mage*, 2003
Barry Hughart, *Bridge of Birds*, 1984
Guy Gavriel Kay, *Under Heaven*, 2010
Marc Laidlaw, *Neon Lotus*, 1988
Chris Willrich, *The Silk Map*, 2013

51

BARB HENDEE

Witches with the Enemy

(London: Penguin Group, 2015)

Series: Mist-Torn Witches Series. Book 3
Story type: Fantasy; Mystery
Subject(s): Psychics; Magic; Murder
Major character(s): Celine Fawe, Psychic (seer), Magician, Sister (of Amelie), Orphan; Amelie Fawe, Psychic (seer), Magician, Sister (of Celine), Orphan; Damek, Royalty (prince); Anton, Royalty (prince)
Locale(s): Shetana, Fictional Location

Summary: Sisters Celine and Amelie Fawe have the ability to see the future, a gift that has also made them some powerful enemies. When they are threatened with death, they leave their homeland of Shetana, intending never to return. But fate and an unexpected summon has altered their plans. The evil prince Damek, the very man who tried to kill them, needs their help. Damek is close to finishing marriage negotiations with a powerful family when his intended bride's sister is murdered. Celine and Amelie's abilities are the only thing that can solve the crime and ensure Damek's marriage takes place. Trust will be in short supply and danger common back in their homeland—danger that may be more than the sisters can handle. This is the third book in Barb Hendee's Mist-Torn Witches series.

Other books by the same author:
Witches in Red, 2014
The Mist-Torn Witches, 2013

Between Their Worlds, 2012
The Dog in the Dark, 2012
Of Truth and Beasts, 2011

Other books you might like:
Joe Abercrombie, *Half the World*, 2015
Kate Forsyth, *The Heart of Stars*, 2007
Glenda Larke, *The Aware*, 2005
Diana L. Paxson, *Ancestors of Avalon*, 2004
M.J. Scott, *The Shattered Court*, 2015

52

BARB HENDEE
J.C. HENDEE, Co-Author

First and Last Sorcerer

(New York: Roc Publishing, 2015)

Series: Noble Dead Series. Book 10
Story type: Alternate World; Fantasy
Subject(s): Fantasy; Friendship; Supernatural
Major character(s): Wynn Hygeorht, Adventurer, Friend (of Magiere, Leesil, Wayfarer, Chap, and Chane); Magiere, Friend (of Wynn, Wayfarer, and Chap), Spouse (of Leesil), Supernatural Being (dhamphir); Leesil, Spouse (of Magiere), Friend (of Wynn, Wayfarer, and Chap); Wayfarer, Friend (of Wynn, Chap, Magiere, and Leesil); Chap, Friend (of Wynn, Wayfarer, Magiere, and Leesil); Chane Andraso, Vampire, Friend (of Wynn); Ghassan il'Sanke, Supernatural Being (domin)
Time period(s): Indeterminate
Locale(s): Suman Empire, Fictional Location

Summary: When her friends are imprisoned wrongly and ordered to be tortured, Wynn Hygeorht rallies a group to go after them and free them. Along with Chane Andraso, a vampire, they head to Suman to request help from a domin named Ghassan il'Sanke. But il'Sanke has a different mission, a quest to find a ghostly spirit that can take over and inhabit the body of a living host. All the while, Wynn's friends Magiere, Leesil, Chap, and Wayfarer are at the mercy of a determined torturer. Magiere, a dhampir, experiences the worst of the pain and suffering as her mysterious captor assaults her telepathically. Though facing almost insurmountable odds, Wynn must free her friends and find a way to fight and defeat this new supernatural enemy that can hide inside anyone. The stakes are high as they struggle to survive this ordeal.

Other books by the same author:
A Wind in the Night, 2014
The Dog in the Dark, 2012
Of Truth and Beasts, 2011
Child of a Dead God, 2008
Dhampir, 2003

Other books you might like:
Steven Brust, *The Book of Taltos*, 2002
Elaine Cunningham, *The Blood Red Harp*, 2006
Susan Griffith, *The Greyfriar*, 2010
Jasper Kent, *Twelve*, 2010
Andy Remic, *Soul Stealers*, 2010

53

RANDY HENDERSON

Finn Fancy Necromancy

(New York: Tor Books, 2015)

Story type: Adventure; Black Magic
Subject(s): Adventure; Alchemy; Betrayal
Major character(s): Phinaeus "Finn" Gramaraye, Supernatural Being (necromancer), Brother (of Mort, Pete, and Samantha), Man, Undertaker (family run Necrotorium business), Narrator (of the novel), Convict (framed of dark necromancy); Mort Gramaraye, Man, Undertaker (in charge of family run necrotorium business), Brother (of Finn, Pete, and Samantha), Supernatural Being (necromancer); Pete Gramaraye, Supernatural Being (necromancer), Brother (of Finn, Mort, and Samantha), Werewolf (or really just thinks he is), Man; Samantha Gramaraye, Sister (of Finn, Mort, and Pete), Woman, Supernatural Being (necromancer); Zeke, Friend (of Finn), Man, Exile (of the Other Realm)
Time period(s): 21st century; 2010s
Locale(s): Washington, United States

Summary: At the age of 15, Phinaeus "Finn" Gramaraye was framed and found guilty for the crime of dark necromancy. He was sentenced to exile in the Other Realm for 25 years. Now, having served his sentence, Finn is released from the Other Realm and finds that whoever framed him the first time is trying to set him up again. Trying to get his life back and find evidence to prove to the Arcane Enforcers he is innocent, Finn returns to his family of magical undertakers and a bunch of magical misfits for help. In his head, Finn is still 15, still experiencing the world as a teen. With the help of his siblings—Mort, who now runs the family necrotorium business; Pete, who thinks he's a werewolf; and, Samantha, who is ironically allergic to magic—and his friend Zeke, a fellow exile and former enforcer, Finn fumbles through culture shock and family issues while he tries to prove his innocence. He has little time if he wants to avoid returning to the Other Realm.

Other books you might like:
Stephen R. Donaldson, *The Runes of the Earth*, 2004
Paul Kearney, *Corvus*, 2010
L.E. Modesitt Jr., *Imager's Battalion*, 2013
Mickey Zucker Reichert, *The Beasts of Barakhai*, 2001
Tad Williams, *Happy Hour in Hell*, 2013

54

LEANNA RENEE HIEBER

The Eterna Files

(New York: Tom Doherty Associates, 2015)

Story type: Alternate History; Gothic
Subject(s): Immortality; Murder; Ghosts
Major character(s): Clare Templeton, Psychic, Advisor (to Mary Todd Lincoln); Mary Todd Lincoln, Widow(er) (of President Abraham Lincoln), Friend (of Clare), Historical Figure; Victoria, Royalty (Queen of

England), Historical Figure; Harold Spire, Investigator (paranormal), Leader (of Omega); Rose Everhart, Researcher (for Omega)

Time period(s): 19th century; 1860s-1880s
Locale(s): London, England; New York, New York

Summary: President Abraham Lincoln has just been assassinated, and Clare Templeton is doing her best to console his grieving widow. In the process of coming to terms with her loss, Mrs. Lincoln becomes convinced the country should never lose another president, and the quest is on for Eterna—a special compound that grants immortality. When England's Queen Victoria becomes aware of Eterna in 1882, she tasks Omega, the special branch of the Metropolitan Police that secretly investigates the paranormal, with finding it first. Harold Spire, who heads up Omega, is skeptical of all things paranormal, but his lead researcher, Rose Everhart, fervently believes things invisible and unexplained do exist. Spire and the Queen want Eterna for England; Clare Templeton, driven by her own private grief over the loss of her true love, wants it just as badly. The search—fraught with supernatural perils such as ghosts and black magic, as well as very mortal dangers including murder and kidnapping—takes place in both New York and London in this novel from award-winning author Leanna Renee Hieber.

Other books by the same author:
The Double Life of Incorporate Things, 2013
The Twisted Tragedy of Miss Natalie Stewart, 2012
Darker Still, 2011
The Darkly Luminous Fight for Persephone Parker, 2010

Other books you might like:
Pip Ballantine, *The Janus Affair*, 2012
Marie Brennan, *A Natural History of Dragons: A Memoir by Lady Trent*, 2013
Gabrielle Charbonnet, *Witch & Wizard*, 2009
Neil Gaiman, *The Graveyard Book*, 2008
Linda Howard, *Killing Time*, 2005
Stephen Hunt, *The Court of the Air*, 2007
Stephen King, *Doctor Sleep*, 2013
Ian R. MacLeod, *The Light Ages*, 2003
George Mann, *The Affinity Bridge*, 2009
David Morrell, *Inspector of the Dead*, 2015
Frank E. Peretti, *The Visitation*, 1999
Anne Perry, *The Angel Court Affair*, 2014
M.J. Rose, *The Witch of Painted Sorrows*, 2015

55

JIM C. HINES

Unbound

(New York: DAW, 2014)

Series: Magic Ex Libris Series. Book 3
Story type: Contemporary; Series
Subject(s): Fantasy; Magic; Books
Major character(s): Isaac Vainio, Librarian, Magician (Libriomancer); Jeneta Aboderin, Student (former, of Peter); Johannes Gutenberg, Historical Figure, Magician (founder of the Porters); Lena Greenwood, War-

rior (dryad); Nidhi Shah, Doctor (psychiatrist); Juan Ponce de Leon, Historical Figure, Sorcerer

Time period(s): 21st century; 2010s
Locale(s): Michigan, United States

Summary: Five hundred years ago Johannes Gutenberg created an organization known as the Porters. The Porters are Libriomancers—magicians who can retrieve concrete objects from the pages of books. Isaac Vainio is a modern-day member of the Porters. His job as a librarian provides cover for his secret magical missions, which have included run-ins with vampires and werewolves. In this novel, the third in the series, Isaac is drawn into a search for a long-lost relic. The spirit of an exiled queen has taken over the body of Isaac's former student, Jeneta Aboderin. Now Jeneta is driven to find the artifact, which has ties to the papacy and has the power to resurrect the dead. Isaac wants to free Jeneta from the queen's control, but Johannes Gutenberg—founder of the Porters—has revoked his magical powers. Isaac has no choice but to use illegal magic, but that course of action comes with great risks.

Other books by the same author:
Codex Born, 2013
Libriomancer, 2012
The Mermaid's Madness, 2009
Goblin War, 2008
Goblin Hero, 2007

Other books you might like:
Ben Aaronovitch, *Broken Homes*, 2014
Ilona Andrews, *Bayou Moon*, 2010
Amber Benson, *How to Be Death*, 2012
Lisa Shearin, *The Grendel Affair*, 2014
Anton Strout, *Dead Matter*, 2010

56

AMANDA HOCKING

Frostfire

(New York: St. Martin's Press, 2014)

Series: Kanin Chronicles Series. Book 1
Story type: Romance; Series
Subject(s): Fantasy; Adventure; Racially mixed people
Major character(s): Bryn Aven, Worker (for Ridley), Outcast (Mixed race, Kanin and Skojare); Ridley Dresden, Military Personnel (Bryn's boss); Konstantin Black, Traitor

Time period(s): Indeterminate
Locale(s): Kanin, Fictional Location

Summary: Bryn Aven longs to become one of the elite guard for the King of the Land of Kanin, but it might be little more than a pipe dream. Her mother was from Skojare, not Kanin, and that makes Bryn a half-breed. She doesn't fit in by race or appearance, and isn't likely to be accepted to the guard. Instead, Bryn serves as a tracker, one sent into the human world to bring back the Kanin changelings after they grow up with their human parents. When the kingdom is attacked, Kanin faces challenges both professional and personal. She must face Konstantin Black, the man who tried to kill her father, and has mixed feelings as she comes to see him in a different light. She must also decide how much she's willing to give to save the land that sees her as an outsider. And she develops growing feelings for her boss, Ridley Dresden—who also develops feelings for Kanin. This is the first book in the Kanin Chronicles.

Other books by the same author:
Crystal Kingdom, 2015
Ice Kissed, 2015
Elegy, 2013
Tidal, 2013
Torn, 2012

Other books you might like:
Jacqueline Carey, *Naamah's Kiss*, 2009
Elizabeth Haydon, *Requiem for the Sun*, 2002
Dennis L. McKiernan, *Once Upon a Spring Morn*, 2006
Jennifer Roberson, *Karavans*, 2006
Chelsea Quinn Yarbro, *Dark Light*, 1999

57

M.K. HUME

The Ice King

(Hatchette, United Kingdom: Headline Book Publishing, 2015)

Series: Twilight of the Celts Series. Book 3
Story type: Adventure; Alternate World
Subject(s): Adventure; Arthurian legend; Fantasy
Major character(s): Arthur, Young Man, Warrior, Royalty (once and future king of Britain); Stormbringer, Royalty (Sae Dene king), Leader
Time period(s): Indeterminate Past
Locale(s): Land of the Denes

Summary: In this continuation of the story of King Arthur as launched in the first two books of the Twilight of the Celts series, Arthur has been away from home and fighting his way through the Land of the Denes. As a result of his many challenging encounters with the brutal and fierce Geats, Arthur has refined his battle skills. He's also learned what it takes to be a leader from the Sae Dene king, Stormbringer, who has taken the young warrior prince who will one day rule Britain under his tutelage. Now, after several long years away from his homeland, it's time for the Last Dragon to sail to Britain and claim his rightful place of leadership.

Other books by the same author:
The Last Dragon, 2014
The Storm Lord, 2014
Web of Deceit, 2013
Death of an Empire, 2012
Warrior of the West, 2009

Other books you might like:
Mark Chadbourn, *World's End*, 2009
J. Robert King, *Mad Merlin*, 2000
Mercedes Lackey, *Gwenhwyfar: The White Spirit*, 2009
Diana L. Paxson, *The Book of the Spear*, 1999
Judith Tarr, *Kingdom of the Grail*, 2000

58

STEPHEN HUNT

In Dark Service

(London: Gollancz, 2014)

Series: Far-Called Trilogy. Book 1
Story type: Adventure; Science Fantasy
Subject(s): Father-son relations; Slavery; Rebellion
Major character(s): Jacob Carnehan, Father (of Carter), Religious (minister); Carter Carnehan, Son (of Jacob), Kidnap Victim, Slave
Time period(s): Indeterminate
Locale(s): Kingdom of Weyland, Fictional Location

Summary: Author Stephen Hunt launches the Far-Called Trilogy with this fantasy novel. Jacob Carnehan is content with his life, willing to follow the rules and live in peace and quiet, leading his congregation and calming troubled waters when he can. His son, Carter, is far less happy and would rather be out in the wide world, experiencing adventures he can only imagine. He gets his wish, but not in the way he wants. Carter gets into a fight and is then kidnapped. The slavers who take him transport him far away to a place with confusing technology where he faces a miserable life of confinement and hard work. While Carter decides whether he'll accept his fate or try to change it through escape or revolt, his father is forced to step out of his life of law-abiding peace and take on all comers as he fights to free his son.

Other books by the same author:
Jack Cloudie, 2011
The Rise of the Iron Moon, 2011
Secrets of the Fire Sea, 2010
The Kingdom Beyond the Waves, 2009
The Court of the Air, 2007

59

ERIN HUNTER

Seekers: Return to the Wild: The Burning Horizon

(New York: HarperCollins, 2015)

Series: Seekers: Return to the Wild Series. Book 5
Story type: Adventure; Series
Subject(s): Fantasy; Animals; Bears
Major character(s): Toklo, Bear (grizzly); Kallik, Bear (polar); Lusa, Bear (black bear); Yakone, Bear (polar)
Time period(s): 21st century; 2010s
Locale(s): Canada; Alaska, United States

Summary: The fifth novel in the Return to the Wild sub-series of Erin Hunter's Seekers series follows four bears as they make their way in the Canadian and Alaska wilderness. The grizzly bear Toklo, black bear Lusa, and polar bears Kallik and Yakone are all bound for Great Bear Lake where the Longest Day Gathering will be held. Lusa still needs to locate a place to live, and Toklo is staying with her until she does, even though he has staked out a home in the mountains. Lusa's adventure takes a turn when she suddenly finds herself alone. While she is apart from her friends, Lusa has time to think about the choices that face her as she moves forward with her life.

Other books by the same author:
Warriors: Dawn of the Clans: Thunder Rising, 2013
Warriors Super Edition: Yellowfang's Secret, 2012
Warriors: Omen of the Stars: Fading Echoes, 2010
Warriors: Omen of the Stars: The Fourth Apprentice, 2009
Warriors: Warrior's Return, 2008

Other books you might like:
Richard Adams, *Shardik*, 1974
Brian Jacques, *Doomwyte: A Tale from Redwall*, 2008
Kij Johnson, *The Fox Woman*, 2000
Gabriel King, *The Wild Road*, 1998
Walter Wangerin, *The Book of the Dun Cow*, 1978

60

ERIN HUNTER

Survivors: Storm of Dogs

(New York: HarperCollins, 2015)

Series: Survivors Series. Book 6
Story type: Adventure; Series
Subject(s): Fantasy; Adventure; Animals
Major character(s): Lucky, Dog; Sweet, Dog (alpha)
Time period(s): 21st century; 2010s

Summary: The sixth novel in Erin Hunter's Survivors series follows the adventures of a wild pack of dogs as they struggle for survival after a devastating earthquake. The "Big Growl," as the dogs call the disaster, changed the landscape and forced even those dogs used to human care and companionship to survive on their own. Since the earthquake, the dogs have formed packs, established a hierarchy, and faced each new danger as it arose. Sweet has now assumed the Alpha role in the Wild Pack, and the dogs believe that they may be able to suspend their worries for a while. Lucky, another member of the pack, refuses to let his guard down, however. He has a feeling that there is another threat on the horizon, and he is right: a Storm of Dogs is on its way.

Other books by the same author:
Warriors: Dawn of the Clans: The Sun Trail, 2013
Warriors Super Edition: Crookedstar's Promise, 2011
Night Whispers, 2010
Warriors: Power of Three: Long Shadows, 2008
Warriors Manga: Graystripe's Trilogy: Warrior's Refuge, 2007

Other books you might like:
Jerry Jay Carroll, *Top Dog*, 1996
Doranna Durgin, *A Feral Darkness*, 2001
Diana Wynne Jones, *Dogsbody*, 1977
Gabriel King, *The Golden Cat*, 1999
Will Shetterly, *Dogland*, 1997

61

MICHAEL JENSEN
DAVID POWERS KING, Co-Author

Woven

(New York: Scholastic, 2015)

Story type: Adventure; Young Adult
Subject(s): Fantasy; Adventure; Magic
Major character(s): Nels, 17-Year-Old, Boy, Impoverished (peasant); Tyra, Young Woman, Royalty (Princess of Averand); Ickabosh, Magician; Rasmus, Apprentice (former, of Ickabosh)
Time period(s): Indeterminate
Locale(s): Averand, Fictional Location

Summary: The world in which the kingdom of Averand resides is woven on a giant loom and cared for by magical weavers. The kingdom is home to both ordinary people and those with supernatural gifts. Seventeen-year-old Nels is of the peasant class, but he wants to better himself by becoming a knight. When he attends the village's annual festival, he seizes the opportunity to prove his strength—and possibly win the affection of Princess Tyra. He wrestles and defeats a knight, but is disappointed when Tyra refuses to kiss him because of his social standing. But when Nels is murdered at the festival, he transforms into a ghost and learns that he is connected to the princess after all. Nels also learns that Averand is in danger, and that Tyra—the only one who can see Nels's apparition—may be the only one who can help him keep the fabric of their world from tearing apart.

Other books you might like:
Ellen Kushner, *The Privilege of the Sword*, 2006
Mercedes Lackey, *Intrigues*, 2010
Ari Marmell, *Covenant's End*, 2015
William Nicholson, *Jango*, 2006
Andre Norton, *Three Hands for Scorpio*, 2005

62

JEFFE KENNEDY

The Talon of the Hawk

(New York: Kensington, 2015)

Series: Twelve Kingdoms Series. Book 3
Story type: Romance; Series
Subject(s): Fantasy; Inheritance and succession; Father-daughter relations
Major character(s): Ursula, Lover (of Harlan), Daughter (eldest, of Uorsine), Warrior, Heir; Uorsine, Royalty (High King of the Twelve Kingdoms), Father (of Ursula); Harlan, Mercenary, Lover (of Ursula)
Time period(s): Indeterminate
Locale(s): Twelve Kingdoms, Fictional Location

Summary: This is the third novel of the Twelve Kingdoms series. Ursula is the eldest daughter of tyrannical High King Uorsin. She has spent her life training as a warrior and heir to the throne, learning to look after its peoples and her two younger sisters. Her abilities and strength are thrown into question when she returns home from a failed military mission and faces the wrath and degradation of her father. She is surprised to see a wealth of foreigners not only in the capital, but also in his court. At the king's side, a foreign witch whispers into his ear, while a hired captain hurls derogatory insults at Ursula, saying she is only a woman not capable of being a warrior. Ursula realizes that her father's grip on his sanity and the kingdom is failing. She realizes that as the heir it is up to her to forge an alliance with her sisters and save the Twelve Kingdoms, even if it means facing down her own father. With the aid of a mercenary named Harlan, she vows to do whatever it takes.

Other books by the same author:
Under His Touch, 2015
Going Under, 2014
The Mark of the Tala, 2014
Rogue's Paradise, 2014
The Tears of the Rose, 2014

Other books you might like:
Lynn Abbey, *Rifkind's Challenge*, 2006
Andre Norton, *Three Hands for Scorpio*, 2005
Joanna Russ, *The Adventures of Alyx*, 1983
Joel Shepherd, *Petrodor*, 2010
Ryk E. Spoor, *Phoenix Rising*, 2013

63

GARY KLOSTER

Firesoul

(Redmond, Washington: Paizo Publishing, 2015)

Series: Pathfinder Tales Series
Story type: Adventure; Series
Subject(s): Orphans; Revenge; Magic
Major character(s): Jiri, Orphan, Warrior, Survivor (of attack), Young Woman
Locale(s): Mwangi Jungle, Fictional Location

Summary: As a baby, Jiri's life nearly ended in fire. Found alive and orphaned in the ashes of her destroyed village, she was rescued by a neighboring tribe and raised to be a formidable jungle druid. When mercenaries from the evil Aspis Consortium unleash an ancient force that incinerates her adopted home, Jiri again escapes a fiery death. Now she must assemble a group of brave warriors to drive the invaders from her home, and gain her revenge in the process. This novel is set in the world of the Pathfinder Roleplaying Game and is one of the many Pathfinder Tales standalone titles.

Other books you might like:
David Gross, *King of Chaos*, 2013
Chris Jackson, *Pirate's Honor*, 2013
Richard A. Knaak, *The Demon Soul*, 2004
Tim Pratt, *Pathfinder Tales: Reign of Stars*, 2014
James L. Sutter, *Pathfinder Tales: The Redemption Engine*, 2014
Josh Vogt, *Forge of Ashes*, 2015

64

CAYLA KLUVER

The Empty Throne

(Don Mills, Ontario, Canada: Harlequin, 2014)

Series: Heirs of Chrior Series. Book 2
Story type: Magic Conflict; Series
Subject(s): Fantasy; Magic; Fairies
Major character(s): Anya, Mythical Creature (fairy), Cousin (of Zabriel and Illumina); Zabriel, Mythical Creature (fairy), Royalty (prince), Cousin (of Anya and Illumina), Young Man (also known as William Wolfram Pyrite), Missing Person; Illumina, Mythical Creature (fairy), Cousin (of Anya and Zabriel)
Time period(s): Indeterminate
Locale(s): Chrior, Fictional Location

Summary: When the queen of the fairy dominion known as Chrior died, Prince Zabriel should have risen to the throne. But Zabriel has been gone from Chrior for a long time. Zabriel's cousin, Anya, is not interested in becoming queen, so she enters the mortal realm to search for Zabriel. Anya makes a terrible discovery there: Prince Zabriel, who is using the name William Wolfram Pyrite, is an accused criminal. Anya is saddened by the fact that she can't bring her beloved cousin back to serve as Chrior's ruler. She is even more distraught by the prospect the realm now faces. Another cousin, Illumina, is now in line for the throne, but Anya doesn't believe she can be trusted. To prove her suspicions about Illumina and protect Chrior, Anya embarks on a dangerous adventure. This novel is the second in the Heirs of Chrior series by Cayla Kluver.

Other books by the same author:
The Queen's Choice, 2014
Allegiance, 2012
Legacy, 2012
Sacrifice, 2012

Other books you might like:
Cinda Williams Chima, *The Demon King*, 2009
Mindy L. Klasky, *The Glasswright's Apprentice*, 2000
William Nicholson, *Noman: Book Three of the Noble Warriors*, 2008
Rick Riordan, *The Serpent's Shadow*, 2012
J.D. Vaughn, *The Second Guard*, 2015

65

LYNN KURLAND (Pseudonym of Lynn Curland)

Dreamer's Daughter

(New York: Berkley Sensation, 2015)

Series: Nine Kingdoms Series. Book 9
Story type: Romance; Series
Subject(s): Fantasy; Romances (Fiction); Magic
Major character(s): Aisling, Seamstress (weaver); Runach, Warrior
Time period(s): Indeterminate
Locale(s): Bruadair, Fictional Location

Summary: This ninth novel in the Nine Kingdoms series by Lynn Kurland is the final story in the trilogy featuring Aisling of Bruadair and Runach of Ceangail. Aisling and Runach are forced to confront their linked destinies. Aisling has long believed that she is nobody of consequence—just a weaver from Bruadair, a country that has inexplicably been losing its magic for many years. But the truth is much different, and Aisling learns that it is up to her to restore the country's magic, the same way Runach has reclaimed his magic since his injury. Together, they will need to let go of the painful events of their past. If they hope to save Bruadair, they must face the evil that is threatening to take over.

Other books by the same author:
Dreamspinner, 2013
One Magic Moment, 2011
One Enchanted Evening, 2010
Princess of the Sword, 2009
Much Ado in the Moonlight, 2006

Other books you might like:
Catherine Asaro, *The Fire Opal*, 2007
Mercedes Lackey, *The Fairy Godmother*, 2004
Sharon Lee, *Carousel Seas*, 2015
Anne McCaffrey, *Black Horses for the King*, 1996
Maria V. Snyder, *Scent of Magic*, 2013

66

NICK LAKE

There Will Be Lies

(New York: Bloomsbury USA, 2015)

Subject(s): Family; Accidents; Mystery
Major character(s): Shelby Jane Cooper, Friend (of Mark), 17-Year-Old, Deaf Person, Accident Victim, Daughter (of Shaylene Cooper); Shaylene Cooper, Mother (of Shelby); Mark, Friend (of Shelby)
Time period(s): 21st century; 2010s
Locale(s): Arizona, United States

Summary: Shelby Jane Cooper's friend Mark offers a cryptic warning before Shelby is hit by an SUV. After the accident that injures her ankle, 17-year-old Shelby—who is deaf—sees a coyote that warns her about lies and a truth she must face. The accident has a strange effect on Shelby's mother, Shaylene, who takes her daughter away from Scottsdale to the Grand Canyon. Lies and truths are revealed on the journey. Shelby learns that her father is alive, and that he poses a danger to both Shelby and her mother. In the desert, Shelby frequently retreats to a fantasy world known as the Dreaming. The coyote appears to Shelby in the Dreaming and explains that she has a mission to fulfill. In the stark and beautiful landscape, Shelby finds that the lines between the real world and the dream world, and between lies and truth, are hard to discern.

Other books by the same author:
Hostage Three, 2013
Betrayal of the Living, 2012
Blood Ninja, 2010
The Revenge of Lord Oda, 2010

Other books you might like:

James P. Blaylock, *The Paper Grail*, 1991
Jonathan Carroll, *Glass Soup*, 2005
Caroline B. Cooney, *The Face on the Milk Carton*, 1990
Richard Grant, *Kaspian Lost*, 1999
Eva Hoffman, *The Secret*, 2001
Stephen King, *The Talisman*, 1984
Tim Powers, *Earthquake Weather*, 1997
Walter Sorrells, *Fake ID*, 2005
Nancy Springer, *Somebody*, 2009
Teri Terry, *Shattered*, 2014

67

GLENDA LARKE

The Dagger's Path

(London: Orbit, 2015)

Series: Forsaken Lands Series. Book 2
Story type: Adventure; Series
Subject(s): Fantasy; Adventure; Magic
Major character(s): Saker, Spy, Religious (priest); Ardhi, Man, Adventurer
Time period(s): Indeterminate
Locale(s): Va-cherished Lands, Fictional Location

Summary: Saker, a priest and spy, is among the party that is sailing with Ardhi to return the item that was stolen from his island by invading sailors. Ardhi must make amends for the role his treachery played in the theft of the magic feather, but his quest will be difficult. The travelers are forced to change ships during their journey, and when they arrive at Ardhi's island with the one stolen feather, they learn that the three remaining feathers are now missing. The island is in turmoil, and Saker and Ardhi must try to gain the islanders' trust and locate the lost feathers. The situation deteriorates when Saker and Ardhi realize that traders have followed them to the island. This novel is the second in the Forsaken Lands series by Glenda Larke.

Other books by the same author:
The Lascar's Dagger, 2014
The Stormlord's Exile, 2011
The Last Stormlord, 2010
Stormlord Rising, 2010
The Aware, 2003

Other books you might like:
Rowena Cory Daniells, *Besieged*, 2012
Mindy L. Klasky, *The Glasswright's Master*, 2004
Juliet E. McKenna, *Dangerous Waters*, 2011
Fiona Patton, *The Golden Tower*, 2008
Jennifer Roberson, *Deepwood*, 2007

68

SHELLY LAURENSTON

The Unleashing

(New York: Kensington, 2015)

Series: Call of Crows Series. Book 1
Story type: Contemporary - Fantasy; Immortality

Subject(s): Mythology; Romances (Fiction); Fantasy
Major character(s): Kera Watson, Veteran (of Afghanistan), Crime Victim, Friend (of Vig), Supernatural Being (Crow); Ludvig "Vig" Rundstrom, Supernatural Being (Crow), Warrior, Friend (of Kera)
Time period(s): 21st century; 2010s
Locale(s): Los Angeles, California

Summary: Kera Watson isn't afraid to fight for what she wants. After ten years as a Marine with two tours in the Middle East, she has returned to Los Angeles to readjust to civilian life. After surviving war zones, however, she meets her death at the hands of a killer, yet her life is not over. She has joined the Crows, an elite fighting warrior group under the service of the Norse god Odin. Ludvig "Vig" Rundstrom, a follower of Odin, is attracted to Kera and knows that her fighting skills make her an excellent addition to the Crows. Kera quickly assimilates, adapting to the power and battle-ready lifestyle. Vig finds himself falling in love with Kera, but the Crows become engaged in an ongoing feud with another warrior clan. This is the first title of the Call of Crows series by Shelly Laurenston.

Other books by the same author:
Wolf with Benefits, 2013
Bear Meets Girl, 2012
The Mane Squeeze, 2009
The Beast in Him, 2008
The Mane Attraction, 2008

Other books you might like:
John Holm, *The Hammer and the Cross*, 1993
Tom Holt, *Expecting Beowulf*, 2002
James Lovegrove, *The Age of Odin*, 2010
J.A. Pitts, *Black Blade Blues*, 2010
Greg van Eekhout, *Norse Code*, 2009

69

VICTORIA LAURIE

Sense of Deception

(New York: Penguin Publishing Group, 2015)

Series: Psychic Eye Series. Book 13
Story type: Mystery; Paranormal
Subject(s): Fantasy; Mystery; Psychics
Major character(s): Abby Cooper, Detective—Amateur, Spouse (of Dutch), Friend (of Candice), Psychic; Dutch Rivers, FBI Agent, Spouse (of Abby); Candice Fusco, Detective—Private, Friend (of Abby)
Time period(s): 21st century; 2010s
Locale(s): Austin, Texas

Summary: Psychic detective Abby Cooper finds herself on the wrong side of the law in the 13th Psychic Eye series entry. Abby is forced to spend a short time in jail when a judge cites her for contempt of court. Before she is released, Abby befriends an inmate who has been convicted of murder. Skylar Miller could be executed for her crime, even though she insists that she is innocent. Skylar's relatives aren't buying her claims, but Abby's psychic insights convince her that Skylar is telling the truth. Abby is determined to exonerate Skylar, and she enlists her detective friend Candice and FBI agent

husband Dutch to help with her investigation. When the last chance for an appeal slips away, Skylar's lawyer makes a desperate attempt to stay her execution. Abby must narrow down the pool of suspects if she's going to find the real killer in time.

Other books by the same author:
When, 2015
Deadly Forecast, 2013
Ghouls, Ghouls, Ghouls, 2011
Doom with a View, 2009
What's a Ghoul to Do?, 2007

Other books you might like:
Juliet Blackwell, *If Walls Could Talk*, 2010
Casey Daniels, *Supernatural Born Killers*, 2012
Justin Gustainis, *Hard Spell*, 2011
Tanya Huff, *The Enchantment Emporium*, 2009
Laura Resnick, *The Misfortune Cookie*, 2013

70

VICTORIA LAURIE

When

(New York: Disney-Hyperion, 2015)

Story type: Paranormal; Young Adult
Subject(s): Fantasy; Parapsychology; Death
Major character(s): Maddie Fynn, 16-Year-Old, 11th Grader, Daughter (of Ma), Friend (of Stubby); Ma, Mother (of Maddie), Widow(er), Alcoholic; Arnold "Stubby" Schroder, 16-Year-Old, 11th Grader, Friend (of Maddie)
Time period(s): 21st century; 2010s
Locale(s): Poplar Hollow, New York

Summary: Maddie Fynn's life changed dramatically when her father, a New York City police officer, was killed on the job. The loss was painful, but her father's death finally revealed to Maddie the meaning of the numbers she sees floating above other people's heads. The numbers that hovered above Dad's head told his death date. Now Maddie realizes that she knows exactly when all of her friends and family members will die. As Maddie's mother grieves and drinks too much, Maddie uses her strange psychic skill to earn some cash. But when she correctly predicts a young boy's death, Maddie ends up a murder suspect. Life is hard enough for Maddie, who deals with bullying at school and her mother's alcoholism at home. Now the authorities think she may be a killer. Maddie's best friend Arnold "Stubby" Schroder also lands on the suspect list until Maddie finds a way to prove that her psychic talents are real.

Other books by the same author:
Sense of Deception, 2015
Fatal Fortune, 2014
Ghoul Interrupted, 2011
Ghouls Gone Wild, 2010
A Vision of Murder, 2005

Other books you might like:
Eoin Colfer, *Artemis Fowl: The Opal Deception*, 2005
Roderick Gordon, *Closer*, 2011
Melinda Metz, *Gifted Touch*, 2001

James Patterson, *The Protectors*, 2009
Darren Shan, *Cirque Du Freak*, 2001

71

MARK LAWRENCE

The Liar's Key

(New York: Ace Books, 2015)

Series: Red Queen's War Series. Book 2
Story type: Series; Sword and Sorcery
Subject(s): Magic; Fantasy; Monarchs
Major character(s): Jalan Kendeth, Royalty (prince); Snorri ver Snagason, Viking; Red Queen, Grandmother (of Jal), Royalty (Queen)
Time period(s): Indeterminate Past
Locale(s): Broken Empire, Fictional Location

Summary: In this second novel in the Red Queen's War trilogy by Mark Lawrence, Prince Jalan Kendeth and the Viking Snorri ver Snagason have acquired the ancient artifact known as Loki's Key. It is capable of opening any door—including the one between the world of the living and the world of the dead. Though Jal wants nothing to do with it—he wishes only to keep it out of the hands of his grandmother, the Red Queen, and her armies—Snorri has other plans. He wants to bring his family back from the dead. However, to do so may mean facing an impossible threat—The Dead King—in whose hands the key would bring certain destruction to the world.

Other books by the same author:
Prince of Fools, 2014
Emperor of Thorns, 2013
King of Thorns, 2012
Prince of Thorns, 2011

Other books you might like:
Peter V. Brett, *The Daylight War*, 2013
Mark Chadbourn, *Always Forever*, 2001
Marjorie M. Liu, *Tiger Eye*, 2005
Brian McClellan, *Promise of Blood*, 2013
Brian Staveley, *The Providence of Fire*, 2015

72

SHARON LEE

Carousel Seas

(Riverdale, New York: Baen, 2015)

Series: Carousel Tides Series. Book 3
Story type: Contemporary; Series
Subject(s): Fantasy; Beaches; Amusement parks
Major character(s): Kate Archer, Businesswoman (owner and operator of carousel), Guardian, Friend (of Borgan); Borgan, Man, Guardian, Friend (of Kate)
Time period(s): 21st century; 2010s
Locale(s): Changing Land, Fictional Location; Archers Beach, Maine

Summary: Kate Archer operates the old carousel in the seaside town of Archers Beach, Maine. Her job is not as straightforward as it appears. The carousel is enchanted, and its animals conceal a dark secret. All of Archers Beach is magic, in fact. It is a supernatural realm known as Changing Land and home to a number of mythical creatures. In addition to being the keeper of the carousel, Kate is a Guardian who is charged with protecting the land. Borgan, a man Kate has recently started dating, is also a Guardian. They seem perfectly suited to one another until another female figure enters the scene. The sea goddess who comes to Archers Beach also has romantic feelings for Borgan, and her attempt to win his heart will have consequences for Kate and the territory she is supposed to protect.

Other books by the same author:
Carousel Sun, 2014
Duainfey, 2014
Korval's Game, 2013
Carousel Tides, 2010
Longeye, 2009

Other books you might like:
David B. Coe, *The Sorcerers' Plague*, 2007
Katharine Kerr, *The Gold Falcon*, 2006
Lynn Kurland, *Dreamer's Daughter*, 2015
Patricia A. McKillip, *The Bards of Bone Plain*, 2010
Sharon Shinn, *Fortune and Fate*, 2008
Jo Walton, *The Just City*, 2014

73

STEPHEN LEIGH

The Crow of Connemara

(New York: DAW, 2015)

Story type: Contemporary - Exotic
Subject(s): Fantasy; Ireland; Mythology
Major character(s): Colin Doyle, Man (Irish-American), Musician; Maeve Gallagher, Woman (Islander)
Time period(s): 21st century; 2010s
Locale(s): Ireland; Chicago, Illinois

Summary: Colin Doyle and Maeve Gallagher are from different places, but they are bound by their Celtic heritage—and perhaps something else. When Colin's father is stricken with a sudden illness, he reunites with his family in Chicago. Colin, a musician, hasn't been home in a while, and he stays with his sister so he can avoid returning to his childhood bedroom, as his mother would prefer. Meanwhile, in Ireland, another vigil takes place by the bedside of an ailing man. A young woman named Maeve Gallagher, who lives on one of the islands off Ireland's western coast, is part of this story. Maeve is an Oileanach, which is a term for "Islander" that carries unpleasant connotations. The mainlanders blame the Islanders for the unexplained events that take place in the coastal region. Although Colin and Maeve are thousands of miles apart as their story begins, they are eventually brought together by Celtic mythology and romance.

Other books by the same author:
Immortal Muse, 2014
Assassins' Dawn, 2013
The Woods, 2012

Heir of Stone, 2005

Other books you might like:
S.L. Farrell, *Holder of Lightning*, 2003
Kenneth C. Flint, *Cromm*, 1990
Gregory Frost, *Tain*, 1986
Morgan Llywelyn, *The Isles of the Blest*, 1989
Juliet Marillier, *Seer of Sevenwaters*, 2010

74

J.F. LEWIS

Oathkeeper

(New York: Pyr, 2015)

Series: Grudgebearer Trilogy. Book 2
Story type: Series; Sword and Sorcery
Subject(s): Wars; Fantasy; Brothers
Major character(s): Kholster, Immortal (Aern), Warrior, Leader (of the Aern, deceased), Father (of Rae'en), Warrior, Slave (former); Rae'en, Daughter (of Kholster), Leader (of the Aern), Warrior; Rivvek, Royalty (Prince, heir of Eldrennai throne), Brother (of Dolvek); Dolvek, Royalty (Prince of Eldrennai), Brother (of Rivvek)
Time period(s): Indeterminate
Locale(s): Fictional Location

Summary: The second volume of the Grudgebearer trilogy focuses on Rae'en, the Freeborn daughter and successor of Kholster. Kholster, the firstborn of the Aern race, is a Grudgebearer. The Aern is an engineered race, designed as warrior-slaves who will protect their creators from their reptilian, magic-resistant enemies known as the Zaur. After the bonds of slavery are broken, it is only Kholster's oath that prevents genocide and war upon his people. Upon his death, all oaths are null and void, leading Rae'en to prevent a war of vengeance upon the Eldrennai, the creators of the Aern. The heir to the Eldrennai throne is Prince Rivvek, who must complete the Test of Four to save his kingdom while his brother, Prince Dolvek, prepares for war with the Zaur. The Zaur are too happy to take advantage of Kholster's death and the disintegration of the oath. Rae'en must decide if she will lead her people into battle against their true enemy.

75

TOM LLOYD

Old Man's Ghosts

(London: Gollancz, 2015)

Series: Empire of a Hundred Houses Series. Book 2
Story type: Adventure; Military
Subject(s): Military life; Fantasy; Infants
Major character(s): Enchei, Military Personnel (Retired); Narin, Investigator, Friend (of Enchei), Lover (of Lady Kine); Lady Kine, Spouse (of House Wyvern nobleman), Lover (of Narin), Noblewoman
Time period(s): Indeterminate
Locale(s): Imperial City, Fictional Location

Summary: The horrors of war can pursue some soldiers far beyond their days of service, but Enchei hopes to escape them and live a quiet, peaceful life. It's been more than ten years and all has been well, until an old mistake rises up to intrude into his otherwise quiet life. His friend, Narin, has become a father through his affair with the married Lady Kine, and the illegitimate child's presence further riles the Imperial City. These events force a reluctant Enchei to face his past. With dark magical forces and evil humans both in pursuit, Enchei will have to find a way to battle ghosts he hoped were long gone and buried. This is the second title of Tom Lloyd's Empire of a Hundred Houses series.

Other books by the same author:
The God Tattoo, 2013
The Dusk Watchman, 2012
The Ragged Man, 2010
The Grave Thief, 2009
The Twilight Herald, 2007

Other books you might like:
Peter V. Brett, *The Warded Man*, 2009
Alan Campbell, *Scar Night*, 2007
David Gemmell, *Lord of the Silver Bow*, 2005
Joel Shepherd, *Haven*, 2011
Adrian Tchaikovsky, *The Guns of the Dawn*, 2015

76

EVIE MANIERI

Fortune's Blight

(New York: Tom Doherty Associates, 2015)

Series: Shattered Kingdoms Series. Book 2
Story type: Alternate World; Series
Subject(s): Wars; Superstition; Supernatural
Major character(s): Daryan, Royalty (King of Shadari); Mongrel, Mercenary (hired to help Shadari)
Time period(s): Indeterminate
Locale(s): Norland, Fictional Location; Shadar, Fictional Location

Summary: In the first novel in the Shattered Kingdoms series, the people of the kingdom of Shadar escaped domination by the Dead Ones. Now, the Shadari are faced with the cost of that victory. Trouble has erupted on many fronts under King Daryan as his people try to cope with the struggles of day to day life in the wake of war. The people respond to shortages and suffering by fighting and clinging to superstition. In Norland, those who once enslaved the Shadari are finding life difficult as well. A mercenary named the Mongrel heads deep into Norland to make good on a promise, one that could drag her and others into a growing conflict that could rip apart the empire. While Shadari and Norland struggle against their separate but related challenges, an old but powerful being waits and watches from the far-off tower of Ravindal Castle for her chance to act.

Other books by the same author:
Blood's Pride, 2013

Other books you might like:
Rowena Cory Daniells, *The King's Bastard*, 2010
Lynn Flewelling, *Casket of Souls*, 2012

Paul Kearney, *Kings of Morning*, 2012
Juliet E. McKenna, *Defiant Peaks*, 2012
Elizabeth Vaughan, *War Cry*, 2011

77

MARSHALL RYAN MARESCA

The Thorn of Dentonhill

(New York: DAW, 2015)

Series: Maradaine Series. Book 1
Story type: Magic Conflict; Series
Subject(s): Fantasy; Magic; Universities and colleges
Major character(s): Veranix Calbert, Young Man, Student—College (University of Maradaine), Vigilante; Willem Fenmere, Criminal, Drug Dealer
Time period(s): Indeterminate
Locale(s): Arduchy of Maradaine, Fictional Location

Summary: The first novel in the Maradaine series introduces Veranix Calbert, a young man who is studying magic at the University of Maradaine. Veranix is not a stellar student; he is distracted by a personal matter that takes up much of his free time. Veranix's family was devastated by the drug known as effitte—and the supplier of that drug, Willem Fenmere. Fenmere operates his drug trade in Dentonhill, a neighborhood that borders the university, and Veranix has made it his mission to dismantle Fenmere's business. He slips away from campus at night to sabotage the transactions that have made Fenmere Dentonhill's top criminal. When Veranix intercepts a pair of powerful objects that were on their way to Fenmere's mage customers, the vigilante college student gets the attention of Maradaine's criminal and magical residents. Things also heat up behind the walls of the university, where the faculty has grown suspicious of Veranix.

Other books you might like:
Steven Erikson, *The Crippled God*, 2011
Simon R. Green, *Wolf in the Fold*, 1991
Juliet E. McKenna, *Banners in the Wind*, 2010
Sarah Monette, *Melusine*, 2005
Fiona Patton, *The Shining City*, 2011

78

ARI MARMELL

Covenant's End

(Amherst, New York: Prometheus Books, 2015)

Series: Widdershins Adventure Series. Book 4
Story type: Adventure; Series
Subject(s): Adventure; Magic; Fantasy
Major character(s): Widdershins "Shins", Girl, Thief, Companion (of Olgun); Olgun, Deity (god), Companion (of Widdershins); Lisette Suvagne, Enemy (of Shins)
Time period(s): Indeterminate
Locale(s): Davillon, Fictional Location

Summary: In the fourth novel in the Widdershins Adventure series, Widdershins—a young woman from an aristocratic family who turned to a life of thievery—returns to the city of Davillon after a lengthy absence. When Shins and Olgun, her companion and personal god, fled Davillon, they left bad feelings in their wake. Now that Shins is back in town, she learns that much has changed. Her foe Lisette Suvagne has used dark magic to influence the workings of the Finder's Guild, an organization whose membership includes Shins and other thieves. Lisette isn't just interested in leading the Finder's Guild; she wants to control Davillon's government and its citizens. Shins may be able to stop Lisette from executing her plot, but she will need help from Olgun and her old friends from Davillon. However, she must first win those friends' forgiveness.

Other books by the same author:
Hot Lead, Cold Iron, 2014
In Thunder Forged, 2013
Thief's Covenant, 2012
The Goblin Corps, 2011
The Warlord's Legacy, 2011

Other books you might like:
Hilari Bell, *Rise of a Hero*, 2005
Holly Black, *Black Heart*, 2012
Michael Jensen, *Woven*, 2015
Diana Wynne Jones, *Dark Lord of Derkholm*, 1998
William Nicholson, *The Wind Singer: An Adventure*, 2000

79

KELLY MCCULLOUGH

Darkened Blade

(New York: Ace Books, 2015)

Series: Fallen Blade Series. Book 6
Story type: Series; Sword and Sorcery
Subject(s): Revenge; Fantasy; Violence
Major character(s): Aral Kingslayer, Assassin, Magician; Triss, Supernatural Being (shade); Namara, Deity, Spirit
Time period(s): Indeterminate
Locale(s): Fictional Location

Summary: In this fantasy novel, the sixth in the Fallen Blade series, once famed assassin Aral Kingslayer lost everything after the murder of his patron goddess, Namara, and the destruction of her temple. He has fought his way back from the darkness, but has never fully recovered from the loss—and has never gotten vengeance for her death. When Namara appears to him in a dream, asking him to get revenge, Aral doesn't hesitate. He'll need to rekindle relationships with the other former Blades, and to call upon his familiar, the Shade Triss. Even then, the battle will be impossible—but Aral knows he'll fight to the death if necessary to avenge Namara.

Other books by the same author:
Drawn Blades, 2014
Blade Reforged, 2013
Bared Blade, 2012
Broken Blade, 2011
CodeSpell, 2008

Other books you might like:
Dave Duncan, *Lord of the Fire Lands*, 1999
Raymond E. Feist, *Exile's Return*, 2004
L.E. Modesitt Jr., *Cyador's Heirs*, 2014
Melanie Rawn, *Touchstone*, 2012
Lawrence Watt-Evans, *Night of Madness*, 2000

80

SEANAN MCGUIRE

Pocket Apocalypse

(New York: DAW, 2015)

Series: InCryptid Series. Book 4
Story type: Contemporary - Exotic; Series
Subject(s): Fantasy; Zoology; Werewolves
Major character(s): Alexander "Alex" Price, Scientist
(cryptozoologist), Boyfriend (of Shelby Tanner);
Shelby Tanner, Girlfriend (of Alex Price), Scientist
(zoologist)
Time period(s): 21st century; 2010s
Locale(s): Australia; Ohio, United States

Summary: In the fourth novel in the InCryptid series,
cryptozoologist Alex Price travels to Australia with his
girlfriend, zoologist Shelby Tanner, to visit Shelby's
family. Alex comes from a long line of cryptozoologists,
and as part of that clan, has investigated a variety of
mysterious creatures. In Australia, Alex encounters
legendary beasts he has not seen before, including a vicious species of werewolf that wants to take over the
country. As Alex adjusts to his unfamiliar surroundings,
he does his best to solve the werewolf problem—even
though he doesn't get a warm welcome from the
Australian cryptozoology community. Meanwhile, he
tries to make inroads with the Shelby's family members,
who don't approve of how much time Shelby spends in
the United States.

Other books by the same author:
Sparrow Hill Road, 2014
The Winter Long, 2014
Midnight Blue-Light Special, 2013
Late Eclipses, 2011
A Local Habitation, 2010

Other books you might like:
Amber Benson, *Death's Daughter*, 2009
John Birmingham, *Ascendance: Dave vs. the Monsters*,
2015
Laurell K. Hamilton, *Dead Ice*, 2015
Ben Macallan, *Desdaemona*, 2011
Devon Monk, *Magic in the Blood*, 2009
Lisa Shearin, *Armed & Magical*, 2007
Carrie Vaughn, *Kitty and the Silver Bullet*, 2008

81

JON F. MERZ

Slavers of the Savage Catacombs

(Riverdale, New York: Baen, 2015)

Series: Shadow Warrior Saga Series. Book 2
Story type: Alternate Universe; Series

Subject(s): Fantasy; Martial arts; Adventure
Major character(s): Ran, Man, Warrior (Shadow Warrior),
Martial Arts Expert
Time period(s): Indeterminate
Locale(s): Igul, Fictional Location; Nehon, Fictional
Location

Summary: In the second novel in the Shadow Warrior
saga, Ran is sent on another dangerous mission in the
fantastic realm he inhabits. He travels to the northern
region with a caravan to see if the reports of an impending incursion there are true. Ran is supposed to serve as
a guard to the caravan, but he ends up being kidnapped
by a band of slavers. Now Ran joins others who are
forced to work as slaves in an underground nightmare.
The leader of the grim operation is a deposed king who
is determined to resume his reign. Ran is now trapped
underground, worrying about the invasion that may be
taking place above him. He hatches a risky escape plan
but quickly learns that the subterranean labyrinth is more
complex and dangerous than he realized.

Other books by the same author:
The Undead Hordes of Kan-Gul, 2013
The Destructor, 2003
The Syndicate, 2003
The Fixer, 2002
The Invoker, 2002

Other books you might like:
Jeff Grubb, *The Last Guardian*, 2002
Chris A. Jackson, *Pirate's Promise*, 2015
Mel Odom, *The Sea Devil's Eye*, 2000
Tim Pratt, *Liar's Blade*, 2013
Chris Willrich, *Pathfinder Tales: The Dagger of Trust*,
2014

82

L.E. MODESITT

Madness in Solidar

(New York: Tom Doherty Associates, 2015)

Series: Imager Portfolio Series. Book 9
Story type: Adventure; Fantasy
Subject(s): Wizards; Magic; Fantasy
Major character(s): Alastar, Leader (new Maitre of the
Collegium), Wizard; Rex Ryen, Royalty (ruler of
Solidar); Desyrk, Wizard (Rogue Imager)
Time period(s): Indeterminate
Locale(s): Solidar, Fictional Location

Summary: Nearly 400 years after its founding, the Collegium of Imagers—wizards—at Solidar has fallen into
shambles. So few of the Imagers are worthy of the title
that, when their leader knows his days are winding down,
he sends for a powerful but virtually unknown Imager
named Alastar to take his place. Alastar has no clue what
he's facing when he takes over the role of Maitre. To
make matters worse in Solidar, ruler Rex Ryen is taxing
the rich and powerful High Holders and the merchants to
fund construction. When they refuse to pay, Ryen orders
them killed one at a time to prove his resolve. An army
so eager to fight they'll side with anyone and a rogue
wizard named Desyrk add to Alastar's troubles as he

tries to save the faltering Collegium and restore it to power. This is the ninth book in the Imager Portfolio series.

Other books by the same author:
The Heritage of Cyador, 2014
Rex Regis, 2014
Antiagon Fire, 2013
Princeps, 2012
Wellspring of Chaos, 2004

Other books you might like:
Kelley Armstrong, *Dime Store Magic*, 2004
Emma Bull, *Finder: A Novel of the Borderlands*, 1994
Charles de Lint, *Forests of the Heart*, 2000
Simon R. Green, *Agents of Light and Darkness*, 2003
Michelle Paver, *The Eye of the Falcon*, 2015
Will Shetterly, *Elsewhere*, 1991

83

DEVON MONK

Infinity Bell

(London: Penguin Group, 2015)

Series: House Immortal Series. Book 2
Story type: Immortality; Series
Subject(s): Immortality; Brothers and sisters; Conspiracy
Major character(s): Matilda Case, Immortal (artificial being), Sister (of Quentin), Friend (of Abraham), Fugitive; Abraham Seventh, Fugitive, Immortal (artificial being), Friend (of Matilda); Quentin, Fugitive, Brother (of Matilda), Genius
Time period(s): Indeterminate Future
Locale(s): Earth

Summary: Matilda Case is one of the "galvanized," powerful, artificial beings pieced together and infused with immortality. After defying the ruling Houses that control the world and triggering a deadly war between them, Matilda, her genius brother, Quentin, and injured fellow galvanized, Abraham Seventh, are on the run, trying to escape the cruel reach of those who wish to control them. They have to find a way to keep forces within the Houses from recreating the time-travel experiment that gave the galvanized their immortality. But the stakes go far beyond their own safety. If the experiment is successful, it could mean the destruction of the world as well. This is the second book in Devon Monk's House Immortal series.

Other books by the same author:
House Immortal, 2014
Cold Copper, 2013
Hell Bent, 2013
Tin Swift, 2012
Magic at the Gate, 2010

Other books you might like:
Simon R. Green, *The Bride Wore Black Leather*, 2012
Mercedes Lackey, *Home from the Sea*, 2012
Sarah Monette, *The Virtu*, 2006
Sharon Shinn, *Mystic and Rider*, 2005
Michelle West, *Skirmish*, 2012

84

MICHAEL MOORCOCK

The Whispering Swarm

(New York: Tom Doherty Associates, 2015)

Series: Sanctuary of the White Friars. Book 1
Story type: Adventure; Alternate History
Subject(s): Alternative worlds; Autobiographies; Writers
Major character(s): Michael Moorcock, Writer, Adventurer, Friend (of Friar Isidore); Friar Isidore, Religious (friar), Friend (of Michael)
Time period(s): 20th century; 1940s-1950s
Locale(s): London, England

Summary: This semi-autobiographical story is Michael Moorcock's first solo effort in nearly a decade. It tells the tale of a young Michael in post-World War II London and combines his real past with fantasy as he meets Friar Isadore and discovers Alsacia, a mysterious and hidden alternate version of London populated by mythical creatures and characters, as well as some of the author's real-life contemporaries. The story moves between real incidents in the author's past that are woven into fantasy adventures in the Sanctuary, as the alternate London is also known. This secret world provides a respite from the real-life challenges of coming of age for the fictional Michael in the early stages of his writing and editing career in post-war London as well as a glimpse into the fantasy life that fueled this career for the character. This is the first novel in the planned three-book Sanctuary of the White Friars series.

Other books by the same author:
Elric in the Dream Realms, 2009
The Skrayling Tree, 2003
Lunching with the Antichrist, 1995
Von Bek, 1995
The Fortress of the Pearl, 1989

Other books you might like:
Elizabeth Bear, *Karen Memory*, 2015
Simon R. Green, *Tales from the Nightside*, 2015
Maureen Johnson, *The Shadow Cabinet*, 2015
Michael Moorcock, *Phoenix in Obsidian*, 2014
Iris Murdoch, *A Severed Head*, 1961
Juliet Nicolson, *Abdication*, 2012
V.E. Schwab, *A Darker Shade of Magic*, 2015
Ian Tregillis, *The Mechanical*, 2015

85

SILVIA MORENO-GARCIA

Signal to Noise

(Oxford, United Kingdom: Solaris, 2015)

Story type: Coming-of-Age; Light Fantasy
Subject(s): Adolescent interpersonal relations; Magic; Music
Major character(s): Meche, 15-Year-Old, Friend (of Sebastian and Daniela), Magician; Sebastian, 15-Year-Old, Friend (of Meche and Daniela); Daniela, 15-Year-Old, Friend (of Meche and Sebastian)

Time period(s): Multiple Time Periods
Locale(s): Mexico City, Mexico

Summary: Fifteen-year-old Meche and her friends, Sebastian and Daniela, are not part of the popular crowd. Very little seems right with their lives in 1988 in Mexico City. One day Meche discovers the magic in her vinyl record collection—literally. Her records show her how to cast spells that make life better for the three pals, at least at first. Eventually the power of the magic causes stress on their relationship. Fast forward 20 years to 2009, and Meche has returned home for the funeral of her father, a disc jockey who fostered her love of music. The former friends meet and rehash their past, resurrecting the conflicts and difficulties of the past. Meche decides her life needs just a little more magic.

Other books by the same author:
Love and Other Poisons, 2014

Other books you might like:
Jeffrey Ford, *The Portrait of Mrs. Charbuque*, 2002
Kate Mosse, *Labyrinth*, 2006
Tim Powers, *Hide Me Among the Graves*, 2012
Catherynne M. Valente, *Under in the Mere*, 2010
Jo Walton, *The Just City*, 2014

86

J.C. NELSON

Armageddon Rules

(New York: Ace Books, 2015)

Series: Grimm Agency Series. Book 2
Story type: Series; Urban
Subject(s): Fantasy; Supernatural; Fairies
Major character(s): Marissa Locks, Woman, Friend (of Princess Ari), Businesswoman (partner in Grimm Agency); Ari, Supernatural Being (Fairy Princess), Friend (of Marissa); Grimm, Employer (former, of Marissa), Businessman (Founder, Grimm Agency), Supernatural Being (Fairy Godfather)
Time period(s): Indeterminate
Locale(s): Kingdom, Fictional Location

Summary: The second book in the Grimm Agency series by J. C. Nelson finds Marissa juggling the responsibilities of her new role as partner in the Grimm Agency, an organization that specializes in magically creating happily-ever-afters. The thrill of a fiery romance and the threat of murderous poodles leave Marissa with little time for peace and quiet. While the Agency's founder, the Fairy Godfather Grimm, remains mysteriously absent and her best friend, Princess Ari, falls prey to a sleeping spell, a violent enemy from Marissa's past shows up in search of revenge. Marissa is forced to take matters into her own hands, and in turn, triggers the Apocalypse. The Agency is known for its ability to solve any problem, but does Marissa have what it takes to protect the land of Kingdom from the end of days?

Other books by the same author:
Free Agent, 2014

Other books you might like:
Keri Arthur, *Bound to Shadows*, 2009
Hannah Jayne, *Under the Gun*, 2013

Victoria Laurie, *Killer Insight*, 2006
Kat Richardson, *Revenant: A Greywalker Novel*, 2014
Lauren M. Roy, *Grave Matters*, 2015

87

NAOMI NOVIK

Uprooted

(New York: Del Rey, 2015)

Story type: Adventure
Subject(s): Adventure; Fairy tales; Romances (Fiction)
Major character(s): Agnieszka, Young Woman, Friend (of Kasia); Kasia, Young Woman, Friend (of Agnieszka); Dragon, Wizard
Time period(s): Indeterminate
Locale(s): Fictional Location

Summary: To protect themselves from the dark forces of the nearby Wood, the residents of a small village have entered a repulsive bargain with a wizard. Dragon, as the wizard is called, selects one young woman from the village to serve him for ten years. In exchange for his chosen girl, Dragon keeps the villagers safe. But for the girl that lives with Dragon, her ten-year stint is a nightmare. The time is approaching for Dragon to make his next selection, and everyone is certain that beautiful Kasia will be the wizard's choice. When Dragon chooses Kasia's friend Agnieszka, all are shocked—including Agnieszka, who was already mourning for Kasia. As Agnieszka assumes her place with Dragon, she makes a surprising discovery. She also has magic powers, and she must put them to use when new challenges arise.

Other books by the same author:
Blood of Tyrants, 2013
Crucible of Gold, 2012
Tongues of Serpents, 2010
Empire of Ivory, 2007
Black Powder War, 2006

Other books you might like:
Philippa Ballantine, *Kindred and Wings*, 2013
Barbara Hambly, *Dragonsbane*, 1985
Mercedes Lackey, *Joust*, 2003
Melanie Rawn, *Sunrunner's Fire*, 1990
Jo Walton, *Tooth and Claw*, 2003

88

NNEDI OKORAFOR

The Book of Phoenix

(New York: DAW Books, 2015)

Story type: Dystopian; Futuristic
Subject(s): Genetic engineering; Love; Prisoners
Major character(s): Phoenix, Prisoner (of Tower Seven), Genetically Altered Being, Lover (of Saeed); Saeed, Genetically Altered Being, Lover (of Phoenix), Prisoner (of Tower Seven)
Time period(s): Indeterminate Future
Locale(s): New York, New York

Summary: Phoenix is a genetically created being, a grown woman in mind and appearance, but was born only two years ago. She has an eidetic memory and remarkable healing powers. Her abilities have been tested to the limit through medical experimentation. Phoenix belongs to Tower 7, one of the genetic technology corporations that run the United States, and has spent her whole life inside the building. She devotes herself to expanding her knowledge and physical prowess and enjoying a blossoming romance with her friend and fellow genetic creation, Saeed. When Saeed takes his own life after witnessing something terrible, Phoenix is devastated. She realizes that the staff of Tower 7 will never reveal the truth behind Saeed's death and that her home is actually her prison. Phoenix flees her captors and embarks upon a search for her identity. This is a prequel to the novel *Who Fears Death*.

Other books by the same author:
Lagoon, 2015
Who Fears Death, 2010
The Shadow Speaker, 2007

Other books you might like:
Octavia E. Butler, *Adulthood Rites*, 1988
Charles de Lint, *Forests of the Heart*, 2000
Ken Liu, *The Grace of Kings*, 2015
Tim Powers, *Declare*, 2001
Jo Walton, *The Just City*, 2014

89

DANIEL JOSE OLDER

Half-Resurrection Blues

(New York: Penguin Publishing Group, 2015)

Series: Bone Street Rumba Series. Book 1
Story type: Series; Urban
Subject(s): Fantasy; Urban life; Afterlife
Major character(s): Carlos Delacruz, Agent (New York Council of the Dead), Young Man
Time period(s): 21st century; 2010s
Locale(s): New York, New York

Summary: In the first novel in the Bone Street Rumba series, author Daniel Jose Older introduces Carlos Delacruz, a Brooklyn resident who works as an agent for the New York Council of the Dead. Carlos is known in the business as an inbetweener. He was brought back to life after dying and now remembers nothing about his previous life or temporary demise. Carlos works to resolve issues that arise between living humans and the deceased. There are other inbetweeners in the city, but as Carlos learns, they are not all as benevolent as he is. One of the inbetweeners has magical abilities, which he's using to assemble a band of demons known as ngks. The ngks pose a threat to the spirit population, and they have targeted some of the Council's agents. Carlos must find and stop the inbetweener who's behind the plot before he succeeds in opening the gates of the Underworld.

Other books by the same author:
Salsa Nocturna, 2012

Other books you might like:
Ann Aguirre, *Blue Diablo: A Corine Solomon Novel*, 2009
Ilona Andrews, *Magic Breaks*, 2014
Laurell K. Hamilton, *A Caress of Twilight*, 2002
Seanan McGuire, *Discount Armageddon*, 2012
Devon Monk, *Magic to the Bone*, 2008

90

REGGIE OLIVER

The Sea of Blood

(Colusa, California: Dark Renaissance Books, 2015)

Story type: Collection; Horror
Subject(s): Horror; Short stories; Ghosts

Summary: This is a collection of short horror fiction from the span of award-winning author Reggie Oliver's career, as well as several new stories. Including works from his previous six volumes, all of which have achieved literary honors, many of the stories are inspired by the darker side of show business, such as "The Skins," while others draw from religion and academe. This collection, winner of the 2012 Children of the Night Award for Best Work of Supernatural Fiction, contains titles such as "Holiday From Hell," "The Baskerville Midgets," and "Mrs. Midnight."

91

ROBIN D. OWENS

Ghost Killer

(New York: Berkley Sensation, 2015)

Series: Ghost Seer Series. Book 3
Story type: Paranormal; Series
Subject(s): Ghosts; Fantasy; Romances (Fiction)
Major character(s): Clare Cermak, Psychic, Girlfriend (of Zach), Accountant; Zach Slade, Detective—Private, Boyfriend (of Clare), Psychic
Time period(s): 21st century; 2010s
Locale(s): Creede, Colorado

Summary: In this third novel in the Ghost Seer series by Robin D. Owens, accountant Clare Cermak is still learning to use her new abilities to see ghosts. She inherited this talent—along with a hefty fortune—from her recently deceased aunt. But when Clare and her boyfriend, private investigator and psychic Zach Slade, encounter an evil presence attacking and threatening to kill a young boy, she knows she can't just stand by, no matter the threat it poses to her. She and Zach get to work looking for a means to fight the evil spirit, but Clare discovers that the entity is much more dangerous than even she realized. She makes an impossible choice that puts Zach's life at risk as she tries to use her abilities to kill the murderous being.

Other books by the same author:
Echoes in the Dark, 2014
Ghost Layer, 2014
Keepers of the Flame, 2008

Protector of the Flight, 2007
Sorceress of Faith, 2006

Other books you might like:
Ilona Andrews, *Fate's Edge*, 2011
Keri Arthur, *Dangerous Games*, 2007
Juliet Blackwell, *Secondhand Spirits*, 2009
E.J. Copperman, *Night of the Living Deed*, 2010
Victoria Laurie, *Better Read than Dead*, 2005

`92`

CARRIE PATEL

Cities and Thrones

(Nottingham, United Kingdom: Angry Robot, 2015)

Series: Buried Life Series. Book 2
Story type: Mystery; Series
Subject(s): Fantasy; Urban life; Mystery
Major character(s): Liesl Malone, Detective—Police (inspector); Arnault, Spy
Time period(s): Indeterminate
Locale(s): Recoletta, Fictional Location

Summary: The city of Recoletta, which lies deep underground, has a social structure all its own. The streets are illuminated with gas lamps, but the shadows conceal dark secrets. The origin of the subterranean city has been unknown by most—until now. The public has learned the truth about Recoletta's history, and the information sends shockwaves throughout the city. A recent coup has also shaken the city's society and prompted a power struggle between rebel and agrarian groups. Liesl Malone, a police inspector, finds herself at the center of the unfolding situation. She must try to maintain order in Recoletta as she keeps tabs on the spies who are at work in the city. This novel is the second in the Buried Life series.

Other books by the same author:
The Buried Life, 2014

Other books you might like:
Joe Abercrombie, *The Blade Itself*, 2006
Alan Campbell, *Iron Angel*, 2008
Jacqueline Carey, *Banewreaker*, 2004
Scott Lynch, *The Republic of Thieves*, 2008
China Mieville, *The Scar*, 2002

`93`

DEN PATRICK

The Boy Who Wept Blood

(Cottonwood, California: Orion Publishing Group, 2015)

Series: Erebus Sequence Series. Book 2
Story type: Adventure; Alternate World
Subject(s): Adventure; Wars; Fantasy
Major character(s): Dino, Young Man, Warrior (swordsman); Anea, Royalty (Queen of Demesne); Lucien de Fontein, Warrior (Dino's mentor), Missing Person
Time period(s): Indeterminate
Locale(s): Demesne, Fictional Location

Summary: Dino is a young swordsman who has found himself facing great challenges. He's sworn an oath to protect the ruler of Demesne, but Queen Anea's efforts on behalf of the fledgling democracy are faltering and a malevolent force is at work against her. Dino struggles to live up to his sworn promise and the example of his mentor, Lucien, though he has been without Lucien's guidance for a decade. Dino is challenged by the powerful families of Landfall, who will do anything to preserve their interests. The young warrior faces a difficult choice: be true to his own values, or resort to spying and murder to honor his vow. This is the second title in the Erebus Sequence series by Den Patrick.

Other books you might like:
Steven Brust, *Tiassa*, 2011
Dave Duncan, *The Alchemist's Apprentice*, 2007
David Eddings, *Guardians of the West*, 1987
Robin Hobb, *Shaman's Crossing*, 2005
Ellen Kushner, *Swordspoint*, 1987

`94`

MICHELLE PAVER

The Eye of the Falcon

(New York: Penguin Young Readers, 2015)

Series: Gods and Warriors Series. Book 3
Story type: Adventure
Subject(s): Ancient Greek civilization; Lions; Falcons
Major character(s): Hylas, Teenager (former goatherder), Friend (of Pirra), Thief, Brother (of Issi); Pirra, Daughter (of high priestess), Friend (of Hylas), Teenager; Telamon, Warrior (leader of the Crows); Issi, Sister (of Hylas)
Locale(s): Keftiu, Greece

Summary: When Hylas began this journey, he was a naive goatherd setting out on a quest to rescue his kidnapped sister, Issi. The trials he has endured have made him stronger, and helped him forge a friendship with Pirra, daughter of the high priestess. When Pirra is taken captive, Hylas travels to the island of Keftiu to rescue her, but it may be Hylas who needs rescuing. Keftiu has been devastated by plague and a volcanic eruption. And to make matters worse, the evil warrior clan known as the Crows is also en route, seeking a prized dagger stolen by Pirra. Reunited, Hylas and Pirra team up with their allies, a lion cub and falcon, to face the Crows in a battle to save what they hold dear. This is the third book in Michelle Paver's Gods and Warriors series.

Other books by the same author:
The Burning Shadow, 2014
A Place in the Hills, 2013
The Shadow Catcher, 2013
Gods and Warriors, 2012
Fever Hill, 2004

Other books you might like:
Janet Lee Carey, *In the Time of the Dragon Moon*, 2015
Robert Jordan, *The Eye of the World*, 1990
George R.R. Martin, *A Game of Thrones*, 1996
L.E. Modesitt, *Madness in Solidar*, 2015
Paula Volsky, *The Grand Ellipse*, 2000

95

LINDSEY PIPER

Hunted Warrior

(New York: Pocket Books, 2015)

Series: Dragon Kings Series. Book 3
Story type: Adventure; Romance
Subject(s): Ancient Greek civilization; Demons; Royalty
Major character(s): Malnefoley, Royalty (leader of the Dragon Kings), Demon, Supernatural Being; The Pet, Woman, Psychic (seer), Fugitive
Locale(s): Greece

Summary: The god-like Dragon Kings have been ruling in the shadows for thousands of years. But now their race is dying. The troubled ruler of the demonic warriors, Malnefoley—known as the Usurper for the questionable way he achieved power—may have found a way to save his people. First he has to track down a dangerous fugitive known as the Pet, a cunning soothsayer who may hold the key to reversing the Dragon King's infertility. Malnefoley's sole objective is to return her and her knowledge to his stronghold. But the Pet has another mission, and when she begins to weave a spell on Malnefoley's heart, he may find himself being swept up in her plans. This is the third book in Lindsey Piper's Dragon Kings series.

Other books by the same author:
Blood Warrior, 2013
Caged Warrior, 2013

Other books you might like:
Keri Arthur, *Moon Sworn*, 2010
Elizabeth Bear, *Range of Ghosts*, 2012
Steve Bein, *Disciple of the Wind*, 2015
Simon R. Green, *From a Drood to a Kill*, 2015
Lisa Shearin, *Con & Conjure*, 2011

96

TERRY PRATCHETT
MARK BEECH, Illustrator

Dragons at Crumbling Castle: And Other Tales

(New York: Clarion Books, 2015)

Story type: Collection; Young Readers
Subject(s): Short stories; Fantasy; Humor

Summary: Before he wrote the best-selling Discworld series and dozens of other novels, Terry Pratchett wrote stories for children and young adults. This anthology collects 14 of those early Pratchett tales, some of which were published by a British newspaper in the 1960s. In "Dragons at Crumbling Castle," a young knight named Ralph becomes an unlikely ambassador for peace when King Arthur sends him to deal with a troublesome dragon family. "Tales of the Carpet People" describes the adventures of the tiny beings that populate the rugs that lie beneath humans' feet. Other stories include "The 59A Bus Goes Back in Time," "Hercules the Tortoise," "The Blackbury Monster," and "Father Christmas Goes to Work." Pen-and-ink drawings by Mark Beech illustrate the collection.

Other books by the same author:
Raising Steam, 2013
Nation, 2008
Making Money, 2007
Monstrous Regiment, 2003
Men at Arms, 1996

Other books you might like:
Piers Anthony, *Air Apparent*, 2007
Robert Asprin, *Dragons Luck*, 2009
Cassandra Clare, *The Lost Herondale*, 2015
Roald Dahl, *Roald Dahl's Book of Ghost Stories*, 1996
Neil Gaiman, *Trigger Warning: Short Fictions and Disturbances*, 2015
Tom Holt, *The Divine Comedies*, 2003
Alan MacDonald, *Trolls, Go Home!*, 2007
Terry Pratchett, *The Carpet People*, 1971
Terry Pratchett, *Good Omens: The Nice and Accurate Prophecies of Agnes Nutter, Witch*, 1990
Jack Prelutsky, *Monday's Troll*, 1996
James Riley, *Story Thieves*, 2015
Angie Sage, *Flyte: Septimus Heap, Book Two*, 2006
Francesca Simon, *Horrid Henry and the Abominable Snowman*, 2007
S. Andrew Swann, *Dragon Thief*, 2015

97

MICKEY ZUCKER REICHERT

Fields of Wrath

(New York: DAW, 2015)

Series: Flight of the Renshai Series. Book 2
Story type: Saga; Series
Subject(s): Wars; Fantasy; Epics
Major character(s): Tae Kahn, Warrior, Father (of Subikahn); Subikahn, Warrior, Son (of Tae Kahn)
Time period(s): Indeterminate
Locale(s): Fictional Location

Summary: This novel, the second in the Renshai Saga, continues the story of the warrior race known as the Renshai, which began with author Mickey Zucker Reichert's Renshai Trilogy. The Great War has ended, and the Renshai once again have possession of their Fields of Wrath. But not all of the Renshai accept their victory with complacency. Tae Kahn is not at ease. He knows how close his people came to defeat, and he suspects that another threat could rise at any moment. The race of giants known as the Kjempemagiska demonstrated the damage just one of their fighters could cause. Tae Kahn knows how devastating a full assault by the Kjempemagiska would be, and he tries to convince others that the Renshai should prepare themselves. The Renshai are weakened from their recent battles, and they will need help from the elves and mages if they are going to defend their territory from an invasion of giants.

Other books by the same author:
Flight of the Renshai, 2009

The Beasts of Barakhai, 2001
The Children of Wrath, 1998
Child of Thunder, 1993
By Chaos Cursed, 1991

Other books you might like:
Linda Evans, *Sleipnir*, 1994
Guy Gavriel Kay, *The Last Light of the Sun*, 2004
James Lovegrove, *The Age of Odin*, 2010
Juliet Marillier, *Wolfskin*, 2003
Fred Saberhagen, *Gods of Fire and Thunder*, 2002

98

ANDY REMIC

The Dragon Engine

(San Francisco: Watkins Media, 2015)

Story type: Adventure; Alternate World
Subject(s): Dragons; Adventure; Deception
Time period(s): Indeterminate Past
Locale(s): Vagandrak, Fictional Location

Summary: An excess of alcohol combined with the lure of fortune and glory has steered more than one otherwise respectable warrior into deep trouble, and it happens again in this novel by British author Andy Remic. Five war heroes from Vagandrak are out together one night when a few too many drinks cloud their collective thinking. They are convinced to sign a contract to go after three Dragon Heads, hidden away in the Five Havens of Karamakkos. The Dragon Heads are reputed to be gems of unbelievable power, with the ability to convey eternal life on their possessors. What's more, the gems are reported to be just part of the hoard of wealth waiting for anyone brave and daring enough to go to the Five Havens and retrieve them. But neither the five would-be fortune seekers nor anyone else is ready for the horrifying truth. This title is set in the same world as Remic's *The Iron Wolves*.

Other books by the same author:
The Iron Wolves, 2014
The White Towers, 2014
Vampire Warlords, 2011
Soul Stealers, 2010
Kell's Legend, 2009

Other books you might like:
David Gemmell, *Ravenheart*, 2001
Richard A. Knaak, *Birthright*, 2006
Peter Orullian, *The Unremembered*, 2011
Michael Swanwick, *The Dragons of Babel*, 2008
Lawrence Watt-Evans, *Dragon Weather*, 1999

99

PETER ROMAN

The Dead Hamlets

(Toronto, Ontario, Canada: ChiZine, 2015)

Series: Book of Cross Series. Book 2
Story type: Literary; Series
Subject(s): Fantasy; Supernatural; Occultism
Major character(s): Cross, Immortal, Man, Rogue; Christopher Marlowe, Historical Figure, Writer, Hunter (demons); Alice, Girl (literary character); William Shakespeare, Historical Figure, Writer, Supernatural Being
Time period(s): Multiple Time Periods
Locale(s): Earth

Summary: In the second novel in the Book of Cross Series, Cross—the soul who inhabits the immortal body of Jesus Christ—is drawn into another incident that demands his unique expertise. This time Cross is concerned with a mass killing that has ties to the supernatural realm and William Shakespeare's *Hamlet*. The victims are faerie folk, and the killer is an otherworldly spirit. Cross has an unpleasant history with the faeries. His own daughter was drawn into their world and now lives among them. When Cross realizes that his daughter is in danger, he begins a search for the sinister spirit. The spirit isn't the only unpleasant character Cross meets. He also has run-ins with supernatural versions of Christopher Marlowe and William Shakespeare, and with literary figures, including Lewis Carroll's Alice and Shakespeare's witches. Cross's investigation leads him to a surprising discovery about *Hamlet*.

Other books by the same author:
The Mona Lisa Sacrifice, 2013

Other books you might like:
Marie Brennan, *In Ashes Lie*, 2009
Diane Duane, *Stealing the Elf-King's Roses*, 2002
Raymond E. Feist, *Faerie Tale*, 1988
Esther M. Friesner, *Elf Defense*, 1988
Laurell K. Hamilton, *A Kiss of Shadows*, 2000

100

DIANA ROWLAND

Vengeance of the Demon

(New York: DAW Books, 2015)

Series: Kara Gillian Series. Book 7
Story type: Paranormal; Series
Subject(s): Detective fiction; Fantasy; Demons
Major character(s): Kara Gillian, Detective—Police, Supernatural Being (Demon summoner); Katashi, Supernatural Being (Demon summoner)
Time period(s): 21st century; 2010s
Locale(s): Louisiana, United States

Summary: This is the seventh novel in the Kara Gillian series by Diana Rowland. Things haven't been going well for Louisiana detective and demon summoner Kara Gillian lately. She has been identified as a murder suspect, and the evidence that points to her seems overwhelming. But that's not the worst of it—Katashi, a master demon summoner, has been working to open a portal that would allow demons to pass through to Earth at will. It's up to Kara to prevent this potentially catastrophic event and protect the friends and family she loves—something she's not going to be able to do if she's behind bars for murder. Kara's also forced to deal with the repercussions of betrayal, though she has little time to dwell on personal losses. She needs to call upon all of her powers now, before it is not just too late for her, but for the whole world.

Other books by the same author:
Fury of the Demon, 2014
White Trash Zombie Apocalypse, 2013
Even White Trash Zombies Get the Blues, 2012
Secrets of the Demon, 2011
Blood of the Demon, 2010

Other books you might like:
Jeaniene Frost, *At Grave's End*, 2008
Laurell K. Hamilton, *Dead Ice*, 2015
Edward Lee, *City Infernal*, 2001
Lilith Saintcrow, *Night Shift*, 2008
Roger Zelazny, *Lord Demon*, 1999

101

LAUREN M. ROY

Grave Matters

(New York: Ace Books, 2015)

Series: Night Owls Series. Book 2
Story type: Horror; Series
Subject(s): Fantasy; Vampires; Supernatural
Major character(s): Elly Garrett, Hunter (former, of vampires), Sister (of Cavale), Worker (at Night Owls Bookstore); Cavale, Brother (of Elly)
Time period(s): 21st century; 2010s
Locale(s): Boston, Massachusetts

Summary: This science fantasy novel is the second installment in the Night Owls series by Lauren M. Roy. Elly Garrett grew up fighting against supernatural beings, a skill she learned from her foster father. Her job at Boston's Night Owls bookstore, however, not only has her working alongside a diverse group of vampires, succubi, and Renfields, but also working to protect the city's most influential vampire, her employer. Elly's brother, Cavale, has reservations about his sister teaming up with vampires, and his worries only increase when a vindictive necromancer sets his sights on Elly and the co-workers she's grown to know and trust. Together, Elly and the Night Owls staff fight to thwart the necromancer's evil plans, but how long will they be able to stay out of harm's way?

Other books by the same author:
The Fire Children, 2015
Night Owls, 2014

Other books you might like:
Jennifer Estep, *By a Thread*, 2012
Yasmine Galenorn, *Blood Wyne*, 2011
Katharine Kerr, *License of Ensorcell*, 2011
Seanan McGuire, *Midnight Blue-Light Special*, 2013
J.C. Nelson, *Armageddon Rules*, 2015

102

DIANNE SALERNI

The Inquisitor's Mark

(New York: HarperCollins, 2015)

Series: Eighth Day Series. Book 2
Story type: Adventure; Series
Subject(s): Fantasy; Adventure; Time
Major character(s): Jax Aubrey, 13-Year-Old, Boy, Friend (of Billy); Riley Pendare, 18-Year-Old, Guardian (of Jax), Relative (descendant of King Arthur); Evangeline Emrys, Girl, Wizard, Relative (of Merlin); Finn Ambrose, Uncle (possibly, of Jax); Billy, Friend (of Jax), Kidnap Victim
Time period(s): 21st century; 2010s
Locale(s): New York, United States; Pennsylvania, United States

Summary: The second novel in the Eighth Day series continues the story of Jax Aubrey, a 13-year-old Transitioner who gets to experience one extra day each week. On Jax's first "eighth day" he met his guardian, an 18-year-old Transitioner named Riley Pendare. Jax also met Evangeline Emrys, a wizard who only lives on the eighth day. Jax and his friends have already survived one encounter with the sinister Kin who want to bring an end to the seven-day world. The Kin are still determined to achieve their goal, and they intend to use Evangline's powerful magic to help them. Meanwhile Jax, who believes he has no surviving family, receives a shock when Finn Ambrose tries to convince Jax that he is his uncle. Finn also makes a stunning revelation about Jax's bloodline. He may actually be part of the clan that is trying to kill Riley and kidnap Evangeline.

Other books by the same author:
The Eighth Day, 2014
The Caged Grave, 2013

Other books you might like:
Victoria Aveyard, *Red Queen*, 2015
Charlie Fletcher, *The London Pride*, 2015
Brandon Mull, *Wild Born*, 2013
Kenneth Oppel, *Silverwing*, 1997
Rick Riordan, *The Red Pyramid*, 2010
Neal Shusterman, *Scorpion Shards*, 1995

103

ROB SANDERS

Archaon: Everchosen

(Nottingham, United Kingdom: Black Library, 2014)

Series: Warhammer 40,000 Series
Story type: Adventure; Science Fantasy
Subject(s): Good and evil; Self awareness; Wars
Major character(s): Archaon, Supernatural Being (Lord of the End Times, Chaos Incarnate), Servant (former, to warrior-god Sigmar), Student (of Father Dagobert); Father Dagobert, Teacher (of Archaon)
Time period(s): Indeterminate
Locale(s): Fictional Location

Summary: Archaon is the Everchosen. He is the incarnation of Chaos and the Lord of End Times. His presence signals the Apocalypse and strikes fear into every living being. Once he was a simple man, seeking only to serve the warrior-god Sigmar. This novel explores Archaon's life before his fall into darkness, as a knowledge-hungry child and eager warrior. Seeking the six treasures of Chaos, Archaon must perform labors to prove his worthiness. His fate is determined once his transformation into the Chaos warrior is complete. Archaon struggles to understand exactly what will become of him with the help of Father Dagobert, a man who is more than a simple tutor and mentor. Father Dagobert eventually becomes Archaon's closest friend.

Other books by the same author:
Legion of the Damned, 2012
Atlas Infernal, 2011
Redemption Corps, 2010

Other books you might like:
Richard Lee Byers, *The Enemy Within*, 2007
David Guymer, *City of the Damned*, 2013
Josh Reynolds, *Road of Skulls*, 2013
C.L. Werner, *The Curse of the Phoenix Crown*, 2015
Chris Wraight, *Luthor Huss*, 2012

104

BRANDON SANDERSON

Firefight

(New York: Random House Children's Books, 2015)

Series: Reckoners Series. Book 2
Story type: Dystopian; Series
Subject(s): Fantasy; Dystopias; Adventure
Major character(s): David, Teenager, Boy (member of Reckoners); Tia, Teenager, Girl (member of Reckoners); Cody, Teenager, Boy (member of Reckoners)
Time period(s): Indeterminate Future
Locale(s): Babylon Restored, Fictional Location; Newcago, Fictional Location

Summary: David and the other Reckoners expand their quest for adventure and vengeance in the second novel in the Reckoners series. The world is a changed place, and David has just completed an unthinkable mission in Newcago. He killed Steelheart, a High Epic who was David's sworn enemy, and the city is supposed to be safer now. But even after his heroic actions, David is not content. He feels driven to search for justice and answers beyond Newcago. David sets his sights on Manhattan, which is now known as Babylon Restored. The flooded region is governed by the High Epic Regalia, and David knows he's putting his life in danger by attempting to enter. But now that he has successfully confronted and defeated a High Epic, David feels ready to take on a new challenge.

Other books by the same author:
Steelheart, 2013
The Emperor's Soul, 2012
Legion, 2012
The Hero of Ages, 2008
Elantris, 2005

Other books you might like:
Joan Aiken, *The Cockatrice Boys*, 1996
Pierce Brown, *Golden Son*, 2015
Joelle Charbonneau, *The Testing*, 2014
Adam Christopher, *Seven Wonders*, 2012
Suzanne Collins, *Catching Fire*, 2009
James Dashner, *The Scorch Trials*, 2010
Peter Dickinson, *The Changes*, 1975
Steven Erikson, *Fall of Light*, 2015
Mark Frost, *Alliance*, 2014
Ryan Graudin, *The Walled City*, 2014
Jeramey Kraatz, *The Cloak Society*, 2012
James Lovegrove, *The Age of Ra*, 2009
Brian McClellan, *The Autumn Republic*, 2015
Peter Moore, *V Is for Villain*, 2014
C.J. Redwine, *Deliverance*, 2014
Madeleine E. Robins, *The Stone War*, 1999
Veronica Roth, *Allegiant*, 2013
Brandon Sanderson, *Words of Radiance*, 2014
John Shirley, *Demons*, 2002
Yvonne Ventresca, *Pandemic*, 2014
Moira Young, *Raging Star*, 2014

105

V.E. SCHWAB (Pseudonym of Victoria Schwab)

A Darker Shade of Magic

(New York: Tom Doherty Associates, 2015)

Series: A Darker Shade of Magic Series. Book 1
Story type: Alternate World; Magic Conflict
Subject(s): Alternative worlds; Magic; Magicians
Major character(s): Kell, Magician (Antari blood magician), Companion (of Lila), Royalty (Prince of Red London), Adoptee; Delilah "Lila" Bard, Thief, Companion (of Kell)
Time period(s): 18th century-19th century; 1760-1820
Locale(s): London, England

Summary: Four versions of London—alternate cities defined by how much or how little magic they contain—are ruled by disparate monarchs. The most familiar version of London, ruled by mad King George, is sooty and magic-free. Red London prospers, thanks to the able rule of the Maresh Dynasty, which encourages proper regard for magic and the lives of its citizens. White London is awash with trouble because regicide is an effective way to acquire power and magic is used as a weapon. But few speak aloud of Black London, where unbridled use of magic caused horrific destruction. Kell passes between all these worlds. He is among the last of a special breed of magicians known as the Travelers who can move between the worlds. Kell is the Red Traveler, a favorite in the Red court and an envoy who transports messages between the worlds' monarchs. But Kell is also a smuggler, and when he's found out and flees to Grey London, he falls into the clutches of Delilah Bard. This opportunistic thief demands passage, and finds trouble in more than one version of London.

Other books by the same author:
Last Wishes, 2014
New Beginnings, 2014

Second Chances, 2014
The Unbound, 2014
The Archived, 2013

Other books you might like:
James P. Blaylock, *Lord Kelvin's Machine*, 1992
Gordon Dahlquist, *The Glass Books of the Dream Eaters: A Novel*, 2006
Diana Gabaldon, *Written in My Own Heart's Blood*, 2014
Stephen Hunt, *Jack Cloudie*, 2011
Kazuo Ishiguro, *The Buried Giant*, 2015
Mercedes Lackey, *The Gates of Sleep*, 2002
Michael Moorcock, *The Whispering Swarm*, 2015
Carol Newsom, *Midnight Soup and a Witch's Hat*, 1987
Douglas Nicholas, *Something Red*, 2012
Tad Williams, *Mountain of Black Glass*, 1999

106

M.J. SCOTT

The Shattered Court

(London: Penguin Group, 2015)

Series: Four Arts Series. Book 1
Story type: Coming-of-Age; Magic Conflict
Subject(s): Magic; Royalty; Knights
Major character(s): Sophia Kendall, Young Woman, Magician, Royalty, Companion (of Cameron); Cameron Mackenzie, Young Man, Guard, Knight, Magician, Companion (of Sophia)
Locale(s): Anglion, Fictional Location

Summary: On the eve of her twenty-first birthday, Sophia Kendall, a woman of high-born blood far down the line of royal succession, faces an age-old ritual that will bind her and her magical powers to a life of service in arranged marriage. But when a brutal terrorist attack devastates the capital, Sophia is forced to flee with her bodyguard Cameron Mackenzie, a member of the royal guard. While running away from home, Sophia's magical powers manifest themselves on her birthday as expected. However, she is far from the required ritual, and her powers bind themselves to her protector, Cameron. Together, Sophia and Cameron's magic is a powerful force, but it is a force the temple wants to suppress and would do anything to keep secret. This is the first book in M.J. Scott's Four Arts series.

Other books by the same author:
Fire Kin, 2014
The Wolf Within, 2014
Iron Kin, 2013
Blood Kin, 2012
Shadow Kin, 2011

Other books you might like:
Lynn Abbey, *Jerlayne*, 1999
Lynn Flewelling, *The Bone Doll's Twin*, 2001
Barb Hendee, *Witches with the Enemy*, 2015
Anne Kelleher, *Silver's Lure*, 2005
Matthew Woodring Stover, *Iron Dawn*, 1997

107

LISA SHEARIN

The Dragon Conspiracy

(New York: Penguin Publishing Group, 2015)

Series: SPI Files Series. Book 2
Story type: Series; Urban
Subject(s): Fantasy; Supernatural; Urban life
Major character(s): Makenna Fraser, Agent (Supernatural Protection and Investigations), Psychic (seer); Ian Byrne, Agent (Supernatural Protection and Investigations)
Time period(s): 21st century; 2010s
Locale(s): New York, New York

Summary: The agents of Supernatural Protection and Investigations deal with magic and mythic mayhem in the second novel in the SPI File series. Makenna Fraser is new to SPI and New York City. She can't believe that she's spending her first Halloween in Manhattan at the Metropolitan Museum of Art with her partner, the gorgeous Ian Byrne. They are there to make sure nothing goes wrong during the opening of the new Mythos exhibit. But something does go very wrong. A group of harpies—frightening mythological monsters—show up and make off with the Dragon Eggs diamonds. The diamonds hold powerful magic, and they can cause severe harm to the metropolitan area's paranormal population. Makenna and Ian must find the harpies before they can execute their deadly plan.

Other books by the same author:
The Grendel Affair, 2014
All Spell Breaks Loose, 2012
Con & Conjure, 2011
Bewitched & Betrayed, 2010
Armed & Magical, 2008

Other books you might like:
Ben Aaronovitch, *Foxglove Summer*, 2014
Amber Benson, *The Witches of Echo Park*, 2015
Simon R. Green, *From Hell with Love*, 2010
Justin Gustainis, *Evil Dark*, 2012
Devon Monk, *Hell Bent*, 2013
Jaye Wells, *Cursed Moon*, 2014

108

RYK E. SPOOR

Phoenix in Shadow

(Riverdale, New York: Baen Books, 2015)

Series: Balanced Sword Series. Book 2
Story type: Series; Sword and Sorcery
Subject(s): Fantasy; Magic; Friendship
Major character(s): Kyri Vantage, Supernatural Being (Phoenix Justiciar of Myrionar), Companion (of Tobimar and Poplock); Tobimar Silverun, Companion (of Kyri); Poplock Duckweed, Companion (of Kyri)
Time period(s): Indeterminate
Locale(s): Moonshade Hollow, Fictional Location

Summary: Kyri Vantage, the Phoenix Justiciar of Myrionar, and her companions Tobimar Silverun of Skysand and Poplock Duckweed find themselves on another dangerous and magical adventure that will make them question everything they thought they knew. Killing Thornfalcon was only the beginning—the Black City is rising, led by the King of All Hells, and it lies just beyond Rivendream Pass in Moonshade Hollow. They must use all their powers to fight this darkness before it consumes them and the world they know—if they are able to survive the journey. This fantasy novel is the second title in the Balanced Sword series by Ryk E. Spoor.

Other books by the same author:
Paradigms Lost, 2014
Phoenix Rising, 2013
Spheres of Influence, 2013
Grand Central Arena, 2010

Other books you might like:
Anne Kelleher, *Silver's Edge*, 2004
Naomi Kritzer, *Freedom's Sisters*, 2006
Lane Robins, *Maledicte*, 2007
Joel Shepherd, *Sasha*, 2009
Jo Walton, *The King's Peace*, 2000

109

JON SPRUNK

Storm and Steel

(New York: Pyr, 2015)

Series: Book of the Black Earth Series. Book 2
Story type: Series; Sword and Sorcery
Subject(s): Slavery; Wars; Freedom
Major character(s): Horace, Slave, Sorcerer, Friend (of Jirom and Alyra); Jirom, Friend (of Horace and Alyra), Mercenary (former), Gladiator (former), Slave; Alyra, Friend (of Horace and Jirom), Spy; Byleth, Royalty (Queen of Erugash)
Time period(s): Indeterminate
Locale(s): Erugash, Fictional Location; Akeshia, Fictional Location

Summary: Horace, the Magician, has destroyed the Temple of the Sun and with it broken his slave chains. Although he joined forces with Byleth, the Queen of Erugash, he realized that no matter how much knowledge he gained about his magical talents from her, the fate of his friends and lovers were tied to Byleth's movements against the slave rebellion. Now Queen Byleth is determined to crush the slave rebellion in her kingdom and maintain order at any price. Horace's best friend, Jirom, is one of the rebels fighting; his lover, Alyra, serves as a spy against Byleth. Horace is torn between the queen and his comrades. His desperate need to understand his elemental magical talents and come into his own right as a magician is at war with his honor, love, and trust for those he cares about most. This is the second book of the Book of the Black Earth series.

110

DIANE STANLEY

The Chosen Prince

(New York: HarperCollins, 2015)

Story type: Historical; Young Adult
Subject(s): Fantasy; Mythology; Ancient Greek civilization
Major character(s): Alexos, Royalty (prince), Brother (older, of Teo); Teo, Brother (younger, of Alexos); Athene, Deity (goddess); Zeus, Deity (god); Suliman, Doctor (court physician)
Locale(s): Greece

Summary: Inspired by William Shakespeare's *The Tempest*, this fantasy novel tells the story of Prince Alexos, who is born for greatness but experiences a life of hardship and tragedy. When Alexos is born, he is decreed to be the champion of the goddess Athene. It is a position of honor, but the responsibility that comes with that honor is daunting. As he grows up, Alexos knows that he is one day supposed to smooth the relationship between Atehene and the god Zeus. In the meantime, he fills his days with ordinary boyhood pursuits and spends time with his younger brother Teo. When Alexos loses the use of this legs and Teo dies—an act for which Alexos is responsible—Alexos must reach deep for the character and courage he needs to fulfill his mission. His quest eventually leads him to a mysterious island, which reveals both answers and new obstacles.

Other books by the same author:
Bella at Midnight, 2014
The Princess of Cortova, 2013
The Cup and the Crown, 2012
The Silver Bowl, 2011

Other books you might like:
Victoria Aveyard, *Red Queen*, 2015
Dave Barry, *Peter and the Shadow Thieves*, 2006
Cinda Williams Chima, *The Enchanter Heir*, 2013
Dave Duncan, *Children of Chaos*, 2006
Sherwood Smith, *Inda*, 2006
Vivian Vande Velde, *The Conjurer Princess*, 1997

111

BRIAN STAVELEY

The Providence of Fire

(New York: Tor Books, 2015)

Series: Chronicle of the Unhewn Throne Series. Book 2
Story type: Adventure; Revenge
Subject(s): Adventure; Assassination; Brothers and sisters
Major character(s): Adare, Lover (former, of Ran il Tornja), Daughter (of the Emperor), Sister (of Kaden and Valyn), Royalty (ruling family of Annurian Empire), Avenger (of her father's murder), Woman; Valyn, Royalty (ruling family of Annurian Empire), Warrior, Mercenary, Man, Adventurer, Avenger (of his father's death), Brother (of Adare and Kaden), Son (of the Emperor); Kaden, Brother (of Adare and

Valyn), Heir (of the Annurian Empire), Royalty (ruling family of Annurian Empire), Son (of the Emperor), Leader (and heir to Annurian Empire); Ran il Tornja, Man, Lover (former, of Adare), Assistant (to the Emperor), Traitor, Murderer (of the Emperor)

Time period(s): Indeterminate

Locale(s): Annurian Empire, Fictional Location

Summary: Siblings Adare, Valyn, and Kaden are still reeling from the murder of their father, the Emperor. They also need to deal with a growing conspiracy to overthrow the Annurian Empire. They embark on divergent paths. Adare realizes the empire's leading general, who has been her lover, was involved in her father's murder, so she leaves the palace to amass an army to defend the empire. Valyn, a renegade member of the elite fighting force, must find a way to keep himself and his brother, Kaden—the heir to the throne—alive while trying to save the empire. Kaden must rely on two unlikely companions on his journey to the Annurian capital to help save the empire. The three are hampered by uncertainty about who can be trusted. Many secret history-shaping events can either save the empire or destroy it. This is the second novel in the Chronicle of the Unhewn Throne series by author Brian Staveley.

Other books by the same author:
The Emperor's Blades, 2014

Other books you might like:
Joe Abercrombie, *Best Served Cold*, 2009
Jim Butcher, *Furies of Calderon*, 2004
Mark Chadbourn, *Kingdom of the Serpent: Burning Man*, 2008
Mark Lawrence, *The Liar's Key*, 2015
Brian McClellan, *Promise of Blood*, 2013
Brandon Sanderson, *The Alloy of Law*, 2011

112

WILLA STRAYHORN

The Way We Bared Our Souls

(New York: Penguin Young Readers, 2015)

Story type: Mystical

Subject(s): Native Americans; Students; Multiple sclerosis

Major character(s): Consuelo "Lo" McDonough, Teenager (suffering from multiple sclerosis), Girlfriend (ex, of Kit), Friend (of Thomas, Kaya, Ellen); Thomas, Teenager (former child soldier), Friend (of Consuelo, Kit, Kaya, Ellen); Kaya, Teenager (ill), Friend (of Consuelo, Kit, Thomas, Ellen); Ellen, Teenager, Addict, Friend (of Consuelo, Kit, Thomas, Kaya); Kit, Teenager, Friend (of Thomas, Kaya, Ellen), Mentally Ill Person (depressed); Jay Walks with Coyotes, Indian, Shaman

Time period(s): 21st century; 2010s

Locale(s): Santa Fe, New Mexico

Summary: Consuelo "Lo" McDonough's newest companion is fear. The high school student is beginning to show symptoms of multiple sclerosis, a disease that runs in her family, and the prospect terrifies her. On her way though the New Mexico desert, she meets a mysterious Native American shaman, who offers to heal her pain.

But to do so, she must bring with her four friends who are also suffering in some way. Lo recruits Thomas, a former child soldier from Liberia; Kaya, who suffers from a numbing physical illness that leaves her unable to feel pain; Ellen, who is mired in a life of drug abuse; and Kit, who is still grieving for his girlfriend, who died in an accident. The ritual enables them to cast off their suffering, but comes with a price—they each take on someone else's pain. For the next week they must carry another's burden, and in the process, find their own healing.

Other books you might like:
James P. Blaylock, *The Rainy Season*, 1999
Richard Grant, *In the Land of Winter*, 1997
Nina Kiriki Hoffman, *Fall of Light*, 2009
Tim Powers, *Expiration Date*, 1995
Nancy Springer, *Metal Angel*, 1994

113

S. ANDREW SWANN

Dragon Thief

(New York: DAW Books, 2015)

Series: Dragon Series. Book 2

Story type: Series; Sword and Sorcery

Subject(s): Humor; Identity; Fantasy

Major character(s): Frank Blackthorne, Thief, Royalty (princess)

Time period(s): Indeterminate

Locale(s): Lendowyn, Fictional Location

Summary: Somewhat mediocre thief Frank Blackthorne inadvertently wound up switching genders when a bit of magic went awry, and now, he's quite sick of being the princess of the Royal Court of Lendowyn. He decides to try using an ancient artifact to return to a more manly form. He succeeds in some respects, but he is now inhabiting the body of a thief on the most-wanted list. Frank can't keep a low profile while he solves his problem because everyone is after him now. He can't change back without help, and his only allies are some teenagers who really believe he is the master thief. Somehow, he must find a way to reclaim his original identity while avoiding all of the people who want to collect the bounty on his borrowed head. Adding to Frank's list of problems is the thief whose body he's taken over—the criminal inhabiting the body of the princess of Lendowyn. This is the second novel in the Dragon series by S. Andrew Swann.

Other books by the same author:
Dragon Princess, 2014
Messiah, 2011
Heretics, 2010
The Dwarves of Whiskey Island, 2005
The Dragons of Cuyahoga, 2001

Other books you might like:
Piers Anthony, *Currant Events*, 2004
Robert Asprin, *Dragons Wild*, 2008
David Bischoff, *Castle Perilous*, 1988
Esther M. Friesner, *Unicorn U*, 1992

Terry Pratchett, *Dragons at Crumbling Castle: And Other Tales*, 2015
Terry Pratchett, *Making Money*, 2007

114

SAM SYKES

The City Stained Red

(London: Orbit, 2015)

Series: Bring Down Heaven Series. Book 1
Story type: Adventure; Series
Subject(s): Fantasy; Adventure; Magic
Major character(s): Lenk, Assassin (swordsman); Miron Evenhands, Religious (priest)
Time period(s): Indeterminate
Locale(s): Cier'Djaal, Fictional Location

Summary: Lenk, a swordsman for hire, is ready to bring his violent career to an end. But first he and his companions must collect payment from the priest Miron Evenhands for a previous mission. Evenhands is not easy to find, however, and when Lenk and his band finally follow the priest's trail to the city of Cier'Djaal, they are drawn into another adventure. Cier'Djaal is a hotbed of conflict. An impending civil war, a religious conflict, restless nonhumans, and an active criminal population have made the city a dangerous place. All Lenk wants to do is find Evenhands and make him pay, but he and his party are finding it impossible to stay out of the fray. The situation becomes more complicated when Lenk confronts Evenhands and learns the truth about the priest's identity. This novel is the first in the Bring Down Heaven series, a sequel to the Aeons' Gate trilogy.

Other books by the same author:
The Skybound Sea, 2012
Black Halo, 2011
Tome of the Undergates, 2010

Other books you might like:
Joe Abercrombie, *Half a King*, 2014
Raymond E. Feist, *A Crown Imperiled*, 2012
Scott Lynch, *The Lies of Locke Lamora*, 2006
Dennis L. McKiernan, *City of Jade*, 2008
R.A. Salvatore, *Gauntlgrym*, 2010

115

ADRIAN TCHAIKOVSKY

The Guns of the Dawn

(New York: Tom Doherty Associates, 2015)

Story type: Alternate History; Fantasy
Subject(s): Wars; Women soldiers; International relations
Major character(s): Emily Marshwic, Woman, Military Personnel
Time period(s): Indeterminate
Locale(s): Lascanne, Fictional Location

Summary: It's been a long and bloody war for the people of Lascanne. Their formerly peaceful neighbors from Denland overthrew their rulers and attacked, and every family has been deeply affected. The fighting drags on, swallowing up all the men of fighting age as the people of Lascanne try valiantly to hold off the rebel Denlanders. With few men left to fight, the military demands families each send one woman to join the battle. Emily Marshwic has already lost her brother and brother-in-law, but she reluctantly answers the call on behalf of her remaining family. She barely knows how to hold a gun. What she sees in the course of battle opens her eyes about her nation and world, and she wonders if her people's cause truly is worth fighting for. When she makes her stand, she'll hold not only her own fate but also the fate of Lascanne in her hands.

Other books by the same author:
The Air War, 2014
The Scarab Path, 2011
The Sea Watch, 2011
Dragonfly Falling, 2010
Empire in Black and Gold, 2008

Other books you might like:
James Enge, *The Wide World's End*, 2015
Jennifer Fallon, *The Lion of Senet*, 2004
David Gemmell, *Stormrider*, 2002
Tom Lloyd, *Old Man's Ghosts*, 2015
Jon Sprunk, *Shadow's Son*, 2010
Harry Turtledove, *Bridge of the Separator*, 2006

116

E.L. TETTENSOR

Master of Plagues

(New York: Penguin Publishing Group, 2015)

Series: Nicolas Lenoir Series. Book 2
Story type: Historical; Series
Subject(s): Fantasy; Diseases; Magic
Major character(s): Nicolas Lenoir, Detective—Police (inspector), Colleague (of Bran Kody); Bran Kody, Detective—Police (sergeant), Colleague (of Nicolas Lenoir)
Locale(s): Kennian, England

Summary: Police inspector Nicolas Lenoir knows that criminals aren't the only threat in Victorian Kennian. He has faced a sinister specter that now haunts his memories. The encounter with darkness changed him, but Lenoir still possess his keen investigative skills. He will need those skills as Kennian faces a new threat. A disease is infecting the residents of the city, and the epidemic doesn't appear to be of natural origin. Lenoir believes someone released the disease on purpose. As sections of the city are quarantined, and the sickness claims victims at an alarming rate, Lenoir and police sergeant Bran Kody must find the madman responsible. But can they stop the epidemic and heal the infected? The Adali, a nomadic sect, may be able to cure the disease with magic. Although Lenoir wants to stop the nightmare, he isn't sure if he should take the risks that come with the Adali's cure. This novel is the second in the Nicolas Lenoir series.

Other books by the same author:
Darkwalker, 2013

Other books you might like:
Dave Duncan, *The Crooked House*, 2000
Barry Hughart, *The Story of the Stone*, 1988
Sarah Monette, *Corambis*, 2009
Mike Resnick, *Stalking the Dragon: A Fable of Tonight*, 2009
Michelle Sagara, *Cast in Flame*, 2014

117

IAN TREGILLIS

The Mechanical

(New York: Orbit Books, 2015)

Series: Alchemy Wars Series. Book 1
Story type: Alternate History; Espionage
Subject(s): Slavery; Espionage; Wars
Major character(s): Jax, Robot (Clakker), Slave; Berenice Charlotte de Mornay-Perigord, Spy, Leader (of French spy ring); Luuk Visser, Religious (Catholic priest), Spy (under Bernice)
Time period(s): 20th century; 1920s
Locale(s): New Amsterdam, Fictional Location

Summary: Long ago, the Dutch used their robotic creations known as the Clakkers to conquer most of the world. Although they appear to be virtually indestructible pieces of technology designed to serve without complaint, the Clakkers are actually self-thinking beings who are kept in line by overwhelming pain and punishment when they refuse to follow orders. The Dutch on North American territory, known as New Amsterdam, have a shaky peace with the neighboring French in Canada. Having been driven out of Europe, the French are determined to understand how the Clakkers work and find a weakness or learn to build their own. They have embraced the study of mechanics and alchemy, but have had limited successes. Bernice Charlotte de Mornay-Perigord is a leader of a spy ring. Luuk Visser is a spy working undercover as a Protestant in New Amsterdam. They recruit a Clakker named Jax who realizes that he wants to break free of his enslavement. Jax is tasked by Luuk with delivering an item as the spy tries to avoid detection. This is the first novel of the Alchemy Wars series.

Other books by the same author:
Necessary Evil, 2013
Something More Than Night, 2013
The Coldest War, 2012
Bitter Seeds, 2010

Other books you might like:
Beth Cato, *The Clockwork Crown*, 2015
Mark Hodder, *The Curious Case of the Clockwork Man*, 2011
Jay Lake, *Escapement*, 2008
George Mann, *The Affinity Bridge*, 2009
Michael Moorcock, *The Whispering Swarm*, 2015
Cherie Priest, *The Inexplicables*, 2012

118

GREG VAN EEKHOUT

Pacific Fire

(New York: Tor Books, 2015)

Series: Daniel Blackland Series. Book 2
Story type: Adventure; Fantasy
Subject(s): Adventure; Coming of age; Deception
Major character(s): Sam, Supernatural Being (golem), Companion (of Daniel), Teenager; Daniel Blackland, Orphan, Man, Wizard (osteomancer), Caregiver (of Sam); Gabriel Argent, Man, Wizard, Criminal (Hierarch); Otis, Man, Criminal, Organized Crime Figure (Hierarch); Sister Tooth, Woman, Sorceress, Criminal (Hierarch)
Time period(s): Indeterminate
Locale(s): Los Angeles, California

Summary: The second novel of Greg van Eekhout's Daniel Blackland series picks up ten years after Daniel killed the Hierarch and ate his heart before escaping with young Sam, a golem and osteomancer. Daniel and Sam have been on the run for a decade, avoiding Los Angeles and never staying in one place for too long. They have been cautiously looking over their shoulders all this time. Daniel is concerned when he learns of a plot by the Trimvirate, the three corrupt ruling powers of LA, to raise a Pacific Firedrake, a powerful dragon. To raise such a magical creature, they need the power of an osteomancer. They need the power of Sam—or more precisely, the power in Sam's bones. Daniel and Sam, along with the help of some friends, travel to LA to spoil the plot and to save the world, while trying to stay alive.

Other books by the same author:
California Bones, 2014
The Boy at the End of the World, 2011
Norse Code, 2009

Other books you might like:
Jim Butcher, *Side Jobs*, 2010
Harry Connolly, *Circle of Enemies*, 2011
Laurell K. Hamilton, *Danse Macabre*, 2006
Anton Strout, *Incarnate*, 2014
S. Andrew Swann, *The Dragons of the Cuyahoga*, 2001

119

J.D. VAUGHN

The Second Guard

(New York: Disney-Hyperion, 2015)

Series: Second Guard Series. Book 1
Story type: Adventure; Series
Subject(s): Fantasy; Adventure; Legends
Major character(s): Talimendra "Tali" Sanchez Kalloryn, Friend (of Zarif and Chey), Girl, 15-Year-Old; Zarif, Boy, 15-Year-Old, Friend (of Tali and Chey); Chey, Boy, 15-Year-Old, Friend (of Tali and Zarif)
Time period(s): Indeterminate
Locale(s): Tequende, Fictional Location

Summary: Talimendra "Tali" Sanchez Kalloryn has just turned 15. According to the rules of Tequende, Tali and all second-born children must leave their families at that age to train for the Second Guard. The preparation is hard, and those who don't qualify become indentured servants until they turn 21. Tali is determined to join the Second Guard as her mother did before her, but she must first navigate the world of the Alcazar, where she and the other candidates train. Tali is a member of the Sun Guild, a guild of merchants. She befriends Zarif, of the intellectual Moon Guild, and Chey, of the agrarian Earth Guild, and begins to understand their similarities and differences. Tali also recognizes that the queen's court is not the upstanding establishment she thought it was. There is a plot in the works that poses a threat to all of Tequende. This novel is the first in the Second Guard series by J.D. Vaughn.

Other books you might like:
Victoria Aveyard, *Red Queen*, 2015
Dave Duncan, *Impossible Odds*, 2003
Simon R. Green, *Beyond the Blue Moon*, 2000
Mindy L. Klasky, *The Glasswright's Test*, 2003
Cayla Kluver, *The Empty Throne*, 2014
L.E. Modesitt Jr., *Imager*, 2009

120

JOSH VOGT

Forge of Ashes

(Redmond, Washington: Paizo Publishing, 2015)

Series: Pathfinder Tales Series
Story type: Adventure; Series
Subject(s): Father-daughter relations; Mountain life; Dwarfs
Major character(s): Akina, Dwarf, Warrior, Companion (of Ondorum), Daughter (of missing person); Ondorum, Mythical Creature (made of stone), Companion (of Akina)
Locale(s): Five Kings Mountains, Fictional Location

Summary: Years ago, the dwarf warrior Akina went off to fight in the Goblinblood Wars. When she returns to her home in the Five Kings Mountains she brings with her a companion, Ondorum, a being of living stone, and a soul transformed by war and her travels. She is no longer satisfied with small-town life and the uninteresting suitors who compete for her affections. When she discovers her father has disappeared, Akina and Ondorum must descend into the recesses beneath the mountains in search of him. It is a journey as dark as it is dangerous. This standalone title is one of the long-running Pathfinder Tales series, which are set in the world of the Pathfinder Roleplaying Game.

Other books you might like:
Ed Greenwood, *The Wizard's Mask*, 2013
Howard Andrew Jones, *Stalking the Beast*, 2013
Gary Kloster, *Firesoul*, 2015
Liane Merciel, *Pathfinder Tales: Nightblade*, 2014
Wendy N. Wagner, *Pathfinder Tales: Skinwalkers*, 2014

121

JAYE WELLS

Deadly Spells

(London: Orbit Books, 2015)

Series: Prospero's War Series. Book 3
Story type: Magic Conflict; Mystery
Subject(s): Magic; Mystery; Witchcraft
Major character(s): Kate Prospero, Police Officer, Magician, Sister (of Danny), Co-worker (partner, of Drew), Girlfriend (ex, of John); Danny Prospero, Young Man, Brother (of Kate); Drew Morales, Police Officer, Co-worker (partner, of Kate), Magician; John Volos, Political Figure (mayor of Babylon), Boyfriend (ex, of Kate)
Locale(s): Babylon, Fictional Location

Summary: Kate Prospero fights crime in a world of spell casters and witches, where magic can be used as a weapon and is as addictive as a drug. Kate and her partner, Drew Morales, work for the Magical Enforcement Agency. They've teamed up with the Babylon Police Department to investigate the murder of a coven leader, a case that could ignite a deadly war between rival covens. As Kate and her partner dig deeper into the dangerous magical underworld, she's being pulled away by outside distractions—particularly her troubled younger brother, Danny, and a nosy reporter who's been snooping into Kate's troubled past. To make matters worse, she finds herself fighting off the affections of both her partner and the new mayor of Babylon, her former boyfriend John Volos. This is the third book in Jaye Wells's Prospero's War series.

Other books by the same author:
Cursed Moon, 2014
Dirty Magic, 2014
Blue-Blooded Vamp, 2012
Green-Eyed Demon, 2011
The Mage in Black, 2010

Other books you might like:
Jim Butcher, *Turn Coat*, 2009
Greg Cox, *A Touch of Fever*, 2011
Kim Harrison, *Black Magic Sanction*, 2010
Seanan McGuire, *An Artificial Night*, 2010
Rob Thurman, *Deathwish*, 2009

122

C.L. WERNER

Deathblade: A Tale of Malus Darkblade

(Nottingham, United Kingdom: Black Library, 2015)

Series: Warhammer: The Chronicles of Malus Darkblade. Book 6
Story type: Magic Conflict; Series
Subject(s): Wars; Fantasy; Elves
Major character(s): Malus Darkblade, Mythical Creature (dark elf), Leader, Warrior, Servant (vassal to Male-

kith); Malekith, Sorcerer (witch king), Royalty
Time period(s): Indeterminate
Locale(s): Naggaroth, Fictional Location

Summary: In the sixth novel of the Warhammer: Chronicles of Malus Darkblade series, dark elf Malus Darkblade has finally become ruler of Hag Graef. Serving as the general to the witch king Malekith, Malus finds his position of power enjoyable and solidifies his grasp on those around him. However, Malekith is determined to wage war against the high elves in Ulthuan and orders Malus to lead the vanguard. Terrible battles at Tiranoc and Eagle's Gate as well as the Battle of Reaver's Mark offer Malus the opportunity to demonstrate his skills both in war and as a leader. He finds that he is presented with opportunity and questions whether the time has come to seize the leadership of Naggaroth. Malus must decide whether to betray his lord, the Witch King, and grasp his destiny as well as the throne. As the battle rages on, Malus finds that even he is fighting for more than just power, he is fighting for his life.

Other books by the same author:
Blighted Empire, 2013
Dead Winter, 2012
The Bounty Hunter, 2010
Blood for the Blood God, 2008
Blood Money, 2003

Other books you might like:
Andy Chambers, *Path of the Dark Eldar*, 2015
David Guymer, *Gotrek and Felix: Slayer*, 2015
William King, *Sword of Caledor*, 2012
Graham McNeill, *Empire*, 2009
Gav Thorpe, *Master of Sanctity*, 2014

123

MICHELLE WEST

Oracle

(New York: DAW Books, 2015)

Series: House War Series. Book 6
Story type: Ancient Evil Unleashed; Chase
Subject(s): Royalty; Magic; Demons
Major character(s): Jewel Markess ATerafin, Ruler (of Terafin)
Time period(s): Indeterminate
Locale(s): Essalieyan Empire, Fictional Location

Summary: In the sixth novel of the House War series, Jewel Markess ATerafin embarks on a quest to save her home and her people. As ruler of Terafin, Jewel experiences visions and glimpses of the future that are beyond her control and understanding. To comprehend what she sees, she must leave the city and seek out the Oracle. Times are dangerous and demons are abroad, wreaking havoc in the city of Averalaan. To stop Jewel from reaching the Oracle, the demons set ancient and terrible monsters after her. Averalaan is troubled by a deeper evil as Jewel departs. The three Princes of the firstborn have been asleep far below ground, but now are stirring. If they should awaken, the city and empire will be destroyed. Jewel's choices will impact her life and her kingdom forever, revealing long-hidden secrets and setting the Essalieyan Empire on a new course.

Other books by the same author:
Skirmish, 2012
City of Night, 2010
The Hidden City, 2008
The Riven Shield, 2003
Sea of Sorrows, 2001

Other books you might like:
Jacqueline Carey, *Kushiel's Dart*, 2001
Kate Elliott, *Traitor's Gate*, 2009
Elizabeth Haydon, *The Assassin King*, 2006
Katharine Kerr, *The Fire Dragon*, 2001
Sharon Shinn, *The Thirteenth House*, 2006

124

KAREN WHIDDON

Shades of the Wolf

(Don Mills, Ontario, Canada: Harlequin Nocturne, 2015)

Story type: Contemporary - Fantasy; Paranormal
Subject(s): Ghosts; Love; Supernatural
Major character(s): Anabel Lee, Shape-Shifter, Widow(er), Friend (of Tyler); Tyler Rogers, Spirit, Brother (of Dena), Friend (of Anabel), Veteran; Dena Rogers, Sister (of Tyler), Kidnap Victim
Time period(s): 21st century; 2010s
Locale(s): Leaning Tree, United States

Summary: Anabel Lee is a shapeshifter who is like catnip to ghosts. Since her husband died 18 months ago in Afghanistan, she has longed to see him again, but he hasn't appeared. Lost in her grief and stubborn bitterness, Anabel ignores the other spirits who ask for help until one ghost won't let her go. Tyler is desperate to save his sister, Dena, who is being held captive. Dena has been captured by an evil warlock shapeshifter. Tyler is determined to get Anabel to help, and she finally agrees. Working closely together to locate Dena, Anabel and Tyler are shocked to discover a passionate attraction forming between them. He is a ghost, so they can never truly be together, and Anabel is still disconsolate over the loss of her husband. Time is running out for Dena, but Anabel and Tyler will never give up and leave her fate to the warlock.

Other books by the same author:
A Secret Colton Baby, 2014
The Lost Wolf's Destiny, 2013
The Wolf Prince, 2013
The Cop's Missing Child, 2012
Lone Star Magic, 2005

Other books you might like:
Jennifer Ashley, *Primal Bonds*, 2011
Patricia Briggs, *Frost Burned*, 2013
Carole Nelson Douglas, *Dancing with Werewolves*, 2007
Constance O'Day-Flannery, *Shifting Love*, 2004
Stephanie Rowe, *Must Love Dragons*, 2006

The Year in Historical Fiction
by
Daniel S. Burt

Katharine Grant in the *New York Times Book Review* wrote in her review of Anna Freeman's *The Fair Fight* (included here) that "Writing any novel involves decisions. In historical novels, these decisions can be agonizing, since readers of this genre are particularly unforgiving. Language? Tense? Voice? Such choices made, you're still left contemplating Henry James's dispiriting judgment that in historical fiction 'the real thing is almost impossible to do, and in its essence the whole effect is as nought.'" Despite Henry James's despairing words about the genre, writers continue to resort to the historical past for their subjects despite the many hard questions historical fiction poses and its unforgiving readers. Besides the questions facing historical novelists mentioned by Grant, there is the biggest question of all: How much must be verifiable? Historical novelists take on the extra burden, not assumed by other novelists, to hold themselves to the standards of the historian, subjugating the imagination to the verifiable evidence of the historical past, and every historical novelist must find the proper balance: Too many facts and a novel may collapse under the weight of dry scholarship; too few (or mistaken) and a novel may be charged with anachronisms or historical unreliability.

Why, therefore, take on this burden? What do historical novelists gain from a genre that seems to forever threaten, in James's word, to come to "nought"? One answer may be found from a writer who set out to recreate the historical past as no other writer had ever done before: James Joyce in his masterwork *Ulysses*. Joyce attempted to reconstruct the action of a single day—June 16, 1904—and such a detailed and accurate depiction of place, Dublin, that Joyce boasted that if the city were destroyed it could be reconstructed using his novel. Joyce, who was living abroad exclusively in Trieste, Zurich, and Paris during the composition of his novel, took on this challenge armed only with his exceptional memory, a Dublin City Directory, and the occasional research forays of relatives who were asked to confirm such details as the kinds of trees surrounding a particular Dublin church. Given his challenge, what is astounding is how few mistakes Joyce made. What is baffling is

why Joyce should have attempted this in the first place. Why not make it easy for himself by inventing his city or blurring the focus so verisimilitude is not such an issue? Perhaps Joyce's answer is contained in his famous declaration, "For myself, I always write about Dublin, because if I can get to the heart of Dublin I can get to the heart of all the cities of the world. In the particular is contained the universal."

"In the particular is contained the universal": that can serve as a credo of the historical novelist as well. Verifiability matters because if you nail the specifics there is hope that you can uncover the universal truths that all worthy literature aspires to discover. Joyce's impossible burden of particularity anchored his work to the real that became his route to reaching larger truths and universality. That serves as a worthy defense of the challenge of the past for the historical novelist. Get the past right, and you reach the real, the true, and the valuable. Why take on the burden? Robert Frost offered a succinct reply to those who asked him why he preferred the formal rigors of meter to free verse: "Writing free verse is like playing tennis with the net down." For the historical novelist, the net is always up.

Before proceeding to the highlights and trends in the historical novels collected here, I need to say a few words about my selection criteria, that is, how I designated a historical novel versus most novels that deal with the past.

Selection Criteria

Since Sir Walter Scott in the early nineteenth century first treated the historical past as if it were the recognizable present, historical fiction has dominated bestseller lists and annual selections of the best works of fiction. The historical past remains irresistible, and apparently inexhaustible, as a literary resource. The form's attraction, however, is even more remarkable because historical fiction is surely one of the most difficult and demanding narrative forms. Historical novelists must serve two contradictory masters: verifiability and invention. A historical novelist must balance the demands of representing the historical record accurately and telling a good story and often imaginatively compensating for gaps and deficiencies in that record. Taking too much latitude with the facts of history shatters the illusion of authenticity; taking too little and the data of history never come to life.

More so than any other fictional genre, it is necessary to define exactly what constitutes a historical novel to justify my selections. All novels deal with the past, except science fiction that is set in the future, or most fantasy novels set in an imagined, alternative world outside historical time. Yet not all novels are truly historical. Central to any workable definition of historical fiction is the degree to which the writer attempts not to recall the past but to recreate it. In some cases the time frame, setting, and customs of a novel's era are merely incidental to its action and characterization. In other cases, period details function as little more than a colorful backdrop for characters and situations that could as easily be played out in a different era with little alteration. So-called historical "costume dramas" could to a greater or lesser degree work as well with a change of costume in a different place and time. The novels that we can identify as truly historical, however, attempt much more than incidental period surface details or interchangeable historical eras. What justifies a designation as a historical novel is the writer's efforts at providing an accurate and believable representation of a particular historical era. The writer of historical fiction shares with the historian a verifiable depiction of past events, lives, and customs. In historical fiction, the past itself becomes as much a subject for the novelist as the characters and action.

Most of us use the phrase "historical novel" casually, never really needing an exact definition to make ourselves understood. We just know it when we see it. This listing, however, requires a set of criteria to determine what's in and what's out. Otherwise the list has no boundaries. If the working definition of historical fiction is too loose, every novel set in a period before the present qualifies, and nearly every novel becomes a historical novel immediately upon publication. If the definition is so strict that only books set in a time before the author's birth, for example, make the cut, then countless works that critics, readers, librarians, and the authors themselves think of as historical novels would be excluded.

The challenge here, therefore, has been to fashion a definition or set of criteria flexible enough to include novels that pass what can be regarded as the litmus test for historical fiction: Did the author use his or her imagination—and often quite a bit of research—to evoke another and earlier time than the author's own? Walter Scott, who is credited with "inventing" the historical novel in English during the early nineteenth century, provides a useful criterion in the subtitle of *Waverley*, his initial historical novel, the story of Scottish life at the time of the Jacobite Rebellion of 1745: "'Tis Sixty Years Since." This supplies a possible formula for separating the created past from the remembered past. What is unique and distinctive about the so-called historical novel is its attempt to imagine a distant period of time before the novelist's lifetime. Scott's sixty-year span between a novel's composition and its imagined era offers an arbitrary but useful means to distinguish between the personal and the historical past. The distance of two generations or nearly a lifetime provides a necessary span for the past to emerge as history and forces the writer to rely on more than recollection to uncover the patterns and textures of the past. I have, therefore, adopted Scott's formula but adjusted it to fifty years, including those books in which the significant portion of their plots is set in a period fifty years or more before the novel was written.

Because a rigid application of this fifty-year rule might disqualify quite a few books intended by their authors and regarded by their readers to be historical novels, another test has been applied to books written about more recent eras: Did the author use actual historical figures and events while setting out to recreate a specific, rather than a general or incidental, historical period? Although it is, of course, risky to speculate about a writer's intention, it is possible by looking at the book's approach, its use of actual historical figures, and its emphasis on a distinctive time and place that enhances the reader's knowledge of past lives, events, and customs to detect when a book conforms to what most would consider a central preoccupation of the historical novel.

I have tried to apply these criteria for the historical novel thoughtfully, and have allowed some exceptions when warranted by special circumstances. I hope I have been able to anticipate what most readers would consider historical novels, but I recognize that I may have overlooked some worthy representations of the past in the interest of dealing with a manageable list of titles. Finally, not every title in the Western, historical mystery, or historical romance genres has been included to avoid unnecessary duplication with the other sections of this book. I have included those novels that share characteristics with another genre—whether fantasy, Western, mystery, or romance—that seem to put the strongest emphasis on historical interest, detail, and accuracy.

Historical Fiction Highlights for the First Half of 2015

What always strikes me in collecting the historical fiction published annually is just how deep and rich the genre remains. Each year I am amazed by how, despite the sense that every era, event, and figure must have already treated, novelists either find the unfamiliar or surprise with new takes on the familiar. This is evident in this collection from the first half of 2015. Some examples chosen randomly: the Tudor court of Henry VIII (Nancy Bilyeau's *The Tapestry*), a journey from Oxford to Viterbo, Italy, in 1267 (David Flusfeder's *John the Pupil*), a post-Civil War Oklahoma outlaw family (Clifford Jackman's *The Winter Family*), a utopian community in nineteenth-century New England (Barbara

Klein Moss's *The Language of Paradise*), eighteenth-century Barcelona (Albert Sanchez Pinol's *Victus*), a nautical adventure in the seventeenth-century (Sean Thomas Russell's *Until the Sea Shall Give Up Her Dead*). There is diversity galore here, as well as fresh perspectives on the historical past.

The novels collected here also demonstrate the richness and persistence of a literary form capacious enough to include such well-regarded literary writers as Kazuo Ishiguro (*The Buried Giant*), Jane Smiley (*Early Warning* and *Some Luck*), Anne Tyler (*A Spool of Blue Thread*), and Steward O'Nan (*West of Sunset*) and reliable stalwarts of the form, such as Anne Perry (*The Angel Court Affair* and *Corridors of the Night*), Bernard Cornwell (*The Empty Throne*), Wilbur A. Smith (*Desert God*), and Barbara Taylor Bradford (*The Cavendon Women*).

Ultimately, however, the sustainability of any literary genre depends on new talent, and represented here is a diverse collection of first-time historical novelists, all of whom have managed to say something new about familiar subjects or to transport their readers to unexpected and unfamiliar events and eras. Examples of each include: India in 1837 and the Thugee Cult (M.J. Carter's *The Strangler Vine*), World War I (Alexis Landau's *The Empire of the Senses*), World War II (Jason Hewitt's *The Dynamite Room*), psychoanalysis in Vienna under the Nazis (Eliza Granville's *Gretel and the Dark*), and an "autobiography" of Jack the Ripper (*I, Ripper*).

Sequels and series further add consistency and continuity to the genre. Examples include Mary Doria Russell's second look at western legend Doc Holliday in *Epitaph*, Bernard Cornwell's ongoing treatment of tenth-century Britain in *The Empty Throne*, the launch of a projected new historical fantasy series set in the thirteenth century (Michael Moorcock's *The Whispering Swarm*), and Julian Stockwin's ongoing Napoleonic Era naval series (*Pasha*).

All of the standard sub-genres of the form—historical mysteries, fictional biography, historical fantasy—are fully represented here.

Historical Mysteries

No other sub-genre of historical fiction is as popular or as extensive as historical mysteries in which writers take on not on the management of secrets and suspense but a historical background that should add to (rather than detract from) the interests. Most important historical periods are represented here, from the Ancient World (Greece in Gary Corby's *Death Ex Machina* and Rome in Rosemary Rowe's *The Fateful Day* and Lindsey Davis's *Deadly Election*), to the Middle Ages (Priscilla Royal's *Satan's Lullaby*, Cora Harrison's *Condemned to Death* and *Verdict of the Court*, Cassandra Clark's *The Dragon of Handale*, Alys Clare's *Blood of the South*, Paul Doherty's *The Book of Fires*, and S.D. Sykes's *Plague Land*). There are mysteries from Tudor and Elizabethan England (C.J. Sansom's *Lamentation* and Kathy Lynn Emerson's *Murder in the Queen's Ward-*

robe), the seventeenth century (Susanna Gregory's *The Cheapside Corpse* and Sam Thomas's *The Witch Hunter's Tale*), the eighteenth century (Robin Blake's *The Hidden Man* and Laura Lebow's *The Figaro Murders*), and the nineteenth century (David Morrell's *Inspector of the Dead*, Ethan J. Wolfe's *The Regulator*, Will Thomas's *Anatomy of Evil*, and Lene Kaaberbol's *Doctor Death*). Of the first half of the twentieth century, every decade is represented: the 1900s (Rhys Bowen's *The Edge of Dreams*), the 1910s (Charles Todd's *A Fine Summer's Day*), the 1920s (Frances Brody's *A Woman Unknown*), the 1930s (Jacqueline Winspear's *A Dangerous Place* and Philip Kerr's *The Lady from Zagreb*), the 1940s (Stephen Kelly's *The Language of the Dead* and David Thomas's *Ostland*), and the 1950s (Lisa Lieberman's *All the Wrong Places*).

Historical figures play a role in the sleuthing as well. These include English poets Chaucer (Bruce Holsinger's *The Invention of Fire*) and John Donne (Bryan Crockett's *Love's Alchemy*), Queen Catherine Parr (C.J. Sansom's *Lamentation*), and writers Thomas De Quincey (David Morrell's *Inspector of the Dead*), Henry James (Dan Simmons's *The Fifth Heart*), and Edna Ferber (Ed Ifkovic's *Cafe Europa*). The notorious Thomas Hare of the grave digging team of Burke and Hare becomes a detective in Peter Ranscombe's *Hare*.

What kind of list of historical mysteries could lack the indomitable Sherlock Holmes? Here he visits Japan in Vasudev Murthy's *Sherlock Holmes: The Missing Years*, comes to America to solve the mystery of the actual death of Clover Adams, wife of historian Henry Adams in Dan Simmons's *The Fifth Heart*, and continues his retirement in the 1920s in Laurie R. King's *Dreaming Spies*.

Among the more intriguing locations for historical mysteries are the court of Camelot in Jay Ruud's *Fatal Feast*, Victorian British Columbia in 1869 in Sean Haldane's *The Devil's Making*, and London's drama scene in the 1950s in Lisa Lieberman's *All the Wrong Places*.

Fictional Biographies

One of the most demanding of the sub-genres of historical are fictional biographies, which re-imagine the lives of historical figures. Freed from the known biographical details, the fictional biographer can embellish and invent, while always risking distortion and falsehood by that invention. The reward is a new perspective on historical figures and possibly a more lively presentation of the familiar or surprising revelations and biographical insights.

Several take up the challenge of re-imagining famous figures. These include: Jesus (Ted Dekker's *A.D. 30*), Shakespeare (Andrea Chapin's *The Tutor*), Abraham Lincoln (Tom Leclair's *Lincoln's Billy*), with two works taking up Lincoln's nemesis, John Wilkes Booth (Jeffrey Francis Pennington's *Lincoln's Assassin* and M.J. Trow's *The Blue and the Grey*), and Charles Darwin (James Morrow's *Galapagos Revisited*). Others take on royals:

English King Stephen and Empress Matilda (Ariana Franklin and Samantha Norman's *The Siege Winter*), Henry VIII and Jane Seymour (Suzannah Dunn's *The May Bride*), Elizabeth I and Lord Robert Dudley (Alison Weir's *The Marriage Game*), and Elizabeth I and the Seymour sisters (Elizabeth Fremantle's *Sisters of Treason*). Non-English royals include Queen Lashmi of India (Michelle Moran's *Rebel Queen*), the seventeenth-century Mogul Emperor Aurangzeb (Alex Rutherford's *Traitors in the Shadows*), Alexander the Great (Colin Falconer's *Colossus*), and Franz Joseph I of Austria and Elizabeth, Empress consort (Allison Pataki's *The Accidental Empress*). American "royalty" depicted include Nat King Cole (Ravi Howard's *Driving the King*), Clark Gable and Carole Lombard (Kate Alcott's *A Touch of Stardust*), and Thomas Edison (Elizabeth Rosner's *Electric City*).

Several works shed light on lesser-known historical figures, such as Emma, queen consort of Canute (Patricia Bracewell's *The Price of Blood*); French fashion designer Coco Chanel (C.W. Gortner's *Mademoiselle Chanel*); American designer Louis Tiffany (Deanne Gist's *Tiffany Girl*); Anglo-Saxon warrior Hereward (James Wilde's *Hereward: End of Days*); Lucy Ann Lobdell, a real-life nineteenth-century woman who sought her fortune disguised as a man (William Klaber's *The Rebellion of Miss Lucy Ann Lobdell*); and Victorian archaeologist Gertrude Lowthian Bell (Ann Gold's *Bell of the Desert*).

Multiple works take up literary subjects, including George Sand (Elizabeth Berg's *The Dream Lover*), Virginia Woolf (Norah Vincent's *Adeline* and Priya Parmar's *Vanessa and Her Sister*), Emily Dickinson (William Nicholson's *Amherst*), Charles Dickens (Thomas Hauser's *The Final Recollections of Charles Dickens*), F. Scott Fitzgerald (Stewart O'Nan's *West of Sunset*), and H.G. Wells (Louisa Treger's *The Lodger*). Artists are not neglected: Van Gogh is the subject of Nellie Hermann's *The Season of Migration* and Manet and his model Victorine are treated in Maureen Gibbon's *Paris Red*. Other writers who make appearances or are central subjects are Ian Fleming (Francine Mathews's *Too Bad to Die*) and Robert Louis Stevenson (Matthew Pearl's *The Last Bookaneer*). Some fictional characters become central in several works, including Leopold and Molly Bloom from Joyce's *Ulysses* in Jessica Stirling's *Whatever Happened to Molly Bloom*, Mammy from *Gone with the Wind* in Donald McCaig's *Ruth's Journey*, and Juliet's nurse from *Romeo and Juliet* in Lois Leveen's *Juliet's Nurse*. Another famous drama provides inspiration: Eliza Doolittle and Henry Higgins from Shaw's *Pygmalion* become Edwardian sleuths in D.E. Ireland's *Wouldn't It Be Deadly*.

Historical Fantasy

One way to overcome the burden of the verifiable in historical fiction is to bend the rules of time and space and incorporate the supernatural and fantasy. This has become one of the more popular sub-genres in recent years, and examples of historical fantasy include vampires during World War II (Marcus Sedgwick's *A Love Like Blood*), the paranormal during the Victorian period (Leanna Renee Hieber's *The Eterna Files*), and witches in 1890s Paris (M.J. Rose's *The Witch of Painted Sorrows*). Alternative histories include Alan Smale's *Clash of Eagles*, in which the Roman Legion invades North America to take on Native Americans; Jeffrey Pennington Francis's *Lincoln's Assassin*, in which John Wilkes Booth survives and tells his side of the Lincoln's assassination; Tony Shumacher's *The Darkest Hour*, depicting a German occupied London in World War II; and Victoria Schwab's *A Darker Shade of Magic*, featuring an alternative London during the eighteenth century.

Historical Fact, the Unusual, and the Exotic

The fundamental burden for historical novelists is facts: how much to use, how much to lose in bringing a story to life. Whereas the data of history can weigh down the imagination, it also can be a great resource for a novel's conflicts. Let me conclude with a selection of novels collected here that make great use of historical facts to ground and discover their stories.

Thomas Keneally in *Shame and the Captives* draws on true events surrounding World War II prison camps in Australia. John Altman in *The Art of the Devil* imagines a plausible plot to assassinate President Eisenhower. Margaret Sweatman in *Mr. Jones* looks at Cold War Canadian politics. Molly Gloss in *Falling from Horses* finds drama in the story of Hollywood stunt riders in the 1930s. Thomas O'Malley and Douglas Graham Purdy in *Serpents in the Cold* find their drama in the details of Boston during the 1950s.

Other novels generate considerable interest and insights from history's overlooked or unusual facts, such as women track athletes in the 1928 Olympics in Carrie Snyder's *Girl Runner*, women boxers in the eighteenth century in Anna Freeman's *A Fair Fight*, women wrestlers in Angelina Mirabella's *The Sweetheart*, women fighting as soldiers in the American Civil War in Kathy Hepinstall's *Sisters of Shiloh*, and gypsies in eighteenth-century Spain in Ildefonso Falcones de Sierra's *The Barfoot Queen*. Among the more exotic locales and customs depicted are Swedish Lapland in 1717 in Cecilia Ekback's *Wolf Winter*, the Ottoman Empire in the sixteenth century in Elif Shafak's *The Architect's Apprentice*, nineteenth-century Iran in Bahiyyih Nakhjavani's *The Woman Who Read Too Much*, Tibet in 1903 in John Wilcox's *Treachery in Tibet*, the 1920s Chicago jazz scene in Marry Morris's *The Jazz Palace*, a freed slave in Post-Civil War San Francisco in Rashad Harrison's *The Abduction of Smith and Smith*, and a Barnum oddity in Joel Fishbane's *The Thunder of Giants*.

These and other historical novels collected here demonstrate both the burden of the factual and the verifiable, as well as their pleasures. As Joyce asserted, "In the particular is contained the universal." Enjoy both from many of these recent historical novels.

Recommendations

Here are my selections of the 25 most accomplished and intriguing historical novels for the first half of 2015:Kate Atkinson, *A God in Ruins*;Bernard Cornwell, *The Empty Throne*;Anita Diamant,*The Boston Girl*;Suzannah Dunn, *The May Bride*;Anna Freeman, *The Fair Fight*;Molly Gloss, *Falling from Horses*;Sara Gruen, *At the Water's Edge*;Kazuo Ishiguro, *The Buried Giant*;Thomas Keneally, *Shame and the Captives*;William Klaber,*The Rebellion of Miss Lucy Ann Lobdell*;Dennis Lehane,*World Gone By*;Jeffrey Lent,*A Slant of Light*;Donald McCaig, *Ruth's Journey*;Stewart O'Nan,*West of Sunset*;Matthew Pearl,*The Last Bookaneer*;Arturo Perez-Reverte, *The Siege*;Ralph Peters, *Valley of the Shadow*;Elizabeth Rosner,*Electric City*;Elif Shafak, *The Architect's Apprentice*;Dan Simmons, *The Fifth Heart*;Jane Smiley,*Early Warning*;Jane Smiley, *Some Luck*;Anne Tyler,*A Spool of Blue Thread*;Sarah Waters, *The Paying Guests*;Jacqueline Winspear, *A Dangerous Place*;

For More Information about Historical Fiction

Printed Sources

Lynda G. Adamson, *American Historical Fiction: An Annotated Guide to Novels for Adults and Young Adults*. Phoenix: Oryx Press, 1999.

Lynda G. Adamson, *World Historical Fiction: An Annotated Guide to Novels for Adults and Young Adults*. Phoenix: Oryx Press, 1999.

Daniel S. Burt, *What Historical Fiction Do I Read Next?* Detroit: Gale, Vols. 1–3, 1997–2003.

Daniel S. Burt, *The Biography Book*. Westport: Oryx/Greenwood Press, 2001.

Mark C. Carnes, *Novel History: Historians and Novelists Confront America's Past (and Each Other)*. New York: Simon & Schuster, 2001.

Donald K Hartman, *Historical Figures in Fiction*. Phoenix: Oryx Press, 1994.

Electronic Sources

The Historical Novel Society (http//www.historicalnovel society.org). Includes articles, interviews, and reviews of historical novels.

Of Ages Past: The Online Magazine of Historical Fiction (http://www.angelfire.com/il/ofagespast/). Includes novel excerpts, short stories, articles, author profiles, and reviews.

Soon's Historical Fiction Site (http://uts.cc.utexas.edu/~soon/histfiction/). A rich source of information on the historical novel genre, including links to more specialized sites on particular authors and types of historical fiction.

Historical Fiction

125

KATE ALCOTT (Pseudonym of Patricia O'Brien)

A Touch of Stardust

(New York: Doubleday, 2015)

Story type: Romance

Subject(s): Movie industry; Movies; Actors

Major character(s): Julie Crawford, Woman, Assistant (to Carole), Worker (for David); Carole Lombard, Lover (of Clark), Employer (of Julie), Historical Figure, Actress; Clark Gable, Historical Figure, Actor, Lover (of Carole); David O. Selznick, Historical Figure, Filmmaker, Employer (of Julie)

Time period(s): 20th century; 1930s (1938)

Locale(s): Los Angeles, California

Summary: Kate Alcott's novel takes place against the backdrop of the filming of *Gone with the Wind* in 1938. Recent college graduate Julie Crawford dreams of becoming a Hollywood screenwriter. She travels from Indiana to California, where she lands a job with one of the film industry's most notorious producers, David O. Selznick. Selznick is obsessed with crafting *Gone with the Wind*, the sweeping Southern romance. He has cast Clark Gable as his leading man, but the married actor is carrying on a secret affair with Carole Lombard, an actress from Julie's hometown of Fort Wayne. Soon Carole asks Julie to work as the actress's personal assistant. Julie experiences first-hand the magic and glamour of Old Hollywood while trying to keep Carole's affair with Clark out of the press. All the while, Julie learns that nothing in Hollywood is as it seems to be.

Other books by the same author:
The Daring Ladies of Lowell, 2014
The Dressmaker, 2012

Other books you might like:
George Baxt, *The Clark Gable and Carole Lombard Murder Case*, 1997
Kristin Hannah, *Angel Falls*, 2000
Stuart M. Kaminsky, *Tomorrow Is Another Day*, 1995
Stewart O'Nan, *West of Sunset*, 2015

Susan Elizabeth Phillips, *Breathing Room*, 2002
Jess Walter, *Beautiful Ruins*, 2012

126

TESSA ARLEN

Death of a Dishonorable Gentleman

(New York: Minotaur Books, 2015)

Story type: Historical - Edwardian; Mystery

Subject(s): Social class; Edwardian age, 1901-1914; Murder

Major character(s): Clementine Elizabeth Talbot, Socialite, Spouse (of Ralph), Noblewoman (Countess of Montfort), Employer (of Edith Jackson); Edith Jackson, Housekeeper; Ralph Cuthbert Talbot, Nobleman (Lord Montfort), Spouse (of Clementine)

Time period(s): 20th century; 1900s

Locale(s): England

Summary: For Lady Montfort, few things in life are more important than the lavish social gatherings she hosts at her sprawling English estate. That is precisely why she has spent months meticulously planning every detail of her upcoming summer costume ball. Unfortunately, all that planning ends up being for naught when her husband's unscrupulous nephew dies unexpectedly at the hands of an unseen murderer. To make matters worse, it soon becomes clear that the young man's death might cost Lady Montfort much more than her party—her son is quickly deemed to be a suspect. Determined to prove his innocence, she launches an investigation with the help of her housekeeper, Mrs. Jackson, that reveals much more about Lady Montfort's esteemed social circle than she ever dreamed possible.

Other books you might like:
John Boyne, *Crippen*, 2006
Marion Chesney, *Hasy Death*, 2004
Tracy Chevalier, *Falling Angels*, 2001
Charles Todd, *A Fine Summer's Day*, 2015
Jacqueline Winspear, *A Dangerous Place*, 2015

127

KATE ATKINSON

A God in Ruins

(New York: Little, Brown and Company, 2015)

Story type: Literary
Subject(s): World War II, 1939-1945; Conduct of life; History
Major character(s): Teddy Todd, Man, Military Personnel (fighter pilot), Brother (of Ursula); Ursula Todd, Woman, Sister (of Teddy)
Time period(s): 20th century
Locale(s): England; Germany

Summary: Kate Atkinson's 2013 novel, *Life After Life*, tells the story of Ursula Todd, a woman whose repeated deaths and births give her a unique perspective on the unfolding of 20th-century history. In this follow-up novel, the focus is on Ursula's brother, Teddy. Unlike his remarkable sister, Teddy lives just one, linear life, but the account of that life reveals much about the realities of World War II and the repercussions the conflict has on those who experience it. Teddy serves as a British fighter pilot, and he is resigned to the likelihood that the war will probably claim his life. When he survives his tour of duty, Teddy goes on to start new phases of his life. He isn't reborn as his sister is, but Teddy still has the opportunity to live several lives, including those of a writer and a family man.

Other books by the same author:
Started Early, Took My Dog, 2011
When Will There Be Good News?, 2008
Our Good Turn, 2006
Case Histories, 2004
Behind the Scenes at the Museum, 1996

Other books you might like:
Jeffrey Archer, *Paths of Glory*, 2009
Bridgett M. Davis, *Into the Go-Slow*, 2014
Sara Gruen, *At the Water's Edge*, 2015
Jason Hewitt, *The Dynamite Room*, 2015
Rachel Joyce, *The Love Song of Miss Queenie Hennessy*, 2015
Dennis Lehane, *World Gone By*, 2015
Jeffrey Lent, *A Slant of Light*, 2015
Daniel Torday, *The Last Flight of Poxl West*, 2015

128

MARTINE BAILEY

An Appetite for Violets

(New York: Thomas Dunne Books, 2015)

Story type: Mystery
Subject(s): Suspense; English (British people); Interpersonal relations
Major character(s): Biddy Leigh, Narrator, Cook, Companion (travel companion for Lady Carinna); Lady Carinna, Employer (of Biddy), Sister (of Kitt); Kitt, Brother (of Lady Carinna); Loveday, Slave (of Lady Carinna)

Time period(s): 18th century; 1770s (1772)
Locale(s): Italy

Summary: Mawton Hall under-cook Biddy Leigh wants nothing more out of life than to marry her longtime sweetheart and become a tavern owner. Instead, she is whisked away from her predictable life when her aged master takes a young wife. Biddy must travel with her young new mistress, Lady Carinna, to Italy. Biddy packs a book of recipes, and records her thoughts on the journey and others in its pages. Lady Carinna says that she selected Biddy because of her talent as a cook, but Biddy soon learns that her mistress might have alternative motives. Biddy gets to know the rest of the party on the journey, and soon finds herself attracted to her mistress's younger brother, Kitt. Once the group arrives in a small villa in Italy, Biddy suddenly finds herself caught up in a murder mystery in which she holds a major key to the puzzle. Included in the book are recipes from the 18th century.

Other books you might like:
Charles Finch, *The Laws of Murder*, 2014
Anna Freeman, *The Fair Fight*, 2015
Sophie Gee, *The Scandal of the Season*, 2007
Constance Heaven, *The Wind from the Sea*, 1991
Elizabeth Hoyt, *Notorious Pleasures*, 2011
Christopher Nicholson, *The Elephant Keeper*, 2009
Andrew Taylor, *The Anatomy of Ghosts*, 2011

129

ELIZABETH BERG

The Dream Lover

(New York: Random House Publishing, 2015)

Story type: Romance
Subject(s): Women's rights; Love; History
Major character(s): George Sand, Historical Figure, Writer, Woman (born Aurore Dupin)
Time period(s): 19th century
Locale(s): Paris, France

Summary: Set in nineteenth century Paris, this is a fictional account of the life of writing legend George Sand. Aurore Dupin leaves her family estate and a bad marriage for a new life in Paris, taking on a new persona as androgynous Sand. That alone would ruffle feathers and raise eyebrows in France's capital, but Sand also leads an adventurous and even wild lifestyle as she pursues her dream of writing. Relationships—platonic and otherwise—with the likes of Frederic Chopin, Gustave Flaubert, Franz Liszt, Eugene Delacroix, Victor Hugo, Marie Dorval, and Alfred de Musset help Sand deal with the pain of her past as well as the nagging doubts about ever reaching her true dream.

Other books by the same author:
The Last Time I Saw You, 2010
Home Safe, 2009
Dream When You're Feeling Blue, 2007
We Are All Welcome Here, 2007
The Year of Pleasures, 2005

Other books you might like:
Julian Barnes, *Flaubert's Parrot*, 1984

Rosalind Brackenbury, *Becoming George Sand*, 2011
Gyles Brandreth, *Oscar Wilde and a Death of No Importance*, 2008
Susanne Dunlap, *Liszt's Kiss*, 2007
Nancy Horan, *Under the Wide and Starry Sky*, 2014
F.W. Kenyon, *The Questing Heart: A Romantic Novel about George Sand*, 1964
Gregory Maguire, *Confessions of an Ugly Stepsister*, 1999
Robin Oliveira, *I Always Loved You*, 2014
Priya Parmar, *Vanessa and Her Sister*, 2014
Matthew Pearl, *The Poe Shadow: A Novel*, 2006
Frances Sherwood, *Vindication*, 1993
Enid Shomer, *The Twelve Rooms of the Nile*, 2012
Colm Toibin, *The Master*, 2004
Gore Vidal, *1876: A Novel*, 1976
Edmund White, *Hotel de Dream*, 2007

130

NANCY BILYEAU

The Tapestry

(New York: Simon and Schuster, 2015)

Series: Joanna Stafford Series. Book 3
Story type: Mystery; Series
Subject(s): British history, 1066-1688; Mystery; Royalty
Major character(s): Joanna Stafford, Religious (former Dominican novice), Artisan (tapestry weaver); Henry VIII, Historical Figure, Royalty (king of England); Catherine Howard, Teenager, Friend (of Joanna); Geoffrey, Lawman (constable); Edmund, Religious (former friar)
Time period(s): 16th century; 1540s
Locale(s): England

Summary: Henry VIII's campaign against the Catholic Church includes the closure of England's monasteries and convents. When Joanna Stafford, a Dominican novice, was forced to leave the nunnery at Dartford, she planned to marry Edmund, a former friar. But that hope was dashed when a law decreed that all former religious must continue to honor their vows of celibacy. Now Joanna spends her days as a tapestry weaver. Her skills eventually impress the king, who invites Joanna to Whitehall Palace. There Joanna is drawn into the court's drama and finds herself dodging kidnappers and would-be assassins. Joanna counsels young Catherine Howard, who is rumored to be the king's next mistress. Familiar with the king's marital history, Joanna fears for the innocent Catherine's life. When Joanna is sent to Europe to acquire tapestries for the palace, she becomes involved in another grave matter: the disappearance of Edmund. This novel is the third in the Joanna Stafford series.

Other books by the same author:
The Chalice, 2013
The Crown, 2012

Other books you might like:
Vanora Bennett, *Portrait of an Unknown Woman*, 2007
Elizabeth Fremantle, *Sisters of Treason*, 2014
Deborah Harkness, *Shadow of Night*, 2012

Brenda Rickman Vantrease, *The Heretic's Wife*, 2010
Alison Weir, *The Lady Elizabeth: A Novel*, 2008

131

RHYS BOWEN (Pseudonym of Janet Quin-Harkin)

The Edge of Dreams

(New York: Minotaur Books, 2015)

Series: Molly Murphy Series. Book 14
Subject(s): Detective fiction; Accidents; Family
Major character(s): Molly Murphy Sullivan, Spouse (of Daniel), Mother (of Liam), Detective—Private (former), Accident Victim, Retiree; Liam Sullivan, Son (of Molly and Daniel), Baby, Accident Victim; Daniel Sullivan, Police Officer, Spouse (of Molly), Father (of Liam)
Time period(s): 20th century; 1900s (1905)
Locale(s): New York, New York

Summary: In the 14th Molly Murphy mystery novel, Molly and her infant son, Liam, are nearly killed in a horrible subway accident. Her husband, Daniel, has been working on a case involving a serial killer who sends mocking notes each time a victim is murdered. Although Molly has retired from her detective business and focuses on her family, Daniel, a captain in the New York Police Department, often discusses his work with her and values both her insight and judgment. Since the notes from the killer are addressed directly to him, Daniel is under a lot of pressure to solve the case quickly. Another note arrives after the subway accident, leaving the Sullivans convinced that the wreck was a deliberate attempt to kill Molly and Liam. Disregarding her injuries, Molly works with her husband to uncover the identity of the serial killer before another note is delivered.

Other books by the same author:
City of Darkness and Light, 2014
Her Royal Spyness, 2007
Death of Riley, 2002
Murphy's Law, 2001
Evans Above, 1997

Other books you might like:
Carol Lea Benjamin, *The Hard Way*, 2006
Alan Bradley, *As Chimney Sweepers Come to Dust*, 2015
Caleb Carr, *The Alienist*, 1994
Caleb Carr, *The Angel of Darkness*, 1997
Anne Perry, *The Angel Court Affair*, 2014
Stefanie Pintoff, *In the Shadow of Gotham*, 2009
Stefanie Pintoff, *Secret of the White Rose*, 2011
S.J. Rozan, *Winter and Night*, 2002
Sandra Scoppettone, *This Dame for Hire*, 2005
Leslie Silbert, *The Intelligencer*, 2004
Ann Stamos, *Bitter Tide*, 2009
Victoria Thompson, *Murder on Astor Place*, 1999

132

PATRICIA BRACEWELL

The Price of Blood

(New York: Viking, 2015)

Series: Emma of Normandy Trilogy. Book 2
Story type: Historical - Medieval; Series
Subject(s): Middle Ages; England; Monarchs
Major character(s): Emma, Royalty (Queen of England), Spouse (of Aethelred), Mother (of Edward), Historical Figure; Aethelred, Historical Figure, Royalty (King of England), Spouse (of Emma), Father (of Edward and other children); Edward, Son (of Emma and Aethelred), Historical Figure
Time period(s): 11th century; 1000s (1006)
Locale(s): England

Summary: The second novel in the Emma of Normandy trilogy continues the fictionalized account of the life of Emma, wife of King Aethelred and queen consort of England. When Emma came to Aethelred's court from Normandy, she learned to navigate the world of English politics and the intricacies of her husband's family. She became stepmother to the many children Aethelred had with his first wife, and she gave her husband a son of their own, Edward. Her relationship with Aethelred is not a loving one, however. Aethelred is a violent ruler, and Emma fears for Edward's safety. Now, in the 11th century, England is being threatened by Viking invaders and internal turmoil. Emma does everything in her power to protect her son and her country, and she works clandestinely to keep a rein on Aethelred.

Other books by the same author:
Shadow on the Crown, 2013

Other books you might like:
Gene Farrington, *The Breath of Kings*, 1982
Cecelia Holland, *Kings of the North*, 2010
Helen Hollick, *The Forever Queen*, 2010
Helen Hollick, *The Hollow Crown*, 2005
Jean Plaidy, *The Bastard King*, 1974

133

BARBARA TAYLOR BRADFORD

The Cavendon Women

(New York: St. Martin's Press, 2015)

Story type: Family Saga
Subject(s): England; History; Family
Major character(s): Charles Ingham, Spouse (former, of Felicity), Father (of Miles, Daphne, Diedre, Dulcie, DeLacy), Nobleman (sixth earl of Mowbray), Spouse (of Charlotte); Charlotte Swann Ingham, Spouse (of Charles); Felicity, Spouse (former, of Charles), Mother (of Miles, Daphne, Diedre, Dulcie, DeLacy); Miles, Spouse (of Clarissa), Son (of Charles and Felicity); Daphne, Daughter (of Charles and Felicity); Diedre, Daughter (of Charles and Felicity); Dulcie, Daughter (of Charles and Felicity); DeLacy, Daughter (of Charles and Felicity); Lady Gwendolyn, Noblewoman, Aunt (of Miles, Daphne, Diedre, Dulcie, DeLacy); Cecily Swann, Entrepreneur (fashion); Clarissa, Spouse (estranged, of Miles)
Time period(s): 20th century; 1920s (1926-1929)
Locale(s): Yorkshire, England

Summary: Author Barbara Taylor Bradford introduced the Ingham and Swann families in the novel *Cavendon Hall*. This follow-up continues the stories of the clans who have lived together for centuries in a Yorkshire manor house—the Inghams as the wealthy owners and the Swanns as their staff. It is 1926, and times are changing in England for the aristocracy, who must now pay steep taxes. Change has also come to Cavendon Hall. Now divorced, Charles Ingham, the sixth Earl of Mowbray, has married Charlotte Swann. His children—Miles, Daphne, Diedre, Dulcie, and DeLacy—welcome the news, as does the elderly Lady Gwendolyn. The family faces new challenges when the members reunite for a summer weekend. The global financial crisis of 1929 is still a few years away, but a more immediate threat prompts the women of Cavendon Hall to take action.

Other books by the same author:
Cavendon Hall, 2014
Just Rewards, 2006
Unexpected Blessings, 2005
Emma's Secret, 2004
Love in Another Town, 1995

Other books you might like:
Paul Elwork, *The Girl Who Would Speak for the Dead*, 2011
Therese Anne Fowler, *Z: A Novel of Zelda Fitzgerald*, 2013
Thomas Mallon, *Bandbox*, 2003
Mary Morris, *The Jazz Palace*, 2015
Jane Smiley, *Early Warning*, 2015
Carrie Snyder, *Girl Runner*, 2015
Genevieve Valentine, *The Girls at the Kingfisher Club*, 2014

134

FRANCES BRODY

A Woman Unknown

(New York: Minotaur Books, 2015)

Series: Kate Shackleton Series. Book 4
Story type: Mystery; Series
Subject(s): Mystery; England; Marriage
Major character(s): Kate Shackleton, Investigator (private), Colleague (of Marcus); Cyril Fitzpatrick, Spouse (of Deirdre); Deirdre Fitzpatrick, Spouse (wife, of Cyril); Marcus Charles, Detective—Police, Colleague (of Kate); Everett Runcie, Crime Victim, Banker
Time period(s): 20th century; 1920s (1923)
Locale(s): England

Summary: Set in 1923 England, this historical mystery novel is the fourth installment in the Kate Shackleton series by Frances Brody. Cyril Fitzpatrick hires private investigator Kate Shackleton to find out what his wife, Deirdre, really does while he's at work. Deirdre's mother is sick, but Cyril isn't convinced that caring for her mother is what keeps Deirdre gone days at a time. Meanwhile, struggling banker Everett Runcie will do anything to speed up his divorce to his American heiress wife. But when Everett is found dead in his hotel room, Kate's investigation turns ominous. Now, with commissions from Cyril to find his missing wife and from Everett's wife to find a murderer, Kate has her hands full. Scotland Yard DCI Marcus Charles is handed the murder case. When he asks Kate for help, but refuses to discuss the details with her, Kate is determined to beat him to the truth.

Other books by the same author:
Murder in the Afternoon, 2014
A Medal for Murder, 2013
Dying in the Wool, 2012

Other books you might like:
William Gibson, *Pattern Recognition*, 2003
P.D. James, *The Skull Beneath the Skin*, 1983
Laurie R. King, *Dreaming Spies*, 2015
Charles Todd, *A Fine Summer's Day*, 2015
Jacqueline Winspear, *Among the Mad*, 2009

135

VITO BRUSCHINI
ANNE MILANO APPEL, Translator

The Prince

(New York: Atria Books, 2015)

Story type: Historical - Mainstream
Subject(s): History; Organized crime; Italy
Major character(s): Ferdinando Licata, Landowner (in Sicily), Organized Crime Figure; Lucky Luciano, Historical Figure, Organized Crime Figure
Time period(s): 20th century; 1920s-1940s (1920-1943)
Locale(s): Sicily, Italy; New York, New York

Summary: In this novel, author Vito Bruschini presents a fictionalized account of the origins of the Mafia. Ferdinando Licata is an important figure in Sicily. He is a rich landowner, and he is working to stop the spread of fascism in his country. As Licata rises to power, he wins the affection of some supporters, but he is reviled by many others. When he is connected to a murder, Licata leaves Sicily and heads to New York City, where Italian and Irish mobsters are vying for dominance. Licata makes a name for himself in America, and he forges an alliance with Lucky Luciano, another mobster. During World War II, Licata and Luciano have the opportunity to help the US military during the invasion of Sicily. Licata eventually returns to his homeland, where more acts of violence and revenge ensue.

Other books you might like:
Nelson DeMille, *The Gate House*, 2008
John Grisham, *The Client*, 1993
Dennis Lehane, *World Gone By*, 2015
Mario Puzo, *The Godfather*, 1969
Mario Puzo, *The Sicilian*, 1984

136

SHANNON BURKE

Into the Savage Country

(New York: Pantheon Books, 2015)

Story type: Historical - American West; Western
Subject(s): Western fiction; History; Adventure
Major character(s): William Wyeth, Young Man, Trapper (fur), Enemy (former, of Henry); Henry Layton, Young Man, Trapper (fur), Enemy (former, of William); Alene Chevalier, Widow(er)
Time period(s): 19th century; 1820s (1826)
Locale(s): United States

Summary: Set in 1826, this historical fiction novel by Shannon Burke is a tale of love, friendship, survival, and adventure in the American West. Seeking his fortune as a fur trapper, 22-year-old William Wyeth travels beyond St. Louis into the open prairies of the West, where a buffalo hunt leaves him badly injured. While recovering in a US Army encampment, William finds hope in the camaraderie of his fellow trappers and love with a young widow named Alene Chevalier. Eventually a former enemy, Henry Layton, shows up and makes William an offer he can't refuse. William joins Henry's newly formed Market Street Fur Company and embarks on an expedition. William finds himself in Crow Indian territory, where he contends with Native American tribes, the British government, and other American trapping companies who are embroiled in a dangerous boundary dispute.

Other books by the same author:
Black Flies, 2008
Safelight, 2004

Other books you might like:
Justin Allen, *Year of the Horse*, 2009
William W. Johnstone, *Forty Guns West*, 1993
Kathleen Kent, *The Outcasts*, 2013
Philip Kimball, *Liar's Moon*, 1999
Jory Sherman, *The Savage Gun*, 2007

137

PAULA RENEE BURZAWA

Tasso's Journey

(Bloomington, Indiana: iUniverse, 2015)

Story type: Historical - World War II
Subject(s): World War II, 1939-1945; History; Greeks
Major character(s): Anastasios "Tasso" Stamatopoulos, Spouse, Military Personnel (Greek soldier)
Time period(s): 20th century; 1940s (1941)
Locale(s): Greece

Summary: Award-winning author Paula Renee Burzawa delivers a tale of love, family, war, and sacrifice. Before the Nazis invade Greece in 1941, Tasso, a Greek soldier, returns home to protect his family, only to learn that his nephew has been stricken with polio. Threatened by an impending attack by the Germans, Tasso's family and fellow villagers make preparations, and Tasso assists the doctors who save his nephew's leg. When Tasso leaves his village to return to his army unit, he and his father-in-law are taken captive by the Germans, and his family is forced to endure a number of hardships at the hands of the invaders. But peace does not follow when Germany and the Axis powers surrender. Greece breaks out in a civil war, and as Greeks are pitted against one another, Tasso's life is forever changed.

Other books by the same author:
Season of Sun, 2010

Other books you might like:
Louis De Bernieres, *Captain Corelli's Mandolin*, 1994
Alan Furst, *Spies of the Balkans*, 2010
Stratis Haviaras, *When the Tree Sings*, 1979
Jack Higgins, *Night Judgement at Sinos*, 1979
Lawrence Norfolk, *In the Shape of a Boar*, 2001

138

ROBERT OLEN BUTLER

The Empire of Night
(New York: Mysterious Press, 2014)

Series: Christopher Marlowe Cobb Thriller Series. Book 3
Story type: Adventure; Historical - World War I
Subject(s): Actors; Deception; Family relations
Major character(s): Chris "Kit" Cobb, Spy (American), Son (of Isabel Cobb), Journalist (newspaper reporter); Isabel Cobb, Actress (stage), Mother (of Kitt Cobb), Spy (American), Lover (of Sir Albert Stockman); Albert Stockman, Spy, Lover (of Isabel Cobb), Nobleman (British/German aristocrat)
Time period(s): 20th century; 1910s (1915)
Locale(s): Cliffs of Dover, England; London, England; Berlin, Germany

Summary: In the third installment of Robert Olen Butler's Christopher Marlowe Cobb Thriller series, Christopher "Kit" Marlowe Cobb is an American journalist turned spy. It is the beginning of World War I and the United States is still considering its involvement in the war. Kit is assigned the mission to go undercover as a German-American newspaper correspondent to reveal the secret German plot to use zeppelins as deadly weapons. Traveling to London and Berlin on this dangerous mission, Kit is unexpectedly paired up with another secret agent: his mother, well-known stage actress Isabel Cobb. Though Kit is uncomfortable with the situation, he must stick to his cover and work with his mother to thwart the Germans, even if it means keeping tabs on a suspected German mole who happens to be Isabel's lover. Facing danger, intrigue, and treachery at every turn, the mother-son spy team struggles to maintain cover and stop the Germans before it's too late.

Other books by the same author:
The Star of Istanbul, 2013
A Small Hotel, 2011
Hell, 2009
Fair Warning, 2002
The Deep Green Sea, 1997

Other books you might like:
Ken Follett, *The Man from St. Petersburg*, 1982
Alan Furst, *Mission to Paris*, 2012
J. Sydney Jones, *The German Agent*, 2015
Yannick Murphy, *Signed, Mata Hari*, 2007
Anne Perry, *Angels in the Gloom*, 2005
Wilbur Smith, *Assegai*, 2009

139

MIRANDA CARTER

The Strangler Vine
(London, United Kingdom: Fig Tree, 2015)

Story type: Historical - Exotic; Historical - Victorian
Subject(s): History; Colonialism; Indians (Asian people)
Major character(s): William Avery, Military Personnel (East India Company's army); Jeremiah Blake, Agent (East India Company); Xavier Mountstuart, Writer (Scottish), Missing Person
Time period(s): 19th century; 1830s (1837)
Locale(s): India

Summary: The East India Company controls much of India in 1837. Tensions are increasing between the native Indians and the British, and the antics of Scottish writer Xavier Mountstuart have only aggravated the situation. He had agreed to leave the country, but failed to make good on his promise. When Mountstuart disappears, two East India Company representatives are dispatched to find him: Jeremiah Blake, a skilled investigative agent, and William Avery, a low-level officer in the company's army. Mountstuart was known to have an interest in India's Thuggees. These gangs, which are deeply rooted in Indian history, prey on travelers, whom they strangle and rob. As Avery and Blake search for Mountstuart, they learn more about the mysterious and dangerous Thuggees and experience the many wonders and dangers of colonial-era India. First novel.

Other books you might like:
Bernard Cornwell, *Sharpe's Triumph*, 1999
David Davidar, *The House of Blue Mangoes*, 2002
Thomas Hoover, *The Moghul*, 1983
David Liss, *The Devil's Company*, 2009
John Masters, *Bhowani Junction*, 1954
Michelle Moran, *Rebel Queen*, 2015
Alex Rutherford, *Traitors in the Shadows*, 2015

140

ANDREA CHAPIN

The Tutor
(New York: Riverhead Books, 2015)

Story type: Literary
Subject(s): British history, 1066-1688; Shakespeare, William; Literature
Major character(s): Katherine de L'Isle, Woman (31 years old), Widow(er), Niece (of Sir Edward); Edward, Nobleman, Uncle (of Katherine), Religious (Catholic); Elizabeth I, Historical Figure, Ruler

(Queen of England); William Shakespeare, Writer, Historical Figure, Tutor; Daulton, Man, Religious (Catholic priest), Crime Victim
Time period(s): 16th century; 1590s (1590)
Locale(s): Lancashire, England

Summary: When 31-year-old widow Katharine de L'Isle goes to live with her Uncle Edward's family in Lancashire, she initially enjoys a calm, bookish life. But in 1590, England is experiencing religious conflict that eventually reaches Edward's estate. When Father Daulton—a priest who had been ministering to Edward's Catholic family secretly—is stabbed to death, Edward escapes to France. He leaves Katharine in Lancashire with his children and the newly arrived tutor, William Shakespeare. Katharine is at first put off by William's forward behavior, and she questions his qualifications as a tutor. But she eventually is impressed with his skills as a poet and enters a romantic relationship with the obviously experienced ladies' man. As Elizabeth I continues her persecution of Catholics, Katharine enjoys the company of the man who is supposed to be her nephew's tutor. But while Katharine is truly smitten, William Shakespeare's motivations remain unclear.

Other books you might like:
Anthony Burgess, *Nothing Like the Sun: A Story of Shakespeare's Love-Life*, 1964
Michael Gruber, *The Book of Air and Shadows: A Novel*, 2007
Karen Harper, *Mistress Shakespeare*, 2009
Faye Kellerman, *The Quality of Mercy*, 1989
Sarah Smith, *Chasing Shakespeares: A Novel*, 2003

141

ALYS CLARE

Blood of the South

(Surrey, England: Severn House, 2015)

Series: Aelf Fen Series. Book 6
Story type: Historical - Medieval; Mystery
Subject(s): England; Detective fiction; Murder
Major character(s): Lassair, Healer, Co-worker (of Rollo), Detective—Amateur; Jack Chevestrier, Police Officer (sheriff's officer); Rollo, Co-worker (of Lassair)
Time period(s): 11th century; 1090s (1093)
Locale(s): Cambridge, England

Summary: In book six of the Aelf Fen mystery series, the sheriff's officer, Jack Chevestrier, requests the assistance of healer Lassair in Cambridge. Lassair helps to rescue a noblewoman and her baby from a mob. The healer lends her assistance in trying to find the extended family of the woman, who has no real information about who her husband's relatives are or where they live. Soon, a torrential rainfall results in wide-scale flooding of the fens. Among the debris, authorities discover the body of a woman. Lassair wonders if the body could be connected to the mystery of the noblewoman, and begins to question the means of death. Could this be a murder investigation? Meanwhile, Lassair's partner, Rollo, is on a mission for King William, and his task is becoming increasingly difficult. Rollo must accept the help of a stranger if he hopes to get out of the Holy Land alive.

Other books by the same author:
The Song of the Nightingale, 2012
The Rose of the World, 2011
Music of the Distant Stars, 2010
Out of the Dawn Light, 2009
The Joys of My Life, 2008

Other books you might like:
Valerie Anand, *The Proud Villeins*, 1990
Simon Beaufort, *Deadly Inheritance*, 2010
Paul Doherty, *The Book of Fires*, 2015
Cora Harrison, *Condemned to Death*, 2015
Cora Harrison, *Verdict of the Court*, 2014
Sharon Kay Penman, *When Christ and His Saints Slept*, 1995
Joan Wolf, *No Dark Place*, 1999

142

CASSANDRA CLARK

The Dragon of Handale

(New York: Minotaur Books, 2015)

Series: Abbess of Meaux Series. Book 5
Story type: Historical - Medieval; Mystery
Subject(s): Mystery; Detective fiction; Crime
Major character(s): Hildegard, Religious (former Cistercian nun), Detective—Amateur; Prioress of Swyne, Religious (Cistercian nun); Basilda, Woman, Religious (Benedictine nun); Fulke, Wealthy (benefactor of Handale Priory)
Time period(s): 14th century
Locale(s): England

Summary: Former Cistercian nun Hildegard returns to her priory at Swyne in the fifth novel in the Abbess Hildegard of Meaux series. Hildegard has been on a year-long pilgrimage in Spain, and she must now decide if she will become part of her religious order again. The prioress suggests a period of discernment and sends Hildegard to Handale Priory, an isolated Benedictine house. Hildegarde, who has solved several mysteries in the past, suspects that her prioress has an ulterior motive in sending her to Handale. When Hildegarde arrives she finds several things amiss. Most notable is the local belief that a dragon lives in the forest near the priory. One of the dragon's alleged victims lies in the morgue, his body covered with deep claw marks. Hildegarde also notices that the prioress, Basilda, treats herself quite well while the penitents in her care suffer excessively. As Hildegarde tries to unravel the mysterious happenings at Handale, she puts her own life in danger.

Other books by the same author:
A Parliament of Spies, 2012
The Law of Angels, 2011
Hangman Blind, 2009
The Red Velvet Turnshoe, 2009

Other books you might like:
Peter Ackroyd, *The Clerkenwell Tales*, 2004
Valerie Anand, *The Ruthless Yeomen*, 1991
Paul Doherty, *The Straw Men*, 2013
Cora Harrison, *Condemned to Death*, 2015

Jean Plaidy, *Passage to Pontefract*, 1982
Priscilla Royal, *Satan's Lullaby*, 2015
Simone Zelitch, *The Confession of Jack Straw*, 1991

143

ACE COLLINS

Hollywood Lost

(Nashville, Tennessee: Abingdon Press, 2015)

Story type: Mystery; Romantic Suspense
Subject(s): Mystery; Detective fiction; Crime
Major character(s): Shelby Beckett, Young Woman, Worker (film studio wardrobe department); Flynn Sparks, Actor; Dalton Andrews, Actor; Clark Gable, Historical Figure, Actor; Cary Grant, Historical Figure, Actor; Bill Barrister, Detective—Homicide
Time period(s): 20th century; 1930s (1936)
Locale(s): Los Angeles, California

Summary: In 1936, Shelby Beckett is a long way from her home in the Oklahoma dust bowl. She has come to Hollywood to find a job, and she discovers a new world of movie stars and millionaires. Shelby takes a position in a movie studio's wardrobe department, and she is soon smitten with two actors—Flynn Sparks and Dalton Andrews. She socializes at Hollywood galas and crosses paths with Cary Grant and other stars. But all is not well in Tinseltown. A murderer is targeting young women in the city, and he may have ties to Shelby's studio. Homicide detective Bill Barrister is on the case, and he has devised a dangerous plan to capture the killer: He wants to use Shelby to lure the strangler out of his hiding place.

Other books by the same author:
The Color of Justice, 2014
Darkness Before Dawn, 2013
The Yellow Packard, 2012
Swope's Ridge, 2009
Farraday Road, 2008

Other books you might like:
Neil Gordon, *The Silent Murders*, 1929
Denise Hamilton, *The Last Embrace*, 2008
Mary Miley, *Silent Murders*, 2014
Nina Revoyr, *The Age of Dreaming*, 2008
Linda L. Richards, *Death Was in the Picture*, 2009
Edward Wright, *While I Disappear*, 2004

144

JOHN CONNELL

Ruins of War

(New York: Berkley, 2015)

Series: Mason Collins Series. Book 1
Subject(s): World War II, 1939-1945; Human psychological experimentation; Germans
Major character(s): Mason Collins, Detective—Homicide (former), Military Personnel (U.S. Army criminal investigator)

Time period(s): 20th century; 1940s (1945)
Locale(s): Germany

Summary: Mason Collins is a former homicide detective from Chicago who joined the US Army during World War II. As the fighting ends in 1945, Collins is in Germany serving as a US Army criminal investigator. The American Zone of Occupation is a mess, with crime and hopelessness everywhere. When a serial killer begins butchering victims and participating in rituals with the corpses, the case is assigned to Collins. Collins must face down Nazi sympathizers and war criminals as well as corrupt US military personnel if he is going to find answers before another body turns up. As he tracks down clues, he draws the attention of many enemies. Soon Collins is in the cross hairs of the serial killer. Collins must navigate bureaucratic and jurisdictional difficulties and snooping reporters, as well as a surly German partner who doesn't trust any Americans. This in the first novel of the Mason Collins series by John Connell.

Other books you might like:
James R. Benn, *Billy Boyle*, 2006
James R. Benn, *The Rest Is Silence*, 2014
Alan Furst, *Red Gold*, 1999
Alan Furst, *The World at Night*, 1996
Alex Grecian, *The Harvest Man*, 2015
Graham Greene, *The Third Man*, 1950
Philip Kerr, *German Requiem*, 1991
Philip Kerr, *The Lady from Zagreb*, 2015
Jason Matthews, *Palace of Treason*, 2015
Charles McCarry, *The Secret Lovers*, 1977
Joyce Carol Oates, *Jack of Spades*, 2015
Matthew Palmer, *Secrets of State*, 2015

145

GARY CORBY

Death Ex Machina

(New York: Soho Crime, 2015)

Series: Athenian Mysteries Series. Book 5
Story type: Mystery; Series
Subject(s): Ancient Greek civilization; Mystery; Murder
Major character(s): Nicolaos, Detective, Spouse (of Diotima); Diotima, Religious (priestess), Spouse (of Nicolaos); Theokritos, Religious (High Priest of Dionysos)
Time period(s): 6th century B.C.
Locale(s): Athens, Greece

Summary: In this novel, the fifth in the Athens Mysteries series by Gary Corby, ancient Athens is preparing to host the Great Dionysia—the premier arts and theater festival. But a "ghost" in the theater is wreaking havoc. Nicolaos and his wife Diotoma are asked to cleanse the theater with an exorcism, and they do so with the help of the High Priest of Dionysos, Theokritos. Much to everyone's surprise, an actor is murdered after the exorcism. Nicolaos and Diotoma begin a more thorough investigation, uncovering some surprising information from the actor's past. Locating the killer is not going to be an easy task, but Nicolaos and Diotoma must track him down before the Great Dionysia is ruined.

Other books by the same author:
The Marathon Conspiracy, 2014
Sacred Games, 2013
The Iona Sanction, 2011
The Pericles Commission, 2010

Other books you might like:
Taylor Caldwell, *Glory and the Lightning*, 1974
Karen Essex, *Stealing Athena: A Novel*, 2008
Colin Falconer, *Colossus*, 2015
Tom Holt, *Goatsong*, 1990
Gray Poole, *The Magnificent Traitor: A Novel of Alcibiades and the Golden Age of Pericles*, 1968

146

BERNARD CORNWELL

The Empty Throne

(New York: HarperCollins, 2014)

Series: Saxon Stories Series. Book 8
Story type: Historical - Medieval; Series
Subject(s): Middle Ages; England; History
Major character(s): Lord Uhtred, Nobleman (Lord of Bebbanburg), Lover (of Lady Aethelflaed); Lady Aethelflaed, Noblewoman, Spouse (of Lord Aethelred), Lover (of Lord Uhtred), Historical Figure; Lord Aethelred, Historical Figure, Nobleman, Administrator (of Kind Edward), Spouse (of Lady Aethelflaed); Edward, Royalty (King of the Anglo-Saxons), Historical Figure; Sigtryggr, Viking
Time period(s): 10th century; 910s (911)
Locale(s): England

Summary: In this novel, the eighth in the Saxon Stories series, author Bernard Cornwell continues his fictionalized account of English history during the tumultuous medieval era. In the year 911, England is a fragmented land that has yet to realize the late King Alfred's vision of unity. In Mercia, the throne is about to be vacated by Aethelred, the land's dying ruler. Although Aethelred has no heir to take his place, he does leave behind a wife, Lady Aethelflaed, who is loved in Mercia and capable of serving as its ruler. The future of the throne is also in question in Wessex, which is currently ruled by King Edward. As Edward worries over which heir will succeed him, Lady Aethelflaed and Lord Uhtred, one of Edward's administrators, join forces to confront the Vikings and other enemies that threaten England.

Other books by the same author:
Agincourt, 2009
The Burning Land, 2009
Sword Song, 2008
The Pale Horseman, 2006
The Last Kingdom, 2004

Other books you might like:
Nancy Bilyeau, *The Chalice*, 2013
Alys Clare, *The Winter King*, 2014
P.C. Doherty, *The Mysterium*, 2012
Paul Doherty, *Candle Flame*, 2014
Susanna Gregory, *Mystery in the Minster*, 2012
Kazuo Ishiguro, *The Buried Giant*, 2015

Guy Gavriel Kay, *The Last Light of the Sun*, 2004
Bernard Knight, *Crowner's Crusade*, 2013
Juliet Marillier, *Foxmask*, 2004
Ian Morson, *Falconer and the Rain of Blood*, 2013
Harry Sidebottom, *Iron and Rust*, 2015
Jessica Sorensen, *The Forever of Ella and Micha*, 2013
Judith Tarr, *King's Blood*, 2005
Joan Wolf, *The Edge of Light*, 1990
Sarah Woodbury, *The Fourth Horseman*, 2013

147

BRYAN CROCKETT

Love's Alchemy

(Waterville, Maine: Five Star, 2015)

Series: John Donne Mystery Series. Book 1
Story type: Mystery; Series
Subject(s): Mystery; Detective fiction; British history, 1066-1688
Major character(s): John Donne, Historical Figure, Writer (poet), Spouse (of Anne More), Spy, Detective; Anne More, Historical Figure, Spouse (of John Donne); Robert Cecil, Historical Figure, Political Figure; James I, Historical Figure, Royalty (king of England); Lady Bedford, Historical Figure, Friend (patron of John Donne); Timothy Burr, Servant (to Lady Bedford)
Time period(s): 17th century; 1600s (1604)
Locale(s): England

Summary: Author Bryan Crockett casts 17th-century English poet John Donne as a detective and spy in this novel, the first in the John Donne Mystery series. It is 1604, and the persecution of Catholics continues under the rule of James I. Although James prefers a policy of religious tolerance, he is overruled by the domineering politician Robert Cecil. John Donne and his family used to be Catholic, but they are now Protestants. Cecil wants to use Donne as a spy to uncover Catholics who are plotting against England. Donne plays along with Cecil's plan, although he has no intention of engaging in espionage. In fact, he plans to turn the tables on Cecil. Meanwhile, Donne is trying to make a living by writing verse. He has married Anne More, but her disapproving father has chosen not to pay her dowry. Lady Bedford, a wealthy patron of the arts, has taken an interest in Donne, but her feelings for him are not entirely professional.

Other books you might like:
Maeve Haran, *The Lady and the Poet*, 2010
Ed O'Connor, *The Yeare's Midnight*, 2002
Garry O'Connor, *Campion's Ghost: The Sacred and Profane Memoirs of John Donne, Poet*, 1994
Jean Plaidy, *The Murder in the Tower*, 1964
Elizabeth Gray Vining, *Take Heed of Loving Me: A Novel about John Donne*, 1963

148

LINDSEY DAVIS

Deadly Election

(London: Hodder & Stoughton, 2015)

Series: Flavia Albia Mystery Series. Book 3
Story type: Amateur Detective; Mystery
Subject(s): Detective fiction; Ancient Roman civilization; Murder
Major character(s): Flavia Albia, Narrator, Friend (of Manlius Faustus), Detective—Amateur; Manlius Faustus, Friend (of Flavia Albia), Political Figure, Government Official
Time period(s): 1st century; 80s (89)
Locale(s): Rome, Italy

Summary: In the third Flavia Albia mystery, the amateur detective must again work with her dear friend Manlius Faustus. Faustus, a magistrate and political figure, remains Flavia's love interest and mystery partner. As she searches through items that her father's auction business is preparing to sell, Flavia discovers a corpse. She is stunned to realize that the chest holding the body has been in warehouse storage for a decade. Meanwhile, Faustus asks her to handle an inquiry into political competitors. The two cases unexpectedly collide, and Flavia and Faustus both find that their lives could be in jeopardy. The political games of ancient Rome can be deadly, and those who seek power are unafraid to play dirty and break the rules. Working around the lingering attraction she feels for Faustus, Flavia dives headlong into her investigations, determined to uncover the truth at any price.

Other books by the same author:
Nemesis, 2010
Alexandria, 2009
See Delphi and Die, 2005
Three Hands in the Fountain, 1997
The Silver Pigs, 1989

Other books you might like:
Robert Harris, *Conspirata: A Novel of Ancient Rome*, 2010
Sara Poole, *Poison*, 2010
John Maddox Roberts, *Saturnalia*, 1999
Steven Saylor, *Arms of Nemesis*, 1992
Peter Tremayne, *Master of Souls*, 2006

149

ANITA DIAMANT

The Boston Girl

(New York: Scribner, 2014)

Story type: Literary
Subject(s): Women; History; Immigrants
Major character(s): Addie Baum, Aged Person (85 years old), Grandmother (of Ava), Sister (of Betty and Celia), Narrator; Betty, Sister (of Addie and Celia); Celia, Sister (of Addie and Betty); Ava, Young Woman (22 years old), Granddaughter (of Addie)
Time period(s): 20th century; 1900s-1980s
Locale(s): Boston, Massachusetts

Summary: In 1985, when 22-year-old Ava asks her elderly grandmother, Addie Baum, how she got to be the woman she is, Addie shares a revealing narrative about life in 20th-century Boston. Addie's parents were Russian Jews who immigrated to the United States with their two daughters, Betty and Celia. Addie was born in the family's Boston tenement in 1900 and went on to experience the social change that swirled around her. Although Addie's parents never adjusted to life in their new country, American-born Addie faced its challenges head-on. She made friends in her bustling North End community, got an education, and established a career in an era that wasn't kind to women. As Addie shares her life story with her beloved granddaughter, she recalls details of her personal life and the historic events she has experienced, including the 1918 flu epidemic.

Other books by the same author:
Day After Night, 2009
The Last Days of Dogtown, 2005
Good Harbor, 2001
The Red Tent, 1997

Other books you might like:
Kevin Baker, *Dreamland*, 1999
Chris Bohjalian, *The Sandcastle Girls*, 2012
Nicholas Delbanco, *The Vagabonds*, 2004
Therese Anne Fowler, *Z: A Novel of Zelda Fitzgerald*, 2013
Jennifer Gilmore, *Golden Country*, 2006
Alice Hoffman, *The Museum of Extraordinary Things*, 2014
William Klaber, *The Rebellion of Miss Lucy Ann Lobdell*, 2015
Paul M. Levitt, *Come with Me to Babylon*, 2008
Susan Meissner, *A Fall of Marigolds*, 2014
Thomas O'Malley, *Serpents in the Cold*, 2015
Belva Plain, *Evergreen*, 1978
Danielle Steel, *A Good Woman*, 2008
Anne Tyler, *A Spool of Blue Thread*, 2015
Katharine Weber, *Triangle*, 2006
Beatriz Williams, *The Secret Life of Violet Grant*, 2014

150

PAUL DOHERTY

The Book of Fires

(Surrey, England: Creme de la Crime, 2015)

Series: Sorrowful Mysteries of Brother Athelstan Series. Book 14
Story type: Mystery; Serial Killer
Subject(s): England; English (British people); British history, 1066-1688
Major character(s): Brother Athelstan, Detective—Amateur, Religious; John Cranston, Detective—Amateur, Nobleman; John of Gaunt, Nobleman (Duke of Lancaster)
Time period(s): 14th century; 1380s (1381)
Locale(s): London, England

Summary: In the 14th book of the Sorrowful Mysteries of Brother Athelstan series, a new killer called the Fire Bringer is terrorizing London. His or her victims are connected to the recent trial and execution of Lady Isolda Beaumont, who was burned at the stake for murdering her husband. As a friend of the Beaumont family, John of Gaunt has ordered Brother Athelstan and Sir John Cranston to investigate the Fire Bringer's murders. The duo learns that one of the victims had a copy of the *Book of Fires* in his possession—a manuscript that is rumored to hold the formula of a deadly weapon. Gaunt is hoping the manuscript is recovered before it falls into the wrong hands. It is up to Brother Athelstan to bring the Fire Bringer to justice and to figure out if the Lady Isolda was really guilty of murder.

Other books by the same author:
Nightshade, 2011
The Magician's Death, 2009
Corpse Candle, 2002
A Tournament of Murders, 1997
The Death of a King, 1985

Other books you might like:
Simon Beaufort, *Deadly Inheritance*, 2010
Alys Clare, *Blood of the South*, 2015
Cora Harrison, *Verdict of the Court*, 2014
C.J. Sansom, *Lamentation*, 2015
S.D. Sykes, *Plague Land*, 2015

151

SUZANNAH DUNN

The May Bride

(New York: Pegasus Books, 2014)

Story type: Historical - Renaissance
Subject(s): Renaissance; England; English (British people)
Major character(s): Jane Seymour, Historical Figure (lady in Queen Katherine's court), Sister (younger, of Edward), Sister (former, sister-in-law of Katherine Filliol); Katherine Filliol, Spouse (former, of Edward), Sister (former, sister-in-law of Jane), Historical Figure; Edward Seymour, Historical Figure, Spouse (former, of Katherine Filliol), Brother (older, of Jane); Queen Katherine, Historical Figure (Queen of England), Spouse (wife, of King Henry VIII)
Time period(s): 16th century; 1530s (1536)
Locale(s): England

Summary: This Tudor-era historical fiction novel by Suzannah Dunn is a tale of family, scandal, power, and self-discovery. In 1536, 15-year-old Jane Seymour is mesmerized by her new sister-in-law, Katherine Filliol, the wife of Jane's eldest brother, Edward. When Edward leaves for the war, however, Katherine appears to get along all too well in his absence. Jane is surprised by the relationship that develops between her father and Katherine, and when Edward returns from the war, the Seymour family is torn apart by scandalous allegations of Katherine's affair with Edward's father. In an effort to rebuild his family's reputation, Katherine is sent away—never to be seen again—and Jane is sent to serve Katharine of Aragon, the first wife of King Henry VIII.

There, in the Queen's court, Jane witnesses first-hand another wife threatened by the power of her husband, and Jane comes to understand the importance of staying true to her own convictions.

Other books by the same author:
The Confession of Katherine Howard, 2010
The Queen's Sorrow, 2008
The Sixth Wife, 2007
The Queen of Subtleties, 2004

Other books you might like:
Carolly Erickson, *The Favored Queen*, 2011
Elizabeth Fremantle, *Queen's Gambit*, 2013
Philippa Gregory, *The Boleyn Inheritance*, 2006
Hilary Mantel, *Bring Up the Bodies*, 2012
Hilary Mantel, *Wolf Hall*, 2009

152

CECILIA EKBACK

Wolf Winter

(New York: Weinstein Books, 2015)

Story type: Mystery
Subject(s): Sweden; Swedes; Mountain life
Major character(s): Maija, Immigrant, Spouse (of Paavo), Mother (of Frederika and Dorotea); Paavo, Spouse (of Maija), Father (of Frederika and Dorotea), Immigrant; Frederika, Immigrant, 14-Year-Old, Daughter (of Maija and Paavo), Sister (of Dorotea); Dorotea, Daughter (of Maija and Paavo), Sister (of Frederika), Immigrant, Child, 6-Year-Old; Eriksson, Crime Victim, Neighbor
Time period(s): 18th century; 1710s (1717-1718)
Locale(s): Sweden

Summary: Hoping to make a fresh start and escape the painful memories of their past, Finnish natives Paavo and Maija, along with their daughters, Frederika and Dorotea, move in the summer of 1717 to the unforgiving but picturesque Swedish Lapland. There they settle at the foot of Blackasen, a large and menacing mountain with a notorious past. Before long, the family finds itself drawn into Blackasen's dark mythos when the girls discover the badly mutilated corpse of a neighbor, Eriksson, high on the mountainside. While many believe Eriksson's demise to be the work of local wolves, Maijia and her kin suspect that he was murdered. As the family investigates their neighbor's untimely death and the harsh winter takes hold, they are inevitably pulled ever deeper into the quiet mountain community's hidden and dangerous underbelly and into a fight for survival that could well end in disaster.

Other books you might like:
Kerstin Ekman, *Under the Snow*, 1961
Ariana Franklin, *The Siege Winter*, 2015
Roger Frison-Roche, *The Raid*, 1964
Paula Hawkins, *The Girl on the Train*, 2015
Tim Johnston, *Descent*, 2015

153

KATHY LYNN EMERSON

Murder in the Queen's Wardrobe

(Sutton, Surrey, England: Severn House Publishers, 2015)

Series: Mistress Jaffrey Mystery Series. Book 1
Subject(s): Mystery; Detective fiction; Crime
Major character(s): Rosamond Jaffrey, Servant (lady-in-waiting), Spy; Elizabeth I, Historical Figure, Royalty (Queen of England), Cousin (of Lady Mary); Francis Walsingham, Historical Figure, Spy; Lady Mary, Noblewoman, Cousin (of Elizabeth I); Ivan IV, Royalty (Russian tsar), Historical Figure
Time period(s): 16th century; 1580s (1582)
Locale(s): London, England

Summary: Mistress Rosamond Jaffrey is a skilled linguist and code-breaker. Sir Francis Walsingham, the head of Queen Elizabeth I's espionage operation, would like Rosamond to also work as a spy. Elizabeth's cousin, Lady Mary, has been spending time with Russia's tsar, Ivan IV, and Walsingham wants to know what's going on between them. He places Rosamond in the position of Mary's lady-in-waiting, where the female spy can keep a close eye on the queen's cousin. The developing relationship between Mary and Ivan has both proponents and detractors, and Rosamond must keep alert for any nefarious plots simmering within the court. The stakes rise when a public official is murdered and Mary and Rosamond are threatened. Now that Rosamond's spy game has become deadly serious, she must risk her own life to keep Lady Mary from harm. This novel is the first in the Mistress Jaffrey Mystery series.

Other books by the same author:
Diana Spaulding #1, 2008
Face Down O'er the Border, 2008
Deadlier than the Pen, 2004
Face Down in the Marrow-Bone Pie, 1997
The Mystery of Hilliard's Castle, 1985

Other books you might like:
Fiona Buckley, *To Shield the Queen*, 1997
P.F. Chisholm, *A Famine of Horses*, 1994
Rory Clements, *Martyr*, 2009
Judith Cook, *Death of a Lady's Maid*, 1997
P.C. Doherty, *The Poison Maiden*, 2007
Patricia Finney, *Firedrake's Eye*, 1992
Philippa Gregory, *The King's Curse*, 2014
Diane Haeger, *The Queen's Rival: In the Court of Henry VIII*, 2011
Karen Harper, *The Last Boleyn*, 1983
Karen Harper, *The Poyson Garden*, 1999
Peg Herring, *Her Highness' First Murder*, 2010
Ross King, *Ex-Libris*, 1998

154

HERMIONE EYRE

Viper Wine

(New York: Horgath, 2015)

Story type: Fantasy
Subject(s): Alchemy; Beauty; Interpersonal relations

Major character(s): Venetia Stanley, Spouse (of Sir Kenelm Digby), Addict (of viper wine), Historical Figure, Noblewoman; Kenelm Digby, Nobleman, Historical Figure, Scientist (alchemist), Diplomat, Political Figure, Explorer, Spouse (of Venetia Stanley)
Time period(s): 17th century; 1640s
Locale(s): England

Summary: In her youth Venetia Stanley was a glorious beauty, renowned for her face to the point of fame. Once captured by the artist Van Dyck on canvas and a muse to playwright Ben Jonson, she has since moved uneasily into middle age. England is simmering on the cusp of civil war. The uneasy women of Charles II's court scrutinize each other's fading beauty, and Venetia soon becomes desperate. Her husband, Sir Kenelm Digby, is an alchemist as well as a politician, explorer, and diplomat. She requests that he prepare a beauty potion for her. Digby sees his wife's beauty beyond her years, and believes that Venetia is simply being vain. He refuses, and Venetia finds herself scrambling for an alternative. She seals an agreement with an apothecary to prepare and sell a potion called viper wine, and launches a decadent trend within the royal court among the noblewomen, who begin looking younger and more beautiful than ever. The political scene is ablaze with arguments between monarchists and puritans, but soon discussion shifts to include arguments about science and magic. Venetia is trapped within the thrall of the viper wine potion, and escape becomes ever more unlikely. First novel.

Other books you might like:
Ella March Chase, *The Queen's Dwarf*, 2014
Jane Feather, *The Silver Rose*, 1997
Philippa Gregory, *Earthly Joys*, 1998
Diane Haeger, *The Perfect Royal Mistress*, 2007
Elizabeth Redfern, *Auriel Rising*, 2004

155

COLIN FALCONER

Colossus

(New York: St. Martin's Press, 2015)

Story type: Military
Subject(s): Ancient Greek civilization; Wars; Alexander the Great
Major character(s): Alexander the Great, Historical Figure, Royalty (King); Colossus, Elephant; Gajendra, Warrior
Time period(s): 4th century B.C.; 320s B.C. (323 B.C.)

Summary: In this novel by Colin Falconer, set in 323 BC Greece, Alexander the Great is plotting his next move and preparing to use the war elephants he obtained in India. When one of the elephants, Colossus, attacks a group of soldiers, one warrior, Gajendra, is able to calm him. Alexander notices and makes Gajendra captain of the elephants. Alexander is rewarded with Gajendra's fierce loyalty until Gajendra adjusts to the privileges of his new station. Gajendra soon has plans of his own, and with the protection of Colossus, he intends to become heir to the throne. It is only when Gajendra sees his dreams within reach that he realizes what he will need to sacrifice to obtain them, even as their army closes in on Rome.

Other books by the same author:
Silk Road, 2011
The Sultan's Harem, 2004
Feathered Serpent, 2002
When We Were Gods, 2002
Rough Justice, 1999

Other books you might like:
Steve Berry, *The Venetian Betrayal*, 2007
Gary Corby, *Death Ex Machina*, 2015
Nikos Kazantzakis, *Alexander the Great*, 1982
Steven Pressfield, *The Virtues of War: A Novel of Alexander the Great*, 2004
Mary Renault, *Fire from Heaven*, 1969
Judith Tarr, *Lord of the Two Lands*, 1993

156

ILDEFONSO FALCONES
MARA FAYE LETHEM, Translator

The Barefoot Queen

(New York: Crown Publishing Group, 2014)

Story type: Adventure; Family Saga
Subject(s): Adventure; Cultural conflict; Crime
Major character(s): Caridad, Slave (freed), Worker (on plantation), Crime Victim (of sexual assualt and rape), Friend (of Melchor and Milagros), Smuggler, Young Woman; Melchor, Grandfather (of Milagros), Smuggler (of tobacco), Friend (of Caridad), Gypsy; Milagros Carmona Vegas, Friend (of Caridad), Granddaughter (of Melchor), Gypsy, Young Woman, Outcast
Time period(s): 18th century; 1740s
Locale(s): Madrid, Spain; Seville, Spain

Summary: Caridad is a former African slave who used to work on a tobacco farm in Cuba. Arriving in Cadiz, Caridad is alone and penniless and not familiar with the dangers of the city and its people. She ends up being abused and forced into prostitution until she is befriended by a gypsy, Melchor, who takes pity upon her situation and takes her in. Melchor lives with his daughter, Ana, and his spirited granddaughter, Milagros. Caridad is welcomed into the gypsy community and she and Milagros quickly become friends. The government of Seville orders the arrest of all gypsies and Caridad and Milagros are able to escape, but the women must overcome misfortune and unhappiness to find the freedom and love that they yearn for and deserve.

Other books by the same author:
Cathedral of the Sea, 2008

Other books you might like:
Isabel Allende, *Zorro*, 2005
Alan Furst, *Midnight in Europe*, 2014
David Liss, *The Day of Atonement*, 2014
Arturo Perez-Reverte, *The Cavalier in the Yellow Doublet*, 2009
Arturo Perez-Reverte, *The Siege*, 2014

157

JOEL FISHBANE

The Thunder of Giants

(New York: St. Martin's Press, 2015)

Story type: Literary
Subject(s): History; Circuses; Women
Major character(s): Anna Swan, Historical Figure (aka Giantess of Nova Scotia); Andorra Kelsey, Actress
Time period(s): 19th century; (1840s-1880s); 20th century; 1930s
Locale(s): Nova Scotia, Canada; United States

Summary: This historical fiction novel from debut author Joel Fishbane chronicles the life of Anna Swan, known as the Giantess of Nova Scotia. A parallel narrative follows Andorra Kelsey, a woman who plays Swan in a Hollywood film. Born in a cabin in Nova Scotia in 1846, Anna Swan grows to be more than seven feet tall. Celebrated for her size, Anna is featured at P.T. Barnum's New York museum and tours the world as a part of Barnum's Human Marvels show. In 1937, Andorra Kelsey, nearly eight feet tall, is asked to star in a film that depicts the life of Anna Swan. Unlike Anna, Andorra is considered a disgrace and embarrassment to her family and, in order to escape poverty, moves to Hollywood. As the double narratives unfold, Anna falls in love with a Civil War veteran. Disappointed by fame, she strives to prove to the world that she's more than a celebrity and a spectacle. First novel.

Other books you might like:
Melanie Benjamin, *The Autobiography of Mrs. Tom Thumb*, 2011
Ellen Bryson, *The Transformation of Bartholomew Fortuno: A Novel*, 2010
Stacy Carlson, *Among the Wonderful*, 2011
Angelina Mirabella, *The Sweetheart*, 2015
Stewart O'Nan, *West of Sunset*, 2015
Harold Schechter, *The Hum Bug*, 2001

158

DAVID L. FLUSFEDER

John the Pupil

(London, England: Fourth Estate, 2015)

Story type: Historical - Medieval
Subject(s): Middle Ages; History; Voyages and travels
Major character(s): John, Student (of Roger Bacon), Young Man; Roger Bacon, Religious (Franciscan friar), Inventor, Scientist, Teacher, Historical Figure; Andrew, Young Man, Religious (Franciscan brother); Bernard, Religious (Franciscan brother); Clement IV, Historical Figure, Religious (pope)
Time period(s): 13th century; 1260s (1267)

Summary: When John, a pupil at the Franciscan monastery near Oxford, is sent on a pilgrimage to Italy, he believes that the journey is meant to be an act of penance. Roger Bacon, the friar who has planned the trek, has been John's trusted teacher for years. But Bacon is an academic, and he has organized the pilgrimage as a ruse to transport scientific equipment and an important document to Pope Clement IV. Two Franciscan novices, Brother Andrew and Brother Bernard, travel with John, although none of the young men know the nature of their mission. In 1267, Europe is a place of wonders and dangers. The travelers, who have to solicit food from strangers on the road, must avoid criminals and temptations. The cargo John and his companions carry from Oxford to Viterbo is powerful, and the trio cannot let it fall into the wrong hands.

Other books by the same author:
A Film by Spencer Ludwig, 2010
The Pagan House, 2009
The Gift, 2003
Like Plastic, 1996
Man Kills Woman, 1993

Other books you might like:
Cassandra Clark, *The Red Velvet Turnshoe*, 2009
Stephen R. Lawhead, *The Iron Lance*, 1998
Ellis Peters, *The Heretic's Apprentice*, 1990
R.F. Tapsell, *The Year of the Horsetails*, 1967
Connie Willis, *Doomsday Book*, 1992

159

SAMANTHA NORMAN
ARIANA FRANKLIN, Co-Author

The Siege Winter

(New York: William Morrow, 2015)

Subject(s): Mystery; Detective fiction; Crime
Major character(s): Emma, 11-Year-Old (also known as Penda), Crime Victim, Apprentice (to Gwil); Gwil, Mercenary (archer for hire), Guardian (of Emma); Stephen, Historical Figure, Royalty (King of England), Cousin (of Matilda); Matilda, Historical Figure, Royalty (empress)
Time period(s): 12th century; 1140s (1141)
Locale(s): England

Summary: In 1141, England is suffering the effects of a protracted civil war and the ongoing fight for the throne between King Stephen and his cousin, Empress Matilda. A young peasant girl, 11-year-old Emma, becomes collateral damage in the violence when she is attacked by a monk and abandoned in a church. The monk presumes that his victim is dead, but Gwil—a mercenary archer traveling through the region—finds Emma and acts as her guardian. He calls the girl Penda, passes her off as a boy, and teachers her how to use a bow and arrow. Penda has no recollection of the attack, but Gwil knows that the girl possesses an incriminating piece of evidence. As Penda hones her skills as an archer, Gwil carries the unsettling knowledge that the monk who assaulted her remains free. This novel was written by Ariana Franklin and her daughter Samantha Norman; Norman completed the book after her mother's death. It was originally published in the United Kingdom in 2014 as *Winter Siege*.

Other books by the same author:
A Murderous Procession, 2010

Grave Goods, 2009
The Serpent's Tale, 2008
Mistress of the Art of Death, 2007
City of Shadows, 2005

Other books you might like:
Maureen Ash, *The Alehouse Murders: A Templar Knight Mystery*, 2007
Alys Clare, *Fortune Like the Moon*, 2000
Cecilia Ekback, *Wolf Winter*, 2015
Ken Follett, *Pillars of the Earth*, 1989
Barbara Reichmuth Geisler, *Other Gods*, 2002
Cora Harrison, *Condemned to Death*, 2015
Ellen Jones, *The Fatal Crown*, 1991
Bernard Knight, *The Sanctuary Seeker*, 1998
    Bernard Knight, co-author
Sharon Kay Penman, *The Queen's Man*, 1996
Sharon Kay Penman, *When Christ and His Saints Slept*, 1995
Ellis Peters, *A Morbid Taste for Bones*, 1978
Jean Plaidy, *The Passionate Enemies*, 1976
Joan Wolf, *No Dark Place*, 1999

160

ANNA FREEMAN

The Fair Fight

(London, United Kingdom: Weidenfeld & Nicolson, 2015)

Story type: Literary
Subject(s): History; Coming of age; Women
Major character(s): Ruth Matchet, Young Woman, Boxer (bare-knuckle fighter), Spouse (of Tom Webber); Tom Webber, Boxer (bare-knuckle fighter), Spouse (of Ruth Matchet); Mr. Granville Dryer, Trainer (of Ruth); Charlotte Sinclair, Woman, Survivor (smallpox)
Time period(s): 18th century
Locale(s): England

Summary: In 18th-century England, bare-knuckle fighting is a spectator sport that draws both men and women to the ring. Ruth Matchet began her life in a brothel, and she has since had to make her own way in the world. She is not beautiful like her sister, so Ruth finds alternate means to secure a living. An unexpected opportunity presents itself when Mr. Granville Dryer persuades Ruth to test her skills as a fighter. Dryer trains Ruth and arranges matches for her in the makeshift fighting ring at the Hatchet Inn. The fights are brutal and bloody, but Ruth is a natural pugilist. When one of Ruth's fights ends badly, Dryer decides to suspend her fighting career. Dryer shifts his attention to Tom Webber, the man Ruth considers to be her husband, although they are not married legally. Ruth's life takes another turn when she forges an alliance with Charlotte Sinclair, a smallpox survivor.

Other books you might like:
Martine Bailey, *An Appetite for Violets*, 2015
Philippa Gregory, *A Respectable Trade*, 1995
Elizabeth Hoyt, *Scandalous Desires*, 2011

Christopher Nicholson, *The Elephant Keeper*, 2009
Andrew Taylor, *The Anatomy of Ghosts*, 2011

161

ESTHER FREUD

Mr. Mac and Me

(New York: Bloomsbury USA, 2015)

Story type: Arts; Historical - World War I
Subject(s): Architecture; Artists; World War I, 1914-1918
Major character(s): Thomas Maggs, Young Man, Friend (of Charles Rennie Mackintosh); Charles "Mac" Rennie Mackintosh, Architect, Friend (of Thomas Maggs), Spouse (of Margaret), Artist; Margaret Mackintosh, Artist, Spouse (of Mac)
Time period(s): 20th century; 1910s (1914)
Locale(s): Suffolk, England

Summary: On the eve of World War I, young Thomas Maggs is enjoying a simple, peaceful life on England's Suffolk coast with his parents and sister when he encounters a strange but kindly man he comes to know as Mac. While Thomas thinks his enigmatic new friend to be something of a Sherlock Holmes-esque detective, Mac's unusual behavior leads the rest of the town to wonder whether he might be more villain than hero. In reality, Mac is Charles Rennie Mackintosh, a colorful architect and artist who quickly forms a close bond with Thomas. Unfortunately, their budding friendship is soon threatened by the abrupt outbreak of war and the seaside community's descent into wartime struggle. As the battle takes its toll on the townspeople, they become increasingly suspicious of Mac's intentions, which, in turn, puts his relationship with Thomas in serious peril.

Other books by the same author:
Lucky Break, 2011
Love Falls, 2007
The Sea House, 2004
Summer at Gaglow, 1998
Peerless Flats, 1993

Other books you might like:
Barbara Taylor Bradford, *Cavendon Hall*, 2014
A.S. Byatt, *The Children's Book*, 2009
James Hilton, *Random Harvest*, 1941
J. Sydney Jones, *The German Agent*, 2015
Anne Perry, *Angels in the Gloom*, 2005
Frances Vieta, *Love in the Land of Barefoot Soldiers*, 2015
Jacqueline Winspear, *Among the Mad*, 2009

162

PATRICK GALE

A Place Called Winter

(London, United Kingdom: Tinder Press, 2015)

Story type: Literary
Subject(s): History; Family; British history, 1815-1914
Major character(s): Harry Cane, Spouse (of Winnie), Father (of Phyllis); Winnie, Spouse (of Harry), Mother (of Phyllis); Phyllis, Girl, Daughter (of Harry and Winnie); Troels Munck, Man, Friend (of Harry)
Time period(s): 20th century; 1900s
Locale(s): Canada; England

Summary: In Edwardian England, Harry Cane lives a quiet life with his wife, Winnie, and their daughter, Phyllis. Harry has feelings for someone else, however, and when his scandalous actions are found out, Harry has to flee his home and family to avoid prosecution. He leaves behind his comfortable lifestyle to live in the Canadian wilderness. On his journey to the unsettled region, Harry crosses paths with Troels Munck, a man who will change the course of his life. Harry settles in a Saskatchewan community called Winter, where he does battle with the rugged environment and Munck's influence. The narrative follows the events of Harry's life as they play out in diverse settings—the suburbs of England, the prairies of Canada, and the Canadian mental hospital where Harry is treated according to the harsh standards of the era. The author based this novel on events from his own family's history.

Other books by the same author:
A Perfectly Good Man, 2012
Notes from an Exhibition, 2007
Rough Music, 2001
Facing the Tank, 1989
Ease, 1986

Other books you might like:
Gil Adamson, *The Outlander: A Novel*, 2008
Richard Ford, *Canada*, 2012
Elizabeth Hay, *Late Nights on Air: A Novel*, 2007
Stef Penney, *The Tenderness of Wolves: A Novel*, 2006
Jane Smiley, *Early Warning*, 2015
Adriana Trigiani, *The Queen of the Big Time*, 2004

163

DAVID GIBBINS

The Sword of Attila

(New York: St. Martin's Press, 2015)

Series: Total War Rome Series. Book 2
Story type: Series
Subject(s): Roman Empire, 30 BC-476 AD; Wars; Espionage
Major character(s): Flavius, Companion (of Macrobius), Nephew (of Aetius), Political Figure; Macrobius, Military Personnel, Companion (of Flavius); Aetius, Military Personnel (commander), Uncle (of Flavius); Arturus, Warrior
Time period(s): 5th century; 430s (439)
Locale(s): Roman Empire; Rome

Summary: In the dying days of the Roman Empire, Flavius, a young political official, and Macrobius, a loyal military officer, are trying to keep the barbarian hordes that surround Rome at bay. After a bitter loss against the Vandals in northern Africa, Flavius's uncle Aetius devises a plan to buy time for the Roman armies. Flavius and Macrobius will be sent up the Danube River, deep into barbarian territory, to forge a treaty with a dangerous ally: the daughter of Attila the Hun. The warrior princess bears little love for her father, who she blames for her mother's death. Success could mean victory over Rome's most feared enemy. Failure will most certainly lead to the destruction of the empire. This is the second book in David Gibbins's Total War Rome series.

Other books by the same author:
The Tiger Warrior, 2009
The Last Gospel, 2008
The Lost Tomb, 2008
Crusader Gold, 2007
Atlantis, 2006

Other books you might like:
Gillian Bradshaw, *The Beacon at Alexandria*, 1986
William Dietrich, *The Scourge of God*, 2005
Philip Hensher, *The Emperor Waltz*, 2014
Valerio Massimo Manfredi, *The Last Legion*, 2003
William Napier, *Attila*, 2008

164

MAUREEN GIBBON

Paris Red

(New York: W. W. Norton & Company, 2015)

Story type: Literary
Subject(s): History; Art; Artists
Major character(s): Edouard Manet, Historical Figure, Artist, Lover (of Victorine Meurent); Victorine Meurent, 17-Year-Old, Young Woman, Historical Figure, Lover (of Edouard Manet), Roommate (of Denise); Denise, Young Woman, Friend (of Victorine)
Time period(s): 19th century; 1860s (1862)
Locale(s): Paris, France

Summary: Author Maureen Gibbon creates a fictionalized account of the relationship of French painter Edouard Manet and his lover and muse, Victorine Meurent. Seventeen-year-old Victorine arrives in 1862 Paris with no money, but she has big dreams. She wants to be part of the city's art scene, and she gets that opportunity when she meets Manet. The artist propositions Victorine and her roommate, Denise, but Victorine makes him choose between them. Manet of course selects Victorine, and she leaves Denise to live with Manet and serve as his model. Although she is young, Victorine is strong and independent. She gets what she wants out of her liaison with Manet, and she is well aware that their relationship is just temporary. During her time with Manet, Victorine makes a big impact on his career. She inspires his bold use of color, and she poses for one of his most famous works, *Olympia*.

Other books by the same author:
Thief, 2010
Swimming Sweet Arrow, 2000
Her Fault, 1988

Other books you might like:
Cathy Marie Buchanan, *The Painted Girls*, 2013
Tracy Chevalier, *Girl with a Pearl Earring*, 1999
Debra Finerman, *Mademoiselle Victorine*, 2007

Elizabeth Robards, *With Violets*, 2008
Kathryn Wagner, *Dancing for Degas*, 2010

165

MOLLY GLOSS

Falling from Horses

(Boston: Houghton Mifflin Harcourt, 2014)

Story type: Historical - American West
Subject(s): Friendship; Movies; Movie industry
Major character(s): Bud Frazer, Rancher, Stuntman (aspiring), Friend (of Lily); Lily Shaw, Writer (aspiring screenwriter), Friend (of Bud)
Time period(s): 20th century; 1930s (1938)
Locale(s): Los Angeles, California

Summary: Best-selling and award-winning author Molly Gloss delivers a historical tale of friendship, adventure, horses, and Hollywood. Nineteen-year-old ranch hand Bud Frazer leaves his home in Echo Creek, Oregon, for Hollywood in 1938, with wide-eyed dreams of becoming a cowboy stunt rider in the movies. Along the way, he meets Lily Shaw, a spirited young woman who dreams of becoming a famous screenwriter, and an unlikely friendship quickly develops between them. Young, naive, and full of hope, Bud and Lily see one another through the ups and downs, glories and disappointments, while they learn what it means to follow their dreams in the world of Hollywood.

Other books by the same author:
The Hearts of Horses, 2007
Wild Life, 2000
The Dazzle of Day, 1997
The Jump-Off Creek, 1989

Other books you might like:
John Byrne Cooke, *South of the Border*, 1989
Loren D. Estleman, *Ragtime Cowboys*, 2014
Glen David Gold, *Sunnyside: A Novel*, 2009
Stewart O'Nan, *West of Sunset*, 2015
Willard Wyman, *Blue Heaven*, 2011

166

ALAN GOLD

Bell of the Desert

(New York: Yucca Publishing, 2015)

Story type: Adventure; Historical
Subject(s): Adventure; Arab-Israeli wars; Cultural conflict
Major character(s): Gertrude Bell, Archaeologist, Linguist, Explorer, Diplomat, Political Figure (with British Civil Service), Writer
Time period(s): 20th century; 1900s-1920s

Summary: This fictional biography of Gertrude Bell—a late 19th and 20th-century archaeologist, explorer and politician—illuminates her travels to the Middle East. Bell was fluid in six languages and a diplomat who helped form and direct British policy during the Great War. She has written several books about her travels and archaeological discoveries and is deemed to be responsible for the preservation of the Baghdad Museum of Ancient Archaeology. She befriends author T.E. Lawrence and contributes to his famous work, *Lawrence of Arabia*. In her travels, Bell is imprisoned by a desert tribal warlord and later brokers discussions that ultimately lead to the formation of Iraq. Throughout her life, Bell achieves great feats challenging the stereotypes the world has placed upon her.

Other books by the same author:
Bloodline, 2013
The Prate Queen, 2006
True Crime, 2005
Warrior Queen, 2005
Jezebel, 2001

Other books you might like:
Elly Griffiths, *The Outcast Dead*, 2014
Carol McCleary, *The Illusion of Murder*, 2011
Elizabeth Peters, *Crocodile on the Sandbank*, 1975
Mary Doria Russell, *Dreamers of the Day*, 2008
Barry Unsworth, *Land of Marvels: A Novel*, 2009

`167`

C.W. GORTNER

Mademoiselle Chanel

(New York: William Morrow, 2015)

Story type: Literary
Subject(s): History; Biographies; Fashion
Major character(s): Gabrielle "Coco" Chanel, Historical Figure, Designer (fashion), Lover (of Arthur Capel); Arthur Capel, Historical Figure, Lover (of Coco Chanel); Jean Cocteau, Historical Figure, Artist, Writer; Pablo Picasso, Historical Figure, Artist
Time period(s): 19th century-20th century; 1880s-1950s
Locale(s): France

Summary: Author C.W. Gortner presents a novelized account of the life of iconic fashion designer and entrepreneur Gabrielle "Coco" Chanel. Gabrielle and her four siblings are born into a working-class family in France. When their mother dies, the children are sent to an orphanage. The girls are later taken in by a relative who owns a millinery business. There Coco hones her skills as a seamstress, and she finds a way to launch a career in fashion. She travels to Paris and meets Arthur Chapel, a wealthy polo player who will change her life. With assistance from Chapel, Coco creates a women's wear collection that attracts prominent clients and establishes Coco in the fashion world. Coco finds great success in her professional life, and she becomes a fixture of 1920s Paris society, hobnobbing with Pablo Picasso, Jean Cocteau, and other luminaries. She also encounters challenges. Coco takes and loses lovers, and she faces difficult decisions when the Nazis arrive in Paris.

Other books by the same author:
The Tudor Vendetta, 2014
The Queen's Vow, 2012
The Tudor Secret, 2011
The Confessions of Catherine de Medici, 2010
The Last Queen, 2008

Other books you might like:
Rhys Bowen, *Naughty in Nice*, 2010
Gioia Diliberto, *The Collection: A Novel*, 2007
Chris Greenhalgh, *Coco Chanel and Igor Stravinsky*, 2009
Jean Marsh, *The House of Eliott*, 1993
Patricia Soliman, *Coco, the Novel*, 1991

`168`

ELIZA GRANVILLE

Gretel and the Dark

(New York: Riverhead Books, 2014)

Story type: Historical
Subject(s): Fairy tales; Imagination; Holocaust, 1933-1945
Major character(s): Josef Breuer, Historical Figure (physician), Doctor (of Lilie); Lilie, Woman, Patient (of Josef); Krysta, Girl, Daughter (of doctor)
Time period(s): 19th century; (1890s); 20th century; 1940s
Locale(s): Vienna, Austria; Germany

Summary: Debut author Eliza Granville follows the mysterious, intertwining paths of a young girl in Nazi Germany and a psychoanalyst in Vienna in this tale of good and evil, loss and redemption. In 1899, prominent Vienna psychoanalyst Josef Breuer is intrigued by his study of a beautiful, nameless woman who, unable to feel and engage emotionally, claims to be a machine. Throughout his psychoanalysis, Josef refers to his patient as Lilie. Years later, a young girl name Krysta lives in Nazi-controlled Germany, where she spends her days at home alone while her father, a doctor, tends to the patients in the infirmary next to their home. As the Nazi forces exert more control and the world around her grows increasingly terrifying, Krysta finds solace in her imagination and retreats into a world of fairy tales, where she learns that her imagination is far more powerful than she ever dreamed. First novel.

Other books you might like:
Martin Amis, *The Zone of Interest*, 2014
Ramona Ausubel, *No One Is Here Except All of Us*, 2012
Carol De Chellis Hill, *Henry James' Midnight Song*, 1993
J. Sydney Jones, *A Matter of Breeding*, 2014
Irving Stone, *The Passions of the Mind*, 1971
D.M. Thomas, *The White Hotel*, 1981
Morris L. West, *The World Is Made of Glass*, 1983

`169`

SUSANNA GREGORY

The Cheapside Corpse

(New York: Little, Brown Book Group, 2015)

Series: Thomas Chaloner Series. Book 10
Story type: Mystery; Series
Subject(s): Mystery; Detective fiction; Crime
Major character(s): Thomas Chaloner, Spy; Charles II,

Historical Figure, Royalty (king of England); Dick Wheler, Crime Victim, Banker

Time period(s): 17th century; 1660s (1665)

Locale(s): London, England

Summary: England faces several threats in 1665. A Dutch invasion is imminent, the dreaded plague is spreading, and financial problems are crippling Charles II's abilities to protect the country. In London, the killing of Dick Wheler attracts the attention of the authorities. Wheler was a successful goldsmith-banker, and his murder could have repercussions. Spy Thomas Chaloner has assisted with investigations in the past, and he is called on now to find out who killed Wheler and why. For this mission, Chaloner acquaints himself with the players in London's financial district. He is shocked to discover how powerful and dangerous the bankers are. As Chaloner carries out his assignment of espionage, a spy from France poses an immediate threat to the city. The man is infected with the plague, and he is delivering the disease wherever he roams. This novel is the tenth in the Thomas Chaloner series.

Other books by the same author:
The Piccadilly Plot, 2012
The Body in the Thames, 2011
A Murder on London Bridge, 2010
The Westminster Poisoner, 2009
The Butcher of Smithfield, 2008

Other books you might like:
Susanna Calkins, *A Murder at Rosamund's Gate*, 2013
Diane Haeger, *The Perfect Royal Mistress*, 2007
Cora Harrison, *Condemned to Death*, 2015
Philip Kerr, *Dark Matter*, 2002
Elizabeth Redfern, *Auriel Rising*, 2004
Priscilla Royal, *Satan's Lullaby*, 2015
Jane Stevenson, *The Shadow King*, 2003

170

SARA GRUEN

At the Water's Edge

(New York: Spiegel and Grau, 2015)

Story type: Adventure; Historical - World War II

Subject(s): Adventure; Courage; Family relations

Major character(s): Madeline "Maddie" Hyde, Young Woman, Spouse (wife of Ellis), Socialite; Ellis Hyde, Son (of retired army colonel), Spouse (of Madeline), Young Man, Socialite, Heir—Dispossessed, Friend (of Hank); Hyde, Father (of Ellis), Retiree (army colonel); Hank, Friend (of Ellis)

Time period(s): 20th century; 1940s (1944-1945)

Locale(s): Scotland; Philadelphia, Pennsylvania

Summary: Maddie, her husband, Ellis Hyde, and their friend Hank are partying socialites, living a materialistic and carefree lifestyle in Philadelphia, Pennsylvania, while World War II is ravaging the world. Both men are exempt from the war because of minor ailments. After a wild party, Ellis's wealthy father is disappointed and embarrassed by his son, and removes financial support from Maddie and Ellis. In an effort to redeem themselves in the eyes of the colonel and their socialite friends, Ellis

and Hank travel to Scotland, dragging Maddie along with them. They plan to complete the colonel's failed mission to find and document the elusive Loch Ness Monster. Ellis and Hank abandon Maddie while they embark upon their drunken excursions. She is not welcomed by the locals, who see the trio as entitled interlopers. In her isolation, Maddie realizes her marriage is falling apart. She eventually discovers valuable friendships and the inner strength to find her own self-worth.

Other books by the same author:
Ape House, 2010
Water for Elephants, 2006
Riding Lessons, 2004

Other books you might like:
Steve Alten, *The Loch*, 2005
Kate Atkinson, *A God in Ruins*, 2015
Jessica Brockmole, *Letters from Skye*, 2013
Anne Douglas, *Dreams to Sell*, 2014
Dominick Dunne, *Too Much Money: A Novel*, 2009
Linda Fairstein, *Bad Blood: A Novel*, 2007
Giles Foden, *Turbulence*, 2009
Pete Hamill, *Tabloid City*, 2011
Jason Hewitt, *The Dynamite Room*, 2015
Gwen Kirkwood, *Dreams of Home*, 2009
Margot Livesey, *Eva Moves the Furniture*, 2001
Susan Meissner, *Secrets of a Charmed Life*, 2015
Susan Meissner, *The Shape of Mercy*, 2008
Jan Moran, *Scent of Triumph*, 2015
Cynthia Swanson, *The Bookseller*, 2015
David Treuer, *Prudence*, 2015

171

SEAN HALDANE

The Devil's Making

(Ottawa, Ontario, Canada: Stone Flower Press, 2015)

Subject(s): Murder; Native North Americans; Detective fiction

Major character(s): Chad Hobbes, Police Officer, Immigrant (English); Dr. McCrory, Doctor, Crime Victim (murdered)

Time period(s): 19th century; 1860s (1869)

Locale(s): British Columbia, Canada

Summary: English police officer Chad Hobbes has recently immigrated to British Columbia. After his arrival, he is pressed to use his investigative skills to solve a murder. It is 1869, and although the white settlers are the minority, they are attempting to impress Victorian values on a seemingly untamable wilderness and the native Indian tribes. The victim, Dr. McCrory, is an American who had been working locally. His methods of phrenology and mesmerism, as well as his promotion of sexual-mystic activities, made him well known but unpopular. His mutilated body causes great concern among other settlers, and an Indian is soon arrested and charged with the crime. There is an incredible lack of evidence, but nobody seems to care. Hobbes must search for a killer while adapting to frontier life, realizing that the savage world he has entered holds very different dangers than what he is used to. This novel is the winner of the Crime Writers of Canada 2014 Arthur Ellis Award for Best Crime Novel.

Awards the book has won:
Arthur Ellis Award: Best Novel, 2014

Other books you might like:
Vicki Delany, *Among the Departed*, 2011
Jody Hedlund, *An Uncertain Choice*, 2015
Julie Klassen, *The Painter's Daughter*, 2015
Jen Turano, *After a Fashion*, 2015
Laurali R. Wright, *A Touch of Panic: A Karl Alberg Mystery*, 1994

▊172

C.S. HARRIS (Pseudonym of Candace Proctor)

Who Buries the Dead

(New York: Penguin Publishing Group, 2015)

Series: Sebastian St. Cyr Series. Book 10
Story type: Historical - Regency; Mystery
Subject(s): Mystery; Detective fiction; Crime
Major character(s): Sebastian St. Cyr, Nobleman (Viscount Devlin), Detective, Spouse (of Hero); Hero, Woman, Spouse (of Sebastian); Stanley Preston, Plantation Owner, Crime Victim; Henry Austen, Historical Figure, Banker, Brother (of Jane Austen); Jane Austen, Historical Figure, Writer (novelist), Sister (of Henry Austen); Henry Lovejoy, Lawman (magistrate); Stanley Oliphant, Military Personnel (Sebastian's former commanding officer), Nobleman, Enemy (of Sebastian)
Time period(s): 19th century; 1810s (1813)
Locale(s): London, England

Summary: When the disembodied head of Stanley Preston is discovered on London's Bloody Bridge, Sebastian St. Cyr, Viscount Devlin, is called in to investigate. Sebastian has proven his skills as a detective on previous cases, and this puzzling crime may benefit from his expertise. As always, Sebastian's wife, Hero, assists in the investigation. A clue is found on the bridge—a strap from a lead coffin that is inscribed "King Charles, 1648." Like Preston, the monarch was decapitated. Preston, a plantation owner, was a collector of morbid antiquities, such as the severed heads of historical figures. As Sebastian and Hero follow their leads, they compile a growing roster of suspects and recognize unsettling connections. Are the victim's familial ties to a British official significant? And what has brought Stanley Oliphant, Sebastian's sworn enemy, to London? This novel is the tenth in the Sebastian St. Cyr Mystery series.

Other books by the same author:
When Maidens Mourn, 2012
What Remains of Heaven, 2009
Where Serpents Sleep, 2008
When Gods Die, 2006
Why Mermaids Sing, 2006

Other books you might like:
Emma Donoghue, *Slammerkin*, 2001
Elizabeth Goudge, *Gentian Hill*, 1949
C.S. Harris, *Who Buries the Dead*, 2015

Laura Lebow, *The Figaro Murders*, 2015
Anne Perry, *The Angel Court Affair*, 2014
Rosemary Stevens, *The Tainted Snuff Box*, 2001
Charles Todd, *A Fine Summer's Day*, 2015

▊173

CORA HARRISON

Condemned to Death

(Sutton, Surrey, England: Severn House Publishers, 2015)

Series: Burren Mystery Series. Book 12
Story type: Historical - Medieval; Mystery
Subject(s): Mystery; Detective fiction; Crime
Major character(s): Mara, Investigator (Brehon of the Burren), Professor (law school dean); Domhnall, Scholar
Time period(s): 16th century
Locale(s): Burren, Ireland

Summary: In the 12th novel in the Burren Mystery series, the discovery of a corpse in an oarless boat prompts an investigation. Mara is the Brehon—the investigating magistrate—of Ireland's Kingdom of the Burren, and when the boat carrying a dead body drifts into her territory, she tries to determine what happened. At first it seems that the man's death was the result of a legal sentence. In 16th-century Burren, those found guilty of killing a family member are left at sea in a vessel without oars. But as Mara and Domhnall, a law student, investigate further, the flaws of that theory are revealed. Domhnall believes he knows the dead man's identity, and that he comes from a region in which kin killers are condemned to death by another means. Mara digs deeper into the mystery and eventually discovers why and how the man in the boat was killed—and who is responsible for the crime.

Other books by the same author:
Deed of Murder, 2011
Scales of Retribution, 2011
Eye of the Law, 2010
The Sting of Justice, 2009
A Secret and Unlawful Killing, 2007

Other books you might like:
Alys Clare, *Blood of the South*, 2015
Cassandra Clark, *The Dragon of Handale*, 2015
Ariana Franklin, *The Siege Winter*, 2015
Susanna Gregory, *The Cheapside Corpse*, 2015
Priscilla Royal, *Satan's Lullaby*, 2015

▊174

RASHAD HARRISON

The Abduction of Smith and Smith

(New York: Atria Books, 2015)

Story type: Historical - Post-American Civil War
Subject(s): American Reconstruction, 1865-1877; Race relations; Interpersonal relations
Major character(s): Jupiter Smith, Slave (former, of Archer), Military Personnel (former Union soldier),

Murderer (of the colonel), Bastard Son (of the colonel), Brother (half, of Archer), Kidnap Victim; Archer Smith, Son (of Colonel Smith), Military Personnel (former Confederate soldier), Kidnap Victim, Brother (half, of Jupiter); Colonel Smith, Father (of Archer), Mentally Ill Person, Crime Victim (murdered by Jupiter)

Time period(s): 19th century; 1860s (1868)
Locale(s): At Sea; San Francisco, California

Summary: The Civil War has ended. Former slave and Union soldier Jupiter Smith has returned to his plantation, where he hopes to find his lover and their child. Instead, he finds his former slave master, who has now gone mad due to syphilis infection. Jupiter takes pity on Colonel Smith and kills him. He does not yet realize the colonel is his father. Jupiter decides to seek a new life in San Francisco. Meanwhile, the Colonel's son, former Confederate soldier Archer Smith, returns home to find his father has been killed. Seeking revenge on Jupiter, Archer follows him out West. However, Archer soon runs into some trouble as his opium habit takes control of his life. He becomes a target for a gang of crimpers, who sell captives to captains of ships. Jupiter tries to save Archer from being shanghaied, but instead both are captured and are taken aboard a ship destined for a dangerous mission. The Smiths must work together to stay alive and make it back home safely.

Other books by the same author:
Our Man in the Dark, 2011

Other books you might like:
Howard Bahr, *The Year of Jubilo: A Novel of the Civil War*, 2000
Thomas Fleming, *A Passionate Girl*, 2004
Jeffrey Lent, *In the Fall*, 2000
Stewart O'Nan, *A Prayer for the Dying*, 1999
Shirley Tallman, *Death on Telegraph Hill: A Sarah Woolson Mystery*, 2012

175

THOMAS HAUSER

The Final Recollections of Charles Dickens

(Berkeley, California: Counterpoint Press, 2014)

Story type: Mystery; Romance
Subject(s): Romances (Fiction); Beauty; Betrayal
Major character(s): Charles Dickens, Writer (author), Journalist, Historical Figure; Geoffrey Wingate, Financier, Spouse (of Amanda Wingate), Crime Suspect; Amanda Wingate, Spouse (of Geoffrey Wingate); Florence Spriggs, Prostitute
Time period(s): 19th century; 1830s-1870s
Locale(s): London, England

Summary: Author Thomas Hauser writes from Charles Dickens's point of view. It is London, England, in the 1870s. Dickens, who is nearing death, embarks on a tale of mystery and intrigue from his past. He takes the reader to 1835 and introduces Amanda Wingate, a beautiful socialite, and her husband, Geoffrey Wingate, a fraudulent financier, as well as Florence Spriggs, a once beauti-

ful but now disfigured prostitute. Dickens becomes enamored of the beautiful Amanda Wingate and remains besotted with her and her beauty for the rest of his life. Researching an article on Amanda's financial adviser husband, Geoffrey, Dickens uncovers some unsettling secrets, not only about Geoffrey but also about his beloved Amanda. An interview with Florence Spriggs brings more suspicions to the surface, and Dickens must decide what to do with this information before his own safety is threatened.

Other books by the same author:
Mark Twain Remembers, 1999
The Hawthorne Group, 1991
Dear Hannah, 1987
The Beethoven Conspiracy, 1984
Ashworth & Palmer, 1981

Other books you might like:
Gaynor Arnold, *Girl in a Blue Dress: A Novel Inspired by the Life and Marriage of Charles Dickens*, 2008
Frederick Busch, *The Mutual Friend*, 1978
Patricia K. Davis, *A Midnight Carol*, 1999
Matthew Pearl, *The Last Dickens*, 2009
Dan Simmons, *Drood*, 2008

176

KATHY HEPINSTALL
BECKY HEPINSTALL HILLIKER, Co-Author

Sisters of Shiloh

(New York: Houghton Mifflin Harcourt, 2015)

Story type: Historical - American Civil War; Literary
Subject(s): United States Civil War, 1861-1865; United States history; Sisters
Major character(s): Josephine Beale, Young Woman (also known as Joseph), Sister (of Libby Beale); Libby Beale, Young Woman (also known as Thomas), Sister (of Josephine Beale), Widow(er) (of Arden Tanner); Arden Tanner, Spouse (deceased, of Libby), Military Personnel (Confederate soldier)
Time period(s): 19th century; 1860s (1862)
Locale(s): United States

Summary: When young bride Libby Beale is widowed soon after her wedding, she sets out on a quest for revenge. Her late husband, Arden Tanner, was fighting with the Confederate Army when he was killed, and Libby is determined to take his place and kill one Yankee for each year of her husband's short life. Libby disguises herself in Arden's clothes and assumes the name Thomas. Libby's older sister, Josephine, also poses as a Confederate soldier so she can protect her grieving sister. As the sisters endure the hardships of battle, Libby becomes increasingly unstable, and Josephine—who calls herself Joseph—falls in love with one of the other soldiers. When Josephine's love interest discovers her true identity, he confesses his mutual attraction, and they run away together. Will Libby, who converses with Arden's ghost, now direct her violent hatred toward her sister?

Other books by the same author:
Blue Asylum, 2012
Prince of Lost Places, 2002

The Absence of Nectar, 2001
The House of Gentle Men, 2000

Other books you might like:
Geraldine Brooks, *March*, 2004
Rita Mae Brown, *High Hearts*, 1986
Charles Frazier, *Cold Mountain*, 1997
Jeffrey Lent, *A Slant of Light*, 2015
Jeff Shaara, *A Blaze of Glory*, 2012
Jane Smiley, *The All-True Travels and Adventures of Lidie Newton*, 1998

177

NELLIE HERMANN

The Season of Migration

(New York: Farrar, Straus and Giroux, 2015)

Story type: Literary
Subject(s): Artists; Painting (Art); Family
Major character(s): Vincent van Gogh, Artist, Brother (of Theo), Historical Figure; Theo van Gogh, Historical Figure, Brother (of Vincent)
Time period(s): 19th century; 1870s (1878-1879)
Locale(s): Petit Wasmes, Belgium

Summary: Before he turned his attention to the canvas and established himself as one of the world's most renowned post-Impressionist painters, Vincent van Gogh was a man of the cloth who preached for a time to the poor and downtrodden locals in a Belgian mining village called Petit Wasmes. His arrival in the town near the end of 1878 marked the beginning of a ten-month period during which little is known of his historical life. In this novel, author Nellie Hermann imagines what might have happened during that critical time when his great artistic creativity was first inspired. She traces van Gogh's conjectural footsteps as he struggles through an inevitable crisis of faith and the realization that his true calling lies not with religion, but with art.

Other books by the same author:
The Cure for Grief, 2008

Other books you might like:
Sheramy D. Bundrick, *Sunflowers*, 2009
Alyson Richman, *The Last Van Gogh*, 2006
Irving Stone, *Lust for Life*, 1934
Frederic Tuten, *Van Gogh's Bad Cafe: A Love Story*, 1997
Carol Wallace, *Leaving Van Gogh*, 2011

178

JASON HEWITT

The Dynamite Room

(New York: Simon & Schuster, 2015)

Story type: Literary
Subject(s): World War II, 1939-1945; Children; Suspense
Major character(s): Lydia, 11-Year-Old, Refugee (World War II); Heiden, Military Personnel (Nazi soldier)

Time period(s): 20th century; 1940s (1940)
Locale(s): Suffolk, England

Summary: Eleven-year-old Lydia is the only passenger who gets off the train when it stops at the station near her Suffolk home. It is 1940, and Lydia—who was previously evacuated to Wales—is determined to make her way back to her family's manor house. She wears a gas mask as she passes through the deserted town and arrives at her home. Although Lydia's family is absent, the house is not empty. A Nazi soldier named Heiden is there, and he claims that he is part of an imminent German invasion. Lydia becomes Heiden's captive, and she agrees to follow the rules he gives her—most importantly, she must not leave the house. As Lydia interacts with Heiden, she tries to understand her situation. She can tell that the soldier is searching for something, and she isn't sure if she should believe everything he says. Gradually the true purpose of Heiden's visit is revealed. First novel.

Other books you might like:
Kate Atkinson, *A God in Ruins*, 2015
Sara Gruen, *At the Water's Edge*, 2015
Jan Moran, *Scent of Triumph*, 2015
Robert Radcliffe, *Under an English Heaven*, 2002
Daniel Torday, *The Last Flight of Poxl West*, 2015
David Treuer, *Prudence*, 2015

179

BRUCE W. HOLSINGER

The Invention of Fire

(New York: William Morrow, 2015)

Series: John Gower Series. Book 2
Story type: Historical - Medieval; Mystery
Subject(s): Mystery; Detective fiction; Crime
Major character(s): John Gower, Historical Figure, Writer (poet), Investigator, Friend (of Geoffrey Chaucer); Geoffrey Chaucer, Historical Figure, Writer (poet), Friend (of John Gower); Ralph Strode, Judge (former), Friend (of John Gower), Historical Figure; Nicholas Brembre, Historical Figure, Government Official (mayor of London); Stephen Marsh, Blacksmith; Richard II, Historical Figure, Royalty (king of England)
Time period(s): 14th century; 1380s (1386)
Locale(s): London, England; Calais, France

Summary: In the second novel in the John Gower series, the corpses of 16 men are discovered near a public privy in London in 1386. The authorities can't determine what weapon caused the victims' piercing wounds, and the city's mayor—Nicholas Brembre—wants the incident covered up. Former judge Ralph Strode asks his friend, the poet and information-gatherer John Gower, to investigate the case. Gower discovers that the men were killed with "handgonnes"—new weapons that fire small projectiles. The portable weapons are sure to transform the way wars are fought. Gower wants to figure out who killed the 16 men and why, and he's also interested in discovering who manufactured the guns. The case is a dangerous one, complicated by greed and politics. As the investigation takes Gower through London and to the port city of Calais, France, the poet-detective must also deal with his failing eyesight.

Other books by the same author:
A Burnable Book, 2014
A Burnable Book, 2014

Other books you might like:
Peter Ackroyd, *The Clerkenwell Tales*, 2004
Mary Devlin, *Murder on the Canterbury Pilgrimage*, 1998
Charles Finch, *The Laws of Murder*, 2014
Ken Follett, *World Without End*, 2007
Margaret Frazer, *The Novice's Tale*, 1992
C.L. Grace, *The Merchant of Death*, 1995
Paul Harding, *The Nightingale Gallery: Being the First of the Sorrowful Mysteries of Brother Athelstan*, 1991
Philippa Morgan, *Chaucer and the House of Fame*, 2004
Candace M. Robb, *A Gift of Sanctuary*, 1998
Anya Seton, *Katherine*, 1954
Jeri Westerson, *Veil of Lies*, 2008

180

RAVI HOWARD

Driving the King

(New York: HarperCollins Publishers, 2015)

Story type: Literary
Subject(s): Civil rights; Civil rights movements; United States history
Major character(s): Nat King Cole, Historical Figure, Singer, Friend (of Nat Weary); Nat Weary, Friend (of Nat King Cole), Bodyguard (of Nat King Cole), Driver (of Nat King Cole)
Time period(s): 20th century; 1950s
Locale(s): Montgomery, United States; Los Angeles, California

Summary: It's the 1950s and Nat King Cole is putting on a special performance in his hometown of Montgomery, Alabama. During the show, his old friend Nat Weary is planning to propose to his girlfriend while Cole sings a special song for them. However, things go awry when a white man tries to attack Cole on stage with a pipe. In defense of his friend, Weary jumps on the stage to stop the attack. His actions send Weary to jail for 10 years, but his bravery is not forgotten. Before he leaves prison, he receives an offer from Cole to become his driver and bodyguard in California. Weary agrees and moves from the segregated South to Los Angeles. Although Los Angeles is much different from Alabama, Weary soon learns that it's still no place for a black man to live in peace—even a talented singer like Cole faces discrimination in the entertainment industry.

Other books by the same author:
Like Trees Walking, 2007

Other books you might like:
O.H. Bennett, *The Lie*, 2009
Carrie Brown, *Confinement*, 2004
Alice Childress, *A Short Walk*, 1979

Toni Morrison, *Jazz*, 1992
Susan Elizabeth Phillips, *Lady Be Good*, 1999

181

STEPHEN HUNTER

I, Ripper

(New York: Simon & Schuster, 2015)

Story type: Mystery; Serial Killer
Subject(s): Mystery; Serial murders; British history, 1815-1914
Major character(s): Jeb, Journalist (newspaper reporter); Thomas Dare, Professor; Jack the Ripper, Historical Figure, Serial Killer; Mairsian, Prostitute, Writer (of letters)
Time period(s): 19th century; 1880s (1888)
Locale(s): London, England

Summary: Jeb, a music critic for the London *Star*, gets his big break when he is assigned to cover a series of murders in London's Whitechapel District. It is 1888, and a murderer who's been dubbed Jack the Ripper has killed several prostitutes and butchered their bodies. Jeb allies himself with Thomas Dare, a college professor who has taken an interest in Jack. The novel follows Jeb as his investigation draws him to the dark, depraved corners of Whitechapel. Fictional excerpts from the murderer's journal provide insights into the killer's mindset. Letters written by a prostitute to her mother convey the terror that grips the city during the Ripper's reign. Jeb and Jack play a dangerous game as they hunt one another. Although the real Jack the Ripper was never caught, the killer's identity in this fictionalized version of his story is revealed.

Other books by the same author:
The Third Bullet, 2013
Soft Target, 2011
Dead Zero, 2010
I, Sniper, 2009
Pale Horse Coming, 2001

Other books you might like:
Robert Bloch, *The Night of the Ripper*, 1984
Kenneth M. Cameron, *The Frightened Man*, 2008
Richard Gordon, *Jack the Ripper*, 1980
Pamela West, *Yours Truly, Jack the Ripper*, 1987
Paul West, *The Women of Whitechapel and Jack the Ripper*, 1991

182

EDWARD IFKOVIC

Cafe Europa

(Scottsdale, Arizona: Poisoned Pen Press, 2015)

Series: Edna Ferber Mystery Series. Book 6
Story type: Mystery; Series
Subject(s): Mystery; Detective fiction; Crime
Major character(s): Edna Ferber, Writer, Journalist, Detective—Amateur, Friend (of Winifred Moss); Winifred Moss, Suffragette, Friend (of Edna Ferber); Harold

Gibbon, Journalist (Hearst newspapers); Cassandra Blaine, Fiance(e) (of Frederic von Erhlich), Crime Victim, Young Woman (American), Heiress, Lover (former, of Endre Molnar); Frederic von Erhlich, Nobleman (count), Fiance(e) (of Cassandra Blaine); Endre Molnar, Young Man (Hungarian), Lover (former, of Cassandra Blaine), Crime Suspect
Time period(s): 20th century; 1910s (1914)
Locale(s): Budapest, Hungary

Summary: In the sixth novel in the Edna Ferber Mystery series, author and journalist Edna travels to Budapest, Hungary, with her friend Winifred Moss, a suffragist. The women book in at the run-down Arpad Hotel and get their scoops on world events and the hotel guests in the Cafe Europa. Political tensions are running high in Europe, and Hearst journalist Harold Gibbon is in Budapest to observe the demise of the Austro-Hungarian Empire. He focuses particularly on the approaching wedding of American heiress Cassandra Blaine to Count Frederic von Erhlich. Gibbon believes such unions between new money and old titles epitomize the deterioration of the status quo. Edna also takes notice of Cassandra, and she believes the young woman is frightened. When Cassandra is murdered, and her former lover—a Hungarian man named Endre Molnar—becomes the suspect, Edna launches her own investigation. She must prove Molnar's innocence by finding out who really killed Cassandra—and why.

Other books by the same author:
Final Curtain, 2014
Downtown Strut, 2013
Make Believe, 2012
Escape Artist, 2011
Lone Star, 2009

Other books you might like:
Vilmos Kondor, *Budapest Noir*, 2012
Elizabeth Kostova, *The Historian*, 2005
Julie Orringer, *The Invisible Bridge*, 2010
Arthur Phillips, *Prague*, 2002
Elizabeth Rosner, *The Speed of Light*, 2001

`183`

KAZUO ISHIGURO

The Buried Giant

(New York: Knopf, 2015)

Story type: Fantasy; Historical - Medieval
Subject(s): Middle Ages; England; Fantasy
Major character(s): Axl, Man (peasant), Aged Person, Spouse (of Beatrice); Beatrice, Woman (peasant), Aged Person, Spouse (of Axl)
Time period(s): 6th century
Locale(s): England

Summary: Axl and Beatrice are an aged husband and wife who live in sixth-century England. Their country is no longer occupied by the Romans, and it is at the moment not engaged in war, but the peace is offset by the harsh living conditions England's peasants must endure. It is a dark place and time, populated with mythical warriors and monsters. Although Axl and Beatrice know that

danger lies beyond their home, they decide to set out on a journey to their son's village. They haven't seen their son for a long time, and they seem to have almost forgotten him. As the husband and wife make their way through the countryside, they meet up with an assortment of characters who are on journeys of their own. Axl and Beatrice's quest prompts them to consider the past as well as the unknown future they face in the afterlife.

Other books by the same author:
Nocturnes: Five Stories of Music and Nightfall, 2009
Never Let Me Go, 2005
When We Were Orphans, 2000
The Unconsoled, 1995
The Remains of the Day, 1989

Other books you might like:
Steve Berry, *The Columbus Affair*, 2012
James Branch Cabell, *Figures of Earth*, 1921
Patrick W. Carr, *A Cast of Stones*, 2013
Bernard Cornwell, *The Empty Throne*, 2014
Nelson DeMille, *The Quest*, 2013
Diana Gabaldon, *Outlander (20th Anniversary Edition): A Novel*, 2011
Leon Garfield, *The Saracen Maid*, 1994
Philippa Gregory, *Stormbringers*, 2013
Tracy Hickman, *Bones of the Dragon*, 2009
Stephen King, *The Talisman*, 1984
Katherine Neville, *The Fire*, 2008
Douglas Nicholas, *The Wicked*, 2014
Jay Ruud, *Fatal Feast*, 2015
V.E. Schwab, *A Darker Shade of Magic*, 2015
Helene Wecker, *The Golem and the Jinni*, 2013
Joan Wolf, *No Dark Place*, 1999

`184`

CLIFFORD JACKMAN

The Winter Family

(New York: Doubleday, 2015)

Story type: Mystery
Subject(s): United States Civil War, 1861-1865; Violence; Gangs
Major character(s): Augustus Winter, Leader (of gang); Quentin Ross, Murderer, Gang Member; Fred Johnson, Gang Member, Slave (former); Lukas Shakespeare, Gang Member
Time period(s): 19th century; 1860s-1890s
Locale(s): American West, United States

Summary: In this novel by Clifford Jackman, the Winter "family"—a brutal gang—meets during the Civil War. The gang, which is led by Augustus Winter over the course of three decades, is made up of murderer Quentin Ross; Fred Johnson, a former slave; and two idiotic and violent brothers. They were formerly Union soldiers, but they quickly turn to violent killing sprees and go up against everyone they encounter, including the Ku Klux Klan. The Winter family is hired to fix an election in Chicago in 1872, then turns to bounty hunting as the gang makes its way across the West. The men raid, rob,

Historical

and kill along the way, even as they begin to turn on each other from within.

Other books you might like:

Edna Buchanan, *A Dark and Lonely Place*, 2011
J. California Cooper, *The Wake of the Wind*, 1998
Patrick deWitt, *The Sisters Brothers*, 2011
Loren D. Estleman, *Black Powder, White Smoke*, 2002
Tom Franklin, *Smonk*, 2006
Ron Hansen, *Desperadoes: A Novel*, 1979
Cormac McCarthy, *Blood Meridian: Or the Evening Redness in the West*, 1985
Larry McMurtry, *Streets of Laredo*, 1993
Thomas Pynchon, *Against the Day: A Novel*, 2006
Mary Doria Russell, *Epitaph*, 2015
Jane Smiley, *The All-True Travels and Adventures of Lidie Newton*, 1998
Daniel Woodrell, *Give Us a Kiss*, 1996

185

ELIZABETH JEFFREY

Meadowlands

(Sutton, Surrey, England: Severn House, 2015)

Story type: Family Saga; Historical - World War I
Subject(s): World War I, 1914-1918; Family sagas; Brothers and sisters
Major character(s): George Barsham, Father (of James, Millie, and Gina), Spouse (of Adelaide); Adelaide Barsham, Spouse (of George), Mother (of James, Millie, and Gina); Millie Barsham, Daughter (of Adelaide and George), Sister (of James and Gina); James Barsham, Son (of George and Adelaide), Brother (of Millie and Gina); Gina Barsham, Daughter (of George and Adelaide), Sister (of Millie and James)
Time period(s): 20th century; 1910s (1914)
Locale(s): England

Summary: In this historical family saga by Elizabeth Jeffrey, it is 1914, and the aristocratic Barsham family—led by George Barsham, a member of parliament, and his wife, Lady Adelaide—are feeling the effects of the war. A number of their estate workers have left, either to fight on the front lines or to work in the munitions factory. Their three children—James, Millie, and Gina—are determined to help their country as well. James decides to enlist, and Millie learns to drive an ambulance, despite Lady Adelaide's protests. Gina works in a soup kitchen, where she learns of the plight of the many local women and children left behind while their husbands and fathers are at the front. Throughout the novel, each of the Barshams moves through challenges and losses, and finds strength in their love for one another and in the people who need them.

Other books by the same author:
For Better, For Worse, 2013
The Thirteenth Child, 2009
Rookhurst Hall, 2008
Travellers' Inn, 2006
Mollie on the Shore, 2005

Other books you might like:

Jennifer Donnelly, *The Wild Rose*, 2011
MacKenzie Ford, *Gifts of War*, 2009
Rosie Harris, *Whispers of Love*, 2010
Cynthia Harrod-Eagles, *Goodbye Piccadilly*, 2014
Stacy Henrie, *Hope Rising*, 2014
Sara Hylton, *Flirting with Destiny*, 2011
Allegra Jordan, *The End of Innocence*, 2014
Alexis Landau, *The Empire of the Senses*, 2015
Doris Lessing, *Alfred and Emily*, 2008
Jennifer Robson, *After the War Is Over*, 2015

186

J. SYDNEY JONES

The German Agent

(Sutton, Surrey, England: Severn House Publishers, 2015)

Subject(s): Mystery; Espionage; Spies
Major character(s): Max Volkman, Spy (German); Adrian Appleby, Courier (British envoy), Uncle (of Catherine); Woodrow Wilson, Historical Figure, Government Official (US president); Edward Fitzgerald, Government Official (senator), Spouse (of Catherine); Catherine Fitzgerald, Spouse (of Edward), Niece (of Adrian Appleby)
Time period(s): 20th century; 1910s (1917)
Locale(s): Washington, District of Columbia

Summary: In 1917, the United States has so far stayed out of World War I. President Woodrow Wilson would like to keep it that way, but an intercepted telegram en route to him may force the president to reconsider. Adrian Appleby, a British envoy, is in possession of the Zimmermann telegram, which contains information about a proposed German alliance with Japan and Mexico. As Appleby makes his way to Wilson, German agent Max Volkman pursues Appleby. Volkman has been ordered to keep the telegram out of the president's hands by any means necessary. But during his time in Washington, DC, Volkman is distracted from his duty by Catherine Fitzgerald—wife of Senator Edward Fitzgerald and niece of Adrian Appleby. The tense mission, which could change the course of the war and history, reaches a climax when Volkman faces an impossible decision.

Other books by the same author:
A Matter of Breeding, 2014
Ruin Value, 2013
The Empty Mirror, 2008
The Hero Game, 1992
Time of the Wolf, 1990

Other books you might like:

Jussi Adler-Olsen, *The Alphabet House*, 2014
Howard Blum, *Dark Invasion: 1915: Germany's Secret War and the Hunt for the First Terrorist Cell in America*, 2014
Robert Olen Butler, *The Empire of Night*, 2014
Robert Olen Butler, *The Hot Country*, 2012
Agatha Christie, *The Secret Adversary*, 1922
Esther Freud, *Mr. Mac and Me*, 2015
Edward Huebsch, *The Last Summer of Mata Hari*, 1979

Graham Ison, *Hardcastle's Mandarin*, 2009
James Morton, *Spies of the First World War*, 2010
Anne Perry, *No Graves As Yet*, 2003
Richard Skinner, *The Red Dancer*, 2002
Charles Todd, *A Fine Summer's Day*, 2015
Lauren Willig, *The Ashford Affair*, 2013

187

LENE KAABERBOL

Doctor Death

(New York: Atria Books, 2015)

Series: Madeleine Karno Mystery Series. Book 1
Subject(s): Mystery; Detective fiction; Crime
Major character(s): Dr. Albert Karno, Doctor (pathologist), Father (of Madeleine Karno); Madeleine Karno, Young Woman, Daughter (of Albert Karno), Apprentice (of Albert Karno); Cecile Montaine, 17-Year-Old, Crime Victim; Father Abigore, Religious (priest)
Time period(s): 19th century; 1890s (1894)
Locale(s): Varbourg, France

Summary: In 1894 France, postmortem examinations are considered desecrations of the dead. Dr. Albert Karno, a pathologist, knows that autopsies yield vital information about the cause of a person's death, but his work his viewed with disapproval by society and the church. Albert's daughter, Madeleine, is aware that her father is known as Doctor Death, but she wants to follow the same career path. When the body of 17-year-old Cecile Montaine is found in the snow outside her home, the corpse is brought to Dr. Karno for examination. A priest, Father Abigore, is present to ensure that nothing unseemly is done to the girl's body. Karno is forced to work with the only clue he can obtain noninvasively—a pair of mites he extracts from Cecile's nasal passages. Madeleine assists her father as he tries to figure out how Cecile died. Unfortunately, more victims are claimed before Doctor Death and his daughter solve the case. This novel is the first in the Madeleine Karno Mystery series.

Other books by the same author:
Death of a Nightingale, 2013
Invisible Murder, 2012
The Boy in the Suitcase, 2011

Other books you might like:
Lisa Appignanesi, *Paris Requiem*, 2004
Caleb Carr, *The Alienist*, 1994
Caleb Carr, *The Angel of Darkness*, 1997
Robin Cook, *Vector*, 1999
Patricia Cornwell, *The Last Precinct*, 2000
Jeffery Deaver, *The Stone Monkey*, 2002
Tess Gerritsen, *The Sinner*, 2003
Anthony Horowitz, *Moriarty*, 2014
Claude Izner, *The Assassin in the Marais*, 2011
D.E. Meredith, *Devoured*, 2010
Kate Mosse, *Sepulchre*, 2008
Karin Slaughter, *Faithless*, 2005
Sarah Smith, *The Vanished Child*, 1992

188

MARY PAT KELLY

Of Irish Blood

(New York: Forge Books, 2015)

Story type: Literary
Subject(s): History; Irish Americans; Abuse
Major character(s): Nora Kelly, Young Woman (24 years old), Designer (fashion), Lover (of Tim); Tim McShane, Gambler, Lover (of Nora); Dolly McKee, Entertainer, Friend (of Nora); Gertrude Stein, Historical Figure; Michael Collins, Historical Figure; James Joyce, Historical Figure; Peter Keeley, Professor
Time period(s): 20th century; 1900s (1903)
Locale(s): Paris, France; Chicago, Illinois

Summary: Nora Kelly lives in an Irish community in Chicago and is involved with Tim McShane, an older man who seems nice at first. But when McShane courts another woman publicly and attempts to strangle Nora, Nora makes an escape to Paris. It is 1903, and Paris is a hub for writers, artists, and political activists. Nora enjoys the heady atmosphere and finds a job as a fashion designer. She crosses paths with James Joyce, Gertrude Stein, and other luminaries, and she is also drawn into the political issues of the era, which include Ireland's fight for independence. As she becomes more involved with the politics of her homeland, Nora dabbles in espionage and uses her own bank account to launder money. Nora also falls for a new man, Professor Peter Keeley, who is deeply involved in the Irish independence movement.

Other books by the same author:
Galway Bay, 2009
Special Intentions, 1997

Other books you might like:
Julie Garwood, *Shadow Dance: A Novel*, 2007
Dennis Lehane, *The Given Day*, 2008
Alice McDermott, *Charming Billy*, 1998
Edwin O'Connor, *The Edge of Sadness*, 1961
Colm Toibin, *Brooklyn*, 2009

189

STEPHEN KELLY

The Language of the Dead

(New York: Pegasus, 2015)

Story type: Historical - World War II; Mystery
Subject(s): Mystery; Detective fiction; Crime
Major character(s): Thomas Lamb, Detective—Police (detective chief inspector), Father (of Vera); Vera Lamb, 18-Year-Old, Worker (air raid warden), Daughter (of Thomas Lamb); David Wallace, Detective—Police (detective sergeant); William Blackwell, Worker (farmhand), Crime Victim; Emily Fordham, Volunteer (infirmary), Woman (pregnant), Crime Victim; Michael Bradford, Farmer, Crime Victim; Peter Wilkins, Teenager, Handicapped (mute)
Time period(s): 20th century; 1940s (1940)

Historical

Locale(s): Quimby, Hampshire

Summary: A murderer is at work in the English village of Quimby, which is already threatened by the Luftwaffe's bombing raids. The first victim is William Blackwell, who is killed with a pitchfork and scythe. The next two victims are pregnant infirmary volunteer Emily Fordham and farmer Michael Bradford, both of whom are murdered savagely. Detective chief inspector Thomas Lamb investigates the cases, which may have a connection to Quimby's occult past. Accused witches were once executed in Quimby, and Blackwell—the first victim—is alleged to have made a deal with a demonic dog as a boy. Lamb comes up with other theories and suspects, but he must solve the case before any more people die. Meanwhile, Nazi airplanes continue to terrorize England, and Lamb worries for the safety of the villagers—particularly his 18-year-old daughter, Vera, who serves as an air raid warden.

Other books you might like:
James R. Benn, *A Mortal Terror*, 2011
John Gardner, *Bottled Spider*, 2002
Maureen Jennings, *Seasons of Darkness*, 2012
Jill Paton Walsh, *A Presumption of Death*, 2003
Sheldon Russell, *The Yard Dog*, 2009

190

THOMAS KENEALLY

Shame and the Captives

(New York: Atria Books, 2015)

Story type: Historical - World War II
Subject(s): World War II, 1939-1945; Prisoners of war; Japanese (Asian people)
Major character(s): Ewan Abercare, Military Personnel (English colonel, prison camp commander); Bernard Suttor, Military Personnel (Australian major); Alice Herman, Woman, Lover (of Giancarlo), Spouse (of prisoner of war); Giancarlo, Prisoner (of war), Lover (of Alice)
Time period(s): 20th century; 1940s (1943-1944)
Locale(s): New South Wales, Australia

Summary: *Schindler's List* author Thomas Keneally delivers a historical fiction novel based on the largest prison escape of World War II, when more than a thousand Japanese prisoners of war attempted to escape from a prison camp in a small farming community in New South Wales, Australia, in 1944. Keneally's account follows the perspectives of the prisoners, camp commanders, and townspeople as they recognize the vast cultural differences between the Japanese prisoners and their Allied captors. While the Japanese prisoners—who consider the shame of being captured far worse than suffering a violent death—prepare their grand escape, the camp's English commander, Ewan Abercare, and his subordinate, Australian major Bernard Suttor, disagree about how to handle their unruly prisoners. Meanwhile, Alice Herman falls in love with Giancarlo, an Italian prisoner of war working on her father-in-law's farm, while her husband is held captive by the Germans in Austria.

Other books by the same author:
The Daughters of Mars, 2013

Office of Innocence, 2003
A River Town, 1995
Woman of the Inner Sea, 1993
Schindler's List, 1982

Other books you might like:
Martin Booth, *Hiroshima Joe*, 1985
Jim Lehrer, *The Special Prisoner*, 2000
Sofi Oksanen, *When the Doves Disappeared*, 2015
Alexander Parsons, *In the Shadow of the Sun*, 2005
Christine Piper, *After Darkness*, 2014
Lilith Saintcrow, *Dead Man Rising*, 2006

191

PHILIP KERR

The Lady from Zagreb

(New York: G.P. Putnam's Sons, 2015)

Series: Bernie Gunther Series. Book 10
Subject(s): Mystery; Detective fiction; Crime
Major character(s): Bernie Gunther, Detective—Homicide (former), Agent (Nazi intelligence); Heinrich Heckholz, Lawyer, Crime Victim; Joseph Goebbels, Political Figure (Nazi propaganda minister), Historical Figure; Dalia Dresner, Actress, Daughter (of Antun Dragun Djurkovic); Antun Dragun Djurkovic, Father (of Dalia Dresner), Missing Person
Time period(s): 20th century; 1940s (1942)
Locale(s): Zagreb, Croatia; Zurich, Switzerland

Summary: In the tenth Bernie Gunther novel, former homicide detective Gunther works as an intelligence agent for the Nazis. The post was not his choice, and Gunther does his best to operate in an ethical manner within the Reich. It is 1942, and Gunther has been charged by Propaganda Minister Joseph Goebbels with locating the missing father of alluring movie actress Dalia Dresner. Gunther follows Antun Dragun Djurkovic's trail to Croatia. Apparently Dalia's father commands a prison camp where he oversees the extermination of Jews and Serbs. When that horrific mission is complete, Gunther returns to Berlin and quickly finds himself in another spot of trouble. His work and connections have attracted the attention of several nations' intelligence agents. Meanwhile, Gunther is also concerned with another case: the unsolved murder of a lawyer who had asked a favor of Gunther before he was killed.

Other books by the same author:
Prayer, 2014
A Man Without Breath, 2013
Field Gray, 2011
If the Dead Rise Not, 2010
Hitler's Peace, 2005

Other books you might like:
David Aaron, *Crossing by Night*, 1993
Rebecca Cantrell, *A Trace of Smoke*, 2009
John Connell, *Ruins of War*, 2015
Jeffery Deaver, *Garden of Beasts*, 2004
David Downing, *Zoo Station*, 2007
Pierre Frei, *Berlin*, 2006
Colin Roderick Fulton, *The Reichsbank Robbery*, 2012

Alan Furst, *The World at Night*, 1996
Paul Grossman, *The Sleepwalkers*, 2010
Ursula Hegi, *Children and Fire*, 2011
Joseph Kanon, *The Good German*, 2001
Joseph Kanon, *Leaving Berlin*, 2015
Philip Kerr, *Berlin Noir*, 1993
John Lawton, *Then We Take Berlin*, 2013
Luke McCallin, *The Man from Berlin*, 2013
Rebecca Pawel, *The Summer Snow*, 2006
Alan Savage, *Partisan*, 2001
Daniel Silva, *A Death in Vienna*, 2004
Simon Tolkien, *Orders from Berlin*, 2012

192

LAURIE R. KING

Dreaming Spies

(New York: Bantam, 2015)

Series: Mary Russell/Sherlock Holmes Series. Book 13
Story type: Mystery
Subject(s): Mystery; Detective fiction; Crime
Major character(s): Sherlock Holmes, Detective, Spouse (of Mary Russell); Mary Russell, Detective, Spouse (of Sherlock Holmes); Lord Darley, Nobleman, Crime Suspect; Haruki Sato, Young Woman (Japanese)
Time period(s): 20th century; 1920s (1924)
Locale(s): At Sea; Oxford, England; Tokyo, Japan

Summary: Husband and wife Sherlock Holmes and Mary Russell become embroiled in a mystery during a pleasure cruise in the 13th series entry. As the couple sails from India to Tokyo on board the *Thomas Carlyle*, Mary is pleased that it is the first visit to Japan for both of them. Mary and Sherlock become acquainted with a young Japanese woman, Haruki Sato, on the steamship. She educates them about her language and culture. Sato asks the couple to help the future Japanese emperor locate an important book. They agree, and Sherlock also busies himself with another matter—exposing fellow passenger Lord Darley as an extortionist. The cases lead Mary and Sherlock on adventures in Japan, but they return to England with the case involving the emperor's book unresolved. The mystery is resurrected months later when Sato journeys to England.

Other books by the same author:
Garment of Shadows, 2012
Touchstone, 2007
A Monstrous Regiment of Women, 1995
The Beekeeper's Apprentice, 1994
A Grave Talent, 1993

Other books you might like:
Isabel Allende, *Ripper*, 2014
Frances Brody, *Dying in the Wool*, 2012
Frances Brody, *A Woman Unknown*, 2015
Caleb Carr, *The Italian Secretary*, 2005
Michael Chabon, *The Final Solution*, 2004
Barbara Cleverly, *The Last Kashmiri Rose*, 2001
Sir Arthur Conan Doyle, *His Last Bow*, 1917
Kerry Greenwood, *Cocaine Blues*, 1987

Anthony Horowitz, *Moriarty*, 2014
Richard Hoyt, *Old Soldiers Sometimes Lie*, 2002
Annette Meyers, *Free Love*, 1999
Soseki Natsume, *Kokoro*, 2010
Charles Todd, *A Fine Summer's Day*, 2015

193

WILLIAM KLABER

The Rebellion of Miss Lucy Ann Lobdell

(New York: St. Martin's Press, 2015)

Story type: Lesbian Historical
Subject(s): History; Sexuality; Women
Major character(s): Lucy Ann Lobdell, Historical Figure, Teacher (music), Mother, Lesbian, Narrator
Time period(s): 19th century
Locale(s): Minnesota, United States; Bethany, Pennsylvania

Summary: Author William Klaber provides a fictionalized account of the journey of Lucy Ann Lobdell, a 19th-century New York woman who blazed a trail in a man's world. During that era, women were severely limited in their choices. Lobdell first works as a music teacher in Bethany, Pennsylvania. She is dissatisfied with the life she is leading, however, and feels stifled by society's expectations. Lobdell abandons her child and dons men's clothing. She passes for a man as she journeys to Minnesota Territory, where she mingles with Native Americans and frontiersmen and survives a bitterly cold winter. She later travels back East, living in Pennsylvania and Delaware. Along the way, Lobdell grapples with her sexual identity. She ultimately ignores the scorn of society and lives as she chooses. First novel.

Other books you might like:
Anita Diamant, *The Boston Girl*, 2014
Kristin Hannah, *The Nightingale*, 2015
Emma Hooper, *Etta and Otto and Russell and James*, 2015
Christina Baker Kline, *Orphan Train*, 2013
Anne Tyler, *A Spool of Blue Thread*, 2015

194

SNORRI KRISTJANSSON

Blood Will Follow

(New York: Jo Fletcher Books, 2015)

Series: Valhalla Saga. Book 2
Story type: Military; Series
Subject(s): Vikings; Immortality; Fantasy
Major character(s): Ulfar Thormodsson, Viking, Immortal, Friend (of Audun); Audun Arngrimsson, Viking, Immortal, Friend (of Ulfar); Valgrad, Healer, Advisor (to King Olav); King Olav, Royalty (King of Stenvik)
Time period(s): 10th century; 990s (996)
Locale(s): Norway

Summary: In the second installment of the Valhalla Saga series, the war between the followers of the White Christ and those of the Norse gods is at an end. After spending many months fighting side by side, Vikings Ulfar Thormodsson and Audun Arngrimsson have gone their separate ways. Ulfar makes his way to Sweden to tell his uncle about the death of his son. Auden, meanwhile, heads south in search of the reason why he and Ulfar have been cursed with immortality. However, the Vikings have not left peace behind. With his new adviser, the healer Valgrad, at his side, King Olav begins to journey north in search of the power that has made Ulfar and Audun immortal. Violence soon catches up to Ulfar and Audun, and both learn that the gods are not yet done interfering with their lives.

Other books by the same author:
Swords of Good Men, 2014

Other books you might like:
Bernard Cornwell, *The Last Kingdom*, 2004
Catherine Coulter, *Lord of Hawkfell Island*, 1993
Michael Crichton, *The Last Eaters of the Dead*, 1976
Cecelia Holland, *The Soul Thief*, 2002
Juliet Marillier, *Foxmask*, 2004

195

DEWEY LAMBDIN

Kings and Emperors

(New York: Thomas Dunne Books, 2015)

Series: Alan Lewrie Series. Book 21
Story type: Series
Subject(s): History; Napoleonic Wars, 1800-1815; England
Major character(s): Alan Lewrie, Military Personnel (navy captain), Sea Captain; Napoleon Bonaparte, Historical Figure (emperor of France); Arthur Wellesley, Historical Figure (Duke of Wellington)
Time period(s): 19th century; 1800s (1807-1808)
Locale(s): Spain

Summary: Dewey Lambdin delivers the 21st installment in his Alan Lewrie historical naval adventures series. Royal Navy Captain Alan Lewrie and his 50-gun HMS *Sapphire* are still stationed in Gibraltar, where Captain Lewrie oversees a flotilla of gunboats in the bay. When Napoleon Bonaparte invades Portugal and leads his attack on Spain, Captain Lewrie and his crew are once again called into action against the king's enemies. As uprisings occur throughout Spain, Lewrie delivers weapons to Spanish patriots, escorts British expeditionary armies who join forces with the Spanish, and witnesses the first battles of the Peninsular War, fought between future Duke of Wellington Sir Arthur Wellesley and Napoleon's finest marshals.

Other books by the same author:
Reefs and Shoals, 2012
King, Ship, and Sword, 2010
Troubled Water, 2008

Havoc's Sword, 2003
King's Captain, 2000

Other books you might like:
Alexander Kent, *Stand into Danger*, 1981
Patrick O'Brian, *The Hundred Days*, 1998
S. Thomas Russell, *Until the Sea Shall Give Up Her Dead*, 2014
Sean Russell, *A Battle Won*, 2010
Julian Stockwin, *Kydd*, 2001
Julian Stockwin, *Pasha: A Kydd Sea Adventure*, 2014
John Wilcox, *Treachery in Tibet*, 2015
Jay Worrall, *Sails on the Horizon*, 2005

196

ALEXIS LANDAU

The Empire of the Senses

(New York: Pantheon, 2015)

Story type: Literary
Subject(s): World War I, 1914-1918; Jews; Family
Major character(s): Lev Perlmutter, Businessman, Religious (assimilated Jew), Spouse (of Josephine), Father (of Franz and Vicki); Josephine Perlmutter, Woman (gentile), Mother (of Franz and Vicki), Spouse (of Lev); Franz Perlmutter, Son (of Lev and Josephine); Vicki Perlmutter, Daughter (of Lev and Josephine); Leah, Woman (peasant), Religious (Jewish)
Time period(s): 20th century; (1910s); 20th century; 1920s (1927-1928)
Locale(s): Berlin, Germany; Riga, Latvia

Summary: Lev Perlmutter has a complicated relationship with his Jewish heritage. A businessman, Lev lives in Berlin with his wife, Josephine, who is not Jewish, and the couple's two children. When the Great War breaks out, Lev joins the army to fight for Germany. But while he is on the Eastern Front, Lev falls in love with Leah, a woman who is the opposite of Josephine. Leah is Jewish and poor, but she delights Lev as Josephine never could. After the war, Lev returns to his family in Berlin. The narrative then moves forward to the late 1920s and finds Lev's children—Franz and Vicki—dealing with their own dilemmas. Franz, a closeted homosexual, is involved with the early Nazi movement. Vicki is smitten with fashion, jazz, and a young man who is related to Lev's former lover, Leah. Meanwhile, Josephine indulges her passion for psychoanalysis and her attraction to her therapist. First novel.

Other books you might like:
Betsy Carter, *The Puzzle King*, 2009
Anna Funder, *All That I Am*, 2012
Paul Grossman, *The Sleepwalkers*, 2010
Elizabeth Jeffrey, *Meadowlands*, 2015
Hans Kellson, *Life Goes On*, 2012
Irmgard Keun, *The Artificial Silk Girl*, 2011

`197`

JOHN LANE

Fate Moreland's Widow

(Columbia, South Carolina: University of South Carolina Press, 2015)

Story type: Literary
Subject(s): Labor; Accidents; Death
Major character(s): Ben Crocker, Friend (of Novie), Accountant, Administrator; George McCane, Businessman, Employer (of Ben), Crime Suspect, Brother (of Angus); Olin Campbell, Labor Leader; Novie Moreland, Widow(er), Young Woman; Angus McCane, Brother (of George), Alcoholic
Time period(s): 20th century; 1930s-1980s
Locale(s): Carlton, South Carolina

Summary: Ben Crocker is in a tough situation. The son of South Carolina mill workers, Ben went to school and worked his way up the ladder until he was hired as an accountant by local cotton mill owner George McCane. In 1935 McCane decides to renovate the mill. In choosing who to lay off, he targets workers who were involved in a bitter strike the previous year. Ben is put in the uncomfortable position of carrying out his boss's wishes. When three people on an overcrowded sighting-seeing boat drown on a lake owned by McCane, the magnate is promptly arrested for their deaths. Trapped between his principals and his position, Ben has to carry the company on his shoulders, negotiate with the labor union, deal with McCane's alcoholic brother, and manage his unexpected feelings for the young widow of one of the drowning victims.

Other books by the same author:
When You Fall, 2001

Other books you might like:
John Bemrose, *The Island Walkers: A Novel*, 2004
Tracy Chevalier, *The Lady and the Unicorn*, 2004
Elizabeth Graver, *Unravelling*, 1997
Kathy Herman, *Day of Reckoning*, 2002
Tracie Peterson, *Daugher of the Loom*, 2003

`198`

ANDREW LATHAM

The Holy Lance

(London: Knox Robinson Publishing, 2015)

Series: English Templars Series. Book 1
Story type: Historical - Medieval; Military
Subject(s): Crusades; Wars; Royalty
Major character(s): Michael Fitz Alan, Military Personnel (of Richard the Lionheart), Knight (Templar); Richard the Lionheart, Royalty (king of England)
Time period(s): 12th century; 1100s (1191)

Summary: English Templar Michael Fitz Alan has distinguished himself in a battle at the city of Acre. His leadership during the counterattack that repels the Saracens has rescued the Third Crusade and drawn the gratitude of King Richard the Lionheart. The king soon entrusts another vital mission to Fitz Alan, a quest that he believes will aid the Christian cause of freeing Jerusalem. He must find a religious relic credited with ensuring the victory of the First Crusade and liberate it from its holders. Fitz Alan has his choice of Templars as he sets out to find the Holy Lance, yet his journey proves arduous. The English band encounters Christians with their own agenda, Saracens, and an assassin. Fitz Alan must also discover who among his chosen soldiers is a traitor. This is the first title of the English Templars series by Andrew Latham.

Other books you might like:
Angus Donald, *Holy Warrior*, 2011
Cecelia Holland, *The King's Witch*, 2011
Zoe Oldenbourg, *The World Is Not Enough*, 1948
Kamran Pasha, *Shadow of the Swords*, 2010
Sharon Kay Penman, *Lionheart*, 2011

`199`

LAURA LEBOW

The Figaro Murders

(New York: Minotaur Books, 2015)

Subject(s): Mystery; Detective fiction; Crime
Major character(s): Lorenzo Da Ponte, Writer (librettist); Joseph II, Historical Figure, Ruler (Habsburg Emperor); Christof Gabler, Nobleman (baron), Political Figure, Employer (former, of Da Ponte), Spouse (of Caroline); Caroline, Spouse (of Baron Gabler); Wolfgang Mozart, Historical Figure, Musician (composer); Florian Auerstein, Servant (Gabler's page), Crime Victim; Johann Vogel, Hairdresser (barber)
Time period(s): 18th century; 1780s (1786)
Locale(s): Vienna, Austria

Summary: Lorenzo Da Ponte is a librettist in 1786 Vienna. Although his work has gained the attention of Emperor Joseph II, Da Ponte struggles to make a living. He hopes that the libretto he is writing for Mozart's *The Marriage of Figaro* will change his fortune, but his life suddenly takes a different turn. When Da Ponte witnesses his barber, Johann Vogel, being arrested and hauled off to debtor's prison, he honors Vogel's request and takes a message to the residence of Baron Gabel, the employer of the barber's fiancee. When Gabel's page, Florian Auerstein, is murdered not long after Da Ponte's visit, Da Ponte is faced with a terrible dilemma. The only way he can avoid execution for a crime he didn't commit is to go undercover at the Palais Gabel and find the real killer. As he plays the role of spy, Da Ponte begins to uncover surprising secrets. First novel.

Other books you might like:
Marjorie Eccles, *Last Nocturne*, 2010
Selden Edwards, *The Little Book*, August 14, 2008
Teresa Grant, *Vienna Waltz*, 2011
C.S. Harris, *Who Buries the Dead*, 2015
Christian Jacq, *The Great Magician*, 2008
Philip Kerr, *German Requiem*, 1991
Beverle Graves Myers, *Interrupted Aria*, 2004
Matt Rees, *Mozart's Last Aria*, 2011

Anthony J. Rudel, *Imagining Don Giovanni*, 2001
Vivien Shotwell, *Vienna Nocturne*, 2014
Joseph Skibell, *A Curable Romantic*, 2010
Juliet Waldron, *Mozart's Wife*, 2001
David Weiss, *The Assassination of Mozart*, 1970

200

TOM LECLAIR

Lincoln's Billy

(Sag Harbor, New York: The Permanent Press, 2015)

Story type: Literary
Subject(s): United States history; Biographies; Presidents (Government)
Major character(s): Abraham Lincoln, Historical Figure, Government Official (US president), Spouse (of Mary Todd Lincoln), Friend (of Billy Herndon); William "Billy" Herndon, Historical Figure, Lawyer, Friend (of Abraham Lincoln), Writer (Lincoln's biographer); Mary Todd Lincoln, Historical Figure, Spouse (of Abraham Lincoln)
Time period(s): 19th century
Locale(s): United States

Summary: William "Billy" Herndon, a longtime colleague and confidante of Abraham Lincoln, set out to write a candid biography of Lincoln after the president's assassination. The book was published but, thanks to Herndon's publisher and collaborators, the biography did not portray Lincoln as Herndon had intended. In this novel, author Tom LeClair gives Herndon the chance to set the record straight. In the fictionalized account, Herndon tells the true story of Lincoln's life and political career. He describes an imperfect man who is not nearly as angelic as history often portrays him. Lincoln is given to bouts of rowdiness and periods of depression. Although Lincoln was opposed to slavery, Herndon reveals the true story behind the president's abolitionist stance. Herndon shares the details of the professional and personal relationship he shared with Lincoln, and he describes the frustrating process of writing Lincoln's biography.

Other books by the same author:
Passing Through, 2008
The Liquidators, 2006
Passing On, 2004
Well-Founded Fear, 2000

Other books you might like:
Steve Berry, *The Lincoln Myth*, 2014
Jerome Charyn, *I Am Abraham*, 2014
Richard Slotkin, *Abe: A Novel of the Young Lincoln*, 2000
Harry Turtledove, *How Few Remain*, 1997
Gore Vidal, *Lincoln: A Novel*, 1984

201

DENNIS LEHANE

World Gone By

(New York: William Morrow, 2015)

Series: Coughlin Series. Book 3
Subject(s): World War II, 1939-1945; Crime; History
Major character(s): Joe Coughlin, Advisor (Bartolo crime family), Widow(er), Father (of Tomas); Tomas, Boy, Son (of Joe); Dion Bartolo, Organized Crime Figure
Time period(s): 20th century; 1940s
Locale(s): Cuba; Tampa, Florida

Summary: In the third novel in the Joe Coughlin series, author Dennis Lehane picks up Coughlin's story a decade after the events of *Live by Night*. Coughlin, who once ruled his own criminal empire, now works as an adviser to the Bartolo family. The end of Prohibition and the start of World War II have changed the landscape of the crime world. Coughlin's wife has been killed, and Joe now raises his son, Tomas, alone. As the war progresses, Coughlin makes his way in the world by using his connections in Tampa society and the military to serve the Bartolo operations in Florida and Cuba. A survivor, Coughlin has established himself in a position of wealth and power. He has taken a new lover, but his contentment will be short-lived when his true identity is revealed.

Other books by the same author:
Live by Night, 2012
Moonlight Mile, 2010
The Given Day, 2006
Mystic River, 2001
A Drink Before the War, 1994

Other books you might like:
Ace Atkins, *The Forsaken*, 2014
Kate Atkinson, *A God in Ruins*, 2015
Vito Bruschini, *The Prince*, 2015
Milton T. Burton, *The Devil's Odds*, 2012
Max Allan Collins, *Road to Perdition*, 2002
Robert Crais, *The Promise*, 2014
Scott M Deitche, *Cigar City Mafia*, 2004
Eric Dezenhall, *The Devil Himself*, 2011
James Ellroy, *American Tabloid*, 1995
T.J. English, *Havana Nocturne*, 2008
Loren D. Estleman, *The Confessions of Al Capone*, 2013
Ed Falco, *The Family Corleone*, 2012
Gillian Flynn, *Gone Girl*, 2012
Adam Foulds, *In the Wolf's Mouth*, 2014
Norberto Fuentes, *The Autobiography of Fidel Castro*, 2010
James W. Hall, *The Big Finish*, 2014
Cathie John, *Little Mexico*, 2000
Zachary Lazar, *I Pity the Poor Immigrant*, 2014
Francine Mathews, *Too Bad to Die*, 2015
Mario Puzo, *The Godfather*, 1969
Kathy Reichs, *Flash and Bones*, 2011
Sebastian Rotella, *The Convert's Song*, 2014
John Sandford, *Mad River*, 2012

Jose Yglesias, *A Wake in Ybor City*, 1963
Sheila York, *Death in Her Face*, 2012

`202`

JEFFREY LENT

A Slant of Light

(New York: Bloomsbury, 2015)

Story type: Historical - American Civil War; Mystery
Subject(s): United States Civil War, 1861-1865; Murder; Agriculture
Major character(s): Malcolm Hopeton, Veteran, Murderer, Spouse (of Bethany); Enoch Stone, Lawyer; Harlan, 15-Year-Old, Orphan, Farmer (employee of August); August Swartout, Farmer, Employer (of Harlan); Bethany, Spouse (of Malcolm); Amos Wheeler, Farmer (employee of Malcolm)
Time period(s): 19th century; 1860s (1865)
Locale(s): New York, United States

Summary: In this novel by Jeffrey Lent, Malcolm Hopeton is a veteran Union soldier who has just returned home to his farm in New York, where he believes that his wife, Bethany, and hired hand, Amos Wheeler, have been having an affair. Malcolm kills them both, despite an unsuccessful attempt by his other farmhand—15-year-old Harlan—to stop him. Malcolm is imprisoned, and Harlan goes to work for another farmer, August Swartout. Harlan remains loyal to Malcolm, however. He had his own experiences with Amos in the past, and he is convinced that both Bethany and Amos had been cheating and stealing from Malcolm. Together with the town's lawyer, Enoch Stone, Harlan is determined to help Malcolm and set things right, even as he learns more about himself and his own strength in impossible situations.

Other books by the same author:
After You've Gone, 2009
A Peculiar Grace, 2007
Lost Nation, 2002
In the Fall, 2000

Other books you might like:
Kate Atkinson, *A God in Ruins*, 2015
Thomas Cobb, *Shavetail: A Novel*, 2008
Kathy Hepinstall, *Sisters of Shiloh*, 2015
Laird Hunt, *Neverhome*, 2014
Jane Smiley, *Early Warning*, 2015

`203`

GEORGE LERNER

The Ambassadors

(New York: Pegasus Books, 2014)

Story type: Political
Subject(s): History; Politics; Genocide
Major character(s): Jacob Furman, Military Personnel, Spouse (husband, of Susanna), Father (of Shalom); Susanna Furman, Holocaust Victim (survivor), Linguist, Spouse (wife, of Jacob), Mother (of Shalom); Shalom Furman, Son (of Jacob and Susanna)
Time period(s): 20th century; 1940s-1990s
Locale(s): Rwanda; New York, New York

Summary: George Lerner's debut novel follows one family's complex and emotional journey through genocide and grief in the 20th century. Since World War II, Jacob Furman has considered it his primary responsibility to rescue survivors from the evils of genocidal hatred. Decades later, he is deployed to the Congo during the Rwandan civil war, where the Tutsis are fighting against the genocidal Hutus. Once again, Jacob's wife, Susanna, and their son, Shalom, are left behind, and the emotional distance between them grows even further. While Susanna, a Holocaust survivor and linguistics academic, busies herself with human language research, Shalom wrestles to find his own identity. But when sickness brings the family back together, they learn that the political events of the 20th century have connected them more deeply than they ever realized. First novel.

Other books you might like:
Ronan Bennett, *The Catastrophist: A Novel*, 1999
W.E.B. Griffin, *The New Breed*, 1987
Barbara Kingsolver, *The Poisonwood Bible*, 1998
Tamar Myers, *The Witch Doctor's Wife: A Novel*, 2009
Marcus Stevens, *The Curve of the World*, 2002

`204`

LOIS LEVEEN

Juliet's Nurse

(New York: Atria Books, 2014)

Story type: Historical - Medieval; Literary
Subject(s): Feuds; Shakespeare, William; Romances (Fiction)
Major character(s): Angelica, Nurse (of Juliet), Spouse (wife, of Pietro); Juliet Cappelletti, Girl (Angelica's charge), Lover (of Romeo), Teenager; Romeo Montecchi, Teenager, Lover (of Juliet); Pietro, Spouse (husband, of Angelica)
Time period(s): 14th century
Locale(s): Verona, Italy

Summary: Lois Leveen reimagines Shakespeare's *Romeo and Juliet* in this novel that retells the famous love story from the perspective of Angelica, Juliet's nurse. The 14th-century plague that afflicted most of Verona claimed the lives of Angelica's six sons. When her daughter dies in infancy, Angelica's husband, Pietro, attempts to distract her from her grief by getting her a position with Verona's high-powered Cappelletti family. Pietro is successful, and Angelica is hired to be the live-in wet nurse to the Cappellettis' newborn daughter, Juliet. Angelica gives herself fully to her role as Juliet's nurse, and for the next 14 years, Angelica becomes Juliet's closest confidante, learns the ins and outs of the political rivalries of Verona, and discovers the dark secrets of the Cappelletti family. Then 14-year-old Juliet meets Romeo, the handsome son of the rival Montecchi family, at a masquerade ball. The days that follow lead to love, loss, and tragedy—not only for the young lovers, but also for Juliet's faithful nurse.

Other books by the same author:
The Secrets of Mary Bowser, 2012

Other books you might like:
Erica Eisdorfer, *The Wet Nurse's Tale*, 2009
Anne Fortier, *Juliet*, 2010
Johanna Lindsey, *Joining*, 1999
Jeanne Ray, *Julie and Romeo: A Novel*, 2000
Elsa Watson, *Maid Marian*, 2004

205

LISA LIEBERMAN

All the Wrong Places

(Waterville, Maine: Five Star, 2015)

Series: Cara Walden Mystery Series. Book 1
Subject(s): Mystery; Detective fiction; Family
Major character(s): Cara Walden, Actress, 17-Year-Old, Sister (half-sister of Gray); Gray Walden, Brother (half-brother of Cara), Writer (blacklisted screenwriter), Homosexual; Geoffrey, Worker (Walden family retainer)
Time period(s): 20th century; 1950s
Locale(s): London, England; Cannes, France; Sicily, Italy; California, United States

Summary: When Gray Walden is blacklisted in 1950s Hollywood for his previous political activities, he relocates to London with his half-sister, 17-year-old Cara, and family retainer Geoffrey. But even though they are thousands of miles from California, they can't escape the past. Cara's mother, a famous actress, died in the pool at her Hollywood home under suspicious circumstances, and Cara still hopes to find out what really happened. In London, the half-siblings pursue different interests. Gray explores the world of politics; Cara takes to the stage as a singer. She eventually becomes an actress and travels to Sicily to shoot a film. As she continues to delve into the mystery of her mother's death, Cara realizes that her curiosity may have personal and professional repercussions. She makes friends and takes lovers as her adventures lead her through Europe and eventually back to the United States. First novel.

Other books you might like:
Kingsley Amis, *Lucky Jim*, 1952
Keith Baker, *Hickory Dickory Dock*, 2007
Joy Fielding, *Lost*, 2003
Pip Granger, *Not All Tarts Are Apple*, 2002
Laura Lippman, *Another Thing to Fall*, 2008
Ngaio Marsh, *Night of the Vulcan*, 1951
Judith McNaught, *Someone to Watch over Me*, 2003
Iris Murdoch, *Under the Net*, 1954
John Osborne, *Look Back in Anger*, 1957
J.D. Robb, *Celebrity in Death*, 2012
Lisa Stapleton, *Absolute Beginner's Guide to Unix*, 1994
Ethan J. Wolfe, *The Regulator*, 2015

206

DAVID LISS

The Day of Atonement

(New York: Random House, 2014)

Story type: Religious
Subject(s): Portuguese (European people); Inquisition; Catholicism
Major character(s): Sebastian Foxx, Man, Survivor (of the Inquisition); Pedro Azinheiro, Religious (Inquisition leader)
Time period(s): 18th century; 1750s (1755)
Locale(s): Lisbon, Portugal

Summary: Set in 1755, this historical thriller from best-selling and award-winning author David Liss follows one man's quest for revenge in the Portuguese Inquisition. At age 13, Sebastian Foxx was sent from Lisbon to London after his Jewish parents were forced to convert to Catholicism and then fell victim to the Inquisition. A decade later, Sebastian returns to Lisbon, Portugal, to find Father Pedro Azinheiro, the Inquisition leader who imprisoned his parents. Sebastian arrives in Lisbon to find a city torn apart by violence and corruption. While attempting to bring his enemies to justice, Sebastian uncovers a web of secrets and arranges a number of escapes to London for others fleeing the Inquisition. But he won't get out of Lisbon before contending with the deadly earthquake that shakes the city on November 1, 1755, reducing it further into rampage and rubble.

Other books by the same author:
The Whiskey Rebels, 2008
The Ethical Assassin, 2006
A Spectacle of Corruption, 2004
The Coffee Trader, 2003
A Conspiracy of Paper, 2000

Other books you might like:
Charmaine Craig, *The Good Men*, 2002
Ildefonso Falcones, *The Barefoot Queen*, 2014
Noah Gordon, *The Last Jew*, 2000
Kathryn Harrison, *Poison*, 1995
S.J. Parris, *Heresy*, 2010
Arturo Perez-Reverte, *Captain Alatriste*, 2005

207

GREER MACALLISTER

The Magician's Lie

(Naperville, Illinois: Sourcebooks Landmark, 2015)

Story type: Mystery
Subject(s): Magic; Magicians; Murder
Major character(s): Arden, Magician; Virgil Holt, Police Officer
Time period(s): 20th century; 1900s (1905)
Locale(s): Waterloo, Iowa

Summary: Whenever the Amazing Arden takes the stage, it's always difficult to tell where the magic ends and reality begins. Such is the case at a show in Waterloo,

Iowa, that appears to go much too far. After a whirlwind performance during which the renowned illusionist unexpectedly replaces her saw with a fire ax in her famous sawing a man in half trick, Arden finds herself the prime suspect in her husband's murder. At the helm of the investigation is Virgil Holt, a police officer who was in attendance at the show. Taking the enigmatic Arden into custody, Holt must use all his wits to determine whether she is truly a master manipulator or simply an innocent victim. With the Amazing Arden's fate hanging in the balance, it's up to Holt to find the truth in a world of illusion.

Other books you might like:
Jim Butcher, *White Night*, 2007
Susanna Clarke, *Jonathan Strange & Mr. Norrell*, 2004
Sara Gruen, *Water for Elephants*, 2007
Erin Morgenstern, *The Night Circus*, 2010
Patrick Rothfuss, *The Wise Man's Fear*, 2011

208

JAMES MACMANUS

Sleep in Peace Tonight

(New York: Thomas Dunne Books, 2014)

Story type: Historical - World War I; Political
Subject(s): Armed forces; Courage; Deception
Major character(s): Harry Hopkins, Advisor (to President Roosevelt), Diplomat (emissary sent to London), Lover (of Leonora Finch); Leonora Finch, Driver (for Harry Hopkins), Spy (British Intelligence officer), Lover (of Harry Hopkins); Franklin Delano Roosevelt, Political Figure (president of the United States), Historical Figure; Winston Churchill, Historical Figure, Political Figure (British prime minister)
Time period(s): 20th century; 1940s (1941)
Locale(s): London, England; Washington, District of Columbia

Summary: It is 1941, and England is being ravaged by the destruction of the Blitz. Prime Minister Winston Churchill is convinced that England will not be able to defeat Hitler without the help of the United States. Political tensions are rising between England and the United States. To relieve tensions, President Franklin Delano Roosevelt sends his trusted adviser and emissary, Harry Hopkins, to London. Leonora Finch, an undercover British Intelligence agent, is assigned to Harry to gauge his views on the war. Romance ensues as she tries to gain his sympathies while exposing him to the plight of the people of England under siege. Hopkins struggles to get President Roosevelt to support the war, however. Hopkins grapples with his appointed mission and his personal feelings about the war, as well as his country's reluctance to become involved in the conflict.

Other books by the same author:
Black Venus, 2013
The Language of the Sea, 2010
On the Broken Shore, 2010

Other books you might like:
Sarah Blake, *The Postmistress*, 2010
Sara Douglass, *Druid's Sword*, 2006
Edward Rutherfurd, *London*, 1997
Sarah Waters, *The Night Watch*, 2006
William Wharton, *Birdy*, 1979

209

FRANCINE MATHEWS

Too Bad to Die

(New York: Riverhead Books, 2015)

Story type: Mystery
Subject(s): Spies; World War II, 1939-1945; Assassination
Major character(s): Ian Fleming, Historical Figure, Writer (novelist), Agent (British Naval Intelligence officer), Friend (of Michael); Michael Hudson, Agent, Friend (of Ian)
Time period(s): 20th century; 1940s (1943)
Locale(s): Tehran, Iran

Summary: It's November 1943, and Winston Churchill, Franklin Roosevelt, and Josef Stalin are meeting in Tehran to discuss the D-Day invasion. Naval intelligence officer Ian Fleming is among the delegation. Fleming is bored with his desk job and spends his down time crafting spy stories. He receives a message that a Nazi assassin has infiltrated the conference and is planning to kill the three world leaders. Throughout his life, Fleming has tried to follow in the steps of his heroic father. After so much time behind a desk, he is itching for some action. He believes this is his big chance to make a difference in the war. With the help of a beautiful Soviet spy, Fleming navigates through the streets of Cairo and Tehran in search of the assassin before it's too late.

Other books by the same author:
Jack 1939, 2012
The Alibi Club, 2006
The Secret Agent, 2002
The Cutout, 2001
Death in the Off-Season: A Merry Folger Mystery, 1994

Other books you might like:
Carlos Davis, *No Dawn for Men*, 2015
Jeffery Deaver, *Garden of Beasts*, 2004
Quinn Fawcett, *Siren Song*, 2003
Alan Furst, *The World at Night*, 1996
Geoffrey Household, *Rogue Male*, 1973
Dennis Lehane, *World Gone By*, 2015
Susan Elia MacNeal, *Mr. Churchill's Secretary*, 2012
Aly Monroe, *The Maze of Cadiz*, 2008
Roger Moorhouse, *Killing Hitler*, 2006
Mitch Silver, *In Secret Service*, 2007
David C. Taylor, *Night Life*, 2015
Herman Wouk, *War and Remembrance*, 1978

210

DONALD MCCAIG

Ruth's Journey: The Authorized Novel of Mammy from Margaret Mitchell's Gone with the Wind

(New York: Atria Books, 2014)

Story type: Historical - Antebellum American South
Subject(s): United States history; Slavery; Literature
Major character(s): Ruth "Mammy", Slave, Caregiver (to Scarlett O'Hara and other children); Solange Escarlette Fornier, Heiress, Spouse (of Augustin Fornier), Mother (of Ellen); Augustin Fornier, Father (of Ellen), Plantation Owner, Spouse (of Solange); Ellen, Spouse (of Gerald O'Hara), Daughter (of Solange and Augustin), Mother (of Scarlett); Gerald O'Hara, Spouse (of Ellen), Father (of Scarlett); Scarlett O'Hara, Southern Belle, Daughter (of Gerald and Ellen)
Time period(s): 19th century; 1820s-1860s
Locale(s): Savannah, Georgia

Summary: In *Rhett Butler's People*, Donald McCaig expanded on Margaret Mitchell's *Gone with the Wind* to tell the story of the man who stole Scarlett O'Hara's heart. In this novel McCaig focuses on another supporting character from Mitchell's classic novel—Mammy. The novel follows the infant Ruth, who will later be known as Mammy, as she is saved from a revolt on a Caribbean plantation and brought to Savannah by Solange and Augustin Fornier. Readers experience the Antebellum South from Ruth's perspective as she becomes a servant in the Fornier household. Ruth witnesses the marriage of Solange and Augustin's daughter, Ellen, to Gerald O'Hara, and eventually serves as Mammy to their daughter, the beautiful and stubborn Scarlett. Although the novel sets the stage for the events of *Gone with the Wind*, this story is about Ruth—her life as a slave, her relationship with her masters and mistresses and their children, and the joys and disappointments of her own life.

Other books by the same author:
Canaan, 2007
Rhett Butler's People, 2007
Jacob's Ladder, 1998
Nop's Trials, 1984

Other books you might like:
Barbara Chase-Riboud, *Sally Hemings: A Novel*, 1979
Hannah Crafts, *The Bondsman's Narrative*, 2002
Toni Morrison, *Beloved*, 1987
Dolen Perkins-Valdez, *Wench: A Novel*, 2010
Alexandra Ripley, *Scarlett*, 1991

211

ANGELINA MIRABELLA

The Sweetheart

(New York: Simon & Schuster, 2015)

Story type: Coming-of-Age
Subject(s): Wrestling; Sports; Interpersonal relations
Major character(s): Leonie Putzkammer, 17-Year-Old, Wrestler, Daughter (of Franz); Franz Putzkammer, Father (of Leonie), Widow(er); Salvatore Costantini, Sports Figure; Joe Pospisil, Trainer; Mimi Hollander, Wrestler; Spider McGee, Wrestler
Time period(s): 20th century; 1950s
Locale(s): Florida, United States; Philadelphia, Pennsylvania

Summary: At just 17 years old, Leonie Putzkammer feels like her life is headed down a dead end road. She feels trapped in the cramped Philadelphia row home she shares with her widowed father and the dingy diner where she works as a waitress. Her outlook abruptly changes, however, when she meets famed professional wrestling promoter Salvatore Costantini and agrees to trade in her apron for wrestling boots. After arriving at trainer Joe Pospisil's School for Lady Grappling in sunny Florida, Leonie reinvents herself as Gorgeous Gwen Davies and forms a tag team with veteran vixen Screaming Mimi Hollander. What's more, as she locks up in the squared circle, she also finds herself falling for the up-and-coming junior heavyweight sensation, Spider McGee. Just when everything seems to be coming together for the dangerous diva, she feels a sudden urge for something more. Leonie transforms herself into a fan favorite heroine known as The Sweetheart, even though doing so means potentially leaving her friendships on the ropes. First novel.

Other books you might like:
Liza Cody, *Bucket Nut*, 1993
Liza Cody, *Musclebound*, 1997
Joel Fishbane, *The Thunder of Giants*, 2015
Bill Morris, *Motor City*, 1992
Thomas O'Malley, *Serpents in the Cold*, 2015
Robert Vaughan, *Cold War*, 1995

212

JAN MORAN

Scent of Triumph

(New York: St. Martin's Griffin, 2015)

Story type: Historical - World War II
Subject(s): World War II, 1939-1945; History; Family
Major character(s): Danielle Bretancourt von Hoffman, Spouse (of Max), Mother (of Nicky), Artisan (perfumer); Max von Hoffman, Spouse (of Danielle), Father (of Nicky); Nicky, Boy, Son (of Danielle and Max); Jonathan Newell-Grey, Military Personnel (captain); Cameron Murphy, Actor
Time period(s): 20th century; 1930s-1940s
Locale(s): Los Angeles, California

Summary: Danielle Bretancourt von Hoffman is uneasy about leaving her young son, Nicky, in Poland when she embarks on a sea voyage in 1939. The successful perfumer could not have predicted how drastically her life was about to change. As England enters the spreading war, Danielle is separated from her husband and their son, who is with his grandmother. She is determined to reunite her family, and she travels throughout Europe to find them. Not all of her family members survive the dangers that are present in so much of Europe, however.

When Danielle gathers together the remnants of her family, she sets out for the United States. In California, Danielle begins to make a new start. She continues her career as a perfumer and establishes herself in the fashion industry. Danielle finds romance, success, and new challenges in Hollywood. The original edition of this novel was published in 2012.

Other books you might like:

Heather Doran Barbieri, *The Lace Makers of Glenmara*, 2009

Michel Faber, *The Crimson Petal and the White*, 2002

Sara Gruen, *At the Water's Edge*, 2015

Jason Hewitt, *The Dynamite Room*, 2015

M.J. Rose, *The Book of Lost Fragrances*, 2012

David Treuer, *Prudence*, 2015

213

MICHELLE MORAN

Rebel Queen

(New York: Touchstone Books, 2015)

Subject(s): Wars; Indian Mutiny, 1857-1858; Indian history

Major character(s): Rani Lakshmi, Royalty (queen), Warrior, Military Personnel; Sita, Narrator, Warrior, Military Personnel (soldier)

Time period(s): 19th century; (1840s-1850s); 20th century; 1910s

Locale(s): Jhansi, India

Summary: When the British Empire sets its sights on India in the mid-nineteenth century, it expects a quick and easy conquest. India is fractured and divided into kingdoms, each independent and wary of one another, seemingly no match for the might of the English. But when they arrive in the Kingdom of Jhansi, the British army is met with a surprising challenge. Instead of surrendering, Queen Lakshmi raises two armies—one male and one female—and rides into battle. Determined to protect her country and her people, she refuses to back down. Also available in Large Print.

Other books by the same author:
The Second Empress, 2012
Madame Tussaud, 2011
Cleopatra's Daughter, 2009
The Heretic Queen, 2008
Nefertiti, 2007

Other books you might like:

Miranda Carter, *The Strangler Vine*, 2015

Barbara Cleverly, *The Damascened Blade*, 2003

Bernard Cornwell, *Sharpe's Fortress*, 2000

David Davidar, *The House of Blue Mangoes*, 2002

John Masters, *Bhowani Junction*, 1954

Bahiyyih Nakhjavani, *The Woman Who Read Too Much*, 2015

Allison Pataki, *The Accidental Empress*, 2015

214

DAVID MORRELL

Inspector of the Dead

(New York: Mulholland Books, 2015)

Series: Thomas De Quincey Mystery Series. Book 2
Story type: Historical - Victorian
Subject(s): Crimean War, 1853-1856; Politics; Murder
Major character(s): Thomas de Quincey, Addict (aka the Opium Eater), Detective—Amateur, Father (of Emily), Writer (essayist), Friend (of Ryan and Becker); Emily de Quincey, Friend (of Ryan and Becker), Daughter (of Thomas); Ryan, Detective (of Scotland Yard), Friend (of Emily, Thomas); Becker, Detective (of Scotland Yard), Friend (of Thomas, Emily); Victoria, Royalty (Queen of England)
Time period(s): 19th century; 1850s (1855)
Locale(s): London, England

Summary: In the second book of the Thomas De Quincey mystery series, war is raging throughout Europe and the English empire is on the verge of collapse. With the government in shambles, London is rocked by a series of murders of the upper class. The deaths are linked to people who have attempted to assassinate Queen Victoria in the past. Could the final target of these murders end with the death of the queen? With the help of his daughter Emily and his Scotland Yard friends Ryan and Becker, Thomas De Quincey, the Opium Eater, searches for the killer before the queen is in the next target on the list. Meanwhile, the queen is forced to ask Lord Palmerston to help form a new government and the help guard her life.

Other books by the same author:
Murder as a Fine Art, 2013
The Protector, 2003
The Brotherhood of the Rose, 1984
First Blood, 1972

Other books you might like:

Wilkie Collins, *The Woman in White*, 1860

Michel Faber, *The Crimson Petal and the White*, 2002

Charles Finch, *A Beautiful Blue Death*, 2007

Ann Granger, *A Rare Interest in Corpses*, 2006

Leanna Renee Hieber, *The Eterna Files*, 2015

Lee Jackson, *A Most Dangerous Woman*, 2007

David Liss, *A Conspiracy of Paper*, 2000

James McGee, *Ratcatcher*, 2006

Anne Perry, *The Angel Court Affair*, 2014

Dan Simmons, *Drood*, 2008

Dan Simmons, *The Fifth Heart*, 2015

Barbara Vine, *The Blood Doctor*, 2002

215

MARY MORRIS

The Jazz Palace

(New York: Nan A. Talese/Doubleday, 2015)

Story type: Historical - Roaring Twenties
Subject(s): Jazz; Family; History

Major character(s): Benny Lehrman, Friend (of Napoleon), Musician, Worker (factory); Pearl Chimbrova, Saloon Keeper/Owner; Napoleon Hill, Musician, Friend (of Benny)
Time period(s): 20th century; 1920s
Locale(s): Chicago, Illinois

Summary: Set in Chicago during the Jazz Age, this novel by Mary Morris follows two Jewish families and their children, who grow up together and suffer unimaginable losses. Benny Lehrman's family runs a hat factory, but he has a much greater interest in jazz, and he is a spectacular piano player. Pearl Chimbrova lost three of her brothers in the sinking of the SS *Eastland*. Her family now runs the Jazz Palace, where Benny occasionally sits in with trumpeter Napoleon Hill. Together, Benny and Napolean begin to get recognition for their talent, and they play at other saloons—including one run by the mob, which brings unexpected trouble into both of their lives. Meanwhile, Benny and Pearl find themselves drawn to each other, but complications in their family lives seem to make it impossible for them to be together.

Other books by the same author:
Revenge, 2004
Acts of God, 2000
A Mother's Love, 1993
The Waiting Room, 1989
The Bus of Dreams, 1985

Other books you might like:
Barbara Taylor Bradford, *The Cavendon Women*, 2015
Roddy Doyle, *Oh, Play That Thing*, 2004
Daniela Kuper, *Hunger and Thirst*, 2004
Adam Langer, *Crossing California*, 2004
Suzanne Rindell, *The Other Typist*, 2013
Carrie Snyder, *Girl Runner*, 2015

216

JAMES MORROW

Galapagos Regained

(New York: St. Martin's Press, 2015)

Story type: Satire
Subject(s): English (British people); Science; Animals
Major character(s): Chloe Bathurst, Actress, Worker (for Charles), Thief; Charles Darwin, Scientist, Employer (of Chloe), Historical Figure, Explorer
Time period(s): 19th century; 1840s-1850s
Locale(s): At Sea; England

Summary: Actress Chloe Bathurst has just been tossed from her theater troupe because of her revolutionary ideas. This state of affairs is doubly difficult, because she needs to raise money quickly to get her father out of debtors' prison. She is hired as a nanny for the children of Charles Darwin. She also has to help care for the collection of animals he collected on his trip to the Galapagos Islands. Chloe soon learns of a contest sponsored by the Percy Bysshe Shelley Society: The first person to prove or disprove the existence of God wins 10,000 pounds. Chloe tries to get Darwin interested, offering to use her acting skills to help prove his theory, but Darwin refuses. Desperate for the money, Chloe decides to steal Darwin's theories and use them as her own. But to prove her purloined theory, she's going to need her own specimens from the Galapagos. Chloe puts together an expedition and braves disaster after disaster in her quest.

Other books by the same author:
The Philosopher's Apprentice, 2008
The Last Witchfinder, 2007
Blameless in Abaddon, 1996
Towing Jehovah, 1994
Only Begotten Daughter, 1990

Other books you might like:
John Darnton, *The Darwin Conspiracy*, 2005
Nicholas Drayson, *Confessing a Murder*, 2002
Roger McDonald, *Mr. Darwin's Shooter*, 1998
Irving Stone, *The Origin*, 1980
Rebecca Stott, *The Coral Thief: A Novel*, 2009

217

BARBARA KLEIN MOSS

The Language of Paradise

(New York: W.W. Norton and Company, 2015)

Story type: Literary
Subject(s): Mysticism; Philosophy; Love
Major character(s): Sophy Hedge, Daughter (of a minister), Artist (painter), Spouse (of Gideon Birdsall), Mother (expecting), Friend (of Leander Solloway); Gideon Birdsall, Spouse (of Sophy Hedge), Student (of theology), Friend (of Leander Solloway), Father (expecting); Leander Solloway, Teacher, Friend (of Sophy Hedge and Gideon Birdsall)
Time period(s): 19th century; 1830s
Locale(s): New England, United States

Summary: Sophy Hedge feels out of place in nineteenth-century New England. She loves to paint and is very free-spirited. However, as the daughter of a minister, she feels stifled. She sees little more than a life of dull domesticity in her future. When theology student Gideon Birdsall arrives to assist her father, Sophy is drawn to his intelligence and spiritualism. The two grow close and Gideon embraces her irregular beliefs and behaviors. After their marriage, Sophy discovers that her husband is restless by nature, and soon his philosophies grow increasingly bizarre. The married couple soon moves into the countryside in Gideon, where they become close to schoolteacher Leander Solloway. He is fixated on re-creating a kind of Eden. Sophy's pregnancy inspires Leander and Gideon to plan an experiment they hope will help them rediscover the language of the Garden of Eden. The decide to build paradise in a greenhouse and use the infant as a test subject. Despite the love she has for her husband and the freedom she enjoys within her marriage, Sophy must choose whether to save her child by fleeing, or fully embrace the life of mysticism and philosophy that allows her to paint and behave as she likes. First novel.

Other books by the same author:
Little Edens: Stories, 2004

Other books you might like:
Robert J. Begiebing, *The Adventures of Allegra Fullerton*, 1999
Esther Forbes, *Rainbow on the Road*, 1954
Charlotte Perkins Gilman, *Herland*, 1979
Anita Shreve, *Fortune's Rocks*, 1999
Susan Sontag, *In America*, 2000

218

MARCIA MULLER
BILL PRONZINI, Co-Author

The Body Snatchers Affair

(New York: Forge Books, 2015)

Series: Carpenter and Quincannon Mystery Series. Book 3
Story type: Historical - Victorian America
Subject(s): Detective fiction; Crime; Missing persons
Major character(s): John Quincannon, Agent (former Secret Service), Co-worker (of Carpenter), Detective—Private; Sabina Carpenter, Co-worker (Quincannon), Detective—Private, Investigator (former, Pinkerton); Sherlock Holmes, Detective—Private
Time period(s): 19th century; 1890s
Locale(s): San Francisco, California

Summary: In the third installment of the Carpenter and Quincannon series, two missing cases have taken the detectives on separate investigations throughout San Francisco. John Quincannon's case takes him into an opium den in Chinatown as he searches for his client's husband. The man has disappeared at the wrong moment, when a tong war is ready to break out over the theft of Bing Ah Kee's body. Meanwhile, Sabina Carpenter is searching for a millionaire corpse that has been taken from his family's crypt. The corpse is now being held for ransom, and Carpenter is afraid her suitor might be involved. Carpenter and Quincannon have little time to find the bodies before the war breaks out, and determine the connection between the conflict and the missing corpses. They also wonder why Sherlock Holmes is watching them from the shadows.

Other books by the same author:
The Bughouse Affair, 2013
The Spook Lights Affair, 2013
The Lighthouse, 1987
Beyond the Grave, 1986
Double, 1984

Other books you might like:
Meredith Blevins, *The Red Hot Empress*, 2005
Kate Bryan, *Murder at Bent Elbow*, 1998
Oakley Hall, *Ambrose Bierce and the Queen of Spades*, 1998
Steve Hockensmith, *Holmes on the Range*, 2006
Anthony Horowitz, *Moriarty*, 2014
Peter King, *The Jewel of the North*, 2001
Michael Kurland, *The Infernal Device*, 1979
Tim Maleeny, *Stealing the Dragon*, 2007
Nicholas Meyer, *The Seven-Per-Cent Solution*, 1974
Peter Ranscombe, *Hare*, 2014

Lisa See, *China Dolls*, 2014
Kelli Stanley, *City of Dragons*, 2010
Shirley Tallman, *Murder on Nob Hill*, 2004

219

VASUDEV MURTHY

Sherlock Holmes, the Missing Years: Japan

(Scottsdale, Arizona: Poisoned Pen Press, 2015)

Series: Missing Years Series. Book 1
Story type: Historical - Victorian; Mystery
Subject(s): Mystery; Detective fiction; Crime
Major character(s): Dr. John Watson, Doctor, Colleague (of Sherlock Holmes); Sherlock Holmes, Detective, Colleague (of John Watson), Enemy (of Moriarty); Moriarty, Professor, Villain, Enemy (of Sherlock Holmes); Shigeo Oshima, Director (intelligence research), Man; Kazushi Hasimoto, Man, Traveler, Crime Victim
Time period(s): 19th century; 1890s (1893)

Summary: In the first novel in the Missing Years series, Dr. John Watson has presumed his colleague Sherlock Holmes dead since he fell from Reichenbach Falls in 1891 with his arch enemy, Professor Moriarty. But now, two years later, Watson learns that the great detective is still alive. Watson receives a note from Holmes inviting him to journey from Liverpool to Bombay on board the *North Star*. En route, Watson's suite mate—Kazushi Hasimoto—is killed, and Watson is sure that Holmes is also on board in disguise. He is wrong. Holmes has been in Japan investigating Operation Kobe55. When the colleagues are united, they are drawn into a series of connected mysteries around the world. Moriarty, who also survived the confrontation at Reichenbach Falls, is the ultimate target of their quest. He is trying to take control of the global opium trade, and he still has some unfinished business with Sherlock Holmes.

Other books by the same author:
The Time Merchants and Other Strange Tales, 2013

Other books you might like:
Isabel Allende, *Ripper*, 2014
Caleb Carr, *The Italian Secretary*, 2005
Michael Chabon, *The Final Solution*, 2004
Anthony Horowitz, *The House of Silk: A Sherlock Holmes Novel*, 2011
Laurie R. King, *The Game*, 2004

220

BAHIYYIH NAKHJAVANI

The Woman Who Read Too Much

(El Segundo, California: Redwood Press, 2015)

Story type: Historical - Exotic; Literary
Subject(s): History; Middle East; Women
Major character(s): poetess of Qazvin, Woman, Writer (poet); Mother of the Shah, Woman, Mother (of the shah), Narrator; Mayor's Wife, Woman, Spouse (of

the mayor), Narrator; Sister of the Shah, Woman, Sister (of the shah), Narrator; Unnamed Character, Woman, Daughter (of the poetess of Qazvin), Narrator; Mullah, Religious, Uncle (of poetess of Qazvin); Shah, Ruler; Mayor, Government Official; Grand Vazir, Political Figure, Advisor

Time period(s): 19th century
Locale(s): Persia

Summary: The central character in this novel, the poetess of Qazvin, is inspired by Tahirih Qurratu'l-Ayn, a poet and religious scholar who was a controversial figure in 19th-century Persia. The novel is divided into four sections, each of which is narrated by a different female contemporary of the poetess—the Shah's mother, the Shah's sister, the Mayor's wife, and the poetess's own daughter. The narrators' accounts reveal the whole of the poetess's experiences. She is intelligent and educated, and she is not afraid to share her opinions. She shocks everyone by refusing to wear a veil. The poetess is admired by some and feared by others. When several prominent men are killed, some wonder if the poetess has the ability to foresee the future. The poetess's actions and opinions eventually result in her imprisonment upon the Shah's orders. After several years of incarceration, the woman believed to be too outspoken for her own good is executed. This novel was written in English and published previously in French, Italian, and Spanish.

Other books by the same author:
Paper, 2005
The Saddlebag: A Fable for Doubters and Seekers, 2000

Other books you might like:
Elena Ferrante, *My Brilliant Friend*, 2012
Jack Higgins, *The Death Trade*, 2013
Linda Howard, *All the Queen's Men*, 1999
David Ignatius, *The Increment*, 2009
Michelle Moran, *Rebel Queen*, 2015

221

WILLIAM NICHOLSON

Amherst

(New York: Simon & Schuster, 2015)

Story type: Historical - Victorian America
Subject(s): Infidelity; Sexual behavior; Brothers and sisters
Major character(s): Alice Dickinson, Advertising (executive), Writer, Lover (of Nick); Nick Crocker, Professor, Lover (of Alice); Mabel Loomis Todd, Spouse (of professor), Young Woman, Lover (of Austin); Austin Dickinson, Lover (of Mabel), Brother (of Emily), Historical Figure; Emily Dickinson, Historical Figure, Writer (poet), Sister (of Austin); Unnamed Character, Professor, Spouse (of Mabel)
Time period(s): 19th century; (1880s); 21st century; 2010s
Locale(s): London, England; Amherst, Massachusetts

Summary: Alice Dickinson takes a leaves of absence from her job as a London advertising executive to write a screenplay based on a scandalous love affair from the 1880s. In order to research her subject matter, she travels to Amherst College in Massachusetts, which was the location of the illicit tryst between Mabel Loomis Todd, young wife of a college faculty member, and Austin Dickinson, the married brother of poet Emily Dickinson. Alice stays at the home of fellow Brit Nick Crocker, a much older and very married academic at Amherst College. Soon, Alice's own life starts to reflect the lives of her subjects as she embarks on her own affair with Nick. William Nicholson's novel, which was originally published in England under the title *The Lovers of Amherst*, weaves the poetry of Emily Dickinson into the narrative, as the plot follows two similar stories of forbidden romance spanning different eras.

Other books by the same author:
Motherland, 2013
Jango, 2007
Seeker, 2006
Slaves of the Mastery, 2001
The Wind Singer: An Adventure, 2000

Other books you might like:
Jerome Charyn, *The Secret Life of Emily Dickinson: A Novel*, 2010
Joanne Dobson, *Quieter than Sleep*, 1997
Anne Edwards, *The Hesitant Heart*, 1974
Jamie Fuller, *The Diary of Emily Dickinson: A Novel*, 1993
Joyce Carol Oates, *Wild Nights!: Stories about the Last Days of Poe, Dickinson, Twain, James, and Hemingway*, 2008

222

THOMAS O'MALLEY
DOUGLAS GRAHAM PURDY, Co-Author

Serpents in the Cold

(New York: Mulholland Books, 2015)

Series: Boston Saga. Book 1
Subject(s): Drug abuse; Crime; Organized crime
Major character(s): Cal O'Brien, Spouse, Alcoholic, Veteran, Police Officer (former), Worker (private security); Dante Cooper, Widow(er), Addict, Friend (of Cal); Butcher, Serial Killer
Time period(s): 20th century; 1950s (1951)
Locale(s): Boston, Massachusetts

Summary: Cal O'Brien and Dante Cooper have lived in Boston all of their lives, but the world has changed, and the city seems stagnant. Cal works for a private security business that's not too picky about its clientele, as long as the customer can afford the service. Cal's drinking too much, trying to forget what he's seen in the war, and what he's lost. . Meanwhile, Dante is struggling to kick his drug addiction, but he cannot seem to stay away from heroin, even though he watched his wife die of an overdose. When Dante's sister-in-law is murdered, apparently by a serial killer called the Butcher, he feels the need to find the killer and enlists Cal in the investigation. It soon becomes clear they are meddling in the affairs of corrupt politicians. When Cal's wife is killed to keep him quiet, the murderer goes too far. Cal and Dante won't stop until they pull down the whole political pyramid and expose the truth.

Other books by the same author:
This Magnificent Desolation, 2013
In the Province of Saints, 2005

Other books you might like:
Benjamin Black, *Christine Falls*, 2007
Anita Diamant, *The Boston Girl*, 2014
Stephanie Grant, *Map of Ireland*, 2009
George V. Higgins, *The Friends of Eddie Coyle*, 1972
Chuck Hogan, *Prince of Thieves*, 2004
Katherine Howe, *The House of Velvet and Glass*, 2012
William Landay, *The Strangler*, 2007
Dennis Lehane, *Live by Night*, 2012
Dennis Lehane, *Mystic River*, 2001
Angelina Mirabella, *The Sweetheart*, 2015
Robert B. Parker, *The Godwulf Manuscript*, 1973
Stephanie Schorow, *Crime of the Century*, 2008

223

SOFI OKSANEN

When the Doves Disappeared

(New York: Knopf Doubleday Publishing Group, 2015)

Story type: Political
Subject(s): Cold War, 1945-1991; World War II, 1939-1945; Russians
Major character(s): Roland, Cousin (of Edgar), Revolutionary; Edgar, Cousin (of Roland), Revolutionary, Spouse (of Juudit); Juudit, Spouse (of Edgar)
Time period(s): 20th century; 1940s-1960s
Locale(s): Estonia

Summary: The year is 1941, and as World War II rages in Europe, the Baltic nation of Estonia strains under Communist rule. Two cousins—Roland, the ethical patriot, and Edgar, the devious opportunist—are trying to stay one step ahead of the Red Army. When German forces capture the country, Roland goes underground so that he cannot be found. Meanwhile, Edgar leaves his wife, Juudit, and willingly sides with the Nazis in order to save his own life. Twenty years later, Estonia is once again burdened by oppression, this time by its Soviet masters. Edgar has forged a new life, yet it shares the same story as before: He's a loyal servant of the KGB and has reunited with Juudit. He also desperately searches for Roland, who seems to have vanished. Edgar's intentions are far from noble, however, because he isn't looking for a reunion with his cousin. Instead, he seeks to ensure that the secrets Roland carries stay buried forever.

Other books by the same author:
Purge, 2010

Other books you might like:
Thomas Keneally, *Shame and the Captives*, 2015
Marcus Sedgwick, *A Love Like Blood*, 2015
Johanna Skibsrud, *Quartet for the End of Time*, 2014
David Thomas, *Ostland*, 2013

Frances Vieta, *Love in the Land of Barefoot Soldiers*, 2015

224

ANN PACKER

The Children's Crusade

(New York: Sribner, 2015)

Story type: Literary
Subject(s): Family; Family history; Sibling rivalry
Major character(s): Bill Blair, Spouse (husband, of Penny), Doctor (pediatrician), Father (of Robert, Rebecca, Ryan, and James); Penny Blair, Spouse (wife, of Bill), Artist, Mother (of Robert, Rebecca, Ryan, and James); Robert Blair, Son (of Bill and Penny), Doctor, Brother (of Rebecca, Ryan, and James); Rebecca Blair, Daughter (of Bill and Penny), Doctor (psychiatrist), Sister (of Robert, Ryan, and James); Ryan Blair, Son (of Bill and Penny), Teacher, Brother (of Robert, Rebecca, and James); James Blair, Son (of Bill and Penny), Brother (youngest, of Robert, Rebecca, and Ryan)
Time period(s): 20th century-21st century; 1950s-2000s (1954-2004)
Locale(s): Portola Valley, California

Summary: Best-selling author Ann Packer explores the power of family bonds in this tale of love, envy, resentment, and forgiveness. In 1954, pediatrician Bill Blair purchases land in Portola Valley, California, where he and his wife, Penny, raise their four children: Robert, Rebecca, Ryan, and James. In an era when women are exploring new roles outside of the home, Penny is a distracted housewife. She finds solace in her art and pottery pursuits and frequently retreats to the family's outdoor shed, which doubles as her studio. Thirty years later, three of the four siblings still live near the family's home. James, the youngest sibling and constant problem child, is the only one who relocates. When James returns home and asks for money, the ensuing conflict stirs up a host of memories and resentments among the siblings. As they recall experiences from their childhoods, the Blair siblings discover how strong a hold the past has on the present.

Other books by the same author:
Swim Back to Me, 2011
Songs Without Words, 2007
The Dive from Clausen's Pier, 2003

Other books you might like:
Jeffrey Archer, *The Sins of the Father*, 2012
Michael Christie, *If I Fall, If I Die*, 2015
Nuruddin Farah, *Hiding in Plain Sight*, 2014
Ann H. Gabhart, *Angel Sister*, 2011
Glen David Gold, *Sunnyside: A Novel*, 2009
Ursula Hegi, *Sacred Time*, 2003
Michael Raleigh, *In the Castle of the Flynns*, 2002
Courtney Miller Santo, *Three Story House*, 2014

Historical

225

PRIYA PARMAR

Vanessa and Her Sister

(New York: Ballantine Books, 2014)

Story type: Literary
Subject(s): History; Literature; Art
Major character(s): Virginia Stephen Woolf, Writer, Sister (of Vanessa), Spouse (of Leonard Woolf), Historical Figure; Vanessa Stephen Bell, Historical Figure, Artist, Sister (of Virginia); Leonard Woolf, Historical Figure, Spouse (of Virginia); Lytton Strachey, Historical Figure, Writer; E.M. Forster, Historical Figure, Writer; John Maynard Keynes, Historical Figure, Economist
Time period(s): 20th century; 1900s-1910s
Locale(s): London, England

Summary: In this novel author Priya Parmar creates a fictionalized account of the complicated relationship shared by Virginia Stephen Woolf and her sister, Vanessa Stephen Bell. Told through a series of diary entries and letters, the novel explores the admiration, jealousy, and devotion that defined Virginia and Vanessa's relationship. Virginia, a writer, and Vanessa, a painter, are founding members of the Bloomsbury group. Born in the early 20th century, the London-based group brings together men and women who share a passion for art, social experimentation, and a bohemian lifestyle. But even in this free-spirited atmosphere, Virginia struggles with the complex feelings she has for Vanessa. In addition to professional jealousies, Virginia also possesses a fierce love for Vanessa that is aggravated by mental health issues. Parmar follows the Stephen sisters as Vanessa marries and becomes a mother, and Virginia eventually finds a husband in Leonard Woolf.

Other books by the same author:
Exit the Actress, 2011

Other books you might like:
Stephanie Barron, *The White Garden: A Novel of Virginia Woolf*, 2009
Elizabeth Berg, *The Dream Lover*, 2015
Michael Cunningham, *The Hours*, 1998
Juliet Gael, *Romancing Miss Bronte*, 2010
Justine Picardie, *Daphne: A Novel*, 2008
Susan Sellers, *Vanessa and Virginia*, 2009
Norah Vincent, *Adeline: A Novel of Virginia Woolf*, 2015

226

ALLISON PATAKI

The Accidental Empress

(New York: Howard Books, 2015)

Story type: Romance
Subject(s): History; Biographies; Romances (Fiction)
Major character(s): Elisabeth "Sisi", Historical Figure, 15-Year-Old, Royalty (Duchess of Bavaria), Sister (of Helene); Franz Joseph, Historical Figure, Royalty (Emperor of Austro-Hungarian Empire); Helene, Sister (older, of Elisabeth)
Time period(s): 19th century; 1850s-1860s
Locale(s): Austria; Germany; Hungary

Summary: In this novel, Allison Pataki, author of *The Traitor's Wife*, follows a 15-year-old Bavarian duchess as she becomes Empress of Austria. When Franz Joseph, the Austro-Hungarian Emperor, reaches marriageable age, his mother arranges a betrothal to a cousin, Helene, in Bavaria. Helene, who has never met Franz, is invited to Vienna to receive a formal proposal. Helene's younger sister Elisabeth—aka Sisi—travels with Helene, but the journey does not go as planned. Sisi is immediately smitten with Franz, and he is with her. Franz voids the arrangement with Helene and proceeds with plans to marry Sisi. Helene never wanted to be empress, so she is happy with the way things work out, but Franz's controlling mother is furious. Sisi becomes Franz's bride and Empress of Austria, but she has much to learn about her new family and her new role.

Other books by the same author:
The Traitor's Wife, 2014

Other books you might like:
William M. Abrahams, *Imperial Waltz*, 1954
Daisy Goodwin, *The Fortune Hunter*, 2014
Kristin Hannah, *The Nightingale*, 2015
Jane Aiken Hodge, *Whispering*, 1995
Freda Lightfoot, *The Duchess of Drury Lane*, 2013
Alison McLeay, *The Dream Maker*, 1999
Susan Meissner, *Secrets of a Charmed Life*, 2015
Fern Michaels, *The Marriage Game*, 2007
Michelle Moran, *Rebel Queen*, 2015
Sophia Nash, *The Once and Future Duchess*, 2014
Elizabeth Sprigge, *The Raven's Wing*, 1940
Fay Weldon, *Habits of the House*, 2013

227

MATTHEW PEARL

The Last Bookaneer

(New York: Penguin Group, 2015)

Subject(s): Books; Publishing industry; Authorship
Major character(s): Pen Davenport, Thief, Publisher; Fergins, Assistant (of Davenport); Belial, Thief, Publisher
Time period(s): 19th century; 1890s (1890)
Locale(s): London, England; Samoa

Summary: For a hundred years, loose copyright laws and a hungry reading public meant that books could be published without an author's permission with extraordinary ease. Authors gained fame but suffered financially. The literary pirates were known as bookaneers. On the eve of the twentieth century, a new international treaty is signed to stop this literary underground. On Samoa, a dying Robert Louis Stevenson labors over a new novel. The thought of one last book from the great author fires the imaginations of the bookaneers, and soon two adversaries, the gallant Pen Davenport—accompanied by bookseller Fergins—and the monstrous Belial, set out for the Pacific island. Also available in Large Print.

Other books by the same author:
The Technologists, 2012
The Last Dickens, 2009
The Poe Shadow: A Novel, 2007
The Dante Club, 2003

Other books you might like:
John Crowley, *Lord Byron's Novel*, 2005
Robert Hellenga, *The Sixteen Pleasures*, 1989
Nancy Horan, *Under the Wide and Starry Sky*, 2014
Alberto Manguel, *Stevenson Under the Palm Trees*, 2004
Justine Picardie, *Daphne: A Novel*, 2008

228

ARTURO PEREZ-REVERTE
FRANK WYNNE, Translator

The Siege

(New York: Random House, 2014)

Story type: Espionage; Mystery
Subject(s): Business enterprises; Crime; Criminals
Major character(s): Rogelio Tizon, Police Officer (police commissioner of Cadiz); Lolita Palma, Heiress, Girlfriend (of Pepe Lobo); Pepe Lobo, Sea Captain (French), Boyfriend (of Lolita Palma)
Time period(s): 19th century; 1810s (1811)
Locale(s): Cadiz, Spain

Summary: It is 1811, and the Spanish port of Cadiz is surrounded by Napoleon's army. The city has lived for a year with the constant threat of a French invasion, but the Spaniards are determined to keep a stronghold. The threat of violence does not exist only outside the port of Cadiz, however—a veil of fear encompasses the city. In the midst of the unrest and the threat of war, a serial killer is randomly murdering young women throughout Cadiz. The police commissioner, Rogelio Tizon, must find and stop the killer before hysteria overwhelms the population. He discovers a troubling pattern to the murders, and races to uncover how the killings are tied to the artillery shells that are landing in the city. Tizon is in a race with time as panic and chaos threaten to overcome the city. He is determined to save other women from meeting a similar fate in Cadiz.

Other books by the same author:
The Painter of Battles, 2008
Captain Alatriste, 2005
The Queen of the South, 2004
The Nautical Chart, 2001
The Seville Communion, 1998

Other books you might like:
Bernard Cornwell, *Sharpe's Fury: Richard Sharpe and the Battle of Barrosa, March 1811*, 2006
Ildefonso Falcones, *The Barefoot Queen*, 2014
Edward Marston, *The Silver Locomotive Mystery*, 2009
David Morrell, *Murder as a Fine Art*, 2013
Anne Perry, *Dorchester Terrace*, 2012
S.K. Tillyard, *Tides of War*, 2011

229

ANNE PERRY

Corridors of the Night

(New York: Ballantine Books, 2015)

Series: William Monk Series. Book 21
Story type: Historical - Victorian; Mystery
Subject(s): Mystery; Detective fiction; Crime
Major character(s): William Monk, Detective—Police (commander, Thames River Police), Spouse (of Hester Monk); Hester Monk, Nurse, Spouse (of William Monk), Kidnap Victim; Magnus Rand, Doctor, Brother (of Hamilton Rand); Hamilton Rand, Scientist (chemist), Brother (of Magnus); Bryson Radnor, Patient (of Magnus and Hamilton Rand); Oliver Rathbone, Lawyer, Friend (of William Monk)
Time period(s): 19th century
Locale(s): London, England

Summary: In Victorian London, brothers Magnus and Hamilton Rand—a doctor and chemist, respectively—are trying to find a cure for leukemia, which is known at that time as "white blood disease." The methods the Rands employ in their research are not ethical, however. They experiment on unwitting patients, and they even kidnap children to use as test subjects. When one of the Rands' patients, Bryson Radnor, comes under the care of nurse Hester Monk, Hester discovers three children who have been held captive by Magnus and Hamilton. Hester, who is married to Thames River Police Commander William Monk, doesn't get the chance to report the Rands to the authorities. The brothers kidnap her to keep their experiments secret. William rounds up colleagues and friends and searches the city streets and beyond for his wife and her captors. This novel is the 21st in the William Monk series.

Other books by the same author:
The Angel Court Affair, 2015
Blood on the Water, 2014
Execution Dock, 2009
Death of a Stranger, 2002
Funeral in Blue, 2002

Other books you might like:
C.S. Harris, *When Maidens Mourn*, 2012
Laurie R. King, *The God of the Hive*, 2010
Marcia Muller, *The Bughouse Affair*, 2013
Jill Paton Walsh, *A Presumption of Death*, 2003
Deanna Raybourn, *The Dark Enquiry*, 2011

230

ANNE PERRY

The Angel Court Affair

(London, United Kingdom: Headline Book Publishing, 2014)

Series: Thomas and Charlotte Pitt Series. Book 30
Story type: Historical - Victorian; Mystery
Subject(s): Mystery; Detective fiction; Crime
Major character(s): Thomas Pitt, Detective—Police (Special Branch), Spouse (of Charlotte); Charlotte

Pitt, Spouse (of Thomas Pitt), Noblewoman, Detective—Amateur; Sofia Delacruz, Young Woman, Religious (preacher)
Time period(s): 19th century; 1890s (1898)
Locale(s): London, England; Spain

Summary: Thomas Pitt, a commander with London's Special Branch, is put off when his superior gives him his new assignment. Thomas is supposed to ensure the safety of Sofia Delacruz, an English-born preacher who has been living in Spain. Sofia's religious views have attracted controversy and death threats. Despite his misgivings, Thomas follows orders and soon realizes that the fears for Sofia's safety are well-founded. She is abducted during the night, and Pitt must now find her before she is harmed by her kidnappers. Pitt is not the only one searching for Sofia, however. Three men who have different motivations and connections to Sofia are also on the lookout for the victim. As the investigation reaches beyond England's shores, Thomas learns that the case could have grave repercussions. This novel is the 30th in the Thomas and Charlotte Pitt series.

Other books by the same author:
Dorchester Terrace, 2012
Long Spoon Lane, 2005
Seven Dials, 2003
Southampton Row, 2002
Pentecost Alley, 1996

Other books you might like:
Tasha Alexander, *A Fatal Waltz*, 2008
Jonathan Barnes, *The Somnambulist*, 2007
Rhys Bowen, *The Edge of Dreams*, 2015
Michel Faber, *The Crimson Petal and the White*, 2002
C.S. Harris, *Who Buries the Dead*, 2015
Leanna Renee Hieber, *The Eterna Files*, 2015
D.E. Ireland, *Wouldn't It Be Deadly*, 2014
David Morrell, *Inspector of the Dead*, 2015
Dan Simmons, *The Fifth Heart*, 2015
Barbara Vine, *The Blood Doctor*, 2002

231

RALPH PETERS

Valley of the Shadow

(New York: Forge, 2015)

Series: Civil War Series. Book 3
Story type: Historical - American Civil War; Series
Subject(s): United States Civil War, 1861-1865; Military life; Wars
Major character(s): Philip Sheridan, Historical Figure, Military Personnel (Union General); Jubal Early, Historical Figure, Military Personnel (Confederate General); George Armstrong Custer, Historical Figure, Military Personnel (Union General); John Brown Gordon, Historical Figure, Military Personnel (Confederate General)
Time period(s): 19th century; 1860s (1864)
Locale(s): Virginia, United States

Summary: In this historical novel, the third in the Civil War series by Ralph Peters, the author retells the story of the months-long battles in 1864 between the Union and Confederate soldiers for the Shenandoah Valley in Virginia. Using accurate historical details, Peters describes the various battles and the generals who led them, including Philip Sheridan and George Armstrong Custer from the Union army and Generals Jubal Early and John Brown Gordon from the Confederates. The novel is detailed and graphic, illustrating the daily life of those fighting on both sides of the battle. Peters explores the choices that were made and the long-lasting ramifications of actions taken on the battlefield.

Other books by the same author:
Cain at Gettysburg, 2012
The Officers' Club, 2011
The War After Armageddon, 2009
The War in 2020, 1991
Red Army, 1989

Other books you might like:
Geraldine Brooks, *March*, 2004
Harold Coyle, *Look Away: A Novel*, 1995
Charles Frazier, *Cold Mountain*, 1997
Jeff Shaara, *Gods and Generals*, 1996
Jeff Shaara, *The Last Full Measure*, 1998

232

SARAH PINBOROUGH

Murder

(New York: Jo Fletcher Books, 2014)

Story type: Historical - Victorian; Horror
Subject(s): Horror; History; Crime
Major character(s): Dr. Thomas Bond, Doctor (police surgeon); Juliana Harrington, Widow(er); Edward Kane, Friend (of Juliana's late husband)
Time period(s): 19th century; 1890s (1896)
Locale(s): London, England

Summary: In Sarah Pinborough's 2013 novel *Mayhem*, police surgeon Thomas Bond investigated the serial murders committed by the Torso Killer, whose spree coincided with that of Jack the Ripper. In this follow-up, Bond is still dealing with the repercussions of that investigation when he is drawn into another horrific case. This time a killer is targeting children. Bond is also dealing with personal issues. He has feelings for Juliana Harrington, a young widow who has connections to his previous case. Juliana may finally be softening to his affections, but the evil that has taken hold in London—and a new man who has entered the scene—could thwart Bond's plans of courtship and marriage. When new evidence and fresh violence emerge, it seems that the child-killer's case and the mystery of Jack the Ripper may be drawing to a close.

Other books by the same author:
Mayhem, 2014
The Chosen Seed, 2012
Feeding Ground, 2009
Tower Hill, 2008
The Taken, 2007

Other books you might like:
Deborah Crombie, *The Sound of Broken Glass*, 2013

Les Daniels, *Yellow Fog*, 1986
P.N. Elrod, *The Hanged Man*, 2015
Elizabeth George, *A Traitor to Memory*, 2001
Clay Griffith, *The Conquering Dark*, 2015
Martha Grimes, *The Old Contemptibles*, 1991
Barbara Hambly, *Renfield: Slave of Dracula*, 2006
Maureen Johnson, *The Shadow Cabinet*, 2015
Ruth Rendell, *The Rottweiler*, 2004
Michael Romkey, *The London Vampire Panic*, 2001

233

ALBERT SANCHEZ PINOL
DANIEL HAHN, Translator
THOMAS BUNSTEAD, Translator

Victus: The Fall of Barcelona
(New York: HarperCollins, 2014)

Story type: Military
Subject(s): Spain; Spaniards; Military life
Major character(s): Marti Zuviria, Engineer (military)
Time period(s): 18th century; 1714
Locale(s): Barcelona, Spain

Summary: This historical tale by best-selling author Albert Sanchez Pinol follows the events of the War of the Spanish Succession in the early 18th century. Military engineer Marti Zuviria knows the truth about the city of Barcelona in the Catalonia region of Spain and its annexation in 1714. Employed by the French and Spanish, both of whom are vying for the Spanish crown, Marti is tasked with both keeping and betraying the Catalan city. His political ambitions drive him into a world of duplicity and intrigue, where he devises a plan that requires all of his combat knowledge if he is to survive. This volume includes a timeline of events, depictions of political figures, battle diagrams, and maps of 18th-century Barcelona.

Other books by the same author:
Cold Skin, 2005
Pandora in the Congo, 2005

Other books you might like:
Bernard Cornwell, *Sharpe's Fury: Richard Sharpe and the Battle of Barrosa, March 1811*, 2006
Ildefonso Falcones, *Cathedral of the Sea*, 2008
Alan Furst, *Midnight in Europe*, 2014
Stephen Hunter, *The Spanish Gambit*, 1985
Carlos Ruiz Zafon, *The Prisoner of Heaven*, 2012

234

PETER RANSCOMBE

Hare
(London: Knox Robinson Publishing, 2014)

Story type: Historical - American Civil War; Mystery
Subject(s): Murder; Crime; Detective fiction
Major character(s): William Hare, Murderer, Crime

Suspect; Alexander Gillespie, Detective—Police; William Burke, Murderer
Time period(s): 19th century; 1820s-1860s
Locale(s): Edinburgh, Scotland; Boston, Massachusetts

Summary: In 1829 serial murderer William Burke was hanged in Edinburgh, Scotland, for his crimes. His accomplice, fellow Irish immigrant William Hare, saved his own life and help convict Burke by testifying for the prosecution. Now free, but despised by the population, Hare moved to London where he reportedly died a gruesome death. More than three decades later, a series of murders shocks the city of Boston. Police Captain Alexander Gillespie, who was part of the Burke investigation in his native Scotland, thinks he has found his killer when he discovers that Hare is not only alive and well, but is working on a canal project in his city. When the killings continue, however, Gillespie realizes Hare is innocent. Now he is forced to do the unthinkable and team up with someone he knows is a cold-blooded killer. In order to track down one murderer, Gillespie must let another murderer lead the way. First novel.

Other books you might like:
Anthony Horowitz, *Moriarty*, 2014
James McGee, *Resurrectionist*, 2007
D.E. Meredith, *Devoured*, 2010
Marcia Muller, *The Body Snatchers Affair*, 2015
Victoria Thompson, *Murder in Chelsea*, 2013

235

KATE RIORDAN

Fiercombe Manor
(New York: Harper, 2015)

Story type: Ghost Story; Gothic
Subject(s): Family history; Ghosts; Pregnancy
Major character(s): Alice Eveleigh, Young Woman (pregnant), Friend (of Tom and Mrs. Jelphs); Mrs. Jelphs, Housekeeper (of Fiercombe Manor), Friend (of Alice), Worker (of Stanton); Tom Stanton, Heir (of Fiercombe Manor), Friend (of Alice); Elizabeth Stanton, Writer (of diary), Relative (of Tom)
Time period(s): 19th century; (1890s); 20th century; 1930s (1933)
Locale(s): England

Summary: Unmarried and pregnant, 22-year-old Alice Eveleigh is forced to move from her London home to the rural estate of Fiercombe Manor. Family friend Mrs. Jelphs, the manor's housekeeper, agrees to look after her until the baby is born. With the home's owners, Lord and Lady Stanton, no longer living there, Alice enjoys the quiet country escape away from her disapproving family. But when she meets Tom, the estate's heir, she learns that the house might not be empty after all— ghosts from the family's tragic past are believed to still haunt the beautiful estate. Alice happens upon the secret diary of Elizabeth Stanton, who lived in the house 30 years earlier. Alice learns that she and Elizabeth have a great deal in common. When tragic secrets from the past are revealed and Alice experiences mysterious phenomena inside the house, she begins to fear for her life—and for her unborn child.

Other books by the same author:
The Girl in the Photograph, 2015

Other books you might like:
Susan Wittig Albert, *The Tale of Hawthorn House*, 2007
Robert Barnard, *A Charitable Body*, 2012
Elizabeth Cadell, *Royal Summons*, 1973
Carola Dunn, *Gunpowder Plot*, 2006
Sadie Jones, *The Uninvited Guests*, 2012

236

M.J. ROSE

The Witch of Painted Sorrows

(New York: Atria Books, 2015)

Series: Daughters of La Lune Series. Book 1
Subject(s): Mystery; Romances (Fiction); History
Major character(s): Sandrine Salome, Woman, Relative (descendant of La Lune), Lover (of Julien); Julien Duplessi, Architect, Lover (of Sandrine); La Lune, Relative (ancestor of Sandrine), Prostitute
Time period(s): 19th century; 1890s (1894)
Locale(s): Paris, France

Summary: Set in 1894 Paris, this supernatural thriller from best-selling author M.J. Rose is the first installment in her Daughters of La Lune series. Sandrine Salome leaves her threatening husband in New York City to seek refuge at her grandmother's mansion in Paris. Upon her arrival, however, Sandrine learns that her grandmother's home has been mysteriously closed for repairs. Against her grandmother's wishes, Sandrine makes her way to the family's mansion, where she meets Julien Duplessi, the young architect her grandmother hired. Together Sandrine and Julien discover hidden paintings left by a couple who lived in the mansion hundreds of years ago. The woman, Sandrine's ancestor and famous courtesan named La Lune, is rumored to have been a witch. Coincidentally, Sandrine soon finds herself consumed by a desire for painting—and for Julien.

Other books by the same author:
The Collector of Dying Breaths, 2014
The Reincarnationist, 2007
Lying in Bed, 2006
The Venus Fix, 2006
The Halo Effect, 2004

Other books you might like:
Cathy Marie Buchanan, *The Painted Girls*, 2013
Gioia Diliberto, *I Am Madame X*, 2003
Alan Furst, *Midnight in Europe*, 2014
Matthew Gallaway, *The Metropolis Case*, 2010
Leanna Renee Hieber, *The Eterna Files*, 2015
Rosalind Laker, *Brilliance*, 2007
Gregory Maguire, *Son of a Witch*, 2005
Kate Mosse, *Sepulchre*, 2008
Christopher Priest, *The Prestige*, 1996
Anne Rice, *The Witching Hour: A Novel*, 1990
Imogen Robertson, *The Paris Winter*, 2013
Emile Zola, *Therese Raquin*, 2011

237

ELIZABETH ROSNER

Electric City

(Berkeley, California: Counterpoint Press, 2014)

Story type: Coming-of-Age; Romance
Subject(s): Coming of age; Courage; Electricity
Major character(s): Charles Proteus Steimetz, Handicapped (severely curved spine), Scholar (mathematician), Immigrant, Inventor, Friend (of Joseph); Joseph Longboat, Indian (Native American), Friend (of Charles); Sophie Levine, Student—High School (at Schenectady High), Girl (Jewish), Classmate (of Martin); Henry Van Curler, Student (at Exeter in New Hampshire), Wealthy; Martin Longboat, Student—High School (at Schenectady High), Classmate (of Sophie), Boy (Native American)
Time period(s): 20th century; (1910s); 20th century; 1960s (1965)
Locale(s): Schenectady, New York

Summary: The story begins in 1919 in Schenectady, New York. Charles Proteus Steimetz and Joseph Longboat are working at Edison Machine Works, where they collaborate to help build the company that will become General Electric. The novel intertwines the history of Schenectady with its rich Native American Mohawk culture, Dutch immigrants, and the history of electricity and the life of a brilliant mathematician who reaches great heights in discovery despite his physical limitations. The story transitions to the 1960s, exploring the friendship and romance between three young people: Martin Longboat, Sophie Levine, and Henry Van Curler. They are struggling to find themselves through the tumult of the era and are also dealing with the economic effects of decisions made by the region's major employers. General Electric and other large companies have decided to leave their hometown, leaving Schenectady to grapple with its future and its very identity.

Other books by the same author:
Blue Nude, 2006
The Speed of Light, 2001

Other books you might like:
Cory Doctorow, *The Rapture of the Nerds*, 2012
Jean Echenoz, *Coverdale Lightning*, 2011
Samantha Hunt, *The Invention of Everything Else*, 2008
Mike Resnick, *The Buntline Special*, 2011
Allen Steele, *V-S Day*, 2014

238

ROSEMARY ROWE

The Fateful Day

(Surrey, England: Severn House Publishers, 2015)

Series: Libertus Mysteries of Roman Britain Series. Book 15
Story type: Mystery; Series
Subject(s): Detective fiction; Roman Empire, 30 BC-476 AD; England

Major character(s): Longinus Flavius Libertus, Detective—Amateur, Artist; Marcus Septimus Aurelius, Landowner
Time period(s): 2nd century; 190s (192)
Locale(s): Glevum, Roman Empire

Summary: In the 15th installment of the Libertus Mysteries of Roman Britain series, Marcus Septimus Aurelius is traveling to Rome and has asked Longinus Flavius Libertus to watch over his lands in his absence. One day, while walking along the road, Libertus sees that a carriage has pulled up near the villa of his patron. Libertus approaches the carriage to let the occupants know the owner is not at home. The carriage driver unexpectedly attacks Libertus and almost runs him down. Libertus is understandably upset and returns to the villa the next day to find out why the gatekeeper let the carriage enter the property. He discovers that the gatekeeper has been murdered and all the house slaves are missing. As Libertus tries to figure out what has happened, terrible news from Rome reaches Britain and shakes the whole Empire to its core.

Other books by the same author:
Dark Omens, 2013
A Whispering of Spies, 2012
The Vestal Vanishes, 2011
Requiem for a Slave, 2010
A Roman Ransom, 2006

Other books you might like:
Lindsey Davis, *A Body in the Bathhouse*, 2001
William Dietrich, *Hadrian's Wall*, 2004
Ruth Downie, *Caveat Emptor*, 2011
Manda Scott, *Dreaming the Eagle*, 2003
Jack Whyte, *The Skystone*, 1996

239

PRISCILLA ROYAL

Satan's Lullaby

(Scottsdale, Arizona: Poisoned Pen Press, 2015)

Series: Medieval Mysteries Series. Book 11
Subject(s): Religion; Murder; History
Major character(s): Eleanor, Religious (prioress), Friend (of Sister Anne); Isabeau, Religious (Abbess), Sister (of Etienne); Etienne Davoir, Religious (priest), Brother (of Isabeau); Anne, Religious (nun), Nurse (infirmarian), Friend (of Eleanor)
Time period(s): 13th century; 1270s (1278)
Locale(s): Norfolk, England

Summary: Suspicions fly when Prioress Eleanor learns that Abbess Isabeau, the head of her order, has asked Father Etienne Davoir to travel from France to perform a thorough inspection of Eleanor's Tyndal Priory in East Anglia, England. Eleanor questions the Abbess's motivation for such an inspection, and things grow more mysterious when Davoir's clerk is poisoned by a potion from Sister Anne, Tyndal's sub-infirmarian. When Davoir's life is threatened, he questions whether the events are Eleanor's attempts of scare him off before he learns the truth behind the allegations that she has broken her vows of celibacy. As the French and the English gather at Tyndal, they know a murderer dwells among them, but can Eleanor prove that she and Sister Anne shouldn't be prime suspects? This novel is the 11th installment in the Medieval Mysteries series by Priscilla Royal.

Other books by the same author:
Covenant With Hell, 2013
Justice for the Damned, 2007
Sorrow Without End, 2006
Tyrant of the Mind, 2004
Wine of Violence, 2003

Other books you might like:
Maureen Ash, *The Alehouse Murders: A Templar Knight Mystery*, 2007
Alys Clare, *Fortune Like the Moon*, 2000
Alys Clare, *The Winter King*, 2014
Cassandra Clark, *The Dragon of Handale*, 2015
P.C. Doherty, *Nightshade*, 2008
Margaret Frazer, *The Novice's Tale*, 1992
Barbara Reichmuth Geisler, *Other Gods*, 2002
Susanna Gregory, *The Cheapside Corpse*, 2015
Susanna Gregory, *A Plague on Both Your Houses*, 1998
Cora Harrison, *Condemned to Death*, 2015
Sharan Newman, *Death Comes as Epiphany*, 1993
Robyn Young, *Insurrection*, 2010

240

MARY DORIA RUSSELL

Epitaph

(New York: HarperCollins, 2015)

Story type: Historical - American West
Subject(s): United States history, 1865-1901; Western fiction; Politics
Major character(s): Doc Holliday, Historical Figure, Friend (of Wyatt Earp), Lawman (deputy US marshal); Wyatt Earp, Historical Figure, Lawman (deputy town marshal), Friend (of Doc Holliday); Josephine "Josie" Sarah Marcus, 18-Year-Old, Lover (of Johnny Behan); Johnny Behan, Lawman (sheriff)
Time period(s): 19th century; 1880s (1881)
Locale(s): Tombstone, Arizona

Summary: Author Mary Doria Russell presents a fictionalized account of the legendary gunfight that took place at the O.K. Corral. The fight—which occurred on October 26, 1881, and lasted less than a minute—was the culmination of a long feud between outlaw cowboys and an assortment of lawmen. The novel focuses particularly on Wyatt Earp, who was one of the officials who came through the skirmish unharmed. An 18-year-old woman named Josephine "Josie" Sarah Marcus is also an important figure in the story. Josie ran away from San Francisco and became involved with politician Johnny Behan. Behan and Earp were political rivals, and they became romantic rivals when Josie left Behan for Earp. Russell writes about Josie and Earp's relationship, and the brief but deadly gunfight that became part of Earp's legacy.

Other books by the same author:
Doc, 2011

Dreamers of the Day, 2008
A Thread of Grace, 2005
Children of God, 1998
The Sparrow, 1996

Other books you might like:
Loren D. Estleman, *Bloody Season*, 1988
Clifford Jackman, *The Winter Family*, 2015
Larry McMurtry, *The Last Kind Words Saloon*, 2014
Robert B. Parker, *Gunman's Rhapsody*, 2001
Paul West, *O.K.: The Corral, the Earps, and Doc Holliday*, 2000
Richard S. Wheeler, *Trouble in Tombstone*, 2004

241

S. THOMAS RUSSELL

Until the Sea Shall Give Up Her Dead

(New York: G.P. Putnam's Sons, 2014)

Series: Charles Hayden Series. Book 4
Story type: Military; Series
Subject(s): Napoleonic Wars, 1800-1815; Wars; Ships
Major character(s): Charles Hayden, Military Personnel, Sea Captain; William Jones, Military Personnel (commanding officer)
Time period(s): 19th century; 1800s
Locale(s): At Sea; Barbados

Summary: This historical adventure novel is the fourth installment in the Charles Hayden series by best-selling author S. Thomas Russell. Royal Navy Captain Charles Hayden and his warship, HMS *Themis*, are en route to the West Indies on the eve of the Napoleonic Wars. On the way to counter the threat of French forces, Hayden happens upon two stranded Spanish sailors, a pair of brothers whose claims stir up suspicions among Hayden and his crew. In Barbados, Hayden is placed under the command of Sir William Jones, the reckless officer whose orders leave Hayden with no favorable options. Refusing Jones's orders will cost Hayden his rank and command, but following them will cost him far more than he's willing to give up.

Other books by the same author:
A Ship of War, 2012
A Battle Won, 2010
Sea Without a Shore, 1996

Other books you might like:
Michael Crichton, *Pirate Latitudes: A Novel*, 2009
Alexander Kent, *Stand into Danger*, 1981
Dewey Lambdin, *Kings and Emperors*, 2015
Patrick O'Brian, *The Unknown Shore*, 1959
Julian Stockwin, *Kydd*, 2001
Julian Stockwin, *Pasha: A Kydd Sea Adventure*, 2014

242

ALEX RUTHERFORD

Traitors in the Shadows

(London: Headline Review, 2015)

Series: Empire of the Moghul Series. Book 6
Story type: Family Saga; Series
Subject(s): Royalty; Inheritance and succession; Family
Major character(s): Aurangzeb, Brother, Father, Ruler (of Moghul Empire), Son (of Jahan), Historical Figure; Jahan, Historical Figure, Ruler (former, of Mughul Empire), Widow(er), Father (of Aurangzeb)
Time period(s): 17th century; 1600s
Locale(s): India

Summary: In the sixth installment of the Empire of the Moghul series, Aurangzeb is the new emperor atop the Peacock Throne. After a bloody civil war in which Aurangzeb eliminated his brothers and nephews, he removed his father, Jahan, to his palace in Agra. Jahan's unexpected recovery from a life-threatening illness did not come soon enough to stop the battle for succession between his chosen heir and his other sons, including Aurangzeb. By 1658, Aurangzeb is able to assume the mantle of Moghul Emperor, following in the long family tradition of warrior-rulers. Jahan lives until 1666 under his son's confinement, mourning the death of his wife, who rests within the Taj Mahal monument. As Emperor, Aurangzeb can't help but reflect on the path he has taken to power and the destruction that the position has wrought upon his family. The devout Muslim wonders how, upon his own death, he will be judged for causing the deaths of his kin and for his treatment of his own wives and children.

Other books by the same author:
The Tainted Throne, 2013
Ruler of the World, 2012
A Kingdom Divided, 2011
Brothers at War, 2010
Raiders from the North, 2010

Other books you might like:
Miranda Carter, *The Strangler Vine*, 2015
Philip Hensher, *The Mulberry Empire*, 2002
Robin Lloyd-Jones, *Lords of the Dance*, 1983
Salman Rushdie, *The Enchantress of Florence: A Novel*, 2008
John Speed, *Tiger Claws: A Novel of India*, 2007

243

JAY RUUD

Fatal Feast

(Farmington Hills, Michigan: Five Star Publishing, 2015)

Series: Merlin Mystery Series. Book 1
Story type: Historical - Fantasy; Historical - Medieval
Subject(s): Arthurian legend; Middle Ages; England
Major character(s): Guenivere, Royalty, Spouse (of Arthur), Crime Suspect; Gawain, Knight; Patrise, Knight, Crime Victim (poisoned); Gildas, Servant,

Narrator; Arthur, Royalty, Spouse (of Guenivere);
Merlin, Wizard; Lancelot, Knight
Time period(s): 5th century-6th century
Locale(s): England

Summary: King Arthur's legendary court is the scene of murder, mystery, and intrigue following the unexpected death of a knight. When Queen Guenivere holds a banquet in celebration of the illustrious Sir Gawain, his fellow knight Sir Patrise abruptly drops dead after eating a poisoned apple given to him by the queen. Upon Patrise's demise, Guenivere is arrested and charged with murder. Certain that his wife is innocent, King Arthur sends Guenivere's servant Gildas to investigate the case with the aid of the great wizard Merlin. With only two weeks until Guenivere is set to face a trial by combat, Gildas and Merlin must do everything they can to uncover the truth behind Patrise's murder and identify the true killer. This is the first Merlin Mystery by literary critic Jay Rudd. First novel.

Other books you might like:
Peter Ackroyd, *The Death of King Arthur*, 2011
Kazuo Ishiguro, *The Buried Giant*, 2015
Mercedes Lackey, *Gwenhwyfar: The White Spirit*, 2009
Jeri Westerson, *Veil of Lies*, 2008
Persia Woolley, *Child of the Northern Spring*, 1987

244

C.J. SANSOM

Lamentation

(New York: Mulholland Books, 2015)

Series: Matthew Shardlake Series. Book 6
Story type: Mystery; Series
Subject(s): History; England; English (British people)
Major character(s): Matthew Shardlake, Lawyer, Employer (of Jack); Catherine Parr, Historical Figure (Queen of England), Spouse (wife, of King Henry VIII); Henry VIII, Historical Figure (King of England), Spouse (husband, of Catherine); Jack Barak, Assistant (to Matthew)
Time period(s): 16th century; 1540s (1546)
Locale(s): London, England

Summary: In 1546 London, attorney Matthew Shardlake is summoned by Queen Catherine Parr, the wife of King Henry VIII, after her secret and controversial manuscript, *Lamentation of a Sinner*, is stolen from her private chamber. The ideas expressed in the Queen's confessional book are so radically Protestant that it would cost her the king's loyalty if he learns of its existence. When the first page of the queen's volume is recovered in the hands of a murdered printer, Shardlake is tasked with finding not only the stolen book, but also the printer's killer. While King Henry VIII is on his deathbed, Protestant and Catholic leaders fight for control of the government. Shardlake and his assistant, Jack Barak, are drawn into a world of murders, conspiracies, and court politics as they fight to save the queen. This historical thriller is the sixth novel in the Matthew Shardlake series by best-selling author C.J. Sansom.

Other books by the same author:
Heartstone, 2011

Revelation, 2009
Winter in Madrid, 2008
Sovereign, 2007
Dissolution, 2003

Other books you might like:
Paul Doherty, *The Book of Fires*, 2015
Carolly Erickson, *The Last Wife of Henry VIII*, 2006
Philippa Gregory, *The Boleyn Inheritance*, 2006
Cora Harrison, *Verdict of the Court*, 2014
Hilary Mantel, *Bring Up the Bodies*, 2012
Judith Merkle Riley, *The Serpent Garden*, 1996

245

TONY SCHUMACHER

The Darkest Hour

(New York: William Morrow, 2014)

Story type: Alternate History
Subject(s): England; English (British people); Jews
Major character(s): John Henry Rossett, Detective—Police, Veteran (World War II), Prisoner (former prisoner of war), Widow(er); Jacob, Religious (Jewish), Orphan
Time period(s): 20th century; 1940s (1946)
Locale(s): London, England

Summary: Set in 1946, this alternate history tale by debut author Tony Schumacher follows the life of a grieving British veteran in Nazi-occupied London. Decorated war hero and London police detective John Henry Rossett returns to the police force after being released from a prisoner of war camp. Still haunted by the deaths of his wife and son in a Resistance bombing, Rossett, under Nazi command, is forced to supervise the roundup of London's Jews for deportation. Many of these are people he has known his whole life. When one of his detainees tips him off about a young Jewish boy named Jacob who is hiding in an abandoned building, Rossett is given the opportunity to save the boy—and also a personal chance at redemption. However, getting Jacob safely into neutral Ireland is a dangerous risk, one that could cost Rossett everything. First novel.

Other books you might like:
Jussi Adler-Olsen, *The Alphabet House*, 2014
Len Deighton, *SS-GB: Nazi-Occupied Britain 1941*, 1978
Robert Harris, *Fatherland*, 1992
Greg Iles, *Black Cross*, 1995
Philip Roth, *The Plot Against America*, 2004
Harry Turtledove, *West and East*, 2010

246

MARCUS SEDGWICK

A Love Like Blood

(New: Pegasus Crime, 2015)

Story type: Historical - World War II; Psychological Suspense

Subject(s): History; World War II, 1939-1945; Revenge
Major character(s): Charles Jackson, Military Personnel (former captain, Royal Army Medical Corps), Researcher (medical); Verovkin, Man, Crime Suspect
Time period(s): 20th century; 1940s-1950s (1944-1951)
Locale(s): Paris, France

Summary: In the days following the liberation of Paris in 1944, Captain Charles Jackson of the Royal Army Medical Corps happens upon a horrific scene while wandering about the city one evening. In an abandoned bunker, Jackson witnesses a man drinking blood from the chest of a woman. Filled with fear, Jackson flees the scene but is later overcome with guilt for not attempting to rescue the young woman. Seven years later, after completing his medical studies at Cambridge University, Jackson is a medical researcher and hematologist. He eagerly accepts an invitation to return to Paris. Once again, Jackson crosses paths with the same man he saw in the bunker. Still tormented by what he witnessed seven years earlier, Jackson follows the man and his beautiful companion, obsessed with uncovering the truth before the mysterious predator strikes again.

Other books by the same author:
Midwinterblood, 2013
White Crow, 2011
Revolver, 2010
The Foreshadowing, 2006
The Book of Dead Days, 2004

Other books you might like:
Cassandra Clare, *City of Glass*, 2009
Justin Cronin, *The Passage*, 2010
Charlaine Harris, *Dead in the Family*, 2010
Elizabeth Kostova, *The Historian*, 2005
Sofi Oksanen, *When the Doves Disappeared*, 2015
James Patterson, *Violets Are Blue*, 2001

247

ELIF SHAFAK

The Architect's Apprentice

(London, United Kingdom: Viking, 2015)

Story type: Historical - Exotic; Literary
Subject(s): Ottoman Empire, ca. 1288-1922; Turkish history; Adventure
Major character(s): Jahan, Boy, 12-Year-Old; Mihrimah, Royalty (princess); Sinan, Architect (royal); Suleiman, Ruler (sultan of Ottoman Empire)
Time period(s): 16th century
Locale(s): Istanbul

Summary: Jahan, a runaway, is only 12 years old when he comes to Istanbul. It is 1540, and the bustling city is the hub of culture in the Ottoman Empire. Jahan has the good fortune of traveling with a white baby elephant, named Chota, that will be a gift to the sultan. The runaway passes himself off as the animal's caregiver, and then assumes that position in the royal palace. As time passes, Jahan travels with Chota when the elephant is needed during wartime. Jahan's experiences beyond the palace open his eyes to a new world. He travels throughout the Ottoman Empire, and his skills as a builder attract the attention of the royal architect Sinan. Jahan and three other young men become Sinan's apprentices, and they assist in the construction of many historic buildings. But while Jahan finds adventure and love, he also witnesses terrible tragedies. He survives plagues and feels the effects of political and cultural upheavals in the 16th-century Ottoman Empire.

Other books by the same author:
Honor, 2013
The Forty Rules of Love, 2010
The Bastard of Istanbul, 2007
The Gaze, 2006
The Saint of Incipient Insanities, 2004

Other books you might like:
Tasha Alexander, *Tears of Pearl*, 2009
Tariq Ali, *The Stone Woman*, 2000
Colin Falconer, *The Sultan's Harem*, 2004
Jean-Christophe Rufin, *The Abyssinian*, 1999
Barry Unsworth, *The Rage of the Vulture*, 1983

248

HARRY SIDEBOTTOM

Iron and Rust

(New York: Overlook Press, 2015)

Series: Throne of the Caesars Series. Book 1
Story type: Military; Series
Subject(s): Roman Empire, 30 BC-476 AD; Politics; Romans
Major character(s): Maximinus Thrax, Ruler (Caesar of Rome), Military Personnel
Time period(s): 3rd century; 200s (235)
Locale(s): Roman Empire

Summary: In the first installment of the Throne of the Caesars series, the murder of Emperor Alexander and his mother has brought Rome's Severan dynasty to an end. With Roman rule now in question, Maximinus Thrax rises up the military ranks to become the new caesar. Although the Senate celebrates the new ruler, the likelihood that the governing body will accept as caesar a former poor shepherd is still in doubt. Meanwhile, a war with the barbarians in the north is taking a toll on the troops as well as depleting the Roman treasury. The threat of rebellion, along with a personal tragedy, drives Maximinus over the edge. He questions his motives for revenge as well as his sanity, yet he is determined to save his civilization.

Other books by the same author:
The Amber Road, 2013
The Caspian Gates, 2012
Lion of the Sun, 2010
King of Kings, 2009
WDIRN1300221513, 2008

Other books you might like:
David Chacko, *The Severan Prophecies*, 2007
Bernard Cornwell, *The Empty Throne*, 2014
Gordon Doherty, *Legionary*, 2015
Simon Scarrow, *Brothers in Blood*, 2014
S. J. A. Turney, *Marius' Mules*, 2014

249

DAN SIMMONS

The Fifth Heart

(New York: Little, Brown and Company, 2015)

Story type: Literary; Mystery
Subject(s): Mystery; Detective fiction; Literature
Major character(s): Henry James, Historical Figure, Writer, Friend (of Henry Adams); Sherlock Holmes, Detective; Henry Adams, Historian, Spouse (of Clover), Friend (of Henry James); Clover Adams, Spouse (of Henry Adams)
Time period(s): 19th century; 1890s (1893)
Locale(s): Paris, France; Washington, District of Columbia

Summary: In 1893, the great detective Sherlock Holmes is presumed dead after the incident at Reichenbach Falls. He is in a period of depression, and he isn't even sure if he's a real person or merely a literary character. As he hovers on the bank of the Seine River in Paris contemplating suicide, Holmes encounters the writer Henry James, who is also suicidal. The meeting diffuses the situation, and Holmes and James form an alliance. They distract themselves with a mystery that involves one of James's American friends. Henry Adams, a historian and member of a prominent political family, lost his wife, Clover, to suicide in 1885. Clover's brother has never accepted that his sister killed herself, and he wants Holmes to uncover the truth. Holmes and James travel to Washington, DC, where they investigate Clover's death and discover its true cause and surprising implications.

Other books by the same author:
Flashback, 2011
Black Hills, 2010
Drood, 2009
The Terror, 2007
Ilium, 2003

Other books you might like:
Isabel Allende, *Ripper*, 2014
Michael Chabon, *The Final Solution*, 2004
Anthony Horowitz, *Moriarty*, 2014
D.E. Ireland, *Wouldn't It Be Deadly*, 2014
Laurie R. King, *The God of the Hive*, 2010
David Morrell, *Inspector of the Dead*, 2015
Anne Perry, *The Angel Court Affair*, 2014

250

JOHANNA SKIBSRUD

Quartet for the End of Time

(New York: W.W. Norton & Company, 2014)

Story type: Political
Subject(s): Betrayal; Brothers and sisters; Class conflict
Major character(s): Arthur Sinclair, Veteran (World War I), Crime Suspect (accused of conspiracy), Father (of Douglas), Missing Person; Douglas Sinclair, Son (of Arthur); Sutton Kelly, Daughter (of US Congressman), Sister (of Alden), Journalist, Friend (of

Douglas), Witness (false); Alden Kelly, Spy (and code breaker), Brother (of Sutton), Son (of US Congressman), Criminal
Time period(s): 20th century; 1920s-1940s
Locale(s): London, England; Germany; Washington, District of Columbia

Summary: This novel is named after composer Olivier Messiaen's hauntingly complicated musical piece *Quartet for the End of Time*. The story begins in the 1930s during the Depression. The Bonus Army, composed of veterans, is preparing to march on Washington, D.C., to demand payment due them. Arthur Sinclair, a World War I veteran, is a working-class man and father of Douglas. Sutton and Alden Kelly are the children of a wealthy and powerful family. All are in Washington, D.C., for the march. Unanticipated events occur and Arthur Sinclair is accused of a crime he did not commit. Fearful of imprisonment, he disappears. Douglas is left to deal with the circumstances of his missing father while both Sutton and Alden, who are responsible for Arthur's situation, must deal with the guilt and the shame that begins to overwhelm them.

Other books by the same author:
The Sentimentalists, 2011

Other books you might like:
Ken Follett, *Winter of the World*, 2012
Laurie R. King, *Touchstone*, 2007
Sofi Oksanen, *When the Doves Disappeared*, 2015
Charles Todd, *Wings of Fire*, 1998
Scott Turow, *Ordinary Heroes*, 2005
Herman Wouk, *The Winds of War*, 1971

251

JANE SMILEY

Early Warning

(New York: Knopf, 2015)

Series: Last Hundred Years Trilogy. Book 2
Story type: Family Saga; Series
Subject(s): Family; Family history; Family relations
Major character(s): Walter Langdon, Farmer, Spouse (of Rosanna), Father (of Frank and four other children); Rosanna Langdon, Spouse (of Walter), Mother (of Frank and four other children); Frank Langdon, Son (of Walter and Rosanna), Brother (of four siblings)
Time period(s): 20th century; 1950s-1980s
Locale(s): United States

Summary: Author Jane Smiley continues the saga of the Langdon clan in the second installment in the Last Hundred Years trilogy. The novel begins in 1953 as five adult siblings are passed the Langdon family torch when their parents, Walter and Rosanna, die. The family and the farm have endured the hardships of the Great Depression and World War II, but most members of the current Langdon generation are looking at life beyond Iowa. As the Cold War era gives way to the cultural revolution of the 1960s and decadence of the 1980s, the siblings deal with personal and professional problems. They marry and become parents, and later grandparents. The Vietnam War, a religious cult, alcoholism, and social changes affect the lives of Walter and Rosanna's children and their offspring, who are now scattered across the country.

Other books by the same author:
Ten Days in the Hills, 2007
Horse Heaven, 2000
The All-True Travels and Adventures of Lidie Newton, 1998
Moo, 1995
A Thousand Acres, 1992

Other books you might like:
Barbara Taylor Bradford, *The Cavendon Women*, 2015
Patrick Gale, *A Place Called Winter*, 2015
Jeffrey Lent, *A Slant of Light*, 2015
Penelope Lively, *Consequences*, 2007
Alice McDermott, *After This*, 2006
David Treuer, *Prudence*, 2015
Anne Tyler, *A Spool of Blue Thread*, 2015

252

WILBUR SMITH

Desert God

(New York: William Morrow, 2014)

Series: Ancient Egypt Series. Book 5
Story type: Adventure; Series
Subject(s): Ancient history; Egyptian antiquities; Adventure
Major character(s): Taita, Slave (eunuch), Advisor (to Pharaoh Tamose); Tamose, Ruler (pharaoh), Father (of Tehuti and Bekatha); Tehuti, Royalty (princess), Daughter (of Tamose), Sister (of Bekatha); Bekatha, Royalty (princess), Daughter (of Tamose), Sister (of Tehuti); Minos, Ruler (King of Crete)
Time period(s): 16th century B.C.
Locale(s): Egypt

Summary: The fifth novel in the Ancient Egypt series is set in the 16th century BC, when the Hyksos people are attempting an incursion into Egypt. The eunuch Taita has established himself as an advisor to Pharaoh Tamose, who relies on the slave's insights. Taita believes that Egypt must ally itself with Sumeria and Crete, but he knows that the Cretans are already engaged in a clandestine alliance with the invading Hyksos. In an attempt to convince Crete's king, Minos, to withdraw from his arrangement with the Hyksos, the pharaoh decides to give the princesses Tehuti and Bekatha to Minos as wives. Taita is charged with taking the young women on the dangerous journey along the Nile to Arabia and into the Mediterranean. Along the way, Taita, Tehuti, and Bekatha encounter robbers, kidnappers, and pirates. But even when the party reaches Crete, the arranged marriages are threatened by a secret Tehuti has been keeping.

Other books by the same author:
Assegai, 2009
The Quest, 2007
Monsoon, 1999
Birds of Prey, 1997
River God, 1994

Other books you might like:
Christian Cameron, *The Great King*, 2014

P.C. Doherty, *The Poisoner of Ptah*, 2007
Brad Geagley, *Year of the Hyenas*, 2005
Lauren Haney, *A Curse of Silence: A Mystery of Ancient Egypt*, 2000
Maria Dahvana Headley, *Queen of Kings*, 2011
Norman Mailer, *Ancient Evenings*, 1983
Michelle Moran, *The Heretic Queen*, 2008
Scott Oden, *Men of Bronze*, 2005
Steven Saylor, *Raiders of the Nile*, 2014
Judith Tarr, *The Shepherd Kings*, 1999

253

CARRIE SNYDER

Girl Runner

(Toronto, Ontario, Canada: House of Anansi Press, 2015)

Story type: Literary
Subject(s): History; Women; Olympics
Major character(s): Aganetha Smart, Woman, Aged Person (104 years old), Patient (nursing home), Runner (former Olympic athlete)
Time period(s): 21st century; 2010s
Locale(s): Canada

Summary: In this novel, author Carrie Snyder casts the fictional character Aganetha Smart as one of the women who competed on Canada's 1928 gold medal-winning Olympic track team. Aganetha is now 104 years old, and she lives in a nursing home where no one knows her amazing story. She developed her running prowess as a young girl and went on to become an Olympian. She and her teammates attracted controversy, but they persevered. When two unexpected visitors come to see Aganetha, it seems that her life story will finally be told. The young man and woman say they are filmmakers, and they persuade Aganetha to share the details of her life with them. As Aganetha revisits the past, she recalls the triumph of her Olympic performance as well as the many challenges and sorrows she experienced in her lifetime. Meanwhile, it becomes clear that the alleged filmmakers have not been entirely forthcoming.

Other books by the same author:
The Juliet Stories, 2012
Hair Hat, 2004

Other books you might like:
Barbara Taylor Bradford, *The Cavendon Women*, 2015
Sandra Brown, *Mean Streak*, 2014
Jennifer Comeaux, *Crossing the Ice*, 2015
Barbara Delinsky, *While My Sister Sleeps*, 2009
Jamie Freveletti, *Running from the Devil*, 2009
Mary Morris, *The Jazz Palace*, 2015

254

JESSICA STIRLING

Whatever Happened to Molly Bloom?

(Sutton, Surrey, England: Severn House Publishers, 2015)

Series: Jim Kinsella Series. Book 1
Story type: Mystery

Subject(s): Mystery; Detective fiction; Crime
Major character(s): Jim Kinsella, Detective—Police (detective inspector), Colleague (of Tom Machin); Tom Machin, Detective—Police (inspector), Colleague (of Jim Kinsella); Molly Bloom, Singer, Spouse (of Leopold Bloom), Mother (of Milly), Lover (of Hugh "Blazes" Boylan), Crime Victim; Leopold Bloom, Spouse (of Molly Bloom), Father (of Milly), Crime Suspect; Hugh "Blazes" Boylan, Colleague (of Molly Bloom), Lover (of Molly Bloom), Crime Suspect; Milly Bloom, Daughter (of Molly and Leopold Bloom)
Time period(s): 20th century; 1900s (1905)
Locale(s): Dublin, Ireland

Summary: Author Jessica Stirling casts characters from James Joyce's novel *Ulysses* in this murder mystery, set in 1905 Dublin. When detective Jim Kinsella is called to a crime scene, he finds the battered corpse of popular performer Molly Bloom and determines that she was killed with a teapot. Leopold Bloom, the victim's husband, becomes the logical suspect, but he claims that he was out of the house at the time of Molly's death. Kinsella eventually sets his sights on another potential killer, Hugh "Blazes" Boylan, who was Molly's colleague and paramour. As Kinsella investigates the clues, which include a perfumed cotton ball, he discovers that Leopold may also have been involved in some extramarital activities. The arrival of Molly and Leopold's daughter, Milly, further complicates the investigation. This novel is the first in the Jim Kinsella series.

Other books by the same author:
The Strawberry Season, 2000
The Island Wife, 1998
Lantern for the Dark, 1992
The Good Provider, 1989
Treasures on Earth, 1985

Other books you might like:
Benjamin Black, *A Death In Summer*, 2011
John Brady, *All Souls*, 1993
Tana French, *Faithful Place*, 2011
Bartholomew Gill, *Death in Dublin*, 2003
D.E. Ireland, *Wouldn't It Be Deadly*, 2014
Gerard O'Donovan, *Dublin Dead*, 2012

255

JULIAN STOCKWIN

Pasha: A Kydd Sea Adventure

(New York: McBook Press, 2014)

Series: Kydd Sea Adventures Series. Book 15
Story type: Adventure; Series
Subject(s): Adventure; Conspiracy; Courage
Major character(s): Thomas Kidd, Sea Captain (British Navy), Friend (of Nicholas Renzi), Co-worker (of Nicholas Renzi); Nicholas Penzi, Secretary (of Thomas Kidd), Spy (British), Friend (of Thomas Kidd), Prisoner (in Turkish prison); Arbuthnot, Government Official (British Ambassador), Diplomat
Time period(s): 18th century-19th century
Locale(s): At Sea; England; Turkey

Summary: This is the 15th installment of the Kydd Sea Adventure series. Captain Thomas Kydd has worked his way up the ranks of the British Navy along with his secretary and friend, Nicholas Renzi. Kydd and Renzi are given new orders and forced to part company. Captain Kydd is assigned to sail for Turkey, where he must help Ambassador Arbuthnot flee in safety. Kydd must rescue the ambassador and try to thwart Napoleon's plot for world dominance. Renzi is assigned to be the British spy within the sultan's court in the Topkapi Palace. After arranging a coup in the palace, Renzi finds himself incarcerated in a Turkish prison. The only hope of rescue is his friend. Will Captain Kydd be able to harness his superior seamanship and sheer bravery to save Renzi?

Other books by the same author:
Conquest, 2011
Quarterdeck, 2005
Seaflower, 2003
Artemis, 2001
Kydd, 2001

Other books you might like:
C.S. Forester, *Lieutenant Hornblower*, 1952
Alexander Kent, *Success to the Brave*, 1983
Dewey Lambdin, *Kings and Emperors*, 2015
S. Thomas Russell, *Until the Sea Shall Give Up Her Dead*, 2014
Barry Unsworth, *Losing Nelson: A Novel*, 1999

256

MARGARET SWEATMAN

Mr. Jones

(Fredericton, New Brunswick, Canada: Goose Lane Editions, 2014)

Story type: Political
Subject(s): Cold War, 1945-1991; Veterans; Communism
Major character(s): Emmett Jones, Veteran (World War II), Colleague (of John); John Norfield, Veteran (World War II), Colleague (of Emmett), Prisoner (former, of war)
Time period(s): 20th century; 1950s (1953)
Locale(s): Canada

Summary: A former World War II pilot struggles to find purpose and identity in this historical fiction novel by award-winning author Margaret Sweatman. Canadian pilot Emmett Jones fought during World War II, and now, in an era of post-war paranoia—and on the edge of the nuclear age—Emmett loses his life's focus, questioning his identity in terms of his family and society at large. John Norfield is a former prisoner of war who commits his life to promoting Communism and encourages Emmett to do the same. Soon, Emmett's relationship with Norfield brings his entire family under the watchful eye of the Canadian government, making them all targets of investigation. And as the Cold War's nuclear arms race intensifies, Emmett puts himself—and everyone he loves—in grave danger.

Other books by the same author:
The Players, 2009
When Alice Lay Down with Peter, 2001

Same and Angie, 1996
Fox, 1991
Private Property, 1988

Other books you might like:
James Carroll, *Firebird*, 1989
Max Allan Collins, *Majic Man*, 1999
Norman Mailer, *Harlot's Ghost*, 1991
Jill Paton Walsh, *A Desert in Bohemia*, 2000
Philip Roth, *I Married a Communist*, 1998

257

S.D. SYKES

Plague Land

(New York: Pegasus Books, 2015)

Subject(s): Middle Ages; Mystery; Murder
Major character(s): Lord Oswald de Lacy, Landowner, Wealthy, Brother (of Clemence), 18-Year-Old; Clemence de Lacy, Sister (of Oswald); Peter, Tutor (of Oswald), Companion (of Oswald); John of Cornwall, Religious (priest)
Time period(s): 14th century; 1350s
Locale(s): Somershill, West Kent

Summary: In a world ravaged by the deaths of millions by plague, one death at the hands of something even more sinister may be the undoing of Oswald de Lacy. Living in a monastery in 14-century England, Oswald has survived the Black Death, a scourge that has claimed the lives of his father and brothers. Now the new Lord of Somerhill Manor, Oswald returns home with no idea how to manage an estate or deal with the changes years of pestilence have had on his village. One of his first tasks is dealing with the murder of a young woman—an act the local priest claims was committed by demons. Oswald knows that's not the case, but finding the human killer may prove to be more deadly than the plague itself. Oswald's mission is made more pressing by the discovery of a second young victim. He relies upon another holy man, a brother, as he fights fear and superstition among the people. First novel.

Other books you might like:
Bernard Cornwell, *1356*, 2013
Bernard Cornwell, *Vagabond*, 2002
P.C. Doherty, *The Nightingale Gallery*, 1991
Paul Doherty, *The Book of Fires*, 2015
Ken Follett, *World Without End*, 2007
Susanna Gregory, *An Unholy Alliance*, 1996
Cora Harrison, *Verdict of the Court*, 2014
Karen Maitland, *Company of Liars*, 2008
Candace M. Robb, *The Riddle of St. Leonard's*, 1997
Barry Unsworth, *Morality Play*, 1995
Brenda Rickman Vantrease, *The Illuminator*, 2005
Jeri Westerson, *Veil of Lies*, 2008
Connie Willis, *Doomsday Book*, 1992

258

DAVID C. TAYLOR

Night Life

(New York: Forge Books, 2015)

Story type: Mystery; Serial Killer
Subject(s): Mystery; Detective fiction; Crime
Major character(s): Michael Cassidy, Detective—Police; Frank Costello, Organized Crime Figure (Mafia boss), Godfather (of Michael); Alexander Ingram, Dancer, Crime Victim; Dylan McCue, Woman, Neighbor (of Michael)
Time period(s): 20th century; 1950s (1954)
Locale(s): New York, New York

Summary: Michael Cassidy is a New York City cop who plays by his own rules. He has a mobster for a godfather, and he has been known to use excessive violence when he feels the situation calls for it. It is 1954, and Joe McCarthy's campaign against American Communists is in full swing. The political atmosphere in the country is tense, and tensions are also rising in the city, where a murderer is targeting young men. Alexander Ingram is the latest victim. A Broadway performer, Ingram was tortured and killed in his Hell's Kitchen apartment. Cassidy investigates the crime, but he isn't the only one involved in the Ingram case. Federal authorities and the Mafia also have an interest in Ingram's death—but why? As Cassidy searches for a serial murderer, he also looks into another mystery. This one concerns a woman named Dylan McCue who has recently become Cassidy's neighbor.

Other books you might like:
Malcolm Brooks, *Painted Horses*, 2014
Pete Hamill, *Loving Women: A Novel of the Fifties*, 1989
Janice Y.K. Lee, *The Piano Teacher: A Novel*, 2008
Francine Mathews, *Too Bad to Die*, 2015
Jayne Anne Phillips, *Lark and Termite: A Novel*, 2009
Philip Roth, *Indignation*, 2008

259

DAVID THOMAS

Ostland

(New York: Quercus, 2013)

Story type: Historical - World War II
Subject(s): Holocaust, 1933-1945; Germans; Suspense
Major character(s): Georg Heuser, Detective—Police (of Murder Squad), Military Personnel (Nazi soldier), Fugitive; Paula Siebert, Lawyer
Time period(s): 20th century; 1940s-1960s
Locale(s): Germany; Russia

Summary: German police detective Georg Heuser joins the Murder Squad in an attempt to rise through the ranks of the SS. On Heuser's first case, he helps to capture a serial killer who has murdered six women on the S-Bahn trains. Thanks to his assistance in the capture, the SS sends him to Ostland, where thousands of Jewish people are killed during the war. In the years following World War II, Heuser attempts to bury his deeds, hoping to forget the atrocities for which he is responsible. However, when searching the Soviet archives, lawyer Paula Siebert learns of the crimes committed by Heuser and his comrades. As Siebert attempts to track him down, Heuser uses the skills he learned as a detective to hide his tracks and distance himself from his former conspirators. This novel by David Thomas is based on a true story.

Other books by the same author:
Blood Relative, 2011
Girl, 1995

Other books you might like:
Jussi Adler-Olsen, *The Alphabet House*, 2014
Harold Nebenzal, *Cafe Berlin*, 1992
Sofi Oksanen, *When the Doves Disappeared*, 2015
Michael Pye, *The Pieces from Berlin*, 2003
David L. Robbins, *The End of War*, 2000
Leonard B. Scott, *The Iron Men*, 1993
Robert Wilson, *The Company of Strangers*, 2001

260

SAM THOMAS

The Witch Hunter's Tale

(London: St. Martin's Press, 2015)

Series: Midwife's Tale Series. Book 3
Story type: Mystery
Subject(s): Puritans; Crime; Murder
Major character(s): Bridget Hodgson, Midwife, Detective—Amateur, Co-worker (of Martha), Aunt (of Will, Joseph); Martha Hawkins, Midwife, Co-worker (of Bridget); Will Hodgson, Nephew (of Bridget), Crime Suspect, Brother (of Joseph); Joseph Hodgson, Brother (of Will), Nephew (of Bridget); Rebecca Hooke, Enemy (of Bridget), Midwife (former)
Time period(s): 17th century; 1645
Locale(s): York, England

Summary: Strange things are afoot in 17th-century England. A harsh winter has whipped the citizens of York into a frenzy, and they are looking to blame their troubles on witchcraft. When a poor, old woman is hanged as a witch, midwife Bridget Hodgson discovers the evidence against the woman was trumped up by Bridget's power-hungry nephew, Joseph, and her nemesis, Rebecca Hooke. Together, Joseph and Rebecca are furthering their ambitions by manipulating a fearful public into believing witches are all around them. As the witch trials continue, Bridget's nephew Will —Joseph's own brother—is accused of murder and sentenced to die. But clearing his name and stopping the slaughter of innocent people proves to be difficult, because one accusation may mean death for Bridget as well. This is the third book in Sam Thomas's Midwife's Tale series.

Other books by the same author:
The Harlot's Tale, 2014
The Midwife's Tale, 2013

Other books you might like:
Ronan Bennett, *Havoc in Its Third Year*, 2004

P.C. Doherty, *Satan's Fire*, 1996
Susanna Gregory, *Mystery in the Minster*, 2012
Margaret Lawrence, *The Burning Bride*, 1998
Margaret Lawrence, *Hearts and Bones*, 1996
Stephen Lewis, *The Dumb Shall Sing*, 1999
Stephen Lewis, *The Sea Hath Spoken*, 2001
James Morrow, *The Last Witchfinder*, 2006
Fiona Mountain, *Lady of the Butterflies*, 2009
Candace M. Robb, *The Cross-Legged Knight*, 2003
Victoria Thompson, *Murder on Astor Place*, 1999
Peter Turnbull, *Fear of Drowning*, 2000

261

WILL THOMAS

Anatomy of Evil

(New York: Minotaur Books, 2015)

Series: Barker and Llewelyn Series. Book 7
Story type: Mystery; Series
Subject(s): Mystery; Murder; History
Major character(s): Cyrus Barker, Detective—Private, Employer (of Llewelyn); Thomas Llewelyn, Assistant (of Barker)
Time period(s): 19th century; 1880s (1888)
Locale(s): London, England

Summary: In this historical mystery by Will Thomas, the seventh in the Barker and Llewelyn series, a murderer known only as the Whitechapel Killer is brutally attacking women in 1888 London. Scotland Yard is having no luck tracking down the perpetrator, so they bring in private investigator Cyrus Barker and his assistant Thomas Llewelyn. Barker and Llewellyn are to consult on the case and act as liaisons with the royal family. The two have never before seen murders quite like this—or faced a killer with such an ability to evade detection. But time is running out, and if Barker and Llewellyn are not able to capture the Whitechapel Killer in time, there may be disastrous consequences.

Other books by the same author:
Fatal Enquiry, 2014
The Hellfire Conspiracy, 2007
The Limehouse Text, 2006
To Kingdom Come, 2005
Some Danger Involved, 2004

Other books you might like:
Tasha Alexander, *A Fatal Waltz*, 2008
Jonathan Barnes, *The Somnambulist*, 2007
Michael Cox, *The Glass of Time*, 2008
Michel Faber, *The Crimson Petal and the White*, 2002
Anne Perry, *Buckingham Palace Gardens: A Novel*, 2008

262

MIKE THOMPSON

Wolf Point

(Farmington Hills, Michigan: Five Star Publishing, 2015)

Series: Andy Larson Frontier Mystery Series. Book 2
Story type: Historical - Roaring Twenties

Subject(s): Prohibition; Law enforcement; Crime
Major character(s): Andy Larson, Lawman
Time period(s): 20th century; 1920s
Locale(s): Wolf Point, Montana

Summary: Wolf Point, Montana, is a dangerous place at the height of Prohibition. An ideal location for bootleggers looking to smuggle their illegal liquor across the Canadian border into the United States, the town has become the scene of an all-out war between different criminal outfits keen on staking their claim on the territory. After Wolf Point's police chief and sheriff are both gunned down, Andy Larson arrives in town determined to restore law and order at long last. Larson, who recently survived a potentially fatal run-in with notorious Chicago mobster Al Capone, takes over the reigns as sheriff alongside a new police chief, who brings his own ideas and methods into the fracas. With continued shootings and bombings, and bootleggers who are willing to try just about anything to move their product and make some dough, Larson is faced with seemingly impossible odds that even he might not be able to overcome.

Other books by the same author:
Curse of Al Capone's Gold, 2008

Other books you might like:
Clive Cussler, *The Bootlegger*, 2014
Nicholas Evans, *The Divide*, 2005
Dorothy Garlock, *By Starlight*, 2012
Dennis Lehane, *Live by Night*, 2012
Nora Roberts, *Chasing Fire*, 2011

263

CHARLES TODD (Pseudonym of Caroline Todd and Charles Todd)

A Fine Summer's Day

(New York: HarperCollins, 2015)

Series: Inspector Ian Rutledge Series. Book 17
Story type: Mystery
Subject(s): World War I, 1914-1918; Detective fiction; Scotland
Major character(s): Ian Rutledge, Detective—Police, Fiance(e) (of Jean); Jean Gordon, Fiance(e) (of Ian); Hamish MacLeod, Military Personnel
Time period(s): 20th century; 1910s (1914)
Locale(s): London, England

Summary: On a June day in 1914, Scotland Yard inspector Ian Rutledge asks his beloved Jean Gordon to marry him. Despite the misgivings of his family and friends of Jean's intentions, Ian in is love and this is one of the happiest moments of his life. But two other events on this day will have profound and tragic impacts on Ian. In another part of England, a woman's death sets off a chain of events that will drag him into a perplexing case of murder. Meanwhile, hundreds of miles away, a political assassination will come to have even more deadly repercussions. As a skittish nation braces for war, Ian must solve one last case before his life changes forever. This is the 17th book in Charles Todd's Inspector Ian Rutledge series.

Other books by the same author:
Hunting Shadows, 2014
The Maharani's Pearls, 2014
A Duty to the Dead, 2009
Wings of Fire, 1998
A Test of Wills, 1996

Other books you might like:
Rennie Airth, *River of Darkness*, 1999
Tessa Arlen, *Death of a Dishonorable Gentleman*, 2015
Alan Bradley, *As Chimney Sweepers Come to Dust*, 2015
Frances Brody, *A Woman Unknown*, 2015
Ken Follett, *Fall of Giants*, 2010
C.S. Harris, *Who Buries the Dead*, 2015
Paula Hawkins, *The Girl on the Train*, 2015
Graham Ison, *Hardcastle's Spy*, 2004
J. Sydney Jones, *The German Agent*, 2015
Laurie R. King, *Dreaming Spies*, 2015
Laurie R. King, *The Beekeeper's Apprentice*, 1994
Edward Marston, *A Bespoke Murder*, 2011
R.N. Morris, *Summon Up the Blood*, 2012
Anne Perry, *No Graves As Yet*, 2003
Jacqueline Winspear, *A Dangerous Place*, 2015

264

DANIEL TORDAY

The Last Flight of Poxl West

(New York: St. Martin's Press, 2015)

Story type: Literary
Subject(s): World War II, 1939-1945; Jews; Family
Major character(s): Poxl West, Veteran (World War II), Writer, Uncle (of Eli Goldstein), Religious (Jewish); Eli Goldstein, Boy, 15-Year-Old, Religious (Jewish), Nephew (of Poxl West)
Time period(s): 20th century; (1980s); 21st century; 2010s
Locale(s): Boston, Massachusetts

Summary: This novel by Daniel Torday tells two stories. In the first, Eli Goldstein looks back on his relationship with his Jewish war hero uncle, Poxl West. Eli is 15 years old in 1986, when Poxl's autobiography—*Skylock: The Memoir of a Jewish RAF Bomber*—is published. Eli worships Poxl and is fascinated by the remarkable story of his escape from Czechoslovakia and his later World War II heroics. The second story in the novel is Poxl's. The text of his memoir alternates with chapters narrated by Eli. Poxl writes about the horrors of the Holocaust, his experiences in Rotterdam, and his adventures as an RAF pilot. But after Poxl's book is published, the validity of his account is questioned. As Eli recalls the events of the book's publication and revisits the memoir as an adult, the truth of Poxl's story is eventually revealed. First novel.

Other books you might like:
Kate Atkinson, *A God in Ruins*, 2015
Jason Hewitt, *The Dynamite Room*, 2015
Stephen Hunter, *Hot Springs*, 2000
Hillary Jordan, *Mudbound*, 2008
Jim Lehrer, *The Special Prisoner*, 2000

James Michael Pratt, *Ticket Home*, 2001
Scott Turow, *Ordinary Heroes*, 2005

265

LOUISA TREGER

The Lodger

(New York: Thomas Dunne Books, 2014)

Story type: Gay - Lesbian Fiction; Literary
Subject(s): Betrayal; British history, 1815-1914; Class conflict
Major character(s): Dorothy Richardson, Suffragette, Writer, Boarder (in boardinghouse), Secretary (at dental office), Friend (of Jane), Lover (of Bertie and Veronica), Feminist; Jane Wells, Friend (of Dorothy), Spouse (of Bertie); Herbert "Bertie" George Wells, Writer, Spouse (of Jane), Lover (of Dorothy); Veronica Leslie-Jones, Lover (of Dorothy), Suffragette, Boarder (in boardinghouse)
Time period(s): 20th century; 1900s
Locale(s): London, England

Summary: Dorothy Richardson is convinced that she can make it in the world without being tied by the bonds of marriage. Yet she finds herself barely scraping by. She is a lodger at a boardinghouse on the seedy side of London and earns a meager wage working in a dentist's office. Dorothy's life begins to change in 1906 when she accepts an invitation to visit an old school friend. Jane has recently married H.G. Wells, an up-and-coming author known as Bertie, who is deeply interested in Dorothy. Despite her friendship with Jane, Dorothy succumbs to Bertie's charms and begins an affair with him. Bertie encourages her in her writing. He also fosters Dorothy's sexual explorations, and in time she begins a relationship with a fellow boarder, Veronica. The women share similar feminist views, yet take different approaches to changing society. Veronica takes the path of activism, while Dorothy pursues her renowned modernist writing, through which she expresses the fear, excitement, and bravery of women's rights during a pivotal time in history. First novel.

Other books you might like:
Sara Gruen, *Water for Elephants*, 2007
David Lodge, *A Man of Parts*, 2011
Carol McCleary, *The Formula for Murder*, 2012
Felix J. Palma, *The Map of Time*, 2011
Susan Sontag, *The Volcano Lover*, 1992
Sarah Waters, *The Paying Guests*, 2014

266

M.J. TROW

The Blue and the Grey

(Sutton, Surrey, England: Creme de la Crime, 2015)

Series: Grand and Batchelor Victorian Mystery Series. Book 1
Story type: Mystery; Series
Subject(s): Detective fiction; Murder; Mystery
Major character(s): Matthew Grand, Detective, Military Personnel (former captain of the 3rd Cavalry of the Potomac); Jim Batchelor, Journalist
Time period(s): 19th century; 1860s (1865)
Locale(s): London, England

Summary: In this first novel in the Grand and Batchelor Victorian Mystery series by M.J. Trow, it is 1865, and Matthew Grand—a former army captain—has been sent to London to locate a person identified as an accessory in the plot to assassinate President Lincoln. Once there, Grand encounters Jim Batchelor, a journalist who has been assigned to cover Grand's investigation and learn the full story of the assassination. But things quickly change when the body of a prostitute is found near the Haymarket Theatre. Grand and Batchelor learn that it is only the most recent murder committed by an individual called the Haymarket Strangler. Grand decides to follow the killer's trail, and it isn't long before he and Batchelor realize there are a few unbelievable connections between the Strangler and Lincoln's assassination.

Other books by the same author:
Traitor's Storm, 2014
Scorpions' Nest, 2013
Silent Court, 2012
Witch Hammer, 2012
Dark Entry, 2011

Other books you might like:
Jan Jordan, *Dim the Flaring Lamps*, 1972
Benjamin King, *A Bullet for Lincoln*, 1993
Jeffrey Francis Pennington, *Lincoln's Assassin*, 2015
David Robertson, *Booth*, 1998
Pamela Redford Russell, *The Woman Who Loved John Wilkes Booth*, 1978

267

FRANCES VIETA

Love in the Land of Barefoot Soldiers

(New York: Yucca Publishing, 2015)

Story type: Historical - World War II; Romance
Subject(s): Archaeology; Africa; Ancient history
Major character(s): Ceseli Larson, Archaeologist, Young Woman
Time period(s): 20th century; 1930s (1935)
Locale(s): Axum, Ethiopia

Summary: Ceseli Larson is a young archaeologist who is determined to unlock the ancient world's greatest secrets even as the modern world is plunging into crisis all around her. In 1935, just after her beloved father's passing, Ceseli sets out for Ethiopia, where she plans to explore the ruins of Axum, an ancient city once ruled by the Queen of Sheba and supposedly home to the long-lost Ark of the Covenant. Unfortunately, her expedition is complicated by Italian dictator Benito Mussolini's forthcoming Ethiopian invasion. The arrival of Mussolini's operatives has unexpected consequences: Much to her surprise, she finds herself falling for an Italian doctor. Though she remains resolute in her desire to make the archaeological breakthrough of a lifetime, doing so will mean somehow balancing her work, her budding romance, and the dangers of the political firestorm that is quickly enveloping Ethiopia.

Other books you might like:
Leslie Epstein, *The Eighth Wonder of the World*, 2006
Irvin Faust, *Jim Dandy*, 1994
Esther Freud, *Mr. Mac and Me*, 2015
Sofi Oksanen, *When the Doves Disappeared*, 2015
Wilbur Smith, *Cry Wolf*, 1976
Evelyn Waugh, *Scoop*, 1938

268

NORAH VINCENT

Adeline: A Novel of Virginia Woolf

(Boston, Massachusetts: Houghton Mifflin Harcourt, 2015)

Story type: Literary
Subject(s): History; Writers; Women
Major character(s): Virginia Woolf, Historical Figure, Writer, Sister (of Vanessa), Spouse (of Leonard); Vanessa Stephen, Sister (of Virginia); Leonard Woolf, Spouse (of Virginia); T.S. Eliot, Historical Figure, Writer; W.B. Yeats, Historical Figure, Writer
Time period(s): 20th century; 1920s-1940s (1925-1941)
Locale(s): Sussex, England

Summary: In this novel, Norah Vincent uses historical details to imagine the life of Virginia Woolf from 1925 to her suicide in the River Ouse in 1941. Vincent considers Virginia's relationship with her family, particularly her sister, Vanessa, and her supportive husband, Leonard. She imagines conversations with the other writers in the Bloomsbury Group, including T.S. Eliot and W.B. Yeats. The author also explores Virginia's perceptions of her own creative process, in particular the struggles she had with her alter ego, Adeline. Adeline was Virginia's birth name, but she separated herself from it after a psychotic break at age 13 when her mother passed away. Virginia had imaginary interactions with Adeline later in life. Through imagined stories and conversations based on actual events, Vincent creates a picture of Virginia's successes and suffering in the last 15 years of her life.

Other books by the same author:
Thy Neighbor, 2012

Other books you might like:
Stephanie Barron, *The White Garden: A Novel of Virginia Woolf*, 2009
Michael Cunningham, *The Hours*, 1998
Clare Morgan, *A Book for All and None*, 2011
Priya Parmar, *Vanessa and Her Sister*, 2014
Susan Sellers, *Vanessa and Virginia*, 2009

269

RONALD J. WALTERS

The Lusitania Conspiracy

(Traverse City, Michigan: Ronald J. Walters, 2015)

Story type: Historical - World War I
Subject(s): World War I, 1914-1918; History; Science

Major character(s): Nikola Tesla, Historical Figure, Scientist; Mark Twain, Historical Figure, Writer, Spirit; Winston Churchill, Historical Figure, Political Figure; Li Yin Huo, Assistant (to Tesla)
Time period(s): 20th century; 1900s-1910s (1909-1915)
Locale(s): *Lusitania*, At Sea; United States

Summary: Author Ronald Walters casts Nikola Tesla, Mark Twain, and Winston Churchill in this novel about the 1915 sinking of the RMS *Lusitania*. Tesla is a scientific genius who intends for his inventions and innovations to be used for the betterment of mankind. But during World War I, the Allies see military potential in Tesla's work. Tesla is assisted by his colleague, Li Yin Huo. Tesla's dearly departed friend, Mark Twain, offers advice to the great scientist from the afterlife. When Tesla and Li find themselves on board the doomed *Lusitania*, they realize they are in a precarious situation. The passenger ship carries civilians, but it also conceals secrets and conspiracies. The British naval authorities may know more than they are letting on about the ship's journey—and the German vessel that is also sailing in the North Atlantic.

Other books you might like:
David Butler, *Lusitania*, 1982
Robert Olen Butler, *The Star of Istanbul*, 2013
Jack Finney, *From Time to Time*, 1995
Anne Perry, *Angels in the Gloom*, 2005
Tad Wise, *Tesla*, 1994

270

ALISON WEIR

The Marriage Game

(New York: Ballantine Books, 2014)

Story type: Historical - Renaissance
Subject(s): History; England; English (British people)
Major character(s): Elizabeth I, Historical Figure (Queen of England), Lover (rumored, of Robert); Lord Robert Dudley, Nobleman (Earl of Leicester), Lover (rumored, of Elizabeth)
Time period(s): 16th century; 1550s (1558)
Locale(s): England

Summary: In this historical fiction novel, best-selling author Alison Weir tells the story of Queen Elizabeth I and her mysterious relationship with Lord Robert Dudley. When Elizabeth is crowned queen at age 25, the unmarried monarch is under constant pressure to marry for the purpose of producing an heir. Determined to rule England alone, however, Elizabeth never intends to marry, but her heart is captured by Lord Robert Dudley, the married Earl of Leicester. Their flirtatious interactions and Robert's appointment to Master of Horse raise speculations throughout the court, fueling rumors of a private romance between Elizabeth and Robert—and whispers of the birth of a secret love child. The scandal intensifies when Robert's wife is found dead, and murder is the suspected cause.

Other books by the same author:
A Dangerous Inheritance, 2012
Captive Queen, 2010
The Lady Elizabeth: A Novel, 2008

Historical

Innocent Traitor, 2006

Other books you might like:
Carolly Erickson, *Rival to the Queen*, 2010
Margaret George, *Elizabeth I*, 2011
Philippa Gregory, *The Virgin's Lover*, 2004
Robin Maxwell, *The Queen's Bastard*, 1999
Jean Plaidy, *Gay Lord Robert*, 1955

271

JOHN WILCOX

Treachery in Tibet

(London: Allison & Busby, 2015)

Series: Simon Fonthill Series. Book 4
Story type: Historical - Edwardian
Subject(s): British Raj, 1858-1947; British history, 1815-1914; Indian history
Major character(s): Simon Fonthill, Military Personnel, Adventurer, Spouse (of Alice Fonthill); Alice Fonthill, Adventurer, Spouse (of Simon Fonthill); Lord Curzon, Ruler (viceroy of India), Nobleman; '352' Jenkins, Sidekick
Time period(s): 20th century; 1900 (1903)

Summary: With the sprawling British Empire veritably at its apex in 1903, it seems unlikely that England could possibly hope to expand its colonial borders any further. At least one ambitious Brit, however, has his mind set on just that. Lord Curzon, the sitting Viceroy of India, is chomping at the bit to invade Tibet, a rugged borderland that is home to the meddlesome Dalai Lama. When Curzon finally grows tired of waging constant border skirmishes with his Tibetan neighbors, he calls in former military expert Simon Fonthill to lead a strike force into the Tibetan capital of Lhasa. With his wife, Alice, at his side, Fonthill heads into the Himalayas and quickly encounters strong resistance from a group of well-armed monks. Worse, after Alice falls into enemy hands, he suddenly realizes that his predicament is far more treacherous that he knew—and in more ways than one.

Other books by the same author:
Bayonets Along the Border, 2014
The War of the Dragon Lady, 2012
The Shangani Patrol, 2010
Siege of Khartoum, 2009
The Guns of El Kebir, 2008

Other books you might like:
Ian Carr, *Sons of Natal*, 2014
Adrian Goldsworthy, *All in Scarlet Uniform*, 2013
Dewey Lambdin, *Kings and Emperors*, 2015
Philip McCutchan, *Soldier of the Raj*, 2014
Wilbur Smith, *The Triumph of the Sun*, 2005

272

JAMES WILDE

Hereward: End of Days

(New York: Bantam, 2015)

Series: Hereward Series. Book 3
Story type: Historical - Medieval; Series

Subject(s): Norman Conquest, 1066; English (British people); Wars
Major character(s): Hereward, Historical Figure (rebel leader), Warrior; William, Historical Figure (William the Conqueror), Royalty (Norman King of England)
Time period(s): 11th century; 1070s (1071)
Locale(s): England

Summary: It's been five years since the Norman victory at the Battle of Hastings, and England is in turmoil, suffering at the hand of William the Conqueror, the country's new and cruel Norman king. England is torn to shreds as villages are destroyed, land is stolen, and innocent lives are taken. The only remaining English stronghold is in the east, and William gathers his army for the final battle of the Norman Conquest. The English have one hope—their fearless warrior, Hereward. He's the only one with the combat tactics to defeat William and reclaim the English crown, but the rebel leader is missing. Will the English find their leader before William makes his final, bloody attack? Set in 1071 England, this is the third installment in James Wilde's Hereward series, a fictional account of the legendary warrior hero.

Other books by the same author:
The Winter Warrior, 2013
The Devil's Army, 2012
The Time of the Wolf, 2012

Other books you might like:
Valerie Anand, *The Disputed Crown*, 1982
Stewart Binns, *Conquest*, 2011
Elizabeth Chadwick, *The Conquest*, 1997
Sile Rice, *The Saxon Tapestry*, 1991
Judith Tarr, *Rite of Conquest*, 2004

273

JACQUELINE WINSPEAR

A Dangerous Place

(New York: Harper, 2015)

Series: Maisie Dobbs Series. Book 11
Story type: Mystery; Series
Subject(s): Mystery; Detective fiction; Crime
Major character(s): Maisie Dobbs, Detective—Private, Widow(er), Daughter (of Frankie Dobbs), Traveler; Frankie Dobbs, Aged Person, Father (of Maisie); Sebastian Babayoff, Photographer, Religious (Sephardic Jew), Crime Victim
Time period(s): 20th century; 1930s (1937)
Locale(s): Gibraltar

Summary: The 11th novel in the Maisie Dobbs series picks up four years after the events of *Leaving Everything Most Loved*. After being widowed and losing the child she was carrying, Maisie has been seeking peace in India. When she gets word that her elderly father is ailing, Maisie decides to return to England. She changes her mind during the journey and disembarks in Gibraltar against the captain's wishes. It is 1937, and Gibraltar is crowded with refugees who are trying to escape the Spanish Civil War. Perched at the entrance to the Mediterranean Sea, the important British territory is also home to a number of Sephardic Jews. When Sebastian Babayoff, a photographer who is a member of that community, is killed, Maisie is drawn into the investigation. As Maisie searches for Sebastian's killer, she attracts the notice of the British Secret Service and is pulled deeper into Gibraltar's complex politics.

Other books by the same author:
Leaving Everything Most Loved, 2013
Messenger of Truth, 2006
Pardonable Lies, 2005
Birds of a Feather, 2004
Maisie Dobbs, 2003

Other books you might like:
Tessa Arlen, *Death of a Dishonorable Gentleman*, 2015
Aileen G. Baron, *A Fly Has a Hundred Eyes*, 2002
Dave Boling, *Guernica: A Novel*, 2008
Rhys Bowen, *Queen of Hearts*, 2014
Alan Bradley, *As Chimney Sweepers Come to Dust*, 2015
Agatha Christie, *Death on the Nile*, 1937
Agatha Christie, *Murder in Three Acts*, 1934
Barbara Cleverly, *A Spider in the Cup*, 2013
Charles Finch, *The Laws of Murder*, 2014
Elizabeth George, *A Place of Hiding*, 2003
Ernest Hemingway, *To Have and Have Not*, 1937
Stephen Hunter, *The Spanish Gambit*, 1985
Laurie R. King, *The Bones of Paris*, 2013
Marek Krajewski, *The Minotaur's Head*, 2012
Rebecca Pawel, *Death of a Nationalist*, 2003
David Plante, *The Foreigner*, 1984
Naomi Ragen, *Ghost of Hannah Mendes*, 1998
David Roberts, *Sweet Poison*, 2001
Dorothy L. Sayers, *Busman's Honeymoon*, 1937
Charles Todd, *A Fine Summer's Day*, 2015
Charles Todd, *Proof of Guilt*, 2013
Nicola Upson, *An Expert in Murder: A New Mystery Featuring Josephine Tey*, 2008

274

ETHAN J. WOLFE

The Regulator

(Waterville, Maine: Five Star, 2015)

Series: Frontier Forensic Mystery Series. Book 1
Story type: Historical - American West; Mystery
Subject(s): Mystery; Detective fiction; Crime
Major character(s): Murphy, Political Figure (Tennessee congressman), Veteran (Civil War); James Garfield, Historical Figure, Political Figure (US president)
Time period(s): 19th century; 1880s (1881)
Locale(s): United States

Summary: The first novel in the Frontier Forensic Mystery series introduces Murphy, a multitalented congressman from Tennessee who works exclusively for President James Garfield. Murphy served as a sharpshooter for the Union Army in the Civil War, and he is familiar with the field of forensic investigation. So when an unknown assailant starts killing off railroad workers in Arizona, Kansas, New Mexico, and Utah, Garfield sends Murphy

to find the murderer. Many victims have already been claimed, and the search area is vast, but Murphy has the skills needed to get the job done. He is an experienced hunter, tracker, and sniper, and he knows how to use the science of his day to solve the crime.

Other books by the same author:
The Last Ride, 2014

Other books you might like:
Howard Bahr, *The Year of Jubilo: A Novel of the Civil War*, 2000
Fred Grove, *Into the Far Mountains*, 1999
Jeffrey Lent, *In the Fall*, 2000
Lisa Lieberman, *All the Wrong Places*, 2015
Stewart O'Nan, *A Prayer for the Dying*, 1999
Stephen Overholser, *West of the Moon*, 2004

275

JENNIFER BORT YACOVISSI

Up the Hill to Home

(Baltimore, Maryland: Apprentice House, 2015)

Story type: Family Saga
Subject(s): History; Family; Social conditions
Major character(s): Emma Miller Beck, Clerk (post office), Spouse (of Charley Beck), Mother (of Lillie); Charley Beck, Technician (US Bureau of Engraving and Printing), Spouse (of Emma), Father (of Lillie); Lillie Beck Voith, Daughter (of Emma and Charley), Spouse (of Ferd Voith), Mother (of nine children); Ferd Voith, Worker (US Bureau of Engraving and Printing), Spouse (of Lillie), Father (of nine children)
Time period(s): 19th century-20th century; 1890s-1930s (1893-1933)
Locale(s): Washington, District of Columbia

Summary: Inspired by the diary of the author's grandmother, this novel follows three generations of a family that lives in the developing city of Washington, DC. When Charley Beck, a technician with the Bureau of Engraving and Printing, marries postal clerk Emma Miller in 1893, he builds a house for his new family. Emma, who is in her late thirties when she weds, has one child with Charley—a daughter named Lillie. When Lillie comes of age, she marries Ferd Voith, and the couple takes up residence in the homestead. Although the house accommodated Emma and Charley's small family easily, it is pushed to its limits over the years as Lillie gives birth to nine children. As the house grows increasingly crowded, and the city and the world change around them, Emma and Charley enjoy happy lives. Emma keeps a record of family events in her diaries, but a tragedy in 1933 changes everything.

Other books you might like:
J. California Cooper, *Some People, Some Other Places*, 2004
Michael Dorris, *Cloud Chamber*, 1997
Louise Erdrich, *The Antelope Wife*, 1998
Alex Haley, *Mama Flora's Family*, 1998
John Updike, *In the Beauty of the Lilies*, 1996

The Tropes of Horror Fiction
by
Don D'Ammassa

No genre can be completely reduced to a small set of storytelling elements. Even such relatively homogeneous forms as romance and westerns include exceptional works that find new ways to rework old themes or even sometimes introduce relatively original concepts. Horror fiction—which largely concerns itself with the supernatural—has become increasingly diverse and sometimes it is even difficult to determine whether or not a particular work should even be included in the genre. Nevertheless, there are various recurring tropes that have persisted through generations of writers and although they may wax or wane in popularity at any given time, they are part of the underlying structure of horror fiction.

The first and probably oldest of these is the ghost story. Ghost stories proliferated in the early works of Oliver Onions, H. Russell Wakefield, M.R. James, August Derleth, even Edith Wharton. They were so common in the late nineteenth and early twentieth centuries in fact that the term "ghost story" was used for almost all horror fiction, including titles that contained nothing remotely like a ghost. Stories such as *The Beckoning Fair One* by Oliver Onions, *The Turn of the Screw* by William James, and *A Christmas Carol* by Charles Dickens made varied uses of the ghost as character. Even *Hamlet* has a ghost. Although immensely popular during the Victorian period and early part of the twentieth century, the ghost story was limited almost exclusively to short forms and as the public taste turned toward novels, they began to fade into a more generalized form of supernatural fiction. In recent years, while ghost stories have declined even further in popularity, a handful of exceptions kept the tradition alive. The most prominent of these was *Ghost Story* by Peter Straub (1979), but there have been several others of note including *Winter Wake* by Rick Hautala and *The Secret of Crickley Hall* by James Herbert (2006).

A distinction needs to be made between ghost stories and haunted house stories. The former refers to a specific individual who has somehow returned from the dead for some specific purpose: vengeance, unfinished business, to watch over a loved one, etc. Haunted houses—or other places—often involve a departed spirit as well, but the supernatural presence is more concerned with location than personality. The disturbances may result from a curse, lingering emotional emanations, or some other cause. A good example of this is *The Shining* by Stephen King (1977). The ghostly presences in the Outlook Hotel are not the spirits of the dead but rather illusions generated by the hotel itself. Some of them represent people who are still alive. Shirley Jackson's *The Haunting of Hill House* (1959) is often incorrectly identified as a ghost story when in fact the strange phenomena are generated by one of the guests/victims rather than ghostly interlopers. Other fine examples of this include *The House That Jack Built* by Graham Masterton (1996) and *Hell House* by Richard Matheson (1971).

The second most popular trope is the vampire, although vampires have changed a great deal since Bram Stoker's *Dracula* appeared in 1897. Vampires appeared intermittently during much of the twentieth century and they were almost always evil, although their nature, powers, and vulnerabilities varied a great deal from one writer to the next. A notable exception was *The Vampire Tapestry* by Suzy McKee Charnas (1980). Her vampire protagonist is a scientist who tries to find more humane ways to satisfy his thirst for blood. Some of the best evil vampire novels from this period include *Fevre Dream* by George R.R. Martin (1982), *Salem's Lot* by Stephen King (1975), *I Am Legend* by Richard Matheson (1954), and *The Hunger* by Whitley Strieber (1982).

The vampire began to undergo a transformation, perhaps starting with the somewhat more sympathetic view taken by Anne Rice in *Interview with the Vampire* (1976) and *Hotel Transylvania* by Chelsea Quinn Yarbro (1979) as well as their many sequels. Vampires began to appear who were tormented by their unnatural desires and sought to ameliorate them in some fashion. P.N. Elrod and Lee Killough inaugurated series about vampire detectives. Other writers posited that vampires were neither evil nor undead but simply another kind of natural creature living secretly among humans. Romance writers adopted the vampire as the symbol of mysterious and powerful eroticism and Stephenie Meyer's Twilight series brought vampire romance to the young adult market. Vampire characters began appearing in urban fantasy series by Laurell K. Hamilton, Charlaine Harris, Tanya Huff, and others. The traditional evil vampire, source of plagues and uncleanliness, has become virtually an endangered species in the modern literature of the supernatural.

The third most popular trope is probably demons and demonic possession, although sometimes the possession is by ghosts. William Peter Blatty's *The Exorcist* (1971), which supposedly is based on real events, led to a shelf load of mostly inferior imitations. One might also include here *Rosemary's Baby* by Ira Levin (1967) and *The Omen* by David Seltzer (1976), which involve manifestations of Satan rather than lesser demons. The demon child is another recurring subtheme used notably in "The Small Assassin" by Ray Bradbury (1946) and several novels by John Saul. Another subset involves the possession of inanimate objects, often dolls—perhaps most notoriously in the series of *Child's Play* movies.

Stories of demonic possession and Satanic creatures almost always are based on Christian beliefs and mythology, but not exclusively. *The Gilgul* by Henry W. Hocherman (1990) is a story of possession told from a Judaic tradition, which is also the basis for *The Sword of the Golem* by Abraham Rothberg (1971) and *The Golem* by Edward Lee (2009). Graham Masterton has featured Native American demons in his Manitou series and Asian mythology for *Tengu* (1983). *Stickman* by Seth Pfefferle (1987) is influenced by African legends as are *The Living Blood* (2001) and *Blood Colony* (2008), both by Tananarive Due. John Ajvice Lindqvist's *Harbor* (2012) makes use of pagan Scandinavian themes.

Zombies are a more difficult subject to discuss because what we currently think of as zombie literature—apocalyptic disasters and flesh eating creatures—is a by-product of George Romero's "Living Dead" movies, which are not about zombies at all. These are more accurately vampires who eat flesh rather than drink blood. The traditional zombie was without will, the slave to the Houngan—a voodoo sorcerer—who restored victims to life in order to use them as servants. Voodoo is a relatively minor theme in supernatural fiction and the only writer who made regular and well researched use of this belief system was Hugh B. Cave, particularly in *Disciples of Dread* (1989), *The Evil* (1981), and *Shades of Evil* (1982). Other interesting novels of voodoo include *Fallen Angel* by William Hjortsberg (1979), which was filmed as *Angel Heart* and *The Darker Saints* by Brian Hodge (1993).

The newer interpretation of the zombie has resulted primarily in slight variations on a theme—a handful of survivors battle against hordes of flesh eating creatures. There have, however, been a few novels that explored the zombie apocalypse from altered viewpoints- often sardonically humorous—or expanded upon the original premise. The best of these include *Dead Sea* by Brian Keene (2007), *Dust* by Joan Frances Turner (2010), *Warm Bodies* by Isaac Marion (2011), and *The Loving Dead* by Amelia Beamer (2010). Younger readers will also find

Never Slow Dance with a Zombie by E. Van Lowe (2009) rewarding.

Werewolves are surprisingly uncommon in horror fiction, perhaps because their nature imposes limits on the plot, which usually consists of a mystery about which of several characters has been infected by the curse. The classic werewolf novel is Guy Endore's *The Werewolf of Paris* (1933), set during the French Revolution. One could also make a good case for including *The Strange Case of Dr. Jekyll and Mr. Hyde* by Robert Louis Stevenson (1886), which is functionally a werewolf novel. Most of the modern werewolf novels of note are those that break away from the conventional story. *The Talisman* by Stephen King and Peter Straub (1984) and *The Wolf's Hour* by Robert McCammon (1989) both have sympathetic werewolf protagonists. Gary Brandner's *The Howling* (1977), Ray Garton's *Bestial* (2009), and Robert Stallman's Orphan trilogy are also excellent. The werewolf, however, has followed the vampire into romance fiction and urban fantasy where they have grown tame and sexy.

Witches and witchcraft also have been been relocated largely to fantasy, in part because there have been good witches and bad witches at least as far back as *The Wizard of Oz* by L. Frank Baum (1900). The classic and still best novel of modern witchcraft is *Conjure Wife* by Fritz Leiber (1952), in which good witches and bad battle for power in an academic setting. Graham Joyce's *Dark Sister* (1992) employs a similar plot for a very different effect. Stories of witchcraft occasionally have made it to the best seller list, as was the case with *The Witches of Eastwick* by John Updike (1984) and the Mayfair Witches series by Anne Rice. They are, however, only a minor element in contemporary horror fiction.

There are several less familiar monsters that recur but which have developed no real tradition within the genre. These include wendigos, gargoyles, doppelgangers, and ghouls. Perhaps surprisingly, mummies too are virtually missing from horror literature. Charles L. Grant's *The Long Night of the Grave* (1986), Joe R. Lansdale's "Bubba Ho-Tep," and Kim Newman's *Seven Stars* stand out but even Anne Rice's attempt—*The Mummy* (1989)—was insignificant. The existence of curses—on families or objects—is a theme used so diversely that it really doesn't constitute a tradition. The most famous example is Edgar Allan Poe's "The Fall of the House of Usher" (1839).

I have avoided two major categories here. Serial killers always were considered a part of mystery and suspense fiction until they became popular in slasher style horror movies, and they now are associated sometimes with horror. Some of the best of these—such as *The Silence of the Lambs* by Thomas Harris (1988) or *Slob* by Rex Miller (1987) evoke many of the emotions of horror fiction, but without the element of the fantastic or supernatural, they are not quite the same thing. The other category omitted is the scientifically rationalized monster—aliens from other worlds, mutations caused by radiation, giant sea monsters or other creatures whose origin is perfectly natural although imaginary. Many of these are in fact effectively horror stories, but they also are science fiction. *The Invasion of the Body Snatchers* by Jack Finney (1954) or *The Tommyknockers* by Stephen King (1987) may be frightening but not in the same way as would be a vampire or a demon.

These stories straddle two genres, as do those involving some variation of nature gone mad. This final category includes suspense, science fiction, and horror and can range from a single creature as in *Cujo* by Stephen King (1982) to a group of associated animals as in Daphne du Maurier's "The Birds" (1952) to nature as a whole in *The Day of the Animal* by Donald Porter (1977). Similarly strange psychic powers may be rationalized as in Stephen King's *Firestarter* (1980) or clearly supernatural as in Charles L. Grant's *In a Dark Dream* (1989).

Although these various tropes rise and fall in popularity, and sometimes shift in some of their details, they remain the basis of the vast majority of modern horror novels. It appears that the things that frighten us most have not basically changed very much over the course of the last couple of centuries, and probably for longer than that.

Recommended Titles

The first half of 2015 has seen a slight resurgence in the number of new novels and story collections involving the supernatural. The popularity of vampires and zombies has diminished noticeably. The best from this period include the following:

The Face of the Earth and Other Imaginings by Algernon Blackwood

Phantoms by Jack Cady

The Doll Collection edited by Ellen Datlow

Harrison Squared by Daryl Gregory

Day Shift by Charlaine Harris

The Shadow Cabinet by Maureen Johnson

Saint Odd by Dean R. Koontz

The Silence by Tim Lebbon

Little Girls by Ronald Malfi

Murder by Sarah Pinborough

Stillwater by Maynard Sims

Positive by David Wellington

Horror Fiction

276

ANIA AHLBORN

Within These Walls

(New York: Simon & Schuster, 2015)

Story type: Supernatural Vengeance
Subject(s): Authorship; Writers; Supernatural
Major character(s): Lucas Graham, Writer; Jeffrey Halcomb, Serial Killer, Leader (cult)
Time period(s): 21st century; 2010s
Locale(s): New York, New York; Washington, United States

Summary: Once upon a time, Lucas Graham was a famous author of biographical crime stories. He was once a household name, but now his career seems to be behind him, just like his marriage, his hopes, and his dreams. When he is given the opportunity to meet with infamous serial killer Jeffrey Halcomb, Lucas is sure he will return to his former glory with a thrilling new tell-all crime book. Lucas is determined to tell the full story about how Jeffrey formed a cult and lured his followers to a remote beach house, so Lucas sets off to that same beach house to soak up the atmosphere. Unfortunately, the souls of Jeffrey's victims are still trapped in the house, and they are angry. Now Lucas must decide how much he is willing to sacrifice to reclaim his fame—is it worth his sanity and maybe even his life?

Other books by the same author:
The Bird Eater, 2014
The Neighbors, 2013
The Shuddering, 2013
Seed, 2012

Other books you might like:
Tananarive Due, *The Good House*, 2003
Stephen Gregory, *The Waking That Kills*, 2013
Graham Masterton, *Picture of Evil*, 1985
Sarah Rayne, *The Whispering*, 2014
Dan Simmons, *Summer of Night*, 1991
Peter Straub, *In the Night Room*, 2004

277

COURTNEY ALAMEDA

Shutter

(New York: Macmillan, 2015)

Story type: Paranormal; Vampire Story
Subject(s): Adolescent interpersonal relations; Supernatural; Extrasensory perception
Major character(s): Micheline Helsing, Young Woman (cursed and possessed), Vampire Hunter, Daughter (of Leonard); Leonard Helsing, Father (of Micheline), Vampire Hunter; Oliver, Computer Expert, Vampire Hunter, Young Man (cursed and possessed); Jude, Young Man (cursed and possessed), Psychic, Vampire Hunter; Ryder, Vampire Hunter, Young Man (cursed and possessed)
Time period(s): 21st century; 2010s
Locale(s): San Francisco, California

Summary: Micheline Helsing comes from a long line of monster hunters, beginning with her most notorious ancestor, Professor Abraham van Helsing, who hunted the infamous Dracula. Now Micheline has followed her heritage to track down and eliminate monsters and ghosts. She has the handy ability to see ghostly sensations surrounding her prey. With the help of a specially designed camera, as well as her teammates—Jude, Oliver, and Ryder—she casts the paranormal out of the realm of the living. When the vampire hunters are stricken with a curse. Micheline must work quickly to cast out the demons within herself and her friends, or they will all perish in just one week. Being possessed causes Micheline serious problems that affect her ability to solve this problem. She is pegged as a rogue and her father, Leonard, takes it upon himself to track her. As she works to convince her dad that she is still on the side of the living, she faces a spirit more sinister than any she has encountered before.

Other books you might like:
Kendare Blake, *Anna Dressed in Blood*, 2011
Bruce Coville, *Amulet of Doom*, 1985
Claudia Gray, *Spellcaster*, 2013
Simon R. Green, *Voices from Beyond*, 2014
Joseph Locke, *Kiss of Death*, 1992
Brian Lumley, *Necroscope: Harry and the Pirates*, 2009
Gretchen McNeil, *Possess*, 2011
Melinda Metz, *Gifted Touch*, 2001

Carol Snow, *Snap*, 2009
Bram Stoker, *Dracula*, 1897

278

KELLEY ARMSTRONG
XAVIERE DAUMARIE, Illustrator

Forsaken

(Burton, Michigan: Subterranean Press, 2015)

Series: Otherworld Stories Series
Story type: Series; Werewolf Story
Subject(s): Werewolves; Fantasy; Horror
Major character(s): Elena Michaels, Werewolf (Alpha), Mother (of Kate); Kate, Missing Person, Daughter (of Elena), Werewolf, Twin, 8-Year-Old; Malcolm Danvers, Werewolf (rogue), Psychopath
Time period(s): 21st century; 2010s
Locale(s): United States

Summary: In this Otherworld series novella by best-selling author Kelley Armstrong, North American pack leader Elena Michaels fights to defeat a rogue werewolf who threatens the safety of her family. Elena was named Alpha of the North American pack three years ago, and even though she's made great strides for women in leadership, some Alphas around the world still question her authority. After difficult negotiations with the European pack leader in London, Elena receives devastating news that one of her eight-year-old twin daughters, Kate, is missing. Malcolm Danvers, a banished pack member with psychotic tendencies, is the prime suspect. Elena and her pack have been tracking Malcom for years, but this time, Elena's not only motivated as a pack leader, but also as a mother—a combination that makes for a wildly dangerous predator. This novella features a number of full-color illustrations by Xaviere Daumarie.

Other books by the same author:
The Calling, 2012
The Hunter and the Hunted, 2012
Frostbitten, 2009
Living with the Dead, 2008
No Humans Involved, 2007

Other books you might like:
Keri Arthur, *Darkness Hunts*, 2012
Patricia Briggs, *River Marked*, 2011
Yasmine Galenorn, *Harvest Hunting*, 2010
Nancy Holzner, *Firestorm*, 2015
Sherrilyn Kenyon, *Instinct*, 2015
Richelle Mead, *Bloodlines*, 2011

279

MINDEE ARNETT

The Nightmare Charade

(New York: Tor Teen, 2015)

Series: Arkwell Academy Series. Book 3
Story type: Fantasy; Young Adult

Subject(s): Boarding schools; Horror; Fantasy
Major character(s): Dusty Everhart, Girl, 16-Year-Old, Supernatural Being (Nightmare), Student—Boarding School (Arkwell Academy)
Time period(s): 21st century; 2010s
Locale(s): Arkwell Academy, Fictional Location

Summary: Sixteen-year-old Dusty Everhart came to Arkwell Academy, a boarding school for the supernaturally gifted, as the school's only Nightmare. To renew her energy stores, Dusty must feed on the dreams of others. She accomplishes this by stealing into strangers' homes and tapping into their nighttime imaginings. Dusty doesn't always like what she sees, however. Since coming to Arkwell, Dusty has been drawn into several mysteries by images she saw in the dreams she stole. Now, in the third and final novel in the Arkwell Academy series, Dusty once again must use her unique skills to prevent a tragedy. This time the enemy is someone Dusty has faced before. At stake are the lives of Dusty's classmates and friends at Arkwell Academy.

Other books by the same author:
Avalon, 2015
The Nightmare Dilemma, 2015
Polaris, 2015
The Nightmare Affair, 2013

Other books you might like:
Rachel Caine, *Black Dawn*, 2012
Steven Charles, *Private School #4: Skeleton Key*, 1986
Melissa de la Cruz, *Lost in Time*, 2011
Rook Hastings, *Immortal Remains*, 2010
Rachel Hawkins, *Miss Mayhem*, 2015
Simon Lake, *Daughter of Darkness*, 1992
Christopher Pike, *The Immortal*, 1993

280

MICHAEL ARONOVITZ

The Witch of the Wood

(New York: Hippocampus Press, 2014)

Story type: Contemporary
Subject(s): Horror; Witches; Witchcraft
Major character(s): Rudy Barnes, Professor (adjunct), Man, Spouse (former, of Pat), Father (of Wolfie); Pat, Woman, Spouse (former, of Rudy); April Orr, Administrator (college), Mother (of Wolfie), Witch; Wolfie, Child (of Rudy and April)
Time period(s): 21st century; 2010s
Locale(s): United States

Summary: When Rudy Barnes, a middle-aged, divorced adjunct professor, arrives at a faculty meeting, he embarrasses himself by ogling the presenter. April Orr is strikingly beautiful, and Rudy can't stop staring at her. After the meeting, Rudy accompanies April to her home where they engage in some rough sex. The encounter leaves Rudy with an unpleasant surprise, however: a painful parasitic infestation. Rudy and April's union also produces a child, Wolfie, but not in the traditional manner. Rudy learns that April is a "witch of the wood," and that she and the other witches are in danger. Now that he has been drawn into April's strange world,

Rudy—along with his former wife and Wolfie—joins the witches' fight against the dark forces that threaten them.

Other books by the same author:
Alice Walks, 2014
The Voices in Our Heads, 2013
Seven Deadly Pleasures, 2009

Other books you might like:
Brenda Jordan, *The Brentwood Witches*, 1987
Graham Joyce, *Dark Sister*, 1999
Fritz Leiber, *Conjure Wife*, 1953
Anne Rice, *Lasher*, 1993
James Robert Smith, *A Confederacy of Horrors*, 2015
Evangeline Walton, *Witchhouse*, 1945

281

DAVID REUBEN ASLIN

Loup Garou: The Beast of Harmony Falls

(North Charleston, South Carolina: Createspace, 2015)

Series: Ian McDermott, Paranormal Investigator Series. Book 1
Story type: Series; Small Town Horror
Subject(s): Monsters; Supernatural; Superstition
Major character(s): Dr. Ian McDermott, Detective—Private, Scientist (cryptozoologist); Bud O'Brien, Lawman (Sheriff); Charlie Redtail, Police Officer (Deputy)
Time period(s): 21st century; 2010s
Locale(s): Harmony Falls, Washington

Summary: A small village in the Cascade Mountains is terrorized by an urban legend that has come to life. The community of Harmony Falls, which lies in the shadow of Mount St. Helens, is shocked when a local lumberjack claims he has been accosted by Bigfoot. Meanwhile, a couple of backpackers disappear, and the townsfolk suspect that the lumberjack's attacker is also responsible for their disappearance. Sheriff Bud O'Brien cannot find a single lead in either case, so he enlists the help of Dr. Ian McDermott. McDermott has a doctoral degree in cryptozoology, and is well-versed in all species of mythological monsters. Sheriff O'Brien isn't convinced that the supernatural is to blame for the crimes in his community, but the evidence soon piles up. Things get even more dangerous and violent in Harmony Falls, and it's up to McDermott to prove that he can handle whatever violent forces are wreaking havoc on the town. This is the first novel of David Reuben Aslin's Ian McDermott, Paranormal Investigator series.

Other books you might like:
Nancy A. Collins, *Walking Wolf*, 1995
Ray Garton, *Bestial*, 2009
Douglas Hawk, *Moonslasher*, 1987
Stephen King, *Silver Bullet*, 1985
Robert R. McCammon, *The Hunter from the Woods*, 2011

282

CHANDLER BAKER

Alive

(New York: Disney-Hyperion, 2015)

Story type: Paranormal; Romantic Suspense
Subject(s): Deception; Friendship; Heart diseases
Major character(s): Stella Cross, Patient (heart transplant), Teenager, Girlfriend (of Levi), Friend (of Henry and Brynn), Young Woman, Student—High School; Levi Zin, Student—High School, Boyfriend (of Stella), Teenager; Henry, Teenager, Friend (of Stella and Brynn), Student—High School; Brynn, Friend (of Stella and Henry), Student—High School, Teenager
Time period(s): 21st century; 2010s
Locale(s): Seattle, Washington

Summary: Teenage Stella Cross has been on the transplant list for years, and despairs of ever receiving the new heart she desperately needs. Finally, though, she receives the organ and recovers from the procedure. With a new heart and a new lease on life, Stella is determined to really live. She starts by dating Levi, the cute and exciting new guy at her Seattle prep school. Unfortunately for Stella, her new heart and boyfriend seem to come with some disturbing side effects. She begins to have dizzy spells, nightmares, and hallucinations. She is in excruciating pain at exactly the same time every day. Because she only feels good, and healthy, when she is with Levi, she craves his presence desperately. She believes they must be together—they are two halves of a whole. Why does Levi affect her this way, and what is really happening with Stella's heart?

Other books you might like:
Aviva Bel'Harold, *Blood Matters*, 2015
Ramsey Campbell, *Creatures of the Pool*, 2010
Stephen King, *Carrie*, 1974
Dean R. Koontz, *Dragon Tears*, 1993
Thomas F. Monteleone, *Serpentine*, 2007

283

CLIVE BARKER

The Scarlet Gospels

(New York: St. Martin's Press, 2015)

Story type: Contemporary
Subject(s): Horror; Good and evil; Supernatural
Major character(s): Harry D'Amour, Paranormal Investigator; Pinhead, Villain, Leader (priest of hell)
Time period(s): Indeterminate
Locale(s): Earth; Hell, Fictional Location

Summary: English horror author Clive Barker pits paranormal investigator Harry D'Amour against demonic villain Pinhead in this horror novel. D'Amour is a detective who specializes in crimes and criminals of the supernatural sort. Pinhead, a character from the Hellraiser franchise, is as evil as they come. But in this confrontation, which according to the author may be Pinhead's last battle, the powers of good and evil will be

Horror

put to the ultimate test. One side will win, but only after a violent and gory struggle. This book is Barker's first novel for adults since *Mister B. Gone*, published in 2007.

Other books by the same author:
Mr. B. Gone, 2007
Coldheart Canyon, 2001
Galilee, 1998
The Thief of Always, 1992
In the Flesh, 1986

Other books you might like:
Richard Kadrey, *Kill the Dead*, 2010
Stephen King, *The Dark Half*, 1989
Edward Lee, *City Infernal*, 2001
Graham Masterton, *Darkroom*, 2004
Peter Straub, *Lost Boy Lost Girl*, 2003

284

AVIVA BEL'HAROLD

Blood Matters

(Calgary, Alberta, Canada: EDGE Science Fiction and Fantasy Publishing, 2015)

Story type: Paranormal; Vampire Story
Subject(s): Vampires; Horror; Friendship
Major character(s): Brittany Watts, Friend (of Emily), Student—High School, Teenager, Vampire; Emily, Friend (of Brittany), Vampire (aka E.V. parasite), Teenager
Time period(s): 21st century; 2010s

Summary: Brittany's friend, Emily, returned at the end of summer a different person. When Brittany finds her friend's corpse, she asks herself why she never asked Emily why she had started cutting, why she seemed so quiet and small—and why she never seemed to eat. Police say Emily committed suicide, and Brittany is emotionally devastated, overcome with grief and regret. She starts to experience odd physical symptoms. She sees Emily everywhere and hears Emily's voice in her head. She is always cold and she has a growing attraction to the smell of blood, along with an overwhelming urge to bite her new boyfriend. Brittany's mere touch raises bruises under others' skin. Her family and friends worry about her strange behavior. Brittany is scared, but she can't stop what is happening to her and what she is becoming.

Other books by the same author:
Safe, 2009

Other books you might like:
Chandler Baker, *Alive*, 2015
Nina Bangs, *Wicked Nights*, 2005
Ray Garton, *Night Life*, 2007
Charlaine Harris, *Day Shift*, 2015
Tanith Lee, *Darkness, I*, 1994

285

ALGERNON BLACKWOOD
MIKE ASHLEY, Co-Editor

The Face of the Earth and Other Imaginings

(Eureka, California: Stark House Press, 2015)

Story type: Collection
Subject(s): Horror; Short stories; Literature
Summary: In this volume, editor Mike Ashley collects 30 short stories and essays by British horror author Algernon Blackwood (1869-1951). The works are representative of Blackwood's early career and demonstrate the scope of the author's mastery of horror fiction and topics. The book's 18 short stories include "The Face of the Earth," which explores the planet as the embodiment of a sentient force, and a ghost tale written in the early years of Blackwood's career. "Down the Danube in a Canadian Canoe" and "The Psychology of Places" are among the 12 essays Ashley chose for the collection.

Other books by the same author:
John Silence: Ancient Sorceries, 2002
The Complete John Silence Stories, 1998
Best Ghost Stories of Algernon Blackwood, 1973
In the Realm of Terror, 1957
The Willows and Other Queer Tales, 1938

Other books you might like:
Joseph Payne Brennan, *Shapes of Midnight*, 1980
M.R. James, *Count Magnus and Other Ghost Stories*, 2005
Stephen King, *Just After Sunset*, 2008
Oliver Onions, *Ghost Stories*, 2001
H. Russell Wakefield, *Reunion at Dawn*, 2000

286

JACK CADY

Phantoms: Collected Writings, Volume 1

(Portland, Oregon: Resurrection House, 2015)

Story type: Collection
Subject(s): Short stories; Writing; Politics
Summary: Resurrection House Publishing remembers award-winning author Jack Cady, author of science fiction novels such as *McDowell's Ghost*, *The Well*, and *Singleton* and short stories such as "The Night We Buried the Road Dog" and "Tattoo," in this posthumous anthology. This collection includes several of Cady's most noted works. In "The Parable of Satan's Adversary," Cady muses on how Satan must go about his work in contemporary times. "The Twenty Pound Canary" looks at the devastating consequences that can occur from experimentation. "Dear Friends" is Cady's letter to the Internal Revenue Service in advance of an audit. The author was the recipient of many awards throughout his career, including the Bram Stoker Award for horror fic-

tion, the World Fantasy Award for fantasy fiction, the Nebula Award for science fiction, and the National Library Anthology Award. Cady died in 2004.

Other books by the same author:
Ghosts of Yesterday, 2003
The Haunting of Hood Canal, 2001
The Night We Buried Road Dog, 1998
The Off Season, 1995
Street, 1994

Other books you might like:
Laird Barron, *The Beautiful Thing That Awaits Us All and Other Stories*, 2013
Tananarive Due, *Ghost Summer: Stories*, 2015
Jack Ketchum, *Closing Time and Other Stories*, 2007
Stephen King, *Everything's Eventual: 14 Dark Tales*, 2002
Robert R. McCammon, *Blue World*, 1989
Thomas Tessier, *Ghost Music and Other Tales*, 2000

287

RAY CLULEY

Probably Monsters

(Toronto, Ontario, Canada: ChiZine Publications, 2015)

Story type: Collection
Subject(s): Short stories; Horror; Literature
Summary: British fantasy and horror writer Ray Cluley presents a collection of short stories that covers a variety of horror themes, from monsters and haunted motels to terrors of the psychological sort. Some of the stories are hardcore horror tales, others are darkly humorous. In "The Festering," the main character conceals her secrets in a drawer—and what a disturbing drawer it is. "Knock Knock" is a traditional ghost tale that takes an unexpected turn; "Shark! Shark!" is a grim but witty account of the making of a shark movie. Set in a creepy motel, "The Travellers Stay" puts an unexpected spin on the haunted hotel story. The collection also includes "All Change," "I Have Heard the Mermaids Sing," "At Night, When the Demons Come," and "Bones of Crow."

Other books by the same author:
Water for Drowning, 2014

Other books you might like:
Dennis Etchison, *Talking in the Dark*, 2001
T.E.D. Klein, *Dark Gods*, 1985
Thomas Ligotti, *Sideshow and Other Stories*, 2003
Scott Nicholson, *Scattered Ashes*, 2008
Jeffrey Thomas, *Doomsdays*, 2007

288

TIM CURRAN

Doll Face

(North Webster, Indiana: DarkFuse, 2015)

Story type: Small Town Horror
Subject(s): Dolls; Supernatural; Rural life

Major character(s): Ramona, Friend (of Soo-Yee, Creep, Chazz, Lex, and Danielle.), Accident Victim; Soo-Yee, Friend (of of Ramona, Creep, Chazz, Lex, and Danielle.), Accident Victim; Creep, Friend (of Soo-Yee, Ramona, Chazz, Lex, and Danielle.), Accident Victim; Chazz, Friend (of Soo-Yee, Creep, Ramona, Lex, and Danielle.), Accident Victim; Lex, Friend (of of Soo-Yee, Creep, Chazz, Ramona, and Danielle), Accident Victim; Danielle, Friend (of Soo-Yee, Creep, Chazz, Lex, and Ramona), Accident Victim
Time period(s): 21st century; 2010s
Locale(s): Stokes, Fictional Location

Summary: The aftermath of a wild party results in an accident that sends a group of friends spiraling toward darkness. Ramona knew that Chazz was too drunk to drive when they first got in the car, but they all let him drive rather than deal with the foul mood Chazz always exhibits when he's told what to do. As they drive into the town of Stokes—a town that seems to pop up right before their eyes—Chazz runs over what he believes to be a person. Now, they are trapped in Stokes, a town they soon learn was destroyed more than a half century ago. As Chazz, Ramona, Soo-Lee, Danielle, Lex, and Creep make their way about the mysterious town, they discover that evil forces are at work. Those forces want to take away their humanity and turn them into dolls.

Other books by the same author:
Leviathan, 2013
Dead Sea, 2007
Hive, 2005
Headhunter, 2003

Other books you might like:
Charlaine Harris, *Midnight Crossroad*, 2014
Nate Kenyon, *Bloodstone*, 2006
Stephen King, *Desperation*, 1996
Dean R. Koontz, *Phantoms*, 1983
Sarah Pinborough, *Tower Hill*, 2008

289

NICK CUTTER (Pseudonym of Craig Davidson)

The Deep

(New York: Gallery Books, 2015)

Story type: Medical; Psychological
Subject(s): Horror; Psychology; Suspense
Major character(s): Luke Nelson, Brother (of Clayton Nelson), Veterinarian; Clayton Nelson, Scientist, Brother (of Luke Nelson)
Time period(s): 21st century; 2010s
Locale(s): Pacific Ocean, At Sea

Summary: The human race is on a path to extinction, thanks to a pandemic known as the 'Gets. The disease cause memory loss that progresses until the body forgets how to function. While the 'Gets spreads across the world, a group of scientists is searching for a cure in the deepest region of the Pacific Ocean. A substance called ambrosia that has been discovered in the Mariana Trench could be a cure. The laboratory, Trieste, which is manned by Clayton Nelson and two other scientists, is eight miles below the ocean's surface. The pressure challenges the lab's construction and the scientist's bodies and minds. When contact is lost with Trieste, Clayton's brother, Luke, joins the team that will travel to the lab to find out what's going on. When Luke gets to the Trieste, he struggles to determine which of the horrors he encounters are real, and which exist only in his mind.

Other books by the same author:
The Troop, 2014

Other books you might like:
Greg Bear, *Quantico*, 2006
Jeff Carlson, *Plague Year*, 2007
Leslie Horvitz, *The Dying*, 1987
John Ringo, *Strands of Sorrow*, 2015
James Rollins, *The Judas Strain*, 2007
Frank Schatzing, *The Swarm*, 2006

290

GINA DAMICO

Hellhole

(New York: Houghton Mifflin Harcourt, 2015)

Subject(s): Horror; Fantasy; Humor
Major character(s): Max Kilgore, 17-Year-Old, Student— High School, Son (of Mom), Friend (of Lore); Mom, Patient (waiting for heart transplant), Mother (of Max); Burg, Demon; Lore, Girl, Student—High School, Friend (of Max)
Time period(s): 21st century; 2010s
Locale(s): Eastville, Massachusetts

Summary: Seventeen-year-old high school student Max Kilgore is a good kid. He cares for his mother, who is waiting for a heart transplant, and he works at a local convenience store. But when Max steals a trinket from the store as a gift for his sick mother, the crime lands him in the unwelcome company of a demon. The evil entity, who is named Burg, takes up residence in Max's basement as punishment for his act of petty thievery. Max decides to make the best of a bad situation and strikes a bargain with his unpleasant guest. If Burg can make Max's mother well again, Max will find Burg a house of his own. Max's friend Lore, who had her own run-in with a demonic visitor, helps Max deal with Burg. As Max works to fulfill his end of the deal, he tries to keep the irascible Burg content in his temporary digs.

Other books by the same author:
Rogue, 2013
Croak, 2012
Scorch, 2012

Other books you might like:
Mario Acevedo, *The Nymphos of Rocky Flats*, 2006
Jim Butcher, *Blood Lite: An Anthology of Humorous Horror Stories Presented by the Horror Writers Association*, 2008
David Macinnis Gill, *Soul Enchilada*, 2009
Andrew Harman, *101 Damnations*, 1995
A.M. Jenkins, *Repossessed*, 2007
Michelle Knudsen, *Evil Librarian*, 2014
Christopher Moore, *You Suck: A Love Story*, 2007
Terry Pratchett, *Good Omens: The Nice and Accurate

Prophecies of Agnes Nutter, Witch, 1990
Tammar Stein, *Spoils*, 2013
Rachel Vail, *Gorgeous*, 2009

291

ELLEN DATLOW

The Doll Collection

(New York: Tor Books, 2015)

Story type: Collection
Subject(s): Horror; Short stories; Dolls

Summary: In this doll-themed anthology, editor Ellen Datlow collects 17 horror stories by prominent genre writers that tap into our fears of human replicas of all sorts. Puppets, ventriloquists' dummies, and children's baby dolls are represented in these short stories, which veer from standard doll horror story lines. "Heroes and Villains" by Stephen Gallagher concerns a frighteningly honest ventriloquist's dummy that has recently acquired a new owner. In "The Doll-Master" by Joyce Carol Oates, the narrator is a collector of dolls that come from a macabre source. Pat Cadigan sets "In Case of Zebras" in an emergency room, where a woman who is fulfilling her community service requirement meets a patient with an eerily realistic doll. The collection also includes "Goodness and Kindness" by Carrie Vaughan, "Skin and Bone" by Tim Lebbon, and "Doll Court" by Richard Bowes.

Other books by the same author:
The Best Horror of the Year Volume Seven, 2015
The Cutting Room, 2014
Fearful Symmetries, 2014
After, 2013
Hauntings, 2013

Other books you might like:
Stephen Gallagher, *Plots and Misadventures*, 2007
Richard Kadrey, *Butcher Bird*, 2007
John Langan, *The Wide, Carnivorous Sky and Other Monstrous Geographies*, 2013
Tim Lebbon, *White and Other Tales of Ruin*, 2002
Carrie Vaughn, *Kitty's Greatest Hits*, 2011

292

GUILLERMO DEL TORO
DANIEL KRAUS, Co-Author

Trollhunters

(New York: Disney-Hyperion, 2015)

Story type: Contemporary; Young Adult
Subject(s): Horror; Adventure; Legends
Major character(s): Jim Sturges, Teenager, Student—High School, Friend (of Tubby); Tubby, Teenager, Boy, Student—High School, Friend (of Jim)
Time period(s): 21st century; 2010s
Locale(s): San Bernardino, California

Summary: When a dark secret that has been concealed in San Bernardino for decades reemerges, two unlikely heroes rise up to fight it. High school student Jim Sturges and his friend Tubby seem to be unlikely heroes when it comes to fending off a monster uprising. But when creatures with a taste for human flesh come out of their hiding places to hunt, Jim and Tubby rise to the challenge and assemble a team to defend San Bernardino from the threat. The band of misfits includes monster hunters of both the human and nonhuman variety. Before the creatures arrived, the boys' major worries were phys-ed class and girls. Now they and their neighbors must face a horrifying new reality.

Other books by the same author:
The Fall, 2011
The Night Eternal, 2011
The Strain, 2011

Other books you might like:
Charles de Lint, *Mulengro: A Romany Tale*, 1985
Christopher Golden, *The Ferryman*, 2002
Dean R. Koontz, *Phantoms*, 1983
Graham Masterton, *The Chosen Child*, 2000
John Saul, *The Devil's Labyrinth*, 2007

293

AMANDA DOWNUM

Dreams of Shreds and Tatters

(Oxford, United Kingdom: Solaris, 2015)

Story type: Fantasy; Occult
Subject(s): Fantasy; Rituals; Occultism
Major character(s): Liz Drake, Friend (of Blake); Blake Enderly, Friend (of Liz), Accident Victim, Homosexual
Time period(s): 21st century; 2010s
Locale(s): Vancouver, British Columbia; dream lands, Fictional Location

Summary: Nightmares warn a woman of the dangers threatening her best friend in this urban fantasy novel by Amanda Downum. Liz Drake hasn't heard from her best friend, Blake Enderly, in months, and the nightmares she's having about him are only making her more suspicious. Concerned for his well-being, Liz flies to Vancouver to see Blake and finds him lying in a coma, the result of a mysterious accident. As Liz spends time with Blake's circle of artists and magic-using friends, she feels certain that she's not getting the whole truth behind the accident that injured Blake and took the life of his boyfriend. If Liz is to uncover the truth and save Blake's life, she must make a dangerous descent into the dream lands. Here, she encounters the Yellow King and risks losing not only her mind, but also her life.

Other books by the same author:
The Kingdoms of Dust, 2012
The Bone Palace, 2010
The Drowning City, 2009

Other books you might like:
Ben Aaronovitch, *Rivers of London*, 2012
Amber Benson, *The Witches of Echo Park*, 2015
Dean Koontz, *Saint Odd*, 2015

Laura Resnick, *The Misfortune Cookie*, 2013
Rob Thurman, *Trick of the Light*, 2009

294

TANANARIVE DUE

Ghost Summer: Stories

(Germantown, Maryland: Prime Books, 2015)

Story type: Collection
Subject(s): African Americans; Fantasy; Ghosts

Summary: Best-selling author Tananarive Due delivers her debut short fiction collection, featuring the Kindred Award-winning title novella and 15 additional short stories. From the many ghosts of Gracetown, Florida, to tales of the future to experiences with Otherness, Due's collection combines black family life and history with Afrofuturism. In addition to the title novella, this collection includes "Patient Zero," "The Lake," "The Knowing," "Herd Immunity," "Free Jim's Mine," "Like Daughter," "Vanishings," and "Carriers."

Other books by the same author:
Blood Colony, 2008
Joplin's Ghost, 2005
The Good House, 2003
The Living Blood, 2001
My Soul to Keep, 1997

Other books you might like:
Jack Cady, *Phantoms: Collected Writings, Volume 1*, 2015
Elizabeth Massie, *The Fear Report*, 2004
Peter Straub, *Houses Without Doors*, 1990
Thomas Tessier, *Ghost Music and Other Tales*, 2000
Lisa Tuttle, *The Mysteries*, 2005

295

DAWN EASTMAN

A Fright to the Death

(New York: Berkley, 2015)

Series: Family Fortune Mystery Series. Book 3
Story type: Fantasy; Ghost Story
Subject(s): Mystery; Detective fiction; Crime
Major character(s): Clyde Fortune, Woman, Police Officer (former), Psychic, Girlfriend (of Mac); Mac, Detective, Boyfriend (of Clyde); Rose Fortune, Psychic (tarot reader), Mother (of Clyde); Vi, Psychic (pets), Aunt (of Clyde)
Time period(s): 21st century; 2010s
Locale(s): Michigan, United States

Summary: Clyde Fortune left her job as a police officer to find some peace in her western Michigan hometown. But life with the Fortune clan—which includes Rose, Clyde's tarot card-reader mother, and Aunt Vi, a pet psychic—has been anything but quiet. Clyde is continually pressured to put her own psychic skills to use to solve the plentiful mysteries of the community. When Clyde and her boyfriend, Mac, plan a trip to Mexico, they believe they'll finally get away from Rose and Vi for a bit. Even when their flight is cancelled because of a snowstorm, Clyde and Mac make the most of the situation and check into the Carlisle Castle, a storied old Michigan hotel. Unfortunately, Rose and Vi are at the venue to attend a knitting convention. The blizzard prevents anyone from leaving the hotel, and when a murder occurs, the guests rightly assume that the killer is snowed in with them. Once again, Clyde uses her sleuthing and psychic skills to investigate.

Other books by the same author:
Be Careful What You Witch For, 2014
Pall in the Family, 2013

Other books you might like:
Madelyn Alt, *The Trouble with Magic*, 2006
Juliet Blackwell, *Secondhand Spirits*, 2009
Heather Blake, *One Potion in the Grave*, 2014
Bailey Cates, *Brownies and Broomsticks: A Magical Bakery Mystery*, 2012
Shirley Damsgaard, *Witch Way to Murder*, 2005
Yasmine Galenorn, *Ghost of a Chance*, 2003
Charlaine Harris, *Dead Until Dark*, 2001
Tanya Huff, *Blood Debt*, 1997
Sofie Kelly, *Curiosity Thrilled the Cat*, 2011
Victoria Laurie, *Crime Seen*, 2007
Fred Saberhagen, *A Question of Time*, 1992

296

P.N. ELROD

The Hanged Man

(New York: Tom Doherty Associates, 2015)

Series: Her Majesty's Psychic Service Series. Book 1
Story type: Series
Subject(s): Detective fiction; Psychics; Extrasensory perception
Major character(s): Alexandrina "Alex" Victoria Pendleton, Psychic, Detective—Private, Daughter (of Father); Lord Richard Desmond, Crime Victim, Psychic, Leader (of the Psychic Service); Queen Victoria, Royalty, Historical Figure, Godmother (of Alex); Father, Father (of Alex), Crime Victim
Locale(s): London, England

Summary: In the first novel of P.N. Elrod's fantasy-mystery series Her Majesty's Psychic Service, the author introduces readers to Alexandrina Victoria Pendleton, a.k.a. Alex. Alex is a psychic with an important job at hand; she serves Queen Victoria—who also happens to be her godmother—as the Royal Psychic. When Alex is called to the scene after the local police discover a body, she is shocked to learn that the corpse belongs to none other than her estranged father. Even worse, she knows that, contrary to what the police believe, her father did not take his own life—he was murdered. When Alex's mentor and head of the Psychic Service, Lord Richard Desmond, is also murdered, she realizes that a conspiracy is afoot. Now it is up to Alex to conjure up all of her powers, psychic and otherwise, to protect not only the Queen but also the very organization that Alex holds most dear.

Other books by the same author:
Song in the Dark, 2005
Cold Streets, 2003
Lady Crymsyn, 2000
The Dark Sleep, 1999
Death and the Maiden, 1994

Other books you might like:
Jonathan Barnes, *The Somnambulist*, 2007
Clay Griffith, *The Conquering Dark*, 2015
Susan Griffith, *The Greyfriar*, 2010
Barbara Hambly, *Traveling with the Dead*, 1995
Valerie Martin, *Mary Reilly*, 1990
Sarah Pinborough, *Mayhem*, 2013
Sarah Pinborough, *Murder*, 2014

297

JG FAHERTY

The Cure

(Cincinnati, Ohio: Samhain Publishing, 2015)

Story type: Supernatural Vengeance
Subject(s): Supernatural; Magic; Murder
Major character(s): Leah DeGarmo, Lover (of unnamed character), Veterinarian, Supernatural Being (healer); Unnamed Character, Supernatural Being (resurrected), Lover (of Leah)
Time period(s): 21st century; 2010s
Locale(s): United States

Summary: Leah DeGarmo has a unique magical ability: she can heal people simply by placing her hands on them. Unfortunately, her magic comes with a price, because she must either then become afflicted with whatever the person suffered, or infect another person with the ailment. When a violent psychopath tries to gain an advantage over Leah, he murders her lover. Leah brings her lover back to life, but now she is possessed by the anger she feels toward the killer—an anger that alters her abilities. Leah sets out on a path of vengeance, determined to bring down anyone who ever tried to hurt her, as well as anyone who stands in her way. Her seething fury could prove to be her undoing, and the more she seeks out her revenge, the more she loses her ability to manage her magic. Will Leah ever be able to maintain control again, or will she lose herself completely to the darkness?

Other books you might like:
John Coyne, *The Piercing*, 1978
K.W. Jeter, *In the Land of the Dead*, 1989
Stephen King, *Pet Sematary*, 1983
Thomas F. Monteleone, *The Resurrectionist*, 1995
J.N. Williamson, *Dead to the World*, 1988

298

CHRISTINE FEEHAN

Cat's Lair

(New York: Little, Brown and Company, 2015)

Series: Leopard People Series. Book 7
Story type: Paranormal

Subject(s): Felidae; Human-animal relationships; Supernatural
Major character(s): Cat Benoit, Shape-Shifter (leopard), Woman; Ridley Cromer, Man, Shape-Shifter (leopard)
Time period(s): 21st century; 2010s
Locale(s): Texas, United States

Summary: In the seventh installment of Christine Feehan's Leopard People series, the author introduces readers to Cat Benoit, a woman with a checkered past. Cat finally has fled from her hometown of New Orleans and is lying low in Texas. She is almost positive that she has shed the attention of the man who haunted her for so many years, but now she is haunted by her developing feelings for a new man in her life. Ridley Cromer teaches Cat martial arts, but he wants to teach her so much more. Unfortunately, Cat can't trust him enough to let down her guard. Yet Ridley can sense that he and Cat share a bond unlike most others, one that delves into a deep and primal part of both of them. Ridley wants nothing more than to show Cat how much they have in common, but will they both be put in danger if they decide to pursue this romance?

Other books by the same author:
Dark Storm, 2012
Savage Nature, 2011
Street Game, 2010
Wild Fire, 2010
Shadow Game, 2003

Other books you might like:
P.D. Cacek, *Canyons*, 2000
Nancy A. Collins, *Wild Blood*, 1994
John Farris, *High Bloods*, 2009
Susan Krinard, *Prince of Wolves*, 1994
Melanie Tem, *Wilding*, 1992

299

RHIANNON FRATER

Dead Spots

(New York: Tor Books, 2015)

Story type: Contemporary
Subject(s): Horror; Fear; Grief
Major character(s): Mackenzie "Mac" Babin, Young Woman (26 years old), Divorced Person; Grant, Guide
Time period(s): 21st century; 2010s
Locale(s): dead spot, Fictional Location; Texas, United States

Summary: A woman's journey to her childhood home leads her to a terrifying alternate realm in this novel by Rhiannon Frater. Twenty-six-year-old Mackenzie "Mac" Babin lost the baby boy she was carrying, and in the aftermath of the stillbirth experienced the collapse of her marriage. Overcome by grief, Mac heads to Texas to visit her mother, but almost wrecks her car when a deer darts onto the road. When she stops at a nearby diner, Mac is welcomed by a man named Grant who tells her that she has entered a dead spot. Mac is now in a shadowy place that lies between life and death. Grant helps Mac navigate the dead spot, which is filled with familiar nightmare elements, including evil clowns and creepy vacant buildings. The dead spot also holds horrors that are unique to Mac's imagination, including the specter of her stillborn son. To escape the dead spot, Mac must rely on Grant and her own strength.

Other books by the same author:
Siege, 2012
Fighting to Survive, 2011
The First Days, 2011
Tale of the Vampire Bride, 2009
Pretty When She Dies, 2008

Other books you might like:
Stephen Blackmoore, *City of the Lost*, 2012
Ray Garton, *Zombie Love*, 2003
Brian Keene, *The Rising*, 2003
Joe McKinney, *The Savage Dead*, 2013
Joseph Nassise, *On Her Majesty's Behalf*, 2014
David Wellington, *Positive*, 2015

300

CECILIA GALANTE

Be Not Afraid

(New York: Random House, 2015)

Story type: Occult; Young Adult
Subject(s): Horror; Occultism; Demons
Major character(s): Marin, 17-Year-Old, Student—High School, Teenager, Classmate (of Cassie), Friend (of Dominic); Cassie Jackson, Student—High School, Teenager, Classmate (of Marin), Sister (of Dominic); Dominic Jackson, Friend (of Marin), Brother (of Cassie)
Time period(s): 21st century; 2010s
Locale(s): United States

Summary: In Cecilia Galante's supernatural thriller for young adults, 17-year-old Marin learns she has a connection to a classmate's mystery illness. After her mother's suicide, Marin develops the supernatural ability to see others' pain, which appears to Marin in various colorful shapes and orbs. To keep from growing overwhelmed by the constant barrage of people's suffering, Marin wears dark sunglasses and avoids looking others in the eye. Marin's approach works well until the day Cassie stands up during Mass at their Catholic high school and singles out Marin in what seems to be a seizure-like episode. Cassie's brother, Dominic, believes that Cassie's condition is something far more sinister than epilepsy, and he's certain Marin is somehow involved. Together, Marin and Dominic uncover the truth behind what's ailing Cassie, and what they find is far more devilish than either of them had imagined.

Other books by the same author:
The Invisibles, 2015
The Patron Saint of Butterflies, 2008

Other books you might like:
Mindee Arnett, *The Nightmare Dilemma*, 2014
Aviva Bel-Harold, *Alive*, 2015

Stephen King, *Carrie*, 1974
Melinda Metz, *Haunted*, 2001
Victoria Schwab, *The Unbound*, 2014
Mary Stewart, *Touch Not the Cat*, 1976
Laurie Faria Stolarz, *Return to the Dark House*, 2015

301

YASMINE GALENORN

Panther Prowling

(New York: Jove, 2015)

Series: Otherworld Series. Book 17
Story type: Paranormal; Romance
Subject(s): Ghosts; Werewolves; Vampires
Major character(s): Delilah D'Artigo, Detective—Private, Sister (of Camille and Menolly), Supernatural Being (werecat), Cousin (of Daniel); Camille D'Artigo, Cousin (of Daniel), Witch, Sister (of Delilah and Menolly); Menolly D'Artigo, Vampire, Sister (of Delilah and Camille), Cousin (of Daniel), Restaurateur; Daniel, Cousin (of Delilah, Camille, and Menolly)
Time period(s): 21st century; 2010s
Locale(s): Earthside, Alternate Universe; Otherworld, Fictional Location

Summary: The half-human, half supernatural D'Artigo sisters return in the 17th Otherworld novel. Witch Camille, vampire Menolly, and werecat Delilah are celebrating the grand reopening of Menolly's bar and grill, with a cadre of Earthside and Otherworld patrons in attendance. Delilah, a private detective, has renamed her agency Cat's Eye Investigations and gains an unexpected first client—the sisters' cousin, Daniel. A band of angry spirits is hot on Daniel's tail, and he blames it on a mysterious sword he recently acquired. Delilah and her sisters attempt to understand the sword and its history. The sword traps in souls, and the ghosts following Daniel are trying to make sure the souls stay put. The spirits are adamant that the soul of an ancient king remain captive. The sisters will have to face the spirits and the king if they want answers.

Other books by the same author:
Crimson Veil, 2014
Autumn Whispers, 2013
Courting Darkness, 2011
Bone Magic, 2010
Ghost of a Chance, 2003

Other books you might like:
Patricia Briggs, *Bone Crossed*, 2009
Scott Chandler, *Ghost Killer*, 2001
Jennifer Estep, *By a Thread*, 2012
Kim Harrison, *The Undead Pool*, 2014
Christine Warren, *Big Bad Wolf*, 2009

302

ADAM GALLARDO

Zombified

(New York: Kensington Teen, 2015)

Series: Zombie Apocalypse Series. Book 2
Story type: Apocalyptic Horror; Coming-of-Age
Subject(s): Zombies; Drugs; Schools
Major character(s): Courtney, Girlfriend (former, of Brandon), Student—High School, Friend (of Phil), Vigilante (zombie fighter), Teenager, Drug Dealer (former); Phil, Friend (of Courtney), Teenager, Student—High School; Brandon, Addict (Z drug), Boyfriend (former, of Courtney)
Time period(s): Indeterminate Future
Locale(s): Zomburbia, Oregon

Summary: Courtney is a high school student by day and a zombie hunter by night. She used to work at Bully Burger and sell Vitamin Z, but she quit to fight zombies in and around her fenced community. Some of her classmates dislike her even though she keeps them safe from the zombies. Courtney wants to move from Oregon to New York to attend Columbia University next year, but her dad doesn't want to even hear about it. The zombies have become faster and even more terrifying, but they are the least of Courtney's problems. She has serious boy trouble. From the new member of her zombie fighting squad to her possible boyfriend, Phil, and her Vitamin Z-addicted former boyfriend, Brandon, Courtney has to deal with three guys. Courtney knows one thing for certain, though; she will root out the Vitamin Z and keep it out of Zomburbia. This is the second Zombie Apocalypse novel by Adam Gallardo.

Other books by the same author:
Zomburbia, 2014

Other books you might like:
Harrison Geillor, *The Zombies of Lake Woebegotten*, 2010
David Lubar, *My Rotten Life*, 2009
Diana Rowland, *Even White Trash Zombies Get the Blues*, 2012
Darren Shan, *Zom-B Bride*, 2015
Joan Frances Turner, *Frail*, 2011
E. Van Lowe, *Never Slow Dance with a Zombie*, 2009

303

ALEX GORDON

Gideon

(New York: Harper Voyager, 2015)

Story type: Paranormal; Supernatural Vengeance
Subject(s): Betrayal; Death; Family history
Major character(s): Lauren Reardon, Daughter (of John), Witch, Young Woman; John Reardon, Father (of Lauren), Warlock
Time period(s): 19th century; (1830s); 21st century; 2010s
Locale(s): Gideon, Illinois

Summary: Lauren Reardon is shocked by what she discovers after her father's death: John Reardon wasn't really John Reardon. He had another name and life before she was born. Lauren has just one real clue about her father's mysterious past: an old photo of a town in Illinois. Lauren decides to visit this town, Gideon, but she finds herself being followed by a strange man. The townspeople are unwelcoming and hostile. When some of them start to disappear, Lauren realizes that the town of Gideon and her father have a history that will not stay buried. Lauren is the latest in a long line of witches. Some witches do good things, while others do not. In 1836, the witches did some very bad things, and an evil entity has haunted Gideon ever since. Lauren discovers hidden power within herself—maybe enough power to affect the horrifying legacy of Gideon. First novel.

Other books you might like:
John Farris, *Fiends*, 1990
Charles L. Grant, *Dialing the Wind*, 1989
Daryl Gregory, *The Devil's Alphabet*, 2009
Dean Koontz, *77 Shadow Street*, 2011
James A. Moore, *Blood Red*, 2005

304

SETH GRAHAME-SMITH

The Last American Vampire
(New York: Grand Central Publishing, 2015)

Story type: Alternate History; Vampire Story
Subject(s): Horror; Vampires; History
Major character(s): Henry Sturges, Vampire; A. Grander VIII, Vampire, Enemy (of Henry Sturges); Adam Plantagenet, Vampire (founder of Union of Vampires); Jack the Ripper, Historical Figure; Arthur Conan Doyle, Historical Figure, Writer; Theodore Roosevelt, Historical Figure, Government Official (US president)
Time period(s): 19th century-20th century; 1860s-1960s
Locale(s): England; United States

Summary: This follow-up to *Abraham Lincoln: Vampire Hunter* continues the story of the vampire Henry Sturges in the aftermath of the president's death. Sturges, who became a vampire in Roanoke Colony, is in pursuit of his enemy, a vampire from Europe known as A. Grander VIII. He follows Grander's trail through the decades and across the Atlantic. As he makes his journey, Sturges feeds his primal needs along the way and crosses paths with a number of historical figures. In Victorian England, he meets Jack the Ripper and Arthur Conan Doyle. Later, he meets Theodore Roosevelt and others. With World War I, the Great Depression, World War II, and the Kennedy assassination serving as backdrops, Sturges tries to protect the American vampires from Grander's European threat.

Other books by the same author:
Unholy Night, 2012
Abraham Lincoln: Vampire Hunter, 2010
Pride and Prejudice and Zombies, 2009

Other books you might like:
Les Daniels, *No Blood Spilled*, 1991

P.N. Elrod, *Quincey Morris, Vampire*, 2001
Tim Powers, *The Stress of Her Regard*, 1989
Michael Romkey, *American Gothic*, 2004
Chelsea Quinn Yarbro, *Midnight Harvest*, 2003

305

MIRA GRANT (Pseudonym of Seanan McGuire)

Rolling in the Deep
(Burton, Michigan: Subterranean Press, 2015)

Story type: Fantasy
Subject(s): Horror; Fantasy; Mermaids
Time period(s): 21st century; 2010s
Locale(s): At Sea

Summary: This horror fantasy novella by Mira Grant follows a documentary film crew on its journey to uncover the truth about the existence of mermaids. When the science fiction cable channel, the Imagine Network, hires the cruise ship *Atargatis* to carry a film crew to the Mariana Trench of the Pacific Ocean to gather footage for a documentary on mermaids, the crews never imagine they will actually find real-life mermaids. While deep at sea, the several hundred people traveling on the *Atargatis*, including a group of professional mermaid actors hired by the network, discover that the myth surrounding mermaids is no myth at all. The tragic voyage leads to a bloody battle between the genuine creatures and the performers who imitate them. And before too long, it becomes clear that no one aboard the *Atargatis* is safe.

Other books by the same author:
Parasite, 2014
Blackout, 2012
Deadline, 2011
An Artificial Night, 2010
Feed, 2010

Other books you might like:
Steve Alten, *The Loch*, 2005
Peter Benchley, *Beast*, 1991
Matthew J. Costello, *Beneath Still Waters*, 1989
Charles de Lint, *Our Lady of the Harbor*, 1991
Jeffrey Konvitz, *Monster: A Tale of Loch Ness*, 1982

306

DARYL GREGORY

Harrison Squared
(New York: Tor Books, 2015)

Story type: Contemporary
Subject(s): Horror; Fantasy; Coming of age
Major character(s): Harrison "H2" Harrison, 16-Year-Old, Student—High School, Amputee (lost one leg in boating accident), Son (of Rosa); Rosa Harrison, Scientist (marine biologist), Widow(er), Mother (of Harrison), Missing Person; Lydia Palwick, Student—High School, Classmate (of Harrison); Lub, Boy (half human, half fish)
Time period(s): 21st century; 2010s

Locale(s): Dunnsmouth, Massachusetts

Summary: Harrison "H2" Harrison has a fear of the water—and for good reason. His father was killed in a boating accident that also claimed one of Harrison's legs. Harrison's mother is a marine biologist, however, so 16-year-old Harrison must accompany Rosa when her research takes her to the coastal community of Dunnsmouth, Massachusetts. Rosa plans to study the giant squid that live in Dunnsmouth's waters. Harrison does his best to acclimate to his new high school, which is spooky and somber. When Rosa disappears just days after their arrival, Harrison tries to find out what's really going on in their new town. Two new friends help Harrison with his mission: Lydia Palwick—a classmate—and Lub—a half-human, half-fish boy who shares Harrison's belief that Rosa is still alive. This contemporary horror novel by Daryl Gregory gives a nod to the fiction of H.P. Lovecraft.

Other books by the same author:
Afterparty, 2014
Raising Stony Mayhall, 2011
Unpossible and Other Stories, 2011
The Devil's Alphabet, 2009

Other books you might like:
Robert Bloch, *Strange Eons*, 1978
Don D'Ammassa, *Servants of Chaos*, 2002
Murray Leinster, *Creatures of the Abyss*, 1961
H.P. Lovecraft, *Waking Up Screaming: Haunting Tales of Terror*, 2003
Brian Lumley, *Dagon's Bell and Other Discords*, 1994

307

CLAY GRIFFITH
SUSAN GRIFFITH, Co-Author

The Shadow Revolution

(New York: Random House Publishing Group, 2015)

Series: Crown and Key Series. Book 1
Story type: Historical - Victorian; Series
Subject(s): Horror; Fantasy; British history, 1815-1914
Major character(s): Simon Archer, Magician (spell-caster), Colleague (of Nick and Kate); Nick Barker, Colleague (of Simon and Kate); Kate Anstruther, Magician (alchemist), Colleague (of Simon and Nick); Malcolm MacFarlane, Hunter (monsters)
Time period(s): 19th century
Locale(s): London, England

Summary: In the first novel in the Crown and Key series, Victorian London is home to a population of werewolves. These lycanthropes pose a danger to the Londoners who encounter them on the streets and in the high-society circles they have accessed. Three people have formed an alliance and use their various paranormal skills to combat the threat. Kate Anstruther is an alchemist; Nick Barker, who is definitely lacking in ambition, helps his protege Simon Archer master the use of magic spells. The group's mission becomes personal when a member of Kate's family attracts the unwanted attention of one of the werewolves. Kate, Nick, and Simon seek additional help from Malcolm MacFarlane, a Scotsman who is a

talented monster slayer. But even so, the werewolf situation may be more than the team can handle.

Other books by the same author:
The Conquering Dark, 2015
The Kingmakers, 2012
The Rift Walker, 2011
The Greyfriar, 2010

Other books you might like:
Les Daniels, *Yellow Fog*, 1986
Barbara Hambly, *Bride of the Rat God*, 1994
Valerie Martin, *Mary Reilly*, 1990
Sarah Pinborough, *Mayhem*, 2013
Brian Stableford, *The Carnival of Destruction*, 1994

308

CLAY GRIFFITH
SUSAN GRIFFITH, Co-Author

The Conquering Dark

(New York: Random House Publishing Group, 2015)

Series: Crown and Key Series. Book 3
Story type: Historical - Victorian; Series
Subject(s): British history, 1714-1815; Horror; Magic
Major character(s): Simon Archer, Magician (scribe), Leader (Crown and Key Society); Malcolm MacFarlane, Hunter (monsters); Kate Anstruther, Magician (alchemist); Penny Carter, Expert (technology); Charlotte, Werewolf; Gaios, Deity (demigod)
Time period(s): 19th century
Locale(s): London, England

Summary: In the third novel in the Crown and Key series, the secret society created to defend Victorian England from supernatural threats faces a powerful opponent. Gaios, a vengeful demigod, is planning the destruction of Great Britain, and the Crown and Key Society may be the empire's only chance for survival. The society now consists of Simon Archer, the magician-scribe who serves as the organization's leader; the alchemist Kate Anstruther; and the monster-hunter Malcolm MacFarlane. Penny Carter, a whiz with Victorian-era technology, and Charlotte, a lycanthrope, also bring their expertise to the team. Their efforts hit a major snag when Simon's powers fail. Before the Crown and Key members can save Britain from Gaios, they must find a way to restore Simon's paranormal skills.

Other books by the same author:
The Shadow Revolution, 2015
The Kingmakers, 2012
The Rift Walker, 2011
The Greyfriar, 2010

Other books you might like:
P.N. Elrod, *The Hanged Man*, 2015
Barbara Hambly, *Those Who Hunt the Night*, 1988
Kim Newman, *Seven Stars*, 2000
Sarah Pinborough, *Murder*, 2014
Michael Romkey, *The London Vampire Panic*, 2001

`309`

PAULA GURAN

New Cthulhu 2: More Recent Weird

(Germantown, Maryland: Prime Books, 2015)

Story type: Collection
Subject(s): Short stories; Horror; Fantasy

Summary: In this volume, Paula Guran collects 19 reprints of modern horror short stories, each of which is inspired by the writings of H.P. Lovecraft. In "Momma Durtt," Michael Shea addresses the realities of toxic waste dumps and organized crime. Politics and terrorism are explored in "The Same Deep Water as You" by Brian Hodge and again in "The Litany of Earth" by Ruthanna Emry. In "Equoid," Charles Stross tells the story of a British government agency tasked with protecting the country from the occult. Also included are entries by Elizabeth Bear and Sarah Monette, among others. All of the works contained in this volume were originally published between 2010 and 2014.

Other books by the same author:
Blood Sisters, 2015
Magic City: Recent Spells, 2014
Time Travel: Recent Trips, 2014
Zombies: The Recent Dead, 2010
Best New Paranormal Romance, 2006

Other books you might like:
Laird Barron, *Occultation and Other Stories*, 2010
Richard Gavin, *Mr. Gaunt and Other Uneasy Encounters*, 2008
Caitlin R. Kiernan, *Alabaster*, 2006
H.P. Lovecraft, *Tales*, 2005
John Shirley, *Darkness Divided*, 2001
Donald Tyson, *The Lovecraft Coven*, 2014

`310`

PAULA GURAN

Blood Sisters: Vampire Stories by Women

(New York: Night Shade Books, 2015)

Story type: Collection; Vampire Story
Subject(s): Horror; Vampires; Fantasy

Summary: Edited by Paula Guran, this short fiction collection of fantasy vampire stories includes entries from 25 of the genre's female authors. Many of the writers represented here have given the vampire story genre their own unique spin. Contained in this volume are the writings of a number of best-selling authors, including Holly Black's "The Coldest Girl in Coldtown," Nancy Holder's "Blood Freak," Catherynne M. Valente's "In the Future When All's Well," and Carrie Vaughn's "A Princess of Spain." Also included are "Renewal" by Chelsea Quinn Yarbro and "La Dame" by Tanith Lee.

Other books by the same author:
New Cthulhu 2: More Recent Weird, 2015
Magic City: Recent Spells, 2014
Time Travel: Recent Trips, 2014
Zombies: The Recent Dead, 2010
Best New Paranormal Romance, 2006

Other books you might like:
Holly Black, *Black Heart*, 2012
Suzy McKee Charnas, *The Vampire Tapestry*, 1980
Nancy Holder, *Buffy the Vampire Slayer: Chosen*, 2003
Tanith Lee, *Dark Dance*, 1992
Chelsea Quinn Yarbro, *Burning Shadows: A Novel of the Count Saint-Germain*, 2009

`311`

LAURELL K. HAMILTON

Dead Ice

(New York: Penguin Publishing Group, 2015)

Series: Anita Blake: Vampire Hunter Series. Book 24
Story type: Fantasy; Series
Subject(s): Fantasy; Horror; Urban life
Major character(s): Anita Blake, Supernatural Being (necromancer), Hunter (vampires), Fiance(e) (of Jean-Claude), Investigator (US Marshal); Jean-Claude, Vampire, Fiance(e) (of Anita)
Time period(s): 21st century; 2010s
Locale(s): United States

Summary: In the 24th novel in Laurell K. Hamilton's Anita Blake: Vampire Hunter series, US Marshal and vampire assassin Anita Blake is experiencing an image problem. She has recently become engaged to vampire Jean-Claude, and now some members of the public think she may have softened. This is, of course, absolutely untrue. Anita gets to prove her skills as a hunter of the paranormal when the FBI seeks her help with a zombie problem. The case involves the production of zombie pornography, which is disturbing in its own right. But what makes the videos even more repulsive is the fact that the women aren't all consenting adults or members of the walking dead. Anita believes that the women are under a dark, dangerous spell. As she investigates the zombie porn case further, the details shock even the hardened Anita.

Other books by the same author:
Affliction, 2013
Bullet, 2010
Blood Noir, 2008
Danse Macabre, 2006
Narcissus in Chains, 2001

Other books you might like:
Patricia Briggs, *Dead Heat*, 2015
Karen Chance, *Hunt the Moon*, 2011
Charlaine Harris, *Dead Ever After*, 2012
Nancy Holzner, *Firestorm*, 2015
Seanan McGuire, *Pocket Apocalypse*, 2015
Chloe Neill, *House Rules*, 2013
Diana Rowland, *Vengeance of the Demon*, 2015

Horror

312

KATHERINE HARBOUR

Briar Queen

(New York: HarperCollins, 2015)

Series: Night and Nothing Series. Book 2
Story type: Fantasy
Subject(s): Fairies; Magic; Suicide
Major character(s): Serafina "Finn" Sullivan, Girlfriend (of Jack), Teenager; Jack Hawthorn, Young Man (former fairy), Boyfriend (of Finn), Supernatural Being, Wealthy (aka Jack Fata); Moth, Supernatural Being; Seth Lot, Supernatural Being, Enemy (of Finn and Jack)
Time period(s): 21st century; 2010s
Locale(s): Ghostlands, Fictional Location; Fair Hollow, New York

Summary: In Katherine Harbour's second Night and Nothing novel, Serafina (Finn) Sullivan is still discovering the secrets of magical Fair Hollow, New York. Finn has begun a relationship with Jack Hawthorn, who was a fairy of the wealthy and powerful Fata clan when she met him. Jack is now mortal, and Finn wants simply to enjoy her relationship and live a quiet life, though she knows neither wish is likely to come easily in Fair Hollow. Their earlier actions have earned Finn and Jack the wrath of a vengeful supernatural being. Seth Lot draws Finn into the terrifying Ghostlands with a secret about Finn's dead sister. With Jack's help, Finn attempts to rally some allies, including a mysterious creature, Moth, who claims to have been sent by Finn's sister. As they navigate the Ghostlands, Finn learns more about her sister's suicide.

Other books by the same author:
Thorn Jack, 2014

Other books you might like:
Simon Clark, *Darkness Demands*, 2001
Nate Kenyon, *The Bone Factory*, 2009
Robert R. McCammon, *Usher's Passing*, 1984
Cherie Priest, *Maplecroft*, 2014
Lisa Tuttle, *The Mysteries*, 2005

313

MOLLY HARPER

The Dangers of Dating a Rebound Vampire

(New York: Pocket Books, 2015)

Series: Half Moon Hollow Series. Book 7
Story type: Romance; Series
Subject(s): Vampires; Romances (Fiction); Family relations
Major character(s): Gigi Scanlon, Worker (at Vampire Headquarters), Young Woman
Time period(s): 21st century; 2010s
Locale(s): Half Moon Hollow, Kentucky

Summary: This paranormal romance novel is the seventh installment in the Half Moon Hollow series by Molly Harper. Now all grown up, Gigi begins her job at the Vampire Headquarters and looks for love in the small Kentucky town of Half Moon Hollow. Gigi's well-meaning family and friends fear Gigi's quest for love, however, might lead her into the arms of a seductive—and dangerous—vampire instead of a safe, trustworthy human. But Gigi is not the naive teenager she once was. She's gained some experience and is willing to fight for what she wants—even if it means going against her family's wishes.

Other books by the same author:
The Care and Feeding of Stray Vampires, 2012
Nice Girls Don't Bite Their Neighbors, 2012
The Art of Seducing a Naked Werewolf, 2011
Nice Girls Don't Have Fangs, 2009
Nice Girls Don't Live Forever, 2009

Other books you might like:
Dakota Cassidy, *Accidentally Demonic*, 2010
E.J. Copperman, *An Uninvited Ghost*, 2011
Casey Daniels, *Tomb with a View*, 2010
MaryJanice Davidson, *Dead and Loving It*, 2006
Victoria Laurie, *Fatal Fortune: A Psychic Eye Mystery*, 2014

314

CHARLAINE HARRIS

Day Shift

(New York: Ace, 2015)

Series: Midnight, Texas Series. Book 2
Subject(s): Fantasy; Mystery; Parapsychology
Major character(s): Olivia Charity, Woman; Lemuel, Vampire; Manfred Bernardo, Psychic
Time period(s): 21st century; 2010s
Locale(s): Midnight, Texas

Summary: The small town of Midnight, Texas, is home to an assortment of unusual characters. Manfred Bernardo, a psychic, is one of those Midnight residents who likes to mind his own business. Yet he can't help but be intrigued by Olivia Charity, who shares a home with a vampire named Lemuel. Manfred crosses paths with the mysterious Olivia when he travels to Dallas to meet with a rich client. He sees Olivia with a man and woman, and then learns the next day that the couple is dead. But Manfred soon has troubles of his own. A client dies in the middle of a reading, and Manfred finds himself in the spotlight. As a scandal grows, Manfred seeks help from Olivia. Although Manfred isn't sure what line of work Olivia is in, he suspects she may be able to solve his unpleasant problem. This novel is the second in the Midnight, Texas series by Charlaine Harris.

Other books by the same author:
Midnight Crossroad, 2014
Dead Ever After, 2013
Deadlocked, 2012
Grave Secret, 2009
Grave Surprise, 2006

Other books you might like:
Aviva Bel'Harold, *Blood Matters*, 2015

Patricia Briggs, *Frost Burned*, 2013
Laurell K. Hamilton, *Hit List*, 2011
Laurell K. Hamilton, *Jason*, 2014
Kim Harrison, *A Perfect Blood*, 2012
Faith Hunter, *Black Arts*, 2014
Chloe Neill, *Dark Debt*, 2015
Eileen Wilks, *Blood Challenge*, 2011

315

CHRISTINA HENRY

Alice

(New York: Penguin Random House, 2015)

Story type: Fantasy; Literary
Subject(s): Fairy tales; Rabbits; Mental disorders
Major character(s): Alice, Amnesiac, Patient, Runaway; Rabbit, Rabbit
Time period(s): Indeterminate
Locale(s): Old City, Fictional Location

Summary: In this reimagined form of Lewis Carroll's classic tale *Alice in Wonderland*, author Christina Henry tells the story of a young woman, stricken with amnesia, who is locked away in a mental hospital. The woman has no knowledge of why she is imprisoned, but she remembers some of the occurrences that preceded her stay. These disjointed memories include a table set for tea and a party that went horrifyingly awry, as well as a mysterious rabbit who may be her ally or her adversary. Alice senses that the rabbit is the key to learning exactly what happened to her, so when the hospital catches fire one fateful night, she takes the opportunity to flee. Alice hides in the Old City, a grey and desolate place filled with downtrodden and dismal people. There, she seeks out the rabbit and the knowledge of her true identity. Unfortunately, sinister forces are tracking Alice, and she must face them if she is ever going to discover the facts about who she is and where she comes from.

Other books by the same author:
Black Spring, 2014
Black City, 2013
Black Howl, 2012
Black Night, 2011
Black Wings, 2010

Other books you might like:
Ramsey Campbell, *The Nameless*, 1981
John Coyne, *Fury*, 1989
Dean R. Koontz, *The Face*, 2003
John Ajvide Lindqvist, *Little Star*, 2012
T.M. Wright, *Cold House*, 2003

316

WILL HILL

Zero Hour

(New York: HarperCollins Children's Books, 2015)

Series: Department 19 Series. Book 4
Story type: Adventure; Series

Subject(s): Horror; Adventure; Vampires
Major character(s): Jamie Carpenter, Teenager, Agent (Department 19); Valentin Rusmanov, Friend (ally of Department 19); Dracula, Vampire; Matt Browning, Agent (Department 19); Larissa Kinley, Agent (Department 19), Vampire
Time period(s): 21st century; 2010s
Locale(s): United States

Summary: When British teenager Jamie Carpenter joined the secret government agency known as Department 19, he entered a world in which figures portrayed in horror novels are very real. Frankenstein's monster and the vampire Dracula have played crucial roles in England's history and continue to do so. Vampirism poses a constant threat, and vampire hunters—such as Jamie's late father—are needed to battle Dracula and his forces. Armed with the truth, Jamie and other Department 19 operatives are on a continual search for a cure for vampirism and a way to neutralize the vampires. In this novel, the fourth in the series, the department finally has a reason to be optimistic. Matt Browning follows one lead to the United States while Jamie and Larissa Kinley travel to Eastern Europe. There they hope to find an ancient remedy to the Dracula problem.

Other books by the same author:
Darkest Night, 2015
Battle Lines, 2013
The Devil in No Man's Land, 2013
The Rising, 2012

Other books you might like:
Carmen Adams, *Song of the Vampire*, 1996
Amelia Atwater-Rhodes, *Demon in My View*, 2000
Justin Gustainis, *Black Magic Woman*, 2008
John Ajvide Lindqvist, *Let the Right One In*, 2007
Kat Richardson, *Vanished*, 2009

317

WILL HILL

Darkest Night

(New York: HarperCollins Children's Books, 2015)

Series: Department 19 Series. Book 5
Story type: Adventure; Series
Subject(s): Horror; Adventure; Vampires
Major character(s): Jamie Carpenter, Teenager, Agent (Department 19); Matt Browning, Agent (Department 19); Larissa Kinley, Agent (Department 19), Vampire; Dracula, Vampire
Time period(s): 21st century; 2010s
Locale(s): England

Summary: In the fifth and final novel in the Department 19 series, the operatives of the agency that deals with supernatural threats face the aftermath of Zero Hour. That deadline has passed, and now the public is aware of the terrifying truth: vampires are real and, led by Dracula, pose a deadly threat to the world's human population. Teenager Jamie Carpenter and other Department 19 agents have fought a long battle against the vampires, but Dracula is now more powerful than ever. The fight has taken its toll on Jamie and his friends, who are also dealing with personal issues. Those who have just learned about the long-kept secret are in a panic. The human race is headed toward a showdown with the bloodthirsty Dracula, and the outcome of the conflict could change the course of history.

Other books by the same author:
Zero Hour, 2015
Battle Lines, 2013
The Devil in No Man's Land, 2013
The Rising, 2012

Other books you might like:
P.N. Elrod, *Lady Crymsyn*, 2000
Christopher Pike, *Night of the Vampire*, 1997
Garfield Reeves-Stevens, *Bloodshift*, 1981
Michael Romkey, *The Vampire Princess*, 1996
Anton Strout, *Deader Still*, 2009

318

NANCY HOLZNER

Firestorm

(New York: Penguin Publishing Group, 2015)

Series: Deadtown Series. Book 6
Story type: Fantasy; Series
Subject(s): Horror; Fantasy; Urban life
Major character(s): Vicky Vaughn, Assassin (demon slayer); Ceridwen, Deity (goddess)
Time period(s): 21st century; 2010s
Locale(s): Boston, Massachusetts

Summary: In the 21st century, Boston is home to an assortment of supernatural entities. A section of the city, called Deadtown, has been set aside especially for this population of monsters, demons, and zombies. Vicky Vaughn, a demon hunter by trade, is familiar with Boston's paranormal happenings. She has taken on many demons in the past, and she made a protective bargain with the deity Ceridwen. Now Vicky is drawn into a battle between the two powerful forces that want to control her. And that's not the only issue that demands Vicky's attention. A demonic presence has let loose a series of supernatural attacks, leaving some of Boston's prominent landmarks infested with goblins, imps, and other unsavory creatures. As the chaos escalates, Vicky realizes she may have to make an impossible choice. This novel is the sixth in the Deadtown series.

Other books by the same author:
Hellhound, 2013
Darklands, 2012
Bloodstone, 2011
Hellforged, 2011
Deadtown, 2010

Other books you might like:
Kelley Armstrong, *Forsaken*, 2015
Jeaniene Frost, *Bound by Flames*, 2015
Chris Marie Green, *The Path of Razors*, 2009
Laurell K. Hamilton, *Dead Ice*, 2015
Sherrilyn Kenyon, *Bad Moon Rising*, 2009

319

RHYS HUGHES

Bone Idle in the Charnel House: A Collection of Weird Stories

(New York: Hippocampus Press, 2014)

Story type: Collection
Subject(s): Horror; Short stories; Literature
Summary: In this volume, Welsh author Rhys Hughes presents a collection of 20 horror stories, some of which are published here for the first time. In "Happiness Leasehold," a rich man is shocked when he learns the true source of his wealth—and that his good fortune has an expiration date. The residents of a small Welsh village face dark supernatural threats in "Sigma Octantis." "The Hydrothermal Reich" revisits the Nazi era and reveals surprising details of Hitler's world takeover plot. The collection also includes "The Old House Under the Snow," "What I Fear Most," "Vampiric Gramps," "Smuggling Old Nick to Newfoundland," and the title story.

Other books by the same author:
Tallest Stories, 2015

Other books you might like:
Gary A. Braunbeck, *Destinations Unknown*, 2006
Dennis Etchison, *The Death Artist*, 2000
Charles L. Grant, *Nightmare Seasons*, 1982
Tim Lebbon, *Fears Unnamed*, 2004
Simon Strantzas, *Nightingale Songs*, 2011
Mark Teppo, *Thirteen: Stories of Transformation*, 2015

320

FAITH HUNTER

Dark Heir

(New York: Roc, 2015)

Series: Jane Yellowrock Series. Book 9
Story type: Series; Urban
Subject(s): Vampires; Supernatural; Fantasy
Major character(s): Jane Yellowrock, Supernatural Being (skinwalker), Shape-Shifter, Hunter (of vampires)
Time period(s): 21st century; 2010s
Locale(s): New Orleans, Louisiana

Summary: This urban fantasy novel by best-selling author Faith Hunter is the ninth book in her Jane Yellowrock series. Jane Yellowrock is no stranger to slaying vampires. A shapeshifting skinwalker, Jane is the best in her field, but when the city of New Orleans is threatened by one of the most powerful vampire witches of the European Council, Jane and her team at Yellowrock Securities might be in over their heads. The witches of the European Council have the power to create wars and control governments, but it doesn't take long for Jane to realize the attack on New Orleans is a personal one—and possibly more than even she can handle.

Other books by the same author:
Black Arts, 2014

Blood Trade, 2013
Death's Rival, 2012
Mercy Blade, 2011
Blood Cross, 2010

Other books you might like:
Anne Bishop, *Murder of Crows*, 2014
Patricia Briggs, *Night Broken*, 2014
Nalini Singh, *Archangel's Storm*, 2012
Carrie Vaughn, *Low Midnight*, 2014
Eileen Wilks, *Death Magic*, 2011

321

CHASE J. JACKSON

Whispers in the Dark

(Atlanta, Georgia: BQB Publishing, 2015)

Story type: Paranormal
Subject(s): Schools; Boarding schools; Twins
Major character(s): Adrian Ramirez, Teacher, Boyfriend (of Lea); Lea, Girlfriend (of Adrian); Robin, Sister (of Raven), Twin (of Raven), Student—Boarding School; Raven, Sister (of Robin), Twin (of Robin), Student—Boarding School
Time period(s): 21st century; 2010s
Locale(s): Newnan, Georgia

Summary: When Adrian Ramirez receives a job offer to teach at a private school in the town in which he grew up, he cannot believe his luck. Adrian moves home with his girlfriend, Lea, and begins his tenure at Finley Academy. The upscale school hides a secret behind its ivy-covered walls, however, and Adrian finds himself troubled by some unusual occurrences. Several students drop out soon after he begins teaching there, and a set of twin sisters named Raven and Robin seem to be behind some of the happenings. Adrian takes it upon himself to uncover the mysteries that haunt the halls of Finley Academy. When he is blamed for a student's mental illness, he realizes the importance of learning exactly what it is that the school, and Robin and Raven, are hiding. Unfortunately, it may be too late, and he may have to risk his life to stop the forces that threaten the academy.

Other books you might like:
Rachel Caine, *Bitter Blood*, 2012
Ramsey Campbell, *Ancient Images*, 1989
Bentley Little, *The Academy*, 2008
Graham Masterton, *Garden of Evil*, 2012
T.M. Wright, *Sleepeasy*, 1993

322

MAUREEN JOHNSON

The Shadow Cabinet

(New York: G.P. Putnam's Sons Books for Young Readers, 2015)

Series: Shades of London Series. Book 3
Subject(s): Horror; Mystery; Ghosts
Major character(s): Rory Deveaux, Girl, Teenager, Student—Boarding School, Hunter (ghosts), Friend (of Charlotte); Charlotte, Friend (of Rory), Kidnap Victim; Jane, Therapist (of Rory and Charlotte), Kidnapper, Cult Member; Stephen, Detective—Police (ghost squad), Spirit (ghost); Callum, Friend (of Rory); Boo, Friend (of Rory)
Time period(s): 21st century; 2010s
Locale(s): London, England

Summary: In the third novel in the Shades of London series, Louisiana native Rory Deveaux and her friends leave their London boarding school to investigate a mystery involving one of their own. Charlotte, a classmate, has been kidnapped by Jane, the woman who was a therapist to both Charlotte and Rory. Jane is a member of a cult, and she wants access to Rory's paranormal talent. A recent encounter with a Jack the Ripper copycat killer gave Rory to ability to destroy ghosts with her touch. Jane believes that skill will be useful in the cult's rituals. As Rory and her friends try to save Charlotte and stay out of Jane's grasp, they also deal with another supernatural situation. Stephen, head of the London police squad that investigates paranormal crimes, recently died and is now caught between the worlds of the living and the dead. Rory may be able to bring him back, but the disappearance of Stephen's body complicates matters.

Other books by the same author:
The Boy in the Smoke, 2014
Devilish, 2013
The Madness Underneath, 2013
The Name of the Star, 2012
Suite Scarlett, 2009

Other books you might like:
Graham Masterton, *The Doorkeepers*, 2001
Michael Moorcock, *The Whispering Swarm*, 2015
Kim Newman, *Anno Dracula*, 1993
Sarah Pinborough, *Murder*, 2014
Brian Stableford, *The Angel of Pain*, 1991

323

S.T. JOSHI

Black Wings of Cthulhu 3

(London: Titan Books, 2015)

Story type: Collection
Subject(s): Horror; Fantasy; Short stories

Summary: Edited by S.T. Joshi, this short fiction collection features 17 original fantasy stories inspired by the writings of H.P. Lovecraft. "Houdini Fish" by Jonathan Thomas is a story of biological horrors set in Lovecraft's hometown of Providence, Rhode Island. Caitlin R Kiernan's "One Tree Hill (The World as Cataclysm)" draws upon Lovecraft's concept of cosmicism, while the idea of alternate worlds is explored in Darrell Schweitzer's "Spiderwebs in the Dark" and in Donald Tyson's "Waller." Also included in this collection are Don Webb's "The Megalith Plague," Peter Cannon's "China Holiday," Mollie L. Burleson's "Hotel del Lago," and Brian Stableford's "Further Beyond."

Other books by the same author:
The Madness of Cthulhu, 2015

Horror

Black Wings of Cthulhu 2, 2014
The Assaults of Chaos, 2013
Black Wings of Cthulhu, 2012

Other books you might like:
Donald R. Burleson, *Wait for the Thunder: Stories for a Stormy Night,* 2010
Richard Gavin, *Charnel Wine,* 2010
Simon Strantzas, *Cold to the Touch,* 2009
Jonathan Thomas, *Thirteen Conjurations,* 2013
Donald Tyson, *The Lovecraft Coven,* 2014

324

JOSH KENT

The Witch at Sparrow Creek

(New York: Hippocampus Press, 2015)

Series: Jim Falk Series. Book 1
Story type: Historical; Series
Subject(s): Witches; Suspense; Magic
Major character(s): Jim Falk, Detective—Amateur, Man, Co-worker (of Spencer Barnhouse); Spencer Barnhouse, Co-worker (of Jim), Librarian (archivist)
Time period(s): Indeterminate Past
Locale(s): Sparrow, Fictional Location

Summary: Jim Falk has been haunted by the childhood memory of watching his father being dragged away by his enemies. Over the years, Jim has been plagued by strange visions about finishing his father's work, which involved ridding the world of evil spirits. Unable to ignore the dreams any longer, Jim seeks the assistance of Spencer Barnhouse. Spencer, who was an archivist for Jim's father, acquires relics and other tools Jim can use in the fight against evil. At the prompting of dreams about a red-headed woman, Jim travels to a town called Sparrow. The woods here are said to be haunted by a magician and a pack of wolves. The local preacher tells Jim of a witch that lives in the woods. When Jim and Spencer investigate the witch, events take a turn for the worse. This is the first installment of the Jim Falk series by Josh Kent. First novel.

Other books you might like:
Charles L. Grant, *The Soft Whisper of the Dead,* 1982
Elizabeth Massie, *Homeplace,* 2007
Michael McDowell, *The Flood,* 1983
Cherie Priest, *Maplecroft,* 2014
Jane Toombs, *Tule Witch,* 1973

325

SHERRILYN KENYON

Instinct

(New York: St. Martin's Press, 2015)

Series: Chronicles of Nick Series. Book 6
Subject(s): Supernatural; Fantasy; Zombies
Major character(s): Nick Gautier, Teenager, Demon (half-demon), Student—High School
Time period(s): 21st century; 2010s

Locale(s): New Orleans, Louisiana

Summary: With a demon sharing his body and a host of people after him, including the dark gods that made him in the first place, Nick Gautier has his hands full. As if it's not bad enough that his father is a demon whose fate is to end the world, that father wants to kill Nick, too. It's a lot for most kids of privilege to deal with, but for Nick it's just another day in private school. He's accepted his life in a world of vampires, shapeshifters, and zombies, and is determined to do whatever he has to to protect his world and his loved ones. He might have made that harder, though, by getting close to the one person who can do him and all he cares about the most harm. This is the sixth book in the Chronicles of Nick series.

Other books by the same author:
Dark Bites, 2014
Infamous, 2012
Bad Moon Rising, 2009
Acheron, 2008
Dark Side of the Moon, 2006

Other books you might like:
Kelley Armstrong, *Forsaken,* 2015
Jim Butcher, *Turn Coat,* 2009
Harry Connolly, *Child of Fire,* 2009
Laurell K. Hamilton, *Micah,* 2006
Kim Harrison, *Black Magic Sanction,* 2010
J.R. Ward, *The Shadows,* 2015

326

VIC KERRY

Revels Ending

(Cincinnati, Ohio: Samhain Publishing, 2015)

Story type: Zombies
Subject(s): Supernatural; Zombies; Demons
Major character(s): Ashe, Fiance(e) (of unnamed character), Man; Unnamed Character, Supernatural Being (resurrected), Fiance(e) (of Ashe)
Time period(s): 21st century; 2010s
Locale(s): Mobile, Alabama

Summary: As Mardi Gras season rolls into Mobile, Alabama, a man named Ashe reflects on his good fortune. His job is going well, and so is his love life. Then his fiancee dies, and before he can even mourn her, she comes back to life—yet she isn't quite the same as before. Even more disturbingly, all of the recently deceased people in town suddenly are roaming around. Ashe suspects that the reanimated dead people are somehow related to some recent actions in which he and his friends participated, and he attempts to put things right. Between the craziness of Mardi Gras and whatever sinister forces have captured the souls of the dead, however, Ashe cannot figure out where to begin. The clock is ticking, and if Ashe can't stop the evil in Mobile, he and his friends could be celebrating the final days of their lives.

Other books you might like:
William Hallahan, *The Search for Joseph Tully,* 1974
Rick Hautala, *Beyond the Shroud,* 1995

Brian Keene, *Dark Hollow*, 2008
Dean Koontz, *77 Shadow Street*, 2011
John Saul, *House of Reckoning*, 2009

327

CAITLIN R. KIERNAN

Cherry Bomb

(New York: Penguin Publishing Group, 2015)

Series: Siobhan Quinn Series. Book 3
Story type: Contemporary; Gay - Lesbian Fiction
Subject(s): Horror; Urban life; Fantasy
Major character(s): Siobhan Quinn, Woman, Vampire
(half), Werewolf (half), Hunter (former, of monsters),
Lesbian; Barbara O'Bryan, Lesbian, Lover (of Siobhan)
Time period(s): 21st century; 2010s
Locale(s): New York, New York

Summary: When Siobhan Quinn left Providence, Rhode
Island, to live in New York City, she thought she was
leaving her monster-hunting days behind her. She was
wrong. Siobhan, who is part vampire and part werewolf,
realizes that she has merely traded one urban horror
show for another. In Manhattan, Siobhan is drawn into
an ancient battle between supernatural forces. At the
center of the conflict is a relic that could have a devastating effect on the modern world. Siobhan must once again
use her monster-hunting skills to set things right.
Meanwhile, she also deals with new developments in her
personal life. She has been in a relationship with Barbara
O'Bryan since she arrived in the city, but everything
changes when another woman introduces herself at a sex
club. This novel is the third in the Siobhan Quinn series.

Other books by the same author:
Blood Oranges, 2013
The Red Tree, 2009
Murder of Angels, 2004
Low Red Moon, 2003
Threshold, 2001

Other books you might like:
Ilona Andrews, *Fate's Edge*, 2011
Elaine Cunningham, *Shadows in the Darkness*, 2004
Laurell K. Hamilton, *Blood Noir*, 2008
Seanan McGuire, *Ashes of Honor*, 2012
Devon Monk, *Stone Cold*, 2014

328

ANDREW KLAVAN

Werewolf Cop

(New York: Pegasus Books, 2015)

Story type: Werewolf Story
Subject(s): Detective fiction; Werewolves; Supernatural
Major character(s): Zach "Cowboy" Adams, Werewolf,
Detective—Homicide; Martin Goulart, Police Officer;
Dominic Abend, Organized Crime Figure
Time period(s): 21st century; 2010s

Locale(s): Germany; Houston, Texas

Summary: Zach Adams, known by his friends as Cowboy,
is one of the top investigators in the United States. He's
the one people call when they want to solve a crime
quickly and efficiently, and he lives and dies by the book
of law. His work ethic and gentle demeanor also make
him a great colleague. When he and his partner, New
York cop Martin Goulart, are assigned to take down the
European mob boss Dominic Abend, Martin has no doubt
that the case will be resolved right away. When clues
lead Zach into the dense forests of Germany, however,
he finds himself attacked—not by a member of the
organization, or by any man for that matter, but by a
horrifying creature. Now Zach feels an animal growing
inside of him. He struggles to manage his inner savage
so he can do his job and stop the crime boss.

Other books by the same author:
Hostage Run, 2015
Nightmare Alley, 2014
Nightmare City, 2013
The Uncanny, 1998
The Animal Hour, 1993

Other books you might like:
Mario Acevedo, *The Undead Kama Sutra*, 2008
Dana Cameron, *Seven Kinds of Hell*, 2013
Guillermo Del Toro, *The Strain*, 2009
Glen Duncan, *The Last Werewolf*, 2011
P.N. Elrod, *Cold Streets*, 2003
Edward Gorman, *Blood Game*, 1989
Charlie Huston, *Already Dead*, 2005
Robert R. McCammon, *The Wolf's Hour*, 1989
Bill Pronzini, *Werewolf!*, 1979
Robert Louis Stevenson, *The Strange Case of Doctor
Jekyll and Mr. Hyde*, 1886
S.A. Swiniarski, *Raven*, 1996
Simon Kurt Unsworth, *The Devil's Detective*, 2015

329

VICTORIA LAURIE

No Ghouls Allowed

(New York: Penguin Publishing Group, 2015)

Series: Ghost Hunter Mysteries Series. Book 9
Story type: Mystery; Series
Subject(s): Horror; Mystery; Detective fiction
Major character(s): M.J. Holliday, Psychic, Television
Personality (*Ghoul Getters*), Friend (of Gilley),
Girlfriend (of Heath), Daughter (of Montgomery
Holliday), Woman; Gilley, Man, Friend (of M.J.),
Television Personality (*Ghoul Getters*); Heath, Man,
Television Personality (*Ghoul Getters*), Boyfriend (of
M.J.); Montgomery Holliday, Wealthy, Widow(er),
Father (of M.J.), Fiance(e) (of Christine Bigelow);
Christine Bigelow, Fiance(e) (of Montgomery)
Time period(s): 21st century; 2010s
Locale(s): Valdosta, Georgia

Summary: In the ninth novel in the Ghost Hunter Mystery
series, psychic M.J. Holliday, her boyfriend, Heath, and
her friend Gilley head south to visit M.J.'s father in Valdosta, Georgia. M.J., Heath, and Gilley host the ghost-

Horror

hunting TV show *Ghoul Getters*, and when they arrive at the stately old home Montgomery Holliday is renovating with his fiancee, they realize that have stumbled upon another supernatural mystery. The contractor has just notified Montgomery that he is pulling his crew from the project. Several unexplained mishaps have occurred on the site, and the workers believe the house is haunted by a dark force. The *Ghoul Getters* team agrees to use its paranormal investigative skills to find out what's really going on at the historic mansion.

Other books by the same author:
The Ghoul Next Door, 2014
Lethal Outlook, 2013
Ghoul Interrupted, 2011
Ghouls, Ghouls, Ghouls, 2011
Doom with a View, 2009

Other books you might like:
Jaci Burton, *The Darkest Touch*, 2008
Dakota Cassidy, *The Accidental Werewolf*, 2008
MaryJanice Davidson, *Undead and Unstable*, 2012
Jeanne C. Stein, *The Becoming*, 2006
Carrie Vaughn, *Kitty Raises Hell*, 2009

330

TIM LEBBON

The Silence

(London: Titan Books, 2015)

Story type: Fantasy
Subject(s): Horror; Supernatural; Human behavior
Major character(s): Ally, Teenager, Girl, Deaf Person
Time period(s): 21st century; 2010s (2016)
Locale(s): England

Summary: Set in 2016, this fantasy thriller by award-winning author Tim Lebbon is a tale of family, fear, desperation, and survival. When carnivorous flying creatures are accidentally released from an underground cave in central Europe, Ally, a deaf teenager, and her family flee to a quiet, rural part of England. The flying creatures, known as vesps, rely on their hearing to hunt and as they make their way toward England, they inspire terror in the people. Ally is accustomed to living in silence, and for her family to survive, they must learn to do the same. As the vesps draw near, Ally and her family witness terrified, desperate humans acting out in ways that rival the violent, gruesome nature of the monsters they're trying to escape.

Other books by the same author:
A Whisper of Southern Lights, 2009
Thirty Days of Night, 2007
Unnatural Selection, 2006
The Nature of Balance, 2001
Mesmer, 1997

Other books you might like:
Sephera Giron, *The Birds and the Bees*, 2002
Frank Herbert, *Lair*, 1977
Donald Porter, *The Day of the Animals*, 1977
Martin Cruz Smith, *Nightwing*, 1977
Donald Thompson, *The Ancient Enemy*, 1979

331

ROBERT LETTRICK

The Murk

(New York: Disney-Hyperion, 2015)

Story type: Fantasy
Subject(s): Good and evil; Swamps; Animals
Major character(s): Piper Canfield, Girl, Friend (of Tad), 14-Year-Old, Sister (of Grace and Monty); Grace Canfield, Baby, Sister (of Piper and Monty), Patient; Tad, Teenager, Boy, Friend (of Piper); Monty "Creeper" Canfield, Brother (of Piper and Grace), Boy
Time period(s): 21st century; 2010s
Locale(s): Okefenokee Swamp, Georgia

Summary: Piper has learned to believe in magic. After all, a wish brought her a new baby sister, Grace. A year later, Piper will stop at nothing to save Grace from dying of an incurable disease. Her friend Tad believes his people may have found the answer ages ago. He and Piper are desperate to save Grace, even if they must venture into dangerous territory to do so. The answer may lie deep within the mystical Okefenokee Swamp, in a mystical silver flower. Piper, Tad, and Piper's brother Monty (aka Creeper) enlist the aid of two guides and head into the murky black water swamp. They encounter animals behaving strangely, and it's easy to understand the rumors that swirl around the mysteries of the swamp. Some say evil spirits live in the Okefenokee. But nothing will stop Piper from finding the flower that is said to cure all diseases—not even an evil presence.

Other books by the same author:
Frenzy, 2014

Other books you might like:
Elizabeth Massie, *Welcome Back to the Night*, 1999
Graham Masterton, *Edgewise*, 2006
Robert R. McCammon, *Boy's Life*, 1991
Michael McDowell, *Cold Moon over Babylon*, 1980
Roland Smith, *Tentacles*, 2009

332

BRIAN LUMLEY

Tales of the Primal Land

(Burton, Michigan: Subterranean Press, 2015)

Story type: Collection; Fantasy
Subject(s): Horror; Fantasy; Supernatural
Major character(s): Mylakhrion, Wizard; Tarra Khash, Barbarian; Cush Gemal, Sorcerer
Locale(s): Theem'hdra, Fictional Location

Summary: Set in the prehistoric era on the primal continent of Theem'hdra, the three works collected in this volume are by award-winning horror fantasy author Brian Lumley. The works were originally published separately in 1991 as the Tales of the Primal Land series. "The House of Cthulhu" comprises ten stories that feature the immortal wizard Mylakhrion, a league of pompous warriors, and a group of vindictive ghosts. "Tarra Khash:

Hrossak" follows the adventures of its title character, a fearless barbarian who challenges a number of supernatural creatures. And in "Sorcery in Shad," Tarra Khash falls into the hands of Cush Gemal, which leaves the entire Primal Land on the brink of danger.

Other books by the same author:
Haggopian and Other Stories, 2009
Harry and the Pirates, 2009
The Nonesuch and Others, 2009
Deadspawn, 1991
Demogorgon, 1987

Other books you might like:
Simon Clark, *Hotel Midnight*, 2005
Thomas Ligotti, *The Spectral Link*, 2014
Adam Niswander, *The Sand Dwellers*, 1998
Clark Ashton Smith, *The Dark Eidolon and Other Fantasies*, 2014
Jeffrey Thomas, *Worship the Night*, 2013

333

RONALD DAMIEN MALFI

Little Girls

(New York: Kensington Publishing, 2015)

Story type: Ghost Story
Subject(s): Suspense; Ghosts; Supernatural
Major character(s): Laurie, Mother, Spouse, Daughter (of Father); Unnamed Character, Father (of Laurie); Abigail, Girl
Time period(s): 21st century; 2010s
Locale(s): United States

Summary: Laurie's father always warned her about staying away from a certain room in their rambling house. As a little girl, the warnings haunted her, but as she grew up she began to regard them as yet another symptom of her father's aloofness. Now, as a married woman with a daughter of her own, Laurie returns to her childhood home after her father's suicide. She tells herself that the chill she feels throughout the home is only the result of the lingering bad memories of her unhappy childhood. Deep in her bones, however, she wonders if it may mean something more. Then she meets her daughter's new friend, Abigail. Abigail reminds Laurie of a girl she knew long ago; a little girl who once lived next door—a little girl long dead. Laurie begins to wonder if the insanity that afflicted her father in the end is taking hold of her. As Laurie gets closer to the truth, she will stop at nothing to keep her family safe. Still, she wonders what became of the little girl next door. Can Laurie save herself, and the little girls, too?

Other books by the same author:
December Park, 2014
Cradle Lake, 2013
The Fall of Never, 2013
Floating Staircase, 2011
Snow, 2010

Other books you might like:
Rick Hautala, *Winter Wake*, 1989
James Herbert, *The Secret of Crickley Hall*, 2006

Shirley Jackson, *The Haunting of Hill House*, 1959
Graham Masterton, *The House That Jack Built*, 1996
Al Sarrantonio, *The Boy with Penny Eyes*, 1987

334

CHLOE NEILL

The Veil

(New York: New American Library, 2015)

Series: Devils Isle Series. Book 1
Story type: Magic Conflict
Subject(s): Magic; Southern United States; Fantasy
Major character(s): Claire Connolly, Human (a Sensitive); Liam Quinn, Human (a Sensitive)
Time period(s): 21st century; 2010s
Locale(s): New Orleans, United States

Summary: In the first book of the Devil's Isle series, Claire Connolly is hiding a dark secret: She is a Sensitive, a human with magical powers. The powers have leaked to humans through the Veil, a border that separates humans from the paranormal. Seven years ago, the Veil fell, causing a supernatural war to erupt. Now those humans who possess magical powers are forced to live in the walled-in community of Devil's Isle. Fearing that her secret would send her to Devil's Isle, Claire has been hiding her skills, but her secret has prevented her from learning to use her powers. When she sees a human in danger, Claire clumsily uses her powers to save the person, drawing the attention of Liam Quinn. Quinn decides to take Claire to Devil's Isle and find her a teacher who can help her control and develop her skills. As more Sensitives begin to use their powers, Claire and Liam team up to control the chaos and save New Orleans before it's too late.

Other books by the same author:
Wild Things, 2014
House Rules, 2013
Drink Deep, 2011
Hard Bitten, 2011
Firespell, 2010

Other books you might like:
Kelley Armstrong, *The Calling*, 2012
Casey Daniels, *Night of the Loving Dead*, 2009
Laurell K. Hamilton, *Affliction*, 2013
Kim Harrison, *Once Dead, Twice Shy*, 2009
Faith Hunter, *Death's Rival*, 2012

335

CHLOE NEILL

Dark Debt

(New York: Penguin Group, 2015)

Series: Chicagoland Vampires Series. Book 11
Subject(s): Fantasy; Vampires; Urban life
Major character(s): Merit, Young Woman, Servant (to Ethan Sullivan); Ethan Sullivan, Vampire (master of Merit)

Horror

Time period(s): 21st century; 2010s
Locale(s): Chicago, Illinois

Summary: When Merit came to Chicago as a grad student, she never expected to get tangled up with the city's vampire clans. But that's exactly what happened when Merit was bitten by a rogue vampire. Although the attacker didn't get much blood, Merit's rescuer—the vampire Ethan Sullivan—thought it best to complete the job. Now Ethan is Merit's Master, and Merit has accepted her role at the House of Cadogan. The arrival of one of Ethan's old foes stirs up trouble in the city. Ethan and Merit are unsure of the man's motives, but it's obvious that evil is afoot. An attempted murder at a high-profile social event is thwarted by Merit and her Master. At first glance, the attack seems connected to the human crime world, but the would-be assassins are actually undead. This novel is the 11th in the Chicagoland Vampires series by Chloe Neill.

Other books by the same author:
Blood Games, 2014
House Rules, 2013
Biting Cold, 2012
Charmfall, 2012
The Dark Elite, 2011

Other books you might like:
Karen Chance, *Fury's Kiss*, 2012
Shannon Drake, *Dead by Dusk*, 2005
Christine Feehan, *Dark Blood*, 2014
Laurell K. Hamilton, *Skin Trade*, 2009
Charlaine Harris, *Day Shift*, 2015

336

SARAH RAYNE

The Whispering

(Surrey, England: Severn House Publishers, 2014)

Series: Michael Flint and Nell West Haunted House Mystery Series. Book 4
Story type: Haunted House; Mystery
Subject(s): Haunted houses; Family history; Supernatural
Major character(s): Michael Flint, Professor (at Oxford), Colleague (of Nell), Detective—Amateur; Nell West, Widow(er), Colleague (of Michael), Antiques Dealer; Luisa Gilmore, Landowner (Fosse House), Recluse
Time period(s): 21st century; 2010s
Locale(s): England

Summary: In the fourth installment of the Michael Flint and Nell West Haunted House mystery series, Oxford professor Michael Flint travels to the Fosse House to research the long-dead Palestrina Choir. Upon arriving at the home, which was once a convent but is now owned by the secretive Luisa Gilmore, Michael is instantly aware that the home houses something menacing. He discovers a strange man who walks the grounds, and learns that Luisa becomes extremely nervous whenever it storms. While researching the home's history back in Oxford, Nell learns the story behind the 1917 "Holziminden sketch"—a legendary drawing from World War I that has been lost for decades. When the weather turns foul, Michael is forced to stay at the home until the storms pass, and must endure a night filled with dark forces and a penetrating whispering.

Other books by the same author:
Deadlight Hall, 2015
The Silence, 2014
What Lies Beneath, 2014
The Sin Eater, 2013
A Dark Dividing, 2012

Other books you might like:
Ania Ahlborn, *Within These Walls*, 2015
Charles L. Grant, *The Orchard*, 1986
Rick Hautala, *Beyond the Shroud*, 1995
Michael Koryta, *Those Who Wish Me Dead*, 2014
Graham Masterton, *The House That Jack Built*, 1996
Maynard Sims, *Stillwater*, 2015

337

SARAH RAYNE

Deadlight Hall

(New York: Severn House, 2015)

Series: Michael Flint and Nell West Haunted House Mystery Series. Book 5
Story type: Ghost Story; Haunted House
Subject(s): Ghosts; Haunted houses; Twins
Major character(s): Dr. Michael Flint, Professor, Paranormal Investigator, Fiance(e) (of Nell); Nell West, Fiance(e) (of Michael), Paranormal Investigator; Dr. Leo Rosendale, Professor; Sophie Reiss, Sister (of Susannah), Twin (of Susannah), Missing Person; Susannah Reiss, Sister (of Sophie), Twin (of Sophie), Missing Person
Time period(s): 21st century; 2010s
Locale(s): Oxford, England

Summary: In the fifth installment from author Sarah Rayne's Michael Flint and Nell West Haunted House Mystery seres, Oxford professor of English Literature Dr. Michael Flint looks into mysterious occurrences at an old house. Dr. Leo Rosendale's childhood was marred by things that happened at Deadlight Hall around the time of the Second World War. He remembers twins named Sophie and Susannah Reiss, who disappeared. Now, Deadlight Hall is scheduled to be renovated into luxury flats, and the construction seems to have stirred up some presence. With the help of Nell West, his fiancee and partner in paranormal investigations, Michael takes a closer look at Deadlight Hall. He discovers that the Reiss twins were not the only children to disappear while living there. Michael and Nell are determined to uncover the truth and set the troubled spirits free, but the more they discover about the house's past, the more they wonder if some secrets might be better forgotten.

Other books by the same author:
The Whispering, 2015
The Silence, 2014
What Lies Beneath, 2014
The Sin Eater, 2013
A Dark Dividing, 2012

Other books you might like:
Rick Hautala, *Cold Whisper*, 1991
James Herbert, *Ash*, 2012
Richard Matheson, *Hell House*, 1971
A.J. Matthews, *Follow*, 2005
J.N. Williamson, *Horror House*, 1981

338

KATIE REUS

Hunter Reborn

(New York: Signet, 2015)

Series: Moon Shifter Series. Book 5
Story type: Paranormal; Romance
Subject(s): Romances (Fiction); Horror; Fantasy
Major character(s): Aiden, Shape-Shifter (wolf), Warrior, Lover (former, of Larissa); Larissa, Vampire, Lover (of Aiden, former)
Time period(s): 21st century; 2010s
Locale(s): United States

Summary: Although Aiden, a lupine shape-shifter, recognizes the beauty of his female pack members, he does not desire them physically. He loved one woman, a vampire named Larissa, who was his bondmate. Larissa has been missing for years, but Aiden has never been able to move on. Now Aiden occupies himself with the business of the pack. At the moment he is investigating the illegal trade of vampire blood, and the case yields some shocking information. Larissa isn't dead, as Aiden presumed. She is alive, but she has undergone a devastating change. Larissa has lost her memory. She doesn't remember recent events or that she was ever involved with Aiden. Aiden is heartbroken that his former lover doesn't know him, but he is determined to protect Larissa from the creature that wants her blood. This novel is the fifth in the Moon Shifter series by Katie Reus.

Other books by the same author:
Beyond the Darkness, 2015
Shattered Duty, 2015

Other books you might like:
Cathy Clamp, *Serpent Moon*, 2010
Christine Cody, *Bloodlands*, 2011
Yasmine Galenorn, *Night Veil*, 2011
Nancy Holzner, *Deadtown*, 2010
Susan Krinard, *Luck of the Wolf*, 2010

339

E.E. RICHARDSON

Disturbed Earth

(Oxford, United Kingdom: Abaddon Books, 2015)

Series: Ritual Crime Unit Series. Book 2
Story type: Paranormal; Police Procedural
Subject(s): Fantasy; Horror; Detective fiction
Major character(s): Claire Pierce, Detective—Police (detective chief inspector)
Time period(s): 21st century; 2010s

Locale(s): North Yorkshire, England
Summary: Based in North Yorkshire, Detective Chief Inspector Claire Pierce heads Northern England's Ritual Crime Unit. After suffering an injury in the line of duty, Claire returns to work to investigate a recent ritual murder and to look into the disappearance of some mysterious artifacts. Although the cases seem at first unrelated, the more Claire uncovers, the more she is convinced that something larger and more threatening is at work—something that could result in complete destruction. Now, Claire must put an end to the ritual before it's too late, but with an insubordinate detective inspector, the unwanted help of a necromancer, mysterious signals coming from the evidence room, and demon-possessed skulls, Claire will have to use all her wits and strength to connect the dots in time. This fantasy thriller by E. E. Richardson is the second installment in the Ritual Crime Unit series.

Other books by the same author:
The Intruders, 2006
Devil's Footsteps, 2005

Other books you might like:
Ann Aguirre, *Agave Kiss*, 2013
Larry Correia, *Monster Hunter Alpha*, 2011
Greg Cox, *A Touch of Fever*, 2011
Simon R. Green, *Spirits from Beyond*, 2013
S. Andrew Swann, *The Dwarves of Whiskey Island*, 2005

340

JONATHAN RYAN

Dark Bride

(New York: Open Road Media, 2015)

Series: 3 Gates of the Dead Series. Book 2
Story type: Religious; Series
Subject(s): Horror; Religion; Demons
Major character(s): Aidan Schaeffer, Religious (associate pastor), Friend (of Brian), Co-worker (of Father Neal); Brian, Friend (of Aidan), Farmer, Father (of daughter); Father Neal, Religious (priest)
Time period(s): 21st century; 2010s
Locale(s): United States
Summary: In the second installment in the 3 Gates of the Dead series by Jonathan Ryan, associate pastor Aidan Schaeffer finds himself questioning his religious beliefs once again. Aidan learns of Father Neal's association with the Order of the Five Sorrows after Father Neal decodes a cryptic voodoo message. According to Father Neal, Aidan is destined to become a fellow member of the Order, a group that uses holy relics from Christ's crucifixion to ward off evil. Puzzled by Father Neal's proclamation, Aidan turns his attention to a string of mysterious events that has occurred on his friend's farm. From inexplicable nighttime lights to Brian's daughter's obsession with her imaginary friend to the appearance of a mystical group of women hunting a witch from the 1600s, Aiden and Brian find themselves in the midst of a supernatural war against evil, a battle that soon turns deadly.

Other books by the same author:
3 Gate of the Dead, 2013

Other books you might like:
Lisa Cantrell, *Boneman*, 1992
Hugh B. Cave, *The Evil*, 1981
Rick Hautala, *Moonwalker*, 1989
James Herbert, *Portent*, 1996
Jay Russell, *Burning Bright*, 1997

341

MARJORIE SANDOR

The Uncanny Reader: Stories from the Shadows

(New York: St. Martin's Press, 2015)

Story type: Collection
Subject(s): Short stories; Horror; Supernatural

Summary: This anthology includes more than 30 short stories from some of the most notable and popular horror fiction writers of the 19th and 20th centuries. Edited by essayist Marjorie Sandor, the collection contains works of such celebrated authors as Edgar Allan Poe, Ambrose Bierce, Anton Chekov, and Edith Wharton, as well as many other award-winning authors from around the world. The stories include "The Sandman," by German author E.T.A. Hoffman, which tells the story of a man who is manipulated by a deceptive lawyer; "Paranoia," by American author Shirley Jackson, in which an office clerk drives himself crazy after convincing himself that he is being stalked; "The Jesters," by Joyce Carol Oates, which chronicles the mysterious noises heard by a husband and wife; French author Jean-Christophe Duchon-Doris's "The Puppets," which questions if a person is really free or controlled by greater forces; and China Mieville's "Foundation," in which a war criminal continues to be haunted by his victims.

Other books by the same author:
Portrait of My Mother, Who Posed Nude in Wartime, 2003

Other books you might like:
Jonathan Carroll, *The Panic Hand*, 1995
Nina Kiriki Hoffman, *Permeable Borders*, 2012
Kelly Link, *Pretty Monsters: Stories*, 2008
Scott Nicholson, *Scattered Ashes*, 2008
Scott Thomas, *Urn & Willow*, 2012

342

VICTORIA SCHWAB

The Unbound

(New York: Disney-Hyperion, 2014)

Series: Archived Series. Book 2
Subject(s): Afterlife; Death; Horror
Major character(s): Mackenzie "Mac" Bishop, Student—High School, Worker (at the Archive), 17-Year-Old
Time period(s): 21st century; 2010s
Locale(s): United States

Summary: Hyde School junior Mackenzie Bishop is trying to get her life back on track. It was only last summer she almost lost her life at her job as a Keeper in the Archive. She works to keep the violent Histories, the dead souls that only a librarian can read, inside the Archive where their bodies rest. Mackenzie is known to be a ruthless Keeper, but nightmares of her near death start creeping into her waking hours. She fears the Histories will try to kill her again, and Mackenzie begins obsessing over them. The teen knows she is safe from the past, but something still seems off. Everyone around her begins disappearing and she's the only link between them all. Only Mackenzie can solve this mystery, she just needs to do it before she loses everything including her life. This is the second title of the Archived series.

Other books by the same author:
A Darker Shade of Magic, 2015
Last Wishes, 2014
New Beginnings, 2014
Second Chances, 2014
The Archived, 2013

Other books you might like:
Mindee Arnett, *The Nightmare Dilemma*, 2014
Bruce Coville, *Eyes of the Tarot*, 1996
Cecilia Galante, *Be Not Afraid*, 2015
Michelle Knudsen, *Evil Librarian*, 2014
Garth Nix, *Lirael: Daughter of the Clayr*, 2001
Mel Odom, *The Rover*, 2001
Thomas Randall, *The Waking: Dreams of the Dead*, 2009
Sean Rodman, *Night Terrors*, 2012
Polly Shulman, *The Grimm Legacy*, 2010
Laurie Faria Stolarz, *Return to the Dark House*, 2015
Joanna Wiebe, *The Wicked Awakening of Anne Merchant*, 2015

343

DARREN SHAN

Zom-B Bride

(New York: Little, Brown and Company, 2015)

Series: Zom-B Series. Book 10
Story type: Series; Young Adult
Subject(s): Zombies; Marriage; Supernatural
Major character(s): B Smith, Supernatural Being (zombie), Teenager, Warrior (Angel); Mr. Dowling, Murderer
Time period(s): 21st century; 2010s
Locale(s): London, England

Summary: This horror fiction novel for young adults is the tenth book in the Zom-B series by best-selling author Darren Shan. In this installment, undead teenage heroine B Smith reconnects with Mr. Dowling, the killer clown who is determined to make B his partner in crime. Although B is completely uninterested in teaming up with Mr. Dowling, she has an idea that will not only allow her to control the evil clown, but also might help her save the world in the process. The price she'll have to pay, however, is more than she's ever considered. Will the sacrifice prove too much for even B to make?

Other books by the same author:
Zom-B City, 2013
Procession of the Dead, 2010
A Living Nightmare, 2009
Demon Thief, 2006
Lord Loss, 2005

Other books you might like:
Adam Gallardo, *Zombified*, 2015
David Lubar, *The Big Stink*, 2010
Isaac Marion, *Warm Bodies: A Novel*, 2011
A. Lee Martinez, *Gil's All Fright Diner*, 2005
Jesse Petersen, *Married with Zombies*, 2010

344

MAYNARD SIMS

Stillwater

(Cincinnati, Ohio: Samhain Publishing, 2015)

Story type: Ghost Story
Subject(s): Ghosts; Rural life; Accidents
Major character(s): Beth Alvarini, Writer, Narrator, Handicapped (a paraplegic); Unnamed Character, Spirit (of drowned girl)
Time period(s): 21st century; 2010s
Locale(s): Sussex, England

Summary: A terrible car accident has left Beth Alvarini a paraplegic who has to spend the rest of her life in a wheelchair. With her family gone and her old life now in tatters, Beth decides to lease Stillwater, a lake house in the country. She hopes she can begin her life again at Stillwater. Although she's looking for a little peace and quiet, Beth soon realizes that Stillwater is anything but that. The home is being haunted by the ghost of a young girl who drowned in the lake. The ghost refuses to leave Stillwater and is unhappy that Beth has moved in. In an effort to subdue the ghost, Beth begins to investigate what happened at the home. She is determined to prove to the spirit that she belongs in Stillwater.

Other books by the same author:
A Plague of Echoes, 2014
Stronghold, 2013
Night Souls, 2010
Black Cathedral, 2008
Demon Eyes, 2007

Other books you might like:
Matthew J. Costello, *Darkborn*, 1992
James Herbert, *Nobody True*, 2005
A.J. Matthews, *Looking Glass*, 2004
Sarah Rayne, *The Whispering*, 2014
T.M. Wright, *The House on Orchid Street*, 2003

345

JAMES ROBERT SMITH

A Confederacy of Horrors

(New York: Hippocampus Press, 2015)

Story type: Collection
Subject(s): Short stories; Southern United States; Ghosts

Summary: Author James Robert Smith presents his first collection of weird short fiction. Several of the tales included here are set in the South. Featured in this collection are 25 short stories, divided into four sections: ghost stories, stories of vengeance, tales of obsession, and violent stories that feature blood. The works in this collection include "On the First Day," which features monsters from space; "Just a Gigolo," which offers a different kind of vampire; "One of Those Days," which takes a look at the end of the world; and "Love and Magick," in which a man uses a different type of magic to battle creatures. Smith, who is the author of several novels, is known for pushing the boundaries of weird fiction. He has also co-edited the 2006 anthology *Evermore*.

Other books by the same author:
The New Ecology of Death, 2013
The Living End, 2011
The Flock, 2006

Other books you might like:
Michael Aronovitz, *The Witch of the Wood*, 2014
Frank Belknap Long, *Night Fear*, 1979
Scott Nicholson, *Scattered Ashes*, 2008
Simon Strantzas, *Nightingale Songs*, 2011
Jonathon Thomas, *Midnight Call and Other Stories*, 2008

346

LAURIE FARIA STOLARZ

Return to the Dark House

(New York: Disney Hyperion, 2015)

Series: Dark House Series. Book 2
Story type: Small Town Horror
Subject(s): Adolescent interpersonal relations; Suspense; Monsters
Major character(s): Ivy Jensen, Teenager, Detective—Amateur; Nightmare Elf, Serial Killer; Taylor Monroe, Teenager
Time period(s): 21st century; 2010s
Locale(s): United States

Summary: In the second novel of author Laurie Stolarz's Dark House series, Ivy Jensen returns to once again face the Nightmare Elf. The local police force proved to be worthless in putting the dreaded serial killer behind bars, and now it's up to Ivy to track the Nightmare Elf down. When a link to a mysterious video clip is e-mailed to her from an unknown source, Ivy thinks that she might finally have the break she needs to stop the murderer in his tracks. Yet as she seeks out justice for the deaths of all of her friends and classmates, she also finds help from an unlikely source. Taylor Monroe has agreed to aid her in her quest for vengeance, but Ivy isn't sure if Taylor is being honest, and time is running out. Now Ivy must decide if she can put her fate in the hands of someone with questionable motives, or if Taylor is really working for the Nightmare Elf after all.

Other books by the same author:
Welcome to the Dark House, 2014
Deadly Little Secret, 2010

Deadly Little Lies, 2009
Project 17, 2009
Red Is for Remembering, 2005

Other books you might like:
Mindee Arnett, *The Nightmare Affair*, 2013
Rachel Caine, *The Dead Girls' Dance*, 2007
Cecilia Galante, *Be Not Afraid*, 2015
Melinda Metz, *Haunted*, 2001
Victoria Schwab, *The Unbound*, 2014
Joanna Wiebe, *The Wicked Awakening of Anne Merchant*, 2015

347

MARK TEPPO

Thirteen: Stories of Transformation

(Portland, Oregon: Underland Press, 2015)

Story type: Anthology
Subject(s): Short stories; Fantasy; Suspense

Summary: The theme running through all the works featured in this anthology revolves around the 13th Tarot card, Death, a symbol of transformation and rebirth. Twenty-eight authors contributed works to this anthology, presenting stories that follow the cycle of life, death, and renewal. Works address the afterlife, loss in this life, and other aspects of death in the past, present, and future. Some of the works included in this collection are the poem "Skin and Paper" by Adrienne Odasso; "Oh, How the Ghost of You Clings" by Richard Bowes; "The Thirteenth Goddess" by Claude Lalumiere; "Feed Me the Bones of Our Saints" by Alex Dally MacFarlane; and "The 13th Ewe" by Lyn McConchie. Editor Mark Teppo is the founder and publisher of the Resurrection House independent publishing company and an author of numerous novels.

Other books by the same author:
The Court of Lies, 2014
Heartland, 2010
Lightbreaker, 2009

Other books you might like:
Laird Barron, *The Imago Sequence and Other Stories*, 2007
Donald R. Burleson, *Beyond the Lamplight*, 1996
Richard Gavin, *At Fear's Altar*, 2012
Rhys Hughes, *Bone Idle in the Charnel House: A Collection of Weird Stories*, 2014
Jeffrey Thomas, *Nocturnal Emissions*, 2010

348

DONALD TYSON

The Lovecraft Coven

(New York: Hippocampus Press, 2014)

Story type: Collection
Subject(s): Horror; Literature; Short stories

Summary: This volume collects two Lovecraftian horror novellas by author Donald Tyson. American horror author H.P. Lovecraft is the central figure in the first story, "The Lovecraft Coven." Although eight decades have passed since Lovecraft's death, the author finds himself in a psychiatric hospital in Providence, Rhode Island. Lovecraft has not reawakened in his own body, but in that of a stranger. When he realizes he is being targeted by shadow walkers, Lovecraft embarks on a quest through the fictional locations in his novels to find a missing magic book. In "Iron Chains," a man who believes the Great Alignment is imminent moves to a Nova Scotia farm to wait for the cosmic event to unfold. When the man finds a buried chain, an ancient windmill, and other oddities on the property, he believes his arrival at the farm is part of a cosmic plan.

Other books by the same author:
The Necronomicon, 2004
The Tortuous Serpent, 1997
The Messenger, 1993

Other books you might like:
Paula Guran, *New Cthulhu 2: More Recent Weird*, 2015
S.T. Joshi, *Black Wings of Cthulhu 3*, 2015
H.P. Lovecraft, *Necronomicon: The Best Weird Tales of H. P. Lovecraft*, 2008
Brian Lumley, *Beneath the Moors and Darker Places*, 2002
Richard A. Lupoff, *Lovecraft's Book*, 1985
Adam Niswander, *The Sand Dwellers*, 1998

349

J.R. WARD

The Shadows

(New York: Penguin Publishing Group, 2015)

Series: Black Dagger Brotherhood Series. Book 13
Subject(s): Fantasy; Romances (Fiction); Occultism
Major character(s): Trez Latimer, Young Man (Shadow), Twin (of iAm), Brother (of iAm); iAm, Young Man (Shadow), Twin (of Trez), Brother (of Trez); Serena, Young Woman (Chosen)
Time period(s): 21st century; 2010s
Locale(s): Caldwell, New York

Summary: Trez and iAm are twin brothers and members of the Shadow race. Although Trez has no surname, he uses the last name Latimer to blend in with the human residents of Caldwell, New York. He works and fulfills his voracious sexual appetite there, but he doesn't let himself get attached to any of the women he sleeps with. Trez's twin worries about his brother's behavior, but iAm notices a change in Trez when Selena, a Chosen, arrives on the scene. But just as it seems Trez may be ready to make big changes in his life, his past catches up with him. Trez was promised to someone else long ago, and he must decide if he will honor that vow or stay with Selena. His faithful brother also faces a crisis. This novel is the 13th in the Black Dagger Brotherhood series.

Other books by the same author:
Lover Reborn, 2012
Lover Unleashed, 2011

Lover Mine, 2010
Lover Revealed, 2007
Lover Unbound, 2007

Other books you might like:
Keri Arthur, *Bound to Shadows*, 2009
Shannon Drake, *Realm of Shadows*, 2002
Jeaniene Frost, *One Grave at a Time*, 2011
Sherrilyn Kenyon, *Instinct*, 2015
Jeanne C. Stein, *Haunted*, 2012

350

FREDA WARRINGTON

The Dark Arts of Blood

(London: Titan Books, 2015)

Series: Blood Wine Series. Book 4
Story type: Series; Vampire Story
Subject(s): Gothic novels; Vampires; Supernatural
Major character(s): Karl, Vampire, Lover (of Charlotte); Charlotte Neville, Vampire, Lover (of Karl); Emil, Dancer, Vampire, Lover (of Fadiya); Fadiya, Vampire, Lover (of Emil), Femme Fatale; Violette Lenoir, Dancer, Vampire; Godric Reiniger, Vampire, Filmmaker
Time period(s): 20th century; 1920s
Locale(s): London, England

Summary: In the fourth novel of Freda Warrington's Blood Wine series, the author continues the horrific yet romantic saga of Charlotte, the daughter of a Cambridge University professor, who has decided to give up her mortality for the everlasting love of her obsession, Karl, a vampire. This time, Karl and Charlotte are called upon to save Emil, a ballet dancer whose relationship with a famous ballerina-turned-vampire named Violette threatens to destroy him. Emil's path of despair leads him to a femme fatale named Fadiya, with whom he seeks comfort after his heartwrenching experience with Violette. Karl and Charlotte know that Fadiya has malevolent intentions, though. As they set out to rescue Emil from the vampire's grasp, they also meet up with Godric Reiniger, who is becoming a powerful force in the vampire community. Karl and Charlotte question this power, however, and they must challenge Godric before their very existence is put in jeopardy.

Other books by the same author:
Pagan Moon, 1997
The Dark Blood of Poppies, 1995
A Dance in Blood Velvet, 1994
A Taste of Blood Wine, 1992
A Blackbird in the Darkness, 1986

Other books you might like:
Suzy McKee Charnas, *The Vampire Tapestry*, 1980
Robert R. McCammon, *The Wolf's Hour*, 1989
Tim Powers, *Hide Me Among the Graves*, 2012
Anne Rice, *Interview with the Vampire*, 1976
Chelsea Quinn Yarbro, *Dark of the Sun*, 2004

351

DAVID WELLINGTON

Positive

(New York: Harper Voyager, 2015)

Story type: Apocalyptic Horror; Zombies
Subject(s): Zombies; Apocalypse; Diseases
Major character(s): Finn, 19-Year-Old, Young Man, Patient (zombie virus carrier)
Time period(s): Indeterminate Future
Locale(s): United States

Summary: A generation has passed since a zombie virus killed off the majority of the American population. Manhattan, which is now inhabited by only 50,000 people, hasn't had a zombie presence for 15 years. Some residents are still carriers of the virus, however. When 19-year-old Finn is identified as one of those potential threats, he is tattooed as a Positive and sent to a government facility. If he survives the incubation period without manifesting the virus, Finn will be released. But Finn never makes it to the military lab. His transport vehicle is attacked, and Finn is forced to go on the run. Now alone in a changed America, Finn must evade the threats posed by both human villains and the roaming zombies. As Finn struggles to survive, he also grapples with the knowledge that the virus he carries could turn him into a flesh-eating monster at any time.

Other books by the same author:
23 Hours, 2009
Frostbite: A Werewolf Tale, 2009
13 Bullets, 2007
99 Coffins, 2007
Monster Island, 2006

Other books you might like:
Mario Acevedo, *Jail-Bait Zombies*, 2009
Rhiannon Frater, *Dead Spots*, 2015
Jonathan Maberry, *Patient Zero*, 2009
Thomas S. Roche, *The Panama Laugh*, 2011
Chuck Wendig, *Double Dead*, 2011

352

DAN WELLS

The Devil's Only Friend

(New York: Tom Doherty Associates, 2015)

Series: John Cleaver Series. Book 4
Story type: Paranormal; Series
Subject(s): Monsters; Demons; Supernatural
Major character(s): John Wayne Cleaver, 17-Year-Old, Hunter (of demons), Friend (of Brooke), Mentally Ill Person (sociopath); Brooke Watson, Friend (of John); The Hunter, Villain (cannibal)
Time period(s): 21st century; 2010s
Locale(s): Clayton, United States

Summary: This book is the fourth installment in author Dan Well's John Cleaver series. This time, John has been enlisted to aid a special team of FBI agents in hunting down a species of demons known as the

Horror

Withered. John has a talent not only for killing demons, but also for attracting them, as well as all other types of evil forces, and this time is no different. All John wants to do is be a normal person and hang out with his friend, Brooke Watson, but Brooke has been hidden away in a psychiatric ward so that the Withered cannot get to her. Unfortunately, as the team closes in on the demons, John and the agents discover too late the bind they are in; all this time, the Withered have been tracking *them*. Meanwhile, John also goes up against a man called the Hunter, who has a taste for human flesh. John must harness all of his sociopathic tendencies to defeat evil once again, but will he lose too much of himself in the process to ever come back?

Other books by the same author:
Partials, 2013
The Hollow City, 2012
I Don't Want to Kill You, 2011
I Am Not a Serial Killer, 2010
Mr. Monster, 2010

Other books you might like:
Clive Barker, *The Damnation Game*, 1985
William Peter Blatty, *Legion: A Novel*, 1983
John Connolly, *The Burning Soul*, 2011
Thomas F. Monteleone, *Eyes of the Virgin*, 2002
John Saul, *Creature*, 1989

353

JOANNA WIEBE

The Wicked Awakening of Anne Merchant

(Dallas, Texas: BenBella Books, 2015)

Series: V Trilogy. Book 2
Story type: Series; Young Adult
Subject(s): Horror; Supernatural; Fantasy
Major character(s): Anne Merchant, Student—Boarding School (Cania Christy Preparatory Academy), Patient (in coma), Friend (of Ben Zin); Ben Zin, Student—Boarding School (Cania Christy Preparatory Academy), Friend (of Anne Merchant); Dia Voletto, Principal (headmaster)
Time period(s): 21st century; 2010s
Locale(s): Wormwood Island, Fictional Location

Summary: In the second entry in the V trilogy, Anne Merchant knows the true nature of Cania Christy Preparatory Academy. The elite boarding school, located on Wormwood Island, is not only for children of wealthy families; it is for rich children who are dead. At Cania Christy, students can compete to win a chance at getting a new life. However, only one student is chosen for the honor each year. Anne's friend and love interest, Ben Zin, is a contestant in the current competition, but dark forces are working to ruin any chance of success. Anne, who is in a coma, may be able to influence the situation from the realm in which she now resides. She seeks the help of some questionable allies to manipulate the contest, but in doing so, she takes great person risks. Anne also faces another dilemma in her subconscious state. She has feelings for Ben, but she is also drawn to

Cania Christy's headmaster, Dia Voletto.

Other books by the same author:
The Unseemly Education of Anne Merchant, 2014

Other books you might like:
Carmen Adams, *The Band*, 1994
Rachel Caine, *Daylighters*, 2013
Steven Charles, *Academy of Terror*, 1986
Melissa de la Cruz, *Bloody Valentine*, 2010
Stephenie Meyer, *Twilight*, 2005
Victoria Schwab, *The Unbound*, 2014
Laurie Faria Stolarz, *Return to the Dark House*, 2015

354

ERIK WILLIAMS

Guardian

(New York: Harper Voyager, 2015)

Story type: Ancient Evil Unleashed
Subject(s): Horror; Angels; Good and evil
Major character(s): Mike Caldwell, Agent (CIA), Assassin; Semyaza, Demon
Time period(s): 21st century; 2010s

Summary: In *Demon*, author Erik Williams introduced Mike Caldwell, a CIA agent assigned to a case involving a deadly pathogen that transforms humans into killers. Caldwell learned that it was not a virus that was causing the outbreaks of violence. A fallen angel named Semyaza, recently released from his burial place in the Middle East, is infecting the world with evil and death. Since Caldwell learned of Semyaza's existence, he has been on a hunt for the demon. In this follow-up novel, Caldwell must face both the fallen angel and the humans that have taken an interest in him. After Caldwell survives one encounter with Semyaza, he expands his desperate mission to protect the human race from the evil force that has been unleashed.

Other books by the same author:
Demon, 2014
Bigfoot Crank Stomp, 2013
Walking Shadows, 2013

Other books you might like:
Brian Lumley, *Titus Crow, Volume One*, 1997
Robert Masello, *The Medusa Amulet*, 2011
Kate Mosse, *Sepulchre*, 2008
James Rollins, *The Blood Gospel*, 2013
Dan Simmons, *Carrion Comfort*, 1989

355

RIO YOUERS

Point Hollow

(Toronto, Ontario: ChiZine Publications, 2015)

Story type: Fantasy; Gothic
Subject(s): Horror; Gothic novels; Fantasy
Major character(s): Oliver Wray, Man (resident of Point

Hollow), Servant (of mountain); Matthew Bridge, Man (former resident of Point Hollow)

Time period(s): 21st century; 2010s

Locale(s): Point Hollow, New York

Summary: Abraham's Faith is a mountain that overlooks the town of Point Hollow, New York. The town is a haven for tourists, who are drawn to its idyllic atmosphere. They don't know that the nearby mountain holds the skeletal remains of many young victims, or that Point Hollow itself conceals a dark secret. Oliver Wray, one of Point Hollow's most respected residents, is part of that secret. He communicates with Abraham's Faith and devotedly does the mountain's bidding. Only one man—Matthew Bridge—has ever suspected Oliver's sinister connection to the mountain, and he has been away from Point Hollow for decades. Matthew is still haunted by a terrifying experience he had in the town, and his personal life is now a shambles. He feels he has no choice but to return to Point Hollow and its evil mountain to set things right.

Other books by the same author:

Westlake Soul, 2012

Other books you might like:

Charlaine Harris, *Midnight Crossroad*, 2014

K.W. Jeter, *In the Land of the Dead*, 1989

Stephen King, *Needful Things*, 1991

John Ajvide Lindqvist, *Harbor*, 2011

Ronald Damien Malfi, *Cradle Lake*, 2013

Inspirational Fiction, Summer 2015
by
Lynda Lee Schab

Fairy Tale Fiction

Once upon a time, there was a genre that took the world by storm. Fairy tales and folktales have been around for thousands of years, first passed on orally, before transitioning to written form. While fairy tales originally were intended for adults, over time most have been reworked into stories for children. Walt Disney has taken many of them to the big screen, in animated and non-animated style, creating everlasting classics that will continue to find their way into every child's DVD collection.

Trending these days are classic fairy tales being used as themes for adult fiction. Princes and princesses are more popular than ever. Author Melanie Dickerson's Medieval Fairy Tale series has been very well received by readers. Her latest release, *The Huntress of Thornbeck Forest*, is described as Swan Lake meets Robin Hood and features a female posing as a poacher in the King's forest in an effort to provide for the poor. Following on its heels is Dickerson's next book, *The Golden Braid*, scheduled for release in late 2015. This one will deliver the story of Rapunzel—in wonderfully imaginative medieval style.

In 2013, Rachel Hauck released her first in the Royal Wedding series with *Once upon a Prince*, followed by *Princess Ever After* in 2014. This year brings readers the third novel, *How to Catch a Prince*. Each book in the series is a unique modernized fairy tale filled with intrigue, enchantment, and, of course, lots of romance and forbidden love.

The Thrill of Romantic Suspense

Speaking of love and intrigue, many romantic suspense novels have been or will be released this year, providing plenty of options for criminal justice and mystery fans who enjoy a thread of romance.

A few of the most talked-about titles include Irene Hannon's *Buried Secrets*, the first in the Men of Valor series; *Taken* by Dee Henderson; *No Place to Hide* by Lynette Eason, the third in the Hidden Identity series;

and *Gone without a Trace* by Patricia Bradley. And definitely worthy of mention is *Sabotaged* by Dani Pettrey, the final installment in the Alaskan Courage series. This series has been a fan favorite, and it will be hard to say goodbye to the endearing McKenna family. Readers undoubtedly are anticipating the fact that Pettrey is working on her next project, and hoping it is as notable as the Alaskan Courage series has been.

A Good, Old Fashioned Love Story

For those who prefer to forego the suspense and settle in for a simple old fashioned love story, there is no shortage of choices in the sweet romance category. Christian fiction has come a long way in this genre, which used to be criticized for being saturated with somewhat predictable storylines and tied-in-a-neat-bow endings. Yes, the fiction formula for love may contain many of the same ingredients, but the sub-plots and underlying themes are a bit more creative and realistic than in years past, in both the contemporary and historical genres.

Love Arrives in Pieces by Betsy St. Amant is a wonderfully written love story of finding beauty from brokenness. Courtney Walsh's *Paper Hearts* tells a tale of a woman who has lost all faith in love, but through a series of unwelcome events learns to open her heart again. Fans of lighthearted historical romance likely will enjoy author Lorna Seilstad's *As Love Blooms*, a charming and delightful account of a woman pursuing her dreams in early twentieth-century Saint Paul, Minnesota. A heavier themed love story involving fetal alcohol syndrome is explored in *Together with You* by Victoria Bylin. This moving romance tugs the heartstrings and touches on the topics of working through guilt and shame and accepting God's grace.

Other noteworthy general romance titles include the humor-laced *Every Bride Needs a Groom* by Janice Thompson; Susan May Warren's fifth Christiansen family series novel, *The Wonder of You*; and Melissa Tagg's *From the Start*, the first in the Walker Family series.

Another Realm of Fiction

The 1980s brought with it a seemingly brief fascination with angels, demons, and the afterlife. While that trend tapered off a bit in the following years, it has returned in full force. More recently, television seems to have become inundated with shows revolving around angels, demons, and the afterlife. These trends have affected the fiction book market, and Christian fiction is no exception. Whereas darker novels addressing spiritual warfare have been appearing on bookstore shelves since Frank Peretti's *Piercing the Darkness* made its debut in the '80s, more and more stories of late have been focusing on angels on earth, similar in tone and theme to the '80s television hit, *Touched by an Angel* starring Roma Downey.

Max Lucado, a well-known and respected preacher and best-selling author with a resume of more than 92 million non-fiction and children's books sold around the world, has just released his first adult fiction title, *Miracle at the Higher Grounds Café*. This charming and heartwarming story centers on Chelsea Chambers, who is separated from her NFL superstar husband and has just re-opened the café her grandmother founded years ago. Chelsea receives a bit of heavenly intervention from "Manny," an angel in employee's clothing.

Best-selling author Karen Kingsbury has also gotten in on "angelic" storytelling. Her recent release, *Angels Walking* the first in a series of the same name, focuses on heavenly beings fulfilling their assignments on earth.

Other recommended titles

Still Life by Christa Parrish

The Art of Losing Yourself by Katie Ganshert

Luther and Katharina by Jody Hedlund

Secrets of a Charmed Life by Susan Meissner

Tiffany Girl by Deeanne Gist

Fatal Trauma by Richard Mabry

A Thing of Beauty by Lisa Samson

As Waters Gone By by Cynthia Ruchti

Finding Me by Kathryn Cushman

The Devil's Game by Daniel Patterson

Like a Flower in Bloom by Siri Mitchell

The Pharaoh's Daughter by Mesu Andrews

Inspirational Fiction

356

TAMERA ALEXANDER

To Win Her Favor

(Grand Rapids, Michigan: Zondervan, 2015)

Series: Belle Meade Plantation Series. Book 2
Story type: Romance; Series
Subject(s): Horse racing; Southern United States; Scandals
Major character(s): Maggie Linden, Daughter (of Mr. Linden), Fiance(e) (of Cullen); Cullen McGrath, Immigrant, Fiance(e) (Maggie); Mr. Linden, Father (of Maggie), Plantation Owner, Aged Person; Bourbon Belle, Horse
Time period(s): 19th century; 1860s (1869)
Locale(s): Nashville, Tennessee

Summary: In the second novel of Tamera Alexander's Belle Meade Plantation series of standalone novels, the author introduces readers to Maggie Linden, a young Southern woman whose passion for horse racing may be the one thing that keeps her family's legacy intact. The War Between the States concluded several years ago, and Maggie and her father have worked their fingers to the bone to keep their plantation, Linden Downs. Maggie's father is in poor health, however, and cannot keep up with his debt. As the Lindens face the possibility of losing their ancestral home, Maggie's father comes up with a plan he believes is their only option: Maggie will marry Irish immigrant Cullen McGrath. Maggie agrees to the terms, but she has another plan. She will race her horse, Bourbon Belle, in Nashville's Drayton Stakes, and use the prize money to save their plantation. Soon, Maggie and Cullen find themselves unexpectedly falling for one another despite their differences. When racial and ethnic tensions come to a head in Nashville, they must help each other to protect everything they hold dear.

Other books by the same author:
To Whisper Her Name, 2012
Belmont Mansion Series, 2011
The Inheritance, 2009
Timber Ridge Reflections Series, 2008
Fountain Creek Chronicles Series, 2006

Other books you might like:
Stephen Bly, *The Mustang Breaker*, 2006

Elizabeth Camden, *Into the Whirlwind*, 2013
Katie Ganshert, *Wildflowers from Winter*, 2012
Sibella Giorello, *The Stars Shine Bright*, 2012
Yvonne L Harris, *A River to Cross*, 2011

357

MESU ANDREWS

The Pharaoh's Daughter

(Colorado Springs, Colorado: Waterbrook Press, 2015)

Series: Treasures of the Nile Series. Book 1
Story type: Historical; Series
Subject(s): Bible stories; Egyptian history, to 642 (Ancient period); Royalty
Major character(s): Anippe, Mother (adoptive, of Moses), Spouse (of Sebak); Sebak, Father (adoptive, of Moses), Spouse (of Anippe), Military Personnel; Moses, Biblical Figure, Adoptee (of Anippe and Sebak), Son (adopted, of Sebak and Anippe); Pharaoh Tut, Royalty, Biblical Figure, Historical Figure
Locale(s): Egypt

Summary: In the first novel from the Treasures of the Nile series, author Mesu Andrews provides a fictionalized account of the life of Moses, the alleged leader of the Israelites and Biblical prophet. An infant boy is found floating in the Nile by Anippe, a daughter of the pharaoh. She is betrothed to Sebak, a military leader, and she is determined to bring him a son. Unfortunately, Anippe is terrified of having a child, having watched her own mother die while giving birth. She knows she must give Sebak a successor to prove her worth as a wife, so she adopts the boy, whom they call Mehy, or Moses, and deceives her husband. Moses clearly descends from the Hebrews, and Tut has declared that all Hebrew boys must killed. Now Anippe must follow her heart and her faith that a greater plan lies ahead for Moses. As she engages in a series of lies and deceit, she convinces herself that she acts for the greater good, and that God will protect her as well as Moses.

Other books by the same author:
In the Shadow of Jezebel, 2014
Love in a Broken Vessel, 2013
Love's Sacred Song, 2012
Love Amid the Ashes, 2011

Other books you might like:
Tessa Afshar, *Pearl in the Sand*, 2010
Antoinette May, *Pilate's Wife*, 2006
Francine Rivers, *Sons of Encouragement*, 2011
Jill Eileen Smith, *Sarai*, 2012
Joan Wolf, *A Reluctant Queen*, 2011

358

JENNIFER BECKSTRAND

Huckleberry Harvest

(New York: Zebra Publishing, 2015)

Series: Matchmakers of Huckleberry Hill Series. Book 5
Story type: Humor; Inspirational
Subject(s): Alcoholism; Amish; Deception
Major character(s): Mandy Helmuth, Granddaughter (of Anna and Felty Helmuth), Friend (of Kristina), Religious (Amish); Noah Mischler, Worker (working at Felty Helmuth's house), Young Man, Handyman, Man (hiding secret family shame), Religious (Amish); Kristina, Friend (brokenhearted friend of Mandy Helmuth), Young Woman (infatuated with Noah Mischler), Religious (Amish); Anna Helmuth, Spouse (of Felthy Helmuth), Grandmother (of Mandy Helmuth), Religious (Amish), Matchmaker (for her granddaughter Mandy); Felty Helmuth, Religious (Amish), Grandfather (of Mandy Helmuth), Spouse (of Anna Helmuth)
Time period(s): 21st century; 2010s
Locale(s): Bonduel, Wisconsin

Summary: This is the fifth installment in the Matchmakers of Huckleberry Hill series by author Jennifer Beckstrand. Anna Helmuth is determined again to play matchmaker. This time she has her sights set on her granddaughter Mandy. Anna gets busy interviewing the young men in town as prospective husbands for her granddaughter. Meanwhile, Mandy returns to Huckleberry Hill to console her brokenhearted friend and give the offending man a piece of her mind. She doesn't expect to lose her own heart, however. Noah Mischler, the town handyman, has a shameful secret. He keeps to himself and to his work until Mandy comes into his life, poking her nose into his personal business and making her way into his heart. Will Noah be able to open himself up to love despite his secrets, or will he let Mandy be married off to one her grandmother's prospects?

Other books by the same author:
Huckleberry Spring, 2015
Huckleberry Christmas, 2014
Huckleberry Hill, 2014
Huckleberry Summer, 2014
Forever in Apple Lake series, 2012

Other books you might like:
Lori Copeland, *A Plain and Simple Heart*, 2012
Mary Ellis, *Love Comes to Paradise*, 2013
Leslie Gould, *Minding Molly*, 2014
Emma Miller, *A Match for Addy*, 2015
Sarah Price, *The Matchmaker*, 2015

359

JENNIFER BECKSTRAND

Huckleberry Spring

(New York: Zebra Books, 2015)

Series: Huckleberry Hill Series. Book 4
Story type: Romance; Series
Subject(s): Christian life; Grandparents; Love
Major character(s): Anna Helmuth, Grandmother (of Ben), Spouse (of Felty); Felty Helmuth, Spouse (of Anna), Grandfather (of Ben); Ben Helmuth, Grandson (of Anna and Felty), Fiance(e) (former, of Emma); Emma Nelson, Fiance(e) (former, of Ben)
Time period(s): 21st century; 2010s
Locale(s): Huckleberry Hill, Wisconsin

Summary: In this inspirational romance by Jennifer Beckstrand, the fourth novel in the Huckleberry Hill series, Ben Helmuth's grandparents Anna and Felty love nothing more than matchmaking in their small town of Huckleberry Hill, Wisconsin—especially for their grandchildren. It broke their hearts to see Ben end his engagement to Emma Nelson. He then moved abruptly to Florida, where he's been living ever since. Emma has continued to help Anna and Felty with their gardens, and they can't understand why Ben would not want to be with such a lovely young woman. When Felty needs surgery, Ben returns home to help care for him, and he is struck once again by Emma's kindness and love. Ben's fear that he can't give Emma what she needs makes him keep his distance, but he soon begins to wonder if he should have a little more faith.

Other books by the same author:
Forever After in Apple Lake Series, 2014
Huckleberry Christmas, 2014
Huckleberry Hill, 2014
Huckleberry Summer, 2014

Other books you might like:
Vannetta Chapman, *A Wedding for Julia*, 2013
Leslie Gould, *Minding Molly*, 2014
Kelly Long, *Lilly's Wedding Quilt*, 2011
Kelly Long, *Sarah's Garden*, 2010
Cindy Woodsmall, *When the Soul Mends*, 2008

360

LORI BENTON

The Wood's Edge

(Colorado Springs, Colorado: WaterBrook Press, 2015)

Series: Pathfinders Series. Book 1
Story type: Historical; Romance
Subject(s): Family relations; Interpersonal relations; United States history, 1600-1775 (Colonial period)
Major character(s): Reginald Aubrey, Father (of Anna), Father (of William), Kidnapper (of William); Anna Aubrey, Sister (of William), Daughter (of Reginald); William Aubrey, Kidnap Victim, Son (of Reginald), Twin (of Two Hawks); Two Hawks, Twin (of William)

Inspirational

Time period(s): 18th century; 1750s-1760s (1757-1768)
Locale(s): New York, United States

Summary: In the first installment of the Pathfinders series, it is a dark day for Major Reginald Aubrey. Fort William Henry has fallen, and his newborn son has died while his wife is sleeping. Desperate to replace the child before his wife wakes, Reginald finds an Oneida mother who has just had twins—one white and one brown. Reginald steals the white baby and leaves his dead son in his place. Although Reginald's family never suspects that the baby named William is not theirs, Reginald is haunted by the guilt of what he has done. Meanwhile, the Oneida family is still suffering from the loss of its child. When the secret is finally revealed, the effect causes severe damage in the two families. But Reginald's other child, Anna, must choose between two loves: her brother William and her brother's twin, Two Hawks, whom she meets in secret.

Other books by the same author:
The Pursuit of Tamsen Littlejohn, 2014
Burning Sky, 2013

Other books you might like:
Jody Hedlund, *Rebellious Heart*, 2013
Allison Pataki, *The Traitor's Wife*, 2014
Tracie Peterson, *A Veiled Reflection*, 2000
Lauraine Snelling, *Daughter of Twin Oaks*, 2000
Bodie Thoene, *Wayward Wind Series*, 1997

361

LISA T. BERGREN

Remnants: Season of Fire

(Grand Rapids, Michigan: Blink, 2015)

Series: Remnants Series
Story type: Dystopian; Fantasy
Subject(s): Dystopias; Good and evil; Prophecy
Major character(s): Andriana, Teenager (Remnant), Friend (of Ronana), Enemy (of Sethos and Keallach); Ronan, Teenager (Knight of the Last Order), Friend (of Andriana); Sethos, Enemy (of Andriana and Ronan); Keallach, Enemy (of Andriana and Ronan), Leader (emperor, of Pacifica)
Time period(s): 21st century; 2090s (2095)
Locale(s): Earth

Summary: Set in 2095, this dystopian novel for young adults is the second installment in the inspirational Remnants series by award-winning author Lisa T. Bergren. Andriana and her fellow Remnants continue their search for the remaining Aileth, prophesied teenagers with special powers who have been chosen and trained since birth. Protected by the Knights of the Last Order, Remnants fight the demonic forces that threaten humanity. Andriana and her knight, Ronan, have confessed their feelings to one another, but challenges rise when Andriana is captured by Sethos and Keallach, the emperor of Pacifica. Does Andriana have the power to convince Keallach to return to the Way and once again follow the Maker's plan, or has Sethos spun a web of evil so thorough that Keallach—and now Andriana—are forever trapped?

Other books by the same author:
Remnants: Season of Wonder, 2015
Grand Tour Series, 2012
River of Time Series, 2011
The Homeward Trilogy, 2009
A Novel of the Gifted Series, 2006

Other books you might like:
Sigmund Brouwer, *Flight of Shadows*, 2010
Shannon Dittemore, *Angel Eyes*, 2012
Krista McGee, *Luminary*, 2014
Robin Parrish, *Vigilante*, 2011
James L. Rubart, *Book of Days*, 2011

362

TERRI BLACKSTOCK
CANDACE CALVERT, Co-Author
SUSAN MAY WARREN, Co-Author

Chance of Loving You

(Carol Stream, Illinois: Tyndale House Publishers, 2015)

Story type: Collection; Romance
Subject(s): Romances (Fiction); Interpersonal relations; Faith

Summary: This inspirational romance collection includes three novellas by best-selling authors Terri Blackstock, Candace Calvert, and Susan May Warren. The theme connecting each work is a contest or competition. In Blackstock's *For Love of Money*, Julie Sheffield works as a waitress while her design firm is getting off the ground. Her head is turned by a handsome man she waits on at the restaurant, but when he leaves her half of a sweepstakes ticket instead of a tip, she's not sure what to think. In Calvert's *The Recipe*, hospital dietary assistant Aimee Curran has high hopes of winning the Vegan Valentine Bake-off, but when she falls for one of her patient's grandsons—a gorgeous CSI photographer—the bake-off victory suddenly pales in comparison to a chance with him. In Warren's *Hook, Line and Sinker*, Abigail Cushman enters the Deep Haven fishing contest, only to learn that her competition is the man who once broke her heart. Will their friendly fishing battle turn into a second chance at love?

Other books you might like:
Wanda E. Brunstetter, *Attic Treasures*, 2005
Colleen Coble, *Smitten Series*, 2011
Katie Lane, *A Match Made in Texas*, 2014
Gail Gaymer Martin, *Romance Across the Globe*, 2015
Beth Wiseman, *The House that Love Built*, 2013

363

TERRI BLACKSTOCK

Twisted Innocence

(Grand Rapids, Michigan: Zondervan, 2015)

Series: Moonlighter Series. Book 3
Story type: Amateur Detective; Romance
Subject(s): Crime; Romances (Fiction); Murder

Major character(s): Holly Cramer, Lover (former, of Creed), Mother (of Lily), Detective—Amateur; Creed Kershaw, Crime Suspect, Lover (former, of Holly), Father (of Lily); Lily Cramer, Daughter (of Holly and Creed)

Time period(s): 21st century; 2010s

Locale(s): Panama City, Florida

Summary: Holly Cramer has made a lot of mistakes in her life, but she's trying her best to put that behind her for the sake of her little girl, Lily. Her partying days are done, her days of running around with bad boys like Creed Kershaw are over. Creed is Lily's father, though no one—not even Creed—knows that. But then the police show up looking for Creed and asking questions. He's wanted in connection with a murder that involved drugs, which is all the more reason for Holly to stay far away from him. She's so determined to keep Creed out of her life that she turns amateur detective and goes looking for him. Creed, protesting his innocence, takes Holly and Lily hostage. She's furious, and yet touched by his gentleness with her little girl—their little girl. The man Creed accuses of the murder is the same man who killed several members of Holly's family. Creed might be innocent, but Holly and Lily are still in danger. Forgiveness and redemption will be required all the way around. This is the third book in the Moonlighters series.

Other books by the same author:
Distortion, 2014
Truth Stained Lies, 2013
The Intervention Series, 2009
Restoration Series, 2005
Cape Refuge Series, 2002

Other books you might like:
Irene Hannon, *Deadly Pursuit*, 2011
Dee Henderson, *The Negotiator*, 2000
DiAnn Mills, *Breach of Trust*, 2009
Lis Wiehl, *Snapshot*, 2014
Karen Young, *Lie for Me*, 2011

364

MAGGIE BRENDAN

The Trouble with Patience

(Ada, Michigan: Baker Publishing Group, 2015)

Series: Virtues and Vices of the Old West Series. Book 1

Story type: Historical - American West

Subject(s): Western fiction; Romances (Fiction); Hotels and motels

Major character(s): Patience Cavanaugh, Innkeeper (of a boarding house), Friend (of Jedidiah); Jedidiah Jones, Lawman (Sheriff), Friend (of Patience)

Time period(s): 19th century; 1860s (1866)

Locale(s): Nevada City, Montana

Summary: One Montana town might be a boon for fortune seekers, but it's a romantic bust for Patience Cavanaugh. She was in love, but the man died as did her hopes of a happy, secure future. Now Patience has thrown herself into repairing an old boarding house, where she'll rent rooms and cook meals to support herself. In exchange for help with the heavy work around the boarding house, she strikes a deal with the sheriff, agreeing to cook for him and the residents in the jail. But Sheriff Jedidiah Jones comes with a little additional baggage: this lawman with a reputation for hanging has a few secrets in his past. As their simple arrangement becomes more complicated, Patience will have to learn to deal with betrayal and reconsider her future and ability to find love. This is the first book in the Virtues and Vices of the Old West series.

Other books by the same author:
The Blue Willow Brides Series, 2011
The Jewel of His Heart: A Novel, 2010
A Love of Her Own, 2010
Heart of the West Series, 2009

Other books you might like:
Maggie Brendan, *The Jewel of His Heart: A Novel*, 2009
Mary Connealy, *Gingham Mountain*, 2009
Lori Copeland, *A Kiss for Cade*, 2009
Deeanne Gist, *Deep in the Heart of Trouble*, 2008
Martha Rogers, *Becoming Lucy*, 2010

365

SIGMUND BROUWER

Nowhere to Hide

(Eugene, Oregon: Harvest House Publishers, 2015)

Story type: Techno-Thriller; Young Adult

Subject(s): Friendship; Technology; Espionage

Major character(s): William King, Mentally Ill Person (PTSD), Teenager, 12th Grader, Volunteer (for CIA), Computer Expert, Friend (of Blake and MJ); Blake Wyatt, Teenager, 12th Grader, Volunteer (for CIA), Friend (of King and MJ), Computer Expert; Michael "MJ" Johnson, Volunteer (for CIA), Teenager, 12th Grader, Computer Expert, Friend (of Blake and King); Evans, Agent (CIA)

Time period(s): 21st century; 2010s

Locale(s): Washington, United States

Summary: This is the sequel to Sigmund Brouwer's young adult novel *Dead Man's Switch*. Teenagers William King, Blake Wyatt, and Michael Johnson (MJ) are seniors in high school who have been tapped by the CIA once again to use their hacking skills to find information. The trio are asked to work with Agent Evans to track down a man who has been missing child support payments. The teens are effectively serving as cyber bounty hunters. Although King suffers from post-traumatic stress disorder after the events in the previous novel and isn't sure that he can trust the CIA or Agent Evans, he is eager to help his friends. The boys quickly realize that more is going on than they were led to believe and they must choose carefully who they can trust and what their real mission is. Blake, King, and MJ must trust in God and each other to uncover the truth before they run out of time.

Other books by the same author:
Dead Man's Switch, 2014
Thief of Glory, 2014
Blood Ties, 2011
Flight of Shadows, 2010

Broken Angel, 2009

Other books you might like:
Ted Dekker, *Hacker: The Outlaw Chronicles*, 2014
Lynette Eason, *No One to Trust*, 2013
Andrew Klavan, *MindWar*, 2014
DiAnn Mills, *Firewall*, 2014
Bill Myers, *The God Hater*, 2010

366

DON BROWN

Detained

(Grand Rapids, Michigan: Zondervan Publishing, 2015)

Series: Navy JAG Series. Book 1
Story type: Legal; Military
Subject(s): Betrayal; Conspiracy; Crime
Major character(s): Hasan Makari, Defendant (terrorism charge), Immigrant (Lebanese), Father (of Najib Makari), Prisoner (at Guantanamo Bay); Najib Makari, Son (of Hasan Makari), Immigrant (Lebanese), Military Personnel (Navy), Defendant (terrorism charge), Prisoner (at Guantanamo Bay); Matt Davis, Lawyer (of Hasan and Najib Makari), Military Personnel (Navy JAG Officer); Emily Gardner, Political Figure (nominee, General Counsel for Homeland Security), Lawyer (Transportation Security Administration)
Time period(s): 21st century; 2010s
Locale(s): Guantanamo Bay, Cuba; Rome, Italy; Washington, District of Columbia; Philadelphia, Pennsylvania; Norfolk, Virginia

Summary: In the first novel of the Navy JAG series, JAG officer Matt Davis is assigned to defend two innocent men accused of terrorism. Hasan and Najib Makari left their homeland of Lebanon with dreams of coming to America and becoming citizens. Their American dream didn't include being arrested, accused of terrorism, and imprisoned in the infamous Guantanamo Bay prison in Cuba. Now Matt must face a powerful federal prosecutor with a hidden agenda and unlimited resources to help save the lives of his clients. While Matt is working to save the Makaris, Emily Gardner, a lawyer with the Transportation Security Administration, is offered the job of a lifetime—to become the general counsel of Homeland Security. As she seeks confirmation to her appointment, Emily uncovers a secret plot that would have devastating effects on the American people. Will Emily be able to unravel the plot and help Matt defend his clients, or will she be eliminated as a threat?

Other books by the same author:
The Malacca Conspiracy, 2010
Black Sea Affair, 2008
Defiance, 2007
Hostage, 2005
Treason, 2005

Other books you might like:
Irene Hannon, *Deadly Pursuit*, 2011
Dee Henderson, *True Devotion*, 2000
Ronie Kendig, *Raptor 6*, 2014

Mel Odom, *Military NCIS Series*, 2006
Joel Rosenberg, *Dead Heat: A Novel*, 2008

367

WANDA E. BRUNSTETTER

The Decision

(Uhrichsville, Ohio: Barbour Publishing, 2015)

Series: Prairie State Friends Series. Book 1
Story type: Romance; Series
Subject(s): Amish; Christian life; Love
Major character(s): Jonah Miller, Religious (Amish), Fiance(e) (of Elaine), Boyfriend (of Sara); Elaine Schrock, Fiance(e) (of Jonah), Friend (of Sara), Religious (Amish); Sara Stutzman, Friend (of Elaine), Religious (Amish), Widow(er), Mother (of Mark), Girlfriend (of Jonah); Mark Stutzman, Son (of Sara), 2-Year-Old, Religious (Amish)
Time period(s): 21st century; 2010s
Locale(s): Arthur, Illinois

Summary: In the first novel from Wande E. Brunstetter's Prairie State Friends series, the author introduces readers to Jonah Miller, a young Amish man who decides to start a new life. Jonah has fled Pennsylvania with a broken heart, and is trying to start over in an Amish community in Illinois. He has taken a chance on love again and becomes engaged to Elaine Schrock, but when deaths and illnesses in Elaine's family cause her to break their engagement, he decides he must move on. When he begins courting Sara Stutzman, a widow with a toddler son, he thinks that his third attempt to find true love just might work out. Yet Elaine is devastated that Jonah is courting one of her friends, and realizes what a mistake she has made in letting Jonah go. When Sara gets some devastating news of her own, Jonah must decide who truly owns his heart.

Other books by the same author:
The Healing Quilt, 2014
Women of Courage, 2014
Goodbye to Yesterday, 2013
Lydia's Charm, 2010
Brides of Lancaster County Series, 2005

Other books you might like:
Annalisa Daughety, *Love Finds You in Charm, Ohio*, 2009
Jerry S. Eicher, *Finding Love at Home*, 2014
Tricia Goyer, *Beyond Hope's Valley*, 2012
Emma Miller, *Leah's Choice*, 2012
Cindy Woodsmall, *For Every Season*, 2013

368

MORGAN L. BUSSE

Heir of Hope

(Phoenix, Arizona: Enclave Publishing, 2015)

Series: Follower of the Word Series. Book 3
Story type: Fantasy; Magic Conflict
Subject(s): Good and evil; Fantasy; Epics

Inspirational

Major character(s): Rowan Mar, Woman, Captive (of the Shadonae); Caleb Tala, Hero (Guardian of mankind), Assassin (formerly); Captain Lore, Military Personnel; Nierne, Writer, Religious (monk)
Locale(s): Tomanin, Fictional Location

Summary: In the third and final book of the Follower of the Word series, the city Thyra has been destroyed and now shadows are starting to invade the world. The Shadonae have captured the Last Truthsayer, Rowen Mar, and hope to make her one of them. She is forced to use her powers to bring in money and struggles with thoughts of revenge. Meanwhile, the former assassin, Caleb Tala, has become the Guardian of mankind. With the scribe Nierne in tow, Caleb had escaped from Temanin and is now heading toward Thyra. Caleb hopes to find answers to who he is and learn more about his mother's past. While searching for Rowen, Captain Lore meets Caleb and Nierne. As Rowan struggles with temptation and tries to do the right thing, Lore and Caleb create a shaky alliance and set out to save humanity.

Other books by the same author:
Son of Truth, 2013
Daughter of Light, 2012

Other books you might like:
Tamera Alexander, *To Whisper Her Name*, 2012
Susan Meissner, *The Shape of Mercy*, 2008
Judith Pella, *A Hope Beyond*, 1997
Tracie Peterson, *The Freedom of the Soul*, 2006
Carla Stewart, *Stardust*, 2012

369

LINDA BYLER

The Witnesses

(New York: Skyhorse Publishing, 2015)

Series: Lancaster Burning Series. Book 3
Story type: Mystery; Series
Subject(s): Amish; Suspense; Arson
Major character(s): Davey Beiler, Religious (Amish minister), Father (of Sarah); Sarah Beiler, Daughter (of Davey), Accident Victim, Religious (Amish)
Time period(s): 21st century; 2010s
Locale(s): Lancaster County, Pennsylvania

Summary: In the third and last installment of Linda Byler's Lancaster Burning series, the author concludes the saga in which the Amish families of Lancaster County, Pennsylvania, have been terrorized by an arsonist. District leader Davey Bieler tries to keep his community from overreacting, especially since some people in his congregation threaten to expose one of the suspects. He asks that they exercise kindness and clemency instead of punishing someone who may not deserve it. When his own daughter is injured while attempting to put out flames in a burning barn, however, he wonders if his leniency is to blame. Now he fears she may never marry, nor achieve her goal of becoming an educator in their community. As Davey comes to terms with his beliefs regarding mercy and justice, he realizes that now, more than ever, he must turn to God if he is to know what is right.

Other books by the same author:
Christmas Visitor, 2013
Lancaster Burning Series, 2013
Sadie's Montana Series, 2012
Lizzie Searches for Love Series, 2010

Other books you might like:
Mindy Starns Clark, *Shadows of Lancaster County*, 2009
Colleen Coble, *Anathema*, 2008
Amanda Flower, *A Plain Scandal*, 2013
Shelley Shepard Gray, *Forgiven*, 2009
Nancy Mehl, *Inescapable*, 2012

370

VICTORIA BYLIN

Together with You

(Bloomington, Minnesota: Bethany House Publishers, 2015)

Story type: Contemporary; Romance
Subject(s): Family relations; Family life; Interpersonal relations
Major character(s): Carly Jo Mason, Social Worker (formerly), Caregiver (nanny to Penny); Dr. Ryan Tremaine, Employer (of Carly), Single Father (of Penny); Penny Tremaine, Daughter (of Ryan), Mentally Challenged Person, 5-Year-Old
Time period(s): 21st century; 2010s
Locale(s): Los Angeles, California

Summary: Carly Mason finds a girl playing with a stuffed rabbit after a lost child alert is blasted throughout the mall. Carly realizes that the little girl, Penny, suffers from fetal alcohol syndrome. As a former social worker, Carly knows better than to get involved with a troubled family, but she finds herself drawn to Penny and her father, Dr. Ryan Tremaine. Meanwhile, Ryan is trying to get his life in order after his ex-wife remarries. Now taking care of three children, Ryan is determined to reconnect with his teenage sons and Penny. Ryan asks Carly to become Penny's nanny. As time progresses, Carly and Ryan are drawn together, despite their attempts at fighting the attraction. Soon Ryan begins to question whether Carly's presence could help rebuild his family or throw a wrench in the works.

Other books by the same author:
Until I Found You, 2014
Midnight Marriage, 2012
West of Heaven, 2012

Other books you might like:
Ginny Aiken, *For Such a Time as This*, 2012
Mindy Starns Clark, *The Amish Nanny*, 2011
Cathy Marie Hake, *Whirlwind*, 2008
Denise Hunter, *A Cowboy's Touch*, 2011
Judith Pella, *A Hope Beyond*, 1997

371

SANDRA BYRD

Mist of Midnight

(New York: Howard Books, 2015)

Series: Daughters of Hampshire Series. Book 1
Story type: Gothic; Series
Subject(s): England; Identity; Missionaries
Major character(s): Rebecca Ravenshaw, Orphan, Heiress; Luke Whitfield, Military Personnel (captain), Heir (presumed)
Time period(s): 19th century; 1850s (1858)
Locale(s): Hampshire, England

Summary: In the aftermath of a rebellion, Rebecca Ravenshaw finds her missionary parents have been killed and she is now an orphan in India. She immediately returns to England, a country she barely recalls from her early childhood. Rebecca journeys to her family estate and makes arrangements to claim her inheritance. She is met with surprise and suspicion upon her arrival, because a woman arrived more than a year ago claiming to be Rebecca. The young woman took over the property, but died unexpectedly. A distant relative, Captain Luke Whitfield, moved into the manor house and assumed control of Rebecca's inheritance. Aghast that an imposter could have taken her place so easily, Rebecca is determined to fight for her bequest. She wonders if Luke was involved in the scheme and planned to steal her home and income. Luke is charming and handsome, and despite her reservations, Rebecca finds herself falling in love with him. This is the first novel of the Daughters of Hampshire series.

Other books by the same author:
Roses Have Thorns, 2013
The Secret Keeper, 2012
To Die For, 2011

Other books you might like:
Tamera Alexander, *Remembered*, 2007
Catherine Richmond, *Through Rushing Water*, 2012
Jen Turano, *A Most Peculiar Circumstance*, 2013
Carrie Turansky, *The Daughter of Highland Hall*, 2014
Lisa Wingate, *Beyond Summer*, 2010

372

AMANDA CABOT

In Firefly Valley

(Grand Rapids, Michigan: Revell, 2015)

Series: Texas Crossroads Series. Book 2
Story type: Romance; Series
Subject(s): Christian life; Romances (Fiction); Interpersonal relations
Major character(s): Marisa St. George, Hotel Worker (business manager); Blake Kendall, Man (hotel guest)
Time period(s): 21st century; 2010s
Locale(s): Firefly Valley, Texas

Summary: In this inspirational romance by Amanda Cabot, the second in the Texas Crossroads series, Marisa St. George has just lost her high-paying job due to the struggling economy. She is forced to return to her hometown of Firefly Valley, Texas, where she takes a job as a business manager at Rainbow's End resort. She's thrown off course by this unexpected change in her life and status, but soon finds herself drawn to one of the guests at her resort, Blake Kendall. She might almost call it love at first sight. But Blake has a secret—and once it's revealed, it could put a stop to their relationship before it's even had a chance to begin. Blake must learn to trust, and Amanda will have to keep her heart open if they are to have a future together.

Other books by the same author:
At Bluebonnet Lake, 2014
Christmas Roses, 2012
Westward Winds Series, 2012
Texas Dreams Series, 2009

Other books you might like:
Tamara Leigh, *Leaving Carolina*, 2009
Beth K. Vogt, *Catch a Falling Star*, 2013
Becky Wade, *My Stubborn Heart*, 2012
Lisa Wingate, *Talk of the Town*, 2008
Alice J. Wisler, *Hatteras Girl*, 2010

373

CANDACE CALVERT

By Your Side

(Carol Stream, Illinois: Tyndale House Publishers, 2015)

Series: Crisis Team Series. Book 1
Story type: Romance; Series
Subject(s): Nursing; Foster home care; Foster children
Major character(s): Macy Wynn, Nurse, Sister (foster, of unnamed character); Unnamed Character, Sister (foster, of Macy), Addict; Fletcher Holt, Police Officer; Unnamed Character, Criminal (sniper)
Time period(s): 21st century; 2010s
Locale(s): Sacramento, California

Summary: In the first novel from Candace Calvert's Crisis Team series, the author introduces readers to Macy Wynn, a nurse who grew up in foster care and has finally found one of her foster sisters. Unfortunately, the girl is struggling with addiction, and Macy has sworn to help her. When Macy is trapped in a pileup on a California freeway as the result of a crazed gunman targeting passing cars, she meets up with deputy Fletcher Holt. Holt has a strong belief in Jesus and the concept that fairness always triumphs. Macy is determined to help everyone involved in the accident, but she doesn't realize that she is the shooter's next target. As Fletcher works to keep Macy safe from the gunman, he also learns that she isn't the type of person who is used to listening to authority. As a romance blossoms between the two of them, they must learn to compromise their steadfast beliefs in order to make it work.

Other books by the same author:
Grace Medical Series, 2012
Mercy Hospital Series, 2009

Inspirational

Other books you might like:
Patricia Bradley, *A Promise to Protect*, 2014
Lynette Eason, *Don't Look Back*, 2010
Serita Ann Jakes, *The Crossing Places*, 2011
Richard L. Mabry, *Critical Condition*, 2014
Jordyn Redwood, *Peril*, 2013

374

ELIZABETH CAMDEN

Beyond All Dreams

(Minneapolis, Minnesota: Bethany House, 2015)

Story type: Romance
Subject(s): Christian life; Mystery; History
Major character(s): Anna O'Brien, Librarian; Luke Callahan, Government Official (Congressman)
Time period(s): 19th century; 1890s (1897)
Locale(s): Washington, District of Columbia

Summary: In this inspirational novel by Elizabeth Camden, the 19th century is in its final years. Anna O'Brien works as a map librarian at the Library of Congress. She happens upon the story of a ship that has vanished at sea, and is immediately captivated by the mystery. She reaches out to Luke Callahan, a handsome congressman, with some questions in her investigation. As the two spend time together, they find that their differences attract them to each other—and despite the rules that prevent Anna from any romantic involvement with members of Congress, they continue to grow closer as they try to solve the mystery of the ship. But what they find is shocking, and revealing what they've learned could put much more than their relationship in danger.

Other books by the same author:
With Every Breath, 2014
Into the Whirlwind, 2013
Against the Tide, 2012
The Rose of Winslow Street, 2012
the Lady of Bolton Hill, 2011

Other books you might like:
Lynn Austin, *Wonderland Creek*, 2011
Mindy Starns Clark, *Echoes of Titanic*, 2012
Amanda Flower, *Maid of Murder*, 2010
Dee Henderson, *True Honor*, 2002
Karen Witemeyer, *To Win Her Heart*, 2011

375

BARBARA CAMERON

One True Path

(Nashville, Tennessee: Abingdon Press, 2015)

Series: Amish Roads Series. Book 3
Story type: Romance; Series
Subject(s): Romances (Fiction); Amish; Family
Major character(s): Rachel Ann, Neighbor (of Abram), Friend (of Michael), Sister (of Sam); Abram Lapp, Neighbor (of Rachel); Michael, Friend (of Rachel); Sam, Brother (of Rachel Ann)

Time period(s): 21st century; 2010s
Locale(s): Goshen, Indiana

Summary: In this Amish romance by Barbara Cameron, the third in the Amish Roads series, Rachel Ann is having a wonderful time during her Rumschpringe—especially spending time with Michael, an Englisch man. Rachel Ann's neighbor, Abram Lapp, has been in love with her for a long time, but he has never confessed his feelings for her. Now he is concerned that Rachel Ann will choose to stay in the Englisch world instead of returning to their small community. But when Rachel Ann's brother is severely injured, Rachel Ann begins to feel guilty for spending this time away from home, and she works hard to earn money for hospital expenses. When she tries to lean on Michael for emotional support, he pulls away. Soon, Rachel Ann is questioning her feelings for Michael and for the Englisch world, and she finds herself drawn back home to the kind, loving Abram.

Other books by the same author:
Crossroads, 2014
A Road Unknown, 2014
Stitches in Time Series, 2012
Quilts of Lancaster County Series, 2010

Other books you might like:
Tricia Goyer, *Beside Still Waters*, 2011
Shelley Shepard Gray, *Wanted*, 2009
Laura V. Hilton, *Patchwork Dreams*, 2011
Beth Shriver, *Rumspringa's Hope*, 2014
Beth Wiseman, *Plain Peace*, 2013

376

JANICE CANTORE

Drawing Fire

(Carol Stream, Illinois: Tyndale House Publishers, 2015)

Series: Cold Case Justice Series. Book 1
Story type: Mystery; Romance
Subject(s): Detective fiction; Mystery; Romances (Fiction)
Major character(s): Abby Hart, Orphan, Detective—Homicide; Luke Murphy, Detective—Private
Time period(s): 21st century; 2010s
Locale(s): Long Beach, California

Summary: This inspirational suspense novel is the first installment in the Cold Case Justice series by Janice Cantore. Long Beach homicide detective Abby Hart is haunted by the mysterious restaurant fire that claimed the lives of her parents years ago. When an investigation of serial murders links one of the victims to the governor, Abby gets the chance to talk to him about the cold case involving the death of her parents. She is surprised to discover a private investigator, Luke Murphy, has an interest in the case as well. Together, Abby and Luke work together to determine who started the fire and why, and Abby learns why Luke is determined to get to the bottom of the case. The more they learn, however, the more questions they have. Is it possible for Abby to make peace with the past when so many questions remain unanswered?

Other books by the same author:
Visible Threat, 2014

Critical Pursuit, 2013
Pacific Coast Justice Series, 2012
A Heart of Justice, 2010

Other books you might like:
Terri Blackstock, *Predator*, 2010
Robin Caroll, *Strand of Deception*, 2013
Brandilyn Collins, *Gone to Ground*, 2012
Lynette Eason, *When the Smoke Clears*, 2012
Dee Henderson, *Taken*, 2015

377

VANNETTA CHAPMAN

Murder Freshly Baked

(Grand Rapids, Michigan: Zondervan, 2015)

Series: Amish Village Mystery Series. Book 3
Story type: Cozy Mystery; Mystery
Subject(s): Detective fiction; Mystery; Amish
Major character(s): Amber Bowman, Manager (of Amish Artisan Village), Friend (of Hannah), Detective—Amateur; Hannah Troyer, Store Owner (storekeeper), Friend (of Amber), Detective—Amateur, Religious (Amish)
Time period(s): 21st century; 2010s
Locale(s): Middlebury, Indiana

Summary: Best-selling author Vannetta Chapman delivers the third novel in her Amish Village Mystery Series. For years, Amber Bowman has managed the Amish Artisan Village in Middlebury, Indiana, but nothing could prepare for the string of poems showing up at the bakery. The threatening notes warn of poisoned pies, and soon, Amber's wondering if a murderer is walking in their midst. Once again, Amber calls upon her friend and storekeeper, Hannah Troyer, to help the police track down the poems' author before someone is targeted. Meanwhile, when a handsome older man makes passes at several of Middlebury's young, single women, Amber and Hannah—as well as the rest of the Village—are on high alert. It will take all their wits and faith to keep Middlebury the peaceful community they've worked so hard to build.

Other books by the same author:
Murder Simply Brewed, 2014
Murder Tightly Knit, 2014
A Promise for Miriam, 2012
Shipshewana Amish Mystery series, 2011
A Simple Amish Christmas, 2010

Other books you might like:
Amanda Flower, *A Plain Death*, 2012
Shelley Shepard Gray, *Secrets of Crittenden County Series*, 2012
Linda Evans Shepherd, *Bake Until Golden: A Novel*, 2011
Amy Wallace, *Hiding in Plain Sight*, 2012
Kit Wilkinson, *Plain Secrets*, 2012

378

MINDY STARNS CLARK
SUSAN MEISSNER, Co-Author

The Amish Clockmaker

(Eugene, Oregon: Harvest House Publishers, 2015)

Series: Men of Lancaster County Series. Book 3
Story type: Mystery; Series
Subject(s): Amish; Mystery; Murder
Major character(s): Matthew Zook, Store Owner; Clayton Raber, Artisan (clockmaker)
Time period(s): 21st century; 2010s
Locale(s): Lancaster County, Pennsylvania

Summary: In this novel by Mindy Starns Clark and Susan Meissner, the third in the Men of Lancaster County series, Matthew Zook is attempting to improve his family's feed and tack store in Lancaster County. But a property dispute has brought the project to a halt and threatened his business. The property used to belong to a clockmaker, Clayton Raber, who was arrested after his wife was found murdered. Though the charges were dropped, everyone still believed he was guilty. Clayton left Lancaster County and has not been heard from since. Matthew will need to track down Clayton in order to resolve the property issue, but he knows he's putting himself in grave danger by going after an alleged murderer who does not want his secrets uncovered.

Other books by the same author:
The Amish Blacksmith, 2014
The Amish Groom, 2014
Lillies on Daybreak Pond, 2014

Other books you might like:
Vannetta Chapman, *Murder Simply Brewed*, 2014
Mary Ellis, *A Plain Man*, 2014
Nancy Mehl, *Inescapable*, 2012
Olivia Newport, *In Plain View*, 2013
Kit Wilkinson, *Plain Secrets*, 2012

379

AMY CLIPSTON

Miles from Nowhere

(Grand Rapids, Michigan: Zondervan, 2015)

Story type: Coming-of-Age; Young Adult
Subject(s): Coming of age; Friendship; Family relations
Major character(s): Chelsea Morris, Student—High School, Teenager, Designer (costume), Friend (of Emily and Dylan), Girlfriend (of Todd); Dylan, Student—College, Actor, Friend (of Chelsea); Todd, Teenager, Boyfriend (of Chelsea); Emily, Friend (of Chelsea)
Time period(s): 21st century; 2010s
Locale(s): Cameronville, North Carolina

Summary: High school senior Chelsea Morris looks forward to spending one last summer in North Carolina with her boyfriend, Todd, and best friend, Emily, before moving to New York City in the fall. An aspiring fashion designer, Chelsea lands the role of lead costume designer at her local theater, but when she attracts the attention of Dylan, a college sophomore and handsome lead actor, her summer takes an unexpected turn. Encouraged by Dylan to make the most of her summer months, Chelsea sneaks off to late-night parties, lies to her family and friends, and questions her feelings for Todd. Chelsea enjoys the freedom and excitement she feels with Dylan, but soon, her wild nights get the best of her. Caught up in a web of lies, Chelsea loses the trust of her parents, is in jeopardy of losing her job, and feels further away from God than she ever has. Now, Chelsea struggles with whether she's the Christian she's always claimed to be and wonders if her reputation and relationships can truly be restored.

Other books by the same author:
Destination Unknown, 2013
Roadside Assistance, 2011
A Place of Peace, 2010
Betrayed, 2009
Kauffman Amish Bakery series, 2009

Other books you might like:
Kristin Billerbeck, *She's All That*, 2005
Mailynn Griffith, *Jade*, 2006
Jenny B. Jones, *The Big Picture*, 2008
Karen Kingsbury, *Fame*, 2005
Alison Strobel, *Worlds Collide*, 2005

380

AMY CLIPSTON

A Simple Prayer

(Grand Rapids, Michigan: Zondervan, 2015)

Series: Hearts of Lancaster Grand Hotel Series. Book 4
Story type: Romance; Series
Subject(s): Romances (Fiction); Amish; Orphans
Major character(s): Linda Zook, Orphan, Niece, Hotel Worker, Accident Victim; Ruth Ebersol, Mother (of Aaron), Aged Person, Patient (stroke), Religious (Amish); Aaron Ebersol, Son (of Ruth)
Time period(s): 21st century; 2010s
Locale(s): Paradise, Pennsylvania

Summary: Linda Zook never really knew her parents, who died in a carriage crash when she was only 4 years old. The accident left Linda seriously injured, and she was left to grow up on her cold and distant uncle's farm. When Linda gets a job at the historic Heart of Paradise Bed and Breakfast, she finally finds a sense of place as well as friends she can call her own. Then Aaron Ebersol checks in. Aaron was banned by the community nearly two decades ago when he deserted the church, and hasn't talked to his family since then. After learning that his mother has had a stroke, Aaron rushes home to help out. Not all of his family wants him there, though. Aaron and Linda connect through their shared longing for familial love, but soon that connection develops into romantic feelings. Now, both Aaron and Linda must struggle with their beliefs and decide whether they belong together. This is the fourth novel of author Amy Clipston's Hearts of Lancaster Grand Hotel series.

Other books by the same author:
A Dream of Home, 2014
A Mother's Secret, 2014
A Hopeful Heart, 2013
Reckless Heart, 2012
The Kauffman Amish Bakery series, 2009

Other books you might like:
Suzanne Woods Fisher, *The Choice*, 2010
Shelley Shepard Gray, *Wanted*, 2009
Kelly Irvin, *To Love and to Cherish*, 2012
Kate Lloyd, *Forever Amish*, 2014
Kim Vogel Sawyer, *When Hope Blossoms*, 2012

381

DEBRA CLOPTON

Betting on Hope

(Nashville, Tennessee: Thomas Nelson, 2015)

Series: Four of Hearts Ranch Series. Book 1
Subject(s): Romances (Fiction); Love; Horses
Major character(s): Maggie Hope, Writer (advice columnist), Mother; Tru Monahan, Cowboy/Cowgirl, Horse Trainer
Time period(s): 21st century; 2010s
Locale(s): Wishing Springs, Texas

Summary: Maggie Hope is an advice columnist whose background leaves her with little advice to give...and it's beginning to show. When she fills in for an interview with champion horse trainer Tru Monahan, the on-camera chemistry between them is undeniable. Maggie's bosses know this is her opportunity to launch her career—and their bank accounts. So Maggie takes Tru up on a bet that he can teach her to ride a cutting horse like any cowgirl. And in the meantime, she can get the scoop on the man under the cowboy hat....Also available in Large Print.

Other books by the same author:
Her Mule Hollow Cowboy, 2014
Her Unexpected Cowboy, 2013
Her Homecoming Cowboy, 2012
Her Rodeo Cowboy, 2011
Yukon Cowboy, 2010

Other books you might like:
Maggie Brendan, *A Love of Her Own*, 2010
Mindy Starns Clark, *The Amish Blacksmith*, 2014
Mary Connealy, *Stuck Together*, 2014
Denise Hunter, *The Trouble with Cowboys*, 2012
Betsy St. Amant, *Rodeo Sweetheart*, 2010

382

COLLEEN COBLE

A Heart's Disguise

(Nashville, Tennessee: Thomas Nelson, 2015)

Series: A Journey of the Heart Series. Book 1
Story type: Romance; Series
Subject(s): United States Civil War, 1861-1865; United

States history, 1865-1901; Romances (Fiction)
Major character(s): Mr. Montgomery, Father (of Sara),
  Aged Person; Sara Montgomery, Daughter (of Mr.
  Montgomery), Fiance(e) (of Ben), Lover (of Rand),
  Kidnap Victim; Rand Campbell, Lover (of Sara),
  Military Personnel; Ben Croftner, Fiance(e) (of Sara),
  Villain, Kidnapper
Time period(s): 19th century; 1860s (1865)
Locale(s): Wabash, Indiana

Summary: In the first novel of Colleen Coble's A Journey
of the Heart series, the author introduces readers to Sara
Montgomery, who continues to grieve for her beau long
after he was lost in battle. Rand Campbell promised to
marry Sara when he returned from fighting in the US
Civil War. When Sara learns that he died in combat, she
knows that she will never be able to love another, yet
her guilt over her father's ill health leads to her engagement to Ben Croftner. Sara decides she will try to be as
happy as she can in the marriage, but just before her
wedding she learns that Rand never died after all, and
Ben has been hiding this fact from her. When Ben
impulsively kidnaps her, she is rescued by none other
than Rand himself. Now that Rand and Sara have recon-
nected, nothing can stop them from sharing their love—
except for Ben, who has sworn revenge on both of them,
and will stop at nothing to get it.

Other books by the same author:
Under Texas Stars Series, 2012
Anathema, 2009
Mercy Falls Series, 2009
Maggie's Mistake, 2002
Red River Bride, 2002

Other books you might like:
Tamera Alexander, *From a Distance*, 2008
Elizabeth Camden, *Against the Tide*, 2012
Judith Miller, *The Brickmaker's Bride*, 2014
Tracie Peterson, *The Icecutter's Daughter*, 2013
Ann Shorey, *Love's Sweet Beginning*, 2014

383

COLLEEN COBLE

The Inn at Ocean's Edge

(Nashville, Tennessee: Thomas Nelson Publishing, 2015)

Series: Sunset Cove Series. Book 1
Story type: Mystery; Romance
Subject(s): Suspense; Murder; Crime
Major character(s): Claire Dellamare, Vacationer; Luke
  Rocco, Vacationer, Brother (of Meg); Meg Rocco,
  Sister (of Luke), Vacationer
Time period(s): 21st century; (2010s); 20th century; 1980s
Locale(s): Folly Shoals Island, Maine

Summary: Claire Dellamare wanted nothing more than to
treat her parents to a relaxing vacation on Folly Shoals
Island off the coast of Maine, but when she walks into
the palatial Hotel Tourmaline, she becomes inexplicably
anxious. She decides she needs to relax and get some
fresh air, so she goes for a walk on the beach. There, she
meets a brother and sister vacationing together. Luke and
Meg Rocco have come to Folly Shoals to figure out

what happened to their mother on that island more than
two decades before. When Claire believes she sees a
murder take place, Luke is the only person who believes
her. No one else will take her seriously because of her
panic attack at the hotel. Luke holds the missing piece to
the mystery of what happened at the hotel, and why
Claire has such a sense of foreboding about it. Now they
must come together to reveal the truth about the past.
This novel is the first book in Colleen Coble's Sunset
Cove series.

Other books by the same author:
Hope Beach Series, 2012
Cry in the Night, 2009
Abomination, 2007
Fire Dancer, 2007
Rock Harbor Mystery Series, 2007

Other books you might like:
Robin Caroll, *Fear No Evil*, 2010
Brandilyn Collins, *Dark Justice*, 2013
Sibella Giorello, *The Mountains Bow Down*, 2011
Dani Pettrey, *Submerged*, 2012
Gayle Roper, *Shadows on the Sand*, 2011

384

COLLEEN COBLE

A Heart's Obsession

(Nashville, Tennessee: Thomas Nelson, 2015)

Series: A Journey of the Heart Series. Book 2
Story type: Historical - Post-American Civil War;
  Romance
Subject(s): Romances (Fiction); Love; Christian life
Major character(s): Sara Montgomery, Fiance(e) (ex, of
  Ben), Lover (of Rand), Sister (of Joel); Joel
  Montgomery, Brother (of Sara); Rand Campbell,
  Lover (of Sara and Jessica), Military Personnel; Ben
  Croftner, Fiance(e) (ex, of Sara), Villain; Jessica
  DuBois, Lover (of Rand)
Time period(s): 19th century; 1860s
Locale(s): Fort Laramie, Wyoming

Summary: In the second novel of Colleen Coble's A
Journey of the Heart series, the author continues the
story of Sara Montgomery, whose erstwhile lover, Rand
Campbell, has come back from the dead. When Sara's
father passes away, her brother insists that she live up to
her promise to marry Ben Croftner. Yet Ben knew that
Sara's true love, Rand, was still alive, even though Sara
thought Rand died during the Civil War. Sara despises
Ben for hiding this secret, and so she takes off for Fort
Laramie, where Rand is stationed. Once there, however,
she learns that Rand may be smitten with another
woman, Jessica DuBois. Sara resolves to stay at Fort
Laramie and claim the man she has fought so hard to
find, but when Ben follows her to Wyoming, he stirs up
a hornet's nest of trouble. Sara isn't willing to let Rand
go so easily, but can she beat Jessica and Ben at their
own games?

Other books by the same author:
Under Texas Stars Series, 2012
Mercy Falls Series, 2009

Fire Dancer, 2007
Distant Echoes, 2005
Red River Bride, 2002

Other books you might like:
Amanda Cabot, *With Autumn's Return*, 2014
Jane Kirkpatrick, *A Light in the Wilderness*, 2014
Judith Miller, *Morning Sky*, 2006
Ann Shorey, *The Dawn of a Dream*, 2011
Lori Wick, *Leave a Candle Burning*, 2006

385

COLLEEN COBLE

A Heart's Danger

(Nashville, Tennessee: Thomas Nelson, Inc., 2015)

Series: A Journey of the Heart Series. Book 3
Story type: Romance; Series
Subject(s): Western fiction; Indian Wars, 1622-1890; Frontier life
Major character(s): Sarah Montgomery, Fiance(e) (former, of Rand), Woman; Rand Campbell, Military Personnel, Fiance(e) (former, of Sarah), Fiance(e) (of Jessica); Ben Croftner, Military Personnel; Jessica DuBois, Fiance(e) (of Rand), Woman
Time period(s): 19th century
Locale(s): Fort Laramie, Wyoming

Summary: As war with the Sioux looms outside the walls of Wyoming's Fort Laramie, Sarah Montgomery is involved in a battle for the heart of the man she loves. Deceived by soldier Ben Croftner, who told her her fiance, Rand Campbell, was killed in the Civil War, Sarah moved on with her life. Only later, when she was about to marry Ben, did she discover the truth. Now bitter over Sarah's subsequent rejection, Ben has allied with Rand's new fiancee to keep the former lovers apart. Ben's actions are even more despicable than anyone realizes: He's conspiring with their Sioux enemies to set a trap for Rand and eliminate him once and for all. Despite all that has gone on, Rand and Sarah are still very much in love, but they may not be able to survive the plots that swirl about them. This is the third book in Colleen Coble's A Journey of the Heart series.

Other books by the same author:
Under Texas Stars Series, 2012
Mercy Falls Series, 2009
Fire Dancer, 2007
Distant Echoes, 2005
Red River Bride, 2002

Other books you might like:
Tammy Barley, *Hope's Promise*, 2010
Melanie Dobson, *Chateau of Secrets*, 2014
Tracie Peterson, *To Dream Anew*, 2004
Murray Pura, *A Bride's Flight from Virginia City, Montana*, 2012
Stephanie Grace Whitson, *Secrets on the Wind*, 2003

386

MARY CONNEALY

Now and Forever

(Bloomington, Minnesota: Bethany House Publishers, 2015)

Series: Wild at Heart Series. Book 2
Story type: Historical
Subject(s): Family; Western fiction; Wilderness survival
Major character(s): Shannon Wilde, Spouse (of Tucker), Rancher; Matthew Tucker, Mountain Man, Spouse (of Shannon)
Time period(s): 19th century; 1860s (1866)
Locale(s): Aspen Ridge, United States

Summary: In book two of the Wild at Heart series, Shannon Wilde—the middle sister of the Wilde clan—has everything set in her life. She has just started a new homestead and begun raising sheep for wool. But one day she crosses paths with Matthew Tucker who, in an attempt to escape a charging grizzly bear, knocks Shannon off a cliff into the river below. When the two escape the rapids and get back to civilization, Shannon's reputation has been soiled, and Tucker is forced to marry her. As the couple learns how to live together, something strange begins to happen on Shannon's land. Shannon and Tucker find out that someone is determined to drive Shannon off her homestead. But that person doesn't realize that Tucker is there to protect the woman he is beginning to fall in love with.

Other books by the same author:
Tried and True, 2014
Trouble in Texas Series, 2013
Sophie's Daughters Series, 2010
Montana Marriages Series, 2009
Lassoed in Texas Series, 2007

Other books you might like:
Margaret Brownley, *Gunpowder Tea*, 2013
Deeanne Gist, *Deep in the Heart of Trouble*, 2008
Cathy Marie Hake, *Fancy Pants*, 2007
Kelly Eileen Hake, *Plots and Pans*, 2014
Karen Witemeyer, *Stealing the Preacher*, 2013

387

LORI COPELAND

My Heart Stood Still

(Eugene, Oregon: Harvest House, 2015)

Series: Sisters of Mercy Flats Series. Book 2
Story type: Romance; Series
Subject(s): Romances (Fiction); Christian life; Native American captivities
Major character(s): Anne-Marie McDougal, Sister (of Abigail and Amelia), Captive, Con Artist; Abigail McDougal, Sister (of Anne-Marie and Amelia), Captive, Con Artist; Amelia McDougal, Sister (of Abigail and Anne-Marie), Captive, Con Artist; Creed Walker, Indian (Crow), Warrior, Spy, Rescuer (of Anne-Marie)
Time period(s): 19th century; 1860s

Locale(s): United States

Summary: In the second novel from Lori Copeland's Sisters of Mercy Flats series, the author continues the story of three sisters who have posed as nuns to con men out of their fortunes. The sisters have been caught and are being taken to prison when three men rescue them. In this novel, Copeland tells the story of Anne-Marie, the middle sister, who has been taken by Creed Walker, a Crow Indian. Anne-Marie at first is grateful that Creed has stepped in and saved her, but the longer she is with him, the more she wonders if he isn't actually her captor. Creed has a secret of his own, however, and Anne-Marie is the only one who can help him with it. Unfortunately, Creed and Anne-Marie find themselves at each other's throats more often than not. As they continue on their journey across the Plains, hiding from marauders and the law, they learn an important lesson about faith and trust in the Lord. Can two con artists change for the better, or are Creed and Anne-Marie doomed to lead lives of sin and deceit? Copeland has rewritten titles from her 1993 Sisters of Mercy Flats romances as inspirational fiction.

Other books by the same author:
Belles of Timber Creek Series, 2011
Now and Always, 2008
Blue Bonnet Belle, 2007
Men of the Saddle Series, 2004
Roses Will Blook Again, 2002

Other books you might like:
Mary Connealy, *Sharpshooter in Petticoats*, 2011
Kelly Eileen Hake, *Plots and Pans*, 2014
Christine Lynxwiler, *Cowgirl at Heart*, 2010
Karen Witemeyer, *Short-Straw Bride*, 2012
Kathleen Y'Barbo, *Anna Finch and the Hired Gun*, 2010

388

KATHRYN CUSHMAN

Finding Me

(Bloomington, Minnesota: Bethany House Publishers, 2015)

Story type: Contemporary
Subject(s): Family; Family relations; Rural life
Major character(s): Kelli Huddleston, Woman
Time period(s): 21st century; 2010s
Locale(s): California, United States; Tennessee, United States

Summary: Throughout her entire life, Kelli Huddleston has believed that her mother and two siblings had died in a fire when she was an infant. But after her father and stepmother die in an auto accident, Kelli finds newspaper clippings that tell a different story: decades earlier, a boating accident claimed the life of a father and his infant daughter. Although the names are different, the man in the photo is clearly her father. Kelli, who has lost her job because she alerted a client to her employer's misdeeds, decides to find out the truth of what happened more than 20 years ago. With only her family name and a few photos, Kelli leaves California and begins her search in a small town in Tennessee. What Kelli finds is something she's not ready to face. Kelli must make a choice that could change her life.

Other books by the same author:
Chasing Hope, 2013
Almost Amish, 2012
Another Dawn, 2011
Leaving Yesterday, 2009

Other books you might like:
Eva Marie Everson, *Slow Moon Rising*, 2013
Tracie Peterson, *House of Secrets*, 2011
Catherine West, *Hidden in the Heart*, 2012
Eric Wilson, *October Baby*, 2012
Lisa Wingate, *Dandelion Summer*, 2011

389

SUSAN PAGE DAVIS

Outlaw Takes a Bride

(Uhrichsville, Ohio: Barbour Publishing, 2015)

Story type: Romance; Western
Subject(s): Western fiction; Crime; Mail order brides
Major character(s): Sally Golding, Widow(er), Spouse (of Johnny), Mail Order Bride; Johnny Paynter, Outlaw, Fugitive, Spouse (of Sally), Brother (of Mark); Mark Paynter, Brother (of Johnny), Crime Victim (deceased); Effie Winters, Spouse (of Reverend Winters); Mr. Winters, Religious (reverend)
Time period(s): 19th century; 1880s (1885)
Locale(s): St. Louis, Missouri; Beaumont, Texas

Summary: Widow Sally Golding lives with the Reverend Winters and his wife, Effie. It's difficult for her to find work in St. Louis, and the Winters have allowed her to stay with them since the death of her husband. Unfortunately, Effie is less than kind to her, and treats her like a slave. When Sally learns about a mail-order bride service, she hatches a plan to marry someone and leave St. Louis far behind. She doesn't realize that the man she believes to be her betrothed, Mark Paynter, is actually his brother, Johnny. Johnny fled to his brother's ranch after being falsely accused of murder, but found his brother dead. Johnny has assumed his dead brother's identity, which means he must go forward with the wedding to Sally. As the lies pile up, Johnny resolves not to add to the deceit by sleeping with Sally on their wedding night, but neither of them can deny the chemistry they feel for each other. Now Johnny must make a choice: come clean and face the consequences of his actions, or continue his deception and hurt the one he loves.

Other books by the same author:
Prairie Dreams, 2012
Captive Trail, 2011
The Crimson Cipher, 2011
Love Finds You in Prince Edwards Island, 2011
Ladie's Shooting Club Series, 2009

Other books you might like:
Ruth Axtell, *Moonlight Masquerade*, 2013
Tracey Victoria Bateman, *Dangerous Heart*, 2008
Amanda Cabot, *Paper Roses*, 2009
Mary Connealy, *Wrangler in Petticoats*, 2010
Lori Copeland, *Outlaw's Bride*, 2009

Inspirational

Laurie Alice Eakes, *A Necessary Deception*, 2011
Mona Hodgson, *The Bride Wore Blue*, 2012
Regina Jennings, *Sixty Acres and a Bride*, 2012
Jill Marie Landis, *Heart of Lies*, 2011
Kathleen Y'Barbo, *Millie's Treasure*, 2013

390

RACHELLE DEKKER

The Choosing

(Carol Stream, Illinois: Tyndale House Publishers, 2015)

Series: Seer Series. Book 1
Story type: Dystopian; Series
Subject(s): Futuristic society; Murder; Social class
Major character(s): Carrington Hale, Spouse, Slave (a Lint), Young Woman
Time period(s): 23rd century; 2250s (2257)
Locale(s): Fictional Location

Summary: In the first installment of the Seer series, Carrington Hale has prepared her entire life for this day, her Choosing ceremony. On this day, she expects to be picked by a man of worth to become his wife and finally receive her identity. However, the worst-case scenario happens and she is not chosen. Now considered a Lint—a nobody—Carrington must become a slave and do the work that no one wants to do. But as Carrington begins her life at the lowest rung of society, a murderer begins killing Lints who fail to obey society's rules. In time, Carrington begins to hear rumors of rebellion, something that goes against everything she believes. When Carrington is offered a chance to leave the Lint and gain a new identity as the second wife of an influential widower, she is fearful of the consequences. Carrington must figure out her place in the world and sort out her complicated beliefs. First novel.

Other books you might like:
Evan Angler, *Swipe Series*, 2012
Heather Burch, *Avenger: A Halfling Novel*, 2013
Bonnie S. Calhoun, *Thunder*, 2014
Sharon Hinck, *The Restorer*, 2007
Krista McGee, *Luminary*, 2014

391

TED DEKKER

A.D. 30

(New York: Hachette Book Group, 2014)

Story type: Historical
Subject(s): Christianity; Middle East; Jewish history
Major character(s): Maviah, Slave, Traveler; Judah, Traveler; Yeshua, Biblical Figure, Teacher; King Herod, Royalty, Biblical Figure
Time period(s): 1st century; 30s (30)

Summary: Having been born the daughter of a Bedouin sheikh, Maviah never imagined that she would become anyone's slave. Yet when her people become subjugated by warring factions, she is sent to throw herself upon the mercy of King Herod in a bid to free them. As she journeys across the desert to find the king, she hears tales of a great man named Yeshua, who will lead the world to peace. Her fellow traveler, Judah, says that Yeshua is the Messiah, also known as the Son of God, and although Maviah doubts Judah's claims, she chooses to see for herself. When Maviah finally meets Yeshua, she begins to learn about faith and fear, and understands that her true course to freedom lies within her heart. Yet not everyone wants Yeshua's words to be known, and Maviah must decide if her faith in his teachings are strong enough to believe in him.

Other books by the same author:
The Sanctuary, 2012
The Priest's Graveyard, 2011
Immanuel's Veins, 2010
Paradise Trilogy, 2006
The Circle Series, 2004

Other books you might like:
Amy Bloom, *Away: A Novel*, 2007
Davis Bunn, *The Centurion's Wife*, 2009
Anthony Burgess, *The Kingdom of the Wicked*, 1985
Lloyd C. Douglas, *The Big Fisherman*, 1948
Jerry B. Jenkins, *I, Paul*, 2014
Tosca Lee, *Iscariat: A Novel of Judas*, 2013
Amin Maalouf, *Leo Africanus*, 1989
Randy Singer, *The Advocate*, 2014
Bodie Thoene, *First Light*, 2003
Robyn Young, *Brethren: An Epic Adventure of the Knights Templar*, 2006

392

VARINA DENMAN

Jaded

(Colorado Springs, Colorado: David C Cook, 2015)

Series: Mended Hearts Series. Book 1
Story type: Romance; Series
Subject(s): Christian life; Christianity; Religion
Major character(s): Ruthie Turner, 20-Year-Old, Young Woman, Friend (of Dodd); Dodd Cunningham, Religious (preacher), Friend (of Ruthie)
Time period(s): 21st century; 2010s
Locale(s): Trapp, Texas

Summary: Debut author Varina Denman delivers the first installment in her Mended Hearts inspirational romance series. Ruthie Turner was seven years old when her family was ostracized from its local church in the small, tight-knit community of Trapp, Texas. For years, Ruthie has resented the Christians in her small town, never understanding why her family was forced to leave the church and never return. Now, 13 years later, Ruthie attracts the attention of the town's new, single preacher, Dodd Cunningham. Dodd's compassion forces Ruthie to rethink her opinions about the church and its members. Rumors of Ruthie and Dodd's relationship circulate throughout Trapp, and their connection is adamantly opposed by the town's closed-minded residents. Soon, secret scandals and long-held grudges resurface and threaten to destroy the church and the community. Can the bitterness and shame that have plagued Trapp for years finally be undone though compassion and forgiveness? First novel.

Other books you might like:
Tamera Alexander, *To Whisper Her Name*, 2012
Amy Lillard, *Saving Gideon*, 2012
Nancy Mehl, *Simple Secrets*, 2010
Jolina Petersheim, *The Outcast*, 2013
Kim Vogel Sawyer, *When Mercy Rains*, 2014

393

MELANIE DICKERSON

The Huntress of Thornbeck Forest

(Nashville, Tennessee: Thomas Nelson, Inc., 2015)

Series: A Medieval Fairy Tale Romance. Book 1
Story type: Romance; Series
Subject(s): Hunting; Poaching; Romances (Fiction)
Major character(s): Odette Menkels, Young Woman, Hunter, Wealthy; Jorgen Hartman, Investigator, Man (forester)
Time period(s): 14th century; 1360s (1363)
Locale(s): Thornbeck Forest, Fictional Location

Summary: Odette Menkels is a sort of female Robin Hood. The daughter of a wealthy businessman, Odette secretly hunts game at night to help feed the poor. Her actions have caught the attention of the region's military commander, who dispatches his forester, Jorgen Hartman, to capture the mysterious poacher. But when Odette and Jorgen meet it is not as enemies. An encounter at a festival dance leaves them both smitten, but neither realizes that they are hunter and prey in another deadly game. As Odette realizes her noble ideals may have been betrayed, the one man she can turn to for help is also sworn to stop her. Faced with the truth, Odette and Jorgen are caught in a battle between love and duty. This is the first book in Melanie Dickerson's Medieval Fairy Tale Romance series.

Other books by the same author:
A Fairy Tale Romance Series, 2010

Other books you might like:
Heather Burch, *Avenger: A Halfling Novel*, 2013
Patrick W. Carr, *A Cast of Stones*, 2013
Angela Elwell Hunt, *The Silver Sword*, 1998
Grace Walton, *Mercy's Heart*, 2013
Mary Weber, *Storm Siren*, 2014

394

LAURIE ALICE EAKES

A Stranger's Secret

(Grand Rapids, Michigan: Zondervan, 2015)

Series: Cliffs of Cornwall Series. Book 2
Story type: Romance; Series
Subject(s): Rural life; England; Mystery
Major character(s): Lady Morwenna Trelawny Penvenan,

Widow(er), Crime Suspect; David Chastain, Carpenter (boat builder)
Time period(s): 19th century; 1810s (1813)
Locale(s): Cornwall, England

Summary: This novel is the second book in the Cliffs of Cornwall series by Laurie Alice Eakes. Lady Morwenna Trelawny Penvenan has worked hard to shed her image as a person of ill repute in Cornwall, and she has finally established herself as a woman of good character. Now that she is widowed, however, no one is left to defend her when she is charged with ransacking ships wrecked along the cliffs nearby. When she sets out to learn who the real thief is, she instead encounters a mysterious man washed ashore. David Chastain has no idea how he ended up in Cornwall, but he does know that someone is trying to kill him. Now Morwenna and David must band together to clear her good name and save his life, but the attraction they feel toward one another may distract them from their mission.

Other books by the same author:
Choices of the Heart, 2013
Heart's Safe Passage, 2012
Highland Crossings, 2012
A Lady's Honor, 2012
The Daughters of Bainbridge House series, 2011

Other books you might like:
Mindy Starns Clark, *Whispers of the Bayou*, 2008
Tracy Groot, *Maggie Bright: A Novel of Dunkirk*, 2015
Lisa Norato, *Prize of My Heart*, 2012
Tracie Peterson, *Morning's Refrain*, 2010
Stephanie Grace Whitson, *A Captain For Laura Rose*, 2014
Kathleen Y'Barbo, *Beloved Castaway*, 2007

395

LYNETTE EASON

No Place to Hide

(Grand Rapids, Michigan: Baker Publishing Group, 2015)

Series: Hidden Identity Series. Book 3
Story type: Mystery
Subject(s): Terrorism; Interpersonal relations; Friendship
Major character(s): Ian Lockwood, Crime Suspect, Friend (of Jackie); Jackie Sellers, Friend (of Ian)
Time period(s): 21st century; 2010s
Locale(s): Georgia, United States

Summary: In the third installment from Lynette Eason's Hidden Identity series, the author introduces readers to Jackie Sellers and Ian Lockwood. When Ian's picture appears on the news, Jackie cannot believe her eyes. He is wanted for terrorism, and Jackie refuses to believe that the boy she used to love has grown into a ruthless assassin. As a worker who specializes in aiding the disenfranchised and unfairly accused in the greater Atlanta area, Jackie knows she must come to the rescue of her longtime friend. She wants to take Ian straight to the police to figure everything out, but Ian knows that is the last thing he should do. Not only is Ian being watched by the FBI, but he is also targeted by the terrorist cell who has framed him. With everyone out to get him and nowhere to turn, Jackie is the only person Ian can trust. He'll have to rely on her to help him save an entire city, but Jackie will need to question her belief in the justice system to do so.

Other books by the same author:
Nowhere to Turn, 2014
No One to Trust, 2013
The Black Sheep's Redemption, 2012
Deadly Reunions Series, 2012
Threat of Exposure, 2011

Other books you might like:
Irene Hannon, *Deadly Pursuit*, 2011
Kathy Herman, *False Pretenses*, 2011
DiAnn Mills, *Firewall*, 2014
Sandra Orchard, *Deadly Devotion*, 2013
Karen Young, *Lie for Me*, 2011

396

JERRY S. EICHER

Miriam's Secret

(Eugene, Oregon: Harvest House, 2015)

Series: Land of Promise Series. Book 1
Story type: Romance; Series
Subject(s): Christian life; Amish; Anabaptists
Major character(s): Miriam Yoder, Fiance(e) (of Wayne), Neighbor (of Ivan); Wayne Yutzy, Fiance(e) (of Miriam); Amos Bland, Wealthy, Aged Person; Ivan Mast, Neighbor (of Miriam)
Time period(s): 21st century; 2010s
Locale(s): Holmes County, Ohio; Oklahoma, United States

Summary: The first installment from Jerry Eicher's Land of Promise series introduces Miriam Yoder, an Amish woman who comes from a large and destitute family. In order to support her family, Miriam seeks employment outside of the home and finds a job taking care of an elderly man named Amos Bland. When Amos dies, Miriam suddenly learns that he has left her a large amount of money—enough to take care of herself and her family for life. Unfortunately, her new wealth makes her a target. The boy she used to love, but who never gave her a second glance, suddenly shows interest in her. Miriam moves to Oklahoma, where no one will know her, and she is sure that her secret will be safe. When she meets Wayne Yutzy, Miriam is certain that he loves her just for her. But as they grow closer, her certainty wanes. Does Wayne know her secret after all, or is he truly interested in her because he loves her?

Other books by the same author:
Katie's Journey to Love, 2013
Fields of Home Series, 2012
Little Valley Series, 2011
Hannah Series, 2009
The Adams County Trilogy, 2008

Other books you might like:
W. Dale Cramer, *Levi's Will: A Novel*, 2005
Mary Ellis, *Love Comes to Paradise*, 2013
Amy Lillard, *Katie's Choice*, 2013

Olivia Newport, *Accidentally Amish*, 2012
Gayle Roper, *A Stranger's Wish*, 2010

397

EVA MARIE EVERSON

Five Brides

(Carol Stream, Illinois: Tyndale House Publishers, 2015)

Story type: Historical
Subject(s): Women; Friendship; Faith
Major character(s): Joan, Young Woman, Roommate (of Evelyn, Betty, Magda, and Inga); Evelyn, Young Woman, Roommate (of Joan, Betty, Magda, and Inga); Betty, Young Woman, Roommate (of Joan, Evelyn, Magda, and Inga); Magda, Young Woman, Roommate (of Joan, Evelyn, Betty, and Inga); Inga, Young Woman, Roommate (of Joan, Evelyn, Betty, and Magda)
Time period(s): 20th century; 1950s (1951)
Locale(s): Chicago, Illinois

Summary: Set in 1950s Chicago, this inspirational romance novel by Eva Marie Everson is a tale of friendship, family, and faith. Betty, Joan, Evelyn, Magda, and Inga live together as roommates in a Chicago apartment. The five independent, career-minded women spend little time with one another, but friendships develop as the working roommates navigate the waters of a mid-century culture that is rapidly changing. When the five women happen to be together in a downtown department store, the acclaimed Carson, Pirie, Scott & Co., they discover a wedding dress that they all love. They agree to jointly purchase and share the dress, though none of them are engaged. The young woman move forward with their lives, each eventually leaving their shared apartment. Will the dress they purchased keep them connected as they experience heartache and happiness?

Other books by the same author:
The Road to Testament, 2014
Cedar Key Series, 2011
This Fine Line, 2010
Things Left Unspoken, 2009

Other books you might like:
Ann Brashares, *Sisterhood of the Traveling Pants Series*, 2001
Robin Jones Gunn, *Sisterchicks Series*, 2003
Rachel Hauck, *The Wedding Dress*, 2012
Denise Hunter, *Dancing with Fireflies*, 2014
Sally John, *The Beach House*, 2006

398

CHRIS FABRY
RICHARD L. RAMSEY, Co-Author
KYLE IDLEMAN, Co-Author

The Song

(Carol Stream, Illinois: Tyndale House Publishers, 2015)

Story type: Romance
Subject(s): Family history; Father-son relations; Romances (Fiction)

Major character(s): Jed King, Musician, Son (of David), Spouse (husband, of Rose); Rose King, Spouse (wife, of Jed); David King, Musician, Father (late, of Jed)
Time period(s): 21st century; 2010s
Locale(s): United States

Summary: Based on the Bible's Song of Solomon and a motion picture screenplay by Richard L. Ramsey, Chris Fabry's inspirational novel is a tale of loss and forgiveness. Jed King lives in the shadow of his famous father, David. The mistakes of his father's past haunt Jed and taint his dreams of having his own successful music career. Things start to look up for Jed, however, when he meets and falls in love with Rose. Inspired by love, Jed writes a song that catapults him into a life of fame and fortune. With the world at his beck and call, Jed faces the same temptations his father faced years ago. Will Jed's commitment to Rose suffer under the pressure of his desire to be successful, or will he stand strong against the seductions of fame? Together, Jed and Rose discover the power of love and forgiveness, and along the way, find fulfillment in being who God created them to be.

Other books by the same author:
Every Waking Moment, 2013
Borders of the Heart, 2012
Almost Heaven, 2010
June Bug, 2009
Dogwood, 2008

Other books you might like:
Mesu Andrews, *Love's Sacred Song*, 2012
Melody Carlson, *Grace Unplugged*, 2013
Karen Kingsbury, *Fifteen Minutes*, 2013
Francine Rivers, *Bridge to Haven*, 2014
Eric Wilson, *Fireproof*, 2008

`399`

SUZANNE WOODS FISHER

Anna's Crossing

(Grand Rapids, Michigan: Baker Publishing, 2015)

Series: Amish Beginnings Series. Book 1
Story type: Romance; Series
Subject(s): Amish; Romances (Fiction); Love
Major character(s): Anna Konig, Young Woman, Religious (Amish), Immigrant (translator); Bairn, Worker (ship)
Time period(s): 18th century; 1730s (1734)
Locale(s): At Sea; Rotterdam, Netherlands

Summary: In the first novel from Suzanne Woods Fisher's Amish Beginning series, the author looks at the journey of Anna Konig, who sets sail one summer day from the Netherlands to the United States and a promise of religious freedom. Anna tells herself she is only embarking on this voyage to help interpret for everyone else, since she is the only person in her community who can speak English. She doesn't want to go, and intends to return as soon as everyone is settled. The trip is long and dismal, and the ship the Amish have commissioned to take them to the New World is manned by a crew that doesn't respect the Amish faith. Anna forms an unlikely kinship with Bairn, the ship's woodworker. Bairn has a

secret that he is keeping from everyone. When he and Anna find themselves in a perilous situation, they both learn a lesson about trust and putting one's faith in others.

Other books by the same author:
The Inn at Eagle Hill Series, 2013
Stony Ridge Seasons Series, 2012
A Lancaster County Christmas, 2011
Lancaster County Secrets Series, 2010

Other books you might like:
Cathy Marie Hake, *Whirlwind*, 2008
Gilbert Morris, *The River Queen*, 2011
Marylu Tyndall, *Forsaken Dreams*, 2013
Dan Walsh, *The Deepest Waters*, 2011
Stephanie Grace Whitson, *A Captain For Laura Rose*, 2014

`400`

KATHLEEN FULLER

A Faith of Her Own

(Nashville: Thomas Nelson, 2015)

Series: Middlefield Amish Series. Book 1
Story type: Contemporary; Series
Subject(s): Amish; Romances (Fiction); Faith
Major character(s): Anna Mae, Young Woman, Religious (Amish), Friend (of Jeremiah); Jeremiah, Man (former Amish), Veterinarian (assistant), Friend (of Anna Mae)
Time period(s): 21st century; 2010s
Locale(s): Middlefield, Ohio

Summary: Anna Mae is a young woman who feels as though she is suffocating within the constrictions of her Amish community. Her childhood friend and the man she had hoped one day to wed chose to leave the community, and since then Anna Mae has been feeling lost and lonely. Jeremiah's departure leads Anna Mae to wonder if she, too, could be destined for a life outside of the plain world. She is afraid to voice her feelings, and grows more despondent as her mother attempts to find her a match within the community. Then Jeremiah returns as to aid the local veterinarian. The pair tentatively rekindles a friendship, despite the rules within the community about such things. As their relationship grows, Anna Mae becomes more haunted by the questions of where she belongs and whether she has the courage to leave the Amish life. She must search within her heart to find God's path and accept her love for Jeremiah. This is the first book of the Middlefield Amish series.

Other books by the same author:
Faithful to Laura, 2012
Hide and Secret, 2011
Middlefield Family Series, 2011
Hearts of Middlefield Series, 2009
The Royal Regency Mystery Series, 2008

Other books you might like:
Barbara Cameron, *Her Restless Heart*, 2012
Olivia Newport, *Accidentally Amish*, 2012
Kim Vogel Sawyer, *When Hope Blossoms*, 2012

Inspirational

Cindy Woodsmall, *When the Morning Comes*, 2007
Dee Yoder, *The Miting*, 2014

401

KATIE GANSHERT

The Art of Losing Yourself

(Colorado Springs, Colorado: WaterBrook Press, 2015)

Story type: Contemporary
Subject(s): Christian life; Sisters; Family
Major character(s): Carmen Hart, Sister (half, of Gracie), Television Personality (meteorologist); Gracie Fisher, 17-Year-Old, Runaway, Sister (half, of Carmen)
Time period(s): 21st century; 2010s
Locale(s): Florida, United States

Summary: In this inspirational novel by Katie Ganshert, television meteorologist Carmen Hart appears to have it all, with a perfect husband, beautiful home, and a supportive and loving church family. Unbeknownst to others, Carmen has been struggling lately. She has been doubting her marriage and her choices in life, and more than ever, she is doubting her faith in God. When Carmen's 17-year-old half-sister, Gracie Fisher, comes back into her life, she gains a new perspective. Gracie has run away from home after one of their mother's drunken episodes, and eventually is found hiding in an old motel. Carmen decides to take the teen in. In reconnecting with her sister, she finds other areas of her life are starting to reconnect as well. Even the old motel, which once belonged to her family, may have a brighter future, if only Carmen has faith.

Other books by the same author:
A Broken Kind of Beautiful, 2014
Wishing on Willows, 2013
Wildflowers from Winter, 2012

Other books you might like:
Sara Evans, *Love Lifted Me*, 2012
Christa Parrish, *Still Life*, 2015
Cynthia Ruchti, *They Almost Always Come Home*, 2010
Carla Stewart, *Broken Wings*, 2011
Beth Wiseman, *Need You Now*, 2011

402

CARRE ARMSTRONG GARDNER

Better All the Time

(Carol Stream, Illinois: Tyndale House Publishers, 2015)

Series: Darlings Series. Book 2
Story type: Series
Subject(s): Sisters; Family relations; Addiction
Major character(s): Seraphina "Sephy" Darling, Sister (older, of Amy); Amy Darling, Sister (younger, of Sephy)
Time period(s): 21st century; 2010s
Locale(s): Maine, United States

Summary: Seraphina "Sephy" Darling struggles with her weight. While she would love to stand out in a crowd, she has grown comfortable taking her place in the background, where she draws the least amount of attention to herself as possible. However, she decides to make some serious changes to her life and appearance when her older brother and best friend announce their engagement. At the same time, Sephy's younger sister, Amy, begins working on the restoration of the community theater's arts programs. In the midst of numerous details and deadlines, she refuses to delegate responsibilities. Unwilling to trust anyone but herself, Amy grows exhausted. As Sephy and Amy live through their own struggles and victories, they discover freedom in being who God intended them to be. This is the second title of Carre Armstrong Gardner's Darlings series.

Other books by the same author:
All Right Here, 2014

Other books you might like:
Melody Carlson, *Love Finds You in Sisters, Oregon*, 2009
Katie Ganshert, *A Broken Kind of Beautiful*, 2014
Irene Hannon, *That Certain Summer*, 2013
Neta Jackson, *Come to the Table*, 2012
Ginny L. Yttrup, *Invisible*, 2013

403

DEEANNE GIST

Tiffany Girl

(New York: Howard Books, 2015)

Story type: Historical; Romance
Subject(s): Artists; Business enterprises; Courage
Major character(s): Flossie Jayne, Young Woman (in love/hate relationship with Reeve Wilder), Artist (glass for Tiffany Glass & Decorating Co.), Woman (part of "New Woman" movement); Reeve Wilder, Journalist (writing about "New Woman" movement), Young Man (in love/hate relationship with Flossie Jayne); Louis Tiffany, Businessman (Tiffany Glass & Decorating Co.), Heir (to Fifth Avenue Jewelry Company)
Time period(s): 19th century; 1890s
Locale(s): New York, New York

Summary: Louis Tiffany, heir to the Fifth Avenue jewelry empire, had grand plans to unveil his groundbreaking stained-glass mosaic temple at the Chicago World's Fair. But he didn't plan for the glassworkers to strike months before the fair. To ensure the completion of his ambitious project, Tiffany hires female students from the Art Students League of New York to finish the work. Flossie Jayne, an aspiring painter and artist, is chosen to be a "Tiffany Girl." She moves away from her sheltered home and tries to build a new life, career, and home for herself. Rebuking the conventional ideals of working women in society, Flossie is faced with disdain and ridicule. Journalist Reeve Wilder is soon assigned to cover the events of the strike and the "New Woman" movement, and he finds himself in a love/hate relationship with the feisty Flossie. Through love, faith, and friendship, Flossie and Reeve find the strength to face the world and all that it presents to them.

Other books by the same author:
Fair Play, 2014
It Happened at the Fair, 2013
Love on the Line, 2011
Maid to Match, 2010
A Bride in the Bargain, 2009

Other books you might like:
Lynn Austin, *A Proper Pursuit*, 2007
Carol Cox, *Fair Game*, 2007
Barbara Croft, *Moon's Crossing*, 2003
Shelley Gray, *Secrets of Sloane House*, 2014
Echo Heron, *Noon at Tiffany's*, 2012
Maureen Lang, *Bees in the Butterfly Garden*, 2012
Grace Mark, *The Dream Seekers*, 1992
Alec Michod, *The White City*, 2004
Olivia Newport, *The Pursuit of Lucy Banning*, 2012
Susan Vreeland, *Clara and Mr. Tiffany*, 2010

404

ELIZABETH GODDARD

Untraceable

(New York: Love Inspired, 2015)

Series: Mountain Cove Series. Book 2
Story type: Contemporary; Romance
Subject(s): Mountaineering; Hostages; Brothers and sisters
Major character(s): Heidi Warren, Sister (of Cade Warren), Co-worker (of Isaiah Callahan), Hostage, Rescuer (search-and-rescue worker); Cade Warren, Rescuer (search-and-rescue worker), Brother (of Heidi Warren), Co-worker (of Isaiah Callahan), Hostage; Isaiah Callahan, Rescuer (search-and-rescue worker), Co-worker (of Heidi and Cade Warren), Hostage
Time period(s): 21st century; 2010s
Locale(s): Alaska, United States

Summary: Heidi Warren is out of practice after an accident left her shaken and afraid to continue her search-and-rescue work. However, her brother Cade and former partner, Isaiah Callahan, need her assistance to rescue stranded hikers from a mountaintop during a blizzard. Heidi pushes away her uneasiness and agrees to help. When they realize that the rescue call was a trap, Heidi feels her world start to slide. The hikers are thieves who have already murdered one of their group. Taking the rescue workers hostage at gunpoint, the criminals insist that the trio guide them through the deadly terrain and weather to safety. Heidi struggles to call upon her faith in God. She turns to Isaiah, a man with whom she once believed she could form a relationship. His own secrets and deceptions prevented anything from happening, but now Heidi must quickly overcome her apprehensions and trust Isaiah with her life if she is to survive this ordeal. This is the second novel of the Mountain Cove series.

Other books by the same author:
Riptide, 2013
Wilderness Peril, 2013
Treacherous Skies, 2012
Freezing Point, 2011

The Camera Never Lies, 2010
Other books you might like:
Robin Caroll, *Deliver Us From Evil*, 2010
Lynette Eason, *Missing*, 2011
Irene Hannon, *Trapped*, 2013
Sandra Orchard, *Perilous Waters*, 2014
Dani Pettrey, *Alaskan Courage Series*, 2012

405

LESLIE GOULD

Amish Promises

(Minneapolis, Minnesota: Bethany House, 2015)

Series: Neighbors of Lancaster County Series. Book 1
Story type: Romance; Series
Subject(s): Amish; Romances (Fiction); Family relations
Major character(s): Joel Beck, Veteran (Iraq War), Spouse (husband, of Shani), Father (of Zane), Neighbor (of the Lehmans), Handicapped; Shani Beck, Spouse (wife, of Joel), Mother (of Zane), Friend (of Eve), Neighbor (of the Lehmans); Eve Lehman, Friend (of Shani), Sister (of Tim), Neighbor (of the Becks), Religious (Amish); Tim Lehman, Brother (of Eve), Widow(er), Religious (Amish), Neighbor (of the Becks); Charlie, Veteran (Iraq War), Friend (of Joel); Zane, 12-Year-Old, Son (of Joel and Shani)
Time period(s): 21st century; 2000s (2004)
Locale(s): Lancaster County, Pennsylvania

Summary: Best-selling author Leslie Gould delivers the first novel in her Neighbors of Lancaster County series. Iraq War veteran Joel Beck and his wife, Shani, expect to find peace and happiness in Lancaster County, Pennsylvania. As they settle into Shani's father's house, all seems well until their son is in an accident that injures one of the Amish boys next door. Eve Lehman has looked after her brother's children since the death of their mother. Her brother, Tim, isn't too keen on interacting with his new neighbors, but Eve and Shani enjoy one another's company, sharing common bonds of faith and family. When Charlie, Joel's old Army friend, arrives in Lancaster and captures the attention of Eve, neighborly relations between the Becks and the Lehmans grow increasingly more complex.

Other books by the same author:
Courtships of Lancaster County Series, 2012
Women of Lancaster County Series, 2011

Other books you might like:
Ann H. Gabhart, *Love Comes Home*, 2014
BJ Hoff, *Rachel's Secret*, 2008
Kelly Long, *Arms of Love*, 2012
Gayle Roper, *An Unexpected Match*, 2014
Elizabeth Byler Younts, *Promise to Return*, 2013

406

SHELLEY SHEPARD GRAY

The Proposal at Siesta Key

(New York: HarperCollins, 2015)

Series: Amish Brides of Pinecraft Series. Book 2
Story type: Romance; Series

Subject(s): Christian life; Amish; Mennonites
Major character(s): Michael Knoxx, Singer, Amputee, Religious (Mennonite); Elizabeth "Lissy" Troyer, Religious (Amish), Sister (of Penny), Crime Victim (murdered), Daughter (of Mamm and Daed); Mamm, Mother (of Lissy and Penny), Spouse (of Daed), Religious (Amish); Daed, Religious (Amish), Spouse (of Mamm), Father (of Lissy and Penny); Penny Troyer, Sister (of Lissy), Daughter (of Mamm and Daed), Religious (Amish)
Time period(s): 21st century; 2010s
Locale(s): Sarasota, Florida

Summary: The second installment of author Shelley Shepard Gray's Amish Brides of Pinecraft series tells the story of Penny Troyer, a young woman whose overprotective parents have stunted her sense of self. Ever since her sister's murder 12 years before, Penny's Mamm and Daed have watched over her day and night, barely allowing her to even go on the porch without their approval. When Penny finds out that Michael Knoxx will lecture at Pinecraft Park's pavilion, she sneaks out of the house without her parents' permission. One of Michael's legs was partially amputated after a horrific disaster, and now he tours the countryside to spread his inspirational message. Michael must stay in Pinecraft after he has surgery, which gives Penny the unexpected opportunity to meet him. Michael and Penny fall for one another, but one thing stands in their way of eternal happiness: Penny's parents. Now, Penny must decide if she will turn away from true love to keep the peace in her household, or break her parents' hearts by pursuing the man of her dreams.

Other books by the same author:
Redemption, 2014
Return to Sugar Creek Series, 2014
Families of Honor Series, 2011
Seasons of Sugar Creek Series, 2010
Sisters of the Heart Series, 2008

Other books you might like:
Vannetta Chapman, *A Wedding for Julia*, 2013
Kathryn Cushman, *Almost Amish*, 2012
Jerry Eicher, *Katie's Journey to Love*, 2013
Leslie Gould, *Courting Cate*, 2012
Stephanie Reed, *The Bargain*, 2013

407

SHELLEY SHEPARD GRAY

The Promise of Palm Grove

(San Diego, California: Center Point Publishing, 2015)

Series: Amish Brides of Pinecraft Series. Book 1
Story type: Contemporary; Romance
Subject(s): Amish; Marriage; Romances (Fiction)
Major character(s): Leona Weaver, Fiance(e) (of Edmund), Religious (Amish); Edmund, Religious (Amish), Fiance(e) (of Leona); Zachary Kaufman, Man, Religious (Amish)
Time period(s): 21st century; 2010s
Locale(s): Pinecraft, Florida

Summary: It should be a joyous time for Leona, a young Amish woman who will soon marry Edmund. She and her friends are on a little vacation in Pinecraft, Florida. Her friends think Leona is so relaxed and happy because she's been under pressure with the wedding plans; only Leona knows it's the distance from the soon-to-be groom, and his need to be in control, that is the cause of her relief. He's a good man, but Leona just can't see herself in a forever life with him, despite the assurances of her family and friends. A chance encounter in this popular Amish vacation spot just complicates things. Leona meets Zachary, who is good looking and lighthearted. He seems to be the opposite of Edmund, and Leona likes what she sees. But can she face the disapproval of her family and disappointment of her fiance to follow where she thinks her heart is leading? This is the first book of the Amish Brides of Pinecraft series.

Other books by the same author:
Redemption, 2014
Return to Sugar Creek Series, 2014
Families of Honor Series, 2011
Seasons of Sugar Creek Series, 2010
Sisters of the Heart Series, 2008

Other books you might like:
Suzanne Woods Fisher, *The Choice*, 2010
Emma Miller, *Leah's Choice*, 2012
Olivia Newport, *Taken for English*, 2014
Anna Schmidt, *A Sister's Forgiveness*, 2012
Lynette Sowell, *A Path Made Plain*, 2014

408

SHELLEY GRAY

Deception on Sable Hill

(Grand Rapids, Michigan: Zondervan, 2015)

Series: Chicago World's Fair Mystery Series. Book 2
Story type: Historical; Mystery
Subject(s): Romances (Fiction); Mystery; Social class
Major character(s): Eloisa Carstairs, Debutante, Wealthy, Girlfriend (of Sean), Crime Victim; Sean Ryan, Detective—Police, Immigrant (son of Irish immigrants), Boyfriend (of Eloisa)
Time period(s): 19th century; 1890s (1893)
Locale(s): Chicago, Illinois

Summary: This historical romance novel is the second installment in the Chicago World's Fair Mystery series by best-selling author Shelley Gray. In 1893, debutante Eloisa Carstairs moves among Chicago's wealthy, high-class society. Though all appears well, Eloisa secretly fears for her life after being assaulted by prominent heir Douglass Sloan. When she shares her secret with Detective Sean Ryan, the son of a poor Irish family, he vows to protect her, and despite their differences in social class, the pair can't deny the attraction between them. Danger increases when three more debutantes are confronted by an attacker, and with the assailant still on the loose, Eloisa fears she could be his next victim. As the romance between Eloisa and Sean grows, they learn that they no longer want to live by the rules and divisions society places upon them. Will they catch the attacker before it's too late?

Other books by the same author:
Secrets of Sloane House, 2014
Days of Redemption Series, 2013
Secrets of Crittenden County Series, 2012
Heart of a Hero Series, 2011
Sisters of the Heart Series, 2008

Other books you might like:
Elizabeth Camden, *Into the Whirlwind*, 2013
Carol Cox, *A Bride So Fair*, 2008
Deeanne Gist, *Fair Play*, 2014
Olivia Newport, *The Pursuit of Lucy Banning*, 2012
Lorna Seilstad, *Making Waves*, 2010

409

JOCELYN GREEN

Spy of Richmond

(Chicago, Illinois: River North Fiction, 2015)

Series: Heroines Behind the Lines Series. Book 4
Story type: Historical - American Civil War; Series
Subject(s): United States Civil War, 1861-1865; Espionage; Spies
Major character(s): Sophie Kent, Spy, Daughter (of Mr. and Mrs. Kent), Abolitionist; Mr. Kent, Editor, Father (of Sophie), Plantation Owner, Spouse (of Sophie), Prisoner; Daphne, Twin (of Bella), Sister (of Bella), Slave (of Sophie); Bella Jamison, Slave (former), Twin (of Daphne), Sister (of Daphne), Spouse (of Mr. Jamison), Spy; Abraham Jamison, Spouse (of Bella), Prisoner; Mrs. Eleanor Kent, Mother (of Sophie); Harrison Caldwell, Journalist, Spy
Time period(s): 19th century; 1860s
Locale(s): Richmond, Virginia

Summary: In the fourth installment of Jocelyn Green's Civil War series Heroines Behind the Lines, the author introduces readers to Sophie Kent, the daughter of a slave owner. When Sophie's mother passes away and her father is imprisoned by the Union Army, she learns that she has inherited her mother's slave, Daphne. Although Sophie wants nothing to do with slavery, her mother's will stipulates that Daphne cannot be freed. Determined to make up for her father's crimes against humanity by becoming an abolitionist, Sophie sneaks behind enemy lines in Richmond, Virginia. She knows she needs some help if she is going to topple the Confederacy, so she turns to Bella Jamison, Daphne's twin sister and a onetime slave whose husband was captured by Confederate soldiers as he fought for the Union. Sophie also relies on Harrison Caldwell, a reporter from a northern state who poses as a secretary for the Confederate government. Soon, Sophie realizes that her actions could have dire consequences for her family, and she must make a choice about which she has the most faith in: her country, or the people she holds most dear.

Other books by the same author:
Yankee in Atlanta, 2014
Widow of Gettysburg, 2013
Wedded to War, 2012

Other books you might like:
Ruth Axtell, *Moonlight Masquerade*, 2013
Laurie Alice Eakes, *A Necessary Deception*, 2011
Siri Mitchell, *The Messenger*, 2012
Allison Pataki, *The Traitor's Wife*, 2014
Roseanna M. White, *Circle of Spies*, 2014

410

TRACY GROOT

Maggie Bright: A Novel of Dunkirk

(Carol Stream, Illinois: Tyndale House Publishers, 2015)

Story type: Historical - World War II
Subject(s): World War II, 1939-1945; England; Faith
Major character(s): Clare Childs, Woman, Shipowner; Winston Churchill, Political Figure (prime minister of Britain), Historical Figure; Adolf Hitler, Historical Figure, Leader (of Nazi Germany)
Time period(s): 20th century; 1940s (1940)
Locale(s): England; Dunkirk, France

Summary: Set against the backdrop of World War II, award-winning author Tracy Groot's inspirational tale draws upon the evacuation of British troops from Dunkirk, France, as Nazi Germany continues in its efforts to invade Western Europe. In 1940 England, Clare Childs inherits the *Maggie Bright*, a 52-foot yacht shrouded in mystery. When a stranger shows up looking for secret documents hidden on the boat, Clare finds herself in the middle of a Scotland Yard investigation that could uncover Hitler's evil schemes and compel America to fight alongside the Allies. Meanwhile, the Nazis trap British troops at Dunkirk, leaving little hope for escape. With large military ships unable to navigate Dunkirk's shallow beaches, British prime minister Winston Churchill calls upon smaller, civilian boats to aid in rescuing British soldiers. Clare answers the call with the *Maggie Bright*, which is being piloted by an American. The vessel carries a detective desperate to uncover the truth.

Other books by the same author:
The Sentinels of Andersonville, 2014
Flame of Resistance, 2012
Madman, 2007
The Brother's Keeper, 2003

Other books you might like:
Mindy Starns Clark, *Echoes of Titanic*, 2012
Laurie Alice Eakes, *A Stranger's Secret*, 2015
Elizabeth Ludwig, *Tide and Tempest*, 2014
Marylu Tyndall, *Forsaken Dreams*, 2013
Roseanna M. White, *Whispers from the Shadows*, 2013

411

IRENE HANNON

Buried Secrets

(Grand Rapids, Michigan: Baker Publishing, 2015)

Series: Men of Valor Series. Book 1
Story type: Mystery; Series

Subject(s): Crime; Law enforcement; Military life
Major character(s): Lisa Grant, Police Officer (chief); Mac McGregor, Detective—Homicide, Military Personnel (former US Navy SEAL)
Time period(s): 21st century; 2010s
Locale(s): Carson, Missouri

Summary: In the first book of Irene Hannon's Men of Valor series, the author introduces readers to Mac McGregor, a former member of the elite US Navy SEAL special forces who has just relocated to Missouri for a quieter life. Lisa Grant had the same idea, which is why she left her intense position with the Chicago Police Department to work as police chief for a small town outside of St. Louis. When a group of construction workers finds a corpse on a building site, Lisa is thrown into a chaotic game of cat and mouse with someone who doesn't want her finding out the victim's identity. When Mac McGregor lends his detective skills to help Lisa crack the case, he realizes that she is the exact type of woman he has been looking for. The killer is determined to stop them from finding answers, so both Mac and Lisa's lives are at risk. Now they must rely on their faith in each other, as well as in God, to help keep them safe.

Other books by the same author:
Deceived, 2014
Trapped, 2013
Vanished, 2013
Lethal Legacy, 2012
Fatal Judgment, 2011

Other books you might like:
Robin Caroll, *Injustice for All*, 2012
Catherine Coulter, *The Cove*, 1996
Catherine Coulter, *Power Play*, 2014
Dee Henderson, *Unspoken*, 2013
Iris Johansen, *The Face of Deception*, 1998
Ronie Kendig, *Nightshade*, 2010
W.W. Lee, *The Good Daughter*, 1994
Melinda Leigh, *Hour of Need*, 2014
S.L. Linnea, *Chasing Eden*, 2007
Chuck Logan, *The Price of Blood*, 1997
DiAnn Mills, *Breach of Trust*, 2009
Mel Odom, *Blood Lines*, 2009

412

LISA HARRIS

Taken

(New York: Love Inspired, 2015)

Story type: Inspirational; Romantic Suspense
Subject(s): Christian life; Romances (Fiction); Mystery
Major character(s): Kate Elliot, Aunt (of Sophie); Sophie, Kidnap Victim, Niece (of Kate); Marcus O'Brian, FBI Agent
Time period(s): 21st century; 2010s
Locale(s): Paris, France

Summary: In this inspirational romance by Lisa Harris, Kate Elliot is horrified when her sister is shot and her young niece, Sophie, is kidnapped. Kate is not sure she can trust the investigators looking into the case, so she decides to defy FBI agent Marcus O'Brian's orders. She

tracks Sophie herself and ends up in Paris. When her own life is threatened, Kate is forced to turn to the handsome FBI agent for help. O'Brian feels a powerful connection to Kate and a desperate need to protect her from harm. That connection is made even stronger when the kidnappers demand a ransom that Kate is not capable of providing. Marcus knows it is up to him to save Sophie and protect Kate before it is too late for both of them.

Other books by the same author:
Deadly Safari, 2014
Fatal Exchange, 2014
Dangerous Passage, 2013
Stolen Identity, 2013
Blood Ransom, 2010

Other books you might like:
Dee Henderson, *Kidnapped*, 2008
Jill Elizabeth Nelson, *Calculated Revenge*, 2010
Sandra Orchard, *Fatal Inheritance*, 2013
Susan Sleeman, *Dead Wrong*, 2012
Camy Tang, *Narrow Escape*, 2013

413

ROBIN LEE HATCHER

Whenever You Come Around

(Nashville, Tennessee: Thomas Nelson, 2015)

Series: Kings Meadow Romance Series. Book 2
Story type: Romance; Series
Subject(s): Writers; Interpersonal relations; Love
Major character(s): Charity Anderson, Writer, Lover (of Buck); Buck Malone, Cowboy/Cowgirl, Lover (of Charity)
Time period(s): 21st century; 2010s
Locale(s): Boise, Idaho; Kings Meadow, Idaho

Summary: This novel is the second book in author Robin Lee Hatcher's Kings Meadow Romance series. Charity Anderson left Kings Meadow, Idaho, far behind long ago, and also abandoned her romantic crush on Buck Malone. Now she's a successful writer living in Boise. When circumstances beyond her control force her to return to her childhood home for a while, Charity finds herself remembering the good and not-so-good times she had in the town. Unfortunately, she also has writer's block, but when she is reunited with Buck, he becomes her muse for a romantic leading man. The more she writes about him, the more she falls back in love with him, and a summer romance begins to bloom. Yet sad moments from her previous time in Kings Meadow keep popping into her head, and she will have to deal with those memories if her relationship with Buck is going to work.

Other books by the same author:
Love Without End, 2014
A Promise Kept, 2014
Where the Heart Lives Series, 2011
When Love Blooms, 2009
The Perfect Life, 2008

Other books you might like:
Katie Ganshert, *Wildflowers from Winter*, 2012

Irene Hannon, *That Certain Summer*, 2013
Denise Hunter, *Dancing with Fireflies*, 2014
Debby Mayne, *Pretty Is as Pretty Does*, 2013
Melissa Tagg, *Here to Stay*, 2014

414

RACHEL HAUCK

How to Catch a Prince

(Grand Rapids, Michigan: Zondervan, 2015)

Series: Royal Wedding Series. Book 3
Story type: Romance; Series
Subject(s): Romances (Fiction); Grief; Afghanistan Conflict, 2001-
Major character(s): Corina Del Ray, Heiress, Journalist; Stephen, Royalty (Prince of Brighton), Brother (of Nathaniel); Nathaniel, Royalty (King), Brother (of Stephen)
Time period(s): 21st century; 2010s
Locale(s): United Kingdom; United States

Summary: In this inspirational romance by Rachel Hauck, heiress and journalist Corina Del Ray and Prince Stephen of Brighton were once very much in love—they were even married. But they had their marriage annulled years ago, and since then, they have both seen their lives torn apart by the war in Afghanistan. Corina's brother was killed in the fighting, and Prince Stephen fought with the Royal Air Command. Now that Stephen has returned home, he has tried to put his past behind him by pursuing a career as a professional rugby player. But when his brother Nathaniel, the king, shows Stephen a document that proves he is still married, Stephen is forced to find Corina so they can appear in court to attempt to annul the marriage again. Stephen isn't prepared for the feelings he experiences when he finally sees Corina again. He knows that he broke Corina's heart when he left her, and that to gain her forgiveness, he will need to have faith in something much greater than the both of them.

Other books by the same author:
Princess Ever After, 2014
Once Upon a Prince, 2013
The Wedding Dress, 2012
Songbird Novel series, 2010
A Lowcountry Romance Series, 2008

Other books you might like:
Sandra D. Bricker, *If the Shoe Fits*, 2013
Lynda Lee Schab, *Mind Over Madi*, 2011
Kathryn Springer, *The Prince Charming List*, 2008
Janice Thompson, *The Dream Dress*, 2014
Susan May Warren, *Happily Ever After*, 2003

415

JODY HEDLUND

An Uncertain Choice

(Grand Rapids, Michigan: Zondervan, 2015)

Story type: Historical - Medieval; Romance
Subject(s): England; History; Middle Ages

Major character(s): Lady Rosemarie, Orphan, Noblewoman, Friend (of Duke of Rivenshire); Duke of Rivenshire, Nobleman (duke), Friend (of Rosemarie)
Time period(s): 14th century; 1390s (1390)
Locale(s): Ashby, England

Summary: According to the Ancient Vow and will of her late parents, in 1390 Lady Rosemarie prepares to enter the convent in four weeks, when she reaches her 18th birthday. When the Duke of Rivenshire, a family friend, arrives at Montfort Castle, Rosemarie's plans to become a nun are put on hold. According to the duke, Rosemarie's parents left one exception to the Ancient Vow—that is, to avoid pledging herself to a religious order, Rosemarie must marry by the eve of her 18th birthday. Rosemarie is soon asked to choose one of three brave knights who contend for her affections, but upon their arrival, mysterious attacks occur throughout the kingdom. When clues from the attacks are traced back to the knights, Rosemarie questions whether finding love is worth the risk—especially when the knight she's most attracted to appears to be the most guilty.

Other books by the same author:
Captured by Love, 2014
Love Unexpected, 2014
A Noble Groom, 2013
Rebellious Heart, 2013
The Preacher's Bride, 2010

Other books you might like:
Heather Burch, *Avenger: A Halfling Novel*, 2013
Melanie Dickerson, *The Fairest Beauty*, 2012
Sean Haldane, *The Devil's Making*, 2015
Julie Klassen, *The Secret of Pembrokoe Park*, 2014
Sarah E. Ladd, *The Heiress of Winterwood*, 2013
Siri L. Mitchell, *A Constant Heart*, 2008

416

JODY HEDLUND

Hearts Made Whole

(Bloomington, Minnesota: Bethany House Publishers, 2015)

Series: Beacons of Hope Series. Book 2
Story type: Historical; Romance
Subject(s): Lighthouses; Employment; Family
Major character(s): Caroline Taylor, Young Woman, Lighthouse Keeper (acting keeper of Windmill Point Lighthouse); Ryan Chambers, Lighthouse Keeper (appointed, of Windmill Point Lighthouse), Veteran (Civil War)
Time period(s): 19th century; 1860s (1865)
Locale(s): Windmill Point, Michigan

Summary: The year is 1865. Caroline Taylor's father has died, and she has taken up the responsibility of supporting her family by running the Windmill Point Lighthouse. Because she is a woman, Caroline is declared unfit to run the lighthouse by the lighthouse inspector, who appoints a new lighthouse keeper. Caroline has nowhere to go, nowhere else to live, and has no job opportunities. She is not prepared when Ryan Chambers, the newly appointed lighthouse keeper, arrives. Ryan, a Civil War veteran battling the haunting memories of the war, is

Inspirational

looking for solitude and peace in his new position. Caroline is not willing to give up her responsibilities on Windmill Point to this man and she questions his ability to assume the role. Ryan, who is emotionally closed off from his past, is reluctant to accept help. As they both face uncertain futures, will Caroline and Ryan must learn to look beyond their painful pasts if they are to see a future together at the lighthouse. This is the second novel of the Beacons of Hope series written by Jody Hedlund.

Other books by the same author:
Captured by Love, 2014
Love Unexpected, 2014
Rebellious Heart, 2013
The Doctor's Lady, 2011
The Preacher's Bride, 2010

Other books you might like:
Colleen Coble, *The Lightkeeper's Bride*, 2010
Jean Thompson Kinsey, *The Lightkeeper's Daughter*, 2013
Serena B. Miller, *The Measure of Katie Calloway*, 2011
Ann Shorey, *When the Heart Heals*, 2013
Elizabeth Byler Younts, *Promise to Cherish*, 2014

417

DEE HENDERSON

Taken

(Grand Rapids, Michigan: Baker Publishing Group, 2015)

Story type: Mystery
Subject(s): Detective fiction; Organized crime; Kidnapping
Major character(s): Shannon Bliss, Kidnap Victim, Young Woman; Becky, Daughter (of Matthew); Matthew Dane, Detective—Private, Father (of Becky)
Time period(s): 21st century; 2010s
Locale(s): Atlanta, Georgia

Summary: Shannon Bliss was kidnapped more than a decade ago, when she was 16, and has finally escaped from her abductors. Now she is on the run, and she knows she can turn to only one person for help. Private detective Matthew Dane shares a similar story. His daughter, Becky, was kidnapped at the age of eight, and he didn't see her again for eight years. Driven by his need to correct past mistakes with his daughter, Matthew desperately wants to help Shannon return to her family. Unfortunately, Shannon's kidnappers belong to the powerful and ruthless Jacoby crime syndicate, and they will stop at nothing to shut her up, including murder. As Matthew unravels the truth about what happened to Shannon, he realizes that if either of them is going to come out of this alive, they are going to have to learn to trust one another.

Other books by the same author:
Undetected, 2014
Unspoken, 2013
Full Disclosure, 2012
Heroes of Quantico series, 2009
The Witness, 2006

Other books you might like:
Franklin Bandy, *Deceit and Deadly Lies*, 1978
Patricia Bradley, *Shadows of the Past*, 2014
Janice Cantore, *Drawing Fire*, 2015
Robin Caroll, *Injustice for All*, 2012
Lynette Eason, *When a Secret Kills*, 2013
Irene Hannon, *Trapped*, 2013

418

CYNTHIA HICKEY

Death by Baking

(North Charleston, South Carolina: CreateSpace, 2015)

Series: Nosy Neighbors Series. Book 4
Story type: Contemporary - Innocent
Subject(s): Detective fiction; Writers; Cooking
Major character(s): Stormi Nelson, Detective—Amateur, Writer, Girlfriend (of Matt), Daughter (of Mrs. Nelson), Neighbor (of Norma); Matt Steele, Boyfriend (of Stormi), Detective—Police; Mrs. Nelson, Mother (of Stormi), Baker; Norma Olson, Neighbor (of Stormi), Aged Person
Time period(s): 21st century; 2010s
Locale(s): Oak Meadows, Arkansas

Summary: In the fourth installment from author Cynthia Hickey's Nosy Neighbors series, Stormi Nelson is back to solve another mystery in the seemingly quaint and quiet town of Oak Meadows, Arkansas. After narrowly escaping her most recent debacle, Stormi has vowed to leave the detecting up to real detectives, such as her boyfriend, Matt. But when Stormi's mother finds a dead person floating in a tub of chocolate at her bakery, Stormi finds herself drawn into another mystery. She soon learns that someone or something wants to drive all of the town's store owners out of business, and she is determined to put a stop to it. Yet with nosy old Norma Olson across the street always trying to stir up trouble, and a bunch of new people moving into the neighborhood, Stormi isn't sure whom she can trust. Stormi must tell Matt what she's been up to, but will she put him in danger when he tries to help her out?

Other books by the same author:
Anything for a Mystery, 2014
Summer Meadows Mystery Series, 2013

Other books you might like:
Vannetta Chapman, *Murder Simply Brewed*, 2014
Sharon Dunn, *Cow Crimes and the Mustang Menace*, 2005
Susan Sleeman, *Nipped in the Bud*, 2010
Virginia Smith, *Murder by Mushroom*, 2007
Chris Well, *Nursing a Grudge*, 2010

419

LYNNE HINTON

The Case of the Sin City Sister

(Nashville: Thomas Nelson, 2015)

Series: Divine Private Detective Agency Mystery Series. Book 2

Story type: Mystery; Series
Subject(s): Christian life; Nuns; Detective fiction
Major character(s): Eve Divine, Religious (nun), Sister (of Dorisanne), Detective—Private; Dorisanne Divine, Missing Person, Sister (of Sister Eve)
Time period(s): 21st century; 2010s
Locale(s): Las Vegas, Nevada

Summary: In the second book of the Divine Private Detective Agency mystery series, after discovering she has a gift for sleuthing, Sister Eve Divine decides to take a leave of absence from her convent. She joins forces with her father and begins investigating the disappearance of a client's missing great-grandfather. But as the case progresses, Sister Eve begins to worry about her younger sister, Dorisanne. It's been weeks since she last heard from her, and Sister Eve has a feeling that something terrible has happened. Sister Eve heads to Las Vegas in search of Dorisanne. With the help of some hidden clues she finds in Dorisanne's address book, Sister Eve is able to follow her sister's trail, which leads her to a dark side of town. She soon realizes that Dorisanne's life is much more complicated than she suspected.

Other books by the same author:
Sister Eve: Private Eye, 2014
Pie Town, 2011
Hope Springs, 2002

Other books you might like:
Christy Barritt, *Hazardous Duty*, 2006
Sharon Dunn, *Death of a Garage Sale Newbie*, 2007
Andrew M. Greeley, *Blackie Ryan Series*, 1985
Lorena McCourtney, *Ivy Malone Series*, 2004
Ralph McInerny, *Father Dowling Series*, 1977

420

DENISE HUNTER

Married 'til Monday

(Nashville, Tennessee: Thomas Nelson, 2015)

Series: Chapel Springs Romance Series. Book 4
Story type: Romance; Series
Subject(s): Romances (Fiction); Marriage; Divorce
Major character(s): Ryan McKinley, Spouse (former husband, of Abby); Abby, Spouse (former wife, of Ryan)
Time period(s): 21st century; 2010s
Locale(s): Summer Harbor, Maine

Summary: Best-selling author Denise Hunter delivers the fourth and final installment in her Chapel Springs Romance series. Ryan McKinley will do anything to win back the love of his ex-wife, Abby. When Abby's parents invite Ryan to their 35th wedding anniversary celebration in Summer Harbor, Maine, Ryan is hopeful that this is God's way of telling him there's still a chance his relationship with Abby can be restored. Abby's strained relationship with her father has kept her from telling her parents about the divorce, and now, the former spouses are forced to attend the anniversary party as man and wife. Abby still finds Ryan irresistible, but the wounds of her broken heart run deep. Is it possible that a week-long road trip to Maine is just what they need to mend their hearts and restore the love between them?

Other books by the same author:
Dancing with Fireflies, 2014
The Wishing Season, 2014
Barefoot Summer, 2013
Game of Love, 2013
The Perfect Match, 2013

Other books you might like:
Eva Marie Everson, *Chasing Sunsets*, 2011
Sharlene MacLaren, *Threads of Joy*, 2014
Deborah Raney, *Home to Chicory Lane*, 2014
Cynthia Ruchti, *They Almost Always Come Home*, 2010
Dan Walsh, *The Dance*, 2013

421

JERRY B. JENKINS

Empire's End

(Franklin, Tennessee: Worthy Books, 2015)

Story type: Historical; Religious
Subject(s): History; Religion; Roman Empire, 30 BC-476 AD
Major character(s): Paul, Biblical Figure (Apostle Paul)
Time period(s): 1st century; 30s
Locale(s): Roman Empire

Summary: In this fictional account of the Apostle Paul, best-selling author Jerry B. Jenkins reimagines the life of the biblical figure as he spreads the gospel of Jesus Christ throughout the Roman Empire. Jenkins follows Paul's early life as a Jewish scholar, his miraculous conversion on the road to Damascus, and the three years he spent in the Arabian wilderness. In Arabia, Paul lives alongside a community of fellow Christian believers and discovers a dreadful connection to his past—a past filled with the persecution of those who preached the same gospel he now preaches. Jenkins's account reconsiders Paul's ever-present "thorn in the flesh," as well as Paul's experiences with romance and fatherhood.

Other books by the same author:
I, Saul, 2013
Precinct 11 Series, 2011
The Jesus Chronicles, 2006
Soon Trilogy, 2003
Left Behind Series, 1995

Other books you might like:
James Cannon, *Apostle Paul*, 2005
Tosca Lee, *Iscariat: A Novel of Judas*, 2013
Joel C. Rosenberg, *Damascus Countdown*, 2013
Randy Singer, *The Advocate*, 2014
Bodie Thoene, *When Jesus Wept*, 2013

422

SALLY JOHN

Heaven Help Heidi

(Eugene, Oregon: Harvest House Publishers, 2015)

Series: Family of the Heart Series. Book 2
Story type: Contemporary; Series

Subject(s): Friendship; Grief; Accidents
Major character(s): Liv McAlister, Businesswoman (owner, Casa de Vida); Heidi Hathaway, Friend (of Piper), Accident Victim; Piper Keyes, Friend (of Heidi)
Time period(s): 21st century; 2010s
Locale(s): Seaside Village, California

Summary: In this inspirational novel by Sally John, the second in the Family of the Heart series, Liv McAllister is the owner of Casa de Vida, which comprises 11 bungalows in a small coastal California town. Heidi Hathaway is Liv's newest tenant. She arrived after a terrible car accident left her unable to drive or walk up the stairs in her condo. She hopes to heal and regain the strength to return to her old life. Heidi's friend Piper Keyes is already living at Casa de Vida. She moved in after her fiance was killed in Afghanistan nearly five years ago. Piper has finally begun to accept her fiance's death, and she starts to explore what her future might look like without him. Together, the women living in Casa de Vida provide support, love, and encouragement to one another as they heal and find their way back to their faith.

Other books by the same author:
Between Us Girls, 2014
Heart Echoes, 2012
Desert Gift, 2011
Safe Harbor Series, 2008
The Beach House Series, 2006

Other books you might like:
Julie Carobini, *Sweet Waters*, 2009
Eva Marie Everson, *Slow Moon Rising*, 2013
Gina Holmes, *Crossing Oceans*, 2010
Trish Perry, *Beach Dreams: A Novel*, 2008
Marybeth Whalen, *The Bridge Tender*, 2014

423

RONIE KENDIG

Falcon

(Uhrichsville, Ohio: Barbour Publishing, Inc., 2015)

Series: Quiet Professionals Series. Book 3
Story type: Military; Series
Subject(s): Military life; Terrorism; Computers
Major character(s): Salvatore Russo, Military Personnel (aka Falcon), Co-worker (of Cassandra); Cassandra Walker, Military Personnel, Co-worker (of Salvatore)
Time period(s): 21st century; 2010s
Locale(s): Afghanistan

Summary: As members of the elite US Army Raptor unit, Salvatore "Falcon" Russo and Lt. Cassandra Walker should be on the same side, but a deadly incident years earlier left a bitter Salvatore vowing to never speak to Cassandra again. War, however, has no room for grudges, and when a terrorist attack leaves several members of Raptor dead, Salvatore and his men are assigned to a strike team led by Cassandra. For the good of the mission, he tries to put his animosity aside, but when he discovers she is hiding secrets from him and his men, Salvatore's anger boils back to the surface. With the respect of command strained and a traitor lurking in their midst, Raptor's mission teeters on ruin. This is the third book in Ronie Kendig's Quiet Professionals series.

Other books by the same author:
Hawk, 2014
Raptor 6, 2014
A Breed Apart Series, 2012
Dead Reckoning, 2010
Discarded Heroes Series, 2010

Other books you might like:
Dee Henderson, *True Honor*, 2002
DiAnn Mills, *Breach of Trust*, 2009
Diane Munson, *Night Flight*, 2012
Mel Odom, *Blood Lines*, 2009
Joel C. Rosenberg, *Damascus Countdown*, 2013

424

KAREN KINGSBURY

Divine

(Carol Stream, Illinois: Tyndale House Publishers, 2006)

Story type: Contemporary
Subject(s): Prostitution; Redemption
Major character(s): Mary Madison, Prostitute (former)
Time period(s): 21st century; 2000s
Locale(s): Washington, District of Columbia

Summary: In this modern version of the story of the Biblical personage Mary Magdalene, author Karen Kingsbury tells the story of Mary Madison. Mary was abused, mistreated, and violated all of her life, finally turning to a life of prostitution and crime. Now reformed, Mary fights for the rights of abused women. She runs five shelters for women throughout the Washington, D.C., area and is a powerful force in Congress, battling for the causes she believes will help women and girls to avoid the life she had, or to escape it.

Other books by the same author:
Fifteen Minutes, 2014
Shades of Blue, 2009
This Side of Heaven, 2009
Every Now and Then, 2008
Between Sundays, 2007

Other books you might like:
Julie Cantrell, *Into the Free*, 2012
Dorothy Clark, *Hosea's Bride*, 2004
Shaunti Feldhahn, *The Lights of Tenth Street*, 2003
Joseph F. Girzone, *Joshua Series*, 1983
Gina Holmes, *Wings of Glass*, 2013
Kenny Kemp, *The Welcoming Door: Parables of the Carpenter*, 2002
Michele Phoenix, *In Broken Places*, 2013
Francine Rivers, *Redeeming Love*, 1991
Darlene Shortridge, *Forever Blessed*, 2012
Ginny L. Yttrup, *Words*, 2011

425

KAREN KINGSBURY

Chasing Sunsets

(New York: Howard Books, 2015)

Series: Angels Walking Series. Book 2
Story type: Contemporary; Religious
Subject(s): Abuse; Adolescence; Counseling
Major character(s): Mary Catherine, Volunteer (with at-risk teens), Wealthy, Patient (heart); Marcus Dillinger, Baseball Player (L.A. Dodgers), Volunteer (works with at-risk teens), Co-worker (of Mary Catherine); Lexy Jones, Abuse Victim (of teen violence), Client (of Last Time In teen program), 16-Year-Old, Gang Member, Girl; Jag, Angel; Aspyn, Angel
Time period(s): 21st century; 2010s
Locale(s): Heaven; Los Angeles, California

Summary: Mary Catherine comes from a wealthy family, but all of her parents' wealth can't buy their daughter more time. Mary Catherine devotes herself to her charity work at the local youth center. She is determined to live her life to the fullest because a congenital heart problem has given her an uncertain future. Mary Catherine; her friend and roommate, Sami; Coach Tyler Ames; and L.A. Dodger Marcus Dillinger work with at-risk teens in the Last Time In program. Mary Catherine finds herself developing feelings for Marcus. She has sworn off love because of her medical diagnosis and tries to avoid her feelings and Marcus, too. In trying to help Lexy Jones, a young gang member and victim of abuse, Mary Catherine encounters issues of faith, love, and loss. Two angels arrive from Heaven to help her to evaluate her life and her true feelings for Marcus. This is the second novel in Karen Kingsbury's Angels Walking series.

Other books by the same author:
Angels Walking, 2015
Fifteen Minutes, 2014
Love Lost series, 2013

Other books you might like:
Mitch Albom, *The First Phone Call from Heaven*, 2013
Kathryn Cushman, *Another Dawn*, 2011
Denise Hunter, *Dancing with Fireflies*, 2014
Karen Kingsbury, *Where Yesterday Lives*, 1998
Max Lucado, *Miracle at the Higher Grounds Cafe*, 2015
Debbie Macomber, *Last One Home*, 2015
Debbie Macomber, *Mr. Miracle*, 2014
Sarah Price, *An Empty Cup*, 2015
Ruth Reid, *Brush of Angel's Wings*, 2012
Lauraine Snelling, *On Hummingbird Wings*, 2011
Nicholas Sparks, *The Last Song*, 2009
Dan A. Stouten, *The Gate*, 2013
Ken Wharton, *Divine Intervention*, 2001

426

STEPHANIE LANDSEM

The Tomb: A Novel of Martha

(New York: Howard Books, 2015)

Series: Living Water Series. Book 3
Story type: Historical; Series
Subject(s): Christianity; Biblical literature; Bible stories
Major character(s): Martha, Friend (of Jesus), Biblical Figure, Sister (of Lazarus), Fiance(e) (of Simon); Lazarus, Biblical Figure, Brother (of Martha), Friend (of Jesus); Simon, Biblical Figure, Fiance(e) (of Martha); Isa, Biblical Figure, Lover (of Martha); Jesus, Religious (messiah), Biblical Figure, Friend (of Martha and Lazarus)
Time period(s): 1st century
Locale(s): Bethany, Israel

Summary: Everyone in the town of Bethany admires Martha, who abides by the Pharisees' laws, provides for her family, and is a dutiful and devout woman with a good reputation. They don't know Martha's secret, a shameful sin that haunts her. Years ago, she innocently fell for a musician at her sister's wedding banquet. Martha believed herself to be in love and allowed him to take her virginity. The musician, Isa, said he would marry Martha but instead he disappeared. Since then he has been roaming the wilderness, mad and lost. Jesus finds him and cures him of his insanity, and he seeks Martha again. Two people know what happens between Isa and Martha, however: her brother, Lazarus, and her fiance, a Pharisee named Simon. When Lazarus becomes ill, Martha knows she can call for Jesus and ask for his help, but Simon has forbidden her to do so. If she defies him, her secret will be revealed. Martha is caught between two agonizing choices and must rely on her faith to see her through.

Other books by the same author:
The Thief, 2014
The Well, 2013

Other books you might like:
Tessa Afshar, *Harvest of Gold*, 2013
Ginny Aiken, *Remember Me When*, 2013
Mesu Andrews, *Love in a Broken Vessel*, 2013
Jill Eileen Smith, *Abigail: A Novel*, 2010
Diana Wallis Taylor, *Martha: A Novel*, 2011

427

BEVERLY LEWIS

The Love Letters

(Bloomington, Minnesota: Bethany House Publishers, 2015)

Story type: Romance
Subject(s): Christian life; Single parent family; Family
Major character(s): Marlena Wenger, Religious (Amish), Sister (of Luella), Fiance(e) (of Nat), Granddaughter (of Mammi Janice); Mammi Janice, Grandmother (of Marlena and Luella), Neighbor (of Ellie), Religious (Beachy Amish-Mennonite); Boston, Man, Vagrant;

Nat Zimmerman, Fiance(e) (of Marlena), Religious (Amish), Young Man; Ellie Bitner, Neighbor (of Mammi Janice); Angela Rose, Baby, Daughter (of Luella); Luella, Sister (of Marlena), Granddaughter (of Mammi Janice)
Time period(s): 20th century; 1960s (1966)
Locale(s): Brownstown, Pennsylvania; Mifflinburg, Pennsylvania

Summary: Marlena Wenger lives in an Old Order Amish community outside of Mifflinburg, Pennsylvania. She is excited about her impending marriage to Nat Zimmerman, but is unexpectedly called away to her grandmother's side after her grandfather passes away. Marlena's grandmother is a Beachy Amish-Mennonite, however, and Marlena has trouble reconciling herself to the community of Brownstown's more liberal ways. Although Marlena believes she will only be in Brownstown for the summer months, life has other plans when her sister, Luella, is in a car accident. Luella was never baptized into the Amish church, and married a non-Amish man who is away fighting in the Vietnam War. Now Marlena must care for her sister's infant daughter, Angela Rose, while Luella recuperates. Luckily, many members of the community are willing to help, including Ellie Bitner, her grandmother's neighbor, as well as a kind homeless man, to whom Marlena offers shelter. As the summer progresses, Marlena begins to question her decision of joining the Old Order, and wonders if she is better suited for her new community.

Other books by the same author:
Child of Mine, 2014
The River, 2014
The Guardian, 2013
The Fiddler, 2012
Home to Hickory Hollow Series, 2012

Other books you might like:
Wanda E. Brunstetter, *A Sister's Test*, 2013
Amy Clipston, *A Gift of Grace*, 2009
Denise Hunter, *Seaside Letters*, 2009
Marta Perry, *Susanna's Dream*, 2014
Cindy Woodsmall, *When the Soul Mends*, 2008

428

HILLARY MANTON LODGE

Reservations for Two

(New York: Crown Publishing Group, 2015)

Series: Two Blue Doors Series. Book 2
Story type: Adventure; Humor
Subject(s): Adventure; Culture; Faith
Major character(s): Juliette D'Alisa, Businesswoman (restaurant owner), Girlfriend (of Neil McLaren), Critic (food), Daughter (of chronically ill mother), Granddaughter (of Mireille); Neil McLaren, Researcher (Medical Immunologist), Boyfriend (of Juliette D'Alisa); Mireille, Grandmother (of Juliette D'Alisa), Woman (with family secrets)
Time period(s): 21st century; 2010s
Locale(s): Provence, France; Italy; Oregon, United States; Memphis, Tennessee

Summary: In the second novel of the Two Blue Doors series, author Hilary Manton Lodge continues to follow the life of Juliette D'Alisa, a former food writer and critic turned restaurateur. When Juliette travels to the family chateau in the South of France to spend time with her family, she is joined by her boyfriend Neil McLaren. They enjoy family, delicious food, and budding romance in their travels through Provence and Tuscany. Returning to Portland to open her new restaurant, Two Blue Doors, Juliette wonders if the romance will be able to withstand the distance that separates her and Neil. Uncertain of her future with Neil, Juliette turns to the mystery of the letters of her beloved grandmother, Mireille. Will discovering the secrets of her grandmother's past offer Juliette the guidance she needs, or will the letters only leave her with more unanswered questions and uncertainty?

Other books by the same author:
A Table by the Window: A Novel of Family Secrets and Heirloom Recipes, 2014
Plain Jayne, 2010
Simply Sara, 2010

Other books you might like:
Kaye Dacus, *Menu for Romance*, 2009
Rachel Hauck, *Dining with Joy*, 2010
Krista Phillips, *Sandwich, with a Side of Romance*, 2012
Lynette Sowell, *A Path Made Plain*, 2014
Betsy St. Amant, *All's Fair in Love and Cupcakes*, 2014

429

KELLY LONG

An Amish Man of Ice Mountain

(New York: Zebra Books, 2015)

Series: Ice Mountain Series. Book 2
Story type: Contemporary; Romance
Subject(s): Abuse; Violence; Interpersonal relations
Major character(s): Joseph King, Oil Industry Worker, Brother (of Edward), Guardian (of Priscilla and Hollie), Religious (Amish); Edward King, Brother (of Joseph), Religious (Amish), Oil Industry Worker; Priscilla Allen, Abuse Victim, Mother (of Hollie), Friend (of Joseph King), Divorced Person; Hollie Allen, Child, Daughter (of Priscilla)
Time period(s): 21st century; 2010s
Locale(s): Ice Mountain, Pennsylvania; West Virginia, United States

Summary: Joseph King's heart lies in Ice Mountain, Pennsylvania, within his Amish community. He has joined his younger brother Edward for work on an oil rig in West Virginia in an attempt to keep Edward out of trouble and close to God. He maintains his home in Ice Mountain and bides his time until he can go home, but Joseph worries that his past mistakes within Amish society might mark him an outsider. While coping with his own problems, Joseph meets Priscilla, a single mother fleeing from an abusive ex. Priscilla and her daughter, Hollie, have been living in their car, and Joseph can't help but feel compassion for them. He offers Priscilla his help through a proposal of platonic marriage. As his wife, she and Hollie would be welcomed into the community of Ice Mountain, where they would be protected and safe. Joseph feels that not only is he doing a good deed, but also that his actions might restore his good reputation. Priscilla and Hollie accept and begin to acclimate to the Amish lifestyle. A tentative trust and relationship begin to build, but secrets and past mistakes threaten to destroy them. This is the second novel of the Ice Mountain series.

Other books by the same author:
The Amish Bride of Ice Mountain, 2014
Amish Beginning Series, 2012
A Marriage of the Heart, 2012
Patch of Heaven Series, 2010

Other books you might like:
W. Dale Cramer, *Levi's Will: A Novel*, 2005
Mary Ellis, *A Plain Man*, 2014
Tricia Goyer, *Along Wooded Paths*, 2011
Beverly Lewis, *The Brethren*, 2006
Beverly Lewis, *The Forbidden*, 2008

430

MAX LUCADO
CANDACE LEE, Co-Author
ERIC NEWMAN, Co-Author

Miracle at the Higher Grounds Cafe

(Nashville, Tennessee: Thomas Nelson, 2015)

Story type: Contemporary
Subject(s): Interpersonal relations; Faith; Religion
Major character(s): Chelsea Chambers, Single Mother, Businesswoman (owner of Higher Grounds Cafe), Friend (of Manny); Manny, Friend (of Chelsea)
Time period(s): 21st century; 2010s
Locale(s): San Antonio, Texas

Summary: Chelsea Chambers is in need of a miracle. Recently separated from her NFL superstar husband—a serial philanderer—she makes a new start in life by taking over operation of her grandmother's old coffee shop, the Higher Grounds Cafe. Despite her greatest efforts and delicious cupcakes, the financial burden of reinventing her grandmother's cafe is too much for Chelsea to bear. When hope is all but lost, Chelsea meets Manny, a man determined to help her succeed. He installs wi-fi in her cafe, but the Internet service will only connect to one site: The God Blog, where questions are asked and God replies. Suddenly, business is booming. Customers fill Chelsea's coffee shop day after day to ask God their most important questions, but is God the one who's really answering?

Other books you might like:
Richard Paul Evans, *The Road to Grace: The Third Journal of the Walk Series*, 2012
Karen Kingsbury, *Chasing Sunsets*, 2015
Karen Kingsbury, *Maggie's Miracle*, 2003
Debbie Macomber, *Mr. Miracle*, 2014
Charles Martin, *When Crickets Cry*, 2006
Rusty Whitener, *A Season of Miracles*, 2010

431

ASHLEY ELIZABETH LUDWIG

Mammoth Secrets

(Aztec, New Mexico: Pelican Ventures, 2015)

Story type: Romance
Subject(s): Deception; Religion; Faith
Major character(s): Jake Gibson, Religious (pastor), Divorced Person, Man (with assumed identity); Lilah Dale, Divorced Person, Twin
Time period(s): 21st century; 2010s
Locale(s): Mammoth, Arkansas

Summary: Jake Gibb in seeking a new life in Mammoth, Arkansas, but the handsome new pastor of the community's church is not all he seems to be. Jake Gibb is not his real name. He has re-created himself to escape a painful divorce. Jake takes over a congregation that fears change and does not trust him. His message of forgiveness over condemnation doesn't sit well with the people in the pews, but it does resonate with one soul. Recovering from her own divorce, Lilah Dale has returned home to Mammoth seeking peace, but finds grief from her family and scorn from her community. Jake and Lilah are kindred souls who may be able to find the peace they seek in each other, but to do that they must first embrace the truth. In Mammoth's judgmental atmosphere, that may not be an easy proposition.

Other books you might like:
Jennifer Allee, *The Pastor's Wife*, 2010
Jerry B. Jenkins, *Riven*, 2008
Kathi Macias, *More than Conquerors*, 2010
Sharlene MacLaren, *Threads of Joy*, 2014
Kathleen Y'Barbo, *Beloved Counterfeit*, 2009

432

RICHARD L. MABRY

Fatal Trauma

(Nashville: Abingdon Press, 2015)

Story type: Contemporary; Romance
Subject(s): Hostages; Hospitals; Gangs
Major character(s): Dr. Mark Baker, Doctor (emergency room), Hostage, Doctor, Boyfriend (former, of Gwen Woodruff), Colleague (of Kelly Atkinson); Kelly Atkinson, Nurse, Colleague (of Mark Baker), Hostage; Gwen Woodruff, Lawyer, Girlfriend (former, of Mark Baker)
Time period(s): 21st century; 2010s
Locale(s): United States

Summary: Dr. Mark Baker is trained to deal with emergency situations and stress. An emergency room doctor, he has dedicated himself to his work. He keeps his social life casual, and has not been in any serious relationships. When a gunman storms the ER and takes Mark, an aide, and nurse Kelly Atkinson—Mark's current girlfriend—hostage, Mark knows what he has to do. The gunman threatens to kill everyone in the ER unless the doctor saves the life of his brother, who has been injured in a gang shootout. A police officer who has just dropped off a patient risks his own life to save the medical staff. The gunman shoots the officer, who dies despite Mark's best efforts. Two gang members are also killed. In the aftermath, Mark and Kelly discover that the gunman and his brother were members of the ruthless Zeta drug cartel. The rest of the gang sets its sights on Mark, who they blame for not saving their members. Desperate for help, Mark contacts his high school sweetheart, attorney Gwen Woodruff, which causes conflict with Kelly.

Other books by the same author:
Critical Condition, 2014
Heart Failure, 2013
Stress Test, 2013
Prescription for Trouble series, 2010

Other books you might like:
Candace Calvert, *Code Triage*, 2010
Shawn Grady, *Tomorrow We Die*, 2010
Harry Kraus, *Lethal Mercy*, 1997
Jordyn Redwood, *Bloodline Trilogy*, 2012
Wm. Paul Young, *Crossroads*, 2012

433

SHARLENE MACLAREN

Gift of Grace

(New Kensington, Pennsylvania: Whitaker House, 2015)

Series: Tennessee Dreams Series. Book 3
Story type: Romance; Series
Subject(s): Christian life; Romances (Fiction); Family
Major character(s): Grace Fontaine, Fiance(e) (of Conrad and Jess), Niece (of Iris); Iris Brockwell, Aunt (of Grace), Aged Person; Jess Travis, Fiance(e) (of Grace), Survivor; Conrad Hall, Lawyer, Fiance(e) (of Grace)
Time period(s): 19th century; 1890s (1894-1897)
Locale(s): Boston, Massachusetts; Paris, Tennessee

Summary: This book is the third novel from author Sharlene MacLaren's Tennessee Dreams series. After the presumed death of her fiance, Jess, Grace Fontaine vowed she would never again give her heart away. When she learns that her great aunt, Iris Brockwell, is on her deathbed, Grace moves from her home in Boston to the rural town of Paris, Tennessee, to take care of her. There, she unexpectedly meets and falls for local attorney Conrad Hall. When Conrad asks for Grace's hand in marriage, Iris wonders if God would want them to wed. After Iris's death, Conrad convinces Grace to move the wedding date up. When Jess turns out to be alive after all, and he shows up in Paris seeking Grace, Grace must determine which man truly loves her, and which man is lying. She must put her faith in the Lord to discover what her heart really wants.

Other books by the same author:
Heart of Mercy, 2014
Threads of Joy, 2014
River of Hope Series, 2011
Tender Vow, 2010
Daughters of Jakob Kane Series, 2008

Other books you might like:
Christina Berry, *The Familiar Stranger*, 2009

Sara Evans, *The Sweet By and By*, 2009
Patricia Hickman, *The Pirate Queen: A Novel*, 2010
Karen Kingsbury, *The Bridge*, 2012
Deborah Raney, *The Face of the Earth*, 2013

434

STEPHENIA H. MCGEE

The Whistle Walk

(By The Vine Press, 2015)

Series: Ironwood Plantation Family Series. Book 1
Story type: Historical; Series
Subject(s): Civil war; United States Civil War, 1861-1865; Slavery
Major character(s): Lydia Harper, Wealthy, Southern Belle; Ruth, Slave
Time period(s): 19th century; 1860s
Locale(s): Mississippi, United States

Summary: In the first novel from Stephenia H. McGee's Ironwood Plantation Family series, the author tells the story of two women who form an unlikely friendship at one of the most sorrowful times in United States history. The nation is in the grips of a bloody civil war, and the South is especially affected by the ongoing battles. Lydia Harper, the daughter of a wealthy plantation owner, doesn't believe that slavery should exist, but when she sees an African American girl being whipped in the town square, she intervenes and purchases the girl from her owner. Ruth has lived her whole life as a field hand, but after Lydia rescues her, she works as Lydia's maid. As the two young women get to know one another, they begin to learn that they have more similarities than they could have imagined. Now they must stand by one another if they are going to make it through the devastation of war and the cruelty of society.

Other books you might like:
Lynn Austin, *A Light to My Path*, 2014
Jocelyn Green, *Yankee in Atlanta*, 2014
Loree Lough, *James's Joy*, 2013
Michael Phillips, *Angels Watching over Me*, 2003
Jennifer Hudson Taylor, *Path of Freedom*, 2013

435

NANCY MEHL

Deadly Echoes

(Bloomington, Minnesota: Bethany House Publishers, 2015)

Series: Finding Sanctuary Series. Book 2
Story type: Romantic Suspense; Series
Subject(s): Christian life; Romances (Fiction); Suspense
Major character(s): Sarah Miller, Sister (of Hannah), Aunt (of Cicely); Hannah Miller, Sister (of Sarah), Mother (of Cicely); Cicely Miller, 10-Year-Old, Daughter (of Hannah), Niece (of Sarah); Paul Gleason, Police Officer (Deputy Sheriff)
Time period(s): 21st century; 2010s
Locale(s): Sanctuary, Missouri

Summary: In this inspirational novel by Nancy Mehl, the second in the Finding Sanctuary series, sisters Sarah and Hannah Miller have spent their lives dealing with the tragedy that struck their family when they were young children—the murder of both their parents. Sarah has only recently had the opportunity to reconnect with her sister after years apart, and then tragedy strikes again. Hannah is murdered in the same manner as her parents, and Sarah is left to care for Hannah's ten-year-old daughter, Cicely. Sarah knows that there must be a connection between the murders, and she asks deputy sheriff Paul Gleason for help in uncovering the truth. As their investigation reveals a series of lies spanning more than two decades, both Sarah and Paul realize that Sarah's life is in danger as well.

Other books by the same author:
Gathering Shadows, 2014
Blown Away, 2011
Harmony Secrets Series, 2010
Missing Mabel, 2010
Ivy Towers Mystery Series, 2008

Other books you might like:
Patricia Bradley, *Shadows of the Past*, 2014
Mindy Starns Clark, *Shadows of Lancaster County*, 2009
Colleen Coble, *Tidewater Inn*, 2012
Irene Hannon, *Vanished*, 2013
Dani Pettrey, *Shattered*, 2013

436

DIANN MILLS

Double Cross

(Carol Stream, Illinois: Tyndale House Publishers, 2015)

Series: FBI: Houston Series. Book 2
Story type: Police Procedural
Subject(s): Law enforcement; Faith; Murder
Major character(s): Laurel Evertson, FBI Agent, Colleague (of Daniel, Morton), Woman; Morton Wilmington, Criminal, Colleague (of Daniel, Laurel); Daniel Hilton, Police Officer, Colleague (of Laurel, Morton)
Time period(s): 21st century; 2010s
Locale(s): Houston, Texas

Summary: When FBI agent Laurel Evertson was called upon to stop a fraud scheme targeting the elderly, she had no idea the assignment would dredge up her past. Laurel discovers evidence linking the case to Morton Wilmington, a convicted felon she helped capture five years ago, and a man who had vowed to kill her. Forced to rely on Morton's assistance, Laurel also teams up with police officer Daniel Hilton, who fears his grandparents are next on the scammer's list. As Laurel, Morton, and Daniel dig into the case, they discover a plot more deadly than simple deceit. Laurel and Daniel are now the targets of a killer and their lives come down to a stark question: Do they trust the supposedly repentant Morton, or are they falling into his trap? This is the second book in DiAnn Mills's FBI: Houston series.

Other books by the same author:
Firewall, 2014

Crime Scene: Houston Series, 2012
Attracted to Fire, 2011
Call of Duty Series, 2009

Other books you might like:
Patricia Bradley, *A Promise to Protect*, 2014
Robin Caroll, *Strand of Deception*, 2013
Lisa Harris, *Fatal Exchange*, 2014
Dee Henderson, *Full Disclosure*, 2012
Sandra Orchard, *Blind Trust*, 2014

437

TYORA MOODY

Hostile Eyewitness

(Wyandanch, New York: Urban Christian, 2015)

Series: Serena Manchester Series. Book 1
Story type: Mystery; Series
Subject(s): Depression (Mood disorder); Family relations; Gangs
Major character(s): Serena Manchester, Journalist (reporter), Accident Victim
Time period(s): 21st century; 2010s
Locale(s): Georgetown County, South Carolina

Summary: Serena Manchester returns to her hometown of Georgetown County, South Carolina, after suffering a traumatic head injury that leaves her out of work and feeling depressed. The former reporter left home 25 years ago, and until now, hasn't had much reason to return. While at home recuperating, Selena witnesses a gang-related crime and thinks she recognizes one of the young men involved. Concerned that her injury has hindered her perception, Serena keeps quiet about the night's events. Soon, danger strikes closer to home, and Serena feels she's to blame. To protect herself and her estranged family, Serena puts her reporter skills to work, and when the local police department refuses her help, she takes matters into her own hands. With this novel, author Tyora Moody launches her Serena Manchester inspirational suspense series.

Other books by the same author:
Deep Fried Trouble, 2013
Victory Gospel Series, 2012

Other books you might like:
Candace Calvert, *Life Support*, 2014
Irene Hannon, *Lethal Legacy*, 2012
Dee Henderson, *The Witness*, 2006
Ronie Kendig, *Trinity: Military War Dog*, 2012
Richard L. Mabry, *Critical Condition*, 2014

438

SARAH E. MORIN

Waking Beauty

(Phoenix, Arizona: Enclave Publishing, 2015)

Story type: Fantasy
Subject(s): Royalty; Fairies; Interpersonal relations
Major character(s): Arpien, Royalty (prince), Rescuer (of

Inspirational

Princess Brierly), Hero; Brierly, Royalty (princess), Captive (cursed by a fairy)
Time period(s): Indeterminate
Locale(s): Fictional Location

Summary: Prince Arpien had planned to gain the throne by waking Princess Brierly from her century-long slumber with a kiss that would break the curse of an evil fairy. But things did not go as planned. After the kiss, the prince has to overcome several obstacles, such as man-eating bugs, poisonous spindles, and a talking lapdog. The kiss does wake Princess Brierly, but something isn't right in her brain. Brierly not only refuses to believe she is awake, she doesn't believe that Prince Arpien is real. Instead, the princess thinks she's still in her sleeping imprisonment and that the rescue is nothing more than a dream doomed to failure. Prince Arpien is drawn to the princess's beauty despite her indifference to him. Will Arpien be able to reclaim the kingdom and prove to Brierly that she is not dreaming?

Other books you might like:
Sandra D. Bricker, *Rise and Shine: A Contemporary Fairy Tale*, 2014
Heather Burch, *Avenger: A Halfling Novel*, 2013
Melanie Dickerson, *The Fairest Beauty*, 2012
Shannon Dittemore, *Angel Eyes*, 2012
Rachel Hauck, *Once Upon a Prince*, 2013

439

OLIVIA NEWPORT

Meek and Mild

(Uhrichsville, Ohio: Shiloh Run Press, 2015)

Series: Amish Turns of Time Series. Book 2
Story type: Romance; Series
Subject(s): Romances (Fiction); Amish; History
Major character(s): Clara Kuhn, Teacher (Sunday School), Friend (of Andrew), Religious (Amish); Andrew Raber, Religious (Amish), Friend (of Clara); Moses Beachy, Religious (Amish)
Time period(s): 20th century; 1910s (1916)
Locale(s): Somerset County, Pennsylvania

Summary: In this inspirational romance by Olivia Newport, the second novel in the Amish Turns of Time series, Clara Kuhn and her family are members of a very conservative Old Order Amish community. It is 1916, and members are required to shun anyone who teaches Sunday school with the Mennonites—something Clara enjoys more than anything else. At the same time, Clara and her family are now required to shun Andrew Raber—a young man who was just about to propose to Clara—because he defies the bishop's authority by continuing to own a car. The community is ready for a change, and when Moses Beachy becomes the new bishop, they all start to move forward to a new Amish-Mennonite faith known today as Beachy Amish.

Other books by the same author:
Wonderful Lonesome, 2014
Avenue of Dreams Series, 2012
Valley of Choice Series, 2012

Other books you might like:
Wanda E. Brunstetter, *The Bishop's Daughter*, 2006
Jerry Eicher, *Katie Opens Her Heart*, 2013
Beverly Lewis, *The Forbidden*, 2008
Kate Lloyd, *Forever Amish*, 2014
Cindy Woodsmall, *The Winnowing Season*, 2013

440

JANETTE OKE
LAUREL OKE LOGAN, Co-Author

Where Trust Lies

(Bloomington, Minnesota: Bethany House Publishers, 2015)

Series: Return to the Canadian West Series. Book 2
Story type: Historical; Romance
Subject(s): Romances (Fiction); Family; Christian life
Major character(s): Beth Thatcher, Teacher; Jarrick Thornton, Police Officer (Royal Canadian Mounted Police)
Time period(s): 19th century
Locale(s): Canada

Summary: In this inspirational romance by Janette Oke and Laurel Oke Logan, the second in the Return to the Canadian West series, Beth Thatcher has been away from her family for the past year, living her dream of becoming a teacher and working in the Canadian West. She has returned to visit with her mother and sisters, but she quickly finds that the distance between them has grown, even as they all embark on a steamship tour along the coast of Canada and the United States. Beth is torn between wanting to reconnect with her family and her desire to return to the Coal Valley to teach—and to be with the man she loves, Canadian Mountie Jarrick Thornton. When Beth's family is caught in a misunderstanding and her faith is tested, Beth is finally forced to confront her choices and decide what is most important in her life.

Other books by the same author:
Where Courage Calls, 2014
A Prairie Legacy Series, 2008
Women of the West Series, 2006
Canadian West Series, 2005
Love Comes Softly Series, 2003

Other books you might like:
Melody Carlson, *A Home at Trail's End*, 2013
Mindy Starns Clark, *Echoes of Titanic*, 2012
Kaye Dacus, *Ransome's Crossing*, 2010
Janice A. Thompson, *Queen of the Waves*, 2012
Karen Witemeyer, *Full Steam Ahead*, 2014

441

SANDRA ORCHARD

Desperate Measures

(Ada, Michigan: Revell Publishing, 2015)

Series: Port Aster Secrets Series. Book 3
Story type: Mystery; Romantic Suspense
Subject(s): Betrayal; Deception; Crime
Major character(s): Kate Adams, Scientist (researcher and

plant expert), Friend (of Tom Parker); Tom Parker, FBI Agent (former), Police Officer (of Port Aster), Friend (of Kate Adams)
Time period(s): 21st century; 2010s
Locale(s): Port Aster, Canada

Summary: In the third and final novel in the Port Aster series, crime and circumstance have scientist and plant expert Kate Adams and detective Tom Parker working together again. Having discovered the medicinal plant that has caused her family turmoil, Kate is desperate to uncover its secrets, hoping it will finally shed light on the circumstances of her father's disappearance. After a mysterious theft, Detective Tom Parker and Kate find themselves working both with and against each other while trying to deny their mutual attraction. Kate and Tom are not the only ones looking for the plant. Other forces are at work, and they are proving to be treacherous. Will Kate and Tom be able to trust each other enough to work together, or will the secrets they are keeping place them in more danger?

Other books by the same author:
Blind Trust, 2014
Identity Withheld, 2014
Perilous Waters, 2014
Deadly Devotion, 2013
Fatal Inheritance, 2013

Other books you might like:
Patricia Bradley, *Shadows of the Past*, 2014
Colleen Coble, *Rosemary Cottage*, 2013
Irene Hannon, *Deceived*, 2014
Nancy Mehl, *Gathering Shadows*, 2014
Dani Pettrey, *Stranded*, 2013

442

CHRISTA PARRISH

Still Life

(Nashville, Tennessee: Thomas Nelson, 2015)

Story type: Contemporary
Subject(s): Marriage; Cults; Infidelity
Major character(s): Ada Goetz, Widow(er), Spouse (of Julian), Cult Member (former); Katherine Walker, Spouse (adulterer), Woman; Julian Goetz, Photographer, Accident Victim, Spouse (former, of Ada)
Time period(s): 21st century; 2010s
Locale(s): United States

Summary: This inspirational novel by award-winning author Christa Parrish is a tale of loss, deception, forgiveness, and hope. Ada grew up in a fringe cult, an extreme religious sect named after her father. When she meets photographer Julian Goetz, she courageously escapes the family compound and turns her back on the only world she has ever known. Julian believes in a gracious and merciful God—nothing like Ada's father taught—and with Julian, Ada realizes how wonderful life can be. Tragedy strikes when Julian is killed in a plane crash, and now, only five months after their marriage, Ada finds herself navigating painful emotions in a strange new world. Meanwhile, Katherine Walker's life is on the

verge of falling apart. Her extramarital affair not only brings escape, but also shame. The plane crash that took Julian's life also affects Katherine and increases her feelings of guilt. Ada and Katherine are left to question where they belong in the world, and they find unexpected answers when the dreams of a young boy lead them to one another.

Other books by the same author:
Stones for Bread, 2013
The Air We Breathe, 2012
Watch Over Me, 2009
Home Another Way, 2008

Other books you might like:
Katie Ganshert, *The Art of Losing Yourself*, 2015
Angela Elwell Hunt, *The Note II: Taking a Chance on Love*, 2009
Karen Kingsbury, *Oceans Apart*, 2004
Susan Meissner, *A Fall of Marigolds*, 2014
Lisa Samson, *Once in a Blue Moon*, 2011
Lisa Wingate, *The Prayer Box*, 2013

443

DANIEL PATTERSON

The Devil's Game

(Ravenwood Way, 2014)

Series: Devil's Game Series. Book 1
Story type: Mystery; Series
Subject(s): Suspense; Devil; Good and evil
Major character(s): James Buchman, Religious (pastor of New Hope Church); Devil, Demon; Charles Griffin, Religious (former pastor of New Hope Church)
Time period(s): 21st century; 2010s
Locale(s): Harmony, New York

Summary: In the first book from Daniel Patterson's Devil's Game series, the author introduces readers to James Buchman, a young minister who recently moved to upstate New York. James has followed his calling into the ministry, and after graduating from religious studies school, has found a church where he can put down roots and build a life. James has taken over for the former pastor of New Hope Church, who became mysteriously ill and died several months earlier. James quickly learns to care for the people of his new town, Harmony, and is devastated when a series of disturbing occurrences rocks the town. These happenings coincide with the arrival of an enigmatic newcomer, for whom James immediately feels distrust. Soon, James realizes that far more violent forces are at work than just bad luck. If he is going to truly shepherd his flock, he will have to face off against the Devil himself.

Other books by the same author:
The Codex, 2014
One Chance, 2013

Other books you might like:
Roger Bruner, *The Devil and Pastor Gus*, 2014
Billy Coffey, *The Devil Walks in Mattingly*, 2014
Mike Duran, *The Telling*, 2012

Inspirational

Dineen Miller, *The Soul Saver*, 2012
Frank E. Peretti, *House*, 2006

444

MARTA PERRY (Pseudonym of Martha Johnson)

Where Secrets Sleep

(Toronto: Harlequin, 2015)

Series: Watcher in the Dark Trilogy. Book 4
Story type: Romance; Series
Subject(s): Amish; Inheritance and succession; Romances (Fiction)
Major character(s): Allison Standish, Designer, Woman, Friend (of Sarah, Nick); Sarah Bitler, Woman, Businesswoman, Friend (of Allison); Nick Whiting, Carpenter, Friend (of Allison)
Time period(s): 21st century; 2010s
Locale(s): Laurel Ridge, Pennsylvania

Summary: Philadelphia interior designer Allison Standish has the big city in her blood. The last place she ever expected to be was heading off to rural Pennsylvania to run a centuries-old mansion in Amish country. But that's exactly where she finds herself when she inherits Blackburn House from a grandmother she never knew she had. The new adventure comes with a catch: She must successfully manage the property for a year, or it goes to another relative. Adjusting to country life takes some doing, but Allison soon makes friends with Sarah, a kindly quilt shop owner, and Nick, a handsome Amish cabinetmaker. As romance simmers between her and Nick, Allison discovers she's also made some enemies. Someone wants her gone from Blackburn and will do anything to drive her out. This is the fourth title of Marta Perry's Watcher in the Dark series.

Other books by the same author:
Abandon the Dark, 2014
Susanna's Dream, 2014
Lydia's Hope, 2013
Search the Dark, 2013
Home by Dark, 2012

Other books you might like:
Wanda E. Brunstetter, *A Sister's Secret*, 2007
Linda Castillo, *Sworn to Silence*, 2009
Colleen Coble, *Anathema*, 2008
Amanda Flower, *A Plain Death*, 2012
Karen Harper, *Fall from Pride*, 2011
Karen Harper, *Finding Mercy*, 2012
Beverly Lewis, *The Reckoning*, 1998
Carla Neggers, *Cold River*, 2009
Olivia Newport, *In Plain View*, 2013
Kit Wilkinson, *Plain Secrets*, 2012

445

TRACIE PETERSON

Steadfast Heart

(Minneapolis, Minnesota: Bethany House, 2015)

Series: Brides of Seattle Series. Book 1
Story type: Historical; Romance

Subject(s): Romances (Fiction); Mail order brides; Family relations
Major character(s): Lenore Fulcher, Young Woman, 20-Year-Old; Kolbein Booth, Young Man, Lawyer, Brother (of missing person)
Time period(s): 19th century; 1880s (1888)
Locale(s): Seattle, Washington

Summary: Set in 1880s Seattle, this inspirational romance novel is the first installment in the Brides of Seattle series by best-selling author Tracie Peterson. Twenty-year-old Lenore Fulcher isn't interested in a marriage of convenience. The well-to-do daughter of a Seattle businessman, Lenore would much rather marry for true love than money. Her father, on the other hand, has his own plans for Lenore's future—plans that include her marriage to one of his business partners, a man 17 years older than Lenore. When Kolbein Booth arrives in Seattle searching for his sister at a finishing school for mail-order brides, the young Chicago attorney meets Lenore and is smitten. With the help of Lenore and the other young women at the Madison Bridal School, Kolbein continues the search for his missing sister, and his attraction to Lenore only grows deeper. Is it possible the true love Lenore has waited for has finally found her?

Other books by the same author:
Land of the Lonestar Series, 2012
Striking a Match Series, 2010
Brides of Gallatin County Series, 2008
Ladies of Liberty Series, 2007
Where My Heart Belongs, 2007

Other books you might like:
Maggie Brendan, *Perfectly Matched*, 2013
Lena Nelson Dooley, *Love Finds You in Golden, New Mexico*, 2010
Mona Hodgson, *Two Brides Too Many: A Novel*, 2010
Melissa Jagears, *Love by the Letter*, 2013
Karen Witemeyer, *To Win Her Heart*, 2011

446

DANI PETTREY

Sabotaged

(San Diego, California: Center Point Publishing, 2015)

Series: Alaskan Courage Series. Book 5
Story type: Mystery; Romance
Subject(s): Dogs; Romances (Fiction); Kidnapping
Major character(s): Kirra Jacobs, Cousin (of missing girl), Rescuer, Friend (of Reef), Niece (of Frank); Reef McKenna, Rescuer, Friend (of Kirra); Frank, Uncle (of Kirra), Father (of missing girl); Unnamed Character, Missing Person, Kidnap Victim, Child, Daughter (of Frank), Cousin (of Kirra)
Time period(s): 21st century; 2010s
Locale(s): Willow, Alaska

Summary: In their past time together, Kirra Jacobs and Reef McKenna didn't get along: She was good, and he was always into some kind of trouble. But now they are a team, working search and rescue for the Iditarod dog race in Alaska, and they are a good team at that. Close contact seems to erase some of the old differences, and

Reef and Kirra are starting to feel a bit of a draw to each other. When Frank, one of the mushers—Kirra's uncle, in fact—goes missing and Reef and Kirra find him, they have a number of questions about what has gone wrong. Frank's daughter has been taken by someone who threatens not only the girl but all of Alaska with an almost unimaginable disaster. Now Kirra and Reef must rely on each other to solve the mystery and rescue Kirra's cousin. This is the fifth book in the Alaskan Courage series.

Other books by the same author:
Silenced, 2014
Shattered, 2013
Stranded, 2013
Submerged, 2012

Other books you might like:
Colleen Coble, *Alaska Twilight*, 2006
Margaret Daley, *The Yuletide Rescue*, 2014
Lynette Eason, *Hide and Seek*, 2013
Lisa Harris, *Fatal Exchange*, 2014
Kristen Heitzmann, *Indelible*, 2011

447

LISA PHILLIPS

Manhunt

(New York: Love Inspired, 2015)

Story type: Romance
Subject(s): Suspense; Law enforcement; Romances (Fiction)
Major character(s): Hailey Shelder, Agent (US marshal), Mother (of Kerry), Single Mother; Eric Hanning, Agent (US marshal), Steve Farrell, Convict, Fugitive; Kerry, 12-Year-Old, Daughter (of Hailey)
Time period(s): 21st century; 2010s
Locale(s): Oregon, United States

Summary: US marshal Hailey Shelder isn't too happy about her new partner. She has spent her career trying to be taken seriously by the men on her force, and now this new, handsome rookie comes along and undermines her at every turn. Hailey's new partner, Eric Hanning, isn't happy about his own career and recent reassignment from Phoenix to rural Oregon. Then, during what should have been a routine prison transfer, ruthless convict Steve Farrell escapes the van he is riding in with Hailey and Eric. Now the new partners must learn to trust each other as they track down Steve, who is determined not only to flee, but also to seek vengeance. Hailey will stop at nothing to protect her daughter, Kerry, but with Steve stalking her at every turn, she will have to rely on Eric to watch out for the both of them. Eric and Hailey find themselves becoming partners in life, but with so much at stake, can they really commit themselves to each other?

Other books by the same author:
Double Agent, 2014
Star Witness, 2014

Other books you might like:
Maggie K. Black, *Killer Assignment*, 2013
Sharon Dunn, *Wilderness Target*, 2014

Shirlee McCoy, *Safe by the Marshall's Side*, 2014
Jill Elizabeth Nelson, *Calculated Revenge*, 2010
Kimberley Woodhouse, *No Safe Haven*, 2011

448

ALLISON PITTMAN

On Shifting Sand

(Carol Stream, Illinois: Tyndale House Publishers, 2015)

Story type: Historical
Subject(s): Droughts; Great Depression, 1929-1934; Christian life
Major character(s): Nola Merrill, Daughter (of Ma and Pa), Spouse (of Russ); Russ Merrill, Spouse (of Nola), Religious (minister)
Time period(s): 20th century; 1930s
Locale(s): Featherling, Oklahoma

Summary: Since the death of her mother, Nola has known she needs to get away from her cold and cruel father at any cost. She marries a local minister, Russ Merrill, thinking marriage will provide the escape she needs. Yet Nola still longs for something more than the stable family life Russ provides. More than a decade later, as Oklahoma faces a crippling drought, Nola confronts her own emotional drought by conducting an affair with Russ's friend Jim. When regret over her infidelity consumes her, Nola knows she must turn to the husband who loves her, confess her indiscretion, and ask for grace. As the dust from thousands of acres of over-farmed land across the Plains whips around them, Nola and Russ face the ultimate test of their marriage. Now, Nola must decide not only if she feels worthy of Russ's forgiveness, but also if she is willing to forgive herself.

Other books by the same author:
All for a Sister, 2014
All for a Song, 2013
All for a Story, 2013
Forsaking All Others, 2011
Lillies in Moonlight, 2011

Other books you might like:
Kathy Harris, *The Road to Mercy*, 2012
Gina Holmes, *Dry as Rain*, 2011
Siri L. Mitchell, *Love's Pursuit*, 2009
Tracie Peterson, *House of Secrets*, 2011
Marybeth Whalen, *The Mailbox: A Novel*, 2010

449

SARAH PRICE

An Empty Cup

(Michigan: Waterfall Press, 2015)

Story type: Inspirational; Romance
Subject(s): Abuse; Alcoholism; Depression (Mood disorder)
Major character(s): Rosanna Zook, Mother (of two children), Abuse Victim (of Timothy Zook), Spouse (of Reuben Troyer), Religious (Amish), Widow(er);

Inspirational

Timothy Zook, Spouse (former, of Rosanna Zook), Alcoholic, Accident Victim (died in buggy accident); Reuben Troyer, Spouse (of Rosanna Zook), Widow(er), Religious (Amish), Businessman (owner of Troyer Harness Shop)
Time period(s): 21st century; 2010s
Locale(s): United States

Summary: Rosanna Zook is a caring and giving Amish woman, one who puts the needs of others before her own. Dealing with the burden of being married to an abusive alcoholic, Rosanna learns to hide her shame and devotes herself to helping others in any way she can. When her husband is killed in a buggy accident, she takes on the all responsibilities of her home and her two children. Later she marries a widower, Reuben Troyer, who owns his own business. Rosanna believes her burdens will be lessened, but as she takes on more responsibilities and evolves into a person who is always taken for granted, Rosanna feels helpless and finds no time for herself. As she struggles with feelings of depression and being overwhelmed, her cup runs empty: She has nothing left to give to her husband, her children, and her community. Will Rosanna be able to ask for and accept the help she needs?

Other books by the same author:
An Amish Buggy Ride, 2014
The Amish Classics Series, 2014
Amish Faith, 2013
The Amish of Lancaster Series, 2012

Other books you might like:
Wanda E. Brunstetter, *Goodbye to Yesterday*, 2013
Sara Evans, *Love Lifted Me*, 2012
Suzanne Woods Fisher, *The Choice*, 2010
Karen Kingsbury, *Chasing Sunsets*, 2015
Kelly Long, *A Marriage of the Heart*, 2012
Cindy Woodsmall, *When the Heart Cries*, 2006

450

SARAH PRICE

Second Chances

(Lake Mary, Florida: Realms Publishing, 2015)

Series: Amish Classics Series. Book 3
Story type: Contemporary; Literary
Subject(s): Amish; Culture; Faith
Major character(s): Anna Eicher, Religious (Amish), Young Woman (25 years old); Freman Whittmore, Businessman (owns large dairy farm), Religious (Amish)
Time period(s): 21st century; 2010s
Locale(s): Lancaster, Pennsylvania

Summary: In the third novel of the Amish Classics series, Author Sarah Price reimagines Jane Austen's *Persuasion* in an Amish setting. Eight years after Anna broke off her engagement to her fiance and best friend, Freman Whittmore, because her father disapproved, she woefully regrets her decision to end their relationship. After the breakup, Freman moved away to Indiana and became a successful dairy farmer. He has returned to Lancaster County to find a wife in his former community. Anna

has never married and still places pleasing and placating her family above her own happiness. When Freman returns, Anna must face her feelings, and she questions the decisions she has made. Will Anna allow Freman to marry another woman without telling him how she really feels? Will she find—and claim—a second chance at love?

Other books by the same author:
The Matchmaker, 2015
First Impressions, 2014
The Plain Fame Trilogy, 2012

Other books you might like:
Shelley Shepard Gray, *Hopeful: Return to Sugarcreek*, 2014
Beverly Lewis, *The Longing: A Novel*, 2008
Kim Vogel Sawyer, *When Mercy Rains*, 2014
Beth Wiseman, *Plain Peace*, 2013
Cindy Woodsmall, *When the Morning Comes*, 2007

451

SARAH PRICE

The Matchmaker

(Lake Mary, Florida: Charisma House, 2015)

Series: Amish Classics Series. Book 2
Story type: Romance; Series
Subject(s): Romances (Fiction); Amish; Christian life
Major character(s): Paul, Son (of bishop), Religious (Amish); Hannah, Religious (Amish), Friend (of Emma); Unnamed Character, Father (of Paul), Religious (Amish bishop); Emma Weaver, Matchmaker, Friend (of Hannah), Religious (Amish)
Time period(s): 21st century; 2010s
Locale(s): Lancaster County, Pennsylvania

Summary: The second novel from Sarah Price's Amish Classics series retells the tale of Jane Austen's *Emma* from the point of view of a young Amish woman living in Lancaster County, Pennsylvania. Emma Weaver enjoys matching the young people in her Amish community up with one another, even though her elders tell her she needs to be careful, or she will anger a lot of people and possibly break a lot of hearts. When Sarah plots to match her friend Hannah up with the bishop's son, Paul, he mistakes her intentions and thinks that Emma wants to court him. Soon the entire town realizes what Emma has been doing, and she faces some serious consequences. Now Emma must attempt to fix her mistakes while trying to get her friends to trust her again. Along the way, she may just find a romance for herself.

Other books by the same author:
An Amish Buggy Ride, 2014
First Impressions, 2014
Amish Faith, 2013
Plain Again, 2013
Valley of Hope, 2012

Other books you might like:
Jennifer Beckstrand, *Huckleberry Harvest*, 2015
Jennifer Beckstrand, *Huckleberry Summer*, 2014
Kaye Dacus, *The Art of Romance*, 2011

Mary Jane Hathaway, *Emma, Mr. Knightley, and Chili-Slaw Dogs*, 2013
Erynn Mangum, *Miss Match*, 2006
Anna Schmidt, *Matchmaker, Matchmaker*, 2006

452

CYNTHIA RUCHTI

As Waters Gone By

(Nashville, Tennessee: Abingdon Press, 2015)

Story type: Contemporary - Innocent
Subject(s): Marriage; Prisons; Christian life
Major character(s): Emmalyn Ross, Spouse (of Max), Cook (Chef), Householder; Max Ross, Prisoner, Spouse (of Emmalyn)
Time period(s): 21st century; 2010s
Locale(s): Madeline Island, Wisconsin

Summary: The fate of Emmalyn Ross's marriage hangs in the balance, all because of one fateful day five years ago. That was the day that her husband, Max, called her to let her know that he'd had too much to drink. Emmalyn didn't get Max's phone call in time, and Max decided to drive home himself. He crashed into the fertility clinic where he and Emmalyn had been trying to conceive, killing a homeless man, and the courts decided the car accident was intentional. Emmalyn has had no contact with Max during his imprisonment. Now, as she contemplates his impending release from prison, she flees town and makes for Madeline Island in Lake Superior. Her savings depleted and her career as a caterer and chef all but over, Emmalyn throws herself into refurbishing an old family cottage. As Emmalyn spends more time on the island, she forms friendships with people just like her, people who sought escape from their former lives. Yet Max will be released from prison soon, and Emmalyn must decide if their relationship is worth saving.

Other books by the same author:
All My Belongings, 2014
When the Morning Glory Blooms, 2013
They Almost Always Come Home, 2010

Other books you might like:
Christa Allan, *Walking on Broken Glass: A Novel*, 2010
Gina Holmes, *Driftwood Tides*, 2014
Karen Kingsbury, *Oceans Apart*, 2004
Marybeth Whalen, *She Makes It Look Easy: A Novel*, 2011
Ginny L. Yttrup, *Words*, 2011

453

LISA SAMSON

A Thing of Beauty

(Nashville, Tennessee: Thomas Nelson, 2015)

Story type: Contemporary
Subject(s): Actors; Addiction; Artists
Major character(s): Fiona Hume, Addict (former), Actress (former child star), Landlord (of Josia); Josia Yeu, Blacksmith, Roommate (tenant, of Fiona)
Time period(s): 21st century; 2010s
Locale(s): Baltimore, Maryland

Summary: It's been ten years since former child star Fiona Hume left Hollywood—and rehab. Reeling from the pain of abuse and betrayal, Fiona sought only to disappear from the rest of the world. Her mansion in downtown Baltimore, purchased to be a renovation project, has become little more than a box in which she can hoard the countless objects she collects from garage sales and thrift stores. Now 32 years old, Fiona is running low on money. To make ends meet, she rents the maid's quarters out to Josia Yeu, a gifted blacksmith. As Josia repurposes Fiona's junk collection into pieces of art, Fiona is influenced by more than his artistry. Peaceful and self-controlled, Josia is everything Fiona isn't. His presence affects her in a way she's never experienced, and soon, Fiona recognizes the power of beauty found within.

Other books by the same author:
Runaway Saint, 2014
The Sky Beneath My Feet, 2013
Resurrection in May, 2010
The Passion of Mary-Margaret, 2009
Club Sandwich, 2005

Other books you might like:
Christa Parrish, *Home Another Way*, 2008
Cynthia Ruchti, *All My Belongings*, 2014
Nancy Rue, *Healing Sands*, 2009
Marybeth Whalen, *The Bridge Tender*, 2014
Lisa Wingate, *The Story Keeper*, 2014

454

KIM VOGEL SAWYER

When Grace Sings

(Colorado Springs, Colorado: Waterbrook Press, 2015)

Series: Zimmerman Restoration Trilogy. Book 2
Story type: Family Saga; Series
Subject(s): Journalism; Mennonites; Christian life
Major character(s): Alexa Zimmerman, Hotel Owner (bed and breakfast owner), Adoptee (of Suzy), Daughter (of Suzy), Cousin (of Anna-Grace), Religious (Mennonite); Suzy Zimmerman, Religious (Mennonite), Mother (adoptive, of Alexa); Anna-Grace Braun, Cousin (of Alexa), Fiance(e) (of Steven), Religious (Mennonite); Steven Brungardt, Religious (Mennonite), Fiance(e) (of Anna-Grace); Briley Forrester, Journalist
Time period(s): 21st century; 2010s
Locale(s): Chicago, Illinois; Arborville, Kansas

Summary: In the second installment of Kim Vogel Sawyer's Zimmerman Restoration Trilogy, the author continues the story of the Zimmerman family with Alexa, who was adopted as a child by Suzy Zimmerman. Alexa has finally come into her own despite never truly feeling as though she fit in with the Old Order Mennonite community in which she lives. Now, she has opened up a bed and breakfast in Arborville, and business is picking up. When Briley Forrester, a reporter from Chicago, comes to town to stay at the B&B indefinitely, Alexa cannot believe her luck. Meanwhile, her cousin Anna-Grace has come to visit her to be closer to the man to whom she is betrothed, Steven Brungardt. The more time Alexa and Anne-Grace spend together, however, the more they discover facts about their family's past that were supposed to stay buried. Unfortunately, they don't realize that their every move is being watched by Briley, who is on assignment to write about the Plain folk and will stop at nothing to get a juicy story.

Other books by the same author:
Echoes of Mercy, 2014
Through the Deep Waters, 2014
When Mercy Rains, 2014
What Once Was Lost, 2013
My Heart Remembers, 2008

Other books you might like:
Shelley Shepard Gray, *Grace: A Christmas Sisters of the Heart Novel*, 2010
Beverly Lewis, *The Secret Keeper*, 2013
Sarah Price, *Plain Fame*, 2012
Deborah Raney, *Home to Chicory Lane*, 2014
Alice J. Wisler, *Hatteras Girl*, 2010

455

ADINA SENFT

Keys of Heaven

(New York: Hachette, 2015)

Series: Healing Grace Series. Book 2
Story type: Romance; Series
Subject(s): Christian life; Amish; Healing
Major character(s): Sarah Yoder, Healer, Neighbor (of Henry), Widow(er), Religious (Amish); Henry Byler, Neighbor (of Sarah), Artist; Eric Parker, Runaway; Silas Lapp, Man, Religious (Amish)
Time period(s): 21st century; 2010s
Locale(s): Whinburg County, United States

Summary: In the second installment of author Adina Senft's Healing Grace series, Amish widow Sarah Yoder continues her journey as the community Dokterfraa, a healer who uses plants to help remedy illnesses. Sarah also continues to deny her true feelings about her neighbor, Henry Byler, who lives within the community after inheriting his family's farm, but was never baptized into the Amish church. Meanwhile, Silas Lapp has come to visit the community, and Sarah's own family wants to match them up. When a non-Amish family comes to stay at a local bed and breakfast and the younger son runs away, Henry and Sarah find themselves working together to try to help the family. Sarah is sure that a certain herb will help the family come together and understand one another, but she isn't sure which herb will help her understand her own heart. Now she must choose between Silas, of whom her family clearly approves, or Henry, which could lead to her being shunned by the entire community.

Other books by the same author:
Herb of Grace, 2014

Amish Quilt Series, 2011
Other books you might like:
Barbara Cameron, *A Time to Love*, 2010
Mary Ellis, *A Plain Man*, 2014
Shelley Shepard Gray, *Forgiven*, 2009
Beth Wiseman, *An Amish Garden*, 2014
Beth Wiseman, *Plain Perfect*, 2008

456

ADINA SENFT

Balm of Gilead

(Nashville, Tennessee: FaithWords Publishing, 2015)

Series: Healing Grace Series. Book 3
Story type: Romance; Series
Subject(s): Amish; Family relations; Friendship
Major character(s): Sarah Yoder, Religious (Amish), Widow(er), Healer (herbal), Mother (of Simon and Caleb), Neighbor (of Henry Byler); Henry Byler, Neighbor (of Sarah Yoder), Artisan (potter), Patient, Religious (Amish); Simon, Brother (of Caleb), Son (returning son of Sarah); Caleb, Son (of Sarah), Brother (of Simon), Religious (Amish)
Time period(s): 21st century; 2010s
Locale(s): Willow Creek, Pennsylvania

Summary: Amish widow Sarah Yoder is denying the feelings that she has developed for her neighbor, Henry Byler. After she hears of Henry's engagement to another woman, Sarah busies herself in her family and her work. She lovingly welcomes her son Simon from Colorado. She makes it her mission to find her sister-in-law a husband, and she continues to learn to create tea and tinctures as an herbal healer. She is doing fine until Henry solicits her to help him with his ailing hands. A successful potter, Henry needs the help and knowledge of Sarah and her herbs to cure his ailment, which threatens his livelihood. Sarah helps create a balm for Henry's hands, but will she be able to find a balm to soothe her broken heart if Henry marries another? This is the third novel in the Healing Grace series by author Adina Senft.

Other books by the same author:
Keys of Heaven, 2015
Herb of Grace, 2014
Amish Quilt Series, 2013

Other books you might like:
Wanda E. Brunstetter, *The Healing Quilt*, 2014
Kathleen Fuller, *A Hand to Hold*, 2010
Laura V. Hilton, *Healing Love*, 2012
Traci Tyne Hilton, *Hearts to God*, 2014
Beverly Lewis, *The Mercy*, 2011

457

DINA L. SLEIMAN

Dauntless

(Bloomington, Minnesota: Bethany House, 2015)

Series: Valiant Hearts Series. Book 1
Story type: Romance

Subject(s): Adventure; Adventurers; Social class
Major character(s): Lady Merry Ellison, Noblewoman, Leader (of the Ghosts of Farthingale Forest); Timothy Grey, Nobleman; King of England, Royalty
Locale(s): England

Summary: In the first installment of the Valiant Hearts series, author Dina L. Sleiman retells the classic literary tale *Robin Hood* with a feminine twist. Lady Merry Ellison was born into the nobility, but a dreadful mistake by her family has cast them out of favor with the Crown. Now Lady Merry finds herself hunted, so she takes to the forest and becomes the leader of a tribe of orphans known as the Ghosts of Farthingale Forest. Timothy Grey also was born into the nobility, but he chooses a different path. He knows that if he can defeat Lady Merry's legendary tribe, he will be celebrated as a hero of England. Timothy meets up with Lady Merry, and is surprised that a young woman can best him at his game. When he learns the truth about the King of England and Lady Merry's ultimate mission, he questions his entire heritage, and turns to his faith to guide him.

Other books by the same author:
Dance from Deep Within, 2013
Love in Three Quarter Time, 2012
Dance of the Dandilion, 2011

Other books you might like:
Patrick W. Carr, *A Cast of Stones*, 2013
Melanie Dickerson, *The Merchant's Daughter*, 2011
Julie Klassen, *The Silent Governess*, 2010
Stephanie Landsem, *The Thief*, 2014
Lynn Morris, *The Baron's Honourable Daughter*, 2014

` 458 `

JILL EILEEN SMITH

The Crimson Cord: Rahab's Story

(Grand Rapids, Michigan: Revell, 2015)

Series: Daughters of the Promised Land Series. Book 1
Story type: Historical; Romance
Subject(s): History; Romances (Fiction); Biblical literature
Major character(s): Rahab, Prostitute, Biblical Figure
Time period(s): 15th century B.C.

Summary: In this inspirational romance, the first in the Daughters of the Promised Land series, author Jill Eileen Smith retells the Bible story of Rahab, imagining how her life might have unfolded. Rahab is forced into an abusive marriage, and she is eventually sold into slavery and prostitution as payment for her husband's gambling debts. When Israelite spies are taken into her home, Rahab sees an opportunity and makes a promise to protect the spies. When the Israelite armies come to Jericho, Rahab has no choice but to put her faith in God and believe the spies will keep the promise they made to her in turn. What Rahab finds outside the city will change her life forever, but what she wants most of all is love, forgiveness, and redemption—something that has seemed impossible until now.

Other books by the same author:
Wives of the Patriarchs Series, 2012

Wives of King David Series, 2009

Other books you might like:
Tessa Afshar, *Pearl in the Sand*, 2010
Mesu Andrews, *Love in a Broken Vessel*, 2013
Stephanie Landsem, *The Well*, 2013
Francine Rivers, *Redeeming Love*, 1991
Joan Wolf, *This Scarlet Cord: The Love Story of Rahab*, 2012

` 459 `

LAURAINE SNELLING

A Harvest of Hope

(Bloomington, Minnesota: Bethany House Publishers, 2015)

Series: Song of Blessing Series. Book 2
Story type: Historical; Romance
Subject(s): Nursing; Norwegian Americans; Romances (Fiction)
Major character(s): Trygve Knutson, Boyfriend (of Miriam); Miriam Hastings, Nurse (in training), Girlfriend (of Trygve), Daughter (of Mrs. Hastings); Mrs. Hastings, Mother (of Miriam), Patient
Time period(s): 20th century; 1900s (1905)
Locale(s): Chicago, Illinois; Blessing, North Dakota

Summary: In the second novel of Lauraine Snelling's Song of Blessing series, young couple Trygve Knutson and Miriam Hastings continue to struggle with their shared sense of place. Miriam is determined to continue her studies at a nursing school in Blessing, North Dakota, but when she must return to Chicago to help care for her mother, who is dying, she questions if her family and community need her more. Meanwhile, Trygve has decides that he wants to ask Miriam for her hand in marriage, but he is uncertain if she loves him as much as he loves her. Trygve writes frequent letters to Miriam and declares his undying love. She looks within her heart and relies on God to provide her with the best course of action. Yet when she finally returns to Blessing, she finds the whole town in turmoil. Is this really the place for her, and more importantly, is Trygve really the man she wants to marry?

Other books by the same author:
To Everything a Season, 2014
A Place to Belong, 2013
Untamed Heart, 2013
Wake the Dawn, 2013
Wild West Wind Series, 2011

Other books you might like:
Andrea Boeshaar, *Unexpected Love*, 2011
Katie Ganshert, *Wildflowers from Winter*, 2012
Joan Johnston, *Maverick Heart*, 1995
Tracie Peterson, *All Things Hidden*, 2014
Martha Rogers, *Autumn Song*, 2011

460

KATHRYN SPRINGER

The Dandelion Field

(Grand Rapids, Michigan: Zondervan, 2015)

Story type: Contemporary; Romance
Subject(s): Christian life; Romances (Fiction); Teenage parents
Major character(s): Ginevieve "Gin" Lightly, Mother (of Raine), Waiter/Waitress, Single Mother; Raine Lightly, Daughter (of Gin), Pregnant Teenager, Student—High School; Cody Bennett, Teenager, Student—High School; Dan Moretti, Fire Fighter
Time period(s): 21st century; 2010s
Locale(s): Banister Falls, Wisconsin

Summary: Ginevieve "Gin" Lightly has moved around ever since the father of her daughter, Raine, left her. It's the only way she can keep herself from remembering the pain. Then their car stops working in Banister Falls, Wisconsin, which is the quintessential American town. Raine begs to stay put, at least until she graduates from high school, and Gin agrees. Gin settles into small-town life and gets a job working as a waitress in a diner, but it isn't long before Raine tells her something that will change both of their lives: she is pregnant. The father of Raine's unborn child is Cody Bennett, whose firefighter father died in the line of duty. Now Cody's father's best friend, Dan Moretti, has taken over as a surrogate dad, and it's up to him to teach Cody about doing the right thing. As Dan and Gin both try to usher Cody and Raine through one of the hardest times in all of their lives, they find themselves falling for one another. This might not be the best time for romance, however, and as things go from hard to impossible, Dan and Gin struggle for cooler heads to prevail.

Other books by the same author:
The Prince Charming List, 2008
Front Porch Princess, 2006

Other books you might like:
Stacy Hawkins Adams, *Lead Me Home*, 2013
Kellie Coates Gilbert, *Mother of Pearl*, 2012
Denise Hunter, *Saving Grace*, 2005
Sally John, *A Journey by Chance*, 2002
Deborah Raney, *Home to Chicory Lane*, 2014

461

NANCY RUE
REBECCA ST. JAMES, Co-Author

One Last Thing

(Nashville, Tennessee: Thomas Nelson, 2015)

Story type: Contemporary
Subject(s): Betrayal; Addiction; Faith
Major character(s): Tara Faulkner, Young Woman, Fiance(e) (of Seth); Seth Grissom, Young Man, Fiance(e) (of Tara); Ned, Religious (priest)
Time period(s): 21st century; 2010s
Locale(s): Savannah, Georgia

Summary: Authors Rebecca St. James and Nancy Rue deliver an inspirational story of hurt and betrayal, hope and strength. Since she was 15 years old, Tara Faulkner has dreamed of marrying Seth Grissom, the boy she grew up next to in the historic district of Savannah, Georgia. However, three weeks before their wedding, Tara's world comes crashing down when she discovers that Seth has a secret addiction. As she wrestles with feelings of hurt and betrayal, Tara questions who Seth really is—and if the real Seth is the man she's grown to love. She's wounded further when she learns that others knew of his habits and kept the truth from her. Tara hastily takes a job at the local cafe, where she finds support and comfort from unexpected sources. With the help of a priest named Ned, she discovers that only Christ can heal the hurts of her past and give her hope for the future.

Other books by the same author:
Sarah's Choice, 2014
The Merciful Scar, 2013

Other books you might like:
Christa Allan, *Walking on Broken Glass: A Novel*, 2010
James Scott Bell, *Presumed Guilty*, 2006
Gina Holmes, *Dry as Rain*, 2011
Gina Holmes, *Wings of Glass*, 2013
Mary Monroe, *God Don't Make No Mistakes*, 2012
Beth Wiseman, *The Promise*, 2014

462

MELISSA TAGG

From the Start

(Grand Rapids, Michigan: Baker Publishing Group, 2015)

Story type: Romance
Subject(s): Romances (Fiction); Family; Football
Major character(s): Kate Walker, Writer, Young Woman; Colton Greene, Football Player (former)
Time period(s): 21st century; 2010s
Locale(s): Maple Valley, United States

Summary: Kate Walker is good at romance—more specifically, she is good at writing about it. As a scriptwriter she's produced scores of happily-ever-afters for the television screen, but can't seem to get her own love life quite right. After another relationship crashes and burns, Kate is mired in a career funk. She retreats to her hometown of Maple Valley to visit her family and stabilize her life. Also in town is former NFL quarterback Colton Greene, who is recovering from a career-ending injury and mending his own romantic wounds. When the play-it-safe Kate and impulsive Colton meet, their attraction is obvious, but their styles don't quite mesh. However, time—and their faith that God will guide them on the right path—may be just what they need to realize they have found something special.

Other books by the same author:
Here to Stay, 2014
Made to Last, 2013

Other books you might like:
Kristin Billerbeck, *Split Ends*, 2007
Karen Kingsburg, *Sunrise*, 2007
Alison Strobel, *Worlds Collide*, 2005

Janice A. Thompson, *Stars Collide*, 2011
Lisa Wingate, *Never Say Never*, 2010

463

SARAH LOUDIN THOMAS

Until the Harvest

(Bloomington, Minnesota: Bethany House, 2015)

Series: Appalachian Blessings Series. Book 2
Story type: Historical; Romance
Subject(s): Family relations; Family; Christian life
Major character(s): Henry Phillips, Student—College (former), Farmer, Friend (of Mayfair, Margaret); Margaret Hoffman, Sister (of Mayfair), Friend (of Henry), Housekeeper; Mayfair Hoffman, Sister (of Margaret), Friend (of Henry)
Time period(s): 20th century; 1970s (1975-1976)
Locale(s): Wise, United States

Summary: After a family tragedy rips him away from college, Henry Phillips feels lost. Now stuck taking care of his family farm, Henry tries to find several ways to escape his grief. He hangs around with the wrong crowd, plays his fiddle, and pals around with his friend Mayfair Hoffman. However, Mayfair's older sister Margaret won't let Henry have a moment's peace. Margaret, who is Henry's grandmother's housekeeper, always seems to be around to annoy him. Henry first thinks that Margaret doesn't care about his loss, but then he learns that Margaret has her own issues to deal with. It turns out that Mayfair has health problems and a unique gift that has Margaret constantly worried about her sister. Henry and Margaret soon find comfort together, and they rely on one another as tragedy strikes.

Other books by the same author:
Miracle in a Dry Season, 2014

Other books you might like:
Irene Hannon, *That Certain Summer*, 2013
Liz Curtis Higgs, *Grace in Thine Eyes*, 2006
Karen Kingsbury, *Coming Home*, 2012
Beverly Lewis, *The Fiddler*, 2012
Ginny L. Yttrup, *Words*, 2011

464

LIZ TOLSMA

Remember the Lilies

(Nashville, Tennessee: Thomas Nelson Publishing, 2015)

Story type: Romance
Subject(s): World War II, 1939-1945; Prisoners of war; Concentration camps
Major character(s): Rand Sterling, Prisoner, Lover (of Irene); Irene Reynolds, Lover (of Rand)
Time period(s): 20th century; 1940s (1943)
Locale(s): Manila, Philippines

Summary: Rand Sterling was once one of the most powerful and influential Americans living in Manila. The owner of several clubs across the city, Rand's reputation was known by local Filipinos as well as former US residents living in the Philippines. That was before World War II broke out in the Pacific, however. Now, Rand is a prisoner at the Santo Tomas Camp, an internment camp for civilians who are enemies of the Japanese. Irene Reynolds is a former missionary who now serves, not entirely willingly, under the Japanese at Santo Tomas. It is her job to get messages to the prisoners of war. When Irene inadvertently ruins Rand's chance to run away from the camp, she watches powerlessly as he is sent off to be tortured. Upon Rand's return, Irene swears she will stop at nothing to make it up to him. The more Rand and Irene get to know one another, the more they find themselves falling in love. But with such dire circumstances surrounding them, they must be careful to keep the ruthless camp authorities from finding out about their feelings for one another.

Other books by the same author:
Daisies Are Forever, 2014
Snow on the Tulips, 2013

Other books you might like:
Lynn Austin, *Candle in the Darkness*, 2002
Kate Breslin, *For Such a Time*, 2014
Murray Pura, *Whispers of a New Dawn*, 2013
Anna Schmidt, *Safe Haven*, 2014
Sarah Sundin, *A Distant Melody*, 2010

465

JEN TURANO (Pseudonym of Jennifer L. Turano)

After a Fashion

(Grand Rapids, Michigan: Baker Publishing, 2015)

Series: Class of Their Own Series. Book 1
Story type: Romance; Series
Subject(s): Christian life; Romances (Fiction); Social class
Major character(s): Miss Harriet Peabody, Designer (Milliner), Fiance(e) (of Ollie); Ollie Addleshaw, Businessman, Wealthy
Time period(s): 19th century; 1880s
Locale(s): New York, New York

Summary: In the first novel of Jen Turano's Class of Their Own series, the author introduces readers to Miss Harriet Peabody, a hatmaker with an eye for fashion and an entrepreneurial spirit. Harriet works in a millinery shop, but would love to open her own shop to display the hats she crafts by hand. She grew up an orphan and works hard for every penny she earns, so her dream is on hold until she saves up enough money. When one of her orders gets mixed up because of a snooty customer, Harriet loses her job. Luckily, shrewd businessman Ollie Addleshaw takes pity on Harriet and comes up with an unusual arrangement. He asks Harriet to pose as his fiancee to win favor with one of his business associates. Soon they discover that they aren't really pretending to be in love after all, but Harriet isn't sure she can fit in with Ollie's elite group. She wonders how she could ever capture the heart of a man who was born into high society.

Other books by the same author:
A Match of Wits, 2014

A Talent for Trouble, 2013
Ladies of Distinction Series, 2012

Other books you might like:
Susan Page Davis, *Love Finds You in Prince Edward Island, Canada*, 2011
Sean Haldane, *The Devil's Making*, 2015
Mona Hodgson, *Too Rich for a Bride*, 2011
Nancy Moser, *An Unlikely Suitor*, 2011
Carla Stewart, *The Hatmaker's Heart*, 2014
Janice Thompson, *The Dream Dress*, 2014

466

BECKY WADE

A Love Like Ours

(Bloomington, Minnesota: Bethany House Publishers, 2015)

Series: Porter Family Series. Book 3
Story type: Religious; Romance
Subject(s): Adolescent interpersonal relations; Courage; Friendship
Major character(s): Jake Porter, Cowboy/Cowgirl (owns race horses), Military Personnel (former marine), Mentally Ill Person (suffers from PTSD), Friend (childhood friend of Lyndie); Lyndie James, Friend (childhood friend of Jake), Horse Trainer (of Jake's horses), Young Woman (single), Neighbor (of Amber), Sister (of Mollie who suffers from cerebral palsy); Amber, Neighbor (of Lyndie), Young Woman (with dating woes); Mollie James, Sister (of Lyndie), Handicapped (suffers from cerebral palsy)
Time period(s): 21st century; 2010s
Locale(s): Holley, Texas

Summary: In the third novel of the Porter Family series, author Becky Wade introduces Jake Porter, a young Iraq War veteran who returns home to his family's horse farm in Holley, Texas. The tortured cowboy bears the scars of war on his face and struggles with the lingering scars of his PTSD. Jake works on the family farm and hires childhood friend Lyndie James to help exercise and train his thoroughbred racing horses. Hardened by his experiences in Iraq, Jake has closed himself off to love and avoids relationships. Lyndie is determined to heal the wounds of both Jake and his spirited but skittish horse Silver Leaf. Lyndie and Jake work together and discover love through their friendship. But will Jake be able to open his heart and trust again? And will Lyndie be able to give her heart to someone who has closed himself off to love and turned away from God?

Other books by the same author:
Meant to Be Mine, 2014
Undeniably Yours, 2013
My Stubborn Heart, 2012

Other books you might like:
Maggie Brendan, *A Love of Her Own*, 2010
Mindy Starns Clark, *The Amish Blacksmith*, 2014
Leslie Gould, *Minding Molly*, 2014
Denise Hunter, *The Trouble with Cowboys*, 2012
Janelle Mowery, *When All My Dreams Come True*, 2011

467

DAN WALSH
GARY SMALLEY, Co-Author

The Legacy

(Grand Rapids, Michigan: Revell, 2015)

Series: Restoration Series. Book 4
Story type: Contemporary; Family Saga
Subject(s): Family; Father-son relations; College environment
Major character(s): Jim Anderson, Father (of Doug Anderson); Doug Anderson, Student—College, Son (of Jim Anderson), Friend (of Christina); Christina, Friend (of Doug Anderson)
Time period(s): 21st century; 2010s
Locale(s): Florida, United States

Summary: The Restoration series follows the members of the Anderson family as they navigate the sometimes murky waters of faith, friendships, and family ties. This fourth installment focuses on the youngest son, Doug. Jim Anderson is concerned for his son and wants to help him grow closer to God and build a strong filial relationship. Doug, a college student, is well mannered and polite and attends church functions and family dinners without any problem when he is home. However, when he is away at school his life descends into chaotic rebellion. Doug keeps secrets from his family, including his drinking, drug use, partying, and the way he neglects his studies to hang out with a troubled crowd. Christina is a young woman who met the Andersons while she was going through a pregnancy crisis. She notices Doug's behavior and new social circle on social media and is determined to help him find God and himself again.

Other books by the same author:
The Desire, 2014
The Dance, 2013
The Promise, 2013

Other books you might like:
Megan DiMaria, *Searching for Spice*, 2008
Karen Kingsbury, *Rejoice*, 2009
Ginger Kolbaba, *Desperate Pastor's Wives*, 2007
Ane Mulligan, *Chapel Springs Revival*, 2014
Marybeth Whalen, *She Makes It Look Easy: A Novel*, 2011

468

BETH WHITE

The Creole Princess

(Grand Rapids, Michigan: Revell, 2015)

Series: Gulf Coast Chronicles. Book 2
Story type: Historical - American Revolution; Series
Subject(s): Romances (Fiction); American Revolution, 1775-1783; Southern United States
Major character(s): Lyse Lanier, Cousin (of Scarlet), Heroine; Rafael Maria Gonzales de Ripparda,

Merchant, Hero, Spy; Scarlet, Slave, Cousin (of Lyse)
Time period(s): 18th century; 1770s (1776)
Locale(s): Mobile, Alabama; New Orleans, Louisiana

Summary: The second Gulf Coast Chronicles novel continues the saga of the Lanier family. Lyse, a young Frenchwoman, is the daughter of a former gentleman and a former slave. She is no stranger to the complicated world of race and heritage in Mobile, Alabama, but she embraces her own culture to the best of her ability. Her cousin, Scarlet, remains a slave; Lyse is smart enough to recognize her own fortune in being free. It is 1776 and the American Revolution is well underway, with the Gulf Coast serving as an important center of trade and espionage. Her loyalties and perceptions are challenged when she meets Don Rafael Maria Gonzales de Ripparda, a Spanish merchant who has been tasked to secretly deliver a load of gold to General Washington's forces. Rafael is dashing, charming, and handsome, and Lyse can't help but become friends with the spy. As the violence escalates, Lyse and Rafael's love grows deeper. Decisions must be made before the British crown takes her life for treason.

Other books you might like:

Elizabeth Camden, *The Lady of Bolton Hill*, 2011
Melanie Dobson, *The Courier of Caswell Hall*, 2013
Laura Frantz, *The Colonel's Lady*, 2011
Allison Pataki, *The Traitor's Wife*, 2014
Roseanna M. White, *Ring of Secrets*, 2013

469

STEPHANIE GRACE WHITSON

Daughter of the Regiment

(New York: Faithwords, 2015)

Story type: Historical; Romance
Subject(s): Civil war; United States Civil War, 1861-1865; Irish Americans
Major character(s): Maggie Malone, Immigrant, Sister (of Jack and Seamus), Lover (of John); Jack Malone, Brother (of Maggie and Seamus), Military Personnel, Immigrant; Seamus Malone, Immigrant, Brother (of Jack and Maggie), Military Personnel; John Coulter, Lover (of Maggie), Military Personnel (sergeant); Elizabeth "Libbie" Blair, Plantation Owner
Time period(s): 19th century; 1860s (1861)
Locale(s): Missouri, United States

Summary: Maggie Malone's family emigrated from Ireland to the United States not long before the Civil War broke out among the Northern and Southern states. Living in the border state of Missouri, the Malones are surrounded by many who favor the Confederacy. Still, Maggie believes that all of that business should be fought among the Americans, until her brothers, Seamus and Jack, choose to join the Irish Brigade of the Union army. When Maggie hears that one of them has been wounded in battle, she rushes to their encampment, where she meets and falls for the dashing Sergeant John Coulter. Meanwhile, Elizabeth "Libbie" Blair opens her home to the Confederate Army. As she does her part to care for the soldiers she shelters, the battle heads on a collision course toward her town. Soon, the soldiers in Maggie's encampment and those under Libbie's watch will take part in a bloody battle, and both women will learn how strong they can be in the face of tragedy.

Other books by the same author:

A Captain for Laura Rose, 2014
The Quilt Chronicles Series, 2012
A Most Unsuitable Match, 2011
Sixteen Brides, 2010
A Claim of Her Own, 2009

Other books you might like:

Lynn Austin, *Candle in the Darkness*, 2002
Jocelyn Green, *Yankee in Atlanta*, 2014
BJ Hoff, *Sons of an Ancient Glory*, 1993
Jane Kirkpatrick, *A Light in the Wilderness*, 2014
Cindy Thomson, *Grace's Pictures*, 2013

470

LIS WIEHL
APRIL HENRY, Co-Author

Lethal Beauty

(Nashville: Thomas Nelson, 2015)

Series: Mia Quinn Mystery Series. Book 3
Story type: Psychological Suspense; Series
Subject(s): Detective fiction; Suspense; Murder
Major character(s): Mia Quinn, Colleague (of Charlie), Friend (of Charlie), Lawyer; Charlie Carlson, Detective—Homicide, Friend (of Mia), Colleague (of Mia); Dandan Yee, Crime Victim (murdered), Prostitute
Time period(s): 21st century; 2010s
Locale(s): Seattle, Washington

Summary: In the third installment of the Mia Quinn mystery series, prosecutor Mia Quinn is preparing to bring justice for a Chinese prostitute who has been found dead, possibly killed by one of her clients. However, what seemed like an open-and-shut case turns out to be anything but. The wealthy client says the victim attacked him first and he stabbed her in self-defense; the tabloids promptly dub the woman a "lethal beauty." Then a witness who is essential to the case goes missing. With the case unraveling before her, the prostitute's mother decides to take justice into her own hands. Meanwhile, homicide detective Charlie Carlson begins to investigate a series of murders. Working with Mia, the pair begins to find a common thread. As they spend more time together, Mia begins to question whether their relationship is becoming something more than just friendship.

Other books by the same author:

A Deadly Business, 2014
A Matter of Trust, 2014
Snapshot, 2014
East Salem Trilogy, 2011
Triple Threat series, 2010

Other books you might like:

Rick Acker, *Dead Man's Rule*, 2005
James Scott Bell, *No Legal Grounds*, 2007
Ace Collins, *The Color of Justice*, 2014

Inspirational

Randy Singer, *Dying Declaration*, 2004
Lee Strobel, *The Ambition*, 2011

471

KAREN WITEMEYER

A Worthy Pursuit

(Minneapolis, Minnesota: Bethany House, 2015)

Story type: Historical; Romance
Subject(s): Western fiction; Teachers; Romances (Fiction)
Major character(s): Charlotte Atherton, Teacher (headmistress), Guardian (of Lily); Lily, Girl, Ward (of Charlotte); Stone Hammond, Bounty Hunter
Time period(s): 19th century; 1890s (1891)
Locale(s): Texas, United States

Summary: Set in 1891 Texas, this historical romance novel by best-selling author Karen Witemeyer is a Western tale of love, trust, and conviction. When Sullivan's Academy for Exceptional Youths closes suddenly, headmistress Charlotte Atherton is left to care for three of her students, including Lily, whose late mother granted Charlotte custody of Lily—and made her promise to protect Lily from her crooked grandfather. When Lily's grandfather hires bounty hunter Stone Hammond to find his grand-daughter, claiming she was abducted, Stone tracks down Charlotte and Lily. Stone quickly learns the situation isn't what he expected—and that Charlotte is Lily's legal guardian. When new dangers present themselves, Charlotte and Stone work together to protect Lily and the other children in Charlotte's care. The feelings that develop between Charlotte and Stone are strong, but can Charlotte really trust the man who came to tear her life apart?

Other books by the same author:
Full Steam Ahead, 2014
Stealing the Preacher, 2013
Short-Straw Bride, 2012
To Win Her Heart, 2011
A Tailor-Made Bride, 2010

Other books you might like:
Margaret Brownley, *Gunpowder Tea*, 2013

Mary Connealy, *Doctor in Petticoats*, 2010
Kelly Eileen Hake, *Plots and Pans*, 2014
Robin Lee Hatcher, *The Heart's Pursuit*, 2014
Christine Lynxwiler, *Cowgirl at Heart*, 2010

472

LORA YOUNG

Once a Thief

(Portland, Oregon: Rivers Edge Publishing, 2015)

Series: O'Neills of Piper Creek Series. Book 1
Story type: Romance; Series
Subject(s): Theft; Crime; Law
Major character(s): Teagan Copperfield, Woman, Thief, Crime Suspect; Jared O'Neill, Lawyer
Time period(s): 19th century; 1870s (1872)
Locale(s): Denver, United States

Summary: The first installment in the O'Neills of Piper Creek series introduces Teagan Copperfield, a professional thief who has been on her own since her parents died when she was young. When Teagan finally gets caught stealing jewels in Denver City, Jared O'Neill—one of the city's best lawyers—agrees to represent her. Jared will keep her from going to jail, and that's all Teagan needs to know to try to get into his good graces. But Teagan doesn't count on getting to know Jared's good Christian family, and she certainly doesn't expect them to take her in as if she were one of their own. The love she feels from the O'Neills is enough to make Teagan want to stop stealing. When Jared's life is threatened, Teagan knows she must be more ruthless than ever if she is going to protect the man she is falling in love with.

Other books by the same author:
Maicious Mischief, 2014

Other books you might like:
Stephanie Landsem, *The Thief*, 2014
Maureen Lang, *Bees in the Butterfly Garden*, 2012
Allison Pataki, *The Traitor's Wife*, 2014
Roseanna M. White, *Ring of Secrets*, 2013
Kathleen Y'Barbo, *Sadie's Secret*, 2014

The Mystery Genre, May 2015:
Diversity or Fragmentation?
by
Clair Lamb

Sara Paretsky, the new President of the Mystery Writers of America, calls it DOLLUS syndrome: They Don't Look Like Us. In an article for *Booklist* published on May 1, Paretsky says that she has been concerned for some time about the scarcity of non-white writers, and specifically African American writers, in crime fiction. While Paretsky noted the success of Walter Mosley and Attica Locke, she named other African-American authors who now are published by small presses, or not at all: Gar Anthony Haywood, Gary Phillips, Barbara Neely, Valerie Wilson Wesley.

In "Colored and Invisible," an article on the new mystery website The Life Sentence (www.thelifesentence.net), author Rachel Howzell Hall is even blunter: "If you're a writer of color and you attend Bouchercon, Malice Domestic, or any of the writing conferences, you already know that there are more robots on Mars than there are colored folks in the banquet room."

This year's Edgar Awards nominees included only one author of color, Nigerian-American Chris Abani, whose book *The Secret History of Las Vegas* was named Best Paperback Original. A quick look at the nominee lists over the award's history shows the peer-judged "best" to be overwhelmingly white. In sixty years of bestowing the recognition, the Mystery Writers of America have never named an African-American Grand Master.

Why is this? Paretsky blames tokenism: Several years ago, she wrties, an African-American friend of hers submitted a fine crime novel to a publisher, only to be told that while the publisher liked her work, they already published Eleanor Taylor Bland, another female African-American author. Apparently the limit was one to a house.

When it comes to awards, authors of color are trapped in their own vicious circle. "Did we have the Whitest [Insert Book Awards] Ever?" Hall wrote. "Did not one writer of color publish anything worthy of nomination or award this year?

"Well, you say, there weren't enough books written by POC to consider. I say, 'You may be right. *Why* weren't there enough to choose from?'"

Fifteen years ago, crime fiction was diverse enough to justify an academic study, *Diversity and Detective Fiction* by Kathleen Gregory Klein, that looked at mystery novels as tools to *teach* diversity. The articles in Klein's book explore crime fiction's depictions of distinctive subcultures, and discuss how these books illustrate subjective definitions of race, ethnicity, gender and other cultural attributes.

Count up the non-white crime writers being published by major houses today, however, and it's hard to reach double digits. Walter Mosley, arguably the most prominent and successful African-American crime novelist, is published by Riverhead Books, a division of Penguin, but has also published extensively through smaller independent presses. Frankie Y. Bailey's second police procedural, *What the Fly Saw*, was published by Minotaur in March. HarperCollins published Attica Locke's third novel, *Pleasantville*, in April. And Rachel Howzell Hall's series, featuring LA detective Elouise Norton, is published in hardcover by Forge. Naomi Hirahara's novels about a Los Angeles bicycle cop are published by Berkley, but only in paperback.

Authors of color have turned increasingly to self-publishing and to smaller presses, which may lack the distribution networks available to the major publishers. Brash Books, a publishing house founded last year by authors Lee Goldberg and Joel Goldman, is bringing old works by Gar Anthony Haywood and Barbara Neely back into print, but neither author has anything new scheduled for publication.

Coincidentally or not, Paretsky's essay in *Booklist* coincided with a Mystery Writers of America survey that asked its members about mystery subgenres. The group identified twenty-eight individual subgenres, and asked members to respond to questions in an effort to distinguish one subgenre from another. They also asked members to identify other subgenres not on the survey list. Subgenres already identified are:

Amateur detective
Con/caper
Cozy
Espionage/spy
Financial
Forensic/Scientific
Hard-boiled
Historical
Humor
Inverted
Legal
Locked Room
Military
Minority population

Noir
Non-fiction/mystery
Paranormal/Supernatural
PI/detective
Political
Police Procedurals
Psychological
Romantic
Serial killer
Technological
Teen
Thriller
True crime

And the ever-popular category "other." The appearance of "minority population" as an individual subgenre seems likely to spur debate, with its implication that mysteries set on native American reservations have much in common with a mystery set in a Haitian community in Miami.

The proliferation of subgenres raises the question of whom these categories benefit, and whether the categories themselves help or hinder the cause of diversity in crime fiction.

"I grew up a poor black child in Los Angeles, and my favorite writers were Stephen King and Jackie Collins," Hall wrote. "[M]y public librarian and English teachers knew that I'd connect with themes of family, greed, fear, angst, alcoholism, and violence. Because I'm not stupid. Because I'm a reader. Because I'm human.

So … why can't it be the other way?"

The diversity problem is most noticeable when it comes to African Americans in crime fiction, but it's not limited to them. Paretsky notes that U.S. readers have little access to crime fiction in translation (despite the efforts of Soho Press), but most of the crime fiction translated into English comes from Scandinavia. "Foreign, exotic, but —like us," Paretsky writes.

How, then, to address this problem? "We need to go back to … good old-fashioned consciousness raising," Paretsky asserts. Paretsky is considered the "founding mother" of Sisters in Crime, which she co-founded in 1987 with a small group of women mystery authors. She points to tactics that had worked for that group, starting with a focus on book reviews and moving on to libraries—"then and now ... the biggest buyers of new and midlist writers' work." Sisters in Crime monitored book reviews and sent lists of books in print directly to libraries and bookstores. Today, writes Paretsky, "the situation for women writers is better, but it is better for the most part for white, non-Latina writers."

The Mystery Writers of America's presidential term lasts only a year, and Paretsky said that she does not expect to see the situation change dramatically within that time. Her essay, however, has opened a conversation within the crime fiction community that will continue.

Mystery Fiction

473

AVERY AAMES (Pseudonym of Daryl Wood Gerber)

As Gouda as Dead

(New York: Berkley Prime Crime, 2015)

Series: Cheese Shop Mystery Series. Book 6
Story type: Contemporary; Cozy Mystery
Subject(s): Murder; Mystery; Weddings
Major character(s): Charlotte Bessette, Store Owner (cheese shop owner), Detective—Amateur, Employer (of Rebecca), Fiance(e) (of Jordan Pace); Rebecca, Worker (for Charlotte), Detective—Amateur; Jordan Pace, Farmer, Fiance(e) (of Charlotte Bessette)
Time period(s): 21st century; 2010s
Locale(s): Providence, Ohio

Summary: In the sixth Cheese Shop Mystery series novel, a wedding is approaching. Charlotte Bessette, amateur detective and owner of Fromagerie Bessette, is about to marry Jordan Pace. Their hometown of Providence, Ohio, is preparing to celebrate Valentine's Day with a week-long series of events known as the Lover's Trail Festival. The wedding is slated to take place at Jordan's cheese-making farm, but the murder of a friend on the property halts everything. Jordan postpones the ceremony out of respect. He eventually realizes that he isn't sure he wants to continue running the farm, after all. Charlotte is determined to solve the mystery and bring her friend justice. She also is determined to punish the person responsible for ruining her wedding plans. During her investigation she discovers another body, this time a local shop owner. With her assistant, Rebecca, who is dating Deputy Devon O'Shea, Charlotte throws herself headlong into danger and intrigue to find the killer. All around her, local politics and Valentines fever wreak havoc in Providence.

Other books by the same author:
Days of Wine and Roquefort, 2014
To Brie or Not to Brie, 2013
Clobbered by Camembert, 2012
Lost and Fondue, 2011
The Long Quiche Goodbye, 2010

Other books you might like:
Claudia Bishop, *A Taste for Murder*, 1994
Sammi Carter, *Candy Apple Dead*, 2005
Laura Childs, *Death by Darjeeling*, 2001

Laura Childs, *Steeped in Evil*, 2014
Cleo Coyle, *On What Grounds*, 2003
Joanne Fluke, *Double Fudge Brownie Murder*, 2015
Wendy Lyn Watson, *I Scream, You Scream*, 2009
Melinda Wells, *Killer Mousse*, 2008

474

J.L. ABRAMO

Circling the Runway

(Lutz, Florida: Down & Out Books, 2015)

Series: Jake Diamond Mystery Series. Book 4
Story type: Contemporary; Private Detective
Subject(s): Mystery; Detective fiction; Crime
Major character(s): Jacob "Jake" Diamond, Detective—Private, Colleague (of Darlene); Roxton "Rocky" Johnson, Detective—Police; Darlene Roman, Colleague (of Jake); Ray Boyle, Detective—Homicide; Roberto Sandoval, Lawyer (assistant district attorney), Crime Victim; Laura Lopez, Detective—Police
Time period(s): 21st century; 2010s
Locale(s): Cayman Islands; Los Angeles, California; Las Vegas, Nevada

Summary: Jacob "Jake" Diamond is a private detective who doesn't always play well with others. But when Roberto Sandoval—an assistant district attorney—is killed, SFPD sergeant Roxton "Rocky" Johnson knows that he needs Jake's assistance—even if the prickly private eye isn't the easiest person to get along with. Rocky thinks someone on the force may be involved in Sandoval's murder, and he knows that Jake will handle the delicate case with integrity and discretion. The investigation—which also involves police detectives Laura Lopez and Ray Boyle, Jake's colleague Darlene Roman, and an assortment of colorful characters—doesn't always go smoothly. Jake and Rocky step on each other's toes, but they manage to get past their differences as they target Sandoval's murderer. This novel is the fourth in the Jake Diamond Mystery series.

Other books by the same author:
Chasing Charlie Chan, 2013
Counting to Infinity, 2004
Clutching at Straws, 2003
Catching Water in a Net, 2001

Other books you might like:

Mark Coggins, *The Immortal Game*, 1999

Stephen Greenleaf, *Grave Error*, 1979

Jerry Kennealy, *Polo Solo*, 1987

Andrew Klavan, *Dynamite Road*, 2003

John T. Lescroart, *The Hunt Club*, 2005

Tim Maleeny, *Stealing the Dragon*, 2007

Marcia Muller, *Wolf in the Shadows*, 1993

475

ELLERY ADAMS (Pseudonym of Jennifer Stanley and J.B. Stanley)

Lemon Pies and Little White Lies

(New York: Penguin Publishing Group, 2015)

Series: Charmed Pie Shoppe Mystery Series. Book 4

Story type: Paranormal; Series

Subject(s): Mystery; Detective fiction; Crime

Major character(s): Ella Mae LeFaye, Woman (has supernatural powers), Baker, Businesswoman (owner of the Charmed Pie Shoppe), Detective—Amateur; Hugh Dylan, Man (love interest of Ella Mae)

Time period(s): 21st century; 2010s

Locale(s): Havenwood, Georgia

Summary: When Ella Mae LeFaye moved to the quaint town of Havenwood, Georgia, she opened the Charmed Pie Shoppe and began sharing her baking skills with the residents of her new community. Ella Mae also gives her customers a little something extra. Her baked goods are charmed, and they have a magical effect on those who eat them. Ella Mae's skills have come in handy in the past, when crimes needed solving in Havenwood. When another mystery develops in town, Ella Mae plays detective once again. This spree has a supernatural angle; the perpetrator leaves symbols at each crime scene that have special meaning to the paranormally gifted baker-detective. As Ella Mae hunts for a killer, she continues to pursue her romantic interest in Hugh Dylan. This novel is the fourth in the Charmed Pie Shoppe Mystery series.

Other books by the same author:

Peach Pies and Homicides, 2014

Peach Pies and Alibis, 2013

Pies and Prejudice, 2012

A Deadly Cliche, 2011

A Killer Plot, 2010

Other books you might like:

Juliet Blackwell, *Secondhand Spirits*, 2009

Jacklyn Brady, *A Sheetcake Named Desire*, 2011

Sue Ann Jaffarian, *Ghost a la Mode*, 2009

Claire M. Johnson, *Beat Until Stiff*, 2002

Connie Shelton, *Sweet Masterpiece*, 2010

L.J. Washburn, *A Peach of a Murder*, 2006

Michael Lee West, *Gone with a Handsomer Man*, 2011

476

SUSAN WITTIG ALBERT

Bittersweet

(New York: Berkley, 2015)

Series: China Bayles Series. Book 23

Subject(s): Mystery; Animals; Holidays

Major character(s): China Bayles, Herbalist, Daughter; Mackenzie "Mack" Chambers, Friend (of China), Police Officer (game warden); Leatha, Mother (of China), Spouse (of Sam); Sam, Spouse (of Leatha), Stepfather (of China); Sue Ellen Krause, Assistant (of Leatha), Crime Victim

Time period(s): 21st century; 2010s

Locale(s): Pecan Springs, Texas; Utopia, Texas

Summary: It's Thanksgiving, and China Bayles is planning to visit her mother, Leatha, and her mother's husband, Sam, who are turning their ranch into a birders' retreat. She's also looking forward to seeing game warden Mack Chambers. Then Sam has had a heart attack. How will Leatha manage if Sam can't work? She does have a helper, Sue Ellen Krause. But China discovers that Sue Ellen, who is leaving her marriage, is in trouble. Before Sue Ellen can tell China the full story, her car veers off a road and she is killed. When a veterinarian is shot in what appears to be a burglary at his clinic, Mack believes his murder could be related to fawns stolen from a nearby ranch. Also available in Large Print.

Other books by the same author:

Death Come Quickly, 2014

Rosemary Remembers, 1995

Hangman's Root, 1994

Witches Bane, 1993

Thyme of Death, 1992

Other books you might like:

Jeff Abbott, *Do Unto Others*, 1994

Nancy Bell, *Restored to Death*, 2003

Bill Crider, *Murder Is an Art*, 1999

Cindy Daniel, *Death Warmed Over...Coming Soon*, 2003

Nancy Fairbanks, *Crime Brulee*, 2001

Ben Rehder, *Buck Fever*, 2002

Mary Willis Walker, *The Red Scream*, 1994

477

BARBARA ALLAN (Pseudonym of Barbara and Max Allan Collins)

Antiques Swap

(New York: Kensington, 2015)

Series: Trash 'n' Treasures Series. Book 9

Story type: Cozy Mystery; Series

Subject(s): Mystery; Detective fiction; Crime

Major character(s): Brandy Borne, Woman (32 years old), Antiques Dealer, Daughter (of Vivian), Detective—Amateur; Vivian Borne, Mentally Ill Person (bipolar disorder), Woman (73 years old), Antiques Dealer, Mother (of Brandy), Detective—Amateur; Wesley

Sinclair III, Businessman, Wealthy, Spouse (of Vanessa); Vanessa Sinclair, Spouse (of Wesley), Crime Victim
Time period(s): 21st century; 2010s
Locale(s): Serenity, Iowa

Summary: In the ninth novel in the Trash 'n' Treasures Mystery series, mother-and-daughter antiques dealers Vivian and Brandy Borne are embarking on a new venture—hosting a television program called *Antiques Sleuths*. A minor mishap during the taping of the first episode sends Brandy tumbling into the arms of Wesley Sinclair III. Brandy and Wesley have a romantic history, but he is now married to Vanessa—who is not happy when she sees the two apparently hugging. Vanessa causes a scene and makes it clear that she is furious with her husband. So when Vanessa is murdered, Wesley becomes the logical suspect. Once again, Brandy and busy-body Vivian put their sleuthing skills to work. Serenity is full of suspects, however, including a snobby bridge club whose members play games that are much racier than cards. Brandy and Vivian put their investigation into high gear when another victim falls.

Other books by the same author:
Antiques Con, 2014
Antiques Bizarre, 2010
Antiques Flee Market, 2008
Antiques Maul, 2007
Antiques Roadkill, 2006

Other books you might like:
Mary Kay Andrews, *Savannah Blues*, 2002
Jane K. Cleland, *Consigned to Death*, 2006
Sharon Fiffer, *Killer Stuff*, 2001
Elaine Flinn, *Dealing in Murder: A Molly Doyle Mystery*, 2003
Tamar Myers, *Larceny and Old Lace*, 1996
J.B. Stanley, *A Killer Collection*, 2006
Lea Wait, *Shadows at the Fair*, 2002

478

JAMES ANDERSON

The Never-Open Desert Diner

(New York: Caravel Mystery Books, 2015)

Story type: Contemporary
Subject(s): Travel; Employment; Friendship
Major character(s): Ben Jones, Truck Driver, Friend (of Claire, Ginny, and Walt), Narrator; Claire, Musician, Friend (of Ben); Ginny, 17-Year-Old, Pregnant Teenager, Friend (of Ben); Walt Butterfield, Businessman (diner owner), Recluse, Friend (of Ben)
Time period(s): 21st century; 2010s
Locale(s): Utah, United States

Summary: This debut novel is narrated by 38-year-old Ben Jones, a trucker who travels desolate Route 117 in Utah making deliveries to the few and far-between residents and businesses along the highway. Ben is single and broke, trapped in the rut of his everyday routines. He suffers from incredible loneliness and a sense of emptiness. One day as he drives, he spots a naked woman playing cello in an empty and deserted housing

development. He befriends her and they begin a tentative relationship. Claire, the cellist, is an orphan like Ben and is also wandering aimlessly through life. Ben also meets Walt, the elderly owner of a once-famous and popular diner. Ben tries to draw him out, but Walt is trapped in his own memories. He preserves the diner and keeps it in pristine shape, but refuses to open the doors. Ben also meets a pregnant teen named Ginny, the daughter of a former girlfriend. The secrets of those along Route 117 could prevent them from finding their way. First novel.

Other books you might like:
Lou Berney, *Gutshot Straight*, 2010
James Lee Burke, *Cimarron Rose*, 1997
Peter Craig, *Blood Father*, 2005
James Crumley, *The Last Good Kiss*, 1978
James D. Doss, *The Shaman Sings*, 1994
Scott Phillips, *The Walkaway*, 2002
John Straley, *The Woman Who Married a Bear*, 1992

479

DONNA ANDREWS

Lord of the Wings

(New York: Minotaur Books, 2015)

Series: Meg Langslow Series. Book 19
Story type: Cozy Mystery; Holiday Themes
Subject(s): Mystery; Detective fiction; Crime
Major character(s): Meg Langslow, Blacksmith, Detective—Amateur; Randall Shiffley, Government Official (mayor of Caerphilly)
Time period(s): 21st century; 2010s
Locale(s): Caerphilly, Virginia

Summary: In the 19th novel in the Meg Langslow Mystery series, the quaint town of Caerphilly, Virginia, is preparing for Halloween. Mayor Randall Shiffley has big plans for the creepiest holiday of the year, and the rest of the town has gotten in on the act. The residents are trimming their houses with spooky decorations and donning scary costumes for the benefit of the visitors expected to flock to Caerphilly. But when fun pranks give way to real crimes, local blacksmith Meg Langslow plays detective again. First, a corpse turns up at the zoo, and then the haunted house suffers a fire that could be arson. Meg must find and stop the perpetrator before Caerphilly's Halloween celebration becomes a real-life horror show.

Other books by the same author:
The Good, the Bad and the Emus, 2014
Crouching Buzzard, Leaping Loon, 2003
Revenge of the Wrought-Iron Flamingos, 2001
Murder with Puffins, 2000
Murder with Peacocks, 1999

Other books you might like:
Miranda Bliss, *Cooking Up Murder*, 2006
Jacklyn Brady, *Murder Takes the Cake*, 2008
Rita Mae Brown, *Wish You Were Here*, 1990
Alyse Carlson, *The Azalea Assault*, 2012
Krista Davis, *The Diva Runs out of Thyme*, 2008
Willard Scott, *Murder under Blue Skies*, 1998
J.B. Stanley, *A Killer Collection*, 2006

480

CONNIE ARCHER

Ladle to the Grave

(New York: Berkley, 2015)

Series: Soup Lover's Mystery Series. Book 4
Story type: Contemporary; Cozy Mystery
Subject(s): Weddings; Murder; Grandfathers
Major character(s): Lucky Jamieson, Store Owner (soup shop owner), Granddaughter (of Jack), Detective—Amateur, Friend (of Sophie), Employer (of Sage); Jack, Crime Suspect, Grandfather (of Lucky); Sophie, Fiance(e) (of Sage), Friend (of Lucky); Sage DuBois, Cook (for Lucky's shop), Fiance(e) (of Sophie)
Time period(s): 21st century; 2010s
Locale(s): Snowflake, Vermont

Summary: The fourth Soup Lover's Mystery series novel continues the amateur detecting of soup shop owner Lucky Jamieson. Lucky's shop in the small town of Snowflake, Vermont, is a hub of all the latest news and gossip. As spring draws near, the town has a new celebration planned to welcome the change of seasons. A pagan-type festival is getting off to a fun start until one of the women involved in the rituals drops dead. The cause of death is traced to an herbal concoction cooked up for the celebration by Lucky's grandfather, Jack, making him the prime suspect in the murder. Aghast and certain that there has been a mistake, Lucky quickly moves to investigate and help Jack. Meanwhile, her chef, Sage, is planning his wedding to Lucky's close friend Sophie. As the wedding spirals out of control, Sophie finds another body in the woods, and Snowflake erupts into chaos. This leaves Lucky trying to solve two murders while still running her business and trying to help Sophie plan the wedding.

Other books by the same author:
A Roux of Revenge, 2014
A Broth of Betrayal, 2013
A Spoonful of Murder, 2012

Other books you might like:
Ellery Adams, *A Killer Plot*, 2010
Sandra Balzo, *Uncommon Grounds*, 2004
Jessica Beck, *A Chili Death*, 2012
Claudia Bishop, *A Taste for Murder*, 1994
JoAnna Carl, *The Chocolate Cat Caper*, 2002
Laura Childs, *Death by Darjeeling*, 2001
Laura Childs, *Eggs in Purgatory*, 2008

481

GRETCHEN ARCHER

Double Mint

(Plano, Texas: Henery Press, 2015)

Series: Davis Way Crime Caper Series. Book 4
Story type: Cozy Mystery; Series
Subject(s): Mystery; Detective fiction; Crime
Major character(s): Davis Way Cole, Woman, Security Officer, Detective, Spouse (of Bradley); Holder Darby, Planner (special events coordinator); Richard Sanders, Employer (of Davis), Spouse (of Bianca); Bianca Sanders, Spouse (of Richard); Bradley Cole, Spouse (of Davis)
Time period(s): 21st century; 2010s
Locale(s): Biloxi, Mississippi

Summary: Davis Way Cole, recently married to Bradley Cole, is a member of the security team at the Belissimo Casino in Biloxi, Mississippi. The popular resort is always busy, so the staff frequently encounters a mystery that needs to be solved. In this fourth novel in the Davis Way Crime Caper series, the casino is preparing for an influx of 500 conventioneers when its special events coordinator—Holder Darby—quits. And Darby isn't the only absence at the resort. A Belissimo guest disappears, leaving a stash of cash in his hotel room, and someone breaks into the casino's vault and makes its contents vanish. While Davis tries to find out how the unsettling events are connected, she also deals with other matters that involve her employer's spouse and her ex-husband's car.

Other books by the same author:
Double Dip, 2014
Double Strike, 2014
Double Whammy, 2013

Other books you might like:
Deborah Coonts, *Wanna Get Lucky?*, 2010
Krista Davis, *The Diva Runs out of Thyme*, 2008
Laura DiSilverio, *Die Buying*, 2011
Janet Evanovich, *One for the Money*, 1994
Jerrilyn Farmer, *Sympathy for the Devil*, 1998
Dorothy Gilman, *The Unexpected Mrs. Pollifax*, 1966
Penny Warner, *How to Host a Killer Party*, 2010

482

PIETER ASPE
BRIAN DOYLE, Translator

From Bruges with Love

(New York: Open Road Media, 2015)

Series: Inspector Van In Mysteries Series. Book 3
Story type: Police Procedural; Serial Killer
Subject(s): Mystery; Detective fiction; Crime
Major character(s): Pieter Van In, Detective—Police (inspector), Spouse (of Hannelore Martens); Hannelore Martens, Lawyer (deputy prosecutor), Spouse (pregnant, of Pieter Van In); Hugo Vermast, Spouse (of Leen Vermast), Father (of Tine Vermast); Leen Vermast, Spouse (of Hugo Vermast), Mother (of Tine Vermast); Tine Vermast, Girl, Daughter (of Hugo and Leen Vermast); Benedict Vervoort, Real Estate Agent; Lodewijk Vandaele, Man, Wealthy, Criminal (pedophile)
Time period(s): 21st century; 2010s
Locale(s): Bruges, Belgium

Summary: Bruges police inspector Pieter Van In wants to go on holiday with his wife, deputy prosecutor Hannelore Martens, before she gives birth to their first child. So when he is called to investigate the discovery of a decades-old skeleton at a farm owned by the Vermast family, Van In hopes he can wrap the case up in short order. He quickly clears the Vermasts, who have only owned the property a short time, and focuses on the farm's previous owner, Lodewijk Vandaele, a child molester. As the case grows more complex, Van In digs deeper into the farm's history. He learns that the property was once the site of a brothel that attracted high-profile visitors, including public officials and members of the law enforcement community. More victims die as Van In tries to determine which suspect is guilty of a 30-year-old murder. This novel is the third in the Pieter Van In Mysteries series, previously published in Belgium, to be translated into English.

Other books by the same author:
The Midas Murders, 2013
The Square of Revenge, 2013

Other books you might like:
Michael Dibdin, *Ratking*, 1989
Nicholas Freeling, *A Dressing of Diamonds*, 1974
Nicholas Freeling, *A Dwarf Kingdom*, 1996
Donna Leon, *Death at La Fenice*, 1992
Barbara Nadel, *Belshazzar's Daughter*, 2004
Louise Penny, *Still Life*, 2006
Martin Walker, *Bruno, Chief of Police*, 2009

483

FRANKIE Y. BAILEY

What the Fly Saw

(New York: Minotaur Books, 2015)

Series: Detective Hannah McCabe Series. Book 2
Story type: Futuristic; Series
Subject(s): Detective fiction; Interpersonal relations; Murder
Major character(s): Hannah McCabe, Detective—Police (partner of Mike Baxter); Mike Baxter, Detective—Police (partner of Hannah McCabe); Kevin Novak, Crime Victim, Client (of Olive Cooper); Olive Cooper, Psychic (medium)
Time period(s): 21st century; 2020s (2020)
Locale(s): Albany, New York

Summary: This is the second Detective Hannah McCabe mystery novel. Hannah and her partner, Mike Baxter, are detectives in Albany, New York in the year 2020. They are working the murder case of a local funeral director who was killed with an arrow. Hannah and Mike are stymied in their investigation of the victim. He was well-liked, successful in business, had a beautiful family, and was active in a local megachurch. The only upheaval in his life was the unexpected death of a close friend recently due to a heart attack. The loss of his friend pushed the funeral director into a deep depression. He had confided in his minister and a psychiatrist while pushing away his wife and children. Hannah's' gut tells her that the deaths are connected somehow and that the victim's church and doctor may be keeping secrets from the detectives. When the various players in their case start to be targeted by the still-unknown killer, Hannah and Mike must place their own lives on the line to stop another murder.

Other books by the same author:
The Red Queen Dies, 2013
You Should Have Died on Monday, 2007
Old Murders, 2003
A Dead Man's Honor, 2001
Death's Favorite Child, 2000

Other books you might like:
Lynn Abercrombie, *The Body Box*, 2005
Jodi Compton, *The 37th Hour*, 2003
J. T. Ellison, *Judas Kiss*, 2009
Rachel Howzell Hall, *Land of Shadows*, 2014
J.D. Robb, *Festive in Death*, 2014
J.D. Robb, *Naked in Death*, 1995
Jess Walter, *Over Tumbled Graves*, 2001

484

SHANNON BAKER

Tattered Legacy

(Woodbury, Minnesota: Midnight Ink, 2015)

Series: Nora Abbott Mystery Series. Book 3
Story type: Amateur Detective; Cozy Mystery
Subject(s): Mystery; Romances (Fiction); Murder
Major character(s): Nora Abbott, Girlfriend (of Cole), Friend (of Lisa), Daughter (of Abigail), Detective—Amateur, Accountant; Abigail Abbott, Mother (of Nora), Detective—Amateur; Lisa, Filmmaker, Lesbian, Crime Victim, Friend (of Nora); Cole Huntsman, Boyfriend (of Nora)
Time period(s): 21st century; 2010s
Locale(s): Moab, Utah

Summary: Nora Abbott may only be an accountant, but she is willing to risk her job and her career to find a way to protect Canyonlands National Park. She convinced her friend Lisa to make a moving documentary film about the park's beauty and resources, hoping that it would help sway people and Congress to vote for an expansion of park lands. The idea is not popular with locals, particularly the ranchers, who are mostly Mormons. While Nora is on vacation with her boyfriend, Cole, she learns that Lisa has been murdered. Lisa's lover, a shunned Mormon, blames Nora for placing the filmmaker in danger. The third Nora Abbott mystery sends Nora and her mother, Abigail, into overdrive as they work to discover who is responsible for the death of Nora's beloved friend. As they search for a killer, it becomes evident that Nora is in danger of losing her life in Canyonlands National Park.

Other books by the same author:
Broken Trust, 2014
Tainted Mountain, 2013
Ashes of the Red Heifer, 2010

Other books you might like:
Sandi Ault, *Wild Indigo*, 2007
Nevada Barr, *Track of the Cat*, 1993
Margaret Coel, *The Eagle Catcher*, 1995
Beth Groundwater, *Deadly Currents*, 2011
Kirk Mitchell, *High Desert Malice*, 1995

Michael Norman, *The Commission*, 2007
Michael Norman, *On Deadly Ground*, 2012

485

DAVID BALDACCI

Memory Man

(New York: Grand Central Publishing, 2015)

Subject(s): Suspense; Murder; Crime
Major character(s): Amos Decker, Detective—Private, Detective—Police (former), Football Player (former), Widow(er)
Time period(s): 21st century; 2010s
Locale(s): Burlington, Vermont

Summary: Ever since he was hit in the head during a high school football game, Amos Decker hasn't been able to forget anything. His perfect memory served him well when he worked as a police detective, but now his memories haunt him. More than a year ago, Amos came home from work to find his wife, daughter, and brother-in-law dead. Although Amos retains every detail of the events of that night, he hasn't been able to find the killer. The incident has all but destroyed him. No longer with the police force, Amos works sporadically as a private detective. But his life is about to take another turn. Someone has come forward to claim responsibility for the triple murder. The unexpected confession coincides with a tragedy that rattles Burlington to its core. When the police call Amos in to help with the case, he resolves to finally solve the mystery of his family's murders.

Other books by the same author:
Zero Day, 2011
The Whole Truth, 2008
The Camel Club, 2005
Split Second, 2003
Absolute Power, 1996

Other books you might like:
R. Scott Bakker, *Disciple of the Dog*, 2010
John Buchan, *The Thirty-Nine Steps*, 1915
Lee Child, *Killing Floor*, 1997
Nelson DeMille, *Plum Island*, 1997
Alison Gaylin, *And She Was*, 2012
William Goldman, *Marathon Man*, 1974
James Grippando, *Cane and Abe*, 2015
James Patterson, *Private Vegas*, 2015
J.D. Robb, *Obsession in Death*, 2015
Stuart Woods, *Hot Pursuit*, 2015
Stuart Woods, *Paris Match*, 2014

486

JEAN-LUC BANNALEC
SORCHA MCDONAGH, Translator

Death in Brittany

(New York: Minotaur Books, 2015)

Series: Commissaire Dupin Series. Book 1
Story type: Police Procedural; Series
Subject(s): Mystery; Detective fiction; Crime
Major character(s): Georges Dupin, Detective—Police (commissaire); Pierre-Louis Pennec, Hotel Owner (Central Hotel), Aged Person (91 years old), Crime Victim
Time period(s): 21st century; 2010s
Locale(s): Pont-Aven, France

Summary: When police commissaire Georges Dupin moves from Paris to the coastal village of Pont-Aven, he anticipates a lighter caseload. But while he is having breakfast one morning in the beautiful setting, he is called to the scene of a murder. The victim is Pierre-Louis Pennec, the elderly proprietor of the landmark Central Hotel. The storied hotel once welcomed the artist Paul Gauguin as a guest, and it is still a popular tourist destination. Although Pont-Aven seems a friendly, peaceful community, Dupin quickly compiles a list of suspects that includes public figures and one of Pennec's friends. Dupin investigates further and discovers secrets about the victim, the suspects, and Pont-Aven itself. As he searches for a solution to the mystery, the irritable detective still manages to enjoy the village's stunning sights and fine cuisine. This novel is the first in the Commissaire Dupin series, which was originally published Germany.

Other books by the same author:
Death in Pont-Aven, 2014

Other books you might like:
Norman Bogner, *To Die in Provence*, 1998
Andrea Camilleri, *The Shape of Water*, 2002
Donna Leon, *Death at La Fenice*, 1992
Pierre Magnan, *Death in the Truffle Wood*, 2005
Barbara Nadel, *Belshazzar's Daughter*, 2004
Georges Simenon, *The Crime of Inspector Maigret*, 1932
Martin Walker, *Bruno, Chief of Police*, 2009

487

MAGGIE BARBIERI

Lies That Bind

(New York: Minotaur Books, 2015)

Series: Maeve Conlon Series. Book 2
Story type: Amateur Detective; Series
Subject(s): Detective fiction; Missing persons; Sisters
Major character(s): Maeve Conlon, Detective—Amateur, Baker, Store Owner, Single Mother, Sister (of Evelyn); Evelyn Conlon, Sister (of Maeve), Mentally Challenged Person, Missing Person
Time period(s): 21st century; 2010s
Locale(s): Farringville, New York

Summary: The second Maeve Conlon novel continues the narrative of Maeve, a single mother who owns a bakery in suburbia. After the events of *Once Upon a Lie*, her family, home, and business have all been under watch by the local police, who are suspicious that there is more to Maeve than meets the eye. When her beloved father dies of an unexpected heart attack, Maeve's world turns upside down. Since her mother died many years ago, she has always relied on her father. She discovers an amazing secret after her father's funeral: she may have a sister. Maeve is determined to learn more about the unexpected sibling and understand why her father hid the information from her. Her sister, Evelyn was born with developmental difficulties and was institutionalized at a young age. The asylum has long since closed, leaving Maeve with few avenues of investigation. A sudden rash of vandalism and theft at her bakery further confounds Maeve as she seeks answers.

Other books by the same author:
Once Upon a Lie, 2013
Final Exam, 2009
Quick Study, 2008
Maeve Conlon #1, 2006
Extracurricular Activities, 2001

Other books you might like:
Linwood Barclay, *No Time for Goodbye*, 2007
Diane Chamberlain, *The Silent Sister*, 2014
Mary Higgins Clark, *A Stranger Is Watching*, 1977
Harlan Coben, *Just One Look*, 2004
Dianne Emley, *The First Cut: A Novel*, 2006
Lisa Gardner, *The Other Daughter*, 1999
Alison Gaylin, *Hide Your Eyes*, 2005
Hank Phillippi Ryan, *The Other Woman*, 2012

488

LORNA BARRETT (Pseudonym of L.L. Bartlett)

A Fatal Chapter

(New York: Berkley, 2015)

Series: Booktown Mystery Series. Book 9
Story type: Amateur Detective; Cozy Mystery
Subject(s): Mystery; Detective fiction; Crime
Major character(s): Tricia Miles, Store Owner (By Hook or By Book), Sister (of Angelica), Detective—Amateur, Friend (of Pete Renquist); Angelica, Sister (of Tricia); Pete Renquist, Leader (president, Stoneham Historical Society), Crime Victim, Friend (of Tricia Miles); Grant Baker, Detective—Police (chief)
Time period(s): 21st century; 2010s
Locale(s): Stoneham, New Hampshire

Summary: Bookseller Tricia Miles investigates the murder of a friend in the ninth novel in the Booktown Mystery series. Tricia—owner of the Stoneham, New Hampshire, bookstore By Hook or By Book—is walking her sister's dog when she finds her friend Pete Renquist suffering a heart attack in the town square. Pete, who is the president of the Stoneham Historical Society, whispers a cryptic sentence to Tricia, and then dies soon afterward at the hospital. Grant Baker, the chief of police, determines the cause of death to be homicide when he learns that Pete suffered a strange puncture wound. Armed with the clue provided by Pete before his death, Tricia launches her own investigation. When another victim, who was also a member of the historical society, is killed, Tricia ignores Baker's advice and puts herself in danger to find the murderer.

Other books by the same author:
Book Clubbed, 2014
Chapter and Hearse, 2010

Bookmarked for Death, 2009
Bookplate Special, 2009
Murder Is Binding, 2008

Other books you might like:
Kate Carlisle, *Homicide in Hardcover*, 2009
Cindy Daniel, *Death Warmed Over...Coming Soon*, 2003
Carolyn G. Hart, *Death on Demand*, 1987
Joan Hess, *Strangled Prose*, 1986
Miranda James, *Murder Past Due*, 2010
Allison Kingsley, *Mind Over Murder*, 2011
Lea Wait, *Shadows at the Fair*, 2002

489

LOU BERNEY

The Long and Faraway Gone

(New York: William Morrow, 2015)

Story type: Contemporary; Private Detective
Subject(s): Detective fiction; Mystery; Murder
Major character(s): Wyatt, Lover (of Julianna), Detective—Private, Survivor (of armed robbery); Julianna, Sister (of missing person), Lover (of Wyatt)
Time period(s): 21st century; 2010s
Locale(s): Oklahoma City, Oklahoma

Summary: Oklahoma City experienced two tragedies in the summer of 1986: an armed robbery led to the death of six movie theater employees, and a teenage girl disappeared without a trace at the annual state fair. Twenty-five years later, both cases are still open and the aftershocks of the two events continue to affect the survivors and their friends and families. Wyatt has struggled with guilt and depression since his friends were killed during the robbery. Now living in Las Vegas and working as a private detective, he finally has a lead on the robbery that changed his life two decades ago. Julianna has spent her life looking for answers about her older sister's disappearance. When a suspect comes back to town, she is determined to find the truth. Wyatt and Julianna's cases collide, and the two decide to work together, leading to a tentative romance. Despite their efforts, even solving the cases may not provide true healing.

Other books by the same author:
Whiplash River, 2012
Gutshot Straight, 2009

Other books you might like:
Kate Atkinson, *Case Histories*, 2004
James Crumley, *The Last Good Kiss*, 1978
Dennis Lehane, *Mystic River*, 2001
Laura Lippman, *What the Dead Know*, 2007
Scott Phillips, *The Walkaway*, 2002
Lori Roy, *Bent Road*, 2011
Willy Vlautin, *Northline: A Novel*, 2008

Mystery

490

STEVE BERRY

The Patriot Threat

(New York: Minotaur Books, 2015)

Series: Cotton Malone Series. Book 10
Story type: Chase; Espionage
Subject(s): Suspense; Mystery; Espionage
Major character(s): Cotton Malone, Agent (former, of Magellan Billet), Retiree, Businessman (bookseller)
Time period(s): 21st century; 2010s
Locale(s): Croatia; Denmark; Venice, Italy

Summary: Cotton Malone, a retired agent of the Magellan Billet, has been summoned from his bookshop in Denmark to chase down a North Korean operative who has potentially acquired documents that could destroy the United States. Having traced the information back to events of 1913, Cotton is briefed on a trail of secrets and deception that began in the 1930s. A new book has revealed that the 16th amendment, which allows the United States to collect taxes, was not properly ratified. Secrets surrounding the amendment could ruin the nation. North Korea's dictator wants the information to bring his enemy to its knees. Malone chases the foreign operative to Italy and Croatia, tracking the spy and rushing to solve the mystery before US enemies can use the information.

Other books by the same author:
The Lincoln Myth, 2014
The Charlemagne Pursuit, 2008
The Alexandria Link, 2007
The Venetian Betrayal, 2007
The Templar Legacy, 2006

Other books you might like:
David Baldacci, *Absolute Power*, 1996
Ben Coes, *Power Down*, 2011
Jack Higgins, *Rain on the Dead*, 2014
Mike Lawson, *The Inside Ring*, 2005
Brad Meltzer, *The Inner Circle*, 2010
Matthew Palmer, *The American Mission*, 2014
Brad Taylor, *No Fortunate Son*, 2014
Brad Thor, *The Lions of Lucerne*, February 27, 2007

491

MARK BILLINGHAM

Time of Death

(New York: Atlantic Monthly Press, 2015)

Series: Tom Thorne Series. Book 13
Story type: Police Procedural; Series
Subject(s): Mystery; Detective fiction; Crime
Major character(s): Tom Thorne, Detective—Police (detective inspector), Boyfriend (of Helen Weeks); Helen Weeks, Detective—Police (detective sergeant), Girlfriend (of Tom Thorne), Classmate (former, of Linda Bates); Linda Bates, Classmate (former, of Helen Weeks), Spouse (of Stephen Bates); Stephen Bates, Crime Suspect, Spouse (of Linda Bates); Jes-

sica Toms, 15-Year-Old, Missing Person, Crime Victim; Poppy Johnston, 15-Year-Old, Missing Person, Crime Victim
Time period(s): 21st century; 2010s
Locale(s): Polesford, Warwickshire

Summary: A kidnapping investigation interrupts DI Tom Thorne's vacation in the 13th novel in the series. Tom and his girlfriend, detective sergeant Helen Weeks, are supposed to travel to the Cotswolds, but they are diverted to Helen's hometown of Polesford when two teenage girls are kidnapped there. The prime suspect is Stephen Bates, who is the husband of Helen's former classmate Linda. When Tom and Helen arrive in Polesford, they find that the evidence against Stephen is overwhelming. But although DNA connects Jessica Toms, one of the victims, to Stephen's car, Tom and Helen believe his claims of innocence. Public opinion is against Stephen, however, and the residents of Polesford resent Helen and Tom's meddling. When the kidnapping case becomes a murder investigation, Tom gets outside help to identify the real killer and find out how someone's manipulating the evidence.

Other books by the same author:
The Bones Beneath, 2014
The Burning Girl, 2004
Lazybones, 2003
Scaredy Cat, 2002
Sleepyhead, 2001

Other books you might like:
Michael Connelly, *The Burning Room*, 2014
Deborah Crombie, *A Share in Death*, 1993
John Harvey, *Flesh and Blood*, 2004
Val McDermid, *The Mermaids Singing*, 1995
Denise Mina, *Garnethill*, 1998
Ian Rankin, *Strip Jack*, 1992
Ruth Rendell, *Sins of the Fathers*, 1976
Peter Robinson, *Gallows View*, 1987

492

CARA BLACK

Murder on the Champ de Mars

(New York: Soho Press, 2015)

Series: Aimee Leduc Series. Book 15
Story type: Private Detective; Series
Subject(s): Murder; Mystery; Detective fiction
Major character(s): Aimee Leduc, Detective—Private, Single Mother
Time period(s): 20th century; 1990s (1999)
Locale(s): Paris, France

Summary: The baptism of Aimee Ludec's six-month-old daughter was supposed to be blissfully celebratory. The arrival of the baby's father and his new wife brought unwanted complicates. The couple is challenging Aimee for custody. Additionally, a distraught Gypsy boy arrives and insists that Aimee accompany him to a nearby hospital where his mother, a longtime informant for Aimee's father, is gravely ill. The woman allegedly has important information related to the murder of Aimee's father ten years ago and will only relay it to Aimee now that she is on her deathbed. When Aimee acquiesces and arrives at the hospital, she is stunned to discover that the woman has been kidnapped. As Aimee struggles to maintain a balance between motherhood, the custody dispute, and rescuing the Gypsy woman, she races all over Paris looking for leads and information. She is closer than ever to solving the mystery of her father's murder, but Aimee's own life is soon in jeopardy. This is the 15th Aimee Leduc novel.

Other books by the same author:
Murder in Pigalle, 2014
Murder in the Bastille, 2003
Murder in the Sentier, 2002
Murder in Belleville, 2000
Murder in the Marais, 1999

Other books you might like:
Marvin Albert, *Stone Angel*, 1986
Linda Barnes, *A Trouble of Fools*, 1987
Pierre Lemaitre, *Alex*, 2013
Jean-Patrick Manchette, *Three to Kill*, 2002
Dominique Manotti, *Dead Horsemeat*, 2006
Tom Mitcheltree, *Blink of an Eye*, 2004
Fred Vargas, *The Chalk Circle Man*, 2009

493

SARA BLAEDEL

The Forgotten Girls

(New York: Grand Central Publishing, 2015)

Series: Louise Rick Series. Book 4
Story type: Police Procedural; Series
Subject(s): Suspense; Mystery; Murder
Major character(s): Louise Rick, Detective—Police, Friend (of Camilla); Camilla Lind, Journalist, Friend (of Louise Rick); Lisemette, Crime Victim, Twin, Abandoned Child
Time period(s): 21st century; 2010s
Locale(s): Copenhagen, Denmark

Summary: Police detective Louise Rick has recently been promoted to the commander of the Missing Persons Department. Her first major case involves a corpse discovered in a local forest. Despite a unique scar located on the woman's face, investigators can find no missing-persons reports matching her description. Louise decides to release a photograph of the woman's face to the media and is shocked to receive a call from a former state employee identifying the dead woman as Lisemette. Relinquished by their parents, Lisemette and her twin sister lived at the state asylum, where they became so-called forgotten girls. As Louise investigates, she is puzzled to discover that both Lisemette and her twin were issued death certificates by the institution more than 30 years earlier. Louise recruits her best friend, Camilla Lind, a journalist, to help discover what happened to Lisemette and her sister in the asylum, as well as the other forgotten girls. However, the secrets surrounding the hospital are buried deeply, and Louise finds her own life in danger. This is the fourth Louise Rick thriller mystery novel.

Other books by the same author:
Call Me Princess, 2012
Farewell to Freedom, 2012
Only One Life, 2012

Other books you might like:
Jussi Adler-Olsen, *The Keeper of Lost Causes*, 2011
Jussi Adler-Olsen, *The Purity of Vengeance*, 2013
Kjell Eriksson, *Black Lies, Red Blood*, 2014
Borge Hellstrom, *Cell 8*, 2011
Anne Holt, *Blind Goddess*, 2012
Lene Kaaberbol, *The Boy in the Suitcase*, 2011
Lars Kepler, *The Hypnotist*, 2011
Camilla Lackberg, *The Ice Princess*, 2010
Asa Larsson, *Until Thy Wrath Be Past*, 2011
Liza Marklund, *Red Wolf*, 2011
Jo Nesbo, *The Redbreast*, 2007
Jo Nesbo, *The Son*, 2014
Ron Rash, *The Cove*, 2012
Helene Tursten, *Detective Inspector Huss*, 2003
Erik Valeur, *The Seventh Child*, 2014

494

HEATHER BLAKE (Pseudonym of Heather Webber)

Some Like It Witchy

(New York: Penguin Publishing Group, 2015)

Series: Wishcraft Mystery Series. Book 5
Story type: Amateur Detective; Paranormal
Subject(s): Mystery; Detective fiction; Crime
Major character(s): Darcy Merriweather, Detective—Amateur, Witch, Friend (of Cherise); Cherise Goodwin, Witch, Friend (of Darcy); Raina Gallagher, Real Estate Agent, Crime Victim
Time period(s): 21st century; 2010s
Locale(s): Salem, Massachusetts

Summary: Darcy Merriweather, a witch who lives in the Enchanted Village neighborhood of Salem, Massachusetts, senses that something wicked is coming to town. She carries the feeling of unease with her when she accompanies her friend, Cherise Goodwin, to visit the house she has put a bid on. The Tavistock house has a long history that includes an unsavory legend. When Darcy and Cherise arrive, they find the cold corpse of Raina Gallagher, the real estate agent, inside. Raina is holding a gemstone, and the wall near her body bears a red letter "A." Darcy must use her sleuthing skills and her magical talents to find Raina's killer before anyone else dies. Was Raina killed by one of her many rivals, or is she the latest victim of the Tavistock house's legend? This novel is the fifth in the Wishcraft Mystery series.

Other books by the same author:
The Goodbye Witch, 2014
The Good, the Bad and the Witchy, 2013
A Potion to Die For, 2013
It Takes a Witch, 2012
A Witch Before Dying, 2012

Other books you might like:
Madelyn Alt, *The Trouble with Magic*, 2006
Juliet Blackwell, *Secondhand Spirits*, 2009

Mystery

Bailey Cates, *Brownies and Broomsticks: A Magical Bakery Mystery*, 2012
Shirley Damsgaard, *Witch Way to Murder*, 2005
Yasmine Galenorn, *Ghost of a Chance*, 2003
Charlaine Harris, *Dead Until Dark*, 2001
Sofie Kelly, *Curiosity Thrilled the Cat*, 2011

495

ROBIN BLAKE

The Hidden Man

(New York: Minotaur Books, 2015)

Series: Cragg and Fidelis Mysteries Series. Book 3
Story type: Historical - Georgian; Series
Subject(s): Mystery; Detective fiction; Crime
Major character(s): Titus Cragg, Investigator (coroner), Friend (of Luke Fidelis); Dr. Luke Fidelis, Doctor, Friend (of Titus Cragg), Spouse (of Elizabeth); Elizabeth, Spouse (of Luke); Preston Guild, Banker, Crime Victim; Ephraim Grimshaw, Government Official (mayor)
Time period(s): 18th century; 1740s (1742)
Locale(s): Preston, England

Summary: The mysterious death of a goldsmith is the central mystery in the third novel in the Cragg and Fidelis series. In 1742, the town of Preston, England, is getting ready for the Preston Guild festival, which is held every 20 years. But the preparations are interrupted by a grim discovery. Philip Pimbo, a goldsmith who had been planning to start a private bank, is found dead of a gunshot in his locked office. When Titus Cragg, the coroner, arrives on the scene, he presumes Pimbo kills himself. But Cragg's friend and colleague, Dr. Luke Fidelis, believes the death could have been accidental—or a homicide. As Cragg and Fidelis investigate Pimbo's death, they find financial dealings that unsettle Ephraim Grimshaw, Preston's mayor. Apparently Pimbo had tied up the Preston Corporation's funds in a slavery scheme. When another man is murdered, Cragg and Fidelis realize they must act quickly to solve the confounding case.

Other books by the same author:
Dark Waters, 2013
A Dark Anatomy, 2012
Trial and Retribution, 1997
The Gwallo, 1992
Fat Man's Shadow, 1990

Other books you might like:
Bruce Alexander, *Blind Justice*, 1994
Bruce Alexander, *Rules of Engagement*, 2005
Faye L. Booth, *Trades of the Flesh*, 2011
Peter Clement, *Mortal Remains*, 2003
C.S. Harris, *Where Shadows Dance*, 2011
Susanna Kearsley, *The Rose Garden*, 2011
Deryn Lake, *Death in the Dark Walk*, 1994
Fidelis Morgan, *Unnatural Fires*, 2000
Chris Nickson, *The Broken Token*, 2010
Oliver Potzsch, *The Dark Monk: A Hangman's Daughter Tale*, 2012
Andrew Taylor, *The Anatomy of Ghosts*, 2011

496

SANDRA BLOCK

Little Black Lies

(New York: Grand Central Publishing, 2015)

Story type: Contemporary; Gothic
Subject(s): Psychiatry; Memory; Adoption
Major character(s): Dr. Zoe Goldman, Therapist (to Sofia), Adoptee, Survivor (of a fire), Doctor (resident); Sofia Vallano, Patient (of Zoe), Murderer
Time period(s): 21st century; 2010s
Locale(s): Buffalo, New York

Summary: Dr. Zoe Goldman is a resident training in a hospital psychiatric ward in Buffalo. She relishes working with the patients despite her own psychological problems, which stem from horrible memories of a childhood fire and a struggle with ADHD. Her birth mother perished in the fire. Zoe was adopted by her mother's best friend and was raised in a loving home. Zoe is now forced to confront the reality that her adoptive mother is suffering from dementia, and she realizes that any chances she might have to learn about her past are rapidly diminishing. Zoe sees a therapist regularly to sort through her recurring nightmares about the trauma. The spark that reignited her questions and dreams is a patient named Sofia Vallano. Sofia has been institutionalized for more than 20 years for murdering her own mother. Zoe has been tasked with getting Sofia to open up and address her mental problems. Long-buried family secrets and deceptions come to light during therapy sessions. First novel.

Other books you might like:
Linwood Barclay, *No Time for Goodbye*, 2007
John Burley, *The Forgetting Place*, 2015
G.H. Ephron, *Amnesia*, 2000
Meg Gardiner, *The Dirty Secrets Club*, 2008
Alison Gaylin, *And She Was*, 2012
Minette Walters, *The Sculptress*, 1993
Kate Wilhelm, *Hamlet Trap*, 1987

497

JANET BOLIN

Seven Threadly Sins

(New York: Berkley, 2015)

Series: Threadville Mystery Series. Book 5
Story type: Cozy Mystery; Series
Subject(s): Mystery; Detective fiction; Crime
Major character(s): Willow Vanderling, Detective—Amateur, Store Owner (In Stitches embroidery boutique), Employer (of Ashley); Ashley, Student—High School, Assistant (to Willow); Antonio, Director (Threadville Academy of Design and Modeling)
Time period(s): 21st century; 2010s
Locale(s): Threadville, Pennsylvania

Summary: Threadville, Pennsylvania, near Erie, is a haven for fiber artists such as Willow Vanderling. Willow is the owner of the embroidery boutique In Stitches, one of the town's many needlework shops. She also plays detective when the need arises. The mystery in this fifth novel in the Threadville Mystery series involves the Threadville Academy of Design and Modeling. The academy could be an asset to the community, but the director—Antonio—has managed to make several enemies. When the academy plans a fashion show to raise funds for scholarships, Willow agrees to be a model. Antonio ruins the event, however, and he then pulls a practical joke on Willow and some of the other models. But the joke is on Antonio, who is found murdered not long after the failed prank. When Willow becomes a suspect, she must find the real killer to prove her own innocence.

Other books by the same author:
Night of the Living Thread, 2014
Thread and Buried, 2013
Threaded for Trouble, 2012
Dire Threads, 2011

Other books you might like:
Elizabeth Lynn Casey, *Sew Deadly*, 2009
Elizabeth Lynn Casey, *Taken In*, 2014
Monica Ferris, *Crewel World*, 1999
Monica Ferris, *The Drowning Spool*, 2014
Earlene Fowler, *Fool's Puzzle*, 1994
Amanda Lee, *The Quick and the Thread*, 2010
Clare O'Donohue, *The Lover's Knot*, 2008

498

JAMES O. BORN (Pseudonym of James O'Neal)

Scent of Murder
(New York: Forge Books, 2015)

Story type: Child-in-Peril; Police Procedural
Subject(s): Mystery; Detective fiction; Crime
Major character(s): Tim Hallett, Police Officer (sheriff's deputy, Canine Assist Team); Arnold Ludner, Criminal (child molester); Claire Perkins, Police Officer (Canine Assist Team); Darren Mori, Police Officer (Canine Assist Team); Rocky, Dog, Police Officer (canine)
Time period(s): 21st century; 2010s
Locale(s): Palm Beach County, Florida

Summary: After Tim Hallett used excessive physical force on suspected child molester Arnold Ludner, he had to give up his job as a police detective in Palm Beach County, Florida. Tim now works on the Canine Assist Team with Rocky, a Belgian malinois, who is easier to work with than a human partner. Like Claire Perkins and Darren Mori, the other members of the canine unit, Tim has a special bond with his dog. Tim uses the unique skills of his canine partner to investigate a disturbing crime spree. A perpetrator is snatching local teenagers, and he has left behind a clue—a sweat-soaked rag. Tim hopes Rocky can get the kidnapper's scent from the rag—and he also hopes that the trail leads to Ludner, who has been released from prison.

Other books by the same author:
Burn Zone, 2008
Field of Fire, 2007
Escape Clause, 2006

Shock Wave, 2005
Walking Money, 2004

Other books you might like:
Robert Crais, *Suspect*, 2013
Alex Kava, *Breaking Creed*, 2015
Lee Charles Kelley, *A Nose for Murder*, 2003
Virginia Lanier, *Death in Bloodhound Red*, 1995
Spencer Quinn, *Dog on It*, 2009
Nora Roberts, *The Search*, 2010
David Rosenfelt, *Dog Tags*, 2010

499

C.J. BOX

Endangered
(New York: G.P. Putnam's Sons, 2015)

Series: Joe Pickett Series. Book 15
Story type: Contemporary; Series
Subject(s): Mystery; Detective fiction; Crime
Major character(s): Joe Pickett, Lawman (game warden), Spouse (of Marybeth), Father (of Sheridan and Lucy), Father (adoptive, of April); Marybeth Pickett, Mother (of Sheridan and Lucy), Mother (adoptive, of April), Librarian, Spouse (of Joe); Sheridan, Young Woman, Student—College, Sister (of Lucy), Daughter (of Joe and Marybeth); Lucy, Student—High School, Sister (of Sheridan), Daughter (of Joe and Marybeth); April, 18-Year-Old, Adoptee (of Joe and Marybeth), Girlfriend (of Dallas Cates), Crime Victim; Dallas Cates, Rodeo Rider, Boyfriend (of April), Crime Suspect
Time period(s): 21st century; 2010s
Locale(s): Wyoming, United States

Summary: As the 15th novel in the Joe Pickett series opens, the Wyoming game warden is taking a count of the grouse he has found slaughtered. A call from the sheriff quickly redirects Joe's attention, however. A young woman has been found beaten nearly to death and left on the side of a road. When Joe meets his wife, Marybeth, at the hospital, their fears are confirmed: the victim is their 18-year-old adopted daughter, April. April ran away with rodeo rider Dallas Cates several months ago. Joe believes that Dallas is the prime suspect, but his parents claim that their son is innocent. As Joe investigates the case, April lies in an induced coma. Another suspect emerges, but Joe is still unsettled by the Cates clan. Meanwhile, Joe gets drawn into another investigation—this one involving an attack on a friend who just got out of jail.

Other books by the same author:
Stone Cold, 2014
Back of Beyond, 2011
Blue Heaven, 2008
Savage Run, 2002
Open Season, 2001

Other books you might like:
Dixie Cash, *Since You're Leaving Anyway, Take Out the Trash*, 2004
Margaret Coel, *Killing Custer*, 2013
Paul Doiron, *The Bone Orchard*, 2014

Paul Doiron, *The Poacher's Son*, 2010
W.E.B. Griffin, *Deadly Assets*, 2015
James W. Hall, *The Big Finish*, 2014
Steve Hamilton, *A Cold Day in Paradise*, 1998
Craig Johnson, *Any Other Name: A Longmire Mystery*, 2014
Craig Johnson, *As the Crow Flies*, 2012
Craig Johnson, *The Cold Dish*, 2005
Craig Johnson, *Dry Bones*, 2015
William Kent Krueger, *Iron Lake*, 1998
D.W. Linden, *Sand Creek*, 2006
Clinton McKinzie, *Badwater*, 2005
Clinton McKinzie, *Crossing the Line*, 2004
John D. Nesbitt, *Trouble at the Redstone*, 2008
Kirk Russell, *Shell Games*, 2003
Dana Stabenow, *Bad Blood*, 2013

500

SUSAN M. BOYER

Lowcountry Boneyard

(Plano, Texas: Henery Press, 2015)

Series: Liz Talbot Mystery Series. Book 3
Story type: Contemporary; Private Detective
Subject(s): Mystery; Detective fiction; Crime
Major character(s): Kent Heyward, Heiress, Woman (23 years old), Missing Person, Daughter (of Colton Heyward); Colton Heyward, Wealthy, Father (of Kent), Client (of Liz Talbot); Liz Talbot, Detective— Private, Southern Belle
Time period(s): 21st century; 2010s
Locale(s): South Carolina, United States

Summary: Private detective Liz Talbot is a mannered Southern lady who happens to carry a gun and solve crimes. For her current case, Liz is summoned from her home on the coastal island of Stella Maris to meet with Colton Heyward in Charleston. Colton's daughter, the 23-year-old heiress Kent Heyward, disappeared a month ago, and Colton wants Liz to find her. Although Liz agrees with the Charleston police department's theory— that Kent left home by choice to get away from her controlling father—she agrees to take the case. Liz begins her investigation and discovers that all is not well in the wealthy Heyward clan. Kent and Colton had heated arguments, and other family members want to get their hands on the Heyward riches. As Liz digs up the secrets of Charleston's most affluent residents, she puts her own life in danger. This novel is the third in the Liz Talbot Mystery series.

Other books by the same author:
Lowcountry Bombshell, 2013
Lowcountry Boil, 2012

Other books you might like:
Mary Kay Andrews, *Savannah Blues*, 2002
Stephanie Bond, *Body Movers*, 2006
Laura Childs, *Death by Darjeeling*, 2001
Nancy Martin, *How to Murder a Millionaire*, 2002
Susan McBride, *Blue Blood*, 2004

Mary Stanton, *Defending Angels*, 2008
Michael Lee West, *Gone with a Handsomer Man*, 2011

501

HARRY BRANDT (Pseudonym of Richard Price)

The Whites

(New York: Henry Holt and Co., 2015)

Story type: Police Procedural
Subject(s): Crime; Murder; Mystery
Major character(s): Billy Graves, Detective—Police (NYPD sergeant), Spouse (of Carmen); Carmen Graves, Woman, Spouse (of Billy); Curtis Taft, Criminal, Murderer
Time period(s): 21st century; 2010s
Locale(s): New York, New York

Summary: The "whites" described here are the criminals who slip through the fingers of law enforcement officials. Like Captain Ahab, each NYPD detective has a nemesis—a white whale—that he pursues relentlessly. For sergeant Billy Graves, that nemesis is Curtis Taft. But Taft isn't the only challenge Billy faces in his career. Billy has spent years trying to redeem himself after an accidental shooting landed him an undesirable position on the city's night watch. Billy performs his job well and responds to late-night felonies all over Manhattan. But when he responds to a deadly knife attack in Penn Station, Billy realizes that he isn't investigating a random killing. The victim is the white of one of Billy's colleagues, and he is connected to an unsolved murder case. The suspense escalates when another nemesis goes missing, and Billy learns his family is in danger.

Other books by the same author:
Lush Life, 2008
Clockers, 1992
Ladies' Man, 1978
Bloodbrothers, 1976
The Wanderers, 1974

Other books you might like:
William Bayer, *Mirror Maze*, 1994
Lawrence Block, *A Long Line of Dead Men*, 1994
Michael Connelly, *The Burning Room*, 2014
Catherine Coulter, *Power Play*, 2014
Brendan DuBois, *Fatal Harbor*, 2014
Lisa Gardner, *Fear Nothing*, 2014
Rachel Howzell Hall, *Land of Shadows*, 2014
Peter May, *Entry Island*, 2013
Ed McBain, *Widows*, 1991
James Patterson, *NYPD Red*, 2012
George P. Pelecanos, *Hard Revolution*, 2004
Ivy Pochoda, *Visitation Street*, 2013
Lawrence Sanders, *The First Deadly Sin*, 1973
Stephen White, *Cold Case*, 2000

502

ALLISON BRENNAN

Compulsion

(New York: Minotaur Books, 2015)

Series: Max Revere Series. Book 2
Story type: Contemporary; Serial Killer
Subject(s): Mystery; Detective fiction; Crime
Major character(s): Maxine "Max" Revere, Journalist (investigative reporter), Television Personality (*Maximum Exposure*); Adam Bachman, Serial Killer (accused); David, Bodyguard (of Max); Sally O'Hara, Detective—Police
Time period(s): 21st century; 2010s
Locale(s): New York, New York

Summary: In the second novel in the Max Revere series, investigative journalist Maxine "Max" Revere lands a big interview for her show, *Maximum Exposure*. Her subject will be Adam Bachman, an accused serial killer who is on trial for five murders. The killer's spree ended when one of his intended victims called the police from the trunk of Bachman's car. The evidence against Bachman seems sure to win a conviction, but Max isn't satisfied. She believes Bachman is responsible for more than five deaths, and she grills him about a missing elderly husband and wife. Max believes that Bachman killed them, too—and that he may not be acting alone. The district attorney isn't happy with Max's interference, which could have a negative effect on the case the department has built against Bachman. Max's bodyguard, David, comes in handy as the investigation grows increasingly dangerous.

Other books by the same author:
Notorious, 2014
Murder in the River City, 2012
Love Me to Death, 2011
Speak No Evil, 2007
The Prey, 2005

Other books you might like:
Jan Brogan, *A Confidential Source*, 2005
Barbara D'Amato, *Hardball*, 1990
Karen E. Olson, *Sacred Cows*, 2005
Brad Parks, *Faces of the Gone*, 2009
Hank Phillippi Ryan, *The Other Woman*, 2012
Hank Phillippi Ryan, *Prime Time*, 2007
Polly Whitney, *Until Death*, 1994

503

EMILY BRIGHTWELL

Mrs. Jeffries and the One Who Got Away

(New York: Berkley, 2015)

Series: Mrs. Jeffries Series. Book 34
Story type: Amateur Detective; Cozy Mystery
Subject(s): Murder; Criminals; Detective fiction
Major character(s): Gerald Witherspoon, Police Officer (inspector), Employer (of Mrs. Jeffries), Friend (of Barnes); Mrs. Jeffries, Widow(er), Housekeeper (of Gerald Witherspoon), Detective—Amateur; Barnes, Police Officer (constable), Friend (of Gerald Witherspoon)
Time period(s): 19th century; 1800s
Locale(s): London, England

Summary: The 34th Mrs. Jeffries novel revisits a previous case, *Mrs. Jeffries Sweeps the Chimney*, in which the murderer eluded justice. When a seemingly innocent citizen is found murdered in a North London cemetery, Inspector Witherspoon recognizes the victim. The quiet boardinghouse matron is actually a wanted killer who escaped him some time ago. A scrap of newspaper in her hand is the only clue that the Inspector and Constable Barnes have to begin their investigation, but the Inspector's housekeeper, Mrs. Jeffries, is always eager to aid her employer in uncovering the truth. This time, however, she can't help but wonder if solving the woman's murder is worth their time and effort. As the pieces of the puzzle begin to come together, Mrs. Jeffries and Inspector Witherspoon continually revisit the older case, hoping to lay both files to rest.

Other books by the same author:
Mrs. Jeffries Pleads the Fifth, 2014
Mrs. Jeffries Takes Stock, 1994
The Ghost and Mrs. Jeffries, 1993
The Inspector and Mrs. Jeffries, 1993
Mrs. Jeffries Dusts for Clues, 1993

Other books you might like:
Tasha Alexander, *And Only to Deceive*, 2005
Donna Fletcher Crowe, *A Most Inconvenient Death*, 2011
Ann Granger, *A Rare Interest in Corpses*, 2006
Sydney Hosier, *Elementary, Mrs. Hudson*, 1996
Kate Parker, *The Vanishing Thief*, 2013
Amanda Quick, *Garden of Lies*, 2015
Will Thomas, *Some Danger Involved*, 2004
Victoria Thompson, *Murder on Astor Place*, 1999

504

DUFFY BROWN (Pseudonym of Dianne Kruetzkamp)

Demise in Denim

(New York: Berkley, 2015)

Series: Consignment Shop Mystery Series. Book 5
Story type: Cozy Mystery; Series
Subject(s): Mystery; Detective fiction; Crime
Major character(s): Reagan Summerside, Store Owner (consignment shop), Detective—Amateur, Divorced Person; Walker Boone, Lawyer, Crime Suspect
Time period(s): 21st century; 2010s
Locale(s): Savannah, Georgia

Summary: Reagan Summerside is the proprietor of a consignment shop that occupies the first story of her Savannah, Georgia, home. At the moment, the top floor is being used to conceal the whereabouts of local attorney Walker Boone. Walker is suspected of murder, and he's hiding out until he and Reagan can figure out who the real killer is. Reagan has mixed feelings about the fugitive she's harboring. Walker handled Reagan's divorce, and although the settlement did not work out as Reagan had hoped, she can't help feeling attracted to him. Reagan and Walker will have to work together if they're going to prove Walker's innocence and remedy their current living arrangement. This novel is the fifth in the Consignment Shop Mystery series.

Other books by the same author:
Geared for the Grave, 2014
Pearls and Poison, 2014
Killer in Crinolines, 2013
Iced Chiffon, 2012

Other books you might like:
Ann Campbell, *Wolf at the Door*, 2000
Sharon Fiffer, *Killer Stuff*, 2001
Elaine Flinn, *Dealing in Murder: A Molly Doyle Mystery*, 2003
Rebecca M. Hale, *How to Wash a Cat*, 2008
Joyce Lavene, *A Timely Vision*, 2010
Tamar Myers, *Larceny and Old Lace*, 1996
Sebastian Stuart, *To the Manor Dead*, 2010

505

LESLIE BUDEWITZ

Assault and Pepper

(New York: Berkley, 2015)

Series: Spice Shop Mystery Series. Book 1
Story type: Amateur Detective; Contemporary
Subject(s): Murder; Business; Divorce
Major character(s): Pepper Reece, Store Owner (Spice Shop), Employer (of Tory), Divorced Person (of Tag), Detective—Amateur; Tag, Police Officer, Divorced Person (of Pepper); Tory Finch, Worker (for Pepper), Crime Suspect
Time period(s): 21st century; 2010s
Locale(s): Seattle, Washington

Summary: The first book of the Spice Shop Mystery series introduces Pepper Reece, a recently divorced businesswoman who has just celebrated the one-year anniversary of her Spice Shop in Seattle's Pike Place Market. Pepper kicked her cheating husband, Tag, to the curb and has been trying to find her own footing. She enjoys her new business immensely, even if her ex-husband, a cop, patrols Pike Place daily. Her foray into amateur detective work begins when a homeless man mysteriously dies on the doorstop of her shop and one of her employees is arrested. Pepper is convinced that Tory is innocent and wants to help clear her name, but Tory is aloof. She is reluctant to talk to anyone about her relationship with the homeless man or explain why the police suspect she may have had a hand in his death. Meanwhile, Tag keeps turning up at the spice shop. He claims he is looking out for Pepper, which leads her to wonder about his true motives.

Other books by the same author:
Crime Rib, 2014
Death Al Dente, 2013

Other books you might like:
Avery Aames, *The Long Quiche Goodbye*, 2010

Mary Kay Andrews, *Savannah Blues*, 2002
Sandra Balzo, *Uncommon Grounds*, 2004
Sammi Carter, *Candy Apple Dead*, 2005
Laura Childs, *Death by Darjeeling*, 2001

506

JOHN BURLEY

The Forgetting Place

(New York: William Morrow, 2015)

Story type: Amateur Detective; Contemporary
Subject(s): Suspense; Murder; Detective fiction
Major character(s): Dr. Lise Shields, Therapist (of Jason Edwards), Doctor (psychiatrist); Jason Edwards, Patient (of Lise), Crime Suspect
Time period(s): 21st century; 2010s
Locale(s): Maryland, United States

Summary: Lise Shields is a psychiatrist who works at Maryland Menaker State Hospital. The hospital is a correctional facility for inmates with mental difficulties who require greater care than a general prison can offer. In the five years that she has been at Menaker, she has come to accept that many of her patients will never be healed and that they will never leave the hospital. Her gut tells her that something is wrong with her new patient, regardless of what her supervisor says. Jason Edwards was admitted to Menaker without any medical history or court orders for commitment, but Lise has been instructed to get Jason to talk to her. Over time, Jason reveals that he suspects his arrival has to do with the murder of his lover and that a conspiracy is afoot. Lise realizes that she is being followed and soon two FBI agents contact her. She begins to wonder how far the corruption spreads within the walls of the hospital, and how far someone will go to keep an innocent man locked up.

Other books by the same author:
No Mercy, 2014
The Absence of Mercy, 2013

Other books you might like:
Keith Ablow, *Denial*, 1997
Sandra Block, *Little Black Lies*, 2015
G.H. Ephron, *Amnesia*, 2000
Alison Gaylin, *And She Was*, 2012
Jonathan Kellerman, *When the Bough Breaks*, 1985
Dennis Lehane, *Shutter Island*, 2003
Minette Walters, *The Dark Room*, 1996
Minette Walters, *The Sculptress*, 1993

507

JEFFREY B. BURTON

The Lynchpin

(Isle of Man, United Kingdom: MP Publishing, 2015)

Story type: Contemporary; Police Procedural
Subject(s): Violence; Murder; Law enforcement
Major character(s): Drew Cady, FBI Agent, Colleague (of

Roland Jund), Fiance(e) (of Terri Ingram); Roland Jund, FBI Agent, Crime Suspect, Colleague (of Drew Cady); Terri Ingram, Fiance(e) (of Drew Cady)
Time period(s): 21st century; 2010s
Locale(s): Minneapolis, Minnesota

Summary: In this sequel to *The Chessman*, FBI Agent Drew Cady has moved to the Minneapolis Medicare Fraud Strike Force. He wanted a break from the dangerous task of hunting down murderous psychopaths, and hoped to work on his relationship with Terri Ingram. Yet murderers never rest, and he is assigned to a homicide case. The perpetrator is brutal and sadistic, leaving his victims in a state of horror. The first victim is a 23-year-old woman whose body was found in Lake Superior. Her blood had been exchanged for embalming fluid while she was still alive. Cady's work relationships also require attention. His former boss and mentor, Roland Jund, an assistant director for the FBI, kills a home invader that turned out to be his wife's lover. Cady is torn between clearing his friend's name and stopping a psychopath. He knows the serial killer could strike again at any time.

Other books by the same author:
The Chessman, 2012
Sleuth Slayer, 2009
Shadow Play, 2005

Other books you might like:
K.J. Erickson, *Third Person Singular*, 2001
Brian Freeman, *Immoral*, 2005
Steve Hamilton, *A Cold Day in Paradise*, 1998
John Sandford, *Dark of the Moon*, 2007
John Sandford, *Rules of Prey*, 1989
Steve Thayer, *The Weatherman*, 1995
John Verdon, *Think of a Number*, 2010

508

RICKY BUSH

Howling Mountain Blues

(Vancouver, Washington: Barking Rain Press, 2015)

Series: Crime Fighting Bluesmen Series. Book 3
Story type: Amateur Detective; Series
Subject(s): Music; Kidnapping; Drugs
Major character(s): Mitty Andersen, Musician (member of The Repeaters), Friend (of Pete Bolden and Lenora Charles), Detective—Amateur; Pete Bolden, Musician (member of The Repeaters), Friend (of Mitty Andersen and Lenora Charles), Detective—Amateur; Lenora Charles, Agent (ATF), Friend (of Mitty Andersen and Pete Bolden), Security Officer (for The Repeaters)
Time period(s): 21st century; 2010s
Locale(s): Belize

Summary: Musicians Mitty Andersen and Pete Bolden return in the third Crime Fighting Bluesmen novel. The Repeaters has been hired to perform in Belize. Their friend Lenora Charles, an ATF agent, thinks she should accompany the band as security personnel. Because the are expecting nothing more than music and relaxation in the sun, Mitty and Pete think Lenora is overreacting. Upon arrival, however, they realize they were very

wrong. A major figure in organized crime is awaiting the concert. He has recently run into trouble with a Mexican cartel over a kidnapping gone wrong and he is hoping to enjoy the blues music while rectifying his business problems. Another kidnapping has Mitty and Pete realizing just how much trouble they have gotten into. They have little time to solve the case if they want to prevent a missing person investigation from becoming a murder case.

Other books by the same author:
The Devil's Blues, 2013
River Bottom Blues, 2013

Other books you might like:
Ace Atkins, *Crossroad Blues*, 1998
Kix Brooks, *The Adventures of Slim and Howdy*, 2008
Tim Dorsey, *Florida Roadkill*, 1999
Bill Fitzhugh, *Fender Benders*, 2001
Kinky Friedman, *Greenwich Killing Time: A Novel*, 1986
Elmore Leonard, *Maximum Bob*, 1991
Bob Morris, *Bahamarama*, 2004

509

IAN CALDWELL

The Fifth Gospel

(New York: Simon & Schuster, 2015)

Story type: Literary; Religious
Subject(s): Mystery; Detective fiction; Catholicism
Major character(s): John Paul II, Religious (Roman Catholic pope), Historical Figure; Alex Andreou, Religious (Greek Catholic priest), Father (of Peter), Brother (of Simon); Peter Andreou, Boy, Son (of Alex), 5-Year-Old; Simon Andreou, Religious (Greek Catholic priest), Brother (of Alex); Ugo Nogara, Man, Museum Curator
Time period(s): 21st century; 2000s (2004)
Locale(s): Vatican City

Summary: The late papacy of John Paul II provides the backdrop for this novel by Ian Caldwell, coauthor of the 2004 best seller, *The Rule of Four*. Ugo Nogara, a curator at the Vatican Museums, is overseeing the installation of a new exhibit. Father Alex Andreou, a Greek Catholic priest who lives in Vatican City with his five-year-old son Peter, is helping Nogara with his research. Father Alex's family has a close association with the Church. Alex's brother Simon is also a priest, as was their father. Alex hopes that Peter will follow the same path, but their lives take a turn when tragedy strikes in the holy city. Nogara is killed just days before his exhibit is to open, and Alex realizes that he and his family are in danger. To find Nogara's killer and keep him from striking again, Alex looks for clues in the museum exhibit, which concerns the Shroud of Turin and a fifth gospel known as the Diatessaron.

Other books by the same author:
The Rule of Four, 2004

Other books you might like:
Steve Berry, *The Templar Legacy*, 2006
Dan Brown, *Angels and Demons*, 2000

Dan Brown, *The Da Vinci Code*, 2003
Ian Caldwell, *The Rule of Four*, 2004
Sean Chercover, *The Trinity Game*, 2012
Umberto Eco, *The Name of the Rose*, 1983
Lev Grossman, *Codex*, 2004
Lev Grossman, *The Magicians*, 2009
Glenn Meade, *The Second Messiah*, 2011
Katherine Neville, *The Eight*, 1988
Matthew Pearl, *The Dante Club*, 2003
Douglas Preston, *Blue Labyrinth*, 2014
James Rollins, *The Eye of God*, 2013
Daniel Silva, *The Fallen Angel*, 2012
Simon Toyne, *The Key*, 2012

510

SUSANNA CALKINS

The Masque of a Murderer

(New York: Minotaur Books, 2015)

Series: Lucy Campion Mysteries Series. Book 3
Story type: Historical; Series
Subject(s): Mystery; Detective fiction; Crime
Major character(s): Lucy Campion, Apprentice (to printer), Detective—Amateur; Sarah Hargrave, Daughter (of Lucy's former employer), Quaker, Friend (of Jacob Whitby), Sister (of Adam); Jacob Whitby, Quaker, Crime Victim, Friend (of Adam, Sarah); Adam Hargrave, Brother (of Sarah), Friend (of Jacob)
Time period(s): 17th century; 1660s (1667)
Locale(s): London, England

Summary: In 1667 London, the city is still recovering from the Great Fire. Lucy Campion, an apprentice to a printer, is reunited with Sarah Hargrave, who is a member of the household in which Lucy was once employed. Sarah, now a Quaker, brings Lucy to the bedside of Jacob Whitby, a fellow Quaker who has suffered fatal injuries in a cart accident. As Lucy writes down Jacob's last statements, she learns that the cart incident was no accident. Someone pushed Jacob and, according to the dying man, that person is posing as a Quaker. The killer was trying to keep Jacob from revealing a secret he had learned. Lucy, who has proven herself a competent detective in the past, sets out to find Jacob's murderer and protect Sarah from harm. This is the third novel in the Lucy Campion Mysteries series by Susanna Calkins.

Other books by the same author:
From the Charred Remains, 2014
A Murder at Rosamund's Gate, 2013

Other books you might like:
Ronan Bennett, *Havoc in Its Third Year*, 2004
John Dickson Carr, *The Devil in Velvet*, 1951
Susanna Gregory, *A Conspiracy of Violence*, 2006
Philip Kerr, *Dark Matter*, 2002
Edward Marston, *The King's Evil*, 2000
Fidelis Morgan, *Unnatural Fires*, 2000
Iain Pears, *An Instance of the Fingerpost*, 1998

511

COLIN CAMPBELL

Snake Pass

(Woodbury, Minnesota: Midnight Ink, 2015)

Series: Resurrection Man Series. Book 4
Story type: Police Procedural; Series
Subject(s): Mystery; Detective fiction; Crime
Major character(s): Jim Grant, Detective—Police (suspended); Jamie Hope, Police Officer (constable); Wendy Rivers, Waiter/Waitress
Time period(s): 21st century; 2010s
Locale(s): Yorkshire, England

Summary: Yorkshire police constable Jim Grant is suspended in the fourth novel in the Resurrection Man series. A fellow constable, Jamie Hope, reports Grant's excessive use of force during a drug bust, and Grant's superiors decide that the constable has bent the rules too far this time. To ease his anger, Grant drives to the Woodlands Truck Stop and Diner, hoping waitress Wendy Rivers will cheer him up. She does, and a calmer Grant heads for his car. When the diner goes dark after Grant leaves, he knows something is wrong. He returns and finds that an apparent robbery is underway. A Ukrainian man is pressing Wendy for information, and Grant soon realizes that the crook is interested in more than the contents of the cash register. Grant takes advantage of the robber's moment of distraction to call for reinforcements. The tension escalates when Jamie Hope arrives as backup and more Ukrainian men enter the diner.

Other books by the same author:
Adobe Flats, 2014
Montecito Heights, 2014
Jamaica Plan, 2013

Other books you might like:
Lee Child, *Killing Floor*, 1997
Lee Child, *Personal*, 2014
John Connor, *Phoenix*, 2003
Bill Kitson, *Depths of Despair*, 2009
Ian Rankin, *Resurrection Men*, 2001
Peter Robinson, *Gallows View*, 1987
Irvine Welsh, *Crime*, 2008

512

KATE CARLISLE

Ripped from the Pages

(New York: Penguin Publishing Group, 2015)

Series: Bibliophile Mystery Series. Book 9
Story type: Amateur Detective; Series
Subject(s): Mystery; Detective fiction; Crime
Major character(s): Brooklyn Wainwright, Expert (book restoration), Detective—Amateur, Girlfriend (of Derek Stone); Derek Stone, Boyfriend (of Brooklyn)
Time period(s): 21st century; 2010s
Locale(s): Sonoma, California

Summary: Brooklyn Wainwright, professional book restorer and amateur sleuth, heads to the Sonoma Valley in the ninth Bibliophile Mystery. She and her boyfriend, Derek Stone, are staying with Brooklyn's parents and taking in some of the local sights. Brooklyn stumbles onto a mystery when she visits a wine cave excavation site. The workers discover an underground room filled with valuable art, jewelry, and books. The chamber also contains a mummified corpse. Brooklyn takes a special interest in the first edition Jules Verne novel that is part of the treasure stash. The book contains a map that shows the whereabouts of another treasure trove. When the discovery attracts the attention of the media, Brooklyn carries out her own investigation and realizes that the treasure and the long-ago murder may have repercussions in the present.

Other books by the same author:
This Old Homicide, 2015
The Book Starts Here, 2014
A High-End Finish, 2014
If Books Could Kill, 2010
Homicide in Hardcover, 2009

Other books you might like:
Lorna Barrett, *Murder Is Binding*, 2008
Lawrence Block, *Burglars Can't Be Choosers*, 1977
John Dunning, *Booked to Die*, 1992
Carolyn G. Hart, *Death on Demand*, 1987
Vincent McCaffrey, *Hound*, 2009
George Sims, *The Last Best Friend*, 1967
Judith Van Gieson, *The Stolen Blue*, 2000

513

ELIZABETH LYNN CASEY (Pseudonym of Laura Bradford)

Wedding Duress

(New York: Berkley, 2015)

Series: Southern Sewing Circle Series. Book 10
Story type: Cozy Mystery; Series
Subject(s): Mystery; Detective fiction; Crime
Major character(s): Tori Sinclair, Seamstress, Fiance(e) (of Milo Wentworth), Detective—Amateur, Friend (of Beatrice); Milo Wentworth, Fiance(e) (of Tori Sinclair); Beatrice, Friend (of Tori Sinclair)
Time period(s): 21st century; 2010s
Locale(s): Sweet Briar, South Carolina

Summary: Tori Sinclair, a member of the Sweet Briar Ladies Society Sewing Circle, moved from up north to make a home in South Carolina. She has fallen in love with Milo Wentworth, and their wedding ceremony is just a few days away. But when Beatrice, one of Tori's friends from the Sewing Circle, needs her help, she adds solving a mystery to her list of things to do. Beatrice is convinced that the death of one of her former employees, which was ruled accidental, is really a homicide. Tori has solved crimes in Sweet Briar before, and Beatrice hopes she can come through again. So as she stitches up wedding favors and prepares for her and Milo's big day, Tori tries to figure out who killed Beatrice's former nanny—and why. This novel is the tenth in the Southern Sewing Circle Mystery series.

Other books by the same author:
Taken In, 2014
Deadly Notions, 2011
Death Threads, 2010
Pinned for Murder, 2010
Sew Deadly, 2009

Other books you might like:
Janet Bolin, *Dire Threads*, 2011
Janet Bolin, *Night of the Living Thread*, 2014
Monica Ferris, *Crewel World*, 1999
Monica Ferris, *The Drowning Spool*, 2014
Earlene Fowler, *Fool's Puzzle*, 1994
Amanda Lee, *The Quick and the Thread*, 2010
Clare O'Donohue, *The Lover's Knot*, 2008

514

LAURA CHILDS (Pseudonym of Gerry Schmitt)

Ming Tea Murder

(New York: Berkley, 2015)

Series: Tea Shop Mysteries Series. Book 16
Story type: Cozy Mystery; Series
Subject(s): Mystery; Detective fiction; Crime
Major character(s): Theodosia Browning, Detective—Amateur, Store Owner (owner of Indigo Tea Shop), Girlfriend (of Max Scofield); Max Scofield, Public Relations (Gibbes Museum), Boyfriend (of Theodosia Browning), Crime Suspect; Edgar Webster, Man (museum donor), Crime Victim
Time period(s): 21st century; 2010s
Locale(s): Charleston, South Carolina

Summary: Tea shop owner Theodosia Browning plays sleuth to clear her boyfriend's name in the 16th novel in the Tea Shop Mysteries series. Theodosia's longtime love interest, Max Scofield, is the public relations direct of Charleston's Gibbes Museum. So when the museum hosts an event to celebrate the opening of a new exhibition—the re-creation of an authentic Shanghai tea house—she attends, even though such events aren't her cup of tea. The gala features food, tea, and a photo booth, where guests can commemorate the evening with a fun snapshot. When Theodosia enters the booth, she finds it occupied by the corpse of Edgar Webster, one of the museum's donors. Theodosia once again puts her detective skills to work and launches her own investigation into the murder. This time her motivation is personal because Max is a suspect.

Other books by the same author:
Steeped in Evil, 2014
English Breakfast Murder, 2003
Shades of Earl Grey, 2003
Gunpowder Green, 2002
Death by Darjeeling, 2001

Other books you might like:
Riley Adams, *Delicious and Suspicious*, 2010
Sandra Balzo, *Uncommon Grounds*, 2004
Jessie Chandler, *Bingo Barge Murder*, 2011
Kate Collins, *Mum's the Word*, 2004

Mystery

Cleo Coyle, *On What Grounds*, 2003
Yasmine Galenorn, *Ghost of a Chance*, 2003
Elizabeth Lee, *A Tough Nut to Kill*, 2014

515

MARY HIGGINS CLARK

The Melody Lingers On

(New York: Simon & Schuster, 2015)

Story type: Contemporary
Subject(s): Mystery; Detective fiction; Crime
Major character(s): Lane Harmon, Interior Decorator, Mother (of Katie); Katie, 5-Year-Old, Daughter (of Lane); Parker Bennett, Financier, Crime Suspect, Missing Person, Spouse (of Anne Bennett), Father (of Eric); Anne Bennett, Spouse (of Parker), Mother (of Eric); Eric Bennett, Son (of Parker and Anne)
Time period(s): 21st century; 2010s
Locale(s): New York, New York

Summary: Interior designer Lane Harmon can't hide her surprise when she learns the identity of her new client. She is Anne Bennett, wife of financier Parker Bennett. Parker went missing in the Caribbean two years ago and is presumed dead. The discovery—after his disappearance—that billions of dollars were missing from a fund he managed has made life miserable for Anne and the couple's son, Eric. The government has seized all of Parker's assets, including the family's opulent home. Anne will now be living in a condo, and she has hired Lane to decorate it. When Lane meets her client, she learns that Anne believes her husband is innocent. Eric would also like to clear Parker's name, but the authorities are out for blood. They want to track down all of Parker's assets—and Parker himself, if he's still alive. Lane gets drawn deeper into the Bennetts' lives and puts her own family in danger in the process.

Other books by the same author:
Daddy's Gone A Hunting, 2013
A Cry in the Night, 1982
The Cradle Will Fall, 1980
A Stranger Is Watching, 1978
Where Are the Children?, 1975

Other books you might like:
Sandra Brown, *Ricochet*, 2006
Lisa Gardner, *Crash and Burn*, 2015
Lisa Gardner, *The Other Daughter*, 1999
James Grippando, *Cane and Abe*, 2015
Tami Hoag, *Kill the Messenger*, 2004
Kay Hooper, *Haunting Rachel*, 1998
Barbara Michaels, *Be Buried in the Rain*, 1985
Nora Roberts, *Homeport*, 1998
Danielle Steel, *Prodigal Son*, 2015
Phyllis A. Whitney, *Woman Without a Past*, 1991

516

ANNE CLEELAND

Murder in Hindsight

(New York: Kensington, 2015)

Series: New Scotland Yard Series. Book 3
Story type: Police Procedural; Series
Subject(s): Mystery; Detective fiction; Crime
Major character(s): Kathleen Doyle, Detective—Police (detective sergeant), Spouse (of Michael Sinclair); Michael Sinclair, Detective—Police (detective chief inspector), Nobleman (Lord Acton), Spouse (of Kathleen Doyle)
Time period(s): 21st century; 2010s
Locale(s): London, England

Summary: A vigilante is at work in London in the third novel in the New Scotland Yard Mystery series. The unknown perpetrator is assassinating criminals who have managed to evade conviction. Detective sergeant Kathleen Doyle and her husband, detective chief inspector Michael Sinclair, Lord Acton, are on the case. Doyle believes that the vigilante has been prompted to action by a specific trigger, and she tries to find ties between the cold cases and current events. The investigation grows more complicated when Doyle learns that she is being followed. The stalker, who appears to be a benevolent figure, is actually working with one of Michael's enemies. As in other cases handled by the husband-and-wife team, the disparity in Doyle and Sinclair's social standings comes into play during the course of the investigation. Doyle is a born detective, however, and she proves her expertise once again.

Other books by the same author:
Murder in Retribution, 2014
Daughter of the God-King, 2013
Murder in Thrall, 2013
Tainted Angel, 2013

Other books you might like:
Elizabeth George, *A Great Deliverance*, 1988
Ann Granger, *Say It with Poison*, 1991
Reginald Hill, *A Clubbable Woman*, 1970
Reginald Hill, *Dialogues of the Dead*, 2001
Ngaio Marsh, *Grave Mistake*, 1978
Carol O'Connell, *Mallory's Oracle*, 1994
Ruth Rendell, *Sins of the Fathers*, 1976

517

HARLAN COBEN

The Stranger

(New York: Dutton, 2015)

Story type: Contemporary
Subject(s): Marriage; Deception; Betrayal
Major character(s): Adam Price, Spouse (of Corinne), Father; Corinne Price, Teacher, Spouse (of Adam), Mother, Missing Person
Time period(s): 21st century; 2010s
Locale(s): New Jersey, United States

Summary: Adam Price thought he had it all: a beautiful wife and two smart, great kids. His world implodes when a stranger confronts him at his son's sixth-grade lacrosse draft. Without revealing his name or purpose, the man simply tells Adam that his wife, Corinne, isn't who he thinks she is and her first pregnancy—which ended in miscarriage—was a lie. Shocked, Adam confronts Corinne, who only asks that Adam wait one day to hear the whole story. The next day, however, Corinne has vanished. She quit her job as a high school teacher, packed a bag, and left a message telling Adam to take care of the kids and not try to contact her. Frantic with worry, Adam tries to uncover his wife's secrets. When Adam connects her to a murder in Ohio, he begins to wonder if he ever knew Corinne at all.

Other books by the same author:
Missing You, 2014
Live Wire, 2011
Deal Breaker, 1995
Miracle Cure, 1991
Play Dead, 1990

Other books you might like:
Jussi Adler-Olsen, *The Alphabet House*, 2014
Linwood Barclay, *Trust Your Eyes*, 2012
Agatha Christie, *Curtain: Hercule Poirot's Last Case*, 1975
Michael Connelly, *The Burning Room*, 2014
Robert Crais, *The Promise*, 2014
Joy Fielding, *Someone Is Watching*, 2015
Joseph Finder, *Paranoia*, 2004
Lisa Gardner, *Crash and Burn*, 2015
Lisa Gardner, *Love You More*, 2011
W.E.B. Griffin, *Deadly Assets*, 2015
Patricia Highsmith, *The Talented Mr. Ripley*, 1955
Laura Lippman, *Hush Hush*, 2015
James Patterson, *Hope to Die*, 2014
Kathy Reichs, *Bones Never Lie*, 2014
Hank Phillippi Ryan, *Truth Be Told*, 2014
John Sandford, *Deadline*, 2014
Lisa Scottoline, *Look Again*, 2009

518

NANCY COCO (Pseudonym of Nancy J. Parra)

Oh Say Can You Fudge

(New York: Kensington, 2015)

Series: Candy-Coated Mystery Series. Book 3
Story type: Contemporary; Cozy Mystery
Subject(s): Crime; Mystery; Detective fiction
Major character(s): Allie McMurphy, Detective—Amateur, Girlfriend (of Trent Jessop), Hotel Owner (McMurphy Hotel and Fudge Shop); Trent Jessop, Wealthy, Boyfriend (of Allie McMurphy); Rodney Rivers, Technician (fireworks), Crime Victim, Colleague (of Henry Schulte); Henry Schulte, Colleague (of Rodney Rivers), Technician (fireworks); Mal, Dog (of Allie)
Time period(s): 21st century; 2010s
Locale(s): Michigan, United States

Summary: Allie McMurphy is getting ready for Mackinac Island's annual Independence Day celebration in the third novel in the Candy-Coated Mystery series. As the new owner of the McMurphy Hotel and Fudge Shop, Allie wants to make sure she has enough fudge to keep visitors happy. She has also hired pyrotechnics experts Rodney Rivers and Henry Schulte to put on a spectacular fireworks display. But when Rodney is killed, and a warehouse full of fireworks goes up in flames, it seems the Fourth of July celebration is doomed. Henry is spooked and refuses to go on with the show, so Allie turns to her rich boyfriend, Trent Jessop, for help. When more fires erupt on the island, amateur detective Allie searches for an arsonist and a murderer. Allie's canine companion, Mal, serves as her faithful partner in crime detection.

Other books by the same author:
Engaged in Murder, 2014
To Fudge or Not to Fudge, 2014
All Fudged Up, 2013
Gluten for Punishment, 2013
Mr. Charming, 2009

Other books you might like:
Avery Aames, *The Long Quiche Goodbye*, 2010
Jessica Beck, *Glazed Murder*, 2010
JoAnna Carl, *The Chocolate Cat Caper*, 2002
Sammi Carter, *Candy Apple Dead*, 2005
Joanne Fluke, *Chocolate Chip Cookie Murder*, 2000
Connie Shelton, *Sweet Masterpiece*, 2010
Wendy Lyn Watson, *I Scream, You Scream*, 2009

519

KATE COLLINS

A Root Awakening

(New York: Penguin Publishing Group, 2015)

Series: Flower Shop Mystery Series. Book 16
Story type: Cozy Mystery; Series
Subject(s): Mystery; Detective fiction; Crime
Major character(s): Abby Knight Salvare, Store Owner (Bloomers), Spouse (of Marco), Detective—Amateur; Marco Salvare, Restaurateur (Down the Hatch Bar and Grill), Spouse (of Abby), Detective—Private; Sergio Marin, Construction Worker, Crime Victim, Spouse (of Rosa); Rosa Marin, Spouse (of Sergio)
Time period(s): 21st century; 2010s
Locale(s): New Chapel, Indiana

Summary: Abby Knight, owner of Bloomers flower shop in New Chapel, Indiana, tacked "Salvare" to the end of her name when she married private detective and tavern owner Marco. Now the newlyweds are shopping for a new house, and they can't seem to agree. Abby wants a house that's move-in ready, and Marco wants a fixer-upper. When they visit a Victorian home that's undergoing repairs, Abby and Marco see one of the workers fall to his death. Evidence indicates that Sergio may have been pushed, and Marco—at the request of Sergio's widow, Rosa—starts searching for a killer and a motive. Meanwhile Abby opens an investigation of her own into the family that owns the house. She can't let Marco

Mystery

know what she's up to, but she has a feeling that the family is hiding something. This novel is the 16th in the Flower Shop Mystery series.

Other books by the same author:
Throw in the Trowel, 2014
Snipped in the Bud, 2006
Dearly Depotted, 2005
Slay it with Flowers, 2005
Mum's the Word, 2004

Other books you might like:
Mary Freeman, *Devil's Trumpet*, 1999
Sarah Graves, *The Dead Cat Bounce*, 1998
Joan Hadley, *The Night-Blooming Cereus*, 1987
Rosemary Harris, *Pushing Up Daisies*, 2008
Rosemary Harris, *Slugfest: A Dirty Business Mystery*, 2011
Janis Harrison, *Bindweed*, 2005
Janis Harrison, *Roots of Murder*, 1999

520

SHEILA CONNOLLY

An Early Wake

(New York: Berkley Prime Crime, 2015)

Series: County Cork Mystery Series. Book 3
Story type: Amateur Detective; Contemporary
Subject(s): Mystery; Murder; Ireland
Major character(s): Maura Donovan, Bartender, Business-woman (owner of Sullivan's), Detective—Amateur
Time period(s): 21st century; 2010s
Locale(s): Leap, Cork

Summary: Maura Donovan, owner of Sullivan's Pub in County Cork, Ireland, has settled well. An American by birth who grew up in pubs around South Boston, Maura took over Sullivan's upon inheriting it and has since dedicated herself to making it a successful business. Now that summer tourist season is drawing to a close, she realizes that she needs to develop a new draw for the lean fall and winter months. When she discovers that Sullivan's once had a wide reputation for music performances, she decides to renew a live-music program. Her first event draws many talented musicians and is a smash hit, and Maura believes she might make it through the winter. Unfortunately, Maura's discovery of a corpse in her pub the following morning has the potential to ruin everything. Maura's detective skills are put to work as she searches for the musician's killer while she keeps her business afloat. This is the third novel of the County Cork Mystery series.

Other books by the same author:
Scandal in Skibbereen, 2014
Buried in a Bog, 2013
Relatively Dead, 2013
Fundraising the Dead, 2010
One Bad Apple, 2008

Other books you might like:
Claudia Bishop, *A Taste for Murder*, 1994
Mary Daheim, *Just Desserts*, 1991

Dicey Deere, *The Irish Cottage Murder*, 1999
Dicey Deere, *The Irish Village Murder*, 2004
Jean Hager, *Blooming Murder*, 1994
Tamar Myers, *Too Many Crooks Spoil the Broth*, 1994
Nancy Means Wright, *Midnight Fires*, 2010

521

AMANDA COOPER (Pseudonym of Donna Lea Simpson)

Shadow of a Spout

(New York: Berkley, 2015)

Series: Teapot Collector Mystery Series. Book 2
Story type: Cozy Mystery; Series
Subject(s): Mystery; Detective fiction; Crime
Major character(s): Rose Freemont, Crime Suspect, Restaurateur (Auntie Rose's Victorian Teahouse), Collector (teapots), Grandmother (of Sophie Taylor); Sophie Taylor, Granddaughter (of Rose Freemont), Worker (Auntie Rose's Victorian Teahouse), Detective—Amateur; Zunia Pettigrew, Crime Victim, Appraiser
Time period(s): 21st century; 2010s
Locale(s): Butterhill, New York; Gracious Grove, New York

Summary: Sophie Taylor has adapted well to life in Gracious Grove, New York, where her grandmother, Rose Freemont, runs Auntie Rose's Victorian Teahouse. Sophie moved to picturesque Gracious Grove after her Manhattan restaurant failed. When Rose travels to Butterhill to attend a convention of the International Teapot Collectors Society, she leaves the shop in Sophie's care. Rose, an avid teapot collector, brings an antique Chinese teapot to the convention for appraisal. But when appraiser Zunia Pettigrew examines the pot, she claims it's a counterfeit. Rose is furious with Zunia, and she becomes the prime suspect when the appraiser is murdered by someone brandishing a teapot. Amateur detective Sophie must close up shop and head for the convention so she can find Zunia's killer and clear Rose's name. This novel is the second in the Teapot Collector Mystery series.

Other books by the same author:
Tempest in a Teapot, 2014
Bran New Death, 2013
A Deadly Grind, 2012
Lady Anne and the Ghost's Revenge, 2009
Lady Anne and the Howl in the Dark, 2009

Other books you might like:
Laura Childs, *Death by Darjeeling*, 2001
Laura Childs, *Steeped in Evil*, 2014
Yasmine Galenorn, *Ghost of a Chance*, 2003
Larry Karp, *The Music Box Murders*, 1999
Deborah Morgan, *Death Is a Cabaret*, 2001
J.B. Stanley, *A Killer Collection*, 2006
Sebastian Stuart, *To the Manor Dead*, 2010

522

TOM COOPER

The Marauders

(New York: Crown, 2015)

Story type: Contemporary; Post-Disaster
Subject(s): Disasters; Neighborhoods; Swamps
Major character(s): Gus Lindquist, Narrator, Addict, Scavenger (treasure hunter); Wes Trench, Fisherman (shrimper), Narrator; Brady Grimes, Narrator, Lawyer
Time period(s): 21st century; 2010s
Locale(s): Jeannette, Louisiana

Summary: The BP oil spill that devastated the Gulf Coast in 2010 has resonating effects among the population of Jeannette, Louisiana. This novel explores the sentiments and traditions of the bayou as people struggle to survive both the lingering effects of Hurricane Katrina and the oil disaster. Gus Lundquist is a one-armed loner who wanders around the swamps with his metal detector while popping pain pills. He is determined to find the long-lost treasure of the pirate Jean Lafitte. His efforts place him in the sights of twin brothers who have a carefully hidden pot farm deep in the bayou. The brothers are also being watched, by of two petty criminals who are determined to gain control of the farm. Wes Trench has followed in his father's footsteps as a shrimp fisherman. Since the spill just about wiped out the shrimping industry, he is no longer sure of his occupation. Brady Grimes, a former resident of Jeannette who now works for BP, is also traveling the bayou. He was ordered to convince locals to accept small settlements in exchange for signing away the right to sue the company in the future. First novel.

Other books you might like:
Ace Atkins, *Crossroad Blues*, 1998
James Lee Burke, *The Neon Rain*, 1987
Carl Hiaasen, *Double Whammy*, 1987
Jonathon King, *The Blue Edge of Midnight*, 2002
Elmore Leonard, *Maximum Bob*, 1991
Dick Lochte, *Blue Bayou*, 1992
Daniel Woodrell, *Under the Bright Lights*, 1986

523

ISIS CRAWFORD (Pseudonym of Barbara Block)

A Catered Mother's Day

(New York: Kensington, 2015)

Series: Mystery with Recipes Series. Book 11
Story type: Cozy Mystery; Series
Subject(s): Mystery; Detective fiction; Crime
Major character(s): Bernie Simmons, Friend (of Ellen Hadley), Detective—Amateur, Woman, Baker, Sister (of Libby Simmons); Libby Simmons, Woman, Baker, Sister (of Bernie), Detective—Amateur, Friend (of Ellen Hadley); Ellen Hadley, Businesswoman (makes pet treats), Spouse (of Bruce), Mother (of Ryan and Ethan), Friend (of Bernie and Libby), Crime Suspect; Bruce Hadley, Spouse (of Ellen), Father (of Ryan and Ethan); Ryan Hadley, Son (of Ellen and Bruce); Ethan Hadley, Son (of Ellen and Bruce)
Time period(s): 21st century; 2010s
Locale(s): Longley, New York

Summary: Ellen Hadley runs a successful pet treat company with little help from her husband, Bruce, and unappreciative sons, Ethan and Ryan. While Ellen juggles her business and the housework, the boys fail to acknowledge her birthday, and Bruce forgets their anniversary. Ellen's friend Bernie suggests jokingly that Ellen should stage her own kidnapping as a wake-up call to her husband and sons. Bernie, who operates A Little Taste of Heaven Bakery with her sister, Libby, forgets about the conversation until Ellen calls on her for help. Apparently Ellen hid out at a remote motel and sent a phony ransom note to Bruce. But the motel room contained a corpse, and by the time Bruce arrived, Ellen was under arrest for murder. The police are not impressed with Ellen's explanation of how she came to be at the crime scene. Bernie and Libby put their Mother's Day preparations on hold so they can do some sleuthing and prove Ellen's innocence. This novel is the 11th in the Mystery with Recipes series.

Other books by the same author:
A Catered Fourth of July, 2014
A Catered Valentine's Day, 2007
A Catered Christmas, 2005
A Catered Wedding, 2004
A Catered Murder, 2003

Other books you might like:
Lucy Burdette, *An Appetite for Murder*, 2012
Diane Mott Davidson, *Catering to Nobody*, 1990
Diane Mott Davidson, *The Whole Enchilada: A Novel of Suspense*, 2013
Jerrilyn Farmer, *Sympathy for the Devil*, 1998
Tim Hemlin, *If Wishes Were Horses . . .*, 1996
Cathie John, *Add One Dead Critic: A Kate Cavanaugh Culinary Mystery*, 1998
Cynthia Lawrence, *Take-Out City*, 1993

524

SUSAN CRAWFORD

The Pocket Wife

(New York: William Morrow, 2015)

Story type: Psychological
Subject(s): Mystery; Detective fiction; Murder
Major character(s): Dana Catrell, Woman, Mentally Ill Person (bipolar disorder), Spouse (of Peter), Mother (of Jamie), Friend (of Celia Steinhauser); Peter Catrell, Lawyer, Spouse (of Dana), Father (of Jamie); Jamie Catrell, Student—College, Son (of Dana and Peter); Celia Steinhauser, Friend (of Dana), Spouse (of Ronald), Crime Victim, Teacher (of Kyle); Ronald Steinhauser, Spouse (of Celia); Jack Moss, Detective—Police, Father (of Kyle); Kyle, Son (of Jack), Student (of Celia)
Time period(s): 21st century; 2010s
Locale(s): Paterson, New Jersey

Summary: When Dana Catrell wakes to the sounds of sirens in her Paterson, New Jersey, neighborhood, she knows something is very wrong. She soon learns that her friend and neighbor, Celia Steinhauser, has been murdered. Dana is unsettled by the news, especially because she thinks she could have had something to do with Celia's death. Dana has bipolar disorder and hasn't been taking her medication. She remembers arguing with Celia, but she can't say for sure what happened after that. Although she doesn't believe she's a killer, Dana begins her own investigation into what really happened in the Steinhauser house. Dana isn't the only suspicious character who has connections to the case, however. Dana's husband, Peter, is acting strangely. And the detective assigned to the case, Jack Moss, is troubled by the fact that his son knew the victim. Dana's deteriorating mental health impedes her search for answers. First novel.

Other books you might like:
Sophie Hannah, *The Truth-Teller's Lie*, 2007
A.S.A. Harrison, *The Silent Wife*, 2013
Elizabeth Haynes, *Into the Darkest Corner*, 2012
Alice LaPlante, *Turn of Mind*, 2011
Pam Lewis, *Speak Softly, She Can Hear*, 2005
Chevy Stevens, *Still Missing*, 2010
S.J. Watson, *Before I Go To Sleep*, 2011

525

JESSIE CROCKETT

A Sticky Situation

(New York: Berkley, 2015)

Series: Sugar Grove Mystery Series. Book 3
Story type: Contemporary; Cozy Mystery
Subject(s): Mystery; Detective fiction; Crime
Major character(s): Dani Greene, Woman, Artisan (syrup maker), Niece (of Hazel), Detective—Amateur; Hazel, Aunt (of Dani); Russ Collins, Contractor; Spooner Duffy, Missing Person, Drifter
Time period(s): 21st century; 2010s
Locale(s): Sugar Grove, New Hampshire

Summary: The Greene family has been producing maple syrup in Sugar Grove, New Hampshire, for four generations. Dani, her siblings, and other relatives are currently getting ready for the town's yearly Maple Festival. The Greenes are also working on the restoration of the local opera house, although Dani is not impressed with the progress contractor Russ Collins is making. Dani is tired of hearing about the problems Russ encounters, but the latest snag can't be ignored. Russ has found the corpse of Spooner Duffy on the site. Spooner disappeared from town years ago—allegedly with funds from the town's coffers, and presumably of his own volition. It's now apparent that Spooner never left Sugar Grove, and that one of the town's residents may be a murderer. Although the Greenes have enough to worry about, a new challenge arrives in the form of Aunt Hazel. This novel is the third in the Sugar Grove Mystery series.

Other books by the same author:
Maple Mayhem, 2014

Drizzled with Death, 2013
Live Free or Die, 2010

Other books you might like:
Judy Clemens, *Till the Cows Come Home*, 2004
Sheila Connolly, *One Bad Apple: An Orchard Mystery*, 2008
Felicia Donovan, *The Black Widow Agency*, 2007
B.B. Haywood, *Town in a Blueberry Jam*, 2010
Hannah Reed, *Buzz Off*, 2010
Paige Shelton, *Farm Fresh Murder*, 2010
Nancy Means Wright, *Mad Season*, 1996

526

ELLEN CROSBY

Ghost Image

(New York: Scribner, 2015)

Series: Sophie Medina Mystery Series. Book 2
Story type: Contemporary; Series
Subject(s): Mystery; Detective fiction; Crime
Major character(s): Sophie Medina, Photojournalist, Friend (of Brother Kevin Boyle); Kevin Boyle, Religious (Franciscan friar), Scientist (environmental), Friend (of Sophie Medina), Crime Victim
Time period(s): 21st century; 2010s
Locale(s): London, England; Washington, District of Columbia

Summary: Brother Kevin Boyle, a Franciscan friar and environmental scientist, is a close friend of photojournalist Sophie Medina. Not long after Boyle hints to Sophie that he has made a significant find in the field of botany, he is murdered in the garden of his Washington, DC, monastery. Boyle had also told Sophie that he was being followed. When Sophie discovers her friend's body, she realizes his concerns were just. Although she has few clues to guide her, Sophie is determined to find Boyle's killer. When she searches Boyle's apartment, she finds an antiquated botany book that leads her to London. As she makes her way to Europe and then back to the States, Sophie comes to realize the significance of Boyle's discovery and why someone wanted him dead. Now she just has to figure out which of her suspects is Boyle's killer. This novel is the second in the Sophie Medina Mystery series.

Other books by the same author:
Multiple Exposure, 2013
The Sauvignon Secret, 2011
The Chardonnay Charade, 2007
The Merlot Murders, 2006
Moscow Nights, 2000

Other books you might like:
Jo Bannister, *Shards*, 1990
Meredith Cole, *Posed for Murder*, 2009
Tom Corcoran, *The Mango Opera*, 1998
Robert Eversz, *Shooting Elvis*, 1996
Alison Gaylin, *Trashed*, 2007
Elizabeth Hand, *Generation Loss*, 2007
Kerry Tucker, *Still Waters*, 1991

527

ANNETTE DASHOFY

Bridges Burned

(Plano, Texas: Henery Press, 2015)

Series: Zoe Chambers Series. Book 3
Story type: Contemporary; Series
Subject(s): Mystery; Detective fiction; Crime
Major character(s): Zoe Chambers, Health Care Professional (paramedic); Pete Adams, Police Officer (chief); Holt Farabee, Father (of Maddie), Widow(er); Maddie Farabee, 10-Year-Old, Daughter (of Holt Farabee)
Time period(s): 21st century; 2010s
Locale(s): Monongahela County, Pennsylvania

Summary: Zoe Chambers works as a paramedic in Vance Township, Pennsylvania. She has witnessed her share of tragedy, but she is especially affected by a fire that kills a wife and mother in a new housing development. In the aftermath, Holt Farabee is left a widower and the lone caregiver to his ten-year-old daughter, Maddie. Although police chief Pete Adams doesn't approve, Zoe invites Holt and Maddie to stay with her while they regain their footing. Pete does some digging and finds out that Holt, who was seen trying to save his wife from the fire, may not be a saint after all. In fact, he may be a killer. Pete tries to convince Zoe that she's in danger, but she refuses to believe him. When Zoe finally accepts the truth about Holt, it may be too late. This novel is the third in the Zoe Chambers series.

Other books by the same author:
Circle of Influence, 2014
Lost Legacy, 2014

Other books you might like:
Terri L. Austin, *Diners, Dives and Dead Ends*, 2012
Christine Barber, *The Replacement Child*, 2008
Judy Clemens, *Till the Cows Come Home*, 2004
Jim Lavene, *That Old Flame of Mine*, 2013
Hannah Miller, *In Dutch Again*, 2002
Tamar Myers, *Too Many Crooks Spoil the Broth*, 1994
Kathryn O'Sullivan, *Foal Play*, 2012

528

JANET DAWSON

Cold Trail

(Palo Alto, California: Perseverance Press, 2015)

Series: Jeri Howard Series. Book 11
Story type: Contemporary; Private Detective
Subject(s): Mystery; Detective fiction; Crime
Major character(s): Jeri Howard, Woman, Detective—Private, Brother (of Brian Howard); Brian Howard, Missing Person, Crime Suspect, Teacher, Spouse (of Sheila), Brother (of Jeri Howard); Sheila Howard, Spouse (of Brian Howard)
Time period(s): 21st century; 2010s
Locale(s): California, United States

Summary: California private detective Jeri Howard investigates the disappearance of her brother in the 11th series entry. Jeri doesn't even know that her brother, Brian, is missing until she is contacted by the Sonoma County coroner. Brian's medical alert bracelet has been found with a burned corpse, and Jeri must identify the body. The dead man, who was shot before he was burned, isn't Brian, but the news is not all good. The presence of Brian's bracelet makes Jeri's brother a suspect in the murder. Jeri begins her investigation with Brian's wife, Sheila, who tells Jeri that Brian left several days ago to go hiking and never came back. Sheila also reveals that she and Brian had been having marital problems. As she searches for answers, Jeri learns that Brian was also having professional problems in his work as a teacher. Jeri apparently doesn't know her brother as well as she thinks she does. This makes the task of finding him and proving his innocence more difficult.

Other books by the same author:
Death Rides the Zephyr, 2013
Bit Player, 2011
Scam and Eggs, 2002
Till the Old Men Die, 1993
Kindred Crimes, 1990

Other books you might like:
Linda Barnes, *A Trouble of Fools*, 1987
Sue Grafton, *"A" Is for Alibi*, 1982
Marcia Muller, *The Cheshire Cat's Eye*, 1983
Diana Orgain, *Bundle of Trouble*, 2009
Sara Paretsky, *Indemnity Only*, 1982
Elizabeth Atwood Taylor, *The Cable Car Murder*, 1981
Gloria White, *Murder on the Run*, 1991

529

JEANNETTE DE BEAUVOIR

Asylum

(New York: Minotaur Books, 2015)

Story type: Contemporary; Serial Killer
Subject(s): Mystery; Detective fiction; Crime
Major character(s): Martine LeDuc, Public Relations (Montreal mayor's office); Julian Fletcher, Detective—Police; Francois Desrocher, Director (Montreal Police Department); Richard Rousseau, Colleague (of Martine LeDuc), Boyfriend (of Danielle Leroux); Danielle Leroux, Librarian, Girlfriend (of Richard Rousseau), Crime Victim
Time period(s): 21st century; 2010s
Locale(s): Montreal, Quebec

Summary: A serial killer is threatening lives and putting a damper on the tourist season in Montreal. Three women have been murdered and raped, and their naked bodies have been displayed on city park benches. When a fourth victim, research librarian Danielle Leroux, is killed, Martine LeDuc, the mayor's public relations director, joins the effort to stop the spree. Working with police detective Julian Fletcher, Martine quickly gets a handle on the case and discovers a connection between the four seemingly unrelated victims. All have ties to a mental asylum that operated in Montreal in the 1950s. The facility used orphaned children in horrifying psychiatric experiments that included electroshock and drug therapies. The government made amends to the survivors long ago, but obviously someone has not forgotten the heinous incident. Martine's investigation leads her to the steam tunnels beneath the site of the former asylum, where she meets the killer and almost becomes his next victim.

Other books by the same author:
Murder Most Academic, 2013
Assignment: Nepal, 2011
The Illusionist, 2000

Other books you might like:
John Farrow, *City of Ice*, 1999
Tess Gerritsen, *The Bone Garden*, 2007
Lene Kaaberbol, *The Boy in the Suitcase*, 2011
Alex Marwood, *The Wicked Girls*, 2012
Louise Penny, *The Beautiful Mystery*, 2012
Kathy Reichs, *Cross Bones*, 2005
Kathy Reichs, *Deja Dead*, 1997

530

ELISABETH DE MARIAFFI

The Devil You Know

(New York: Touchstone, 2015)

Story type: Amateur Detective
Subject(s): Mystery; Detective fiction; Crime
Major character(s): Evie Jones, Young Woman (in her twenties), Friend (of David Patton), Journalist (newspaper reporter); David Patton, Friend (of Evie); Lianne Gagnon, Crime Victim (murdered), Friend (deceased, of Evie and David); Robert Nelson Cameron, Crime Suspect
Time period(s): 20th century; 1990s (1993)
Locale(s): Toronto, Ontario

Summary: Evie Jones works as a crime reporter at the *Toronto Free Press*, but she still suffers the effects of a murder that touched her personally. Eleven years ago, in 1982, Evie's then best friend Lianne Gagnon, age 11, was raped and killed. Robert Nelson Cameron was named as the suspect, but he was never apprehended. Evie lives with the constant fear that Lianne's killer will return and target her. She sometimes sees a strange man watching her, but Evie isn't sure if he's real or a product of her anxious imagination. When a work assignment leads Evie to cold case files, she opens her own investigation into Lianne's death. With help from her old friend, David Patton, Evie begins to put the pieces of the case together. They are shocked when they realize Cameron may be innocent after all. First novel.

Other books by the same author:
How to Get Along with Women, 2012

Other books you might like:
Peter Abrahams, *End of Story*, 2006
Linwood Barclay, *No Time for Goodbye*, 2007
Gillian Flynn, *Sharp Objects*, 2006
Alison Gaylin, *And She Was*, 2012
A.S.A. Harrison, *The Silent Wife*, 2013
Caroline Kepnes, *You*, 2014

Laura Lippman, *Hush Hush*, 2015
Alex Marwood, *The Wicked Girls*, 2012
Minette Walters, *The Sculptress*, 1993

531

JEFFREY DEAVER

Solitude Creek

(New York: Grand Central Publishing, 2015)

Series: Kathryn Dance Series. Book 4
Subject(s): Suspense; Crime; Detective fiction
Major character(s): Kathryn Dance, Agent (California Bureau of Investigation)
Time period(s): 21st century; 2010s
Locale(s): California, United States

Summary: California Bureau of Investigation agent Kathryn Dance searches for a uniquely dangerous killer in the fourth series entry. The perpetrator Kathryn is looking for didn't kill with a gun or a bomb. He incited panic among a crowd of concertgoers about a nonexistent fire, and then barred the doors so people would be trampled to death. This twisted murderer has learned how to claim lives by using fear and the power of suggestion to his advantage. The attack at the concert is just the first of many killings the assailant has planned. Kathryn must figure out which location he'll target next before another deadly mass panic is set in motion.

Other books by the same author:
XO, 2012
Roadside Crosses, 2009
The Sleeping Doll, 2007
Garden of Beasts, 2004
The Bone Collector, 1997

Other books you might like:
Robin Burcell, *Every Move She Makes*, 1999
Lincoln Child, *The Forgotten Room*, 2015
Robert Crais, *Demolition Angel*, 2000
Robert Ellis, *City of Fire*, 2007
Dianne Emley, *The First Cut: A Novel*, 2006
Rochelle Majer Krich, *Fair Game*, 1993
Carol O'Connell, *Mallory's Oracle*, 1994
T. Jefferson Parker, *The Blue Hour*, 1999
James Patterson, *Hope to Die*, 2014
Douglas Preston, *Blue Labyrinth*, 2014
John Sandford, *Deadline*, 2014

532

HANNAH DENNISON

Deadly Desires at Honeychurch Hall

(New York: Minotaur Books, 2015)

Series: Honeychurch Hall Mystery Series. Book 2
Story type: Cozy Mystery; Series
Subject(s): Mystery; Detective fiction; Crime
Major character(s): Kat Stanford, Daughter (of Iris),

Detective—Amateur, Television Personality (formerly of *Fakes and Treasures*), Antiques Dealer; Iris Stanford, Widow(er), Mother (of Kat), Writer (also known as Krystalle Storm); Valentine Prince-Avery, Consultant (Department of Transport); Trudy Wynne, Journalist (tabloid)

Time period(s): 21st century; 2010s
Locale(s): Little Dipperton, Devon

Summary: Kat Stanford, formerly of the television antiques show *Fakes and Treasures*, now lives in Little Dipperton, Devon, with her mother, Iris. Without consulting Kat, Iris sold the family home in London and purchased a carriage house on the grounds of the grand estate Honeychurch Hall. There, Iris pursues her clandestine career as the romance writer Krystalle Storm, and Kat continues her work in the antiques trade—when she isn't solving local murders, that is. When Kat and her mother meet Valentine Prince-Avery, a visitor who claims to be in town for an auction, they quickly discover the real reason for his presence in Little Dipperton. Valentine, a consultant for the Department of Transport, is assessing the area for the construction of a high-speed rail line. Kat is soon investigating another murder, and realizes many suspects wanted a representative from the Department of Transport dead. As Kat searches for a killer, tabloid reporter Trudy Wynne looks for a story that will ruin Kat and Iris.

Other books by the same author:
Accused!, 2015
Murder at Honeychurch Hall, 2014
Expose!, 2009
Scoop!, 2009
A Vicky Hill Exclusive!, 2008

Other books you might like:
M.C. Beaton, *Agatha Raisin and the Quiche of Death*, 1992
Agatha Christie, *The Mysterious Affair at Styles*, 1921
Carola Dunn, *Death at Wentwater Court*, 1994
Julie Hyzy, *Grace Under Pressure*, 2010
Ngaio Marsh, *Last Ditch*, 1977
Dorothy L. Sayers, *Clouds of Witness*, 1925
Minette Walters, *The Ice House*, 1992

533

BRUCE DESILVA

A Scourge of Vipers

(New York: Forge Books, 2015)

Series: Liam Mulligan Series. Book 4
Story type: Contemporary; Series
Subject(s): Mystery; Detective fiction; Crime
Major character(s): Liam Mulligan, Journalist (investigative, *The Providence Dispatch*); Charles Twisdale, Editor (*The Providence Dispatch*); Fiona McNerney, Political Figure (governor of Rhode Island); Dominic "Whoosh" Zerelli, Gambler (bookmaker)
Time period(s): 21st century; 2010s
Locale(s): Providence, Rhode Island

Summary: Investigative reporter Liam Mulligan continues his struggle against the mores of 21st-century newspaper

journalism in the fourth series entry. Now that General Communications Holdings International owns *The Providence Dispatch*, the reporting of hard news is less important than accommodating advertisers and making profits. Mulligan is one of the last members of the staff interested in getting the story and making a difference. When Rhode Island's governor, Fiona McNerney, suggests the state legalize sports gambling to remedy budget woes, Mulligan's editor gives the story low priority, so Mulligan investigates on his own. The organized crime community wants to kill the proposal, which would eat into their bookmaking profits, and sports organizations fear the effect legalized gambling would have on the integrity of their games. Interested parties come to Providence prepared to persuade legislators with cash. Murders occur, and Mulligan investigates, but he ends up becoming a suspect.

Other books by the same author:
Providence Rag, 2014
Cliff Walk, 2012
Rogue Island, 2010

Other books you might like:
Mark Arsenault, *Gravewriter*, 2006
Thomas Gately Briody, *Rogue's Isles*, 1995
Jan Brogan, *A Confidential Source*, 2005
Eric Dezenhall, *Money Wanders*, 2002
Laura Lippman, *Baltimore Blues*, 1997
Karen E. Olson, *Sacred Cows*, 2005
Howard Owen, *Oregon Hill*, 2012

534

CHRISTINE DESMET

Five-Alarm Fudge

(New York: Penguin Publishing Group, 2015)

Series: Fudge Shop Mystery Series. Book 3
Story type: Contemporary; Cozy Mystery
Subject(s): Mystery; Detective fiction; Crime
Major character(s): Ava Oosterling, Cook (fudge maker), Store Owner, Friend (of Pauline Mertens and Laura Rousseau), Detective—Amateur; Pauline Mertens, Friend (of Ava Oosterling); Laura Rousseau, Friend (of Ava Oosterling); Arnaud Van Damme, Royalty (prince from Belgium), Son (of Amandine); Amandine Van Damme, Royalty (princess from Belgium), Mother (of Arnaud)
Time period(s): 21st century; 2010s
Locale(s): Fishers' Harbor, Wisconsin

Summary: In the third novel in the Fudge Shop Mystery series, Ava Oosterling—proprietor of Oosterlings' Live Bait, Bobbers & Belgian Fudge & Beer—is searching a church attic for a missing recipe. Belgium's Prince Arnaud Van Damme and his mother, Princess Amandine, are coming to Fishers' Harbor, Wisconsin, for the yearly harvest festival, and Ava wants to have a special treat on hand. The old family recipe for the divine white fudge is supposedly hidden in the church, and Ava convinces her friends Pauline Mertens and Laura Rousseau to help with the hunt. But when a fire strikes the historic building, another secret is exposed—the body of a murdered man. Are the murder and the missing fudge recipe related? Ava plays amateur detective to find answers and a killer, but she puts her own life in danger in the process.

Other books by the same author:
Hot Fudge Frame-Up, 2014
First-Degree Fudge, 2013
Mischief in Moonstone, 2008
Spirit Lake, 2000
Men of Moonstone Series, 2009-

Other books you might like:
Avery Aames, *The Long Quiche Goodbye*, 2010
Jessica Beck, *Glazed Murder*, 2010
JoAnna Carl, *The Chocolate Cat Caper*, 2002
Sammi Carter, *Candy Apple Dead*, 2005
Joanne Fluke, *Chocolate Chip Cookie Murder*, 2000
Connie Shelton, *Sweet Masterpiece*, 2010
Wendy Lyn Watson, *I Scream, You Scream*, 2009

535

LAURA DISILVERIO

The Readaholics and the Falcon Fiasco

(New York: Penguin Publishing Group, 2015)

Series: Book Club Mystery Series. Book 1
Story type: Contemporary; Cozy Mystery
Subject(s): Mystery; Detective fiction; Crime
Major character(s): Amy-Faye Johnson, Planner (events), Leader (Readaholics book club), Girlfriend (former, of Doug Elvaston), Detective—Amateur; Doug Elvaston, Boyfriend (former, of Amy-Faye Johnson), Fiance(e) (of Madison Taylor); Madison Taylor, Lawyer, Fiance(e) (of Doug Elvaston), Client (of Amy-Faye); Ivy, Friend (of Amy-Faye), Crime Victim
Time period(s): 21st century; 2010s
Locale(s): Heaven, Colorado

Summary: The first novel in the Book Club Mystery series introduces Amy-Faye Johnson, an event planner and member of the Readaholics book club. Amy-Faye lives in Heaven, Colorado, near her parents. She is meeting with her new client—bride-to-be Madison Taylor—when she gets an unpleasant surprise. Madison's fiance is Amy-Faye's former boyfriend, Doug Elvaston. The situation is awkward, but Amy-Faye soon has other things to worry about. Her friend Ivy, who is also a member of the mystery-loving Readaholics, dies unexpectedly, and Amy-Faye disagrees when the death is ruled a suicide. Amy-Faye believes someone poisoned Ivy deliberately, and she launches her own investigation to find the truth. But as Amy-Faye digs into Ivy's personal life, she realizes that Ivy had enemies who might want her dead. Amy-Faye draws on her knowledge of literary detectives to find the killer and protect her own life.

Other books by the same author:
All Sales Fatal, 2012
Swift Run, 2012
Die Buying, 2011
Swift Edge, 2011

Swift Justice, 2010

Other books you might like:
Sammi Carter, *Candy Apple Dead*, 2005
Diane Mott Davidson, *Catering to Nobody*, 1990
Jo Dereske, *Miss Zukas and the Library Murders*, 1994
John Dunning, *Booked to Die*, 1992
Jerrilyn Farmer, *Sympathy for the Devil*, 1998
Beth Groundwater, *A Real Basket Case*, 2007
Maggie Sefton, *Knit One, Kill Two*, 2005

536

CLAIRE DONALLY

Hiss and Tell

(New York: Berkley, 2015)

Series: Sunny and Shadow Mystery Series. Book 4
Story type: Cozy Mystery; Series
Subject(s): Mystery; Detective fiction; Crime
Major character(s): Sunny Coolidge, Detective—Amateur, Journalist, Girlfriend (of Will Price); Will Price, Police Officer (constable), Boyfriend (of Sunny Coolidge); Priscilla Kingsbury, Heiress, Fiance(e) (of Carson de Kruk); Carson de Kruk, Fiance(e) (of Priscilla Kingsbury), Son (of Augustus de Kruk); Augustus de Kruk, Businessman, Wealthy, Father (of Carson de Kruk); Shadow, Cat
Time period(s): 21st century; 2010s
Locale(s): Kittery Harbor, Maine

Summary: When journalist Sunny Coolidge moved from New York City to Kittery Harbor, Maine, she didn't anticipate covering many crime stories. But so far the town has produced more than its share of murder cases. In this fourth novel in the Sunny and Shadow Mystery series, Sunny is drawn into another criminal investigation. This one is connected to a high-profile wedding that was set to take place in the coastal town. The bride- and groom-to-be are heiress Priscilla Kingsbury and the wealthy Carson de Kruk. The discovery of a dead body puts a damper on the festivities, however, even though the cause of death is ruled accidental. Sunny is skeptical and, with assistance from her police constable boyfriend, Will Price, and inquisitive cat, Shadow, she conducts her own investigation.

Other books by the same author:
Last Licks, 2014
Cat Nap, 2013
The Big Kitty, 2012
Celebrity Sudoku, 2010
Death by Sudoku, 2007

Other books you might like:
Lorna Barrett, *Murder Is Binding*, 2008
Lilian Jackson Braun, *The Cat Who Could Read Backwards*, 1966
Rita Mae Brown, *Wish You Were Here*, 1990
Carole Nelson Douglas, *Catnap*, 1992
Miranda James, *Murder Past Due*, 2010
Shirley Rousseau Murphy, *Cat on the Edge*, 1996

Clea Simon, *Mew is for Murder*, 2005

537

ELIZABETH J. DUNCAN

Slated for Death

(New York: Minotaur Books, 2015)

Series: Penny Brannigan Series. Book 6
Story type: Cozy Mystery; Series
Subject(s): Mystery; Detective fiction; Crime
Major character(s): Penny Brannigan, Businesswoman (spa owner), Colleague (of Victoria Hopkirk), Detective—Amateur; Victoria Hopkirk, Businesswoman (spa owner), Colleague (of Penny Brannigan); Glenda Roberts, Leader (organizer of St. David's Day concert), Daughter (of Doreen), Mother (of Peris), Sister (of Rebeccah), Crime Victim; Doreen, Aged Person, Mother (of Glenda and Rebeccah); Peris, Son (of Glenda); Rebeccah, Daughter (of Doreen), Sister (of Glenda); Gareth Davies, Detective—Police
Time period(s): 21st century; 2010s
Locale(s): Llanelen, Wales

Summary: In the sixth novel in the Penny Brannigan Mystery series, the Wales town of Llanelen is preparing for the annual St. David's Day concert. Glenda Roberts is in charge of the event, which is to be held in a local slate mine that has been transformed into a tourist attraction. When Glenda's corpse is discovered in the mine, the local authorities begin a murder investigation. Penny Brannigan, who owns the popular Llanelen Spa with Victoria Hopkirk, takes over for Glenda because the town simply cannot afford to cancel the concert. As Penny carries on with the concert preparations, she finds time to help her longtime admirer, DCI Gareth Davies, with his investigation into Glenda's murder. Penny looks to Glenda's surviving family members, including her elderly mother, Doreen, for clues. When Doreen dies, Penny focuses her sleuthing on the nursing home where Doreen resided. She begins to believe that the murders are rooted in the victims' family history.

Other books by the same author:
Never Laugh as a Hearse Goes By, 2013
A Small Hill to Die On, 2012
A Killer's Christmas in Wales, 2011
A Brush with Death, 2010
The Cold Light of Mourning, 2009

Other books you might like:
Nancy Atherton, *Aunt Dimity's Death*, 1992
M.C. Beaton, *Agatha Raisin and the Quiche of Death*, 1992
Rhys Bowen, *Evanly Bodies*, 2006
Rhys Bowen, *Evans Above*, 1997
Simon Brett, *The Body on the Beach*, 2000
Dorothy Cannell, *The Thin Woman*, 1984
Julie Hyzy, *Grace Under Pressure*, 2010

Alexander McCall Smith, *The Handsome Man's De Luxe Cafe*, 2014

538

CAROLA DUNN

Superfluous Women

(New York: Minotaur Books, 2015)

Series: Daisy Dalrymple Series. Book 22
Story type: Historical; Series
Subject(s): Mystery; Detective fiction; Crime
Major character(s): Daisy Dalrymple, Journalist, Spouse (of Alec Fletcher), Detective—Amateur, Friend (of Willie Chandler); Alec Fletcher, Detective—Police (detective inspector), Spouse (of Daisy); Wilhelmina "Willie" Chandler, Accountant, Friend (of Daisy), Roommate (housemate of Isabel Sutcliffe, Vera Leighton); Isabel Sutcliffe, Roommate (housemate of Willie Chandler, Vera Leighton); Vera Leighton, Roommate (housemate Willie Chandler, Isabel Sutcliffe); Mrs. Gray, Landowner (former owner of Cherry Trees), Crime Victim
Time period(s): 20th century; 1920s (1927)
Locale(s): Beaconsfield, England

Summary: In 1927 a noxious fog prompts journalist Daisy Dalrymple to spend some time at the country home of her friend, Wilhelmina "Willie" Chandler. Willie lives at Cherry Trees with Vera Leighton and Isabel Sutcliffe, two women whose marriage prospects have been greatly diminished by the Great War. When Daisy's husband, Scotland Yard detective Alec Fletcher, comes to dinner at Cherry Trees, he agrees to break into the locked cellar to look for wine. But instead of a delightful vintage, Alec finds a corpse. The dead woman is most likely Mrs. Gray, the former owner of Cherry Trees. But who killed her—and why? Willie, Vera, and Isabel become suspects, and Alec agrees to help the local authorities with the murder investigation. Amateur detective Daisy assists, too, and she manages to dig up many of the old manor house's secrets. This novel is the 22nd in the Daisy Dalrymple series.

Other books by the same author:
Heirs of the Body, 2013
Manna from Hades, 2009
The Winter Garden Mystery, 1995
Death at Wentwater Court, 1994
Miss Hartwell's Dilemma, 1989

Other books you might like:
Rhys Bowen, *Her Royal Spyness*, 2007
Simon Brett, *Blotto, Twinks and the Ex-King's Daughter*, 2011
Agatha Christie, *The Secret Adversary*, 1922
Jill Churchill, *Anything Goes*, 1999
Kerry Greenwood, *Cocaine Blues*, 1987
Catriona McPherson, *After the Armistice Ball*, 2005
Jacqueline Winspear, *Maisie Dobbs*, 2003

Mystery

539

KATE DYER-SEELEY

Slayed on the Slopes

(New York: Kensington, 2015)

Series: Pacific Northwest Series. Book 2
Story type: Amateur Detective; Series
Subject(s): Mystery; Detective fiction; Crime
Major character(s): Meg Reed, Journalist (*Northwest Extreme* magazine); Greg Dixon, Editor (*Northwest Extreme* magazine); Ben Rogers, Rescuer (Ridge Ranger), Crime Victim
Time period(s): 21st century; 2010s
Locale(s): Oregon, United States

Summary: Meg Reed wasn't exactly honest when she applied for a writing job at *Northwest Extreme* magazine. She convinced editor Greg Dixon that she was an outdoorswoman and proved her journalistic dedication and sleuthing skills on her first assignment at Angel's Rest. Now she is at the Silcox Hut on Mount Hood to do a story on the Ridge Rangers, a mountain rescue team. The Rangers are gathering for a winter training session, but Meg doesn't plan on getting involved in any of their adventures. Meg's visions of a relaxing retreat in a mountain lodge are shattered by a violent snowstorm and the sound of gunfire. When the frigid corpse of Ben Rogers, one of the Rangers, is found outside, Meg knows she must play detective again. A killer is with them on the mountain, and he or she may not be satisfied with just one victim. This is the second title of the Pacific Northwest series.

Other books by the same author:
Scene of the Climb, 2014

Other books you might like:
Shannon Baker, *Tainted Mountain*, 2013
Joan Bartlett, *Nice Shows*, 2000
Nancy Bush, *Candy Apple Red*, 2005
Lynn Cahoon, *Guidebook to Murder*, 2014
Mary Daheim, *The Alpine Advocate*, 1992
Mary Daheim, *The Alpine Yeoman*, 2014
April Henry, *Circles of Confusion*, 1999

540

KEVIN EGAN

The Missing Piece

(New York: Forge Books, 2015)

Story type: Legal
Subject(s): Mystery; Law; Trials
Major character(s): Oliver Johnstone, Judge; Linda Conover, Judge; Gary Martin, Lawman (court officer), Crime Victim, Handicapped; Foxx, Lawman (court officer); Mike McQueen, Lawman (court officer); Ivan Zoltar, Worker (custodian); Paul Douglas Leonard White, Nobleman (Earl of Leinster)
Time period(s): 21st century; 2010s
Locale(s): New York, New York

Summary: It's been three years since gunmen barged into Judge Oliver Johnstone's courtroom and stole a valuable silver urn. The artifact was part of the ancient Roman trove known as the Salvus Treasure, and Johnstone was supposed to decide who should have rightful ownership—Croatia, Hungary, or Paul Douglas Leonard White, the Earl of Leinster. Gary Martin, a court officer, was paralyzed by one of the gunmen's bullets, and the hearing ended in a mistrial. Now Judge Linda Conover, Johnstone's former clerk, is hearing the case. Ownership of the Salvus Treasure still hasn't been determined, and the missing urn has not been recovered. As Judge Conover presides over the court proceedings, the New York County Courthouse is steeped in intrigue. Martin, whose life was changed by the courtroom attack, believes the priceless urn is hidden somewhere in the building. Others connected to the case have their own theories.

Other books by the same author:
Midnight, 2013
Outside Agency, 1997
Buried Lies, 1996
Local Knowledge, 1995
The Perseus Breed, 1988

Other books you might like:
Steve Berry, *The Templar Legacy*, 2006
Dan Brown, *The Da Vinci Code*, 2003
Ian Caldwell, *The Rule of Four*, 2004
Lincoln Child, *Relic*, 1995
Chris Kuzneski, *Sign of the Cross*, 2006
Ben Mezrich, *Seven Wonders*, 2014
Arturo Perez-Reverte, *The Club Dumas*, 1997

541

HALLIE EPHRON

Night Night, Sleep Tight

(New York: William Morrow, 2015)

Story type: Historical
Subject(s): Mystery; Detective fiction; Crime
Major character(s): Deirdre Unger, Woman, Daughter (of Arthur Unger), Friend (of Joelen Nichol), Handicapped; Arthur Unger, Writer (screenwriter), Father (of Deirdre); Joelen Nichol, Friend (of Deirdre), Murderer (confessed)
Time period(s): 20th century; 1980s (1986)
Locale(s): Los Angeles, California

Summary: When Deirdre Unger travels from San Diego to her father's Hollywood home in 1986, she is shocked to find Arthur Unger dead in the swimming pool. Arthur's days as a successful screenwriter are over, and Deirdre was going to help her father prepare the house for sale. Although Deirdre initially presumes that Arthur's death was accidental, she soon begins to think otherwise. This is not the first questionable death Deirdre has been connected to. Twenty years ago, Deirdre's childhood friend, Joelen Nichol, confessed to the stabbing death of her mother's boyfriend. The killing took place after a party at the Nichols' house. Deirdre was sleeping over that night, and when Arthur was driving her home, they were involved in an accident that left Deirdre handicapped. As

Deirdre revisits the past in search of answers, she begins to realize that her father's death may be connected to the tragic events of two decades ago.

Other books by the same author:
There Was an Old Woman, 2013
Come and Find Me, 2011
Never Tell a Lie, 2009
Guilt, 2005
Amnesia, 2000

Other books you might like:
Megan Abbott, *The Song Is You*, 2007
Cheryl Crane, *The Bad Always Die Twice*, 2011
Carrie Fisher, *Postcards from the Edge*, 1987
Cliff Jahr, *Detour: A Hollywood Story*, 1988
R.T. Jordan, *Remains to be Scene*, 2007
Rochelle Majer Krich, *Blues in the Night*, 2002
Terrill Lee Lankford, *Earthquake Weather*, 2004

`542`

ALEX ERICKSON

Death by Coffee

(New York: Kensington, 2015)

Series: Bookstore Cafe Mystery Series. Book 1
Story type: Amateur Detective; Contemporary
Subject(s): Mystery; Detective fiction; Crime
Major character(s): Krissy Hancock, Store Owner (Death by Coffee bookstore cafe), Friend (of Vicki Patterson), Detective—Amateur; Vicki Patterson, Store Owner (Death by Coffee bookstore cafe), Friend (of Krissy Hancock); Brendon Lawyer, Crime Victim; Paul Dalton, Police Officer
Time period(s): 21st century; 2010s
Locale(s): Pine Hills, United States

Summary: In the first novel in the Bookstore Cafe Mystery series, best friends and California natives Krissy Hancock and Vicki Patterson move to the Midwest and open a bookstore/cafe in Pine Hills. The young women name the shop Death by Coffee in honor of Krissy's novelist father, who wrote a book of the same title. Their business gets off to a rough start, however. One of their first customers, the disagreeable Brendon Lawyer, orders a cup of coffee to go and dies soon thereafter. Brendon had a severe peanut allergy, but Krissy and Vicki are certain that their coffee wasn't the culprit. Krissy decides to put her knowledge of literary mysteries to work, and she acquaints herself with local cop Paul Dalton. She learns that several residents of Pine Hills had a grudge against Brendon—but is one of them a killer?

Other books you might like:
Laura Alden, *Murder at the PTA*, 2011
Sandra Balzo, *Uncommon Grounds*, 2004
Lorna Barrett, *Murder Is Binding*, 2008
Michael Bowen, *Washington Deceased*, 1990
Jessie Chandler, *Bingo Barge Murder*, 2011
Cleo Coyle, *On What Grounds*, 2003
Cindy Daniel, *Death Warmed Over...Coming Soon*, 2003

`543`

JOHN FARROW

The Storm Murders

(New York: Minotaur Books, 2015)

Series: Emile Cinq-Mars Series. Book 4
Story type: Police Procedural; Series
Subject(s): Mystery; Detective fiction; Crime
Major character(s): Emile Cinq-Mars, Detective—Police, Retiree, Spouse (of Sandra); Sandra, Spouse (of Emile)
Time period(s): 21st century; 2010s
Locale(s): Montreal, Quebec; New Orleans, Louisiana

Summary: Emile Cinq-Mars is a retired Montreal police detective, but he hasn't left his career behind completely. When a husband and wife are found murdered in their remote farmhouse after a major winter storm, Cinq-Mars is called in as a consultant on the puzzling case. The victims are located in different parts of the house, and each is missing a finger. Somehow the person who committed the crime managed to get away without leaving footprints in the snow. Meanwhile, the FBI is investigating similar murders in New Orleans. Cinq-Mars accepts the FBI's request to help with that case, and he travels to Louisiana with his wife, Sandra. While Sandra and Emile work together on the investigation, they find time to enjoy some of the city's sights. The case takes an unexpected turn when Sandra is kidnapped and held for ransom. This novel is the fourth in the Emile Cinq-Mars series.

Other books by the same author:
The River Burns, 2014
River City, 2011
Ice Lake, 2001
City of Ice, 1999
High Water Chants, 1977

Other books you might like:
Giles Blunt, *Forty Words for Sorrow*, 2001
Ann Cleeves, *Raven Black*, 2006
Steve Hamilton, *A Cold Day in Paradise*, 1998
Anne Holt, *1222*, 2011
Catriona McPherson, *The Day She Died*, 2014
Louise Penny, *A Fatal Grace*, 2007
Julia Spencer-Fleming, *Through the Evil Days*, 2013

`544`

TRICIA FIELDS

Firebreak

(New York: Minotaur Books, 2015)

Series: Josie Gray Mysteries Series. Book 4
Story type: Police Procedural; Series
Subject(s): Mystery; Detective fiction; Crime
Major character(s): Josie Gray, Detective—Police (chief); Otto Podowski, Police Officer; Billy Nix, Musician (country), Spouse (of Brenda); Brenda Nix, Spouse (of Billy)
Time period(s): 21st century; 2010s

Locale(s): Artemis, Texas

Summary: When fierce wildfires threaten the Texas community of Artemis, police chief Josie Gray orders an evacuation. In the aftermath of the fires, as Josie surveys the property damage in the area, she learns that one person was killed in the disaster. The body of an unidentified man is found burned in the home of country singer Billy Nix and his wife, Brenda. It's unclear why the victim was in the house while the Nixes were out of town, but Josie soon learns that the man's death was not an accident. The discovery of a syringe at the scene indicates that someone drugged the victim so he would be trapped in the house when the fire hit. Billy and Brenda Nix have an alibi, but that doesn't immediately eliminate them from Josie's list of suspects. This novel is the fourth in the Josie Gray Mysteries series.

Other books by the same author:
Wrecked, 2014
Scratchgravel Road, 2013
The Territory, 2011

Other books you might like:
Lori Armstrong, *No Mercy*, 2009
Nevada Barr, *Borderline*, 2009
Nevada Barr, *Track of the Cat*, 1993
Nancy Herndon, *Acid Bath*, 1995
Craig Johnson, *The Cold Dish*, 2005
Michael McGarrity, *Tularosa*, 1996
Terry Shames, *A Killing at Cotton Hill*, 2013

545

JOSEPH FINDER

The Fixer

(Boston, Massachusettes: Dutton Publishing, 2015)

Story type: Amateur Detective; Contemporary
Subject(s): Betrayal; Criminals; Deception
Major character(s): Rick Hoffman, Journalist (former investigative reporter), Son (of Leonard Hoffman), Man (down on his luck); Leonard Hoffman, Father (of Rick Hoffman), Aged Person (suffering from dementia); Jeff, Neighbor (of Rick), Contractor (building)
Time period(s): 21st century; 2010s
Locale(s): Boston, Massachusetts

Summary: Rick Hoffman's fiance has left him, he has been fired from his job, and he can't afford the rent on his apartment. When Rick is forced to move back into his rundown family home to save on expenses, he plans to renovate the house and sell it. The house has stood empty for almost 20 years, since Rick's father had a stroke and moved into a nursing home. The rent is free, and Rick has some unusual roommates. When Rick is trying to locate those roommates—squirrels that are running amok in the walls—he happens upon a large pile of money. Rick investigates where the money came from and whose money it is, and he uncovers secrets about his attorney father's past. He doggedly pursues the truth and follows the money trail. While inching himself closer and closer to danger with each answer, Rick realizes how far his father had gone to protect his family.

Other books by the same author:
Suspicion, 2014
Company Man, 2005
Paranoia, 2004
High Crimes, 1998
Red Carpet, 1983

Other books you might like:
Linda Barnes, *The Big Dig*, 2002
Linda Barnes, *Lie Down with the Devil*, 2008
Terry Devane, *Uncommon Justice*, 2001
Edwin O'Connor, *The Last Hurrah*, 1970
Daniel Palmer, *Helpless*, 2012
Robert B. Parker, *All Our Yesterdays*, 1994
Robert B. Parker, *Small Vices*, 1997

546

JESSICA FLETCHER (Pseudonym of Donald Bain)

Murder She Wrote: Killer in the Kitchen

(New York: Penguin Publishing Group, 2015)

Series: *Murder, She Wrote* Mystery Series. Book 43
Story type: Amateur Detective; Contemporary
Subject(s): Crime; Interpersonal relations; Murder
Major character(s): Jessica Fletcher, Writer, Detective— Amateur, Friend (of Brad and Marcie Fowler); Brad Fowler, Restaurateur (owns Leg and Claw Restaurant), Crime Suspect (accused of murder), Spouse (of Marcie); Gerard "Pepe" Lebeouf, Restaurateur (Chef), Crime Victim (stabbed in the chest with a knife); Marcie Fowler, Restaurateur (owns Leg and Claw Restaurant), Spouse (of Brad Fowler)
Time period(s): 21st century; 2010s
Locale(s): Cabot Cove, Maine

Summary: Brad and Marcie Fowler always dreamed of opening their own restaurant. Finally, their dreams are coming true. With the help of family and friends, they will be opening the Leg and Claw restaurant in Cabot Cove. But their dream doesn't include culinary competition with the likes of Gerard "Pepe" Lebeouf, a famous New York City chef who is opening a restaurant next door to the Leg and Claw. When Lebeouf ends up dead with a kitchen knife in his chest, Brad is the prime suspect. Not knowing where to turn, Brad and Marcie ask family friend and mystery writer Jessica Fletcher for help. Jessica uncovers some of Lebeouf's underhanded dealings and knows there are many people who may have wanted the chef dead. She just has to figure out which of them actually killed Lebeouf.

Other books by the same author:
Murder, She Wrote: Death of a Blue Blood, 2014
Murder, She Wrote: Brandy and Bullets, 1995
Murder, She Wrote: Rum and Razors, 1995
Murder, She Wrote: Manhattans and Murder, 1994
Murder, She Wrote: Gin and Daggers, 1989

Other books you might like:
Gilbert Adair, *The Act of Roger Murgatroyd: An Entertainment*, 2006

Agatha Christie, *The Murder at the Vicarage*, 1930
Judy Fitzwater, *Dying to Get Published*, 1998
Susan Kandel, *I Dreamed I Married Perry Mason*, 2004
Kris Neri, *Revenge of the Gypsy Queen*, 1999
Julie Smith, *True-Life Adventure*, 1985
Nicola Upson, *An Expert in Murder: A New Mystery Featuring Josephine Tey*, 2008

547

AMANDA FLOWER

The Final Reveille

(Woodbury, Minnesota: Midnight Ink, 2015)

Series: Living History Museum Mystery Series. Book 1
Story type: Amateur Detective; Series
Subject(s): Civil war; Crime; Deception
Major character(s): Kelsey Cambridge, Detective—Amateur (out to prove her innocence), Director (of Barton Farm), Crime Suspect (suspected of murdering Maxwell), Mother (of Hayden), Divorced Person; Cynthia Cherry, Businesswoman (benefactress of Barton Farms), Friend (of Kelsey), Aged Person (with deteriorating health), Administrator (of Cherry Charity Foundation); Maxwell, Nephew (of Cynthia Cherry), Heir (to Cherry Foundation), Crime Victim (murdered); Hayden, 5-Year-Old, Son (of Kelsey)
Time period(s): 21st century; 2010s
Locale(s): Barton Farms, Ohio

Summary: Kelsey Cambridge is pulling out all the stops to keep Barton Farm, the living history museum where she works as director, operating. To impress her most generous benefactress and to drum up business for Barton Farm, Kelsey has planned a long weekend of Civil War reenactments, along with the First Annual Blue and Gray Ball. The reenactment takes a murderous turn when the nephew of the benefactress, Maxwell, is found dead on the farm. Because Maxwell had recently threatened to cut funding to the museum, Kelsey becomes the prime suspect in his murder. Kelsey must battle to find the real killer or her dreams for the farm and her future will soon be history. This is the first novel in the Living History Museum Mystery series by Amanda Flower.

Other books by the same author:
Andi Unstoppable, 2015
A Plain Malice, 2014
Andi Unexpected, 2013
A Plain Death, 2012
Maid of Murder, 2010

Other books you might like:
Sheila Connolly, *Fundraising the Dead*, 2010
Kathleen Ernst, *Old World Murder*, 2010
Beth Groundwater, *Deadly Currents*, 2011
Charlotte Hinger, *Deadly Descent*, 2009
Maddy Hunter, *Alpine for You*, 2003
Karen MacInerney, *Murder on the Rocks*, 2006
G.M. Malliet, *Death of a Cozy Writer*, 2008

548

JOANNE FLUKE

Double Fudge Brownie Murder

(New York: Kensington, 2015)

Series: Hannah Swensen Series. Book 18
Story type: Contemporary; Cozy Mystery
Subject(s): Mystery; Detective fiction; Crime
Major character(s): Hannah Swensen, Baker, Sister (of Michelle and Andrea), Daughter (of Delores), Crime Suspect, Detective—Amateur; Michelle, Sister (of Hannah and Andrea), Daughter (of Delores); Andrea, Sister (of Hannah and Michelle), Daughter (of Delores); Delores, Mother (of Hannah, Michelle, and Andrea), Spouse (of Doc Knight); Doc Knight, Spouse (of Delores); Ross Barton, Filmmaker, Boyfriend (former, of Hannah)
Time period(s): 21st century; 2010s
Locale(s): Lake Eden, Minnesota; Las Vegas, Nevada

Summary: The Las Vegas wedding of Delores Swensen and Doc Knight complicates Hannah Swensen's already complicated love life in the 18th series entry. When Hannah, a bakery owner, travels from Lake Eden, Minnesota, for the ceremony, she discovers that her former flame Ross Barton is Doc's best man. Hannah returns to Lake Eden planning to sever ties with her two current love interests, but she is quickly distracted by more pressing matters. Hannah is scheduled to face vehicular homicide charges. When Hannah finds the body of the judge who was to hear the charges, the well-liked Lake Eden baker becomes a suspect in the murder. To prove her innocence to her friends and neighbors, Hannah plays detective. As she searches for a killer and a motive, Hannah juggles the attentions of her two suitors—and of Ross, who shows up in Lake Eden unexpectedly. This novel includes 28 recipes.

Other books by the same author:
Blackberry Pie Murder, 2004
Blueberry Muffin Murder, 2001
Lemon Meringue Pie Murder, 2001
Strawberry Shortcake Murder, 2001
Chocolate Chip Cookie Murder, 2000

Other books you might like:
Avery Aames, *As Gouda as Dead*, 2015
Jessica Beck, *Custard Crime*, 2014
Jacklyn Brady, *Murder Takes the Cake*, 2008
Kate Carlisle, *A Cookbook Conspiracy*, 2013
Bailey Cates, *Brownies and Broomsticks: A Magical Bakery Mystery*, 2012
Bailey Cates, *Some Enchanted Eclair: A Magical Bakery Mystery*, 2014
Laura Childs, *Eggs in a Casket*, 2014
Diane Mott Davidson, *Catering to Nobody*, 1990
Diane Mott Davidson, *The Whole Enchilada: A Novel of Suspense*, 2013
Kerry Greenwood, *Earthly Delights*, 1992
Victoria Hamilton, *Bran New Death*, 2013
Mary Ellen Hughes, *The Pickled Piper*, 2014
Julie Hyzy, *Home of the Braised*, 2014
Jenn McKinlay, *Dark Chocolate Demise*, 2015

Mystery

Jenn McKinlay, *Sprinkle with Murder*, 2010
Denise Swanson, *Dying for a Cupcake*, 2015

549

JACK FREDRICKSON

Silence the Dead

(Sutton, Surrey, England: Severn House Publishers, 2015)

Story type: Contemporary
Subject(s): Mystery; Detective fiction; Crime
Major character(s): Mac Bassett, Government Official (mayor); Betty Jo Dean, 17-Year-Old, Crime Victim (murdered 30 years ago)
Time period(s): 21st century; (2010s); Multiple Time Periods; 20th century; 1980s (1982)
Locale(s): Grand Point, Illinois

Summary: Betty Jo Dean was 17 years old when she was murdered in 1982. Now, more than three decades later, Betty Jo's body has been exhumed. Her killer was never found, and Mac Bassett—mayor of Grand Point, Illinois—wants to reopen the case. The medical examiners are shocked when they unzip the black vinyl bag in the casket and find Betty Jo's corpse dressed only in underwear. Her head is missing; a skull has been put in the bag in its place. The reopening of the murder investigation is off to an unsettling start, and Mac encounters increasing resistance as he digs deeper into the cold case. It becomes obvious that the truth was suppressed at the time of Betty Jo's death, and that someone wants to keep those secrets buried. Mac realizes the gravity of the decades-old conspiracy when new victims are claimed in the present.

Other books by the same author:
The Dead Caller from Chicago, 2013
Hunting Sweetie Rose, 2012
Honestly Dearest, You're Dead, 2009
A Safe Place for Dying, 2006

Other books you might like:
Giles Blunt, *Forty Words for Sorrow*, 2001
Truman Capote, *In Cold Blood*, 1965
Gillian Flynn, *Dark Places*, 2009
Jim Harrison, *The Great Leader*, 2011
Donald Harstad, *Eleven Days: A Novel of the Heartland*, 1998
Greg Iles, *Natchez Burning*, 2014
Alex Kava, *A Perfect Evil*, 2001

550

BRIAN FREEMAN

Season of Fear

(London: Quercus, 2014)

Series: Cab Bolton Series. Book 2
Story type: Police Procedural; Series
Subject(s): Mystery; Detective fiction; Crime
Major character(s): Cab Bolton, Detective—Police, Son (of Tarla Bolton); Tarla Bolton, Actress, Mother (of Cab); Diane Fairmont, Political Figure (candidate for governor), Widow(er); Peach Piper, Worker (Diane Fairmont's campaign)
Time period(s): 21st century; 2010s
Locale(s): Lake Wales, Florida

Summary: Diane Fairmont is the Common Way Party's candidate in the gubernatorial race in Florida. A decade ago, Diane's husband was assassinated at a fund-raiser while he was running for the same office. When Diane receives a threatening letter that appears to have been sent by her husband's killer, police detective Cab Bolton is called in to investigate. As Cab looks into the case, he realizes that something strange is going on in the Common Way Party. His suspicions are confirmed when Peach Piper, one of Diane's campaign workers, asks Cab to look into the recent death of her boyfriend, who was also on the campaign staff. As Cab digs deeper into the party, he becomes entangled in Florida politics. The approach of a tropical storm complicates Cab's investigation. This novel is the second in the Cab Bolton series.

Other books by the same author:
The Cold Nowhere, 2014
Spilled Blood, 2012
The Bone House, 2011
Stripped, 2006
Immoral, 2005

Other books you might like:
E.C. Ayres, *Hour of the Manatee*, 1994
Thomas B. Cavanagh, *Head Games*, 2007
Harlan Coben, *Long Lost*, 2009
Jonathon King, *The Blue Edge of Midnight*, 2002
Tom Lowe, *A False Dawn*, 2009
John D. MacDonald, *The Deep Blue Good-by*, 1964
Randy Wayne White, *Captiva*, 1996

551

JAMIE FREVELETTI

Robert Ludlum's The Geneva Strategy

(New York: Grand Central Publishing, 2015)

Series: Covert-One Series. Book 11
Story type: Political
Subject(s): Kidnapping; Politics; Political prisoners
Major character(s): Jon Smith, Military Personnel (Lieutenant, Covert-One special operations team); Randi Russell, Agent (CIA); Chang Ying Peng, Political Prisoner (former), Scientist (biologist)
Time period(s): 21st century; 2010s
Locale(s): Washington, District of Columbia

Summary: A party for a microbiologist rescued from a Chinese prison takes a dangerous twist when Covert-One team member Lt. Col. Jon Smith is attacked by unknown assailants outside the venue. He soon learns that several high-level government officials were kidnapped the night of the party for Chang Ying Peng. Smith discovers it may all be part of a plot to gain information needed to seize control of US drones while they are in operation. Smith and CIA operative Randi Russell form a team to go after the kidnapped officials, but they may have more on their hands than they bargained for when disharmony among the kidnappers leads to plans for a terror attack with a dangerous drug. His investigation is hindered by the plight of the scientist who developed the memory drug—she remains locked in a mental institution. This is author Jamie Freveletti's second book in the multi-author Covert-One series.

Other books by the same author:
Dead Asleep, 2012
Robert Ludlum's The Janus Reprisal, 2012
The Ninth Day, 2011
Running Dark, 2010
Running from the Devil, 2009

Other books you might like:
Alex Berenson, *Twelve Days*, 2015
James H. Cobb, *Target Lock*, 2001
Jeffery Deaver, *The Skin Collector*, 2014
Joseph Finder, *The Zero Hour*, 1996
Vince Flynn, *American Assassin: A Thriller*, 2010
Vince Flynn, *Last Man*, 2012
Lisa Gardner, *Crash and Burn*, 2015
Mark Greaney, *Tom Clancy Full Force and Effect*, 2014
W.E.B. Griffin, *The Assassination Option*, 2014
W.E.B. Griffin, *Top Secret*, 2014
Jack Higgins, *Rain on the Dead*, 2014
Anthony Horowitz, *Moriarty*, 2014
John Le Carre, *Our Kind of Traitor*, 2010
Gayle Lynds, *Masquerade*, 1996
Kyle Mills, *Rising Phoenix*, 1997
Daniel Silva, *The Heist*, 2014
Brad Thor, *The Lions of Lucerne*, February 27, 2007

552

DANIEL FRIEDMAN

Riot Most Uncouth

(New York: Minotaur Books, 2015)

Story type: Amateur Detective; Historical
Subject(s): Mystery; Mystery fiction; Murder
Major character(s): Lord Byron, Historical Figure, Student—College (at Trinity College in Cambridge), Detective—Amateur, Rake (troublemaker)
Time period(s): 19th century; 1800s (1807)
Locale(s): Cambridge, England

Summary: It is 1807, and Lord Byron is enjoying the easy life of a student at Trinity College in Cambridge, England. Unbeknownst to the college, he shares his dorm room with "the Professor," a large bear. Despite his juvenile antics, Byron's interest is piqued when a young woman is found murdered in a nearby boarding house. There are no police investigators, and private investigators are very expensive. Byron takes it upon himself to prove his genius and solve the case. He must somehow do this while keeping up his habits of drinking, carousing with married women, and causing mayhem wherever he goes. But will his genius prove adequate to solve the murder, or will it only lead him into more danger?

Other books by the same author:
Don't Ever Look Back, 2014
Don't Ever Get Old, 2012

Other books you might like:
Peter Ackroyd, *The Casebook of Victor Frankenstein*, 2008
Stephanie Barron, *Jane and the Madness of Lord Byron*, 2010
John Crowley, *Lord Byron's Novel*, 2005
David Liss, *The Twelfth Enchantment*, 2011
Benjamin Markovits, *Imposture*, 2007
Tim Powers, *Hide Me Among the Graves*, 2012
Miranda Seymour, *Count Manifred*, 1977

553

SUSAN FROETSCHEL

Allure of Deceit

(Amherst, New York: Seventh Street Books, 2015)

Story type: Contemporary - Exotic
Subject(s): Mystery; Cultural conflict; Charity
Major character(s): Michael Sendry, Entrepreneur, Crime Victim (killed in terrorist attack), Spouse (of Rose), Son (of Lydia); Rose Sendry, Crime Victim (killed in terrorist attack), Spouse (of Michael); Lydia Sendry, Manager (GlobalConnect), Mother (of Michael); Parsaa, Man, Leader (of Laashekoh); Leila, Young Woman, Crime Suspect
Time period(s): 21st century; 2010s
Locale(s): Afghanistan; United States

Summary: When Michael Sendry's will was read after he and his wife were killed in a terrorist attack, his family was shocked to learn that much of the entrepreneur's fortune would go to charity. Michael provided funds to found GlobalConnect, an international aid organization that would distribute money to needy communities around the world. Michael's mother, Lydia Sendry, now serves as GlobalConnect's director and helps decide where the funding will go each year. Not everyone earmarked for GlobalConnect funding is pleased, however. In the Afghanistan village of Laashekoh, two women have caught the attention of Sendry's organization. One provides reproductive health care to women; the other may have been convicted of crimes she didn't commit. The residents don't want Americans meddling in their affairs, and village leader Parsaa wants to handle a local criminal case on his own. The conflict between the villagers and the outsiders escalates when visiting orphanage workers disappear in Laashekoh.

Other books by the same author:
Fear of Beauty, 2013
Royal Escape, 2008
Interruptions, 2004
Alaska Gray, 1994

Other books you might like:
Nadeem Aslam, *The Wasted Vigil*, 2008
Alex Carr, *The Prince of Bagram Prison*, 2008
Deborah Ellis, *The Breadwinner*, 2000
Dan Fesperman, *The Warlord's Son*, 2004
Khaled Hosseini, *And the Mountains Echoed*, 2013

Khaled Hosseini, *The Kite Runner*, 2003
Paul Pickering, *Over the Rainbow*, 2012

Evelyn Piper, *Bunny Lake Is Missing*, 1957
Douglas Preston, *Two Graves*, 2012
J.D. Robb, *Festive in Death*, 2014
David Rosenfelt, *Airtight*, 2013
Tina Seskis, *One Step Too Far*, 2015
S.J. Watson, *Before I Go To Sleep*, 2011
Stuart Woods, *Insatiable Appetites*, 2015

554

LISA GARDNER

Crash and Burn

(New York: Penguin Group, 2015)

Series: Tessa Leoni Series. Book 3
Story type: Psychological; Series
Subject(s): Identity; Missing persons; Memory disorders
Major character(s): Nicole "Nicky" Frank, Accident Victim, Spouse (of Thomas); Thomas Frank, Spouse (of Nicky); Wyatt Foster, Police Officer (sergeant)
Time period(s): 21st century; 2010s
Locale(s): United States

Summary: When Nicole "Nicky" Frank awakens after a car wreck, her only concern is locating the missing child she believes she was searching for. But once the police investigate Nicky's claims, they cannot find any evidence that the girl is even real. Sergeant Wyatt Foster has seen his share of confused accident victims before, but something about Nicky's situation makes him take her seriously. Then Nicky's husband, Thomas, comes to the police station and tells Wyatt that Nicky has a past head injury that affects her memory. Wyatt isn't sure that Thomas is telling the whole story, however, and he soon discovers that this accident isn't the only one Nicky has had lately. Now Wyatt can't help but wonder if—and why—someone wants Nicky dead. Wyatt has his work cut out for him. He knows he has to get to the bottom of this case if he wants to save Nicky's life and possibly the life of the enigmatic little girl.

Other books by the same author:
Fear Nothing, 2014
Touch & Go, 2013
Catch Me, 2012
Love You More, 2011
Live to Tell, 2010

Other books you might like:
Peter Abrahams, *Oblivion*, 2005
Linwood Barclay, *No Time for Goodbye*, 2007
Mary Higgins Clark, *The Cinderella Murder*, 2014
Mary Higgins Clark, *The Melody Lingers On*, 2015
Harlan Coben, *The Stranger*, 2015
Harlan Coben, *Tell No One*, 2001
Liz Coley, *Pretty Girl-13*, 2013
Michael Collins, *The Resurrectionists*, 2002
Catherine Coulter, *The Lost Key*, 2014
Jamie Freveletti, *Robert Ludlum's The Geneva Strategy*, 2015
Alison Gaylin, *And She Was*, 2012
Tess Gerritsen, *Die Again*, 2014
Paula Hawkins, *The Girl on the Train*, 2015
Alex Kava, *Breaking Creed*, 2015
Owen Laukkanen, *The Professionals*, 2012
Michael Ledwidge, *Worst Case*, 2010
Sandra Parshall, *The Heat of the Moon*, 2006
James Patterson, *Hope to Die*, 2014

555

P.L. GAUS

Whiskers of the Lion

(New York: Penguin Publishing Group, 2015)

Series: Amish-Country Mystery Series. Book 9
Story type: Contemporary; Series
Subject(s): Crime; Mystery; Detective fiction
Major character(s): Bruce Robertson, Lawman (sheriff); Stan Armbruster, Detective—Police; Fannie Helmuth, Drug Dealer, Fugitive, Religious (Amish); Howie Dent, Companion (of Fannie), Crime Victim; Teresa Molina, Murderer, Organized Crime Figure; Rachel Ramsayer, Computer Expert; Mike Branden, Professor, Spouse (of Caroline); Caroline Branden, Spouse (of Mike); Parker, FBI Agent
Time period(s): 21st century; 2010s
Locale(s): Holmes County, Ohio

Summary: In the ninth novel in the Amish-Country Mystery series, sheriff Bruce Robertson continues to deal with the repercussions of a drug-related killing. Two residents of Holmes County, Ohio, brought cocaine to their community from an Amish vacation spot in Florida. One of the reluctant drug mules was killed by mobster Teresa Molina; the other is now running for her life. Robertson wants to find Fannie Helmuth before Molina does. He enlists the help of Mike and Caroline Branden, who go undercover among the Amish. Robertson is not the only one looking for Fannie, however. Police detective Stan Armbruster and FBI agent Parker are also involved in the case. The feds want Fannie as a witness in Molina's trial. Fannie knows that Robertson, Armbruster, and Parker are searching for her, but she doesn't know if she can trust any of them. Meanwhile, Robertson receives unexpected help with the investigation from a dream.

Other books by the same author:
The Names of Our Tears, 2013
Cast a Blue Shadow, 2003
Clouds Without Rain, 2001
Broken English, 2000
Blood of the Prodigal, 1999

Other books you might like:
Elizabeth Lynn Casey, *Hearse and Buggy*, 2012
Linda Castillo, *The Dead Will Tell*, 2014
Linda Castillo, *Sworn to Silence*, 2009
Judy Clemens, *Different Paths*, 2008
Judy Clemens, *Till the Cows Come Home*, 2004
Mette Ivie Harrison, *The Bishop's Wife*, 2014
Anna Dee Olson, *Growing Up Amish: Insider Secrets from One Woman's Inspirational Journey*, 2008

556

CHRISTOPHER GOLDEN

Tin Men

(New York: Ballantine Books, 2015)

Story type: Adventure; Dystopian
Subject(s): Betrayal; Criminals; Deception
Major character(s): Danny Kelso, Military Personnel (Private in Remote Infantry Corp), Android (controls avatar, Tin Men); Kate Wade, Military Personnel (Corporal), Android (controls avatar, Tin Men), Director (of Remote Infantry Corp)
Time period(s): Indeterminate Future
Locale(s): Heidelberg, Germany; Greece; Damascus, Syria

Summary: In the near future, amid political turmoil, economic collapse, and environmental catastrophes, the United States is trying to keep peace across the globe. The US military is out of options and must turn to its Remote Infantry Corps—robot soldier avatars known as Tin Men that are remotely controlled by human operators to police the violence. The deployment is showing success until anarchists known as Bot-Killers unleash an electromagnetic pulse. The EMP short-circuits all electrical technology, trapping Private Danny Kelso, Corporal Kate Wade, and the Remote Infantry Corps platoon in their avatars. Meanwhile in Greece, the G-20 Summit is compromised, and the president's life is in danger. The Tin Men must carry out their mission to secure the president's safety. They must face danger and violence to confront those who resent the US military's policing mission and somehow save their own lives in the process.

Other books by the same author:
When Rose Wakes, 2010
Poison Ink, 2008
Straight on 'til Morning, 2001
Strangewood, 1999
Bikini, 1995

Other books you might like:
Mark Alpert, *Final Theory*, 2008
Tom Clancy, *Red Rabbit*, 2002
Jim DeFelice, *Dale Brown's Dreamland: Revolution*, 2008
Michael DiMercurio, *Terminal Run*, 2002
Tom Doyle, *American Craftsmen*, 2014
Robert Gandt, *With Hostile Intent*, 2001
Matt Richtel, *The Cloud*, 2013

557

SALLY GOLDENBAUM

A Finely Knit Murder

(New York: Penguin Publishing Group, 2015)

Series: Seaside Knitters Mystery Series. Book 9
Story type: Amateur Detective; Humor
Subject(s): Crime; Deception; Family relations
Major character(s): Birdie Favazza, Grandmother (of Gabby), Detective—Amateur (of Seaside Knitters Club); Gabby Marietti, Granddaughter (of Birdie Favazza), Student (at Sea Harbor Community Day School); Elizabeth Hartley, Principal (Headmistress of Sea Harbor Community Day School), Crime Suspect (of murdering Blythe Westerland); Blythe Westerland, Administrator (school board member), Crime Victim (murdered); Izzy Chambers Perry, Detective—Amateur (of Seaside Knitters Club), Businesswoman (owns Knitting Shop), Niece (of Nell); Nell Endicott, Detective—Amateur (of Seaside Knitters Club), Aunt (of Izzy), Aged Person; Cass, Fisherman (Lobster fisherwoman), Detective—Amateur (of Seaside Knitters Club)
Time period(s): 21st century; 2010s
Locale(s): Sea Harbor, Massachusetts

Summary: The ladies of the Seaside Knitters Club—Nell, Cass, and Birdie—return in the ninth novel in the Seaside Knitters Mystery Series by Sally Goldenbaum. The ladies are thrilled that Birdie's granddaughter Gabby will be visiting and attending the Sea Harbor Community Day School, where the Seaside Knitters teach a popular knitting class. Gabby loves the school and its progressive curriculum. Disgruntled board member Blythe Westerland is not happy with the new direction the school is taking, and she is vocal about her intentions to have the headmistress fired. Before she can follow through on her intentions, Blythe is found murdered near the school boathouse. With the headmistress as the prime suspect, the Seaside Knitters set down their knitting needles and try to solve the murder and prove the headmistress's innocence.

Other books by the same author:
Murder in Merino, 2014
Patterns in the Sand, 2009
Death by Cashmere, 2008
Murder on a Starry Night, 2005
Murder on Elderberry Road, 2003

Other books you might like:
Anne Canadeo, *While My Pretty One Knits*, 2009
Betty Hechtman, *Hooked on Murder*, 2008
Mary Kruger, *Died in the Wool: A Knitting Mystery*, 2005
Hannah Miller, *In Dutch Again*, 2002
Clare O'Donohue, *The Lover's Knot*, 2008
Nancy Pickard, *Generous Death*, 1984
Maggie Sefton, *Knit One, Kill Two*, 2005

558

MARGARET GRACE (Pseudonym of Camille Minichino)

Manhattan in Miniature

(Palo Alto, California: Perservearance Press, 2015)

Series: Miniature Mystery Series. Book 8
Story type: Amateur Detective; Series
Subject(s): Murder; Mystery; Mystery fiction
Major character(s): Geraldine "Gerry" Porter, Assistant (of Bebe at miniatures booth), Retiree (school teacher), Grandmother (of Maddie Porter), Detective—Amateur (of friend Cynthia's aunt's murder); Maddie Porter, Granddaughter (of Gerry), Detective—Amateur, Assistant (at miniatures booth), 11-Year-

Old; Bebe Mellon, Friend (of Gerry Porter), Businesswoman (Manager of SuperKrafts store), Director (of miniatures booth at craft fair); Cynthia Bishop, Friend (of Gerry Porter), Niece (of Elsie); Elsie, Aunt (of Cynthia Bishop), Crime Victim (believed to be murdered)

Time period(s): 20th century; 2010s
Locale(s): New York, New York

Summary: Gerry Porter and her granddaughter Maddie travel to New York City in the eighth novel in the Miniature Mystery series by Margaret Grace. Gerry and Maddie are excited about visiting Manhattan at Christmastime. They plan to see the sights of the city together, including Rockefeller Center and Radio City Music Hall. When Gerry and Maddie travel from California, they promise to help Gerry's friend Bebe, a manager of a SuperKrafts store, run a miniatures craft booth at an important fair. They do not expect that on their trip they will craft their way into a murder mystery. Will Gerry and Maddie be able to help out with the craft fair while they investigate a suspicious death? Will their sleuthing place Maddie in grave danger? And will Gerry be able to solve a murder and save her granddaughter before it's too late?

Other books by the same author:
Madness in Miniature, 2014
Malice in Miniature, 2009
Mourning in Miniature, 2009
Mayhem in Miniature, 2008
Murder in Miniature, 2008

Other books you might like:
Sharon Fiffer, *Killer Stuff*, 2001
Elaine Flinn, *Dealing in Murder: A Molly Doyle Mystery*, 2003
Rebecca M. Hale, *How to Wash a Cat*, 2008
Larry Karp, *Scamming the Birdman*, 2000
Tamar Myers, *Larceny and Old Lace*, 1996
J.B. Stanley, *A Killer Collection*, 2006
Sebastian Stuart, *To the Manor Dead*, 2010

559

JAMES GRADY

Last Days of the Condor
(New York: Forge Books, 2015)

Series: Condor Series. Book 3
Story type: Espionage; Series
Subject(s): Mystery; Espionage; Spies
Major character(s): Vin, Agent (CIA, also known as Condor), Worker (Library of Congress); Faye Dozier, Agent (Homeland Security); Bald Peter, Agent (Homeland Security), Crime Victim
Time period(s): 21st century; 2010s
Locale(s): Washington, District of Columbia

Summary: Author James Grady introduced CIA agent Condor in his 1974 novel, *Six Days of the Condor*. In this third novel in the series, Condor—who now also uses the name Vin—has been released from a secret government psychiatric facility. He is placed in a job at the Library of Congress, where his handler—Homeland Security agent Faye Dozier—keeps tabs on him. While Vin is adjusting to his new situation, he is quickly drawn back into the world of espionage. The body of Faye's partner, a fellow Homeland Security agent known as Bald Peter, is found nailed to a wall of Vin's apartment. Vin is the obvious suspect, but Faye is certain that the Condor is innocent. As in his past adventures, Condor goes on the run. This time Faye accompanies him, and the two navigate the threats they encounter in Washington, DC, as they try to evade Bald Peter's killer.

Other books by the same author:
Mad Dogs, 2006
Razor Game, 1985
Runner in the Street, 1984
Shadow of the Condor, 1975
Six Days of the Condor, 1974

Other books you might like:
Alex Berenson, *The Faithful Spy*, 2006
Ben Coes, *Power Down*, 2011
Frederick Forsyth, *The Day of the Jackal*, 1971
W.E.B. Griffin, *Top Secret*, 2014
Stephen Hunter, *Point of Impact*, 1993
David Ignatius, *Agents of Innocence*, 1987
Daniel Silva, *The Kill Artist*, 2000
Thomas W. Young, *The Mullah's Storm*, 2010

560

HEATHER GRAHAM (Pseudonym of Heather Graham Pozzessere)

The Dead Play On
(Buffalo, New York: Mira Books, 2015)

Series: Cafferty and Quinn Series. Book 3
Story type: Fantasy; Mystery
Subject(s): Crime; Deception; Friendship
Major character(s): Arnie Watson, Veteran, Crime Victim (murdered), Friend (of Tyler Anderson), Musician (saxophone player), Classmate (former, of Tyler and Danni); Tyler Anderson, Musician (saxophone player), Friend (of Arnie Watson), Classmate (former, of Arnie and Danni); Danni Cafferty, Detective—Amateur (paranormal), Girlfriend (of Michael Quinn), Colleague (of Michael Quinn), Classmate (former, of Arnie and Tyler), Businesswoman (owner of antiques shop); Michael Quinn, Detective—Private, Colleague (of Danni Cafferty), Boyfriend (of Danni Cafferty)
Time period(s): 21st century; 2010s
Locale(s): New Orleans, Louisiana

Summary: Tyler Anderson doesn't believe his friend Arnie Watson killed himself. He believes Arnie was murdered. Other musicians throughout New Orleans are being murdered, too, and Tyler believes that Arnie's saxophone is the key to the killings. When Tyler plays the instrument, he sees visions of Arnie's life. Tyler is unable to convince the police that his friend has been murdered; instead, authorities have classified it a drug overdose. Tyler turns to Danni Cafferty and Michael Quinn, who have a reputation for solving unusual cases. Danni and Michael must put aside their personal involvement and learn to trust each other's instincts in solving the musicians' murders. Delving into the New Orleans music scene, they uncover secrets of Arnie's past that may lead them to the murderer and begin to unravel the threads of deceit behind the music. This is the third title of the Cafferty and Quinn mystery series.

Other books by the same author:
The Betrayed, 2015
The Forgotten, 2015
The Silenced, 2015
Waking the Dead, 2015
When Irish Eyes Are Haunting, 2015

Other books you might like:
Justine Davis, *Enemy Waters*, 2011
Laura Griffin, *One Last Breath*, 2007
Daniel Hecht, *City of Masks*, 2003
Kay Hooper, *Stealing Shadows*, 2000
Martha C. Lawrence, *Murder in Scorpio*, 1995
Kat Martin, *Against the Storm*, 2011
Brenda Novak, *Killer Heat*, 2010
Terri Persons, *Blind Spot*, 2007
Karen Rose, *Watch Your Back*, 2014
Julie Smith, *Louisiana Hotshot*, 2001
Julie Smith, *New Orleans Mourning*, 1990
Erica Spindler, *Last Known Victim*, 2007

561

ANDREW GROSS

One Mile Under

(New York: William Morrow, 2015)

Series: Ty Hauck Series. Book 4
Story type: Psychological Suspense
Subject(s): Detective fiction; Ranch life; Murder
Major character(s): Ty Hauck, Police Officer (former), Godfather (of Dani), Detective—Private; Dani Whalen, Guide (of whitewater rapids), Friend (of Trey), Stepdaughter (former, of Wade); Wade Dunn, Police Officer (chief, of Aspen), Stepfather (former, of Dani); Trey Watkins, Crime Victim, Friend (of Dani)
Time period(s): 21st century; 2010s
Locale(s): Aspen, Colorado

Summary: In the fourth installment of the Ty Hauck series, whitewater guide Dani Whalen is leading a tour group down the rapids in Colorado. She finds the body of her friend, Trey Watkins, in the river. Although his death is ruled an accident, Dani believes it was murder. She pleads with Wade Dunn, the local police chief and her former stepfather, to reopen the case. Even after a witness dies in a suspicious accident before he can tell anyone what he saw, Dunn refuses, and instead puts Dani behind bars. Dani's father asks his old friend, detective Ty Hauck, to investigate. Ty, who's also Dani's godfather, comes to Dani's rescue, but Trey's murder is even more complicated than the two suspected. Soon they are involved in a scheme that involves big energy corporations and ranchers whose land is in desperate need of water.

Other books by the same author:
Everything to Lose, 2014
Reckless, 2010
Don't Look Twice, 2009
The Dark Tide, 2008
The Blue Zone: A Novel, 2007

Other books you might like:
Lee Child, *Nothing to Lose*, 2008
Lincoln Child, *Terminal Freeze*, 2009
James W. Hall, *Under Cover of Daylight*, 1987
Jonathon King, *The Blue Edge of Midnight*, 2002
T. Jefferson Parker, *California Girl*, 2004
Douglas Preston, *Thunderhead*, 1999
Randy Wayne White, *Captiva*, 1996

562

NICHOLAS GUILD

Blood Ties

(New York: Forge Books, 2015)

Story type: Family Saga; Psychological Suspense
Subject(s): Betrayal; Childhood; Crime
Major character(s): Ellen Ridley, Detective—Homicide (San Francisco Police Department), Colleague (of Sam); Sam, Detective—Homicide (San Francisco Police Department), Colleague (of Ellen Ridley); Stephen Tregear, Military Personnel (US Naval Intelligence), Computer Expert (hacker and code breaker), Son (of Walter Rayne); Walter Rayne, Crime Suspect, Criminal (serial killer), Father (of Stephen)
Time period(s): 21st century; 2010s
Locale(s): San Francisco, California

Summary: Homicide Detective Ellen Ridley and her partner, Sam, are assigned to hunt down a serial killer who is butchering young women across the San Francisco Bay area. Ridley's prime suspect, Stephen Tregear, is a computer hacker and code-breaker who works for US Navy Intelligence. Although Tregear proves not to be the killer, he has important information about the case. He points Ridley in an unexpected direction: his father, Walter Rayne. Tregear has been hiding from his sordid past and his father for more than 20 years and fears for his own life and safety. Ready to confront his past, Tregear agrees to cooperate with Ridley to stop his father and put an end to the killings. As Rayne continues to terrorize the women of the San Francisco area, Ridley and Tregear piece together the clues of the past. They are playing a dangerous game with a killer as they try to find a way to stop Rayne.

Other books by the same author:
The Moonlight, 2012
The Assyrian, 1987
The President's Man, 1982
The Summer Soldier, 1978
The Lost and Found Man, 1975

Other books you might like:
Robin Burcell, *Every Move She Makes*, 1999
Meg Gardiner, *The Dirty Secrets Club*, 2008
Alex Kava, *A Perfect Evil*, 2001

Laurie R. King, *A Grave Talent*, 1993
James Patterson, *1st to Die*, 2001
Clyde Phillips, *Fall from Grace: A Noir Thriller*, 1998
Kirk Russell, *A Killing in China Basin*, 2011

563

DAVID HAGBERG

Retribution

(New York: Forge Books, 2015)

Series: Kirk McGarvey Series. Book 18
Story type: Espionage; Series
Subject(s): Mystery; Espionage; Spies
Major character(s): Kirk "Mac" McGarvey, Director (CIA); Wolfhardt Weiss, Police Officer (Interpol); Pam Schlueter, Leader (of mercenaries)
Time period(s): 21st century; 2010s
Locale(s): Germany; Pakistan; United States

Summary: When members of the Navy's SEAL Team Six entered Pakistan in 2011 to assassinate Osama bin Laden, they angered many Pakistanis. In this novel, the 18th in the Kirk McGarvey series, Pakistani officials still hold a grudge over the intrusive military operation, and they intend to take revenge. They assemble a band of German mercenaries to kill off all 24 members of the SEAL Team responsible for bin Laden's death. The assassins claim the life of one SEAL, but Interpol police officer Wolfhardt "Wolf" Weiss is soon on their trail. CIA director Kirk "Mac" McGarvey joins the investigation and traces the operation to Germany and Pakistan. He hopes to find out who is in charge of the operation before any more SEAL Team Six members die. For Pam Schlueter, the German woman who negotiated the deal between the Pakistanis and the mercenaries, the mission is personal. Her ex-husband was a SEAL, and she wants payback for the abuse he inflicted on her.

Other books by the same author:
Blowout, 2012
Burned, 2009
Without Honor, 1989
The Capsule, 1976
Twister, 1975

Other books you might like:
Tom Clancy, *The Sum of All Fears*, 1991
Vince Flynn, *American Assassin: A Thriller*, 2010
James Grady, *Six Days of the Condor*, 1974
W.E.B. Griffin, *Top Secret*, 2014
Don Mann, *Hunt the Wolf*, 2012
Kyle Mills, *Rising Phoenix*, 1997
A.J. Tata, *Sudden Threat*, 2008
Brad Thor, *The Lions of Lucerne*, February 27, 2007
Joakim Zander, *The Swimmer*, 2015

564

CAROLYN HAINES

Bone to Be Wild

(New York: Minotaur Books, 2015)

Series: Sarah Booth Delaney Series. Book 15
Story type: Mystery; Paranormal
Subject(s): Courage; Crime; Deception
Major character(s): Sarah Booth Delaney, Southern Belle, Detective—Private, Fiance(e) (former, of Graf Milieu); Graf Milieu, Fiance(e) (former, of Sarah Booth Delaney); Scott Hampton, Businessman (club owner); Jitty, Spirit (ghost living in Sarah's house), Friend (of Sarah Booth Delaney); Tinkie, Friend (best friend of Sarah Booth Delaney), Southern Belle, Assistant (to Sarah Booth Delaney), Wealthy
Time period(s): 21st century; 2010s
Locale(s): Zinnia, Mississippi

Summary: In the 15th novel of the Sarah Booth Delaney Mystery Series, Sarah Booth Delaney is left to pick up the pieces of her broken heart after her fiance, Graf Milieu, left her and moved to Hollywood. Trying to keep herself busy and avoid dwelling on her heartbreak, she dives into her work as a private detective. Her new case involves an old flame, Scott Hampton, a popular guitarist and leader of a blues band. Scott has returned to Zinnia, Mississippi, to open a blues club called Playin' the Bones. He has received ominous messages threatening his life and those of his fellow musicians. When the threats become too real and a bartender is shot outside Scott's club, Sarah must work overtime with the help of her friends Tinkie, Jitty, and Sheriff Coleman Peters to stop a killer.

Other books by the same author:
Booty Bones, 2014
Crossed Bones, 2003
Splintered Bones, 2002
Buried Bones, 2000
Them Bones, 1999

Other books you might like:
Mary Kay Andrews, *Savannah Blues*, 2002
Dorothy Cannell, *The Thin Woman*, 1984
Carol Higgins Clark, *Decked*, 1992
Susan Kandel, *I Dreamed I Married Perry Mason*, 2004
Susan McBride, *Blue Blood*, 2004
Katy Munger, *Legwork*, 1997
Elaine Viets, *Shop Till You Drop: A Dead-End Job Mystery*, 2003

565

PARNELL HALL

Puzzled Indemnity

(New York: Minotaur Books, 2015)

Series: Puzzle Lady Mysteries Series. Book 16
Story type: Amateur Detective; Series
Subject(s): Crime; Mystery; Detective fiction
Major character(s): Cora Felton, Detective—Amateur,

Writer (crossword puzzles), Lover (of Crowley), Friend (of Becky Baldwin); Crowley, Police Officer (sergeant), Lover (of Cora); Becky Baldwin, Lawyer, Friend (of Cora); Hank Wells, Insurance Agent, Spouse (of Brittany); Brittany Wells, Spouse (of Hank)

Time period(s): 21st century; 2010s
Locale(s): Bakerhaven, Connecticut

Summary: In the 16th Puzzle Lady Mystery novel, Cora Felton is looking for some excitement as the long winter drags on in Bakerhaven, Connecticut. Cora is the famous syndicated columnist the Puzzle Lady, although her niece is the real author of the puzzles, and she has played amateur detective on a number of cases. She is currently involved in the investigation of a liquor store robbery, but her lawyer friend—Becky Baldwin—has just presented her with another case. Brittany Wells is concerned that her husband, insurance agent Hank Wells, is having an affair. Worse, she suspects that Hank may by plotting her murder. Cora agrees to investigate and quickly finds that Hank is indeed cheating on Brittany. When Brittany won't accept Cora's findings, the Puzzle Lady takes extreme measures and uses puzzles to solve the case. This novel includes crossword and Sudoku puzzles by Will Shortz.

Other books by the same author:
NYPD Puzzle, 2014
Safari, 2014
A Clue for the Puzzle Lady, 1999
Baxter Trust, 1988
Detective, 1987

Other books you might like:
Nero Blanc, *The Crossword Murder*, 1999
Nero Blanc, *Death on the Diagonal*, 2006
Shelley Freydont, *The Sudoku Murder*, 2007
Casey Mayes, *Deadly Row*, 2010
Kaye Morgan, *Death by Sudoku*, 2007
Herbert Resnicow, *The Crossword Hunt*, 1987
Herbert Resnicow, *Murder Across and Down*, 1985

566

GLEN ERIK HAMILTON

Past Crimes

(New York: William Morrow, 2015)

Series: Van Shaw Series. Book 1
Story type: Contemporary; Series
Subject(s): Mystery; Detective fiction; Crime
Major character(s): Van Shaw, Veteran (former Army Ranger), Criminal (former), Grandson (of Donovan Shaw); Donovan "Dono" Shaw, Criminal, Grandfather (of Van), Crime Victim; Hollis Brant, Smuggler, Criminal; Jimmy Corcoran, Expert (technology), Criminal

Time period(s): 21st century; 2010s
Locale(s): Seattle, Washington

Summary: In the first novel in the Van Shaw series, Van—a former Army Ranger—is summoned to the home of Donovan Shaw, the grandfather who raised him. Van and Dono's relationship was troubled. Dono, a lifelong criminal, taught his grandson how to make a living by stealing and scamming. Van turned his back on his grandfather and his criminal lifestyle at the age of 18, choosing a career in the US Army instead. But now, a decade later, Van can't ignore a message from Dono, asking him to come back to Seattle. Van makes the trip, but he never gets to speak with his grandfather. Dono is bleeding to death from a gunshot wound when Van gets to his house. Van becomes a suspect in Dono's murder, but he is determined to find out who really killed his grandfather—and why. He hooks up with Dono's former colleagues and uses his criminal and military skills in his search for answers. First novel.

Other books you might like:
Lee Child, *Killing Floor*, 1997
Harlan Coben, *No Second Chance*, 2003
Steve Hamilton, *The Lock Artist*, 2010
Ross Macdonald, *The Blue Hammer*, 1976
Duane Swierczynski, *Expiration Date*, 2010
Newton Thornburg, *Cutter and Bone*, 1976
Don Winslow, *The Winter of Frankie Machine*, 2006

567

DAVID HANDLER

Phantom Angel

(New York: Minotaur Books, 2015)

Series: Benji Golden Series. Book 2
Story type: Contemporary; Private Detective
Subject(s): Mystery; Detective fiction; Crime
Major character(s): Benji Golden, Man (25 years old), Detective—Private; Morrie Frankel, Producer (Broadway), Client (of Benji); R.J. Farnell, Wealthy, Financier, Missing Person, Boyfriend (of Jonquil Beausoleil); Jonquil "Boso" Beausoleil, Young Woman, Actress (aspiring), Girlfriend (of Farnell)

Time period(s): 21st century; 2010s
Locale(s): New York, New York

Summary: Twenty-five-year-old private detective Benji Golden had wanted to be an actor. Now he works for his family's business, Golden Legal Services. His current case takes him to the theater district, where Broadway producer Morrie Frankel needs to find missing billionaire R.J. Farnell fast. Frankel is trying to get his musical adaptation of *Wuthering Heights* off the ground, but the show is plagued with problems that include a lack of financial support. Farnell was supposed to contribute $12 million to the production, but he and his money are suddenly nowhere to be found. Benji follows Farnell's trail to his girlfriend, wannabe actress Jonquil "Boso" Beausoleil. The case takes a turn when Morrie is killed in the theater district. Benji refocuses on the investigation, following clues that lead him to an odd assortment of New York City characters. This is the second novel in the Benji Golden series.

Other books by the same author:
The Coal Black Asphalt Tomb, 2014
Runaway Man, 2013
Click to Play, 2009
The Cold Blue Blood, 2001
The Man Who Died Laughing, 1988

Mystery

Other books you might like:

Linda Barnes, *Blood Will Have Blood*, 1982

Richard Ellington, *Shoot the Works*, 1948

Gillian B. Farrell, *Alibi for an Actress*, 1992

Kinky Friedman, *Greenwich Killing Time: A Novel*, 1986

Parnell Hall, *Detective*, 1987

Parnell Hall, *Safari*, 2014

Carol O'Connell, *It Happens in the Dark*, 2013

568

JENNIFER HARLOW

Witch upon a Star

(Woodbury, Minnesota: Midnight Ink, 2015)

Series: Midnight Magic Mystery Series. Book 3

Story type: Paranormal; Series

Subject(s): Mystery; Vampires; Romances (Fiction)

Major character(s): Anna Olmstead West, Spouse (of Nathan), Mother (of Joe and Max), Lover (former, of Asher), Witch; Nathan West, Spouse (of Anna), Father (of Joe and Max); Asher, Vampire, Lover (former, of Anna); Joe West, 7-Year-Old, Son (of Anna and Nathan); Max West, 5-Year-Old, Son (of Anna and Nathan)

Time period(s): 21st century; 2010s

Locale(s): Garland, Texas

Summary: As Anna West sits in a Garland, Texas, park watching her sons play, she seems like any other young mother. She is married to a man named Nathan West, and she is looking forward to celebrating her 29th birthday with her small family that evening. But Anna is a witch who has never escaped her past. She was taken by a vampire named Asher when she was a girl. She initially played the role of Asher's surrogate daughter, but then Anna became the vampire's lover. When Asher's passion and obsession became too much for Anna, she left the supernatural world and eventually made a place for herself in the mortal world. But Anna has never forgotten Asher. And when Anna is targeted by a mysterious kidnapper, she realizes that Asher hasn't forgotten her, either. He wants to possess her again. This novel is the third in the Midnight Magic Mystery series.

Other books by the same author:

Werewolf Sings the Blues, 2014

Galilee Rising, 2013

Justice, 2013

What's a Witch to Do?, 2013

Mind Over Monsters, 2011

Other books you might like:

Kelley Armstrong, *Bitten*, 2001

Jim Butcher, *Storm Front*, 2000

Simon R. Green, *Something from the Nightside*, 2003

Laurell K. Hamilton, *Guilty Pleasures*, 1993

Alma Katsu, *The Taker*, 2011

Sherrilyn Kenyon, *Night Pleasures*, 2002

Chelsea Quinn Yarbro, *Hotel Transylvania*, 1978

569

CAROLYN G. HART

Don't Go Home

(New York: Berkley Publishing, 2015)

Series: Death on Demand Series. Book 25

Story type: Amateur Detective; Cozy Mystery

Subject(s): Anger; Betrayal; Crime

Major character(s): Annie Darling, Store Owner (of Death on Demand Mystery Bookstore), Detective—Amateur, Friend (of Marian Kenyon); Alex Griffith, Crime Victim (murdered), Writer (novelist); Marian Kenyon, Journalist, Friend (of Annie Darling), Crime Suspect

Time period(s): 21st century; 2010s

Locale(s): Broward Rock, South Carolina

Summary: In the 25th novel in the Death by Demand series by Carolyn Hart, former Broward's Rock resident and best-selling author Alex Griffith returns to town to promote his new book, *Don't Go Home*. Annie Darling is excited to host a party and book signing at her bookstore, Death on Demand, for the Southern literary icon. Alex is planning more than just signing books; he intends to expose certain people of Broward's Rock as the real-life inspirations for the characters in his book. The people of Broward's Rock are less than pleased and not afraid to express their displeasure. But when Alex turns up dead, Annie's best friend is the prime suspect in his murder. Despite promising to abstain from meddling, Annie cannot sit idly on the sidelines and watch her friend go to jail when the real killer may still be among them.

Other books by the same author:

Death at the Door, 2014

Ghost at Work, 2008

Dead Man's Island, 1993

Design for Murder, 1988

Death on Demand, 1987

Other books you might like:

Lorna Barrett, *Murder Is Binding*, 2008

Susan M. Boyer, *Lowcountry Boil*, 2012

Cindy Daniel, *Death Warmed Over...Coming Soon*, 2003

Jo Dereske, *Miss Zukas and the Library Murders*, 1994

Joan Hess, *Strangled Prose*, 1986

Allison Kingsley, *Mind Over Murder*, 2011

Louise Penny, *A Trick of the Light*, 2011

570

SAMANTHA HAYES

What You Left Behind

(New York: Crown Publishing Group, 2015)

Story type: Police Procedural; Psychological Suspense

Subject(s): Suicide; Mystery fiction; Mystery

Major character(s): Lorraine Fisher, Aunt (of Freddie), Detective—Police (Detective Inspector), Sister (of Jo); Jo, Mother (of Freddie), Sister (of Lorraine); Freddie, Bullied Child, Son (of Jo), Teenager,

Nephew (of Lorraine), Mentally Ill Person (depressed); Greg Burnley, Detective—Police (detective inspector)
Time period(s): 21st century; 2010s
Locale(s): Radcote, England

Summary: The village of Radcote is finally starting to recover from a rash of teenage suicides that occurred two years earlier. When a young man is killed in a motorcycle accident and a suicide note is found, however, the threat of more suicides again casts a pall over the village. Detective Inspector Lorraine Fisher decides she is in desperate need of a vacation, so she decides to visit her sister and nephew in Radcote. Lorraine is troubled by her teenage nephew's behavior and disturbed by the unsettling deaths that have plagued the village. She is not truly convinced that they were suicides and is determined to uncover the truth behind the teen deaths. While trying to reveal the secret behind the deaths, Lorraine may stumble upon something more dangerous than she bargained for.

Other books by the same author:
You Belong to Me, 2015
Before You Die, 2014
Until You're Mine, 2013

Other books you might like:
Megan Abbott, *The Fever*, 2014
Chelsea Cain, *One Kick*, 2014
Agatha Christie, *Crooked House*, 1949
Erin Kelly, *The Poison Tree*, 2011
J. Wallis Martin, *The Bird Yard*, 1998
Alex Marwood, *The Wicked Girls*, 2012
Kimberly McCreight, *Reconstructing Amelia*, 2013
Denise Mina, *The End of the Wasp Season*, 2011

571

ELIZABETH HAYNES

Behind Closed Doors

(New York: Harper Paperbacks, 2015)

Series: Briarstone Crime Series. Book 2
Story type: Police Procedural; Series
Subject(s): Crime; Criminals; Deception
Major character(s): Louisa "Lou" Smith, Detective—Police (Detective Chief Inspector of Major Crimes Division), Consultant (for Scarlett Rainsford case); Scarlett Rainsford, Crime Victim (human trafficking), Young Woman, Missing Person; Sam Hollands, Detective—Police (Detective Sergeant with Briarstone Police), Co-worker (of Louisa Smith)
Time period(s): 21st century; 2010s
Locale(s): Briarstone, England

Summary: In the second novel of the DCI Louisa Smith series, 15 years ago, Scarlett Rainsford disappeared when on a family vacation in Greece. At the time, investigators could not determine if she was abducted or if she ran away and could find no trace of the 15-year-old. Lou Smith worked the Rainsford case, and it has haunted her for years. Now Scarlett is found during a raid on a brothel in Briarstone. Lou is busy working with her major crime team on two disturbing cases, a brutal teen

beating and a robbery/murder. While Lou tries to find the connection between these crimes, Detective Sergeant Sam Hollands questions Scarlett about her disappearance and how she ended up in a brothel back in Briarstone. When the evidence in each case starts to stitch together all of the cases, Scarlett may be their only lead. Now the investigators must work even harder to get the abused young woman to tell them the painful truth.

Other books by the same author:
Human Remains, 2013
Under a Silent Moon, 2013
Dark Tide, 2012
Into the Darkest Corner, 2011

Other books you might like:
Harry Bingham, *Talking to the Dead*, 2012
S.J. Bolton, *Now You See Me*, 2011
Jane Casey, *The Burning*, 2011
Lynda LaPlante, *Prime Suspect*, 1993
Denise Mina, *Still Midnight*, 2010
Carol O'Connell, *Mallory's Oracle*, 1994
Neil White, *Fallen Idols*, 2007

572

JULIA HEABERLIN

Black-Eyed Susans

(New York: Random House Publishing Group, 2015)

Story type: Psychological Suspense; Serial Killer
Subject(s): Murder; Memory; Crime
Major character(s): Tessa Cartwright, Single Mother, Crime Victim, Mentally Ill Person; Terrell Darcy, Serial Killer (accused)
Time period(s): 20th century; (1990s); 21st century; 2010s
Locale(s): Texas, United States

Summary: In 1995, 16-year-old Tessa Cartwright nearly became the victim of a killer. She was found in a Texas field clinging to life, covered with black-eyed Susans and lying upon the corpses of the killer's previous victims. Although her memory of how she got there was a half-remembered mess, Tessa testified at the trail of the murder suspect and was instrumental in his conviction. Twenty years later, Tessa is a single mother who still has no clear memory of her ordeal. One winter's day she finds some freshly planted black-eyed Susans outside her home. If the real killer is still at large and taunting her, that means she helped put an innocent man on death row. To find the truth and save a man's life, Tessa must unlock secrets her mind is desperately fighting to keep hidden.

Other books by the same author:
Lie Still, 2013
Playing Dead, 2012

Other books you might like:
Megan Abbott, *The End of Everything*, 2011
Gillian Flynn, *Sharp Objects*, 2006
Sara J. Henry, *Learning to Swim*, 2011
Shirley Jackson, *We Have Always Lived in the Castle*, 1962
Pam Lewis, *Speak Softly, She Can Hear*, 2005

Laura Lippman, *What the Dead Know*, 2007
Jennifer McMahon, *Promise Not to Tell*, 2006

573

JOAN HESS

Pride v. Prejudice

(New York: St. Martin's Press, 2015)

Series: Claire Malloy Series. Book 20
Story type: Amateur Detective; Cozy Mystery
Subject(s): Murder; Law; Detective fiction
Major character(s): Claire Malloy, Store Owner, Detective—Amateur, Mother (of Caron), Spouse (of Peter); Peter Rosen, Police Officer (chief), Spouse (of Claire); Caron, Teenager, Daughter (of Claire); Sarah Swift, Crime Suspect
Time period(s): 21st century; 2010s
Locale(s): Farberville, Arkansas

Summary: Much has changed in Claire Malloy 's life recently. She has married her police chief boyfriend Peter, her daughter Caron has grown into a rambunctious teenager, and she's ready to turn over daily operations of her bookstore to her loyal employees. However, one thing remains constant: Claire can still get herself in a heap of trouble. When she is called to jury duty, she is publicly humiliated and dismissed by a prosecutor who holds a grudge against her husband. To get her revenge, Claire seeks out the defendant in the case, intending to prove the woman's innocence. The problem is, the more she digs into the case, the more signs she finds that point to the woman's guilt. The bigger issue on her plate, though, may just be the impending visit of her new mother-in-law. This is the 20th book in Joan Hess's Claire Malloy series.

Other books by the same author:
Murder as a Second Language, 2013
The Merry Wives of Maggody, 2010
Busy Bodies, 1995
Malice in Maggody, 1987
Strangled Prose, 1986

Other books you might like:
Lorna Barrett, *Murder Is Binding*, 2008
Ali Brandon, *Double Booked for Death*, 2011
Jon L. Breen, *The Gathering Place*, 1984
Jill Churchill, *Grime and Punishment*, 1989
Cindy Daniel, *Death Warmed Over...Coming Soon*, 2003
Carolyn G. Hart, *Death Walked In: A Death on Demand Mystery*, 2008
Allison Kingsley, *Mind Over Murder*, 2011

574

SUSAN HILL

The Soul of Discretion

(London: Chatto & Windus, 2014)

Series: Chief Superintendent Simon Serrailler Mysteries Series. Book 8

Story type: Police Procedural; Series
Subject(s): Mystery; Detective fiction; Crime
Major character(s): Simon Serrailler, Detective—Police (chief superintendent), Brother (of Cat), Boyfriend (of Rachel), Stepson (of Judith); Cat, Sister (of Simon), Stepdaughter (of Judith); Rachel, Girlfriend (of Simon); Judith, Stepmother (of Simon and Cat); Kieran Bright, Detective—Police (chief constable)
Time period(s): 21st century; 2000s-2010s
Locale(s): Lafferton, England

Summary: Chief Superintendent Simon Serrailler's current case takes him away from his home turf of Lafferton, England, to work undercover in another town. He is informed of his assignment by chief constable Kieran Bright, who is new to Lafferton. On Bright's orders, Simon leaves without telling his family or live-in girlfriend where he is going. Simon's mission is dangerous and depressing. He is supposed to play the role of a depraved criminal, a charade that Simon finds quite unsettling. While he is away on his secret assignment, those close to Simon face challenges of their own. His sister, Cat, is dealing with professional and personal problems. Their stepmother, Judith, is also experiencing difficulties. As Simon is drawn deeper into his undercover case, its repercussions threaten the seemingly peaceful Lafferton. This is the eighth novel in the Chief Superintendent Simon Serrailler Mysteries series.

Other books by the same author:
Black Sheep, 2013
A Question of Identity, 2012
The Pure in Heart, 2005
The Various Haunts of Men, 2004
The Woman in Black, 1983

Other books you might like:
Margery Allingham, *The Tiger in the Smoke*, 1952
Ann Cleeves, *Raven Black*, 2006
Deborah Crombie, *A Share in Death*, 1993
Elly Griffiths, *The Crossing Places*, 2010
Ruth Rendell, *From Doon with Death*, 1964
Ruth Rendell, *The Monster in the Box*, 2009
Peter Robinson, *Gallows View*, 1987

575

NAOMI HIRAHARA

Grave on Grand Avenue

(New York: Penguin Publishing Group, 2015)

Series: Officer Ellie Rush Mystery Series. Book 2
Story type: Contemporary; Series
Subject(s): Law enforcement; Bicycles; Detective fiction
Major character(s): Ellie Rush, Police Officer (bicycle officer); Fang Xu, Crime Suspect; Eduardo, Gardener
Time period(s): 21st century; 2010s
Locale(s): Los Angeles, California

Summary: Los Angeles bicycle cop Ellie Rush starts her day on a typical patrol near a famed concert hall. She ends it caught up in a possible case of murder with international implications. Moments after Ellie stops to chat up local gardener Eduardo, he is found seriously injured at the bottom of a flight of stairs. The prime suspect is Fang Xu, father of a famous Chinese musician, who claims Eduardo was trying to steal his son's prized cello. When the gardener dies of his injuries, and Xu disappears, the authorities get involved. But Ellie can't just let the case go. Her investigation would go a lot easier, however, if she didn't get her car stolen and end up on the bad side of her superiors. This is the second book in Naomi Hirahara's Officer Ellie Rush Mystery series.

Other books by the same author:
Murder on Bamboo Lane, 2014
Strawberry Yellow, 2013
Snakeskin Shamisen, 2006
Gasa-Gasa Girl, 2005
Summer of the Big Bachi, 2004

Other books you might like:
Paul Bishop, *Citadel Run*, 1988
Howard Fast, *Samantha*, 1967
Rachel Howzell Hall, *Land of Shadows*, 2014
Rochelle Majer Krich, *Fair Game*, 1993
Sujata Massey, *The Salaryman's Wife*, 1997
Joseph Wambaugh, *Hollywood Station: A Novel*, 2006
Paula L. Woods, *Inner City Blues: A Charlotte Justice Novel*, 1999

`576`

PHIL HOGAN

A Pleasure and a Calling

(New York: Doubleday, 2014)

Story type: Psychological
Subject(s): Psychology; Real estate; Crime
Major character(s): William Heming, Real Estate Agent, Employer (of Katya), Narrator; Katya, Consultant (real estate)
Time period(s): 21st century; 2010s
Locale(s): England

Summary: William Heming is a successful real estate agent in a picturesque English town, and he conducts his life with a certain sense of morality. No one suspects that Heming is hiding an unusual collection in his home. He owns a set of keys for every property he has sold or leased, and he uses them to gain access to his clients' lives. At first it seems that Heming's illegal intrusions are relatively benign. He leaves secret evidence of his visits behind, but he doesn't steal anything or harm anyone. As the novel progresses, and Heming shares more of his back story, his reliability as a narrator falters. He uses his keys to avenge neighborhood misdeeds—for instance, depositing dog droppings in the home of a dog-walker who fails to clean up after his animal. As Heming's dark side is revealed, it becomes clear that the deranged real estate agent may have been involved in past and present murders.

Other books by the same author:
All This Will Be Yours, 2005
The Freedom Thing, 2003
Hitting the Groove, 2001

Other books you might like:
Deb Caletti, *He's Gone*, 2013
Emma Donoghue, *Room*, 2010
Gillian Flynn, *Gone Girl*, 2012
John Fowles, *The Collector*, 1963
Graham Greene, *Brighton Rock*, 1938
Patricia Highsmith, *The Talented Mr. Ripley*, 1955
Shirley Jackson, *We Have Always Lived in the Castle*, 1962
Herman Koch, *The Dinner*, 2013
Jeffry P. Lindsay, *Darkly Dreaming Dexter*, 2004
Patrick McGrath, *Spider*, 1990
Ruth Rendell, *The Water's Lovely*, 2007
Charlotte Rogan, *The Lifeboat*, 2012
Adam Ross, *Mr. Peanut*, 2010
Dan Simmons, *Drood*, 2008
Chevy Stevens, *Still Missing*, 2010
Norah Vincent, *Thy Neighbor*, 2012
S.J. Watson, *Before I Go To Sleep*, 2011

`577`

LEE HOLLIS (Pseudonym of Rick Copp and Holly Simason)

Death of a Cupcake Queen

(New York: Kensington Books, 2015)

Series: Hayley Powell Food and Cocktails Mystery Series. Book 6
Story type: Amateur Detective; Cozy Mystery
Subject(s): Murder; Detective fiction; Reunions
Major character(s): Hayley Powell, Writer (food columnist), Detective—Amateur, Classmate (former, of Sabrina, Nykki, Ivy); Sabrina Merryweather, Classmate (former, of Hayley, Nykki, Ivy); Nykki Temple, Classmate (former, of Hayley, Sabrina, Ivy); Ivy Foster, Crime Victim, Classmate (former, of Hayley, Sabrina, Nykki)
Time period(s): 21st century; 2010s
Locale(s): Bar Harbor, Maine

Summary: Being the food columnist at a Maine newspaper is a delicious job for Hayley Powell, who gets invited to all the best parties. One she'd rather not be attending, however, is her own high school reunion. The presence of Sabrina, Nykki, and Ivy—three of the nastiest girls from the old days—is enough to sour any fun the event has to offer. When self-centered beauty queen Ivy is found dead at the reunion, Hayley dusts off her sleuthing skills and begins looking into the case. If she wants to find the killer, she better be careful. The high school's mean girls have apparently made an enemy, and that person may not stop at one murder. This is the sixth book in the Hayley Powell Food and Cocktails Mystery series by Lee Hollis.

Other books by the same author:
Death of a Chocoholic, 2014
Death of a Christmas Caterer, 2014
Death of a Coupon Clipper, 2013
Death of a Country Fried Redneck, 2012
Death of a Kitchen Diva, 2012

Other books you might like:

Claire Donally, *The Big Kitty*, 2012
Vicki Doudera, *A House to Die For*, 2010
Kathy Lynn Emerson, *Kilt Dead*, 2007
Sarah Graves, *The Dead Cat Bounce*, 1998
Lee Charles Kelley, *A Nose for Murder*, 2003
Allison Kingsley, *Mind Over Murder*, 2011
Leslie Meier, *Mail-Order Murder*, 1991

578

MARY ELLEN HUGHES

License to Dill

(New York: Berkley, 2015)

Series: Pickled and Preserved Mystery Series. Book 2
Story type: Amateur Detective; Cozy Mystery
Subject(s): Mystery; Detective fiction; Crime
Major character(s): Piper Lamb, Woman, Store Owner, Cook (pickles and preserves), Girlfriend (of Will Burchett); Will Burchett, Farmer (Christmas trees), Boyfriend (of Piper Lamb); Gerald Standley, Farmer (herbs), Crime Suspect; Raffaele Conti, Manager (soccer team), Crime Victim
Time period(s): 21st century; 2010s
Locale(s): Cloverdale, New York

Summary: In the second novel in the Pickled and Preserved Mystery series, Piper Lamb plays detective when crime strikes in Cloverdale, New York. Piper moved from Albany to Cloverdale to get away from her ex. She sells her culinary creations at her new shop, Piper's Picklings, and she is romantically involved with local Christmas tree farmer Will Burchett. But Piper's former boyfriend threatens to ruin everything when he follows her to Cloverdale. Piper is also busy with another matter. A European soccer team has come to town, and there's bad blood between Raffaele Conti, the team's manager, and Gerald Standley, the herb farmer who provides dill for Piper's pickles. When Raffaele turns up dead on Gerald's property, the herb farmer becomes the logical suspect. Piper uses her sleuthing skills to find the real killer and stop him from striking again.

Other books by the same author:
The Pickled Piper, 2014
Paper-Thin Alibi, 2008
Wealth of Deception, 2006
A Taste of Death, 2003
Resort to Murder, 2000

Other books you might like:
Avery Aames, *The Long Quiche Goodbye*, 2010
Susan Wittig Albert, *Death Comes Quickly*, 2014
Susan Wittig Albert, *Thyme of Death*, 1992
Laura Childs, *Death by Darjeeling*, 2001
Heather Vogel Frederick, *Pies and Prejudice*, 2010
Mary Freeman, *Devil's Trumpet*, 1999
Victoria Hamilton, *Bran New Death*, 2013

579

CHRISTINE HUSOM

Snow Way Out

(New York: Berkley, 2015)

Series: Snow Globe Shop Mystery Series. Book 1
Story type: Amateur Detective; Series
Subject(s): Mystery; Detective fiction; Crime
Major character(s): Camryn "Cami" Brooks, Store Owner (Curio Finds), Detective—Amateur, Friend (of Pinky); Alice "Pinky" Nelson, Restaurateur (coffee shop), Friend (of Cami); Jerrell Powers, Convict (former)
Time period(s): 21st century; 2010s
Locale(s): Brooks Landing, Minnesota

Summary: The first novel in the Snow Globe Shop Mystery series introduces Camryn "Cami" Brooks, a curio shop owner in Brooks Landing, Minnesota. Cami's Curio Finds shop adjoins a coffee shop that is owned by her friend, Alice "Pinky" Nelson. The women share resources and ideas, and they have decided to cohost a class about one of Cami's favorite curios—snow globes. Participants gather at Cami's shop to make their own snow globes. The class is a success, and the newly made snow globes go home with their owners. One of the globes is left behind, however. Its scene contains a figure dozing on a bench. When Cami walks home through the park, she sees a man who has been stabbed and posed similarly on a bench. Cami becomes a suspect in the strange murder, and she plays detective to prove her innocence and find the real killer.

Other books by the same author:
A Death in Lionel's Woods, 2013
The Noding Field Mystery, 2012
An Altar by the River, 2010
Buried in Wolf Lake, 2009
Murder in Winnebago County, 2008

Other books you might like:
Jane K. Cleland, *Consigned to Death*, 2006
Margaret Grace, *Madness in Miniature*, 2014
Margaret Grace, *Murder in Miniature*, 2008
Larry Karp, *The Music Box Murders*, 1999
Tamar Myers, *Larceny and Old Lace*, 1996
J.B. Stanley, *A Killer Collection*, 2006
Sebastian Stuart, *To the Manor Dead*, 2010

580

JULIE HYZY

All the President's Menus

(New York: Berkley, 2015)

Series: White House Chef Mystery Series. Book 8
Story type: Amateur Detective; Series
Subject(s): Mystery; Detective fiction; Crime
Major character(s): Olivia Paras, Spouse (of Leonard Gavin), Cook (White House executive chef); Marcel, Cook (pastry chef); Leonard Gavin, Agent (Secret Service), Spouse (of Olivia Paras)

Time period(s): 21st century; 2010s
Locale(s): Washington, District of Columbia

Summary: Olivia Paras's official job at the White House is that of executive chef. But she has also played detective when criminals or terrorists threatened the First Family or members of the staff. Not all of the White House Secret Service agents appreciate Olivia's sleuthing, but one smitten agent—Leonard Gavin—has recently become her husband. Now, as the Secret Service deals with safety concerns, Olivia deals with staff cutbacks in the kitchen. White House functions have been scaled back, so Olivia is looking forward to one event that hasn't been cancelled—a dinner for a presidential candidate from Saardisca. While Olivia and the other chefs prepare for the dinner, trouble brews in the kitchen. First, pastry chef Marcel faints after being drugged, and then another chef dies. Olivia must identify the killer in her kitchen before another victim falls. This novel is the eighth in the White House Chef Mystery series.

Other books by the same author:
Home of the Braised, 2014
Grace Under Pressure, 2010
Hail to the Chef, 2008
State of the Onion, 2008
Deadly Blessings, 2005

Other books you might like:
Claudia Bishop, *A Taste for Murder*, 1994
Miranda Bliss, *Cooking Up Murder*, 2006
Dorothy Cannell, *The Thin Woman*, 1984
Virginia Rich, *The Cooking School Murders*, 1982
Phyllis Richman, *The Butter Did It*, 1997
Al Roker, *The Morning Show Murders*, 2009
Michael Lee West, *Gone with a Handsomer Man*, 2011

581

ARNALDUR INDRIDASON
VICTORIA CRIBB, Translator

Reykjavik Nights
(New York: St. Martin's Press, 2015)

Series: Reykjavik Murder Mystery Series. Book 10
Story type: Police Procedural; Series
Subject(s): Murder; Law enforcement; Mystery
Major character(s): Erlendur Sveinsson, Police Officer, Detective—Police
Time period(s): 20th century; 1970s (1974)
Locale(s): Reykjavik, Iceland

Summary: In Reykjavik, Iceland, Erlendur Sveinsson does what most young police officers do: he patrols the night streets, writing tickets and escorting wayward drunks to the station. That all changes when a homeless man is found dead on his beat, the victim of an apparent accidental drowning. Something doesn't sit right with Erlendur, but because of the dead man's status, no one in the department seems to care about the case. Erlendur begins his own investigation and makes a connection between the man's death and that of a young woman who recently went missing. As he travels through the dark inner circles of the city's underworld, Erlendur finds more than the answers he's looking for. He's also

developing the foundation for a successful career as an investigator. This is the tenth book in Arnaldur Indridason's Reykjavik Murder Mystery series.

Other books by the same author:
Strange Shores, 2013
The Draining Lake, 2007
Voices, 2006
Silence of the Grave, 2005
Jar City, 2004

Other books you might like:
Quentin Bates, *Frozen Out*, 2011
Kjell Eriksson, *The Princess of Burundi*, 2006
Karin Fossum, *Don't Look Back*, 2002
Jo Nesbo, *The Redbreast*, 2007
Michael Ridpath, *Where the Shadows Lie*, 2011
Yrsa Sigurdardottir, *Last Rituals*, 2007
Yrsa Sigurdardottir, *Someone to Watch Over Me*, 2015
Ami Thorarinsson, *Season of the Witch*, 2012

582

SUE ANN JAFFARIAN

Ghost in the Guacamole
(New York: Berkley, 2015)

Series: Ghost of Granny Apples Mystery Series. Book 5
Story type: Paranormal; Series
Subject(s): Mystery; Detective fiction; Crime
Major character(s): Emma Whitecastle, Psychic, Granddaughter (great-great-great-granddaughter of Granny Apples), Detective—Amateur; Granny Apples, Spirit (ghost), Detective—Amateur, Grandmother (great-great-great-grandmother of Emma); Lucinda "Lucy" Ricardo, Sister (of Ricarda), Daughter (of Felix), Businesswoman (Roble Foods); Ricarda "Rikki" Ricardo, Sister (of Lucinda), Daughter (of Felix), Businesswoman (Roble Foods); Felix Ricardo, Father (deceased, of Lucinda and Ricarda), Spirit (ghost)
Time period(s): 21st century; 2010s
Locale(s): Los Angeles, California

Summary: Emma Whitecastle is a psychic who has a unique relationship with the spirit of her ancestor, Granny Apples. The two women—one mortal, one supernatural—work together to help Emma's clients solve mysteries and crimes that are troubling them. Lucinda "Lucy" and Ricarda "Rikki" Ricardo come to Emma when they need to make an important business decision. The two sisters inherited Roble Foods when their father, Felix, died, and they disagree on what to do with the family business. Rikki wants to keep the business, and Lucy wants it off her hands. When Emma communicates with Felix, the sisters learn that their father agrees with Lucy. In fact, he believes that they'll be risking their lives if they don't sell. Felix should know; he was murdered, and his killer could strike again. Emma and Granny Apples use their psychic and sleuthing skills to keep that from happening. This is the fifth novel in the Ghost of Granny Apples Mystery series.

Other books by the same author:
Ghost of a Gamble, 2014
The Rabbit Died, 2011

Murder in Vein, 2010
Ghost a la Mode, 2009
Too Big to Miss: An Odelia Grey Mystery, 2001

Other books you might like:
P.J. Alderman, *Haunting Jordan*, 2009
Susan M. Boyer, *Lowcountry Boil*, 2012
Helen Chappell, *Slow Dancing with the Angel of Death*, 1996
E.J. Copperman, *Night of the Living Deed*, 2010
Jim Lavene, *That Old Flame of Mine*, 2013
Thorne Smith, *Topper*, 1926

583

MIRANDA JAMES (Pseudonym of Dean James)

Arsenic and Old Books

(New York: Berkley, 2015)

Series: Cat in the Stacks Mystery Series. Book 6
Story type: Cozy Mystery; Series
Subject(s): Mystery; Detective fiction; Crime
Major character(s): Charlie Harris, Librarian (Athena College), Widow(er); Lucinda Beckwith Long, Political Figure (mayor of Athena), Mother (of Beck); Beck Long, Man, Political Figure (candidate for state senate), Son (of Lucinda); Jasper Singletary, Political Figure (candidate for state senate); Marie Steverton, Professor, Crime Victim; Diesel, Cat
Time period(s): 21st century; 2010s
Locale(s): Athena, Mississippi

Summary: College librarian Charlie Harris and his cat, Diesel, investigate another case of murder in the sixth Cat in the Stacks mystery. When Lucinda Long, mayor of Athena, Mississippi, donates family diaries from the Civil War era to Athena College, she wants Charlie to take charge of their verification and preservation. Lucinda's son, Beck, is planning a run for the state senate, and Lucinda believes that promoting the Long family history can only help his campaign. She is wrong. Another potential candidate, Jasper Singletary, wants to get his hands on the diaries to prove the claims his clan has made for generations about the Longs' sullied past. Marie Steverton, an unpopular professor at the college, also shows a suspicious interest in the diaries. When Marie is killed, and the diaries disappear and reappear, Charlie must find the murderer and the motive before he becomes the next victim.

Other books by the same author:
Bless Her Dead Little Heart, 2014
The Silence of the Library, 2014
File M for Murder, 2012
Classified as Murder, 2011
Murder Past Due, 2010

Other books you might like:
Garrison Allen, *Desert Cat*, 1994
Lorna Barrett, *Murder Is Binding*, 2008
Ali Brandon, *Double Booked for Death*, 2011
Kate Carlisle, *Homicide in Hardcover*, 2009
Carole Nelson Douglas, *Catnap*, 1992
Joan Hess, *Strangled Prose*, 1986

Allison Kingsley, *Mind Over Murder*, 2011
Ann B. Ross, *Miss Julia Lays Down the Law*, 2015

584

J.A. JANCE

Cold Betrayal

(New York: Touchstone, 2015)

Series: Ali Reynolds Series. Book 10
Story type: Contemporary; Series
Subject(s): Mystery; Detective fiction; Crime
Major character(s): Ali Reynolds, Television Personality (former newscaster), Spouse (of B. Simpson), Mother (of Chris), Mother (mother-in-law of Athena), Friend (of Sister Anselm); B. Simpson, Technician (security expert), Spouse (of Ali); Chris, Son (of Ali), Spouse (of Athena); Athena, Spouse (of Chris), Granddaughter (of Betsy Peterson), Daughter (daughter-in-law of Ali); Betsy Peterson, Grandmother (of Athena); Anselm Becker, Religious (nun), Friend (of Ali); Enid Tower, Pregnant Teenager, Cult Member, Runaway, Accident Victim
Time period(s): 21st century; 2010s
Locale(s): Sedona, Arizona; Bemidji, Minnesota

Summary: Ali Reynolds juggles two cases in two states in the tenth series entry. Ali is adjusting happily to life in Sedona, Arizona, with her new husband, B. Simpson, but her daughter-in-law needs her help. Athena, who is married to Ali's son, Chris, believes that someone is trying to harm her grandmother, Betsy Peterson. She believes she has found evidence that someone entered Betsy's Minnesota home at night and tried to kill her. When the local authorities won't help, B. installs a security system. Ali gets involved in another case when her friend, Sister Anselm Becker, cares for an accident victim in the hospital. The victim, a pregnant teenager named Enid Tower, was struck on a highway while she was escaping from a cult compound. Sister Anselm and Ali learn that "The Family" forces Enid and other young girls into polygamous marriages. Ali continues her search for Betsy's would-be killer while she exposes the cult's dark secrets.

Other books by the same author:
Moving Target, 2014
Edge of Evil, 2005
Desert Heat, 1993
Hour of the Hunter, 1991
Until Proven Guilty, 1985

Other books you might like:
Mary Higgins Clark, *The Cinderella Murder*, 2014
Tess Gerritsen, *Die Again*, 2014
Darrell James, *Nazareth Child*, 2011
Kelly Lange, *The Reporter*, 2002
Sylvia Nobel, *Deadly Sanctuary*, 1998
Twist Phelan, *Heir Apparent*, 2007
    Twist Phelan, co-author
Kathy Reichs, *Bones Never Lie*, 2014
Hank Phillippi Ryan, *The Other Woman*, 2012
Hank Phillippi Ryan, *Prime Time*, 2007
Betty Webb, *Desert Noir*, 2001

585

MAUREEN JENNINGS

No Known Grave

(Toronto, Ontario, Canada: McClelland & Stewart, 2014)

Series: Tom Tyler Mystery Series. Book 3
Story type: Historical - World War II; Series
Subject(s): Mystery; Detective fiction; Crime
Major character(s): Tom Tyler, Detective—Police (detective inspector); Daisy Stevens, Nurse; Dr. Beck, Doctor (psychiatrist)
Time period(s): 20th century; 1940s (1942)
Locale(s): Ludlow, Shropshire

Summary: Detective Inspector Tom Tyler investigates murders at a veterans' convalescent home in the third series entry. It is 1942, and a manor house in Ludlow, Shrophire, is being used to house soldiers who have been physically and psychologically injured in the war. Anglican sisters run the facility, nursing the blinded and maimed men back to some semblance of health. St. Anne's Convalescent Hospital is the last place in his jurisdiction that Tom Tyler would expect a crime to occur. When he is called in to investigate two homicides that were committed on the property, Tyler is at a loss as to the murderer's means and motives. The hospital is isolated and secure; most of its residents are physically incapable of carrying out such an act. As Tyler launches his investigation, he starts receiving disturbing letters that reveal the true nature of the crime.

Other books by the same author:
Beware This Boy, 2012
Season of Darkness, 2011
A Journeyman to Grief, 2007
Does Your Mother Know?, 2006
Except the Dying, 1997

Other books you might like:
Agatha Christie, *Towards Zero*, 1944
   Agatha Christie, co-author
Brian Cooper, *The Cross of San Vicente*, 1988
John Gardner, *Bottled Spider*, 2002
John Lawton, *Black Out*, 1995
Ngaio Marsh, *Colour Scheme*, 1943
Laura Wilson, *Stratton's War*, 2008

586

IRIS JOHANSEN

Your Next Breath

(New York: St. Martin's Press, 2015)

Series: Catherine Ling Series. Book 4
Subject(s): Espionage; Crime; Mother-son relations
Major character(s): Catherine Ling, Agent (CIA), Mother (of Luke), Friend (of Hu Chang); Luke, 11-Year-Old, Son (of Catherine); Hu Chang, Friend (mentor of Catherine)
Time period(s): 21st century; 2010s
Locale(s): China

Summary: In the fourth novel in the Catherine Ling series, Catherine continues to become reacquainted with her son Luke, who was recently rescued after years of captivity. Catherine has been with the CIA since she was a teenager in Hong Kong. When Luke was kidnapped at the age of two, it took nine long years to attain his release. Now Catherine and Luke's reunion is threatened by a new danger. An unknown killer is claiming victims who are connected to Catherine. A fellow CIA operative, a former streetwalker, and a trusted colleague have all been murdered, and the perpetrator shows no interest in stopping his spree. Catherine fears that the next targets will be the two people who are most important to her—her son and Hu Chang, her mentor. Before she can stop the killer, Catherine must figure out which of her enemies is behind the crimes.

Other books by the same author:
Shadow Play, 2015
Live to See Tomorrow, 2014
What Doesn't Kill You, 2012
Chasing the Night, 2010
The Face of Deception, 1998

Other books you might like:
Jeff Abbott, *Adrenaline*, 2011
Larry Bond, *The Enemy Within*, 1996
Christopher Chambers, *Sympathy for the Devil*, 2001
Catherine Coulter, *The Cove*, 1996
Tess Gerritsen, *Die Again*, 2014
Francine Mathews, *The Cutout*, 2001
Taylor Smith, *Guilt by Silence*, 1995
Amanda Kyle Williams, *Club Twelve*, 1990

587

MERRY JONES

In the Woods

(Sutton, Surrey, England: Severn House Publishers, 2015)

Series: Harper Jennings Mystery Series. Book 5
Story type: Contemporary; Series
Subject(s): Mystery; Detective fiction; Crime
Major character(s): Harper Jennings, Mother (of Chloe), Woman, Veteran (Iraq War), Spouse (of Hank), Archaeologist; Hank Harper, Scientist (geologist), Spouse (of Harper), Father (of Chloe); Chloe, Baby, Daughter (of Harper and Hank); Phil Russo, Hunter, Crime Victim; Albert Rogers, Worker (pipeline), Crime Victim; Joe Slader, Police Officer (chief)
Time period(s): 21st century; 2010s
Locale(s): Black Moshannon State Park, Pennsylvania

Summary: Harper Jennings has mixed feelings about the camping trip she and her husband have planned. Harper, an Iraq War vet, is pleased to have some alone time with Hank, who survived a recent brain injury, but she doesn't like being away from their infant daughter, Chloe. Their venture into Black Moshannon State Park in Pennsylvania proves more dangerous than Harper and Hank expected. Harper finds the body of a murder victim, and their camping group receives a hostile welcome from the Hunt Club, a survivalist group that considers the forest its private property. The club's members are vehemently

Mystery

opposed to the gas fracking that is taking place in the region. When a camper disappears, and another murder takes place, Harper uses her proven skills to search for a killer. This novel is the fifth in the Harper Jennings Mystery series.

Other books by the same author:
Outside Eden, 2013
The Trouble with Charlie, 2013
Summer Session, 2011
The Borrowed and Blue Murders, 2008
The Nanny Murders, 2005

Other books you might like:
Mary Anna Evans, *Rituals*, 2013
Mary Anna Evans, *Artifacts*, 2003
Elly Griffiths, *The Crossing Places*, 2010
Jamie Harrison, *The Edge of the Crazies*, 1995
Cara Hoffman, *Be Safe I Love You*, 2014
Sharyn McCrumb, *Sick of Shadows*, 1984
Julia Spencer-Fleming, *One Was a Soldier*, 2011

588

DAVID JOY

Where All Light Tends to Go

(New York: G.P. Putnam's Sons, 2015)

Story type: Literary
Subject(s): Crime; Drugs; Murder
Major character(s): Jacob McNeely, 18-Year-Old, Son (of Charlie and Laura), Boyfriend (former, of Maggie), Worker (crystal meth operation); Charlie McNeely, Drug Dealer (crystal meth), Spouse (of Laura), Father (of Jacob); Laura McNeely, Addict (crystal meth), Spouse (of Charlie), Mother (of Jacob); Maggie, Girlfriend (former, of Jacob); Robbie, Drug Dealer (supplier to Charlie)
Time period(s): 21st century; 2010s
Locale(s): Cashiers, North Carolina

Summary: The way 18-year-old Jacob McNeely sees it, he is trapped in his life in the Appalachian community of Cashiers, North Carolina. He quit school when he was 16 to work for his father, Charlie, a crystal meth dealer. His mother, Laura, is addicted to the drugs Charlie sells. Jacob used to have a girlfriend, Maggie, but he ended their relationship so he wouldn't tangle her up with his sorry family. Meth dealing is a dangerous business, and Charlie has no qualms about killing those who cross him. When Charlie orders the murder of one of his suppliers, the two employees he charges with the task fail and put everyone involved with the meth business in danger. Charlie takes matters into his own hands, and then seals Jacob's fate by making him get rid of the corpses. When Maggie comes back into Jacob's life, it seems he may have a chance to get away from the mountains and the bleak future he anticipates. First novel.

Other books by the same author:
Growing Gills: A Fly Fisherman's Journey, 2011

Other books you might like:
Wiley Cash, *A Land More Kind Than Home*, 2012
Harry Crews, *A Feast of Snakes*, 1976

Charles Frazier, *Nightwoods*, 2011
Sharyn McCrumb, *She Walks These Hills*, 1994
Steve Weddle, *Country Hardball*, 2013
Daniel Woodrell, *Winter's Bone: A Novel*, 2006

589

MICHAEL A. KAHN

The Sirena Quest

(Scottsdale, Arizona: Poisoned Pen Press, 2015)

Story type: Amateur Detective
Subject(s): Mystery; Detective fiction; Crime
Major character(s): Lou Solomon, Lawyer, Widow(er), Friend (of Ray, Gordie, Billy), Graduate (Barrett College, 1974); Gordie Cohen, Graduate (Barrett College, 1974), Friend (of Lou, Ray, Billy); William "Bronco Billy" McCormick, Friend (of Lou, Gordie, Ray), Graduate (Barrett College, 1974); Ray Gorman, Graduate (Barrett College, 1974), Friend (of Lou, Gordie, Billy); Robert Godwin, Graduate (Barrett College, 1959), Wealthy
Time period(s): 20th century; 1990s (1994)
Locale(s): United States

Summary: Lou Solomon, Gordie Cohen, Ray Gorman, and William "Bronco Billy" McCormick became fast friends while they were undergrads at Barrett College in New England. They called themselves the James Gang— after their dorm, James Hall—and they were inseparable until they graduated in 1974. The men's 20th reunion is approaching, and another alumnus—Robert Godwin, '59— has made an intriguing challenge to the Barrett community. The college was once home to *Sirena*, a Greco-Roman sculpture that disappeared from the school in 1959. The person who finds and returns the statue to Barrett will receive a $2 million prize. Godwin will also endow the school with $23 million. Lou, Gordie, Ray, and Billy reunite to embark on a quest for *Sirena*. With the June 17 deadline looming, the members of the James Gang follow clues across the country and renew old friendships.

Other books by the same author:
Face Value, 2014
The Mourning Sexton, 2005
Due Diligence, 1995
Death Benefits, 1992
The Canaan Legacy, 1988

Other books you might like:
Lawrence Block, *Burglars Can't Be Choosers*, 1977
W.R. Burnett, *The Asphalt Jungle*, 1949
Ian Caldwell, *The Rule of Four*, 2004
Michael Crichton, *The Great Train Robbery*, 1975
Janet Evanovich, *The Chase*, 2014
Lev Grossman, *Codex*, 2004
Donald E. Westlake, *The Hot Rock*, 1970

590

JOSEPH KANON

Leaving Berlin

(New York: Atria Books, 2015)

Story type: Espionage; Historical
Subject(s): Cold War, 1945-1991; Espionage; Spies
Major character(s): Alex Meier, Writer, Religious (Jewish), Immigrant, Spy
Time period(s): 20th century; 1940s (1948)
Locale(s): Berlin, Germany

Summary: In the aftermath of World War II, Alex Meier finds that he is no longer safe in his adopted country. Meier came to America before the Nazis rose to power in Germany, his homeland. Now it is 1948—the dawn of the McCarthy era—and Meier's political history has made him a candidate for deportation. To earn the right to stay in the United States for himself and his family, Meier strikes a dangerous deal with the CIA: Meier will return to Berlin to gather intelligence for the Americans. Meier finds his city a changed place that is divided physically, politically, and culturally. His mission gets off to a bad start when an East German operative dies, and Meier has to go on the run. As Meier navigates the complex, corrupt landscape of postwar Berlin, he discovers the shocking truth about his mission.

Other books by the same author:
Stardust, 2009
Alibi, 2005
The Good German, 2001
The Prodigal Spy: A Novel, 1998
Los Alamos, 1997

Other books you might like:
David Downing, *Lehrter Station*, 2012
David Downing, *Masaryk Station*, 2013
Tom Gabbay, *The Tehran Conviction*, 2009
Graham Greene, *The Third Man*, 1950
W.E.B. Griffin, *Top Secret*, 2014
David John, *Flight from Berlin*, 2012
Denis Johnson, *The Laughing Monsters*, 2014
Philip Kerr, *German Requiem*, 1991
Philip Kerr, *The Lady from Zagreb*, 2015
Philip Kerr, *A Quiet Flame*, 2009
Robert Littell, *The Company: A Novel of the CIA*, 2002
Charles McCarry, *Christopher's Ghosts*, 2007
Ian McEwan, *The Innocent*, 1990
Olen Steinhauer, *The Bridge of Sighs*, 2003

591

MICHAEL KARDOS

Before He Finds Her

(New York: Mysterious Press, 2015)

Story type: Contemporary
Subject(s): Mystery; Crime; Detective fiction
Major character(s): Ramsey Miller, Crime Suspect, Fugitive, Spouse (of Allison), Father (of Meg), Truck Driver; Allison Miller, Spouse (of Ramsey), Mother (of Meg), Crime Victim; Meg Miller, Girl (also known as Melanie Denison), Crime Victim, Daughter (of Ramsey and Allison), Pregnant Teenager; Wayne, Uncle (of Meg)
Time period(s): 21st century; 2010s
Locale(s): Silver Bay, New Jersey; Fredonia, West Virginia

Summary: When truck driver Ramsey Miller murdered his wife in 1991, the public and the Millers' neighbors in Silver Bay, New Jersey, were led to believe that he also killed the couple's three-year-old daughter, Meg. But Meg survived and was relocated to West Virginia under the Witness Protection Program. Ramsey was never caught. For 15 years, Meg has been living with her aunt and uncle as Melanie Denison, and she is tired of the restrictive conditions that are supposed to keep her safe. In an ill-advised attempt to assert her independence, Melanie gets involved with a teacher and becomes pregnant. She wants to make a new start for her child, and to do that, Melanie believes she must find Ramsey. Melanie heads back to Silver Bay, hoping to finally confront the man who killed her mother.

Other books by the same author:
The Art and Craft of Fiction, 2012
The Three-Day Affair, 2012
One Last Good Time, 2010

Other books you might like:
David Baldacci, *Split Second*, 2003
Kate Brian, *Shadowlands*, 2013
David Cristofano, *The Exceptions*, 2012
Jeffery Deaver, *The Edge*, 2011
Tom Epperson, *Sailor*, 2012
Gillian Flynn, *Dark Places*, 2009
Lisa Gardner, *The Survivors Club*, 2001
Andrew Gross, *The Blue Zone: A Novel*, 2007
Iris Johansen, *The Perfect Witness*, 2014
Pam Lewis, *Speak Softly, She Can Hear*, 2005
John Lutz, *In for the Kill*, 2007
Alex Marwood, *The Wicked Girls*, 2012
Jax Miller, *Freedom's Child*, 2015
Ridley Pearson, *Cut and Run*, 2005
Daniel Pyne, *Fifty Mice*, 2014
Chevy Stevens, *Never Knowing*, 2011
Lisa Unger, *Black Out*, 2008

592

DIANE KELLY

Death, Taxes, and Cheap Sunglasses

(New York: St. Martin's Paperbacks, 2015)

Series: Tara Holloway Series. Book 8
Story type: Contemporary; Series
Subject(s): Mystery; Detective fiction; Crime
Major character(s): Tara Holloway, Agent (IRS), Girlfriend (of Nick Pratt); Nick Pratt, Agent (IRS), Boyfriend (of Tara Holloway)
Time period(s): 21st century; 2010s

Mystery

Locale(s): Dallas, Texas

Summary: In the eighth Tara Holloway novel, Dallas IRS agent Tara works a case that gets personal. Tara's skills with numbers and guns make her a valuable player in the government's fight against con artists and tax cheats. But her talent and nerve are tested when the IRS teams up with the DEA to target a big drug operation. IRS agent Nick Pratt, who recently became Tara's boyfriend, is also involved in the case. He must go undercover among the bad guys, and Tara knows that the assignment is putting Nick's life in danger. Tara wants to protect Nick, but she has to be careful she doesn't let her concern interfere with the success of the mission. She must also try not to put her own life in jeopardy.

Other books by the same author:
Death, Taxes and Silver Spurs, 2014
Paw Enforcement, 2014
Love, Luck and Little Green Men, 2013
Death, Taxes and a Skinny No-Whip Latte, 2012
Death, Taxes and a French Manicure, 2011

Other books you might like:
Connie Feddersen, *Dead in the Water*, 1993
Maggie Sefton, *Knit One, Kill Two*, 2005
Connie Shelton, *Deadly Gamble*, 1995
Patricia Smiley, *Cool Cache: A Tucker Sinclair Mystery*, 2008
Patricia Smiley, *False Profits*, 2004
Malinda Terreri, *A Tax Deductible Death*, 2001
Maggie Toussaint, *In for a Penny*, 2008

593

TRACY KIELY

Murder with a Twist

(Woodbury, Minnesota: Midnight Ink, 2015)

Series: Nic and Nigel Mystery Series. Book 1
Story type: Cozy Mystery; Series
Subject(s): Detective fiction; Family; Dogs
Major character(s): Nic Martini, Detective—Police (former), Spouse (of Nigel), Woman; Nigel Martini, Spouse (of Nic), Cousin (of Daphne), Nephew (of Olive); Daphne Beasley, Cousin (of Nigel), Daughter (of Olive); Olive, Aunt (of Nigel), Mother (of Daphne); Leo, Missing Person
Time period(s): 21st century; 2010s
Locale(s): New York, New York

Summary: Nic and Nigel Martini are a couple of high-society big shots from Los Angeles, trying New York City on for size while they are attending a relative's birthday party. The Big Apple is not unfamiliar territory to Nic, who used to be an NYPD detective before she met Nigel and was spirited off to the West Coast. When Leo, the philandering husband of one of Nigel's cousins, goes missing, his pampered relatives beg Nic to investigate, even though the consensus is that Nigel's cousin would be better off if Leo stayed gone. To track the missing man, Nic will have to reacquaint herself with some lowlifes from her old line of work—a proposition that is becoming deadlier by the minute. This is

the first book in Tracy Kiely's Nic and Nigel Mystery series.

Other books by the same author:
Murder Most Austen, 2012
Murder Most Persuasive, 2011
Murder on the Bride's Side, 2010
Murder at Longbourn, 2009

Other books you might like:
Agatha Christie, *The Secret Adversary*, 1922
Dashiell Hammett, *The Thin Man*, 1934
Laurie R. King, *The Beekeeper's Apprentice*, 1994
Ngaio Marsh, *Night of the Vulcan*, 1951
Robin Paige, *Death at Bishop's Keep*, 1994
Dorothy L. Sayers, *Gaudy Night*, 1935
Thorne Smith, *Topper*, 1926

594

SHANNON KIRK

Method 15/33

(Longboat Key, Florida: Oceanview Publishing, 2015)

Story type: Contemporary
Subject(s): Mystery; Psychology; Kidnapping
Major character(s): Unnamed Character, Narrator, Girl, 16-Year-Old, Pregnant Teenager, Kidnap Victim; Unnamed Character, Kidnapper; Doctor, Doctor; Mr. Obvious, Man; Mrs. Obvious, Woman; Roger Liu, FBI Agent
Time period(s): 21st century; 2010s
Locale(s): United States

Summary: When the narrator of this novel, a 16-year-old pregnant girl, is abducted and held at a remote farmhouse, she does not surrender to her fate. She knows that the couple who visits her, whom she refers to as Mr. and Mrs. Obvious, intend to take her baby when it's born. She also knows that her repulsive kidnapper has underestimated her. The girl is smart, resourceful, and possibly a sociopath. Despite the frightening conditions of her captivity, she is able to take a meticulous inventory of the items in her surroundings that could be used in her escape. A blanket, a window, a loose floorboard, a keyhole—these features in her surroundings could serve a purpose if the girl thinks and acts carefully. As the days pass, the girl does more than plan her escape, however. She also thinks about how she will make her captor pay for what he has done. First novel.

Other books you might like:
Chelsea Cain, *Heartsick*, 2007
Gillian Flynn, *Gone Girl*, 2012
Lisa Gardner, *Alone*, 2005
John Katzenbach, *What Comes Next*, 2012
Cody McFadyen, *Shadow Man*, 2006
Jennifer McMahon, *Promise Not to Tell*, 2006
Stuart Neville, *Stolen Souls*, 2011

595

ED KOVACS

The Russian Bride

(New York: St. Martin's Press, 2015)

Story type: Contemporary; Espionage
Subject(s): Military life; Marriage; Espionage
Major character(s): Kit Bennings, Agent (undercover), Military Personnel, Spouse (of Yulana); Yulana Petkova, Woman, Spouse (of Kit), Engineer, Mother; Viktor Popov, Organized Crime Figure
Time period(s): 21st century; 2010s
Locale(s): Moscow, Russia; Los Angeles, California; Las Vegas, Nevada

Summary: Military intelligence officer Major Kit Bennings is working undercover to flush out a mole at the US embassy in Moscow. As he watches his fellow Americans, trying to find the spy, he is being watched himself and is soon dragged into a deadly game. A Russian mob boss with ties to the KGB kidnaps Kit's sister and blackmails Kit into marrying a Russian bride. With his loyalty compromised, Kit is forced to go rogue. He takes his new wife to the United States, where she follows her own agenda. When he realizes he's part of the mobster's scheme to acquire a devastating pulse weapon from the United States, Kit must tread carefully. Enlisting the help of the few friends who still trust him, Kit tries to find a way to stop the mobster's plot and find his sister before it's too late.

Other books by the same author:
Burnt Black, 2013
Good Junk, 2012
Storm Damage, 2011
Unseen Forces, 2004

Other books you might like:
Joseph Finder, *The Moscow Club*, 1991
John Le Carre, *The Spy Who Came in from the Cold*, 1963
Robert Littell, *Legends*, 2005
Charles McCarry, *The Miernik Dossier*, 1973
Martin Cruz Smith, *Gorky Park*, 1981
Keith Thomson, *Once a Spy: A Novel*, 2010
John Trenhaile, *The Mahjong Spies*, 1986

596

JON LAND

Black Scorpion

(New York: Tom Doherty Associates, 2015)

Series: Michael Tiranno the Tyrant Series. Book 2
Story type: Revenge; Series
Subject(s): Conspiracy; Kidnapping; Human rights
Major character(s): Michael Tiranno, Businessman (casino owner), Wealthy, Boyfriend (of Scarlett); Scarlett Swan, Archaeologist, Kidnap Victim, Girlfriend (of Michael); Vladimir Dracu, Leader (of Black Scorpion), Organized Crime Figure
Time period(s): 21st century; 2010s
Locale(s): Las Vegas, Nevada

Summary: Las Vegas casino owner and financial giant Michael Tiranno is not a man to be messed with. An orphan raised by a Sicilian mob boss, Michael has already used his power and heroism to thwart a terrorist attack on Las Vegas. Now he faces another deadly menace when the leader of an international human trafficking cartel known as the Black Scorpion makes him a target. Vladimir Dracu claims a linage back the infamous Vlad the Impaler, but it's a grudge born in a connection with Michael's past that fuels his quest for revenge. When Black Scorpion kidnaps Michael's girlfriend, he must again draw upon his vast resources and his ruthless determination to bring down a deadly threat. This is the second book in author Jon Land's Michael Tiranno the Tyrant series.

Other books by the same author:
Strong Enough to Die, 2009
The Seven Sins: The Tyrant Ascending, 2008
The Walls of Jericho, 1997
The Eighth Trumpet, 1989
The Omega Command, 1986

Other books you might like:
Robert Ferrigno, *Prayers for the Assassin: A Novel*, 2006
Victor Gischler, *Go-Go Girls of the Apocalypse*, 2008
Stephen King, *The Stand*, 1978
Douglas Preston, *Blasphemy*, 2008
Mario Puzo, *The Godfather*, 1969
James Rollins, *Sandstorm*, 2004
Neal Stephenson, *Snow Crash*, 1992

597

AMANDA LEE (Pseudonym of Gayle Trent)

Wicked Stitch

(New York: Penguin Publishing Group, 2015)

Series: Embroidery Mystery Series. Book 8
Story type: Cozy Mystery; Series
Subject(s): Mystery; Detective fiction; Crime
Major character(s): Marcy Singer, Detective—Amateur, Store Owner (The Seven Year Stitch), Girlfriend (of Ted Nash), Crime Suspect; Ted Nash, Detective—Police, Boyfriend (of Marcy Singer); Nellie Davis, Store Owner (Scentsibilities), Sister (of Clara); Clara, Store Owner (Knitted and Needled), Sister (of Nellie), Crime Victim
Time period(s): 21st century; 2010s
Locale(s): Tallulah Falls, Oregon

Summary: Amateur detective Marcy Singer has investigated several murders in Tallulah Falls, Oregon, but she becomes the suspect in the eighth Embroidery Mystery. Marcy, proprietor of the needlework shop The Seven Year Stitch, is busy setting up her booth for the town's upcoming Renaissance Faire. She isn't too busy to notice that Nellie Davis and her annoying sister have booths flanking hers. Nellie owns an aromatherapy store; Clara is in the process of opening Knitted and Needled, a needlework shop that will compete directly with Marcy's. So when Marcy finds Clara strangled to death with a scarf, she becomes the obvious suspect. As in previous Tallulah Falls cases, Marcy plays detective, but this time she's trying to clear her own name. With help from her boyfriend, police detective Ted Nash, Marcy learns that she is not the only person who had a motive for killing Clara.

Other books by the same author:
Thread End, 2014
The Long Stitch Goodnight, 2012
Stitch Me Deadly, 2011
Thread Reckoning, 2011
The Quick and the Thread, 2008

Other books you might like:
Janet Bolin, *Dire Threads*, 2011
Elizabeth Lynn Casey, *Sew Deadly*, 2009
Monica Ferris, *Crewel World*, 1999
Monica Ferris, *The Drowning Spool*, 2014
Earlene Fowler, *Fool's Puzzle*, 1994
Amanda Lee, *The Quick and the Thread*, 2010
Clare O'Donohue, *The Lover's Knot*, 2008

598

PATRICK LEE

Signal

(New York: Minotaur Books, 2015)

Series: Sam Dryden Series. Book 2
Story type: Contemporary; Series
Subject(s): Mystery; Detective fiction; Technology
Major character(s): Sam Dryden, Veteran (former Special Forces operative), Friend (of Claire Dunham); Claire Dunham, Security Officer (security chief at Bayliss Labs), Friend (of Sam)
Time period(s): 21st century; 2010s
Locale(s): United States

Summary: Sam Dryden is no longer active as a Special Forces operative, but he still puts his skills to work when the need arises. He responds without question when his former colleague, Claire Dunham, makes a late-night call seeking Dryden's help. Claire is in charge of internal security at Bayliss Labs, an operation that has ties to a defense contractor. Bayliss has developed a machine that harnesses the power of neutrino particles and allows users to manipulate time and, in a sense, predict the future. The technology has already attracted the attention of some groups who want to use the device for their own purposes. Others are determined to destroy the device, as evidenced by a fire at Bayliss Labs. Together, Dryden and Claire must try to keep the device safe and out of enemy hands. This novel is the second in the Sam Dryden series.

Other books by the same author:
Runner, 2014
Deep Sky, 2011
Ghost Country, 2010
The Breach, 2009

Other books you might like:
Mark Alpert, *Final Theory*, 2008
Greig Beck, *Beneath the Dark Ice*, 2010

Joseph Finder, *Paranoia*, 2004
Philip Kerr, *The Grid*, 1995
Kira Peikoff, *No Time to Die*, 2014
Matt Richtel, *Hooked*, 2007

599

DONNA LEON

Falling in Love

(New York: Atlantic Monthly Press, 2015)

Series: Guido Brunetti Series. Book 24
Story type: Police Procedural; Series
Subject(s): Mystery; Detective fiction; Crime
Major character(s): Guido Brunetti, Detective—Police (commissario), Spouse (of Paola); Paola Brunetti, Spouse (of Guido Brunetti); Flavia Petrelli, Singer (opera)
Time period(s): 21st century; 2010s
Locale(s): Venice, Italy

Summary: Commissario Guido Brunetti helped prove opera singer Flavia Petrelli's innocence in the first murder mystery in the series. In the 24th Brunetti novel, Flavia needs the commissario's help again. Flavia is now a renowned opera diva who has attracted an impressive following throughout Europe. But one of her fans has crossed a line and become her stalker. At venues in St. Petersburg, London, and Amsterdam, Flavia has received extravagant gifts of flowers and jewelry. In Venice she returns to her dressing room to find it overflowing with yellow roses. When she has dinner with her old friend Brunetti and his wife, Flavia voices her concerns about her unknown admirer. Brunetti isn't convinced that the fan's behavior is sinister until two of Flavia's acquaintances are injured by a violent assailant. The scenario is a new one for Brunetti, who educates himself on the psychology of stalking so he can understand what Flavia is up against.

Other books by the same author:
By Its Cover, 2014
Death and Judgment, 1995
Dressed for Death, 1994
Death in a Strange Country, 1993
Death at La Fenice, 1992

Other books you might like:
Grace Brophy, *The Last Enemy*, 2007
Andrea Camilleri, *Game of Mirrors*, 2015
Andrea Camilleri, *The Shape of Water*, 2002
Stephen J. Cannell, *At First Sight: A Novel of Obsession*, 2008
Massimo Carlotto, *The Colombian Mule*, 2003
Jeffery Deaver, *XO*, 2012
Michael Dibdin, *Ratking*, 1989
Clare Donoghue, *Never Look Back*, 2014
Charles Dubow, *Indiscretion*, 2013
Conor Fitzgerald, *The Dogs of Rome*, 2010
George Harrar, *Reunion at Red Paint Bay*, 2013
Beverle Graves Myers, *Whispers of Vivaldi*, 2014
Magdalen Nabb, *Death of an Englishman*, 1981
Hilary Norman, *Eclipse*, 2012

J.D. Robb, *Obsession in Death*, 2015
Thomas Sterling, *The Evil of the Day*, 1955
Martin Walker, *The Children Return*, 2015

600

JOHN T. LESCROART

The Fall

(New York: Atria Books, 2015)

Series: Dismas Hardy Series. Book 16
Subject(s): Crime; Murder; Law
Major character(s): Dismas Hardy, Man, Lawyer, Father (of Rebecca); Rebecca Hardy, Lawyer, Daughter (of Dismas); Tanya Morgan, 17-Year-Old, Foster Child, Crime Victim; Greg Treadway, Teacher (middle school), Volunteer (foster children advocate), Crime Suspect
Time period(s): 21st century; 2010s
Locale(s): San Francisco, California

Summary: When 17-year-old foster child Tanya Morgan dies after falling from a San Francisco overpass, the case is quickly ruled a homicide. City law enforcement officials, who have been criticized for their lax approach to cases involving African American victims, feel pressured to come up with a suspect fast. Greg Treadway, a teacher who also serves as a foster child advocate, met with Tanya not long before her death. He is arrested and charged with Tanya's murder, and he enlists the help of Rebecca Hardy in proving his innocence. Rebecca, daughter of the respected attorney Dismas Hardy, works in her father's firm. She is certain of Greg's innocence and begins searching for other possible suspects. Rebecca and Dismas's investigation uncovers an abusive stepfather and a mentally ill mother, but it also reveals information about Greg that may keep him on the suspect list. This novel is the 16th in the Dismas Hardy series.

Other books by the same author:
Sunburn, 2009
The Suspect, 2007
The Hunt Club, 2006
A Certain Justice, 1995
Dead Irish, 1989

Other books you might like:
Alafair Burke, *Close Case*, 2005
Michael Connelly, *The Gods of Guilt*, 2013
Michael Connelly, *The Lincoln Lawyer*, 2005
Joel Goldman, *Motion To Kill*, 2011
John Grisham, *Sycamore Row*, 2013
Jonnie Jacobs, *Shadow of Doubt*, 1996
William Lashner, *Hostile Witness*, 1995
John T. Lescroart, *A Certain Justice*, 1995
Maxine Paetro, *14th Deadly Sin*, 2015
Richard North Patterson, *No Safe Place*, 1998
David L. Robbins, *Scorched Earth*, 2002
Lisa Scottoline, *Devil's Corner*, 2005
Lisa Scottoline, *Lady Killer*, 2008
Troy Soos, *Hanging Curve*, 1999
Robert Traver, *Anatomy of a Murder*, 1958

601

DAVID LEVIEN

Signature Kill

(New York: Doubleday, 2015)

Series: Frank Behr Series. Book 4
Story type: Private Detective; Serial Killer
Subject(s): Mystery; Detective fiction; Crime
Major character(s): Frank Behr, Detective—Private, Detective—Police (former); Kerry Gibbons, Mother (of Kendra), Widow(er); Kendra Gibbons, Missing Person, Daughter (of Kerry); Gary Breslau, Detective—Police; Lisa Mistretta, Psychologist; Django Quinn, Photographer (crime scene)
Time period(s): 21st century; 2010s
Locale(s): Indianapolis, Indiana

Summary: Private detective Frank Behr hunts for a serial killer in the fourth series entry. Behr has alienated many of his friends and colleagues, and he is running low on funds. He decides to try his luck at locating Kendra Gibbons, a girl who has been missing for a year. Her mother, Kerry, is offering a big reward, and Behr desperately needs the cash. As Behr investigates Kendra's disappearance, a killer begins targeting other young women in Indianapolis. The victims are sexually assaulted and dismembered; the serial killer leaves behind disturbing displays of his handiwork. Behr knows that Kendra could be one of the killer's victims, but finding the serial killer isn't going to be easy. He enlists the help of criminal psychologist Lisa Mistretta and crime scene photographer Django Quinn to stop the spree as the death toll continues to climb.

Other books by the same author:
Thirteen Million Dollar Pop, 2011
Where the Dead Lay, 2009
City of the Sun, 2008
Swagbelly: A Pornographer's Tale, 2003
Rounders, 1998

Other books you might like:
G.M. Ford, *Fury*, 2001
Alex Kava, *A Perfect Evil*, 2001
Michael Koryta, *Tonight I Said Goodbye*, 2004
Michael Z. Lewin, *Ask the Right Question*, 1971
Richard Montanari, *The Rosary Girls*, 2005
John Sandford, *Rules of Prey*, 1989
Jess Walter, *Over Tumbled Graves*, 2001

602

ROBERT S. LEVINSON

The Evil Deeds We Do

(Waterville, Maine: Five Star, 2015)

Story type: Contemporary
Subject(s): Mystery; Detective fiction; Murder
Major character(s): Lainie Davis Gardner, Producer (former), Widow(er), Mother (of Sara), Crime Suspect, Lover (former, of Thom); Roy, Spouse (deceased, of Lainie), Organized Crime Figure,

Father (of Sara); Sara, Teenager, Daughter (of Lainie and Roy); Harry Roman, Lawyer (assistant district attorney); Thom Newberry, Lover (former, of Lainie)
Time period(s): 21st century; 2010s
Locale(s): California, United States

Summary: Lainie Davis Gardner used to be an influential record producer in Los Angeles, but her circumstances have changed. Her gangster husband is dead, and assistant DA Harry Roman is working hard to prove that Lainie paid someone to kill him. Before Roy's death, Lainie was facing numerous criminal charges related to her business, but thankfully, they have been dropped. She focuses now on keeping her teenage daughter, Sara, in line. But Lainie may be facing new charges soon, if Roman gets his way. The ADA says that he has fresh evidence against Lainie, but she initially ignores his claims. When a former boyfriend, Thom Newberry, tells Lainie that Roman is telling the truth, Lainie pays attention. Lainie is worried that she will lose custody of Sara, and Thom says he can keep that from happening—if Lainie performs one favor. Unfortunately, Thom's favor could land Lainie in more trouble.

Other books by the same author:
Finders Keepers Losers Weepers, 2014
Where the Lies Begin, 2006
Ask a Dead Man, 2004
Hot Paint, 2002
The Elvis and Marilyn Affair, 1999

Other books you might like:
Stephen J. Cannell, *Hollywood Tough*, 2003
Marcia Clark, *Guilt by Association*, 2011
Michael Connelly, *The Lincoln Lawyer*, 2005
Gabrielle Kraft, *Bullshot*, 1987
Dick Lochte, *Croaked!*, 2007
Keith Snyder, *Show Control*, 1996
Joseph Wambaugh, *Hollywood Station: A Novel*, 2006

603

ROBERT K. LEWIS

Innocent Damage

(Woodbury, Minnesota: Llewellyn Worldwide, Ltd., 2015)

Series: Mark Mallen Series. Book 3
Story type: Child-in-Peril; Contemporary
Subject(s): Drug abuse; Mystery; Missing persons
Major character(s): Mark Mallen, Detective—Police (former), Addict (former); Gwen Saunders, Detective—Police
Time period(s): 21st century; 2010s
Locale(s): San Francisco, California

Summary: At one time, Mark Mallen was a trusted member of the San Francisco Police Department, working as an undercover narcotics officer. One assignment changed all that by transforming his life into a drug-addicted hell. He was dismissed from the force as a result of his heroin dependence. While he has begun to put his heroin habit behind him, he can't suppress his instincts as a cop. When a detective asks Mark to help investigate the disappearance of a three-year-old girl, he takes on the case. To find her, Mark must call upon the underworld connections he has made, both as a cop and during his days as an addict. In doing so, he uncovers something much bigger than one missing girl. The plot that he reveals leads him to his fellow brothers in blue, as he discovers the case may involve several members of San Francisco's finest. This is the third book in Robert K. Lewis's Mark Mallen series.

Other books by the same author:
Critical Damage, 2014
Untold Damage, 2013

Other books you might like:
William Babula, *St. John's Baptism*, 1988
Linda Fairstein, *Hell Gate*, 2010
Ross Macdonald, *Underground Man*, 1971
Stephen Jay Schwartz, *Boulevard*, 2009
Nichelle D. Tramble, *The Dying Ground: A Hip-Hop Noir Novel*, 2001
Andrew Vachss, *Flood*, 1985
Andrew Vachss, *Terminal: A Burke Novel*, 2007

604

LAURA LIPPMAN

Hush Hush

(New York: William Morrow, 2015)

Series: Tess Monaghan Series. Book 12
Story type: Private Detective; Series
Subject(s): Mystery; Detective fiction; Crime
Major character(s): Tess Monaghan, Detective—Private, Girlfriend (of Crow), Mother (of Carla Scout); Crow, Boyfriend (of Tess), Father (of Carla Scout); Carla Scout, 3-Year-Old, Daughter (of Tess and Crow); Tyner Gray, Lawyer; Sandy Sanchez, Colleague (Tess's partner); Melisandre Harris Dawes, Criminal (acquitted of killing daughter), Mentally Ill Person, Spouse (former, of Stephen), Mother (of Alanna and Ruby); Stephen, Spouse (former, of Melisandre), Father (of Alanna and Ruby); Alanna, Daughter (of Stephen and Melisandre), 17-Year-Old; Ruby, 15-Year-Old, Daughter (of Melisandre and Stephen)
Time period(s): 21st century; 2010s
Locale(s): Baltimore, Maryland

Summary: Baltimore private detective Tess Monaghan finds her current assignment particularly disturbing. At the request of an old friend, Tess is consulting on the security arrangements for Melisandre Harris Dawes. Dawes has been out of the country since she was found not guilty by reason of insanity in the death of her two-year-old daughter 12 years ago. Dawes convinced the judge and jury that when she caused her baby's death by deliberately leaving her in a hot car, she was experiencing extreme postpartum depression. Now Dawes wants to re-establish a relationship with the two teenage daughters she left behind, and she has brought a film crew to document their reunion. The girls aren't interested in reconciling with their mother, however, and Tess senses immediately that Melisandre is still manipulating those around her. When Melisandre is implicated in a new murder, Tess re-examines the previous case in a search for answers. This novel is the 12th in the Tess Monaghan series.

Other books by the same author:
After I'm Gone, 2014
And When She Was Good, 2012
The Girl in the Green Raincoat, 2011
The Most Dangerous Thing, 2011
I'd Know You Anywhere, 2010

Other books you might like:
Megan Abbott, *The End of Everything*, 2011
Harlan Coben, *The Stranger*, 2015
Tim Cockey, *The Hearse You Came in On*, 2000
Elisabeth de Mariaffi, *The Devil You Know*, 2015
Robert Dugoni, *My Sister's Grave*, 2014
Sara Gran, *Claire DeWitt and the Bohemian Highway*, 2013
James Grippando, *Cane and Abe*, 2015
Elizabeth Gunn, *Red Man Down*, 2014
Mo Hayder, *Hanging Hill*, 2012
Karen Keskinen, *Black Current*, 2014
Dennis Lehane, *Moonlight Mile*, 2010
Jassy MacKenzie, *The Fallen*, 2012
Alex Marwood, *The Wicked Girls*, 2012
Jennifer McMahon, *The One I Left Behind*, 2013
Preston Pairo III, *Bright Eyes*, 1996
Sara Paretsky, *Body Work*, 2011
Sara Paretsky, *Brush Back*, 2015
Matthew Pearl, *The Poe Shadow: A Novel*, 2006
Thomas Pynchon, *Bleeding Edge*, 2013
J.M. Redmann, *Water Mark*, 2010
Kathy Reichs, *Bones Are Forever*, 2012
Robert Rotenberg, *The Guilty Plea*, 2011
Lori Roy, *Until She Comes Home*, 2013
Ayelet Waldman, *Nursery Crimes*, 2000
Stuart Woods, *Santa Fe Edge*, 2010

605

ATTICA LOCKE

Pleasantville

(New York: HarperCollins Publishers, 2015)

Series: Jay Porter Series. Book 2
Story type: Legal; Series
Subject(s): Law; Political campaigns; Elections
Major character(s): Jay Porter, Widow(er), Single Father, Widow(er), Lawyer (environmental), Activist (former), Father; Neal Hathorne, Crime Suspect, Grandson (of Sam); Sam Hathorne, Wealthy, Political Figure, Grandfather (of Neal)
Time period(s): 20th century; 1990s (1996)
Locale(s): Houston, Texas

Summary: As the city of Houston votes on election night in 1996, a young election worker is kidnapped and murdered in the African American suburb of Pleasantville. Neal Hathorne, a member of a powerful, old-money family, and nephew of a mayoral candidate, is accused of the crime. Environmental lawyer Jay Porter is unexpectedly approached and asked to take on the case. It's not the type of work he would normally accept, but Jay's biggest courtroom success was 15 years ago, and he needs the money. Defending a client the

evidence suggests is guilty may be tough enough, but Jay also has other obstacles to navigate. Hathorne's uncle is facing a runoff election against the district attorney, leaving Jay and his case struggling against competing forces of political ambition and manipulation. This is the second book in Attica Locke's Jay Porter Series.

Other books by the same author:
The Cutting Season, 2012
Black Water Rising, 2009

Other books you might like:
Jay Brandon, *Fade the Heat*, 1991
Stephen L. Carter, *The Emperor of Ocean Park*, 2002
Tim Green, *The Letter of the Law*, 2000
Greg Iles, *The Quiet Game*, 1999
David Lindsey, *Body of Truth*, 1992
D.R. Meredith, *Murder by Impulse*, 1987
Pamela Samuels-Young, *Every Reasonable Doubt*, 2006

606

BILL LOEHFELM

Doing the Devil's Work

(New York: Sarah Crichton Books, 2015)

Series: Maureen Coughlin Series. Book 3
Story type: Police Procedural; Series
Subject(s): Detective fiction; Southern United States; Murder
Major character(s): Maureen Coughlin, Police Officer; Caleb Heath, Crime Suspect, Young Man
Time period(s): 21st century; 2010s
Locale(s): New Orleans, Louisiana

Summary: In the third book of the Maureen Coughlin mystery series, Maureen has completed her police training and is a rookie New Orleans cop. She is on patrol when she notices a foul smell. She explores an abandoned house and discovers a body. The victim, whose tattoos identify him as a white supremacist, had his throat cut. Later that night, Maureen pulls over a suspicious couple in a car filled with stolen purses. The couple is taken into custody and the woman, who seems ill, is taken to the hospital. The woman is released, and later is discovered with her throat cut in the same fashion as the first victim. Maureen begins to suspect the murders are connected, and all signs point to the son of a wealthy real estate developer, who happens to own the house in which Maureen found the first body. As she tries to figure out who is responsible for the murders, she must also deal with the police corruption and the criminal underbelly of New Orleans.

Other books by the same author:
The Devil in Her Way, 2013
The Devil She Knows, 2011
Bloodroot, 2009
Fresh Kills, 2008
Osama Bin Laden, 2003

Other books you might like:
James Lee Burke, *The Tin Roof Blowdown*, 2007
Rachel Howzell Hall, *Land of Shadows*, 2014
P.J. Parrish, *A Thousand Bones*, 2007

Julie Smith, *New Orleans Mourning*, 1990
Daniel Woodrell, *The Ones You Do*, 1992
Daniel Woodrell, *Under the Bright Lights*, 1986
Paula L. Woods, *Inner City Blues: A Charlotte Justice Novel*, 1999

607

JESS LOUREY

February Fever

(Woodbury, Minnesota: Midnight Ink, 2015)

Series: Murder-by-Month Mystery Series. Book 10
Story type: Cozy Mystery; Series
Subject(s): Trains; Murder; Detective fiction
Major character(s): Mira James, Investigator, Co-worker (of Mrs. Berns), Girlfriend (of Johnny); Mrs. Burns, Co-worker (of Mira); Johnny Leeson, Boyfriend (of Mira)
Time period(s): 21st century; 2010s
Locale(s): United States

Summary: In the 10th installment of the Murder-by-Month mystery series, Mira James's relationship with Johnny Leeson is doing great. But then Johnny takes a month-long internship in Portland, Oregon. Mira would like to visit him, but is paralyzed by fear when she thinks about getting into a plane. Her friend Mrs. Berns convinces her to visit Johnny for Valentine's Day and even attend an international conference for private investigators, and plans a trip that circumvents airports. Mrs. Berns books them seats on the Valentine Train, a train for singles. At first Mira is apprehensive, but after a couple of glasses of champagne, she's ready to relax. As Mira tries to enjoy the excursion, a snowstorm stops the train in its tracks. Suddenly, a passenger is murdered and the victim's family disappears. Mira must catch the murderer before he or she claims another victim.

Other books by the same author:
January Thaw, 2014
August Moon, 2008
June Bug, 2007
Knee High by the Fourth of July, 2007
May Day, 2006

Other books you might like:
Jeff Abbott, *Do Unto Others*, 1994
Jo Dereske, *Farewell, Miss Zukas*, 2011
Jo Dereske, *Miss Zukas and the Library Murders*, 1994
Charlaine Harris, *Real Murders*, 1990
Marion Moore Hill, *Bookmarked for Murder*, 2002
Fran Stewart, *Orange as Marmalade*, 2003

608

ALICE LOWEECEY

Nun Too Soon

(Plano, Texas: Henery Press, 2015)

Series: Giulia Driscoll Mystery Series. Book 1
Story type: Cozy Mystery; Series
Subject(s): Mystery; Murder; Detective fiction
Major character(s): Giulia Falcone-Driscoll, Religious (former nun), Investigator (private), Spouse (wife, of Frank); Frank Driscoll, Detective—Police, Spouse (husband, of Giulia); Roger Fitch, Crime Suspect (aka Silk Tie Killer)
Time period(s): 21st century; 2010s
Locale(s): Cottonwood, Pennsylvania

Summary: Alice Loweecey delivers the first installment in her Giulia Driscoll Mystery series. Former nun Giulia Falcone-Driscoll is a private investigator in Cottonwood, Pennsylvania. She heads Driscoll Investigations while her husband, Frank Driscoll, works as a detective in the local police department. Giulia's up against the clock with her latest client. She's only got 13 days to prove that Roger Fitch, also known as the Silk Tie Killer, didn't strangle his girlfriend with one of his neckties. Roger's girlfriend has enough enemies to make room for a number of suspects, but Roger has a motive. Giulia's investigation is challenged by a local tabloid reporter; her client Roger, who claims she's not trying hard enough to find a lead on another suspect; and Frank, who believes Roger is guilty. Soon, Giulia questions whether she is fighting for justice or defending a murderer.

Other books by the same author:
Veiled Threat, 2013
Back in the Habit, 2012
Force of Habit, 2011

Other books you might like:
Lee Harris, *The Good Friday Murder*, 1992
Alison Joseph, *Sacred Hearts*, 1994
Nancy Martin, *How to Murder a Millionaire*, 2002
Sister Carol Anne O'Marie, *A Novena for Murder*, 1984
Monica Quill, *Not a Blessed Thing*, 1981
Winona Sullivan, *A Sudden Death at the Norfolk Cafe*, 1993

609

DIXIE LYLE

Marked Fur Murder

(New York: St. Martin's Press, 2015)

Series: Whiskey, Tango and Foxtrot Series. Book 3
Story type: Amateur Detective; Contemporary
Subject(s): Animals; Mystery; Supernatural
Major character(s): Deirdre "Foxtrot" Lancaster, Detective—Amateur, Friend (of Tango and Whiskey), Girlfriend (of Ben), Worker (for Zelda); Zelda "ZZ" Zoransky, Woman, Eccentric, Wealthy, Employer (of Foxtrot); Tango, Cat (spirit), Friend (of Foxtrot and Whiskey), Telepath; Whiskey, Shape-Shifter (Dog), Friend (of Foxtrot and Tango); Ben, Boyfriend (of Foxtrot), Brother (of Ann), Indian (part Cowichan); Ann, Crime Victim, Sister (of Ben), Indian (part Cowichan)
Time period(s): 21st century; 2010s
Locale(s): Hartville, New York

Summary: Deirdre "Foxtrot" Lancaster and her unusual animal colleagues, Tango the dead and telepathic cat and

Whiskey the shape-shifting dog, have a new mystery. Once again, Foxtrot's rich and eccentric boss, Zelda "ZZ" Zoransky, is throwing a huge party for the rich and famous on the grounds of her mansion, animal sanctuary, and private zoo. Ann, the sister of Foxtrot's boyfriend, Ben, is found dead in the mansion's pool. Early indications are that she was zapped when a hairdryer fell into the pool, but Ben insists that's not possible. His family has the blood of the Cowichan tribe, and they can control lightning, Ben tells her, so a little hairdryer wouldn't have killed his sister. Foxtrot and her extrasensory pets will have to figure out which of the guests killed Ann in this third book in the Whiskey, Tango and Foxtrot series.

Other books by the same author:
A Taste Fur Murder, 2014
To Die Fur, 2014

Other books you might like:
Ali Brandon, *Double Booked for Death*, 2011
Charlaine Harris, *Dead Until Dark*, 2001
Jayne Ann Krentz, *Light in Shadow*, 2002
Victoria Laurie, *Abby Cooper, Psychic Eye*, 2005
Judi McCoy, *Hounding the Pavement*, 2009
Clea Simon, *Dogs Don't Lie*, 2011
Helen Smith, *Invitation to Die*, 2013

610

BECKY MASTERMAN

Fear the Darkness

(New York: Minotaur Books, 2015)

Series: Brigid Quinn Series. Book 2
Story type: Private Detective; Series
Subject(s): Suspense; Detective fiction; Family relations
Major character(s): Brigid Quinn, FBI Agent (retired), Investigator, Aunt (of Gemma-Kate), Spouse (of Carlo); Gemma-Kate, 17-Year-Old, Niece (of Brigid and Carlo); Carlo, Spouse (of Brigid), Uncle (of Gemma-Kate)
Time period(s): 21st century; 2010s
Locale(s): Tucson, Arizona

Summary: In the second book of the Brigid Quinn series, the retired FBI agent is settling into her new life as a private investigator in Tucson, Arizona. Her calm life is soon interrupted by a life-changing event: The death of her sister-in-law. Brigid's 17-year-old niece, Gemma-Kate, comes to live with her in Tucson for a few months so she can qualify for in-state tuition at the University of Arizona. Brigid soon learns that something isn't right about Gemma-Kate. First, one of Brigid's dogs nearly dies after eating a poisonous toad. Then Brigid starts to hallucinate and feels weak. Could Gemma-Kate be behind her sudden illness? Meanwhile, Brigid reluctantly takes on an investigation of a drowning that does not appear to be accidental. That leaves two distinct possibilities for Brigid to explore. Did the boy commit suicide, or did someone kill him?

Other books by the same author:
Rage Against the Dying, 2013

Other books you might like:
Lisa Gardner, *Alone*, 2005
Alan Jacobson, *The 7th Victim: A Novel*, 2008
Andrea Kane, *Twisted*, 2008
Alex Kava, *A Perfect Evil*, 2001
Cody McFadyen, *Shadow Man*, 2006
Kirk Mitchell, *Cry Dance*, 1999
Jonathan Nasaw, *The Girls He Adored*, 2000

611

JEANNE MATTHEWS

Where the Bones are Buried

(Scottsdale, Arizona: Poisoned Pen Press, 2015)

Series: Dinah Pelerin Mystery Series. Book 5
Story type: Psychological Suspense; Series
Subject(s): Native Americans; Germans; Murder
Major character(s): Dinah Pelerin, Professor (of Native American studies), Girlfriend (of Thor), Daughter (of Swan); Swan Calms, Mother (of Dinah), Crime Suspect, Indian (Seminole), Criminal (blackmailer), Spouse (former, of drug dealer); Thor Ramberg, Boyfriend (of Dinah), Agent (counterintellegence agent); Margaret, Criminal (blackmailer), Spouse (former, of drug dealer)
Time period(s): 21st century; 2010s
Locale(s): Berlin, Germany

Summary: In the fifth book of the Dinah Pelerin mystery series, American anthropologist Dinah is finally happy in her life. She has a loving boyfriend, secret agent Thor Ramberg, and is living with him in Berlin, where she teaches Native American studies to university students. Her happiness is soon shattered by the arrival of her mother, Swan. Swan's presence reminds Dinah of a secret she's been hiding from Thor. Swan, a Seminole, is teaming up with Margaret, another of her former husband's ex-wives. Swan has been invited to a pow-wow organized by a club of American Indian-obsessed Germans. She and Margaret are attending the event to get to a club member who is a tax dodger so they can blackmail him. When one of the club members is found dead and scalped after a drumming ceremony, Swan is the prime suspect. Dinah begins to search for the killer, but her investigation just uncovers more lies.

Other books by the same author:
Her Boyfriend's Bones, 2013
Bonereapers, 2012
Bet Your Bones, 2011
Bones of Contention, 2010

Other books you might like:
Christine Andreae, *Trail of Murder*, 1992
Aaron Elkins, *Fellowship of Fear*, 1982
Mary Anna Evans, *Artifacts*, 2003
Linda French, *Talking Rain*, 1998
Tom Mitcheltree, *Katie's Will*, 1997
David D. Nolta, *Grave Circle*, 2003
Sarah Stewart Taylor, *O' Artful Death*, 2003

Mystery

612

ALYSSA MAXWELL

Murder at Beechwood

(New York: Kensington, 2015)

Series: Gilded Newport Mystery Series. Book 3
Story type: Amateur Detective; Historical - Victorian America
Subject(s): Murder; Infants; Wealth
Major character(s): Emma Cross, Writer (society page reporter), Detective—Amateur; Derrick Andrews, Crime Suspect; Jesse Whyte, Detective—Police
Time period(s): 19th century; 1890s (1896)
Locale(s): Newport, Rhode Island

Summary: Emma Cross, a society reporter in 1896 Rhode Island, has just turned down a marriage proposal and certainly has no plans to become a mother any time soon. Yet that is the role she finds herself playing when someone abandons a baby at her doorstep. Using her newspaper connections, Emma begins a search for the child's parents by asking questions at several society functions. When a well-to-do businessman is killed during a sailboat race, accusations of murder fly. The suspect is the man who recently asked Emma to marry him, and evidence found at the scene connects the dead man to the abandoned baby. It's a mystery Emma can't help trying to solve, but as she pokes around she risks uncovering secrets some powerful people want to keep buried. This is the third book in Alyssa Maxwell's Gilded Newport Mystery series.

Other books by the same author:
Murder Most Malicious, 2015
Murder at the Breakers, 2014
Murder at the Marble House, 2014

Other books you might like:
Lawrence Alexander, *The Big Stick*, 1986
Tasha Alexander, *And Only to Deceive*, 2005
Kenneth M. Cameron, *The Frightened Man*, 2008
Megan Chance, *An Inconvenient Wife*, 2004
Paula Cohen, *Gramercy Park*, 2002
Daisy Goodwin, *The American Heiress*, 2011
Edith Wharton, *The House of Mirth*, 1905

613

EDITH MAXWELL

Farmed and Dangerous

(New York: Kensington Publishing Corporation, 2015)

Series: Local Foods Mystery Series. Book 3
Story type: Amateur Detective; Cozy Mystery
Subject(s): Agriculture; Murder; Detective fiction
Major character(s): Cam Flaherty, Farmer, Detective—Amateur, Crime Suspect, Mother, Girlfriend (of Pete); Pete Pappas, Detective—Police, Boyfriend (of Cam)
Time period(s): 21st century; 2010s
Locale(s): Westbury, Massachusetts

Summary: Organic farmer Cam Flaherty is doing her best to get through the temperamental New England winter. As the snow piles up outside, she's trying to keep her greenhouse from collapsing and fulfill her commitment to the local community-supported agriculture project. The last thing she needs is to be accused of murder. When an abrasive elderly resident at an assisted-living facility is poisoned, Cam's produce is linked to the death. To clear her name she begins looking into the case, though digging around begins to endanger her romance with a local police detective who's also investigating. Cam's curiosity nearly proves her undoing, as a blizzard strands her in a building with the murder suspects—one of whom is a killer who does not want to be discovered. This is the third book in Edith Maxwell's Local Foods Mystery series.

Other books by the same author:
Til Dirt Do Us Part, 2014
A Tine to Live, a Tine to Die, 2013

Other books you might like:
Judy Clemens, *Till the Cows Come Home*, 2004
Sheila Connolly, *One Bad Apple: An Orchard Mystery*, 2008
Jessie Crockett, *Drizzled with Death*, 2013
B.B. Haywood, *Town in a Blueberry Jam*, 2010
Hannah Reed, *Buzz Off*, 2010
Paige Shelton, *Farm Fresh Murder*, 2010
Nancy Means Wright, *Mad Season*, 1996

614

KIMBERLY MCCREIGHT

Where They Found Her

(New York: HarperCollins Publishers, 2015)

Story type: Contemporary; Family Saga
Subject(s): Murder; Infants; Detective fiction
Major character(s): Molly Sanderson, Journalist, Spouse, Mother; Sandy Mendelson, 16-Year-Old (high school dropout), Daughter (of Jenna); Barbara, Mother, Woman (PTA president); Jenna, Mother (of Sandy)
Time period(s): 21st century; 2010s
Locale(s): Ridgedale, New Jersey

Summary: When the body of a newborn is found in the New Jersey woods, the case threatens to unearth very painful memories for reporter Molly Sanderson. Two years earlier, Molly suffered a miscarriage, and the traumatic experience drove her into a deep depression and extensive therapy sessions. As she investigates the death of the infant found close to a respected university, the lives of other women in the well-to-do college town begin to weave into the story. Sandy, a 16-year-old dropout, is trying to find her missing, hard-partying mother, and Barbara, the almost-too-perfect PTA president, might also be involved in something. Eventually the pieces begin to fall into place, and as the identity of the child is revealed, years of secrets that have lingered below the community's surface come bubbling up. Author Kimberly McCreight reveals the events unfolding in Ridgedale through the voices of four main female characters.

Other books by the same author:
Reconstructing Amelia, 2013

Other books you might like:
Chelsea Cain, *One Kick*, 2014
Gillian Flynn, *Sharp Objects*, 2006
Cara Hoffman, *So Much Pretty*, 2011
Rebecca James, *Sweet Damage*, 2014
Pam Lewis, *Speak Softly, She Can Hear*, 2005
Laura Lippman, *What the Dead Know*, 2007
Jennifer McMahon, *Promise Not to Tell*, 2006
Lori Roy, *Bent Road*, 2011
Chevy Stevens, *Still Missing*, 2010

615

G.A. MCKEVETT (Pseudonym of Sonja Massie)

Killer Gourmet

(New York: Kensington, 2015)

Series: Savannah Reid Series. Book 20
Story type: Cozy Mystery
Subject(s): Murder; Detective fiction; Restaurants
Major character(s): Savannah Reid, Spouse (of Dirk), Detective—Private, Friend (of Ryan, John); Baldwin Norwood, Crime Victim, Cook; Ryan Stone, Friend (of Savannah), Restaurateur; John Gibson, Restaurateur, Friend (of Savannah); Dirk Coulter, Detective—Police (detective sergeant), Spouse (of Savannah)
Time period(s): 21st century; 2010s
Locale(s): Los Angeles, California

Summary: In the 20th installment of the Savannah Reid mystery series, Savannah and her colleagues at the Moonlight Magnolia Detective Agency are excited to help their friends Ryan Stone and John Gibson plan their new restaurant. When head chef Baldwin Norwood is found dead in the kitchen of the restaurant, Savannah's attention turns from food to crime solving. She soon discovers that although Norwood was a talented cook, the people he worked with did not love him. The suspects begin to line up: a former business partner whose career was ruined by Norwood; a girlfriend who didn't get enough love and attention; a jealous sous chef who wants Norwood's job. Savannah is working to discover who is responsible for Norwood's death, but this time she's not doing it for a check—she's helping her husband, Detective Sergeant Dirk Coulter, collar the killer.

Other books by the same author:
Killer Physique, 2014
Cooked Goose, 1998
Killer Calories, 1997
Bitter Sweets, 1996
Just Desserts, 1995

Other books you might like:
Carol Lea Benjamin, *This Dog for Hire*, 1996
Susan M. Boyer, *Lowcountry Boil*, 2012
Nancy Bush, *Candy Apple Red*, 2005
Krista Davis, *The Diva Runs out of Thyme*, 2008
Alton Gansky, *A Small Dose of Murder*, 1999

Sue Ann Jaffarian, *Hell on Wheels*, 2014
Sue Ann Jaffarian, *Too Big to Miss: An Odelia Grey Mystery*, 2006

616

JENN MCKINLAY

Dark Chocolate Demise

(London: Penguin Publishing Group, 2015)

Series: Cupcake Bakery Mystery Series. Book 7
Story type: Amateur Detective; Cozy Mystery
Subject(s): Murder; Food; Mystery
Major character(s): Mel Cooper, Girlfriend (ex, of Joe), Businesswoman (bakery owner), Co-worker (of Angie), Detective—Amateur; Angie DeLaura, Businesswoman (bakery owner), Co-worker (of Mel), Brother (of Joe); Joe DeLaura, Lawyer (prosecutor), Brother (of Angie), Boyfriend (ex, of Mel)
Time period(s): 21st century; 2010s
Locale(s): Scottsdale, Arizona

Summary: Fairy Tale Cupcake owners Mel and Angie are undertaking a gruesome promotion to celebrate their town's upcoming Old Town Zombie Walk. In addition to dressing up like the undead and doing their best zombie impersonations, the pair are also baking up some treats for the ravenous hordes to devour. In the midst of the undead fun, Mel gets a shock when she discovers a real corpse stuffed into a prop casket. Joe—Angie's prosecutor brother and Mel's former boyfriend—is working on a dangerous mob case, so the women deduce the killer may have been targeting him. As Mel investigates, her search may be about more than finding a killer—it may mean the difference between becoming a victim and staying alive. This is the seventh book in Jenn McKinlay's Cupcake Bakery Mystery series.

Other books by the same author:
Red Velvet Revenge, 2012
Buttercream Bump Off, 2011
Death by the Dozen, 2011
Sprinkle with Murder, 2010

Other books you might like:
Jacklyn Brady, *Murder Takes the Cake*, 2008
Jacklyn Brady, *A Sheetcake Named Desire*, 2011
JoAnna Carl, *The Chocolate Cat Caper*, 2002
Sammi Carter, *Candy Apple Dead*, 2005
Bailey Cates, *Brownies and Broomsticks: A Magical Bakery Mystery*, 2012
Joanne Fluke, *Chocolate Chip Cookie Murder*, 2000
Joanne Fluke, *Double Fudge Brownie Murder*, 2015
Victoria Hamilton, *Bran New Death*, 2013

617

STACI MCLAUGHLIN

A Healthy Homicide

(New York: Kensington, 2015)

Series: Blossom Valley Mystery Series. Book 4
Story type: Cozy Mystery; Mystery

Mystery

Subject(s): Murder; Small business; Crime
Major character(s): Dana Lewis, Businesswoman, Detective—Amateur, Crime Suspect
Time period(s): 21st century; 2010s
Locale(s): Blossom Valley, California

Summary: Dana Lewis is successfully running the O'Connell Organic Farm and Spa in Blossom Valley, California. However, the operation gains some competition with the opening of the Pampered Life nearby. This spa features a variety of luxurious treatments as well as a staff that is incredibly pleasing to the eye. At first, Dana is not worried; she has regular customers and things seem fine. Eventually, Dana becomes worried that the lavish new spa could start hurting the farm's income. Once the owner of The Pampered Life is killed, everyone suspects Dana had something to do with the death. In order to save the O'Connell business,and herself, Dana must find out who killed the owner of the rival spa. This is the fourth novel in the Blossom Valley Mysteries series.

Other books by the same author:
Green Living Can Be Deadly, 2014
All Natural Murder, 2013
Going Organic Can Kill You, 2012

Other books you might like:
Judy Clemens, *Till the Cows Come Home*, 2004
Sheila Connolly, *One Bad Apple: An Orchard Mystery*, 2008
Diana Killian, *Corpse Pose*, 2008
Kathryn Lilley, *Dying to Be Thin*, 2007
Hannah Reed, *Buzz Off*, 2010
Paige Shelton, *Farm Fresh Murder*, 2010
Tracy Weber, *Murder Strikes a Pose*, 2014

618

CATRIONA MCPHERSON

The Child Garden

(Woodbury, Minnesota: Midnight Ink, 2015)

Story type: Contemporary
Subject(s): Mother-son relations; Suicide; Murder
Major character(s): Gloria Harkness, Mother, Detective—Amateur
Time period(s): 21st century; 2010s
Locale(s): Scotland

Summary: Years ago an alternative school called Eden was forced to close after a student committed suicide. The school was converted into a personal care home, but the scandal still lingers over the place. Its grounds and buildings are now neglected and are gradually but clearly falling into disrepair. Gloria Harkness is one of the few people willing to live close to the facility, but it's not entirely her choice. Her special-needs son is a patient there. One day, a childhood friend of Gloria's shows up claiming a former classmate at Eden is harassing him to meet her at the site of the suicide.The woman claims the death was really a murder. Fueled by the desire to keep her son safe, Gloria agrees to help investigate the mystery, even if it's more than she can handle. As she encounters Scottish myths and superstitions, Gloria

becomes more and more concerned with discovering the truth about Eden.

Other books by the same author:
Come to Harm, 2015
Dandy Gilver and the Reek of Red Herrings, 2014
The Day She Died, 2014
As She Left It, 2013
After the Armistice Ball, 2005

Other books you might like:
Agatha Christie, *Cat Among the Pigeons*, 1959
Lois Duncan, *Down a Dark Hall*, 1974
Kazuo Ishiguro, *Never Let Me Go*, 2005
Serena Mackesy, *Hold My Hand*, 2008
J. Wallis Martin, *A Likeness in Stone*, 1997
Josephine Tey, *Miss Pym Disposes*, 1948
Kevin Wignall, *Among the Dead*, 2002

619

JENNY MILCHMAN

As Night Falls

(New York: Random House Publishing Group, 2015)

Story type: Contemporary; Family Saga
Subject(s): Prisoners; Family; Mother-daughter relations
Major character(s): Sandy Tremont, Woman, Mother (of Ivy), Spouse (of Ben), Sister (of Nick); Ben, Guide (wilderness), Spouse (of Sandy), Father (of Ivy); Ivy, 15-Year-Old, Daughter (of Sandy, Ben); Harlan, Prisoner (escaped), Murderer, Companion (of Nick); Nick, Prisoner (escaped), Murderer, Brother (of Sandy), Companion (of Harlan)
Time period(s): 21st century; 2010s
Locale(s): New York, United States

Summary: As a snowstorm looms in New York's Adirondack Mountains, the Tremont household is brimming with tension. Sandy Tremont and her 15-year-old daughter have had another fight, and once again are not speaking to each other. Sandy's husband, Ben, returns from work to this poisoned atmosphere. The real trouble, however, is approaching through the trees. Two escaped convicts are making a desperate push to reach Canada and need supplies for the trip. Harlan and Nick have been cellmates for two decades and both are extremely violent. Their destination is the Tremont home. Their goal is to regroup, stock up, and leave no witnesses. The men invade the home and take the family hostage, but the brewing storm delays their escape. As the situation deteriorates, a dangerous secret is brought to light that pushes things further into chaos: Sandy and Nick are sister and brother. The Tremonts and their captors are caught in a swirling storm of secrets and lies that threatens to consume them.

Other books by the same author:
Ruin Falls, 2014
Cover of Snow, 2013

Other books you might like:
Linwood Barclay, *No Time for Goodbye*, 2007
Chris Bohjalian, *A Killing in the Real World*, 1988
Gillian Flynn, *Sharp Objects*, 2006

Pam Lewis, *Speak Softly, She Can Hear*, 2005
Jennifer McMahon, *Promise Not to Tell*, 2006
Nancy Pickard, *The Virgin of Small Plains*, 2006
Julia Spencer-Fleming, *Through the Evil Days*, 2013

620

LEE MIMS

Saving Cecil

(Woodbury, Minnesota: Llewellyn Worldwide, Ltd., 2015)

Series: Cleo Cooper Series. Book 3
Story type: Amateur Detective; Series
Subject(s): Murder; Geology; Agriculture
Major character(s): Cleo Cooper, Scientist (geologist), Detective—Amateur, Fiance(e) (of Bud), Crime Suspect, Spouse (ex, of Bud); Clyde Stuckey, Lawman (sheriff); Bud, Fiance(e) (of Cleo), Spouse (ex, of Cleo); Chris Bryant, Lawman (sheriff's deputy)
Time period(s): 21st century; 2010s
Locale(s): North Carolina, United States

Summary: As a geologist, Cleo Cooper is used to digging things up, and her latest job is no exception. Her consulting work for a North Carolina natural gas company leads her to a dead body near a drilling site. While it's obvious Cleo had nothing to do with the murder, a local sheriff with a longstanding grudge against her family declares she is the prime suspect. Determined to clear her name and indulge her passion for detective work, Cleo sets out to find the real killer. To do so she'll have to find a way to juggle her impending marriage and all the planning it entails while getting knee-deep in a conspiracy involving illegal hunting, hog farming, and the unexpected romantic attention of a young deputy. This is the third book in Lee Mims's Cleo Cooper series.

Other books by the same author:
Trusting Viktor, 2014
Hiding Gladys, 2013

Other books you might like:
Sarah Andrews, *In Cold Pursuit*, 2007
Sarah Andrews, *Tensleep*, 1994
Dana Cameron, *Site Unseen*, 2002
Jack DuBrul, *Vulcan's Forge*, 1998
Mary Anna Evans, *Artifacts*, 2003
Jamie Harrison, *The Edge of the Crazies*, 1995
Susan Cummins Miller, *Death Assemblage*, 2003

621

ADAM MITZNER

Losing Faith

(New York: Gallery Books, 2015)

Story type: Contemporary; Legal
Subject(s): Law; Organized crime; Terrorism
Major character(s): Aaron Littman, Lawyer, Lover (former, of Faith), Spouse, Father (of daughters); Faith Nichols, Spouse, Judge, Lover (former, of Aaron); Nicolai Garkov, Organized Crime Figure, Crime Suspect
Time period(s): 21st century; 2010s
Locale(s): New York, New York

Summary: Aaron Littman has worked his way up the ladder to become head of one of the most prestigious law firms in New York and one of the most powerful attorneys in the nation. His latest case, however, threatens to tear all of that down. He is representing Russian mob financier Nicolai Garkov, whose disclosed connection to a terrorist bombing has made him a reviled public figure. To ensure his acquittal, Nicolai has threatened to reveal a secret affair the married Aaron had with Faith Nichols, the presiding judge in the case, who is also married. Now Aaron and Faith both have a lot to lose. She's on the verge of being nominated for the Supreme Court, while Aaron risks the loss of his wife, daughters, and career in law. Torn between their sworn duties to the law and desire to protect their careers and families, Aaron and Faith must figure out how to outwit the unrepentant Nicolai in a chess game in which he controls the most powerful piece.

Other books by the same author:
A Case of Redemption, 2013
A Conflict of Interest, 2011

Other books you might like:
David Ellis, *The Hidden Man*, 2009
James Grippando, *The Pardon: A Novel*, 1994
John Grisham, *The Partner*, 1997
William Lashner, *Hostile Witness*, 1995
Steve Martini, *Compelling Evidence*, 1992
Christopher Reich, *Rules of Deception*, 2008
Lisa Scottoline, *Accused*, 2013

622

FREDERIQUE MOLAY

The City of Blood

(New York: Le French Book, 2015)

Series: Paris Homicide Mystery Series. Book 3
Story type: Contemporary; Police Procedural
Subject(s): Murder; Mystery; French (European people)
Major character(s): Nico Sirsky, Police Officer (chief); Samuel Cassian, Artist, Father (of missing person)
Time period(s): 21st century; 2010s
Locale(s): Paris, France

Summary: Performance artist Samuel Cassian's latest project has been 30 years in the making. Three decades ago, he buried the leftovers of a banquet at a Paris museum, and now he has unearthed his "creation." His artistic endeavor hits a snag when the unveiling reveals a mystery. A human skeleton is found among the remains of the feast, prompting Chief of Police Nico Sirsky and his investigative team to look into the case. His first task is to determine if the corpse is the body of the artist's son, who disappeared around the time the feast was buried. Soon the city is rocked by a series of nightclub murders, and as Nico begins to piece together the clues, he begins to suspect a connection between the corpse and the killings. This is the third book in Frederique

Mystery

Molay's Paris Homicide Mystery series.

Other books by the same author:
Crossing the Line, 2014
The 7th Woman, 2013

Other books you might like:
Cara Black, *Murder in the Marais*, 1998
Pierre Lemaitre, *Alex*, 2013
Donna Leon, *Death at La Fenice*, 1992
Vincent McConnor, *The Provence Puzzle*, 1980
Barbara Nadel, *Belshazzar's Daughter*, 2004
Georges Simenon, *The Crime of Inspector Maigret*, 1932
Fred Vargas, *The Chalk Circle Man*, 2009

623

SHIRLEY ROUSSEAU MURPHY
PAT J.J. MURPHY, Co-Author

The Cat, the Devil, the Last Escape

(New York: William Morrow, 2015)

Series: Cat and the Devil Mystery Series. Book 2
Story type: Paranormal; Series
Subject(s): Ghosts; Supernatural; Crime
Major character(s): Morgan Blake, Crime Suspect, Friend (of Lee), Father (of Sammie); Sammie Blake, 9-Year-Old, Daughter (of Morgan), Friend (former owner of Misto), Psychic; Misto, Cat, Spirit; Lee Fontana, Criminal, Friend (of Morgan)
Time period(s): 20th century; 1940s
Locale(s): California, United States

Summary: One of the devil's closest associates, Brad Falon, commits a fatal robbery and lays the blame on his friend Morgan Blake. Morgan is found guilty of the crime and is sentenced to life in prison, much to the dismay of his family. Looking for some comfort, Morgan's daughter Sammie turns to the ghost of her deceased cat, who watches over the child. The spirit, Misto, suspects Sammie has something that the devil wants to possess. Meanwhile, Morgan becomes friends with a longtime prisoner, Lee Fontana, who has outsmarted Satan in the past, thanks to Misto's help. Satan has been targeting Fontana's family for generations. Morgan and Lee begin to plan an escape. Morgan intends to bring the real criminal to justice and clear his name. All they need to do is outwit the devil. Meanwhile, Misto is working to understand how and why Sammie is connected to Lee. This is the second book of the Cat and the Devil mystery series by Pat and Shirley Murphy.

Other books by the same author:
The Cat, the Devil, and Lee Fontana, 2014
Cat Bearing Gifts, 2012
Cat Under Fire, 1998
Cat on the Edge, 1996
The Catswold Portal, 1992

Other books you might like:
Lilian Jackson Braun, *The Cat Who Could Read Backwards*, 1966
Lilian Jackson Braun, *The Cat Who Had 60 Whiskers*, 2007

Rita Mae Brown, *Nine Lives to Die*, 2014
Rita Mae Brown, *Wish You Were Here*, 1990
Carole Nelson Douglas, *Cat in a Yellow Spotlight*, 2014
Carole Nelson Douglas, *Catnap*, 1992
Clea Simon, *Mew is for Murder*, 2005

624

JO NESBO
NEIL SMITH, Translator

Blood on Snow

(New York: Knopf Doubleday Publishing, 2015)

Story type: Psychological Suspense
Subject(s): Abuse; Assassination; Criminals
Major character(s): Olav Johansen, Murderer (for hire, fixer), Criminal (works for Daniel Hoffmann); Daniel Hoffmann, Drug Dealer, Criminal (crime boss), Spouse (of Corina Hoffmann); Corina Hoffmann, Spouse (of Daniel Hoffmann)
Time period(s): 20th century; 1970s (1976)
Locale(s): Oslo, Norway

Summary: It is 1976 in Oslo, Norway. Olav Johansen works for heroin kingpin and crime boss Daniel Hoffmann. Olav is not good at many things. He is unsuccessful as a petty criminal. He is dyslexic and he is too soft-hearted. But he is good at one thing, one specific skill that Hoffmann finds invaluable. Olav is good at making people disappear. He is a killer known as a fixer. Eventually, however, even a fixer as skilled as Olav finds his work challenging. Hoffmann orders his fixer to make his wife, Corina Hoffmann, go away. This is a problem Olav doesn't want to solve. He begins watching Corina and soon becomes entranced by the unsuspecting woman. Olav realizes he has a problem of his own—he must figure out how to avoid killing Corina and find a way to keep them both alive when Hoffmann discovers his betrayal.

Other books by the same author:
The Cockroaches, 2014
The Bat, 2012
Nemesis, 2008
The Redbreast, 2006
The Devil's Star, 2005

Other books you might like:
Jorgen Brekke, *Where Monsters Dwell*, 2014
K. O. Dahl, *The Fourth Man*, 2006
Ake Edwardson, *Death Angels*, 2009
Thomas Enger, *Burned*, 2011
Kjell Eriksson, *The Hand that Trembles*, 2011
Kjell Eriksson, *The Princess of Burundi*, 2006
Karin Fossum, *Bad Intentions*, 2011
Karin Fossum, *Don't Look Back*, 2002
Anne Holt, *1222*, 2011
Anne Holt, *Blessed Are Those Who Thirst*, 2013
Jan Kjaerstad, *The Seducer*, 2006
Camilla Lackberg, *Buried Angels*, 2014
Henning Mankell, *An Event in Autumn*, 2014
Kristina Ohlsson, *Unwanted*, 2012
Gunnar Staalesen, *Yours Until Death*, 1993

625

T.J. O'CONNOR

Dying for the Past

(Woodbury, Minnesota: Midnight Ink, 2015)

Series: Gumshoe Ghost Mystery Series. Book 2
Story type: Ghost Story; Series
Subject(s): Suspense; Detective fiction; Murder
Major character(s): Oliver "Tuck" Tucker, Spirit, Detective—Police (formerly), Spouse (of Angela); Dr. Angela "Angel" Hill-Tucker, Spouse (of Oliver), Niece (of Andre), Professor; Andre Cartier, Uncle (of Angela), Crime Suspect; Vincent Calaprese, Criminal (mobster), Crime Victim (murdered), Spirit
Time period(s): 21st century; (2010s); 20th century; 1930s (1939)
Locale(s): Winchester, Virginia

Summary: During a fundraising gala for the local university, one of the attendees is shot on the dance floor while everyone is watching. In addition to the murder, the money that was raised during the event has disappeared. Although no one knows for sure who pulled the trigger, the main suspect is Andre Cartier, uncle to the gala organizer, Angela Tucker. In an attempt to clear the name of his wife's uncle, former police detective Oliver "Tuck" Tucker searches for the real killer. His investigation takes him to the 1930s, where he meets gangster Vincent Calabrese. Tuck must read Vincent's journal, which is filled with secrets on spies still active decades later. Tuck also learns of a family secret that could explain why he is still around, even though he has died. This in the second novel of the Gumshoe Ghost Mystery series by T.J. O'Connor.

Other books by the same author:
Dying to Know, 2014

Other books you might like:
Casey Daniels, *Don of the Dead*, 2006
Carolyn G. Hart, *Ghost at Work*, 2008
Sharon Pape, *Sketch Me If You Can*, 2010
Thorne Smith, *Topper*, 1926
Thorne Smith, *Topper Takes a Trip*, 1932
Simone St. James, *The Haunting of Maddy Clare*, 2012
Karen White, *The House on Tradd Street*, 2008

626

TIM O'MARA

Dead Red

(New York: Minotaur Books, 2015)

Series: Raymond Donne Mystery Series. Book 3
Story type: Series
Subject(s): Murder; Crime; Friendship
Major character(s): Raymond "Ray" Donne, Friend (of Ricky), Police Officer (former), Teacher; Ricky Torres, Crime Victim, Detective—Private, Friend (of Ray); Jack Knight, Friend (of Ricky), Detective—Private, Police Officer (former)
Time period(s): 21st century; 2010s

Locale(s): New York, New York

Summary: Teacher Raymond Donne's relaxing summer vacation comes to an abrupt halt with a single phone call. His pal from his days as an NYPD cop, Ricky Torres, wants to meet him in the middle of the night. Before Ray can get answers, someone guns Ricky down and nearly takes Ray out as well. Ricky's been working as a private investigator for another former cop, Jack Knight. As Ray looks for answers about Ricky's murder, he reluctantly takes over his friend's missing-person case. The 16-year-old daughter of a bigwig has disappeared, and Ray believes the killer he seeks is tied up in the case. He's puzzled by what he finds in Ricky's recent history, too. Ricky had applied for reinstatement to the police force, and seemed to have a lot of cash with no explanation of where it came from. Ray's inquiries just seem to raise more questions and few answers. This is the third title in the Raymond Donne Mystery series.

Other books by the same author:
Crooked Numbers, 2013
Sacrifice Fly, 2012

Other books you might like:
Jim Fusilli, *Closing Time*, 2001
Alison Gaylin, *And She Was*, 2012
Alison Gaylin, *Hide Your Eyes*, 2005
Merry Jones, *Summer Session*, 2011
Kimberly McCreight, *Reconstructing Amelia*, 2013
Carol O'Connell, *The Chalk Girl*, 2012
Peter Spiegelman, *Black Maps*, 2003

627

CARLENE O'NEIL

One Foot in the Grape

(New York: Berkley Prime Crime, 2015)

Series: Cypress Cove Mystery Series. Book 1
Story type: Amateur Detective; Cozy Mystery
Subject(s): Women; Suspense; Detective fiction
Major character(s): Penny Lively, Narrator, Detective—Amateur, Aunt (of Hayley), Employer (of Connor), Neighbor (of Antonia); Hayley, Niece (of Penny), Crime Suspect; Antonia Martinelli, Neighbor (of Penny); Connor, Worker (of Penny's winery)
Time period(s): 21st century; 2010s
Locale(s): Cypress Cove, California

Summary: In the first installment of the Cypress Cove Mystery series, Penny Lively has just lost her job as a photographer. As she considers what her next should be, she inherits a winery from her late aunt. With the help of her niece Hayley and winery manager Connor, Penny believes that the winery will give her the fresh start that she needs. Right before the Autumn Festival, neighboring winery owner Antonia Martinelli comes to Penny asking for help. Antonia believes that someone is intentionally spoiling her wine, and she needs Penny to use her sleuthing skills to find out who the culprit is. As Penny begins her investigation, a staff member is found dead beside the grape crusher. All eyes turn to Hayley, who was the last person to see the victim before he was

Mystery

murdered. It's up to Penny to find the murderer and clear her niece's name.

Other books you might like:

Tony Aspler, *Blood is Thicker than Beaujolais*, 1993

Linda Barnes, *Blood Will Have Blood*, 1982

Lucy Burdette, *An Appetite for Murder*, 2012

Sheila Connolly, *One Bad Apple: An Orchard Mystery*, 2008

Ellen Crosby, *The Merlot Murders*, 2006

Nadia Gordon, *Sharpshooter: A Sunny McCoskey Napa Valley Mystery*, 2002

Michele Scott, *Murder Uncorked*, 2005

628

KATHRYN O'SULLIVAN

Neighing with Fire

(New York: Minotaur Books, 2015)

Series: Colleen McCabe Series. Book 3
Story type: Contemporary; Series
Subject(s): Women; Detective fiction; Murder
Major character(s): Colleen McCabe, Fire Fighter (fire chief of Corolla), Girlfriend (of Bill); Bill Dorman, Police Officer (Sheriff of Corolla), Boyfriend (of Colleen); Denny Custis, Crime Victim; Antonio "Pinky" Salvatore, Crime Suspect
Time period(s): 21st century; 2010s
Locale(s): Corolla, North Carolina

Summary: In the third book of the Colleen McCabe mystery series, a dead body is disinterred from beneath a vacation home's boardwalk after a tropical storm rips through Corolla, North Carolina. As fire chief Colleen McCabe and sheriff Bill Dorman investigate, land developer Denny Custis dies in a fire. Colleen believes the fire is suspicious and the deaths are connected. Colleen and Bill soon learn that everyone in Corolla had a problem with Denny—including Colleen. Rival land developer Pinky Salvatore becomes the prime suspect in Denny's murder, yet Colleen feels he is innocent and tries to clear his name. As the suspect list continues to grow, Bill and Colleen soon become involved in a battle between a touring company and animal rights protesters who are set on protecting Corolla's wild horses and an endangered shore bird.

Other books by the same author:
Murder on the Hoof, 2014
Foal Play, 2013

Other books you might like:

Ellery Adams, *A Killer Plot*, 2010

Ellen Block, *The Language of Sand*, 2010

Marguerite Henry, *Misty of Chincoteague*, 1947

Jody Jaffe, *Horse of a Different Killer*, 1995

Jim Lavene, *That Old Flame of Mine*, 2013

Joyce Lavene, *A Timely Vision*, 2010

Michele Scott, *Saddled with Trouble*, 2006

629

DANIEL PALMER

Constant Fear

(New York: Kensington Books, 2015)

Story type: Psychological Suspense
Subject(s): Survival; Suspense; Hostages
Major character(s): Jake Dent, Father (of Andy), Worker (custodian at Pepperell Academy); Andy Dent, Son (of Jake), Diabetic, Student
Time period(s): 21st century; 2010s
Locale(s): Winston, United States

Summary: Jake Dent's life falls apart after he is arrested for drunk driving. Not only did his dream of becoming a great baseball player disappear, but his marriage crumbled as well. Now a survivalist and school custodian, Jake spends his time preparing his son Andy to be ready for any emergency. Andy, meanwhile, has a secret he keeps from his father. A student at Pepperell Academy, Andy is a member of a computer club that steals from wealthy people and gives the money to the poor. After the club steals money from a drug cartel, the cartel strikes back. Using a chemical truck spill as cover, the cartel invades the school and takes Andy and his computer club friends hostage. However, the cartel doesn't know that Jake is hiding in the school's tunnel system. Jake knows what will happen next and, with a plethora of supplies and a limited amount of time, he sets out to save his son and the other students from the cartel.

Other books by the same author:
Trauma, 2015
Desperate, 2014
Stolen, 2013
Helpless, 2012
Delirious, 2011

Other books you might like:

Linwood Barclay, *Trust Your Eyes*, 2012

Harlan Coben, *The Innocent*, 2005

Joseph Finder, *Buried Secrets*, 2010

Lisa Gardner, *Love You More*, 2011

Gregg Hurwitz, *You're Next*, 2011

Chris Mooney, *Remembering Sarah*, 2004

Lisa Unger, *Black Out*, 2008

630

GIGI PANDIAN

The Accidental Alchemist

(Woodbury, Minnesota: Midnight Ink, 2015)

Series: Accidental Alchemist Mystery Series. Book 1
Story type: Fantasy; Paranormal
Subject(s): Alchemy; Mystery; Murder
Major character(s): Zoe Faust, Supernatural Being (alchemist), Woman; Dorian Robert-Houdin, Supernatural Being (gargoyle); Brixton, 14-Year-Old, Neighbor (of Zoe)
Time period(s): 21st century; 2010s

Locale(s): Portland, Oregon

Summary: Herbalist Zoe Faust has packed her things and moved to a rundown house in Portland, Oregon. She's making a fresh start, far from the alchemy trade—or so she believes. While unpacking, she discovers a stone gargoyle among her things. Zoe is astonished to discover the gargoyle is more than decorative—in fact, it's alive. He introduces himself as Dorian Robert-Houdin and he requests Zoe's skills as an alchemist. She's reluctant to dabble, though Dorian's very life is at stake. A day later, a repairman is murdered in her house and Zoe discovers that the killer has stolen some of her alchemical texts. As she works to learn who else has followed her to Portland, Zoe encounters some locals, including 14-year-old neighbor Brixton. She also spends time cooking vegan feasts, with a little assistance in the kitchen from her gargoyle gourmet. This is the first title in Gigi Pandian's Accidental Alchemist Mystery series, which includes recipes.

Other books by the same author:
Pirate Vishnu, 2014
Artifact, 2012

Other books you might like:
Madelyn Alt, *The Trouble with Magic*, 2006
Barbra Annino, *Opal Fire*, 2012
Juliet Blackwell, *Secondhand Spirits*, 2009
Heather Blake, *It Takes a Witch*, 2012
Dana Cameron, *Seven Kinds of Hell*, 2013
Shirley Damsgaard, *Witch Way to Murder*, 2005
CC Dragon, *A Mansion, A Drag Queen, and a New Job*, 2015

631

NANCY J. PARRA

Flourless to Stop Him

(New York: Berkley Prime Crime, 2015)

Series: Baker's Treat Mystery Series. Book 3
Story type: Amateur Detective; Cozy Mystery
Subject(s): Cooking; Murder; Drugs
Major character(s): Toni Holmes, Narrator, Sister (of Tim), Baker, Detective—Amateur; Tim Holmes, Brother (of Toni), Crime Suspect; Grandma Ruth, Journalist
Time period(s): 21st century; 2010s
Locale(s): Oiltop, Kansas

Summary: In the third book of the Baker's Treat Mystery series, it's the busy season for gluten-free baker Toni Holmes. She's hard at work creating delicious treats for the holiday season when she learns a dead body has been found in the bathtub of a local hotel. What's more suspicious is that hotel room is registered to her brother Tim. With her brother as a prime suspect in the murder, Toni begins an investigation. She soon learns that someone has been using her brother's name to check into several hotels in the area and then sell drugs from the rooms. After her brother is arrested, Toni gets some unwanted help from Grandma Ruth, a nonagenarian investigative reporter who will stop at nothing to find the truth. Together, they set about to clear Tim's name before the holiday season ends.

Other books by the same author:
Engaged in Murder, 2014
Murder Gone A-Rye, 2014
Gluten for Punishment, 2013
Saving Samantha, 2002
A Wanted Man, 2002

Other books you might like:
Jacklyn Brady, *Murder Takes the Cake*, 2008
Jacklyn Brady, *A Sheetcake Named Desire*, 2011
JoAnna Carl, *The Chocolate Cat Caper*, 2002
Sammi Carter, *Candy Apple Dead*, 2005
Bailey Cates, *Brownies and Broomsticks: A Magical Bakery Mystery*, 2012
Joanne Fluke, *Chocolate Chip Cookie Murder*, 2000
Victoria Hamilton, *Bran New Death*, 2013

632

JAMES PATTERSON
MARSHALL KARP, Co-Author

NYPD Red 3

(New York: Little, Brown and Company, 2015)

Series: NYPD Red Series. Book 3
Story type: Contemporary; Series
Subject(s): Mystery; Detective fiction; Crime
Major character(s): Zach Jordan, Detective—Police (NYPD Red); Kylie MacDonald, Detective—Police (NYPD Red); Hunter Hutchinson Alden Jr., Businessman, Wealthy, Father (of Tripp), Spouse (of Janelle); Janelle Alden, Spouse (of Hunter), Mother (of Tripp); Hunter "Tripp" Hutchinson Alden III, 18-Year-Old, Son (of Hunter and Janelle), Missing Person; Peter, Driver
Time period(s): 21st century; 2010s
Locale(s): New York, New York

Summary: Wealthy Manhattan businessman Hunter Hutchinson Alden Jr. celebrates the start of the new year by breaking his resolution to quit drinking. He is reluctantly in attendance at his father's annual gala, and he is impatiently awaiting the arrival of his 18-year-old son, Tripp. Peter, the family's driver, has apparently gone to retrieve the teenager, who had car trouble in Harlem. Hunter makes his way to the garage and finds Tripp's camera case on the floor. Tripp's initials are painted on the case in blood, but the item Hunter finds inside is even more disturbing. Detectives Zach Jordan and Kylie MacDonald, members of the detail known as NYPD Red, are called to investigate. Their unit's specialty is handling crimes that involve the city's richest and most influential residents. As Zach and Kylie search for Hunter and a killer, they are drawn into a shocking high-society conspiracy. This is the third novel in the NYPD Red series.

Other books by the same author:
NYPD Red 2, 2014
NYPD Red, 2012
Kill Me if You Can, 2011
The Rabbit Factory, 2006
Along Came a Spider, 1993

Mystery

Other books you might like:
Janice Cantore, *Critical Pursuit*, 2013
Reed Farrel Coleman, *Robert B. Parker's Blind Spot*, 2014
Douglas Corleone, *Payoff*, 2014
Linda Fairstein, *Final Jeopardy*, 1996
Linda Fairstein, *Terminal City*, 2014
Tricia Fields, *Wrecked*, 2014
Tami Hoag, *Cold Cold Heart*, 2014
Alice Loweecey, *Veiled Threat*, 2013
Ed McBain, *Lady Killer*, 1958
Maxine Paetro, *14th Deadly Sin*, 2015
James Patterson, *Private Vegas*, 2015
James Patterson, *Unlucky 13*, 2014
Lawrence Sanders, *The First Deadly Sin*, 1973
Jonathan Santlofer, *The Death Artist*, 2002
Stuart Woods, *New York Dead*, 1991

633

PAULA PAUL

Medium Dead

(New York: Alibi, 2015)

Series: Alexandra Gladstone Series. Book 4
Story type: Amateur Detective; Historical - Victorian
Subject(s): Murder; Suspense; England
Major character(s): Dr. Alexandra Goodwin, Doctor, Friend (of Nicholas), Detective—Amateur; Alvina Elwold, Psychic, Crime Victim; Nicholas Forsyth, Friend (of Alexandra), Nobleman (Lord Dunsford)
Locale(s): Newton-upon-Sea, England

Summary: Dr. Alexandra Gladstone, a female doctor, takes up the practice that her father had left behind in Newton-upon-Sea in the fourth installment of the Alexandra Gladstone Mystery series. With her faithful yet sometimes overprotective dog Zack by her side, Alexandra spends her days tending to the sick villagers. When the village's psychic, Alvina Elwold, is found dead in the church cemetery, rumors of her murder begin to spread. Some believe that Alvina is now conversing with other spirits and is cursing her enemies. Others believe that a royal visitor may be involved in the murder. The rational Alexandra dismisses the rumors, but she does believe Alvina was murdered. With the help of her friend—Nicholas Forsyth, Lord Dunsford—Alexandra must find the truth before the murderer strikes again.

Other books by the same author:
Forgetting Tommie, 2014
Half a Mind to Murder, 2003
An Improper Death, 2002
Symptoms of Death, 2002
Geronimo Chino, 1980

Other books you might like:
Evelyn Anthony, *Victoria and Albert*, 1958
Stephanie Barron, *A Flaw in the Blood*, 2008
Emily Brightwell, *The Inspector and Mrs. Jeffries*, 1993
C.S. Harris, *What Angels Fear*, 2005
Emma Jameson, *Ice Blue*, 2011
Edward Marston, *Peril on the Royal Train*, 2013

Christine Trent, *A Virtuous Death*, 2014

634

GEORGE P. PELECANOS

The Martini Shot

(New York: Little, Brown and Company, 2015)

Story type: Collection; Mystery
Subject(s): Crime; Deception; Mystery

Summary: Television scriptwriter George Pelicanos provides a collection of eight hard-boiled crime stories: a novella and seven shorter works. The theme throughout the work is the struggle for survival. In the title novella, a television scriptwriter who greatly resembles Pelecanos is startled by the sudden change in his life—it is beginning to conform to the scripts he writes. In one story, an investigator is interrupted by a young boy while he is searching for a deceased man. In "The Confidential Informant," a man tries to impress his impassive father by relaying information to the police. In "The Dead Their Eyes Implore Us," Pelecanos explores the clash between a Pinkerton Agent and an immigrant during the Great Depression. Most of these works have been published in a variety of anthologies.

Other books by the same author:
The Cut, 2011
The Way Home, 2009
Right as Rain, 2001
Shoedog, 1994
A Firing Offense, 1992

Other books you might like:
Earl Emerson, *Deviant Behavior*, 1988
Edward P. Jones, *All Aunt Hagar's Children: Stories*, 2006
Edward P. Jones, *Lost in the City: Stories*, 1992
Dennis Lehane, *Coronado: Stories*, 2006
Laura Lippman, *Hardly Knew Her: Stories*, 2008
Dinaw Mengestu, *The Beautiful Things That Heaven Bears*, 2007
Richard Powers, *The Time of Our Singing*, 2003

635

CAROL J. PERRY

Tails, You Lose

(New York: Kensington, 2015)

Series: Witch City Mystery Series. Book 2
Story type: Cozy Mystery; Paranormal
Subject(s): Mystery; Murder; Psychics
Major character(s): Lee Barrett, Psychic, Television Personality, Teacher (Tabitha Trumbull Academy of the Arts)
Time period(s): 21st century; 2010s
Locale(s): Salem, Massachusetts

Summary: In this second novel in the Witch City Mystery series by Carol J. Perry, former television psychic Lee

Barrett is now volunteering as an instructor at the Tabitha Trumbull Academy of the Arts—or "The Tabby"—in Salem, Massachusetts. All seems well until the school's handyman is found murdered on Christmas, and Lee begins to get the impression that her psychic abilities may be coming back to her. Lee and her students decide to make a documentary about the history of the academy building, which was formerly a department store. What they find is nothing short of chilling. From a mystifying labyrinth of tunnels under Salem to spooky visions appearing in Lee's classroom, the building has a truly creepy history—and it seems to be bleeding into the present.

Other books by the same author:
Caught Dead Handed, 2014
Going Overboard, 1991
13 and Loving It, 1989
Make-Believe Love, 1989
Sand Castle Summer, 1988

Other books you might like:
Heather Blake, *It Takes a Witch*, 2012
Victoria Laurie, *Abby Cooper, Psychic Eye*, 2005
T.J. MacGregor, *The Hanged Man*, 1998
Kris Neri, *High Crimes on the Magical Plane*, 2009
Shari Shattuck, *Eye of the Beholder*, 2007
Clea Simon, *Dogs Don't Lie*, 2011
Heather Webber, *Truly, Madly*, 2010

636

CATE PRICE

Lie of the Needle

(New York: Berkley Prime Crime, 2015)

Series: Deadly Notions Series. Book 3
Story type: Cozy Mystery; Series
Subject(s): Murder; Sewing; Antiques
Major character(s): Daisy Buchanan, Businesswoman (antique shop owner), Detective—Amateur, Friend (of Cyril); Cyril, Friend (of Daisy), Man, Missing Person
Time period(s): 21st century; 2010s
Locale(s): Millbury, Pennsylvania

Summary: Best-selling author Cate Price returns with the third installment in her Deadly Notions cozy mystery series. Daisy Buchanan, owner of Sometimes a Great Notion, a vintage sewing and antique store in Millbury, Pennsylvania, joins forces with the town's Historical Society to save a 200-year-old farmhouse. Daisy and the society have put together a fund-raiser in an effort to stop an eager developer from taking over the historic property. The most anticipated item for sale is a pinup calendar featuring the local hunks from Millbury. But when Daisy's friend Cyril misses his photo shoot and the calendar photographer turns up dead, Daisy discovers that someone isn't as keen on preserving the farmhouse as she is. Will Daisy piece the clues together in time to find her friend and stop the killer before he or she claims another victim?

Other books by the same author:
A Dollhouse to Die For, 2014

Going Through the Notions, 2013

Other books you might like:
Janet Bolin, *Dire Threads*, 2011
Elizabeth Lynn Casey, *Sew Deadly*, 2009
Elizabeth Lynn Casey, *Taken In*, 2014
Monica Ferris, *And Then You Dye*, 2012
Monica Ferris, *Crewel World*, 1999
Amanda Lee, *The Quick and the Thread*, 2010
Amanda Lee, *Thread End*, 2014

637

DAVID PUTNAM

The Replacements

(Longboat Key, Florida: Oceanview Publishing, 2015)

Series: Bruno Johnson Series. Book 2
Story type: Police Procedural; Series
Subject(s): Detective fiction; Mystery; Kidnapping
Major character(s): Bruno Johnson, Detective—Police (former), Convict (former), Colleague (former, of Barbara), Spouse (husband, of Marie); Jonas Mabry, Kidnapper; Marie, Spouse (wife, of Bruno); Barbara Wicks, Police Officer (Chief, of Montclair, California), Colleague (former, of Bruno)
Time period(s): 21st century; 2010s
Locale(s): California, United States

Summary: David Putnam delivers the second novel in his Bruno Johnson mystery series. Ex-convict and ex-detective for the Los Angeles County Sheriff's Department, Bruno Johnson escapes to Costa Rica with his wife, Marie, and the eight children they saved—illegally—from domestic abuse. When Barbara Wicks, Johnson's former associate and police chief for Montclair, California, shows up at the bar Johnson tends, he's certain she's there to arrest him. Instead, she asks for his assistance with a kidnapper named Jonas Mabry, who was rescued as a child from an abusive home by Johnson. Jonas has kidnapped two young girls, and, in addition to a million-dollar ransom, has demanded that he only deal with Johnson. Willing to risk arrest to help, Johnson returns to California to answer Jonas's dangerous demands. But does he have what it takes to save the young girls' lives—and his own?

Other books by the same author:
The Disposables, 2014

Other books you might like:
Richard Barre, *The Innocents*, 1995
Baron Birtcher, *Roadhouse Blues*, 2000
Paul Bishop, *Kill Me Again*, 1994
Stephen J. Cannell, *The Tin Collectors*, 2001
T. Jefferson Parker, *L.A. Outlaws*, 2008
John Shannon, *The Concrete River*, 1996
Don Winslow, *The Winter of Frankie Machine*, 2006

Mystery

638

BRYON QUERTERMOUS

Murder Boy

(New York: Polis Books, 2015)

Story type: Contemporary; Psychological Suspense
Subject(s): Crime; Kidnapping; Writers
Major character(s): Dominick Prince, Student (of Parker Farmington), Kidnapper, Writer (aspiring); Parker Farmington, Professor (adviser to Dominick), Kidnap Victim
Time period(s): 21st century; 2010s
Locale(s): Detroit, Michigan

Summary: Aspiring writer Dominick Prince dreams of leaving Detroit for a writing fellowship in New York City. Only one thing is standing in his way: his thesis adviser, Parker Farmington. An academic elitist, Farmington is concerned that Dominick's low-rate crime novel might hinder his chances at tenure, and for that reason, he refuses to sign off on Dominick's work. Determined not to let Farmington keep him from pursuing his literary dreams, Dominick devises a plan to kidnap the professor. Dominick solicits the help of Farmington's disgruntled mistress and her reckless brother, a bounty hunter. Unlike Dominick's fictional plots, this real-life conspiracy falls to pieces quickly. A fast-paced adventure through the streets of Detroit ensues, and Dominick will be lucky to come out alive. First novel.

Other books you might like:
Linwood Barclay, *Bad Move*, 2004
Ray Bradbury, *Death Is a Lonely Business*, 1985
Max Allan Collins, *No Cure for Death*, 1983
Harry Dolan, *Bad Things Happen*, 2009
Tim Dorsey, *The Stingray Shuffle*, 2003
Duane Swierczynski, *Severance Package*, 2008
Jess Walter, *Citizen Vince*, 2005

639

BRYAN REARDON

Finding Jake

(New York: William Morrow, 2015)

Story type: Literary; Psychological Suspense
Subject(s): Father-son relations; Family relations; High schools
Major character(s): Simon Connelly, Father (of Jake and Laney), Spouse (husband, of Rachel); Jake Connelly, Teenager, 17-Year-Old, Student—High School, Crime Suspect, Missing Person, Brother (of Laney), Son (of Simon and Rachel); Rachel Connelly, Spouse (wife, of Simon), Mother (of Jake and Laney), Lawyer; Laney Connelly, Teenager, Student—High School, Sister (of Jake), Daughter (of Simon and Rachel)
Time period(s): 21st century; 2010s
Locale(s): Wilmington, Delaware

Summary: This psychological thriller by Bryan Reardon follows one father's quest to find his son, the suspected gunman in a high school shooting. Stay-at-home dad Simon Connelly looks after his teenage son and daughter, Jake and Laney, while his wife, a successful attorney, works to support the family. When Simon receives a text about a shooting at his kids' suburban Delaware high school, he reports to the designated meeting area and learns that 17-year-old Jake is not only missing, but also one of the suspected gunmen. As Simon recalls moments from Jake's childhood, he questions whether his quiet, reserved son is capable of such violent actions and wonders if his own child-rearing is part of the cause. As the search for Jake continues into the weeks following the shooting, Simon confronts what he knows—and doesn't know—about Jake. First novel.

Other books you might like:
Wally Lamb, *The Hour I First Believed*, 2008
William Landay, *Defending Jacob*, 2012
Joyce Maynard, *To Die For*, 1992
Alissa Nutting, *Tampa*, 2013
Jodi Picoult, *Nineteen Minutes*, 2007
Francine Prose, *After*, 2003
Lionel Shriver, *We Need to Talk about Kevin*, 2003

640

KATHY REICHS

Speaking in Bones

(New York: Bantam, 2015)

Series: Temperance Brennan Series. Book 18
Story type: Police Procedural; Series
Subject(s): Mystery; Detective fiction; Crime
Major character(s): Dr. Temperance "Tempe" Brennan, Anthropologist (forensic)
Time period(s): 21st century; 2010s
Locale(s): Charlotte, North Carolina

Summary: Temperance "Tempe" Brennan is one of a few dozen forensic anthropologists who work in the United States. When law enforcement officials have to deal with severely compromised human remains—or even just bones—that are beyond a coroner's expertise, they call on Tempe to figure out how the victim died. Tempe's latest case involves a missing person, but her seemingly run-of-the-mill investigation ends up being far from ordinary. The case leads her to some buried bones, and Tempe must figure out who put them there. The remains may belong to a serial killer's victims, or they may be evidence of cult-related murders. This novel is the 18th in the Temperance Brennan series by Kathy Reichs.

Other books by the same author:
Bones Never Lie, 2014
Fatal Voyage, 2001
Deadly Decisions, 2000
Death du Jour, 1999
Deja Dead, 1997

Other books you might like:
Jefferson Bass, *Carved in Bone*, 2006
Patricia Cornwell, *Postmortem*, 1990
Kathryn Fox, *Malicious Intent*, 2006
Jonathan Hayes, *Precious Blood: A Novel*, 2007
Jonathan Kellerman, *Motive*, 2015

Thomas Noguchi, *Unnatural Causes*, 1988
Karin Slaughter, *Blindsighted*, 2001
Robert W. Walker, *Killer Instinct*, 1992

641

LINDA REILLY

Fillet of Murder

(New York: Berkley Prime Crime, 2015)

Series: Deep Fried Mystery Series. Book 1
Story type: Cozy Mystery; Series
Subject(s): Mystery; Murder; Restaurants
Major character(s): Talia Marby, Friend (of Bea), Waiter/
   Waitress (Lambert's Fish & Chips); Bea Lambert,
   Friend (of Talia), Restaurateur (Lambert's Fish &
   Chips); Phil Turnbull, Store Owner
Time period(s): 21st century; 2010s
Locale(s): Massachusetts, United States

Summary: In this novel, the first in the Deep Fried
Mystery series by Linda Reilly, Talia Marby is ready to
start a new life in her hometown in the Berkshires after
she leaves her old job and boyfriend behind. She's working at her friend Bea's shop, Lambert's Fish and Chips,
and she is thoroughly enjoying herself until town
busybody Phil Turnbull gets in the way. He wants Bea to
sign a petition against a new business, and he keeps
bothering her, no matter how many times she refuses.
But when Phil is found dead in his shop, the police name
Bea as the primary suspect based on a comment she
muttered in frustration about boiling him in oil. Talia
takes it upon herself to prove Bea's innocence. She
launches her own investigation into the other people in
town and is shocked by what she uncovers. This novel
also includes a few recipes for deep-fried feasts.

Other books by the same author:
Some Enchanted Murder, 2013

Other books you might like:
Riley Adams, *Delicious and Suspicious*, 2010
Mary Kay Andrews, *Savannah Blues*, 2002
Connie Archer, *A Spoonful of Murder*, 2012
Jessica Beck, *A Chili Death*, 2012
Claudia Bishop, *A Taste for Murder*, 1994
Chris Cavender, *A Slice of Murder*, 2009
Judith Cutler, *The Food Detective*, 2005

642

J.D. RHOADES

Devils and Dust

(New York: Polis Books, 2015)

Series: Jack Keller Series. Book 4
Story type: Psychological Suspense; Series
Subject(s): Suspense; Illegal immigrants; Mystery
Major character(s): Jack Keller, Bounty Hunter,
   Mercenary, Lover (former, of Angela), Friend (of
   Oscar); Angela, Spouse (wife, of Oscar), Lover
   (former, of Jack); Oscar Sanchez, Missing Person,
Friend (of Jack), Spouse (husband, of Angela)
Time period(s): 21st century; 2010s
Locale(s): United States

Summary: This psychological thriller is the fourth installment in the Jack Keller series by J. D. Rhoades. Bounty
hunter Jack Keller leads a quiet life in a small southwestern town until his former employer—and ex-lover—
Angela shows up asking for help. Angela's husband and
Keller's best friend, Oscar Sanchez, has gone missing.
He was trying to uncover what happened to his sons
after he arranged for them to cross the Mexican border
illegally. Keller's search leads him to the crime lord who
arranged for the transport of Oscar's sons, and from
there, Keller confronts human traffickers, drug lords, and
a white supremacist group running a forced labor camp
in the South Carolina swamps. Along the way, Keller
faces down demons from his past and comes to terms
with the feelings he still has for Angela.

Other books by the same author:
Storm Surge, 2010
Breaking Cover, 2008
Safe and Sound, 2007
Good Day in Hell, 2006
The Devil's Right Hand, 2005

Other books you might like:
Brett Battles, *The Cleaner*, 2007
Anthony Bruno, *Devil's Food*, 1997
Lee Child, *Killing Floor*, 1997
Ed Gorman, *Guild*, 1987
Chris Rogers, *Bitch Factor*, 1998
Michael Stone, *The Low End of Nowhere*, 1996
Michael Stone, *Totally Dead*, 1999

643

KATE RHODES

The Winter Foundlings

(New York: Minotaur Books, 2015)

Series: Alice Quentin Series. Book 3
Story type: Child-in-Peril; Police Procedural
Subject(s): Mystery; Suspense; Kidnapping
Major character(s): Dr. Alice Quentin, Psychologist
   (forensic), Researcher, Colleague (of Don); Don
   Burns, Detective—Police, Colleague (of Alice);
   Louis Kinsella, Serial Killer, Prisoner
Time period(s): 21st century; 2010s
Locale(s): London, England

Summary: Award-winning author Kate Rhodes returns
with the third novel in her Alice Quentin series. After
swearing off police work indefinitely, forensic psychologist Alice Quentin looks forward to peace and quiet and
to letting go of the feelings she has for Detective Don
Burns. Alice begins a research sabbatical at a high-
security hospital outside of London. When four young
girls go missing in the area and three turn up dead,
Detective Burns once again turns to Alice for help. The
recent string of kidnappings and murders has an obvious
connection to the crimes of Louis Kinsella, England's
most notorious child murderer, who is currently imprisoned at the facility where Alice conducts research. Now

Mystery

Alice is given the chance to get inside the mind of a killer, but Kinsella doesn't give up information easily. It's a race against the clock, and to save the life of the fourth little girl, Alice must risk her own.

Other books by the same author:
A Killing of Angels, 2014
Crossbones Yard, 2013

Other books you might like:
Lindsay Ashford, *Frozen*, 2003
N.J. Cooper, *No Escape*, 2009
G.H. Ephron, *Amnesia*, 2000
Nicci French, *Blue Monday*, 2012
Michael Robotham, *Suspect*, 2005
Minette Walters, *The Sculptress*, 1993
Shirley Wells, *Into the Shadows: Introducing Forensic Psychologist Jill Kennedy and DCI Max Trentham*, 2007

644

CYNTHIA RIGGS

Poison Ivy

(New York: Minotaur Books, 2015)

Series: Martha's Vineyard Mystery Series. Book 11
Story type: Amateur Detective; Cozy Mystery
Subject(s): Mystery; Universities and colleges; Murder
Major character(s): Victoria Trumbull, Aged Person, Professor (adjunct), Writer (poet), Detective—Amateur, Colleague (of Thackery); Thackery Wilson, Colleague (of Victoria); Brownie, Dog
Time period(s): 21st century; 2010s
Locale(s): Massachusetts, United States

Summary: Acclaimed poet Victoria Trumbull begins her first day as an adjunct professor at Ivy Green College, a small school on Martha's Vineyard. She arrives to find a corpse in her classroom and quickly learns that a second body has been found buried under poison ivy. Victoria and her colleagues are certain the murders are connected, but they have little evidence to lead them to a suspect. The college's founder, Thackery Wilson, knows that if news of the campus murders leaks, the school's weakening ties with a partner campus could break altogether. As the death toll of tenured faculty members continues to rise, Victoria and the groundskeeper's dog, Brownie, team up with Thackery and the police to stop the killer from putting an end to Ivy College. This is the 11th novel in the Martha's Vineyard Mystery series by Cynthia Riggs.

Other books by the same author:
The Bee Balm Murders, 2011
Jack in the Pulpit, 2004
The Cemetery Yew, 2003
The Cranefly Orchid Murders, 2002
Deadly Nightshade, 2001

Other books you might like:
Linda Castillo, *Sworn to Silence*, 2009
Philip R. Craig, *A Beautiful Place to Die*, 1989
Philip R. Craig, *Vineyard Chill: A Martha's Vineyard Mystery*, 2008

Tricia Fields, *The Territory*, 2011
Joan Hess, *Malice in Maggody*, 1987
Francine Mathews, *Death in a Cold Hard Light*, 1998
Francine Mathews, *Death in the Off-Season: A Merry Folger Mystery*, 1994

645

MICHAEL ROBOTHAM

Life or Death

(New York: Mulholland Books, 2015)

Story type: Police Procedural; Psychological Suspense
Subject(s): Theft; Murder; Conspiracy
Major character(s): Audie Palmer, Brother (of Carl), Prisoner, Friend (of Moss); Desiree Furness, FBI Agent; Moss Webster, Prisoner, Friend (of Audie); Carl, Brother (of Audie)
Time period(s): 21st century; 2010s
Locale(s): Texas, United States

Summary: After pleading guilty to his involvement in an armored-truck robbery that resulted in the deaths of four people and left $7 million unaccounted for, Audie Palmer was sentenced to ten years in a Texas prison. Now, just one day before he's scheduled to be released, Audie vanishes. His prison friend Moss Webster—not to mention FBI Special Agent Desiree Furness and a host of other high-profile officials—are looking for answers—and for Audie. As Audie attempts to out-run his pursuers, he recalls painful memories of his past, including his relationship with his brother, Carl, and his undying affection for the only woman he has ever loved. Will Audie's brave escape lead to the truth about the infamous robbery, and how long will it take his pursuers to realize he's running to protect someone else's life and not his own?

Other books by the same author:
Watching You, 2013
Bombproof, 2008
The Night Ferry, 2007
Lost, 2006
Suspect, 2005

Other books you might like:
Peter Craig, *Blood Father*, 2005
Joseph Finder, *Vanished*, 2009
Tim Green, *Exact Revenge*, 2005
Chuck Hogan, *Prince of Thieves*, 2004
Gregg Hurwitz, *You're Next*, 2011
Stephen King, *The Green Mile*, 1999
Tim Willocks, *Green River Rising*, 1994

646

BARBARA ROSS

Musseled Out

(New York: Kensington Books, 2015)

Series: Maine Clambake Mystery Series. Book 3
Story type: Cozy Mystery; Series

Subject(s): Mystery; Murder; Restaurants
Major character(s): Julia Snowden, Restaurateur (Snowden Family Clambake Company), Sister (in-law, of Sonny); Sonny, Brother (in-law, of Julia), Restaurateur (Snowden Family Clambake Company); David Thwing, Restaurateur (Mussel King)
Time period(s): 21st century; 2010s
Locale(s): Busman's Harbor, Maine

Summary: In this novel, the third in the Maine Clambake Mystery series by Barbara Ross, Julia Snowden has gone back to her hometown of Busman's Harbor on the coast of Maine to help her family—owners of the Snowden Family Clambake Company—manage their restaurant. Things are going well until David Thwing, the "Mussel King," starts scouting out a new location for his business in their area and threatens to put them out of business. But when Thwing is found murdered a few days later, trapped underneath a lobster boat, the police immediately suspect Julia's brother-in-law, Sonny, as the killer. Julia is convinced Sonny didn't do it, but she needs to find a way to prove it with scant evidence to the contrary.

Other books by the same author:
Boiled Over, 2014
Clammed Up, 2013
The Death of an Ambitious Woman, 2010

Other books you might like:
Claire Donally, *The Big Kitty*, 2012
Vicki Doudera, *A House to Die For*, 2010
Kathy Lynn Emerson, *Kilt Dead*, 2007
Sarah Graves, *The Dead Cat Bounce*, 1998
Lee Charles Kelley, *A Nose for Murder*, 2003
Allison Kingsley, *Mind Over Murder*, 2011
Leslie Meier, *Mail-Order Murder*, 1991

647

MARK RUBINSTEIN

The Lovers' Tango

(Laguna Hills, California: Thunder Lake Press, 2015)

Story type: Romance
Subject(s): Mystery; Marriage; Love
Major character(s): Bill Shaw, Lover (of Nora), Writer; Nora Reyes, Actress, Lover (of Bill)
Time period(s): 21st century; 2010s
Locale(s): United States

Summary: In this novel by Mark Rubinstein, Bill Shaw, a successful writer, and Nora Reyes, a sought-after actress, fell head over heels for each other the moment they met. Their passionate relationship led to a wonderful marriage. Then Nora unexpectedly became very ill and passed away. The DA rules her death a homicide, and Bill—to his horror—is named as the prime suspect. The rest of the novel follows the process of the trial, with Bill attempting to deal with his grief over the loss of the love of his life, and the lawyers attempting to unravel the mystery and find out what really happened at the end of Nora's life. A novel that Bill was working on becomes the catalyst for the jury's decision, as it strangely parallels Nora's illness and death.

Other books by the same author:
Mad Dog Justice, 2014
Return to Sandara, 2014
The Foot Soldier, 2013
Love Gone Mad, 2013
Mad Dog House, 2012

Other books you might like:
Linda Barnes, *The Perfect Ghost*, 2013
Gregg Hurwitz, *The Crime Writer*, 2007
Paul Johnston, *The Death List*, 2007
Susan Kelly, *The Gemini Man*, 1985
Rochelle Majer Krich, *Blues in the Night*, 2002
Lisa Miscione, *Angel Fire*, 2002
Nancy Pickard, *The Whole Truth*, 2000

648

ANNELISE RYAN (Pseudonym of Beth Amos)

Stiff Penalty

(New York: Kensington Books, 2015)

Series: Mattie Winston Series. Book 6
Story type: Amateur Detective; Cozy Mystery
Subject(s): Mystery; Detective fiction; Murder
Major character(s): Mattie Winston, Scientist (coroner), Detective—Amateur; Derrick Ames, Teacher, Crime Victim
Time period(s): 21st century; 2010s
Locale(s): Sorenson, Wisconsin

Summary: No stranger to the dead, deputy coroner Mattie Winston is on the case when local high school math teacher Derrick Ames is murdered with a barbecue fork. As clues pile up and a variety of motives are exposed, pregnant and hormonal Mattie can't believe that the prime suspect is the teacher's own teenage son. Whatever the case, a killer is still at large, and Mattie must uncover the truth before the death toll rises in Sorenson, Wisconsin. Meanwhile, Mattie is concerned that the man who has been stalking her is actually her estranged father. Much of the story is revealed through therapy sessions with a psychiatrist. These are appointments Mattie must keep because the unplanned pregnancy is ample proof that she's still seeing a colleague, in direct violation of department rules. A decidedly mundane third mystery is whether Mattie will marry the father. This cozy mystery is the sixth novel in Annelise Ryan's Mattie Winston series.

Other books by the same author:
Board Stiff, 2014
Lucky Stiff, 2013
Frozen Stiff, 2011
Scared Stiff, 2010
Working Stiff, 2009

Other books you might like:
Noreen Ayres, *A World the Color of Salt*, 1992
Victoria Houston, *Dead Angler*, 2000
Sarah Kemp, *No Escape*, 1984
Mary Logue, *Blood Country*, 1999
David Williams, *Prescription for Murder*, 1990
Mark Zuehlke, *Hands Like Clouds*, 2000
Mark Zuehlke, *Sweep Lotus*, 2004

Mystery

649

PATRICIA TWOMEY RYAN

Rising Tide

(Sutton, Surrey, England: Severn House, 2015)

Story type: Police Procedural
Subject(s): Detective fiction; Romances (Fiction); Murder
Major character(s): Emily Harrington, Woman (wedding guest), Friend (of Thomas and Sarah), Crime Suspect; Thomas Moller, Detective—Police, Friend (of Emily); Ariana Van Meeterens, Teenager, Girl, Crime Victim; Sarah Maitland, Bride, Friend (of Emily)
Time period(s): 21st century; 2010s
Locale(s): Aruba

Summary: This mystery novel by Patricia Twomey Ryan is the sequel to the author's 2014 novel, *Windswept*. Emily Harrington returns to Aruba for the wedding of Sarah Maitland, the daughter of the owners of the Island Bluffs resort. Emily is happy to reunite with Chief Inspector Thomas Moller, but a romantic weekend turns grim when the body of teenager Ariana Van Meeterens washes up on the beach the morning after the wedding. As Moller and his colleagues investigate the crime scene, their primary piece of evidence is the gold bangle bracelet found on the victim's wrist—a bracelet that everyone recognizes as belonging to Emily. As they narrow in on the mysterious bracelet, Emily is once again thrust into danger. Things only get worse when a resort guest reports false information to the media, and Emily becomes the next target.

Other books by the same author:
Windswept, 2014

Other books you might like:
Kathy Brandt, *Swimming with the Dead*, 2003
Agatha Christie, *A Caribbean Mystery*, 1964
Jerrilyn Farmer, *The Flaming Luau of Death*, 2005
Quinn Fawcett, *Death to Spies*, 2002
Stella Whitelaw, *Second Sitting*, 2008
Stella Whitelaw, *A Wide Berth*, 2010
Phyllis A. Whitney, *Columbella*, 1966

650

SOFIE RYAN (Pseudonym of Darlene Ryan)

Buy a Whisker

(New York: Penguin Publishing Group, 2015)

Series: Second Chance Cat Mystery Series. Book 2
Story type: Cozy Mystery; Series
Subject(s): Mystery; Pets; Murder
Major character(s): Sarah Grayson, Store Owner (Second Chance); Lily Carter, Baker; Elvis, Cat
Time period(s): 21st century; 2010s
Locale(s): North Harbor, Maine

Summary: In this cozy mystery by Sofie Ryan, the second in the Second Chance Cat Mystery series, Sarah Grayson is enjoying a nice, calm life in North Harbor, Maine. She lives there with her cat, Elvis, and runs her secondhand shop, Second Chance. Sarah solved a murder just a few months ago and, unfortunately, the peace doesn't last long. A developer comes to town, hoping to make some changes to the waterfront. Many of the local business owners are fine with it, except baker Lily Carter. She doesn't get a chance to put a stop to it, however; she's found dead in her bakery soon after voicing her refusal to sell her business. Sarah and Elvis use their unique skills to investigate the murder, and they put themselves in the killer's crosshairs in the process.

Other books by the same author:
The Whole Cat and Caboodle, 2014

Other books you might like:
Garrison Allen, *Desert Cat*, 1994
Lorna Barrett, *Murder Is Binding*, 2008
Ali Brandon, *Double Booked for Death*, 2011
Rebecca M. Hale, *How to Wash a Cat*, 2008
Miranda James, *Murder Past Due*, 2010
Fran Stewart, *Orange as Marmalade*, 2003
Carrie Vaughn, *Kitty's Big Trouble*, 2011

651

VANESSA A. RYAN

A Palette for Murder

(Waterville, Maine: Five Star, 2015)

Series: Lana Davis Mystery Series. Book 1
Story type: Contemporary; Series
Subject(s): Mystery; Murder; Insurance
Major character(s): Lana Davis, Insurance Agent; Antonio Chavez, Heir (insurance beneficiary)
Time period(s): 21st century; 2010s
Locale(s): Santa Fe, New Mexico

Summary: In this novel, the first in the Lana Davis Mystery series by Vanessa A. Ryan, Lana Davis is sent by her insurance company to Santa Fe, New Mexico. She is supposed to track down Antonio Chavez, the beneficiary of a sizable life insurance policy. It's important that she find him because another heir has come out of the woodwork, claiming that he is the rightful recipient. He's causing a headache for Lana's company, and he's threatening Lana's job. Though she expects this to be a relatively straightforward task, Lana soon realizes that Antonio is not going to be very easy to find. The information she has on him leads her into the arts community in Santa Fe, where extreme wealth—and extreme greed—lead to desperate actions. When Lana uncovers a dead body, she realizes that she stands to lose a lot more than her job if she doesn't get to the bottom of things.

Other books by the same author:
The Blood of Redemption, 2015
The Legacy of Fear, 2015
The Trail of Terror, 2015
A Blue Moon, 2013

Other books you might like:
Gwen Freeman, *Murder...Suicide...Whatever...*, 2007
Sue Grafton, *"A" Is for Alibi*, 1982
Gabrielle Lord, *Feeding the Demons*, 1999
Lise McClendon, *The Bluejay Shaman*, 1994

Sara Paretsky, *Indemnity Only*, 1982
Connie Shelton, *Deadly Gamble*, 1995
Maggie Toussaint, *In for a Penny*, 2008

652

JOHN SANDFORD
Gathering Prey
(New York: G.P. Putnam's Sons, 2015)

Series: Lucas Davenport Series. Book 25
Story type: Contemporary; Series
Subject(s): Mystery; Missing persons; Detective fiction
Major character(s): Lucas Davenport, Detective, Father (of Letty); Letty Davenport, Daughter (of Lucas); Pilate, Gang Member (leader); Henry, Streetperson; Skye, Streetperson
Time period(s): 21st century; 2010s
Locale(s): North Dakota, United States

Summary: In this 25th novel in the Lucas Davenport mystery series by John Sandford, Lucas finds himself in a case involving a dangerous gang when his daughter, Letty, befriends Skye and Henry, two homeless panhandlers who travel around the country. When one of the travelers calls Letty for help, saying that her boyfriend has gone missing, Letty agrees to go back to North Dakota to help her. Lucas goes with Letty, and when they arrive, they learn more about the gang. Led by a man known as Pilate, the group is made up of brutally violent murderers who target travelers. Lucas and Letty suspect that Henry is their latest victim. Lucas is determined to track down Pilate and his gang before they take any other lives—including theirs.

Other books by the same author:
Field of Prey, 2014
Dark of the Moon, 2007
Shadow Prey, 1990
The Fool's Run, 1989
Rules of Prey, 1989

Other books you might like:
Michael Connelly, *The Burning Room*, 2014
Michael Connelly, *City of Bones*, 2002
Robert Crais, *The Promise*, 2014
Jeffery Deaver, *The Bone Collector*, 1997
K.J. Erickson, *Third Person Singular*, 2001
W.E.B. Griffin, *Deadly Assets*, 2015
Steve Hamilton, *A Cold Day in Paradise*, 1998
William Kent Krueger, *Iron Lake*, 1998
Owen Laukkanen, *The Professionals*, 2012
J.D. Robb, *Obsession in Death*, 2015
P.J. Tracy, *Monkeewrench*, 2003
Urban Waite, *Sometimes the Wolf*, 2014

653

LISA SCOTTOLINE
Every Fifteen Minutes
(New York: St. Martin's Press, 2015)

Story type: Psychological Suspense
Subject(s): Mental health; Murder; Suspense

Major character(s): Dr. Eric Parrish, Psychologist (psychiatrist), Spouse (separated); Max Jakubowski, Patient (of Dr. Parrish), Grandson (of Virginia), 17-Year-Old, Mentally Ill Person; Virginia Teichner, Grandmother (of Max)
Time period(s): 21st century; 2010s
Locale(s): Pennsylvania, United States

Summary: Dr. Eric Parrish is the chief psychiatrist at one of the top psychiatric hospitals in the United States. Although his personal life is in shambles because his marriage is falling apart, Eric's professional life has never been better. Then he meets Max, a teenager with a dying grandmother and numerous mental issues that make him one of Eric's most difficult patients. Obsessive ritualization is the only thing that keeps Max from going overboard most days, and he must complete each of his routines every quarter hour. Then a girl with whom Max is obsessed turns up dead, and Max disappears from the psych ward. As Eric goes out on his own to try to figure out what happened, he finds himself not only a suspect but also charged with sexual misconduct. Eric is sure that none of these things are coincidence, but he must prove it before his life completely falls apart.

Other books by the same author:
Keep Quiet, 2014
Accused, 2013
Final Appeal, 1995
Running from the Law, 1995
Everywhere that Mary Went, 1993

Other books you might like:
Chris Abani, *The Secret History of Las Vegas*, 2014
Iain M. Banks, *The Wasp Factory*, 1984
G.H. Ephron, *Delusion*, 2002
Nicci French, *Blue Monday*, 2012
Nicci French, *Waiting for Wednesday*, 2014
Camilla Grebe, *Some Kind of Peace*, 2012
Daryl Gregory, *We Are All Completely Fine*, 2014
April Henry, *The Girl Who Was Supposed to Die*, 2013
Jonathan Kellerman, *Killer*, 2014
Jonathan Kellerman, *The Murderer's Daughter*, 2015
William Landay, *Defending Jacob*, 2012
Tawni O'Dell, *One of Us*, 2014
Jodi Picoult, *Nineteen Minutes*, 2007
Lionel Shriver, *We Need to Talk about Kevin*, 2003
Stephen White, *Line of Fire*, 2012

654

MICHAEL SEARS
Long Way Down
(New York: G. P. Putnam's Sons, 2015)

Series: Jason Stafford Series. Book 3
Story type: Contemporary; Series
Subject(s): Finance; Biotechnology; Mystery
Major character(s): Jason Stafford, Investigator (financial); Philip Haley, Engineer (biotechnology), Crime Suspect (insider trading)
Time period(s): 21st century; 2010s
Locale(s): New York, New York

Mystery

Summary: Award-winning author Michael Sears returns with the third novel in his Jason Stafford series. Financial investigator Jason Stafford learned a lot during his two-year stint in federal prison, primarily who can be trusted—and who can't. So when millionaire engineer Philip Haley comes to him for help, Stafford offers his services. Haley, the CEO of a biotechnology company on the brink of a major biofuel development, is accused of insider trading, and Stafford believes him when he claims it's all a setup. From the Chinese government to Haley's estranged wife, Stafford uncovers a series of lies and cover-ups, secrets and betrayals that lead him on a deadly hunt for the truth. The stakes are higher than ever for Stafford, and he'll have to stay one step ahead of everyone involved if he—and his family—have any chance of staying alive.

Other books by the same author:
Mortal Bonds, 2013
Black Fridays, 2012

Other books you might like:
Mike Cooper, *Clawback*, 2012
Joseph Finder, *Paranoia*, 2004
Andrew Grant, *Run*, 2014
John Grapper, *A Fatal Debt*, 2012
Christopher Reich, *Numbered Account*, 1998
Peter Spiegelman, *Black Maps*, 2003
Norb Vonnegut, *Top Producer*, 1997
Urban Waite, *Sometimes the Wolf*, 2014

655

L.J. SELLERS

Wrongful Death

(Seattle, Washington: Thomas and Mercer, 2015)

Series: Detective Wade Jackson Mystery Series. Book 10
Story type: Police Procedural; Series
Subject(s): Detective fiction; Mystery; Law enforcement
Major character(s): Wade Jackson, Detective—Police
Time period(s): 21st century; 2010s
Locale(s): Eugene, Oregon

Summary: This mystery thriller is the tenth novel in the Detective Jackson series by best-selling author L.J. Sellers. Detective Wade Jackson is called to the scene when an officer from the Eugene Police Department is found murdered near a homeless camp. The night before the incident, the policeman was seen handing out blankets throughout the homeless community. Homeless twins are named prime suspects, and when arrests are made, tensions rise between the police department and the homeless community. As Eugene's homeless citizens continue to riot and revolt against the police, new evidence connects a series of sexual assaults with the officer's death. The killer is still at large, and catching him or her will mean putting another innocent life at risk—a decision Jackson and his team will have to make very quickly.

Other books by the same author:
Deadly Bonds, 2014
The Trigger, 2013
Secrets to Die For, 2009

The Sex Club, 2007
Beyond Conception, 2001

Other books you might like:
Alafair Burke, *Judgment Calls*, 2003
Bill Cameron, *Lost Dog*, 2007
J.A. Jance, *Until Proven Guilty*, 1985
Kenneth R. Lewis, *Little Blue Whales*, 2006
Ridley Pearson, *Undercurrents*, 1988
Jess Walter, *Land of the Blind*, 2003
Jess Walter, *Over Tumbled Graves*, 2001

656

TERRY SHAMES

A Deadly Affair at Bobtail Ridge

(Amherst, New York: Seventh Street Books, 2015)

Series: Samuel Craddock Mystery Series. Book 4
Story type: Contemporary; Police Procedural
Subject(s): Mystery; Detective fiction; Brothers and sisters
Major character(s): Samuel Craddock, Lawman, Neighbor (of Jenny); Jenny Sandstone, Lawyer (prosecutor), Neighbor (of Samuel), Daughter (of Vera), Sister (of Eddie); Vera Sandstone, Mother (of Jenny and Eddie); Eddie Sandstone, Brother (of Jenny), Son (of Vera)
Time period(s): 21st century; 2010s
Locale(s): Texas, United States

Summary: In this novel by Terry Shames, the fourth in the Samuel Craddock Mystery series, Samuel was ready to retire from his career as a Texas lawman, but he's now back as acting chief of police. He has lived next door to county prosecutor Jenny Sandstone and her mother, Vera, for a long time. When Vera is on her deathbed, Samuel goes to visit and is given a vague warning about Jenny being in danger. Shortly after Vera passes away, Jenny is involved in a mysterious accident, her precious horses are attacked, and her estranged brother Eddie shows up after years away. Samuel is determined to protect Jenny, but Jenny seems equally determined to keep her past buried. She drinks to excess and avoids Samuel at all costs. Samuel looks into Jenny's past on his own. He wants to respect her privacy and maintain her friendship, but he is concerned for her life. What he uncovers reveals a shocking and dangerous secret.

Other books by the same author:
Dead Broke in Jarrett Creek, 2014
The Last Death of Jack Harbin, 2014
A Killing at Cotton Hill, 2013

Other books you might like:
Milton T. Burton, *The Rogues' Game*, 2005
Bill Crider, *Too Late to Die*, 1986
Tricia Fields, *The Territory*, 2011
Steve Hamilton, *A Cold Day in Paradise*, 1998
James Hime, *The Night of the Dance*, 2003
Ben Rehder, *Buck Fever*, 2002
Anne Wingate, *Death by Deception*, 1988

657

WILLIAM SHAW

The Kings of London

(New York: Mulholland Books, 2015)

Series: Breen and Tozer Series. Book 2
Story type: Historical; Police Procedural
Subject(s): Mystery; Crime; Detective fiction
Major character(s): Cathal Breen, Detective—Police, Colleague (partner, of Helen); Helen Tozer, Detective—Police, Colleague (partner, of Cathal); Francis Pugh, Crime Victim, Son (of politician)
Time period(s): 20th century; 1960s (1968)
Locale(s): London, England

Summary: Still mourning the death of his father, Detective Sergeant Cathal Breen has just returned to work. He is called to the scene of a gas explosion, where the remains of a badly burned, unidentifiable body have been found. Soon, Breen finds himself on the scene of a second mysterious fire, where the victim is identified as Francis Pugh, the son of a high-ranking government minister. Breen and his partner, Temporary Detective Constable Helen Tozer, follow the clues into London's evolving 1960s bohemian subculture. As they unravel a web of lies, police cover-ups, and abuses of power, they are further alienated from London's corrupt police department. Determined to get to the bottom of the case, Breen and Tozer go out on their own and follow the investigation into the center of London's art world and hippie communes. This is the second book in the Breen and Tozer series by journalist William Shaw.

Other books by the same author:
She's Leaving Home, 2014

Other books you might like:
Jake Arnott, *The Long Firm*, 1999
Patricia Hall, *Dead Beat*, 2011
June Hampson, *Trust Nobody*, 2006
P.D. James, *Unnatural Causes*, 1967
John Lawton, *A Little White Death*, 1998
Margaret Moore, *Kiss Me Quick*, 2003
Ruth Rendell, *The Secret House of Death*, 1968

658

STAV SHEREZ

Eleven Days

(New York: Europa Editions, 2014)

Story type: Police Procedural
Subject(s): Detective fiction; Mystery; Fires
Major character(s): Jack Carrigan, Detective; Geneva Miller, Detective
Time period(s): 21st century; 2010s
Locale(s): London, England

Summary: In this mystery by Stav Sherez, the sequel to *A Dark Redemption*, detective inspectors Jack Carrigan and Geneva Miller are investigating a fire at a London convent that killed ten nuns. The nuns were found seated at the kitchen table, as though they did not attempt to escape. A mysterious 11th woman was found dead in a confessional booth on another floor. In the course of the investigation, the detectives discover that these nuns were part of the Liberation Theology movement in the 1970s. They had served time and been tortured in Peru. Carrigan and Miller realize that a series of other crimes in the city might be connected to this fire—and to the nuns' ongoing activism. The nuns helped young girls escape prostitution, and in the process attracted the attention of a group of very dangerous men.

Other books by the same author:
A Dark Redemption, 2012
The Black Monastery, 2009
The Devil's Playground, 2004

Other books you might like:
Mark Billingham, *Sleepyhead*, 2001
S.J. Bolton, *Now You See Me*, 2011
Jane Casey, *The Burning*, 2011
Martina Cole, *The Ladykiller*, 1993
Deborah Crombie, *A Share in Death*, 1993
Elizabeth George, *For the Sake of Elena*, 1992
Mo Hayder, *Birdman*, 1999

659

CLEA SIMON

Kittens Can Kill

(Scottsdale, Arizona: Poisoned Pen Press, 2015)

Series: Pru Marlowe Pet Noir Series. Book 5
Story type: Amateur Detective; Cozy Mystery
Subject(s): Detective fiction; Animals; Pets
Major character(s): Pru Marlowe, Animal Trainer, Psychic (animal psychic); Ernesto, Cat, Companion (of David); David Canaday, Animal Lover (owner, of Ernesto), Lawyer
Time period(s): 21st century; 2010s
Locale(s): Beauville, Massachusetts

Summary: Clea Simon delivers the fifth installment in her Pru Marlowe Pet Noir cozy mystery series. Pet behavior specialist Pru Marlowe arrives at a client's home to discover a playful kitten named Ernesto bouncing around the body of his dead owner, David Canaday, a distinguished attorney in Beauville, Massachusetts. Investigators find no obvious cause of death, but Canaday's adult daughters have their own ideas about what killed their father, blaming everything from allergies to drug interactions. When David's partner reads his will, the fighting among David's daughters intensifies. Pru must use her special—and secret—ability to read animals' minds if she plans to find out what really happened to David that morning. Ernesto is the only one who knows the truth about David's death and his feuding daughters. But can Pru solve the mystery and keep her secret ability under wraps?

Other books by the same author:
Panthers Play for Keeps, 2014
Cats Can't Shoot, 2012
Dogs Don't Lie, 2011
Shades of Grey, 2009
Mew is for Murder, 2005

Mystery

Other books you might like:

Rita Mae Brown, *Wish You Were Here*, 1990
Carole Nelson Douglas, *Cat in a Yellow Spotlight*, 2014
Carole Nelson Douglas, *Catnap*, 1992
Patricia Fry, *Catnapped*, 2013
Mildred Gordon, *Undercover Cat*, 1963
Shirley Rousseau Murphy, *Cat on the Edge*, 1996
Akif Pirincci, *Felidae Series*, 1993

660

ROB SINCLAIR

Rise of the Enemy

(New York: Clink Street Publishing, 2015)

Series: Enemy Series. Book 2
Story type: Espionage; Series
Subject(s): Espionage; Mystery; Betrayal
Major character(s): Carl Logan, Agent (Joint Intelligence Agency)
Time period(s): 21st century; 2010s
Locale(s): Russia

Summary: In this thriller by Rob Sinclair, the second in the Enemy series, Joint Intelligence agent Carl Logan is sent to Russia on what appears to be a routine mission: infiltrating a military technology manufacturer. But things go horribly wrong. Logan's cover is blown, his colleague is killed, and he is taken prisoner and tortured. During his ordeal, Logan starts to see patterns and similarities where he never expected to. He realizes that the people he thought were his allies are something else altogether. He soon comes to believe that he's been set up by his own agency. Even if he manages to escape the Russians, Logan knows he will never be able to escape the watchful eye of the JIA—not unless he takes drastic action.

Other books by the same author:
Dance with the Enemy, 2014

Other books you might like:

Alex Berenson, *The Faithful Spy*, 2006
Robert Ferrigno, *Prayers for the Assassin: A Novel*, 2006
Vince Flynn, *American Assassin: A Thriller*, 2010
David Hagberg, *Without Honor*, 1989
William Hallahan, *Foxcatcher*, 1986
Matthew Reilly, *Ice Station*, 1999
Brad Thor, *The Lions of Lucerne*, February 27, 2007

661

KAREN ROSE SMITH

Gilt by Association

(New York: Kensington Publishing Corporation, 2015)

Series: Caprice De Luca Mystery Series. Book 3
Story type: Amateur Detective; Cozy Mystery
Subject(s): Detective fiction; Real estate; Decorative arts
Major character(s): Caprice De Luca, Interior Decorator, Detective—Amateur; Louise Downing, Crime Victim
Time period(s): 21st century; 2010s
Locale(s): Kismet, Pennsylvania

Summary: Karen Rose Smith returns with the third novel in her Caprice De Luca cozy mystery series. Home-stager Caprice De Luca is all set for her Valentine's Day-themed open house at the frilly residence of her client, Louise Downing, in snowy Kismet, Pennsylvania. But when Louise is found murdered in the greenhouse on the day of the open house, stager-turned-sleuth Caprice is on the hunt for a motive and a suspect. Caprice looks for answers among friends and family, including a mysterious male friend of Louise's who claims their relationship was nothing more than a friendship. But the more Caprice uncovers, the more she learns about Louise's past—a past that her husband of 30 years knows nothing about.

Other books by the same author:
Deadly Dècor, 2014
Staged to Death, 2013
The Bracelet, 2007
Which Child is Mine?, 2004
A Man Worth Loving, 1992

Other books you might like:

Ginny Aiken, *Design on a Crime*, 2005
Jennie Bentley, *Fatal Fixer-Upper*, 2008
Mary Branham, *Little Green Man in Ireland*, 1997
Leslie Caine, *Death by Inferior Design*, 2004
Dorothy Cannell, *The Thin Woman*, 1984
Paula Carter, *Leading an Elegant Death*, 1999
Denise Osbourne, *Deadly Arrangement*, 2001

662

STEPHEN SOLOMITA

The Striver

(Sutton, Surrey, England: Severn House, 2015)

Story type: Police Procedural
Subject(s): Detective fiction; Crime; Organized crime
Major character(s): Boots Littlewood, Detective—Police (NYPD), Colleague (partner, of Jill); Teddy Winuk, Organized Crime Figure; Johnny Piano, Organized Crime Figure (mob boss), Father (of Carlo); Jill Kelly, Police Officer (NYPD), Colleague (partner, of Boots); Carlo Pianetti, Crime Victim, Organized Crime Figure, Criminal (rapist), Son (of Johnny)
Time period(s): 21st century; 2010s
Locale(s): New York, New York

Summary: This crime thriller by Stephen Solomita is the sequel to his 2013 novel, *Dancer in the Flames*. NYPD Detective Boots Littlewood is called to the Brooklyn neighborhood of Greenpoint, where Carlo Pianetti, the son of mobster Johnny Piano, has been killed with a shot to the head. Boots pieces together events that took place just before Carlo's death. Teddy Winuk, a young up-and-coming criminal, discovered Carlo under the Pulaski Bridge raping a young woman. Teddy's only response was to shoot Carlo in the head. Boots is looking for both Carlo's victim and his killer, but he's not alone in his search for the gunman. Johnny is also determined to find his son's killer. Because of the volatile history Johnny has with Boots, quick-tempered "Crazy" Jill Kelly, Boots's police partner, is around to make sure both men stay in line.

Other books by the same author:
Dancer in the Flames, 2012
Trick Me Twice, 1998
Damaged Goods, 1996
A Good Day to Die, 1993
A Twist of the Knife, 1988

Other books you might like:
Lorenzo Carcaterra, *Gangster*, 2001
Richard Condon, *Prizzi's Honor*, 1982
Eric Dezenhall, *Money Wanders*, 2002
Gary Phillips, *High Hand*, 2000
Nicholas Pileggi, *Wiseguy: Life in a Mafia Family*, 1987
Richard Price, *Clockers*, 1992
Mario Puzo, *The Godfather*, 1969

663

MICKEY SPILLANE
MAX ALLAN COLLINS, Co-Author

Kill Me, Darling
(London: Titan Books, 2015)

Series: Mike Hammer Series. Book 20
Story type: Series
Subject(s): Crime; Mystery; Detective fiction
Major character(s): Mike Hammer, Investigator (private), Lover (former, of Velda); Velda, Lover (former, Mike), Police Officer, Missing Person; Nolly Quinn, Drug Dealer, Organized Crime Figure
Time period(s): 20th century; 1950s (1954)
Locale(s): Miami, Florida; New York, New York

Summary: Set in 1954, this crime thriller is the 20th novel that features private investigator Mike Hammer, the signature character created by hard-boiled crime writer Mickey Spillane. In this installment, Hammer drowns his sorrows in the bottle when Velda, his long-time partner and love, walks out on him, leaving nothing more than a one-word note. Hammer resurfaces to find that a cop who once worked with Velda on the NYPD Vice Squad has been murdered. When Hammer learns that Velda has gone to Miami with gangster Nolly Quinn, he's hot on her trail. With the help of a journalist and a Miami police detective, Hammer is determined to rescue Velda, but does Velda want to be rescued? Is it possible Velda's move to Miami has anything to do with the recent murder of her former colleague?

Other books by the same author:
King of the Weeds, 2014
The Goliath Bone, 2008
My Gun is Quick, 1950
Vengeance is Mine, 1950
I, the Jury, 1947

Other books you might like:
Lawrence Block, *Eight Million Ways to Die*, 1982
Robert Crais, *The Monkey's Raincoat*, 1987
Robert Crais, *The Promise*, 2014
James Crumley, *The Last Good Kiss*, 1978

Elmore Leonard, *Rum Punch*, 1992
John D. MacDonald, *The Deep Blue Good-by*, 1964
Ross Macdonald, *The Drowning Pool*, 1950
Urban Waite, *Sometimes the Wolf*, 2014
Charles Willeford, *Miami Blues*, 1984

664

ERICA SPINDLER

The First Wife
(New York: St. Martin's Press, 2015)

Story type: Contemporary; Romance
Subject(s): Mystery; Romances (Fiction); Marriage
Major character(s): Bailey Browne, Spouse (wife, of Logan); Logan Abbott, Spouse (husband, of Bailey); Billy Ray, Police Officer (Chief); True Abbott, Missing Person, Spouse (former, of Logan)
Time period(s): 21st century; 2010s
Locale(s): Wholesome, Louisiana

Summary: This romantic thriller by best-selling author Erica Spindler follows a young bride as she searches for the truth about the man she loves but isn't sure she should trust. Bailey Browne accepts Logan Abbott's marriage proposal only ten days after meeting him on a beach in Grand Cayman. When the newlyweds return to Logan's 90-acre horse farm in the small town of Wholesome, Louisiana, the tragic events of Logan's past begin to unfold. Soon, Bailey learns of Logan's first wife, True, who apparently disappeared, as well as other young women in the area who have gone missing. Their disappearances all trace back to Logan. Although he's been unable to convict Logan, Police Chief Billy Ray is certain Logan killed True and the other women. Now, as Bailey realizes she barely knows the man she married, she must decide whether to trust her heart or to believe the mounting evidence.

Other books by the same author:
Justice for Sara, 2013
Copycat, 2006
See Jane Die, 2004
A Winter's Rose, 1993
Heaven Sent, 1988

Other books you might like:
Daphne du Maurier, *Rebecca*, 1938
Tami Hoag, *Still Waters*, 1992
Linda Howard, *Veil of Night*, 2010
Jane Moore, *The Second Wives Club*, 2006
Tina Seskis, *One Step Too Far*, 2015
Anya Seton, *Dragonwyck*, 1944
Danielle Steel, *Vanished*, 1993
Mary Stewart, *Airs Above the Ground*, 1965

665

WENDY CORSI STAUB

The Black Widow
(New York: HarperCollins Publishers, 2015)

Story type: Serial Killer
Subject(s): Dating (Social customs); Divorce; Computers

Major character(s): Gaby Duran, Mother (of deceased child), Divorced Person, Woman, Spouse (ex, of Ben); Ben Duran, Spouse (ex, of Gaby), Man, Father (of deceased child), Divorced Person; Alex Jones, Mother (of deceased child), Serial Killer, Woman

Time period(s): 21st century; 2010s

Locale(s): New York, New York

Summary: Gaby Duran is trying to navigate through the rubble left of her life after the death of her child and her subsequent divorce. To help get Gaby's mind off of her losses, her cousin suggests she try her hand at online dating. Gaby agrees to give it a shot, even though she is well aware the Internet dating pool has more Mr. Wrongs than Mr. Rights. Gaby's jarred by the profile of her former husband, Ben, which she finds on a dating website, but pushes through. Meanwhile, another single woman with a heartbreaking history is also sifting through the online profiles, making her choices and looking for a connection. Alex's goal is decidedly singular, and she has no qualms about doing whatever it takes to acquire what she wants. It doesn't take long for the authorities to notice a series of missing men, all of whom have gone missing after heading out for a first date. Gaby and Alex are worlds apart, but still find themselves on a collision course.

Other books by the same author:
The Perfect Stranger, 2014
Nightwatcher, 2012
Live to Tell, 2010
The Awakening, 2007
Summer Lightning, 1993

Other books you might like:
Mary Higgins Clark, *A Stranger Is Watching,* 1977
Meg Gardiner, *Ransom River,* 2012
Lisa Gardner, *The Survivors Club,* 2001
Alison Gaylin, *Hide Your Eyes,* 2005
Tami Hoag, *Kill the Messenger,* 2004
Lisa Scottoline, *Dirty Blonde,* 2006
Lisa Unger, *Die for You,* 2009

666

OLEN STEINHAUER

All the Old Knives

(New York: Minotaur Books, 2015)

Story type: Contemporary

Subject(s): Mystery; Espionage; Terrorism

Major character(s): Henry Pelham, Agent (CIA), Lover (former, of Celia Harrison); Celia Harrison, Lover (former, of Henry Pelham), Agent (former, CIA)

Time period(s): 21st century; 2010s

Locale(s): Carmel-by-the-Sea, California

Summary: When former lovers Henry Pelham and Celia Harrison meet for dinner at a restaurant in Carmel-by-the-Sea, they discuss more than their failed relationship. While they were together, Henry and Celia both worked in the CIA's Vienna office. They played a part in the 2006 tragedy now referred to as "Flughafen," in which 172 airline passengers died when terrorists took over their plane in Vienna. Celia left the agency in the

aftermath of the incident, and has made a new life in California. She is married now and has two children. Henry is still an agent in Vienna, and he is still trying to uncover the intelligence failure that led to that past tragedy. As Henry and Celia reconnect over dinner, they revisit the events of 2006 and consider how the rescue plan was compromised. Their conversation gradually yields surprising revelations.

Other books by the same author:
The Cairo Affair, 2014
On the Lisbon Disaster, 2014
The Tourist, 2009
Victory Square, 2007
The Bridge of Sighs, 2003

Other books you might like:
Charles Cumming, *A Foreign Country,* 2012
Len Deighton, *Berlin Game,* 1983
Ken Follett, *Eye of the Needle,* 1978
W.E.B. Griffin, *Top Secret,* 2014
John Le Carre, *The Spy Who Came in from the Cold,* 1963
Robert Littell, *Vicious Circle,* 2006
Charles McCarry, *The Secret Lovers,* 1977
Chris Pavone, *The Expats,* 2012

667

FRAN STEWART

A Wee Murder in My Shop

(London: Penguin Group, 2015)

Series: ScotShop Mystery Series. Book 1

Story type: Cozy Mystery; Ghost Story

Subject(s): Scotland; Scots (British people); Murder

Major character(s): Peggy Winn, Businesswoman, Detective—Amateur, Cousin (of Shoe), Friend (of Dirk); Dirk, Spirit, Friend (of Peggy); Shoe, Cousin (of Peggy), Crime Suspect

Time period(s): 21st century; 2010s

Locale(s): Scotland; Hamelin, Vermont

Summary: Aye, 'tis a fine day to solve a mystery for Peggy Winn. Peggy is the owner of a small Vermont shop that specializes in selling Scottish wares. On a trip to Scotland to hunt for new items, she buys an old tartan shawl, which comes with a mysterious ability. When she wraps it around her shoulders, she conjures up the ghost of a 14th-century Scotsman she nicknames Dirk. Returning to Vermont, Peggy finds herself in the presence of another dead person, this one of the more recently killed variety. The body of her former boyfriend is sprawled on the floor of her shop and her cousin is arrested for murder. Now Peggy and her otherworldly ally must find the real killer and clear her cousin's name. This is the first book in Fran Stewart's ScotShop Mystery series.

Other books by the same author:
Gray as Ashes, 2014
A Slaying Song Tonight, 2011
Green as a Garden Hose, 2005
Yellow as Legal Pads, 2004
Orange as Marmalade, 2003

Other books you might like:
Barbara Bretton, *Casting Spells*, 2008
Ann Campbell, *Wolf at the Door*, 2000
Jane K. Cleland, *Consigned to Death*, 2006
Melissa Glazer, *A Murderous Glaze*, 2007
Sue Ann Jaffarian, *Ghost a la Mode*, 2009
Joyce Lavene, *A Timely Vision*, 2010
Amy Patricia Meade, *Well-Offed in Vermont*, 2011

668

JONATHAN STONE

The Teller

(North Charleston, South Carolina: CreateSpace Independent Publishing Platform, 2012)

Story type: Contemporary; Police Procedural
Subject(s): Finance; Crime; Organized crime
Major character(s): Elaine Kelly, Banker; Antonio Desirio, Aged Person
Time period(s): 21st century; 2010s
Locale(s): New York, New York

Summary: Elaine Kelly is a young woman who could really use a break. Stuck working as a teller at a Queens bank, she seems to have little hope of ever moving up in the world—especially since most of what she makes pays her dying mother's medical bills. Things take an unexpected turn when one of Elaine's regular customers, a lonely old man named Antonio Desirio, is hit and killed by a truck after he makes one of his weekly deposits. In the aftermath of Antonio's abrupt demise, Elaine checks his account and finds what just might be her ticket to the good life: $1 million that she can easily transfer into her own account without anyone knowing. But when she goes through with the scheme, she quickly learns that Antonio may not have just been the elderly loner she thought he was. Apparently, Antonio's fortune belongs to someone else—and that "someone else" is determined to get it back by any means necessary.

Other books by the same author:
Moving Day, 2014
Parting Shot, 2006
Breakthrough, 2003
The Heat of Lies, 2001
The Cold Truth, 1999

Other books you might like:
Felicia Donovan, *The Black Widow Agency*, 2007
James Grippando, *Found Money*, 1998
Jesse Kellerman, *The Executor*, 2010
Daniel Palmer, *Delirious*, 2011
Marcus Sakey, *Good People*, 2008
Michael Sears, *Black Fridays*, 2012
Norb Vonnegut, *Top Producer*, 1997

669

VIDAR SUNDSTOL
TIINA NUNNALLY, Translator

The Ravens

(Minneapolis, Minnesota: University Of Minnesota Press, 2015)

Series: Minnesota Trilogy. Book 3
Story type: Contemporary; Series
Subject(s): Murder; Native Americans; Dreams
Major character(s): Lance Hansen, Ranger, Relative (son-in-law of Willy); Swamper Caribou, Indian, Healer; Willy Dupree, Relative (father-in-law of Lance)
Time period(s): 21st century; 2010s
Locale(s): Minnesota, United States

Summary: US forest ranger Lance Hansen has been investigating the murder of a Norwegian tourist in Minnesota for some time, and now it seems he may be able to crack the case at last. In the aftermath of a hunting trip gone wrong, Lance has a late night vision of Swamper Caribou, an Ojibwe healer who died under mysterious circumstances a hundred years ago. Looking for answers, Lance consults with his former father-in-law, who has a special talent for interpreting dreams. To Lance's surprise, the session reveals some important information that may be the key to solving the mystery surrounding the tourist's death and the death of Swamper Caribou. While this breakthrough proves vital to Lance's quest for justice, it also exposes a darker truth that he never expected or wanted to know.

Other books by the same author:
Only the Dead, 2014
The Land of Dreams, 2013

Other books you might like:
Giles Blunt, *Forty Words for Sorrow*, 2001
C.J. Box, *Open Season*, 2001
Paul Doiron, *The Poacher's Son*, 2010
L.L. Enger, *Comeback*, 1990
William Kent Krueger, *Iron Lake*, 1998
Kirk Mitchell, *High Desert Malice*, 1995
Yrsa Sigurdardottir, *Someone to Watch Over Me*, 2015
Steve Thayer, *The Weatherman*, 1995

670

PETER SWANSON

The Kind Worth Killing

(New York: William Morrow, 2015)

Story type: Literary
Subject(s): Psychology; Suspense; Marriage
Major character(s): Ted Severson, Businessman, Wealthy, Spouse (of Miranda); Miranda Severson, Artist, Spouse (of Ted), Lover (of Brad Daggett); Lily Kintner, Researcher (archivist); Brad Daggett, Contractor, Lover (of Miranda)
Time period(s): 21st century; 2010s
Locale(s): London, England; Boston, Massachusetts

Summary: Two passengers on a transatlantic flight plot a murder in this novel by Peter Swanson. Well-to-do

Mystery

Boston businessman Ted Severson and archivist Lily Kintner meet on a plane and, over cocktails, share the darkest secrets of their lives. Ted tells the tale of his marriage to Miranda, an artist type who he suspects is having an affair. In an alcohol-induced moment of truth, Ted confesses to Lily that he'd like to kill his wife. When Lily offers to assist, the two strangers on a plane begin planning Miranda's murder. Back in Boston, Ted's suspicions are confirmed; Miranda is involved with the couple's contractor, Brad Daggett. But as the murder plot moves forward, it becomes obvious that Lily hasn't been completely forthcoming about her past. Ted and Lily's dark game escalates when they attract the attention of a clever detective.

Other books by the same author:
The Girl with a Clock for a Heart, 2014

Other books you might like:
Chelsea Cain, *One Kick*, 2014
Agatha Christie, *4:50 from Paddington*, 1957
Dick Francis, *The Edge*, 1988
Paula Hawkins, *The Girl on the Train*, 2015
Patricia Highsmith, *Strangers on a Train*, 1950
Christopher Isherwood, *Mr. Norris Changes Trains*, 1935
J.D. Robb, *Strangers in Death*, 2008
Stuart Woods, *Choke: A Novel*, 1995

671

DUANE SWIERCZYNSKI

Canary

(New York: Little, Brown and Company, 2015)

Story type: Family Saga; Police Procedural
Subject(s): Law enforcement; Drugs; Family relations
Major character(s): Sarie Holland, 19-Year-Old, Student—College, Crime Suspect, Sister (of Marty), Writer (diary); Ben Wildey, Detective—Police; Marty Holland, Brother (of Sarie)
Time period(s): 21st century; 2010s
Locale(s): Philadelphia, Pennsylvania

Summary: Sarie Holland is a highly intelligent college student who makes a stupid mistake. While giving a ride to a friend, Sarie is caught up in a drug deal and arrested. To avoid going to jail, she agrees to become a confidential informant for the police. The officer in charge of the operation is eager to catch the big fish and pushes Sarie too hard to reel him him. In the process she narrowly escapes getting killed, and realizes her place in the undercover food chain. Now wise to their ways and pursued by the bad guys on both sides of the law, Sarie uses her intelligence to play the cops and criminals against each other and tries to stay one step ahead of her pursuers. Her interest in removing herself from the roster of confidential informants is largely driven by the frequent disappearance of other informants in the gritty streets of Philly. Much of what happens is revealed through Sarie's diary, in which addresses entries to her dead mother.

Other books by the same author:
Point and Shoot, 2013

Fun and Games, 2011
Hell and Gone, 2011
Expiration Date, 2010
Secret Dead Men, 2005

Other books you might like:
Megan Abbott, *Queenpin*, 2007
Jodi Compton, *Hailey's War*, 2010
Solomon Jones, *C.R.E.A.M.*, 2006
Joe R. Lansdale, *Sunset and Sawdust*, 2004
George P. Pelecanos, *Drama City*, 2005
Richard Price, *Clockers*, 1992
Don Winslow, *Savages*, 2010

672

VICTORIA THOMPSON

Murder on Amsterdam Avenue

(New York: Berkley, 2015)

Series: Gaslight Mystery Series. Book 17
Story type: Historical; Series
Subject(s): Murder; Detective fiction; Civil war
Major character(s): Sarah Brandt, Midwife, Fiance(e) (of Frank); Frank Malloy, Detective—Police, Fiance(e) (of Sarah); Charles Oakes, Son (of Gerald); Gerald Oakes, Father (of Charles)
Time period(s): 19th century; 1890s
Locale(s): New York, New York

Summary: Midwife Sarah Brandt and detective sergeant Frank Malloy, a pair of mystery-solving sleuths, are busy making arrangements for their upcoming wedding when they learn of the unexpected death of Charles Oakes, the son of close friends. On the surface, it appears that Charles's death is the result of a sudden illness, but all may not be what it seems. Suspecting foul play, Charles's father, Gerald, asks Sarah and Frank to investigate what he believes might be a case of poisoning. As they look into Charles' untimely demise, Sarah and Frank quickly find themselves in a dangerous world of secrets—some of which date back to the Civil War—that some powerful parties want to keep quiet at any cost. Will Sarah and Frank be able to shed some light on Charles's death, or will their nuptials be indefinitely postponed?

Other books by the same author:
Murder in Murray Hill, 2014
Murder on Washington Square, 2002
Murder on Gramercy Park, 2001
Murder at St. Mark's Place, 2000
Murder on Astor Place, 1999

Other books you might like:
Lawrence Alexander, *The Big Stick*, 1986
Tasha Alexander, *And Only to Deceive*, 2005
Lyndsay Faye, *The Gods of Gotham*, 2012
C.S. Harris, *What Angels Fear*, 2005
Allan Levine, *Evil of the Age*, 2008
Miriam Grace Monfredo, *Seneca Falls Inheritance*, 1992
Anne Perry, *The Face of a Stranger*, 1990

673

DAVID THURLO
AIMEE THURLO, Co-Author

Grave Consequences

(New York: Minotaur Books, 2015)

Series: Charlie Henry Mystery Series. Book 2
Story type: Private Detective; Series
Subject(s): Native Americans; Murder; Jewelry
Major character(s): Charlie Henry, Businessman, Brother (of Alfred), Veteran; Alfred Henry, Police Officer, Brother (of Charlie); Gordon Sweeney, Businessman, Veteran
Time period(s): 21st century; 2010s
Locale(s): Albuquerque, New Mexico

Summary: Charlie Henry has retired from the Special Forces and opened an Albuquerque pawn shop with his partner and fellow veteran, Gordon Sweeney. He's ready to enjoy the peaceful retirement he always dreamed of. Unfortunately, it might take just a bit longer for that dream to come true. A young Navajo man arrives at the shop one day, claiming that his girlfriend accidentally pawned a family heirloom turquoise necklace. He pleads for its return. Since the man cannot produce a claim ticket, however, Charlie has no choice but to deny his request. When the man returns a short time later, he comes armed to the teeth and with plenty of backup. Charlie realizes that this is about much more than just a necklace. He is thrust into a web of intrigue and lies he will somehow have to navigate if he is to learn the truth—or even just survive.

Other books by the same author:
The Pawnbroker, 2014
Bad Faith, 2002
Second Sunrise, 2002
Her Destiny, 1997
Blackening Song, 1995

Other books you might like:
David Cole, *Butterfly Lost*, 2000
Brian Garfield, *Relentless*, 1972
Anne Hillerman, *Spider Woman's Daughter*, 2013
Tony Hillerman, *Skinwalkers*, 1986
Kirk Mitchell, *Cry Dance*, 1999
Susan Slater, *The Pumpkin Seed Massacre*, 1999
Richard Martin Stern, *Murder in the Walls*, 1971

674

HELENE TURSTEN

The Beige Man

(New York: Soho Crime, 2015)

Series: Detective Inspector Huss Series. Book 7
Major character(s): Irene Huss, Detective—Police (inspector), Mother, Spouse; Torleif "Muesli" Sandberg, Crime Victim (of a hit-and-run); Juan Rejon Rejon, Detective—Police (inspector); Heinz Becker, Crime Suspect; Anders Pettersson, Crime Suspect, Drug Dealer

Time period(s): 21st century; 2010s
Locale(s): Tenerife, Canary Islands; Goteborg, Sweden

Summary: Goteborg, Sweden: The high-speed chase of a stolen BMW takes a chilling turn when the officers witness a gruesome hit-and-run. After they finally locate the abandoned vehicle, search dogs uncover an entirely different horror: the half-naked corpse of a young girl in a nearby root cellar. As Detective Inspector Irene Huss and her colleagues struggle to put the pieces together, they discover the owner of the stolen car—a retired police officer—is the victim in the hit-and-run. Could it be coincidence? Or is something larger at play? Also available in Large Print.

Other books by the same author:
The Fire Dance, 2014
Night Rounds, 2012
The Glass Devil, 2007
The Torso, 2006
Detective Inspector Huss, 2003

Other books you might like:
Karin Alvtegen, *Missing*, 2008
Kerstin Ekman, *Under the Snow*, 1961
Kjell Eriksson, *The Princess of Burundi*, 2006
Inger Frimansson, *Good Night, My Darling*, 2007
Lars Kepler, *The Hypnotist*, 2011
Liza Marklund, *Red Wolf*, 2011
Kristina Ohlsson, *Unwanted*, 2012

675

WENDY TYSON

Dying Brand

(Plano, Texas: Henery Press, 2015)

Series: Allison Campbell Mystery Series. Book 3
Story type: Amateur Detective; Series
Subject(s): Murder; Suspense; Conspiracy
Major character(s): Allison Campbell, Consultant, Detective—Amateur
Time period(s): 21st century; 2010s
Locale(s): Philadelphia, Pennsylvania

Summary: Image consultant Allison Campbell is no stranger to murder mysteries and whodunits. But when the victim in her latest case turns out to be her ex-boyfriend, her quest for justice becomes personal. From the outset, the case is anything but straightforward. Though the amateur sleuth had not seen or heard from her ex in years, his widow claims that he was on his way to meet Allison when he was killed. Then, when compromising photos of Allison and her now-deceased former lover surface, the mystery only deepens. Determined to clear her name and bring the real killer to justice, Allison sets out to uncover the truth about her old flame's life since they went their separate ways. What she finds, however, may be much more dangerous than she expects.

Other books by the same author:
Deadly Assets, 2014
Killer Image, 2013

Other books you might like:

M.C. Beaton, *Agatha Raisin and the Quiche of Death*, 1992

Carl Brookins, *Inner Passages*, 2000

Alyse Carlson, *The Azalea Assault*, 2012

Carole Nelson Douglas, *Catnap*, 1992

Anne Underwood Grant, *Multiple Listing*, 1998

Patricia Sprinkle, *Murder at Markham*, 1988

Pari Noskin Taichert, *The Clovis Incident*, 2004

676

DIANE VALLERE

With Vics You Get Eggroll

(Plano, Texas: Henery Press, 2015)

Series: Mad for Mod Mystery Series. Book 3
Story type: Amateur Detective; Cozy Mystery
Subject(s): Decorative arts; Murder; Detective fiction
Major character(s): Madison Night, Designer, Detective—Amateur; Tex Allen, Detective—Police
Time period(s): 21st century; 2010s
Locale(s): Lakewood, Texas

Summary: Interior decorator extraordinaire and amateur sleuth Madison Night is on the case once again, and this time it's personal. While restoring an old ranch home, Madison finds herself drawn into a mystery surrounding several recent abductions and an apparent murder. When evidence found at the scene implicates her police lieutenant friend Tex Allen as the prime suspect, Madison jumps into action in an earnest effort to uncover the truth. At the same time, she is also faced with the arduous task of both appeasing her particularly difficult client and managing her own complicated personal life. Eventually, Madison's sly sleuthing reveals that the crimes are more complex than they appear. One of her loved ones may be in danger, and a copycat criminal may be at work. Will Madison be able to solve the mystery and clear Tex's name, or will the case—and her remodeling project—come crashing down around her?

Other books by the same author:
Some Like It Haute, 2015
Buyer, Beware, 2013
That Touch of Ink, 2013
Designer Dirty Laundry, 2012
Pillow Stalk, 2012

Other books you might like:
Ginny Aiken, *Design on a Crime*, 2005
Leslie Caine, *Death by Inferior Design*, 2004
Dorothy Cannell, *The Thin Woman*, 1984
Paula Carter, *Leading an Elegant Death*, 1999
Jayne Ann Krentz, *Light in Shadow*, 2002
Denise Osbourne, *Deadly Arrangement*, 2001
Linda Shirley Robertson, *Murder Swings the Tide*, 2003

677

ELAINE VIETS

Checked Out

(New York: Penguin Publishing Group, 2015)

Series: Dead-End Job Mysteries. Book 14
Story type: Private Detective; Series
Subject(s): Libraries; Art; Detective fiction
Major character(s): Helen Hawthorne, Detective—Private, Spouse (of Phil); Elizabeth Cateman Kingsley, Socialite, Client; Phil Sagemont, Spouse (of Helen), Detective—Private; Paris, Cat
Time period(s): 21st century; 2010s
Locale(s): Fort Lauderdale, Florida

Summary: Private sleuth Helen Hawthorne's latest case finds her playing librarian, searching for a lost masterpiece, and trying desperately to avoid falling victim to a killer in the stacks. Hired by the elite socialite Elizabeth Cateman Kingsley to find a priceless watercolor that was accidently left in a book, Helen takes a job as a volunteer at Flora Park Library. She quickly learns that she may not be the only one in search of the valuable prize. At first, Helen's biggest obstacles include Paris, the library's mischievous calico cat, and an alleged ghost that has a habit of making things disappear. Before long, however, things take a turn for the worse. After a corpse is discovered in the parking lot, Helen realizes that the stakes are much higher than she imagined. If she does not find the watercolor soon, she might just be next murder victim.

Other books by the same author:
Catnapped!, 2014
Just Murdered, 2005
Dying to Call You, 2004
Murder Between the Covers, 2003
Shop Till You Drop: A Dead-End Job Mystery, 2003

Other books you might like:
Jeff Abbott, *Do Unto Others*, 1994
Jo Dereske, *Miss Zukas and the Library Murders*, 1994
Laura DiSilverio, *Die Buying*, 2011
Charlaine Harris, *Real Murders*, 1990
Miranda James, *Murder Past Due*, 2010
Jess Lourey, *May Day*, 2006
Karen E. Olson, *The Missing Ink*, 2009

678

LEA WAIT

Twisted Threads

(New York: Kensington Books, 2015)

Series: Mainely Needlepoint Mysteries. Book 1
Story type: Cozy Mystery; Series
Subject(s): Hobbies; Sewing; Mystery
Major character(s): Angie Curtis, Granddaughter (of Charlotte), Detective—Amateur, Woman, Crime Suspect; Charlotte, Aged Person, Businesswoman, Grandmother (of Angie), Crime Suspect
Time period(s): 21st century; 2010s

Locale(s): Harbor Haven, Maine

Summary: After a decade away, Angie Curtis returns to the the beautiful seaside community of Harbor Haven, Maine, to complete a somber task. She was raised in the town by her grandmother after her mother's disappearance 19 years earlier. Now, Angie receives word that her mother's body has been found and that she was the victim of murder. Angie reconnects with her grandmother, Charlotte, who has started a needlepoint supplies shop. Angie agrees to help Charlotte check up on a client, who owes Charlotte a debt. When the client ends up dead, Angie and Charlotte are the prime suspects. To clear their names, Angie begins her own investigation into the death. As the case begins to unravel, she discovers it may have a connection to her mother's death as well. This is the first book in Lea Wait's Mainely Needlepoint Mystery series.

Other books by the same author:
Shadows of a Down East Summer, 2011
Shadows at the Spring Show, 2005
Shadows on the Ivy, 2004
Shadows on the Coast, 2003
Shadows at the Fair, 2002

Other books you might like:
Janet Bolin, *Dire Threads*, 2011
Elizabeth Lynn Casey, *Sew Deadly*, 2009
Elizabeth Lynn Casey, *Taken In*, 2014
Monica Ferris, *Crewel World*, 1999
Monica Ferris, *The Drowning Spool*, 2014
Amanda Lee, *The Quick and the Thread*, 2010
Leslie Meier, *Mail-Order Murder*, 1991

679

TRACY WEBER

A Killer Retreat

(Woodbury, Minnesota: Midnight Ink, 2015)

Series: Downward Dog Mysteries. Book 2
Story type: Cozy Mystery; Series
Subject(s): Exercise; Teaching; Murder
Major character(s): Kate Davidson, Woman, Girlfriend (of Michael), Teacher (yoga instructor), Friend (of Rene), Crime Suspect, Detective—Amateur, Companion (of Bella); Michael, Boyfriend (of Kate); Rene, Friend (of Kate); Bella, Dog (German shepherd), Companion (of Kate)
Time period(s): 21st century; 2010s
Locale(s): Orcas Island, Washington

Summary: Kate Davidson thought she'd be able to help her students relieve their stress when she accepted a job teaching yoga at the Elysian Springs resort near Seattle. Little did she know the experience would actually ratchet up her own stress level. While attending the wedding of the resort's caretakers, Kate gets into a public argument with an annoying fellow guest, who is later found floating dead in a hot tub. Naturally, the police immediately suspect Kate. Out of jail for the time being, she teams up with her boyfriend, best friend, and pet German shepherd, Bella, to investigate. Kate and her team must discover who the real killer is, or her next pose will be

for a police mug shot. This is the second book in Tracy Weber's Downward Dog Mysteries series.

Other books by the same author:
Murder Strikes a Pose, 2014

Other books you might like:
Linda Howard, *To Die For*, 2005
Diana Killian, *Corpse Pose*, 2008
Diana Killian, *Death in a Difficult Position*, 2011
Kathryn Lilley, *Dying to Be Thin*, 2007
Staci McLaughlin, *Going Organic Can Kill You*, 2012
Natalie M. Roberts, *Tutu Deadly*, 2007
Sarah Steding, *A Diet to Die For*, 2013

680

ANDREW WELSH-HUGGINS

Slow Burn

(Athens, Ohio: Ohio University Press, 2015)

Series: Andy Hayes Mysteries. Book 2
Story type: Contemporary; Series
Subject(s): Arson; Death; Football
Major character(s): Andy Hayes, Detective—Private, Football Player (former), Fiance(e) (former, of Suzanne); Aaron Custer, Crime Suspect, Grandson (of Dorothy); Suzanne Gregory, Television Personality, Journalist, Fiance(e) (former, of Andy); Dorothy Custer, Grandmother (of Aaron)
Time period(s): 21st century; 2010s
Locale(s): Columbus, Ohio

Summary: Private investigator Andy Hayes was a star quarterback for the Ohio State Buckeyes, until one bad decision destroyed his career and legacy forever. Still dealing with the fallout from his past, Andy takes up the seemingly hopeless case of Aaron Custer. Aaron has been sentenced to life in prison for setting a fire that left three Ohio State students dead. When Andy starts digging deeper he finds Aaron may not have committed the crime after all, but the real culprits' motives may be deadlier than he can handle. To make things worse, Andy may be forced to rely on his former fiancee for help, and that is a path he never wanted to travel down again. This is the second book in Andrew Welsh-Huggins's Andy Hayes Mysteries series.

Other books by the same author:
Fourth Down and Out, 2014
Hatred at Home, 2011
No Winners Here Tonight, 2009

Other books you might like:
Ace Atkins, *Crossroad Blues*, 1998
Franklin Bandy, *Deceit and Deadly Lies*, 1978
Earl Emerson, *Thomas Black Series*, 1985
Robert Irvine, *Baptism for the Dead*, 1988
Michael Koryta, *Tonight I Said Goodbye*, 2004

Mike Resnick, *Dog in the Manger*, 1995
John Maddox Roberts, *A Typical American Town*, 1994

681

RANDY WAYNE WHITE

Cuba Straits

(New York: G.P. Putnam's Sons, 2015)

Series: Doc Ford Series. Book 22
Story type: Adventure; Humor
Subject(s): Adventure; Cuban Revolution, 1953-1959; Cuban history
Major character(s): Marion "Doc" Ford, Scientist (marine biologist), Retiree (NSA Agent); Juan Garcia, Smuggler (of Cuban baseball players), Collector (of historical collectibles), Friend (of Doc Ford); Sighurdhr Tomilson, Hippie, Sidekick (of Doc Ford); Figueora "Figgy" Cassanova, Baseball Player, Missing Person, Man (Cuban)
Time period(s): 21st century; 2010s
Locale(s): Cuba; Key West, Florida

Summary: In author Randy Wayne White's 22nd installment of the Doc Ford Series, Doc Ford, a Florida marine biologist and retired NSA agent, is called upon to help his old friend General Juan Garcia. Garcia buys and sells high-profile historical collectibles. He also is a smuggler, who turns a profit sneaking Cuban baseball players into the United States. Garcia's Cuban shortstop, Figueova Cassanova, has gone missing along with a briefcase that contains private letters written by Fidel Castro to his mistress. These historical documents may contain invaluable information about Cuban military and political activities. Doc Ford and his hipster side-kick, Tomilson, travel from Florida to Cuba as they chase both the historical documents and the missing baseball player. But Doc and Tomilson are not alone on their mission to find the Castro letters. Against the modern Cuban backdrop they encounter a Russian Spy, a Santeria priest, and a young girl. All these players increase the suspense, mayhem, and chaos of the investigation.

Other books by the same author:
Bone Deep, 2014
Captiva, 1996
The Man Who Invited Florida, 1993
The Heat Islands, 1992
Sanibel Flats, 1990

Other books you might like:
Peggy Blair, *The Beggar's Opera*, 2012
Tom Corcoran, *The Mango Opera*, 1998
W.E.B. Griffin, *Deadly Assets*, 2015
James W. Hall, *Under Cover of Daylight*, 1987
Jose Latour, *Outcast*, 1999
Dennis Lehane, *Live by Night*, 2012
Bob Morris, *Bahamarama*, 2004
Leonardo Padura, *Havana Blue*, 2007

682

STUART WOODS

Hot Pursuit

(New York: G.P. Putnam's Sons, 2015)

Series: Stone Barrington Series. Book 33
Story type: Political; Revenge
Subject(s): Suspense; Adventure; Airplanes
Major character(s): Stone Barrington, Friend (of Holly and Kate), Lover (of Pat), Lawyer; Pat Frank, Pilot, Lover (of Stone), Girlfriend (former, of stalkers); Holly Barker, Friend (of Stone), Advisor (national security); Millicent Martindale, Assistant (of Holly Barker); Kate Lee, Political Figure (US president), Friend (of Stone)
Time period(s): 21st century; 2010s
Locale(s): England; Washington, District of Columbia; Wichita, Kansas

Summary: This is the 33rd novel in Stuart Wood's Stone Barrington series. Stone Barrington, a successful Manhattan attorney, picks up a new Citation M2 plane in Wichita, Kansas. He also embarks upon a new journey—a fresh romance with the copilot, the beautiful Pat Frank. Stone's new girlfriend brings quite a bit of baggage to the relationship, however. She has two stalker ex-boyfriends with shady pasts. While Stone and Pat are jetting to new adventures in Europe, the stalker ex-boyfriends are never far behind the pair. Meanwhile, Stone's friend Holly Barker has become the new national security adviser for newly elected US president Kate Lee. When a conspiracy plot to assassinate the president is uncovered, Holly and her new quirky assistant, Millicent Martindale, must race against time to discover the identity of the terrorists to protect the president. In true Stone style, the international intrigue remains classy.

Other books by the same author:
Insatiable Appetites, 2015
Swimming to Catalina, 1998
Dead in the Water, 1997
Dirt, 1996
New York Dead, 1991

Other books you might like:
Jeff Abbott, *The Inside Man*, 2014
David Baldacci, *Memory Man*, 2015
David Baldacci, *Zero Day*, 2011
Dale Brown, *Drone Strike: A Dreamland Thriller*, 2014
Joseph Finder, *Vanished*, 2009
George Galdorisi, *Tom Clancy's Op-Center: Out of the Ashes*, 2014
Paul Garrison, *Robert Ludlum's The Janson Option*, 2014
Andrew Gross, *The Dark Tide*, 2008
Michael Ledwidge, *Step on a Crack*, 2007
Brad Meltzer, *The Inner Circle*, 2010
Scott O'Connor, *Half World*, 2014
James Patterson, *Honeymoon*, 2005
James Patterson, *NYPD Red 2*, 2014
Christopher Reich, *Rules of Deception*, 2008
Brad Thor, *Hidden Order*, 2013

Go Ahead and Judge That Book by Its Cover!
by
Holly Hibner and Mary Kelly

The old phrase "don't judge a book by its cover" is a plea to not rush to judgment, not least of all when it comes to books. Generally, this is good advice. Librarians often are found promoting a book in less than stellar condition by suggesting that it is worn out from all the folks who have loved it. "A well-loved book is a good book!" Those folks in the communication world of publishing, multimedia presentations, Internet communication, and other web design understand that visuals are a key point in both marketing the book to potential readers and communicating the essence of the book in a single image. In fact, these two concepts of the written and the visual image are inextricably tied together in how we consume information, art, and literature.

Book design is about much more than just its cover. It is the art of assembling the entire physical experience of the reading material. This can be everything from the layout of the cover art to the placement of the author's name, right down to the actual font and binding. All of this matters to the book designer. The written word or story can stand alone, but the entire experience relies on the book designer to communicate and "sell" a book to a reader. Otherwise, what is the point if the book is never picked up and read?

Book design is also more than a sales pitch for a book. Of course the marketing implications are obvious: Good covers sell books. However, there is more than marketing at work. Good book design is about the reading experience. A good story or information is the author's message, but it doesn't fly all by itself. The reader is expecting to have a physical reaction to a book. Depending on the story or the author's words, this physical experience is what the author wants the reader to feel. The readers, as well, want a visceral experience. Readers probably credit this entire experience to content, but clearly there is more going on than just good writing or the author's message.

Cover art for a book is ground zero for marketing a book to its reader. Readers get a "feel" for a book in an instant by looking at the cover. Images, colors, and design elements come together in a single moment and invite the reader to investigate further. It is that single feeling or impression that needs to communicate the essence of the book to then become our visceral experience. Readers remember book covers, and many authors understand that a cover can make or break a book. Many people will remember a cover when trying to recall a book title. To this day, there are covers that are considered iconic, and absolutely part and parcel of the book's popularity. Think about the *Great Gatsby*'s overly large eyes (Francis Cugot design, 1925) or the cover of *Clockwork Orange* (David Pellam design, 1972) with its colorful single cog eye. These iconic covers have designs that transcend time and are inextricably tied to the written word. The mind's eye will flash to the cover when remembering the book.

Given that books and book design are so important, what does this mean for e-book readers? Is design still a factor in the brave new world of electronic information? Is it possible to invoke the same physicality of books in the world of electronic books? E-books and other virtual information still must deliver some kind of cue to the reader to engage.

Although e-books and other virtual information are subject to the same marketing impulses as traditional materials to get people to choose a particular title, the landscape is challenging. Traditional "browseable" book stores use an entire array of sensual experiences from store layout and ambience to attractive, eye-catching book displays, and even the smell of coffee and pastries can persuade the casual browser to become a paying reader. Libraries, as well, have begun staging a more bookstore feel and marketing to customers in this way.

However, in a virtual environment, how can booksellers and librarians get people interested in materials when they don't exist is a physical way? E-readers offer a distinct and important advantage over traditional book formats by giving readers instantaneous availability. No effort is required! However, the e-book still has to be selected by the reader. Within the constraints of a catalog or website of virtual electronic space, design needs to entice a reader to click on a selection. In this brave new world, does cover art still matter? Emphatically, yes!

As with the traditional book, e-books have to catch attention with their virtual covers. In addition, the electronic format now gives everyone access to publishing the written word. Writers are cutting out the middleman of publishers and flying solo by publishing on a blog, website, or any other e-book self-publishing platform. Publishers no longer are the sole gatekeepers of what is published and marketed to consumers. Everyone has virtually unlimited access to everything. The result is a crowded playing field of many media choices for readers.

This becomes a good news/bad news situation. The good news is that anyone can publish and the bad news is that anyone can publish. Yes, that means more choices for readers, but the reality is that there isn't an editing process or quality control. Any book of any quality is released into the wilds of Internet publishing. Poor cover design in the virtual setting can ruin a book's chances with readers, regardless of the quality of the written word. Anyone with a computer and basic software can create an e-book. Graphics and artwork also are easily managed by computers. That said, the reality is that not everyone is a writer or a book cover designer.

The bookstore browse is now a virtual browse. Within the confines of computer screen catalogs and websites, the entirety of reading choices must be communicated. They create a visually appealing way to encourage browsing or help users find a suitable item. Cover art takes on a new role when presented in a thumbnail-size square. Web design and book design collide in helping consumers of e-books navigate choices. Can there be great book cover designs in such a restricted space?

It also isn't just the computer screen: Tablets, e-readers, and smartphones all have e-reader potential, and readability of material can vary greatly depending on the sophistication of the device. Again, the design goals are the same, but what works in printed material can fail in the e-book format. Fonts, page layout, and covers have new significance with the space restrictions of screens.

Design must communicate the book in a small size, and yet stand out in a field of potentially millions of choices. Categories, genres, metatags, and other ways of organizing book collections have become foremost in the minds of book designers. How does a reader choose a book when staring at a blank computer screen, or have to create a search to find something to read?

Since the introduction of the online catalog in libraries, browsing or "accidently" finding a title is one of the joys of library users and bookstore customers. Translating this into a virtual experience is a new challenge for designers, as well as the librarians and booksellers that are charged with connecting readers to media. Most readers need art and design to assist in their enjoyment of reading materials, even if they don't readily acknowledge its power in the their decision-making process.

Book Covers worth Revisiting:

Seamus Haney's *Beowulf* (2001)

Mario Puzo's *The Godfather* (1969)

Truman Capote's *In Cold Blood* (1966)

Michael Crighton's *Jurassic Park* (1990)

Sylvia Plath's *The Bell Jar* (1966)

V.C. Andrews's *Flowers in the Attic* (1979)

Ralph Ellison's *The Invisible Man*(1952)

Ray Bradbury's *Fahrenheit 451* (1953)

Popular Fiction

683

SALAR ABDOH

Tehran at Twilight

(Brooklyn, New York: Akashic Books, 2014)

Story type: Contemporary; Modern
Subject(s): Islam; Middle East; Friendship
Major character(s): Reza Malek, Expatriate, Journalist (former), Teacher, Friend (of Sina); Sina Vafa, Friend (of Reza)
Time period(s): 21st century; 2000s (2008)
Locale(s): Tehran, Iran

Summary: Reza Malek fled Tehran with his father before the revolution and has been living in the United States for several years. After college he became an interpreter for war correspondents in the Middle East, reporting on the conflicts between religious factions and the efforts of American military forces. It was dangerous, but Reza was with his best friend, Sina Vafa. Reza eventually published a book about his experiences and was offered a job at a university in New York City. Sina remained in Iran and the two friends grew apart. In 2008, Reza receives a phone call from Sina begging for help. The ties of friendship are strong and Reza travels to Tehran, where he is surrounded by corrupt politicians and religious leaders. He realizes that Sina is involved with anti-American groups and that both of their lives may be in danger. Sina offers one comfort: He has located Reza's long-lost mother, who apparently abandoned her family 30 years ago. As mother and son tentatively reunite, Reza will finally demand answers for all of his questions.

Other books by the same author:
Tehran Noir, 2014
Tel Aviv Noir, 2014
The Poet Game, 2000

Other books you might like:
Dale Brown, *Drone Strike: A Dreamland Thriller*, 2014
Ben Coes, *Independence Day*, 2015
Brian Haig, *The Night Crew*, 2015
Richard House, *The Kills*, 2014
David Ignatius, *The Increment*, 2009
Gina B. Nahai, *The Luminous Heart of Jonah S.*, 2014
Patrick Robinson, *Diamondhead*, 2009

Joel C. Rosenberg, *Damascus Countdown*, 2013
Mahbod Seraji, *Rooftops of Tehran*, 2009
Dalia Sofer, *The Septembers of Shiraz*, 2007

684

ELLIOT ACKERMAN

Green on Blue

(New York: Scribner, 2015)

Story type: Literary; Military
Subject(s): Afghanistan Conflict, 2001-; Wars; Family
Major character(s): Aziz Iqtbal, Boy, Brother (of Ali); Ali Iqtbal, Boy, Brother (of Aziz); Garzan, Leader (Taliban); Atal, Leader (village of Gomal), Guardian (of Fareeda); Fareeda, Girl, Ward (of Atal)
Time period(s): 21st century; 2010s
Locale(s): Afghanistan

Summary: War changes the lives of two young Afghan brothers in this novel by Elliot Ackerman. Aziz and Ali Iqtbal are poor, but they enjoy a stable home life until a military incursion kills the rest of their family. The orphaned brothers make their way to the nearby city, where they find work and save their money. Ali wants Aziz to attend school, but their fortune turns again when a bomb strikes the city. Ali is permanently maimed and requires extensive medical care. Aziz agrees to serve in a US-sponsored militia unit known as the Special Lashkar so that Ali will receive the treatment he needs. Aziz then enters a murky world of violence and corruption. As he carries out the missions of the Special Lashkar, Aziz also carries out his own quest for vengeance against the Taliban leader who caused Ali's injuries. Ackerman is a veteran of the Iraq and Afghan conflicts. First novel.

Other books you might like:
Sebastian Barry, *The Temporary Gentleman*, 2014
Fatima Bhutto, *The Shadow of the Crescent Moon*, 2015
Paolo Giordano, *The Human Body*, 2014
Aaron Gwyn, *Wynne's War*, 2014
Masha Hamilton, *What Changes Everything*, 2013
Khaled Hosseini, *A Thousand Splendid Suns*, 2007
Ron Lealos, *Pashtun*, 2014
Valerie O. Patterson, *Operation Oleander*, 2013
Joydeep Roy-Bhattacharya, *The Watch*, 2012
Suzanne Fisher Staples, *Under the Persimmon Tree*, 2005

685

ELIZABETH ADLER

Last to Know

(New York: Minotaur Books, 2014)

Story type: Mystery
Subject(s): Mystery; Detective fiction; Crime
Major character(s): Harry Jordan, Detective—Police;
Lacey Havnel, Mother (of Bea), Crime Victim; Bea
Havnel, 21-Year-Old, Crime Victim, Daughter (of
Lacey); Wally Osborne, Writer (suspense novelist),
Spouse (of Rose), Father (of Roman, Madison,
Frazer, and Diz); Rose Osborne, Spouse (of Wally),
Mother (of Roman, Madison, Frazer, and Diz); Ro-
man Osborne, Son (of Wally and Rose), Brother (of
Madison, Frazer, and Diz), 18-Year-Old; Madison
Osborne, Girl, 16-Year-Old, Twin (of Frazer),
Daughter (of Wally and Rose), Sister (of Roman and
Diz); Frazer Osborne, Girl, 16-Year-Old, Twin (of
Madison), Daughter (of Wally and Rose), Sister (of
Roman and Diz); Diz Osborne, Boy, 11-Year-Old,
Son (of Wally and Rose), Brother (of Roman,
Madison, and Frazer)
Time period(s): 21st century; 2010s
Locale(s): Evening Lake, Massachusetts

Summary: Boston police detective Harry Jordan comes to
Evening Lake, Massachusetts, to take a break from the
world of big-city crime. But Harry's vacation is interrupted by a house explosion that kills a woman—or so it
seems. Twenty-one-year-old Bea Havnel escapes the
blaze, but her mother, Lacey, is found dead in the ruined
house. She was killed by a stab wound, not the fire.
Harry can't help but investigate the strange case, and as
he does so, he becomes acquainted with Evening Lake's
residents. The Osbornes, neighbors of the Havnels, invite
Bea to stay with them during the investigation. Wally
Osborne, a crime novelist, and his wife, Rose, are the
parents of four children: 18-year-old son Roman, 16-
year-old twin girls Madison and Frazer, and 11-year-old
son Diz. At least one of the Osbornes is keeping a secret
about the night of the explosion. As Harry searches for
Lacey's killer, he discovers surprising information about
the Havnel family.

Other books by the same author:
Please Don't Tell, 2013
A Place in the Country, 2012
From Barcelona, with Love, 2011
It All Began in Monte Carlo, 2010
There's Something About St. Tropez, 2009

Other books you might like:
Mary Higgins Clark, *Daddy's Gone A Hunting*, 2013
Patricia Cornwell, *Flesh and Blood*, 2014
Lisa Gardner, *Fear Nothing*, 2014
Judith Guest, *The Tarnished Eye*, 2004
Tami Hoag, *The 9th Girl*, 2013
Lisa Jackson, *Deserves to Die*, 2014
Iris Johansen, *The Perfect Witness*, 2014
Alex Kava, *Fireproof*, 2012
Lora Leigh, *Deadly Sins*, 2012
Charlotte Link, *The Watcher*, 2014

686

JUSSI ADLER-OLSEN

The Alphabet House

(New York: Penguin Group, 2014)

Story type: Historical
Subject(s): World War II, 1939-1945; Military life;
Adventure
Major character(s): James Teasdale, Military Personnel
(British pilot), Patient (psychiatric); Bryan Young,
Patient (psychiatric), Military Personnel (British
pilot)
Time period(s): 20th century; 1940s
Locale(s): Germany

Summary: During World War II, the British suspect that
the Germans are constructing factories near Dresden.
Pilots James Teasdale and Bryan Young are dispatched
to the region to investigate. The Nazis spot their plane
and bring it down, leaving James and Bryan with little
hope for escape. When they encounter a moving train,
the pilots hop on board and find that the cars are carrying wounded SS personnel. They pose as patients and
pretend to have psychiatric problems. When James and
Bryan are sent to the notorious psychiatric facility known
as the Alphabet House, they realize that their nightmare
has just begun. They become test subjects for the German doctors, who treat them with shock therapy and
medications. Their plan is to ride out the war at Alphabet
House, but an unsettling discovery poses a new threat.

Other books by the same author:
The Marco Effect, 2014
A Conspiracy of Faith, 2013
The Purity of Vengeance, 2013
The Absent One, 2012
The Keeper of Lost Causes, 2011

Other books you might like:
Michael Baden, *Remains Silent*, 2005
Harlan Coben, *The Stranger*, 2015
Ken Follett, *Hornet Flight*, 2002
James Grady, *Mad Dogs*, 2006
Jack Higgins, *Thunder Point*, 1993
Christopher Hyde, *The House of Special Purpose*, 2004
J. Sydney Jones, *The German Agent*, 2015
Ward Larsen, *Stealing Trinity*, 2008
Francine Mathews, *The Alibi Club*, 2006
Bernard Minier, *The Frozen Dead*, 2014
Tony Schumacher, *The Darkest Hour*, 2014
Chevy Stevens, *Always Watching*, 2013
David Thomas, *Ostland*, 2013
Scott Turow, *Ordinary Heroes*, 2005

687

YELENA AKHTIORSKAYA

Panic in a Suitcase

(New York: Riverhead Books, 2014)

Story type: Literary
Subject(s): Immigrants; Russian Americans; Family

Major character(s): Pasha Nasmertov, Man (Russian), Writer (poet), Uncle (of Frida); Frida Nasmertov, Young Woman, Niece (of Pasha)
Time period(s): 20th century-21st century; 1990s-2010s
Locale(s): Ukraine; New York, New York

Summary: In the 1990s, many members of the extended Nasmertov family have immigrated to the United States from Russia. They live in an enclave in Brighton Beach, Brooklyn, with other immigrants from Russia and Ukraine. When Pasha, a relative who chose to remain in the Old Country, visits, he is puzzled by the contradictions in the Russian-American lifestyle. The relatives who came to the United States live in a Russian neighborhood and shop at Russian grocery stores. Now that the Soviet Union has collapsed, they can travel freely back to the homeland whenever they choose. The novel follows both the Nasmertov family in Brighton Beach and Pasha, as he travels twice from Ukraine to New York. As the years pass, Pasha's niece Frida considers her own place in the world. She came to America as a young girl, but she still feels a connection to her homeland, where Pasha still lives. First novel.

Other books you might like:
Chimamanda Ngozi Adichie, *Americanah*, 2013
Gurjinder Basran, *Everything Was Good-Bye*, 2010
Amy Bloom, *Away: A Novel*, 2007
NoViolet Bulawayo, *We Need New Names*, 2013
Edwidge Danticat, *The Dew Breaker*, 2004
Nafisa Haji, *The Writing on My Forehead: A Novel*, 2009
Cristina Henriquez, *The Book of Unknown Americans*, 2014
Jean Kwok, *Mambo in Chinatown*, 2014
Jhumpa Lahiri, *The Namesake*, 2003
Ellen Litman, *The Last Chicken in America*, 2007
Laura McBride, *We Are Called to Rise*, 2014
Gary Shteyngart, *The Russian Debutante's Handbook*, 2002

688

ELISA ALBERT

After Birth

(Boston: Houghton Mifflin Harcourt, 2015)

Story type: Contemporary; Family Saga
Subject(s): Mothers; Pregnancy; Infants
Major character(s): Ari, Mother (of Walker), Spouse (of Paul), Student—Graduate, Friend (of Mina); Paul, Spouse (of Ari), Father (of Walker), Professor; Mina, Mother (expectant), Friend (of Ari), Musician
Time period(s): 21st century; 2010s
Locale(s): Utrecht, New York

Summary: When she was six months pregnant, Ari left the big city behind and moved to upstate New York, where she hoped to become a mother on her own terms. But when little Walker entered the world, Ari found herself living in a bizarre nightmare called motherhood. Dealing with a C-section scar, a newborn's dysfunctional sleep patterns, and the pressure of finishing her doctorate dissertation, Ari is long past her wit's end. Into this landscape comes Mina, a former musician and poet who is about to give birth to her own little bundle of woe. Normally mistrustful of women, Ari welcomes Mina to their little town and the women strike up a friendship. As the women bond, they discover in each other an unexpected pillar of support that can help them traverse the pitfalls of motherhood.

Other books by the same author:
The Book of Dahlia, 2008
How This Night Is Different: Stories, 2006

Other books you might like:
Pete Dexter, *Spooner*, 2009
Mary Gaitskill, *Veronica: A Novel*, 2005
Zoe Heller, *What Was She Thinking?: Notes on a Scandal*, 2003
Amy Koppelman, *A Mouthful of Air*, 2003
Courtney Maum, *I Am Having So Much Fun Here Without You*, 2014
Claire Messud, *The Emperor's Children*, 2006
David Nicholls, *Us*, 2014
Tom Rachman, *The Imperfectionists: A Novel*, 2010
Jose Saramago, *Death with Interruptions*, 2008
Kate Walbert, *Our Kind*, 2004

689

SARAH ADDISON ALLEN

First Frost

(New York: St. Martin's, 2015)

Series: Waverley Family Series. Book 2
Story type: Coming-of-Age; Contemporary
Subject(s): Southern United States; Adolescent interpersonal relations; Pregnancy
Major character(s): Claire Waverley, Mother (of Mariah), Aunt (of Bay), Businesswoman, Sister (of Sydney); Sydney Waverley, Sister (of Claire), Mother (of Bay), Aunt (of Mariah); Mariah, Daughter (of Claire), Child, Cousin (of Bay), Niece (of Sydney); Bay, 15-Year-Old, Daughter (of Sydney), Niece (of Claire), Cousin (of Mariah)
Time period(s): 21st century; 2010s
Locale(s): Bascom, North Carolina

Summary: Author Sarah Addison Allen continues the homespun Southern story of Claire and Sydney Waverley. Sydney's daughter, Bay, is now 15 years old and struggling with teen angst and her first crush, as well as navigating the murky waters of high school. Sydney, now a popular hair stylist at Whitedoor, desperately wants to have another baby with her husband, while Claire has begun a new business venture. Claire has decided to turn her talent for creating botanical candies into a business, leaving her catering job behind her. Claire's 9-year-old daughter, Mariah, misses the time she had formerly spent with her mother, and Claire can feel her control over her family life slipping away. Bay discovers that her own special talent lies in her ability to fit things together, making her a prime recruit for the prom committee. However, when a mysterious man arrives in Bascom threatening to spill Waverley family secrets, the women and girls must pull together to protect what is most important.

Other books by the same author:
Lost Lake, 2014
The Peach Keeper, 2011
The Girl Who Chased the Moon, 2010
The Sugar Queen, 2008
Garden Spells, 2007

Other books you might like:
Tiffany Baker, *The Gilly Salt Sisters*, 2012
Maeve Binchy, *Evening Class*, 1996
Maeve Binchy, *A Week in Winter*, 2012
Tracy Chevalier, *Remarkable Creatures*, 2010
Gail Godwin, *Flora*, 2013
Posie Graeme-Evans, *Wild Wood*, 2015
Alice Hoffman, *Practical Magic*, 1995
Morag Joss, *Our Picnics in the Sun*, 2013
Elizabeth Kostova, *The Swan Thieves: A Novel*, 2010
Debbie Macomber, *Love Letters*, 2014
Susan Mallery, *Barefoot Season*, 2012
Lydia Netzer, *How to Tell Toledo from the Night Sky*, 2014
Deborah Raney, *Home to Chicory Lane*, 2014
Ilie Ruby, *The Language of Trees*, 2010
Danielle Steel, *Hotel Vendome*, 2011
Anne Tyler, *A Spool of Blue Thread*, 2015
Luis Alberto Urrea, *Queen of America*, 2011

690

MARTIN AMIS

The Zone of Interest

(New York: Knopf Doubleday Publishing Group, 2014)

Story type: Historical - World War II; Romance
Subject(s): Holocaust, 1933-1945; Germans; Jews
Major character(s): Golo Thomsen, Lover (of Hannah), Office Worker, Narrator; Hannah Doll, Spouse (of Paul), Lover (of Golo); Paul Doll, Military Personnel (German commander), Spouse (of Hannah), Narrator; Szmul, Narrator, Prisoner (Jewish), Worker
Time period(s): 20th century; 1940s
Locale(s): Poland

Summary: Amid the chaos of brutality and death in a World War II concentration camp, three people are struggling to gain what they desire. One man seeks love, another wants to hold on to what he has, and a third wants his life. German officer Golo Thomsen, who got his position through family connections, has set his sights on Hannah, the beautiful wife of the camp commander. Commander Paul Doll, a weak-willed drunk, and is on the verge of losing his position—either to his German superiors or the encroaching Allied forces. As Golo and Hannah try to undermine Paul's leadership, the paranoid commander enlists the help of Szmul, a Jew forced into disposing of bodies from the gas chamber, to uncover their affair. But the wily Szmul knows the camp's secrets and is willing to use them to stay alive.

Other books by the same author:
Lionel Asbo: State of England, 2012

The Pregnant Widow, 2010
House of Meetings, 2007
Yellow Dog, 2003
Heavy Water and Other Stories, 1998

Other books you might like:
Chris Bohjalian, *The Light in the Ruins*, 2013
Michel Faber, *The Book of Strange New Things*, 2014
Eliza Granville, *Gretel and the Dark*, 2014
Helen Humphreys, *The Evening Chorus*, 2015
Ismail Kadare, *The Fall of the Stone City*, 2013
Alison McLeod, *Unexploded*, 2013
Sean Michaels, *Us Conductors*, 2014
Francine Prose, *Guided Tours of Hell: Novellas*, 1997
Ruta Sepetys, *Between Shades of Gray*, 2011
Goce Smilevski, *Freud's Sister*, 2012

691

LILI ANOLIK

Dark Rooms

(New York: HarperCollins Publishers, 2015)

Story type: Mystery
Subject(s): Murder; Sisters; Detective fiction
Major character(s): Grace Baker, Young Woman, Detective—Amateur, Sister (of Nica); Nica Baker, Sister (of Grace), Crime Victim, 16-Year-Old
Time period(s): 21st century; 2010s
Locale(s): Hartford, Connecticut

Summary: Sisters Grace and Nica have always been opposites. The quiet, reserved Grace has always lived in the shadow of her younger, effervescent sister. When 16-year-old Nica is murdered, the identity of the killer is a foregone conclusion. A loner classmate of hers has committed suicide and left behind a note confessing to the crime. But this resolution doesn't sit well with Grace, who slides deep into grief and drugs as she tries to focus on her first year of college. Just as Grace decides to drop out of school, she stumbles onto some information that leads her to question her sister's death. She becomes obsessed with tracking Nica's final days and unmasking her true killer. Now the sister who always felt inferior is discovering something about herself as she searches for justice for Nica.

Other books you might like:
Patricia Cornwell, *Scarpetta*, 2008
Hilary Davidson, *Evil in All Its Disguises*, 2013
Brian Evenson, *Last Days*, 2009
Stephen King, *Full Dark, No Stars*, 2010
Laura Lippman, *What the Dead Know*, 2007
Kimberly McCreight, *Reconstructing Amelia*, 2013
Denise Mina, *A Sickness in the Family*, 2010
Kate Morton, *The Secret Keeper*, 2012
Rob Scott, *Asbury Park*, 2012
Dan Simmons, *Drood*, 2008

692

JERRY APPS

The Great Sand Fracas of Ames County

(Madison, Wisconsin: Terrace Books, 2014)

Story type: Contemporary
Subject(s): Community relations; Environmental engineering; Mining
Major character(s): Emily Higgins, Leader (of the Link Lake Historical Society), Aged Person; Marilyn Jones, Leader (of Link Lake Economic Development Council); Stony Field, Journalist, Writer; Ambrose Adler, Recluse, Farmer, Aged Person
Time period(s): 21st century; 2010s
Locale(s): Link Lake, Wisconsin

Summary: A small Wisconsin town is divided by the potential destruction of an ancient tree and local landmark. Known as the Trail Marker Oak, the tree has stood for centuries and is a part of the historical Menominee trail. When the Link Lake Economic Development Council pushes for a proposed sand mine that would require the oak's demolition, the Link Lake Historical Society isn't willing to give up without a fight. Determined and stubborn women lead both groups, and each believes that her perspective is the correct one. Marilyn Jones leads the Economic Development Council and argues that the project would provide jobs, income, and opportunity for Link Lake and the surrounding county. Octogenarian Emily Higgins is the head of the Historical Society and she is horrified at the proposed demolition and how it would alter the town and landscape irrevocably. While the conflict mounts, a nationally recognized environmental columnist by the pen name of Stony Field swoops in on the story, offering commentary which draws the battle into the media spotlight. In the middle of everything is a reclusive farmer named Ambrose Adler who carries a secret.

Other books by the same author:
Letters from Hillside Farm, 2013
Tamarack River Ghost, 2012
Cranberry Red, 2010
Blue Shadows Farm, 2009
In a Pickle, 2007

Other books you might like:
Nickolas Butler, *Shotgun Lovesongs*, 2014
Fannie Flagg, *The All-Girl Filling Station's Last Reunion*, 2013
Joshilyn Jackson, *A Grown-Up Kind of Pretty*, 2012
Ann Leary, *The Good House*, 2013
Jason Mott, *The Wonder of All Things*, 2014
David Rhodes, *Driftless*, 2008
Nora Roberts, *The Perfect Hope*, 2012
Nicholas Sparks, *Safe Haven*, 2010
Adriana Trigiani, *The Supreme Macaroni Company*, 2013
Jeanette Walls, *The Silver Star*, 2013

693

URSULA ARCHER

Five

(London: St. Martin's Press, 2014)

Story type: Mystery
Subject(s): Mystery; Games; Law
Major character(s): Beatrice Kaspary, Detective—Homicide, Colleague (of Florin); Florin Wenninger, Detective—Homicide, Colleague (of Beatrice); Owner, Serial Killer
Time period(s): 21st century; 2010s
Locale(s): Austria

Summary: It begins with a dead body. Austrian homicide detective Beatrice Kaspary is called out to investigate a woman's corpse found in a cow pasture. What makes this case strange is a set of numbers tattooed on the bottom of the body's feet. Beatrice and her partner, Florin Wenninger, soon figure out the numbers are coordinates for a Global Positioning System. When they arrive at the location, they discover human body parts sealed in a plastic bag, along with another set of coordinates. Soon the detectives are being led around in a bloody treasure hunt by a killer dubbed the Owner. The more they investigate, the deeper they become involved in the Owner's plot. When the killer makes the case personal for Beatrice, she must decide how much she is willing to risk to catch a murderer.

Other books you might like:
Donato Carrisi, *The Whisperer*, 2012
Robert Ellis, *The Lost Witness*, 2009
Tami Hoag, *The 9th Girl*, 2013
Henning Mankell, *Troubled Man*, 2011
Richard Montanari, *The Doll Maker*, 2015
Frank Muir, *Hand for a Hand*, 2012
Jo Nesbo, *The Son*, 2014
James Patterson, *Hope to Die*, 2014
John Sandford, *Deadline*, 2014
Erica Spindler, *Last Known Victim*, 2007

694

MICHAEL ARDITTI

The Breath of Night

(Mount Pleasant, South Carolina: Arcadia Books, 2014)

Story type: Contemporary; Mystery
Subject(s): Religion; Saints; Family
Major character(s): Julian Tremayne, Missing Person, Religious (missionary priest); Philip Seward, Investigator
Time period(s): 20th century; (1970s-1980s); 21st century; 2010s
Locale(s): Philippines

Summary: Julian Tremayne was a priest and a missionary in the Marcos-controlled Philippines during the 1970s and 1980s. His outspoken criticism of oppression and support of Marcos's enemies landed him in prison and reportedly led to his death. Thirty years later, at the request of Tremayne's family, Philip Seward travels to the Philippines to research the priest's life and death. Philip's goal is to determine whether Tremayne is a worthy candidate for sainthood. As he investigates, Philip soon learns that while Marcos may be long gone, corruption and violence are still a way of life on the island. His mission to find answers leads him into a world where truth resides under a mountain of deceit and things are never what they seem.

Other books by the same author:
The Celibate, 1997
Pagan's Father, 1996

Other books you might like:
Nadeem Aslam, *The Blind Man's Garden*, 2013
NoViolet Bulawayo, *We Need New Names*, 2013
Sherko Fatah, *The Dark Ship*, 2015
Richard Flanagan, *The Unknown Terrorist*, 2007
Thomas Keneally, *The Tyrant's Novel*, 2004
Adam Mansbach, *Rage Is Back*, 2013
Frederic Rich, *Christian Nation*, 2013
Jose Saramago, *Raised from the Ground*, 2012
Willy Vlautin, *The Free*, 2014
Jess Walter, *The Zero*, 2006

695

EMILY ARSENAULT

What Strange Creatures

(New York: William Morrow, 2014)

Story type: Literary; Mystery
Subject(s): Brothers and sisters; Mystery; Murder
Major character(s): Theresa Battle, Student—Graduate, Writer (copy), Sister (of Jeff); Jeff Battle, Genius, Boyfriend (of Kim Graber), Crime Suspect, Brother (of Theresa); Kim Graber, Waiter/Waitress, Girlfriend (of Jeff), Crime Victim
Time period(s): 21st century; 2010s
Locale(s): Thompsonville, Massachusetts

Summary: Theresa Battle and her brother Jeff are intelligent underachievers. Theresa is writing copy while she works on her never-ending thesis on a medieval mystic. She is divorced and lives with an assortment of pets in her home in Thompsonville, Massachusetts. Jeff is adrift in his career, but he has had some recent success in his personal life. He is involved with a waitress, Kim Graber, who seems to adore him. When Kim asks Theresa to watch her dog while she is away, Theresa agrees. Kim never returns, however; she is murdered, and her corpse is discovered in the nearby woods. Jeff becomes the obvious suspect, and Theresa comes to his defense unquestioningly. To prove Jeff's innocence, Theresa looks into Kim's past to find other potential suspects. When Theresa discovers Kim's ties to a political scandal, she realizes that she also may be in danger.

Other books by the same author:
Miss Me When I'm Gone, 2012
In Search of the Rose Notes, 2011
The Broken Teaglass, 2009

Other books you might like:
Jo Bannister, *Perfect Sins*, 2014

David Bell, *The Forgotten Girl*, 2014
Maureen Carter, *Child's Play*, 2014
Thomas H. Cook, *Sandrine's Case*, 2013
Catherine Coulter, *Bombshell*, 2013
James Grippando, *Cane and Abe*, 2015
Sophie Hannah, *The Carrier*, 2015
John T. Lescroart, *The Keeper*, 2014
James Patterson, *The Beach House*, 2002
John Sandford, *Uncaged*, 2014

696

QUAN BARRY

She Weeps Each Time You're Born

(New York: Penguin Random House, 2015)

Story type: Ethnic; Psychic Powers
Subject(s): Vietnamese (Southeast Asian people); Family; Psychics
Major character(s): Rabbit, Psychic, Girl, Orphan
Time period(s): 20th century; 1970s
Locale(s): Vietnam

Summary: In the first novel from poet Quan Barry, the author tells the story of a girl coming of age in a land filled with violence and despair. Rabbit is a Vietnamese girl born during the height of the Vietnamese conflict, which is yet another devastating blemish in her embattled country's history. Rabbit is born against all odds to a deceased woman, and becomes part of a family related to her only in spirit. The dead haunt Rabbit's psyche as her family drifts across Vietnam, searching for a chance to survive or an escape from the country. Meanwhile, the girl discovers the ancestry that made her who she is, from the French occupation to her own family's magical connection to the ethereal world. As the ghosts in Rabbit's mind tell her more about what has happened in Vietnam's past, she retains a glimmer of hope that she will be able to find a future, even in the perilous circumstances that constantly surround her.

Other books you might like:
T.C. Boyle, *The Harder They Come*, 2015
Lan Cao, *The Lotus and the Storm*, 2014
Anthony Doerr, *All the Light We Cannot See*, 2014
Thu Huong Duong, *The Zenith*, 2012
Michel Faber, *The Book of Strange New Things*, 2014
Adam Foulds, *In the Wolf's Mouth*, 2014
Indira Ganesan, *The Journey*, 1990
Violet Kupersmith, *The Frangipani Hotel*, 2014
Marie Manilla, *The Patron Saint of Ugly*, 2014
Yann Martel, *Beatrice and Virgil*, 2010

697

FREDERICK BARTHELME

There Must Be Some Mistake

(New York: Little, Brown and Company, 2014)

Story type: Contemporary
Subject(s): Old age; Retirement; Interpersonal relations

Major character(s): Wallace Webster, Aged Person, Divorced Person, Artist (former graphic artist), Father (of Morgan), Friend (of Jilly); Morgan Webster, Young Woman, Daughter (of Wallace); Jilly, Divorced Person, Artist (graphic artist), Friend (of Wallace Webster)
Time period(s): 21st century; 2010s
Locale(s): Kemah, Texas

Summary: Forced to accept early retirement, graphic designer Wallace Webster finds himself struggling to adapt to the sudden changes in his life. He lives in a condo complex called Forgetful Bay in Kemah, Texas. Though divorced, he nonetheless maintains contact with his ex-wife as well as his grown daughter, Morgan. Going through the motions as he aimlessly looks for a new focus, Wallace examines his family relationships as well as the one he has with his lover and with Jilly, a former colleague to whom he has always been attracted. His parents, brother, and first wife are all deceased and as he dwells on his own mortality, he realizes that many of his neighbors at Forgetful Bay are dying steadily in a series of bizarre freak accidents. Consumed with observing and understanding the world around him, Wallace offers commentary on pop culture, his neighbors' choices in lawn ornamentation, and whether his life has turned out the way he expected.

Other books by the same author:
Waveland, 2009
Elroy Nights, 2003
The Law of Averages: New and Selected Stories, 2000
Bob the Gambler, 1997
Painted Desert, 1995

Other books you might like:
Joe Hill, *Horns: A Novel*, 2010
Shane Kuhn, *The Intern's Handbook*, 2014
Linda Francis Lee, *The Ex-Debutante*, 2008
Leila Meacham, *Roses*, 2010
Michael Parker, *All I Have in This World*, 2014
Tom Perrotta, *The Abstinence Teacher*, 2007
Cynthia Robinson, *The Dog Park Club*, 2010
Rene Steinke, *Friendswood*, 2014
Cordelia Strube, *Milosz*, 2012

698

RICHARD BAUSCH

Before, During, After

(New York: Knopf, 2014)

Story type: Contemporary; Literary
Subject(s): Interpersonal relations; Love; Psychology
Major character(s): Natasha Barrett, Young Woman, Fiance(e) (of Michael Faulk), Artist; Michael Faulk, Religious (Episcopalian priest), Fiance(e) (of Natasha Barrett)
Time period(s): 21st century; 2000s
Locale(s): Jamaica; New York, New York; Memphis, Tennessee

Summary: Natasha Barrett and Michael Faulk seem an unlikely couple, but when they meet, they fall in love immediately and become engaged after knowing each other just a short time. In September of 2001, Natasha, an artist, and Michael, an Episcopalian priest, are separated by previous obligations. Natasha travels to Jamaica with a friend. Michael goes to New York City to attend a wedding and is caught up in the terror of the 9/11 attacks. He is unharmed, but he has difficulty getting out of the city. When Natasha hears the news in Jamaica, she is distraught and fears the worst about her fiance. She gets drunk and is sexually assaulted, but she can't bring herself to tell Michael what happened when they finally reunite in Memphis. Michael suspects something happened in Jamaica. Both he and Natasha realize that the events of September 11 have changed them and their relationship.

Other books by the same author:
Something Is Out There: Stories, 2010
Peace, 2008
Thanksgiving Night, 2006
Wives and Lovers: Three Short Novels, 2004
The Stories of Richard Bausch, 2003

Other books you might like:
Don DeLillo, *Falling Man*, 2007
Jeffrey Eugenides, *The Marriage Plot*, 2011
Julia Glass, *Whole World Over*, 2006
Stephen May, *Life! Death! Prizes!*, 2012
Ian McEwan, *On Chesil Beach*, 2007
Joyce Carol Oates, *The Falls*, 2004
Reynolds Price, *The Good Priest's Son*, 2005
Marilynne Robinson, *Lila*, 2014
Edward St. Aubyn, *On the Edge*, 2014
Donna Tartt, *The Goldfinch*, 2013

699

NED BEAUMAN

Glow

(New York: Knopf Doubleday Publishing Group, 2015)

Story type: Contemporary
Subject(s): Drugs; English (British people); Conspiracy
Major character(s): Raf, Young Man, Designer (web), Boyfriend (of Cherish); Cherish, Young Woman, Girlfriend (of Raf); Theo, Friend (of Raf), Kidnap Victim, Immigrant
Time period(s): 21st century; 2010s (2010)
Locale(s): London, England

Summary: The life of a young slacker in London is never easy—especially when he has an unusual sleep disorder and becomes involved in a bizarre conspiracy. Raf is a twenty-something web designer and operator of a pirate radio station whose body works on odd sleep rhythms. He spends his nights bouncing around London clubs and raves. On one such adventure, he hears about a new drug making the rounds called Glow. Raf is interested in trying it and begins searching for a way to get some Glow. When his best friend, a Burmese immigrant named Theo, is kidnapped, Raf realizes he may have found something more. Soon Raf is immersed in a drug ring run by a Burmese chemist and a shady mining corporation. And what about that beautiful girl he's starting to fall in love with? She may be part of the scheme as well.

Other books by the same author:
The Teleportation Accident, 2013
Boxer, Beetle, 2010

Other books you might like:
Margaret Atwood, *The Year of the Flood*, 2009
Justin Cartwright, *Lion Heart*, 2013
Hilary Mantel, *Bring Up the Bodies*, 2012
Anthony McCarten, *Death of a Superhero*, 2012
Lorrie Moore, *A Gate at the Stairs: A Novel*, 2009
Marisha Pessl, *Special Topics in Calamity Physics*, 2006
Karen Russell, *Swamplandia*, 2011
Robin Sloan, *Mr. Penumbra's 24-Hour Bookstore*, 2012
Amor Towles, *Rules of Civility*, 2011
Sarah Waters, *The Paying Guests*, 2014

700

CHRISTOPHER R. BEHA

Arts and Entertainments

(New York: HarperCollins Publishers, 2014)

Story type: Contemporary
Subject(s): Popular culture; Television programs; Entertainment industry
Major character(s): Eddie Hartley, Actor, Teacher (acting class), Spouse (of Susan), Lover (former, of Martha); Susan Hartley, Spouse (of Eddie); Martha Martin, Actress, Lover (former, of Eddie)
Time period(s): 21st century; 2010s
Locale(s): New York, United States

Summary: Once upon a time, Eddie Hartley believed he was destined to be the next big thing in Hollywood, but at the age of 33 he has finally come to terms with the fact that his acting career is all but over. These days, Eddie makes his living teaching acting to students at the same college preparatory school he attended as a kid. Then Eddie learns that his wife, Susan, is infertile. Deciding he cannot handle any more failure in his life, Eddie resolves to raise the money for Susan's fertility treatments any way he can. He follows a friend's advice and sells to the highest bidder an intimate video of Eddie and his ex-girlfriend, a hot actress. What ensues is a series of mishaps that not only tears Eddie's marriage apart, but also delves him deep into the world of celebrity gossip. Now that Eddie finally has all the fame he dreamed about, but has lost his wife and unborn children in the process, will he decide that it wasn't worth the price?

Other books by the same author:
What Happened to Sophie Wilder, 2012

Other books you might like:
Amy Bloom, *Lucky Us*, 2014
Halle Butler, *Jillian*, 2015
Susan Coll, *The Stager*, 2014
Eric Jerome Dickey, *Friends and Lovers*, 1997
Dave Eggers, *The Circle*, 2013
Joshua Ferris, *To Rise Again at a Decent Hour*, 2014

Herman Koch, *Summer House with Swimming Pool*, 2014
Farran Smith Nehme, *Missing Reels*, 2014
Amy Sohn, *Motherland*, 2012
John Warner, *The Funny Man*, 2011
Meg Wolitzer, *The Position*, 2005

701

R.G. BELSKY

The Kennedy Connection

(New York: Atria Books, 2014)

Series: Gil Malloy Series. Book 1
Story type: Mystery
Subject(s): Journalism; Mystery; Detective fiction
Major character(s): Gil Malloy, Journalist (newspaper reporter); Lee Harvey Oswald Jr., Son (of Lee Harvey Oswald); Nikki Reynolds, Agent (literary)
Time period(s): 21st century; 2010s
Locale(s): New York, New York; Dallas, Texas

Summary: New York City newspaper reporter Gil Malloy came very close to losing his job when he was accused of falsifying sources for a story. Now Malloy is waiting for the big story that will let him prove his journalistic integrity. Several options present themselves, including a story idea proposed by his literary agent Nikki Reynolds that seems downright outlandish—at first. According to Nikki, Lee Harvey Oswald Jr. claims to have proof his father did not kill President John F. Kennedy. Malloy passes on the idea until two murders occur in the city that may have ties to the Kennedy assassination. Two victims are shot at different locations, and a Kennedy half-dollar is found at each crime scene. Malloy believes that the murders are somehow tied to Oswald's claims, and he travels to Dallas to find the connection. This novel is the first in the Gil Malloy series by R.G. Belsky.

Other books you might like:
David Baldacci, *The Camel Club*, 2005
Lee Child, *Personal*, 2014
Mary Higgins Clark, *I've Got You Under My Skin*, 2014
Stephen Hunter, *The Third Bullet*, 2013
Stephen King, *11/22/1963*, 2011
Jim Lehrer, *Top Down: A Novel of the Kennedy Assassination*, 2013
James Patterson, *Burn*, 2014
John Sandford, *Deadline*, 2014
Stuart Woods, *Standup Guy*, 2014

702

ALEX BERENSON

Twelve Days

(New York: G.P. Putnam, 2015)

Series: John Wells Series. Book 9
Story type: Contemporary; Espionage
Subject(s): Suspense; Politics; International relations

Major character(s): John Wells, Spy (former CIA); Salome, Spy (Israeli agent)
Time period(s): 21st century; 2010s
Locale(s): Iran; Israel; United States

Summary: In the ninth John Wells novel, the protagonist returns to prevent war between the United States and Iran. A former CIA agent, Wells has uncovered a scheme that has the two countries at each other's throats. War between the two nations would be expensive, violent, and disastrous. Wells has traced the plot to an Israeli agent known as Salome. Salome is a trained killer who seeks to send the United States false information about Iran possessing materials to build nuclear weapons. As Israel's main enemy, if Iran were to go to war with the United States, then Israel would benefit exponentially. Exploding two commercial airlines kills more than 300 people, notching up the tension between powers. Wells and his colleagues work frantically with the CIA to prevent the American attempt on Iran in 12 days' time, while Salome is determined to prevent interference at any cost.

Other books by the same author:
The Counterfeit Agent, 2014
The Midnight House, 2010
The Silent Man, 2009
The Ghost War, 2008
The Faithful Spy, 2006

Other books you might like:
Jeff Abbott, *Collision*, 2008
David Baldacci, *Zero Day*, 2011
Dale Brown, *Drone Strike: A Dreamland Thriller*, 2014
Marc Cameron, *National Security*, 2011
Jack Coughlin, *Time to Kill*, 2013
Gerard de Villiers, *The Madmen of Benghazi*, 2014
Matthew Dunn, *Dark Spies*, 2014
Barry Eisler, *The Detachment*, 2011
Vince Flynn, *American Assassin: A Thriller*, 2010
Jamie Freveletti, *Robert Ludlum's The Geneva Strategy*, 2015
Mark Greaney, *The Gray Man*, 2009
Mark Greaney, *Tom Clancy Full Force and Effect*, 2014
W.E.B. Griffin, *Hazardous Duty*, 2013
W.E.B. Griffin, *Top Secret*, 2014
Mark Henshaw, *Cold Shot*, 2014
Jack Higgins, *The Death Trade*, 2013
Jack Higgins, *Rain on the Dead*, 2014
David Ignatius, *Bloodmoney*, 2011
Don Mann, *SEAL Team Six: Hunt the Falcon*, 2013
Joel C. Rosenberg, *Damascus Countdown*, 2013
Daniel Silva, *The Heist*, 2014
Daniel Silva, *The Kill Artist*, 2000
Olen Steinhauer, *An American Spy*, 2012
Brad Taylor, *No Fortunate Son*, 2014
Brad Taylor, *One Rough Man*, 2011
Brad Thor, *The Lions of Lucerne*, February 27, 2007

703

FATIMA BHUTTO

The Shadow of the Crescent Moon
(London: Penguin Publishing Group, 2015)

Story type: Family Saga; Literary
Subject(s): Afghanistan Conflict, 2001-; Family sagas; Terrorism
Major character(s): Aman Erum, Brother (of Sikandar, Hayat); Sikandar, Doctor, Spouse (of Mina), Brother (of Aman, Hayat); Mina, Spouse (of Sikandar); Hayat, Brother (of Aman, Sikandar), Boyfriend (of Samarra); Samarra, Young Woman, Girlfriend (of Hayat)
Time period(s): 21st century; 2000s
Locale(s): Mir Ali, Pakistan

Summary: Living under the shadow of Taliban oppression in a small Pakistani village, three brothers have existed with war and violence as part of their everyday reality. The eldest, Aman Erum, escaped to the United States to get an education and returned with ambitions of becoming a successful businessman. Sikandar, a doctor whose son was killed by the Taliban, now cares for his wife, Mina, who is suffering from mental illness. Hayat is the youngest and continues in the activist footsteps of their father by joining with a separatist group. On a fateful Friday morning, with the Americans invading neighboring Afghanistan and the threat of Taliban violence always present, the brothers make the decision to pray at different mosques. In the hours that follow, their lives will be touched by tragedy and bravery will come from unlikely places.

Other books you might like:
Pearl Abraham, *American Taliban: A Novel*, 2010
Elliot Ackerman, *Green on Blue*, 2015
Nadeem Aslam, *The Blind Man's Garden*, 2013
Don DeLillo, *Falling Man*, 2007
Amit Majmudar, *Partitions*, 2011
Ann Patchett, *Bel Canto*, 2001
Naomi Ragen, *The Covenant*, 2004
James Robertson, *The Professor of Truth*, 2013
Bina Shah, *A Season for Martyrs*, 2014
Bilal Tanweer, *The Scatter Here Is Too Great*, 2014
John Updike, *Terrorist*, 2006

704

FRANCESCA LIA BLOCK

Beyond the Pale Motel
(New York: St. Martin's Press, 2014)

Story type: Mystery; Serial Killer
Subject(s): Sexual behavior; Serial murders; Friendship
Major character(s): Catt, Alcoholic, Hairdresser, Spouse (former, of Dash), Friend (of Bree); Bree, Hairdresser, Alcoholic, Friend (of Catt), Mother (of Skylar); Dash, Spouse (former, of Catt), Musician; Skylar, Son (of Bree)
Time period(s): 21st century; 2010s

Locale(s): Los Angeles, California

Summary: Catt and her best friend, Bree, are recovering alcoholics who spend their days working together at a Southern California hair salon, and working out at a local gym. Staying sober has been a struggle for the women, but a successful one, and they share their experiences on a popular blog. But Catt's world is thrown into chaos when her husband leaves her for another woman. She copes by running into the arms, and the beds, of an almost endless string of men. When Los Angeles is rocked by a series of brutal murders, Catt sees that the victims bear a striking resemblance to Bree, and she is convinced her friend will be the killer's next target. As Catt edges toward a confrontation with a killer, it may be her own demons that prove to be most dangerous.

Other books by the same author:
The Island of Excess Love, 2014
Teen Spirit, 2014
Love in the Time of Global Warming, 2013
The Elementals, 2012
Pink Smog: Becoming Weetzie Bat, 2012

Other books you might like:
Jackie Collins, *Confessions of a Wild Child*, 2014
Clare Donoghue, *Never Look Back*, 2014
Linda Fairstein, *Terminal City*, 2014
Joy Fielding, *Someone Is Watching*, 2015
Lisa Gardner, *Fear Nothing*, 2014
David Jackson, *Marked*, 2013
Fern Michaels, *In Plain Sight*, 2015
Barbara Palmer, *Claudine*, 2014
J.D. Robb, *Festive in Death*, 2014
Harold Robbins, *The Devil to Pay*, 2006

705

HILARY BOYD

Tangled Lives

(New York: Quercus, 2014)

Story type: Literary
Subject(s): Family; Family relations; Parent-child relations
Major character(s): Annie Delancey, Spouse (of Richard), Mother (of Ed, Marsha, Lucy, and Daniel); Richard Delancey, Spouse (of Annie), Father (of Ed, Marsha, and Lucy); Ed Delancey, Restaurateur, Son (of Annie and Richard), Brother (of Marsha and Lucy), Boyfriend (of Emma); Marsha Delancey, Daughter (of Annie and Richard), Sister (of Ed and Lucy); Lucy Delancey, Daughter (of Annie and Richard), Sister (of Ed and Marsha); Emma, Girlfriend (of Ed); Daniel, Adoptee, Son (of Annie)
Time period(s): 21st century; 2000s
Locale(s): London, England

Summary: Richard and Annie Delancey live in the North London home they bought just before the arrival of their first child Ed. Ed is now 26, and his sisters, Marsha and Lucy, are also adults. Annie enjoys spending time with her family on the rare occasion when they are all together, but a secret from the past is about to change Annie's relationship with her husband and children.

Richard doesn't know it, but Annie gave birth to a baby boy in Kent in 1967 and gave him up for adoption. Annie thinks often about the baby she surrendered, but she is shocked when she learns from the social service agency that Daniel—her son—is interested in finding his birth mother. She wants desperately to meet Daniel even though she knows the news of his existence will be a surprise to Richard and her other children. However, Annie is not prepared for the repercussions of her revelation.

Other books by the same author:
Thursdays in the Park, 2013

Other books you might like:
Leslie Carroll, *Choosing Sophie*, 2008
Kim Edwards, *The Memory Keeper's Daughter: A Novel*, 2005
Judith Frank, *All I Love and Know*, 2014
Carre Armstrong Gardner, *All Right Here*, 2014
Elin Hilderbrand, *Winter Street*, 2014
Lisa Jewell, *The House We Grew Up In*, 2014
Wally Lamb, *We Are Water*, 2013
Mary McNear, *Butternut Summer*, 2014
Liane Moriarty, *The Husband's Secret*, 2013
Jodi Picoult, *Lone Wolf*, 2012
Joanna Trollope, *Brother and Sister*, 2004
Menna van Praag, *The Dress Shop of Dreams*, 2014
Penny Vincenzi, *Sheer Abandon*, 2005

706

KARA BRADEN

The Longest Night

(Naperville, Illinois: Sourcebooks Casablanca, 2014)

Series: Longest Night Series. Book 1
Subject(s): Romances (Fiction); Veterans; Love
Major character(s): Cecily Knight, Military Personnel (former Marine Captain); Ian Fairchild, Lawyer
Time period(s): 21st century; 2010s
Locale(s): Canada

Summary: In this romance by Kara Braden, former Marine Captain Cecily Knight has fled to her cabin in the Canadian wilderness to live alone and avoid triggering her PTSD. When unexpected circumstances arise, criminal defense lawyer Ian Fairchild must share some of the space in Cecily's cabin. Ian has his own demons. He became addicted to painkillers following an injury and is in recovery, but he's trying to avoid relapse. Initially, the two are polite, but choose to avoid one another. They soon find that they have a mutual respect for and interest in each other. Their tentative friendship grows into something much deeper as their emotional and physical attraction becomes impossible to ignore. This novel is the first in the Longest Night series. First novel.

Other books you might like:
Donna Alward, *Treasure on Lilac Lane*, 2014
Sara Arden, *Return to Glory*, 2014
Toni Blake, *Holly Lane*, 2011
Susan Donovan, *The Sweetest Summer*, 2014
Rachel Gibson, *What I Love About You*, 2014

Shirley Jump, *The Sweetheart Secret*, 2014
Donna Kauffman, *Sandpiper Island*, 2014
Catherine Mann, *Shelter Me*, 2014
Christie Ridgway, *Take My Breath Away*, 2014
Emily Snow, *Tidal*, 2013

707

HALLE BUTLER

Jillian

(Chicago: Curbside Splendor Publishing, 2015)

Story type: Contemporary; Psychological
Subject(s): Medical professions; Single parent family; Dogs
Major character(s): Jillian, Office Worker (manager), Single Mother (of Adam), Co-worker (of Megan); Megan, Young Woman, Office Worker, Co-worker (of Jillian), Secretary; Adam, Son (of Jillian)
Time period(s): 21st century; 2010s
Locale(s): Chicago, Illinois

Summary: In a doctor's office in an upper-middle-class Chicago suburb, a battle is brewing. On one side is officer manager Jillian, a single mother in her mid-thirties who wears a mask of blind optimism to cover up feelings of unhappiness. On the other is Megan, a bitter twenty-something who channels her deep-seated feelings of boredom and discontent into hatred of Jillian. The women coexist in a state of smoldering resentment, with Jillian's constant can-do world view grating on Megan's every nerve. As the underlying sadness and selfishness in Jillian and Megan's lives begins to bubble up, the ordinary turns awkward and their paths bring them closer to an inevitable conflict. In the end, it is a conflict that will prove they are not so different from each other as they believe. First novel

Other books you might like:
Theresa Alan, *Who You Know*, 2003
Max Barry, *Company*, 2006
Christopher R. Beha, *Arts and Entertainments*, 2014
Connie May Fowler, *How Clarissa Burden Learned to Fly*, 2010
Laurie Frankel, *Goodbye for Now*, 2012
Robert Glancy, *Terms and Conditions*, 2014
Suzanne Greenberg, *Lesson Plans*, 2014
Joshilyn Jackson, *Someone Else's Love Story*, 2013
Lucy Kellaway, *In Office Hours*, 2011
Joshua Mohr, *Fight Song: A Novel*, 2013

708

CHELSEA CAIN

One Kick

(New York: Simon and Schuster, 2014)

Series: Kick Lannigan Series. Book 1
Story type: Mystery
Subject(s): Kidnapping; Martial arts; Women
Major character(s): Kit "Kick" Lannigan, Kidnap Victim, Martial Arts Expert, Friend (of Bishop); John Bishop, Friend (of Kit), Detective—Amateur, Wealthy
Time period(s): 21st century; 2010s
Locale(s): Portland, Oregon

Summary: Chelsea Cain, author of the Archie Sheridan/Gretchen Lowell thrillers, here kicks off a new series about a young woman, Kit "Kick" Lannigan, who has acquired a unique set of skills after a traumatic childhood experience. Kick was six years old when she was kidnapped. She was held for five years by a pedophile who taught her to shoot, pick locks, and make bombs. After being rescued at age 11, she began taking martial arts and other defense classes. Now 21, she spends most of her time practicing. When two children disappear from the Portland area where she lives, a man who spends his time working to find missing kids asks for her help. John Bishop knows Kick has a perspective on such crimes unlike any other. Kick reluctantly agrees. She soon realizes that to find the children, she's going to have to confront the terror of her own past.

Other books by the same author:
Let Me Go, 2013
Kill You Twice, 2012
The Night Season, 2011
Evil at Heart, 2009
Sweetheart, 2008

Other books you might like:
Lee Child, *Persuader*, 2003
Liza Cody, *Bucket Nut*, 1993
Patricia Cornwell, *Postmortem*, 1990
Sophie Hannah, *The Carrier*, 2015
Samantha Hayes, *What You Left Behind*, 2015
Tami Hoag, *Cold Cold Heart*, 2014
Alex Kava, *A Perfect Evil*, 2001
Jonathan Kellerman, *Motive*, 2015
Caroline Kepnes, *You*, 2014
Jeff Lindsay, *Dexter Is Dead*, 2015
Kimberly McCreight, *Where They Found Her*, 2015
Michael Robotham, *Lost*, 2005
Greg Rucka, *Keeper*, 1996
Zoe Sharp, *Killer Instinct*, 2010
Karin Slaughter, *Blindsighted*, 2001
Taylor Stevens, *The Informationist*, 2011
Peter Swanson, *The Kind Worth Killing*, 2015

709

STEPHEN L. CARTER

Back Channel

(New York: Knopf Doubleday Publishing Group, 2014)

Subject(s): United States history; Nuclear weapons; Russians
Major character(s): Margo Jensen, 19-Year-Old, Student—College, Friend (of Bobby Fischer), Spy (for American government); Vasily Smyslov, Chess Player (Russian), Spy, Historical Figure; Bobby Fischer, Historical Figure, Chess Player, Friend (of Margo)

Time period(s): 20th century; 1960s (1962)
Locale(s): Russia; Washington, District of Columbia; Ithaca, New York

Summary: It's 1962 and the world is poised on the brink of a nuclear war. The Soviets have missiles in Cuba and tense negotiations are under way to diffuse the potential disaster that could cost tens of thousands of lives. Two world leaders are caught between advisers who want to see war and two nations that want peace and safety. Their best hope of solving this is to negotiate through an unofficial back channel. They find that in the unlikely form of Margo Jensen, a 19-year-old black Cornell student. A Soviet chess champion, Vasily Smyslov, has tipped off the Americans to a Soviet strategy in Cuba. This chess expert will be playing in a tournament in Russia with Bobby Fischer, and Fischer wants Margo along as his lucky charm. The suspense builds as the young American woman weaves her way through international intrigue to bring about resolution in this fictionalized account of the Cuban missile crisis.

Other books by the same author:
The Impeachment of Abraham Lincoln, 2012
Jericho's Fall, 2009
Palace Council, 2008
New England White, 2007
The Emperor of Ocean Park, 2002

Other books you might like:
William F. Buckley, *Getting It Right*, 2003
John Crowley, *The Translator*, 2002
Brendan DuBois, *Resurrection Day*, 1999
Clive Egleton, *Pandora's Box*, 2008
W.E.B. Griffin, *The Assassination Option*, 2014
John T. Lescroart, *The Keeper*, 2014
Florencia Mallon, *Beyond the Ties of Blood*, 2012
Brad Meltzer, *The Fifth Assassin*, 2013
Richard North Patterson, *Loss of Innocence*, 2013
David L. Robbins, *The Betrayal Game*, 2008
Daniel Silva, *The English Girl*, 2013
Martin Cruz Smith, *Tatiana*, 2013
Jim Walker, *October Dawn*, 2001

710

DIANE CHAMBERLAIN

The Silent Sister

(New York: St. Martin's Press, 2014)

Story type: Mystery
Subject(s): Family; Sisters; Suicide
Major character(s): Riley MacPherson, Sister (of Lisa and Danny), Psychologist, Daughter (of Mr. MacPherson); Mr. MacPherson, Father (of Lisa, Danny, and Riley); Lisa MacPherson, Crime Suspect, Daughter (of Mr. MacPherson), Sister (of Danny and Riley), Missing Person; Danny MacPherson, Brother (of Lisa and Riley), Military Personnel, Son (of Mr. MacPherson)
Time period(s): 20th century; (1980s); 21st century; 2010s
Locale(s): New Bern, North Carolina

Summary: Riley MacPherson has always thought that her sister, Lisa, killed herself when they were young. She remembers grieving her sister's death, and it has shaped the woman she has become. When her father passes away decades later, Riley gets to work organizing his house, which is her childhood home. There, she uncovers something that changes her entire life: Lisa is not dead. In fact, Lisa went into hiding after killing someone, and she changed her name to circumvent the law. Riley wants to reach out to Lisa and tell her that Riley knows her secret, but no one will help her. Riley's brother, Danny, wants to tell the police the truth about Lisa because he believes Lisa's crime ruined everything for him. Now Riley must find out the truth about why Lisa killed someone so that she can get what is left of her family back. With most of the evidence in Lisa's favor gone, however, Riley isn't sure where to begin.

Other books by the same author:
Necessary Lies, 2013
The Good Father, 2012
The Midwife's Confession, 2011
The Lies We Told, 2010
The Shadow Wife, 2010

Other books you might like:
Maggie Barbieri, *Lies That Bind*, 2015
Jillian Cantor, *Margot*, 2013
Caroline B. Cooney, *No Such Person*, 2015
Robert Dugoni, *My Sister's Grave*, 2014
Joshilyn Jackson, *The Girl Who Stopped Swimming*, 2008
E. Lockhart, *We Were Liars*, 2014
Patricia MacDonald, *I See You*, 2014
Lauren Oliver, *Vanishing Girls*, 2015
Jodi Picoult, *Leaving Time*, 2014
Nora Roberts, *The Liar*, 2015
Jessica Warman, *The Last Good Day of the Year*, 2015

711

DARCIE CHAN

The Mill River Redemption

(New York: Ballantine Books, 2014)

Series: Mill River Series. Book 2
Story type: Contemporary; Series
Subject(s): Sisters; Family; Inheritance and succession
Major character(s): Rose, Sister (of Emily), Daughter (of Josie); Emily, Sister (of Rose), Daughter (of Josie); Josie DiSanti, Mother (deceased, of Emily and Rose); Ivy Collard, Store Owner (bookstore), Aunt (of Josie)
Time period(s): 21st century; 2010s
Locale(s): Mill River, Vermont

Summary: When Josie DiSanti moved to Mill River, Vermont, in the 1980s with her daughters, Rose and Emily, she planned to make a new start. Josie didn't know that a painful feud would be born in the pretty little town. Years later, Rose and Emily remain estranged since the event that tore them apart. While she was alive, Josie tried to get her daughters to reconcile. Before she died, Josie hatched a plan that would ensure that the girls would spend time together again. According to the terms of Josie's will, Rose and Emily must live next to one another in Mill River and find the key that opens the safe deposit box that holds their inheritance. Although Rose and Emily are grown women, they continue their feud through petty acts of vandalism. A crisis finally prompts the sisters to reconsider their relationship. This novel is the second in the Mill River series by Darcie Chan.

Other books by the same author:
The Mill River Recluse, 2014

Other books you might like:
Jeffrey Archer, *Mightier than the Sword*, 2015
Lucy Clarke, *Swimming at Night*, 2013
C.J. Darlington, *Thicker Than Blood*, 2009
Lily Everett, *Sanctuary Island*, 2013
Kristin Hannah, *Between Sisters*, 2003
Irene Hannon, *That Certain Summer*, 2013
Debbie Macomber, *Love Letters*, 2014
Mary Alice Monroe, *The Summer Wind*, 2014
Jojo Moyes, *Silver Bay*, 2007
Luanne Rice, *Little Night*, 2012
Danielle Steel, *One Day at a Time*, 2009
Susan Rebecca White, *A Soft Place to Land*, 2010

712

MICHAEL CHRISTIE

If I Fall, If I Die
(New York: Hogarth, 2015)

Story type: Coming-of-Age
Subject(s): Mother-son relations; Mental disorders; Coming of age
Major character(s): Will, Boy, Son (of Diane), Friend (of Marcus); Diane, Mentally Ill Person (agoraphobe), Mother (of Will); Marcus, Friend (of Will), Skater (skateboarder)
Time period(s): 21st century; 2010s
Locale(s): Ontario, Canada

Summary: Will's agoraphobic mother, Diane, has led him to believe that the outside world is a terrifying, dangerous place. Diane keeps Will indoors with her at all times. And although she has created a fulfilling interior world and exposed her son to science and the arts, Diane can't allow Will to experience the outside world first-hand. When Will finally ventures beyond the door of his home by himself, he does so dressed in protective gear. He is shocked and relieved that he survives the journey unharmed, and he eventually leaves his mother's insular world to experience life as a normal boy. Because of his years of isolation, Will has no social skills and no idea how to carry on a conversation. As he deals with adolescent challenges that are complicated by his unusual upbringing, Will makes an unlikely friend and finds joy in the sport of skateboarding.

Other books you might like:
Jenn Crowell, *Etched on Me*, 2014
Karen Harrington, *Courage for Beginners*, 2014
Rebecca James, *Sweet Damage*, 2014
Miranda July, *The First Bad Man*, 2015
Joyce Maynard, *After Her*, 2013
Ann Packer, *The Children's Crusade*, 2015

Angela Pneuman, *Lay It on My Heart*, 2014
Adam Rapp, *Know Your Beholder*, 2015
Alice Sebold, *The Almost Moon*, 2007
David Vann, *Dirt*, 2012
Jeanette Walls, *The Silver Star*, 2013

713

MARY HIGGINS CLARK
ALAFAIR BURKE, Co-Author

The Cinderella Murder
(New York: Simon & Schuster, 2014)

Series: Under Suspicion Series. Book 1
Story type: Contemporary Realism
Subject(s): Television programs; Murder; Detective fiction
Major character(s): Laurie Moran, Producer (of reality TV show); Alex Buckley, Lawyer, Television Personality (show host); Susan Dempsey, Student—College, Crime Victim
Time period(s): 21st century; 2010s
Locale(s): California, United States

Summary: In this first-time collaboration between authors Mary Higgins Clark and Alafair Burke, a reality television program serves as the backdrop of a murder investigation. Laurie Moran is the producer of a new reality show that tries to solve cold case murders by reenacting them with the people who were originally involved. The show is an immediate success and Laurie decides to feature the unsolved murder of UCLA student Susan Dempsey, whose body was found without a shoe. With many intriguing questions surrounding the beautiful young woman's death and with big names from Hollywood and the tech industry on the suspect list, Laurie and show host Alex Buckley, who is also a lawyer, see the ratings soaring. However, the murderer may have other ideas. This book, the first in the Under Suspicion series by these authors, features characters first introduced in Clark's *I've Got You Under My Skin*.

Other books by the same author:
I've Got You Under My Skin, 2014
Daddy's Gone A Hunting, 2013
The Lost Years, 2012
I'll Walk Alone, 2011
The Shadow of Your Smile, 2010

Other books you might like:
Barbara Allan, *Antiques Chop*, 2013
Charles Atkins, *Done to Death*, 2014
Allison Brennan, *Notorious*, 2014
Mary Jane Clark, *Footprints in the Sand*, 2013
Patricia Cornwell, *Flesh and Blood*, 2014
Lisa Gardner, *Crash and Burn*, 2015
J.A. Jance, *Cold Betrayal*, 2015
Camilla Lackberg, *The Stranger*, 2013
Sophie Littlefield, *A Bad Day for Pretty*, 2010
Alex Marwood, *The Killer Next Door*, 2014
Peter May, *Freeze Frame*, 2010
Dennis Palumbo, *Phantom Limb*, 2014
Cath Staincliffe, *Dead to Me*, 2014
Brian Thomsen, *The Reel Stuff*, 1998

Lisa Unger, *Fragile*, 2010
Kate Wilhelm, *Cold Case*, 2008

714

PAUL CLEAVE

Five Minutes Alone

(New York: Atria Books, 2014)

Series: Christchurch Noir Crime Series. Book 8
Story type: Mystery
Subject(s): Law enforcement; Murder; Detective fiction
Major character(s): Carl Schroder, Detective—Police, Vigilante, Co-worker (former, of Theodore); Theodore Tate, Detective—Police, Father (of Emily), Spouse (of Bridget), Co-worker (former, of Carl); Kelly Summers, Young Woman, Crime Victim
Time period(s): 21st century; 2010s
Locale(s): Christchurch, New Zealand

Summary: When the body of a convicted rapist is found dismembered by a train, Detective Theodore Tate begins to suspect the man's victim may be responsible. Tate is onto something, but the truth he uncovers leads him to a place he never thought it would. A former colleague, Carl Schroder, recently recovered from a gunshot wound to the head that has left him incapable of feeling emotion, has been helping crime victims get revenge by giving them five minutes alone with their attackers. Tate and others in the police force are torn between the law and the desire for well-deserved punishment. But when Schroder's exercise in vigilante justice goes wrong, the two men end up on opposite sides of a very deadly moral dilemma. This is the eight book in Paul Cleave's Christchurch Noir Crime series.

Other books by the same author:
Joe Victim, 2013
The Cleaner, 2012
The Laughterhouse, 2012
Collecting Cooper, 2011
Blood Men, 2010

Other books you might like:
Gillian Flynn, *Gone Girl*, 2012
Tana French, *The Secret Place*, 2014
Lisa Gardner, *The Survivors Club*, 2001
Greg Iles, *The Death Factory*, 2014
Jonathan Kellerman, *Motive*, 2015
William Landay, *Defending Jacob*, 2012
Perri O'Shaughnessy, *Dreams of the Dead*, 2011
Joyce Carol Oates, *Rape: A Love Story*, 2004
James Patterson, *Hope to Die*, 2014
Louise Penny, *The Long Way Home*, 2014

715

JENNY COLGAN

Sweetshop of Dreams

(London: Sphere, 2014)

Story type: Family Saga; Romance
Subject(s): Family; Nursing; Old age

Major character(s): Rosie Hopkins, Young Woman, Niece (great, of Lilian), Girlfriend (of Gerard), Caregiver, Nurse; Lilian, Aunt (great, of Rosie), Businesswoman (shop owner); Gerard, Boyfriend (of Rosie); Stephen, Young Man, Friend (of Rosie)
Time period(s): 21st century; 2010s
Locale(s): Lipton, England; London, England

Summary: Rosie Hopkins has a nice job as a nurse, a nice boyfriend, and a nice life in London. Problem is, "nice" is a bit boring for Rosie. When she temporarily finds herself without a job, Rosie's mother offers her the opportunity to care for an elderly relative in the countryside. Wanting nothing more than to get the job done and return to London, Rosie accepts and travels to the tiny village of Lipton. There she meets her feisty great-aunt, Lilian, who owns an old-fashioned candy store, and soon finds herself taking care of the business. As her reluctance melts away, Rosie begins to fall for Lipton and its charming residents, including the mysterious and handsome Stephen. This wasn't the life she expected, but Rosie is discovering she may finally have found the life she wants.

Other books by the same author:
The Loveliest Chocolate Shop in Paris, 2014
Meet Me at the Cupcake Cafe, 2013
Christmas at the Cupcake Cafe, 2012
The Boy I Loved Before, 2004
Amanda's Wedding, 2001

Other books you might like:
Cecelia Ahern, *The Time of My Life*, 2011
Tilly Bagshawe, *Fame*, 2013
Carolyn Brown, *The Red-Hot Chili Cook-Off*, 2014
Sarah Dunn, *Secrets to Happiness: A Novel*, 2009
Emily Giffin, *The One and Only*, 2014
Gil McNeil, *A Good Year for the Roses*, 2014
Naomi Neale, *The Mile-High Hair Club*, 2005
Sarah Pekkanen, *Catching Air*, 2014
Adriana Trigiani, *The Supreme Macaroni Company*, 2013
Menna van Praag, *The Dress Shop of Dreams*, 2014

716

SUSAN COLL

The Stager

(New York: Sarah Crichton Books, 2014)

Story type: Literary
Subject(s): Family; Family life; Humor
Major character(s): Lars Jorgenson, Tennis Player (former), Spouse (of Bella), Father (of Elsa); Bella, Spouse (of Lars), Mother (of Elsa); Elsa, Girl, Daughter (of Lars and Bella); Nabila, Caregiver (Elsa's nanny); Eve Brenner, Real Estate Agent (home stager)
Time period(s): 21st century; 2010s
Locale(s): Bethesda, Maryland

Summary: Lars and Bella Jorgenson are frustrated because they haven't gotten any acceptable offers on their Bethesda house. Lars, a former tennis player, is an overweight, drug-addled version of his former self. Bella wants desperately to escape their Maryland suburb. The couple's daughter, Elsa, is a precocious observer of all that goes on in the house. She spends her days with her nanny, Nabila, and witnesses the comings and goings of real estate agents and potential buyers. When a stager is called in to make the Jorgensons' home more appealing, Elsa gets to know her. Eve is not happy in her current career as a stager; she wants to be a journalist. When she arrives at the Jorgenson house, she realizes that she has a connection to her new clients. Eve and Bella were once friends, which means that Eve knows many of Bella's secrets. Eve's presence adds a new dimension to the already strained family dynamic.

Other books by the same author:
Beach Week, 2010
Rockville Pike: A Suburban Comedy of Manners, 2005
Acceptance, 2003
Karlmarx.com, 2001

Other books you might like:
Wilton Barnhardt, *Lookaway, Lookaway*, 2013
Christopher R. Beha, *Arts and Entertainments*, 2014
Craig Ferguson, *Between the Bridge and the River*, 2006
Hans Keilson, *Comedy in a Minor Key*, 2010
Kevin Kwan, *Crazy Rich Asians*, 2013
Merrill Markoe, *The Psycho Ex Game*, 2004
Christopher Moore, *A Dirty Job*, 2006
Chuck Palahniuk, *Doomed*, 2013
Amy Sohn, *Motherland*, 2012
John Warner, *The Funny Man*, 2011

717

JEFFREY CONDRAN

Prague Summer

(Berkeley, California: Counterpoint Press, 2014)

Story type: Contemporary; Mystery
Subject(s): Czechs; Marriage; Political prisoners
Major character(s): Stephanie, Diplomat (US state department), Spouse (of Henry), Friend (of Selma); Henry, Dealer (of rare books), Spouse (of Stephanie); Selma Al-Khateeb, Friend (of Stephanie), Spouse (of Mansour); Mansour Al-Khateeb, Spouse (of Selma), Political Prisoner
Time period(s): 21st century; 2010s
Locale(s): Prague, Czech Republic

Summary: Stephanie and Henry have a good life in the Czech Republic capital of Prague. Stephanie works for the US State Department and Henry is a rare books dealer. They spend their days in a predictable but satisfying existence, awash in the literary charms of the Old World city. Crashing into their world comes Selma, an old friend of Stephanie's, whose Muslim husband has been arrested by the US government. The couple initially sees Selma's visit as a chance for her to get away from her troubles and enjoy Europe. But Selma has her own agenda, and when she begs Henry for help in freeing Mansour, he lets himself get drawn into her plans. In the process, Henry gets dangerously close to Selma, a situation that threatens to tear apart the very life he and

Stephanie have created. First novel.

Other books you might like:
Steve Berry, *The Lincoln Myth*, 2014
Sharon Bolton, *A Dark and Twisted Tide*, 2014
Sophie Hannah, *The Carrier*, 2015
Kelly Jones, *Lost and Found in Prague*, 2015
Laura Lippman, *The Most Dangerous Thing*, 2011
Lee Martin, *Break the Skin*, 2011
Gustavo Faveron Patriau, *The Antiquarian*, 2014
Chris Pavone, *The Accident*, 2014
Paul Robertson, *According to Their Deeds*, 2009
Lisa Unger, *Crazy Love You*, 2015

718

MICHAEL CONNELLY

The Burning Room

(New York: Little, Brown and Company, 2014)

Series: Harry Bosch Series. Book 19
Story type: Mystery
Subject(s): Mystery; Detective fiction; Crime
Major character(s): Harry Bosch, Veteran, Detective—Police (LAPD), Colleague (partner of Lucia Soto); Lucia "Lucky" Soto, Detective—Police (LAPD), Colleague (partner of Harry Bosch); Orlando Merced, Musician (mariachi), Crime Victim
Time period(s): 21st century; 2010s
Locale(s): Los Angeles, California

Summary: As the 19th novel in the Harry Bosch series opens, mariachi musician Orlando Merced has just died from injuries sustained in a shooting ten years ago. LAPD detective Harry Bosch and his new partner, Lucia "Lucky" Soto, take the unusual cold case, which involves a warm body but sparse evidence. Bosch and Soto begin their investigation by revisiting the circumstances of Merced's shooting. He was playing with his band in a city plaza when a drive-by gunman put a bullet in his back, but the detectives suspect that it was not a random incident. Merced was connected to an LA politician who eventually used the injured musician's tale for political purposes. Further digging takes Bosch and Soto to a fatal fire 20 years ago that is tied to Merced's murder. As seasoned detective Bosch tries to make sense of the complicated cold case, he must also guide Lucky through her first homicide investigation.

Other books by the same author:
The Gods of Guilt, 2013
The Black Box, 2012
The Drop, 2011
The Fifth Witness, 2011
The Reversal, 2010

Other books you might like:
Jussi Adler-Olsen, *The Keeper of Lost Causes*, 2011
David Baldacci, *The Escape*, 2014
Mark Billingham, *Time of Death*, 2015
Harry Brandt, *The Whites*, 2015
Edna Buchanan, *Cold Case Squad*, 2004
Robin Burcell, *Cold Case*, 2004
Jan Burke, *Nine*, 2002

Lee Child, *Personal*, 2014
Harlan Coben, *The Stranger*, 2015
Max Allan Collins, *Criminal Minds: Finishing School*, 2008
John Darnton, *Black and White and Dead All Over*, 2008
Sue Grafton, *"O" Is for Outlaw*, 1999
W.E.B. Griffin, *Deadly Assets*, 2015
Rachel Howzell Hall, *Land of Shadows*, 2014
Jonathan Kellerman, *Motive*, 2015
Peter Lovesey, *Down Among the Dead Men*, 2015
Peter May, *The Blackhouse*, 2012
Jo Nesbo, *The Bat*, 2013
James Patterson, *Hope to Die*, 2014
Ian Rankin, *Saints of the Shadow Bible*, 2014
Charles Rosenberg, *Long Knives*, 2014
Hank Phillippi Ryan, *Truth Be Told*, 2014
John Sandford, *Deadline*, 2014
John Sandford, *Gathering Prey*, 2015
Stephen White, *Cold Case*, 2000
Michael Wiley, *Blue Avenue*, 2014
Kate Wilhelm, *Cold Case*, 2008

719

PATRICIA CORNWELL

Flesh and Blood

(New York: HarperCollins Publishers, 2014)

Series: Kay Scarpetta Series. Book 22
Story type: Series
Subject(s): Serial murders; Murder; Detective fiction
Major character(s): Dr. Kay Scarpetta, Aunt (of Lucy), Doctor, Detective (forensics), Spouse (of Benton); Benton Wesley, Spouse (of Kay), FBI Agent; Lucy, Niece (of Kay), Crime Suspect
Time period(s): 21st century; 2010s
Locale(s): United States

Summary: In this 22nd novel from author Patricia Cornwall's series featuring Kay Scarpetta, Dr. Scarpetta becomes entrenched in another mystery when she finds pennies behind her home near Boston. Scarpetta is just about to leave for a much-needed holiday with her husband, FBI agent Benton Wesley, when she finds these mysterious items. She then gets a call about a murder that has occurred not far from her house. Soon a serial killer is at large, and none of the subsequent murders have anything in common except that the murderer leaves copper at all of the crime scenes. Scarpetta is taken around the country, chasing the killer at large, until she finally uncovers proof that indicates the killer is her own niece. Scarpetta is reluctant to accept that her niece could be the murderer, but she must work extra hard to clear her family member's name. The body count is climbing, and Scarpetta could be next.

Other books by the same author:
Dust, 2013
The Bone Bed, 2012
Red Mist, 2011
Port Mortuary, 2010

The Scarpetta Factor, 2009
Other books you might like:
Elizabeth Adler, *Last to Know*, 2014
Jefferson Bass, *Carved in Bone*, 2006
Benjamin Black, *Christine Falls*, 2007
Mary Higgins Clark, *The Cinderella Murder*, 2014
Beverly Connor, *One Grave Too Many*, 2003
Robin Cook, *Foreign Body*, 2008
Tess Gerritsen, *The Bone Garden*, 2007
Carolyn Haines, *Booty Bones*, 2014
Terry Hayes, *I Am Pilgrim*, 2013
Greg Iles, *Blood Memory*, 2005
Margaret Maron, *Three-Day Town*, 2011
Leslie Meier, *English Tea Murder*, 2011
James Patterson, *Tick Tock*, 2011
Jodi Picoult, *House Rules*, 2010
Kathy Reichs, *Bones Never Lie*, 2014
Karin Slaughter, *Unseen*, 2013
Helen Smith, *Beyond Belief*, 2014
Marcia Dutton Talley, *Dark Passage*, 2013

720

ROBERT CRAIS

The Promise

(New York: Penguin Group, 2014)

Series: Elvis Cole Series. Book 16
Story type: Mystery; Series
Subject(s): Missing persons; Detective fiction; Mystery
Major character(s): Elvis Cole, Detective—Private, Colleague (of Joe), Veteran; Joe Pike, Veteran, Detective—Private, Colleague (of Elvis); Scott James, Police Officer, Trainer (of Maggie), Colleague (of Maggie); Maggie, Police Officer (K-9), Colleague (of Scott), Dog
Time period(s): 21st century; 2010s
Locale(s): Los Angeles, California

Summary: In this sixteenth installment in the long-running Elvis Cole and Joe Pike series, author Robert Crais brings back a pair of heroes from his book *Suspect*. A female employee of a defense contractor has gone missing. Elvis Cole discovers the woman is being blackmailed, but instead of money, the blackmailer demands explosives. Meanwhile, Los Angeles police officer Scott James and his K-9 companion, Maggie, chase a suspect into an apparently empty building and are attacked. They discover their suspect is dead and the building he fled into is not at all empty—it is full of explosives. Here Scott and Maggie cross paths with private investigator Elvis. Their case seems to have a lot in common with the investigation being conducted by Elvis and PI Joe Pike. In an investigation that involves drug dealers, war veterans, and terrorists, all four—Elvis, Joe, Scott, and Maggie—must work together to hunt for the woman before she gets killed, or the killer gets them.

Other books by the same author:
Suspect, 2013
Taken, 2012
The Sentry, 2011

The First Rule, 2010
Chasing Darkness, 2008

Other books you might like:
Ace Atkins, *The Forsaken*, 2014
Ace Atkins, *Robert B. Parker's Kickback*, 2015
James Lee Burke, *Light of the World*, 2013
Stephen J. Cannell, *The Prostitutes' Ball*, 2010
Lee Child, *Personal*, 2014
Harlan Coben, *The Stranger*, 2015
Max Allan Collins, *Supreme Justice*, 2014
Michael Connelly, *City of Bones*, 2002
Michael Connelly, *The Lincoln Lawyer*, 2005
Tim Dorsey, *Shark Skin Suite*, 2015
Dennis Lehane, *World Gone By*, 2015
Maxine Paetro, *14th Deadly Sin*, 2015
T. Jefferson Parker, *L.A. Outlaws*, 2008
John Sandford, *Deadline*, 2014
John Sandford, *Gathering Prey*, 2015
Barbara Seranella, *No Human Involved*, 1997
John Shannon, *The Concrete River*, 1996
Mickey Spillane, *Kill Me, Darling*, 2015
Various Authors, *Inherit the Dead: A Novel*, 2013
Joseph Wambaugh, *Hollywood Station: A Novel*, 2006

721

MAYA SLOAN
CREATOR OF RICH KIDS OF INSTAGRAM, Co-Author

Rich Kids of Instagram
(New York: Gallery Books, 2014)

Story type: Contemporary; Satire
Subject(s): Satire; Wealth; Adolescence
Major character(s): Annalise Hoff, Teenager, Wealthy;
  Miller Crawford, Teenager, Wealthy; Desdemona
  Goldberg, Teenager, Wealthy; Philip Atwater,
  Teenager, Wealthy; Christian Rixen, Teenager,
  Wealthy; Cordelia Derby, Teenager, Wealthy; April
  Holiday, Teenager, Wealthy
Time period(s): 21st century; 2010s
Locale(s): United States

Summary: On the Instagram feed "Rich Kids of Insta-gram," super wealthy teenagers share photos of them-selves at wild parties, on exotic vacations, and engaged in extravagant shopping sprees. This novel provides a fictionalized version of the money-fueled, privileged lives of some of these super rich kids. The characters include Annalise Hoff, Miller Crawford, Desdemona Goldberg, Philip Atwater, Christian Rixen, Cordelia Derby, and April Holiday. Some are from old-money families; others are offspring of the newly rich, and as such, have more to prove in their social stratosphere. In this satirical coming-of-age novel, the rich kids take turns narrating the events of their lives, from driving Italian sports cars and throwing bashes in the Hamptons to hooking up with their significant others in their parents' Manhattan apartments.

Other books by the same author:
High Before Homeroom, 2010

Other books you might like:
Barbara Delinsky, *Looking for Peyton Place*, 2006
Dominick Dunne, *Too Much Money: A Novel*, 2009
Rachel Van Dyken, *Elite*, 2013
David Freeman, *It's All True*, 2004
Daniel Handler, *The Basic Eight*, 1999
Walter Kirn, *Mission to America*, 2005
Nicola Kraus, *Nanny Returns*, 2009
Alix Kates Shulman, *Menage*, 2012
Susan Waggoner, *Better than Chocolate*, 2005

722

DAVID CRONENBERG

Consumed
(New York: Scribner, 2014)

Story type: Literary
Subject(s): Horror; Science fiction; Technology
Major character(s): Naomi, Journalist; Nathan, Journalist;
  Celestine Arosteguy, Philosopher (Marxist), Spouse
  (of Aristide); Aristide Arosteguy, Philosopher (Marx-ist), Spouse (of Celestine); Herve Blomqvist,
  Student—Graduate; Zoltan Molnar, Doctor
  (unlicensed surgeon); Dr. Barry Roiphe, Doctor
Time period(s): 21st century; 2010s
Locale(s): Toronto, Canada; Paris, France; Budapest,
  Hungary

Summary: Journalists Naomi and Nathan travel the world searching for sensational stories. They are rivals, but that doesn't keep them from sleeping together when they are in the same city. Naomi is now in Paris, following a high-profile murder. Celestine Arosteguy has been found dead—and partially consumed—in the apartment she shared with her husband, Aristide. Since Aristide is nowhere to be found, he is the prime suspect. Naomi, accompanied by grad student Herve Blomqvist, searches for Aristide and discovers unsettling information about the couple's relationship. Meanwhile, Nathan is in Budapest researching another disturbing story. This one involves Zoltan Molnar, a surgeon who operates illegally and may be involved in the trafficking of human organs. When an ill-advised sexual encounter leaves Nathan with an uncommon disease, he seeks help from the Canadian doctor who is an expert on the condition. Eventually Naomi and Nathan realize that their stories are connected. First novel.

Other books by the same author:
The Brood, 1979

Other books you might like:
Cynthia Bond, *Ruby*, 2014
Douglas Clegg, *Dinner with the Cannibal Sisters*, 2014
Thomas Christopher Greene, *The Headmaster's Wife*,
  2014
Pete Hamill, *Tabloid City*, 2011
Herman Koch, *Summer House with Swimming Pool*,
  2014
Joyce Carol Oates, *High Crime Area*, 2014
Michael Palmer, *The Fifth Vial*, 2007
Tom Rachman, *The Imperfectionists: A Novel*, 2010
Anita Shreve, *Testimony*, 2008
Bryan Smith, *Depraved*, 2009

Popular Fiction

723

MICHAEL CRUMMEY

Sweetland

(New York: Liveright Publishing Corporation, 2015)

Story type: Contemporary
Subject(s): Islands; Neighborhoods; Family relations
Major character(s): Moses Sweetland, Man (Sweetland resident)
Time period(s): 21st century; 2010s
Locale(s): Sweetland, Newfoundland and Labrador

Summary: Positioned on a small island off the coast of Newfoundland, the sparsely-populated village of Sweetland is deteriorating. When the provincial government offers residents of the struggling island community resettlement money, there's only one condition: everyone must leave. Sixty-nine-year-old Moses Sweetland, a descendent of the island's founders, is the town's only holdout. While Sweetland's residents pack up and move out, Moses chooses to stay in his family's home, refusing to give in to neighbors' pressures and government bribes. Unable to imagine another way of life, Moses examines the island's weathered history, its quirky community of residents, family legends, and his own deep connection to land and sea. Moses's supplies diminish, and he struggles to survive, all the while observing the steady decline of his beloved village and its surroundings.

Other books by the same author:
Galore, 2009
The Wreckage, 2005
River Thieves, 2002
Flesh and Blood: Selected Short Fiction, 1998

Other books you might like:
Amy Bloom, *Lucky Us*, 2014
Marjorie Celona, *Y*, 2013
Tatiana de Rosnay, *The House I Loved*, 2012
Junot Diaz, *The Brief Wondrous Life of Oscar Wao*, 2007
Louise Erdrich, *The Round House*, 2012
Nuruddin Farah, *Knots*, 2007
Alice Hoffman, *Blackbird House*, 2004
Steena Holmes, *Stillwater Rising*, 2014
Emma Hooper, *Etta and Otto and Russell and James*, 2015
Deborah Levy, *Swimming Home*, 2012
Emily St. John Mandel, *Station Eleven*, 2014
Margaret Mazzantini, *Morning Sea*, 2015
Per Petterson, *I Refuse*, 2014
Caryl Phillips, *The Lost Child*, 2015
Marilynne Robinson, *Lila*, 2014
Paulo Scott, *Nowhere People*, 2014
Mary Helen Specht, *Migratory Animals*, 2015
Edward St. Aubyn, *On the Edge*, 2014
Alex Taylor, *The Marble Orchard*, 2014
Denis Theriault, *The Peculiar Life of a Lonely Postman*, 2015
Zoe Wicomb, *October*, 2014

724

RACHEL CUSK

Outline

(New York: Farrar, Straus and Giroux, 2015)

Story type: Literary
Subject(s): Interpersonal relations; Women; Writers
Major character(s): Faye, Writer, Teacher, Narrator; Ryan, Professor; Paniotis, Friend (of Faye); Angeliki, Friend (of Faye)
Time period(s): 21st century; 2010s
Locale(s): Athens, Greece

Summary: This novel by Rachel Cusk is presented through a series of ten conversations. The first is between Faye, the writer who is the central figure and narrator of the novel, and the Greek businessman she is seated next to on a flight from London to Athens. Faye does most of the listening as the man tells the story of his personal and professional life. She is well aware that she is hearing a carefully edited version of the truth. In Athens, where she is teaching a summer writing class, Faye interacts again with her former seatmate and also with students, faculty, and her local friends, Paniotis and Angeliki. It is through the conversations Faye has with this diverse cast of characters that the reader comes to understand Faye's backstory.

Other books by the same author:
The Bradshaw Variations, 2010
Arlington Park, 2006
In the Fold, 2005
The Lucky Ones, 2003
The Country Life, 1997

Other books you might like:
Paul Auster, *The Red Notebook*, 2013
Russell Banks, *Lost Memory of Skin*, 2011
Don DeLillo, *The Angel Esmeralda: Nine Stories*, 2011
Andre Dubus III, *The Garden of Last Days: A Novel*, 2008
Sebastian Faulks, *A Week in December*, 2009
Paolo Giordano, *The Solitude of Prime Numbers*, 2010
Hari Kunzru, *Gods Without Men*, 2011
Reif Larsen, *I Am Radar*, 2015
Ian McEwan, *The Children Act*, 2014
Jose Saramago, *Skylight*, 2014
Lionel Shriver, *Big Brother*, 2013
Laura van den Berg, *Find Me*, 2015

725

CLIVE CUSSLER
DIRK CUSSLER, Co-Author

Havana Storm

(New York: Penguin Group, 2014)

Series: Dirk Pitt Series. Book 23
Story type: Psychological Suspense; Series
Subject(s): Communism; Politics; Suspense
Major character(s): Dirk Pitt, Adventurer, Father (of Dirk

Jr. and Summer); Summer Pitt, Daughter (of Dirk), Sister (of Dirk Jr.), Scientist (oceanographer); Dirk Pitt Jr., Brother (of Summer), Son (of Dirk), Scientist (marine biologist)

Time period(s): 21st century; 2010s
Locale(s): At Sea; Cuba

Summary: Marine adventurer Dirk Pitt is probing an incident off the coast of Cuba. During his investigation into the tragedy, which could eventually put the United States in jeopardy, Dirk finds himself embroiled in Cuban politics when the death of Fidel Castro sends the country into a tailspin. As Dirk attempts to extricate himself from the situation, his son and daughter—Dirk Jr., a marine biologist, and Summer, an oceanographer—have troubles of their own. They are trying to track down an ancient artifact that could lead them to untold wealth. When they learn that the artifact might have sunk prior to the Spanish-American War in 1898, they head to the coast of Cuba and land in the middle of the clash. Now the Pitts must figure out how to talk their way out of a situation that may not only put their own lives at stake, but also bring the United States in direct conflict with Cuba. This novel is the 23rd in the Dirk Pitt series.

Other books by the same author:
The Assassin, 2015
Piranha, 2015
The Bootlegger, 2014
The Eye of Heaven, 2014
Ghost Ship, 2014

Other books you might like:
Will Adams, *The Alexander Cipher*, 2007
Steve Berry, *The Templar Legacy*, 2006
Paul Christopher, *Secret of the Templars*, 2015
Clive Cussler, *Lost City*, 2004
Charles Flemingz, *After Havana*, 2004
Carolina Garcia-Aguilera, *Havana Heat: A Lupe Solano Mystery*, 2000
Mark Greaney, *Tom Clancy Full Force and Effect*, 2014
Eric L. Haney, *No Man's Land*, 2010
Iris Johansen, *Fatal Tide*, 2003
Jose Latour, *Comrades in Miami*, 2005
Leonardo Padura, *Havana Red*, 2005
Barbara Parker, *Suspicion of Rage*, 2005
Ridley Pearson, *The Risk Agent*, 2012
David Poyer, *The Whitness of the Whale*, 2013
Matthew Reilly, *The Five Greatest Warriors: A Novel*, 2010
James Rollins, *Sandstorm*, 2004
Peter Tonkin, *Mariner's Ark*, 2015

726

JOHN DARNIELLE

Wolf in White Van

(New York: Farrar, Straus and Giroux, 2014)

Story type: Literary; Psychological
Subject(s): Psychology; Games; Accidents
Major character(s): Sean Phillips, Narrator, Recluse, Accident Victim (disfigured), Inventor (game); Lance,

Student—High School; Carrie, Student—High School
Time period(s): 21st century; 2010s
Locale(s): California, United States; Florida, United States

Summary: A reclusive game inventor narrates this novel by John Darnielle, a musician with the American band the Mountain Goats. Sean Phillips is the author of Trace Italian, a fantasy game played through the mail that draws participants into imaginary realms. Phillips created the game to fill the time he spent recovering from an accident he suffered in his teens. His facial scars prompted him to withdraw from society for more than a decade. Now in his thirties, Phillips connects with the outside world through Trace Italian. But Phillips's isolated world is compromised when two of Trace Italian's players are harmed while playing the game. As a trial looms, truths about Phillips's story begin to come to light. It seems that the narrator may have had a greater hand in creating his insular world than he first let on. First novel.

Awards the book has won:
Alex Awards, 2015

Other books you might like:
Ellery Adams, *Murder in the Mystery Suite*, 2014
Isabel Allende, *Ripper*, 2014
Madison Smartt Bell, *The Color of Night*, 2011
Sarah Bird, *Above the East China Sea*, 2014
Chris Bohjalian, *Close Your Eyes, Hold Hands*, 2014
John Brandon, *A Million Heavens*, 2012
James Dashner, *The Eye of Minds*, 2013
Cory Doctorow, *Makers*, 2009
Austin Grossman, *You*, 2013
Bret Anthony Johnston, *Remember Me Like This*, 2014
Courtney Elizabeth Mauk, *Orion's Daughters*, 2014
Celeste Ng, *Everything I Never Told You*, 2014
Joyce Carol Oates, *Mudwoman*, 2012
Michael Olson, *Strange Flesh*, 2012
Robert Rotstein, *Reckless Disregard*, 2014
Zadie Smith, *NW: A Novel*, 2012
David Vann, *Dirt*, 2012

727

LINDA DAVIES

Ark Storm

(New York: Tom Doherty Associates, 2014)

Story type: Science Fiction; Techno-Thriller
Subject(s): Weather; Terrorism; Meteorology
Major character(s): Gwen Boudain, Scientist (meteorologist), Companion (of Dan); Dan Jacobsen, Companion (of Gwen), Journalist; Gabriel Messenger, Businessman; Ali Al Baharna, Wealthy, Terrorist
Time period(s): 21st century; 2010s
Locale(s): California, United States

Summary: Meteorologist Gwen Boudain sees more than storms brewing off the California coast: She sees devastation. Gwen has discovered a weather phenomenon known as an ARK storm, rivers of super moist air in the atmosphere capable of spawning catastrophic weather conditions. But nature is not the only deadly force at work. The company funding Gwen's research has developed a cloud-seeding technology capable of creating man-made rain, and a wealthy Arab jihadist wants to use it to turn the ARK storm into a weapon. When Gwen and newspaper reporter Dan Jacobsen discover the conspiracy, they find themselves on the run and their lives in danger. Together they must stay alive long enough to uncover the truth behind the deadly plan, and put a stop to it before millions are killed.

Other books by the same author:
Into the Fire, 1999
Wilderness of Mirrors, 1996
Nest of Vipers, 1995

Other books you might like:
Tom Clancy, *Against All Enemies*, 2011
Michael Crichton, *Micro*, 2011
Jim DeFelice, *Rogue Warrior: Curse of the Infidel*, 2014
Tom Grace, *The Secret Cardinal*, 2007
James W. Hall, *The Big Finish*, 2014
Anthony Horowitz, *Oblivion*, 2013
Robert Knott, *Robert B. Parker's The Bridge*, 2014
James Rollins, *The Kill Switch: A Tucker Wayne Novel*, 2014
John Sandford, *Deadline*, 2014
Brad Thor, *Act of War*, 2014

728

BRIDGETT M. DAVIS

Into the Go-Slow

(New York: The Feminist Press at CUNY, 2014)

Story type: Literary
Subject(s): Sisters; Interpersonal relations; Africa
Major character(s): Angie, 21-Year-Old, Sister (of Ella), Traveler; Ella, Sister (of Angie, deceased)
Time period(s): 20th century; 1960s-1980s
Locale(s): Nigeria; Detroit, Michigan

Summary: The year is 1986, and Angie has been mourning the death of her sister, Ella, for four years. Angie feels that she cannot find closure without taking radical steps, so the 21-year-old woman packs her bags and leaves Detroit for Nigeria, the place where Ella died. Although Ella was beautiful and brilliant, she had some radical ideas and struggled with addiction, which ultimately took her life. The novel explores the sisters' lives in Detroit from the 1960s to the 1980s, and Ella's time in Nigeria during the 1980s. As Angie follows her sister's footsteps, she learns a great deal about herself as well. She eventually realizes that she might be able to move forward in life after all. The political atmosphere of Nigeria as well as the issues of race and the culture of "being black" are coupled with grief, loss, love, and forgiveness on Angie's journey.

Other books by the same author:
Shifting through Neutral, 2004

Other books you might like:
Chimamanda Ngozi Adichie, *Americanah*, 2013
Kate Atkinson, *A God in Ruins*, 2015

J.M. Coetzee, *Diary of a Bad Year*, 2007
Teju Cole, *Every Day Is for the Thief*, 2014
Jeffrey Eugenides, *The Marriage Plot*, 2011
Karen Joy Fowler, *We Are All Completely Beside Ourselves*, 2013
Claire Messud, *The Last Life*, 1999
Zadie Smith, *NW: A Novel*, 2012
Amy Tan, *The Valley of Amazement*, 2013
S.J. Watson, *Second Life*, 2015

729

BROOKE DAVIS

Lost and Found

(New York: Dutton, 2015)

Story type: Contemporary
Subject(s): Children; Grief; Reunions
Major character(s): Millie Bird, 7-Year-Old, Abandoned Child; Agatha Pantha, Aged Person, Rescuer (of Millie Bird), Traveler (with Karl), Widow(er); Karl, Aged Person, Runaway (from nursing home), Rescuer (of Millie Bird), Traveler (with Agatha Pantha), Widow(er)
Time period(s): 21st century; 2010s
Locale(s): Australia

Summary: Millie Bird, who is seven years old, has bright red hair and boots to match. She lives in Australia with her mother, who has been suffering from intense grief and depression since the death of Millie's father. One day her mother abandons Millie in a department store. It is only by chance that Millie is rescued by two people who are just as much in need of a savior as she is. Agatha Pantha is 82 years old. Since the death of her husband seven years ago, Agatha has become a shut-in, consumed by grief and bitterness. Karl is a widower as well. He used to communicate with his wife by finger-typing messages onto her skin. He has been living in a nursing home, wallowing in his memories and loss, until he finally escapes. When the three lost souls connect, the adults are determined to return Millie to her mother and reunite the broken family. As they make this journey, Millie's youthful exuberance and mischievous heart bring healing to her new friends.

Other books you might like:
Fannie Flagg, *The All-Girl Filling Station's Last Reunion*, 2013
Rachel Joyce, *The Love Song of Miss Queenie Hennessy*, 2015
Sandra Kring, *The Book of Bright Ideas*, 2006
Joyce Carol Oates, *Missing Mom*, 2005
Carolyn Parkhurst, *Lost and Found*, 2006
Per Petterson, *I Refuse*, 2014
Francine Prose, *Goldengrove*, 2008
Ann B. Ross, *Miss Julia's Marvelous Makeover*, 2014
Neil Smith, *Boo*, 2015
Lolly Winston, *Happiness Sold Separately*, 2006
Desiree Zamorano, *The Amado Women*, 2014

730

PAULA TREICK DEBOARD

The Fragile World

(Toronto: Mira Publishing, 2014)

Story type: Family Saga
Subject(s): Death; Family; Father-daughter relations
Major character(s): Curtis Kaufman, Teacher, Father (of Olivia and Daniel), Spouse (former, of Kathleen); Olivia Kaufman, Teenager, Daughter (of Curtis, Kathleen), Sister (of Daniel); Kathleen Kaufman, Spouse (former, of Curtis), Mother (of Olivia and Daniel); Daniel Kaufman, Son (of Curtis and Kathleen), Accident Victim, Brother (of Olivia), Student—College
Time period(s): 21st century; 2010s
Locale(s): United States; Sacramento, California

Summary: On the surface, the Kaufmans seem to be the picture-perfect image of a family. Curtis is a high school science teacher; Kathleen restores furniture; their daughter, Olivia, is a typical 12-year-old; and their son, Daniel, is attending college on a music scholarship. But the family's world is shattered when Daniel is killed in a bizarre hit-and-run accident. The grief of his death destroys the family, inside and outside. Five years later, Curtis and Kathleen are divorced, and Olivia is consumed by her phobias. When Curtis hears the man responsible for Daniel's death is being released from prison, he breaks down. Packing up Olivia in the car, he hits the road, intent on revenge. As the pair get closer to their goal, and father and daughter begin to bond, they may just rediscover something they thought they lost.

Other books by the same author:
The Mourning Hours, 2013

Other books you might like:
Dorothea Benton Frank, *Folly Beach*, 2010
Pete Hamill, *North River*, 2007
Wally Lamb, *We Are Water*, 2013
Jandy Nelson, *I'll Give You the Sun*, 2014
Jodi Picoult, *Lone Wolf*, 2012
Christopher Scotton, *The Secret Wisdom of the Earth*, 2015
Elizabeth Strout, *Olive Kitteridge*, 2008
Joanna Trollope, *The Other Family: A Novel*, 2010
Anne Tyler, *A Spool of Blue Thread*, 2015
David Wroblewski, *The Story of Edgar Sawtelle: A Novel*, 2008

731

LUCY DILLON

A Hundred Pieces of Me

(London: Hodder & Stoughton Ltd., 2014)

Story type: Contemporary; Literary
Subject(s): Divorce; Cancer; Conduct of life
Major character(s): Gina Bellamy, Divorced Person, Spouse (ex, of Stuart), Cancer Patient (former); Stuart Bellamy, Divorced Person, Spouse (ex, of Gina)
Time period(s): 21st century; 2010s
Locale(s): England

Summary: When Gina Bellamy's husband announces to her that he is leaving her for another woman, she becomes melancholy but is not devastated by the news. After all, she recently beat breast cancer, so she's certain she can weather a divorce from a man from whom she has grown apart over the past several years. Gina leaves her marriage and her home behind, and moves into a small apartment with very little space to spare. There, she realizes that many of her belongings are just items to which she feels no personal connection, things that are just taking up space. She makes a solemn vow to part with all but 100 of her most prized possessions, yet letting go of objects proves to be more difficult than she imagines. Now, as Gina notes each item she keeps, she remembers its importance and how it symbolizes specific times in her life that have shaped who she was, and who she wants to become.

Other books by the same author:
The Secret of Happy Ever After, 2013
Lost Dogs and Lonely Hearts, 2011
Walking Back to Happiness, 2011

Other books you might like:
Mary Kay Andrews, *Ladies' Night*, 2013
Laura Dave, *Eight Hundred Grapes*, 2015
Wendy Francis, *Three Good Things*, 2013
Emily Giffin, *The One and Only*, 2014
Beth Harbison, *Driving with the Top Down*, 2014
Elin Hilderbrand, *The Matchmaker*, 2014
Gil McNeil, *A Good Year for the Roses*, 2014
Kristina Riggle, *Keepsake*, 2012
Anne Rivers Siddons, *Off Season*, 2008
Haywood Smith, *Queen Bee Goes Home Again*, 2014
Kristin von Kreisler, *An Unexpected Grace*, 2013

732

KEITH DONOHUE

The Boy Who Drew Monsters

(New York: Picador, 2014)

Story type: Ghost Story; Horror
Subject(s): Family; Parent-child relations; Monsters
Major character(s): Jack Peter Keenan, 10-Year-Old, Boy, Autistic (Asperger syndrome), Son (of Holly and Tim), Friend (of Nick); Holly Keenan, Spouse (of Tim), Mother (of Jack); Tim Keenan, Spouse (of Holly), Father (of Jack); Nick, Boy, Friend (of Jack); Miss Tiramaku, Housekeeper
Time period(s): 21st century; 2010s
Locale(s): Maine, United States

Summary: Since Jack Peter Keenan nearly drowned in the ocean three years earlier, the 10-year-old autistic boy has been afraid to leave home. His parents hope their son's new interest in drawing will be a successful means of therapy and help him to overcome his fear. But something strange begins to happen. The monsters Jack draws begin appearing in their Maine community, manifesting

Popular Fiction

themselves as horrifying visions of beast-men, deformed children, and mysterious apparitions. As Jack's drawings begin to take a darker turn, those closest to him are caught in the growing insanity. His mother hears strange sounds emanating from the ocean at night, his father wanders the beach chasing ghosts, and his best friend is getting dangerously close to the truth. In desperation, his mother seeks answers from a mysterious woman, who may know the roots of Jack's ability.

Other books by the same author:
Centuries of June, 2011
Angels of Destruction, 2009
The Stolen Child, 2006

Other books you might like:
Jonathan Aycliffe, *The Silence of Ghosts*, 2015
John Boyne, *This House Is Haunted*, 2013
Justin Evans, *The White Devil*, 2011
Joe Hill, *Heart-Shaped Box*, 2007
Ann Hite, *The Storycatcher*, 2013
Rebecca James, *Sweet Damage*, 2014
Simone St. James, *An Inquiry into Love and Death*, 2013
Garth Stein, *A Sudden Light*, 2014
Peter Straub, *Mrs. God*, 2012
Martyn Waites, *The Woman in Black*, 2014
Sarah Waters, *The Little Stranger*, 2009

733

TIM DORSEY

Shark Skin Suite

(New York: HarperCollins, 2015)

Series: Serge Storms Series. Book 18
Story type: Contemporary; Humor
Subject(s): Law; Friendship; Humor
Major character(s): Serge Storms, Historian, Serial Killer, Lawyer (unlicensed); Brook Campanella, Lawyer, Friend (of Serge)
Time period(s): 21st century; 2010s
Locale(s): Florida, United States

Summary: The eighteenth Serge Storms novel continues the hijinks of the charming serial killer and psychopathic Floridian. Serge, an avid local historian, has realized that he has the potential to be a successful lawyer crusading against corrupt banks. Despite the fact that he is not educated in law or certified by the Bar, he throws his talents and passion into the experience. He trains for the occupation through extensive viewings of television crime dramas and law-oriented films. Uncovering scams and cons across the state is a thrill for Serge and he jumps into the mortgage fraud fray. His former girlfriend, Brook Campanella, has recently passed the Bar and taken up a criminal case against the power banking company Consolidated Financial. Consolidated Financial isn't afraid to fight dirty to dodge punishment. Brook is struggling in court until Serge shows up to help her out and dispense his own particular brand of justice and wisdom.

Other books by the same author:
Tiger Shrimp Tango, 2014
The Riptide Ultra-Glide, 2013

Pineapple Grenade, 2012
Electric Barracuda, 2011
When Elves Attack, 2011

Other books you might like:
H. Lee Barnes, *Cold Deck*, 2013
Dave Barry, *Insane City*, 2013
Jim Butcher, *Skin Game: A Novel of the Dresden Files*, 2014
Paul Cleave, *Joe Victim*, 2013
Robert Crais, *The Promise*, 2014
Michael Dibdin, *Cosi Fan Tutti*, 1996
Rick Gavin, *Nowhere Nice*, 2013
Dennis Hart, *Gulf Boulevard*, 2014
Carl Hiassen, *Skink—No Surrender*, 2014
Steve Israel, *The Global War on Morris*, 2015
Jeff Lindsay, *Dexter Is Dead*, 2015
Lydia Millet, *Mermaids in Paradise*, 2014

734

MARK DOTEN

The Infernal

(Minneapolis, Minnesota: Graywolf Press, 2015)

Story type: Political
Subject(s): Middle East; Wars; Terrorism
Major character(s): L. Paul Bremer, Historical Figure, Military Personnel, Political Figure; Dick Cheney, Political Figure, Historical Figure; Condoleezza Rice, Historical Figure, Political Figure; Mark Zuckerberg, Computer Expert, Inventor, Historical Figure; Osama bin Laden, Historical Figure, Terrorist; Akkad Boy, Boy, Psychic; Mark Doten, Narrator
Time period(s): 21st century; 2000s
Locale(s): Iraq

Summary: This debut novel by Mark Doten is a unique look at the history of the war on terror through the eyes of an unlikely subject. It is the beginning of the 21st century, and the events of 9/11 have incited a war between the United States and Iraq. One sweltering day, a young boy is found deep within the Akkad Valley. He has burns all over his body, and the US troops who find him have no idea where he came from. An expert is brought in to torture the child under the guise of interrogating him. Out of this experience, the boy gives voice to significant personalities of the era, including political figures such as Dick Cheney and Condoleezza Rice, military personnel like L. Paul Bremer, who led the US invasion of Iraq, people in popular culture like Facebook inventor Mark Zuckerberg, and some of the world's most notorious terrorists, including Osama bin Laden. Doten includes his own persona as a narrator of the novel. First novel.

Other books you might like:
Pearl Abraham, *American Taliban: A Novel*, 2010
Hassan Blasim, *The Corpse Exhibition and Other Stories of Iraq*, 2014
Marilyn Bowering, *What it Takes to Be Human*, 2006
Peter Hoeg, *The Elephant Keepers' Children*, 2012
Adam Johnson, *The Orphan Master's Son*, 2012

Mike McCormack, *Notes From a Coma*, 2013
Mike Meginnis, *Fat Man and Little Boy*, 2014
Ana Menendez, *The Last War*, 2009
David Mitchell, *Cloud Atlas*, 2004
Haruki Murakami, *IQ84*, 2011

735

DAVID DUCHOVNY

Holy Cow

(New York: Farrar, Straus, and Giroux, 2015)

Story type: Humor; Satire
Subject(s): Cows (Cattle); Freedom; Social conditions
Major character(s): Elsie Bovary, Cow; Unnamed Character, Farmer; Shalom, Pig; Tom, Bird (turkey)
Time period(s): 21st century; 2010s
Locale(s): New York, United States

Summary: Elsie Bovary spends much of her time standing in a field nibbling grass and gossiping with a pal. Her life isn't wasted, however; she is, after all, a cow. Elsie contends that cows are pretty smart, and she proves it one night when she wanders over to her farmer's home. Elsie spies on him through the window as he watches a lighted cube in his living room. While peeking into the farmer's window, Elsie sees a documentary about factory farms, and she is horrified to realize that she, and probably the other animals in the barnyard as well, are destined for the same fate as the animals on television. Now, with the help of a Jewish pig named Shalom and a technologically savvy turkey named Tom, Elsie flees from the farm. Yet she realizes that her work isn't finished when she saves only herself, so she sets off on a mission to create a better world for all humans, as well as all of bovine-kind.

Other books you might like:
W. Bruce Cameron, *A Dog's Purpose*, 2010
Son-mi Hwang, *The Hen Who Dreamed She Could Fly*, 2013
Andrew Kaufman, *The Tiny Wife*, 2014
Mark Laxer, *The Monkey Bible*, 2010
George Orwell, *Animal Farm*, 1954
Laline Paull, *The Bees*, 2014
Robert Rankin, *The Hollow Chocolate Bunnies of the Apocalypse*, 2004
Robert Repino, *Mort(e)*, 2015
Josh Ritter, *Bright's Passage*, 2011
Sam Savage, *Firmin: Adventures of a Metropolitan Lowlife*, 2006

736

MARIA DUENAS

The Heart Has Its Reasons

(New York: Atria Books, 2014)

Story type: Literary
Subject(s): Infidelity; College environment; Writers
Major character(s): Blanca Perea, Woman, Professor (linguistics), Divorced Person, Friend (of Daniel); Daniel Carter, Professor, Friend (of Blanca)
Time period(s): 20th century; 1990s (1999)
Locale(s): Madrid, Spain; California, United States

Summary: With a job as a linguistics professor at Madrid university, a husband, and two grown children, Blanca Perea's life seems to be on solid ground. But that life comes to a crashing halt when her husband of 20 years runs off with another woman—a woman who is carrying his child. Suddenly questioning everything about her life, the devastated Blanca decides she needs a change. She accepts a job at a university in California to research the life of Andres Fontana, a Spanish writer who has been dead for 30 years. As she becomes immersed in Fontana's world, a charming professor named Daniel Carter enters hers. The two men, she discovers, share a connection, and as she continues to investigate both their lives, she just may find answers for her own.

Other books by the same author:
The Time In Between, 2011

Other books you might like:
Carellin Brooks, *One Hundred Days of Rain*, 2015
Richard Ford, *Let Me Be Frank with You*, 2014
Amy Greene, *Long Man*, 2014
Stephanie Kallos, *Language Arts*, 2015
Ian McEwan, *The Children Act*, 2014
Per Petterson, *I Refuse*, 2014
Melissa Pritchard, *Palmerino*, 2014
Marilynne Robinson, *Lila*, 2014
Zadie Smith, *NW: A Novel*, 2012
Mario Vargas Llosa, *The Discreet Hero*, 2015

737

ROBERT DUGONI

My Sister's Grave

(Seattle, Washington: Thomas & Mercer, 2014)

Series: Tracy Crosswhite Series. Book 1
Story type: Mystery; Police Procedural
Subject(s): Law enforcement; Sisters; Murder
Major character(s): Tracy Crosswhite, Detective—Homicide, Sister (of Sarah); Sarah Crosswhite, Sister (of Tracy), Crime Victim; Edmund House, Convict
Time period(s): 21st century; 2010s
Locale(s): Washington, United States; Seattle, Washington

Summary: In the first installment of the Tracy Crosswhite series, author Robert Dugoni introduces readers to a homicide investigator for the Seattle Police Department. More than two decades ago, Tracy Crosswhite's sister, Sarah, was murdered. A local man named Edmund House was tried and convicted of the crime, but Tracy never really believed that Edmund was the killer. Her continued quest for justice was the impetus behind joining the Seattle Police Department, and it led Tracy on her career path to investigate murders. When Sarah's skeleton is found in the mountains surrounding the city, Tracy finally gets a break in the one cold case she is determined to solve. She is certain that she will not only be able to prove that Edmund is innocent, but that she will also find out what happened all those years ago. Unfortunately, someone wants to keep the truth buried, and he or she is willing to kill again to keep the facts from being unearthed.

Other books by the same author:
The Conviction, 2012
Murder One, 2011
Bodily Harm, 2010
Wrongful Death, 2009
Damage Control, 2007

Other books you might like:
C.J. Box, *The Highway*, 2013
Allison Brennan, *Playing Dead*, 2008
Diane Chamberlain, *The Silent Sister*, 2014
Alison Gaylin, *Stay with Me*, 2014
Tess Gerritsen, *Die Again*, 2014
Valentina Giambanco, *The Gift of the Darkness*, 2014
Lisa Jackson, *Deserves to Die*, 2014
J.A. Jance, *Dead Wrong*, 2006
Laura Lippman, *Hush Hush*, 2015
Maxine Paetro, *14th Deadly Sin*, 2015

738

DAVE EGGERS

Your Fathers, Where Are They? And the Prophets, Do They Live Forever?

(New York: Alfred A. Knopf, 2014)

Story type: Contemporary; Political
Subject(s): Hostages; Politics; Economics
Major character(s): Thomas, Man (captor); Kev, Captive, Astronaut
Time period(s): 21st century; 2010s
Locale(s): California, United States

Summary: Best-selling author Dave Eggers delivers a tale about one man's attempt to resolve his personal, political, and economic grievances with the US government. A troubled man named Thomas holds Kev, a NASA astronaut, hostage on an abandoned military base in California. Bound by chains, Kev screams for help as Thomas begins his interrogation. Thomas, who considers himself a moral, principled man, asks Kev questions about various abuses of the US government and its institutions. While Thomas resents the government for its biased priorities, he depends on its institutions to provide his life with purpose. Thomas's questioning of Kev leads to subsequent interrogations of additional captives, some with whom Thomas is abusive. Among the additional captives are a former congressman, an elementary school teacher, a police officer, and Thomas's mother. Composed entirely of dialogue, this novel raises questions about war, education, pedophilia, police brutality, and justice.

Other books by the same author:
The Circle, 2013
The Wild Things, 2009

What Is the What, 2006
How We Are Hungry: Stories, 2004

Other books you might like:
John Brandon, *Further Joy*, 2014
Aaron Elkins, *The Worst Thing*, 2011
Chris Ewan, *Dead Line*, 2014
Joshua Ferris, *To Rise Again at a Decent Hour*, 2014
Michael Gruber, *The Book of Air and Shadows: A Novel*, 2007
S.M. Hulse, *Black River*, 2015
Denis Johnson, *The Laughing Monsters*, 2014
Chuck Klosterman, *The Visible Man*, 2011
Cormac McCarthy, *The Sunset Limited*, 2006
Donna Tartt, *The Goldfinch*, 2013

739

JILL ALEXANDER ESSBAUM

Hausfrau

(New York: Random House, 2015)

Story type: Literary; Psychological
Subject(s): Women; Marriage; Family
Major character(s): Anna Benz, Woman (American), Spouse (of Bruno), Mother (of three children); Bruno Benz, Banker, Spouse (of Anna), Father (of three children); Dr. Messerli, Psychologist
Time period(s): 21st century; 2010s
Locale(s): Zurich, Switzerland

Summary: Anna Benz has been living in Zurich for nine years with her banker husband, Bruno, and their three children. But in that time Anna, who is American, has not made any friends in her neighborhood or made an attempt to learn Swiss German, the local language. Anna's life looks ideal to outsiders, but she feels empty and disconnected. Things change when she sees a psychologist, Dr. Messerli, and takes a language course. Anna's world opens up, but she shocks herself when she finds out how far she is willing to go to change her life. She takes several lovers, but she struggles emotionally when each affair comes to an end. Being unfaithful to Bruno is easier than Anna expected, but she now must face the fact that she is no longer the good wife she believed herself to be. First novel.

Other books you might like:
Anita Brookner, *Hotel Du Lac*, 1984
Anthony Doerr, *All the Light We Cannot See*, 2014
Janet Fitch, *White Oleander*, 1999
Gustave Flaubert, *Madame Bovary*, 1857
Paula Hawkins, *The Girl on the Train*, 2015
Cathy Lamb, *What I Remember Most*, 2014
Liane Moriarty, *Big Little Lies*, 2014
Liane Moriarty, *What Alice Forgot*, 2011
Leo Tolstoy, *Anna Karenina*, 1877
Ellen Marie Wiseman, *What She Left Behind*, 2013

740

MICHEL FABER

The Book of Strange New Things

(New York: Hogarth, 2014)

Subject(s): Space colonies; Missionaries; Romances (Fiction)
Major character(s): Peter, Religious (Christian missionary), Spouse (husband, of Bea); Beatrice "Bea", Spouse (wife, of Peter)
Time period(s): Indeterminate Future
Locale(s): Oasis, Outer Space; United Kingdom

Summary: This futuristic tale from award-winning and best-selling author Michel Faber is a story of faith, love, suffering, and redemption. Christian missionary Peter travels to a distant galaxy to share his faith with the inhabitants of the planet Oasis, while his wife, Beatrice "Bea," remains at home on Earth. Peter quickly immerses himself in his new mission field, a land owned by a mysterious company known as USIC. While the natives of the planet, called Oasans, battle a fatal, widespread sickness, Bea sends word to Peter of the horrific apocalyptic events occurring on Earth. The Oasans find hope in Peter's teachings from the Bible, but back home, in the midst of devastation and destruction, Bea questions the beliefs she once held firmly. Threatened by the distance between them, the love between Peter and Bea is tested on all fronts, and Peter must choose between his two worlds—the old and the new.

Other books by the same author:
The Apple: Crimson Petal Stories, 2011
The Fire Gospel, 2008
Vanilla Bright Like Eminem, 2007
The Courage Consult, 2004
The Crimson Petal and the White, 2002

Other books you might like:
Martin Amis, *The Zone of Interest*, 2014
Margaret Atwood, *MaddAddam*, 2013
Quan Barry, *She Weeps Each Time You're Born*, 2015
Jim Crace, *The Pesthouse*, 2007
Nomi Eve, *Henna House*, 2014
Tom McCarthy, *Satin Island*, 2015
Walter M. Miller, *A Canticle for Leibowitz*, 1959
David Mitchell, *The Bone Clocks*, 2014
Sandra Newman, *The Country of Ice Cream Star*, 2014
Benjamin Percy, *The Dead Lands*, 2015
Marilynne Robinson, *Lila*, 2014
Mary Doria Russell, *The Sparrow*, 1996
Karen Thompson Walker, *The Age of Miracles*, 2012
Jeanette Winterson, *The Stone Gods*, 2007

741

NURUDDIN FARAH

Hiding in Plain Sight

(New York: Penguin Random House, 2014)

Story type: Contemporary; Ethnic
Subject(s): Africa; Photography; Women

Major character(s): Bella, Sister (half, of Aar), Photographer, Aunt (of Salif and Dahaba); Salif, Nephew (of Bella), Son (of Aar and Valerie), Brother (of Dahaba); Dahaba, Niece (of Bella), Sister (of Salif), Daughter (of Aar and Valerie); Valerie, Mother (of Salif and Dahaba), Spouse (of Aar); Aar, Spouse (of Valerie), Man (deceased), Brother (half, of Bella), Father (of Salif and Dahaba)
Time period(s): 21st century; 2010s
Locale(s): Nairobi, Kenya

Summary: Bella is a world-renowned, globe-trotting fashion photographer. Her lifestyle affords her all the luxuries she can imagine, which makes her far removed from her mother's homeland of Somalia. When she learns that her half-brother, Aar, has died in a terrorist bombing, she is called to his home in Nairobi to take charge of his children, Salif and Dahaba. Bella reluctantly accepts her responsibility to her family, but soon learns what beautiful and wonderful children her niece and nephew are. Then their estranged mother, Valerie, returns to the city, and throws the family into chaos once again. Meanwhile, the region experiences unrest at the hands of forces rebelling against the government, and staying in Nairobi becomes a security issue. As Bella struggles with her new life, she must also make a choice about how much of an influence she wants to be to Aar's children, and how much she can protect them.

Other books by the same author:
Crossbones, 2011
Knots, 2007
Links, 2004
Gifts, 1999
Maps, 1999

Other books you might like:
Molly Antopol, *The UnAmericans*, 2014
Nawal El Saadawi, *Zeina*, 2011
Nathan Englander, *The Ministry of Special Cases*, 2007
Adam Foulds, *In the Wolf's Mouth*, 2014
Ru Freeman, *On Sal Mal Lane*, 2013
Amina Gautier, *Now We Will Be Happy*, 2014
Wendy Guerra, *Everyone Leaves*, 2012
Okey Ndibe, *Foreign Gods, Inc.*, 2014
Ann Packer, *The Children's Crusade*, 2015
Rachel Seiffert, *The Walk Home*, 2014

742

DAN FESPERMAN

Unmanned

(New York: Knopf Doubleday Publishing Group, 2014)

Story type: Military
Subject(s): Airplanes; Air travel; Aircraft accidents
Major character(s): Darwin Cole, Pilot (former), Military Personnel
Time period(s): 21st century; 2010s
Locale(s): United States

Summary: Former Air Force pilot Darwin Cole will forever remember the moment his life changed because his greatest mistake cannot be forgotten. After gunning down an innocent Afghan child while piloting a drone,

Popular Fiction

Cole was discharged from the military and has since lived in shame. Then a group of reporters comes to Cole with some new information about that horrible day. They reveal that Cole's mistake actually may have been ordered from above. Unfortunately, cracking the case is not as easy as Cole thinks. The military is not eager to admit its mistakes, nor is it willing to clear Cole's name as the scapegoat. Cole learns that the drones and other military weapons that he always believed worked toward the greater good are in fact working against him. Even worse, he finds out that he is constantly being watched by the very hi-tech equipment that he thought would save the world.

Other books by the same author:
The Double Game, 2012
Layover in Dubai, 2010
The Arms Maker of Berlin, 2009
The Amateur Spy, 2007
The Small Boat of Great Sorrows, 2003

Other books you might like:
Alex Berenson, *The Faithful Spy*, 2006
Larry Bond, *Larry Bond's Red Dragon Rising: Blood of War*, 2013
Dale Brown, *Starfire*, 2014
Dale Brown, *Strike War*, 2004
Richard Clarke, *Sting of the Drone*, 2014
Michael Connelly, *The Black Echo*, 1992
Stephen Coonts, *Deep Black: Jihad*, 2007
Nelson DeMille, *Up Country*, 2002
Clive Egleton, *The Renegades*, 2006
David Finkel, *Thank You for Your Service*, 2013
James Hannibal, *Shadow Catcher*, 2013
Jack Higgins, *The Death Trade*, 2013
Cara Hoffman, *Be Safe I Love You*, 2014
David Ignatius, *Body of Lies*, 2007
John Le Carre, *A Delicate Truth*, 2013
Mike Maden, *Blue Warrior*, 2014
Stewart O'Nan, *The Names of the Dead*, 1996
Matthew Reilly, *Scarecrow Returns*, 2012
Daniel Suarez, *Kill Decision*, 2012

743

CHARLES FINCH

The Laws of Murder

(New York: St. Martin's Press, 2014)

Series: Charles Lenox Mysteries Series. Book 8
Story type: Mystery
Subject(s): Murder; Detective fiction; Conspiracy
Major character(s): Charles Lenox, Nobleman, Colleague (of John, Polly, LeMaire), Detective—Private, Political Figure (former); Lord John Dallington, Colleague (of Charles, Polly, LeMaire), Nobleman, Detective—Private; Polly Buchanan, Detective—Private, Widow(er), Colleague (of Charles, John, LeMaire); LeMaire, Colleague (of Charles, John, Polly), Detective—Private
Time period(s): 19th century; 1870s (1876)
Locale(s): London, England

Summary: After trying his hand at politics, Charles Lenox gives up his seat in Parliament to return to his former career as a private investigator. With the help of three colleagues, he forms his own agency. But business in 1876 London certainly isn't booming. A series of newspaper articles critical of Lenox's venture has kept the clients away in droves. When the man responsible for the scathing attacks, a police inspector and former friend, is murdered, Scotland Yard turns to Lenox for help. This case strains his already frayed relationship with his partners, however. His prime suspect is a man already suspected in a number of other crimes, but when the man is also found dead, Lenox realizes he's embroiled in a case more deadly than he imagined. This is the eighth book in Charles Finch's Charles Lenox Mysteries series.

Other books by the same author:
The Last Enchantments, 2014
An Old Betrayal, 2013
A Death in the Small Hours, 2012
A Burial at Sea, 2011
A Stranger in Mayfair, 2010

Other books you might like:
Martine Bailey, *An Appetite for Violets*, 2015
Alan Bradley, *As Chimney Sweepers Come to Dust*, 2015
Charles Finch, *A Beautiful Blue Death*, 2007
Ariana Franklin, *The Serpant's Tale*, 2008
Bruce W. Holsinger, *The Invention of Fire*, 2015
D.E. Ireland, *Wouldn't It Be Deadly*, 2014
Graham Moore, *The Sherlockian*, 2010
Matthew Pearl, *The Poe Shadow: A Novel*, 2006
Iain Pears, *Stone's Fall*, 2009
Deanna Raybourn, *Silent in the Grave*, 2007
Marcus Sedgwick, *Revolver*, 2010
Jacqueline Winspear, *A Dangerous Place*, 2015

744

RICHARD FORD

Let Me Be Frank with You

(New York: HarperCollins, 2014)

Series: Frank Bascombe Series
Story type: Literary
Subject(s): Conduct of life; Men; Aging (Biology)
Major character(s): Frank Bascombe, Retiree (real estate business), Spouse (former, of Ann); Ann, Patient (Parkinson's disease), Spouse (former, of Frank)
Time period(s): 21st century; 2010s (2012)
Locale(s): New Jersey, United States

Summary: Richard Ford introduced his best-known character, Frank Bascombe, in the 1986 novel *The Sportswriter*, and continued his story in *Independence Day* and *The Lay of the Land*. In this novel, presented as four connected novellas, Bascombe is a 68-year-old retiree dealing with personal and universal challenges. It is 2012, and Hurricane Sandy has recently devastated the New Jersey coastline, including the beach house Bascombe used to own. He visits the site of destruction and encounters the current owner of the demolished property.

In another scenario, Bascombe revisits another significant element in his life: his former wife, Ann, who now has Parkinson's disease and is living in a nursing home. Bascombe also deals with the impending death of an old friend. As he experiences various manifestations of loss, Bascombe considers the inevitability of his own demise and begins to make practical preparations.

Other books by the same author:
Canada, 2012
The Lay of the Land, 2006
A Multitude of Sins: Stories, 2001
Women With Men: Three Stories, 1997
Independence Day, 1995

Other books you might like:
Fredrik Backman, *A Man Called Ove*, 2014
Muriel Barbery, *The Elegance of the Hedgehog*, 2008
T.C. Boyle, *The Harder They Come*, 2015
Maria Duenas, *The Heart Has Its Reasons*, 2014
John Gould, *Seven Good Reasons Not to Be Good*, 2010
Miranda July, *The First Bad Man*, 2015
Thomas E. Kennedy, *Beneath the Neon Egg*, 2014
Reif Larsen, *I Am Radar*, 2015
Armistead Maupin, *The Days of Anna Madrigal*, 2014
Ian McEwan, *The Children Act*, 2014
Darragh McKeon, *All That Is Solid Melts into Air*, 2014
David Mitchell, *The Bone Clocks*, 2014
Anna Quindlen, *Still Life with Bread Crumbs*, 2014
Philip Roth, *Nemesis*, 2010
Jane Somers, *The Diaries of Jane Somers*, 1984
Rene Steinke, *Friendswood*, 2014
Ted Thompson, *The Land of Steady Habits*, 2014
Beatriz Williams, *A Hundred Summers*, 2013

745

PETE FROMM

If Not for This

(Pasadena, California: Red Hen Press, 2014)

Story type: Literary
Subject(s): Interpersonal relations; Love; Marriage
Major character(s): Maddy, Young Woman, Adventurer (rafter), Spouse (of Dalt), Patient (multiple sclerosis); Dalt, Young Man, Adventurer, Spouse (of Maddy)
Time period(s): 21st century; 2010s
Locale(s): Oregon, United States; Wyoming, United States

Summary: Maddy is usually only interested in older men, but when she meets Dalt, she falls in love immediately. Dalt is also smitten, and the two whitewater rafters marry on a riverbank and begin a life of adventure together. They start a rafting business and take clients on river excursions at destinations around the world. Their seemingly charmed lives take a turn when Maddy learns simultaneously that she is pregnant and that she has multiple sclerosis. Although they receive the diagnosis with determination, Maddy and Dalt are gradually forced to face the realities of Maddy's disease. Their first child is born without complications, and Maddy eventually surrenders to Dalt's desire to have another child. It is

after the birth of the second baby that Maddy's health declines. Maddy and Dalt must deal with the disease and its effects on their marriage and family.

Other books by the same author:
As Cool as I Am, 2003
How All This Started, 2000
Night Swimming: Stories, 1999
Blood Knot, 1998
Dry Rain: Stories, 1997

Other books you might like:
Elizabeth Berg, *We Are All Welcome Here: A Novel*, 2006
Jenn Crowell, *Etched on Me*, 2014
Maddie Dawson, *The Opposite of Maybe*, 2014
Jonathan Evison, *The Revised Fundamentals of Caregiving*, 2012
Zoe Fishman, *Driving Lessons*, 2014
Ann Lewis Hamilton, *Expecting*, 2014
Jojo Moyes, *Me Before You*, 2012
Colleen Oakley, *Before I Go*, 2015
Ann Packer, *The Dive from Clausen's Pier*, 2002
Jonathan Tropper, *One Last Thing Before I Go*, 2012

746

AMINA GAUTIER

Now We Will Be Happy

(Lincoln, Nebraska: University of Nebraska Press, 2014)

Story type: Collection; Contemporary
Subject(s): Puerto Ricans; Hispanic Americans; Race relations

Summary: This is a short fiction collection focused on selections of the Puerto Rican population: Afro, US mainland-born, and displaced Puerto Ricans. These three groups often find themselves struggling within their cultural identity and finding their place within Puerto Rican culture as a whole. Bi-cultural Puerto Rican protagonists and narrators define the 11 short stories within this text, which won the 2013 Prairie Schooner Book Prize in Fiction. Stories by Amina Gautier included here include "Bodega," "Only Son," "How to Make Flan," and the title story. Some of the works are interrelated and explore characters' lives in greater detail.

Other books by the same author:
At-Risk: Stories, 2011

Other books you might like:
Uwem Akpan, *Say You're One of Them*, 2008
Austin Clarke, *They Never Told Me and Other Stories*, 2013
Junot Diaz, *This Is How You Lose Her*, 2012
Cary Fagan, *My Life among the Apes*, 2012
Nuruddin Farah, *Hiding in Plain Sight*, 2014
Dagoberto Gilb, *Before the End, After the Beginning*, 2011
Ha Jin, *A Good Fall: Stories*, 2009
Phil Klay, *Redeployment*, 2014
Alice Munro, *Dear Life: Stories*, 2012

Edith Pearlman, *Binocular Vision: New and Selected Stories*, 2011

747

LISA GENOVA

Inside the O'Briens

(New York: Simon & Schuster, 2015)

Story type: Literary
Subject(s): Diseases; Medical care; Family life
Major character(s): Joe O'Brien, Police Officer, Spouse (of Rosie), Father (of JJ, Patrick, Meghan, and Katie); Rosie O'Brien, Spouse (of Joe), Mother (of JJ, Patrick, Meghan, and Katie); JJ O'Brien, Brother (of Katie, Patrick, and Meghan), Son (of Joe and Rosie), Teenager; Meghan O'Brien, Sister (of Patrick, Katie, and JJ), Daughter (of Joe and Rosie); Katie O'Brien, Sister (of JJ, Meghan, and Patrick), Daughter (of Joe and Rosie); Patrick O'Brien, Brother (of JJ, Meghan, and Katie), Son (of Joe and Rosie)
Time period(s): 21st century; 2010s
Locale(s): Charlestown, Massachusetts

Summary: Even-tempered Joe O'Brien shocks his family when he begins having flareups of anger and forgetfulness. At the age of 44, Joe has always been a good family man, but now he has his wife and four children walking on eggshells around him. Joe blames his issues on his work as a cop with the Charlestown, Massachusetts, police department, until his family finally forces him to see a doctor. Test results change the O'Briens' lives forever. They learn that Joe has a terminal brain disorder called Huntingdon's disease—even worse, the disease is genetic and cannot be cured or treated. As each of his children wrestles with the decision of whether to explore genetic testing to find out if they will get the disease, they work to support Joe's failing health and each other. Author Lisa Genova tells the story of a family rocked by the news of a fatal illness, and how they all learn to cope together and individually.

Other books you might like:
Angela Elwell Hunt, *The Face*, 2008
Harry Kraus, *Could I Have This Dance?*, 2002
Harry Kraus, *For the Rest of My Life*, 2003
Alison Leonard, *Tina's Chance*, 1988
Hilary Mantel, *The Giant, O'Brien*, 1998
Richard Powers, *Generosity: An Enchantment*, 2009
Jill Rubalcaba, *Saint Vitus' Dance*, 1996
Barbara Vine, *The Blood Doctor*, 2002
Jonathan Weiner, *His Brother's Keeper: A Story from the Edge of Medicine*, 2004

748

TESS GERRITSEN

Die Again

(New York: Penguin Random House, 2014)

Series: Rizzoli and Isles Series. Book 11
Story type: Mystery

Subject(s): Law enforcement; Medicine; Medical professions
Major character(s): Jane Rizzoli, Detective—Homicide; Dr. Maura Isles, Doctor (medical examiner)
Time period(s): 21st century; 2010s
Locale(s): Botswana; Boston, Massachusetts

Summary: In the 11th installment of Tess Gerritsen's Rizzoli and Isles series, homicide detective Jane Rizzoli and her colleague, medical examiner Maura Isles, are on the case when a wealthy man known for his penchant for hunting big game turns up dead. The man recently had been asked to obtain a rare snow leopard for a local museum, and the dead animal also turns up at the crime scene. As Isles looks for similar cases, Rizzoli must follow the evidence all the way to Africa. There, she discovers that this recent death could be connected to a mass murder. As Rizzoli searches for the only person who lived through that horrific event four years ago, she hopes to find out the answers she is looking for and solve the case. The more she digs into the clues she finds, however, the closer she brings the killer to her.

Other books by the same author:
Last to Die, 2012
The Silent Girl, 2011
Ice Cold, 2010
The Keepsake, 2008
The Bone Garden, 2007

Other books you might like:
Nevada Barr, *Destroyer Angel*, 2014
C.J. Box, *Below Zero*, 2009
Robin Cook, *Host*, 2015
Robert Dugoni, *My Sister's Grave*, 2014
Janet Evanovich, *Top Secret Twenty-One*, 2014
Lisa Gardner, *Crash and Burn*, 2015
James W. Hall, *Silencer*, 2010
Parnell Hall, *Safari*, 2014
J.A. Jance, *Cold Betrayal*, 2015
Iris Johansen, *Your Next Breath*, 2015
Alex Kava, *Silent Creed*, 2015
Jonathan Kellerman, *Motive*, 2015
Evan McNamara, *Fair Game*, 2006
Maxine Paetro, *14th Deadly Sin*, 2015
Michael Palmer, *Trauma*, 2015
Douglas Preston, *Cold Vengeance*, 2011
Kathy Reichs, *Bones Never Lie*, 2014
Karen Robards, *Hush*, 2014
Urban Waite, *Sometimes the Wolf*, 2014

749

WILLIAM GIRALDI

Hold the Dark

(New York: Liveright, 2014)

Story type: Literary
Subject(s): Wilderness areas; Wolves; Suspense
Major character(s): Medora Slone, Woman, Spouse (of Vernon), Mother (of Bailey); Vernon Slone, Military Personnel, Spouse (of Medora), Father (of Bailey), Friend (of Cheeon); Bailey Slone, Boy, 6-Year-Old,

Son (of Medora and Vernon), Missing Person; Russell Core, Expert (wolves); Cheeon, Hunter, Friend (of Vernon); Donald Marium, Detective—Police
Time period(s): 21st century; 2010s
Locale(s): Keelut, Alaska

Summary: As the long Alaskan winter begins, Medora Slone is alone in her home in Keelut with her six-year-old son, Bailey. Medora's husband, Vernon, is serving overseas in the military. When Bailey goes missing, Medora believes the boy has been taken by the wolves that surround the village in the dark. She contacts wolf expert Russell Core for help in finding out what happened to her son. When Russell arrives, he is unable to confirm that the local wolf pack had anything to do with Bailey's disappearance. In fact, he discovers evidence that indicates that human evil, not natural instinct, is at work in Keelut. Russell sets out after Medora, who has also gone missing. When Vernon returns home, he embarks on a violent spree as he also searches for his wife. Detective Donald Marium joins the hunt as he tries to stop Vernon.

Other books by the same author:
Busy Monsters, 2011

Other books you might like:
Jay R. Bonansinga, *Frozen*, 2005
Kenneth Calhoun, *Black Moon*, 2014
Lincoln Child, *Terminal Freeze*, 2009
Stephen Fry, *Arctic Fire*, 2012
Ryan David Jahn, *Acts of Violence*, 2009
Henning Mankell, *Troubled Man*, 2011
Robert Masello, *The Romanov Cross*, 2013
Richard Price, *Lush Life*, 2008
James Rollins, *Ice Hunt*, 2003
Kimberley Woodhouse, *No Safe Haven*, 2011

750

OLIVIA GLAZEBROOK

Never Mind Miss Fox

(New York: Little, Brown and Company, 2014)

Subject(s): Scandals; Marriage; Suspense
Major character(s): Martha Barkes, Spouse (of Clive), Mother (of Eliza); Clive Barkes, Spouse (of Martha), Father (of Eliza); Eliza Barkes, Daughter (of Martha and Clive); Eliot Fox, Musician, Teacher
Time period(s): 21st century; 2010s
Locale(s): England

Summary: By outward appearances, Martha and Clive Barkes seem to be the perfect couple. They were college sweethearts at Oxford University and have been happily raising a daughter, Eliza, for the past few years. Yet Martha does not know that Clive hides a devastating mystery deep within his past. That mystery rears its ugly head one day in the form of Eliza's new music teacher, Eliot Fox, with whom Eliza is instantly taken. Much to Clive's horror, Eliot weaves herself more and more into the fabric of the Barkes' lives. Clive constantly worries that their secret will be revealed to Martha. Now Clive must decide exactly what he is willing to do to protect the life he has so carefully cultivated for himself. Will

he be able to keep Eliot at arm's length from his family, or will Eliot continue to hold Clive in her thrall until she tears his life apart?

Other books by the same author:
The Trouble with Alice, 2011

Other books you might like:
Elizabeth Benedict, *The Practice of Deceit: A Novel*, 2005
Deb Caletti, *He's Gone*, 2013
Meg Donohue, *All the Summer Girls*, 2013
Gillian Flynn, *Gone Girl*, 2012
Jennifer Handford, *Acts of Contrition*, 2014
Zoe Heller, *What Was She Thinking?: Notes on a Scandal*, 2003
Laura Lippman, *After I'm Gone*, 2014
Laura Lippman, *The Most Dangerous Thing*, 2011
Claire Messud, *The Woman Upstairs*, 2013
Sue Miller, *The Arsonist*, 2014
Alissa Nutting, *Tampa*, 2013
Chad Pelley, *Every Little Thing*, 2013
Lionel Shriver, *We Need to Talk about Kevin*, 2003
Lisa Unger, *In the Blood*, 2014
Carter Wilson, *The Boy in the Woods*, 2014
Meg Wolitzer, *The Ten-Year Nap*, 2008

751

ABBI GLINES

You Were Mine

(New York: Atria Books, 2014)

Series: Rosemary Beach Series. Book 9
Story type: Romance
Subject(s): Romances (Fiction); Sexual behavior; Wealth
Major character(s): Tripp Newark, Young Man, Boyfriend (former, of Beth), Cousin (of Jace); Beth Lowry, Young Woman, Girlfriend (former, of Tripp), Girlfriend (of Jace); Jace, Cousin (of Tripp), Boyfriend (of Beth)
Time period(s): 21st century; 2010s
Locale(s): Rosemary Beach, Florida

Summary: Tripp Newark was born into wealth, but didn't want to be obsessed by it. Dating the girl he was expected to, and preparing to attend Yale University, Tripp was destined for a life consumed with money and status—a burden he did not want. So he made his decision to ride off and leave it all behind at the end of summer. Then he meets Beth, and he rethinks his future. The barmaid from the wrong side of the tracks captures his heart, and even though he cannot give up on his plan, he promises her he will return. But life gets in the way, and when Tripp finally returns, years have passed. While Tripp followed the path he wanted, Beth followed her own. Now she is involved with Tripp's cousin, and once again, Tripp's future is in doubt. This is the ninth book in Abbi Glines's Rosemary Beach series.

Other books by the same author:
Forever Too Far, 2014
Misbehaving, 2014
One More Chance, 2014

Rush too Far, 2014
Sometimes It Lasts, 2014

Other books you might like:
Rochelle Alers, *Haven Creek*, 2013
Suzanne Brockmann, *No Ordinary Man*, 2014
Sandra Brown, *Mean Streak*, 2014
Janet Chapman, *Stranger in Her Bed*, 2007
Claire Cook, *Time Flies*, 2013
Jennifer Crusie, *Maybe This Time*, 2010
Christina Dodd, *Just the Way You Are*, 2003
Penelope Douglas, *Falling Away*, 2015
Jancee Dunn, *Don't You Forget About Me*, 2008
Linda Howard, *Shadow Woman*, 2012
Julia London, *Return to Homecoming Ranch*, 2014
Debbie Macomber, *Fairy Tale Weddings*, 2009
Judith McNaught, *Every Breath You Take*, 2005
Olivia Miles, *Recipe for Romance*, 2014
Carla Neggers, *Cider Brook*, 2014
Kristen Proby, *Forever with Me*, 2014
Nora Roberts, *Irish Rebel*, 2000
Nicholas Sparks, *The Best of Me*, 2011
Danielle Steel, *Until the End of Time*, 2013
Patricia Thayer, *Texas Ranger Takes a Bride*, 2008

752

YANNICK GRANNEC
WILLARD WOOD, Translator

The Goddess of Small Victories
(New York: Other Press, 2014)

Story type: Historical
Subject(s): Death; Mathematics; Family relations
Major character(s): Anna Roth, Friend (of Adele), Young Woman (translator); Adele Godel, Widow(er) (of Kurt), Dancer (former), Aged Person, Historical Figure; Kurt Godel, Historical Figure, Spouse (of Adele), Mentally Ill Person, Professor (mathematician), Genius
Time period(s): 20th century; 1920s-1980s
Locale(s): Vienna, Austria; Princeton, New Jersey

Summary: When famed mathematician Kurt Godel dies in 1978, he leaves behind a complicated legacy. The troubled genius had spent his later years at Princeton University beset with paranoia and had wasted away of anorexia. To acquire the rights to his precious research records, in 1980 officials at the school send young archivist Anna Roth to a nursing home to talk to Godel's reluctant widow, Adele. Despite a frosty first encounter, the two women begin to connect. As the two become friends, Adele opens up to Anna. She describes her life with Kurt, from their youth in Vienna, to his friendship with luminaries including Albert Einstein, and his descent into mental illness and death. Adele's story is that of a bright life lived in the shadow of another, and helps Anna understand and learn how to take control of her own life. First novel.

Other books you might like:
Dominique Fortier, *Wonder*, 2014
Gail Godwin, *Flora*, 2013

Nancy Moser, *Washington's Lady*, 2008
Sylvia Nasar, *A Beautiful Mind*, 1998
Zia Hader Rahman, *In the Light of What We Know*, 2014
Paul Robertson, *An Elegant Solution*, 2013
Stuart Rojstaczer, *The Mathematician's Shiva*, 2014
Simon Spurrier, *Numbercruncher*, 2014
Colm Toibin, *Nora Webster*, 2014
Susan Vreeland, *Clara and Mr. Tiffany*, 2010

753

MIKE GREENBERG

My Father's Wives
(New York: William Morrow, 2015)

Story type: Contemporary
Subject(s): Family; Father-son relations; Self knowledge
Major character(s): Jonathan Sweetwater, Son (of Percy), Spouse (of Claire), Financier; Percival "Percy" Sweetwater III, Father (of Jonathan, deceased), Political Figure (senator), Divorced Person; Claire Sweetwater, Spouse (of Jonathan)
Time period(s): 21st century; 2010s
Locale(s): United States

Summary: Jonathan Sweetwater is a successful Wall Street financier living in a Connecticut mansion with his beloved wife, Claire, and their beautiful children. They are wealthy and Jonathan is pleased with his life. The only flaw that he focuses on is his complicated relationship with his deceased father, Percy. After inadvertently stumbling into a troubling family problem, Jonathan begins to question his marriage and his life. He realizes that to face his present issues and move into the future, he must learn more about Percy. Percy was a US senator who left when Jonathan was only nine years old. He remarried and divorced five times, and never bothered to keep in touch with his only son. Jonathan tracks down each former wife in search of understanding and healing. He hopes to find information that will guide him through his current predicaments and help him become a better man and husband. Ultimately, Jonathan must decide whether to return to Claire and his children or follow in his father's footsteps.

Other books by the same author:
All You Could Ask For, 2013

Other books you might like:
Iain M. Banks, *The Quarry*, 2013
Elizabeth Berg, *Once Upon a Time, There Was You*, 2011
Joshua Henkin, *The World Without You*, 2012
Tom Perotta, *Nine Inches: Stories*, 2013
Anna Quindlen, *Still Life with Bread Crumbs*, 2014
Austin Ratner, *In the Land of the Living*, 2013
Rainbow Rowell, *Landline*, 2014
Emma Straub, *The Vacationers*, 2014
Jonathan Tropper, *One Last Thing Before I Go*, 2012
Martha Woodroof, *Small Blessings*, 2014

754

WILLIAM E. BUTTERWORTH IV
W.E.B. GRIFFIN, Co-Author

Deadly Assets

(New York: Penguin Publishing Group, 2015)

Series: Badge of Honor Series. Book 12
Story type: Contemporary; Police Procedural
Subject(s): Crime; Murder; Law enforcement
Major character(s): Matt Payne, Police Officer (Homicide Sergeant), Friend (of Mickey O'Hara); Mickey O'Hara, Journalist (Pulitzer Prize winning), Friend (of Matt Payne)
Time period(s): 21st century; 2010s
Locale(s): Philadelphia, Pennsylvania

Summary: In this 12th novel of the Badge of Honor Series, the city of Philadelphia has the dubious honor of leading the nation in murders, and the Citizen's Oversight Committee is looking for answers from the police department. When the committee focuses on shootings involving the police, the actions of Matt Payne, a sergeant with the homicide unit, come under question. The questions and accusations start to run deep when the committee's chairperson is murdered and Payne is ordered to remain quietly on the side. He concentrates on the murder of a reporter and his family, a crime that appears to be related to a drug series the young man was working on for esteemed journalist Mickey O'Hara. Payne knows the deaths of the young reporter, his wife, and their child were meant as a warning to O'Hara, but he also knows that O'Hara won't back down—nor will Payne remain silent for long in the face of his accusers.

Other books by the same author:
The Assassination Option, 2014
Top Secret, 2014
Hazardous Duty, 2013
The Last Witness, 2013
Empire and Honor, 2012

Other books you might like:
C.J. Box, *Endangered*, 2015
Harlan Coben, *The Stranger*, 2015
Michael Connelly, *The Burning Room*, 2014
Jeffery Deaver, *The Skin Collector*, 2014
Stephen Hunter, *Sniper's Honor*, 2014
James Patterson, *Private Vegas*, 2015
Douglas Preston, *Blue Labyrinth*, 2014
John Sandford, *Gathering Prey*, 2015
Eric Van Lustbader, *Robert Ludlum's The Bourne Ascendancy*, 2014
Randy Wayne White, *Cuba Straits*, 2015

755

W.E.B. GRIFFIN
WILLIAM E. BUTTERWORTH IV, Co-Author

Top Secret

(New York: Putnam, 2014)

Series: Clandestine Operations Series. Book 1
Story type: Espionage

Subject(s): Espionage; Spies; Military life
Major character(s): James D. Cronley Jr., Military Personnel (second lieutenant), Spy, Widow(er); Reinhard Gehlen, Military Personnel (German major general), Historical Figure
Time period(s): 20th century; 1940s (1945)
Locale(s): Argentina; Germany; United States

Summary: In the first novel in the Clandestine Operations series, father and son authors W.E.B. Griffin and William E. Butterworth IV introduce James D. Cronley Jr., a newly recruited agent of the fledgling CIA. It is 1945, just months after the official end of World War II, and the United States is shifting its focus from warfare to espionage. Although the Nazis have been defeated, some survivors who have so far escaped justice come to Argentina to regroup. When Cronley thwarts the Nazis' efforts to stockpile weapons-grade uranium in Argentina, he is recognized for his service and recruited by a new agency. Cronley's first assignment involves obtaining intelligence from Nazi and Soviet personnel. As he plies enemy agents for information, Cronley deals with power struggles between the OSS, FBI, and other organizations presumably playing for the same team. Cronley's personal life is no more stable; he is married and widowed within the span of days.

Other books by the same author:
The Assassination Option, 2014
Hazardous Duty, 2013
The Last Witness, 2013
Empire and Honor, 2012
The Spymasters, 2012

Other books you might like:
Alex Berenson, *Twelve Days*, 2015
Laurent Binet, *HHhH: A Novel*, 2012
Robert Conroy, *Red Inferno: 1945: A Novel*, 2010
David Downing, *Lehrter Station*, 2012
Ken Follett, *Edge of Eternity*, 2014
Jamie Freveletti, *Robert Ludlum's The Geneva Strategy*, 2015
Alan Furst, *Blood of Victory*, 2002
James Grady, *Last Days of the Condor*, 2015
Mark Greaney, *Tom Clancy Full Force and Effect*, 2014
David Hagberg, *Retribution*, 2015
Jack Higgins, *Rain on the Dead*, 2014
Joseph Kanon, *Leaving Berlin*, 2015
Philip Kerr, *Hitler's Peace*, 2005
Gary Kriss, *The Zodiac Deception*, 2014
Aly Monroe, *Washington Shadow*, 2011
James Naughtie, *The Madness of July*, 2014
Daniel Silva, *The Heist*, 2014
Olen Steinhauer, *All the Old Knives*, 2015

756

JAMES GRIPPANDO

Cane and Abe

(New York: Harper, 2015)

Story type: Legal; Mystery
Subject(s): Mystery; Detective fiction; Crime

Popular Fiction

Major character(s): Abe Beckham, Lawyer, Widow(er) (of Samantha Vine), Spouse (of Angelina), Crime Suspect; Samantha Vine, Spouse (deceased, of Abe), Lawyer, Sister (of J.T.); Angelina, Spouse (of Abe); J.T., Mentally Ill Person (bipolar disorder), Brother (of Samantha); Tyla Tomkins, Lawyer, Lover (former, of Abe), Crime Victim (murdered); Victoria Santos, FBI Agent
Time period(s): 21st century; 2010s
Locale(s): Miami, Florida

Summary: Even though prominent attorney Abe Beckham remarried after the death of his first wife, he is still deeply in love with Samantha Vine. Angelina, Abe's current wife, knows that Abe hasn't let go of Samantha, and she disapproves of the relationship he maintains with Samantha's family. Before Abe married Angelina, he had a brief affair with Tyla Tomkins, a Miami attorney. So when Tyla's body is found in the Everglades, Abe keeps close tabs on the case. Tyla may be the victim of a serial killer who's been stalking women in the area, but she doesn't seem to fit the profile, and the evidence at the crime scene doesn't exactly match the others. Abe tries to downplay his involvement with the victim, but when FBI agent Victoria Santos learns that Abe hasn't been forthcoming, she puts him at the top of the suspect list. Abe finds himself in deeper trouble when Angelina disappears.

Other books by the same author:
Black Horizon, 2014
Blood Money, 2013
Need You Now, 2012
Afraid of the Dark, 2011
Money to Burn, 2010

Other books you might like:
Emily Arsenault, *What Strange Creatures*, 2014
David Baldacci, *Memory Man*, 2015
Mary Higgins Clark, *The Melody Lingers On*, 2015
Harlan Coben, *Tell No One*, 2001
David Ellis, *Line of Vision*, 2001
Joseph Finder, *Suspicion*, 2014
Gillian Flynn, *Gone Girl*, 2012
Tana French, *The Secret Place*, 2014
Jilliane P. Hoffman, *Retribution*, 2004
Greg Iles, *The Bone Tree*, 2012
Dean Koontz, *Saint Odd*, 2015
William Landay, *Defending Jacob*, 2012
Paul Levine, *To Speak for the Dead*, 1990
Laura Lippman, *Hush Hush*, 2015
E. Lockhart, *We Were Liars*, 2014
Richard North Patterson, *Degree of Guilt*, 1992
Scott Turow, *Presumed Innocent*, 1987
Lisa Unger, *Die for You*, 2009
Stuart Woods, *Paris Match*, 2014

757

CLAIRE HAJAJ

Ishmael's Oranges

(London: Oneworld Publications, 2014)

Story type: Historical; Literary
Subject(s): History; Jews; Arab-Israeli wars

Major character(s): Salim, 7-Year-Old, Boy (Palestinian); Judith "Jude", Girl (Jewish)
Time period(s): 20th century; 1940s-1970s
Locale(s): London, England; Jaffa, Palestine

Summary: As this novel by Claire Hajaj opens, Salim, a seven-year-old Palestinian boy, is looking forward to an upcoming rite of passage: He is going to help his father with the orange harvest. But it is April of 1948, and the harvest in Jaffa is about to be postponed by the outbreak of war. Miles away another child, a Jewish girl named Jude, is experiencing a childhood that has also been touched by war. Her family has survived the Holocaust, and they are under the mistaken belief that their struggle is over. Years later, Salim and Jude meet in London and, despite their very different backgrounds, fall in love. Although their heritage should make them enemies, Salim and Jude defy convention and marry. The novel follows the Palestinian man and his Jewish wife from childhood in the 1940s through their college days in the 1960s to later years when they become parents to twins, revealing the challenges they encounter.

Other books you might like:
Chimamanda Ngozi Adichie, *Americanah*, 2013
Amy Bloom, *Away: A Novel*, 2007
Junot Diaz, *This Is How You Lose Her*, 2012
Charles Finch, *The Last Enchantments*, 2014
Peg Kingman, *Not Yet Drown'd*, 2007
Jhumpa Lahiri, *Unaccustomed Earth*, 2008
Chris McCourt, *Cleansing of Mahommed*, 2012
Julie Orringer, *The Invisible Bridge*, 2010
Ellen Marie Wiseman, *The Plum Tree*, 2013
Margaret Wurtele, *The Golden Hour*, 2012

758

JAMES W. HALL

The Big Finish

(London: St. Martin's Press, 2014)

Series: Thorn Series. Book 11
Story type: Mystery
Subject(s): Father-son relations; Detective fiction; Ecology
Major character(s): Thorn, Detective—Private, Friend (of Sugarman), Father (of Flynn); Flynn Moss, Son (of Thorn), Activist (environmental); Sugarman, Detective—Private, Friend (of Thorn); Tina Gathercole, Girlfriend (of Sugarman); Madeline Cruz, FBI Agent; X-88, Activist (environnmental)
Time period(s): 21st century; 2010s
Locale(s): Florida, United States; Pine Haven, North Carolina

Summary: Florida private investigator Thorn recently discovered he had a son. Now that son, Flynn Moss, a environmental activist, has gone missing while undercover on a North Carolina hog farm. Thorn's only clue to his whereabouts is a postcard with the words "Help Me" on the back. On his way to Carolina, Thorn is contacted by a person claiming to be an FBI agent who says Flynn has been murdered. She says she needs Thorn's help in catching the killers. Enraged, Thorn accepts the task, bent on bringing his son's murderers to justice. As he confronts the hog farm owners and a brutal ex-con with the strange ability to track by smell, Thorn also discovers a sobering truth—everything he was told about the case is a lie. This is the 11th book in author James W. Hall's Thorn series.

Other books by the same author:
Going Dark, 2013
Dead Last, 2011
Silencer, 2010
Hell's Bay, 2008
Magic City, 2006

Other books you might like:
David Baldacci, *King and Maxwell*, 2013
Steve Berry, *The King's Deception*, 2013
C.J. Box, *Endangered*, 2015
James Lee Burke, *Wayfaring Stranger*, 2014
Michael Crichton, *State of Fear*, 2004
Clive Cussler, *The Storm*, 2012
Linda Davies, *Ark Storm*, 2014
Mark Greaney, *Tom Clancy Full Force and Effect*, 2014
Mike Lawson, *House Reckoning*, 2014
Dennis Lehane, *World Gone By*, 2015

759

DANIEL HANDLER

We Are Pirates

(New York: Bloomsbury USA, 2015)

Story type: Literary
Subject(s): Violence; Pirates; Human behavior
Major character(s): Phil Needle, Producer (radio), Spouse (of Marina), Father (of Gwen); Marina Needle, Spouse (of Phil), Mother (of Gwen); Gwen Needle, 14-Year-Old, Daughter (of Phil and Marina), Friend (of Amber and Cody), Swimmer; Cody Glasserman, Boy, Friend (of Gwen); Amber, Girl, Teenager, Friend (of Gwen)
Time period(s): 21st century; 2010s
Locale(s): San Francisco, California

Summary: A radio producer and his rebellious teenage daughter embark on separate, very different ventures in this novel by Daniel Handler. Phil Needle and his assistant are in the process of making a business deal that Phil hopes will finance the purchase of his San Francisco Bay condo. His 14-year-old daughter, Gwen, a synchronized swimmer who has recently befriended wild girl Amber, is also engaged in a mission that involves the Bay. She and Amber round up a band of misfits, steal a boat, and establish themselves as modern-day pirates. Like her father, Gwen is in search of a big payoff, and she is willing to partake in unimaginable acts of violence to achieve her goal. As Gwen and her pirates terrorize the San Francisco Bay area, Phil focuses his attention on bringing his daughter's ill-advised adventure to an end. Handler, aka Lemony Snicket, is also the author of the Series of Unfortunate Events novels.

Other books by the same author:
Why We Broke Up, 2011
Adverbs, 2006
Watch Your Mouth, 2000

The Basic Eight, 1999

Other books you might like:
Isabel Allende, *Zorro*, 2005
Jeffery Deaver, *Carte Blanche*, 2011
Jonas Jonasson, *The 100-Year-Old Man Who Climbed Out the Window and Disappeared*, 2012
Elmore Leonard, *Djibouti*, 2010
Robert Low, *The Whale Road*, 2007
Andrew Motion, *Silver: Return to Treasure Island*, 2012
Johnny Shaw, *Plaster City*, 2014
Dan Simmons, *The Terror*, 2007
Harry Turtledove, *The Gryphon's Skull*, 2002
Jeff VanderMeer, *Fast Ships, Black Sails*, 2008

760

JAMES HANNAHAM

Delicious Foods

(New York: Little, Brown and Company, 2015)

Story type: Literary
Subject(s): Family; Grief; African Americans
Major character(s): Darlene, Widow(er) (of Nat), Mother (of Eddie), Addict; Nat, Spouse (deceased husband of Darlene), Father (deceased, of Eddie); Eddie, Boy, Son (of Darlene and Nat); Scotty, Object (personification of crack cocaine)
Time period(s): 21st century; 2010s
Locale(s): Louisiana, United States

Summary: When Darlene's husband, Nat, dies, Darlene is inconsolable. She loves their young son, Eddie, and knows she must take care of him, but crack cocaine becomes her only source of comfort. Darlene finds a glimmer of hope when she is offered a job on a farm run by Delicious Foods. She hopes that the farm will give her the opportunity to provide for Eddie, but Darlene soon realizes that it is a prison. In exchange for drugs, she and other addicts are forced to work long hours to pay for debts fabricated by their Delicious Foods employers. No one knows where Darlene has been taken, so she has little chance of being rescued. The story is told from the perspectives of both Darlene and Eddie, who searches desperately for his missing mother. The drug that keeps Darlene a captive also narrates the novel as a character named Scotty.

Other books by the same author:
God Says No, 2009

Other books you might like:
Sheila Banks, *Bittersweet*, 2010
Cynthia Bond, *Ruby*, 2014
John Brandon, *Citrus County*, 2010
Ginnah Howard, *Night Navigation*, 2009
Stephanie Kegan, *Golden State*, 2015
Toni Morrison, *A Mercy*, 2008
Anna Quindlen, *Every Last One*, 2010
Matt Sumell, *Making Nice*, 2015

Donna Tartt, *The Goldfinch*, 2013
Aaron Thier, *The Ghost Apple*, 2014

761

BETH HARBISON

Driving with the Top Down

(New York: St. Martin's Press, 2014)

Story type: Coming-of-Age; Family Saga
Subject(s): Family life; Friendship; Women
Major character(s): Colleen Bradley, Companion (of Tamara and Bitty), Businesswoman, Mother (of teenage son), Spouse, Aunt (of Tamara); Tamara, Niece (of Colleen), 16-Year-Old, Companion (of Colleen and Bitty), Dysfunctional Family Member; Bitty Camalier, Woman, Companion (of Colleen and Tamara)
Time period(s): 21st century; 2010s
Locale(s): United States; Florida, United States

Summary: Colleen Bradley should be happy. She has a husband, teenage son, and successful antique business, but something in her life just feels out of place. When a business opportunity gives her the chance to take an East Coast road trip, she relishes the time as a way to find inner peace. Her plans go askew, however, when she inherits her troubled niece, Tamara, as a traveling partner. The 16-year-old turns out to be better company than expected, but she is not the last unexpected guest on the journey. Stopping at a diner, they run into Colleen's old friend, Bitty, an unhappy woman contemplating suicide. Bitty finds her way into the traveling party, and together they head to Florida. Along the way, the women confront the pain in their lives and realize the friendships they have formed will help get them through it.

Other books by the same author:
Chose the Wrong Guy, Gave Him the Wrong Finger, 2013
When in Doubt, Add Butter, 2012
Always Something There to Remind Me, 2011
Thin, Rich, Pretty, 2010
Hope in a Jar, 2009

Other books you might like:
Elizabeth Berg, *Tapestry of Fortunes*, 2013
Marie Bostwick, *Apart at the Seams*, 2014
Bethany Chase, *The One That Got Away*, 2015
Claire Cook, *Time Flies*, 2013
Lucy Dillon, *A Hundred Pieces of Me*, 2014
Colleen Faulkner, *As Close as Sisters*, 2014
Karen McQuestion, *The Long Way Home*, 2012
Susan Elizabeth Phillips, *Heroes Are My Weakness*, 2014
Emilie Richards, *No River Too Wide*, 2014
Courtney Miller Santo, *Three Story House*, 2014
Nancy Thayer, *The Guest Cottage*, 2015
Jamie Langston Turner, *To See the Moon Again*, 2014
Susan Wiggs, *The Goodbye Quilt*, 2011

762

SAMANTHA HARVEY

Dear Thief

(New York: HarperCollins Publishers, 2014)

Story type: Contemporary; Family Saga
Subject(s): Friendship; Letters (Correspondence); Marriage
Major character(s): Unnamed, Narrator, Woman, Divorced Person, Friend (former, of Nina), Caregiver; Nina, Woman (aka Butterfly), Friend (former, of narrator)
Time period(s): 21st century; 2010s
Locale(s): London, England

Summary: Sometimes the hurt, bitterness, and resentment left behind in a wounded marriage never heals. Years have passed since the ultimate act of betrayal destroyed a family and a friendship. In one woman's heart, the anger and pain has not receded with time, prompting her to put pen to paper and write a series of letters to her former best friend, Nina. Known to the writer as Butterfly, Nina had an affair with the writer's husband and eventually lured him away. As the thoughts flow into words, the writer relives her story, dredging up raw emotions and mixing them with fantasies of revenge. Written over the span of months, the woman's letters are never meant to be delivered, but they become sharp stabs at the past from a strong and damaged soul.

Other books by the same author:
The Wilderness, 2009

Other books you might like:
Annie Barrows, *The Guernsey Literary and Potato Peel Pie Society*, 2008
Claire Cook, *Best Staged Plans*, 2011
Connie May Fowler, *The Problem with Murmur Lee: A Novel*, 2005
Mary Gaitskill, *Veronica: A Novel*, 2005
Tessa Hadley, *Clever Girl*, 2014
Barbara Kingsolver, *The Lacuna: A Novel*, 2009
Amelie Nothomb, *Life Form*, 2013
Jennifer Scott, *The Accidental Book Club*, 2014
Kathrine Kressman Taylor, *Address Unknown*, 2001
Rufi Thorpe, *The Girls from Corona del Mar*, 2014

763

SARAH HEALY

House of Wonder

(London: Penguin Group, 2014)

Story type: Contemporary; Family Saga
Subject(s): Family; Mentally disabled persons; Twins
Major character(s): Jenna Parsons, Businesswoman, Single Mother (of Rose), Sister (of Warren), Twin, Daughter (of Priscilla), Divorced Person; Warren Parsons, Brother (of Jenna), Twin, Mentally Challenged Person, Son (of Priscilla); Priscilla Parsons, Beauty Pageant Contestant (former), Mother (of Jenna and Warren); Rose, 4-Year-Old, Daughter (of Jenna)
Time period(s): 21st century; 2010s

Locale(s): New Jersey, United States

Summary: Thirtysomething single mother Jenna Parsons has carved out a nice career for herself, far away from the family drama she grew up with in her New Jersey neighborhood. But her past reels her back when her aging mother begs her to come home to care for her and Jenna's mentally-challenged twin brother, Warren. Jenna returns to her old neighborhood, but it is not the same place she left. Her beloved brother, once seen as just a little different, is beaten after being suspected in a string of neighborhood burglaries. And to the neighbors, her quirky, shopaholic mother has become a crazy old lady with a hoarding problem. As Jenna tries to uncover the truth about her family, an old flame reenters her life, and may just provide the spark to reignite love and keep her in her true home

Other books by the same author:
Can I Get an Amen?, 2012

Other books you might like:
Elizabeth Berg, *Tapestry of Fortunes*, 2013
Elinor Lipman, *The Family Man*, 2009
Jo-Ann Mapson, *Owen's Daughter*, 2014
Hannah Pittard, *Reunion*, 2014
Luanne Rice, *The Lemon Orchard*, 2013
Kimberla Lawson Roby, *The Perfect Marriage*, 2013
Cathleen Schine, *The Three Weissmanns of Westport*, 2010
Nancy Thayer, *The Guest Cottage*, 2015
Joanna Trollope, *Balancing Act*, 2014
Penny Vincenzi, *More Than You Know*, 2012

764

BRADEN HEPNER

Pale Harvest

(Salt Lake City, Utah: Torrey House Press, 2014)

Story type: Literary
Subject(s): Family; Western fiction; Agriculture
Major character(s): Jack Selvedge, Orphan, 20-Year-Old, Farmer (dairy), Grandson (of Blair Selvedge), Friend (of Heber); Blair Selvedge, Farmer (dairy), Grandfather (of Jack); Heber, Friend (of Jack); Rebekah Rainsford, Young Woman
Time period(s): 21st century; 2010s
Locale(s): Juniper Scrag, Utah

Summary: Twenty-year-old Jack Selvedge has lived with his grandparents on their dairy farm since his parents died ten years ago. The clan has worked the land in Juniper Scrag, Utah, for generations, but each generation finds it harder to make a living on the arid farm. Jack knows the challenges of caring for the family's 100 cows, but he loves the work and looks forward to the day when he will be a partial owner of the farm. Jack's world changes when he learns that his imposing grandfather, Blair, has changed his mind about the future ownership of the farm. Feeling hurt and betrayed, Jack turns his attentions to Rebekah Rainsford, a beautiful young woman who has recently come back to Juniper Scrag with her mother. Rebekah is trying to escape a painful past, but Jack can't get her to talk about it. Jack seeks support from his close friend Heber as he considers his future. First novel.

Other books you might like:
Julian Barnes, *The Sense of an Ending*, 2011
Raymond Carver, *Call If You Need Me: The Uncollected Fiction and Other Prose*, 2001
Amanda Coplin, *The Orchardist*, 2012
Lin Enger, *The High Divide*, 2014
Amy Greene, *Long Man*, 2014
Jane Hamilton, *A Map of the World*, 1994
Brian Hart, *The Bully of Order*, 2014
Colum McCann, *TransAtlantic*, 2013
Phillip Meyer, *The Son*, 2013
Katy Simpson Smith, *The Story of Land and Sea*, 2014

765

SALLY HEPWORTH

The Secrets of Midwives

(New York: St. Martin's Press, 2015)

Story type: Contemporary
Subject(s): Women; Mother-daughter relations; Grandmothers
Major character(s): Neva Bradley, Woman (pregnant), Midwife, Daughter (of Grace), Granddaughter (of Floss); Grace Bradley, Midwife, Mother (of Neva), Daughter (of Floss); Floss, Woman, Midwife (retired), Mother (of Grace), Grandmother (of Neva), Lesbian, Lover (of Lil); Lil, Woman, Lover (of Floss); Patrick, Doctor (pediatrician); Sean, Doctor (obstetrician)
Time period(s): 21st century; 2010s
Locale(s): Providence, Rhode Island

Summary: Like her mother, Grace, and grandmother, Floss, Neva Bradley is a midwife in Providence, Rhode Island. Floss is retired, but she remains a strong presence in Neva and Grace's lives. Although the three women share a common vocation, they do not share everything with one another. Neva has been keeping her pregnancy a secret for seven months, and when she can't conceal her condition any longer, she still withholds the identity of her baby's father from Grace and Floss. Grace, who was raised by a single mother, wants her grandchild to have a father and pushes Neva to tell the truth. Neva responds to her mother's prying by withdrawing further from Grace. Floss, who lives with her lover, Lil, is empathetic to Neva's situation. Floss has been keeping a secret for decades about the circumstances of Grace's birth, and she is beginning to think it may be time to reveal the story to her daughter and granddaughter. First novel.

Other books you might like:
Elizabeth Berg, *Home Safe*, 2009
Claire Cook, *Life's a Beach*, 2007
Kristin Hannah, *Winter Garden*, 2010
Elin Hilderbrand, *The Love Season*, 2006
Beth Hoffman, *Looking for Me*, 2013
Joshilyn Jackson, *Between, Georgia*, 2006
Luanne Rice, *The Geometry of Sisters*, 2010
J. Courtney Sullivan, *Maine*, 2011

Karen White, *The Time Between*, 2013
Lauren Willig, *That Summer*, 2014

Brad Taylor, *Days of Rage*, 2014
Brad Taylor, *No Fortunate Son*, 2014
Brad Thor, *Act of War*, 2014

766

JACK HIGGINS

Rain on the Dead

(New York: Penguin Group, 2014)

Series: Sean Dillon Series. Book 21
Story type: Series
Subject(s): Terrorism; Politics; Suspense
Major character(s): Sean Dillon, Agent (Black Ops); Sara Gideon, Military Personnel (captain); Jake Cazalet, Political Figure (former US president)
Time period(s): 21st century; 2010s
Locale(s): Massachusetts, United States

Summary: This book is the 21st installment of author Jack Higgins's Sean Dillon series. When two Chechen terrorists working with al Qaeda arrive on Nantucket to assassinate former US president Jake Cazalet, they don't bank on their mission being thwarted by special agent Sean Dillon and his companion, Captain Sara Gideon. Even though it's easy for Sean and Sara to neutralize the terrorists, they can't help but wonder how the interlopers knew about the former president's location in the first place. When Sean learns who is behind the assassination attempt, he knows he must act fast. This name from Sean's past is so terrifying that he knows if he doesn't stop the culprit, more attempts will ensue. Jack's life and the security of the entire nation will be at risk. Now Sean must use everything he knows about this secret operative to bring him down.

Other books by the same author:
The Death Trade, 2013
A Devil Is Waiting, 2012
The Judas Gate, 2011
First Strike, 2010
The Wolf at the Door, 2010

Other books you might like:
David Baldacci, *Hell's Corner*, 2010
Alex Berenson, *Twelve Days*, 2015
Steve Berry, *The Patriot Threat*, 2015
Dale Brown, *Target Utopia*, 2015
Ben Coes, *Independence Day*, 2015
Vince Flynn, *Last Man*, 2012
Jamie Freveletti, *Robert Ludlum's The Geneva Strategy*, 2015
Stephen Fry, *Kodiak Spy*, 2014
Mark Greaney, *Tom Clancy Full Force and Effect*, 2014
W.E.B. Griffin, *The Assassination Option*, 2014
W.E.B. Griffin, *Top Secret*, 2014
Brian Haig, *The Night Crew*, 2015
Ward Larsen, *Assassin's Game*, 2014
Jonathan Maberry, *Code Zero*, 2014
Leo Maloney, *Silent Assassin*, 2013
Brad Meltzer, *The President's Shadow*, 2015
James Rollins, *The Kill Switch: A Tucker Wayne Novel*, 2014
Sebastian Rotella, *The Convert's Song*, 2014

767

STEVE HIMMER

Fram

(Brooklyn, New York: Ig Publishing, 2015)

Story type: Adventure
Subject(s): Cold War, 1945-1991; Voyages and travels; Spies
Major character(s): Oscar, Government Official, Spouse (of Julia); Alexi, Government Official; Julia, Spouse (of Oscar)
Time period(s): 21st century; 2010s

Summary: Oscar works for the US government on a top secret, and extremely vague, mission for the Bureau of Ice Prognostication. Since the Cold War, Oscar and his coworker, Alexi, have mapped out the theoretical geography of the Arctic Circle. It is Oscar's job to essentially guess what ice formations might be in the region, and therefore save the government billions of dollars in federal funding since no one will have to physically explore the Arctic. Then, Oscar and Alexi are presented with an assignment to actually go on an expedition to the Arctic Circle. As Oscar learns more about the fact that the Cold War between the United States and the Soviet Union never truly ended, he realizes the bureaucratic lie that he has been living all this time. Meanwhile, he also rekindles his marriage to his wife, Julia, who never quite understood what his job was until now.

Other books you might like:
Kingsley Amis, *The Anti-Death League*, 1966
Vince Flynn, *Last Man*, 2012
Simon R. Green, *Daemons Are Forever*, 2008
Graham Greene, *Our Man in Havana*, 2007
Andrew Marr, *Head of State*, 2015
Ian McEwan, *Solar*, 2010
Daniel Silva, *The Heist*, 2014
Elizabeth Stuckey-French, *Revenge of the Radioactive Lady*, 2011
Keith Thomson, *Twice a Spy*, 2011
Peter Warner, *The Mole*, 2013

768

ANN HOOD

An Italian Wife

(New York: W. W. Norton & Company, 2014)

Story type: Family Saga
Subject(s): Family; Italy; Italian Americans
Major character(s): Josephine Rimaldi, 14-Year-Old, Spouse (of Vincenzo Rinaldo), Mother (Carmine, Elisabetta, Valentina, and four others), Grandmother (of Francesca), Grandmother (great-grandmother of

Aida); Vincenzo Rimaldi, Worker (mill), Spouse (of Josephine), Father (of Carmine, Elisabetta, and four other children); Carmine, Son (of Josephine and Vincenzo); Elisabetta, Daughter (of Josephine and Vincenzo); Valentina, Daughter (of Josephine), Adoptee (given up by Josephine); Francesca, Granddaughter (of Josephine); Aida, Granddaughter (great-granddaughter of Josephine)
Time period(s): 19th century-20th century; 1880s-1990s
Locale(s): Italy; United States

Summary: As this novel by Ann Hood opens, 14-year-old Josephine Rimaldi is married to the much-older Vincenzo Rinaldo according to a family arrangement. It is the late 1890s, and Josephine lives as Vincenzo's wife for just a few days before he immigrates to the United States. Years later Vincenzo is able to send for Josephine, and she leaves her familiar village to live in an Italian neighborhood in Rhode Island. Although theirs is a loveless marriage, Josephine and Vincenzo have six children together, including Carmine and Elisabetta. Josephine also gives birth to another child, Valentina, who is fathered by a lover, but she surrenders the child for adoption and tells Vincenzo the baby is dead. The novel follows Josephine in 20th-century America, as her children, grandchildren, and great-grandchildren experience the effects of world wars and social change. Like Josephine, her descendants search for love and fulfillment.

Other books by the same author:
The Obituary Writer, 2013
The Red Thread, 2010
The Knitting Circle, 2007
An Ornithologist's Guide to Life, 2004
Ruby, 1998

Other books you might like:
Kate Atkinson, *Behind the Scenes at the Museum*, 1996
Francisco Azevedo, *Once Upon a Time in Rio*, 2014
Christopher Castellani, *All This Talk of Love*, 2013
Sandra Cisneros, *Caramelo*, 2002
Suellen Dainty, *After Everything*, 2014
Ursula Hegi, *The Worst Thing I've Done*, 2007
Khaled Hosseini, *And the Mountains Echoed*, 2013
Lloyd Jones, *Hand Me Down World*, 2010
Matthew Thomas, *We Are Not Ourselves*, 2014
Rufi Thorpe, *The Girls from Corona del Mar*, 2014
Adriana Trigiani, *Lucia, Lucia: A Novel*, 2003

769

EMMA HOOPER

Emma and Otto and Russell and James

(New York: Simon & Schuster, 2015)

Story type: Contemporary; Quest
Subject(s): Old age; Marriage; Travel
Major character(s): Etta, Aged Person, Housewife, Spouse (of Otto), Friend (of Russell), Companion (of James); Otto, Aged Person, Spouse (of Etta), Veteran; Russell, Aged Person, Friend (of Etta); James, Coyote, Companion (of Etta)
Time period(s): 20th century-21st century; 1940s-2010s

Locale(s): Canada; Saskatchewan, Canada
Summary: At the age of 82, Etta realizes she has never seen the ocean. So she puts on her walking boots, straps on her rifle, and sets out from her home in Saskatchewan, Canada, for the distant shores of the Atlantic. She leaves a note to her husband, Otto, promising to "try to remember to come back." Otto understands, having seen the ocean many years ago when he fought in World War II. He will wait. But neighbor Russell will not. Russell has long been in love with Etta and has watched her and Otto from his nearby farm, so he begins his own journey to find her. As Etta's quest continues, she is accompanied by a magical talking coyote named James, and the joys and sorrows of a lifetime of fleeting memories.

Other books you might like:
John Banville, *The Sea*, 2005
Julian Barnes, *The Sense of an Ending*, 2011
J.M. Coetzee, *Slow Man*, 2005
Kent Haruf, *Our Souls at Night*, 2015
Jonas Jonasson, *The 100-Year-Old Man Who Climbed Out the Window and Disappeared*, 2012
Rachel Joyce, *The Unlikely Pilgrimage of Harold Fry*, 2012
William Kowalski, *The Hundred Hearts*, 2013
Ron McLarty, *The Memory of Running*, 2004
Brian Panhuyzen, *The Sky Manifest*, 2013
Alice Walker, *Now Is the Time to Open Your Heart*, 2004

770

NICK HORNBY

Funny Girl

(London: Penguin UK, 2014)

Story type: Historical; Literary
Subject(s): England; Television programs; Humor
Major character(s): Barbara Parker, Young Woman (aka Sophie Straw), Beauty Pageant Contestant, Actress; Clive, Actor; Tony, Writer (television); Bill, Writer (television); Dennis, Director (television)
Time period(s): 20th century; 1960s
Locale(s): London, England

Summary: Barbara Parker—Miss Blackpool 1964—is the belle of her northern England town, but she dreams of making it big in London. She moves to the city, changes her name to Sophie Straw, and auditions for a role in a TV comedy. Sophie doesn't get that role, but she does catch the attention of writers Tony and Bill and director Dennis. They create a show just for Sophie, titled *Funny Girl*, and cast an actor named Clive to play her on-screen spouse. The show is a hit, and Sophie finds the success she wanted. Tony and Bill write episode after episode for their charming star, and Dennis tries to maintain control of the show while he deals with personal problems—namely, his affection for Sophie and his decreasing interest in his wife. The novel follows both the on-screen and off-screen lives of the characters as *Funny Girl* peaks and falls in popularity.

Other books by the same author:
Juliet, Naked, 2009

Slam, 2007
A Long Way Down, 2005
How to Be Good, 2001
About a Boy, 1998

Other books you might like:
Erica Bauermeister, *The Lost Art of Mixing*, 2013
Elizabeth Berg, *Say When*, 2003
Maeve Binchy, *Chestnut Street*, 2014
Eleanor Brown, *The Weird Sisters*, 2011
Michael Callahan, *Searching for Grace Kelly*, 2015
Julia Darling, *Crocodile Soup*, 2000
Helen Fielding, *Bridget Jones's Diary*, 1996
Nick Hornby, *Juliet, Naked*, 2009
John Kenney, *Truth in Advertising*, 2013
Penelope Lively, *How It All Began*, 2012
Alexander McCall Smith, *The Importance of Being Seven: A 44 Scotland Street Novel*, 2010
Liane Moriarty, *What Alice Forgot*, 2011
Jojo Moyes, *One Plus One*, 2014
Andrew O'Hagan, *The Life and Opinions of Maf the Dog, and of His Friend Marilyn Monroe*, 2010
Andrew O'Hagan, *Personality*, 2003
Cathleen Schine, *Fin and Lady*, 2013
Lionel Shriver, *The Post-Birthday World: A Novel*, 2007
Helen Simonson, *Major Pettigrew's Last Stand*, 2011
Jess Walter, *Beautiful Ruins*, 2012

771

ANTHONY HOROWITZ

Moriarty

(New York: Harper, 2014)

Subject(s): Mystery; Detective fiction; Crime
Major character(s): Frederick Chase, Detective (Pinkerton); Athelney Jones, Detective (Scotland Yard inspector); Sherlock Holmes, Detective, Colleague (of John Watson), Enemy (of James Moriarty); James Moriarty, Villain, Enemy (of Sherlock Holmes); John Watson, Doctor, Colleague (of Sherlock Holmes); Clarence Devereux, Criminal
Time period(s): 19th century; 1890s (1891)
Locale(s): London, England

Summary: In his second full-length Sherlock Holmes redux, author Anthony Horowitz creates a mystery set in the aftermath of the great detective's presumed death. During a fateful meeting at Switzerland's Reichenbach Falls, Holmes and his arch enemy, James Moriarty, are believed to have plunged to their deaths. Holmes's colleague, Dr. John Watson, discovered evidence of a struggle, and he has described the events he witnessed to Scotland Yard. Pinkerton detective Frederick Chase remains interested in Moriarty, even though the criminal mastermind is apparently dead. Chase has been following Clarence Devereux, an American criminal and suspected colleague of Moriarty, who is in Europe to claim the territory left by the "Napoleon of crime." In London, Chase allies himself with Athelney Jones of Scotland Yard, and the two scour the city's backstreets in search of Moriarty's heir apparent. Jones proves to be a skilled practitioner of Holmes's methods.

Other books by the same author:
Oblivion, 2013
Russian Roulette, 2013
Death and the Underworld, 2011
The House of Silk: A Sherlock Holmes Novel, 2011
Scorpia Rising, 2011

Other books you might like:
Adam Christopher, *The Ghost Line*, 2015
David Stuart Davies, *The Devil's Promise*, 2014
Jamie Freveletti, *Robert Ludlum's The Geneva Strategy*, 2015
Neil Gaiman, *Trigger Warning: Short Fictions and Disturbances*, 2015
John Gardner, *Moriarty*, 2008
Barry Grant, *The Strange Return of Sherlock Holmes*, 2010
Alex Grecian, *The Devil's Workshop*, 2014
Anthony Horowitz, *The House of Silk: A Sherlock Holmes Novel*, 2011
Jamyang Norbu, *Sherlock Holmes: The Missing Years*, 1999
H. Paul Jeffers, *The Forgotten Adventures of Sherlock Holmes*, 2005
Lene Kaaberbol, *Doctor Death*, 2015
Laurie R. King, *Dreaming Spies*, 2015
Kieran Lyne, *The Last Confession of Sherlock Holmes*, 2014
Larry Millett, *The Disappearance of Sherlock Holmes*, 2002
Marcia Muller, *The Body Snatchers Affair*, 2015
Peter Ranscombe, *Hare*, 2014
Michael Robertson, *Moriarty Returns a Letter*, 2014
Kieran Shields, *A Study in Revenge*, 2013
Sam Siciliano, *The Further Adventures of Sherlock Holmes: The Grimswell Curse*, 2013
Dan Simmons, *The Fifth Heart*, 2015
Donald Thomas, *Sherlock Holmes and the Ghosts of Bly*, 2010
Charles Valey, *The Last Moriarty: A Sherlock Holmes Thriller*, 2014
Alan Vanneman, *Sherlock Holmes and the Hapsburg Tiara*, 2004

772

STEVE ISRAEL

The Global War on Morris

(New York: Simon & Schuster, 2015)

Story type: Contemporary; Humor
Subject(s): Humor; United States; Espionage
Major character(s): Morris Feldstein, Salesman, Crime Suspect, Father, Spouse (of Rona); Rona Feldstein, Doctor, Spouse (of Morris), Mother; Dick Cheney, Political Figure, Colleague (of Karl Rove), Historical Figure; Karl Rove, Historical Figure, Political Figure, Colleague (of Dick Cheney)
Time period(s): 21st century; 2000s (2004)

Locale(s): New York, New York

Summary: Morris and Rona Feldstein are a typical Long Island Jewish couple. Morris is a medical salesman who likes his quiet existence and routines. He watches baseball, is a good father, and maintains a timeshare in Florida. Rona, a doctor, keeps on top of national and international events, and expresses her opinions loudly. When Morris is seduced by a secretary on his sales route, in a moment of weakness he uses his company credit card to pay for a motel room. This act triggers the attention of NICK, the government supercomputer that tracks national security threats. As Dick Cheney and Karl Rove drum up fear of terrorism and traitors, NICK begins to draw connections between various, unconnected aspects within Morris and Rona's lives, and Morris finds himself the number-one suspect in the nation. Rona's medical practice and friendship with a Muslim boy at their timeshare, his daughter's political beliefs, his sales route, and some traffic violations are only the tip of the iceberg. Written by a US Congressman, this novel humorously explores the American government's approach to home security in 2004. First novel.

Other books you might like:
Dave Barry, *Insane City*, 2013
Tim Dorsey, *Shark Skin Suite*, 2015
Carl Hiassen, *Skink—No Surrender*, 2014
James Hynes, *Next: A Novel*, 2010
Chuck Palahniuk, *Beautiful You*, 2014
Tom Robbins, *Villa Incognito*, 2003
Matt Ruff, *The Mirage*, 2012
Lionel Shriver, *The New Republic*, 2012
L. Neil Smith, *The American Zone*, 2001
Jerry Stahl, *Happy Mutant Baby Pills*, 2013

773

REBECCA JAMES

Sweet Damage

(New York: Random House Publishing Group, 2014)

Story type: Gothic; Mystery
Subject(s): Landlord-tenant relations; Mystery; Housing
Major character(s): Tim Ellison, Cook, Caregiver (to Anna); Anna London, 20-Year-Old, Young Woman, Recluse
Time period(s): 21st century; 2010s
Locale(s): Sydney, Australia

Summary: Tim Ellison feels like he lucked out. When he was looking to move to downtown Sydney, Australia, he found what seemed like the perfect place. He's discovered a room for a great price near his workplace and his favorite beach. The catch? The home he'll be staying at is a gloomy, foreboding mansion, and he will be caring for the house's enigmatic resident. Anna London is a beautiful 20-year-old but carries herself like an old woman. A slave to her fears, she keeps herself holed up in her mansion and never leaves. As Tim adjusts to life in the house, strange things start to happen. Mysterious noises and shadowy figures rattle through the night, and disturbing messages appear on the walls. As Tim begins to fall for Anna, he begins to wonder if it's the house that's haunted, or if it all comes back to Anna.

Other books by the same author:
Cooper Bartholomew Is Dead, 2014
Beautiful Malice, 2010

Other books you might like:
Michael Christie, *If I Fall, If I Die*, 2015
Keith Donohue, *The Boy Who Drew Monsters*, 2014
Brendan Duffy, *House of Echoes*, 2015
Stephen King, *Full Dark, No Stars*, 2010
Kimberly McCreight, *Where They Found Her*, 2015
Jennifer McMahon, *The Winter People*, 2014
Madeleine Roux, *Asylum*, 2013
Frank Tallis, *The Sleep Room*, 2013
Anna Todd, *After We Fell*, 2014
Lisa Unger, *Crazy Love You*, 2015
Carly Anne West, *The Bargaining*, 2015

774

HA JIN

A Map of Betrayal

(New York: Knopf Doubleday Publishing Group, 2014)

Story type: Espionage; Family Saga
Subject(s): China; Chinese Americans; Chinese (Asian people)
Major character(s): Gary Shang, Spy, Father (of Lilian); Lilian Shang, Professor, Daughter (of Gary)
Time period(s): 21st century; (2010s); 20th century; 1940s-1980s
Locale(s): China; United States

Summary: Lilian Shang has grown up knowing she is the daughter of a Chinese spy. Her father, Gary Shang, was convicted and jailed decades earlier for spying against the United States. But there is much more to his story that she never knew. After the death of her parents, Lilian receives her father's diary. She discovers he had another life in his native China before he became a spy, and the world she entered into was part of his deception. She travels to China to investigate who her father really was, and to meet the family he left behind to do his duty to his homeland. She uncovers a man forced to choose between devotion to family or country. In the end, the man who betrayed his adopted nation was also betrayed by the one of his birth.

Other books by the same author:
Nanjing Requiem, 2011
A Good Fall: Stories, 2009
A Free Life, 2007
War Trash, 2004
The Crazed, 2002

Other books you might like:
John Banville, *The Untouchable*, 1997
Graham Greene, *The Human Factor*, 1978
Mai Jia, *Decoded*, 2014
Denis Johnson, *The Laughing Monsters*, 2014
Joseph Kanon, *The Prodigal Spy: A Novel*, 1998
Chang-Rae Lee, *Native Speaker*, 1995
Ian McEwan, *The Innocent*, 1990
Anchee Min, *Pearl of China: A Novel*, 2009
Yan Mo, *Frog*, 2014

Popular Fiction

Yannick Murphy, *Signed, Mata Hari*, 2007
Joakim Zander, *The Swimmer*, 2015

775

SARAH JIO

The Look of Love

(New York: Plume, 2014)

Story type: Contemporary; Romance
Subject(s): Romances (Fiction); Magic; Love
Major character(s): Jane Williams, Businesswoman (florist), Companion (of Sam); Sam, Dog, Companion (of Jane)
Time period(s): 21st century; 2010s
Locale(s): Seattle, Washington

Summary: Jane Williams has all but given up on love. From an early memory of her father walking out on her family she developed a blurred vision of love and has never found a successful relationship. Instead she dedicates herself to her beloved dog and her flower shop in Pike Place Market. On Christmas Eve, the day before her 29th birthday, Jane receives a card that claims she was born with the gift to see love in all its forms. She is told that her gift comes with a price: she must identify the six types of love in detail within her journal. She is given until the full moon after her 30th birthday—failure to complete the task means she will never find love for herself. Diving into the lives and relationships of her family and friends, Jane is surprised to find herself falling for a science writer, but is disappointed to find out that he doesn't believe in love at all. It is up to her to convince him that love is a possibility, or else her own future is sealed. This novel by Sarah Jio was inspired by the song "The Look of Love."

Other books by the same author:
The Last Camellia, 2013
Morning Glory, 2013
Blackberry Winter, 2012
The Bungalow, 2011
The Violets of March, 2011

Other books you might like:
Cecelia Ahern, *Rosie Dunne*, 2005
Mary Kay Andrews, *Save the Date*, 2014
Jenny Colgan, *The Loveliest Chocolate Shop in Paris*, 2014
Jessica Q. Fox, *Hard to Get*, 2010
Emily Giffin, *The One and Only*, 2014
Jill Mansell, *Don't Want to Miss a Thing*, 2013
Emma McLaughlin, *The First Affair*, 2013
Laurie Viera Rigler, *Confessions of a Jane Austen Addict: A Novel*, 2007
Plum Sykes, *The Debutante Divorcee*, 2006
Gemma Townley, *The Hopeless Romantic's Handbook*, 2007

776

DENIS JOHNSON

The Laughing Monsters

(New York: Farrar, Straus and Giroux, 2014)

Story type: Contemporary; Political
Subject(s): Suspense; Politics; Culture
Major character(s): Roland Nair, Agent (U.S. Intelligence, rogue), Friend (of Michael); Michael Adriko, Orphan (African war orphan), Friend (of Roland), Fiance(e) (of Davidia); Davidia, Student—Graduate, Fiance(e) (of Michael)
Time period(s): 21st century; 2010s
Locale(s): Freetown, Sierra Leone

Summary: Set in West Africa, this suspense thriller by award-winning author Denis Johnson is a tale of politics and culture, loyalty and deception. Though he claims to be Scandinavian, Roland Nair travels with a U.S. passport. When Roland is invited by his old friend, Michael Adriko, to return to Freetown, Sierra Leone, Roland arrives with the hopes that history will repeat itself. Roland and Michael, an African war orphan, made a fortune ten years earlier during Sierra Leone's civil war. And now, even though Roland was invited for the purpose of meeting Michael's new fiance, Davidia, Roland can't help but think Michael's true motivation involves another money-making scheme. As Roland, Michael, and Davidia travel deep into the Congo in search of Michael's clan near the Newada Mountain, Michael's dangerous plan unfolds. But all three travelers have secrets they are keeping, and no one knows who can be trusted.

Other books by the same author:
Train Dreams, 2011
Nobody Move, 2009
Tree of Smoke, 2007
The Name of the World, 2000
Already Dead: A California Gothic, 1997

Other books you might like:
Anthony Capella, *The Various Flavors of Coffee*, 2008
Joseph Conrad, *Heart of Darkness*, 1899
Dave Eggers, *Your Fathers, Where Are They? And the Prophets, Do They Live Forever?*, 2014
Richard Flanagan, *The Narrow Road to the Deep North*, 2014
Alan Furst, *Mission to Paris*, 2012
Damon Galgut, *The Impostor*, 2008
Ian Holding, *Of Beasts and Beings*, 2011
Ha Jin, *A Map of Betrayal*, 2014
Joseph Kanon, *Leaving Berlin*, 2015
Barbara Kingsolver, *The Poisonwood Bible*, 1998
Dan Mayland, *The Colonel's Mistake*, 2012
Charles McCarry, *The Shanghai Factor*, 2013
Todd Moss, *The Golden Hour*, 2014
Adaobi Tricia Nwaubani, *I Do Not Come to You by Chance*, 2009
Matthew Palmer, *The American Mission*, 2014
Ridley Pearson, *The Red Room*, 2014
Daniel Silva, *The English Spy*, 2015
Paul Theroux, *The Lower River*, 2012

777

RACHEL JOYCE

The Love Song of Miss Queenie Hennessy

(New York: Penguin Random House, 2015)

Story type: Literary
Subject(s): Letters (Correspondence); Friendship; Diseases
Major character(s): Miss Queenie Hennessy, Aged Person, Friend (of Harold); Harold Fry, Friend (of Queenie)
Time period(s): Indeterminate
Locale(s): Berwick-on-Tweed, England

Summary: In this companion novel to *The Unlikely Pilgrimage of Harold Fry*, author Rachel Joyce tells the story of the letter that Queenie never sent Harold. Queenie lies in wait at her final resting place, a hospice in the English countryside. There, she is supposed to be awaiting Harold, but she knows he will never come. She begins writing a letter confessing to Harold all she needs to tell him about her life, including her feelings about him and the relationships she has had since they parted ways. Meanwhile, Queenie forms new relationships with the nuns who care for her in her final days, and with the other patients of the hospice. Yet Queenie has a darker reason for putting her pen to paper. She has a long hidden secret that she has never told anyone, and she hopes if she shares it with her dearest friend, Harold, she will finally put her soul to rest.

Other books by the same author:
Perfect, 2014
The Unlikely Pilgrimage of Harold Fry, 2012

Other books you might like:
Kate Atkinson, *A God in Ruins*, 2015
Fredrik Backman, *My Grandmother Asked Me to Tell You She's Sorry*, 2015
Brooke Davis, *Lost and Found*, 2015
Jonas Jonasson, *The 100-Year-Old Man Who Climbed Out the Window and Disappeared*, 2012
Alexander McCall Smith, *Bertie's Guide to Life and Mothers: A 44 Scotland Street Novel*, 2013
David Nicholls, *Us*, 2014
Matthew Quick, *The Good Luck of Right Now*, 2014
Robin Sharma, *The Secret Letters of the Monk Who Sold His Ferrari*, 2011
Lionel Shriver, *So Much for That*, 2010
Jess Walter, *Beautiful Ruins*, 2012
Martha Woodroof, *Small Blessings*, 2014

778

MIRANDA JULY

The First Bad Man

(New York: Scribner, 2015)

Story type: Contemporary
Subject(s): Women; Friendship; Sexuality
Major character(s): Cheryl Glickman, Roommate (of Clee), Colleague (of Phillip); Clee, Daughter (of Cheryl's boss), Roommate (of Cheryl), 21-Year-Old; Phillip Bettelheim, Colleague (of Cheryl)
Time period(s): 21st century; 2010s
Locale(s): United States

Summary: Cheryl Glickman is convinced that her life is supposed to be different. Her colleague at work, Phillip, doesn't seem to recognize her although she is sure that they have been lovers in a dozen past lives—if he would only open his eyes they could both be very happy. She is a hard worker at a small nonprofit that offers self-defense training as exercise routines, but otherwise is muddling her way through life. Cheryl is always on the lookout for a baby she feels should be hers, a soul who appears in the guise of other children. When Cheryl's employers ask if their wayward 21-year-old daughter, Clee, can move in with her for a while, Cheryl can't say no. Clee is a spoiled, narcissistic brat who shocks Cheryl with her rudeness and poor attitude. Cheryl's carefully ordered life is thrown into upheaval. Clee works to draw Cheryl out of her shell and encourages her to make her own happiness, question her sexuality, and understand her desires. The two women forge an intense bond. In time Cheryl helps Clee understand what it is to be truly loved. First novel.

Other books by the same author:
No One Belongs Here More Than You: Stories, 2007

Other books you might like:
Sam Byers, *Idiopathy*, 2013
Michael Christie, *If I Fall, If I Die*, 2015
Junot Diaz, *The Brief Wondrous Life of Oscar Wao*, 2007
Andre Dubus III, *Dirty Love*, 2013
Fannie Flagg, *The All-Girl Filling Station's Last Reunion*, 2013
Richard Ford, *Let Me Be Frank with You*, 2014
Chad Harbach, *The Art of Fielding*, 2011
Miranda July, *No One Belongs Here More than You: Stories*, 2007
Steve Martin, *The Pleasure of My Company*, 2003
Liz Moore, *Heft*, 2012
Jenny Offill, *Last Things*, 1999
Ann Packer, *Songs Without Words*, 2007
Tom Rachman, *The Imperfectionists: A Novel*, 2010
George Saunders, *Tenth of December: Stories*, 2013
Julie Schumacher, *Dear Committee Members*, 2014
Maria Semple, *Where'd You Go, Bernadette*, 2012
Graeme Simsion, *The Rosie Project*, 2013
Jane Somers, *The Diaries of Jane Somers*, 1984

779

ALEX KAVA

Breaking Creed

(New York: G.P. Putnam's Sons, 2015)

Series: Ryder Creed Series. Book 1
Story type: Mystery
Subject(s): Mystery; Detective fiction; Crime
Major character(s): Ryder Creed, Veteran (Marine),

Popular Fiction

Trainer (search-and-rescue dogs); Maggie O'Dell, FBI Agent

Time period(s): 21st century; 2010s

Locale(s): Alabama, United States; Washington, District of Columbia; Florida, United States

Summary: In the first novel in the Ryder Creed series, author Alex Kava pairs Ryder, a K9 search-and-rescue dog trainer, with FBI agent Maggie O'Dell, the star of a long-running suspense series. Ryder, a former Marine, uses the skills he learned in the military to train K9 dogs for law enforcement. His dogs can sniff out drugs and other contraband, but when Ryder is called to search a fishing boat off Florida's Gulf Coast, the dogs find five children concealed on board. In the process of exposing a human trafficking operation, Ryder puts his own life in danger. Meanwhile in Washington, DC, Maggie is trying to find out who tortured and killed several victims who have been found in the Potomac River. Maggie eventually learns that her case is connected to Ryder's, but her discovery may have come too late.

Other books by the same author:
Stranded, 2013
Fireproof, 2012
Hotwire, 2011
Black Friday, 2010
Damaged, 2010

Other books you might like:
James O. Born, *Scent of Murder*, 2015
Allison Brennan, *Dead Heat*, 2014
Robert Crais, *Suspect*, 2013
Clive Cussler, *Ghost Ship*, 2014
Lisa Gardner, *Crash and Burn*, 2015
Iris Johansen, *The Search*, 2000
Lee Charles Kelley, *A Nose for Murder*, 2003
Andrew Klavan, *A Killer in the Wind*, 2013
Virginia Lanier, *Death in Bloodhound Red*, 1995
Nicole Maggi, *The Forgetting*, 2015
Ridley Pearson, *Choke Point*, 2013
Jodi Picoult, *Vanishing Acts*, 2005
Spencer Quinn, *Dog on It*, 2009
Nora Roberts, *The Search*, 2010
James Rollins, *The Kill Switch: A Tucker Wayne Novel*, 2014
David Rosenfelt, *Dog Tags*, 2010
Taylor Stevens, *The Doll*, 2013

780

JONATHAN KELLERMAN

Motive

(New York: Penguin Random House, 2015)

Series: Alex Delaware Series. Book 30
Story type: Psychological Suspense
Subject(s): Detective fiction; Serial murders; Crime
Major character(s): Milo Sturgis, Detective—Homicide; Alex Delaware, Psychologist; Ursula Corey, Crime Victim; Katherine Hennepin, Crime Victim
Time period(s): 21st century; 2010s
Locale(s): Los Angeles, California

Summary: In the 30th installment from author Jonathan Kellerman's Alex Delaware series, criminal psychologist Alex Delaware must stop a clever serial killer who appears to have a grudge against him. When Lieutenant Milo Sturgis of the Los Angeles Police Department examines the crime scene following the murder of Katherine Hennepin, he is certain it will be an open-and-shut case. When he can't find a suspect, however, he rethinks that belief. Then Sturgis and Delaware are assigned the case of Ursula Corey, and they soon see that the case is eerily similar to that of Hennepin. Both women were killed execution style, and in both cases the obvious suspects can account for their whereabouts at the time of each murder. When they learn of another murder under similar circumstances, Sturgis and Delaware know that they have a serial killer on their hands. Now they have to figure out what makes this killer tick before the murderer takes another life.

Other books by the same author:
The Golem of Hollywood, 2014
Killer, 2014
Guilt, 2013
Victims, 2012
Mystery, 2011

Other books you might like:
Chelsea Cain, *One Kick*, 2014
Paul Cleave, *Five Minutes Alone*, 2014
Michael Connelly, *The Burning Room*, 2014
Jennifer DuBois, *Cartwheel*, 2013
Tana French, *The Secret Place*, 2014
Tess Gerritsen, *Die Again*, 2014
Sophie Hannah, *The Carrier*, 2015
Kay Hooper, *Haunted*, 2014
Phillip Margolin, *Woman with a Gun*, 2014
Cuyler Overholt, *A Deadly Affection*, 2012
James Patterson, *Hope to Die*, 2014
James Patterson, *Private Vegas*, 2015
Louise Penny, *The Long Way Home*, 2014
Kathy Reichs, *Speaking in Bones*, 2015
J.D. Robb, *Obsession in Death*, 2015
Michael Robotham, *Say You're Sorry*, 2012
Michael Robotham, *Watching You*, 2014
Lisa Unger, *In the Blood*, 2014
Kate Waterson, *Fractured*, 2015
Stephen White, *Line of Fire*, 2012
Stuart Woods, *Insatiable Appetites*, 2015

781

JAMES KELMAN

If It Is Your Life

(London: Hamish Hamilton, 2010)

Story type: Collection
Subject(s): Short stories; Literature; International relations

Summary: Novelist, playwright, and essayist James Kelman presents a collection of 19 short stories that explore the concerns and dilemmas that permeate everyday life. In "If It Is Your Life," a college student spends his time commuting by bus and pondering his current worries. In

"The Gate," a much older man—a grandfather—has trouble finding his way home after purchasing a bike for his grandchild. "The Third Man, or Else the Fourth" also focuses on elderly characters. In this case, older men who have come to see a horse race share stories and opinions while they wait. The collection also includes "Tricky Times Ahead Pal," "The Later Transgression," "Justice for One," and "I Am Putty."

Other books by the same author:
Mo Said She Was Quirky, 2013
Kieron Smith, Boy, 2008
You Have to Be Careful in the Land of the Free, 2004
Translated Accounts, 2001
The Good Times: Stories, 1998

Other books you might like:
Jimmy Buffett, *A Salty Piece of Land*, 2004
Ian Frazier, *The Cursing Mommy's Book of Days: A Novel*, 2012
Alasdair Gray, *The End of Our Tethers: 13 Sorry Stories*, 2003
Peter Hoeg, *The Elephant Keepers' Children*, 2012
Kazuo Ishiguro, *Nocturnes: Five Stories of Music and Nightfall*, 2009
B.J. Novak, *One More Thing: Stories and Other Stories*, 2014
Betsey Osborne, *The Natural History of Uncas Metcalfe*, 2006
Maggie Shipstead, *Seating Arrangements: A Novel*, 2012
Luke Williams, *The Echo Chamber*, 2011

782

CAROLINE KEPNES

You

(New York: Atria/Emily Bestler Books, 2014)

Story type: Psychological Suspense
Subject(s): Stalking; Murder; Friendship
Major character(s): Guinevere Beck, Boyfriend (of Joe), Writer, Young Woman, Crime Victim; Joe Goldberg, Young Man, Boyfriend (of Guinevere), Worker (at bookstore), Murderer
Time period(s): 21st century; 2010s
Locale(s): New York, New York

Summary: The day Guinevere Beck walked into a New York City bookstore she didn't realize she also was walking into Joe Goldberg's life. Instantly smitten, the bookstore clerk and aspiring writer bond over their love of literature. A later chance encounter only furthers Guinevere's slide into Joe's life. As the pair begin a relationship, things are not all as they seem. Joe has been orchestrating things from the start, watching Guinevere's every move, following her through social media, and becoming the man he thinks she wants him to be. As Joe's obsession deepens, his obstacles to Guinevere begin to vanish. First, her cheating boyfriend disappears. Next, it's her best friend. And all along, Joe's waiting arms are there to comfort Guinevere. First novel.

Other books you might like:
Sandra Brown, *Low Pressure*, 2012
Chelsea Cain, *One Kick*, 2014
Catherine Coulter, *Power Play*, 2014
Elisabeth de Mariaffi, *The Devil You Know*, 2015
Lynette Eason, *Nowhere to Turn*, 2014
Nicci French, *Secret Smile*, 2004
Elizabeth Haynes, *Into the Darkest Corner*, 2012
Lindsey Hunter, *Ugly Girls*, 2014
Claire Kendal, *The Book of You*, 2014
Jayne Ann Krentz, *Trust No One*, 2015
J.D. Robb, *Obsession in Death*, 2015

783

STEPHEN KING

Revival

(New York: Scribner, 2014)

Story type: Horror
Subject(s): Religion; Faith; Family
Major character(s): Charles Jacobs, Religious (minister), Outcast; Jamie Morton, Musician, Addict, Traveler
Time period(s): 20th century-21st century; 1960s-2010s
Locale(s): New England, United States

Summary: Horror author Stephen King addresses the issues of faith and fanaticism in this story. Spanning five decades of Jamie Morton's life, the tale begins with the arrival of a charismatic reverend who takes over the local church. The Reverend Charles Jacobs and his beautiful wife are embraced by the town. Jamie, despite his young age, forms a friendship with Jacobs. However, tragedy soon strikes Jamie's family and the community is dumbfounded when the beloved minister falls from grace. In a tirade against God and Christianity, he mocks the tenets of organized faith and flees town. Decades later, Jamie is a transient musician, moving from gig to gig as his heroin addiction costs him jobs, relationships, and a meaningful life. A chance encounter with Jacobs allows the pair to reforge their friendship in a dark fashion.

Other books by the same author:
Mr. Mercedes, 2014
Doctor Sleep, 2013
Joyland, 2013
The Wind through the Keyhole, 2012
11/22/1963, 2011

Other books you might like:
Ann Aguirre, *Mortal Danger*, 2014
Douglas Clegg, *Isis*, 2006
Nancy A. Collins, *Looks Could Kill*, 2006
Gemma Files, *Hexslinger Series*, 2010
Gemma Files, *A Tree of Bones*, 2012
Nate Kenyon, *Bloodstone*, 2006
Stephen King, *Needful Things*, 1991
Dean R. Koontz, *Life Expectancy*, 2004
Michael Laimo, *The Demonologist*, 2005
Sarah Langan, *The Keeper*, 2006
Stephen Leather, *Nightfall*, 2012
Weston Ochse, *Scarecrow Gods*, 2005
Tom Piccirilli, *November Mourns*, 2005

Gary Raisor, *Sinister Purposes*, 2006
Marcus Sedgwick, *The Book of Dead Days*, 2003
Peter Straub, *A Dark Matter*, 2010
Jeff VanderMeer, *Area X*, 2014
Pat Walsh, *The Crowfield Demon*, 2012
Wrath James White, *The Resurrectionist*, 2009

784

SOPHIE KINSELLA (Pseudonym of Madeleine Wickham)

Shopaholic to the Stars

(New York: Random House, 2014)

Series: Shopaholic Series. Book 7
Story type: Contemporary; Series
Subject(s): Women; Fashion; Romances (Fiction)
Major character(s): Rebecca "Becky" Bloomfield Brandon, Expert (fashion), Spouse (of Luke), Mother (of Minnie), Friend (of Suze and Tarquin); Luke Brandon, Consultant (public relations), Spouse (of Becky), Father (of Minnie); Minnie, 2-Year-Old, Daughter (of Becky and Luke); Sage Seymour, Actress, Client (of Luke); Lois Kellerton, Actress (rival of Sage); Suze, Friend (of Becky); Tarquin, Friend (of Becky)
Time period(s): 21st century; 2010s
Locale(s): Los Angeles, California

Summary: Fashionista Becky Brandon and her family travel to Hollywood in the seventh novel in Sophie Kinsella's Shopaholic series. Becky's husband, Luke, is doing PR work for actress Sage Seymour, and Becky wants in on the Tinseltown action. When she misses out on a personal shopper job, Becky decides to put her considerable fashion skills to work as a stylist to the rich and famous. Sage seems a logical candidate for Becky's client list, but when the fickle actress makes her disinterest known, Becky accepts an offer from another celebrity. Lois Kellerton is also a big-name actress; unfortunately, she is Sage's big-time rival. Becky's excitement about her new career is somewhat dampened by the strained relationship between her and Luke's clients. As Becky navigates her new social scene, she encounters one amusing problem after another.

Other books by the same author:
Wedding Night, 2013
I've Got Your Number, 2012
Mini-Shopaholic, 2010
Twenties Girl, 2009
Remember Me?, 2008

Other books you might like:
Roz Bailey, *Retail Therapy*, 2004
Melissa de la Cruz, *Girl Stays in the Picture*, 2009
Amanda Goldberg, *Beneath a Starlet Sky*, 2011
Lauren Graham, *Someday, Someday, Maybe*, 2013
Jane Green, *Saving Grace*, 2014
Mimi Hare, *The Second Assistant*, 2004
Wendy Holden, *Beautiful People*, 2008
Rachel Hollis, *Party Girl: The Ugly Side of Hollywood's Prettiest Parties*, 2014
Allie Kingsley, *The Liar, the Bitch, and the Wardrobe*, 2012

Jen Lancaster, *Bitter Is the New Black: Confessions of a Condescending, Egomaniacal, Self-Centered Smartass, Or, Why You Should Never Carry a Prada Bag to the Unemployment Office*, 2006
Kimberla Lawson Roby, *The Best of Everything*, 2009
Emma McLaughlin, *Between You and Me*, 2012
Melissa Pimentel, *Love by the Book*, 2015
Lisa Rinna, *Starlit: A Novel*, 2010
Babe Walker, *Psychos*, 2014
Lauren Weisberger, *Last Night at Chateau Marmont*, 2010
Lauren Weisberger, *Revenge Wears Prada: The Devil Returns*, 2013

785

DEAN KOONTZ

Saint Odd

(New York: Bantam Books, 2015)

Series: Odd Thomas Series. Book 7
Story type: Paranormal
Subject(s): Fantasy; Death; Supernatural
Major character(s): Odd Thomas, Eccentric, Young Man, Cook, Child of Divorced Parents, Psychic (former, of Stormy); Bronwen "Stormy" Llewellyn, Spirit, Woman, Girlfriend (former, of Odd), Psychic
Time period(s): 21st century; 2010s
Locale(s): Pico Mundo, California

Summary: In the seventh and final installment of the Odd Thomas series, Odd Thomas is drawn back home to his hometown of Pico Mundo for his final confrontation with evil. His dreams show him a glimpse of what evil lies ahead. He keeps seeing Pico Mundo submerged underwater and all the townspeople dead. A satanic cult that Thomas has crossed paths with before has plans to wreak death and destruction on his hometown and the people he cares for. Thomas reconnects with some of his old friends. The carnival is back in town and sets the stage for the mayhem, which involves a devastating virus. Thomas both faces off against his enemies and once again encounters his late soul mate and girlfriend, Stormy Llewellyn.

Other books by the same author:
Deeply Odd, 2013
Odd Interlude, 2013
Odd Apocalypse, 2012
In Odd We Trust, 2008
Odd Hours, 2008
The Good Guy, 2007
Brother Odd: A Novel, 2006
Forever Odd, 2005
The Face, 2003
Odd Thomas, 2003
Seize the Night, 1999
Strange Highways, 1995

Other books you might like:
Amanda Downum, *Dreams of Shreds and Tatters*, 2015
Dennis Etchison, *Shadow Man*, 1993

Seth Grahame-Smith, *Abraham Lincoln: Vampire Hunter*, 2010
S.L. Grey, *The New Girl*, 2014
James Grippando, *Cane and Abe*, 2015
Joe Hill, *Horns: A Novel*, 2010
Kay Hooper, *Chill of Fear*, 2005
John Irving, *A Prayer for Owen Meany: A Novel*, 1989
John Irving, *The World According to Garp*, 1978
Stephen King, *The Dead Zone*, 1979
Stephen King, *Firestarter*, 1980
Stephen King, *Full Dark, No Stars*, 2010
Brian Lumley, *Necroscope Defilers*, 2000
Jonathan Maberry, *Fall of Night*, 2014
Graham Masterton, *Darkroom*, 2004
Thomas F. Monteleone, *Eyes of the Virgin*, 2002
Christopher Moore, *The Stupidest Angel*, 2004
Douglas Preston, *Blue Labyrinth*, 2014
Kat Richardson, *Greywalker*, 2006
Robin Riopelle, *Deadroads*, 2014
Mags Storey, *Dead Girls Don't*, 2015
Jeff VanderMeer, *Area X*, 2014
Dan Wells, *I Am Not a Serial Killer*, 2010
Colson Whitehead, *Zone One*, 2011
F. Paul Wilson, *Bloodline: A Repairman Jack Novel*, September 18, 2007
David Wong, *John Dies at the End*, 2007

786

JAYNE ANN KRENTZ

Trust No One

(New York: Putnam Adult, 2015)

Subject(s): Romances (Fiction); Murder; Crime
Major character(s): Grace Elland, Worker (employee of Sprague Witherspoon); Sprague Witherspoon, Motivational Speaker, Employer (of Grace), Crime Victim; Julius Arkwright, Financier (venture-capitalist), Veteran (former Marine)
Time period(s): 21st century; 2010s
Locale(s): United States

Summary: The death of Grace Elland's employer, motivational speaker Sprague Witherspoon, changes the course of Grace's life. Grace is the one who finds the corpse, and she knows that the liquor bottle at the scene is a message for her. In an attempt to recover from the shock of the event, Grace returns to the town she was raised in and tries to make a new start. Although Grace has learned a thing or two about optimism from Sprague, she is hard pressed to find anything good about her blind date with financier Julius Arkwright. The two see eye to eye on almost nothing, but when Grace finds herself in danger, Julius becomes her surprising ally. Grace is being followed by someone who obviously has evil intent. Now Sprague, who was a Marine before he became a wealthy businessman, may have to put his fighting skills to the test.

Other books by the same author:
River Road, 2014
Dream Eyes, 2013

Copper Beach, 2012
In Too Deep, 2010
Fired Up, 2009
Other books you might like:
D.D. Ayres, *Irresistible Force*, 2014
Allison Brennan, *Notorious*, 2014
Suzanne Brockmann, *Into the Storm: A Novel*, 2006
Sandra Brown, *Low Pressure*, 2012
Shelley Coriell, *The Broken*, 2014
Christina Dodd, *Virtue Falls*, 2014
Cynthia Eden, *Scream for Me*, 2014
Christine Feehan, *Predatory Game*, 2008
Lori Foster, *No Limits*, 2014
Kay Hooper, *Sleeping with Fear*, 2006
Caroline Kepnes, *You*, 2014
Elizabeth Lowell, *Dangerous Refuge*, 2013
Kat Martin, *Against the Storm*, 2011
Carla Neggers, *The Whisper*, 2010
Susan Elizabeth Phillips, *Heroes Are My Weakness*, 2014
Karen Robards, *Hush*, 2014
J.D. Robb, *Obsession in Death*, 2015
Karen Rose, *Closer Than You Think*, 2015
Karen Rose, *Silent Scream*, 2010

787

LORNA LANDVIK

Best to Laugh

(Minneapolis: University of Minnesota Press, 2014)

Story type: Contemporary; Humor
Subject(s): Entertainment industry; Comedians; Comedy
Major character(s): Candy Pekkala, Entertainer (stand-up comedian)
Time period(s): 21st century; 2010s
Locale(s): Los Angeles, California; Minnesota, United States

Summary: Candy Pekkala leaps at the chance to expand her horizons when her cousin calls from Hollywood offering her apartment to sublet. Half Korean, half Norwegian, Candy has been raised by her grandmother and recently graduated from college. She has no plans for the future, so she is all too glad to flee Minnesota in search of an interesting future. She accepts her cousin's offer and moves into Peyton Hall, where she quickly makes friends with a variety of neighbors including a gypsy fortune-teller and a female bodybuilder. The complex is full of individuals who have tried to make it in show business and those who have made it but lost everything. With encouragement from her grandmother and new friends, Candy steps into the world of stand-up comedy. She is determined to bring her own brand of Minnesota humor to the stage and find fame. She will have to overcome sexism and critics who argue that female comedians simply do not know how to be funny.

Other books by the same author:
Mayor of the Universe, 2014
'Tis the Season, 2008
The View from Mount Joy, 2007

Oh My Stars, 2005
Angry Housewives Eating Bon Bons, 2003

Other books you might like:
Elizabeth Berg, *The Last Time I Saw You*, 2010
Fannie Flagg, *I Still Dream About You*, 2010
Billie Letts, *Made in the U.S.A.: A Novel*, 2008
Elinor Lipman, *The View from Penthouse B*, 2013
Jennifer Ross, *The Icing on the Cupcake*, 2010
Adriana Trigiani, *The Supreme Macaroni Company*, 2013
Amy Wallen, *Moonpies and Movie Stars*, 2006
Jess Walter, *Beautiful Ruins*, 2012
Rebecca Wells, *The Crowning Glory of Calla Lily Ponder*, 2009
Meg Wolitzer, *The Interestings*, 2013

788

DENNIS LEHANE

The Drop

(New York: William Morrow, 2014)

Story type: Contemporary Realism; Family Saga
Subject(s): Criminals; Organized crime; Bars (Drinking establishments)
Major character(s): Bob Saginowski, Bartender, Cousin (of Marv), Friend (of Nadia); Marv, Businessman, Cousin (of Bob); Nadia, Friend (of Bob)
Time period(s): 21st century; 2010s
Locale(s): Boston, Massachusetts

Summary: Bob Saginowski endures a lonely existence working as a bartender for his cousin Marv in a seedy Boston neighborhood. A few days after Christmas, Bob finds an abused puppy in a trash can and adopts him. This seemingly small act, however, brings big consequences for Bob. While rescuing the puppy, Bob meets Nadia, a woman with a tragic past. He also gets the unwanted attention of a local thug who claims to be the puppy's rightful owner. Bob is further dragged into the plots swirling around him when the bar is robbed and Marv faces the wrath of the Chechen mafia—the real owners of the bar who use it as a drop for their ill-gotten money. With love and violence in the air, Bob must decide which path to take to avoid conflict.

Other books by the same author:
World Gone By, 2015
Live by Night, 2012
Moonlight Mile, 2010
Shutter Island, 2010
The Given Day, 2008

Other books you might like:
Ace Atkins, *The Forsaken*, 2014
Ace Atkins, *Robert B. Parker's Cheap Shot*, 2014
Lawrence Block, *Hit Me*, 2013
Joe Clifford, *Lamentation*, 2014
Michael Connelly, *The Black Box*, 2012
Robert Crais, *Suspect*, 2013
Tana French, *The Secret Place*, 2014
Donna Leon, *Beastly Things*, 2012
John T. Lescroart, *The Ophelia Cut*, 2013

Archer Mayor, *The Price of Malice*, 2009
Robert B. Parker, *Blue-Eyed Devil*, 2010
T. Jefferson Parker, *Full Measure*, 2014
John Sandford, *Deadline*, 2014

789

EDAN LEPUCKI

California

(New York: Little, Brown and Company, 2014)

Story type: Science Fiction
Subject(s): Apocalypse; Survival; Class conflict
Major character(s): Cal, Survivor, Spouse (of Frida); Frida, Survivor, Spouse (of Cal)
Time period(s): Indeterminate Future
Locale(s): California, United States

Summary: With the world gone, Cal and Frida still have each other. They left Los Angeles after a catastrophe destroyed most of civilization, and retreated to a cabin in the wilderness. When Frida discovers she's pregnant, she and Cal realize they need the safety found in numbers to raise a child. They set out for a nearby community of survivors, and find a place steeped in mistrust of the outside world. As Cal and Frida struggle to fit in, they realize the world they have stepped into may harbor dangers greater than the one they left. Various factions have different, secretive agendas. With their child on the way, Cal and Frida have to decide who to trust, and whether the shelter they so desperately sought is safe. First novel.

Other books you might like:
Margaret Atwood, *The Handmaid's Tale*, 1985
Margaret Atwood, *MaddAddam*, 2013
Glenn Beck, *Agenda 21: Into the Shadows*, 2015
Jenna Black, *Revolution*, 2014
Laura Bynum, *Veracity*, 2010
Mark Z. Danielewski, *The Familiar, Volume 1: One Rainy Day in May*, 2015
Alena Graedon, *The Word Exchange: A Novel*, 2014
Sarah Hall, *Daughters of the North*, 2007
Hugh Howey, *Sand*, 2014
Paul Antony Jones, *Extinction Point*, 2014
Stephen King, *The Stand*, 1978
Peyton Marshall, *Goodhouse*, 2014
Kate L. Mary, *Broken World*, 2014
Marcus Sakey, *A Better World*, 2014
Cheryl Taylor, *Gone to Ground*, 2014
John Twelve Hawks, *Spark*, 2014
Laura van den Berg, *Find Me*, 2015
Carol Lynch Williams, *The Haven*, 2014

790

BEN LERNER

10:04

(New York: Faber & Faber, 2014)

Story type: Literary
Subject(s): Urban life; Death; Conduct of life

Major character(s): Unnamed Character, Narrator, Writer, Friend (of Alex); Alex, Woman, Friend (of narrator)
Time period(s): 21st century
Locale(s): New York, New York

Summary: In this novel an unnamed narrator considers the unpredictability of his own life in a near-future New York City that is facing its own gradual demise. The novel's lead character has made a name for himself in the literary world, but his personal life is not so rosy. He is currently undergoing testing for a heart condition, and he is considering the possibility of fatherhood. His friend Alex has asked him to impregnate her, and he must decide how he will respond. The narrator describes his daily experiences in a New York that is quite recognizable but is increasingly affected by both climate and social changes. For the protagonist, every encounter seems to present an opportunity for introspection and contemplation of an unsettled future.

Other books you might like:
John Banville, *The Sea*, 2005
Amy Bloom, *Away: A Novel*, 2007
Michael Chabon, *The Amazing Adventures of Kavalier and Clay: A Novel*, 2000
E.L. Doctorow, *City of God*, 2000
Hari Kunzru, *Gods Without Men*, 2011
Emily St. John Mandel, *Station Eleven*, 2014
David Mitchell, *Cloud Atlas*, 2004
Jenny Offill, *Dept. of Speculation*, 2014
Michael Ondaatje, *Divisadero*, 2007
Philip Roth, *Everyman*, 2006
Juan Gabriel Vasquez, *The Sound of Things Falling*, 2013

791

EMILY LIEBERT

When We Fall

(New York: Penguin Random House, 2014)

Story type: Literary
Subject(s): Friendship; Women; Grief
Major character(s): Allison Parker, Widow(er), Friend (of Charlotte), Mother (of Logan); Logan Parker, Son (of Allison), 10-Year-Old; Gia Crane, 9-Year-Old, Daughter (of Charlotte and Charlie); Charlie Crane, Father (of Gia), Spouse (of Charlotte), Wealthy; Charlotte Crane, Spouse (of Charlie), Mother (of Gia), Friend (of Allison)
Time period(s): 21st century; 2010s
Locale(s): Wincourt, New York

Summary: Widow Allison Parker is tired of the fast pace of New York City. She moves herself and her son, Logan, to the suburbs, where she plans to finally fulfill her fantasy of living the life of a bohemian artist. Charlotte Crane lives the good life, with a wealthy husband, a sweet daughter, and a wardrobe filled with designer labels. When Allison and Charlotte's lives intersect, they feel blessed with the good fortune of at last finding a best friend with whom they can share everything, particularly among the gossip-loving women who live in their town. Yet the more time they spend together, the more they unwittingly expose the truth about themselves to each other. When Charlotte realizes that her marriage is not the ideal relationship she always thought, she begins to question what else in her life she may not quite understand. When both women are forced to face the facts about what their lives have become, they don't necessarily like what they see.

Other books by the same author:
You Knew Me When, 2013

Other books you might like:
Elizabeth Berg, *Tapestry of Fortunes*, 2013
Robyn Carr, *Four Friends*, 2014
Jude Deveraux, *The Mulberry Tree*, 2002
Sherri Wood Emmons, *The Weight of Small Things*, 2013
Jane Green, *Saving Grace*, 2014
Danielle Steel, *Sisters*, 2007
Jennifer Weiner, *Certain Girls*, 2008
Karen White, *The Beach Trees*, 2011
Lauren Willig, *That Summer*, 2014
Lisa Wingate, *The Story Keeper*, 2014

792

ELIZABETH LITTLE

Dear Daughter

(New York: Viking Books, 2014)

Subject(s): Murder; Rural life; Family history
Major character(s): Janie Jenkins, Narrator, Convict (former), Crime Suspect, Model
Time period(s): 21st century; 2010s
Locale(s): South Dakota, United States

Summary: It's been 10 years since "It Girl" Janie Jenkins was charged with the death of her mother. At the time of the murder, Janie had been at the top of her game. She had great looks, fame, and many rich suitors. Janie is finally released from prison after her lawyer proves some evidence in her case had been mishandled. Janie is determined to discover who the real killer is. Avoiding the press and celebrity stalkers, Janie goes undercover and follows her one lead to a small South Dakota town. With the help of a few friendly locals, including the town's police chief, Janie soon learns how the town is connected to her mother. But the town is full of dark secrets, and many of the residents do everything they can to keep Janie and the world from learning the truth.

Other books you might like:
Jami Alden, *Hide from Evil*, 2011
Patricia Cornwell, *Dust*, 2013
Bret Easton Ellis, *Less than Zero*, 1985
Gillian Flynn, *Dark Places*, 2009
Alison Gaylin, *Trashed*, 2007
Tami Hoag, *Cold Cold Heart*, 2014
Gregg Hurwitz, *The Crime Writer*, 2007
Lisa Jackson, *Tell Me*, 2013
Iris Johansen, *The Perfect Witness*, 2014
Stieg Larsson, *The Girl Who Kicked the Hornet's Nest*, 2009
Robert S. Levinson, *The Elvis and Marilyn Affair*, 1999

Popular Fiction

Sara Paretsky, *Critical Mass*, 2013
David Rosenfelt, *Heart of a Killer*, 2011
Maria Semple, *Where'd You Go, Bernadette*, 2012
Elizabeth L. Silver, *The Execution of Noa P. Singleton*, 2013
Kate White, *If Looks Could Kill*, 2002
Ellen Marie Wiseman, *What She Left Behind*, 2013

Crista McHugh, *Falling for the Wingman*, 2014
Sarah Rayner, *One Moment, One Morning*, 2010
Emilie Richards, *No River Too Wide*, 2014
Rainbow Rowell, *Attachments*, 2011
Jodi Thomas, *Chance of a Lifetime*, 2013
Marybeth Whalen, *The Mailbox: A Novel*, 2010
Karen White, *On Folly Beach*, 2010
Susan Wiggs, *The Beekeeper's Ball*, 2014
Sherryl Woods, *Swan Point*, 2014

793

DEBBIE MACOMBER

Love Letters

(New York: Random House Publishing Group, 2014)

Series: Rose Harbor Series. Book 3
Subject(s): Romances (Fiction); Interpersonal relations; Hotels and motels
Major character(s): Jo Marie Rose, Hotel Owner (Rose Harbor Inn), Widow(er); Mark Taylor, Handyman; Ellie Reynolds, Young Woman (23 years old), Vacationer (Rose Harbor Inn); Maggie Porter, Spouse (of Roy), Vacationer (Rose Harbor Inn); Roy Porter, Spouse (of Maggie), Vacationer (Rose Harbor Inn)
Time period(s): 21st century; 2010s
Locale(s): Cedar Cove, Washington

Summary: In the third novel in the Rose Harbor series, new guests arrive at Jo Marie Rose's bed-and-breakfast establishment in Cedar Cove, Washington. Against her mother's wishes, 23-year-old Ellie Reynolds has traveled alone to Rose Harbor Inn. She is finally going to meet the man she's been talking to online in person, but she may find that her mother's concerns about the stranger are justified. Maggie and Roy Porter are having romantic problems of a different sort. They are married with children, but their relationship is in a rocky place. Maggie hopes a restful getaway will give them a new start, but Roy seems to remain distant. Meanwhile, Jo Marie continues to grieve for the husband she lost two years ago as she tries to discern her feelings for the inn's handyman, Mark Taylor. Love letters from the past may deliver what all three women need.

Other books by the same author:
Last One Home, 2015
Blossom Street Brides, 2014
North to Alaska, 2014
The Gift of Christmas, 2013
Marriage Between Friends, 2013

Other books you might like:
Sarah Addison Allen, *First Frost*, 2015
Elizabeth Berg, *Tapestry of Fortunes*, 2013
Marie Bostwick, *Apart at the Seams*, 2014
Heather Burch, *One Lavender Ribbon*, 2014
Robyn Carr, *The Homecoming*, 2014
Darcie Chan, *The Mill River Redemption*, 2014
Jennifer Chiaverini, *The Giving Quilt*, 2012
Genell Dellin, *Sweet Tea for Two*, 2012
Linda Goodnight, *The Memory House*, 2015
Kristin Hannah, *Fly Away*, 2013
Jan Karon, *Somewhere Safe with Somebody Good*, 2014
Timothy Lewis, *Forever Friday*, 2013

794

DEBBIE MACOMBER

Last One Home

(New York: Ballantine Books, 2015)

Story type: Contemporary
Subject(s): Sisters; Family; Forgiveness
Major character(s): Cassie Carter, Spouse (of Duke), Mother (of Aimee), Daughter (of Sandra Judson), Sister (of Karen and Nichole); Duke Carter, Spouse (of Cassie), Father (of Aimee); Aimee Carter, 12-Year-Old, Daughter (of Cassie and Duke); Karen Goodwin, Sister (of Cassie and Nichole), Spouse (of Garth), Daughter (of Sandra Judson); Garth Goodwin, Spouse (of Karen); Nichole Patterson, Spouse (of Jake), Daughter (of Sandra Judson), Sister (of Cassie and Karen); Jake Patterson, Spouse (of Nichole); Sandra Judson, Mother (of Cassie, Karen, and Nichole)
Time period(s): 21st century; 2010s
Locale(s): Washington, United States

Summary: Cassie is only 31, but she has experienced more than her share of heartache. She foolishly abandoned her college plans to marry a man who turned out to be abusive. She now has a 12-year-old daughter, Aimee, whom she adores, but Cassie has alienated her family—especially her sisters, Karen and Nichole, who still resent how Cassie treated their parents. With her bad marriage behind her, Cassie is starting a new phase in her life. When she learns that she may have a chance to reconcile with her sisters, Cassie returns to the Washington State community where they grew up. But Cassie soon realizes that reconnecting with Karen and Nichole isn't going to be easy. Both women have husbands and lives of their own, and they have never been able to get over the hurt of knowing that Cassie was their father's favorite. As Cassie works to make amends with her sisters, she also considers her romantic future.

Other books you might like:
Caroline B. Cooney, *Janie Face to Face*, 2013
Lily Everett, *Sanctuary Island*, 2013
Karen Kingsbury, *Chasing Sunsets*, 2015
Mary McNear, *Butternut Summer*, 2014
Fern Michaels, *The Blossom Sisters*, 2013
Mary Alice Monroe, *The Summer Wind*, 2014
Brenda Novak, *Come Home to Me*, 2014
Luanne Rice, *Little Night*, 2012
Joni Rodgers, *The Secret Sisters: A Novel*, 2006
Danielle Steel, *Prodigal Son*, 2015

795

MIKE MADEN
Blue Warrior
(New York: G.P. Putnam, 2014)

Series: Troy Pearce Series. Book 2
Story type: Chase; Contemporary
Subject(s): Africa; Wars; Weapons
Major character(s): Troy Pearce, Contractor, Businessman, Agent (former CIA), Friend (of Margaret Myers); Margaret Myers, Political Figure (former president of United States), Friend (of Troy Pearce); Mossa Ag Alla, Warrior (aka Blue Warrior), Leader
Time period(s): 21st century; 2010s
Locale(s): Mali

Summary: In the second Troy Pearce novel, the CEO of Pearce Systems has received a request from an old friend that can't be ignored. Former US president Margaret Myers has contacted the ex-CIA agent and skilled mountaineer in hopes that he will undertake a rescue mission in Northern Africa. His private contracting company focuses on remotely piloted vehicles (drones) and technological weaponry. A friend and former lover of Pearce has been injured and trapped in Mali amidst extensive civil and political war while on a top-secret assignment. Other dangers there include Chinese forces who are protecting a Lanthanum mine investment, an al-Qaida Sahara group of jihadists, and a regiment from the French Foreign Legion. Pearce uses his arsenal to defend his friends and searches for his former lover, becoming embroiled in the political upheaval of the region. Mossa Ag Alla, also known as the Blue Warrrior, is the leader of the rebel troops and nationalist effort.

Other books by the same author:
Drone, 2013

Other books you might like:
Dale Brown, *Strike Zone*, 2004
Richard Clarke, *Sting of the Drone*, 2014
Stephen Coonts, *Deep Black: Jihad*, 2007
Clive Cussler, *Sacred Stone: A Novel of the* Oregon Files, 2004
Dan Fesperman, *Unmanned*, 2014
Mark Greaney, *Tom Clancy Full Force and Effect*, 2014
Mischa Hiller, *Disengaged*, 2015
James Patterson, *Private Berlin*, 2013
Barrett Tillman, *Vulcan's Fire: Harold Coyle's Strategic Solutions, Inc.*, 2008
Daniel H. Wilson, *Amped*, 2012

796

EMILY ST. JOHN MANDEL
Station Eleven
(New York: Knopf, 2014)

Story type: Dystopian; End of the World
Subject(s): Actors; Prophecy; Apocalypse
Major character(s): Arthur Leander, Actor; Jeevan Chaudhary, Man, Worker (EMT); Kirsten Raymonde, Traveler, Survivor (of Georgia Flu), Actress

Time period(s): Multiple Time Periods
Summary: Emily St. John Mandel follows three lives that intersect on one snowy night in this post-apocalyptic tale. Accomplished actor Arthur Leander is performing as King Lear in a theater production in Canada when he has a heart attack and collapses. Kirsten Raymonde, a child actor, gazes in shock at the scene. Jeevan Chaudhary, an ex-paparazzo now working as an EMT, is in attendance and quickly tries to resuscitate Arthur, but it is too late and Arthur dies. The horrible scene onstage foreshadows events outside. The same night, a horrific flu begins spreading all over the world. Jeevan holes up with his brother, barely escaping contamination, and attempts to wait out the pandemic. Fifteen years later, Kirsten has survived and is traveling between sparse settlements of survivors with an acting and orchestral troupe, the Traveling Symphony. As they arrive in St. Deborah by the Water, the performers encounter a prophet who threatens them with violence if they leave. Arthur, Jeevan, and Kirsten have very differing experiences, but fate will connect them all.

Other books by the same author:
The Lola Quartet, 2012
The Singer's Gun, 2010
Last Night in Montreal, 2009

Awards the book has won:
Arthur C. Clarke Award, 2015

Other books you might like:
Margaret Atwood, *The Year of the Flood*, 2009
David Brin, *The Postman*, 1985
John L. Campbell, *Ship of the Dead*, 2014
Eleanor Catton, *The Luminaries*, 2013
Michael Crummey, *Sweetland*, 2015
E.L. Doctorow, *City of God*, 2000
Shaunta Grimes, *Rebel Nation*, 2014
Peter Heller, *The Dog Stars*, 2012
Rajan Khanna, *Falling Sky*, 2014
Stephen King, *The Stand*, 1978
Stephen King, *The Stand: The Complete and Uncut Edition*, 1990
Hari Kunzru, *Gods Without Men*, 2011
Maya Lang, *The Sixteenth of June*, 2014
Ben Lerner, *10:04*, 2014
Adriana Lisboa, *Crow Blue*, 2013
Demitria Lunetta, *In the End*, 2014
David Mitchell, *The Bone Clocks*, 2014
David Mitchell, *Cloud Atlas*, 2004
Sandra Newman, *The Country of Ice Cream Star*, 2014
Michael Ondaatje, *Divisadero*, 2007
Benjamin Percy, *The Dead Lands*, 2015
Laura van den Berg, *Find Me*, 2015
Rick Yancey, *The 5th Wave*, 2013

797

PHILLIP MARGOLIN
Woman with a Gun
(New York: HarperCollins Publishers, 2014)

Story type: Mystery
Subject(s): Photography; Murder; Weapons

Major character(s): Stacey Kim, Writer, Detective—Amateur; Kathy Moran, Photographer
Time period(s): 21st century; 2010s
Locale(s): New York, New York; Palisades Heights, Oregon

Summary: Stacey Kim is a writer looking for inspiration. She finds it while viewing an exhibit by noted photographer Kathy Moran. One of Moran's photos, entitled *Woman with a Gun*, is a stark, black-and-white image of a woman in a wedding dress holding a weapon behind her back. Stacey begins to wonder who the woman is and what story surrounds her. She begins investigating and discovers the woman is a newlywed bride suspected in the decade-old murder of her millionaire husband. Now obsessed with the crime, Stacey travels to the Oregon town where the picture was taken and begins asking questions. When another body turns up, it becomes apparent that someone doesn't want her snooping around. And the one person who may know the truth—photographer Kathy Moran—isn't about to give up her secrets.

Other books by the same author:
Worthy Brown's Daughter, 2014
Sleight of Hand, 2013
Capitol Murder, 2012
Vanishing Acts, 2011
Supreme Justice, 2010

Other books you might like:
Michael Blair, *Depth of Field*, 2009
C.J. Box, *Cold Wind*, 2010
Megan Chance, *The Spiritualist*, 2008
Vicki Delany, *Negative Image*, 2010
Robert Eversz, *Zero to the Bone*, 2006
Jonathan Kellerman, *Motive*, 2015
Alice LaPlante, *A Circle of Wives*, 2014
Chuck Logan, *South of Shiloh: A Thriller*, 2008
Walter Mosley, *All I Did Was Shoot My Man*, 2012
James Patterson, *10th Anniversary*, 2011
Peter Turnbull, *Trophy Wife*, 2006

798

PEYTON MARSHALL

Goodhouse

(New York: Farrar, Straus and Giroux, 2014)

Subject(s): Biotechnology; Dystopias; Futuristic society
Major character(s): James, 17-Year-Old, Crime Suspect (potential); Bethany, Teenager, Friend (of James), Daughter (of Goodhouse Administrator)
Time period(s): 21st century; 2090s-2100s
Locale(s): United States

Summary: Seventeen-year old James has been sent to Goodhouse—not because he committed a crime, but because he might. As the 22nd century approaches, science has found a way to identify a portion of DNA that indicates criminal tendencies, and James has it. Kids like James are sent to Goodhouse, a place not quite a prison, but much harsher than the worst boarding school. There, authorities work to train these potential criminals to curb their worst tendencies. But when James finally does com-mit his first crime—stealing a barrette from the room of a girl named Bethany—he sets off a string of consequences. His retraining is intensified, and Bethany grows increasingly attracted to him. Bethany's father is on the school staff. He may be a friend, or he may be James's worst enemy. As the staff uses drugs to control James, he has a harder time sorting out what is going on around him, and the dangers of Goodhouse increase. First novel.

Other books you might like:
Margaret Atwood, *The Year of the Flood*, 2009
Anthony Burgess, *A Clockwork Orange*, 1962
Cory Doctorow, *The Rapture of the Nerds*, 2012
Robert Ferrigno, *Prayers for the Assassin: A Novel*, 2006
Alena Graedon, *The Word Exchange: A Novel*, 2014
Walter Greatshell, *Mad Skills*, 2010
Gregg Hurwitz, *The Program: A Novel*, 2004
Kazuo Ishiguro, *Never Let Me Go*, 2005
P.D. James, *The Children of Men*, 1993
Sophie Jordan, *Uninvited*, 2014
Edan Lepucki, *California*, 2014
Lois Lowry, *The Giver*, 1993
Sean Murphy, *Punk Rock Jesus*, 2013
Lauren Oliver, *Delirium*, 2011
J.D. Robb, *Naked in Death*, 1995
John Twelve Hawks, *Spark*, 2014
Ben H. Winters, *Last Policeman Series*, 2012

799

TOM MCCARTHY

Satin Island

(London: Knopf Doubleday Publishing Group, 2015)

Story type: Contemporary; Psychological
Subject(s): Social history; Culture; Writing
Major character(s): U, Anthropologist (corporate), Researcher, Narrator, Writer
Time period(s): 21st century; 2010s
Locale(s): Earth

Summary: Years ago, U, who calls himself a corporate anthropologist, published a paper on nightclub culture. In the corporate world and academic circles, the project made him famous. Now he's been hired by a corporation he calls the Company. U has been given the task of writing something even more ambitious: a comprehensive study of modern human culture. The project is named the Great Report, but completing it will be no easy task. In an era when trends evaporate soon after they form and the whims of the masses change like shifting quicksand, U is soon drowning in a murky sea of data. Overwhelmed by theories, fleeting concepts, and ambiguous constants, U begins to wonder if he will ever finish the Great Report. Or maybe, in his infinite failure, he's been succeeding all along.

Other books by the same author:
Men in Space, 2012

Other books you might like:
Marcel Beyer, *Spies*, 2005

T. Coraghessan Boyle, *The Inner Circle*, 2004
John Darnton, *The Darwin Conspiracy*, 2005
Aaron Elkins, *Little Tiny Teeth*, 2007
Michel Faber, *The Book of Strange New Things*, 2014
Lily King, *Euphoria*, 2014
Jonathan Lethem, *Lucky Alan and Other Stories*, 2015
Javier Marias, *The Infatuations*, 2013
Joyce Carol Oates, *Little Bird of Heaven*, 2009
Marisha Pessl, *Special Topics in Calamity Physics*, 2006

800

IAN MCEWAN

The Children Act

(New York: Nan A. Talese, 2014)

Story type: Legal; Literary
Subject(s): Law; England; Child care
Major character(s): Fiona Maye, Judge (High Court), Spouse (of Jack); Jack, Spouse (unfaithful, of Fiona); Adam, 17-Year-Old, Cancer Patient (leukemia), Religious (Jehovah's Witness)
Time period(s): 21st century; 2010s
Locale(s): London, England

Summary: Medical ethics, social responsibility, and religion clash in this novel by Ian McEwan. Seventeen-year-old Adam is a leukemia patient in a London hospital whose staff wants to administer life-saving blood transfusions. Adam has refused the treatment on religious grounds, however, and his parents—also Jehova's Witnesses—agree with their son's choice. High Court judge Fiona Maye becomes involved in the case when the hospital seeks a court order allowing them to treat Adam. As Fiona struggles with the complexities of the case, she also deals with turmoil at home. Her longtime husband, Jack, has moved out after Fiona refused to agree to an open marriage. When Fiona meets with Adam at the hospital, she is moved by the experience. She later makes her ruling, which has unexpected consequences for Adam, his family, and Fiona.

Other books by the same author:
Sweet Tooth, 2012
Solar, 2010
On Chesil Beach, 2007
Saturday, 2005
Atonement, 2002

Other books you might like:
Elizabeth Bass, *Miss You Most of All*, 2011
Carla Buckley, *The Deepest Secret*, 2014
Michael Cunningham, *The Snow Queen*, 2014
Rachel Cusk, *Outline*, 2015
Maria Duenas, *The Heart Has Its Reasons*, 2014
Richard Ford, *Let Me Be Frank with You*, 2014
Adam Foulds, *In the Wolf's Mouth*, 2014
John Grisham, *Sycamore Row*, 2013
Chad Harbach, *The Art of Fielding*, 2011
Kent Haruf, *Benediction*, 2013
William Landay, *Defending Jacob*, 2012
Yannick Murphy, *This Is the Water*, 2014
Jodi Picoult, *Handle with Care*, 2009

Jodi Picoult, *My Sister's Keeper*, 2004
Jodi Picoult, *Nineteen Minutes*, 2007
Marilynne Robinson, *Lila*, 2014
Lionel Shriver, *So Much for That*, 2010
Randy Singer, *Dying Declaration*, 2004
Darin Strauss, *More Than It Hurts You*, 2008
Colm Toibin, *Nora Webster*, 2014

801

LAURA MCNEAL

Dollbaby

(New York: Viking Books, 2014)

Subject(s): Civil rights; Vietnam War, 1959-1975; Family history
Major character(s): Liberty "Ibby" Bell, 12-Year-Old, Granddaughter (of Fannie), Friend (of Dollbaby, Queenie); Fannie Bell, Grandmother (of Ibby), Employer (of Queenie, Dollbaby); Queenie, Mother (of Dollbaby), Servant (of Fannie), Friend (of Ibby); Dollbaby, Daughter (of Queenie), Friend (of Ibby), Servant (of Fannie)
Time period(s): 20th century; 1960s-1970s (1964-1972)
Locale(s): New Orleans, United States

Summary: When her father dies after a freak accident, 12-year-old Liberty Bell is sent to stay with her eccentric grandmother, Fannie. Taking her father's ashes with her, Ibby moves from Olympia, Washington, to New Orleans. The South is very different from Washington, especially in 1964. Although civil rights and war protests are happening in the streets, tradition is the way of life in Fannie's home. The home is run by two black servants, Queenie and her daughter Dollbaby. Fannie treats these servants like family, and they help Ibby adjust to Southern life. As the years progress, Ibby and her family experience the changing times together. In addition, Ibby learns about Fannie's life before she became a mother and grandmother—a life that included several trips to an asylum.

Other books by the same author:
Dark Water, 2010

Other books you might like:
Elizabeth Berg, *We Are All Welcome Here: A Novel*, 2006
Susan Crandall, *Whistling Past the Graveyard*, 2013
Fannie Flagg, *Fried Green Tomatoes at the Whistle-Stop Cafe*, 1987
Susan Gregg Gilmore, *The Improper Life of Bezellia Grove*, 2010
Minrose Gwin, *The Queen of Palmyra*, 2010
Beth Hoffman, *Saving CeeCee Honeycutt: A Novel*, 2010
Sue Monk Kidd, *The Secret Life of Bees*, 2002
Kiese Laymon, *Long Division*, 2013
Sena Jeter Naslund, *Four Spirits*, 2003
Joyce Carol Oates, *Black Girl/White Girl*, 2006
Nancy Peacock, *Home Across the Road*, 1999
Kathryn Stockett, *The Help*, 2009
Karen Stolz, *World of Pies*, 2000

802

MARY MCNEAR

Butternut Summer

(New York: HarperCollins Publishing, 2014)

Series: Butternut Lake Trilogy. Book 2
Story type: Contemporary; Romance
Subject(s): Divorce; Father-daughter relations; Family relations
Major character(s): Caroline Keegan, Businesswoman (owner of Pearl's Coffee Shop), Mother (of Daisy), Divorced Person (from Jack); Daisy Keegan, 21-Year-Old, Student—College (senior), Daughter (of Caroline and Jack), Girlfriend (of Will); Jack Keegan, Divorced Person (from Caroline), Father (of Daisy); Will Hughes, Mechanic, Boyfriend (of Daisy)
Time period(s): 21st century; 2010s
Locale(s): Butternut Lake, Minnesota

Summary: This second book in a trilogy further explores the life of Caroline, a coffee shop owner introduced in the first book, *Up at Butternut Lake*. With her shop, Pearl's, in deep financial trouble, and her daughter, Daisy, about to start her senior year of college, Caroline doesn't need a visit from her ex-husband, Jack. Daisy has recently reestablished a relationship with her dad, who shows up at the lake for a visit. Daisy also has a new relationship with an old high school friend named Will, a mechanic with a reputation for trouble. Although Daisy will leave the lake to return to college at summer's end, the young couple's relationship deepens. At the same time, Caroline wrestles with her financial struggles and the feelings left unresolved after her separation from Jack 18 years before.

Other books by the same author:
Moonlight on Butternut Lake, 2015
The Night Before Christmas, 2014
Up at Butternut Lake, 2014

Other books you might like:
Caroline Adderson, *Ellen in Pieces*, 2014
Elizabeth Berg, *The Last Time I Saw You*, 2010
Hilary Boyd, *Tangled Lives*, 2014
Dorothea Benton Frank, *The Hurricane Sisters*, 2014
Lorna Landvik, *Mayor of the Universe*, 2014
Penelope Lively, *How It All Began*, 2012
Debbie Macomber, *Last One Home*, 2015
Jojo Moyes, *One Plus One*, 2014
Luanne Rice, *The Lemon Orchard*, 2013
Susan Wiggs, *The Beekeeper's Ball*, 2014
Martha Woodroof, *Small Blessings*, 2014

803

PETER MEHLMAN

It Won't Always Be This Great

(Baltimore, Maryland: Bancroft Press, 2014)

Story type: Contemporary; Ethnic
Subject(s): Jews; Vandalism; Marriage
Major character(s): Unnamed Character, Narrator, Doctor (podiatrist, of Audra Uziel), Spouse (of Alyse), Father (of Esme and Charlie), Criminal (vandal); Alyse, Spouse (of narrator), Mother (of Esme and Charlie); Esme, Daughter (of narrator and Alyse), Sister (of Charlie); Charlie, Son (of narrator and Alyse), Brother (of Esme); Audra Uziel, Patient (of narrator), Daughter (of Nat Uziel); Nat Uziel, Leader (of Jewish community), Store Owner (of vandalized store), Father (of Audra Uziel)
Time period(s): 21st century; 2010s
Locale(s): New York, New York

Summary: An unnamed podiatrist in Long Island has a successful practice and is happily married to his college sweetheart, Alyse. Together they have two children, Esme and Charlie. The podiatrist (and narrator) isn't sure what inspires him to break a storefront window one night as he walks home. The store belongs to Nat Uziel, a leader in the local Jewish community. The podiatrist treats Nat's daughter, Audra, who is a beautiful and brilliant 19-year-old woman. She is also determined to seduce her doctor. The act of vandalism enrages Nat, who insists the criminals are anti-Semitic. His demands for justice create a media storm and a frenzied search for the perpetrator. As his life crumbles around him and the media circus swarms during the hunt for the perpetrator, the narrator struggles with his despair and the real reasons he might have broken Nat's window.

Other books you might like:
T.C. Boyle, *The Harder They Come*, 2015
E.L. Doctorow, *Andrew's Brain*, 2014
Sara Gruen, *Ape House*, 2011
Jonathan Lethem, *Dissident Gardens*, 2013
Elinor Lipman, *The Family Man*, 2009
Ann-Marie MacDonald, *Adult Onset*, 2014
Tom Perrotta, *The Leftovers*, 2011
Alex Shearer, *This Is the Life*, 2015
Lionel Shriver, *Big Brother*, 2013
Anne Tyler, *A Spool of Blue Thread*, 2015

804

RANDY SUSAN MEYERS

Accidents of Marriage

(New York: Atria Books, 2014)

Story type: Contemporary
Subject(s): Abuse; Accidents; Marriage
Major character(s): Maddy Illica, Social Worker, Accident Victim, Abuse Victim, Spouse (of Ben), Mother (of Emma, Gracie, and Caleb), Narrator; Ben Illica, Lawyer, Father (of Emma, Gracie, and Caleb), Spouse (of Maddy), Narrator; Emma Illica, 14-Year-Old, Sister (of Caleb and Gracie), Daughter (of Maddy and Ben), Narrator; Caleb Illica, Son (of Maddy and Ben), Brother (of Gracie and Emma); Gracie Illica, Daughter (of Maddy and Ben), Sister (of Emma and Caleb)
Time period(s): 21st century; 2010s
Locale(s): Boston, Massachusetts

Summary: Maddy Illica, a social worker, spends her days counseling abused women and children and helping them to build a better life. What she cannot admit to herself is that her own marriage and spousal relationship are less than perfect. Her husband, Ben, is a lawyer with an intense temper. He often exhibits wild mood swings and bursts of rage. Their three children, Emma, Gracie, and Caleb, are used to their father's attitudes and their mother's placating demeanor. It isn't until Ben's temper causes a terrible car accident—which leaves Maddy in a coma with potential brain damage—that the Illicas' world screeches to a halt. Ben is positive that he is not to blame, while Emma can't help but be furious at her father's actions, which have left her responsible for her two younger siblings while her mother suffers. As Maddy struggles to recover, it becomes apparent that their marriage will never be the same again, and she and Ben must question where they will go from here.

Other books by the same author:
The Comfort of Lies, 2013
The Murderer's Daughters, 2010

Other books you might like:
Barbara Delinsky, *Escape*, 2011
Julia Glass, *Whole World Over*, 2006
Amy Hatvany, *Safe with Me*, 2014
Sue Miller, *The Senator's Wife*, 2008
Liane Moriarty, *Big Little Lies*, 2014
Jodi Picoult, *Lone Wolf*, 2012
Laura Pritchett, *Stars Go Blue*, 2014
Emilie Richards, *No River Too Wide*, 2014
Anita Shreve, *Rescue*, 2010
Anne Tyler, *The Amateur Marriage*, 2004

805

LYDIA MILLET

Mermaids in Paradise

(New York: W. W. Norton, 2014)

Story type: Satire
Subject(s): Mermaids; Marriage; Weddings
Major character(s): Deb, Spouse (of Chip), Bride, Traveler; Chip, Bridegroom, Traveler, Spouse (of Deb)
Time period(s): 21st century; 2010s
Locale(s): Virgin Islands

Summary: Cynical and sardonic Deb is honeymooning with her new husband, the affable and sociable Chip, when they hear that a marine biologist has seen mermaids off the coast of their island. When the scientist is found dead the following day, Deb realizes that she and Chip must fight to keep the discovery safe. Unfortunately, the resort at which they are staying learns about the mermaids, and puts a plan into motion to make the creatures an international attraction. Chip and Deb enlist the help of some of the other people staying at the resort to stop the owners from carrying out their plan, but some of the vacationers take the mission a little too far. As Deb spends her vacation fighting for the mermaids' cause, she realizes that she finally feels like she has a purpose in life. Unfortunately, a series of events makes her wonder if the mermaids ever really existed, or if they were just figments of everyone's imagination.

Other books by the same author:
Pills and Starships, 2014
Magnificence, 2012
The Shimmers in the Night, 2012
The Fires Beneath the Sea, 2011
Ghost Lights, 2011

Other books you might like:
Max Barry, *Company*, 2006
Libba Bray, *Beauty Queens*, 2011
Lesley Choyce, *The Republic of Nothing*, 1994
Eric Dezenhall, *Turnpike Flameout*, 2006
Tim Dorsey, *Shark Skin Suite*, 2015
Mark Helprin, *Freddy and Fredericka*, 2005
Carl Hiaasen, *Star Island*, 2010
Merry Jones, *Elective Procedures*, 2014
Bob Morris, *Bahamarama*, 2004
Jesmyn Ward, *Salvage the Bones*, 2011

806

KANAE MINATO
STEPHEN SNYDER, Translator

Confessions

(Boston: Little, Brown and Company, 2014)

Subject(s): Murder; Revenge; Mystery
Major character(s): Yuko Moriguchi, Teacher (middle school science), Mother (of Manami); Manami, 4-Year-Old, Daughter (of Yuko), Crime Victim (murdered)
Time period(s): 21st century; 2010s
Locale(s): Japan

Summary: Four-year-old Manami was the light of middle school science teacher Yuko Moriguchi's life. When her little daughter died, Yuko initially accepted the police department's determination that it was an unfortunate accident. But then Yuko discovers that the child was murdered by two of her students. So before she resigns, Yuko delivers one last lesson and sets her revenge in motion. Her class learns the lesson well, and their actions punish the two young murderers more harshly than any court would have allowed. Yuko's revenge may cost more lives along the way. First novel.

Awards the book has won:
Alex Awards, 2015

Other books you might like:
Holly Brown, *Don't Try to Find Me*, 2014
Amber Dermont, *The Starboard Sea*, 2012
Gillian Flynn, *Gone Girl*, 2012
Keigo Higashino, *The Devotion of Suspect X*, 2011
Iris Johansen, *Chasing the Night*, 2010
Natsuo Kirino, *Out*, 2005
Patricia MacDonald, *Cast into Doubt*, 2011
Lee Martin, *The Bright Forever: A Novel*, 2005
Kimberly McCreight, *Reconstructing Amelia*, 2013
Miyuki Miyabe, *All She Was Worth*, 1997
Miyuki Miyabe, *The Devil's Whisper*, 2007
Haruki Murakami, *1Q84*, 2009
Ryu Murakami, *Coin Locker Babies*, 1995

Popular Fiction

Marisha Pessl, *Night Film*, 2012
Wendy Corsi Staub, *The Good Sister*, 2013
P. D. Viner, *The Last Winter of Dani Lancing*, 2013
Shuichi Yoshida, *Villian*, 2010

807

DAVID MITCHELL

The Bone Clocks
(New York: Random House, 2014)

Story type: Contemporary; Literary
Subject(s): Psychics; Science fiction; Interpersonal relations
Major character(s): Holly Sykes, Runaway, Psychic, 15-Year-Old
Time period(s): 20th century-21st century; 1980s-2040s
Locale(s): Australia; Iraq; United States

Summary: Realism and fantasy intertwine in this novel from best-selling and award-winning author David Mitchell. Told in six narratives, the story of Holly Sykes begins in 1984 in North Kent, England, where the 15-year-old runs away following an argument with her mother. As Holly makes her way further into the English countryside, the voices known only as the Radio People, which contacted Holly once before, begin to speak again. Soon Holly, who is gifted with psychic abilities, finds herself in the middle of a mysterious spiritual war between the Radio People and the Horologists. From this point, Holly moves back and forth in time, place, and states of reality. From a Cambridge student who meets Holly in Switzerland to a war reporter dispatched to Baghdad to a once-famous novelist, Holly's mysterious experiences affect lives throughout the years—even the lives of those not yet born. They all have their parts to play in this conflict, but how long will it take Holly to find out what her role is?

Other books by the same author:
The Thousand Autumns of Jacob De Zoet, 2010
Black Swan Green, 2006
Cloud Atlas, 2004
Number9Dream, 2001
Ghostwritten, 2000

Other books you might like:
Margaret Atwood, *Stone Mattress: Nine Tales*, 2014
T.C. Boyle, *The Harder They Come*, 2015
Mark Z. Danielewski, *The Familiar, Volume 1: One Rainy Day in May*, 2015
Anthony Doerr, *All the Light We Cannot See*, 2014
Michel Faber, *The Book of Strange New Things*, 2014
Richard Flanagan, *The Narrow Road to the Deep North*, 2014
Jonathan Safran Foer, *Everything Is Illuminated*, 2002
Richard Ford, *Let Me Be Frank with You*, 2014
Howard Jacobson, *J: A Novel*, 2014
Emily St. John Mandel, *Station Eleven*, 2014
David Mitchell, *Cloud Atlas*, 2004
Haruki Murakami, *1Q84*, 2009
Haruki Murakami, *Colorless Tsukuru Tazaki and His Years of Pilgrimage*, 2014

Michael Ondaatje, *Divisadero*, 2007
Tom Rachman, *The Imperfectionists: A Novel*, 2010
Philip Roth, *Everyman*, 2006
Maggie Shipstead, *Astonish Me*, 2014
Jo Walton, *My Real Children*, 2014

808

YAN MO
HOWARD GOLDBLATT, Co-Author

Frog
(New York: Penguin, 2014)

Story type: Family Saga; Historical
Subject(s): China; Communism; Chinese Civil War, 1945-1949
Major character(s): Gugu, Midwife, Aunt (of Wan Zu), Doctor (obstetrician); Wan Zu, Writer, Nephew (of Gugu)
Time period(s): 20th century-21st century; 1940s-2010s
Locale(s): China

Summary: Wan Zu is a struggling playwright who is writing the story of his aunt Gugu's life. Gugu is a noted obstetrician who has endured through the Cultural Revolution and the communist era in China. As a young girl, she learned her trade from a visiting western professional and dedicated herself to women's health and the birthing process, surpassing all of the regional midwives in skill and ability. The novel is organized by the political changes and atmosphere in China. It begins at the struggle for power between the communists and nationalists, when a young Gugu firmly embraces communism and Mao's doctrines. By 1979, the Cultural Revolution is ended and Gugu remains a firm Communist who strictly embraces the one-child policy. By 2005, Gugu has mellowed and her opinions are tinged with regret. Wan Zu's own life experiences are interspersed with Gugu's and the inspiration for his new play, *The Frog.*

Other books by the same author:
Pow!, 2012
Sandalwood Death, 2012
Life and Death Are Wearing Me Out, 2008
Big Breasts and Wide Hips, 2004
Shifu, You'll Do Anything for a Laugh, 2001

Other books you might like:
Joan Didion, *Play It as It Lays*, 1970
Graham Greene, *The Quiet American*, 1955
Ma Jian, *The Dark Road*, 2014
Ha Jin, *A Map of Betrayal*, 2014
Doris Lessing, *The Good Terrorist*, 1985
Yan Lianke, *The Four Books*, 2015
Zadie Smith, *NW: A Novel*, 2012
Vladimir Sorokin, *Day of the Oprichnik*, 2011
Amy Tan, *The Valley of Amazement*, 2013
Zechen Xu, *Running through Beijing*, 2014

809

BETH MORAN

Making Marion

(Oxford, United Kingdom: Lion Fiction, 2014)

Story type: Contemporary
Subject(s): Family; Family history; Romances (Fiction)
Major character(s): Marion Miller, Young Woman, Receptionist; Scarlett, Manager (Peace and Pigs Holiday Park); Reuben, Young Man
Time period(s): 21st century; 2010s
Locale(s): Nottinghamshire, England

Summary: Marion Miller comes to Nottinghamshire looking for answers about her father's past. Through a series of miscommunications, she finds herself employed at the reception desk at Peace and Pigs Holiday Park. The family campsite is run by an American woman, Scarlett, who is more interested in staffing the desk than she is in listening to Marion's back story. Marion has memories of watching an animated film about Robin Hood with her father. She has a photo of her father wearing a Robin Hood costume; she was named for the legendary Maid Marion. With these scant clues to guide her, Marion searches for information about her father. Meanwhile, she occupies herself with the daily adventures Peace and Pigs offers and the handsome young man who could become a love interest.

Other books you might like:
Melody Carlson, *Dating, Dining, and Desperation*, 2014
Robin Lee Hatcher, *Love Without End*, 2014
Karen Kingsbury, *Angels Walking*, 2014
Tamara Leigh, *Restless in Carolina*, 2011
Tracie Peterson, *A Moment in Time*, 2014
Pam Rhodes, *If You Follow Me*, 2014
Katherine Spencer, *Harbor of the Heart*, 2014
Laura Jensen Walker, *Becca by the Book*, 2010
Courtney Walsh, *Paper Hearts*, 2014
Lori Wick, *Jessie*, 2008

810

CAITLIN MORAN

How to Build a Girl

(New York: Harper, 2014)

Story type: Coming-of-Age; Literary
Subject(s): Coming of age; Women; Culture
Major character(s): Johanna Morrigan, 14-Year-Old (also known as Dolly Wilde), Writer, Daughter (of Dadda and Mum), Sister (of Krissi, Lupin, and the twins); Dadda, Father (of Johanna, Krissi, Lupin, and the twins); Mum, Mother (of Johanna, Krissi, Lupin, and the twins); Krissi, Son (of Dadda and Mum), Brother (of Johanna, Lupin, and the twins); Lupin, Son (of Dadda and Mum), Brother (of Johanna, Krissi, and the twins)
Time period(s): 20th century; 1990s
Locale(s): London, England

Summary: Fourteen-year-old Johanna Morrigan doesn't get much guidance from her father and mother. It is the 1990s, and Dadda is still trying to become a rock star. Mum deals with their growing brood, which increased to five children after the birth of the "Unexpected Twins." Johanna realizes how on her own she is after a humiliating experience is broadcast on local television. She decides to make a fresh start and adopts the name Dolly Wilde. As Dolly, she spends her teenage years smoking, drinking, and sleeping around. She also launches a journalism career by writing scathing music reviews. Although she finds independence and adventure, Johanna's attempt to re-create herself falls short. Her parents didn't give her what she needs to make her way in the world, but neither do the bands and books on which she has based her new identity. First novel.

Other books you might like:
Meagan Brothers, *Supergirl Mixtapes*, 2012
Sarah Dessen, *What Happened to Goodbye*, 2011
John Green, *Looking for Alaska*, 2005
Judy Juanita, *Virgin Soul*, 2013
Joe Meno, *Hairstyles of the Damned*, 2004
Curtis Sittenfeld, *Prep: A Novel*, 2005
Marc Spitz, *How Soon Is Never?*, 2003
Natalie Standiford, *How to Say Goodbye in Robot*, 2009
Lili Wilkinson, *Pink*, 2011
Kate Zambreno, *Green Girl*, 2014

811

COURTNEY MORENO

In Case of Emergency

(San Francisco: McSweeney's, 2014)

Story type: Contemporary; Lesbian Contemporary
Subject(s): Medical care; Medical professions; Occupations
Major character(s): Piper Gallagher, Health Care Professional (EMT), Lesbian, Abandoned Child, Sister (of Ryan), Girlfriend (of Ayla); Ayla, Lesbian, Veteran, Girlfriend (of Piper); Ryan Gallagher, Brother (of Piper)
Time period(s): 21st century; 2010s
Locale(s): Los Angeles, California

Summary: Piper Gallagher is a 29-year-old woman working as an EMT in South Central Los Angeles. She has spent her life wandering from one job to the next, suffering vestigial trauma from being abandoned by her mother as a child, and searching for a meaningful relationship. She has recently found a new girlfriend, Ayla, who is an Iraq war veteran who struggles with post-traumatic stress disorder. As an EMT, Piper is struggling to find her footing. She is unsure of her actions and uncomfortable on calls. Her knowledge of emergency medicine and human biology improves over the first few weeks and she begins to feel more confident. After one particular call, she begins to question her own abilities. She leans on her brother, Ryan, as well as her partners in the ambulance to build up her own self-confidence and embrace her desire to soothe her patients. First novel.

Other books you might like:
LaShonda K. Barnett, *Jam on the Vine*, 2015

Jove Belle, *Love and Devotion*, 2013
Bebe Moore Campbell, *72 Hour Hold: A Novel*, 2005
Erin Celello, *Learning to Stay*, 2013
Jenn Crowell, *Etched on Me*, 2014
Lynne Hinton, *Welcome Back to Pie Town*, 2012
Arleen Pare, *Leaving Now*, 2012
Heidi Jon Schmidt, *The Bride of Catastrophe*, 2003
Anita Shreve, *Rescue*, 2010
Jesse J. Thoma, *Seneca Falls*, 2014

812

JASON MOTT

The Wonder of All Things

(Don Mills, Ontario, Canada: Mira, 2014)

Story type: Literary
Subject(s): Miracles; Friendship; Accidents
Major character(s): Ava Campbell, 13-Year-Old, Daughter (of Macon), Stepdaughter (of Carmen), Friend (of Wash), Healer; Macon Campbell, Lawman (sheriff), Spouse (of Carmen), Father (of Ava); Carmen, Woman (pregnant), Spouse (of Macon), Stepmother (of Ava); Wash, Boy, Friend (of Ava), Accident Victim
Time period(s): 21st century; 2010s
Locale(s): Stone Temple, North Carolina

Summary: Thirteen-year-old Ava Campbell has so far been able to keep her healing powers a secret. But when an air show accident seriously injures Ava's friend, Wash, she has no choice but to heal his wounds on the spot. When video of the event is recorded on a spectator's phone and uploaded to the Internet, Ava becomes known as the Miracle Child. Her small town of Stone Temple, North Carolina, soon attracts the curious and those seeking cures for ailments. Ava's facing pressure close to home, too. Her stepmother, Carmen, would like some divine assistance with her pregnancy. She can't bear the thought of suffering another miscarriage. Ava's father, Macon, the local sheriff, deals with the assortment of characters that have flocked to Stone Temple, including celebrity preacher Isaiah Brown. As Ava struggles to adjust to her unwanted fame, she also becomes weaker with each healing she performs.

Other books by the same author:
The Returned, 2013

Other books you might like:
Mitch Albom, *The First Phone Call from Heaven*, 2013
Jerry Apps, *The Great Sand Fracas of Ames County*, 2014
Tiffany Baker, *Mercy Snow*, 2014
Aimee Bender, *Particular Sadness of Lemon Cake*, 2011
Sandra Cisneros, *Have You Seen Marie?*, 2012
Elizabeth Collison, *Some Other Town*, 2015
Katelyn Detweiler, *Immaculate*, 2015
Janis Hallowell, *The Annunciation of Francesca Dunn: A Novel*, 2004
Ursula Hegi, *The Worst Thing I've Done*, 2007
James Kimmel Jr., *The Trial of Fallen Angels*, 2012
James L. Rubart, *The Chair*, 2011

813

YANNICK MURPHY

This Is the Water

(New York: HarperCollins Publishing, 2014)

Subject(s): Serial murders; Swimming; Murder
Major character(s): Annie, Mother (Swim mom), Friend (of Paul and Chris); Paul, Father (Swim Dad), Spouse (of Chris), Friend (of Annie); Chris, Mother (Swim mom), Spouse (of Paul), Friend (of Annie)
Time period(s): 21st century; 2010s
Locale(s): New England, United States

Summary: Annie is a typical suburban swim mom with typical suburban swim-mom problems. She worries about her kids, she worries about her marriage, and she's just a bit attracted to Paul, who is the dad of another one of the swimmers. Paul is also married to Annie's friend, Chris. The swim parents aren't the only ones watching the girls in the pool, but they are too busy with their own personal distractions to notice the man looking on from the bleachers. When one of the girls is found dead at a rest stop, the incident brings back memories of another terrible discovery Paul made there a long time ago. The repercussions of this latest in a string of killings will shatter the swim parents and force them to make some hard decisions.

Other books by the same author:
The Call, 2011
In a Bear's Eye: Stories, 2008
Signed, Mata Hari, 2007
Here They Come, 2006
The Sea of Trees, 1997

Other books you might like:
Megan Abbott, *The End of Everything*, 2011
Paul Auster, *Invisible*, 2009
Iain M. Banks, *Complicity*, 1993
Julian Barnes, *The Sense of an Ending*, 2011
Rajorshi Chakraborti, *Shadow Play*, 2010
Jan Ellison, *A Small Indiscretion*, 2014
Tana French, *Broken Harbor*, 2012
Siri Hustvedt, *The Blazing World*, 2014
Bret Anthony Johnston, *Remember Me Like This*, 2014
Laura Lippman, *What the Dead Know*, 2007
Ian McEwan, *The Children Act*, 2014
Jay McInerney, *Bright Lights, Big City*, 1984
Jennifer McMahon, *Promise Not to Tell*, 2006
Joyce Carol Oates, *Carthage*, 2014
Tom Perrotta, *Little Children*, 2004
Christos Tsiolkas, *Barracuda*, 2014
Mark Yakich, *A Meaning for Wife*, 2011

814

GINA B. NAHAI

The Luminous Heart of Jonah S.

(New York: Akashic Books, 2014)

Story type: Family Saga; Mystery
Subject(s): Jews; Middle East; Immigrants

Major character(s): Raphael's Son, Son (of the Black Bitch of Bushehr), Wealthy, Crime Victim, Criminal; Raphael Soleyman, Man (elderly), Spouse (of the Black Bitch of Bushehr), Wealthy; Black Bitch of Bushehr, Spouse (of Raphael), Mother (of Raphael's Son); Elizabeth, Aunt (of Raphael's Son)

Time period(s): 20th century; (1950s); 21st century; 2010s (2013)

Locale(s): Tehran, Iran; Los Angeles, California

Summary: The head of the wealthy Soleyman family has been hated his whole life, so it was no surprise when he turned up dead. An Iranian Jew born in 1950s Tehran, he was called Raphael's Son—but he most certainly wasn't. Despite his questionable parentage, he was named heir to the family fortune, leading to deadly consequences. When the Iranian revolution engulfed the country, Raphael's Son fled to Los Angeles, where he continued to accumulate wealth and enemies. He fostered enmity among his family and in the community when he emerged unscathed and considerably richer from a Ponzi scheme that ruined many of his clients. His murder seemed inevitable, and when he was finally found with his throat slashed, there was no shortage of suspects. However, after his body vanishes, some begin to wonder if he is really dead.

Other books by the same author:
Caspian Rain, 2007
Sunday's Silence, 2001
Moonlight on the Avenue of Faith, 1999
Cry of the Peacock, 1991

Other books you might like:
Salar Abdoh, *Tehran at Twilight*, 2014
Naomi Alderman, *Disobedience*, 2006
Jami Attenberg, *The Middlesteins*, 2012
Michael Chabon, *The Yiddish Policemen's Union: A Novel*, 2007
Stephen Dixon, *Phone Rings*, 2005
Dara Horn, *The World to Come*, 2006
Tova Mirvis, *The Outside World*, 2004
Peter Orner, *Love and Shame and Love*, 2011
Philip Roth, *Everyman*, 2006
Christopher Tilghman, *The Right-Hand Shore*, 2012
Jonathan Tropper, *This Is Where I Leave You*, 2009

815

DAVID CONNERLEY NAHM

Ancient Oceans of Central Kentucky

(Columbus, Ohio: Two Dollar Radio, 2014)

Story type: Literary

Subject(s): Family; Brothers and sisters; Kidnapping

Major character(s): Leah Shepard, Director (nonprofit organization), Sister (of Jacob); Jacob Shepard, Brother (of Leah), Missing Person

Time period(s): 21st century; 2010s

Locale(s): Crow Station, Kentucky

Summary: Leah Shepard is executive director of a nonprofit organization in Crow Station, Kentucky. She has lived in Crow Station her whole life. It is where she spent a happy childhood with her little brother, Jacob, and it's where Jacob disappeared years ago, when he was just five. Leah reminisces often about her rural Kentucky upbringing—outings, picnics, and trips to county fairs with Jacob and her parents. She also recalls the guilt she still feels about her brother's disappearance. It is obvious that Crow Station is not as perfect as it seems. Someone stole Jacob away from his happy little life there long ago, and that someone has never brought him back. When a man comes to Leah's workplace and says that he is her long-lost little brother, Leah is forced to face the past. First novel.

Other books you might like:
Emma Donoghue, *Room*, 2010
Gail Godwin, *Unfinished Desires*, 2009
Jennifer Haigh, *Faith*, 2011
Ursula Hegi, *The Worst Thing I've Done*, 2007
Morag Joss, *The Night Following*, 2008
Ian McEwan, *Saturday*, 2005
Richard Powers, *The Echo Maker*, 2006
Clara Sanchez, *The Scent of Lemon Leaves*, 2014
Elizabeth Strout, *The Burgess Boys*, 2013
Donna Tartt, *The Goldfinch*, 2013

816

SANDRA NEWMAN

The Country of Ice Cream Star

(London: Chatto & Windus, 2014)

Story type: Dystopian; Literary

Subject(s): Dystopias; Plague; Social conditions

Major character(s): Ice Cream Star, Girl, Narrator, Sister (of Driver), 15-Year-Old; Driver, 18-Year-Old, Young Man, Brother (of Ice Cream); Pasha, Man, Survivor (Posies plague)

Time period(s): Indeterminate Future

Locale(s): Massa, Massachusetts

Summary: The survivors of a plague they call the Posies make their way in their changed world by scavenging. Their lives are short, because the disease kills most of its victims before they turn 20. Fifteen-year-old Ice Cream Star and her 18-year-old brother, Driver, are members of the Sengles, a tribe of African American survivors. The Sengles inhabit Massa, which was once known as Massachusetts, and they speak a form of English that has mutated in the years since the plague began. Ice Cream emerges as the leader of the Sengles when Driver exhibits the first symptoms of the infection. When the children and teens are on a scavenging expedition, they find and capture a white man who has somehow reached the age of 30. Pasha, who is Russian, tells Ice Cream and the Sengles that he knows of a cure for the Posies. Desperate to save her brother, Ice Cream embarks on a dangerous quest.

Other books by the same author:
The Only Good Thing Anyone Has Ever Done, 2003

Other books you might like:
Margaret Atwood, *MaddAddam*, 2013
Paul Auster, *In the Country of Last Things*, 1988

Jim Crace, *The Pesthouse*, 2007
Michel Faber, *The Book of Strange New Things*, 2014
Peter Heller, *The Dog Stars*, 2012
Laura Kasischke, *Mind of Winter*, 2014
Chang-Rae Lee, *On Such a Full Sea*, 2014
Emily St. John Mandel, *Station Eleven*, 2014
Cormac McCarthy, *The Road*, 2006
Susan Beth Pfeffer, *Life as We Knew It*, 2006
John Ringo, *Strands of Sorrow*, 2015
Laura van den Berg, *Find Me*, 2015

817

DAVID NICHOLLS

Us

(New York: HarperCollins Publishers, 2014)

Story type: Family Saga
Subject(s): Family; Travel; Marriage
Major character(s): Douglas Petersen, Scientist (biochemist), Spouse (of Connie), Father (of Albie); Connie Petersen, Spouse (of Douglas), Mother (of Albie); Albie Petersen, 17-Year-Old, Son (of Douglas, Connie)
Time period(s): 21st century; 2010s
Locale(s): London, England; Paris, France; Venice, Italy; Amsterdam, Netherlands; Madrid, Spain

Summary: It seemed an unlikely match, but somehow reserved biochemist Douglas Petersen managed to land the beautiful, artistic Connie as his wife. Almost 30 years of apparently happy marriage and one son later, Connie hits Douglas with some devastating news. Their life together, she says, has run its course, and she wants a divorce. The news comes at a bad time for the family, as the Petersens are preparing to embark on a tour of Europe. Douglas decides to go ahead with the trip. He sees it as a last chance to save his marriage and bridge the emotional distance with his son, Albie. But his plan seems to go off the rails when the experience starts off bad and gets worse. To keep his family together, Douglas discovers the one person who needs to change the most may be himself.

Other books by the same author:
One Day, 2010
The Understudy, 2005
A Question of Attraction, 2004

Other books you might like:
Elisa Albert, *After Birth*, 2015
Anne Enright, *Yesterday's Weather*, 2008
Elin Hilderbrand, *Silver Girl*, 2011
Nick Hornby, *Juliet, Naked*, 2009
Lisa Jewell, *After the Party*, 2011
Rachel Joyce, *The Love Song of Miss Queenie Hennessy*, 2015
Liane Moriarty, *The Husband's Secret*, 2013
Jennie Nash, *The Last Beach Bungalow*, 2008
David Park, *The Light of Amsterdam*, 2012
Emily Perkins, *Novel about My Wife*, 2008
Anne Tyler, *The Amateur Marriage*, 2004
Nell Zink, *The Wallcreeper*, 2014

818

JOHN NIVEN

Straight White Male

(New York: Grove/Atlantic, 2014)

Story type: Satire
Subject(s): Entertainment industry; Interpersonal relations; Dating (Social customs)
Major character(s): Kennedy Marr, Teacher, Immigrant, Man, Writer
Time period(s): 21st century; 2010s
Locale(s): England; Los Angeles, California

Summary: Kennedy Marr has come a long way from the Ireland he was raised in as a boy. He now lives in Hollywood, where he made a fortune as a screen writer and spends much of his downtime partying as hard as he can. Unfortunately, Kennedy has had a lot of downtime lately due to a lack of ideas, but that hasn't stopped him from constantly imbibing in drink, drugs, and illicit sex—all of which has eaten away at his financial reserves. When the IRS demands he pay $1 million in back taxes, he fears that the party is finally over for him. Yet Kennedy has luck on his side, because a university in England is bestowing a prominent award upon him. The award comes with a 500,000 pound stipend that will allow him to clear his tax debt, but to receive it, he must agree to teach at the school for one school year. As Kennedy struggles in the academic world, he also must confront some relationships from the past that he never expected to encounter again.

Other books by the same author:
Cold Hands, 2012
Kill Your Friends, 2009

Other books you might like:
Louis Begley, *Schmidt Steps Back*, 2012
Jude Cook, *Byron Easy*, 2014
Don DeLillo, *Cosmopolis*, 2003
Jonathan Franzen, *The Corrections*, 2001
Siri Hustvedt, *The Blazing World*, 2014
James Kelman, *You Have to Be Careful in the Land of the Free*, 2004
Ian McEwan, *Amsterdam*, 1998
Lydia Millet, *Everyone's Pretty*, 2005
Salman Rushdie, *Shalimar the Clown*, 2005
Jose Saramago, *Death with Interruptions*, 2008

819

STEWART O'NAN

West of Sunset

(New York: Viking, 2015)

Subject(s): Writers; Biographies; History
Major character(s): F. Scott Fitzgerald, Historical Figure, Writer, Spouse (of Zelda), Lover (of Sheilah Graham); Zelda Fitzgerald, Historical Figure, Spouse (of F. Scott Fitzgerald), Patient (psychiatric hospital); Sheilah Graham, Historical Figure, Journalist (gossip columnist); Ernest Hemingway, Historical Figure,

Writer; Dorothy Parker, Historical Figure, Writer; Humphrey Bogart, Historical Figure, Actor
Time period(s): 20th century; 1930s-1940s (1937-1940)
Locale(s): Los Angeles, California

Summary: In this novel author Stewart O'Nan creates a fictionalized account of the final years of F. Scott Fitzgerald's life. The story begins in 1937 Hollywood, where Fitzgerald is working as a screenwriter and trying to pick up the pieces of his professional and private lives. Devastating reviews of his recent work have beaten down the Jazz Age novelist, who is writing a new novel—*The Last Tycoon*—that he hopes will resurrect his career. Fitzgerald's wife, Zelda, is in a North Carolina psychiatric facility, which is one of the reasons Fitzgerald is in such dire financial straits. Although it is Hollywood's golden age, Fitzgerald is not content. He crosses paths with such luminaries as Humphrey Bogart and Ernest Hemingway and has an affair with well-known gossip columnist Sheilah Graham, but he never regains his footing. Before he can complete and publish his new novel, Fitzgerald dies of heart failure in 1940.

Other books by the same author:
The Odds, 2012
Emily, Alone, 2011
Songs for the Missing, 2008
Last Night at the Lobster, 2007
The Good Wife, 2005

Other books you might like:
Kate Alcott, *A Touch of Stardust,* 2015
James Aldridge, *One Last Glimpse,* 1977
Joel Fishbane, *The Thunder of Giants,* 2015
Therese Anne Fowler, *Z: A Novel of Zelda Fitzgerald,* 2013
Molly Gloss, *Falling from Horses,* 2014
Ian McEwan, *Atonement,* 2002
Caroline Preston, *Gatsby's Girl,* 2006
Erika Robuck, *Call Me Zelda,* 2013
Lee Smith, *Guests on Earth,* 2013
R. Clifton Spargo, *Beautiful Fools: The Last Affair of Zelda and Scott Fitzgerald,* 2013
Emma Straub, *Laura Lamont's Life in Pictures,* 2012
George Zucker, *The Last Flapper,* 1969

820

COLLEEN OAKLEY

Before I Go

(New York: Gallery Books, 2015)

Story type: Contemporary; Medical
Subject(s): Marriage; Cancer; Death
Major character(s): Daisy Richmond, Student—Graduate, Cancer Patient, Spouse (of Jack), Friend (of Kayleigh); Jack Richmond, Student—Graduate, Spouse (of Daisy); Kayleigh, Friend (of Daisy)
Time period(s): 21st century; 2010s
Locale(s): Athens, Georgia

Summary: Four years ago, Daisy and Jack suffered the biggest hurdle of their young lives when Daisy was

diagnosed with cancer. She fought the disease and won, and now at age 27 she is ready to celebrate her fourth year cancer free—an occasion she calls her "cancerversary." But her hope is crushed when doctors tell her the cancer has returned, and this time she can't fight it. The news is hard enough on her, but she knows her loving but helpless husband will struggle without her. So she embarks on her life's last mission: to find a new wife for Jack. As she checks out possible matches and the reality of her husband with someone else hits her, Daisy wonders if she'd doing the right thing. Maybe she should live for today and not try to dictate a future she will never see.

Other books you might like:
Cecelia Ahern, *PS, I Love You,* 2004
David Baldacci, *One Summer,* 2011
Kimberly Belle, *The Last Breath,* 2014
Francesca Lia Block, *The Elementals,* 2012
Paula Marantz Cohen, *Suzanne Davis Gets a Life,* 2014
Catherine Coulter, *Whiplash,* 2010
Pete Fromm, *If Not for This,* 2014
Brian Keene, *Terminal,* 2005
Lisa Scottoline, *Betrayed,* 2014
Anne Tyler, *The Beginner's Goodbye,* 2012
Meg Wolitzer, *The Ten-Year Nap,* 2008

821

JOYCE CAROL OATES

The Sacrifice

(New York: Ecco Press, 2015)

Story type: Historical; Literary
Subject(s): Race relations; Racism; Kidnapping
Major character(s): Sybilla Frye, Kidnap Victim, Daughter (of Ednetta), 14-Year-Old; Ednetta Frye, Mother (of Sybilla)
Time period(s): 20th century; 1980s
Locale(s): New Jersey, United States

Summary: Sybilla Frye has been missing for days. As Ednetta Frye frantically searches for her daughter, a neighbor discovers the girl bound and covered in feces. The 14-year-old has been severely injured and racial slurs have been written on her body. According to Sybilla, several white men, including a police officer, abducted, beat, and raped her. Although Ednetta believes Sybilla and tries to protect her from the authorities, the social workers who interview the teen in the hospital doubt her story. Meanwhile, the black community believes Sybilla's story is just another example of racial hostility and the injustices the community experiences from the all-white police department. Sybilla's story, true or false, exposes the longstanding racial divide in the New Jersey town.

Other books by the same author:
Carthage, 2014
High Crime Area, 2014
Lovely, Dark, Deep: Stories, 2014

The Accursed, 2013

Evil Eye: Four Novellas of Love Gone Wrong, 2013

Other books you might like:

Andre Dubus III, *The Garden of Last Days: A Novel,* 2008

Ralph Ellison, *Three Days Before the Shooting...,* 2010

Karen Joy Fowler, *We Are All Completely Beside Ourselves,* 2013

Michiel Heyns, *The Children's Day,* 2009

Michael Hiebert, *Dream with Little Angels,* 2013

Deborah Johnson, *The Secret of Magic,* 2014

Tim Johnston, *Descent,* 2015

Toni Morrison, *Home,* 2012

Marilynne Robinson, *Lila,* 2014

Garth Stein, *A Sudden Light,* 2014

Christopher Tilghman, *The Right-Hand Shore,* 2012

822

SHAWN LAWRENCE OTTO

Sins of Our Fathers

(Minneapolis, Minnesota: Milkweed Editions, 2014)

Story type: Mystery

Subject(s): Suspense; Native American reservations; Business enterprises

Major character(s): John "JW" White, Banker, Gambler, Thief; Johnny Eagle, Banker

Time period(s): 21st century; 2010s

Locale(s): Minnesota, United States

Summary: JW works for a small regional bank in Minnesota. JW had a pretty decent life, but it begins to spiral out of control after his son's death. JW turns his back on his wife and teenage daughter and succumbs to a gambling addiction. When he steals a large sum of money from the bank, JW is caught. His boss offers him a deal: he will not be prosecuted if he participates in a game of corporate espionage. JW moves to a Native American reservation and sets to work spying on and disrupting the business of Johnny Eagle, a successful Native American financier. Johnny recently left the business world to work on the Ojibwe reservation. He wants nothing more than to bring financial security to his community. When he and JW face off with one another, the undercurrent of racial conflict is brought to the forefront of their respective communities. Now JW must choose between the person he wants to be, and the devil's bargain that he made with his employer. First novel.

Other books you might like:

Cristina Alger, *The Darlings,* 2012

Justin Cartwright, *Other People's Money,* 2011

Harlan Coben, *The Woods,* 2007

David Ellis, *Breach of Trust,* 2011

David Ignatius, *The Director,* 2014

David Kent, *The Blackjack Conspiracy,* 2005

Julie Kramer, *Delivering Death,* 2014

John Le Carre, *Our Kind of Traitor,* 2010

Kate Rhodes, *A Killing of Angels,* 2014

John Sandford, *Deadline,* 2014

823

CHUCK PALAHNIUK

Beautiful You

(New York: Doubleday, 2014)

Story type: Literary; Satire

Subject(s): Satire; Sexual behavior; Marketing

Major character(s): Penny Harrigan, Worker (law firm); Cornelius Linus Maxwell, Entrepreneur, Wealthy; Alouette D'Ambrosia, Actress; Clarissa Hind, Government Official (US President)

Time period(s): 21st century; 2010s

Locale(s): Paris, France; New York, New York

Summary: A billionaire entrepreneur tries to take over the world with a new line of sex toys in this novel by Chuck Palahniuk. Cornelius Linus Maxwell, known as "Climax-well" to the women who have experienced his sexual prowess, chooses plain-Jane law firm worker Penny Harrigan as his latest conquest. Although Penny is surprised by Maxwell's attention, she travels with him to Paris and surrenders to the power of his sex toys. Penny falls hard for Maxwell and his Beautiful You products, but Maxwell is only using Penny as the final test subject before the toys go on the market. When they do, women buy them up and share Penny's sexual ecstasy. Unfortunately, the addictive power of Maxwell's toys prompts female consumers to give up on men and even their families and careers. Penny begins to realize that battery-powered domination of women was Maxwell's plan all along.

Other books by the same author:

Doomed, 2013

Invisible Monsters Remix, 2012

Damned, 2011

Tell-All, 2010

Pygmy, 2009

Other books you might like:

Paul Beatty, *The Sellout,* 2015

Helen DeWitt, *Lightning Rods,* 2011

Lolita Files, *Sex.Lies.Murder.Fame,* 2006

Steve Israel, *The Global War on Morris,* 2015

Cherie Jeffrey, *Turn Me On,* 2007

Larry Kramer, *Search for My Heart,* 2015

Peter Lefcourt, *The Woody: A Novel,* 1998

Sam Lipsyte, *The Fun Parts,* 2013

Henry Miller, *Tropic of Cancer,* 1934

Will Self, *Cock and Bull,* 1992

Christopher Ward, *Dead Brilliant,* 2013

Irvine Welsh, *The Sex Lives of Siamese Twins,* 2015

824

JAMES PATTERSON

Hope to Die

(New York: Little, Brown and Company, 2014)

Series: Alex Cross Series. Book 22
Story type: Mystery; Psychological Suspense
Subject(s): Detective fiction; Kidnapping; Family relations
Major character(s): Alex Cross, Grandson (of Nana Mama), Detective, Spouse (of Bree), Father (of Damon, Jannie, and Alex Jr.); Brianna "Bree" Stone Cross, Spouse (of Alex), Stepmother (of Damon, Jannie, and Alex Jr.), Kidnap Victim; Damon Cross, Kidnap Victim, Son (of Alex), Stepson (of Bree), Brother (of Jannie), Stepbrother (of Alex Jr.); Janelle "Jannie" Cross, Daughter (of Alex), Stepdaughter (of Bree), Sister (of Damon), Stepsister (of Alex Jr.), Kidnap Victim; Alex Cross Jr., Kidnap Victim, Son (of Alex), Stepson (of Bree), Stepbrother (of Damon and Jannie); Nana Mama, Grandmother (of Alex), Kidnap Victim
Time period(s): 21st century; 2010s
Locale(s): Washington, District of Columbia

Summary: In this twenty-second installment of the Alex Cross series, the detective finds himself facing a challenge unlike any he's ever had. In the previous novel, *Cross my Heart*, Cross's family—his wife, Bree; children Damon, Jannie, and Alex, Jr.; and Nana Mama—were kidnapped. Now, the psychopath who is holding Cross's loved ones reveals the price of getting them back: Cross himself. With the lives of everyone he cares about most on the line, Cross will have to find a way to defeat the kidnapper's plans and rescue his family. He stands a good chance of having to give up his own life in the bargain.

Other books by the same author:
Burn, 2014
Homeroom Diaries, 2014
Invisible, 2014
Private Down Under, 2014
Private India, 2014

Other books you might like:
Ursula Archer, *Five*, 2014
Ace Atkins, *Robert B. Parker's Cheap Shot*, 2014
Lee Child, *Personal*, 2014
Marcia Clark, *Killer Ambition*, 2013
Paul Cleave, *Five Minutes Alone*, 2014
Harlan Coben, *The Stranger*, 2015
Michael Connelly, *The Burning Room*, 2014
Jeffrey Deaver, *Solitude Creek*, 2015
Tricia Fields, *Wrecked*, 2014
Lisa Gardner, *Crash and Burn*, 2015
Lisa Gardner, *Touch & Go*, 2013
W.E.B. Griffin, *The Last Witness*, 2013
Mo Hayder, *Wolf*, 2014
Greg Iles, *The Bone Tree*, 2012
Christine T. Jorgensen, *Missing*, 2013
Jonathan Kellerman, *Motive*, 2015
Ridley Pearson, *The Red Room*, 2014
Kathy Reichs, *Bones Never Lie*, 2014

John Sandford, *Uncaged*, 2014
Brad Thor, *Hidden Order*, 2013

825

JAMES PATTERSON
PETER DE JONGE, Co-Author

Miracle at Augusta

(New York: Little, Brown and Company, 2015)

Story type: Contemporary
Subject(s): Golf; Sports; Conduct of life
Major character(s): Travis McKinley, Golfer
Time period(s): 21st century; 2010s
Locale(s): Augusta, Georgia

Summary: In this novel, authors James Patterson and Peter de Jonge continue the story of Travis McKinley, the character they introduced in *Miracle on the 17th Green*. Travis defied the odds and became a golf pro when he was 50 and, through a miraculous turn of events, won the PGA Senior Open. The success made him uneasy, however, and now his career and personal life are on a downswing. Travis isn't playing well, and he drinks too much. When he gets in an alcohol-fueled fight with another golfer, pictures of the brawl surface, and Travis is disgraced. He wants to find a way to redeem himself, but the USPGA has banned him from the tour. Instead of trying to resurrect his own career, Travis focuses his attention on a misfit teenager who has the potential to be a great golfer.

Other books you might like:
Lee K. Abbott, *The Putt at the End of the World*, 2000
Michael Bamberger, *The Swinger*, 2012
Nicola Barker, *The Yips*, 2012
John R. Corrigan, *Cut Shot*, 2001
William Miller, *Night Golf*, 1999
Steven Pressfield, *The Legend of Bagger Vance*, 1995
Don J. Snyder, *Winter Dreams*, 2004
Michael Tucker, *After Annie*, 2012

826

JAMES PATTERSON
MAXINE PAETRO, Co-Author

Private Vegas

(New York: Little, Brown and Company, 2015)

Series: Private Series. Book 9
Story type: Mystery
Subject(s): Mystery; Detective fiction; Crime
Major character(s): Jack Morgan, Detective—Private; Lester Olsen, Businessman, Assassin (trainer)
Time period(s): 21st century; 2010s
Locale(s): Las Vegas, Nevada

Summary: Jack Morgan leads his international investigative agency, Private, from its headquarters in Los Angeles. His latest case draws him to Las Vegas, Nevada, where businessman Lester Olsen is using beautiful women as assassins. Olsen has found Sin City's resources ideal for his operation. There's no shortage of young ladies looking for the attention Olsen can give. And after he treats them to expensive meals and Vegas shows, Olsen trains the young women to be murderers. In a city where everyone has something to hide, Morgan knows he has his work cut out for him. Olsen's assassins blend in with all of the other beautiful people who are seduced by Vegas's glitz. This novel is the ninth in the Private series by James Patterson and Maxine Paetro.

Other books by the same author:
Burn, 2014
Confessions: The Paris Mysteries, 2014
Hope to Die, 2014
The Lost, 2014
Private Down Under, 2014

Other books you might like:
Chris Abani, *The Secret History of Las Vegas*, 2014
Cathy Ace, *The Corpse with the Platinum Hair*, 2014
Rennie Airth, *The Reckoning*, 2014
Jeffrey Archer, *Mightier than the Sword*, 2015
David Baldacci, *Memory Man*, 2015
Ken Bruen, *Purgatory*, 2013
Roy Chaney, *The Ragged End of Nowhere*, 2009
Deborah Coonts, *Lucky Stiff*, 2011
Mick Farren, *Vickers*, 1988
W.E.B. Griffin, *Deadly Assets*, 2015
J.A. Jance, *Fire and Ice*, 2009
Faye Kellerman, *The Beast*, 2013
Jonathan Kellerman, *Motive*, 2015
Jonathan Kellerman, *Victims*, 2012
Lynda La Plante, *Blind Fury*, 2010
Owen Laukkanen, *Kill Fee*, 2014
Maxine Paetro, *Confessions: The Paris Mysteries*, 2014
Sara Paretsky, *Critical Mass*, 2013
James Patterson, *NYPD Red 2*, 2014
James Patterson, *NYPD Red 3*, 2015
J.D. Robb, *Obsession in Death*, 2015
Vince Van Patten, *The Picasso Flop*, 2007
Stuart Woods, *Insatiable Appetites*, 2015

827

THOMAS PERRY

A String of Beads

(New York: Mysterious Press, 2014)

Series: Jane Whitefield Series. Book 8
Subject(s): Suspense; Native Americans; Missing persons
Major character(s): Jane Whitefield, Vigilante, Friend (of Jimmy Sanders); Jimmy Sanders, Fugitive, Crime Suspect, Missing Person, Friend (of Jane Whitefield)
Time period(s): 21st century; 2010s
Locale(s): Amherst, New York

Summary: In the eighth book of the Jane Whitefield series, the master tracker and hand-to-hand combat expert is approached by a force that she cannot deny. All eight clan mothers from her father's Seneca tribe request her assistance. Despite the fact that she is now a suburban homemaker, tradition dictates that she must comply. Her past profession and abilities in helping people flee

dangerous situations and create new, anonymous lives is something that the clan mothers are relying on. A childhood friend from the reservation, Jimmy Sanders, is in trouble. The police suspect Jimmy in a murder case, but he is being framed. The criminals who are framing him hunt him relentlessly and his trail has vanished. Jane must backtrack into her own memories of life on the reservation and draw upon all of her skills to save her friend before both of them end up dead.

Other books by the same author:
The Boyfriend, 2013
Poison Flower, 2012
The Informant, 2011
Strip, 2010
Runner, 2009

Other books you might like:
Linwood Barclay, *No Time for Goodbye*, 2007
Colin Bateman, *Maid of the Mist*, 2013
Edna Buchanan, *Legally Dead*, 2008
Sam Cabot, *Skin of the Wolf*, 2014
Lee Child, *Personal*, 2014
Margaret Coel, *Blood Memory*, September 2, 2008
Robert Crais, *Suspect*, 2013
James D. Doss, *Stone Butterfly*, 2006
CJ Lyons, *Black Sheep*, 2013
M.J. McGrath, *White Heat*, 2011
Carol O'Connell, *Find Me*, 2006
Thomas Perry, *Poison Flower*, 2012
Anna Quindlen, *Black and Blue*, 1998
Julia Spencer-Fleming, *Out of the Deep I Cry*, 2004
Dana Stabenow, *A Cold Day for Murder*, 1992
John Verdon, *Think of a Number*, 2010
Randy Wayne White, *Bone Deep*, 2014

828

SUSAN ELIZABETH PHILLIPS

Heroes Are My Weakness

(New York: William Morrow, 2014)

Subject(s): Adolescence; Interpersonal relations; Love
Major character(s): Annie Hewitt, Impoverished, Actress, Neighbor (of Theo); Theo Harp, Writer, Wealthy, Neighbor (of Annie)
Time period(s): 21st century; 2010s
Locale(s): Peregrine Island, Maine

Summary: Annie is broke and desperate. She has been eking out a living as a puppeteer for children's shows and as a ventriloquist, but her career as an actress has stalled completely. Upon the death of her mother, Annie inherits an old family cabin on an island off the coast of Maine. She reluctantly heads there to hammer out a plan for the future, praying that she will not reawaken adolescent memories of her last trip to the island. A sadistic neighbor, Theo Harp, almost killed her when they were teens and Annie would prefer to steer clear of him now. She is surprised to find that the evil and sadistic young man she remembers is nowhere to be found. Theo has matured and is intrigued by Annie's return. During the long winter on a bitterly cold Maine island, a relationship begins to develop between Annie and Theo. Annie may finally learn the truth about Theo's past actions and alleged villainous deeds.

Other books by the same author:
The Great Escape, 2012
Call Me Irresistible, 2011
What I Did for Love, 2009
Natural Born Charmer, 2007
Match Me If You Can, 2005

Other books you might like:
Sarah Abbot, *Destiny Bay*, 2008
Catherine Anderson, *Silver Thaw*, 2015
Jennifer Crusie, *Maybe This Time*, 2010
Janet Dailey, *Texas Tough*, 2015
Jude Deveraux, *Ever After*, 2015
Emily Giffen, *The One and Only*, 2014
Ginna Gray, *Pale Moon Rising*, 2004
Beth Harbison, *Driving with the Top Down*, 2014
Kay Hooper, *Haunting Rachel*, 1998
Donna Kauffman, *Sandpiper Island*, 2014
Jayne Ann Krentz, *Trust No One*, 2015
Elizabeth Lowell, *Night Diver*, 2014
Susan Mallery, *The Girls of Mischief Bay*, 2015
Linda Lael Miller, *The Marriage Season*, 2015
Marta Perry, *Abandon the Dark*, 2014
Jennifer Weiner, *All Fall Down*, 2014
Phyllis A. Whitney, *Spindrift*, 1975

`829`

JODI PICOULT

Leaving Time

(New York: Ballantine Books, 2014)

Story type: Psychic Powers
Subject(s): Animals; Animal rights; Elephants
Major character(s): Jenna Metcalf, 13-Year-Old, Daughter, Detective—Amateur; Alice Metcalf, Mother, Scientist, Missing Person; Serenity Jones, Psychic; Virgil Stanhope, Investigator (private); Thomas Metcalf, Father, Mentally Ill Person
Time period(s): 21st century
Locale(s): Kenya; New Hampshire, United States

Summary: Thirteen-year-old Jenna Metcalf is desperate to find her mother, who vanished ten years earlier on the same night a tragic death occurred on the New Hampshire elephant sanctuary run by Jenna's parents, Alice and Thomas Metcalf. For years Jenna has monitored missing person websites and studied her scientist mother's journals searching for some clue as to why she disappeared the same night one of the sanctuary keepers was found crushed to death in the elephant enclosure. Eventually enlisting the help of a once-famous psychic and a former police detective with a failing private practice, Jenna embarks on an investigation into the events surrounding the fateful evening of her mother's disappearance hoping to find not only if her mother is still alive, and if so, where she is, but why she failed to take Jenna with her or at least return for her. Characters Jenna, Serenity Jones (the psychic), and Virgil Stanhope (private

investigator) take turns telling the story from their points of view, interspersed with entries from Alice Metcalf's journal, which primarily details her research on elephant grieving.

Other books by the same author:
The Storyteller, 2013
Between the Lines, 2012
Lone Wolf, 2012
Sing You Home, 2011
House Rules, 2010

Other books you might like:
Diane Chamberlain, *The Silent Sister*, 2014
Mary Higgins Clark, *Daddy's Gone A Hunting*, 2013
Sarah Cornwell, *What I Had Before I Had You*, 2014
Beth Hoffman, *Looking for Me*, 2013
Jenny Jagerfeld, *Me on the Floor, Bleeding*, 2014
Lisa Jewell, *The House We Grew Up In*, 2014
Iris Johansen, *Bonnie*, 2011
Laura McHugh, *The Weight of Blood*, 2014
Jennifer McMahon, *Don't Breathe a Word*, 2011
Jennifer McMahon, *The Winter People*, 2014
Maggie O'Farrell, *Instructions for a Heatwave*, 2013
Mary Rickert, *The Memory Garden*, 2014
Maria Semple, *Where'd You Go, Bernadette*, 2012
Jeri Smith-Ready, *This Side of Salvation*, 2014
Anna Stothard, *The Pink Hotel*, 2013
Elizabeth Strout, *The Burgess Boys*, 2013
Jennifer Sturman, *And Then I Found Out the Truth*, 2010
M.O. Walsh, *My Sunshine Away*, 2015

`830`

MELISSA PIMENTEL

Love by the Book

(New York: Penguin Books, 2015)

Story type: Contemporary; Romance
Subject(s): Women; Romances (Fiction); Dating (Social customs)
Major character(s): Lauren Cunningham, Woman (28 years old)
Time period(s): 21st century; 2010s
Locale(s): London, England

Summary: At the end of March, 28-year-old Lauren Cunningham is still adjusting to single life in London. She left her home in Portland, Maine, after striking out romantically in the United States and moved to England to have some no-strings-attached fun with British men. Although she insists she isn't looking for a relationship, Lauren isn't able to hang on to any of her lovers for very long. So on April 1, she begins an experiment. Each month, she follows the advice in a different dating manual to determine which book provides the best results. As she works her way through *The Rules*, *The Technique of the Love Affair*, and *The Art of Dating*, Lauren keeps a record of her dating experiences with men she nicknames Top Hat, Bike Guy, and Sleepy Eyes. Lauren is surprised when some of the books' advice

Popular Fiction

proves to be valid. She's even more surprised when she realizes she may be looking for a real relationship after all.

Other books you might like:

Carolyn Brown, *The Red-Hot Chili Cook-Off*, 2014

Hester Browne, *The Runaway Princess*, 2012

Meg Cabot, *The Bride Wore Size 12*, 2013

Jennifer Crusie, *The Cinderella Deal*, 1996

Erin Duffy, *On the Rocks*, 2014

Janet Evanovich, *Wicked Charms*, 2015

Jessica Grose, *Sad Desk Salad*, 2012

Beth Kendrick, *Cure for the Common Breakup*, 2014

Sophie Kinsella, *Shopaholic to the Stars*, 2014

Jen Lancaster, *Here I Go Again*, 2013

Jill Mansell, *Thinking of You*, 2013

Ali McNamara, *From Notting Hill with Love...Actually*, 2012

Rainbow Rowell, *Attachments*, 2011

Susan Schneider, *The Wedding Writer*, 2011

Alison Sweeney, *The Star Attraction*, 2013

831

JERRY PINTO

Em and the Big Hoom

(New Delhi, India: Aleph Book Company, 2012)

Story type: Literary

Subject(s): Family; Mental disorders; Parent-child relations

Major character(s): Em, Woman, Mentally Ill Person, Spouse (of Big Hoom), Mother (of Susan and narrator); Big Hoom, Man, Spouse (of Em), Father (of Susan and narrator); Susan, Daughter (of Em and Big Hoom), Sister (of narrator); Unnamed Character, Boy, Narrator, Son (of Em and Big Hoom), Brother (of Susan), 15-Year-Old

Time period(s): 20th century; 1980s-1990s

Locale(s): Bombay, India

Summary: The unnamed narrator of this novel, a 15-year-old boy, lives in late-20th-century Bombay with his family. "Big Hoom," the father, is a salesman. The mother, Em, deals with recurring bouts of severe mental illness that began after the narrator's birth. The boy and his older sister, Susan, are familiar with Em's eccentric behavior and her periods of mania and depression. They also know that their mother has tried several times to kill herself. It was the children who discovered Em in the bathroom after one particularly bloody suicide attempt. The narrative follows the family as its members deal with Em's fragile health. As the years pass, the narrator struggles with the conflicting feelings he has for his mother—feelings that are complicated by the boy's worry that he will become mentally unstable himself.

Other books you might like:

Aravind Adiga, *Last Man in Tower*, 2011

Russell Banks, *The Reserve*, 2008

Muriel Barbery, *The Elegance of the Hedgehog*, 2008

Juliann Garey, *Too Bright to Hear Too Loud to See*, 2012

Pete Hamill, *Snow in August*, 1997

Lynne Hinton, *The Order of Things*, 2009

Claire Messud, *The Woman Upstairs*, 2013

Joyce Carol Oates, *The Gravedigger's Daughter*, 2007

Matthew Quick, *The Silver Linings Playbook*, 2008

Manil Suri, *The City of Devi*, 2013

Miriam Toews, *All My Puny Sorrows*, 2014

832

MICHAEL PITRE

Fives and Twenty-Fives

(New York: Bloomsbury USA, 2014)

Story type: Literary; Military

Subject(s): Wars; Military life; Interpersonal relations

Major character(s): Peter Donovan, Military Personnel (lieutenant), Veteran (Iraq War); Lester "Doc" Pleasant, Military Personnel (medic), Veteran (Iraq War); Kateb "Dodge" el-Hariti, Student—College (former, Baghdad University), Young Man, Linguist (interpreter)

Time period(s): 21st century; 2010s

Locale(s): Iraq; United States

Summary: Peter Donovan is back in the United States after serving in the Iraq War. He is trying to adjust to civilian life, but memories of his war experiences fill his thoughts day and night. Flashbacks transport Peter to Iraq, where his unit worked on the seemingly mundane task of filling potholes. But the job was actually quite dangerous, because any of the holes could hide a bomb. Lester "Doc" Pleasant was also a member of the unit. He served as a medic, but was overwhelmed by the injuries and deaths he witnesses. Doc used drugs as an escape, but that decision had dire consequences. Kateb "Dodge" el-Hariti, an interpreter for the Americans, found his loyalty tested every day. Back in the States, Peter still carries Dodge's copy of *The Adventures of Huck Finn*. It is one of the mementos that keeps the war ever present as Peter tries to move forward. First novel.

Other books you might like:

James Brady, *The Marines of Autumn: A Novel of the Korean War*, 2000

Ben Fountain, *Billy Lynn's Long Halftime Walk*, 2012

Phil Klay, *Redeployment*, 2014

Patricia McCormick, *Purple Heart*, 2009

Walter Dean Myers, *Sunrise over Fallujah*, 2008

Richard North Patterson, *In the Name of Honor*, 2010

Kevin Powers, *The Yellow Birds*, 2012

Ross Ritchell, *The Knife*, 2015

Joydeep Roy-Bhattacharya, *The Watch*, 2012

Julia Spencer-Fleming, *One Was a Soldier*, 2011

Minette Walters, *The Chameleon's Shadow: A Novel*, 2008

833

HANNAH PITTARD

Reunion

(New York: Hachette Book Group, 2014)

Story type: Contemporary
Subject(s): Family; Grief; Death
Major character(s): Kate Pulaski, Sister (of Nell and Elliot), Writer, Daughter (of Dad); Dad, Father (of Nell, Elliot, and Kate), Mentally Ill Person (suicide); Elliot, Brother (of Kate and Nell), Son (of Dad); Nell, Daughter (of Dad), Sister (of Kate and Elliot)
Time period(s): 21st century; 2010s
Locale(s): Atlanta, Georgia

Summary: Kate Pulaski's life is falling apart. Her career as a writer is in shambles, her marriage is ending, her bank account is nearly empty, and, while sitting on the runway waiting for her plane to be rerouted, she learns that her father has committed suicide. Kate's relationship with her father has been nearly non-existent since her mother died when Kate was still a child, but her brother and sister insist that she travel to Atlanta to attend the funeral. Kate is reunited not only with her immediate family—Elliot and Nell—but also with the extended family her father created. As Elliot, Nell, and Kate each attempt to grieve a man they never really knew, all of them are faced with some facts about their lives. Elliot must admit that his own marriage and family are not as perfect as he publicly portrays, Nell must face her own discontent, and Kate must deal with the wreckage of her life. Meanwhile, they all struggle with their feelings about their father's other children and multiple wives, and the myriad of emotions that his death has left behind.

Other books by the same author:
The Fates Will Find Their Way, 2011

Other books you might like:
John Michael Cummings, *Don't Forget Me, Bro*, 2015
Annie Dillard, *The Maytrees: A Novel*, 2007
Elizabeth Gaffney, *When the World Was Young*, 2014
Julia Glass, *I See You Everywhere*, 2008
Kristin Hannah, *Winter Garden*, 2010
Sarah Healy, *House of Wonder*, 2014
Sarah Klassen, *The Wittenbergs*, 2013
Jennifer Scott, *The Sister Season*, 2013
Leah Stewart, *The History of Us*, 2013
J. Courtney Sullivan, *Maine*, 2011
Jonathan Tropper, *This Is Where I Leave You*, 2009
Anne Tyler, *A Spool of Blue Thread*, 2015

834

ANGELA PNEUMAN

Lay It on My Heart

(New York: Mariner Books, 2014)

Story type: Coming-of-Age; Literary
Subject(s): Coming of age; Religion; Family
Major character(s): Charmaine Peake, 13-Year-Old, Daughter (of David and Phoebe), Granddaughter (of Daze); David Peake, Religious (claims to be prophet), Spouse (of Phoebe), Father (of Charmaine), Son (of Daze), Mentally Ill Person; Phoebe Peake, Spouse (of David), Mother (of Charmaine); Daze Peake, Mother (of David), Grandmother (of Charmaine)
Time period(s): 21st century; 2010s
Locale(s): East Winder, Kentucky

Summary: Thirteen-year-old Charmaine Peake's grandfather was a revered preacher. Her father, David, claims to be a prophet. Charmaine unquestioningly adheres to her family's rigid religious lifestyle, praying all the time and following the Lord's path. But things change when David returns from a pilgrimage to the Holy Land. He injures himself and is admitted to a psychiatric hospital where he is treated for bipolar disorder. The medication David is given quells the voice in his head that he believed was God. Meanwhile, Charmaine and her mother Phoebe are left on their own to deal with David's medical bills. They rent their home to a missionary family and move into a tiny trailer. When Phoebe starts middle school, she is exposed to a world beyond her father's religious fanaticism. She questions her beliefs further when she discovers that the boy who is living in her former bedroom may not be as pious as he seems.

Other books by the same author:
Home Remedies, 2007

Other books you might like:
Sarah Addison Allen, *Garden Spells*, 2007
Elizabeth Berg, *Home Safe*, 2009
Amy Bloom, *Lucky Us*, 2014
Bebe Moore Campbell, *72 Hour Hold: A Novel*, 2005
Michael Christie, *If I Fall, If I Die*, 2015
Jenn Crowell, *Etched on Me*, 2014
Penelope Lively, *How It All Began*, 2012
Travis Nichols, *The More You Ignore Me*, 2013
Sheri Reynolds, *Firefly Cloak*, 2006
Sheila Roberts, *Better than Chocolate*, 2012
Rebecca Wells, *Ya-Yas in Bloom*, 2004

835

MARK POWELL

The Sheltering

(Columbia, South Carolina: University of South Carolina Press, 2014)

Story type: Contemporary Realism; Family Saga
Subject(s): Family; Wars; Veterans
Major character(s): Luther Redding, Military Personnel, Pilot (of military drone), Spouse (of Pamela), Father (of Katie and Lucy); Pamela Redding, Spouse (of Luther), Mother (of Katie and Lucy); Katie Redding, Sister (of Lucy), Daughter (of Luther and Pamela); Lucy Redding, Sister (of Katie), Daughter (of Luther and Pamela); Bobby Rosen, Veteran (of war in Iraq), Dysfunctional Family Member, Divorced Person, Brother (of Donny); Donny Rosen, Prisoner (released), Brother (of Bobby)
Time period(s): 21st century; 2010s
Locale(s): Afghanistan; Iraq; United States; Miami, Florida; Tampa, Florida; Georgia, United States; New

Orleans, Louisiana; Charleston, South Carolina

Summary: While war is usually fought on the battlefield, sometimes the most devastating conflicts are those the warriors bring home with them. Luther Redding is a drone pilot, remotely bringing death to the enemy from his post at a Florida air base. Veteran Bobby Rosen has returned home to a hopelessly damaged marriage and is burdened by his terrible actions in Iraq. When a sudden death strikes the Redding household, Luther's grief-stricken daughter, Katie, impulsively flees down a path of self-destruction. Lost in the reality of their new lives, Bobby and his former convict brother, Donny, take their own journey into darkness, setting off on a drug-addled road trip. In time Katie and Bobby's paths will cross and lead either to a deadly resolution, or a last chance at redemption.

Other books you might like:
Greg Baxter, *The Apartment*, 2013
Lea Carpenter, *Eleven Days: A Novel*, 2013
Paolo Giordano, *The Human Body*, 2014
Siri Hustvedt, *The Sorrows of an American*, 2008
Thomas Keneally, *Office of Innocence*, 2003
Kevin Powers, *The Yellow Birds*, 2012
Roxana Robinson, *Sparta*, 2013
Dalton Trumbo, *Johnny Got His Gun*, 1939
Thrity Umrigar, *The Story Hour*, 2014
Evie Wyld, *After the Fire, a Still Small Voice*, 2009

836

DAVID POYER

The Cruiser

(London: St. Martin's Press, 2014)

Series: Dan Lenson Series. Book 14
Story type: Military; Series
Subject(s): Military life; Ships; Death
Major character(s): Dan Lenson, Military Personnel, Sea Captain
Time period(s): 21st century; 2010s
Locale(s): At Sea

Summary: Dan Lenson's first command as captain is a ship stuck on land. He's called in to relieve the captain of the USS *Savo Island*, a naval vessel carrying a new missile system, which has run aground in the Mediterranean Sea. Lenson takes command and embarks on a secret mission to the Middle East. The journey is no easy task. With battle looming, Lenson must find a way to motivate a crew low on morale and solve a mysterious death aboard ship. As conflict flares between Israel and Iraq, Lenson is put in a position where the cost of his decisions could be measured in lives. This is the fourteenth book in David Poyer's Dan Lenson series.

Other books by the same author:
The Whiteness of the Whale, 2013
The Towers, 2011
Ghosting, 2010
The Crisis, 2009
The Weapon, 2008

Other books you might like:
Larry Bond, *Larry Bond's Red Dragon Rising: Blood of War*, 2013
Dale Brown, *Edge of Battle*, 2006
Sandra Brown, *Lethal*, 2011
Lee Child, *A Wanted Man*, 2012
Martha Cooley, *Ice Shear*, 2014
Don Mann, *SEAL Team Six: Hunt the Jackal*, 2014
Ross Ritchell, *The Knife*, 2015
Patrick Robinson, *The Delta Solution*, 2011
James Rollins, *The Kill Switch: A Tucker Wayne Novel*, 2014
Brad Taylor, *No Fortunate Son*, 2014
Brad Thor, *The Last Patriot: A Thriller*, 2008

837

LINCOLN CHILD
DOUGLAS PRESTON, Co-Author

Blue Labyrinth

(New York: Grand Central Publishing, 2014)

Series: Aloysius Pendergast Series. Book 14
Story type: Mystery; Series
Subject(s): Mystery; Crime; Murder
Major character(s): Aloysius Pendergast, FBI Agent, Friend (of Vincent); Vincent D'Agosta, Police Officer (NYPD), Friend (of Aloysius Pendergast)
Time period(s): 21st century; 2010s
Locale(s): California, United States; New York, New York

Summary: This mystery thriller is the 14th installment in the Aloysius Pendergast series from best-selling authors Douglas Preston and Lincoln Child. FBI Special Agent Aloysius Pendergast finds the body of a long-time enemy on the doorstep of his home on the Upper West Side of Manhattan. When the autopsy reveals a turquoise gem wedged in the murder victim's stomach, the search for the killer leads Pendergast to the Salton Sea, a deserted mine on California's shore. Pendergast's discoveries unearth a long-kept family secret, and soon, the agent is on the trail of his own murderous stalker, a killer seeking revenge for an age-old offense. But as Pendergast digs deeper into his family's sordid past, he is plagued mentally and physically. Meanwhile, his friend and NYPD associate, Vincent D'Agosta, investigates the gruesome murder of a technician at the New York Museum of Natural History.

Other books by the same author:
The Lost Island, 2014
White Fire, 2013
Gideon's Corpse, 2012
The Third Gate, 2012
Two Graves, 2012

Other books you might like:
Neil Albert, *The January Corpse*, 1991
Ace Atkins, *The Forsaken*, 2014
David Baldacci, *The Escape*, 2014
Dan Brown, *Inferno*, 2013
Ian Caldwell, *The Fifth Gospel*, 2015
John Case, *Ghost Dancer: A Novel*, 2006
Clive Cussler, *Spartan Gold: A Fargo Adventure*, 2009

Jeffrey Deaver, *Solitude Creek*, 2015
Nelson DeMille, *The Panther*, 2012
Colin Dexter, *The Remorseful Day*, 2000
W.E.B. Griffin, *Deadly Assets*, 2015
Tami Hoag, *Cold Cold Heart*, 2014
Raymond Khoury, *The Devil's Elixir*, 2011
Andrew Klavan, *A Killer in the Wind*, 2013
Dean Koontz, *Saint Odd*, 2015
Ken Kuhlken, *The Good Know Nothing*, 2014
Michael Kurland, *Sherlock Holmes: The Hidden Years*, 2004
Douglas Preston, *The Lost Island*, 2014
Bill Pronzini, *Strangers*, 2014
Sebastian Rotella, *The Convert's Song*, 2014
Hank Phillippi Ryan, *Truth Be Told*, 2014
John Searles, *Help for the Haunted*, 2013
Brad Taylor, *No Fortunate Son*, 2014

838

DANIEL PYNE

Fifty Mice

(London: Penguin Publishing Group, 2014)

Story type: Mystery
Subject(s): Memory; Kidnapping; Family
Major character(s): Jay Johnson, Kidnap Victim, Captive
Time period(s): 21st century; 2010s
Locale(s): Catalina Island, California; Los Angeles, California

Summary: Jay Johnson's life resides squarely in the ordinary. He has a good job, an active group of friends, and a loving girlfriend. That all changes one day when Jay is abducted in a Los Angeles subway station by the government. Whisked off to a hidden enclave on Catalina Island, Jay is told he is part of a murder investigation and is placed in the Federal Witness Protection Program. Unfortunately, he has no recollection of any of the events they insist he should know about. Forced to adjust to his new life, complete with an agency-provided family, Jay begins to question his own memories, and wonders which reality is the truth and which is an invention. But as much as he wants to escape the island, his emotions are complicated when he starts to have feelings for his new family.

Other books by the same author:
Twentynine Palms, 2010

Other books you might like:
Lisa Gardner, *Fear Nothing*, 2014
Heather Graham, *The Silenced*, 2015
Emma Healey, *Elizabeth Is Missing*, 2014
Tami Hoag, *Cold Cold Heart*, 2014
Lisa Jackson, *Never Die Alone*, 2015
Iris Johansen, *The Perfect Witness*, 2014
Michael Kardos, *Before He Finds Her*, 2015
Mary Kubica, *The Good Girl*, 2014
Dennis Lehane, *Shutter Island*, 2003
Kristen Lippert-Martin, *Tabula Rasa*, 2014
Joyce Maynard, *After Her*, 2013

Isla Morley, *Above*, 2014
Susan May Warren, *You Don't Know Me*, 2012

839

CAISEY QUINN

Loving Dallas

(New York: HarperCollins, 2015)

Series: Neon Dreams Series. Book 2
Story type: Romance
Subject(s): Romances (Fiction); Musicians; Country music
Major character(s): Dallas Lark, Musician; Robyn Breeland, Businesswoman (promotions manager), Manager (promotions, Midnight Bay Bourbon)
Time period(s): 21st century; 2010s
Locale(s): Nashville, Tennessee; Texas, United States

Summary: This novel is the second book from author Caisey Quinn's Neon Dreams series. Robyn Breeland has worked hard to get where she is. Her job as a promotions manager for one of the top bourbon companies in the country doesn't allow her much time for romance, and she likes it that way. Then her boss announces that their company is signing on with up-and-coming country star Dallas Lark's national tour. Once upon a time, Dallas was the love of Robyn's life. But then he left her and tore her heart to pieces. When Dallas and Robyn start spending time together again, they realize that they still have the same passion for each other they had before. Unfortunately, neither one of them is sure if they are getting another shot at love or another opportunity to have their hearts broken.

Other books by the same author:
Kylie Ryans Trilogy, 2015
Leaving Amarillo, 2015
Falling for Fate, 2014
Girl with a Guitar, 2014
Last Second Chance, 2014

Other books you might like:
Jay Crownover, *Rule*, 2013
Colleen Hoover, *Maybe Someday*, 2014
J. Lynn, *Be with Me*, 2014
Megan Mulry, *A Royal Pain*, 2012
Jane Porter, *She's Gone Country*, 2010

840

ROSA RANKIN-GEE

The Last Kings of Sark

(London: Virago Press, 2013)

Story type: Literary
Subject(s): Coming of age; Islands; Interpersonal relations
Major character(s): Jude, Young Woman, Graduate (college), Tutor (of Pip); Pip Defoe, Boy, 16-Year-Old, Son (of Eddy and Esme), Student (of Jude); Eddy Defoe, Spouse (of Esme), Father (of Pip); Esme Defoe, Spouse (of Eddy), Mother (of Pip); Sofi, Young

Popular Fiction

Woman (Polish), 19-Year-Old, Cook (for Defoe family)
Time period(s): 21st century; 2010s
Locale(s): Sark, England

Summary: When Jude is hired to tutor 16-year-old Pip Defoe, the Defoe family presumes Jude is a man. But when Jude arrives on the Channel island of Sark, Eddy and Esme Defoe realize that Jude is definitely female. After all parties recover from the initial confusion, Jude adjusts to her strange new surroundings. Sark has no cars, and it was until recent years a fiefdom. The Defoe clan is also unusual. Eddy is often absent; Esme isolates herself in her bedroom. Pip is bright, but he has no intention of spending the summer studying. Jude, Pip, and the 19-year-old cook, Sofi, quickly form a friendship. They drink wine, explore the island, and engage in a number of questionable adventures. Their time together is brief, however, and when summer ends, they go their separate ways. Even as they lose touch over the years, Jude, Pip, and Sofi remain affected by their summer on Sark.

Other books you might like:
Isabel Allende, *Maya's Notebook*, 2013
Carol Rifka Brunt, *Tell the Wolves I'm Home*, 2012
Elin Hilderbrand, *The Love Season*, 2006
Joyce Maynard, *The Good Daughters*, 2010
Colum McCann, *TransAtlantic*, 2013
Sigrid Nunez, *Salvation City*, 2010
Lucinda Riley, *The Girl on the Cliff*, 2012
Maxine Swann, *Flower Children*, 2007
Donna Tartt, *The Goldfinch*, 2013
Meg Wolitzer, *The Interestings*, 2013

841

JAMES WESLEY RAWLES

Liberators

(New York: Penguin Random House, 2014)

Series: Coming Collapse Series. Book 5
Subject(s): Dystopias; Apocalypse; Survival
Major character(s): Ray McGregor, Veteran; Phil Adams, Agent (former, Defense Intelligence Agency)
Time period(s): 21st century
Locale(s): Canada; United States

Summary: In the fifth novel of James Wesley Rawles's Coming Collapse series, the author continues his novelization of what could happen if the first world were to experience a financial catastrophe in the near future. Rawles chronicles the journey of Ray McGregor, a veteran from the Afghanistan-U.S. war who is attempting to travel from Michigan into the remote regions of British Columbia, Canada, to reach his parents. McGregor's progress is stymied by worsening conditions throughout the United States, and he must navigate around the mass hysteria and total chaos that has taken hold of most major U.S. cities. McGregor's friend Phil Adams, who is a former government agent, helps him along the way, and soon they find themselves banding together when the country is taken over by a totalitarian regime. Now it is up to these two men, both of whom once fought to free other countries from dictatorial rule, to fight against the very country they had always sworn to protect.

Other books by the same author:
Expatriates, 2013
Founders, 2012
Survivors, 2011
Patriots, 1998

Other books you might like:
Richard A. Clarke, *Pinnacle Event*, 2015
Sarah Crossan, *Resist*, 2013
Stephanie Diaz, *Rebellion*, 2015
James Jaros, *Burn Down the Sky*, 2011
Lee Kelly, *City of Savages*, 2015
Oliver North, *Counterfeit Lies*, 2014
Kate Ormand, *Dark Days*, 2014
Joel C. Rosenberg, *The Third Target*, 2015
Michael Savage, *A Time for War*, 2013
John Twelve Hawks, *Spark*, 2014
Carol Lynch Williams, *The Haven*, 2014

842

SARAH RAYNER

Getting Even

(New York: Picador, 2014)

Story type: Contemporary; Revenge
Subject(s): Betrayal; Friendship; Revenge
Major character(s): Orianna, Advertising, Friend (of Ivy), Girlfriend (of Dan); Ivy, Advertising, Friend (of Orianna); Dan, Boyfriend (of Orianna), Colleague (of Orianna and Ivy)
Time period(s): 21st century; 2010s
Locale(s): New York, New York

Summary: Author Sarah Rayner has created a modern adaptation of Shakespeare's play *Othello*. Though polar opposites, Ivy and Orianna are best friends and colleagues at an advertising firm. Together, they form a slam-dunk creative team that has helped put their employer on the map. Sweet and naive Orianna accepts a promotion, which makes her the calculating Ivy's new boss. Shocked and bitter, Ivy feels the betrayal even deeper when she realizes that the promotion has been in the works for months and Orianna has kept it a secret from everyone, including her. Ivy decides that Orianna is due for a setback and uses her intimate knowledge of her former friend's life and relationships in an attempt to ruin her life. Orianna has been involved with another colleague, Dan, in a low-key relationship, so Ivy begins to spread rumors about Dan and other women in the office. Office rumors and lies send Orianna's life on a downhill spiral, but she has no idea that her best friend is responsible. Ivy becomes careless in her glee at tearing down Orianna, however, and soon her own secrets may be spilled all over the office.

Other books by the same author:
Another Night, Another Day, 2014
The Other Half, 2014
The Two Week Wait, 2012
One Moment, One Morning, 2011

Other books you might like:
Tamar Cohen, *War of the Wives*, 2015
Eric Jerome Dickey, *The Other Woman*, 2003
Sean Dixon, *The Many Revenges of Kip Flynn*, 2011
Ann Leary, *The Good House*, 2013
Mary McNear, *Up at Butternut Lake*, 2014
Leila Meacham, *Roses*, 2010
Eleanor Moran, *The Last Time I Saw You*, 2013
Jojo Moyes, *Silver Bay*, 2007
Waubgeshig Rice, *Legacy*, 2014
Daryl Sneath, *All My Sins*, 2014
Joanna Trollope, *Second Honeymoon*, 2006

843

KATHY REICHS

Bones Never Lie

(New York: Bantam Books, 2014)

Series: Temperance Brennan Series. Book 17
Story type: Mystery; Police Procedural
Subject(s): Detective fiction; Law enforcement; Serial murders
Major character(s): Dr. Temperance "Tempe" Brennan, Anthropologist (forensic), Co-worker (former partner, of Andrew); Andrew Ryan, Detective, Co-worker (former partner, of Tempe); Anique Pomerleau, Serial Killer
Time period(s): 21st century; 2010s
Locale(s): Charlotte, North Carolina

Summary: Best-selling author Kathy Reichs delivers the seventeenth novel in her series featuring forensic anthropologist Temperance Brennan. Suspicions rise when Dr. Temperance "Tempe" Brennan is called in to Charlotte's Police Department to meet with a homicide cop from Vermont over a cold case that has been reopened. The unsolved murder of an 11-year-old girl from Charlotte is linked to the notorious Canadian serial killer Anique Pomerleau, the murderer who slipped through the hands of Tempe and her ex-partner, lead detective Andrew Ryan, years ago. New evidence suggests that Pomerleau is responsible for two recent murders in North Carolina and Vermont. When another young girl goes missing, authorities fear she's Pomerleau's next victim. The second chance Tempe has longed for has finally come around, but to get Andrew back on the case, she'll have to convince him to come out of hiding.

Other books by the same author:
Terminal, 2015
Exposure, 2014
Bones of the Lost, 2013
Code, 2013
Bones are Forever, 2012

Other books you might like:
Sarah Andrews, *Rock Bottom*, 2012
Jefferson Bass, *Carved in Bone*, 2006
Jefferson Bass, *Cut to the Bone*, 2013
Simon Beckett, *The Chemistry of Death*, 2006
Harlan Coben, *The Stranger*, 2015
Patricia Cornwell, *Flesh and Blood*, 2014

Patricia Cornwell, *Postmortem*, 1990
Jeffery Deaver, *The Skin Collector*, 2014
Susan Dunlap, *Pious Deception*, 1989
Linda Fairstein, *Terminal City*, 2014
Tess Gerritsen, *Die Again*, 2014
Tess Gerritsen, *The Sinner*, 2003
Ron Goulart, *One Grave Too Many*, 1974
J.A. Jance, *Cold Betrayal*, 2015
Iris Johansen, *Silencing Eve*, 2013
Faye Kellerman, *Murder 101*, 2014
Sharyn McCrumb, *Sick of Shadows*, 1984
Maxine Paetro, *14th Deadly Sin*, 2015
James Patterson, *Hope to Die*, 2014
John Sandford, *Deadline*, 2014
Karin Slaughter, *Cop Town*, 2014

844

RUTH RENDELL

The Girl Next Door

(New York: Scribner, 2014)

Subject(s): Interpersonal relations; Mystery; Suspense
Major character(s): Daphne Jones, Wealthy, Widow(er), Lover (former, of Alan); John "Woody" Winwood, Father (of Michael); Michael Winwood, Son (of Woody); Alan, Lover (former, of Daphne); Lewis, Nephew (of James); James, Uncle (of Lewis), Military Personnel
Time period(s): 21st century; 2010s
Locale(s): London, England

Summary: This mystery novel by Ruth Rendell is set in contemporary Britain, although the story begins much earlier, toward the end of World War II when a group of young friends in London discover a hidden tunnel and use it to play in. Now, nearly 60 years later, a construction crew has uncovered a box that contains two skeletal hands—one from a woman, one from a man. The investigators call the friends together: Daphne Jones, now a wealthy widow; her former lover, Alan, who is trapped in a passionless marriage and immediately recalls his former attraction to Daphne; Lewis, who remembers his uncle James's interest in the tunnel; and Michael, the son of the horrible John "Woody" Winwood, who abandoned the boy when he was young. Someone in the group knows the truth about the hands. They must take a hard look at their choices in the past and uncover long-hidden secrets.

Other books by the same author:
No Man's Nightingale, 2013
The Saint Zita Society, 2012
The St. Zita Society, 2012
The Vault, 2011
Portobello, 2010

Other books you might like:
Margery Allingham, *The Tiger in the Smoke*, 1952
Kate Atkinson, *Case Histories*, 2004
Alan Bradley, *The Sweetness at the Bottom of the Pie*, 2009
Gillian Flynn, *Gone Girl*, 2012

Nicci French, *Tuesday's Gone*, 2013
Tana French, *Faithful Place*, 2011
Elly Griffiths, *The Crossing Places*, 2010
Sophie Hannah, *The Dead Lie Down*, 2010
A.S.A. Harrison, *The Silent Wife*, 2013
Jonathan Kellerman, *Killer*, 2014
J. Wallis Martin, *A Likeness in Stone*, 1997
Kate Morton, *The Distant Hours*, 2010
Kate Morton, *The Secret Keeper*, 2012
Perri O'Shaughnessy, *Keeper of the Keys*, 2006
Tina Seskis, *One Step Too Far*, 2015
Tom Rob Smith, *The Farm*, 2014
Jeff Somers, *Chum*, 2013
Minette Walters, *The Ice House*, 1992

845

ANNE RICE

Prince Lestat

(New York: Knopf, 2014)

Series: Vampire Chronicles. Book 11
Subject(s): Horror; Fantasy; Vampires
Major character(s): Lestat de Lioncourt, Vampire; Louis de Pointe du Lac, Vampire; Armand, Vampire; Mekare, Vampire, Twin (of Maharet); Maharet, Vampire, Twin (of Mekare); David Talbot, Vampire, Investigator (supernatural)
Time period(s): 21st century; (2010s); Multiple Time Periods
Locale(s): Earth

Summary: Anne Rice resurrects her Vampire Chronicles, which she had previously concluded with the 2003 novel *Blood Canticle*, in this 11th series entry. The story centers on the vampire Lestat, but it draws characters from previous novels into a complex plot that involves a crisis unfolding in the vampire world. A voice of unknown origin is ordering vampires to kill others of their kind. The Voice stirs the oldest of vampires to slaughter their younger counterparts, resulting in massacres around the world. As the Voice incites widespread bloodshed in the modern world, the characters relate their personal histories in ancient Africa, medieval Europe, and other distant times and places. Although the vampires expect Lestat to solve the mystery of the Voice and stop the slaughter, the self-absorbed vampire chooses his own timetable for entering the fray.

Other books by the same author:
The Wolves of Midwinter, 2013
Interview with the Vampire: Claudia's Story, 2012
The Wolf Gift, 2012
Of Love and Evil, 2010
Angel Time, 2009

Other books you might like:
Christopher Buehlman, *The Lesser Dead*, 2014
Lee Carroll, *The Shape Stealer*, 2013
Justin Cronin, *The Twelve*, 2012
Peter David, *Artful*, 2014
Tananarive Due, *My Soul to Take*, 2011
Barbara Hambly, *Kindred of Darkness*, 2014

Charlaine Harris, *Dead Ever After*, 2012
Julie Kagawa, *The Eternity Cure*, 2013
Jeanne Kalogridis, *Covenant with the Vampire: The Diaries of the Family Dracul*, 1994
Nikki Kelly, *Lailah*, 2014
Ira Levin, *Son of Rosemary*, 1997
Rebecca Maizel, *Infinite Days: A Vampire Queen Novel*, 2010
Kim Newman, *Johnny Alucard: Anno Dracula 1976-1991*, 2013
Lauren Owen, *The Quick*, 2014
Josh Reynolds, *Master of Death: The Blood of Nagash*, 2014
Erica Stevens, *Redemption*, 2014
Chelsea Quinn Yarbro, *Hotel Transylvania*, 1978

846

ROSS RITCHELL

The Knife

(New York: Blue Rider Press, 2015)

Story type: Military
Subject(s): Military life; Afghanistan Conflict, 2001- ; Middle East
Major character(s): Dutch Shaw, Military Personnel
Time period(s): 21st century; 2000s

Summary: In his debut novel, Ross Ritchell tells the story of a US Special Forces unit and its commander, and the tough choices he must make to fulfill his call of duty. As the team leader for his unit, Dutch Shaw doesn't think much about killing his enemies. He understands that the cutthroat world he lives in means that he either must kill, or be killed. When he learns about his grandmother's death, he realizes he has lost the last person who connected him to the outside world. Still, he must put his grief aside when his squad is redeployed deep into the enemy's terrain. Their target is a new group called Al Ayeela, which has already claimed its share of US soldiers' lives. As Dutch leads his unit toward their destination, he meets very little opposition. Soon he understands that the ease of their journey is intentional, and that the enemy is luring him closer on purpose. First novel.

Other books you might like:
Ben Coes, *Independence Day*, 2015
Paolo Giordano, *The Human Body*, 2014
Aaron Gwyn, *Wynne's War*, 2014
James Hannibal, *Shadow Catcher*, 2013
Ron Lealos, *Pashtun*, 2014
Scott McEwan, *The Sniper and the Wolf*, 2014
Michael Pitre, *Fives and Twenty-Fives*, 2014
Kevin Powers, *The Yellow Birds*, 2012
David Poyer, *The Cruiser*, 2014
Brad Taylor, *The Insider Threat*, 2015

847

J.D. ROBB (Pseudonym of Nora Roberts)

Obsession in Death
(New York: Putnam Adult, 2015)

Series: In Death Series. Book 40
Story type: Mystery
Subject(s): Mystery; Murder; Crime
Major character(s): Eve Dallas, Detective—Police (NYPSD), Spouse (of Roarke); Roarke, Wealthy, Spouse (of Eve)
Time period(s): 21st century; 2060s
Locale(s): New York, New York

Summary: In the second half of the twenty-first century, crime still runs rampant in New York City. This time, the case hits too close to home for Eve Dallas, a detective with the New York City Police and Security Department. Eve's success on previous cases has made her a bit of a celebrity, but that fame has put lives in danger. A stalker has become obsessed with Eve; he has created a fantasy world in which he shares a special bond with the detective. To prove his devotion, the deranged fan goes on a murder spree and delivers each victim to Eve as a present. To stop the killing, Eve must play along with her stalker's game of obsession and retain his trust until she gets the opportunity to make her move. This novel is the 40th in the In Death series by J.D. Robb.

Other books by the same author:
Festive in Death, 2014
Thankless in Death, 2013
Delusion in Death, 2012
Fantasy in Death, 2010
Creation in Death, 2007

Other books you might like:
David Baldacci, *Memory Man,* 2015
K.A. Bedford, *Orbital Burn,* 2003
Richard Bowker, *Dover Beach,* 1987
Eric Brown, *New York Dreams,* 2004
Lee Child, *Make Me,* 2015
Emma Cole, *Every Secret Thing,* 2006
Christine Feehan, *Predatory Game,* 2008
Tess Gerritsen, *The Keepsake,* 2008
Merry Jones, *The River Killings,* 2006
Jonathan Kellerman, *Motive,* 2015
Caroline Kepnes, *You,* 2014
Jayne Ann Krentz, *Trust No One,* 2015
Tim Lebbon, *London Eye,* 2012
Donna Leon, *Falling in Love,* 2015
Paul Levinson, *The Pixel Eye,* 2003
Kat Martin, *Against the Storm,* 2011
James Patterson, *Private Vegas,* 2015
Karen Rose, *Scream for Me,* 2008
Karen Rose, *Silent Scream,* 2010
Alan Russell, *Guardians of the Night,* 2015
John Sandford, *Gathering Prey,* 2015
Patrick Swenson, *The Ultra Thin Man,* 2014
Debra Webb, *Revenge,* 2013
Tina Whittle, *The Dangerous Edge of Things,* 2011

848

ANN B. ROSS

Etta Mae's Worst Bad-Luck Day
(New York: Viking, 2014)

Series: Miss Julia Series. Book 16
Story type: Contemporary; Series
Subject(s): Southern United States; Rural life; Interpersonal relations
Major character(s): Etta Mae Wiggins, Young Woman (30 years old), Divorced Person (twice), Nurse (home care), Spouse (former, of Skip), Girlfriend (former, of Bobby Lee), Friend (of Miss Julia), Fiance(e) (of Howard Sr.); Howard Connard Sr., Fiance(e) (of Etta Mae), Patient (of Etta Mae), Wealthy, Father (of Howard Connard Jr.); Howard Connard Jr., Son (of Howard Connard Sr.); Skip, Spouse (former, of Etta Mae); Bobby Lee, Police Officer, Boyfriend (former, of Etta Mae); Miss Julia Springer, Widow(er), Friend (of Etta Mae), Detective—Amateur
Time period(s): 21st century; 2010s
Locale(s): Abbotsville, North Carolina

Summary: The sixteenth novel in the Miss Julia series focuses on the romantic adventures of Julia's unlucky-in-love friend, Etta Mae Wiggins. With two failed marriages in her past, 30-year-old Etta Mae is looking for a good husband and a better life. When she becomes a home health nurse to Howard Connard Sr., who's recovering from a stroke, Etta turns on her considerable female charms. Howard is rich, and he could be Etta Mae's ticket out of the trailer park. When Howard proposes, Etta Mae accepts eagerly, but obstacles soon arise on her path to happiness. Howard Sr.'s son, Howard Jr., wants to keep his inheritance out of Etta Mae's hands. Etta Mae's first husband, Skip, has just won the lottery, but he must hide the lucky ticket from the crooks who are chasing him. Police officer Bobby Lee, another former love interest, also distracts Etta Mae from her mission of marrying her patient.

Other books by the same author:
Miss Julia's Marvelous Makeover, 2014
Miss Julia Stirs Up Trouble, 2013
Miss Julia to the Rescue, 2012
Miss Julia Rocks the Cradle, 2011
Miss Julia Renews Her Vows, 2010

Other books you might like:
Susan Wittig Albert, *Thyme of Death,* 1992
Mignon F. Ballard, *Miss Dimple Picks a Peck of Trouble,* 2014
Elizabeth Lynn Casey, *Taken In,* 2014
Monica Ferris, *The Drowning Spool,* 2014
B.B. Haywood, *Town in a Sweet Pickle,* 2015
Margaret Maron, *Bootlegger's Daughter,* 1992
Maggie Sefton, *Yarn over Murder,* 2014
Deborah Smith, *Mossy Creek,* 2001
Patricia Sprinkle, *When Did We Lose Harriet?,* 1997
Rebecca Wells, *Little Altars Everywhere,* 1992

Popular Fiction

849

SEBASTIAN ROTELLA

The Convert's Song

(New York: Little, Brown and Company, 2014)

Story type: Mystery

Subject(s): Terrorism; Law enforcement; Friendship

Major character(s): Valentine Pescatore, Detective—Private, Agent (former, US Border Patrol), Friend (of Raymond), Colleague (of Fatima); Raymond Mercer, Friend (of Valentine), Crime Suspect; Fatima Belhaj, Colleague (of Valentine), Agent (French)

Time period(s): 21st century; 2010s

Locale(s): Buenos Aires, Argentina; Paris, France; Baghdad, Iraq

Summary: Valentine Pescatore was weary of his life as a US Border Patrol agent, so he left his job and became a private investigator in Buenos Aires, Argentina. There he meets an old friend, Raymond Mercer, a former singer who converted to Islam. As the two catch up, Raymond shifts the conversation away from what he does for a living and why he's in Argentina. When hundreds of people are killed in a terrorist bombing at a crowded shopping mall, Raymond is the immediate suspect. As he is accused of the crime, Valentine is implicated by association. Valentine teams up with a French agent to prove his innocence and discover the truth behind his friend's actions. They pursue Raymond from South America, to Europe, and eventually to Baghdad. Valentine wants answers, but when he finds them, they may not be the ones he expected.

Other books by the same author:

Finding Oscar: Massacre, Memory, and Justice in Guatemala, 2012

Pakistan and the Mumbai Attacks, 2011

Triple Crossing, 2011

Twilight on the Line, 1998

Other books you might like:

David Baldacci, *King and Maxwell*, 2013

Alex Berenson, *The Faithful Spy*, 2006

Alex Carr, *The Prince of Bagram Prison*, 2008

Jack Coughlin, *An Act of Treason*, 2011

Mark Greaney, *Tom Clancy Full Force and Effect*, 2014

Derek Haas, *The Silver Bear*, 2008

Jack Higgins, *Rain on the Dead*, 2014

Stephen Hunter, *Dead Zero*, 2011

Dennis Lehane, *World Gone By*, 2015

Gayle Lynds, *The Assassins*, 2015

Douglas Preston, *Blue Labyrinth*, 2014

S.J. Rozan, *On the Line*, 2010

Olen Steinhauer, *The Tourist*, 2009

Brad Taylor, *The Insider Threat*, 2015

Brad Thor, *Act of War*, 2014

Don Winslow, *The Power of the Dog*, 2005

Tom Young, *The Renegades*, 2012

850

DONAL RYAN

The Thing About December

(Hanover, New Hampshire: Steerforth Press, 2014)

Story type: Contemporary; Family Saga

Subject(s): Ireland; Parent-child relations; Irish (European people)

Major character(s): Johnsey Cunliffe, Friend (of Siobhan and Mumbly Dave), Farmer, Young Man, Son, Mentally Challenged Person; Packie Collins, Co-worker (boss, of Johnsey); Eugene Penrose, Bully; Mumbly Dave, Patient, Friend (of Johnsey); Siobhan, Friend (of Johnsey), Nurse

Time period(s): 21st century; 2010s

Locale(s): Tipperary, Ireland

Summary: Johnsey Cunliffe is a simple man living under the protection of his parents on their farm in rural Ireland. When his father dies of cancer and his devastated mother soon follows, Johnsey is left to fend for himself in a world of bullies and schemers out to gain control of his family land. The introverted Johnsey gets by, relying on the quiet wisdom he learned from his father to make sense of a world that moves at a pace he can't match. However, peace is not his lot in life. After a brutal beating puts him in the hospital, Johnsey is befriended by a fellow patient and a nurse, who continue to visit him after he is released. Their friendship seems true, but do they really want what is best for Johnsey, or are they after just the valuable pieces of his life?

Other books by the same author:

The Spinning Heart, 2013

Other books you might like:

Lindsey Barraclough, *Long Lankin*, 2011

Sebastian Barry, *The Secret Scripture*, 2008

Roddy Doyle, *Wilderness*, 2007

Anne Enright, *The Gathering*, 2007

Kent Haruf, *Benediction*, 2013

Ian McEwan, *Atonement*, 2002

Per Petterson, *I Refuse*, 2014

Marilynne Robinson, *Lila*, 2014

Elizabeth Strout, *The Burgess Boys*, 2013

Colm Toibin, *Nora Webster*, 2014

851

HANK PHILLIPPI RYAN

Truth Be Told

(New York: Forge Books, 2014)

Series: Jane Ryland Series. Book 3

Story type: Contemporary; Police Procedural

Subject(s): Detective fiction; Journalism; Housing

Major character(s): Jane Ryland, Journalist, Lover (of Jake Brogan); Jake Brogan, Detective—Police, Lover (of Jane Ryland)

Time period(s): 21st century; 2010s

Locale(s): Boston, Massachusetts

Summary: In the third Jane Ryland mystery novel, the journalist and detective duo is working on two cases: a foreclosure scheme and a possible false confession. Jane is investigating a rash of foreclosures and evictions in the Boston area, sniffing out the story after several murders are committed inside recently foreclosed homes. As she moves deeper into her investigation, those responsible lash out, determined to keep their crimes a secret from the dogged reporter and from law enforcement. While Jane searches for the truth, her friend and lover, Detective Jake Brogan, is wrapped up in a cold case known as the Lilac Sunday killing. The crime occurred 20 years ago while Jake's grandfather was working as the police commissioner, and Jake is grateful for the original crime notes when an individual confesses. Jake isn't sure whether the man could actually be the killer, however. When Jane and Jake realize that their cases are on a collision course, they must race to find a killer before time runs out.

Other books by the same author:
The Wrong Girl, 2013
The Other Woman, 2012
Drive Time, 2010
Air Time, 2009
Face Time, 2007

Awards the book has won:
Agatha Award: Best Novel, 2014

Other books you might like:
C.J. Box, *The Highway*, 2013
Sandra Brown, *Mean Streak*, 2014
Harlan Coben, *The Stranger*, 2015
Michael Connelly, *The Burning Room*, 2014
Tami Hoag, *Cold Cold Heart*, 2014
Iris Johansen, *Silencing Eve*, 2013
James Patterson, *Invisible*, 2014
Douglas Preston, *Blue Labyrinth*, 2014
Lisa Scottoline, *Accused*, 2013
Daniel Silva, *The Heist*, 2014

852

JOHN SANDFORD

Deadline

(New York: Putnam, 2014)

Series: Virgil Flowers Series. Book 8
Subject(s): Crime; Murder; Mystery
Major character(s): Virgil Flowers, Agent (Minnesota Bureau of Criminal Apprehension), Friend (of Johnson Johnson); Johnson Johnson, Friend (of Virgil); Lucas Davenport, Employer (of Virgil); Clancy Conley, Journalist, Crime Victim; Jeff Purdy, Lawman (sheriff); McKinley Ruff, 12-Year-Old
Time period(s): 21st century; 2010s
Locale(s): Trippton, Minnesota

Summary: In the eighth novel in the Virgil Flowers series, the Minnesota Bureau of Criminal Apprehension agent investigates a series of dog thefts in the small town of Trippton. Virgil's friend Johnson Johnson has information about the dognappings, which are apparently being carried out by local men. The case is more complicated that Virgil first suspects, but he must turn his attention to another matter when his supervisor, Lucas Davenport, assigns him to a murder investigation. The victim is Clancy Conley, a reporter who was planning to expose the questionable financial activities of the Buchanan County Consolidated School Board. Virgil eventually discovers that the board members took an official vote to decide if Conley should be eliminated. The vote was not in Conley's favor, and the board members are willing to kill again if necessary. Meanwhile, the dog theft case escalates, and Virgil uncovers a meth operation.

Other books by the same author:
Gathering Prey, 2015
Field of Prey, 2014
Uncaged, 2014
Silken Prey, 2013
Storm Front, 2013

Other books you might like:
Ursula Archer, *Five*, 2014
Ace Atkins, *The Forsaken*, 2014
David Baldacci, *The Escape*, 2014
Josh Bazell, *Wild Thing*, 2012
R.G. Belsky, *The Kennedy Connection*, 2014
James Lee Burke, *Wayfaring Stranger*, 2014
Harlan Coben, *The Stranger*, 2015
Michael Connelly, *The Burning Room*, 2014
Robert Crais, *The Promise*, 2014
Linda Davies, *Ark Storm*, 2014
Jeffrey Deaver, *Solitude Creek*, 2015
Janet Evanovich, *The Job*, 2014
Joanne Fluke, *Red Velvet Cupcake Murder*, 2013
Brian Freeman, *The Cold Nowhere*, 2014
John Katzenbach, *Red 1-2-3*, 2014
Faye Kellerman, *Murder 101*, 2014
Annie Knox, *Paws for Murder*, 2014
Julie Kramer, *Delivering Death*, 2014
Owen Laukkanen, *Kill Fee*, 2014
Owen Laukkanen, *The Stolen Ones*, 2015
Dennis Lehane, *The Drop*, 2014
Thomas Maltman, *Little Wolves*, 2013
Shawn Lawrence Otto, *Sins of Our Fathers*, 2014
Douglas Preston, *White Fire*, 2013
Kathy Reichs, *Bones Never Lie*, 2014
Karin Slaughter, *Unseen*, 2013
Wendy Webb, *The Vanishing*, 2014

853

COURTNEY MILLER SANTO

Three Story House

(New York: William Morrow, 2014)

Story type: Literary
Subject(s): Family; Cousins; Friendship
Major character(s): Lizzie, Soccer Player (former), Cousin (of Elyse and Isobel); Elyse, Cousin (of Lizzie and Isobel); Isobel, Actress (former child star), Cousin (of Lizzie and Elyse)
Time period(s): 21st century; 2010s
Locale(s): Memphis, Tennessee

Summary: When cousins Lizzie, Elyse, and Isobel were girls, they shared such a close bond that their family referred to them as the "triplins." Each of the girls had her own dreams, and now that they are adults, they are forced to face their missteps and failings. Lizzie was a promising soccer player until she was sidelined by an injury. Elyse is in love with the man her sister is going to marry, and Isobel hasn't been able to resurrect an acting career that peaked when she was a child. The three cousins and best friends are reunited when they take on the project of restoring their grandmother's run-down Memphis home. The ancient house, which overlooks the Mississippi River, is in need of some TLC. The women are also in need of support, and as they share their stories, they revisit memories and reveal long-held secrets.

Other books by the same author:
The Roots of the Olive Tree, 2012

Other books you might like:
Donna Alward, *The House on Blackberry Hill*, 2014
Heather Burch, *One Lavender Ribbon*, 2014
Beth Harbison, *Driving with the Top Down*, 2014
Elin Hilderbrand, *Winter Street*, 2014
Joshilyn Jackson, *A Grown-Up Kind of Pretty*, 2012
Shelley Noble, *Breakwater Bay*, 2014
Ann Packer, *The Children's Crusade*, 2015
Danielle Steel, *44 Charles Street*, 2011
J. Courtney Sullivan, *Maine*, 2011
Wendy Wax, *Ocean Beach*, 2012
Lauren Willig, *That Summer*, 2014

854

JOSE SARAMAGO
MARGARET JULL COSTA, Translator

Skylight

(Boston: Houghton Mifflin Harcourt, 2014)

Story type: Literary
Subject(s): Marriage; Apartments; Family relations
Major character(s): Silvestre, Spouse (of Mariana), Landlord; Mariana, Spouse (of Silvestre); Abel, Young Man; Caetano, Spouse (of Justina); Justina, Spouse (of Caetano); Emilio, Spouse (of Carmen); Carmen, Spouse (of Emilio); Isaura, Young Woman, Sister (of Adriana); Adriana, Sister (of Isaura), Young Woman; Lidia, Woman (mistress)
Time period(s): 20th century; 1950s
Locale(s): Lisbon, Portugal

Summary: Lives and stories intersect and weave together in a Lisbon, Portugal, apartment complex in the 1950s. Elderly couple Silvestre and Mariana take in a young boarder, Abel, and delve into the philosophical divide between generations. In another corner of the building, two couples—Caetano and Justina, and Emilio and Carmen—watch as their marriages crumble under a landslide of conflict. Young sisters Isaura and Adriana are on the threshold of womanhood and experiencing a sexual awakening. They soon wake up to the complications their indiscretions can bring. Another woman, Lidia, begins to doubt her married lover's intentions. This is the English translation of author Jose Saramago's novel, written in 1953 and first published in his native Portuguese in 2011.

Other books by the same author:
The Lives of Things: Short Stories, 2012
The Manual of Painting and Calligraphy, 2012
Raised from the Ground, 2012
Cain, 2011
The Elephant's Journey, 2010

Other books you might like:
Muriel Barbery, *The Elegance of the Hedgehog*, 2008
Greg Baxter, *The Apartment*, 2013
Rachel Cusk, *Outline*, 2015
Jonathan Franzen, *Freedom*, 2011
Kent Haruf, *Our Souls at Night*, 2015
Jessica Francis Kane, *This Close: Stories*, 2013
John Lanchester, *Capital*, 2012
Tova Mirvis, *Visible City*, 2014
Irene Nemirovsky, *Suite Francaise*, 2006
Donal Ryan, *The Spinning Heart*, 2013
Sarah Waters, *The Paying Guests*, 2014

855

REBECCA SCHERM

Unbecoming

(New York: Viking, 2015)

Story type: Contemporary; Femme Fatale
Subject(s): Betrayal; Deception; Theft
Major character(s): Grace Graham, Expatriate, Woman (aka Julie), Friend (of Alls), Spouse (of Riley), Artist, Lover (of Alls); Riley Graham, Spouse (of Grace), Friend (of Alls), Wealthy, Convict (on parole); Alls, Friend (of Riley and Grace), Convict (on parole), Lover (of Grace)
Time period(s): 21st century; 2010s
Locale(s): Paris, France; Garland, Tennessee

Summary: Grace has been living in Paris for three years under an assumed name and history. She tells everyone that her name is Julie and that she is from California, not the small town of Garland, Tennessee. She is working above a small shop repairing and restoring antiques, most of which she suspects are stolen. That doesn't bother her because she keeps to herself, hoping that the men she betrayed never find her. Growing up in Garland, Grace's family was not close. In the fourth grade, she met wealthy Riley Graham and his best friend, Alls. Eventually Riley and Grace got married and she went to university to study art history. At her suggestion and following her plan, Alls and Riley rob a local heritage home. Grace manages to escape with a valuable canvas, but the men are caught and imprisoned. Three years later, they are both out on parole, and Grace is certain that they will come for her. First novel.

Other books you might like:
Kate Atkinson, *Life After Life*, 2013
Sonya Cobb, *The Objects of Her Affection*, 2015
Tana French, *The Likeness*, 2008

Sara Gran, *Claire DeWitt and the City of the Dead*, 2011
Penny Hancock, *Kept in the Dark*, 2011
Cynthia Harrod-Eagles, *Star Fall*, 2015
Lisa Lutz, *How to Start a Fire*, 2015
David Morrell, *Long Lost*, 2002
Bradford Morrow, *The Forgers*, 2014
Carla Neggers, *Harbor Island*, 2014
Iris Owens, *After Claude*, 1973
Marisha Pessl, *Night Film*, 2012
Sylvain Reynard, *The Raven*, 2015
Daniel Silva, *The Heist*, 2014
Wallace Stroby, *Shoot the Woman First*, 2013
Barbara Vine, *The Child's Child*, 2012
Kevin Wignall, *Who Is Conrad Hirst?*, 2007

Lucy Kellaway, *Who Moved My Blackberry?*, 2006
James Kincaid, *A History of the African-American People [Proposed] by Strom Thurmond: A Novel as Told to Percival Everett and James Kinkaid*, 2004
Sam Lipsyte, *Home Land: A Novel*, 2004
Alexander McCall Smith, *Unusual Uses for Olive Oil: A Professor Dr. von Igelfeld Entertainment Novel*, 2012
John Moe, *Dear Luke, We Need to Talk, Darth: And Other Pop Culture Correspondences*, 2014
Liz Moore, *Heft*, 2012
Francine Prose, *Blue Angel*, 2000
Rainbow Rowell, *Attachments*, 2011
Diane Smith, *Letters from Yellowstone*, 1999
Aaron Thier, *The Ghost Apple*, 2014

856

JULIE SCHUMACHER

Dear Committee Members

(New York: Doubleday, 2014)

Story type: Literary; Satire
Subject(s): Satire; Letters (Correspondence); College environment
Major character(s): Jason Fitger, Professor (creative writing); Darren Browles, Student—College (of Fitger)
Time period(s): 21st century; 2010s
Locale(s): United States

Summary: At Payne University, a fictional college in the American Midwest, the liberal arts curriculum is suffering at the hands of the school's business departments. Jason Fitger, a professor of creative writing, struggles with budget cuts and inadequate facilities while the faculty in the economics department enjoys copious compensation and renovated offices. Fitger feels that his career is circling the drain, but he has high hopes for his sole grad student, Darren Browles, who is working on a novel. Fitger is certain that Browles is a literary genius, and he takes a special interest in the student. This epistolary novel comprises the many letters of recommendation that Fitger writes for Browles and other students and colleagues. Candid to the point of offense, the letters reveal what the disillusioned professor really thinks about other members of the Payne community. Fitger also discloses the details of his unsettled personal life in letters to his former spouse and lover.

Other books by the same author:
The Unbearable Book Club for Unsinkable Girls, 2012
Black Box, 2008
The Book of One Hundred Truths, 2006
The Chain Letter, 2005
Grass Angel, 2004

Other books you might like:
Aravind Adiga, *The White Tiger: A Novel*, 2008
Terry Fallis, *The Best Laid Plans: A Novel*, 2007
Jonathan Safran Foer, *Everything Is Illuminated*, 2002
Alyson Foster, *God Is an Astronaut*, 2014
Lars Iyer, *Dogma*, 2012
Miranda July, *The First Bad Man*, 2015

857

LISA SCOTTOLINE

Betrayed

(New York: St. Martin's Press, 2014)

Series: Rosato & Associates Series. Book 13
Story type: Mystery
Subject(s): Law; Murder; Illegal immigrants
Major character(s): Judy Carrier, Lawyer, Niece (of Vicky); Vicky, Aunt (of Judy), Cancer Patient, Friend (of Emelia); Emelia Juarez, Immigrant, Crime Victim, Friend (of Vicky)
Time period(s): 21st century; 2010s
Locale(s): Philadelphia, Pennsylvania

Summary: In the 13th of Lisa Scottoline's Rosato and Associates novels, Philadelphia attorney Judy Carrier is going through a personal crisis as her closest colleague makes partner. Judy feels left behind in her career, and even worse, she learns that her dear Aunt Vicky has cancer. Soon Judy leaves Philadelphia to help her aunt, and soon learns that one of Vicky's friends, Emelia, has been murdered. Emelia, an immigrant who was in the United States illegally, is shrouded in mystery, and now it's up to Judy to put her personal issues aside and help Vicky out by discovering Emelia's killer. Unfortunately, the more Judy learns about Emelia's secret life, the more she learns about her own family's skeletons, and soon a target is on Judy's back as she delves deeper into the mysterious circumstances surrounding Emelia's death.

Other books by the same author:
Every Fifteen Minutes, 2015
Have a Nice Guilt Trip, 2014
Keep Quiet, 2014
Accused, 2013
Don't Go, 2013

Other books you might like:
Lorie Blundon, *Rattlesnake Fever*, 2012
Sandra Brown, *Smash Cut*, 2009
Michael Connelly, *The Gods of Guilt*, 2013
Catherine Coulter, *Whiplash*, 2010
Janet Evanovich, *To the Nines*, 2003
Linda Fairstein, *Terminal City*, 2014
Nancy Grace, *The Eleventh Victim*, 2009

Popular Fiction

John Grisham, *The Racketeer*, 2012
John Grisham, *The Rainmaker*, 1995
Greg Iles, *The Death Factory*, 2014
John T. Lescroart, *The Ophelia Cut*, 2013
Malcolm MacPherson, *Deadlock*, 1998
Steve Martini, *Trader of Secrets*, 2010
Janet Neel, *Ticket to Ride*, 2005
Colleen Oakley, *Before I Go*, 2015
Karen E. Olson, *Dead of the Day*, 2007
Mary-Ann Tirone Smith, *Dirty Water*, 2008
Julia Spencer-Fleming, *I Shall Not Want*, 2008
Tony Spinosa, *Hose Monkey*, 2006
Kate Wilhelm, *Heaven Is High*, 2011

858

WILL SELF

Shark

(New York: Grove Press, 2014)

Story type: Literary
Subject(s): Vietnam War, 1959-1975; Drugs; Movies
Major character(s): Dr. Zack Busner, Psychologist (psychiatrist)
Time period(s): 20th century; 1970s (1970-1975)
Locale(s): Willisden, England

Summary: In this prequel to his 2013 novel *Umbrella*, author Will Self revisits the life of Dr. Zack Busner, a therapist who dabbles in popular and alternative psychiatry at his clinic, Concept House. When some of his patients embark on an acid trip, they encourage Zack to join them, a request to which he unwillingly obliges. At the same time, across the ocean in the United States, students at Kent State University face off against the Ohio National Guard to protest President Richard Nixon's Cambodian Campaign. It isn't until five years later, while watching the movie *Jaws*, that Zack realizes exactly what happened the day he decided to drop acid with his patients. Self mixes prose with post-modernist writing to tell the story of how Zack is affected by historical and psychological events. Self is also the author of *How the Dead Live*, *Great Apes*, *Dorian*, and *The Book of Dave*.

Other books by the same author:
Umbrella, 2012
Walking to Hollywood, 2011
What the Hell Are You Doing?, 2011
The Undivided Self, 2010
The Liver, 2009

Other books you might like:
Andre Aciman, *Harvard Square*, 2013
Sebastian Faulks, *Human Traces*, 2006
Denis Johnson, *Tree of Smoke: A Novel*, 2007
Yannick Murphy, *Here They Come*, 2006
David Rhodes, *Rock Island Line*, 2008
Alyson Richman, *The Rhythm of Memory*, 2012
Will Self, *Umbrella*, 2012
Jeet Thayil, *Narcopolis*, 2012
David Vann, *Goat Mountain*, 2013
Sarah Waters, *The Paying Guests*, 2014

859

TINA SESKIS

One Step Too Far

(New York: William Morrow, 2015)

Story type: Contemporary; Urban
Subject(s): Twins; Family; Runaways
Major character(s): Emily Coleman, Woman (alias Cat Brown), Spouse, Mother, Secretary, Twin (of Caroline), Friend (of Angel), Lawyer; Angel, Friend (of Cat); Caroline Brown, Twin (of Emily)
Time period(s): 21st century; 2010s
Locale(s): London, England

Summary: Emily Coleman, a beautiful and successful lawyer, is happily married with a young son and fabulous house. She was always the good girl growing up, doted upon by her mother but ignored by her womanizing father. Emily's twin sister, Caroline, has not fared so well in life. Surprised by a second infant, their mother rejected Caroline and focused instead on Emily. Caroline's life has been marred by disappointment and trouble. It isn't until Emily experiences something terrible that she begins to move away from her carefully constructed existence. She walks out of her life and forges a new one in the sprawl of London. Emily gets a job as a receptionist in a small marketing company and calls herself Cat. She moves into a shared flat with several odd personalities and begins drinking heavily and using drugs. Her new best friend, Angel, senses that Emily is vulnerable and tries to protect her in the low-rent district. Emily finds that she can't escape her memories no matter how hard she tries. She must decide whether she wants to face her responsibilities or continue burying her feelings. First novel.

Other books by the same author:
A Serpentine Affair, 2013

Other books you might like:
Gillian Flynn, *Gone Girl*, 2012
Lisa Gardner, *Crash and Burn*, 2015
Niven Govinden, *All the Days and Nights*, 2014
Sophie Hannah, *The Carrier*, 2015
Jenny Milchman, *Ruin Falls*, 2014
Joyce Carol Oates, *Jack of Spades*, 2015
Ruth Rendell, *The Girl Next Door*, 2014
Erica Spindler, *The First Wife*, 2015
Lisa Unger, *Crazy Love You*, 2015
Nell Zink, *Mislaid*, 2015

860

DAVID SHAFER

Whiskey Tango Foxtrot

(New York: Mulholland Books, 2014)

Story type: Techno-Thriller
Subject(s): Technology; Interpersonal relations; Suspense
Major character(s): Leo Crane, Friend (of Mark), Writer; Mark Deveraux, Friend (of Leo), Worker (for the Committee); Leila Majnoun, Worker (of a non-profit)

Time period(s): 21st century; 2010s
Locale(s): Myanmar; Oregon, United States

Summary: Leo Crane and Mark Deveraux have been best friends since college. But now that they are in the real world, they find themselves taking different roads. Mark is working for the Committee, a group of international capitalists who are preparing to privatize all online information. The Committee's information takeover does have one obstacle: Dear Diary, which uses technology, espionage, and politics to prevent the Committee's plans. Leo, fed up with Mark's ideals, has begun posting political rants online that criticize the Committee. However, the Committee has been reading what Leo is writing and is making sure to erase it. Meanwhile, nonprofit employee Leila Majnoun stumbles upon the Committee's true plan for the information takeover. If she tells anyone of their plans, then those closest to her could suffer.

Other books you might like:
Wilhelmina Baird, *Crashcourse*, 1993
Stephen Baker, *The Boost*, 2014
Max Barry, *Lexicon*, 2013
Drew Chapman, *The Ascendant*, 2014
Jeffery Deaver, *The Blue Nowhere*, 2001
Cory Doctorow, *Homeland*, 2013
Brian Falkner, *Brain Jack*, 2009
John C. Ford, *The Cipher*, 2015
William Gibson, *Pattern Recognition*, 2003
Lev Grossman, *The Magicians*, 2009
David Mitchell, *Cloud Atlas*, 2004
Chuck Palahniuk, *Choke*, 2001
Thomas Pynchon, *The Crying of Lot 49*, 1966
Mark Russinovich, *Rogue Code*, 2014
Neal Stephenson, *Reamde*, 2011
P.J. Tracy, *Shoot to Thrill*, 2010
Connie Willis, *Doomsday Book*, 1992

861

DAVID SHAPIRO

You're Not Much Use to Anyone

(New York: New Harvest, 2014)

Story type: Literary
Subject(s): Coming of age; Urban life; Internet
Major character(s): David, Clerk, Graduate (college), Writer (blogger)
Time period(s): 21st century; 2000s
Locale(s): New York, New York

Summary: David Shapiro models the protagonist of this coming-of-age novel on himself. Like Shapiro, the David in the novel graduates from college and takes a filing job for which he is overqualified. David knows that his parents expect him to go to law school, but he decides to hold off on that move. He tells his parents he's studying for the LSAT exams, but he instead launches a music review blog—*Pitchfork Reviews Reviews*, which is the name of Shapiro's real-life Tumblr blog. The blog becomes more successful than David ever hoped, and he gets a major mention in the *New York Times*. This unexpected moment of fame does little to improve David's station in life, however. He is still without a girlfriend or high-paying job, and he still isn't sure what he really wants to do with his life. First novel.

Other books you might like:
Courtney Cole, *If You Leave*, 2013
Rebecca Donovan, *What If*, 2015
Laura Hemphill, *Buying In*, 2013
Nick Hornby, *High Fidelity*, 1995
Jill Knapp, *What Happens to Men When They Move to Manhattan?*, 2014
Yvonne Prinz, *The Vinyl Princess*, 2010
Karen Rizzo, *Famous Baby*, 2014
Leigh Stein, *The Fallback Plan*, 2012
S.C. Stephens, *Thoughtful*, 2015
Zoe Sugg, *Girl Online: The First Novel by Zoella*, 2014

862

ALEX SHEARER

This Is the Life

(New York: Washington Square Press, 2015)

Story type: Family Saga; Medical
Subject(s): Brothers; Family; Cancer
Major character(s): Louis, Cancer Patient, Brother (of unnamed character); Unnamed Character, Narrator, Brother (of Louis), Caregiver
Time period(s): 21st century; 2010s
Locale(s): Brisbane, Queensland

Summary: Louis and his younger brother are family, but they have never been friends. The intelligent and restless Louis was never able to stay in one place, which made it difficult for his brother to get close to him. As the years went by, the two drifted further and further apart, until the day Louis is diagnosed with an inoperable brain tumor. To help care for Louis, his brother moves from England to Australia, and begins the task of trying to bridge the great emotional distance between them. As the brothers try to navigate the realities of living in the present with cancer, they revisit a past laced with bitterness and unmet expectations. Still, they are family, and as Louis's condition deteriorates, together they discover the things that really matter in the end.

Other books by the same author:
The Cloud Hunters, 2013
Canned, 2006
Sea Legs, 2005
The Great Blue Yonder, 2002
The Summer Sisters and the Dance Disaster, 1998

Other books you might like:
John Michael Cummings, *Don't Forget Me, Bro*, 2015
Jonathan Evison, *The Revised Fundamentals of Caregiving*, 2012
A.M. Homes, *May We Be Forgiven*, 2012
Stephen King, *Full Dark, No Stars*, 2010
Scott Lasser, *The Year That Follows*, 2009
Peter Mehlman, *It Won't Always Be This Great*, 2014
Heather Newton, *Under the Mercy Trees*, 2011

Popular Fiction

Vivian R. Probst, *Death by Roses*, 2015
Austin Ratner, *In the Land of the Living*, 2013
Jonathan Tropper, *One Last Thing Before I Go*, 2012
Michelle Wildgen, *Bread and Butter*, 2014

863

YRSA SIGURDARDOTTIR
PHILIP ROUGHTON, Translator

Someone to Watch Over Me

(London: Hodder & Stoughton Ltd., 2015)

Series: Thora Gudmundsdottir Legal Series. Book 5
Story type: Psychological Suspense
Subject(s): Law; Down syndrome; Suspense
Major character(s): Jakob, Mentally Challenged Person, Crime Suspect, Friend (of Josteinn); Thora Gudmundsdottir, Lawyer; Josteinn Karlsson, Criminal (pedophile), Convict, Friend (of Jakob), Mentally Ill Person
Time period(s): 21st century; 2000s-2010s (2008-2010)
Locale(s): Iceland

Summary: In the fifth book of the Thora Gudmundsdottir series by author Yrsa Sigurdardottir, Icelandic attorney Thora Gudmundsdottir is called upon to defend an intellectually delayed client accused of arson. Jakob, the only survivor of a devastating fire at his former nursing facility, has Down syndrome. He has been convicted of setting the deadly blaze. Now Jakob resides in a mental hospital, and one of his fellow patients wants Thora to attempt to retry his court case. Jakob continues to claim that he didn't set the fire, but that he witnessed an angel do it. If Thora is going to get Jakob released from psychiatric care, she needs to know exactly what happened the night of the fire. Unfortunately, because all of the other victims are dead, and because Jakob lacks the ability to understand the consequences he faces, Thora isn't sure she will be able to help Jakob win his freedom.

Other books by the same author:
I Remember You, 2014
The Day Is Dark, 2013
Ashes to Dust, 2012
My Soul to Take, 2009
Last Rituals, 2007

Other books you might like:
Quentin Bates, *Chilled to the Bone*, 2013
Mark Billingham, *Sleepyhead*, 2001
Fridrik Erlings, *Boy on the Edge*, 2014
Arnaldur Indridason, *Reykjavik Nights*, 2015
Lars Kepler, *The Fire Witness*, 2013
Jodi Picoult, *House Rules*, 2010
Michael Ridpath, *Sea of Stone*, 2014
Vidar Sundstol, *The Ravens*, 2015
Lisa Unger, *In the Blood*, 2014

864

ALEXANDER MCCALL SMITH

The Handsome Man's De Luxe Cafe

(New York: Knopf Publishing Group, 2014)

Series: No. 1 Ladies' Detective Agency Series. Book 15
Subject(s): Detective fiction; Mystery; Friendship
Major character(s): Precious Ramotswe, Spouse (of J.L.B.), Detective—Private, Co-worker (of Grace); Grace Makutsi, Detective—Private, Restaurateur, Mother, Co-worker (of Precious); J.L.B. Matekoni, Businessman, Spouse (of Precious); Mrs., Amnesiac, Immigrant
Time period(s): 21st century; 2010s
Locale(s): Gaborone, Botswana

Summary: The No. 1 Ladies' Detective Agency is an institution in the town of Gaborone, Botswana. Run by Precious Ramotswe and her new partner, Grace Makutsi, the agency is a place where things are found and problems are solved. Their latest case has them trying to discover the identity of a woman with no memory of who she is or how she ended up in Botswana. Adding to the challenge, Grace has just opened a new restaurant and is dealing with the unique personalities of her new staff. Meanwhile, Precious's husband, J.L.B. Matekoni, has his own staffing decision to make—a decision that will lose him an employee, and give his wife a new investigator. This is the 15th book in Alexander McCall Smith's No. 1 Ladies' Detective Agency series.

Other books by the same author:
Emma, 2014
The Forever Girl, 2014
The Mystery of the Missing Lion, 2014
Bertie Plays the Blues, 2013
The Minor Adjustment Beauty Salon, 2013

Other books you might like:
Colin Cotterill, *The Axe Factor*, 2014
Cleo Coyle, *Once Upon a Grind*, 2014
Elizabeth J. Duncan, *Slated for Death*, 2015
Clyde Edgerton, *The Night Train*, 2011
Christy Fifield, *Murder Ties the Knot*, 2015
Dorothy Gilman, *Mrs. Pollifax and the Lion Killer*, 1996
Jane Haddam, *Fighting Chance*, 2014
Tarquin Hall, *The Case of the Missing Servant*, 2009
John Hassler, *The New Woman*, 2005
Armistead Maupin, *The Days of Anna Madrigal*, 2014

865

TATJANA SOLI

The Last Good Paradise

(New York: St. Martin's Press, 2015)

Story type: Contemporary - Exotic
Subject(s): Islands; Pacific Islanders; Vacations
Major character(s): Ann, Spouse (of Richard), Wealthy,

Vacationer (at the resort); Richard, Vacationer (at the resort), Spouse (of Ann), Wealthy; Dex Cooper, Musician, Lover (of Wende), Vacationer (at the resort); Wende, Vacationer (at the resort), Lover (of Dex Cooper); Loren, Businessman (owner of the resort); Titi, Heiress—Dispossessed (Tahitian royalty), Worker (at the resort), Spouse (of Cooked); Cooked, Worker (at the resort), Spouse (of Titi)
Time period(s): 21st century; 2010s

Summary: A remote island paradise in the South Pacific seems like the perfect place to escape the realities of life. This novel follows the experiences of several visitors and residents of the atoll's resort and how they have come to be there, the problems they face, and the relationships they maintain. Dex Cooper, a famous musician, is hiding out on the island with his latest muse, a girl named Wende, while he explores the future of his career. Richard and Ann are married but have recently suffered a fall from societal grace. They fled to the resort in hopes of finding a simpler life. Also weighing in is Loren, the owner of the resort, and two members of his staff, spouses Cooked and Titi. Titi is a descendant of Tahitian royalty and expects to one day inherit the resort from Loren.

Other books by the same author:
The Forgetting Tree, 2012
The Lotus Eaters, 2010

Other books you might like:
David Baldacci, *One Summer*, 2011
Chris Bohjalian, *Before You Know Kindness*, 2004
Jude Deveraux, *First Impressions*, 2005
Eric Jerome Dickey, *The Other Woman*, 2003
Kristin Hannah, *Comfort and Joy*, 2005
Jim Harrison, *The English Major*, 2008
Benilde Little, *Acting Out*, 2003
Fern Michaels, *The Blossom Sisters*, 2013
Anita Shreve, *Rescue*, 2010
Maureen Millea Smith, *When Charlotte Comes Home: A Novel*, 2006

866

NINA SOLOMON

The Love Book

(New York: Akashic Books, 2015)

Story type: Romance
Subject(s): Love; Magic; Friendship
Major character(s): Emily, Writer, Mother, Divorced Person; Max, Woman, Trainer (personal); Cathy, Teacher, Woman; Beatrice, Aged Person, Woman
Time period(s): 21st century; 2010s
Locale(s): France; New York, New York

Summary: When four women meet up on a singles' bicycle trip through France, they have no idea what fate has set in motion for them. In a bookshelf on a stop along their route, they discover *The Love Book*, a mysterious work of magical spells and incantations designed to help the reader find his or her soul mate. Or perhaps the book has found them. In any case, most of the women are skeptical of the book's magic, but superstitious Cathy believes and takes the book with her when the women return to New York. Back home in the United States, *The Love Book* begins to weave its spell. Circumstances and coincidences align to propel Cathy, Emily, Max, and Beatrice into romantic situations. The book is seemingly guiding each of them on a journey to find her soul mate, even if the women's destinations are not the ones they expected.

Other books by the same author:
Single Wife, 2003

Other books you might like:
Ann Brashares, *Sisterhood Everlasting*, 2011
Erin Duffy, *On the Rocks*, 2014
Emily Giffen, *The One and Only*, 2014
Jane Green, *Swapping Lives*, 2006
Beth Harbison, *Chose the Wrong Guy, Gave Him the Wrong Finger*, 2013
Eliza Kennedy, *I Take You*, 2015
Marian Keyes, *Last Chance Saloon*, 2002
Sophie Kinsella, *Wedding Night*, 2013
Liz Tuccillo, *How to Be Single*, 2008
Lauren Weisberger, *Chasing Harry Winston*, 2008

867

EDWARD ST. AUBYN

On the Edge

(New York: Picador, 2014)

Story type: Contemporary; Modern
Subject(s): Spiritualism; Interpersonal relations; Marriage
Major character(s): Adam, Man (guru), Teacher (of Brooke, Kenneth, Peter, Sabine, and Crystal); Brooke, Student (of Adam), Wealthy; Kenneth, Student (of Adam); Peter, Banker, Spouse, Lover (of Sabine and Crystal), Student (of Adam); Sabine, Lover (of Peter), Student (of Adam); Crystal, Lover (of Peter), Student (of Adam)
Time period(s): 21st century; 2010s
Locale(s): Big Sur, California

Summary: A New Age community located in California is full of unique characters. Adam is the guru who runs the place. Brooke, an incredibly wealthy woman who hopes to use her finances to gain spiritual enlightenment, subsidizes him financially. Kenneth, the self-proclaimed shaman of "Streamism," is hoping for a relationship with Brooke. Individuals looking for a new direction in life or some other form of escape end up at their compound. Peter, a banker from England, has thrown aside his ordinary life as a husband and father to chase the illuminating Sabine all the way to California. Sabine is a flamboyant personality with an unorthodox sexuality, but Peter ultimately ends up in a relationship with Crystal, another lonely figure seeking enlightenment from Adam's wisdom. As these individuals come together, their spiritual journeys and education provide them with parallel experiences—if not outcomes—while they question happiness, relationships, the lessons of Eastern religions, and more.

Other books by the same author:
Lost for Words, 2014

At Last, 2012
Mother's Milk, 2005
Some Hope, 2003

Other books you might like:
Isabel Allende, *Maya's Notebook*, 2013
Richard Bausch, *Before, During, After*, 2014
Aimee Bender, *An Invisible Sign of My Own*, 2000
Nina Berkhout, *The Gallery of Lost Species*, 2015
Elizabeth Collison, *Some Other Town*, 2015
Michael Crummey, *Sweetland*, 2015
Junot Diaz, *The Brief Wondrous Life of Oscar Wao*, 2007
Hari Kunzru, *Gods Without Men*, 2011
Norman Mailer, *The Castle in the Forest*, 2007
Rebecca Makkai, *The Hundred-Year House*, 2014
Philip Roth, *Nemesis*, 2010

Laura Benedict, *Bliss House*, 2014
Chris Bohjalian, *The Night Strangers*, 2011
Matt Bondurant, *The Night Swimmer*, 2011
Edgar Cantero, *The Supernatural Enhancements*, 2014
Keith Donohue, *The Boy Who Drew Monsters*, 2014
Patricia Reilly Giff, *Gingersnap*, 2013
Adele Griffin, *Tighter*, 2011
Joe Hill, *Heart-Shaped Box*, 2007
Joe Hill, *Horns: A Novel*, 2010
Rosemary McLoughlin, *Tyringham Park*, 2012
Joyce Carol Oates, *The Sacrifice*, 2015
Madeleine Roux, *Asylum*, 2013
Jane Smiley, *Some Luck*, 2014
Peter Straub, *Mrs. God*, 2012
Christopher Tilghman, *The Right-Hand Shore*, 2012
Wendy Webb, *The Tale of Halcyon Crane*, 2010
Alexi Zentner, *The Lobster Kings*, 2014

868

GARTH STEIN

A Sudden Light

(New York: Simon & Schuster, 2014)

Story type: Coming-of-Age; Family Saga
Subject(s): Family history; Family relations; Identity
Major character(s): Trevor Riddell, 14-Year-Old, Son (of Jones), Grandson (of Samuel), Nephew (of Serena); Jones Riddell, Brother (of Serena), Son (of Samuel), Father (of Trevor); Serena Riddell, Aunt (of Trevor), Sister (of Jones), Daughter (of Samuel); Samuel "Grandpa" Riddell, Father (of Jones and Serena), Grandfather (of Trevor); Unnamed Character, Spirit
Time period(s): 20th century; 1990s (1990)
Locale(s): Seattle, Washington

Summary: This coming-of-age tale from *New York Times* best-selling author Garth Stein introduces Trevor Riddell, who experiences a lot by the age of 14. His parents are bankrupt and have decided to separate after their marriage fails. Trevor's father, Jones, moves Trevor to the family mansion, the Riddell House. The family timber fortune allowed for this mansion in the forest to be built. Jones and his sister, Serena, are determined to put their elderly and sick grandfather, Samuel, in a home. They then intend to sell the Riddell House and property for development and split the profits. However, as Trevor explores the mansion, he comes across a ghost carrying a message from the family patriarch, Elijah. Elijah Riddell wants the property to be returned to natural forest in reparation for the trees felled by the Riddell Timber Company. The ghost is adamant in carrying out Elijah's wish and Trevor may be the only person to settle the family dilemma. The spirit brings more than a message, however; it sends Trevor down a path that brings to light many painful family secrets.

Other books by the same author:
The Art of Racing in the Rain, 2008
How Evan Broke His Head and Other Secrets, 2004
Raven Stole the Moon, 1998

Other books you might like:
Alexandra Adornetto, *Ghost House*, 2014

869

RENE STEINKE

Friendswood

(New York: Penguin Group, 2014)

Story type: Literary
Subject(s): Community relations; Interpersonal relations; Family
Major character(s): Lee, Woman (middle-aged), Mother (of deceased teenage daughter); Willa, Teenager, Crime Victim (gang raped), Classmate (of Dex); Dex, Classmate (of Willa), Trainer (football team); Hal, Real Estate Agent, Religious (born-again Christian)
Time period(s): 20th century; 1990s
Locale(s): Friendswood, Texas

Summary: The community of Friendswood, Texas, situated on the Gulf Coast, is dominated by the residents' devotion to their Christian faith and football. But something sinister lurks beneath the surface of the town. A nearby factory has been dumping toxic waste near Friendswood for years, and although residents have long suspected the company's illegal actions, a hurricane has recently uncovered the evidence. The exposure of the chemical waste prompts some of Friendswood's citizens to take action. Lee, mother of a deceased teenage girl, is especially interested in the incident; she is sure her daughter's death was caused by the toxic waste. Meanwhile, Willa, a girl who attends the local high school, faces a crisis of her own after she is raped by members of the school's beloved football team. Across Friendswood, Lee, Willa, and other residents deal with the personal and communal issues that are part of daily life in their Texas town.

Other books by the same author:
Holy Skirts, 2005
The Fires, 1999

Other books you might like:
Frederick Barthelme, *There Must Be Some Mistake*, 2014
Rick Bass, *All the Land to Hold Us*, 2013

Erin Brockovich, *Rock Bottom*, 2011
James Browning, *The Fracking King*, 2014
Carla Buckley, *Invisible*, 2012
Edwidge Danticat, *Claire of the Sea Light*, 2013
Richard Ford, *Let Me Be Frank with You*, 2014
Peter Heller, *The Dog Stars*, 2012
Barbara Kingsolver, *Flight Behavior*, 2012
Creston Mapes, *Poison Town*, 2014
George Shaffner, *In the Land of Second Chances*, 2004
Tim Winton, *Eyrie*, 2014

870

SUSAN STRECKER

Night Blindness

(New York: Thomas Dunne Books, 2014)

Story type: Contemporary
Subject(s): Interpersonal relations; Parent-child relations; Romances (Fiction)
Major character(s): Jensen Reilly, Girlfriend (former, of Ryder), Sister (of Will), Daughter (of Sterling), Spouse (of Nic); Ryder, Boyfriend (former, of Jensen), Friend (of Will), Doctor; Sterling Reilly, Father (of Jensen and Will), Cancer Patient; Will Reilly, Brother (of Jensen), Son (of Sterling), Friend (of Ryder), Accident Victim (deceased); Nic, Artist, Spouse (of Jensen)
Time period(s): 21st century; 2010s
Locale(s): Connecticut, United States; Santa Fe, New Mexico

Summary: Jensen Reilly is nervous to return to Connecticut after a 13-year absence. Her father, Sterling, has been diagnosed with a brain tumor and Jensen knows that she must go to be with him. Returning to her family home in New England reminds her of her brother, Will, and the tragedy of his death. She has avoided her family for all these years because of her feelings of guilt and grief. She also left her true love, her high school sweetheart Ryder, when she left New England for Santa Fe. Now Jensen is married to Nic, an artist who travels to the Greek isles while she tends to her father. Ryder was Will's best friend and now is a doctor who is helping Sterling seek special care. Jensen is torn between her past and her present. She wonders if it is too late to reconnect with Ryder and her parents, and come to terms with what happened to Will.

Other books you might like:
Elizabeth Berg, *Tapestry of Fortunes*, 2013
Marie Bostwick, *The Second Sister*, 2015
Elin Hilderbrand, *Winter Street*, 2014
Lynne Hugo, *A Matter of Mercy*, 2014
Cassandra King, *Moonrise*, 2013
Emily Liebert, *You Knew Me When*, 2013
Sue Miller, *The Arsonist*, 2014
Katherine Reay, *Lizzy and Jane*, 2014
J. Courtney Sullivan, *Maine*, 2011
Karen White, *A Long Time Gone*, 2014

871

MIRIAM TOEWS

All My Puny Sorrows

(San Francisco: McSweeney's Publishing, 2014)

Story type: Literary
Subject(s): Sisters; Family; Suicide
Major character(s): Elfrieda "Elf" Von Riesen, Woman, Musician (pianist), Wealthy, Sister (of Yoli); Yolandi "Yoli" Von Riesen, Woman, Divorced Person, Mother (of two teenagers), Sister (of Elf)
Time period(s): 21st century; 2010s
Locale(s): Canada

Summary: Two sisters struggle with the issue of suicide in this novel by Miram Toews. Life is not easy for Yolandi, who is known as Yoli. She is raising two teenagers as a single mother with little money, but she has no desire to leave the world any time soon. It is Yoli's sister, Elfrieda—called Elf—who has tried multiple times to kill herself. Although Elf is married, a talented concert pianist, and financially comfortable, she is determined to end her life on her own terms. Despite their obvious differences, Yoli and Elf, who were raised Mennonite, share a close relationship. When Elf makes another suicide attempt, the burden of healing the family falls on Yoli. Canadian author Toews also wrote *The Flying Troutmans* and *Summer of My Amazing Luck*.

Other books by the same author:
Irma Voth, 2011
The Flying Troutmans, 2008
A Complicated Kindness, 2004
A Boy of Good Breeding, 1998
Summer of My Amazing Luck, 1996

Other books you might like:
Carrie Arcos, *There Will Come a Time*, 2014
Tiffany Baker, *The Gilly Salt Sisters*, 2012
Louis Begley, *Memories of a Marriage*, 2013
Anita Brookner, *Strangers*, 2009
Holly Chamberlin, *The Friends We Keep*, 2015
Kathryn Craft, *The Art of Falling*, 2014
Eileen Goudge, *Once in a Blue Moon*, 2009
Rachel Howzell Hall, *A Quiet Storm: A Novel*, 2002
Ursula Hegi, *The Worst Thing I've Done*, 2007
RM Johnson, *The Million Dollar Deception*, 2008
Tim Pears, *Landed: A Novel*, 2010
Per Petterson, *I Refuse*, 2014
Jerry Pinto, *Em and the Big Hoom*, 2012
Luanne Rice, *Dance with Me*, 2004
Michelle Richmond, *Golden State*, 2014
Elisabeth Robinson, *The True and Outstanding Adventures of the Hunt Sisters*, 2004
Alice Sebold, *The Almost Moon*, 2007
Kate Walbert, *Our Kind*, 2004
Jeanette Walls, *The Silver Star*, 2013

872

DAVID TREUER

Prudence

(New York: Riverhead Books, 2015)

Subject(s): World War II, 1939-1945; Native Americans; Interpersonal relations
Major character(s): Frankie Washburn, Friend (of Billy), Young Man, Military Personnel (bomber pilot), Son (of Jonathan and Emma); Billy, Friend (of Frankie), Young Man (Native American); Prudence, Girl (Native American); Felix, Handyman (Native American); Jonathan Washburn, Spouse (of Emma), Father (of Frankie); Emma Washburn, Spouse (of Jonathan), Mother (of Frankie)
Time period(s): 20th century; 1940s
Locale(s): Minnesota, United States

Summary: It is 1942, and Frankie Washburn is visiting his parents at the family's Minnesota retreat before he leaves for bomber pilot training. Emma and Jonathan Washburn are already at the resort, which lies across the river from a recently established POW camp. Emma hates that the camp was built so close to their property, and she is distraught when a German prisoner escapes. Frankie joins the search party and is drawn into a chain of events that will change the course of several lives. He shoots into the brush, thinking he has found the escaped prisoner, but Frankie ends up killing a young Indian girl. Her companion, Prudence, survives and is taken in by Felix, the Washburns' Native American handyman. Frankie goes off to war, but the incident has lasting consequences. The novel follows Prudence and Frankie in the aftermath of the shooting. The story also explores the complex relationship Frankie shares with a young Native American man named Billy.

Other books by the same author:
The Translation of Dr. Appelles, 2006
The Hiawatha, 1999
Little, 1995

Other books you might like:
Elizabeth Berg, *Dream When You're Feeling Blue*, 2007
Geraldine Brooks, *Caleb's Crossing*, 2011
Louise Erdrich, *The Antelope Wife*, 1998
Louise Erdrich, *The Plague of Doves: A Novel*, 2008
Julia Franck, *Blindness of the Heart*, 2010
Gail Godwin, *Flora*, 2013
Sara Gruen, *At the Water's Edge*, 2015
Jason Hewitt, *The Dynamite Room*, 2015
Thomas Keneally, *The Daughters of Mars*, 2013
William Kent Krueger, *Northwest Angle*, 2011
Jan Moran, *Scent of Triumph*, 2015
Yannick Murphy, *Signed, Mata Hari*, 2007
Julie Orringer, *The Invisible Bridge*, 2010
Francine Prose, *Lovers at the Chameleon Club, Paris 1932*, 2014
Danny Scheinmann, *Random Acts of Heroic Love*, 2009
Steve Sem-Sandberg, *The Emperor of Lies*, 2011
Jane Smiley, *Early Warning*, 2015
Alice Walker, *By the Light of My Father's Smile*, 1998

873

SYLVIA TRUE

The Wednesday Group

(New York: St. Martin's Press, 2015)

Story type: Contemporary
Subject(s): Women; Psychology; Infidelity
Major character(s): Gail, Judge, Spouse (of unfaithful man), Woman (in therapy); Lizzy, Spouse (of unfaithful man), Woman (in therapy), Teacher; Kathryn, Counselor, Student—Graduate; Hannah, Housewife, Spouse (of unfaithful man), Woman (in therapy); Bridget, Spouse (of unfaithful man), Woman (in therapy), Nurse; Flavia, Librarian, Spouse (of unfaithful man), Woman (in therapy)
Time period(s): 21st century; 2010s
Locale(s): Boston, Massachusetts

Summary: Five women from different walks of life have one thing in common: their husbands all are sex addicts who, in one way or another, have been unfaithful to their wives. The women meet in a counseling group, and their lives intertwine as they learn how much they have in common, despite coming from different backgrounds: Gail is a judge, Hannah is a housewife, Bridget is a nurse, Lizzy is a teacher, and Flavia is a librarian. Each woman must decide which path she wants to follow toward wellness and forgiveness. Some of them may choose to remain in their marriages, while some may choose to leave. Along the way, they are shepherded by Kathryn, a graduate student in psychology who leads the group. Slowly but surely, Kathryn realizes that she may be in over her head. First novel.

Other books you might like:
Marie Bostwick, *Apart at the Seams*, 2014
Barbara Delinsky, *Sweet Salt Air*, 2013
Liz Fenton, *Your Perfect Life*, 2014
Kristin Hannah, *Fly Away*, 2013
Anita Hughes, *Monarch Beach*, 2012
Susan Mallery, *The Girls of Mischief Bay*, 2015
Karen McQuestion, *The Long Way Home*, 2012
Sue Miller, *The Senator's Wife*, 2008
Liza Palmer, *Girl Before a Mirror*, 2015
Danielle Steel, *A Perfect Life*, 2014

874

JOHN TWELVE HAWKS

Spark

(New York: Penguin Random House, 2014)

Story type: Psychological Suspense
Subject(s): Assassination; Dystopias; Business enterprises
Major character(s): Jacob Underwood, Assassin, Mentally Ill Person; Emily Buchanan, Missing Person, Worker (former, of DBG)
Time period(s): 21st century; 2010s
Locale(s): London, England; Paris, France; New Delhi, India; New York, New York

Summary: Jacob Underwood is on a special assignment for DBG, a global company stationed in New York City. His job is to hunt and kill people who threaten the success of DBG, and his mental disorder makes him the perfect candidate for the position. Jacob has a brain malady caused by a motorcycle crash; because of that, he believes he is dead, and therefore his actions have no meaning or consequences. His syndrome also sorts his life into neat, organized compartments, but soon he will learn that all he thinks he knows is false. When he is charged with the task of locating Emily Buchanan, a former employee of DBG who has taken off—ostensibly with millions of dollars of trade secrets that could destroy DBG—his entire belief system is challenged. Now, Jacob must deal with the truth: The reality that exists within his mind may not be real, and the destruction that he leaves in his wake truly does matter.

Other books by the same author:

The Golden City, 2009

The Dark River, 2007

The Traveler, 2005

Other books you might like:

Margaret Atwood, *The Handmaid's Tale*, 1985

Albert Brooks, *2030: The Real Story of What Happens to America*, 2011

Pierce Brown, *Red Rising*, 2014

Tobias S. Buckell, *Hurricane Fever*, 2014

Melvin Burgess, *The Hit*, 2014

Lee Child, *Personal*, 2014

Linda Fairstein, *Terminal City*, 2014

Edan Lepucki, *California*, 2014

Peyton Marshall, *Goodhouse*, 2014

James Wesley Rawles, *Liberators*, 2014

Jeff Somers, *The Electric Church*, 2007

Tarun J. Tejpal, *The Valley of Masks*, 2014

⬛ 875

ANNE TYLER

A Spool of Blue Thread

(New York: Knopf Publishing, 2015)

Story type: Family Saga

Subject(s): Brothers and sisters; Family history; Family

Major character(s): Abby Whitshank, Spouse (of Red Whitshank), Mother (of Amanda, Douglas, Jeannie and Denny), Retiree, Aged Person; Red Whitshank, Spouse (of Abby Whitshank), Father (of Amanda, Douglas, Jeannie and Denny), Son (of Junior and Linnie Mae Whitshank), Retiree, Aged Person; Junior Whitshank, Spouse (of Linnie Mae Whitshank), Contractor, Father (of Red Whitshank); Linnie Mae Whitshank, Mother (of Red Whitshank), Spouse (of Junior Whitshank); Denny Whitshank, Brother (of Douglas, Amanda and Jeannie), Son (of Red and Abby Whitshank); Douglas "Stem", Son (of Red and Abby Whitshank), Brother (of Amanda, Jeannie and Denny); Amanda, Daughter (of Red and Abby Whitshank), Sister (of Douglas, Jeannie and Denny); Jeannie, Daughter (of Red & Abby Whitshank), Sister (of Amanda, Douglas and Denny)

Time period(s): Multiple Time Periods; 20th century-21st century; 1950-2010 (1950-2015)

Locale(s): Baltimore, Maryland

Summary: Abby and Red Whitshank are growing older. Abby has been experiencing mental confusion and wandering away from her home. Red has recently suffered a mild heart attack. They are adamant that they do not need or want any help, but their children return home to decide how to care for their ailing parents. There is Douglas, the one that always put everyone before himself; Amanda, the take charge one; Jeannie, the one who usually gets lost amongst the family chaos; and Denny, the youngest, selfish, and rebellious one. Once back in Baltimore, the siblings—along with their children—must determine how to care for both their parents and the family home that was built by Red's father, Junior Whitshank. The siblings bring their own problems, adding to the past issues and new issues that arise during the visit. Three generations of stories and secrets are revealed along with the love that ties the family together.

Other books by the same author:

The Beginner's Goodbye, 2012

Noah's Compass, 2009

Digging to America, 2006

The Amateur Marriage, 2004

Back When We Were Grownups, 2001

Other books you might like:

Sarah Addison Allen, *First Frost*, 2015

Elizabeth Berg, *Tapestry of Fortunes*, 2013

Maeve Binchy, *Heart and Soul*, 2009

Meg Waite Clayton, *The Wednesday Sisters*, 2008

Pat Conroy, *South of Broad*, 2009

Paula Treick DeBoard, *The Fragile World*, 2014

Anita Diamant, *The Boston Girl*, 2014

Kim Edwards, *The Lake of Dreams*, 2010

Kristin Hannah, *The Nightingale*, 2015

Kent Haruf, *Eventide*, 2004

Elin Hilderbrand, *Winter Street*, 2014

Sarah Jio, *Good Night June*, 2014

Eddie Joyce, *Small Mercies*, 2015

William Klaber, *The Rebellion of Miss Lucy Ann Lobdell*, 2015

Alice McDermott, *After This*, 2006

Monica McInerney, *Hello from the Gillespies*, 2014

Peter Mehlman, *It Won't Always Be This Great*, 2014

Toni Morrison, *God Help the Child*, 2015

Shelley Noble, *Breakwater Bay*, 2014

Hannah Pittard, *Reunion*, 2014

Henriette Lazaridis Power, *The Clover House*, 2013

Anna Quindlen, *Still Life with Bread Crumbs*, 2014

Marilynne Robinson, *Home*, 2008

Rachel Seiffert, *The Walk Home*, 2014

Jane Smiley, *Early Warning*, 2015

876

JOHN VAILLANT

The Jaguar's Children

(Boston: Houghton Mifflin Harcourt, 2015)

Story type: Ethnic; Psychological Suspense
Subject(s): Voyages and travels; International relations; Mexican Americans
Major character(s): Hector Gonzales, Narrator, Impoverished, Immigrant (undocumented), Traveler (stranded)
Time period(s): 21st century; 2010s
Locale(s): Oaxaca, Mexico; United States

Summary: Seeking freedom from Oaxaca, Mexico, 15 people have paid passage to be smuggled into the United States. Eleven men and four women are hidden in an empty water tanker truck, which has broken down en route. The smugglers left them sealed and hidden in the water tanker and promised to return with someone to fix the truck, but they haven't come back. Trapped within the sealed tank, they are forced to face the fear and reality of the heat, cold, thirst, and possible starvation. Hector, one of the trapped young men, narrates the story. Using his injured friend's cell phone, he desperately sends his story to the only number that works, a US number labeled "annimac." Hector describes his culture and the suffocating politics and policies of Oaxaca. He can only hope that someone is receiving the messages and trying to help them, or the 15 undocumented immigrants will remain trapped and surely will die.

Other books by the same author:
The Panther on the Prowl, 2012
The Tiger: A True Story of Vengeance and Survival, 2012
The Golden Spruce: A True Story of Myth, Madness and Greed, 2006

Other books you might like:
Luis Alberto Urrea, *Into the Beautiful North*, 2009
Jimmy Santiago Baca, *A Glass of Water*, 2009
Rick Bass, *The Diezmo*, 2005
Philip Caputo, *Crossers*, 2009
Ann Jaramillo, *La Linea: A Novel*, 2006
Swifty Lang, *Feeding Ground*, 2011
Norah McClintock, *Nothing to Lose*, 2012
Michel Stone, *The Iguana Tree*, 2012
Amanda Eyre Ward, *The Same Sky*, 2015
Don Waters, *Sunland*, 2013

877

LAURA VAN DEN BERG

Find Me

(New York: Farrar, Straus and Giroux, 2015)

Story type: Literary; Science Fiction
Subject(s): Psychology; Diseases; Social conditions
Major character(s): Joy Jones, Young Woman, Patient (the Hospital), Roommate (of Louis); Louis, Patient (the Hospital), Roommate (of Joy); Sam, Patient (the Hospital), Twin (of Christopher); Christopher, Patient (the Hospital), Twin (of Sam); Dr. Bek, Doctor
Time period(s): 21st century; 2010s
Locale(s): United States

Summary: Joy Jones lives with other survivors of a mysterious disease at a facility in Kansas known as the Hospital. Until the illness—which manifests in silver blisters, memory loss, and death—devastated the country, Joy lived a dull life as a grocery clerk near Boston. Her immunity to the disease earned her a spot at the Hospital, where she is subjected to Dr. Bek's experiments and meets other patients who also display immunity. Pilgrims visit the facility, but they aren't allowed through the doors. Dr. Bek has established a strict structure and routine at the Hospital, which includes designated floor groups and copious staff supervision. But when the Hospital's systems fail, Joy is able to leave the facility and set out on a personal quest. As she makes her way from Kansas to Florida, Joy experiences the realities of her changed world. First novel.

Other books by the same author:
The Isle of Youth: Stories, 2013
What the World Will Look Like When All the Water Leaves Us, 2009

Other books you might like:
Margaret Atwood, *MaddAddam*, 2013
Rachel Cusk, *Outline*, 2015
Jennifer Egan, *A Visit from the Goon Squad*, 2011
Lauren Groff, *Arcadia*, 2012
Kazuo Ishiguro, *Never Let Me Go*, 2005
Emmi Itaranta, *Memory of Water*, 2014
Chang-Rae Lee, *On Such a Full Sea*, 2014
Edan Lepucki, *California*, 2014
Emily St. John Mandel, *Station Eleven*, 2014
Sandra Newman, *The Country of Ice Cream Star*, 2014

878

MENNA VAN PRAAG

The Dress Shop of Dreams

(New York: Random House Publishing Group, 2014)

Story type: Fantasy
Subject(s): Magic; Romances (Fiction); Clothing
Major character(s): Cora Sparks, Scientist, Granddaughter (of Etta), Orphan, Friend (of Walt); Etta Sparks, Businesswoman (dress shop owner), Grandmother (of Cora); Walt, Businessman (book store owner), Friend (of Cora)
Time period(s): 21st century; 2010s
Locale(s): Oxford, England

Summary: Ever since her parents died in a mysterious fire 20 years ago, Cora Sparks has immersed herself in work at her Oxford University science lab, or on visits to her grandmother Etta's dress shop. Etta wants her granddaughter to find happiness, and she thinks she has the answer. Her dress shop is no ordinary boutique, it's infused with magic, and with just a few stitches, Etta has the power to release a person's most passionate desires. So she sets her sights on local bookseller, Walt, who has been in love with Cora for ages. But the secret she sews into Walt's collar doesn't have the effect she intended. Instead, it sets off a romantic chain reaction that will change the lives of everyone involved, and possibly bring answers to the mystery that has shaped Cora's life.

Other books by the same author:
The House at the End of Hope Street, 2013

Other books you might like:
Cecelia Ahern, *PS, I Love You*, 2004
Lisa Van Allen, *The Wishing Thread*, 2013
Sarah Addison Allen, *Garden Spells*, 2007
Hilary Boyd, *Tangled Lives*, 2014
Jenny Colgan, *Sweetshop of Dreams*, 2014
Sarah Creech, *Season of the Dragonflies*, 2014
Laura Esquivel, *The Law of Love*, 1995
Alice Hoffman, *Green Heart*, 2012
Ilie Ruby, *The Salt God's Daughter*, 2012
Adriana Trigiani, *The Shoemaker's Wife*, 2012

879

DEB VANASSE

Cold Spell

(Fairbanks, Alaska: University of Alaska Press, 2014)

Story type: Literary
Subject(s): Family; Mother-daughter relations; Wilderness areas
Major character(s): Ruth Sanders, Mother (of Sylvie and Anna), Lover (of Kenny); Sylvie, 11-Year-Old, Daughter (of Ruth), Sister (of Anna); Anna, 5-Year-Old, Daughter (of Ruth), Sister (of Sylvie); Kenny, Lover (of Ruth)
Time period(s): 21st century; 2010s
Locale(s): Alaska, United States; Minnesota, United States

Summary: Sylvie is just 11 when her mother, Ruth, first becomes obsessed with the glacier. Ruth tears a picture of the glacier out of a magazine in the pediatrician's waiting room, while Sylvie and her younger sister, Anna, see the doctor. Ruth learns all she can about the glacier, which is in Alaska, and her fascination with the icy wilderness in the picture increases as the years past. It seems that Ruth's destiny is sealed when a man named Kenny recognizes the glacier in the photo when he happens to visit Ruth's office. Ruth takes Sylvie and Anna to live near the glacier that has consumed her for so long. But the facts Ruth has accumulated about Alaska and the glacier don't prepare her for the reality of living in the frigid landscape. As the women adjust to their new surroundings, they deal with conflicts in their community and within their family.

Other books by the same author:
Out of the Wilderness, 1999
A Distant Enemy, 1997

Other books you might like:
Wayne Harrison, *The Spark and the Drive*, 2014
Adriana Lisboa, *Crow Blue*, 2013
Benjamin Lytal, *A Map of Tulsa*, 2013
Cyndi Sand-Eveland, *Tinfoil Sky*, 2012

Cathleen Schine, *The Three Weissmanns of Westport*, 2010
Gary D. Schmidt, *Okay for Now*, 2011
Sharon Short, *My One Square Inch of Alaska*, 2013
Rufi Thorpe, *The Girls from Corona del Mar*, 2014

880

JEFF VANDERMEER

Area X

(New York: Farrar, Straus and Giroux, 2014)

Series: Southern Reach Trilogy
Story type: Collection
Subject(s): Monsters; Dystopias; Death
Locale(s): Area X, Fictional Location

Summary: Area X is a deadly mystery. Where mankind once thrived, nature has reclaimed territory, wiping out any trace of civilization. The first team sent to explore Area X discovers a strange world full of creatures and vegetation that defy explanation. Those that follow are not so lucky. Subsequent expeditions end in death, madness, or both. A government agency known as the Southern Reach is charged with monitoring the region, but the secrets it uncovers are answers it may not wish to find. When one more team is dispatched on a rescue mission, they encounter new terrain and new dangers. When the explorers finally uncover the ultimate truth about Area X, it only contains terrifying implications for the outside world. This is a compilation of Jeff Vander-Meer's Southern Reach Trilogy.

Other books by the same author:
Acceptance, 2014
Annihilation, 2014
Authority, 2014
The Third Bear, 2010
Finch, 2009

Other books you might like:
A.J. Colucci, *Seeders*, 2014
Justin Cronin, *The Twelve*, 2012
Nick Cutter, *The Troop*, 2014
Mira Grant, *Symbiont*, 2014
Stephen King, *Revival*, 2014
Dean Koontz, *Saint Odd*, 2015
Angelo Peluso, *Mount Misery*, 2014
F.J.R. Titchenell, *Splinters*, 2014
Joseph Wallace, *Invasive Species*, 2013
Chris Wooding, *Silver*, 2013

881

DONNA VANLIERE

The Christmas Light

(New York: St. Martin's Press, 2014)

Story type: Holiday Themes
Subject(s): Christmas; Christian life; Friendship
Major character(s): Kaylee, Pregnant Teenager; Stephen,

Popular Fiction

Spouse (of Lily); Lily, Spouse (of Stephen); Jennifer, Mother (of six-year-old), Widow(er); Ryan, Father (of daughter), Divorced Person
Time period(s): 21st century; 2010s
Locale(s): United States

Summary: In this novel inspired by the Christmas season, author Donna VanLiere tells the story of a group of unlikely companions who find unexpected love and joy just in time for the holidays. Jennifer is trying hard to raise her young daughter, but the memories of the untimely death of her husband still hurts their little family, particularly at this time of year. Meanwhile, Ryan also grapples with single parenthood after his divorce, and he must find a new place where he and his daughter can live. Newlyweds Steven and Lily seem to have everything, but they want nothing more than to add a baby to their family. Then they meet Kaylee, a teenager who just learned that she is pregnant. Soon, these five strangers discover that they can help one another to make their lives complete. Their chance meetings may be the Christmas miracle they longed for.

Other books by the same author:
The Good Dream, 2012
The Christmas Note, 2011
The Christmas Journey, 2010
The Christmas Secret, 2009
The Christmas Promise, 2007

Other books you might like:
Mary Kay Andrews, *Christmas Bliss*, 2013
Davis Bunn, *Prayers of a Stranger*, 2012
Melody Carlson, *The Christmas Shoppe*, 2011
Vannetta Chapman, *The Christmas Quilt*, 2013
Richard Paul Evans, *The Mistletoe Promise*, 2014
Richard Paul Evans, *A Winter Dream*, 2012
Robin Jones Gunn, *Finding Father Christmas*, 2007
June McCrary Jacobs, *A Holiday Miracle in Apple Blossom*, 2013
Thomas Kincade, *A Season of Angels*, 2012
Katherine Spencer, *Thomas Kinkade's Cape Light: All Is Bright*, 2014
Dan Walsh, *Remembering Christmas*, 2011

882

URBAN WAITE

Sometimes the Wolf

(New York: William Morrow, 2014)

Story type: Psychological Suspense
Subject(s): Father-son relations; Crime; Murder
Major character(s): Patrick Drake, Lawman (former sheriff), Father (of Bobby), Widow(er), Convict; Bobby Drake, Spouse, Lawman (deputy sheriff), Son (of Patrick)
Time period(s): 21st century; 2010s
Locale(s): Silver Lake, Washington

Summary: Twelve years ago, sheriff Patrick Drake hit rock bottom after the death of his wife. He spiraled out of control financially and emotionally, and he went to jail after stealing a large sum of money. Now Patrick finally has been released, and he goes to work and live with his son, Bobby, who is employed by the same sheriff's department that Patrick worked for. Bobby has his own problems: his marriage is on the rocks, and the town of Silver Lake remembers his father not for the good he did as sheriff, but for being a thief and a liar. When a group of outlaws comes to town searching for the cash that Patrick stole more than a decade before, he must fight for his life to keep the past from catching up with him. Yet this time he also has his son to protect, and he isn't willing to let Bobby down again.

Other books by the same author:
The Carrion Birds, 2013
The Terror of Living, 2011

Other books you might like:
Ken Bruen, *Merrick*, 2014
Linda Castillo, *After the Storm*, 2015
Tess Gerritsen, *Die Again*, 2014
Roger Hobbs, *Ghostman*, 2013
Joe R. Lansdale, *Dead Aim*, 2013
Stuart Neville, *The Final Silence*, 2014
David Putnam, *The Disposables*, 2014
John Sandford, *Gathering Prey*, 2015
Michael Sears, *Long Way Down*, 2015
Mickey Spillane, *Kill Me, Darling*, 2015

883

CASEY WALKER

Last Days in Shanghai

(Berkeley, California: Counterpoint Press, 2014)

Story type: Mystery
Subject(s): China; Politics; Money
Major character(s): Luke Slade, Young Man, Assistant (to Leonard); Leonard Fillmore, Political Figure (US Congressman)
Time period(s): 21st century; 2010s
Locale(s): China

Summary: Luke Slade is a young, ambitious aide to congressman Leonard Fillmore—the boorish, verbally abusive statesman who is tagged with the nickname Leo the Lyin. Luke knows the congressman's trip to China will be a real test of patience, but he has no idea how bad things will get. When they arrive in China, Fillmore promptly takes off on a drunken bender, then disappears just as quickly. A frazzled Luke now has the double duty of trying to track down his boss and keeping up the appearance that everything's fine with their Chinese contacts. Luke soon realizes the congressman was involved in some shady dealings, and if he wants to find Fillmore he'll have to wade into a sea of corruption. Now Luke runs the risk of being made a scapegoat for murder.

Other books you might like:
Lisa Brackmann, *Rock Paper Tiger*, 2010
F.J. Chase, *Darkness Under Heaven*, 2009
Lee Child, *Personal*, 2014
Linda Fairstein, *Hell Gate*, 2010
Michael Ledwidge, *Step on a Crack*, 2007
Jo Nesbo, *The Son*, 2014
Ridley Pearson, *The Risk Agent*, 2012

Douglas Preston, *The Kraken Project*, 2014
Cliff Ryder, *Out of Time*, 2008
John Sandford, *Wicked Prey*, 2009

884

M.O. WALSH

My Sunshine Away

(New York: G.P. Putnam's Sons, 2015)

Story type: Mystery
Subject(s): Coming of age; Crime; Rape
Major character(s): Lindy Simpson, 15-Year-Old, Girl, Runner (track star), Crime Victim (raped); Unnamed Character, Narrator, Boy, 14-Year-Old
Time period(s): 20th century; 1980s (1989)
Locale(s): Baton Rouge, Louisiana

Summary: A brutal crime destroys the innocence of a 1989 Baton Rouge neighborhood in this novel by M.O. Walsh. An unknown assailant, who is never apprehended, rapes 15-year-old Lindy Simpson in her home. A 14-year-old boy, the unnamed narrator of this novel, is in love with Lindy, and he is devastated by the attack. The boy's feelings for Lindy are well known, and his preoccupation with her puts him on the suspect list for a time. In his narrative the boy reveals what life is like for the residents of Piney Creek Road during that era. The truth doesn't always agree with the neighborhood's idyllic image, however. When the boy looks back on the events of that terrible summer as an adult, he realizes how memory and perspective change over time. First novel.

Other books you might like:
Isabel Allende, *Maya's Notebook*, 2013
Francesca Lia Block, *The Elementals*, 2012
Holly Brown, *Don't Try to Find Me*, 2014
Louise Erdrich, *The Round House*, 2012
Gillian Flynn, *Dark Places*, 2009
Herman Koch, *Summer House with Swimming Pool*, 2014
Kimberly McCreight, *Reconstructing Amelia*, 2013
Joyce Carol Oates, *We Were the Mulvaneys*, 1996
Jodi Picoult, *Leaving Time*, 2014
Alice Sebold, *The Lovely Bones*, 2002

885

IRVINE WELSH

The Sex Lives of Siamese Twins

(New York: Penguin Random House, 2015)

Story type: Contemporary
Subject(s): Exercise; Psychology; Mental disorders
Major character(s): Lucy Brennan, Trainer; Lena Sorenson, Artist
Time period(s): 21st century; 2010s
Locale(s): Miami Beach, Florida

Summary: In this novel, author Irvine Welsh tells the story of Lucy Brennan, a personal trainer who lives in Miami. Lucy is consumed by her own image, and she spends every waking moment attempting to be beautiful on the outside, yet spends no time worrying about the beauty of her soul. When a rare act of heroism brings her into the public spotlight, she attracts the attention of Lena Sorenson, an obese artist who becomes preoccupied with being just like Lucy. Yet as Lucy harangues Lena about her weight problem, Lena begins to reveal exactly what happened to her in her life that made her pack on the pounds. Unfortunately, Lucy is unyielding in her judgment of Lena, and her cruel and harsh treatment of the obese woman and others like her creates a series of events that spiral both women toward darkness. Welsh is also the author of *Trainspotting*, *Porno*, and *Filth*.

Other books by the same author:
Skagboys, 2012
Because I Am a Girl, 2011
Reheated Cabbage: Tales of Chemical Degeneration, 2009
Crime, 2008
If You Liked School, You'll Love Work, 2007

Other books you might like:
S.G. Browne, *Big Egos*, 2013
Amanda Filipacchi, *The Unfortunate Importance of Beauty*, 2015
Larry Kramer, *Search for My Heart*, 2015
Ian McEwan, *Amsterdam*, 1998
Chuck Palahniuk, *Beautiful You*, 2014
Chuck Palahniuk, *Make Something Up: Stories You Can't Unread*, 2015
Kit Reed, *Thinner than Thou*, 2004
Yazmina Reza, *Happy are the Happy*, 2015
Gary Shteyngart, *Super Sad True Love Story*, 2010
Bradley Somer, *Imperfections*, 2012
T.E. Stazyk, *Identities*, 2012

886

MARCIA WILLETT

The Sea Garden

(New York: Bantam Press, 2012)

Story type: Literary
Subject(s): Family; Family history; Artists
Major character(s): Jess Penhaligon, Young Woman, Artist, Friend (of Kate); Kate Porteous, Widow(er) (of artist), Friend (of Jess)
Time period(s): 21st century; 2010s
Locale(s): England

Summary: Jess Penhaligon lost her father eight years ago when he was killed in Bosnia. Although she finished university and is about to receive a prestigious art award, Jess wonders how things might have been different if both her parents were still alive. Jess, who does botanical paintings, must travel to London for the award presentation. She stays in Devon with Kate Porteous, widow of a famous artist; Jess's mother is not able to make the journey. As Jess gets to know her gracious hostess, who spends most of her time in Cornwall, the women begin to discover connections between them. When Jess gets to know Kate's relatives and friends, she becomes further convinced that her family is somehow

Popular Fiction

tied to this welcoming group of people. The past gradually reveals itself, but its old secrets may have serious repercussions in the present.

Other books by the same author:
Christmas in Cornwall, 2012
The Summer House, 2010
The Prodigal Wife, 2009
The Way We Were, 2009
Memories of the Storm, 2007

Other books you might like:
Elizabeth Adler, *Invitation to Provence*, 2004
Chris Bohjalian, *The Sandcastle Girls*, 2012
Rachel Gibson, *Tangled Up in You*, 2007
Rosie Harris, *Whispers of Love*, 2010
Jayne Ann Krentz, *White Lies*, 2007
Jodi Ellen Malpas, *This Man Confessed*, 2014
Jojo Moyes, *One Plus One*, 2014
Tasmina Perry, *Daddy's Girls*, 2007
Carly Phillips, *Kiss Me If You Can*, 2010
Haley Tanner, *Vaclav and Lena*, 2011
Susan Wiggs, *The Beekeeper's Ball*, 2014

887

LISA WINGATE

The Story Keeper

(Carol Stream, Illinois: Tyndale House Publishers, Inc., 2014)

Story type: Contemporary; Historical - Americana
Subject(s): Family; Appalachian people (Southern States); Appalachian Mountains
Major character(s): Jen Gibbs, Editor (Vida House), Daughter (of a minister), Sister; Sarra, Young Woman (Melungeon)
Time period(s): Multiple Time Periods; 21st century; (2010s); 20th century; 1900s
Locale(s): New York, New York; North Carolina, United States

Summary: Jen Gibbs left her family and her past behind in Appalachia when she headed to New York City. Her father is a strict and intensely conservative preacher, and her sister is married with more children than she can feed. Dutifully sending money home is the extent of Jen's famiy involvement until a partial manuscript crosses her desk. Now an editor at the prestigious Vida Publishing House, Jen isn't supposed to handle items from the slush pile, but this one called out to her. It is about Sarra, a Melungeon girl held captive by hill folk in Appalachia at the turn of the century. Called home by Sarra's story, Jen is determined to discover the origins of the manuscript and find a way to publish the book. She returns home to the Blue Ridge Mountains and explores her own roots as well as the truth behind Sarra and the manuscript.

Other books by the same author:
Wildwood Creek, 2014
Firefly Island, 2013
The Prayer Box, 2013
Blue Moon Bay, 2012
Dandelion Summer, 2011

Other books you might like:
Kate Lord Brown, *The Perfume Garden*, 2015
Davis Bunn, *Book of Dreams*, 2011
Fred Chappell, *Look Back All the Green Valley*, 1999
Jim Fergus, *One Thousand White Women: The Journals of May Dodd*, 1998
Rene Gutteridge, *Ghost Writer*, 2000
Robin Lee Hatcher, *Whispers from Yesterday*, 1999
Rachel Hauck, *The Wedding Dress*, 2012
Angela Elwell Hunt, *The Emerald Isle*, 1999
Annie Jones, *Deep Dixie*, 1999
Rachel Joyce, *Perfect*, 2014
Emily Liebert, *When We Fall*, 2014
Colum McCann, *TransAtlantic*, 2013
Sena Jeter Naslund, *The Fountain of St. James Court; or, Portrait of the Artist as an Old Woman*, 2013
Diane Noble, *The Last Storyteller*, 2004
Marta Perry, *Anna's Return*, 2010
Melissa Pritchard, *Palmerino*, 2014
Francine Rivers, *Leota's Garden*, 1999
Lisa Samson, *A Thing of Beauty*, 2015
Danielle Steel, *Legacy: A Novel*, 2010
Travis Thrasher, *Ghostwriter*, 2009
Nancy E. Turner, *These Is My Words: The Diary of Sarah Agnes Prine, 1881-1901: Arizona Territories: a Novel*, 1998
Lauren Willig, *That Summer*, 2014

888

BETH WISEMAN

The Promise

(Nashville, Tennessee: Thomas Nelson, 2014)

Subject(s): Missing persons; Indians (Asian people); Christian life
Major character(s): Mallory Hammond, Girlfriend (of Tate), Friend (pen pal of Abdul), Religious (Christian), Receptionist (for a doctor); Tate Webber, Musician, Boyfriend (of Mallory); Abdul, Man (Pakistani), Friend (pen pal of Mallory)
Time period(s): 21st century; 2010s
Locale(s): Pakistan; United States

Summary: Mallory lost her best friend and cousin when they were 17. Mallory begged her parents to allow her to donate a kidney to save her life, but they would not agree to it. When her cousin passed away, Mallory promised her that she would save someone in her honor. Mallory is searching for the opportunity to make good on that promise. Now that she is an adult, she will not let her parents, her adoring boyfriend, Tate, or anyone else stand in the way of her good intentions. When her pen pal in Pakistan asks her for help in finding his missing daughter, Mallory takes a leap of faith and flies to the Middle East to join in the search. When she arrives, Mallory learns her mission is clouded by deception and evil intentions. She is held against her will and must put her faith in God even as she descends into despair. This novel, which includes a study guide, is based on the true experience of a friend of author Beth Wiseman.

Other books by the same author:
Daughters of the Promise Series, 2013
The House that Love Built, 2013
Plain Peace, 2013
Land of Canaan Series, 2012
Need You Now, 2012

Other books you might like:
Lynn Austin, *Candle in the Darkness*, 2002
Terri Blackstock, *Word of Honor*, 1999
Davis Bunn, *The Turning*, 2014
Brandilyn Collins, *Deceit*, 2010
Lori Copeland, *Under the Summer Sky*, 2013
Jody Hedlund, *The Doctor's Lady*, 2011
Julie Lessman, *Dare to Love Again*, 2014
Cathy Liggett, *Beaded Hope*, 2010
Elizabeth Ludwig, *No Safe Harbor*, 2012
Tim Owens, *The Search Committee*, 2012
Christine Pountney, *Sweet Jesus*, 2012
Catherine Richmond, *Through Rushing Water*, 2012
Lauraine Snelling, *A Heart for Home*, 2011
Rebecca St. James, *One Last Thing*, 2015
Susan May Warren, *Expect the Sunrise*, 2006

`889`

STUART WOODS

Paris Match

(New York: Putnam, 2014)

Series: Stone Barrington Series. Book 31
Subject(s): Mystery; Detective fiction; Suspense
Major character(s): Stone Barrington, Lawyer, Consultant (CIA), Hotel Owner, Friend (of Katharine Lee), Lover (of Mirabelle Chance); Katharine Lee, Political Figure (presidential candidate), Friend (of Stone); Ann Keaton, Director (Katharine Lee's campaign); Lance Cabot, Director (CIA); Yevgeny Majorov, Enemy (of Stone); Mirabelle Chance, Designer (fashion), Lover (of Stone)
Time period(s): 21st century; 2010s
Locale(s): Paris, France; United States

Summary: The 31st novel in the Stone Barrington series takes the New York attorney and businessman to Paris, where he is opening a new hotel. While in the City of Light, Stone enjoys the company of fashion designer Mirabelle Chance. But Stone's Paris romp is rudely interrupted by a gunman who obviously has a grudge against Stone—or works for someone who does. Although Mirabelle handily disposes of the armed intruder, Stone must still deal with an enemy who is bent on revenge. Meanwhile in the United States, Stone's good friend, presidential candidate Katharine Lee, is facing her own problems. Like Stone, Katharine has enemies who want to do her harm. She is also trying to fend off attacks by members of the press, who are scrutinizing her campaign and her pregnancy.

Other books by the same author:
Hot Pursuit, 2015
Insatiable Appetites, 2015
Carnal Curiosity, 2014

Cut and Thrust, 2014
Standup Guy, 2014

Other books you might like:
Jeffrey Archer, *Only Time Will Tell*, 2011
David Baldacci, *Memory Man*, 2015
Harlan Coben, *Deal Breaker*, 1995
Jeffery Deaver, *The Kill Room*, 2013
Nelson DeMille, *The Quest*, 2013
Vince Flynn, *Kill Shot*, 2011
Marie Force, *Fatal Jeopardy*, 2014
John Gardner, *Day of Absolution*, 2000
James Grippando, *Cane and Abe*, 2015
Michael Ledwidge, *Step on a Crack*, 2007
Steve Martini, *Trader of Secrets*, 2010
Brad Meltzer, *The Inner Circle*, 2010
Lawrence Sanders, *McNally's Secret*, 1992
R. F. Sharp, *No Regrets, No Remorse*, 2012
Tiffany Snow, *Out of Turn*, 2013
Robert K. Tanenbaum, *Corruption of Blood*, 1995
Scott Turow, *Identical*, 2013

`890`

STUART WOODS

Insatiable Appetites

(New York: Penguin Group, 2015)

Series: Stone Barrington Series. Book 32
Story type: Legal; Series
Subject(s): Social class; Money; Inheritance and succession
Major character(s): Stone Barrington, Lawyer
Time period(s): 21st century; 2010s
Locale(s): Washington, District of Columbia; New York, New York

Summary: This novel is the 32nd installment of the Stone Barrington series, which is written by Stuart Woods. In this book, NYPD detective-turned-lawyer Stone Barrington has fallen into a large amount of money after making some shrewd decisions. Of course for a guy with Stone's kind of luck, that means it isn't long before the situation takes a turn for the worse. Now he has someone gunning for his newfound wealth. In the meantime, Stone has been given the role of executor for a friend's estate, but each heir proves to be even shadier than the last one. Stone's quest takes him to some of the toniest neighborhoods on the East Coast, including the suburbs of District Columbia and the elite sections of New York City, where he finds himself entangled in a web of deceit, lies, and even death.

Other books by the same author:
Carnal Curiosity, 2014
Cut and Thrust, 2014
Paris Match, 2014
Standup Guy, 2014
Doing Hard Time, 2013

Other books you might like:
David Baldacci, *King and Maxwell*, 2013
Ted Bell, *Hawke*, 2003
William Bernhardt, *Capitol Offense*, 2009

Henry Chang, *Death Money*, 2014
Reed Farrel Coleman, *Robert B. Parker's Blind Spot*, 2014
Catherine Coulter, *Bombshell*, 2013
Catherine Coulter, *Power Play*, 2014
Clive Cussler, *Spartan Gold: A Fargo Adventure*, 2009
Linda Fairstein, *Hell Gate*, 2010
Rory Flynn, *Third Rail*, 2014
Lisa Gardner, *Crash and Burn*, 2015
Chuck Greaves, *The Last Heir*, 2014
W.E.B. Griffin, *Covert Warriors*, 2011
Jonathan Kellerman, *Motive*, 2015
Adam LeBor, *The Geneva Option*, 2013
Michael Ledwidge, *Step on a Crack*, 2007
John D. MacDonald, *The Deep Blue Good-by*, 1964
Michael Palmer, *Political Suicide*, 2012
Robert B. Parker, *Night Passage*, 1997
James Patterson, *Cross Fire*, 2010
James Patterson, *Private Vegas*, 2015
James Patterson, *Sail*, 2008
John Sandford, *Silken Prey*, 2013
Martin Cruz Smith, *Tatiana*, 2013
Randy Wayne White, *Dead of Night*, 2005

891

ERIKA T. WURTH

Crazy Horse's Girlfriend

(Chicago: Curbside Splendor Publishing, 2014)

Story type: Coming-of-Age; Contemporary Realism
Subject(s): Drug abuse; Native Americans; Poverty
Major character(s): Margaritte, 16-Year-Old, Indian, Drug Dealer, Pregnant Teenager, Daughter (of alcoholic), Girlfriend (of Mike); Mike Walker, Boyfriend (of Marguerite), Addict
Time period(s): 21st century; 2010s
Locale(s): Idaho Springs, Colorado

Summary: Margaritte is a 16-year-old girl hemmed into a hopeless existence by the poverty and dysfunction of her Native American community in Colorado. Angry at the misery around her and the alcoholism rampant in her family, Margaritte has adopted a tough-as-nails attitude and turns to a life of dealing drugs. She sees the distant, bright lights of faraway Denver as a way out of this life, but she doesn't know how to get there. When she falls for a drug-addled, ne'er-do-well named Mike, she sees him as her latest ticket out of her hellish town. Instead, he just adds one more bar to her prison when she discovers she's pregnant. Margaritte must now face her worst fear as she attempts to salvage a life from the wreckage around her. First novel.

Other books you might like:

Sherman Alexie, *The Absolutely True Diary of a Part-Time Indian*, 2007
Judy Chicurel, *If I Knew You Were Going to Be This Beautiful, I Never Would Have Let You Go*, 2014
Louise Erdrich, *The Round House*, 2012
Jim Fergus, *The Wild Girl*, 2005
Tupelo Hassman, *Girlchild*, 2012

Ellen Hopkins, *Crank*, 2004
Kerry Hudson, *Tony Hogan Bought Me an Ice-Cream Float Before He Stole My Ma*, 2014
Kim McCullough, *Clearwater*, 2013
Larry Watson, *American Boy*, 2011
Annie Weatherwax, *All We Had*, 2014

892

DESIREE ZAMORANO

The Amado Women

(El Paso, Texas: Cinco Puntos Press, 2014)

Story type: Literary
Subject(s): Women; Hispanic Americans; Family
Major character(s): Mercedes "Mercy" Amado, Woman (Latina), Divorced Person, Mother (of Celeste, Sylvia, and Nataly); Celeste, Sister (of Sylvia and Nataly), Manager (financial), Daughter (of Mercy); Sylvia, Spouse (of abusive husband), Daughter (of Mercy), Sister (of Celeste and Nataly); Nataly, Daughter (of Mercy), Artist, Sister (of Celeste and Sylvia)
Time period(s): 21st century; 2010s
Locale(s): California, United States

Summary: Mercedes "Mercy" Amado has moved past her marriage to an unfaithful, alcoholic husband and now enjoys a comfortable lifestyle in Southern California. She raised three daughters—Celeste, Sylvia, and Nataly—but Mercy is disappointed that the women are not closer. Each of the sisters has followed her own path in search of her vision of happiness. Celeste, the eldest, has found success in her financial career, but underlying problems prevent her from finding contentment. Sylvia married a wealthy white man and moved to the suburbs, where she raises her two children and endures the consequences of her husband's violent temper. The youngest sister, Nataly, lives the life of an artist and seems reluctant to grow up. The fragile relationships shared by the women are tested when a single event changes their world.

Other books you might like:

Isabel Allende, *Maya's Notebook*, 2013
Julia Alvarez, *How the Garcia Girls Lost Their Accents*, 1991
Brooke Davis, *Lost and Found*, 2015
Louise Erdrich, *The Painted Drum*, 2005
Maya Lang, *The Sixteenth of June*, 2014
Alice McDermott, *After This*, 2006
Joyce Carol Oates, *The Falls*, 2004
Marge Piercy, *Three Women*, 1999
Marilynne Robinson, *Gilead*, 2004
Jane Smiley, *A Thousand Acres*, 1991
Zadie Smith, *On Beauty*, 2005
Therese Walsh, *The Moon Sisters*, 2014

893

JOAKIM ZANDER
ELIZABETH CLARK WESSEL, Translator

The Swimmer

(New York: HarperCollins, 2015)

Story type: Psychological Suspense
Subject(s): Suspense; Espionage; Spies
Major character(s): Klara Walldeen, Government Official (aide), Daughter (of Unnamed character); Unnamed Character, Father (of Klara), Spy
Time period(s): 21st century; (2010s); 20th century; 1980s
Locale(s): Brussels, Belgium

Summary: Klara Walldeen never knew her father. He left her to be raised by relatives more than three decades ago. Klara's father, a spy, believes he did this for her own safety as well as for his, but when his enemies follow Klara to Europe, he realizes that some things cannot be undone. The lack of a father figure in her life didn't stop Klara from becoming successful, however, and she works as an aide for the European Union's Parliament. When Klara inadvertently learns some classified information, she finds herself the target of a ruthless international villain. Now, the only person who can come to her rescue is her father, a retired agent for the CIA who never wanted Klara to know about the world he lives in. As Klara becomes more embroiled in international intrigue, her father must give up his hope for a better life for his daughter so that he can protect and save her.

Other books you might like:
Alex Berenson, *The Night Ranger*, 2012
Andrew Britton, *Threatcon Delta*, 2014
Gerard de Villiers, *Revenge of the Kremlin*, 2015
Brian Freemantle, *Red Star Falling*, 2013
David Hagberg, *Retribution*, 2015
Ha Jin, *A Map of Betrayal*, 2014
Andrew Kaplan, *Scorpion Deception*, 2013
Chris Pavone, *The Expats*, 2012
James Rollins, *The Kill Switch: A Tucker Wayne Novel*, 2014
Daniel Silva, *The Heist*, 2014

894

NELL ZINK

The Wallcreeper

(London: Fourth Estate Ltd., 2014)

Story type: Contemporary; Literary
Subject(s): Marriage; Sexual behavior; Birds
Major character(s): Tiffany, Young Woman, Spouse (of Stephen), Environmentalist; Stephen, Young Man, Spouse (of Tiffany), Researcher (pharmaceutical), Environmentalist
Time period(s): 21st century; 2010s
Locale(s): Albania; Germany; Bern, Swaziland

Summary: Tiffany and Stephen threw their lives together without thinking. Young, shallow, and impulsive, they married after only three weeks and moved to Europe when Stephen got a job at a Swiss medical firm. Out driving one day, the couple hits a small bird called a wallcreeper, causing a crash that results in a pregnant Tiffany miscarrying. The bird-loving Stephen adopts the injured wallcreeper to care for it, seemingly more concerned with its well-being than his wife's. Together they bounce through their nonchalant marriage, openly having affairs, and eventually drift through Europe and away from each other to become environmental activists. Yet through all this, somehow their strange relationship finds a way to endure the trials they inflict on it. As they set out to save the environment, can they muster the effort to save themselves? First novel.

Other books you might like:
Julian Barnes, *Love, Etc.*, 2001
Thomas Christopher Greene, *The Headmaster's Wife*, 2014
Christina Baker Kline, *Bird in Hand*, 2009
Ian McEwan, *On Chesil Beach*, 2007
Tessa McWatt, *Vital Signs*, 2011
David Nicholls, *Us*, 2014
Tom Perotta, *Little Children*, 2004
Sheila Schwartz, *Lies Will Take You Somewhere*, 2009
Lionel Shriver, *The Post-Birthday World: A Novel*, 2007
Sarah Tucker, *The Last Year of Being Married*, 2004

Romance Fiction in Review
by
Kristin Ramsdell

"Romance has been elegantly defined as the offspring of fiction and love." —Benjamin Disraeli

"We were born to unite with our fellow men, and to join in community with the human race." —Cicero

"I think tolerance and acceptance and love is something that feeds every community." —Lady Gaga

Have you noticed? Lately, it's been all about community—at least when it comes to the romance world. Whether it's the super-abundance of charming small-town community series romances lining the shelves, as well as the best-sellers lists; the sudden popularity of writer online communities critiquing and voting on each other's works in progress and in some cases even allying themselves with publishers, as Avon and JukePop (a writers' crowdfunding platform) have done recently; or the surprising ways in which the opinions expressed in online reading communities (e.g. GoodReads) and other more general social media groups are influencing the ways in which books are acquired by libraries and even bookstores, community in its many forms is alive, active, and impacting the genre as never before.

It's logical, of course, because we humans are social creatures, biologically programmed to need each other. While we all need our time alone, we do tend sort ourselves into groups, essentially forming communities, whether it's by geography/location, family/clan/tribe, profession, interest, or merely pure chance—and we've been doing this since time began. So actually this all makes sense. But the difference this time around is that we are connected, both remotely and instantaneously, as never before, and the impact that this is having already is remarkable, and I have a feeling it is just the beginning.

An Industry Overview

Romance, as a whole, continues its bumpy, but successful, path as tech and self-publishing continue to disrupt (current ubiquitous buzzword!) the market.

With the ongoing chaos in the traditional publishing arena as the big name publishers try to plan for the future and catch up, it's no surprise that romance writers continue to explore independent options, in many cases with significant success. A prime example is Barbara Freethy, Rita Award-winning, best-selling author. Although traditionally published, Freethy opted to go the indie route with exceptional success. Recently she inked a deal with Ingram to market her print books through them directly, something that usually is impossible without an arrangement with one of the large New York publishers (http://www.barbarafreethy.com/new-print-venture-with-ingram/). This appears to be an important breakthrough for indie authors (many of whom are romance writers), and it will be interesting to see if others follow suit.

That being said, more and more romance writers are experimenting with the indie route. Technology is providing ways for authors to navigate the complexities of online publishing more easily, and a growing number of independent editors, artists, and web experts, some of whom were originally employed by the major publishing houses, are appearing to meet the need. A growing number of writers also are taking the hybrid path (being both traditionally and indie published), something that seems to be working well for many writers, especially if they have gotten back the rights to their backlists.

Publishers are trying valiantly to deal with the new and ever-changing landscape in a variety of ways. In addition to the classic merger and acquisition business move (the sale of Harlequin Enterprises to HarperCollins, which resulted in a number of top level people losing their jobs in a cost-cutting measure and was discussed in a previous essay, is a prime example), publishers also are ramping up their electronic capabilities. Most now have e-original imprints and typically release print and ebook titles concurrently. Many are exploring more innovative measures and the collaboration between Avon and JukePop (see above) is only one example. Publishers have also realized the benefits of wooing successful indie authors who already have a guaranteed readership, and they have had a good deal of success. Recently, there have been rumblings of rewriting the standard book sale contract, but these are early days, and as of this writing, they are just rumors.

The idea of ebook subscription services, mentioned in an earlier essay, continues to attract interest; and while it's still too early to predict success, the fact that Harlequin recently has decided to make 15,000 of its ebook titles available through Scribd should help. Oyster and Kindle Unlimited are the other major players in this field. How all of this impacts the library world remains to be seen.

Despite the current chaos, the romance industry is alive and well, and given its resiliency and ability to eventually adapt to change, it is likely to remain so.

A Genre Overview

As mentioned above, it's all about community, and nowhere is that more evident than in the contemporary romance market. Community series still reign supreme, and whether the setting is a coastal fishing village, a quaint mountain hamlet, a laid back Southern town, or a small farming community in America's heartland, readers can't seem to get enough and the writers are happy to oblige. Robyn Carr's Thunder Point (*One Wish*), Emily March's Eternity Springs (*Teardrop Lane*), Jill Shalvis's Lucky Harbor (*One in a Million*), Brenda Novak's Whiskey Creek (*The Heart of Christmas*), Christie Ridgway's Cabin Fever (*Make Me Lose Control*), Kimberly Kincaid's Pine Mountain (*Stirring Up Trouble*), LuAnn McLane's Cricket Creek (*Sweet Harmony*), and Maisey Yates's Copper Ridge (*Part Time Cowboy*) are some of the current examples included in this volume. Although the vast majority of community series are set in the present, the historical market claims a few, including Linda Broday's Bachelors of Battle Creek series (*Texas Mail-Order Bride* and *Twice a Texas Bride*) set in the Old West.

Similar in concept to the community series, books linked by character, family, friendship, or theme are more popular than ever. Grace Burrowes's Sweetest Kisses contemporary trilogy (*A Single Kiss*, *The First Kiss*, and *Kiss Me Hello*), Eileen Dreyer's Regency-set Drake's Rakes series (*Twice Tempted*), Regina Scott's inspirational Frontier Bachelors series (*The Bride Ship* and *Would-Be Wilderness Wife*), and Bec McMasters paranormal Steampunk London books (*Of Silk and Steam*) are a few of the many examples. Note: Approximately half of the romance titles included in this volume are parts of series or linked in some way.

Although not represented among the current titles, novellas and short stories of various kinds and lengths continue to attract interest. Until recently, these shorter romances usually were included in print anthologies or collections, but with the ebook making it possible to publish them separately, they've become much more popular, especially when they are linked to existing series.

As usual, romances (except for Inspirationals, which generally remain sweet) continue to run the gamut when it comes to sex. With some so racy or kinky that you expect the pages to go up in smoke, others so chaste that a single kiss seems almost erotic, and the vast majority on the spectrum somewhere in between, there's a sensuality level to please everyone.

Readers (and writers, as well) continue their love affair with military heroes and heroines. Although real battle scenes may be included, sometimes even in flashbacks, more often these stories focus on the difficulties faced by those returning from war and readjusting to non-military life. Not surprisingly, dealing with PTSD is a common theme. Whereas most of these titles are contemporary, there are historical examples as well. One of the best in the current volume is *Only Enchanting*, the fourth in Mary Balogh's exceptional Survivors Series that deals with a group of wounded characters variously affected by the Napoleonic Wars.

Speaking of Napoleon, it's worth noting that June 18, 2015, was the 200th anniversary of his ultimate defeat at Waterloo. (He was permanently exiled to St. Helena after that where he remained until his death.) The Napoleonic Wars and the Battle of Waterloo are traditional background fodder for late Georgian and Regency romances; and while most of them typically limit the war references to characters returning from the battlefield, a few take readers to the front lines. Georgette Heyer's classic *An Infamous Army* and Eileen Dreyer's *Barely a Lady* (2010) have Brussels and Waterloo settings, while Marjorie Farrell's *Red, Red Rose* (1999) and Evelyn Richardson's *Lord Harry's Daughter* (2001) give realistic accounts of the Peninsular conflicts.

And we can't forget the cowboys! These rugged heroes, whether historical or modern day, continue to enthrall readers as *Part Time Cowboy* by Maisey Yates, *Kissed by a Cowboy*, *The Cowboy SEAL* by Laura Marie Altom, and *Texas Mail-Order Bride* nicely demonstrate.

Subgenres in Brief

As expected, contemporaries, those romances set in the present, continue to dominate the market. Though series titles continue to take top honors in numbers, single titles are more than holding their own. As discussed above, many of the current popular titles are part of community series; nevertheless, there are plenty of others to explore. The contemporary subgenre is broad and includes everything from tender, heartwarming charmers such as Grace Burrowes's Sweetest Kisses Trilogy to sexy, fast-paced romps such as Julia Harper's *Once and Always*, and everything in between. Although the focus is always on the primary hero and heroine, many of the longer books have a number of supporting characters and sometimes secondary plots, as well; and humor, secrets, and light mystery or suspense elements may also add to the mix.

Historicals continue to draw fans, treating them to romantic adventures that include everything from ninth-century Sweden (e.g., Michelle Styles's *Taming His Viking Woman*), Renaissance adventures (e.g., Amanda

McCabe's *Betrayed by His Kiss*) and fast-paced early-to-mid eighteenth-century adventures (e.g., Paula Quinn's pirate adventure, *The Wicked Ways of Alexander Kidd* and Elizabeth Hoyt's realistic, sexy, London-set Maiden Lane tales) to witty Regency romps (e.g., Anne Gracie's *The Spring Bride*, Jo Beverley's *Too Dangerous for a Lady*, Sarah MacLean's *Never Judge a Lady by Her Cover*), lively Victorians (e.g., Victoria Alexander's *The Shocking Secret of a Guest at the Wedding*, Lorraine Heath's *The Duke and the Lady in Red*), and gritty tales of the Old West (e.g., Jo Goodman's *This Gun for Hire*, Linda Broday's *Twice a Texas Bride*). In addition, with the changes in the historical time period definitions for the genre, a growing number of romances with early twentieth-century settings are beginning to appear (e.g., Elizabeth Jeffrey's *Meadowlands* and Sharon Page's *An American Duchess*).

Paranormals—edgy, inventive, and diverse—continue to please their fans with stories ranging from humor-dusted vampire tales (e.g., Lynsay Sands' *The Immortal Who Loved Me* [Argeneau series]) and myth-based stories with a good helping of sass (e.g., Gena Showalter's *The Darkest Touch* [Lords of the Underworld series]) to dark, intense stories (e.g., Christine Feehan's *Viper Game* [GhostWalker)]), sexy, engaging shifter tales (e.g., Jennifer Ashley *Mate Bond* [Shifters Unbound]), and a particularly engaging paranormal historical with an unusual Roaring Twenties setting, Jenn Bennett's *Grave Phantoms* (Roaring Twenties).

With its classic combination of danger, suspense, and romance, Romantic Suspense continues to keep readers engaged and asking for more. Although the majority of these are set in the present (e.g., Jayne Ann Krentz's *Trust No One*, Karen Robard's *Hush*, Mary Burton's *Cover Your Eyes*, and Nora Roberts's *The Liar*), Historical Romantic Suspense is becoming a favorite with Regency and Victorian Era gems such asJoanna Bourne's *Rogue Spy* and Amanda Quick's *Garden of Lies*.

Inspirational Romance continues to appeal to its devoted fan base with a variety of sweet, faith-based stories. Settings can be either contemporary or historical, and there can be some mystery and suspense involved, but they generally are grounded in conservative Christian theology, although the intensity and method of presentation will vary widely, depending on the writer and the romance imprint. Regina Scott's engaging Frontier Bachelors Series is a delightful example of gently religious Inspirational Romance that would also appeal to fans of sweet, non-inspirational romances.

New Adult romances, focusing on 18- to 25-year-olds, are attracting fans with lively, often sexy, stories of characters experiencing life on their own for the first time. College settings and first jobs are typical settings, but these stories can take place anywhere post-adolescents are learning to cope with the realities of life without the benefit of parents or home. Jennifer L. Armentrout's *Fall with Me*, Erin McCarthy's *Believe*, and Caisey Quinn's *Leaving Amarillo* and *Loving Dallas* are some current examples.

Romance Statistics Update

RWA's official ROMStat Report for 2013 is finally available, but it has undergone something of a change. Because the data from Simba Information used in making up the report is no longer being sold, RWA now is relying only on information from Bookstats and Nielsen Bookscan. As a result, the report is slightly less informative than before. Nevertheless, we do have some new 2013 figures! According to Bookstats, romance fiction generated $1.079 billion in sales (topped only by Thrillers, which came in at $1.088 billion) and accounts for 21 percent of the adult fiction market. Sales for the other adult fiction categories are as follows: General ($810.8 million), Literary ($548.5 million), Mystery & Detective ($442.1 million), and Fantasy ($377.3 million). Bookscan reported that 9,513 romance ISBNs were published during 2013, but because each version of a title requires a separate ISBN, that probably isn't the actual number of romance titles published. Bookstats also reported that sales for romances were divided evenly by physical and ebooks (49 percent each), with 2 percent assigned to other digital formats, but for the trade market as a whole, physical format accounted for 77 percent of revenues and ebooks for 21 percent, with the remaining 2 percent being picked up by other digital formats. For more information on the romance genre, check out the Industry Statistics webpage at Romance Writers of America (www.rwa.org/p/cm/ld/fid=580). Statistics for the overall publishing industry in 2013 were discussed in the romance essay of the previous issue of *What Do I Read Next?* Finally, a bit of 2014 news: According to Bookscan, sales of print books rose by 2.4 percent over 2013, although of particular interest to romance readers, mass market title sales declined by 10.3 percent for the year. This slight rise in print sales has been seen by some as an indication that print is not as dead as had been predicted (Milliot, Jim. "For Books, Print Is Back," *Publishers Weekly*, January 2, 2015.)

Conferences, Grants, Awards, and other News of Interest

Although romance writers, librarians, fans, and industry professionals attend any number of excellent conventions, workshops, and conferences each year, it is the annual conference of the Romance Writers of America that is the year's most important event. Primarily a working conference (as opposed to a fan/reader conference) for the genre's professionals, this event provides the opportunity for writers, librarians, agents, editors, and booksellers to network with colleagues, improve their craft, learn from their peers, and advance their careers in a fast-paced, intense conference that typically begins with a charity book signing event that is open to the public and ends with the spectacular Rita Awards ceremony. The details of the 2014 conference are included in the previous volume and will not be repeated here. The 2015 RWA conference will be held July 23–26th in San Antonio, Texas, and will feature Barbara Freethy as Keynote Speaker, Julia Quinn and

Nalini Singh as featured speakers, and Lisa Kleypas as the Rita Awards Ceremony Emcee.

As usual, this year's conference will be preceded by Librarians' Day on July 22, 2015, a day-long, intensive event that targets local librarians and booksellers and is jam-packed with lively, wide-ranging presentations by best-selling authors and savvy librarians. An afternoon networking sessions gives attendees a chance to interact with each other as well as meet a number of romance authors. This year's presentations include panels on the appeal of the romantic suspense novel, the particular challenges of writing holiday-themed romances, trends in romance fiction from several editors' points of view, and an interactive session on creating effective partnerships in the new publishing environment. The luncheon speaker will be best-selling author Jude Deveraux. For more information and registration forms, check the link www.rwa.org/p/cm/ld/fid=795.

RWA's Cathie Linz Librarian of the Year Award is presented to a librarian "who demonstrates outstanding support of romance authors and the romance genre." This year's recipient is librarian Lisa Schimmer, a Senior Cataloger at NoveList, who will receive the award at the Awards luncheon during the annual conference. This award was renamed this year in honor of librarian and romance author Cathie Linz, RWA's first Library Liaison.

RWA's Academic Research Grant Committee was especially productive this year, awarding grants for three different research projects. Recipients were Jonathan Andrew Allan, Ph.D. (Brandon University), for "The Optimism of Happily Ever After," an exploration of romance's happy, or satisfactory, ending via Affect Theory; Drs. Beth Driscoll (University of Melbourne), Lisa Fletcher (University of Tasmania), and Kim Wilkins (University of Queensland) for "The Genre World of Romance in 21st Century Australia," a study of the romance genre in Australia through in-depth case studies of three authors in different stages of their careers; and Jessica Taylor, Ph.D. (University of Toronto) for "Professional Business Women: Romance Writers, Feminism and 'Women's Work,'" an examination of the ways in which romance writers choose to define their work and its value and negotiate the relationship between the artistic/creative and professional/commercial aspects.

In addition, RWA's Library $4500 Grant established to "provide a public library the opportunity to build or expand its romance fiction collection and/or host romance fiction programming" has been awarded to the Auburn Public Library (Georgia). The Library plans to use the grant "to develop an outstanding collection of romance fiction, both single-selling titles and series titles."

Finally, the romance community was saddened by the deaths of legendary historical author Bertice Small, and contemporary romance writer and RWA's first Library Liaison, Cathie Linz. Small was one of the original ground-breaking "Avon Ladies" and her *Skye O'Malley* is a classic to this day. Linz, noted for humorous, sexy

contemporaries, was a driving force in fostering effective relationships between the library and romance communities. As mentioned above, the Librarian of the Year Award has been renamed in her honor.

Future Trends

Peering into a crystal ball has never been one of my strengths, as a glance at some of the predictions I've made over time will show. Nevertheless, we have to try; and since the past often contains the seeds of the future—although we may not know just how they will grow up—we do have a shot at getting it right—maybe. With that (and romance) in mind, let's consider the following:

Tech and the Industry

1) Technology will continue to disrupt the publishing industry at large and romance along with it, but romance will survive better than most.

2) More and more writers will continue to go the indie or hybrid route.

3) Traditional publishers will continue to court successful indie authors with varying degrees of success.

4) The relationship between ebooks and print will reach equilibrium, but audio books will claim a larger share of the market as authors discover the benefits of audio. Mass market paperbacks will feel any decline the most because of the way in which romance readers have adopted ebooks.

5) Publishers will continue to try to stay ahead of the tech and social changes (including indie/self-publishing) that are occurring and affecting their sales and ways of operation.

7) Libraries will struggle to deal with issues of format and access, as well as the fledgling subscription lending programs (Scribd, Oyster, Kindle Unlimited, etc.) that could be an issue.

8) Copyright and fair use will continue to be an issue for libraries.

The Romance Genre

1) Romance will adapt to change and continue to thrive.

2) Community series and other kinds of linked books will continue to be strong.

3) Academic interest in popular romance fiction will increase and more institutions will begin to recognize its importance.

4) New Adult romances will continue to be popular for the moment, but, like chick-lit, will fade as its readers grow beyond the genre.

5) Military and all public safety heroes (and occasionally heroines) will remain popular.

6) Western settings, complete with cowboys, will continue to attract fans for the moment.

7) Early twentieth-century settings for romance (Edwardian, WW I, Roaring Twenties, Depression Era,

WW II) will attract more interest.

8) Diversity of all kinds will continue to become an integral, accepted part of romance.

9) Novellas and short stories enable writers to accommodate fans who want shorter forms.

Once again, these are just possibilities, projections based loosely on the past. Some may happen, others will not; but things are changing in the romance world at lightning speed and it's a pretty safe bet that the second half of 2015 will be just as fascinating, if not more so, than the first.

Romance in Review

Romance review coverage remains a vibrant combination of print and online resources. The major mainstream players, *Booklist* (www.ala.org/offices/publishing/productsandpublications/periodicals/periodicals), *Library Journal* (lj.libraryjournal.com), *Publishers Weekly* (www.publishersweekly.com), and *Kirkus Reviews* (www.kirkusreviews.com), continue their coverage of the romance genre, as do several newspapers across the country. *Library Journal* publishes a regular bimonthly romance review column, which includes forthcoming e-original as well as print titles; *Booklist* has a separate romance fiction category in each issue, as do the other genres; and *Publishers Weekly* and *Kirkus Reviews* both have a romance review section as well. In addition to print, all four provide online review coverage that varies in amount and delivery method, including supplemental material such as *Library Journal*'s weekly Xpress reviews, and most are making increased use of Facebook, Twitter, Tumblr, and other social media platforms to connect with selectors, as well as readers. With the explosion of e-original titles from established romance publishers, e-only publishers, and digitally self-published authors, mainstream review publications now are covering digital romances of all varieties at an increasing rate. Many of these reviews are also picked up various indexing services and are available in standard databases, bookseller's websites, vendor websites, and library online catalogs.

The traditional mainstream review sources definitely have stepped up their coverage in recent years; but as improved as they are, it is still the sources that focus on genre fiction, and romance in particular, that provide the most comprehensive coverage. Even though it now reviews all kinds of genre fiction, *RT Book Reviews* (www.rtbookreviews.com), originally named *Romantic Times*, is the most complete. It is published monthly, includes an assortment of reviews and articles, and makes many of its reviews available online.

Affaire de Coeur (www.affairedecoeur.com) is another long-time magazine that features romance-related articles and reviews. Many of its reviews are also available online.

In addition, there are a many exclusively-online review sites. For a variety of reasons libraries often are reluctant to rely on these alone; however, classic sites such as All About Romance (www.likesbooks.com), Romance Reviews Today (www.romrevtoday.com), and Romance in Color (www.romanceincolor.com/) definitely are worth checking out. Online reading communities such as GoodReads (www.goodreads.com) and Library Thing (www.librarything.com) are becoming more important, as are the growing number of romance-related blogs (Smart Bitches Love Trashy Books [smartbitchestrashybooks.com] is one of many). Lists such as RRA-L (Romance Readers Anonymous—groups.yahoo.com/neo/groups/rra-l/info) and the more general Fiction-L (www.mgpl.org/read-listen-view/fl/flmenu/) are also still active, adding to the ability of readers and fans to exchanged opinions and recommendations at record speed and impact bookstores and libraries as never before. In addition, many of the groups mentioned above have a presence on FaceBook and Twitter and most can be followed via Twitter, Tumblr, an RSS feed, or any of the growing number of social media websites and apps.

Just as tech is changing publishing, it is changing how books—in all their various formats (print, electronic, audio)—are reviewed. Many libraries still rely on the classic print/online sources for selecting materials, but a significant number are exploring the online-only environment, as well—and they are discovering a growing group of often credible resources that could be useful when it comes to meeting the modern needs of their readers.

Recommendations for Romance

Reading tastes vary greatly. What makes a book appeal to one person may make another reject it. By the same token, two people may like the same book for totally different reasons. Obviously, reading is a highly subjective and personal undertaking. For this reason, the recommended readings attached to each entry have tried to cast as broad a net as was reasonably possible. Suggested titles have been chosen on the basis of similarity to the main entry in one or more of the following areas: historical time period, geographic setting, theme, character types, plot pattern or premise, writing style, or overall mood or "feel." All suggestions may not appeal to the same person, but it is to be hoped that at least one would appeal to most.

Because romance reading tastes do vary so widely and readers (and writers) often apply vastly differing criteria in determining what makes a romance good, bad, or exceptional, I cannot claim that the following list of recommendations consists solely of the "best" romance novels of the year. (In fact many of these received no awards or special recognition at all.) It is simply a selection of books that the romance contributors, John Charles, Shelley Mosley, Sandra Van Winkle, and I found particularly interesting; perhaps some of these will appeal to you, too.

Silver Thaw by Catherine Anderson

Kissing under the Mistletoe by Bella Andre

No One Like You by Kate Angell

Only Enchanting by Mary Balogh

Rogue Spy by Joanna Bourne

The Viscount Who Lived Down the Lane by Elizabeth Boyle

Texas Mail Order Bride by Linda Broday

The Sweetest Kisses Trilogy by Grace Burrowes

Twice Tempted by Eileen Dreyer

Broken by Cynthia Eden

What a Woman Gets by Judi Fennell

This Gun for Hire by Jo Goodman

The Spring Bride by Anne Gracie

Dearest Rogue by Elizabeth Hoyt

Meadowlands by Elizabeth Jeffrey

If the Viscount Falls by Sabrina Jeffries

Trust No One by Jayne Ann Krentz

Never Judge a Lady by Her Cover by Sarah MacLean

Final Lap by Erin McCarthy

Taking Fire by Lindsay McKenna

Of Silk and Steam by Bec McMaster

Echo Lake by Carla Neggers

This Heart of Mine by Brenda Novak

Garden of Lies by Amanda Quick

The Courtesan Duchess by Joanna Shupe

The Bedding Proposal by Anne Warren

For Further Reference

Publisher Websites and Book Clubs

In addition to going to the general websites of online book suppliers such as Amazon.com and traditional bookstores such as Barnes & Noble, readers now can order romances in print and/or e-book, and in some cases downloadable audio, formats directly from a number of individual publishers' websites. Many of these websites also feature reviews, information on any subscription book clubs the publisher has, and ways for readers to connect with each other. Some of these target the library market and have standing order plans available. Services vary from website to website; several of the more popular are listed below.

Note: Self-publishing continues its drive into the romance market and there are many platforms and programs available for authors to use. Amazon's CreateSpace and KDP programs, mentioned briefly below, and Smashwords are examples of current popular options.

Publishers

Amazon. www.amazon.com In addition to selling books by other publishers on its website, Amazon has launched its own romance imprint, Montlake Romance (www.apub.com/imprint-detail?imprint=6) It also has a variety of programs that allow authors to publish their own works in a variety of formats, including its print program, CreateSpace (www.createspace.com/), its audio program, Audible Audiobook Creation Exchange (www.acx.com/), and its various KDP (Kindle Direct Publishing) ebook programs (kdp.amazon.com/).BelleBooks/Bell Bridge Books. www.bellebooks.com/ (Choose the Romance link in the column at the left-hand side of the page.)

Buroughs Publishing Group. boroughspublishinggroup.com/

Grand Central Publishing (Grand Central, Forever, Forever Yours). http://www.hachettebookgroup.com/publishers/grand-central-publishing/ (Click on the imprint links on the right-hand side of the page.)

HarperCollins/Avon Books (Avon, Avon Impulse, Avon Inspire). www.avonromance.com

Harper Collins/Harlequin Books (Harlequin [classic Harlequin and Silhouette series line], Love Inspired, Heartsong Presents, Mira, Luna, HQN, Kimani Press, Cosmo Red Hot Reads, Spice, Worldwide Library, etc.). www. harlequin.com

Note: HarperCollins acquired Harlequin Enterprises in 2014.

Kensington Books (Zebra, Dafina, Brava, Aphrodisia, KTeen, KTeen Dafina, eKensington, Lyrical Press). www.kensingtonbooks.com (Click on the Books link at the top of the page and then on the link for Romance on the left side of the page.)

Medallion Press. www.medallionpress.com (Choose the "Genres" link under the Books button at the top of the page to get to the Romance listings.)

Penguin Group (Berkley, Putnam, Signet, NAL, Jove, Plume, Dutton). www.penguingroup.com (Choose the link for Romance on the right-hand side of the page.)

Red Sage Publishing. www.eredsage.com

Riptide Publishing. www.riptidepublishing.com/ (Scroll down and click on the Browse & Search Link; then choose the Genre filter on the right to limit by romance.)

Samhain Publishing. www.samhainpublishing.com/

Simon and Schuster (Pocket). www.simonandschuster.com (Choose Books by Category on the upper left and then the link for Romance.)

Sourcebooks, Inc. (Sourcebooks Casablanca). www.sourcebooks.com (Choose Shop Our Books in the left hand column, then Fiction, and then Romance.)

St. Martin's Press. www.heroesandheartbreakers.com/

This community site for romance fans is probably the easiest way to find the romances St. Martin's Press publishes. The main website (us.macmillan.com/smp) is less helpful. Note: the Heroes and Heartbreakers site also includes titles from other publishers, as well. The Wild Rose Press. http://www.thewildrosepress.com/ (The romance link is on the left.)

Selected Book Clubs and Mail Order Services

Although waning in popularity, several publishers still have book club and mail order options. Check their links for more information.

Doubleday Book Club—Romance. www.doubledaybookclub.com/browse-books/romance.html

Harlequin's Reader Service. Provides books in many of the Harlequin lines on a monthly subscription basis. www.readerservice.com/

Rhapsody Book Club. www.rhapsodybookclub.com

Selected Subscription Services

A number of subscription services for borrowing ebooks, similar to Netflix for films and videos, have sprung up. The content of each varies widely, and their success is yet to be determined. The better known ones are:

Scribd. www.scribd.com/ Note: Scribd and Harlequin have recently announced that 15,000 Harlequin ebook titles will be available through Scribd's subscription service.

Oyster Unlimited. www.oysterbooks.com/?p=ASQ2219

Kindle Unlimited. www.amazon.com/kindleunlimited

Conferences

Numerous conferences are held each year for writers, readers, and scholars of romance fiction. Four of the more important and/or interesting national ones are listed below. For a more complete listing, particularly of regional or local conferences designed primarily for romance writers, consult the *Romance Writers' Report*, a monthly publication of The Romance Writers of America or visit their website (www.rwa.org).

The Annual RT Book Lovers Convention is sponsored by *RT Book Reviews Magazine*. The 2015 Book Lover's Convention was held in Dallas, Texas, May 12–17, and as usual, this reader-focused conference was a lively, fast-paced event enjoyed by the many authors and fans who attended. The 2016 Convention is slated to be held in Las Vegas, Nevada, April 12–17. The Romantic Times organization also sponsors a number of romance-related tours for readers and writers.

The RWA Annual Conference is sponsored by Romance Writers of America (RWA) and usually held in July. As mentioned previously, the 2014 conference was held in San Antonio, Texas, July 23–26, and the 2015 conference is scheduled for July 22–25 in New York City. This is RWA's working conference and is aimed at romance writers, editor, librarians, and other romance professionals, rather than fans and readers. Traditionally, it is preceded by a day-long Librarians' Day Event that focuses on librarians and library staff in the local area.

RomCon will hold its 2015 Reader Weekend/University event, a combined reader and author convention, September 25–27 in Denver, Colorado. For more information see RomCon's website (www.romcon.com/about-reader-weekend).

Traditions and Trajectories of Love: The Sixth Conference of the International Association for the Study of Popular Romance (IASPR) will be held June 23–26, 2015, in Salt Lake City, Utah. This conference targets the international academic community and welcomes popular fiction scholars to submit proposals for presentation in the subsequent conference by October 9, 2015. More information can be found on IASPR's website (www.iaspr.org).

Popular Romances

895

VICTORIA ALEXANDER (Pseudonym of Cheryl Griffin)

The Shocking Secret of a Guest at the Wedding

(New York: Zebra Books, 2014)

Series: Millworth Manor Series. Book 4
Story type: Historical - Victorian America; Series
Subject(s): Marriage; Weddings; Family relations
Major character(s): Jackson Quincy Graham Channing, Banker; Lady Theodosia "Teddy" Winslow, Planner (wedding), Noblewoman
Time period(s): 19th century; 1880s
Locale(s): England; New York, New York

Summary: Lady Theodosia "Teddy" Winslow is doing everything she can to keep up appearances as she struggles to maintain her place in late 19th-century English high society. Since her father's passing, Teddy and her mother have only barely been able to make ends meet and hold on to their place among the social elite. While her mother insists that Teddy should marry a wealthy man who can support her, Teddy is far more interested in pursuing her blossoming career as a wedding planner. Eventually, Teddy's eagerness to succeed leads her to an important wedding job and an encounter with Jackson Quincy Graham Channing. A well-to-do city banker, Channing is presently contemplating his own career path. During the celebration, Jackson comes to Teddy's rescue at an uncomfortable moment and claims that he is her fiance. What begins as a convenient white lie quickly turns into a real romance that might change both parties' futures forever.

Other books by the same author:
The Scandalous Adventures of the Sister of the Bride, 2014
The Importance of Being Wicked, 2013
My Wicked Little Lies, 2012
What Happens at Christmas, 2012
His Mistress by Christmas, 2011

Other books you might like:
Connie Brockway, *The Bridal Season,* 2001
Juliana Gray, *A Lady Never Lies,* 2012
Laura Lee Guhrke, *Wedding of the Season,* 2011
Judith Ivory, *The Indiscretion,* 2001

Sarah MacLean, *Never Judge a Lady by Her Cover,* 2014
Sherry Thomas, *Beguiling the Beauty,* 2012

896

VICTORIA ALEXANDER (Pseudonym of Cheryl Griffin)

The Daring Exploits of a Runaway Heiress

(New York: Kensington, 2015)

Series: Millworth Manor Series. Book 5
Story type: Historical - Victorian; Series
Subject(s): Inheritance and succession; Romances (Fiction); England
Major character(s): Lucy Merryweather, Heiress; Cameron Effington, Journalist
Time period(s): 19th century; 1880s (1888)
Locale(s): England

Summary: In this fifth installment in the Millworth Manor series by best-selling author Victoria Alexander, American heiress Lucy Merryweather inherits a fortune and escapes to England to make good on her aunt's last wishes. In 1888, Lucy inherits more than money from her Aunt Lucinda. She also receives Aunt Lucinda's book of regrets—a list of adventures and escapades she wish she'd had the courage to pursue. Now, Lucy decides the best way to honor the memory of her aunt is to accomplish as many unfulfilled wishes as she can. From swimming naked under a moonlit sky to riding an elephant to being painted in the nude, the list is as wild as it is vast. Away from family and the prying eyes of New York, Lucy expects that England will offer her the freedom she desires. But will the handsome private investigator hired to follow her put an end to Lucy's antics, or will he join in on the fun?

Other books by the same author:
The Scandalous Adventures of the Sister of the Bride, 2014
The Shocking Secret of a Guest at the Wedding, 2014
The Importance of Being Wicked, 2013
My Wicked Little Lies, 2012
What Happens at Christmas, 2012

Other books you might like:
Juliana Gray, *A Lady Never Lies,* 2012

Laura Lee Guhrke, *How to Lose a Duke in Ten Days*, 2014

Betina Krahn, *The Unlikely Angel*, 1996

Donna MacMeans, *The Education of Mrs. Brimley*, 2007

Sherry Thomas, *Tempting the Bride*, 2012

897

LAURA MARIE ALTOM

The Cowboy SEAL

(Don Mills, Ontario, Canada: Harlequin, 2014)

Series: Operation: Family Series. Book 7
Story type: Contemporary; Series
Subject(s): Romances (Fiction); Love; Family
Major character(s): Cooper Hansen, Son (of Clint), Brother (of Peg), Military Personnel (Navy SEAL), Brother (brother-in-law of Millie); Clint Hansen, Father (of Cooper and Peg), Father (father-in-law of Millie), Widow(er), Patient (had stroke); Peg, Daughter (of Clint), Sister (of Cooper), Sister (sister-in-law of Millie); Millie Hansen, Widow(er), Mother (of LeeAnn and JJ), Sister (sister-in-law of Peg, Cooper), Daughter (daughter-in-law of Clint); Lee-Ann Hansen, 11-Year-Old, Daughter (of Millie), Granddaughter (of Clint), Niece (of Peg, Cooper); JJ Hansen, 7-Year-Old, Son (of Millie), Grandson (of Clint), Nephew (of Peg, Cooper)
Time period(s): 21st century; 2010s
Locale(s): Brewer's Falls, Colorado

Summary: When US Navy SEAL Cooper Hansen returns to Brewer's Falls, Colorado, he realizes the pain his family has experienced during his ten-year absence. Cooper's brother died, leaving behind a wife, Millie, and their children, LeeAnn and JJ. Cooper's father, Clint, is currently recovering from a stroke. Cooper's sister, Peg, has been staying at the ranch to help Millie care for Clint, but it's time for her to return to her own family. The members of the Hansen clan have been at odds since Cooper's mother died. Clint has always held Cooper responsible for her death. Now that Cooper is back, he realizes that it might not be too late to make amends. He gets to know the niece and nephew he'd never met before, and he helps Millie try to turn the struggling ranch around. In the process, a romance begins to grow between Cooper and his brother's widow. This novel is the seventh in the Operation: Family series.

Other books by the same author:
The SEAL's Baby, 2014
The SEAL's Stolen Child, 2014
The SEAL's Christmas Twins, 2013
The SEAL's Valentine, 2013
A Navy SEAL's Secret Baby, 2012

Other books you might like:
Pamela Britton, *A Cowboy's Christmas Wedding*, 2013
Janice Maynard, *A Touch of Persuasion*, 2012
Cathy McDavid, *His Christmas Sweetheart*, 2013
Trish Milburn, *The Cowboy Sheriff*, 2012
Rebecca Winters, *Her Wyoming Hero*, 2013

898

CATHERINE ANDERSON

Silver Thaw

(New York: Signet, 2015)

Series: Mystic Creek Series. Book 1
Story type: Contemporary; Series
Subject(s): Romances (Fiction); Single parent family; Mothers
Major character(s): Amanda Banning, Abuse Victim, Mother (of Chloe), Neighbor (of Jeb); Jeb Sterling, Neighbor (of Amanda and Chloe); Chloe Banning, Girl, 6-Year-Old, Daughter (of Amanda), Neighbor (of Jeb)
Time period(s): 21st century; 2010s
Locale(s): Mystic Creek, Oregon

Summary: Best-selling author Catherine Anderson delivers the first novel in her Mystic Creek contemporary romance series. Amanda Banning escapes to Mystic Creek, Oregon, after gathering the courage to leave the husband she's feared for years. Desperate to make a fresh start in a new city, Amanda struggles to provide for herself and Chloe, her six-year-old daughter. She finds solace in writing her deepest desires on small pieces of paper and releasing them into the wind. Amanda's neighbor, Jeb Sterling, swore off love a long time ago, but when he finds Amanda's notes all over his property, he is inspired by her courage and drawn to her beauty. When harsh temperatures leave Amanda and Chloe homeless, Jeb welcomes them into his home. Soon, he is devoted to making all of Amanda's dreams come true. But can Amanda receive his kindness and learn to trust—and love—again?

Other books by the same author:
Walking on Air, 2014
Perfect Timing, 2013
Lucky Penny, 2012
Here to Stay, 2011
Early Dawn, 2009

Other books you might like:
Barbara Delinsky, *Montana Man*, 1995
Linda Lael Miller, *Sierra's Homecoming*, 2006
Debbie Macomber, *The Snow Bride*, 2003
Susan Elizabeth Phillips, *Heroes Are My Weakness*, 2014
Susan Wiggs, *Candlelight Christmas*, 2013

899

BELLA ANDRE

Kissing Under the Mistletoe

(Richmond, Virginia: Mills & Boon, 2013)

Series: Sullivans Series. Book 10
Story type: Holiday Themes; Series
Subject(s): Romances (Fiction); Love; Holidays
Major character(s): Mary Sullivan, Mother (of eight), Spouse (of Jack); Jack Sullivan, Spouse (of Mary), Father (of eight)

Time period(s): 21st century; 2010s
Locale(s): Lake Tahoe, California

Summary: In this tenth romance in the Sullivans series by Bella Andre, matriarch Mary Sullivan is getting ready for all eight of her children and their current partners to come home to Lake Tahoe for Christmas. As she decorates the tree with ornaments collected over the years and made by her children, she reminisces. One of the oldest ornaments reminds her of her very first Christmas with her husband, Jack. She begins to recall their early time getting to know one another, the first days they spent together, and the story of how they fell in love and began the life that led to their beautiful family. Though they took things slowly, neither one could ignore their undeniable chemistry—and how it grew into the strong and unshakeable bond that they built over the years together, shared now in this holiday-themed story.

Other books by the same author:
It Must Be Your Love, 2015
All for You, 2014
Always on My Mind, 2014
Kiss Me Like This, 2014
The Way You Look Tonight, 2014

Other books you might like:
Carolyn Brown, *Honky Tonk Christmas*, 2010
Carolyn Brown, *Mistletoe Cowboy*, 2012
Donna Kauffman, *The Naughty List*, 2010
Susan Mallery, *Christmas on 4th Street*, 2013
Brenda Novak, *The Heart of Christmas*, 2014
Susan Wiggs, *Candlelight Christmas*, 2013

900

ILONA ANDREWS (Pseudonym of Ilona and Andrew Gordon)

Burn for Me

(New York: Avon, 2014)

Series: Hidden Legacy Series. Book 1
Story type: Fantasy; Paranormal
Subject(s): Romances (Fiction); Parapsychology; Magic
Major character(s): Nevada Baylor, Detective—Private (Baylor Investigative Agency), Woman; Connor "Mad" Rogan, Wealthy (billionaire), Magician (has paranormal powers)
Time period(s): 21st century; 2010s
Locale(s): United States

Summary: The first novel in the Hidden Legacy series centers on an alternative world order that was brought about by the 1863 discovery of the Osiris serum. The serum awakened paranormal abilities that had long been dormant in human bloodlines. Over the years, the most powerful families established themselves as the Houses and now control the workings of the world. Nevada Baylor has no magical skill. She is a detective with Baylor Investigative Agency. When she is hired to track a subject who is a member of the most powerful magic order, she accepts despite her misgivings. The mission could either make her career or get her killed. Nevada hits a snag when she realizes that she isn't the only one on the trail of the Prime. Connor "Mad" Rogan, who has money and magic powers, is after the same subject, and

he wants Nevada's help. When Nevada is kidnapped by Mad, she is surprised by the attraction she feels for her captor.

Other books by the same author:
Magic Breaks, 2014
Magic Rises, 2013
Gunmetal Magic, 2012
Steel's Edge, 2012
Fate's Edge, 2011

Other books you might like:
Lara Adrian, *Kiss of Midnight*, 2007
Christina Dodd, *Chains of Ice*, 2010
Christine Feehan, *Spirit Bound*, 2011
Larissa Ione, *Bound by Night*, 2013
Pamela Palmer, *A Blood Seduction*, 2012

901

KATE ANGELL

No One Like You

(New York, New York: Kensington Publishing Corp., 2015)

Story type: Contemporary
Subject(s): Romances (Fiction); Baseball; Love
Major character(s): Rylan Cates, Baseball Player; Beth Avery, Assistant
Time period(s): 21st century; 2010s
Locale(s): Barefoot William, Florida

Summary: The fourth installment of Angell's Barefoot William Beach series set in the titular bucolic seaside Florida town sees pro baseball player Rylan Cates move to the small community as part of an eight week spring training program. As his personal assistant has recently become married, he hires Beth Avery, who is also new to town, to care for his four beloved dogs. For her part, Beth had come to Barefoot William to escape the failure of her business and a pained relationship with her family. Though Beth only took the job as a temporary respite from her troubles, she comes to enjoy both the company of Rylan and his exuberant pack of dogs—especially Atlas, a lovable Great Dane who seems to have his own plans for Beth and Rylan.

Other books by the same author:
No Sunshine When She's Gone, 2014
No Strings Attached, 2013
No Tan Lines, 2012
Sweet Spot, 2012
Sliding Home, 2009

Other books you might like:
Jennifer Crusie, *Getting Rid of Bradley*, 1994
Janet Evanovich, *Love in a Nutshell*, 2012
Carly Phillips, *Hot Stuff*, 2004
Susan Elizabeth Phillips, *Heaven, Texas*, 1995
Deborah Shelley, *Talk about Love*, 1999

Romances

902

JENNIFER L. ARMENTROUT

Fall with Me

(New York, New York: HarperCollins Publishers, 2015)

Story type: Romantic Suspense
Subject(s): Romances (Fiction); Suspense; Mystery
Major character(s): Roxanne "Roxy" Ark, Bartender, Artist; Reece Anders, Police Officer; Charlie, Friend, Crime Victim
Time period(s): 21st century; 2010s
Locale(s): United States

Summary: Book five in Armentrout's "Wait for You" series focuses on the story of Roxanne "Roxy" Ark, a passionate artist and part time bartender who has had a crush on her childhood friend, officer Reece Anders, for years. Sadly, a misunderstanding has caused a rift to form between them, and Roxy is left hoping for a chance to somehow repair their fractured relationship. Though Reece remains cool around Roxy, he still maintains a fierce protectiveness for her safety. So when the man who put Roxy's best friend, Charlie, into a long-term care facility begins to contact Roxy after his release from prison, Reece finds himself by her side once again. The situation becomes even more frightening when Roxy begins receiving upsetting messages—threats she believes comes from Charlie's attacker, though Reece remains determined to find their true source, even as he tries to deny his own growing feelings for Roxy.

Other books by the same author:
Dead List, 2015
Forever with You, 2015
Don't Look Back, 2014
Stone Cold Touch, 2014
Wicked, 2014

Other books you might like:
Amanda Berry, *His Small-Town Sweetheart*, 2015
Cora Carmack, *Losing It Series*, 2013
C.C. Cartwright, *My Mr. London*, 2014
Inglath Cooper, *Nashville: Ready to Reach*, 2012
Carla Coxwell, *Secrets Revealed*, 2014
Caisey Quinn, *Leaving Amarillo*, 2015

903

KATHARINE ASHE (Pseudonym of Katharine Brophy Dubois)

I Loved a Rogue

(New York: Avon, 2015)

Series: Prince Catchers Series. Book 3
Story type: Historical - Regency; Series
Subject(s): History; Sisters; Family history
Major character(s): Eleanor Caulfield, Lover (former, of Taliesin), Foster Child, Companion (traveling, of Taliesin); Taliesin, Companion (traveling, of Eleanor), Lover (former, of Eleanor), Gypsy
Time period(s): 19th century; 1810s (1819)
Locale(s): England

Summary: Award-winning author Katharine Ashe delivers the third novel in her Prince Catchers historical romance series. In 1819 England, Eleanor Caulfield is the oldest of three sisters who are desperate to learn the truth of their family heritage. When the minister who served as the girls' foster father finally marries, Eleanor, the only unmarried sister, is free to leave the home. With the support of her sisters, Eleanor plans to embark on an adventure that will lead her to the truth about their parents. Her sisters insist that she take an escort: Taliesin, the handsome gypsy who broke her heart 11 years ago. While Taliesin is determined to undo the hurt he caused Eleanor in the past, Eleanor is ready to break free from the repressed and sheltered life she's known, but neither is prepared for the adventure that lies ahead.

Other books by the same author:
I Adored a Lord, 2014
I Married the Duke, 2013
How a Lady Weds a Rogue, 2012
How to Be a Proper Lady, 2012
When a Scot Loves a Lady, 2012

Other books you might like:
Suzanne Enoch, *Taming an Impossible Rogue*, 2012
Anne Gracie, *The Spring Bride*, 2015
Anne Gracie, *To Catch a Bride*, 2009
Eloisa James, *Midnight Pleasures*, 2000
Mary Jo Putney, *Nowhere Near Respectable*, 2011

904

JANE ASHFORD (Pseudonym of Jane LeCompte)

Married to a Perfect Stranger

(Naperville, Illinois: Sourcebooks Casablanca, 2015)

Story type: Historical - Regency
Subject(s): Romances (Fiction); History; Marriage
Major character(s): Mary Fleming, Artist (painter), Spouse (of John Bexley); John Bexley, Diplomat, Spouse (of Mary Fleming)
Time period(s): 19th century; 1810s (1816)
Locale(s): London, England

Summary: John Bexley and Mary Fleming were married according to an arrangement made by their families. They had hardly gotten to know one another when John left for a two-year diplomatic assignment. It is now 1816, and John has returned to London and his wife. His government work has taught him to be secretive, and he isn't prepared to share the details of his time in China with Mary. When the couple is reunited, John is surprised to find that the reserved young woman he married has changed. Confident and independent, she has achieved success as an artist. They must get acquainted all over again, and this process does not go smoothly at first. But as John and Mary spend time together, they appreciate how they both have grown, and they find their bond strengthening. Now it is the relatives and friends who initially supported their marriage who are skeptical about the couple's unconventional relationship.

Other books by the same author:
The Bride Insists, 2014
Once Again a Bride, 2013

Bride to Be, 1999
The Bargain, 1997
The Marriage Wager, 1996

Other books you might like:
Lily Dalton, *Never Desire a Duke*, 2013
Erin Knightley, *A Taste for Scandal*, 2012
Jade Lee, *What the Groom Wants*, 2014
Christine Merrill, *Two Wrongs Make a Marriage*, 2012
Diane Perkins, *The Marriage Bargain*, 2005

905

JENNIFER ASHLEY

Rules for a Proper Governess
(New York: Berkley Publishing, 2014)

Series: Mackenzies/McBrides Series. Book 7
Story type: Historical; Series
Subject(s): Class conflict; Family relations; Romances (Fiction)
Major character(s): Sinclair McBride, Father (of Caitlin and Andrew), Lawyer (Scottish Barrister), Widow(er); Roberta "Bertie" Frasier, Thief (pickpocket), Governess (for Sinclair McBride), Young Woman (from London's East Side); Caitlin McBride, Daughter (of Sinclair McBride); Andrew McBride, Son (of Sinclair McBride)
Time period(s): 19th century; 1880s (1885)
Locale(s): London, England

Summary: Author Jennifer Ashley returns with the seventh book in the Mackenzies/McBrides series. Seven years after the death of his wife, Sinclair McBride is still mourning and struggling with her passing. As a barrister, he buries himself in his work, earning the nickname "Basher McBride" because of his exceptional conviction record. But as a widower and father of two young children, McBride is bereft. The children are a handful, and McBride can't seem to keep his house staff and governess from quitting. Everything changes the day he meets Bertie Frasier, a beautiful, spirited young woman who was raised in the low end of London. The streetwise pickpocket Bertie stumbles into McBride's life, stealing his watch along with his heart. Bertie's refreshing and somewhat unconventional ways breathe new life into the family, but will a blackmail plot ruin their newly found happiness? Will Bertie and McBride's pasts ruin the future they could have together?

Other books by the same author:
The Wicked Deeds of Daniel MacKenzie, 2013
The Duke's Perfect Wife, 2012
The Many Sins of Lord Cameron, 2011
Lady Isabella's Scandalous Marriage, 2010
The Madness of Lord Ian Mackenzie, 2009

Other books you might like:
Geralyn Dawson, *Her Outlaw*, 2007
Julie Garwood, *For the Roses*, 1995
Julia London, *Highlander in Disguise*, 2005
Cathy Maxwell, *Adventures of a Scottish Heiress*, 2003
Teresa Medeiros, *Some Like It Wicked*, 2008

906

TESSA BAILEY

Need Me
(New York: Avon Impulse, 2015)

Series: Broke and Beautiful Series. Book 2
Story type: Contemporary; Series
Subject(s): Romances (Fiction); College environment; Universities and colleges
Major character(s): Honey Perribow, Student—College (medical), Student (of Ben); Ben Dawson, Professor (English, of Honey)
Time period(s): 21st century; 2010s
Locale(s): New York, New York

Summary: In the second novel in the Broke and Beautiful series by best-selling author Tessa Bailey, Kentucky native Honey Perribow breaks all the rules and falls in love with her professor. Honey moved to New York City to go to Columbia University and pours all of her energy into her medical degree pursuit, until she meets dreamy English professor Ben Dawson. Teacher-student relationships are strictly prohibited at the university, but Honey is determined to get his attention. When a mishap at an off-campus gathering lands Ben and Honey in a locked closet, their attraction is uncontrollable. Ben knows he can't date a student, but as much as tries to avoid her, his desire for her only grows. Now, Ben's ready to break all the rules to show Honey how he feels about her.

Other books by the same author:
Chase Me, 2015
Risking It All, 2015
Baiting the Maid of Honor, 2014
Exposed by Fate, 2014
Owned by Fate, 2014

Other books you might like:
Gemma Burgess, *Brooklyn Girls*, 2013
Cora Carmack, *Faking It*, 2013
Jay Crownover, *Better When He's Bad*, 2014
J. Lynn, *Be with Me*, 2014
Molly McAdams, *Deceiving Lies*, 2014

907

MARY BALOGH

Only Enchanting
(New York: Penguin Publishing Group, 2014)

Series: Survivors' Club Series. Book 4
Story type: Historical
Subject(s): Napoleonic Wars, 1800-1815; Veterans; Romances (Fiction)
Major character(s): Agnes Keeping, Widow(er), Spouse (of Flavian); Flavian, Spouse (of Agnes), Nobleman (Viscount Ponsonby)
Time period(s): 19th century
Locale(s): England

Summary: Agnes Keeping has been married, but she has never been in love. Oh, there was fondness for her young husband, who died a few years ago of a winter chill, but what they had was not love or passion. That was fine with Agnes then, and a life free from love and passion is fine with her now. That is before she meets Viscount Ponsonby—Flavian, to his friends. He is one of seven survivors of the Napoleonic Wars who became friends during their recovery at Penderris Hall in Cornwall. When his fiancee deserts him and then comes back, Flavian tries to avoid the woman by turning to Agnes. Agnes falls for the charming Flavian and accepts his proposal of marriage, only to discover that he is only trying to get revenge against his fickle fiancee. Agnes leaves, but she is then pursued by her new husband, who desires her for who she is. This is the fourth book in the Survivors Club series.

Other books by the same author:
The Escape, 2014
The Arrangement, 2013
The Proposal, 2012
A Secret Affair, 2010
Seducing an Angel, 2009

Other books you might like:
Grace Burrowes, *The Traitor*, 2014
Sarah Elliott, *The Earl and the Governess*, 2010
Gaelen Foley, *My Notorious Gentleman*, 2013
Erin Knightley, *The Baron Next Door*, 2014
Tracy Anne Warren, *Seduced by His Touch*, 2009

908

MAYA BANKS (Pseudonym of Sharon Long)

Keep Me Safe

(New York: HarperCollins Publishers, 2014)

Series: Slow Burn Trilogy. Book 1
Story type: Contemporary; Series
Subject(s): Kidnapping; Telepathy; Brothers and sisters
Major character(s): Ramie St. Claire, Empath; Caleb Devereaux, Wealthy, Brother (of Tori), Employer (of Ramie); Tori Devereaux, Kidnap Victim, Sister (of Caleb)
Time period(s): 21st century; 2010s
Locale(s): United States

Summary: Ramie St. Claire has a gift, but this gift comes with a terrible cost. She can find missing and abducted people by sensing their pain. But their pain becomes her pain, and every time Ramie uses her power to help, it hurts her. This time, it's worse than usual. Caleb Devereaux's younger sister Tori has been kidnapped, and he will stop at nothing to find her. The Devereaux family has money and status, and Caleb is used to getting his way. He pushes Ramie to find his sister until it nearly destroys her. The search is painful, and it's made even harder because Ramie has to deal with her growing feelings for Caleb. Caleb realizes this and wants to make it up to Ramie. But when Caleb's sister is at last found, Ramie is shattered and seeks a place far away from the source of all her pain. Then she finds herself in trouble, and it's her turn to seek Caleb's help. The question now is—how much is he willing to risk for the woman who risked so much for him? This is the first book in the Slow Burn trilogy.

Other books by the same author:
In His Keeping, 2015
After the Storm, 2014
When Day Breaks, 2014
Forged in Steele, 2013
Highlander Most Wanted, 2013

Other books you might like:
Nina Bruhns, *If Looks Could Chill*, 2009
Pamela Clare, *Breaking Point*, 2011
Gemma Halliday, *The Perfect Shot*, 2010
Christy Reece, *Last Chance*, 2010
Stephanie Tyler, *Promises in the Dark*, 2010

909

SOPHIE BARNES

Lady Sarah's Sinful Desires

(New York: Avon Books, 2015)

Series: Secrets at Thorncliff Manor Series. Book 1
Story type: Historical - Regency; Series
Subject(s): Romances (Fiction); Marriage; England
Major character(s): Lord Christopher Spencer, Nobleman; Lady Sarah, Noblewoman
Time period(s): 19th century; 1820s (1820)
Locale(s): England

Summary: Lord Christopher Spencer has never met a woman he could trust, and the last thing he wants to do is look for a bride. However, when he and his family arrive at Thorncliff Manor for the summer, he meets Lady Sarah and is instantly captivated by her charm and passion. Sarah didn't come to Thorncliff Manor to find love—she came to make plans for her future. She tries at first to ignore Christopher, but she can't deny what she feels when he's around. As her feelings for Christopher deepen, the secrets of her tarnished past resurface. Sarah fears there's no hope for their future, but will Christopher find the courage to believe the love between them is real? This historical romance novel is the first installment in the Secrets at Thorncliff Manor series by Sophie Barnes.

Other books by the same author:
The Danger of Tempting an Earl, 2014
The Scandal in Kissing an Heir, 2013
The Trouble with Being a Duke, 2013
How Miss Rutherford Got Her Groove Back, 2012
Lady Alexandra's Excellent Adventure, 2012

Other books you might like:
Kathryn Caskie, *How to Seduce a Duke*, 2006
Jane Feather, *An Unsuitable Bride*, 2012
Jo Goodman, *Let Me Be the One*, 2002
Olivia Parker, *At the Bride Hunt Ball*, 2008
Jennifer St. Giles, *Darkest Dreams*, 2006

910

TAMRA BAUMANN

It Had to Be Him

(Seattle, Washington: Montlake Romance, 2015)

Story type: Contemporary; Romantic Suspense
Subject(s): Romances (Fiction); Reunions; Family
Major character(s): Meg Anderson, Mother (of Haley), Lover (of Josh Granger); Josh Granger, FBI Agent, Father (of Haley), Lover (of Meg Anderson); Haley Anderson, Daughter (of Meg and Josh)
Time period(s): 21st century; 2010s
Locale(s): Anderson Butte, Colorado

Summary: In the first novel in the It Had to Be series, Meg Anderson returns to the mountain resort town of Anderson Butte, Colorado in hopes of finding relief from the troubles that have plagued her. It may not have been her best plan, however, as Anderson Butte was largely founded by her family and her disapproving father is its powerful mayor. Oh, and it also happens to the place where, as a pregnant mom-to-be, she was abandoned by the love of her life, Josh Granger. But despite being largely MIA for the last three years, Josh has begun to try and get in contact with Meg again, much to her dismay. However, Josh is desperate. He knows that Meg may never be able to forgive him for disappearing, but he hopes to be able to tell her soon that it was done for her protection. And even though he's still not supposed to reveal the truth behind his deception yet, he simply must see Meg and their daughter Haley even if it means that his deception might catch up with all of them—and his secrets have the power to kill them all

Other books you might like:
Jaci Burton, *The Perfect Play*, 2011
Robyn Carr, *Sunrise Point*, 2012
Jessica Lemmon, *Bringing Home the Bad Boy*, 2015
Candis Terry, *Sweet Surprise*, 2015
RaeAnne Thayne, *A Cold Creek Reunion*, 2012

911

MACY BECKETT

Make You Remember

(New York: Penguin Publishing Group, 2014)

Series: Dumont Bachelors Series. Book 2
Story type: Contemporary; Series
Subject(s): Romances (Fiction); River boats; Child care
Major character(s): Beau Dumont, Wealthy (former bad boy), Boyfriend (high school boyfriend of Devyn); Devyn Mauvais, Girlfriend (high school girlfriend of Beau), Child-Care Giver (on Dumont family riverboat)
Time period(s): 21st century; 2010s
Locale(s): New Orleans, Louisiana

Summary: There's a lot Devyn Mauvais wants to leave behind. Her legacy as a descendent of a voodoo queen would be one thing; her job leading ghost tours in New Orleans would be another. And her high school relationship with bad-boy Beau Dumont would absolutely make the list of things Devyn is happy to see in the rearview mirror. When Beau offers her a job in the day care on his family's riverboat, Devyn sees it as a chance to shake off her family's voodoo past and ditch the ghost tours—nothing more. For Beau, though, the offer has an ulterior motive. Now that he's reformed his bad-boy ways, he's determined to fix the biggest mistake he ever made: letting Devyn walk away. He's sure that he can change her all-business attitude towards him, if only he can make her remember when they first loved each other. This is the second book in the Dumont Bachelors series.

Other books by the same author:
Make You Mine, 2014
A Shot of Sultry, 2013
Surrender to Sultry, 2013
Sultry with a Twist, 2012

Other books you might like:
Chelsea M. Cameron, *My Favorite Mistake*, 2013
Marie Force, *And I Love Her*, 2015
Jill Gregory, *Sunflower Lane*, 2014
Katie Lane, *Make Mine a Bad Boy*, 2011
Susan Lyons, *Sex on the Slopes*, 2010
Jill Shalvis, *Still the One*, 2015

912

JENN BENNETT

Grave Phantoms

(New York: Berkley Sensation, 2015)

Series: Roaring Twenties Series. Book 3
Story type: Fantasy; Historical - Roaring Twenties
Subject(s): Romances (Fiction); Race relations; Psychics
Major character(s): Astrid Magnusson, Student—College, Wealthy, Psychic; Bo Yeung, Assistant (to the Magnusson family)
Time period(s): 20th century; 1920s (1928)
Locale(s): San Francisco, California

Summary: This historical paranormal romance is the third novel in the Roaring Twenties series by Jenn Bennett. College student and daughter of a wealthy bootlegger Astrid Magnusson returns home to San Francisco, where she can't wait to see Bo Yeung, the young Chinese man who has worked for the Magnusson family for years. Their reunion is made difficult when a yacht that's been missing for one year crashes into the family's docks, bringing with it a group of mysterious survivors. When an ancient turquoise sculpture gives Astrid visions about the yacht's mysterious disappearance, she and Bo are thrust into a world of dark magic and age-old riches. Danger lurks at every corner, but at a time when mixed-race marriages are outlawed, resisting their strong desires for one another may prove to be the greatest challenge for Astrid and Bo.

Other books by the same author:
Grim Shadows, 2014
Binding the Shadows, 2013
Bitter Spirits, 2013
Summoning the Night, 2012
Kindling the Moon, 2011

Other books you might like:
Kresley Cole, *Dark Needs at Night's Edge*, 2008
Barbara Freethy, *Golden Lies*, 2004
Deanna Raybourn, *The Dead Travel Fast*, 2010
Simone St. James, *The Haunting of Maddy Clare*, 2012
Simone St. James, *The Other Side of Midnight*, 2015

913

JENNIFER BERNARD

The Night Belongs to Fireman

(New York: Avon Publishing, 2014)

Series: Bachelor Firemen Novels. Book 6
Story type: Romantic Suspense; Series
Subject(s): Kidnapping; Father-daughter relations; Romances (Fiction)
Major character(s): Fred Breen, Fire Fighter (at San Gabriel Fire Department), Bodyguard (of Rachel Kessler); Rachel Kessler, Kidnap Victim (at age eight), Daughter (of tech billionaire, Rob Kessler); Rob Kessler, Businessman (succesful), Father (of Rachel Kessler)
Time period(s): 21st century; 2010s
Locale(s): San Gabriel, California

Summary: Author Jennifer Bernard returns with the sixth novel in the Bachelor Fireman series. Fred Breen is a hunky fireman at the San Gabriel Fire Department. He's just ending a relationship, and he isn't looking for a girlfriend. But when he rescues raven-haired beauty Rachel Kessler from a limousine crash, Fred may have found that special someone he wasn't looking for. After the San Gabriel Fire Department is called to save Rachel and her friends, Fred is labeled the "Bachelor Hero," and Rachel's past kidnapping is revisited by the media. Rachel's successful and powerful father, Rob, is afraid that the man who kidnapped Rachel when she was a child will return to hurt her. Rob hires Fred Breen to protect his daughter. As Rachel tries to overcome issues from her past, will she be able to deal with her feelings for Fred? And will the "Bachelor Hero" be able to rescue Rachel again from danger?

Other books by the same author:
Four Weddings and a Fireman, 2014
How to Tame a Wild Fireman, 2013
Sex and the Single Fireman, 2013
The Fireman Who Loved Me, 2012
Hot for Fireman, 2012

Other books you might like:
Charlotte Maclay, *Bold and Brave-Hearted*, 2001
Sylvia Mendoza, *On Fire/Al Rojo Vivo*, 1999
Allie Pleiter, *The Fireman's Homecoming*, 2013
Susan Wiggs, *Just Breathe*, 2008
Sherryl Woods, *A Love Beyond Words*, 2001

914

AMANDA BERRY

His Small-Town Sweetheart

(Don Mills, Ontario, Canada: Harlequin, 2015)

Story type: Contemporary
Subject(s): Romances (Fiction); Friendship
Major character(s): Nicole "Nikki" Baxter, Lover (of Sam Ward); Sam Ward, Lover (of Nicole Baxter)
Time period(s): 21st century; 2010s
Locale(s): Tawnee Valley, United States

Summary: The newest chapter in Berry's Ward Brother series, *His Small-Town Sweetheart* relates the story of how Nicole Baxter and Sam Ward's childhood friendship threatens to turn into something more intimate now that Nicole has returned to Tawnee Valley after a twenty year absence. To her surprise, however, the sweet boy that Nikki remembers has instead turned into a quiet and isolated loner who is selling his beloved home. Though his brothers have managed to find love, Sam feels lonely and embittered after his childhood love left town. But now that Nikki has come back, can the couple rekindle the old sparks between them?

Other books by the same author:
One Night with the Best Man, 2014
Father by Choice, 2013
L.A. Cinderella, 2010

Other books you might like:
Jennifer L. Armentrout, *Fall with Me*, 2015
Leanne Banks, *A Maverick for Christmas*, 2011
Kathleen Eagle, *Never Trust a Cowboy*, 2014
Marie Ferrarella, *The Baby Wore a Badge*, 2014
Crystal Green, *The Hard-to-Get Cowboy*, 2011
Diana Palmer, *Texas Born*, 2014

915

JO BEVERLEY

Too Dangerous for a Lady

(New York: Signet Select, 2015)

Series: Company of Rogues Series. Book 16
Story type: Historical - Regency; Series
Subject(s): Romances (Fiction); Revolutions; England
Major character(s): Lady Hermione Merryhew, Noblewoman, Traveler; Mark Thayne, Military Personnel (Lieutenant), Agent (government, secret)
Time period(s): 19th century; 1810s (1817)
Locale(s): England

Summary: In the 16th novel of the Company of Rogues series by best-selling author Jo Beverley, Lady Hermione Merryhew gets a second chance at love and finds herself in the midst of a dangerous plot involving a group of English radicals. On the way to her great-uncle's estate, Lady Hermione and her nephews find rest at an inn, where Lieutenant Mark Thayne begs her to help hide him from the law. Hermione recognizes the man she assumes to be a thief. Six years earlier, she met Mark at a ball, and since that night she's dreamed of enjoying the kiss they never shared. Now Viscount Faringay, Mark is a secret government agent who has infiltrated a group of extreme revolutionaries who seek to wreak havoc in London. He's content to keep Hermione thinking he's a fugitive thief, afraid that the truth will only increase her risk of danger. But when Mark's forced to trust her with an ominous letter, Hermione finds herself in the line of fire.

Other books by the same author:
A Shocking Delight, 2014
Seduction in Silk, 2013
A Scandalous Countess, 2012
An Unlikely Countess, 2011
The Secret Duke, 2010

Other books you might like:
Elizabeth Essex, *Almost a Scandal*, 2012
Madeline Hunter, *The Counterfeit Mistress*, 2013
Sabrina Jeffries, *How the Scoundrel Seduces*, 2014
Stephanie Laurens, *The Lady Risks All*, 2012
Mary Jo Putney, *Not Quite a Wife*, 2014

916

LISA BINGHAM

Desperado

(New York, New York: Berkley Books, 2015)

Story type: Ranch Life; Western
Subject(s): Romances (Fiction); Ranch life; Love
Major character(s): Prairie Dawn "P.D." Raines, Lover (of Elam), Store Owner, Restaurateur; Elam Taggart, Rancher
Time period(s): 21st century; 2010s
Locale(s): Bliss, Utah

Summary: The first entry in Bingham's new Taggart Brothers series, *Desperado* relates the story of the eldest Taggart brother, Elam. To date, his life has been filled with tragedy: his parents and sister were killed in a tragic accident that left his brother Barry mentally disabled, he is haunted by the horrors he witnesses during his military service, and he is still grieving the loss of his wife. The very last thing he is looking for is romance. Prairie Dawn, or P.D. as she prefers to be called, has seen her own share of hardship. The daughter of hippies, she was largely forced to raise herself, and despite harboring feelings of abandonment, she managed to gain degrees in business and physics. After discovering that a career in the sciences was not really what she was searching for, she dropped everything to move to Bliss, Utah, where she bought a restaurant. Short on cash, she organizes a contest during Bliss's Wild West fair that she hopes will enable her to remodel the building. She enlists the help of Elam, who is stunned to learn his partner in this enterprise is a woman—a beautiful woman to whom he is becoming increasingly attracted.

Other books by the same author:
Twins Times Two, 2001
Man Behind the Voice, 2000
And Babies Make Ten, 1999
When Night Draws Near, 1999
Wild Masquerade, 1997

Other books you might like:
Rochelle Alers, *Breakaway*, 2010
Rachel Lee, *Defending the Eyewitness*, 2014
Merline Lovelace, *Hot as Ice*, 2002
Carla Neggers, *Heron's Cove*, 2012
Dallas Schulze, *Addie and the Renegade*, 1996

917

TONI BLAKE (Pseudonym of Toni Herzog)

Love Me If You Dare

(New York: Avon, 2015)

Series: Coral Cove Series. Book 2
Story type: Contemporary; Series
Subject(s): Romances (Fiction); Hotels and motels; Real estate
Major character(s): Camille Thompson, Real Estate Agent; Reece Donovan, Hotel Owner (Happy Crab Motel)
Time period(s): 21st century; 2010s
Locale(s): Coral Cove, Florida

Summary: The Vanderhook Company wants to construct a new development—Windchime Resorts—in Coral Cove, Florida. But one stubborn hotel owner there refuses to sell his property. Vanderhook decides to send special acquisitions negotiator Camille Thompson to meet with Reece Donovan, owner of the Happy Crab Motel. Camille never fails to convince even the most reluctant property owners to accept her offers. But Reece is committed to his low-key life in Coral Cove, and he's determined to keep Vanderhook and Windchime Resorts from ruining the place that means so much to him. Camille is impressed by Reece's tenacity, although she's sure she'll win in the end. However, their long negotiations are complicated by the mutual attraction that grows between them. This novel is the second in the Coral Cove series.

Other books by the same author:
All I Want Is You, 2014
Half Moon Hill, 2013
Willow Springs, 2012
Holly Lane, 2011
Whisper Falls, 2010

Other books you might like:
Jennifer Bernard, *The Fireman Who Loved Me*, 2012
Jacquie D'Alessandro, *Summer at Seaside Cove*, 2011
Susan Donovan, *Sea of Love*, 2013
Rachel Gibson, *Rescue Me*, 2012
R.L. Mathewson, *Double Dare*, 2015
Candis Terry, *Sweetest Mistake*, 2013

918

MARIE BOSTWICK

The Second Sister

(New York: Kensington Books, 2015)

Subject(s): Sisters; Death; Friendship
Major character(s): Lucy Toomey, Political Figure

Romances

(campaigner), Sister (of Alice); Alice Toomey, Mentally Challenged Person (impaired), Sister (of Lucy)
Time period(s): 21st century; 2010s
Locale(s): Nilson's Bay, Wisconsin

Summary: Best-selling author Marie Bostwick delivers a tale of family, friendship, and second chances. Lucy Toomey left the small town of Nilson's Bay, Wisconsin, years ago. Alice, her older sister, became mentally impaired after an accident in her teens, and never left town. In her Wisconsin home she developed a sense of community and stability among a close group of friends who share an interest in quilting. Lucy, a political campaigner, lives a fast-paced life in Washington, DC, for many years. But when Alice suddenly dies, Lucy travels back to her quiet hometown. In Nilson's Bay, in accordance with Alice's will, Lucy moves into her sister's cottage and soon sees Alice's life in a new light. Soon, Alice's circle of friends shares the same affection for Lucy that the women had for Alice. As the women tell stories and share struggles, Lucy finds acceptance and support, and she realizes that Alice's gift to her is one that will last a lifetime.

Other books by the same author:
Apart at the Seams, 2014
Between Heaven and Texas, 2013
Ties That Bind, 2012
Threading the Needle, 2011
A Thread So Thin, 2010

Other books you might like:
Deborah Cloyed, *The Summer We Came to Life*, 2011
Meg Donohue, *How to Eat a Cupcake*, 2012
Jennifer Greene, *Sparkle*, 2006
Tanya Michaels, *The Good Kind of Crazy*, 2006
Camille Noe Pagan, *The Art of Forgetting*, 2011
Susan Strecker, *Night Blindness*, 2014

919

JOANNA BOURNE

Rogue Spy

(New York: Penguin Publishing Group, 2014)

Series: Spymaster Series. Book 5
Story type: Historical - Regency; Series
Subject(s): French Revolutionary Wars, 1792-1799; Espionage; Romances (Fiction)
Major character(s): Camille Leyland, Spy, Friend (Childhood friend of Pax); Thomas "Pax" Paxton, Friend (childhood friend of Camille), Spy
Time period(s): 19th century; 1810s
Locale(s): England

Summary: Camille Leyland and Thomas Paxton have a secret—and a secret past. As children, they were taken from their French homes and planted in English families as spies during the French Revolution. Thomas—Pax—has decided his honor will no longer allow him to live with what he did in the past, and he's come to England to face the consequences. Instead of execution, however, he's offered an opportunity to prove he truly is sorry for his past. This puts him squarely in the path of his child-

hood friend, Camille, who is on the trail of the same person Pax is seeking. Old feelings and new intrigue combine as Pax and Camille try to find their way through their complicated situation and back to each other. This is the fifth book in the Spymaster series.

Other books by the same author:
The Black Hawk, 2011
The Forbidden Rose, 2010
My Lord and Spymaster, 2008
The Spymaster's Lady, 2008

Other books you might like:
Zoe Archer, *Wicked Temptation*, 2014
Juliana Gray, *How to Tame Your Duke*, 2013
Marguerite Kaye, *Rumors That Ruined a Lady*, 2013
Vanessa Kelly, *How to Plan a Wedding for a Royal Spy*, 2015
Kate Moore, *Blackstone's Bride*, 2012

920

KELLY BOWEN

I've Got My Duke to Keep Me Warm

(New York: Forever, 2014)

Series: Lords of Worth Series. Book 1
Story type: Historical - Regency; Series
Subject(s): Romances (Fiction); History; England
Major character(s): Gisele Whitby, Woman, Spouse (estranged, of Adam Levire); Adam Levire, Nobleman (Marquess of Valence), Spouse (estranged, of Gisele Whitby), Fiance(e) (of Lady Julia Hextall); Lady Julia Hextall, Noblewoman (daughter of a duke), Fiance(e) (of Adam Levire); James "Jamie" Montcrief, Military Personnel (former cavalry officer), Bastard Son (of a duke)
Time period(s): 19th century; 1810s (1816)
Locale(s): England

Summary: In the first novel in the Lords of Worth series, a young lady plots revenge against her husband in 1816 England. Four years ago, Gisele Whitby was living with her abusive husband, Adam Levire, the Marquess of Valence, waiting for a chance to get away. When a fire broke out in London, Gisele took advantage of the opportunity and escaped. She was presumed dead, but in reality has started a new life away from her horrid husband. When Gisele learns that Levire is going to marry again, she decides she must protect his unsuspecting bride-to-be, Lady Julia Hextall, from the abuse she will suffer if the wedding takes place. Gisele employs Jamie Montcrief, a former cavalry officer, as an accomplice in her mission of vengeance. Although Gisele tries to keep her relationship with Jamie professional, she finds it hard not to mix business and pleasure. First novel.

Other books by the same author:
A Good Rogue Is Hard to Find, 2015
You're the Earl That I Want, 2015

Other books you might like:
Mary Balogh, *The Escape*, 2014

Liz Carlyle, *Never Deceive a Duke*, 2007
Eileen Dreyer, *Barely a Lady*, 2010
Julie Anne Long, *A Notorious Countess Confesses*, 2012
Mary Jo Putney, *No Longer a Gentleman*, 2012

921

KELLY BOWEN

A Good Rogue Is Hard to Find

(New York: Forever, 2015)

Series: Lords of Worth Series. Book 2
Story type: Historical - Regency; Series
Subject(s): England; Money; Wealth
Major character(s): William Somerhall, Nobleman, Son (of the Duchess of Worth); Eleanor, Noblewoman (Duchess of Worth), Mother (of William), Widow(er), Employer (of Jenn); Jenna Hughes, Companion (to Eleanor)
Time period(s): 19th century; 1810s (1817)
Locale(s): London, England

Summary: Kelley Bowan returns with the second Regency novel in her Lords of Worth historical romance series. Well-to-do William Somerhall moves in with his mother, Eleanor, the Dowager Duchess of Worth, to temper her recent eccentric behavior and save her from social ruin. He meets her young companion, Miss Jenna Hughes, and becomes suspicious of the young woman's motives in being with the duchess. William begins to closely monitor his mother's financial dealings. Jenna knows first-hand about poor merchants who struggle at the hand of wealthy nobles who refuse to pay their accounts. Now, with the help of William's mother, Jenna runs a successful undercover redistribution scheme: they swindle money from the wealthy to pay off the very merchants the nobles owe. Jenna is worried that William will uncover their secret, so she uses the art of seduction to distract him from the truth. To her surprise, William's willing to play along.

Other books by the same author:
I've Got My Duke to Keep Me Warm, 2014

Other books you might like:
Connie Brockway, *So Enchanting*, 2009
Manda Collins, *Why Earls Fall in Love*, 2014
Anne Gracie, *The Autumn Bride*, 2013
Anne Gracie, *His Captive Lady*, 2008
Sarah MacLean, *Ten Ways to Be Adored When Landing a Lord*, 2010

922

VALERIE BOWMAN

The Unlikely Lady

(New York: St. Martin's Press, 2015)

Series: Playful Brides Series. Book 3
Story type: Historical - Regency; Series
Subject(s): Romances (Fiction); Marriage; England
Major character(s): Jane Lowndes, Spinster; Lord Garrett Upton, Nobleman, Military Personnel
Time period(s): 19th century; 1810s (1816)
Locale(s): London, England

Summary: This Regency-era romance is the third novel in the Playful Brides series by Valerie Bowman. Jane Lowndes has no desire to marry. She's finds joy and contentment in her books alone. She's spent years trying to convince her mother that she's destined to stay a spinster—and that's the way she wants it. Lord Garrett Upton looks forward to enjoying life as a bachelor before settling down. When he meets Jane at a friend's wedding celebration, she doesn't hesitate to let Garrett know exactly how she feels about men of his kind. However, when the pair unknowingly crosses paths at a masquerade ball and shares a passionate kiss, their intentions of staying unattached and single are threatened by the mutual attraction they feel toward one another. Headstrong Jane is determined to stay far from the marriage altar, but when a beautiful widow seeks the attention of Garrett, she decides she might be ready to join the game of love after all.

Other books by the same author:
The Accidental Countess, 2014
The Unexpected Duchess, 2014
Secrets of a Runaway Bride, 2013
Secrets of a Scandalous Marriage, 2013
Secrets of a Wedding Night, 2012

Other books you might like:
Elizabeth Boyle, *If Wishes Were Earls*, 2014
Tessa Dare, *Romancing the Duke*, 2014
Vicky Dreiling, *How to Marry a Duke*, 2011
Jillian Hunter, *The Countess Confessions*, 2014
Kate Noble, *Follow My Lead*, 2011

923

VALERIE BOWMAN

The Accidental Countess

(New York: St. Martin's, 2014)

Series: Playful Brides Series. Book 2
Story type: Historical - Regency; Series
Subject(s): Romances (Fiction); British history, 1714-1815; Family
Major character(s): Lady Cassandra Monroe, Young Woman, Cousin (of Penelope); Penelope, Cousin (of Cassandra), Fiance(e) (intended, of Julian Swift); Julian Swift, Military Personnel (captain), Veteran (Napoleonic War), Fiance(e) (intended, of Penelope)
Time period(s): 19th century; 1810s (1815)
Locale(s): London, England

Summary: While Captain Julian Swift was away fighting against Napoleon's forces, he received meager correspondence from Penelope, the woman he intends to marry. Penelope's cousin, Cassandra Monroe, did write faithfully, however. And Cassandra has not given up hope that she can win Julian's heart before it's too late. When Julian arrives in London in 1815, he presents himself at Penelope's home. Cassandra intercepts him, however, and concocts a plot to steer Julian away from Penelope. She directs Julian to a house party, where he

Romances

presumes he will meet his reluctant future wife. Meanwhile, Cassandra assumes the role of the fictitious Patience Bunbury and proceeds to use her charms on Julian. Cassandra succeeds in distracting Julian from Penelope, but now Julian is falling in love with a woman who doesn't exist. She must reveal her true identity eventually, but Cassandra fears how Julian will react when he knows he's been duped. This novel is the second in the Playful Brides series.

Other books by the same author:
The Accidental Countess, 2014
The Unexpected Duchess, 2014
Secrets of a Runaway Bride, 2013
Secrets of a Scandalous Marriage, 2013
Secrets of a Wedding Night, 2012

Other books you might like:
Sophie Barnes, *The Scandal in Kissing an Heir*, 2013
Tessa Dare, *A Night to Surrender*, 2011
Kieran Kramer, *Dukes to the Left of Me, Princes to the Right*, 2010
Kate Noble, *The Game and the Governess*, 2014
Olivia Parker, *At the Bride Hunt Ball*, 2008

924

ELIZABETH BOYLE

The Viscount Who Lived Down the Lane

(New York: Avon Publishing, 2014)

Series: Rhymes with Love Series. Book 4
Story type: Historical; Series
Subject(s): Interpersonal relations; Loneliness; Romances (Fiction)
Major character(s): Louisa Tempest, Young Woman, Heroine, Sister (of Lavinia); Pierson Stratton, Nobleman (Viscount Wakefield), Recluse, Veteran (injured in war); Lavinia Tempest, Sister (of Louisa), Debutante (of the London Season); Hannibal, Cat (of Louisa)
Time period(s): 19th century; 1810s
Locale(s): London, England

Summary: Author Elizabeth Boyle returns with the fourth novel in the Rhymes with Love series. At the behest of their late godmother, Louisa Tempest and her twin sister, Lavinia, travel to London to be introduced to society and find suitable husbands. Shrouded by a family scandal, Louisa hopes for the best for her sister, but she willingly resigns herself to the lonely life of a spinster. Louisa's well-laid plans are derailed when her cat, Hannibal, continually harasses their neighbor Pierson Stratton, Viscount Wakefield. A war injury and the death of his best friend have left Pierson physically and emotionally crippled. Louisa feels guilty for the mayhem her cat has caused and, sensing how isolated and lonely Pierson is, takes it upon herself to help. Her meddling causes havoc in Pierson's life, his home, and his heart. Will Louisa be able to heal Pierson, or will her family scandal threaten to ruin their budding happiness?

Other books by the same author:
And the Miss Ran Away with the Rake, 2013

If Wishes Were Earls, 2013
Along Came a Duke, 2012
Lord Langley Is Back in Town, 2011
Mad about the Duke, 2010

Other books you might like:
Liz Carlyle, *Never Lie to a Lady*, 2007
Tessa Dare, *A Week to be Wicked*, 2012
Shana Galen, *If You Give a Rake a Ruby*, 2013
Sally MacKenzie, *Surprising Lord Jack*, 2013
Sarah MacLean, *Never Judge a Lady by Her Cover*, 2014
Regina Scott, *The Courting Campaign*, 2013

925

TERRI BRISBIN (Pseudonym of Theresa S. Brisbin)

Rising Fire

(New York: Signet Eclipse, 2015)

Series: Stone Circles Series. Book 1
Story type: Fantasy; Historical - Medieval
Subject(s): Middle Ages; Fantasy; Supernatural
Major character(s): Brienne, Woman (gifted, fire manipulator), Lover (of William); William de Brus, Spy, Lover (of Brienne)
Time period(s): 13th century; 1280s (1286)
Locale(s): Scotland

Summary: Set in 1286 Scotland, this romantic fantasy novel is the first book in the Stone Circles series by award-winning author Terri Brisbin. For as long as she can remember, Brienne of Yester has had the ability to manipulate fire, but when her powers suddenly intensify, her life is forever changed. William de Brus is sent by the king to uncover the truth about an alleged connection between a nobleman and the fabled fire goddess, and along the way, he meets Brienne. He is captivated by her innocence and beauty, but William soon learns that she possess the very power he's been sent to destroy. Now, he is torn between honoring the king's orders and following his heart. As he fights to protect Brienne from the forces controlling her, darkness closes in on every side. Can the young lovers overcome the evil forces that threaten to destroy all of humanity?

Other books by the same author:
Yield to the Highlander, 2014
At the Highlander's Mercy, 2013
The Highlander's Dangerous Temptation, 2013
The Highlander's Stolen Touch, 2012
His Enemy's Daughter, 2011

Other books you might like:
Coreene Callahan, *Knight Avenged*, 2014
Mary Jo Putney, *Kiss of Fate*, 2004
Nora Roberts, *Dance of the Gods*, 2006
Nora Roberts, *Morrigan's Cross*, 2006
Nora Roberts, *Valley of Silence*, 2006

926

PAMELA BRITTON

Kissed by a Cowboy

(Don Mills, Ontario, Canada: Harlequin, 2015)

Story type: Contemporary; Ranch Life
Subject(s): Romances (Fiction); Animals; Ranch life
Major character(s): Wesley "Wes" Landon, Rancher; Jillian Thacker, Veterinarian
Time period(s): 21st century; 2010s
Locale(s): Via Del Caballo, California

Summary: Jillian Thacker has always had an uncanny ability to sense the needs of animals, a gift that has led to her job as the town vet for Via Del Caballo, California. Her talents brings her in contact with handsome rancher Wes Landon, the father to a newborn baby. He feels an almost instant connection to the beautiful veterinarian and hopes that perhaps she can become the final piece to completing his family. But can he reach her in the same way that she is able to communicate with her animal charges?

Other books by the same author:
A Cowboy's Angel, 2014
The Texan's Twins, 2014
A Cowboy's Christmas Wedding, 2013
A Cowboy's Pride, 2013
The Rancher's Bride, 2013

Other books you might like:
Carolyn Brown, *Just a Cowboy and His Baby*, 2012
Roz Denny Fox, *A Texas-Made Family*, 2008
Pamela Morsi, *Red's Hot Honky-Tonk Bar*, 2009
Diana Palmer, *Iron Cowboy*, 2008
Ann Roth, *A Rancher's Redemption*, 2014

927

LINDA BRODAY

Texas Mail Order Bride

(Naperville, Illinois: Sourcebooks, Incorporated, 2015)

Story type: Historical - American West
Subject(s): Romances (Fiction); Ranch life; Western fiction
Major character(s): Delta Dandridge, Southern Belle; Cooper Thorne, Rancher
Time period(s): 19th century; 1870s
Locale(s): Battle Creek, Texas

Summary: Set in 1878 Battle Creek, Texas, *Texas Mail Order Bride* is the first novel in Broday's Bachelors of Battle Creek series of historical westerns. When sassy Southern belle Delta Dandridge steps off the stagecoach, she insists that she is the mail order bride that straitlaced rancher Cooper Thorne has sent for. Though he denies ever having signed on for a marriage, Delta is desperate to leave her past behind and refuses to leave. Instead, she takes a position at a mercantile store and has soon charmed everyone in town—even Cooper Thorne. However, before the couple can commit themselves to one another, they must face threats created by the deliber-

ate slaughter of Cooper's cattle, an abusive neighbor, and their own fears about commitment.

Other books by the same author:
Redemption, 2005
The Cowboy Who Came Calling, 2003
Knight on the Texas Plains, 2002

Other books you might like:
Sandra Chastain, *The Mail Order Groom*, 2002
Leigh Greenwood, *The Reluctant Bride*, 2005
Lorraine Heath, *Texas Destiny*, 1997
Jill Marie Landis, *Summer Moon*, 2001
Bobbi Smith, *Runaway*, 2009

928

LINDA BRODAY

Twice a Texas Bride

(Naperville, Illinois: Sourcebooks, Incorporated, 2015)

Story type: Historical - American West; Western
Subject(s): Romances (Fiction); Western fiction; Ranch life
Major character(s): Callie Quinn, Lover (of Rand Sinclair); Rand Sinclair, Lover (of Callie Sinclair), Rancher
Time period(s): 19th century; 1870s
Locale(s): Battle Creek, Texas

Summary: The second novel in the Bachelors of Battle Creek series, *Twice a Texas Bride* focuses on the middle of the Sinclair brothers, Rand, a strong-willed rancher who spent much of his childhood in an orphanage and has become resistant to the touch of a woman. Callie Quinn has seen her own share of suffering and has good reason to not trust men, having been betrayed at various times by her stepfather, stepbrother, and boyfriend. When her twin sister dies, she grabs her nephew and flees, looking for the treasure box left to her by her mother that she hopes holds the key to their future. She returns to her childhood home —the same ranch recently purchased by Rand—with her sister's outlaw boyfriend in pursuit. When Rand finds the pair hiding in one of his buildings, he agrees to let them stay in exchange for Callie working as a cook on the ranch. However, before long, the pair begin to let their respective guards down and find surprising comfort and security in each other's company.

Other books by the same author:
Texas Mail Order Bride, 2015
Redemption, 2005
The Cowboy Who Came Calling, 2003
Knight on the Texas Plains, 2002

Other books you might like:
Lorraine Heath, *Texas Destiny*, 1997
Jill Marie Landis, *Come Spring*, 1992
Maggie Osborne, *Prairie Moon*, 2002
Kaki Warner, *Pieces of Sky*, 2010
Penelope Williamson, *The Outsider*, 1996

Romances

929

CAROLYN BROWN

Cowboy Boots for Christmas:
(Cowboy Not Included)

(Naperville, Illinois: Sourcebooks Casablanca, 2014)

Series: Burnt Boot, Texas Series. Book 1
Story type: Contemporary; Holiday Themes
Subject(s): Romances (Fiction); Western fiction; Ranch life
Major character(s): Finn O'Donnell, Veteran (Army sniper), Rancher, Friend (of Callie); Callie Brewster, Veteran, Friend (of Finn), Aunt (of Martin); Martin, Nephew (of Callie), Witness (of murder)
Time period(s): 21st century; 2010s
Locale(s): Burnt Boot, Texas

Summary: This holiday romance novel is the first book in the Burnt Boot, Texas series from best-selling author Carolyn Brown. Retired army sniper Finn O'Donnell looks forward to celebrating a quiet and peaceful holiday season at his new ranch on the outskirts of Burnt Boot, Texas. His peaceful plans are interrupted, however, when former soldier and friend Callie Brewster shows up with her nephew Martin in tow. Martin, who witnessed a murder, is seeking protection. Instead of entering Martin into a witness protection program, Callie turns to the only man she can trust—Finn. But the anonymity they're looking for is hard to come by in a small town like Burnt Boot, where rumors and rumblings spread quickly throughout the community. When Finn, Callie, and Martin find themselves in the middle of an ongoing feud between two of Burnt Boot's families, the quiet Christmas Finn was hoping for turns into one spirited holiday season.

Other books by the same author:
The Cowboy's Mail Order Bride, 2014
Daisies in the Canyon, 2014
How to Marry a Cowboy, 2014
Long, Hot Texas Summer, 2014
The Red-Hot Chili Cook-Off, 2014

Other books you might like:
Janet Dailey, *Calder Pride*, 1999
Linda Lael Miller, *Montana Creeds: Tyler*, 2009
Pamela Morsi, *Red's Hot Honky-Tonk Bar*, 2009
Vicki Lewis Thompson, *Bachelor Father*, 2012
Pat Warren, *Stranded on the Ranch*, 1998

930

KARMA BROWN

Come Away with Me

(Toronto, Canada: Mira, 2015)

Story type: Family Saga
Subject(s): Marriage; Grief; Death
Major character(s): Tegan Lawson, Mother (Wife of Tegan); Gabe Lawson, Father (Husband of Tegan)
Time period(s): 21st century; 2010s

Locale(s): Italy; Thailand; Hawaii, United States; Chicago, Illinois

Summary: Tegan Lawson and her husband, Gabe, are enjoying an idyllic life together—a happiness that is about to expand with the addition of their first child. However, after a tragic car accident on Christmas Eve changes everything, their marriage comes under enormous stress, and Tegan blames Gabe for their suffering. Brown's novel charts the couple's emotional and physical paths toward healing as they take an around-the-world tour (which they call their "Jar of Spontaneity") to try to recapture the love that originally brought them together. Together, they ride elephants in Thailand, sample Italy's best wines, and relax on the beaches of Hawaii. Over time Tegan and Gabe begin to overcome their grief and re-experience the joys of being married again. First novel.

Other books you might like:
Rochelle Alers, *Beyond Business*, 2005
Suzanne Brockmann, *Into the Fire: A Novel*, 2008
Sandra Brown, *A Secret Splendor*, 1983
Kristi Gold, *The Only Man for Her*, 2012
Susan Wiggs, *Table for Five*, 2005

931

HESTER BROWNE

Honeymoon Hotel

(New York: Gallery Books, 2014)

Story type: Contemporary
Subject(s): Hotels and motels; Weddings; Work environment
Major character(s): Rosie McDonald, Planner; Joe Bentley Douglas, Hotel Worker, Manager
Time period(s): 21st century; 2010s
Locale(s): London, England

Summary: Rosie McDonald has done much to turn around the declining reputation of the once-renowned Bonneville Hotel since she joined the staff as a wedding planner. With her fastidious attention to detail, Rosie has all but single-handedly reinvented an aging hotel that once played host to the social elite and was one of London's most sought-after wedding venues. Regardless of her accomplishments, however, ambitious Rosie is still eager to advance her career. She's well on her way to doing just that when the Bonneville's owner appoints his son Joe as the hotel's new manager. Almost instantly, Rosie and the freewheeling Joe find themselves butting heads. Worst of all, this monkey wrench in Rosie's plans comes right on the verge of the biggest, most important wedding the hotel has ever held. Will Rosie be able to keep it together and stay on her high-trajectory career path, or will Joe's meddling send her crashing back to square one?

Other books by the same author:
The Runaway Princess, 2012
Swept Off Her Feet, 2011
The Finishing Touches, 2009
The Little Lady Agency and the Prince, 2008
Little Lady, Big Apple, 2007

Other books you might like:
Dana Bate, *The Girls' Guide to Love and Supper Clubs*, 2013
Megan Caldwell, *Vanity Fare: A Novel of Lattes, Literature, and Love*, 2013
Laura Florand, *The Chocolate Heart*, 2013
Ali McNamara, *From Notting Hill with Love...Actually*, 2012
Linda Yellin, *What Nora Knew*, 2014

932

GRACE BURROWES

The First Kiss

(Naperville, Illinois: Sourcebooks Casablanca, 2015)

Series: Sweetest Kisses Series. Book 2
Story type: Contemporary; Series
Subject(s): Romances (Fiction); Single parent family; Musicians
Major character(s): Vera Waltham, Musician (classical pianist), Divorced Person, Spouse (former, of Donal MacKay), Mother (of Twyla), Widow(er) (of Alexander Waltham); Alexander Waltham, Spouse (deceased, of Vera), Father (of Twyla); Twyla Waltham, 8-Year-Old, Daughter (of Vera and Alexander); Trent Knightley, Lawyer, Brother (of James Knightley); James Knightley, Lawyer, Brother (of Trent Knightley); Donal MacKay, Spouse (former, of Vera)
Time period(s): 21st century; 2010s
Locale(s): Maryland, United States

Summary: Vera Waltham, a classic pianist and single mother of eight-year-old Twyla, has not been lucky in love. Her first husband—Twyla's father, Alexander—died. Her second marriage—to Donal MacKay—ended in divorce. Vera's lawyer Trent Knightley, whom she trusts implicitly, has guided her through the long and painful divorce process. She is not interested in starting another relationship any time soon, but Trent's brother James, who is also an attorney, falls for Vera and pursues her relentlessly. As Vera cares for Twyla and focuses on her career, she endures James's advances and continued harassment from Donal. When Vera begins receiving unsettling threats, however, she seeks help from James even though she knows about his questionable past. This novel is the second in the Sweetest Kisses series.

Other books by the same author:
Kiss Me Hello, 2015
A Single Kiss, 2015
The Captive, 2014
The Laird, 2014
The Traitor, 2014

Other books you might like:
Robyn Carr, *The Homecoming*, 2014
Robyn Carr, *One Wish*, 2015
Brenda Novak, *Come Home to Me*, 2014
Hope Ramsay, *Last Chance Family*, 2014
JoAnn Ross, *Castaway Cove*, 2013
Susan Wiggs, *Candlelight Christmas*, 2013

933

GRACE BURROWES

Kiss Me Hello

(Naperville, Illinois: Sourcebooks Casablanca, 2015)

Series: Sweetest Kisses Series. Book 3
Story type: Contemporary; Series
Subject(s): Romances (Fiction); Rural life; Foster children
Major character(s): Sidonie Lindstrom, Woman, Foster Parent (of Luis); Luis, Boy, Foster Child (of Sidonie); MacKenzie "Mac" Knightley, Lawyer, Worker (farrier), Neighbor (of Sidonie)
Time period(s): 21st century; 2010s
Locale(s): Maryland, United States

Summary: Sidonie Lindstrom is definitely not looking for love when she moves to the Maryland countryside with her foster son, Luis. She just wants to make a new start, but that is proving difficult since she was relying on money that hasn't been made available to her yet. Sidonie is not fond of lawyers, and she shares this opinion readily with her new neighbor, MacKenzie Knightley, who comes to shoe her horses. Mac, who enjoys his solitude and privacy, doesn't reveal to Sidonie that he's a lawyer as well as a farrier. Mac isn't interested in romance, but he can't help being attracted to Sidonie. He makes his feelings known, but Sidonie seems resistant to his advances. As Sidonie tries to discern her feelings for Mac, she also deals with Luis's problematic caseworker. This novel is the third in the Sweetest Kisses series.

Other books by the same author:
The First Kiss, 2015
A Single Kiss, 2015
The Captive, 2014
The Laird, 2014
The Traitor, 2014

Other books you might like:
Robyn Carr, *The Hero*, 2013
Marcia Evanick, *Mistletoe Bay*, 2007
Marcia Evanick, *A Misty Harbor Wedding*, 2006
Kieran Kramer, *You're So Fine*, 2015
Hope Ramsay, *Last Chance Family*, 2014
Christie Ridgway, *Make Me Lose Control*, 2014

934

GRACE BURROWES

The Duke's Disaster

(Naperville, Illinois: Sourcebooks Casablanca, 2015)

Story type: Historical - Regency
Subject(s): Romances (Fiction); Courtship; Marriage
Major character(s): Araminthea "Thea" Collins, Lady; Noah Winters, Gentleman (Duke of Anselm)
Time period(s): 19th century; 1810s
Locale(s): England

Summary: Noah Winters, the handsome Duke of Anselm, has a aristocratic duty to produce an heir, a tiresome chore that he decides to approach with clinical logic. After preparing a list of suitable candidates, he finally

Romances

winnows down the list to a single eligible woman. Unfortunately, he discovers that his chosen wife has already become engaged to another. Rather than go through the whole miserable process again, he decides instead to simply court the newly engaged woman's paid companion, Araminthea "Thea" Collins, who luckily happens to be the daughter of an earl. While Thea is not immediately enamored of either the Duke or his marriage proposal, she quickly recognizes that with his help, she can enable her own sister to avoid marrying against her wishes as she must do. The couple is married within the week, though their growing rapport is soon badly damaged by the revelation of a set of secrets held by both Thea and Noah. Can the estranged lovers find the strength needed to forgive the other's transgressions and ultimately find happiness in each other's arms?

Other books by the same author:
The First Kiss, 2015
Kiss Me Hello, 2015
Must Love Highlanders, 2015
A Single Kiss, 2015
The Sweetest Kiss, 2015

Other books you might like:
Suzanne Enoch, *Taming an Impossible Rogue*, 2012
Tina Gabrielle, *A Perfect Scandal*, 2010
Anne Gracie, *To Catch a Bride*, 2009
Amelia Grey, *The Duke in My Bed*, 2014
Lavinia Kent, *Bound by Temptation*, 2010
Kieran Kramer, *The Trouble with Princesses*, 2013

935

GRACE BURROWES

What a Lady Needs for Christmas

(Naperville, Illinois: Sourcebooks, Incorporated, 2014)

Series: MacGregor Series. Book 4
Story type: Historical - Victorian; Holiday Themes
Subject(s): Single parent family; Scotland; Scandals
Major character(s): Lady Joan Flynn, Heiress, Spouse (of Dante); Dante Hartwell, Widow(er), Businessman (mill owner), Single Father, Spouse (of Lady Joan)
Locale(s): Scotland

Summary: Lady Joan Flynn is eager to get out of Edinburgh and away from the looming scandal nipping at her heels. She has no memory of what happened after she met with a male acquaintance, but she fears evidence of the experience may soon become visible. Though the train out of town is full, a business owner she knows offers her space in the compartment he's taken for himself and his children. Dante Hartwell, a mill owner and single father, is on his way to the same holiday party in the country that Lady Joan will attend. He also has a problem, though a less dire one: He needs a high-born wife to improve the lot of his family and his business. The two soon hit upon a practical idea that solves both their problems: They will marry. Despite the circumstances, they are well-matched and seem destined for a comfortable relationship, until a blackmail threat puts their happiness at risk. This is the fourth book in the MacGregor series.

Other books by the same author:
A Duke's Disaster, 2015
The First Kiss, 2015
Kiss Me Hello, 2015
Must Love Highlanders, 2015
A Single Kiss, 2015

Other books you might like:
Suzanne Enoch, *The Devil Wears Kilts*, 2013
Suzanne Enoch, *Rogue with a Brogue*, 2014
Tina Gabrielle, *A Perfect Scandal*, 2010
Donna Grant, *Wicked Highlander*, 2010

936

JACI BURTON

Hope Burns

(New York: Jove Books, 2014)

Series: Hope Series. Book 3
Story type: Contemporary; Series
Subject(s): Family relations; Interpersonal relations; Love
Major character(s): Molly Burnett, Young Woman, Girlfriend (ex-girlfriend of Carter), Sister (of Emma); Carter Richards, Young Man, Boyfriend (ex-boyfriend of Molly); Emma Burnett, Bride (to be), Sister (of Molly)
Time period(s): 21st century; 2010s
Locale(s): Hope, Oklahoma

Summary: Author Jaci Burton returns to Hope, Oklahoma, in the third entry in the Hope series. This novel explores the relationship between Molly Burnett and Carter Richards. Molly has successfully avoided going back home to Hope—and seeing Carter, her ex-high school sweetheart—for 12 years. When Molly's sister announces she is getting married, Molly must return home and inevitably face Carter and the secret she fled from so long ago. And when Molly's mom gets injured, and Molly stays in Hope to help, she can't avoid Carter any longer. The chemistry between the couple reignites, and Molly and Carter can't resist each other. But will the secret Molly is keeping and the heartbreak of the past prompt her to run away again?

Other books by the same author:
Hope Flames, 2014
Hope Ignites, 2014
Straddling the Line, 2014
One Sweet Ride, 2013
Thrown by a Curve, 2013

Other books you might like:
Victoria Alexander, *The Prince's Bride*, 2001
Sylvia Day, *Entwined with You*, 2013
Abbi Glines, *When I'm Gone*, 2015
Jo Leigh, *Tangled Sheets*, 1999
Kate Meader, *Feel the Heat*, 2013
Vicki Lewis Thompson, *After Hours*, 2003

937

JACI BURTON

Love After All

(New York, New York: Jove, 2015)

Story type: Contemporary - Mainstream
Subject(s): Romances (Fiction); Dating (Social customs)
Major character(s): Chelsea Gardner, Teacher, Lover (of Sebastian Palmer); Sebastian "Bash" Palmer, Restaurateur, Lover (of Chelsea Gardner), Divorced Person
Time period(s): 21st century; 2010s
Locale(s): United States

Summary: High school math teacher Chelsea feels likes she been out with enough guys that she knows what makes them tick, and, frankly, she's tired of the dating carousel; she won't settle for anything less than husband material in her next partner. So she compiles a ten-point list of qualities that any potential boyfriend must absolutely have—almost none of which can be used to describe bar owner Sebastian "Bash" Palmer. Recognizing that Chelsea's list is a dead end, he nonetheless signs on to help her find the "perfect" man to prove that she is going about relationships the wrong way. Though he himself is not in the market for a long term relationship, he cannot deny the chemistry that exists between them—chemistry that makes him wonder if perhaps he is the one with the skewed priorities.

Other books by the same author:
Play by Play, 2015
Quarterback Draw, 2015
Hope Burns, 2014
Hope Ignites, 2014
Hope Flames, 2013

Other books you might like:
Susan Andersen, *No Strings Attached*, 2014
Lorelei Brown, *Ahead in the Heat*, 2015
Susan Mallery, *Chasing Perfect*, 2010
Jill Shalvis, *Simply Irresistible*, 2010
Shannon Stacey, *All He Ever Desired*, 2013

938

MARY BURTON

Cover Your Eyes

(New York: Zebra Books, 2014)

Series: Morgans of Nashville Series. Book 1
Story type: Mystery; Police Procedural
Subject(s): Serial murders; Law enforcement; Law
Major character(s): Rachel Wainwright, Lawyer (defense attorney for Jeb), Colleague (of Deke); Deke Morgan, Detective—Homicide, Colleague (of Rachel); Jeb Jones, Convict, Client (of Rachel)
Time period(s): 21st century; 2010s
Locale(s): Nashville, Tennessee

Summary: This romantic thriller is the first installment in the Morgans of Nashville series by best-selling author Mary Burton. Defense attorney Rachel Wainwright is convinced her client, Jeb Jones, isn't guilty of the crime he was convicted of 30 years ago, but Detective Deke Morgan is reluctant to run the DNA test Rachel has requested. His late father was the police officer who arrested Jones for the brutal murder of Annie Dawson, and he's confident the tests will confirm Jones's guilt. But when several women are murdered in the same fashion as Annie, Rachel and Deke both believe Annie's real killer is still on the loose. Rachel and Deke work to uncover the truth and quickly learn that someone is just as determined to keep the truth hidden—and will do anything to make sure it stays that way. Meanwhile, a mutual respect between Rachel and Deke turns into shared attraction.

Other books by the same author:
Be Afraid, 2015
You're Not Safe, 2014
No Escape, 2013
The Seventh Victim, 2013
Before She Dies, 2012

Other books you might like:
Allison Brennan, *See No Evil*, 2007
Pamela Callow, *Damaged*, 2010
Kendra Elliot, *Bridged*, 2015
Laura Griffin, *Unforgivable*, 2010
Brenda Novak, *Trust Me*, 2008
Sharon Sala, *Wild Hearts*, 2015
Debra Webb, *Anywhere She Runs*, 2010

939

SHANNON K. BUTCHER

Edge of Betrayal

(New York: Signet Eclipse, 2014)

Series: Edge Series. Book 4
Story type: Contemporary; Series
Subject(s): Romances (Fiction); Interpersonal relations; Mystery
Major character(s): Mira Sage, Mercenary (undercover), Colleague (of Adam); Adam Brink, Mercenary (undercover), Colleague (of Mira)
Time period(s): 21st century; 2010s
Locale(s): Dallas, Texas

Summary: This romantic suspense novel is the fourth book in the Edge series by best-selling author Shannon K. Butcher. Mira Sage works for the Edge, an undercover operation working to stop the threats of the deadly Threshold Project. At the hands of the evil Dr. Stynger, the experiments carried out by the Threshold Project have ruined the lives of countless people. Mira has developed a database of the project's victims—victims she's desperately trying to save. But to help them, she'll need the aid of a former Threshold employee, Adam Brink, a man she's never trusted. She believes Adam is a traitor, but when she learns their goals are more similar than she thought, Mira realizes the man she can't trust is now the man she can't resist.

Other books by the same author:
Binding Ties, 2015
Willing Sacrifice, 2014

Romances

Falling Blind, 2013
Edge of Sanity, 2012
Razor's Edge, 2011

Other books you might like:
Maya Banks, *Long Road Home*, 2011
Shannon K. Butcher, *Razor's Edge*, 2011
Elle Kennedy, *Midnight Rescue*, 2012
Lindsay McKenna, *Wolf Haven*, 2014
Sharon Sala, *Wild Hearts*, 2015
Stephanie Tyler, *Unbreakable*, 2013

940

CANDACE CAMP

Pleasured

(New York, New York: Pocket Books, 2015)

Subject(s): Romances (Fiction); Scotland
Major character(s): Damon, The Earl of Mardoun, Leader, Widow(er); Meg Munro, Healer
Time period(s): 19th century; 1800s
Locale(s): Kinclannoch, Scotland

Summary: The second book of the Secrets of the Loch Trilogy by Candace Camp, *Pleasured* begins with the arrival of Damon, the Earl of Mardoun, to his family estate in the small community of Kinclannoch in the Scottish highlands. There he meets the village healer, Meg Munro, a stubborn and fiery woman who has yet to meet the man she believes to be worthy of her love. When the Earl's daughter grows desperately sick, he calls upon Meg to heal her. Their time together is electric and before long, he begins a lengthy pursuit of the free-spirited Scotswoman. Eventually, she begins to return his affection, but can their mutual love overcome his obligation to marry someone of his own status?

Other books by the same author:
Treasured, 2014
Impetuous, 2013
The Marrying Season, 2013
A Summer Seduction, 2012
A Winter Scandal, 2011

Other books you might like:
Diana Gabaldon, *The Scottish Prisoner*, 2011
Susan King, *The Raven's Wish*, 2011
Julianne MacLean, *Claimed by a Highlander*, 2011
Lynsay Sands, *To Marry a Scottish Laird*, 2014
Joan Wolf, *The Scottish Lord*, 2014

941

ANNA CAMPBELL

A Scoundrel by Moonlight

(New York: Forever, 2015)

Series: Sons of Sin Series. Book 4
Story type: Historical - Regency; Series
Subject(s): Romances (Fiction); Sisters; Scandals
Major character(s): Nell Trim, Sister (of Dorothy); James Fairbrother, Nobleman (Marquess of Leath); Dorothy, Sister (of Nell)
Time period(s): 19th century; 1820s (1828)
Locale(s): Yorkshire, England

Summary: Set in 1828 England, this Regency romance novel is the fourth installment in the Sons of Sin series by award-winning author Anna Campbell. Nell Trim is desperate to expose the wild ways of James Fairbrother, the Marquess of Leath. After breaking the hearts of countless young women—and bringing scandal to her sister Dorothy—Nell wants nothing more than to bring James to justice. When James finds Nell in his family's library looking for his diary of secret love affairs, he wants to throw her out immediately, but his mother takes Nell in as her personal companion. Sparks fly as Nell gets to know the man she thought she hated. Soon, Nell questions whether he's the scoundrel Dorothy made him out to be, or if he's trying to lure her in as part of another one of his schemes.

Other books by the same author:
What a Duke Dares, 2014
Days of Rakes and Roses, 2013
A Rake's Midnight Kiss, 2013
Seven Nights in a Rogue's Bed, 2012
Midnight's Wild Passion, 2011

Other books you might like:
Liz Carlyle, *The Earl's Mistress*, 2014
Eileen Dreyer, *Barely a Lady*, 2010
Elizabeth Essex, *After the Scandal*, 2014
Cecilia Grant, *A Lady Awakened*, 2012
Lisa Kleypas, *Devil in Winter*, 2006

942

ROBYN CARR

One Wish

(Don Mills, Ontario, Canada: Mira, 2015)

Series: Thunder Point Series. Book 7
Story type: Contemporary; Series
Subject(s): Romances (Fiction); Ice skating; Flowers
Major character(s): Grace Dillon, Woman (also known as Izzy Banks), Skater (former), Store Owner (florist); Troy Headly, Teacher (high school)
Time period(s): 21st century; 2010s
Locale(s): Thunder Point, Oregon

Summary: In the seventh novel in the Thunder Point series, Grace Dillon has come to the coastal community of Thunder Point, Oregon, to make a fresh start. She used to be the professional ice skater known as Izzy Banks, but now Grace just wants to run her flower shop and enjoy a peaceful life away from the crazy world of competitive skating. The move also serves another purpose—it puts her far from her mother, with whom Grace shares a strained relationship. Grace isn't interested in a serious romance, but when high school teacher Troy Headly proposes that they date casually, she can't resist. Their no-strings-attached arrangement proves to be more complicated than they expected, however. Grace and Troy realize they have true feelings for one another, but Grace's mother may ruin everything when she arrives in Thunder Point.

Other books by the same author:
A New Hope, 2015
The Chance, 2014
The Homecoming, 2014
The Promise, 2014
The Hero, 2013

Other books you might like:
Grace Burrowes, *The First Kiss*, 2015
Kieran Kramer, *You're So Fine*, 2015
Susan Mallery, *Hold Me*, 2015
Brenda Novak, *Come Home to Me*, 2014
Jill Shalvis, *Forever and a Day*, 2012
Sherryl Woods, *Harbor Lights*, 2009

943

KENDRA LEIGH CASTLE

Every Little Kiss

(New York, New York: Signet, 2015)

Story type: Contemporary
Subject(s): Romances (Fiction); Weddings; Love
Major character(s): Emma Henry, Lover (of Seth Andersen), Sister (of Sam Henry), Planner; Seth Andersen, Veteran, Police Officer, Lover (of Emma Henry)
Time period(s): 21st century; 2010s
Locale(s): Harvest Cove, United States

Summary: In the second book of Kendra Leigh Castle's Harvest Cove series, event planner Emma Henry is considered to be the most normal—albeit tense—member of her family, which is a role she adopted after the death of her father at twelve. His untimely death also contributed to her controlling nature and fear of commitment. So when she unwinds in dramatic fashion at her sister's bachelorette party, she is unprepared for the consequences—especially the news that everyone in town now thinks she spent the night with police officer Seth Andersen. For his part, Seth was relieved to find a small town to settle down in after his military service ended, but he is unprepared for the realities of small town gossip and particularly the beautiful woman at the center of all the talk. But to his surprise, he begins to believe there might be something to a possible romance with Emma after all.

Other books by the same author:
One of These Nights, 2015
For the Longest Time, 2014
Immortal Craving, 2013
Midnight Reckoning, 2012
Shadow Rising, 2012

Other books you might like:
Catherine Bybee, *Not Quite Dating*, 2012
Brenda Jackson, *One Winter's Night*, 2012
Susan Mallery, *Before We Kiss*, 2014
Candis Terry, *Something Sweeter*, 2014
Teri Wilson, *Unmasking Juliet*, 2014

944

MANDA COLLINS

A Good Rake Is Hard to Find

(New York: St. Martin's Press, 2015)

Series: Lords of Anarchy Series. Book 1
Story type: Mystery; Regency
Subject(s): Accidents; Gangs; British history, 1815-1914
Major character(s): Leonora "Nora" Craven, Sister (of Jonathan), Fiance(e) (of Freddy); Jonathan Craven, Accident Victim, Brother (of Nora); Lord Frederick "Freddy" Lisle, Fiance(e) (of Nora), Rake, Nobleman
Time period(s): 19th century; 1810s
Locale(s): England

Summary: This novel is the first installment from the Lords of Anarchy series by Manda Collins. Miss Leonora "Nora" Craven still grieves for her beloved brother, Jonathan, who was killed in a carriage accident. Nora feels certain that the driving club to which her brother belonged, the Lords of Anarchy, had something to do with his death—if only she could figure out what. Fortunately, Nora knows someone who can help her. Unfortunately, that someone is Lord Frederick "Freddy" Lisle, to whom she was once engaged. Freddy agrees to come to Nora's aid, and he has a plan: they will pose as an engaged couple once again to give Nora access to the Lords of Anarchy. The Lords are not to be messed with, however, and Nora soon puts herself in danger. Even more dangerous are the old feelings that Nora notices bubbling up inside her. But she isn't sure she can trust Freddy with her heart again.

Other books by the same author:
Why Earls Fall in Love, 2014
Why Lords Lose Their Hearts, 2014
How to Entice an Earl, 2013
Why Dukes Say I Do, 2013
How to Romance a Rake, 2012

Other books you might like:
Jo Beverley, *To Rescue a Rogue*, 2006
Madeline Hunter, *The Surrender of Miss Fairbourne*, 2012
Sabrina Jeffries, *To Wed a Wild Lord*, 2011
Vanessa Kelly, *Secrets for Seducing a Royal Bodyguard*, 2014
Sarah MacLean, *No Good Duke Goes Unpunished*, 2013

945

JAY CROWNOVER (Pseudonym of Jennifer M. Voorhees)

Rowdy

(New York: HarperCollins Publishers, 2014)

Series: Marked Men Series. Book 5
Story type: Contemporary; Series
Subject(s): Sisters; Art; Romances (Fiction)
Major character(s): Salem Cruz, Manager (Tattoo shop), Friend (childhood, of Rowdy), Sister (of Poppy); Rowland "Rowdy" St. James, Artist (Tattoo), Friend

(sidebar) Romances

(Childhood friend of Salem and Poppy); Poppy Cruz, Sister (of Salem), Friend (childhood friend of Rowdy)
Time period(s): 21st century; 2010s
Locale(s): Denver, Colorado

Summary: Salem Cruz was raised to be the quintessential minister's daughter—sweet, quiet, obedient. But Salem had the heart of a rebel and was never good enough to please her father. As soon as she was able, she fled Loveless, Texas, and left her parents and little sister Poppy behind. The break was so complete she didn't even go back when Poppy got married. After wandering around the country gathering experience and tattoos, Salem is offered a dream gig managing one of the hottest tattoo shops around—The Marked in Denver, Colorado. She almost passes it up until she sees the profile of one of the artists there—a young man she grew up next to, who taught her how to draw, and is now quite grown up and handsome. Rowland St. James—nicknamed Rowdy—makes a living from his drawing hobby now, but he does his nickname credit. He also headed out of Loveless after the girl he loved—Salem's little sister, Poppy—told him he wasn't good enough for her. Since then he's been living wild and free, with no interest in women. When Salem and Rowdy are reunited, she's interested but he's not. But he could be—at least until Poppy shows up. This is the fifth book in the Marked Men series.

Other books by the same author:
Asa, 2015
Better When He's Bold, 2015
Better When He's Bad, 2014
Nash, 2014
Rome, 2014

Other books you might like:
Chelsea M. Cameron, *My Sweetest Escape*, 2014
Jennifer Dawson, *Take a Chance on Me*, 2014
Katie Lane, *Make Mine a Bad Boy*, 2011
Kelsie Leverich, *A Beautiful Distraction*, 2014
Susan Lyons, *Sex on the Slopes*, 2010

946

VICTORIA DAHL (Pseudonym of Victoria Grondahl)

Flirting with Disaster

(Don Mills, Ontario, Canada: Harlequin, 2015)

Story type: Contemporary
Subject(s): Romances (Fiction); Suspense; Deception
Major character(s): Isabelle West, Artist, Lover (of Tom Duncan); Tom Duncan, Lover (of Isabelle West), Agent (of the US Marshall's Office)
Time period(s): 21st century; 2010s
Locale(s): Jackson Hole, Wyoming

Summary: US Deputy Marshall Tom Duncan is in Jackson Hole, Wyoming to help protect the safety of a judge presiding over an important case. As part of his duties, he goes door-to-door in the judge's neighborhood to notify the residents of the judge's presence. However, when he meets prickly artist Isabelle West, he senses that she is hiding something, which instantly puts her on his radar. For Isabelle, the Marshall's operation is a disaster, as she had sought out remote Jackson Hole as a means of starting over and getting away from her past—a past that sneakily clever Tom has every chance of uncovering. Nonetheless, despite the danger he represents to her, she can't help feeling a strong emotional connection to him. When he finally does learn her secret, will he protect her, or be forced to do his duty as an officer of the law? *Flirting with Disaster* is the second book in the Jackson: Girls' Night Out series.

Other books by the same author:
Taking the Heat, 2015
Looking for Trouble, 2014
So Tough to Tame, 2013
Too Hot to Handle, 2013
Close Enough to Touch, 2012

Other books you might like: *Justice at Cardwell Ranch*, 2012
Pamela Clare, *Breaking Point*, 2011
Cynthia Eden, *Fear for Me: A Novel of the Bayou Butcher*, 2013
Kendra Elliott, *Chilled*, 2012
Aimee Thurlo, *Secrets of the Lynx*, 2012

947

B.J. DANIELS (Pseudonym of Barbara Heinlein)

Wild Horses

(Don Mills, Ontario, Canada: Harlequin, 2015)

Series: Montana Hamiltons Series. Book 1
Story type: Ranch Life; Series
Subject(s): Western fiction; Ranch life; Romances (Fiction)
Major character(s): Olivia "Livie" Hamilton, Fiance(e) (of Cooper), Abuse Victim; Cooper Barnett, Rancher, Fiance(e) (of Livie)
Time period(s): 21st century; 2010s
Locale(s): Beartooth, Montana

Summary: This romantic suspense novel is the first installment in the Montana Hamiltons series by best-selling author B.J. Daniels. Olivia "Livie" Hamilton is engaged to hard-working Cooper Barnett, but she's keeping a secret that could change their lives forever. Livie was caught in a terrible snow storm and rescued by a man who took advantage of the situation by drugging her. Several months later, when Livie learns she's pregnant, she's worried about what she doesn't remember about that night and uncertain who the father is. Threats from an anonymous blackmailer force Livie to tell Cooper the truth about what happened the night of her accident—and that the baby she's carrying might not belong to him. Livie is hopeful that Cooper will protect her despite the outcome, but when the blackmailer's scheme takes on new facets, even a love as strong as the bond Livie and Cooper share is tested. This is the first title in the Montana Hamiltons series.

Other books by the same author:
Lone Rider, 2015
Atonement, 2014
Mercy, 2014
Forsaken, 2013

Justice at Cardwell Ranch, 2012

Other books you might like:
Cindy Dees, *Close Pursuit*, 2014
Kat Martin, *Desert Heat*, 2004
Karen Robards, *Heartbreaker*, 1997
Jennifer Ryan, *At Wolf Ranch*, 2015
Jennifer Ryan, *When It's Right*, 2015

948

B.J. DANIELS (Pseudonym of Barbara Heinlein)

Deliverance at Cardwell Ranch

(Don Mills, Ontario, Canada: Harlequin, 2014)

Series: Cardwell Ranch Series. Book 7
Story type: Contemporary; Ranch Life
Subject(s): Ranch life; Romances (Fiction); Memory
Major character(s): Austin Cardwell, Police Officer (deputy sheriff); Unnamed Character, Patient, Amnesiac, Woman
Time period(s): 21st century; 2010s
Locale(s): Big Sky, Montana

Summary: Best-selling author B.J. Daniels delivers the seventh installment of the Cardwell Ranch contemporary romance series. During the worst blizzard Montana has seen in years, deputy sheriff Austin Cardwell rescues a mysterious—and beautiful—traveler. She has no recollection of who she is, where she's from, or why she's running. When a man arrives at the hospital claiming to be her husband, the fear in her eyes lets Austin know that her life is in danger. Now, determined to protect the beauty he rescued, Austin keeps a constant watch over her, and feelings of trust—and passion—develop between them. Can Austin uncover the truth of her identity before her dangerous past catches up with them?

Other books by the same author:
Wild Horses, 2015
Atonement, 2014
Mercy, 2014
Wedding at Cardwell Ranch, 2014
Forsaken, 2013

Other books you might like:
Carolyn Brown, *Mistletoe Cowboy*, 2012
Susan Donovan, *I Want Candy*, 2012
Katie Lane, *A Match Made in Texas*, 2014
Julia London, *Return to Homecoming Ranch*, 2014
Tawny Weber, *A SEAL's Salvation*, 2014

949

ELLE DANIELS

He's No Prince Charming

(New York: Forever, 2014)

Series: Ever After Series. Book 1
Story type: Historical - Regency; Romantic Suspense
Subject(s): Brothers and sisters; Deception; Fairy tales
Major character(s): Marcus Bradley, Fiance(e) (jilted), Nobleman (Marquis of Fleetwood), Abuse Victim (by his father), Hero (scarred); Danielle "Danni" Strafford, Heroine (witty), Heiress (in disguise), Businesswoman (of elopement agency/bookstore); Caroline Bradley, Sister (of Marcus)
Locale(s): Gretna Green, England

Summary: This is Elle Daniel's debut novel and the first book in the Ever After Series. Inspired by the "Beauty and the Beast" fairy tale, this book features the Marquis of Fleetwood, Marcus Bradley, as the Beast, and Danielle "Danni" Strafford as "Beauty"—an heiress with a secret identity. True to tale, Marcus is a physically and emotionally scarred man due to the cruelty of his late father. To protect his family's fortune and save his sister from an arranged marriage, Marcus must find a bride who is also an heiress. When Marcus's wealthy intended runs away and elopes with her true love—with the help of Danni and her secret elopement business—Marcus blackmails Danni to help him find a new bride. As they try to acquire an heiress by any means, Danni starts to understand the wounds underneath Marcus's harsh behavior and begins to fall in love with the beast. Having been unloved and mistreated all his life, Marcus is resistant to Danni. Will Danni be able to make Marcus overcome his past and make him believe he is truly worthy of love? Or will Danni's secret ultimately tear them apart?

950

TESSA DARE (Pseudonym of Eve Ortega)

Say Yes to the Marquess

(New York: Avon, 2014)

Series: Castles Ever After Series. Book 2
Story type: Historical - Regency; Series
Subject(s): Romances (Fiction); History; Family
Major character(s): Clio Whitmore, Woman, Fiance(e) (of Piers Brandon); Piers Brandon, Diplomat, Fiance(e) (of Clio Whitmore), Nobleman (Marquess of Granville), Brother (of Rafe Brandon); Rafe Brandon, Boxer, Rake, Brother (of Piers Brandon)
Time period(s): 19th century; 1810s
Locale(s): England

Summary: When Clio Whitmore inherits a castle from an uncle, she decides it is time to end her eight-year engagement to Piers Brandon, Marquess of Granville. She is a woman of means now, and she doesn't have to rely on a husband's social and financial standing. Because Piers is away on a diplomatic assignment, Clio asks his brother, Rafe, who has control of Piers's affairs, to end the engagement officially. Rafe, a boxer, wants the marriage to proceed, however. He is in love with Clio, and he knows that his brother can give her a good life. To persuade Clio to marry Piers, Rafe promises that he will set a date and plan a perfect wedding down to the tiniest detail. But as the wedding plans proceed for Clio and her absent groom-to-be, Rafe finds it harder to keep his feelings for his brother's fiancee a secret. This is the second novel in the Castles Ever After series.

Other books by the same author:
Romancing the Duke, 2014
Any Duchess Will Do, 2013

A Lady by Midnight, 2012
A Week to Be Wicked, 2012
A Night to Surrender, 2011

Other books you might like:
Sophie Barnes, *The Danger of Tempting an Earl*, 2014
Elizabeth Boyle, *Along Came a Duke*, 2012
Kieran Kramer, *If You Give a Girl a Viscount*, 2011
Elizabeth Michels, *How to Lose a Lord in 10 Days or Less*, 2014
Tracy Anne Warren, *The Princess and the Peer*, 2012

951

JO DAVIS

On the Run

(New York, New York: Signet, 2015)

Story type: Romantic Suspense
Subject(s): Romances (Fiction); Criminals; Gangs
Major character(s): Angel Silva, Sister (of Rab Silva), Criminal, Lover (of Tonio Salvatore); Tonio Salvatore, Detective, Lover (of Angel Silva); Rab Silva, Brother (of Angel Silva), Criminal, Gang Member
Time period(s): 21st century; 2010s
Locale(s): Sugarland, Tennessee

Summary: Police detective Tonio Salvatore is focused on his job as an officer in the Sugarland police department after his fiancee left him at the altar and ran off with his best friend. Burned by love, he releases his sexual frustrations through brief romantic encounters—one of which leads to his introduction to dangerous gang leader Rab Silva. As the Sugarland Police Department has been trying to investigate Silva for years without success, they seize upon Tonio's chance meeting by having him go undercover as "Tonio Reyes" within Rab's gang to find evidence of his crimes. Though Tonio is committed to getting the job done, he finds himself distracted by Rab's beautiful sister despite the danger this creates for the both of them. Angel Silva finds herself equally attracted to the newest member of her brother's gang, but has long harbored the desire to leave her criminal life behind her. So what will she do when she discovers Tonio's real identity? This is the fourth book in the Sugarland Blue series.

Other books by the same author:
In His Sights, 2014
Hot Pursuit, 2013
Sworn to Protect, 2013
Line of Fire, 2010
Ride the Fire, 2010

Other books you might like:
Pamela Callow, *Damaged*, 2010
Laura Griffin, *Far Gone*, 2014
Brenda Novak, *Trust Me*, 2008
Karen Rose, *Count to Ten*, 2007
Marylu Tyndall, *Forsaken Dreams*, 2013

952

JUSTINE DAVIS (Pseudonym of Justine Dare)

Operation Power Play

(Don Mills, Ontario, Canada: Harlequin Paperback, 2015)

Story type: Romantic Suspense
Subject(s): Romances (Fiction); Murder; Crime
Major character(s): Brett Dunbar, Detective, Widow(er); Sloan Burke, Widow(er); Cutter, Dog
Time period(s): 21st century; 2010s
Locale(s): United States

Summary: Book five of Davis's Cutter's Code series once again features the intuitive dog Cutter and his attempts to unite lost souls in love connections. The figures in question here are police officer Brett Dunbar and Sloan Burke, two emotionally scarred figures who each lost their spouses in tragic circumstances. Brett's wife was murdered by a criminal he had pursued, while Sloan's husband died in the line of duty as a war hero. As a result, Brett is unwilling to put anyone else he cares for in danger, while Sloane is frightened about becoming involved with someone in a potentially dangerous profession. Nonetheless, circumstances conspire to bring them together—initially just to resolve some simple paperwork issues, but larger threats force them to uncover the identity of a murderer. While both Brett and Sloan struggle to overcome their fears about falling in love again, luckily they are working with a highly perceptive dog who seems determined to bring them together.

Other books by the same author:
Heart of the Hawk, 2015
Rebel Prince, 2015
Wild Hawk, 2015
Operation Unleashed, 2014
Skypirate, 2014

Other books you might like:
Sharon Hamilton, *SEAL of My Heart*, 2014
Elle James, *SEAL's Honor*, 2014
Geri Krotow, *Navy Rescue*, 2014
Anne Marsh, *Burns So Bad*, 2013
Dana Marton, *Guardian Agent*, 2011

953

SIERRA DEAN

Perfect Catch

(Cincinnati, Ohio: Samhain Publishing, 2015)

Story type: Contemporary - Mainstream
Subject(s): Romances (Fiction); Baseball
Major character(s): Alice Darling, Lover (of Alex Ross), Sports Figure, Single Mother; Alex Ross, Baseball Player, Lover (of Alice Darling)
Time period(s): 21st century; 2010s
Locale(s): Lakeside, Florida

Summary: As a baseball umpire in the minor leagues, Alice Darling is a woman in a traditionally male field, so she knows that mixing romance with business is career suicide. In addition, having grown up in a town with a minor league team, Alice already has made the mistake of trying to date a baseball player—an error she has no intention of repeating. So why does Alex Ross, the newly demoted catcher for the San Francisco Felons, distract her so much? Against her better judgment, she allows herself to fall for Alex, though when rumors begin to spread about their possible relationship, it puts both her job and their potential future at risk. Can Alice allow herself to trust a baseball player—especially one who may only be in town for a short while—when giving into her desires may destroy her career? This is the second book in the Boys of Summer series.

Other books by the same author:
Bayou Blues, 2015
Winter, 2014
Autumn, 2013
Pitch Perfect, 2013
Secret Unleashed, 2013

Other books you might like:
Bella Andre, *Let Me Be The One*, 2013
Jaci Burton, *Changing the Game*, 2011
Jaci Burton, *Straddling the Line*, 2014
LuAnn McLane, *Pitch Perfect*, 2012
RaeAnne Thayne, *Willowleaf Lane*, 2013

954

HELENKAY DIMON

Falling Hard

(New York: HarperCollins, 2015)

Series: Bad Boys Undercover Series. Book 2
Story type: Adventure; Series
Subject(s): Espionage; Military life; Adventurers
Major character(s): Weston "West" Brown, Military Personnel, Agent (Special Ops); Alex Palmer, Doctor, Father (of Lexi); Lexi Turner, Daughter (of Alex)
Time period(s): 21st century; 2010s
Locale(s): Pakistan

Summary: In the second installment from HelenKay Dimon's Bad Boys Undercover series, the author continues the saga of the Alliance, a special task force comprising members of the CIA and Great Britain's MI-6. West Brown is ready for some rest and relaxation after the Alliance's last mission. But when he gets a call to save an American doctor in the mountains of Pakistan, West reluctantly goes to the doctor's rescue. When he arrives at the clinic, he finds the doctor's daughter instead. Lexi Turner has noticed movement in the hills surrounding the clinic, and she knows that something suspicious is going on. She notifies the Alliance, per her father Alex's instructions, but doesn't expect a man like West to show up. Now West must get Lexi out of Pakistan before criminal forces strike. But he and Lexi are distracted by the attraction they feel for each other—an attraction that puts them both in harm's way.

Other books by the same author:
Cornered, 2015
Playing Dirty, 2015
Running Hot, 2015

Only, 2014
Traceless, 2014

Other books you might like:
Cherry Adair, *Hush*, 2011
Suzanne Brockmann, *Flashpoint*, 2004
M.L. Buchman, *The Night Is Mine*, 2012
Dee Davis, *Double Danger*, 2012
Julie Ann Walker, *Hell on Wheels*, 2012

955

SIERRA DONOVAN

No Christmas Like the Present

(New York: Kensington Books, 2014)

Story type: Contemporary; Holiday Themes
Subject(s): Christmas; Romances (Fiction); Holidays
Major character(s): Lindsay Miller, Businesswoman; Fred, Man (messenger)
Time period(s): 21st century; 2010s
Locale(s): Lakeside, Colorado

Summary: Lindsay Miller discovers the magic of Christmas in this tale of family, forgiveness, and romance by Sierra Donovan. Lindsay stays busy each holiday season by making fudge, sending holiday cards, and giving gifts, but each year she finds that her long list of activities keeps her from enjoying a season meant to be filled with magic and wonder. When Fred, a strangely dressed man with a British accent, shows up at her front door, skeptical Lindsay isn't sure what to believe. Fred insists that he's a messenger sent to help her find the joy of Christmas. His mission is to help Lindsay right the wrongs of her past so she can fully enjoy her future, and he only has until midnight on Christmas Eve to do it. Along the way, Fred and Lindsay discover a deep attraction to one another, but falling in love is not a part of Fred's assignment.

Other books by the same author:
Meg's Confession, 2007
Love on the Air, 2004

Other books you might like:
Robyn Carr, *A Virgin River Christmas*, 2008
Richard Paul Evans, *The Mistletoe Promise*, 2014
Christine Flynn, *Her Holiday Prince Charming*, 2013
Anne Oliver, *Mistletoe Not Required*, 2013
RaeAnne Thayne, *A Cold Creek Noel*, 2012

956

EILEEN DREYER

Twice Tempted

(New York: Forever, 2014)

Series: Drake's Rakes Series. Book 5
Story type: Historical - Regency; Series
Subject(s): Romances (Fiction); British history, 1714-1815; Family
Major character(s): Lady Fiona Hawes, Young Woman, Twin (of Mairead), Sister (of Ian), Granddaughter (of

Romances

Marquess of Dourne); Mairead, Granddaughter (of Marquess of Dourne), Twin (of Fiona), Sister (of Ian); Ian, Brother (of Fiona and Mairead), Grandson (of Marquess of Dourne), Friend (of Alex Knight); Marquess of Dourne, Grandfather (of Fiona, Mairead, and Ian); Alex Knight, Nobleman (Lord Whitmore), Spy, Friend (of Ian)

Time period(s): 19th century; 1810s
Locale(s): England

Summary: When Alex Knight rescued twin sisters Fiona and Mairead Hawes and delivered them to the home of their grandfather, he thought he was doing what was best for the girls. But the Marquess of Dourne proved to be a heartless guardian, and he forced Fiona and Mairead from his home when their brother, Ian, was revealed to be a traitor to England. Although the twins are now entirely on their own, they make a meager living as teachers and have become self-sufficient. But Alex—a spy who was Ian's great friend— feels responsible for Fiona and Mairead's predicament, and he still remembers the single kiss he and Fiona shared long ago. He decides that he should find the sisters and return them to their proper place in society, even though that may not be what Fiona and Mairead want. Meanwhile, surprising news about Ian comes to light. This novel is the fifth in the Drake's Rakes series.

Other books by the same author:
Once a Rake, 2013
Always a Temptress, 2011
Never a Gentleman, 2011
Barely a Lady, 2010

Other books you might like:
Nita Abrams, *The Spy's Reward*, 2006
Joanna Bourne, *The Black Hawk*, 2011
Anna Campbell, *What a Duke Dares*, 2014
Elizabeth Essex, *After the Scandal*, 2014
Mary Jo Putney, *Not Quite a Wife*, 2014

957

CYNTHIA EDEN (Pseudonym of Cindy Roussos)

Confessions

(Don Mills, Ontario, Canada: Harlequin, 2015)

Series: Battling McGuire Boys Series. Book 1
Story type: Contemporary; Romantic Suspense
Subject(s): Romances (Fiction); Suspense; Love
Major character(s): Grant McGuire, Detective—Private, Veteran (former US Army Ranger), Lover (former, of Scarlett Stone); Scarlett Stone, Crime Suspect, Lover (former, of Grant McGuire)
Time period(s): 21st century; 2010s
Locale(s): Austin, Texas

Summary: It's been ten years since Scarlett Stone and Grant McGuire last saw one another. She had just graduated high school and was looking forward to college— and continuing her relationship with Grant. He was four years older and had decided he wanted to experience life beyond Texas. Grant went on to serve as a US Army Ranger, and he's now back in Austin working as a private detective. He's closing up the office after a long day

when Scarlett appears and asks desperately for his help. She tells Grant that she is being followed, and when the police show up and handcuff her, Grant finally understands Scarlett's predicament. She is being charged with a murder she swears she didn't commit, and she needs Grant to prove her innocence by identifying the real murderer. Grant's investigation is complicated by his romantic history with his beautiful client. This is the first novel in the Battling McGuire Boys series.

Other books by the same author:
Broken, 2015
Secrets, 2015
Twisted, 2015
Evidence of Passion, 2014
Once Bitten, Twice Burned, 2014

Other books you might like:
Laura Caldwell, *Claim of Innocence*, 2011
Suzanne Forster, *The Private Concierge*, 2008
Julie Garwood, *The Ideal Man*, 2011
Julie Garwood, *Sweet Talk*, 2012
Cindy Gerard, *Over the Line*, 2006

958

CYNTHIA EDEN

Twisted

(New York: Avon Books, 2015)

Series: LOST Series. Book 2
Story type: Contemporary; Mystery
Subject(s): Romances (Fiction); Suspense; Missing persons
Major character(s): Dean Bannon, FBI Agent (former), Agent (of Last Operation Search Team); Emma Castille, Con Artist
Time period(s): 21st century; 2010s
Locale(s): New Orleans, Louisiana

Summary: Best-selling author Cynthia Eden delivers the second novel in her LOST romantic suspense series. Former FBI agent Dean Bannon is a member of the Last Option Search Team (LOST), an organization that specializes in finding missing persons. When he travels to New Orleans to find a missing 16-year-old girl, he meets Emma Castille, a beautiful con artist with an uncanny sense of intuition. Independent Emma tempts no-nonsense Dean in more ways than one, and although he's wary because of Emma's sordid past, the chemistry between them is undeniable. When an intruder leaves a threatening message in Emma's home, suggesting that she's the abductor's next victim, Dean vows to protect her. As he watches Emma's every move, their attraction to one another deepens, and as more secrets are revealed, they realize they're both being targeted.

Other books by the same author:
Broken, 2015
Confessions, 2015
Midnight Sins, 2015
Secrets, 2015
Eternal Flame, 2014

Other books you might like:
Beverly Barton, *The Fifth Victim*, 2003

Tess Gerritsen, *The Surgeon*, 2001
Heather Graham, *Deadly Night*, 2008
Laura Griffin, *Twisted*, 2012
Hunter Morgan, *She'll Never Live*, 2004

959

CYNTHIA EDEN

Broken

(New York: HarperCollins, 2015)

Series: LOST Series. Book 1
Story type: Contemporary; Series
Subject(s): Serial murders; Memory disorders; Identity
Major character(s): Gabe Spencer, Agent (LOST team), Detective—Private, Veteran (former US Navy SEAL); Eve Gray, Amnesiac; Lady Killer, Murderer, Serial Killer
Time period(s): 21st century; 2010s
Locale(s): Dauphin Island, Alabama; Atlanta, Georgia

Summary: In the first novel from Cynthia Eden's LOST series, the author introduces readers to Gabe Spencer. A former US Navy SEAL, Gabe now leads the Last Option Search Team, or LOST, a group of agents to whom others turn when they have no other hope. When Eve Gray wakes up with no idea who she is, she seeks out Gabe to help her uncover her identity. Yet when Gabe sets eyes on Eve, he is chilled to his core because she looks exactly like a woman who was murdered. As Gabe helps Eve try to find out who she really is, he must also protect her from the Lady Killer, a murderer who is killing women who resemble Eve. Meanwhile, Gabe and Eve must fight their growing passion for each other, because it could put both of them at risk of being the Lady Killer's next victim.

Other books by the same author:
Confessions, 2015
Midnight Sins, 2015
Secrets, 2015
Eternal Flame, 2014
Playing with Fire, 2014

Other books you might like:
Shelley Coriell, *The Broken*, 2014
Tess Gerritsen, *The Surgeon*, 2001
Laura Griffin, *Twisted*, 2012
Linda Howard, *Dying to Please*, 2002
Anne Stuart, *The Widow*, 2001

960

KENDRA ELLIOT

Bridged

(Seattle, Washington: Montlake Romance, 2015)

Story type: Romantic Suspense
Subject(s): Romances (Fiction); Mystery; Serial murders
Major character(s): Ava McLean, Twin (of Jayne), Agent (of the FBI); Mason Callahan, Police Officer; Jayne McLean, Twin (of Ava), Mentally Ill Person

Time period(s): 21st century; 2010s
Locale(s): Portland, Oregon

Summary: In *Bridged*, the second book in the Mason Callahan series, a serial killer seems to be on the loose in Portland, Oregon, leaving his victims hanging from bridges throughout the city. After a congressman becomes his latest victim, the Oregon State Police are baffled by the lack of evidence at the crime scenes. FBI agent Ava McLean and her romantic partner, detective Mason Callahan, are both called in to help with the investigation, and together they try to unravel the many twists and mysteries that seem to surround the case. Adding to Ava's problems is the reemergence of Ava's mentally disturbed and drug addicted sister, whose boyfriend is somehow connected to the case. Battling through both the mystery of the murders, her insecurities about her sister, and her still-evolving relationship with Mason, Ava realizes that she has her hands full.

Other books by the same author:
Spiraled, 2015
Alone, 2014
Vanished, 2014
Buried, 2013
Chilled, 2012

Other books you might like:
Allison Brennan, *See No Evil*, 2007
Jaci Burton, *The Heart of a Killer*, 2011
Mary Burton, *Cover Your Eyes*, 2014
Jo Davis, *Sworn to Protect*, 2013
Lori Foster, *Run the Risk*, 2012
Maggie Shayne, *Deadly Obsession*, 2014

961

CHRISTINE FEEHAN

Viper Game

(New York: Penguin Group, 2015)

Series: GhostWalker Series. Book 11
Story type: Paranormal; Series
Subject(s): Romances (Fiction); Fantasy; Parapsychology
Major character(s): Wyatt Fontenot, Experimental Subject (GhostWalker), Brother (of Gator); Gator Fontenot, Experimental Subject (GhostWalker), Brother (of Wyatt); Le Poivre "Pepper" de Cayenne, Woman, Guardian (of three young girls)
Time period(s): 21st century; 2010s
Locale(s): United States

Summary: The 11th novel in the GhostWalker series follows the story of Wyatt Fontenot, a GhostWalker who attained psychic powers in a clandestine military experiment. Wyatt now possesses feline instincts and behaviors, but those talents have cost him dearly. Although he submitted to the government's experiment willingly, he underestimated the toll the experience would take on him or the underlying ambitions of those behind it. Now he is back in the swampland that is his home territory, reacquainting himself with the bayou's many secrets. He crosses paths with a beautiful woman named Le Poivre de Cayenne, aka Pepper, who may be able to put Wyatt's skills to use. Pepper is serving as guardian to three young girls, and although Wyatt doesn't know the nature of the threat, he helps Pepper in her mission to keep them safe. In the course of fulfilling their duty, Pepper and Wyatt recognize a dangerous attraction growing between them.

Other books by the same author:
Air Bound, 2014
Dark Wolf, 2014
Leopard's Prey, 2013
Magic Before Christmas, 2013
Samurai Game, 2012

Other books you might like:
Jennifer Ashley, *Shifter Mates*, 2015
Shannon K. Butcher, *Finding the Lost*, 2009
Jayne Castle, *Siren's Call*, 2015
Isabel Cooper, *Legend of the Highland Dragon*, 2013
Christina Dodd, *Wilder*, 2012
Jeaniene Frost, *The Beautiful Ashes*, 2014
Heather Graham, *The Dead Room*, 2007
Sherrilyn Kenyon, *Unleash the Night*, 2006
Lora Leigh, *Lion's Heat*, 2010
Lora Leigh, *The Man Within*, 2005
Kathleen Nance, *Phoenix Unrisen*, 2007
Terry Spear, *Jaguar Hunt*, 2014
Terry Spear, *Silence of the Wolf*, 2014

962

JUDI FENNELL

What a Woman Gets

(New York: Penguin Publishing Group, 2014)

Series: Manley Maids Series. Book 3
Story type: Contemporary; Romance
Subject(s): Romances (Fiction); Wealth; Employment
Major character(s): Liam Manley, Worker (Manley Maids), Brother; Cassidy Davenport, Heir—Dispossessed, Worker (for Liam), Socialite
Time period(s): 21st century; 2010s
Locale(s): California, United States

Summary: It started when the three Manley brothers lost a bet to their sister and were forced to join her housecleaning business. This means that Liam Manley must put up with women he would not normally go anywhere near, like the stuck-up, free-spending Cassidy Davenport. Liam grits his teeth and does his job, cleaning the house of the detestable woman, until her father cuts off her allowance. No income means no home, so the move could mean Liam is rid of Cassidy. Instead, he gives her a job. With the employer-employee tables turned, Liam gleefully anticipates teaching Cassidy a lesson or two. Free of her father's influence and able to let the real Cassidy loose for the first time, the young woman ends up surprising Liam. Still, things could get more messy than a maid can handle in this third book in the Manley Maids series.

Other books by the same author:
What a Woman, 2015
If the Shoe Fits, 2014
What a Woman Needs, 2014
What a Woman Wants, 2014

Beauty and the Best, 2012

Other books you might like:
Chelsea M. Cameron, *My Favorite Mistake*, 2013
Dakota Cassidy, *Burning Down the Spouse*, 2011
June Gray, *Surrender*, 2014
Deirdre Martin, *Straight Up*, 2010
Christina Skye, *A Home By the Sea*, 2011

963

MARIE FORCE

And I Love Her

(New York, New York: Berkley, 2015)

Story type: Contemporary - Mainstream
Subject(s): Romances (Fiction); Love; Family
Major character(s): Megan Kane, Waiter/Waitress; Hunter Abbott, Businessman, Accountant
Time period(s): 21st century; 2010s
Locale(s): Butler, Vermont

Summary: Megan Kane's life seems to be falling apart: first, Will Abbott, the man she thought she loved, fell for another woman, and now her sister has announced plans to move out of town and possibly close the diner where Megan works. This combination of news leaves Megan shattered, leading to an epic crying fest outside the diner one day. This is where Hunter Abbott finds her, and he recognizes an opportunity when he sees one. Hunter has been in love with Megan for as long as he can remember, but she has only ever had eyes for his younger brother. As the family "fixer"—that is, the man called in to fix all the personal and business problems that seem to constantly arise—Hunter has always worked to make sure that his family was taken care of, but now maybe it's time to take care of himself. *And I Love Her* is the fourth book in the Green Mountain series.

Other books by the same author:
Ask Me Why, 2015
Fatal Mistake, 2015
I Saw Her Standing There, 2014
Kisses After Dark, 2014
Let Me Hold Your Hand, 2014

Other books you might like:
Lacey Baker, *Homecoming*, 2013
Macy Beckett, *Make You Remember*, 2014
Jill Gregory, *Sunflower Lane*, 2014
Sydney Landon, *No Denying You*, 2014
LuAnn McLane, *Wildflower Wedding*, 2014

964

MARIE FORCE

I Saw Her Standing There

(New York: Berkley Sensation, 2014)

Series: Green Mountain Series. Book 3
Story type: Contemporary; Series
Subject(s): Friendship; Rural life; Family relations

Major character(s): Lucy Mulvaney, Lover (of Colton), Friend (of Cameron); Colton Abbott, Lover (of Lucy), Brother (of Will); Cameron, Friend (of Lucy), Girlfriend (of Will); Will Abbott, Boyfriend (of Cameron), Brother (of Colton)
Time period(s): 21st century; 2010s
Locale(s): Butler, United States

Summary: In the third book of the Green Mountain series, Colton Abbott and Lucy Mulvaney have kept their relationship a secret from their friends and family for some time now. New Yorker Lucy doesn't enjoy keeping things from her best friend, Cameron; however, Lucy is reluctant to tell Cameron that she is having an affair with the brother of Cameron's new boyfriend, Will. Meanwhile, Colton's family is starting to become suspicious. When Lucy and Colton decide to spend a long weekend at his family's lake house in Vermont, they are finally caught by Cameron and Will. Now that their relationship is no longer a secret, will they continue on as they once did? Or has the relationship lost its appeal now that it's out in the open? Included in this book is a short story based on the Green Mountain series.

Other books by the same author:
And I Love Her, 2015
Chance for Love, 2014
Gansett After Dark, 2014
Kisses After Dark, 2014
Meant for Love, 2013

Other books you might like:
Bella Andre, *From This Moment On*, 2011
Stephanie Bond, *Baby, Drive South*, 2011
Carolyn Brown, *Mistletoe Cowboy*, 2012
Catherine Bybee, *Single by Saturday*, 2014
Chelsea M. Cameron, *My Sweetest Escape*, 2014
Melody Carlson, *Once Upon a Winter's Heart*, 2014
Jill Gregory, *Sunflower Lane*, 2014
Karina Halle, *The Pact*, 2015
Karen Harper, *Forbidden Ground*, 2014
Megan Hart, *Precious and Fragile Things*, 2011
Crista McHugh, *Falling for the Wingman*, 2014
Christie Ridgway, *Take My Breath Away*, 2014
Nora Roberts, *Whiskey Beach*, 2013
Sherryl Woods, *Dogwood Hill*, 2014

965

LORI FOSTER

Holding Strong

(Don Mills, Ontario, Canada: Harlequin, 2015)

Story type: Contemporary
Subject(s): Romances (Fiction); Martial arts
Major character(s): Cherry Peyton, Lover (of Denver Lewis); Denver Lewis, Lover (of Cherry Peyton), Boxer (MMA fighter)
Time period(s): 21st century; 2010s
Locale(s): Warfield, Ohio

Summary: Featured as secondary characters in *No Limits*, the first book in Lori Foster's Ultimate series, Cherry Peyton and Denver Lewis are the focus of *Holding Strong*. Denver is a mixed martial arts fighter whose reputation is growing fast, enabling him to sign with a professional fighting organization, the SBC. Cherry, meanwhile, is a bubbly flirt whose outgoing exterior belies the pain that she feels inside as a result of a difficult childhood. Denver has long paid attention to Cherry, though he finds her flirtatious nature off-putting. Nevertheless, after a night together, they begin to rely on one another to a degree that neither has ever experienced before—a connection that will prove invaluable when Cherry's painful past begins to catch up with her once again. This is the second book in Lori Foster's Ultimate series.

Other books by the same author:
No Limits, 2015
Dash of Peril, 2014
Getting Rowdy, 2013
A Perfect Storm, 2012
Run the Risk, 2012

Other books you might like:
Jaci Burton, *Straddling the Line*, 2014
Rachel Gibson, *See Jane Score*, 2003
Deirdre Martin, *Icebreaker*, 2010
Melanie Scott, *Angel in Armani*, 2015
Jill Shalvis, *Slow Heat*, 2010

966

ADDISON FOX (Pseudonym of Frances Karkosak)

Silken Threats

(Don Mills, Ontario, Canada: Harlequin Paperback, 2015)

Story type: Romantic Suspense
Subject(s): Romances (Fiction)
Major character(s): Cassidy Tate, Store Owner; Tucker Buchanan, Engineer, Military Personnel; Violet Richardson, Store Owner, Friend; Lilah Castle, Friend, Store Owner; Max Baldwin, Businessman, Friend
Time period(s): 21st century; 2010s
Locale(s): Dallas, Texas

Summary: When Tucker Buchanan first encounters Cassidy Tate, he offers a comforting presence to Cassidy after the wedding store she co-owns with several friends is seemingly burgled. Though there is lot of minor damage, nothing seems to have been stolen. Nonetheless, she is grateful for the strong presence of Tucker, who although an ex-soldier, now works at a nearby engineering firm. Together, the pair deduce that the crime was likely the work of someone searching for something, rather than a robbery. As Tucker and his partner elect to help the bridal store owners help with cleanup, he also assists Cassidy uncover the decades-old mystery behind the initial break-in. Although at first just partners in an investigation, the pair find themselves developing feelings for one another, even as their investigation places them in ever-growing danger. First book in the Dangerous in Dallas series.

Other books by the same author:
Secret Agent Boyfriend, 2015

Tempting Target, 2015
The Manhattan Encounter, 2014
Just in Time, 2013
The London Deception, 2013

Other books you might like:
Jana DeLeon, *The Lost Girls of Johnson's Bayou*, 2012
Cynthia Eden, *Glitter and Gunfire*, 2013
Paula Graves, *Secret Assignment*, 2012
Rita Herron, *Cowboy in the Extreme*, 2012
Mallory Kane, *Gone*, 2013

967

MEGAN FRAMPTON

The Duke's Guide to Correct Behavior

(New York: Avon, 2014)

Series: Dukes Behaving Badly Series. Book 1
Story type: Historical - Victorian; Series
Subject(s): Romances (Fiction); British history, 1815-1914; Parenthood
Major character(s): Marcus, Nobleman (Duke of Rutherford), Single Father (of Rose); Rose, 4-Year-Old, Bastard Daughter (of Marcus); Lily Russell, Governess (to Rose)
Time period(s): 19th century; 1840s (1840)
Locale(s): London, England

Summary: Marcus is floundering in his new role as Duke of Rutherford. He has no interest in hosting proper parties, getting married, or starting a family. His reputation as a womanizer is well known, and he has fathered at least one illegitimate child. But Marcus's attitude begins to change when one of his unknown offspring—a four-year-old girl named Rose—is placed in his care after her mother dies. Marcus had paid Rose's mother a sum of money when he learned she was pregnant, but he didn't want to know anything about the child. Now Rose is a member of the duke's household, and Marcus must find a governess to take care of her. Lily Russell applies for the job and is immediately charmed by Rose and smitten with Marcus. The duke is also attracted to Lily and, with her help, he tries to change his rakish ways. This novel is the first in the Dukes Behaving Badly series.

Other books by the same author:
A Singular Lady, 2005

Other books you might like:
Sophie Barnes, *The Trouble with Being a Duke*, 2013
Elizabeth Boyle, *And the Miss Ran Away with the Rake*, 2013
Tessa Dare, *Any Duchess Will Do*, 2013
Elizabeth Michels, *Must Love Dukes*, 2014
Sophia Nash, *Between the Duke and the Deep Blue Sea*, 2012

968

ELYSSA FRIEDLAND

Love and Miss Communication

(New York: HarperCollins, 2015)

Story type: Contemporary
Subject(s): Computers; Technology; Interpersonal relations
Major character(s): Evie Rosen, Lawyer, Granddaughter (of Bette); Bette Rosen, Grandmother (of Evie)
Time period(s): 21st century; 2010s
Locale(s): New York, New York

Summary: Evie Rosen is an up-and-coming attorney who seems to be forever single. When she gets bad news about her career and an ex-boyfriend, she realizes how tired she is of always looking at a screen. She decides to put away her Blackberry, stay away from social media, shut down her laptop, and live her life technology-free. Soon, her computer-free plan works: she begins to meet people and starts to cherish the friends and family she already has. When her grandmother, Bette, is diagnosed with cancer, Evie makes a special point to spend time with her instead of calling and texting her. Now that Evie has learned to appreciate real life rather than the virtual world, she opens herself up to finding her true path and a man who will walk it with her.

Other books you might like:
Meg Cabot, *Boy Meets Girl*, 2004
Megan Caldwell, *Vanity Fare: A Novel of Lattes, Literature, and Love*, 2013
Beth Kendrick, *My Favorite Mistake*, 2004
Rainbow Rowell, *Attachments*, 2011
Linda Yellin, *What Nora Knew*, 2014

969

JEANIENE FROST

Bound by Flames

(New York: HarperCollins Publishing, 2015)

Series: Night Prince Series. Book 3
Story type: Vampire Story
Subject(s): Vampires; Marriage; Revenge
Major character(s): Vlad, Vampire, Spouse (of Leila); Leila, Spouse (of Vlad), Vampire
Time period(s): 21st century; 2010s
Locale(s): Romania

Summary: Being married to the world's most famous vampire, Vlad, isn't easy, but that's what Leila is facing. Nothing in her past, not even her years with the carnival, has prepared Leila for being a freshly minted vampire and the bride of the Prince of Darkness. And nothing prepared her for the danger she would face when Vlad's old enemy realizes Leila is the famed vampire's weakness. As strong and dangerous as Vlad himself, this enemy will stop at nothing to get at Vlad. At the same time, the vampire's desire to protect his wife is driving her away. Vlad truly loves his new wife, and that might be the end of both of them. This is the third book in the Night Prince series.

Other books by the same author:
Twice Tempted, 2013
Once Burned, 2012
Devil to Pay, 2011
Happily Never After, 2011
One Foot in the Grave, 2008

Other books you might like:
Lara Adrian, *Crave the Night*, 2014
Sharon Ashwood, *Possessed by an Immortal*, 2014
Sharon Ashwood, *Ravenous*, 2009
Elaine Bergstrom, *Blood Alone*, 1990
Christine Feehan, *Air Bound*, 2014
Nancy Holzner, *Firestorm*, 2015
Linda Howard, *Blood Born*, 2010
Larissa Ione, *Immortal Rider*, 2011
Kristen Painter, *Blood Rights*, 2011
Mimi Jean Pamfiloff, *Accidentally Married to...a Vampire?*, 2013
Kate Pearce, *Kiss of the Rose*, 2010
Lynsay Sands, *The Immortal Who Loved Me*, 2015
Maggie Shayne, *Bloodline*, 2009
Nalini Singh, *Archangel's Shadows*, 2014
Susan Sizemore, *Blood2Blood*, 2014
Kerrelyn Sparks, *Wild About You*, 2012
J.R. Ward, *The King*, 2014
J.R. Ward, *Lover Awakened*, 2006
J.R. Ward, *Lover Mine*, 2010
J.R. Ward, *The Story of Son*, 2015

970

SHANA GALEN (Pseudonym of Shane Bolks)

Earls Just Want to Have Fun

(Naperville, Illinois: Sourcebooks Casablanca, 2015)

Series: Covent Garden Cubs Series. Book 1
Story type: Historical - Regency; Series
Subject(s): Romances (Fiction); British history, 1714-1815; Social class
Major character(s): Marlowe, Young Woman (also known as Elizabeth), Thief (member of Covent Garden Cubs); Brook Derring, Investigator, Brother (of Maxwell Derring); Maxwell Derring, Nobleman (Earl of Dane), Brother (of Brook Derring), Guardian (of Marlowe); Satin, Criminal, Leader (of Covent Garden Cubs)
Time period(s): 19th century; 1810s
Locale(s): London, England

Summary: Marlowe makes a living in Regency-era London as a member of the Covent Garden Cubs. Led by a man known as Satin, the Cubs are pickpockets and con artists. They are hungry and dirty, and they have little hope of escaping the streets. But when Brook Derring, an investigator, finds Marlowe and takes an interest in her, Marlowe gets a chance to make a new start. Brook puts Marlowe in the care of his brother, Maxwell Derring, Earl of Dane. Maxwell reluctantly takes the wild girl in and tries to educate and tame her. As Maxwell

teaches Marlowe how to act like a lady, he is surprised to find that he is attracted to the former pickpocket. But Marlowe—who may be the long-lost Lady Elizabeth Grafton—teaches Maxwell a few lessons of her own when they return to London's underbelly to confront Satin. This novel is the first in the Covent Garden Cubs series.

Other books by the same author:
Love and Let Spy, 2014
Sapphires Are an Earl's Best Friend, 2014
If You Give a Rake a Ruby, 2013
True Spies, 2013
When You Give a Duke a Diamond, 2012

Other books you might like:
Jo Beverley, *Tempting Fortune*, 1995
Sabrina Jeffries, *Dance of Seduction*, 2003
Johanna Lindsey, *A Loving Scoundrel*, 2004
Julie Anne Long, *To Love a Thief*, 2005
Rachelle Morgan, *A Scandalous Lady*, 2003

971

JESSICA GILMORE

His Reluctant Cinderella

(Don Mills, Ontario, Canada: Harlequin, 2014)

Story type: Contemporary
Subject(s): Family relations; Single parent family; Parent-child relations
Major character(s): Castor Rafferty, Businessman (Vice CEO of Rafferty's Stores), Brother (of Polly); Clara Castleton, Businesswoman (owner of Castleton Concierge Consultancy), Single Mother (to daughter Summer); Summer, Daughter (of Clara); Polly Rafferty, Sister (of Castor), Client (of Clara), Missing Person
Time period(s): 21st century; 2010s
Locale(s): London, England

Summary: In this contemporary romance novel by author Jessica Gilmore, Castor Rafferty is the globetrotting Vice CEO of Rafferty's Stores. The only thing he values more than his business reputation is his personal freedom. Commitment is not for Castor until he meets single mom and businesswoman Clara Castleton. Clara has no time for men. She has no time to waste on a relationship because she is too busy raising her daughter, Summer, and running Castleton Concierge Consultancy. Despite both their issues with commitment, Castor and Clara find themselves falling in love. Clara doubts that she will be able to fit into Castor's jet-setting, socialite lifestyle, however, and Castor doubts his ability to become a stepfather to Clara's daughter. Will the couple be able to overcome their fears of commitment? Will their love be enough?

Other books by the same author:
The Return of Mrs. Jones, 2014
Summer with the Millionaire, 2014

Other books you might like:
Stacy Connelly, *Small-Town Cinderella*, 2014
Caroline Cross, *Cinderella's Tycoon*, 1999
Shelley Galloway, *Cinderella Christmas*, 2014

Romances

Jessica Hart, *Cinderella's Wedding Wish*, 2009
Karen Rose Smith, *His Country Cinderella*, 2011

972

ABBI GLINES

When I'm Gone

(New York: Atria Paperbacks, 2015)

Series: Rosemary Beach Series. Book 11
Story type: Contemporary; Series
Subject(s): Family; Abuse; Sexual abuse
Major character(s): Mase Colt-Manning, Young Man, Rancher; Reese Ellis, Young Woman, Housekeeper
Time period(s): 21st century; 2010s
Locale(s): Rosemary Beach, United States

Summary: Mase Colt-Manning and Reese Ellis have been searching their whole lives for a place where they can fit in and just feel comfortable. Little did either of them know that that place was with one another. After finally fleeing from an abusive family situation, Reese is thrilled to land a job working as a housemaid for a wealthy couple in Rosemary Beach. As it happens, Reese's new employers are Mase's parents. Though he enjoys his blue-collar life as a Texas rancher and rarely keeps in contact with his family, Mase decides to pay a visit to his parents' sprawling beach home. It is there that he is awakened one morning by a beautiful young maid named Reese, who is startled to find a barely clothed cowboy in the house. They hit it off immediately, but Reese finds her livelihood on the line when she causes an accident from which Mase must rescue her. Though her past experience with men leave her feeling a little leery about Mase's intentions, Reese wonders if she's finally found a guy with a real heart of gold.

Other books by the same author:
Misbehaving, 2014
One More Chance, 2014
Rush Too Far, 2014
Take a Chance, 2014
You Were Mine, 2014

Other books you might like:
Kate Angell, *No Strings Attached*, 2013
Jaci Burton, *Hope Burns*, 2014
Lori Foster, *No Limits*, 2014
Susan Mallery, *Sweet Spot*, 2008
Erin McCarthy, *Final Lap*, 2014

973

JO GOODMAN (Pseudonym of Joanne Dobrzanski)

This Gun for Hire

(New York: Berkley Sensation, 2015)

Story type: Historical; Western
Subject(s): Miners; Romances (Fiction); Family relations
Major character(s): Quill McKenna, Lawyer (for Ramsey), Bodyguard (for Ramsey), Lover (of Calico); Katherine "Calico" Nash, Bounty Hunter, Bodyguard (for Ann), Lover (of Quill); Ramsey Stonechurch, Mine Owner, Client (of Quill), Father (of Ann); Ann Stonechurch, 17-Year-Old, Student, Daughter (of Ramsey), Client (of Calico)
Time period(s): 19th century; 1880s (1888)
Locale(s): Stonechurch, Colorado

Summary: Set in 1888 Colorado, this Western romance novel follows the repercussions of death threats against a wealthy mining family. Quill McKenna serves as attorney and bodyguard for wealthy mine owner Ramsey Stonechurch. Having survived a number of attempts against his life, Ramsey fears his enemies might soon come for his 17-year-old daughter, Ann. Quill arranges for renowned bounty hunter Katherine "Calico" Nash to move to the family's estate and guard Ann under the guise of being an academic tutor. As Quill and Calico spend time together at the Stonechurch estate, the attraction between them grows. Their secret affair continues as threats against the Stonechurch dynasty increase. Quill and Calico investigate labor issues at the mine and gain insight into the growing unrest throughout the community, and soon, they discover that the family's enemies are far closer than they thought.

Other books by the same author:
In Want of a Wife, 2014
True to the Law, 2013
The Last Renegade, 2012
A Place Called Home, 2011
Never Love a Lawman, 2009

Other books you might like:
Lori Austin, *Beauty and the Bounty Hunter*, 2012
Lori Austin, *An Outlaw in Wonderland*, 2013
Millie Criswell, *Dangerous*, 1998
Maggie Osborne, *The Seduction of Samantha Kincade*, 1995
Patricia Potter, *Defiant*, 1995

974

LINDA GOODNIGHT

The Memory House

(Don Mills, Ontario, Canada: Harlequin, 2015)

Story type: Contemporary; Historical - American Civil War
Subject(s): Romances (Fiction); Hotels and motels; Fathers
Major character(s): Julia Presley, Hotel Owner, Mother; Eli Donovan, Father, Criminal; Alex Donovan, Son (of Eli Donovan); Charlotte Reed Portland, Farmwife, Mother (of Benjamin Portland); Edgar Portland, Farmer, Father (of Benjamin Portland), Military Personnel; William "Will" Gadsden, Military Personnel (Union Army Captain); Benjamin Portland, Son (of Charlotte and Edgar)
Time period(s): 21st century; (2010s); 19th century; 1860s
Locale(s): Honey Ridge, Tennessee

Summary: Linda Goodnight's *The Memory House* relates two interconnected stories, one in present day and one taking place during the Civil War. Set in Honey Ridge, Tennessee, both stories chart the unlikely romantic connections between disparate men and women suffering through personal crises. The Civil War-era story is concerned with the tale of Charlotte Portland, the bride of a Confederate soldier. Mother to Benjamin and wife of Edgar, Charlotte is charged with caring for Edgar's family business, the Peach Orchard Farm. As the War escalates, the farm is forced to serve as the local residence of several Union soldiers, including the kindly Captain William Gadsen. Though a Yankee, William is everything Charlotte's husband is not: attentive, interested, and affectionate. Despite their mutual attraction, the couple recognizes that they cannot act upon their feelings, and Will heads back to war. A century and a half later, the Peach Orchard Farm has become Julia Presley's Peach Farm Inn, her home and business. Into her life comes Eli Donovan, a newly released ex-con, who comes to town to be near the son he only recently discovered existed. Julia hires Eli to help her renovate the Inn, and the couple discovers they are developing feelings for one another. However, a tragedy forces Eli to become a larger factor in his son's life, complicating the burgeoning emotional connection between Eli and Julia. Adding insight to their complicated relationship is a cache of letters they discover during the renovation that date back to the Civil War and relates the secret and intimate correspondence between a certain Charlotte Portland and Union Captain William Gadsden.

Other books by the same author:
Cowboy under the Mistletoe, 2014
The Lawman's Honor, 2014
Rancher's Refuge, 2013
Sugarplum Homecoming, 2013
A Touch of Grace, 2010

Other books you might like:
Robyn Carr, *The Hero*, 2013
Debbie Macomber, *Love Letters*, 2014
Curtiss Ann Matlock, *Love in a Small Town*, 1997
Emilie Richards, *Rising Tides*, 1997
LaVyrle Spencer, *Small Town Girl*, 1997

975

ANNE GRACIE

The Spring Bride
(New York: Berkley Sensation, 2015)

Series: Chance Sisters Series. Book 3
Story type: Historical - Regency; Series
Subject(s): Social class; Marriage; Poverty
Major character(s): Jane Chance, Woman, Fiance(e) (of Lord Cambury); Zachary Black, Crime Suspect, Spy (former), Nobleman; Lord Cambury, Nobleman, Fiance(e) (of Jane), Wealthy
Time period(s): 19th century; 1810s (1817)
Locale(s): London, England

Summary: Anne Gracie delivers the third novel in her Chance Sisters historical romance series. Jane Chance makes preparations for her entrance into London's high society. Jane's parents married for love, but were disowned by their families and died in poverty. Determined to move past a life of hardship, Jane is willing to sacrifice love for the promise of stability. Her plans are interrupted, however, when she happens upon a stray dog and meets the mysterious and attractive Zachary Black. A former spy, Zachary is facing murder charges, and until his name is cleared, he's on strict orders to lay low—but he's also a man used to getting what he wants. When Jane accepts the proposal of wealthy Lord Cambury, Zachary is forced to make his move. Will Jane do the very thing she swore she wouldn't and marry for love instead of money?

Other books by the same author:
The Autumn Bride, 2014
The Winter Bride, 2014
The Accidental Wedding, 2013
To Catch a Bride, 2009
His Captive Lady, 2008

Other books you might like:
Katharine Ashe, *I Loved a Rogue*, 2015
Liz Carlyle, *A Woman of Virtue*, 2001
Eloisa James, *Midnight Pleasures*, 2000
Eloisa James, *The Ugly Duchess*, 2012
Tracy Anne Warren, *Her Highness and the Highlander*, 2012

976

DONNA GRANT

Hot Blooded
(New York: St. Martin's Press, 2014)

Series: Dark Kings Series. Book 4
Story type: Contemporary - Fantasy; Series
Subject(s): Romances (Fiction); Dragons; Scotland
Major character(s): Iona Campbell, Heir (to her father's secret responsibility), Daughter (of John); Laith, Mythical Creature (Dragon King); John Campbell, Man (Keeper of the gateway), Father (of Iona)
Time period(s): 21st century; 2010s
Locale(s): Dreagan, Scotland

Summary: After the loss of her father, Iona travels to Scotland to try to learn more about his past. She discovers there is a dark secret in her ancestral home of Dreagan, and she is part of it. Her father was the guardian of the doorway to another land, one where the Dragon Kings had sent the dragons ages ago. The Dragon Kings couldn't touch the magical doorway; that task had to be entrusted to a human. But now John Campbell is dead—murdered—and while the Dragon Kings mourn the loss of their ally and friend, their attention now turns to his daughter, the heir to his responsibility. Laith is one of the Dragon Kings, and though most in the town think him no more than a bar owner, he and the other Dragon Kings have long been their protectors. But now Iona has arrived, and Laith finds himself falling for her in ways that could be dangerous to them and many others in this fourth book in the Dark Kings series.

Other books by the same author:
Masters of Seduction, 2015
Night's Blaze, 2015
The Seduced, 2015
The Tempted, 2015
Midnight's Promise, 2013

Other books you might like:
Heather Graham, *The Cursed*, 2014
Sandra Hill, *Kiss of Pride*, 2012
Pamela Palmer, *A Kiss of Blood*, 2013
Gena Showalter, *The Darkest Touch*, 2014
J.D. Tyler, *Wolf's Fall*, 2014

977

JUNE GRAY

Surrender

(New York: Penguin Publishing Group, 2014)

Series: Disarm Series. Book 8
Story type: Contemporary; Military
Subject(s): Military life; Deception; Romances (Fiction)
Major character(s): Julie Keaton, Fiance(e) (of Jason), Friend (of Neal), Mother (of Will); Jason Sherman, Military Personnel (killed in Afghanistan), Fiance(e) (of Julie); Neal, Surfer, Friend (of Julie); Will, Child (son of Julie)
Time period(s): 21st century; 2010s
Locale(s): Monterey, California

Summary: Julie Keaton was just starting to trust her heart to Jason Sherman—to believe that they could make a life together after his deployment was over. He loved her; that she knew for sure. But then he was killed in action, and nothing was certain. Julie is finally starting to get over the uncertainty left after Jason's death and make a new life for herself and her son, Will. She goes back home for the wedding of friends and meets Neal, a handsome stranger. He is so easy to talk to that after just minutes Julie is hoping to see him again—soon. She starts to take down the walls she built around her heart to protect herself after Jason's death. But just as she dares to dream of a new life, Julie discovers Neal has been keeping a secret—one that could come between them. This is the eighth novel in the Disarm series.

Other books by the same author:
Arrest, 2014
Heading East, 2014

Other books you might like:
Lauren Christopher, *The Red Bikini*, 2014
Judi Fennell, *What a Woman Gets*, 2014
Jessica Lemmon, *Bringing Home the Bad Boy*, 2015
Emily March, *Nightingale Way*, 2012
Jodi Thomas, *Can't Stop Believing*, 2013
Julie Ann Walker, *Rev It Up*, 2012

978

JILL GREGORY

Sunflower Lane

(New York: Penguin Publishing Group, 2014)

Series: Lonesome Way Series. Book 4
Story type: Contemporary - Mainstream; Series
Subject(s): Interpersonal relations; Orphans; Romances (Fiction)

Major character(s): Annabelle Harper, Classmate (former high school classmate of Wes), Aunt (to two orphaned nieces and one nephew); Wes McPhee, Agent (former, DEA), Classmate (former high school classmate of Annabelle)
Time period(s): 21st century; 2010s
Locale(s): Lonesome Way, Montana

Summary: Annabelle Harper had a reputation as a troublemaker when she was younger, and she lit out of Lonesome Way right after high school. But when her sister and brother-in-law are killed in a plane crash, Annabelle sets aside her life to come back home to care for her two nieces and nephew. Wes McPhee also left town right after graduation to get away from his difficult, adulterous, and abusive father. Even though his father has been dead for years, only Wes's concern for his grandmother—who recently fell and broke her wrist—can make Wes, a hardened former DEA agent, come back to his hometown for even a few days. Wes remembers Annabelle —and her reputation for being easy and getting physical when she was angry. But Annabelle is different now, and that means that she has to stay away from Wes, no matter how attracted they are to each other. It isn't until danger shows up in town that the two can move beyond the past and into each others' arms in this fourth novel in the Lonesome Way series.

Other books by the same author:
Blackbird Lane, 2013
Larkspur Road, 2012
Sage Creek, 2011
Wolf River, 2007
Thunder at Dawn, 2005

Other books you might like:
Kate Angell, *Sweet Spot*, 2010
Macy Beckett, *Make You Remember*, 2014
Robyn Carr, *Angel's Peak: A Virgin River Novel*, 2010
Susan Donovan, *I Want Candy*, 2012
Marie Force, *And I Love Her*, 2015
Marie Force, *I Saw Her Standing There*, 2014
Kristan Higgins, *Waiting on You*, 2014
Susan Mallery, *Barefoot Season*, 2012

979

AMELIA GREY (Pseudonym of Gloria Dale Skinner)

The Duke in My Bed

(New York: St. Martin's Paperbacks, 2014)

Series: Heirs Club Series. Book 1
Story type: Historical - Regency; Series
Subject(s): Romances (Fiction); History; England
Major character(s): Bray Drakestone, Gambler, Nobleman (future duke), Heir, Fiance(e) (of Louisa); Louisa Prim, Fiance(e) (of Bray), Noblewoman
Time period(s): 19th century; 1810s (1815)
Locale(s): London, England

Summary: Set in Regency-era London, this romance novel is the first installment in the Heirs Club series by best-selling author Amelia Grey. Bray, the future Duke of Drakestone, never refuses a challenge, but the wildly confident heir is in over his head when a harmless dare turns deadly. As a result, Bray is forced to marry the oldest of his opponent's sisters, Miss Louisa Prim—a woman he's never met. At first reluctant to commit himself to marriage, Bray is pleasantly surprised when he meets the beautiful, strong-willed Louisa. And when Louisa lets Bray know she has no intention of marrying a careless rogue like him, Bray accepts the challenge to win her over. Louisa is determined to put up a fight, but how long can her defenses stand against the romantic advances of the handsome future duke?

Other books by the same author:
The Rogue Steals a Bride, 2013
A Gentleman Says "I Do", 2012
A Gentleman Never Tells, 2011
An Earl to Enchant, 2010
A Marquis to Marry, 2009

Other books you might like:
Grace Burrowes, *The Duke's Disaster*, 2015
Claudia Dain, *Daring a Duke*, 2010
Gaelen Foley, *My Dangerous Duke*, 2010
Jenna Petersen, *The Unclaimed Duchess*, 2010
Melody Thomas, *Beauty and the Duke*, 2009
Tracy Anne Warren, *The Bedding Proposal*, 2015

| 980 |

LAURA GRIFFIN

Beyond Limits

(New York, New York: Pocket Books, 2015)

Story type: Romantic Suspense
Subject(s): Romances (Fiction); Military life; Terrorism
Major character(s): Elizabeth LeBlanc, FBI Agent; Derek Vaughn, Military Personnel, Lover (of Elizabeth LeBlanc)
Time period(s): 21st century; 2010s
Locale(s): Texas, United States

Summary: Back on the job after suffering an injury in the line of duty, FBI agent Elizabeth LeBlanc is eager to jump into the thick of her new assignment in Texas. Intel has indicated the possibility of a terrorist attack there from a foreign source, and to prevent such a scenario, Elizabeth is forced to work with a Navy SEAL with whom she has a history. As awkward as it for Derek Vaughn for to see Elizabeth again, it was his team's mission that uncovered the intelligence upon which this investigation is centered—a reconnaissance mission that cost him the life of one of his men. Additionally, his entire family lives in Texas and he is not going to sit idly on the sidelines while their lives are threatened. Together, Elizabeth and Derek investigate the source of the threat while simultaneously exploring their developing feelings for one another. This is the eighth book in Griffin's Tracers series.

Other books by the same author:
Far Gone, 2014
Exposed, 2013
Scorched, 2012
Twisted, 2012
Snapped, 2011

Other books you might like:
Maya Banks, *Long Road Home*, 2011
Alexis Grant, *Sizzle and Burn*, 2011
Catherine Mann, *Protector*, 2012
Katie Reus, *Targeted*, 2013
Julie Ann Walker, *Full Throttle*, 2014

| 981 |

LAURA LEE GUHRKE

Catch a Falling Heiress

(New York: HarperCollins, 2015)

Series: American Heiress in London Series. Book 3
Story type: Historical - Victorian; Series
Subject(s): Romances (Fiction); History; Social class
Major character(s): Linnet Holland, Heiress (American), Girlfriend (of Frederick); Frederick, Boyfriend (of Linnet); Jack Featherstone, Nobleman (earl), Impoverished
Time period(s): 19th century; 1880s
Locale(s): England; Rhode Island, United States

Summary: A rogue tries to play the romantic hero in this third novel in the American Heiress in London series. Jack, Earl of Featherstone, has a title but no fortune. He is just the type of suitor American heiress Linnet Holland is trying to avoid. She knows England is crowded with poor noblemen looking for wealthy brides, so Linnet sets her sights instead on Frederick, a New Yorker. But Frederick is not as respectable as Linnet thinks. When Frederick plans to ensnare her in a scandal, Jack intervenes. To save Linnet from an inappropriate encounter with Frederick, Jack shows up at the rendezvous spot, kisses Linnet, and proposes. The plan backfires when Linnet refuses and hurries off to England to find a husband before news of her indiscretion with Jack spreads. Jack, who is smitten with the feisty American, does not give up easily. He follows Linnet to England to convince her to be his bride.

Other books by the same author:
How to Lose a Duke in Ten Days, 2014
When the Marquess Met His Match, 2013
Scandal of the Year, 2011
Trouble at the Wedding, 2011
Wedding of the Season, 2010

Other books you might like:
Victoria Alexander, *The Perfect Mistress*, 2011
Connie Brockway, *The Bridal Season*, 2001
Juliana Gray, *A Lady Never Lies*, 2012
Carrie Lofty, *Starlight*, 2012
Sherry Thomas, *Not Quite a Husband*, 2009

| 982 |

JULIA HARPER (Pseudonym of Elizabeth Hoyt)

Once and Always

(New York: Forever, 2015)

Story type: Contemporary
Subject(s): Romances (Fiction); Suspense; Crime

Romances

Major character(s): Maisa Burnsey, Woman, Traveler; Sam West, Police Officer
Time period(s): 21st century; 2010s
Locale(s): Coot Lake, Minnesota

Summary: Sam West, a police officer in Coot Lake, Minnesota, is well acquainted with Maisa Burnsey. He pulls her over every time she drives her VW Beetle through town. Sam has warned Maisa repeatedly about her speeding, but he actually appreciates each traffic stop that gives him the opportunity to admire Maisa's striking beauty. While Sam is issuing Maisa's latest warning on the side of the road, he is forced to leap onto the hood of her car when a driver deliberately tries to hit him. The town of Coot Lake is suddenly not as quiet as it once was. It has attracted the attention of organized crime figures from Russia, who believe the town is connected to a stash of missing diamonds. As Sam deals with Coot Lake's new criminals, he also tries to find out what Maisa is hiding.

Other books by the same author:
For the Love of Pete, 2009
Hot, 2008

Other books you might like:
Jennifer Crusie, *Faking It*, 2002
Jana DeLeon, *Unlucky*, 2007
Christina Dodd, *Tongue in Chic*, 2007
Julie James, *A Lot Like Love*, 2011
Susan Sey, *Money Honey*, 2010

983

KAREN HAWKINS

The Prince Who Loved Me

(New York: Pocket Books, 2014)

Series: Oxenburg Princes Series. Book 1
Story type: Historical - Regency; Series
Subject(s): Family relations; Interpersonal relations; Marriage
Major character(s): Alexsey Romanovin, Grandson (of Alexsey), Royalty (Prince), Young Man (unmarried); Bronwyn Murdoch, Spinster (24 year old), Assistant (father's patent); Natasha Nikolaevna, Royalty (Grand Duchess), Grandmother (of Prince Alexsey)
Locale(s): Oxenburg, Fictional Location; Scotland

Summary: This is the first novel in the Oxenburg Princes series by author Karen Hawkins. This fairy tale-inspired historical romance novel features the intelligent, attractive 24-year-old Bronwyn Murdoch, who would rather read a book than be married, and Prince Alexsey Romanovin, whose grandmother, the Grand Duchess Natasha Nikolaevna, is hell-bent on finding him a wife despite his misgivings. To placate his grandmother, Alexsey devises a plan to court and have his way with Bronwyn while he's visiting the Scottish Highlands. Bronwyn overhears the prince's plan and devises her own. She decides to seduce the cad Alexsey, have him fall in love with her, and then dump him. In their ploys of seduction, Prince Alexsey and Bronwyn do not expect to fall in love. But now they must decide what they want of each other and of their future.

Other books by the same author:
How to Entice an Enchantress, 2013
How to Pursue a Princess, 2013
How to Capture a Countess, 2012
The Taming of a Scottish Princess, 2012
A Most Dangerous Profession, 2011

Other books you might like:
Catherine Coulter, *The Duke*, 1995
Julie Garwood, *The Bride*, 1989
Cathy Maxwell, *Adventures of a Scottish Heiress*, 2003
Julia Quinn, *Just Like Heaven*, 2011
Jaclyn Reding, *The Adventurer*, 2002

984

ELIZABETH HAYLEY

The Best Medicine

(New York, New York: Penguin, 2015)

Story type: Contemporary
Subject(s): Romances (Fiction); Hospitals; Sex roles
Major character(s): Lauren "Lo" Hastings, Graduate, Lover (of Scott Jacobs); Dr. Scott Jacobs, Doctor, Lover (of Lauren Hastings)
Time period(s): 21st century; 2010s
Locale(s): United States

Summary: Newly graduated Lauren Hastings has a problem. With her master's degree finally in hand, she is excited about finally moving into the professional ranks, until a bit of trouble leaves her in debt to a bar and she instead needs an immediate job. She's forced to take a position at Dr. Scott Jacob's medical practice, though she resents being once again being stuck in part-time menial work when she could be pursuing her ambitions. What doesn't help is how attractive and infuriating she finds her new boss. As neither Lauren or Scott is looking for a relationship, they fall into a sexual arrangement with no strings attached. Over time, however, it eventually evolves into a friendship as well—but can it turn into something more? This is the first book in Elizabeth Hayley's Strictly Business series.

Other books by the same author:
Perfectly Ever After, 2014
Picking up the Pieces, 2014
Pieces of Perfect, 2014
Sex Snob, 2013

Other books you might like:
Stella Bagwell, *His Medicine Woman*, 2011
Jennifer Greene, *Lucky*, 2005
Virginia Kantra, *Guilty Secrets*, 2004
Teresa Southwick, *Holding Out for Doctor Perfect*, 2012
Sherryl Woods, *The Christmas Bouquet*, 2014

985

LORRAINE HEATH (Pseudonym of Jan Nowasky)

The Duke and the Lady in Red

(New York: HarperCollins, 2015)

Series: Scandalous Gentlemen of St. James Series. Book 3

Story type: Historical - Victorian; Series

Subject(s): Romances (Fiction); England; History

Major character(s): Rosalind Sharpe, Young Woman; Duke of Avendale, Nobleman

Time period(s): 19th century; 1870s

Locale(s): London, England

Summary: A woman strikes an outrageous bargain in the third and final novel in the Scandalous Gentlemen of St. James Place series. The Duke of Avendale is known as a womanizer, but that doesn't impede his ability to attract new conquests. The latest lady to catch his eye is Rosalind Sharpe, who in turn has her eye on the duke's fortune. She needs money and concocts a devious plan to get her hands on Avendale's stash of coins. When Avendale catches Rosalind in the act, he doesn't throw her out of his house. He is attracted to the obviously cunning woman, despite her thievery, and proposes a scandalous way for her to earn the cash she needs. Avendale will pay Rosalind any sum she likes if she gives herself to him for a week. Rosalind agrees, but she and Avendale are both surprised by the repercussions of their romantic romp.

Other books by the same author:
The Last Wicked Scoundrel, 2014
Once More, My Darling Rogue, 2014
When the Duke Was Wicked, 2014
Lord of Wicked Intentions, 2013
Lord of Temptation, 2012

Other books you might like:
Jennifer Ashley, *The Wicked Deeds of Daniel Mackenzie*, 2013
Manda Collins, *Why Earls Fall in Love*, 2014
Christina Dodd, *Rules of Engagement*, 2000
Julie Anne Long, *A Notorious Countess Confesses*, 2012
Kathryn Smith, *When Marrying a Scoundrel*, 2010

986

ELIZABETH HEITER

Disarming Detective

(Don Mills, Ontario, Canada: Harlequin, 2015)

Story type: Romantic Suspense

Subject(s): Romances (Fiction); Serial murders; Mystery

Major character(s): Isabella "Ella" Cortez, FBI Agent; Logan Greer, Detective

Time period(s): 21st century; 2010s

Locale(s): Oakville, Florida; Quantico, Virginia

Summary: About to leave for a long-deserved vacation, FBI profiler Ella Cortez finds detective Logan Greer waiting for her in the parking lot. He has been pursuing a case in his native Florida that he believes involves a serial killer, though his bosses don't agree. Looking over his information, Ella sees striking similarities to a case that she has been investigating for years—the case that led her to become a profiler in the first place. Giving up her vacation with her friends, she accompanies Logan to his home town of Oakville, Florida. As they investigate the twists in the case, they find themselves connecting on more than a professional level—a development that has the potential to distract them from the dangers to their lives that are circling around them. First book in the Lawmen series.

Other books by the same author:
Seduced by the Sniper, 2015
SWAT Secret Admirer, 2015
Vanished, 2014
Hunted, 2013

Other books you might like:
Mallory Kane, *Gone*, 2013
Beverly Long, *Dead by Wednesday*, 2014
Joanna Wayne, *Son of a Gun*, 2012
Debra Webb, *High Noon*, 2012
Rebecca York, *Sudden Insight*, 2012

987

STACY HENRIE

Hope Rising

(New York: Forever, 2014)

Series: Of Love and War Series. Book 2

Story type: Historical - World War I; Series

Subject(s): Romances (Fiction); World War I, 1914-1918; Nursing

Major character(s): Evelyn Gray, Nurse (US Army Nurse Corps), Fiance(e) (of Ralph Kelley), Military Personnel (US Army Nurse Corps); Ralph Kelley, Military Personnel (private), Fiance(e) (of Evelyn); Joel Campbell, Military Personnel (corporal)

Time period(s): 20th century; 1910s (1918)

Locale(s): France

Summary: When US Army nurse Evelyn Gray is sent to France during World War I to care for the injured troops, she knows that she and the other nurses aren't supposed to get involved with the soldiers. But Private Ralph Kelley is persistent, and he and Evelyn begin a romantic relationship. When Evelyn becomes pregnant, Ralph promises that he will marry her. But everything changes when Ralph is killed in battle. Now Evelyn must deal with the unplanned pregnancy on her own. She focuses on her work and becomes particularly interested in one patient, corporal Joel Campbell. He is recovering from injuries that may affect his ability to father a child. Evelyn has feelings for Joel, and the couple eventually begins to consider options for their future. Meanwhile Joel, who knew Ralph, must decide if he should tell Evelyn what he knows about her fiance's death. This novel is the second in the Of Love and War series.

Other books by the same author:
Hope at Dawn, 2014
Lady Outlaw, 2012

Romances

Other books you might like:
Amanda Harte, *Laughing At The Thunder*, 2004
Elizabeth Jeffrey, *Meadowlands*, 2015
Elizabeth Ludwig, *No Safe Harbor*, 2012
Pamela Morsi, *Something Shady*, 1995
Jennifer Robson, *Somewhere in France*, 2013
LaVyrle Spencer, *That Camden Summer*, 1996

988

HANNAH HOWELL

If He's Daring

(New York: Zebra, 2014)

Series: Wherlocke Series. Book 6
Story type: Historical - Regency; Paranormal
Subject(s): Adventure; Class conflict; Extrasensory perception
Major character(s): Lady Catryn Gryffin de Warrene, Widow(er), Mother (of Alwyn), Crime Victim (son Alwyn kidnapped), Thief (steals carriage), Psychic (has premonitions); Alwyn Gryffin de Warrene, Son (of Catryn), Kidnap Victim, Psychic (sees dead spirits); Sir Orion Wherlocke, Psychic (a tracker), Father (of Giles), Crime Victim (carriage stolen); Giles Wherlocke, Son (of Sir Orion Wherlocke), Empath, Passenger (in stolen carriage); Morris de Warren, Brother (in-law of Catryn), Kidnapper (of Alwyn), Heir—Dispossessed
Time period(s): 18th century; 1790s (1790)
Locale(s): London, England

Summary: This sixth historical paranormal romance novel in Hannah Howell's Wherlocke series continues the Wherlocke family saga of adventure, mystery, and romance. Widow Lady Catryn Gryffin de Warrene would never steal, but she has no choice when her brother-in-law Morris kidnaps her son Alwyn. She must get her son back at any cost. Stealing Sir Orion Wherlocke's carriage, but leaving her lame horse as collateral, Catryn recklessly pursues Alwyn. Unbeknownst to Lady Catryn, Sir Orion's son Giles is still a passenger in the stolen carriage. When Orion tracks down Catryn, with Giles inside the stolen carriage, he is furious. However, Orion is persuaded by Giles to help the fiery redhead, Catryn, save Alwyn. During their mishap-filled chase, Catryn stirs feelings within Orion that he would rather ignore. He has avoided love all his life, but now Catryn is making him feel reckless and daring him to open his heart to love.

Other books by the same author:
Highland Master, 2013
If He's Tempted, 2013
Highland Avenger, 2012
If He's Dangerous, 2011
Stolen Ecstasy, 2011

Other books you might like:
Shana Abe, *The Smoke Thief*, 2005
Madeline Hunter, *The Surrender of Miss Fairbourne*, 2012
Kathryne Kennedy, *Double Enchantment*, 2008

Patricia Rice, *Merely Magic*, 2000
Ciji Ware, *A Cottage by the Sea*, 1997

989

ELIZABETH HOYT

Darling Beast

(New York: Grand Central Publishing, 2014)

Series: Maiden Lane Series. Book 7
Story type: Historical - Georgian; Series
Subject(s): Romances (Fiction); British history, 1714-1815; Single parent family
Major character(s): Lily Stump, Actress, Mother (of Indio); Indio, Boy, Son (of Lily), 7-Year-Old; Maude Ellis, Servant (maid); Apollo Greaves, Crime Suspect (accused of murder), Nobleman (Viscount Kilbourne), Fugitive (escapee from Bedlam)
Time period(s): 18th century; 1740s (1741)
Locale(s): London, England

Summary: An abandoned theater provides sanctuary for a troubled woman and an escaped convict in the seventh novel in the Maiden Lane series. Lily Stump was a celebrated London actress, but in 1741, she finds her circumstances have changed. Lily is now living in a fire-damaged theater with her seven-year-old son, Indio, and her maid, Maude Ellis. Although Lily doesn't know it, the theater is also home to Apollo Greaves, Viscount Kilbourne. Greaves has also experienced a change of fortune. He was arrested for murder and beaten so savagely he cannot speak. After escaping from Bedlam, Greaves hides from the authorities at the theater and busies himself by tending its gardens. Indio is the first one to detect Greaves's presence, and the boy at first mistakes the large man for a monster. Lily's initial fear of Greaves turns to affection when she discovers the gentle, intelligent soul that lies within his gruff exterior.

Other books by the same author:
Duke of Midnight, 2013
Lord of Darkness, 2013
Thief of Shadows, 2012
Notorious Pleasures, 2011
Scandalous Desires, 2011

Other books you might like:
Jo Beverley, *A Scandalous Countess*, 2012
Eloisa James, *When Beauty Tamed the Beast*, 2011
Laura Kinsale, *Flowers from the Storm*, 1992
Kate Moore, *To Save the Devil*, 2010
Julia Ross, *The Seduction*, 2002

990

ELIZABETH HOYT

Dearest Rogue

(New York: Grand Central Publishing, 2015)

Series: Maiden Lane Series. Book 8
Story type: Historical; Series
Subject(s): Romances (Fiction); England; English (British people)
Major character(s): Lady Phoebe Batten, Noblewoman, Blind Person, Ward (of James); James Trevillion,

Military Personnel (former soldier), Bodyguard (of Phoebe)
Time period(s): 18th century; 1740s (1741)
Locale(s): England

Summary: Set in 1741 England, this historical romance novel is the eighth book in the Maiden Lane series by best-selling author Elizabeth Hoyt. Lady Phoebe Batten is the lively sister of a prominent duke. Like her peers, she longs for love and the excitement of a social life. Phoebe's eyesight is badly impaired, however, and her brother insists that she be escorted by an armed bodyguard at all times. Captain James Trevillion, a former member of the king's cavalry, considers himself well prepared to oversee the safety of his beautiful charge. But when Lady Phoebe is targeted by kidnappers, James faces a set of challenges different from any he's known. On the run from danger, Phoebe and James escape to a remote location outside of London, where James's tough exterior softens. As a more gentle side of James emerges, Phoebe's attraction to her bodyguard grows, and their friendship soon turns into a passionate romance.

Other books by the same author:
Darling Beast, 2014
Duke of Midnight, 2013
Lord of Darkness, 2013
Thief of Shadows, 2012
Scandalous Desires, 2011

Other books you might like:
Jo Beverley, *A Scandalous Countess*, 2012
Liz Carlyle, *Never Lie to a Lady*, 2007
Sylvia Day, *Pride and Pleasure*, 2011
Eloisa James, *Duchess by Night*, 2008
Courtney Milan, *Proof by Seduction*, 2010

991

JILLIAN HUNTER (Pseudonym of Maria Hoag)

Forbidden to Love the Duke

(New York: Penguin Group, 2015)

Series: Fenwick Sisters Affairs Series. Book 1
Story type: Historical - Regency; Series
Subject(s): Romances (Fiction); History; England
Major character(s): Lady Ivy Fenwick, Governess, Noblewoman, Impoverished; James, Nobleman (Duke of Ellsworth), Employer (of Ivy)
Time period(s): 19th century; 1810s
Locale(s): England

Summary: When Lady Ivy Fenwick's father is killed in a duel, she and her sisters are forced to find their own means of support. Although they sell every item of value from the estate, they still don't have the funds they need. Ivy realizes that she must take drastic measures. She takes a governess position in the household of James, Duke of Ellsworth, where she will care for his wards. James knows that he probably shouldn't bring Lady Ivy into his home or his life, but he finds her irresistible. As expected, James begins to fall in love with Ivy, but he is not the only man interested in her. Another suitor has made his intentions known, and James must decide how far he is willing to go to win Ivy for his own.

Other books by the same author:
The Countess Confessions, 2014
The Mistress Memoirs, 2013
The Duchess Diaries, 2012
A Bride Unveiled, 2011
A Duke's Temptation, 2010

Other books you might like:
Valerie Bowman, *Secrets of a Wedding Night*, 2012
Lecia Cornwall, *How to Deceive a Duke*, 2012
Tessa Dare, *Romancing the Duke*, 2014
Elizabeth Essex, *A Breath of Scandal*, 2012
Madeline Hunter, *Ravishing in Red*, 2010
Julia Quinn, *The Secrets of Sir Richard Kenworthy*, 2015

992

MADELINE HUNTER

His Wicked Reputation

(New York: Jove, 2015)

Series: Wicked Trilogy. Book 1
Story type: Historical - Regency; Series
Subject(s): Romances (Fiction); British history, 1714-1815; Social class
Major character(s): Gareth Fitzallen, Bastard Son (of a duke), Art Dealer; Eva Russell, Artist (painter), Sister (of Rebecca); Rebecca, Sister (of Eva)
Time period(s): 19th century; 1810s
Locale(s): England

Summary: Gareth Fitzallen, the illegitimate son of a duke, is an art dealer known for his sexual prowess. He has lured many beautiful women to his bed, but he is not prepared for the feelings he has for Eva Russell. Gareth meets Eva, a painter, when he travels to Langdon's End to assess a house he has inherited. He is also looking into a big art heist that took place in the area. Eva has no romantic aspirations of her own. She is resigned to life as a single woman, and she focuses on finding a suitable husband for her sister, Rebecca. Her friends assure Eva that Gareth is no such man, so Eva tries to keep Rebecca away from him. Gareth is smitten with Eva, however, who is much less experienced in love than the women he's used to. Eva surrenders easily to Gareth's charms, but their relationship is threatened by Gareth's search for the stolen art. This novel is the first in the Wicked Trilogy.

Other books by the same author:
The Accidental Duchess, 2014
The Conquest of Lady Cassandra, 2013
The Counterfeit Mistress, 2013
The Surrender of Miss Fairbourne, 2012
Dangerous in Diamonds, 2011

Other books you might like:
Christina Brooke, *The Greatest Lover Ever*, 2014
Loretta Chase, *Silk Is for Seduction*, 2011
Sabrina Jeffries, *How to Woo a Reluctant Lady*, 2011
Lisa Kleypas, *Devil in Winter*, 2006
Julia London, *The Seduction of Lady X*, 2012

Romances

993

ELOISA JAMES (Pseudonym of Mary Bly)

Four Nights with the Duke

(New York: HarperCollins, 2015)

Series: Desperate Duchesses Series. Book 8
Story type: Historical; Series
Subject(s): Romances (Fiction); History; Marriage
Major character(s): Emilia "Mia" Gwendolyn Carrington, Young Woman, Spouse (of Evander); Evander "Vander" Septimus Brody, Nobleman (Duke of Pindar), Spouse (of Emilia)
Time period(s): 18th century
Locale(s): England

Summary: Even though Evander "Vander" Septimus Brody was in line to be Duke of Pindar, Emilia "Mia" Gwendolyn Carrington had no romantic interest in him. When she was young she rebuffed his attentions and stated outright that she would never marry him. Now they are adults. Vander has his title, but Mia finds herself in a desperate situation she never anticipated. When she realizes that Vander is her only option for a husband, Mia does the unthinkable and asks him to marry her. Vander accepts on the condition that Mia agrees to the terms he proposes. He will spend only four nights a year with her—and only if she begs for his company. Mia is certain she will never beg to see Vander, but Vander is gambling that the unconventional marriage will grow into a real romance. This novel is the eighth in the Desperate Duchesses series by Eloisa James.

Other books by the same author:
Three Weeks with Lady X, 2014
Once Upon a Tower, 2013
The Lady Most Willing, 2012
The Ugly Duchess, 2012
The Duke Is Mine, 2011

Other books you might like:
Sophie Barnes, *The Danger of Tempting an Earl*, 2014
Loretta Chase, *Not Quite a Lady*, 2007
Tessa Dare, *Romancing the Duke*, 2014
Kate Noble, *The Game and the Governess*, 2014
Maya Rodale, *Seducing Mr. Knightly*, 2012

994

LORELEI JAMES

Cowgirls Don't Cry

(Macon, Georgie: Samhain Publishing, 2011)

Story type: Series; Western
Subject(s): Erotica; Romances (Fiction); Western fiction
Major character(s): Jessie McKay, Widow(er), Spouse (of Luke); Luke McKay, Spouse (of Jessie), Brother (of Brandt), Father (of baby); Brandt McKay, Brother (of Luke)
Time period(s): 21st century; 2010s

Summary: In *Cowgirls Don't Cry* by Lorelei James, Jessie McKay has rebounded from the death of her husband to marry Luke McKay, who has no respect for her or their marriage. Luke is willing to share his wife with other participants in his alcohol-fueled sex games, and Jessie surrenders any hopes for true love in her life. Luke's brother Brandt has made his feelings for Jessie known, but the jaded young woman is not interested in romance—especially with another McKay. When Jessie strikes out on her own, Brandt follows, seeking her help in caring for Luke's illegitimate child. Jessie takes the baby and Brandt in, intending to use her brother-in-law for her own pleasure. *Cowgirls Don't Cry* is the 10th book in the Rough Riders series.

Other books by the same author:
The Cowgirl's Little Secret, 2015
Night Shift, 2015
Secrets, 2015
Blue Moon, 2014
Christmas Moon, 2013

Other books you might like:
Marina Adair, *Autumn in the Vineyard*, 2013
Maya Banks, *Letting Go*, 2014
Carolyn Brown, *Long, Hot Texas Summer*, 2014
Sadie Callahan, *Lone Star Woman*, 2009
Lauren Dane, *Drawn Together*, 2013
Kat Martin, *Against the Storm*, 2011
Lindsay McKenna, *The Defender*, 2012
Cathy Gillen Thacker, *The Inherited Twins*, 2008

995

SABRINA JEFFRIES (Pseudonym of Deborah Gonzales)

If the Viscount Falls

(New York: Pocket Books, 2015)

Series: Duke's Men Series. Book 4
Story type: Historical - Regency; Series
Subject(s): Romances (Fiction); History; Family
Major character(s): Dominick Manton, Heir (presumptive, to Rathmoor viscountcy), Brother (of George), Fiance(e) (former, of Jane Vernon); George Manton, Brother (of Dominick), Spouse (of Nancy); Jane Vernon, Fiance(e) (former, of Dominick), Cousin (of Nancy); Nancy, Spouse (of George), Cousin (of Jane), Widow(er), Missing Person
Time period(s): 19th century; 1810s
Locale(s): England

Summary: The fourth novel in the Duke's Men series centers on a plot of family intrigue and betrayal. Dominick Manton's future looked bright before his brother's act of betrayal changed everything. Dom was engaged to Jane Vernon and in line to be viscount when George revealed information that caused Dom to lose his title, his inheritance, and his fiancee. Dom protected Jane as well as he could from the scandal, but he has never let go of the love he feels for her. George assumed the life that was supposed to be Dom's and married Jane's cousin, Nancy. When George dies, it seems Dom finally has the opportunity to set things right. Because George and Nancy had no children, the viscountcy reverts to Dom. But will he get a second chance with Jane? The opportunity arises when Dom and Jane are reunited by a crisis—Nancy's disappearance.

Other books by the same author:
How the Scoundrel Seduces, 2014
When the Rogue Returns, 2014
What the Duke Desires, 2013
A Lady Never Surrenders, 2012
'Twas the Night After Christmas, 2012

Other books you might like:
Katharine Ashe, *In the Arms of a Marquess*, 2011

Cara Elliott, *Too Wicked to Wed*, 2011

Madeline Hunter, *The Accidental Duchess*, 2014

Vanessa Kelly, *Confessions of a Royal Bridegroom*, 2014

Stephanie Laurens, *The Masterful Mr. Montague*, 2014

996

RACHAEL JOHNS

Jilted

(Don Mills, Ontario, Canada: Harlequin, 2014)

Story type: Contemporary; Romantic Suspense
Subject(s): Betrayal; Community relations; Courage
Major character(s): Ellie Hughes, Actress (soap opera star), Fiance(e) (ex-fiancee of Flynn), Relative (god-daughter of Matilda); Flynn Quatermaine, Fiance(e) (ex-fiance of Ellie), Hero (small town), Rancher (runs family ranch); Matilda, Godmother (of Ellie)
Time period(s): 21st century; 2010s
Locale(s): Hope Junction, Australia

Summary: It has been more than ten years since television soap opera star Ellie Hughes has been back to Hope Springs—more than ten years since she left her ex-fiance, Flynn Quatermaine, standing alone at the altar without any explanation. Returning to Hope Springs was not part of Ellie's plans, but when her godmother Matilda is injured, she has no choice. By choosing to return to her small hometown, Flynn must face her past with Flynn—and the scorn and disapproval of the townspeople. It is inevitable that Ellie will run into Flynn, but neither she nor Flynn expects the unresolved feelings they experience when they meet. Will Ellie and Flynn be able to overcome the hurts of the past, or will Ellie's secret cause her to run again?

Other books by the same author:
The Kissing Season, 2014
Man Drought, 2013
Outback Dreams, 2013
One Perfect Night, 2011

Other books you might like:
Michelle Conder, *Socialite's Gamble*, 2014

Barbara Hannay, *A Very Special Holiday Gift*, 2014

Kelly Hunter, *Wife for a Week*, 2007

Carol Marinelli, *An Indecent Proposition*, 2012

Nicola Marsh, *Overtime in the Boss's Bed*, 2010

997

VANESSA KELLY

How to Plan a Wedding for a Royal Spy

(New York, New York: Zebra, 2015)

Story type: Historical - Regency
Subject(s): Romances (Fiction); Spies; Espionage
Major character(s): Evie Whitney, Fiance(e) (to Michael), Twin (to Edie); Captain William "Wolf" Endicott, Bastard Son (illegitimate son of the Duke of York), Spy; Alastair "Alec" Gilbride, Cousin (of William), Spy; Eden "Edie" Whitney, Twin (of Evie); Sir Dominic Hunter, Spy; Michael Beaumont, Fiance(e) (of Evie)
Time period(s): 19th century; 1810s
Locale(s): England

Summary: In Vanessa Kelly's *How to Plan a Wedding for a Royal Spy*, William "Will" Endicott, a veteran of the Battle of Waterloo, is called back to England to help his royal father, the Duke of York, uncover a potential assassination plot. Though illegitimate, Will is an invaluable piece in the plans of his father to expose the suspected Catholic Irish conspiracy, because the man they believe to be at the center of the plot is Michael Beaumont, the fiancé of Will's childhood sweetheart, Evie Whitney. Using his charm and Evie's lingering feelings towards him, Will attempts to uncover the details of the plot while denying his own submerged feelings for his now-beautiful former love.

Other books by the same author:
How to Marry a Royal Highlander, 2015
Confessions of a Royal Bridegroom, 2014
Secrets for Seducing a Royal Bodyguard, 2014
Sex and the Single Earl, 2010
Mastering the Marquess, 2009

Other books you might like:
Joanna Bourne, *Rogue Spy*, 2014

Gayle Callen, *Redemption of the Duke*, 2014

Anna Campbell, *Seven Nights in a Rogue's Bed*, 2012

Marguerite Kaye, *Rumors That Ruined a Lady*, 2013

Kate Moore, *Blackstone's Bride*, 2012

998

BETH KENDRICK (Pseudonym of Beth Lavin)

New Uses for Old Boyfriends

(New York: Penguin Publishing Group, 2015)

Series: Black Dog Bay Series. Book 2
Story type: Contemporary; Series
Subject(s): Romances (Fiction); Family; Finance
Major character(s): Lila Alders, Divorced Person, Television Personality (former), Daughter (of Daphne); Daphne, Mother (of Lila), Widow(er), Model (former); Ben, Manager (property), Friend (of Lila); Malcolm, Military Personnel, Friend (of Lila)
Time period(s): 21st century; 2010s
Locale(s): Black Dog Bay, Delaware

Romances

Summary: When Lila Alders returns to her family home in Black Dog Bay, Delaware, her life is definitely on a downswing. She and her wealthy husband recently divorced, and she lost her job on a television shopping network. Back in Black Dog Bay, she finds her recently widowed mother, Daphne, struggling with her late husband's business debts. But Lila's hometown holds some pleasant surprises, too. She forges a friendship with Ben, who used to be her boyfriend. And she opens a vintage clothing shop with her mother, a former model. By selling items from Daphne's extensive wardrobe, the women are able to improve their financial situation. Malcolm, another man from Lila's past, is a military man with some serious sewing skills. Although Lila barely remembers Malcolm from her younger days, he makes a big impression on her now. This novel is the second in the Black Dog Bay series.

Other books by the same author:
Cure for the Common Breakup, 2014
The Week Before the Wedding, 2013
The Lucky Dog Matchmaking Service, 2012
The Bake-off, 2011
Second Time Around, 2010

Other books you might like:
Stacey Ballis, *Out to Lunch*, 2013
Kim Gruenenfelder, *Keep Calm and Carry a Big Drink*, 2013
Beth Harbison, *Always Something There to Remind Me*, 2011
R.L. Mathewson, *Double Dare*, 2015
Melissa Senate, *The Love Goddess' Cooking School*, 2010
Linda Yellin, *What Nora Knew*, 2014

999

ELLE KENNEDY

Midnight Action

(New York: Penguin Publishing Group, 2014)

Series: Killer Instinct Series. Book 5
Story type: Contemporary; Military
Subject(s): Military life; Romances (Fiction); Assassination
Major character(s): Noelle Phillips, Stepdaughter (of Rene), Assassin (hired to kill Jim Morgan), Lover (former, of Jim); Jim Morgan, Mercenary, Lover (former, of Noelle); Rene Laurent, Stepfather (of Noelle)
Time period(s): 21st century; 2010s
Locale(s): France

Summary: Eighteen years ago, Noelle fell for an incredibly handsome American soldier in a Paris cafe. Her life was in turmoil because of her violent stepfather, and she'd allowed Jim Morgan to help her. Noelle was not quite 18 at the time, and she didn't know that Jim had ulterior motives: he was after her criminal father and using Noelle as a way to get to him. Now fate has given Noelle an opportunity for payback. The team of assassins she leads has been given a new target—Jim Morgan. No longer in the military, Jim now heads up a team of mercenaries. To fulfill his latest assignment, he's going to need the help of the woman he once used, but has never been able to forget. Noelle and Jim have no reason to trust each other, but they are going to need to get past that and back into each others' hearts if they are going to survive. This is the fifth book in the Killer Instincts series.

Other books by the same author:
Midnight Pursuits, 2014
Midnight Alias, 2013
Midnight Games, 2013
Special Ops Exclusive, 2013
Midnight Rescue, 2012

Other books you might like:
Vivian Arend, *High Passion*, 2013
Maya Banks, *When Day Breaks*, 2014
Laura Kaye, *Hard as You Can*, 2014
Lindsay McKenna, *Down Range*, 2013
Anna Sullivan, *Temptation Bay*, 2013

1000

KIMBERLY KINCAID

Stirring Up Trouble

(New York: Kensington Books, 2014)

Series: Pine Mountain Series. Book 3
Story type: Contemporary - Mainstream; Series
Subject(s): Writers; Writing; Family relations
Major character(s): Sloane Russo, Writer (novelist), Tutor (to Bree); Gavin Carmichael, Employer (of Sloane), Brother (half-brother of Bree); Bree, 13-Year-Old, Sister (half-sister of Gavin), Student (of Sloane)
Time period(s): 21st century; 2010s
Locale(s): Pine Mountain

Summary: New York born-and-raised Sloane Russo has a master's degree in creative writing and three best-sellers to her credit, but right now, she's a little down on her financial luck. She's tucked away, not in the European hostels that inspired her first novels, but in the Blue Ridge Mountains where she is helping a friend. Sloane needs to make a little money, and the best way to do that in her temporary home is to work as a tutor/nanny for Gavin Carmichael. Gavin is good looking, but he's stubbornly determined to take care of his 13-year-old half-sister and doesn't think that Sloane is up to the task. Gavin is firmly convinced that taking care of his sister means denying himself any fun in life. But crazy, beautiful Sloane might be just the kind of fun Gavin should be having. This is the third book in the Pine Mountain series.

Other books by the same author:
Fire Me Up, 2015
Gimme Some Sugar, 2014
Stirring Up Trouble, 2014
Turn Up the Heat, 2014

Other books you might like:
Chelsea M. Cameron, *My Favorite Mistake*, 2013
Donna Hill, *Secret Attraction*, 2011
Erin McCarthy, *Final Lap*, 2014

Christie Ridgway, *Make Me Lose Control*, 2014
Christie Ridgway, *Take My Breath Away*, 2014

1001

ERIN KNIGHTLEY

The Earl I Adore

(New York: Penguin Publishing Group, 2015)

Series: Prelude to a Kiss Series. Book 2
Story type: Regency; Series
Subject(s): Romances (Fiction); Social class; Marriage
Major character(s): Sophie Wembley, Debutante, Sister (of Penelope); Penelope, Sister (of Sophie); John "Evan" Fairfax, Nobleman (Earl of Evansleigh)
Time period(s): 19th century
Locale(s): Bath, England

Summary: This novel is the second installment from author Erin Knightley's Prelude to a Kiss series. When Sophie Wembley learns that her sister Penelope has gone off and married a commoner, she takes matters into her own hands before word gets around their village. When the gentlemen in Bath find out what Sophie's sister has done, Sophie will be deemed unworthy of marriage. She has to act fast to find a willing suitor. Luckily, John "Evan" Fairfax, Earl of Evansleigh, has arrived in town. As Sophie and Evan spend more time together, Sophie is sure that he is the perfect man for her. But Evan has a scandal in his past as well, and he isn't sure that Sophie will accept him once she hears it. Now, both Sophie and Evan must decide how much they are willing to risk for love, and how to forgive each other's past transgressions.

Other books by the same author:
The Baron Next Door, 2014
Flirting with Fortune, 2013
More Than a Stranger, 2012
A Taste for Scandal, 2012

Other books you might like:
Valerie Bowman, *The Unexpected Duchess*, 2014
Kathryn Caskie, *Rules of Engagement*, 2004
Caroline Linden, *Love and Other Scandals*, 2013
Julia Quinn, *The Sum of All Kisses*, 2013
Maya Rodale, *The Wicked Wallflower*, 2013

1002

KIERAN KRAMER

You're So Fine

(New York: St. Martin's, 2015)

Story type: Contemporary
Subject(s): Romances (Fiction); Adoption; Single parent family
Major character(s): Lacey Clark, Mother (adoptive, of Henry), Actress (aspiring); Henry, Adoptee, Son (adopted, of Lacey), 5-Year-Old; Beau Wilder, Actor
Time period(s): 21st century; 2010s
Locale(s): Indigo Beach, South Carolina

Summary: Lacey Clark's return to her home state of South Carolina is less than triumphant. She had moved to Los Angeles hoping to find success as an actress. Now she is the adoptive mother of Henry, the five-year-old son of a former boyfriend. She is low on cash, and she has left her shattered dreams behind in California. Though Lacey is happy to be away from the movie business, she doesn't escape her past completely. Back in South Carolina, she takes a job at a film studio and becomes housemates with Beau Wilder, an actor. Lacey tries to resist, but realizes she is attracted to Beau. She suspects Beau might not be a good influence on a five-year-old boy, but the handsome actor is actually wonderful with Henry. Although Beau can't believe it, he is becoming attached to his housemate and her son.

Other books by the same author:
Sweet Talk Me, 2014
The Earl Is Mine, 2013
Say Yes to the Duke, 2013
Loving Lady Marcia, 2012
If You Give a Girl a Viscount, 2011

Other books you might like:
Grace Burrowes, *Kiss Me Hello*, 2015
Robyn Carr, *One Wish*, 2015
Julie James, *It Happened One Wedding*, 2014
Lisa Kleypas, *Sugar Daddy*, 2007
Julia London, *Extreme Bachelor*, 2006
Susan Elizabeth Phillips, *The Great Escape*, 2012
Tracy Anne Warren, *The Man Plan*, 2014

1003

RACHEL LACEY

For Keeps

(New York: Grand Central Publishing, 2015)

Series: Love to the Rescue Series. Book 2
Story type: Contemporary; Series
Subject(s): Romances (Fiction); Camping; Children
Major character(s): Merry Atwater, Rescuer (animals), Therapist (animal); TJ Jameson, Rancher, Leader (Camp Blue Sky), Uncle (Noah); Noah, Boy, Autistic, Nephew (of TJ)
Time period(s): 21st century; 2010s
Locale(s): United States

Summary: An unlikely romance develops between an animal lover and a rancher in the second novel in the Love to the Rescue series. Merry Atwater has taken a job at Camp Blue Sky, where she uses her expertise in animal therapy to help the camp's young visitors. Noah, a boy with autism, is one of the children who benefits from Merry's program. Noah is the nephew of the camp's manager, TJ Jameson. Family is everything to TJ, and he is thrilled to see how Noah is responding to Merry and her animals. Merry is not exactly thrilled with TJ, however. She finds working with him difficult, no matter how good-looking he is. TJ wants a family of his own, but he knows Merry isn't interested in anything serious. The cowboy doesn't give up on his dream easily, however, and he does his best to win Merry over.

Other books by the same author:
Unleashed, 2014

Other books you might like:
Kristan Higgins, *My One and Only*, 2011
Robin Kaye, *Call Me Wild*, 2012
Jill Shalvis, *Rumor Has It*, 2013
Kandy Shepherd, *Home Is Where the Bark Is*, 2010
Teri Wilson, *Unleashing Mr. Darcy*, 2014

1004

SYDNEY LANDON

No Denying You

(New York: Penguin Publishing Group, 2014)

Series: Danvers Series. Book 5
Story type: Contemporary; Series
Subject(s): Work environment; Romances (Fiction); Reunions
Major character(s): Emma Davis, Assistant (Administrative assistant to Brant); Brant Stone, Employer (Emma's boss)
Time period(s): 21st century; 2010s
Locale(s): United States

Summary: Emma Davis can't stand her job—or more accurately, she can't stand her boss. A tense, demanding workaholic, Brant Stone is as attractive as he is infuriating. Emma tries to get transferred. Brant refuses the request. She tries acting up to make him want to transfer her. He is unmoved. At last Emma gains an edge when she finds some information she can use to blackmail Brant. Unfortunately, there is one thing she wants more than getting away from Brant—not having her mother fix her up with a date for her high school reunion. Instead, Emma blackmails Brant into accompanying her and playing the perfect boyfriend. That's when the sexual tension really starts to build in this fifth book of the Danvers series of romances.

Other books by the same author:
Always Loving You, 2015
Fighting for You, 2014
Fractured, 2014
Pierced, 2014
Fall for Me, 2013

Other books you might like:
Bella Andre, *Let Me Be The One*, 2013
Carolyn Brown, *Billion Dollar Cowboy*, 2013
Catherine Bybee, *Single by Saturday*, 2014
Marie Force, *And I Love Her*, 2015
Donna Hill, *Secret Attraction*, 2011
Lorelei James, *Hillbilly Rockstar*, 2014

1005

STEPHANIE LAURENS

The Tempting of Thomas Carrick

(Don Mills, Ontario, Canada: Mira, 2015)

Series: Cynster Series. Book 22
Story type: Historical; Series
Subject(s): Romances (Fiction); Scotland; History
Major character(s): Thomas Carrick, Businessman, Wealthy; Lucilla Cynster, Woman (from powerful clan), Healer
Time period(s): 19th century; 1830s
Locale(s): Scotland

Summary: Thomas Carrick doesn't know it yet, but he is destined to marry Lucilla Cynster. He loved her once, but now he tries to keep his distance. Instead, the powerful businessman searches for a suitable bride in Glasgow society. Lucilla bides her time on her clan's estate, which borders the Carrick property, certain that Thomas will eventually return to her. Lucilla's patience is answered when a crisis draws Thomas home. Illness has struck Thomas's uncle, the estate's current laird, and Lucilla may be the only one who can help. Thomas reluctantly reaches out to Lucilla, but he only wants her to help his uncle heal. Although Lucilla knows the terms of the arrangement, she has no intention of letting Thomas slip away from her again. She believes they are supposed to be together, and she will do everything in her power to make Thomas hers. This novel is the 22nd in the Cynster series by Stephanie Laurens.

Other books by the same author:
By Winter's Light, 2014
Loving Rose, 2014
The Masterful Mr. Montague, 2014
And Then She Fell, 2013
The Taming of Ryder Cavanaugh, 2013

Other books you might like:
Jennifer Ashley, *The Seduction of Elliot McBride*, 2012
Manda Collins, *Why Earls Fall in Love*, 2014
Sabrina Jeffries, *Beware a Scot's Revenge*, 2007
Karen Ranney, *The Devil of Clan Sinclair*, 2013
Anne Stuart, *Never Kiss a Rake*, 2013

1006

STEPHANIE LAURENS

By Winter's Light

(Don Mills, Ontario: Harlequin, 2014)

Series: Cynster Series. Book 21
Story type: Holiday Themes; Series
Subject(s): Scotland; Holidays; Christmas
Major character(s): Daniel Crosbie, Tutor; Claire Meadows, Governess
Time period(s): 19th century; 1830s (1837)
Locale(s): Scotland

Summary: Author Stephanie Laurens continues her series featuring the Cynsters, a Scottish family, and their many romances. The winter holidays make the perfect setting for love to bloom. When Daniel Crosbie, tutor to one of the Cynsters' young sons, first encounters Claire Meadows, governess to another of the Cynster siblings, he is certain that he has met the woman of his dreams. Yet Claire has been burned before, and she is determined not to have her heart broken again. Claire should know by now, however, that the Cynsters are one family determined to dabble in matchmaking. With the family's help, Daniel sets out to win Claire's heart once and for all, and convince her that he is worth her time. When a tragedy puts a damper on the holiday festivities, Claire finally learns that sometimes she must let her guard down, especially when it comes to Daniel and his feelings for her.

Other books by the same author:
Loving Rose, 2014
The Masterful Mr. Montague, 2014
And Then She Fell, 2013
The Taming of Ryder Cavanaugh, 2013
The Lady Risks All, 2012

Other books you might like:
Jennifer Ashley, *The Duke's Perfect Wife*, 2012
Grace Burrowes, *Once Upon a Tartan*, 2013
Christina Dodd, *Some Enchanted Evening*, 2004
Susan King, *Waking the Princess*, 2003
Jennifer McQuiston, *What Happens in Scotland*, 2013

1007

JADE LEE (Pseudonym of Katherine Ann Grill)

50 Ways to Ruin a Rake

(Naperville, Illinois: Sourcebooks Casablanca, 2015)

Series: Rakes and Rogues Series. Book 1
Story type: Regency; Series
Subject(s): Science; Women; Marriage
Major character(s): Melinda "Mellie" Smithson, Fiance(e) (of Trevor), Daughter (of Mr. Smithson), Inventor; Mr. Smithson, Scientist, Father (of Mellie), Tutor (of Trevor); Trevor Anaedsley, Fiance(e) (of Mellie), Student (of Mr. Smithson)
Time period(s): 19th century
Locale(s): England

Summary: This novel is the first book in author Jade Lee's Rakes and Rogues series. Melinda "Mellie" Smithson grew up watching her father invent and create, and she longs to one day be as successful a scientist as he is. When she devises a formula for a woman's facial cream, she knows that the invention will make her a mint. Unfortunately, her father doesn't believe that women should have their own money or run their own businesses. Luckily, Mellie's longtime suitor Trevor Anaedsley steps in. He suggests that they marry, and he agrees to pass every cent that Mellie's cream makes along to her. For his part, Trevor will finally gain access to the trust fund that he was promised once he marries. This marriage isn't much of a sham for Trevor, however. He cannot deny the love he has for Mellie. Does she feel the same way, or is she truly only marrying him for convenience?

Other books by the same author:
What the Groom Wants, 2014
What the Bride Wore, 2013
Wedded in Scandal, 2012
Wedded in Sin, 2012
Wicked Seduction, 2011

Other books you might like:
Jayne Fresina, *Miss Molly Robbins Designs a Seduction*, 2014

Samantha Grace, *Lady Amelia's Mess and a Half*, 2012
Kieran Kramer, *If You Give a Girl a Viscount*, 2011
Elizabeth Michels, *Must Love Dukes*, 2014
Sophia Nash, *Between the Duke and the Deep Blue Sea*, 2012

1008

RACHEL LEE

Undercover Hunter

(Don Mills, Ontario, Canada: Harlequin, 2015)

Story type: Romantic Suspense
Subject(s): Romances (Fiction)
Major character(s): DeeJay Dawkins, Investigator; Cade Bankston, Investigator
Time period(s): 21st century; 2010s
Locale(s): Wyoming, United States

Summary: A serial killer has invaded the sanctuary of Conard County, Wyoming in the 20th installment of Lee's Conard County: The Next Generation. Assigned to catch the killer are detectives Cade Bankston and Dee-Jay Dawkins, two ace detectives with strong motivations not to trust the opposite sex. In the past, Cade was falsely accused of sexual harassment, while DeeJay was pressured to cover up a rape during her time in the military. To make matters worse, while posing as a pair of travel writers on assignment, they are forced to pose as a married couple. Despite their misgivings about one another, eventually their protective walls begin to fall, but can they put aside their growing attraction to in time to prevent the killer from kidnapping another young boy?

Other books by the same author:
Deadly Hunter, 2014
Defending the Eyewitness, 2014
Snowstorm Confessions, 2014
A Very Maverick Christmas, 2014
Thanksgiving Daddy, 2013

Other books you might like:
Carla Cassidy, *Mystic Lake*, 2012
Justine Davis, *Operation Blind Date*, 2013
Franklin W. Dixon, *The London Deception*, 1999
Marie Ferrarella, *Cavanaugh Undercover*, 2014
Carla Neggers, *Harbor Island*, 2014

1009

RACHEL LEE

Snowstorm Confessions

(Don Mills, Ontario, Canada: Harlequin, 2014)

Series: Conard County: The Next Generation Series. Book 21
Story type: Contemporary; Series
Subject(s): Infidelity; Marriage; Family history
Major character(s): Brianna Cole, Nurse, Spouse (ex-wife of Luke Masters), Neighbor (of Jack Milkin); Luke Masters, Spouse (ex-husband of Brianna Cole),

Businessman (developer); Jack Milkin, Neighbor (of Brianna Cole)

Time period(s): 21st century; 2010s
Locale(s): Conard County, Wyoming

Summary: Author Rachel Lee returns to Conard County, where she brings together former spouses to face their past and a new peril. Brianna Cole is finally getting her life on track after her divorce from Luke Masters. She has a rewarding nursing career and a home that she can call her own. The last person she expects to see is her ex-husband, but when Luke is injured on a job in Conard County, Brianna volunteers to look after him at her home. When they find themselves snowed in, Brianna and Luke can't deny the feelings they still have for each other, but they may not be able to overcome problems of the past. Will they be able to rekindle their relationship, or will Brianna's obsessed neighbor be more of an issue than they can both handle?

Other books by the same author:
Deadly Hunter, 2014
Defending the Eyewitness, 2014
A Very Maverick Christmas, 2014
Thanksgiving Daddy, 2013
The Widow of Conard County, 2013

Other books you might like:
Carla Cassidy, *Return to Bachelor Moon*, 2013
Delores Fossen, *Renegade Guardian*, 2013
Cassie Miles, *Snow Blind*, 2014
Carla Neggers, *Saint's Gate*, 2011
Marilyn Pappano, *Forbidden Stranger*, 2009

1010

JESSICA LEMMON

Bringing Home the Bad Boy

(New York, New York: Forever, 2015)

Story type: Contemporary Realism
Subject(s): Romances (Fiction); Death; Love
Major character(s): Charlotte "Charlie" Harris, Friend (of Rae Downey), Lover (of Evan Downey); Evan Downey, Artist, Father (of Lyon Downey), Widow(er) (of Rae Downey), Lover (of Charlotte Harris); Lyon Downey, Son (of Evan and Rae Downey); Rae Downey, Spouse (of Evan Downey), Mother (of Lyon Downey)
Time period(s): 21st century; 2010s
Locale(s): Evergreen Cove, United States

Summary: Since the death of Rae—his wife and the mother of his son—five years ago, tattoo artist Evan Downey has struggled to adapt to her absence. Though he has been able to work through his grief by focusing on his son and his career, he knows that Lyon needs more than what Evan has been able to give. So he hopes that the quiet, friendly security of Evergreen Cove—where Evan spent his childhood summers—might help bring the boy out of his shell. Charlotte "Charlie" Harris understands Evan's grief, as she had been Rae's best friend. Now that the pair are back in Evergreen Cove, she wants to help them move forward, just as her friend would have wanted. But what was she didn't expect was

how strong her feelings for Evan would become. Charlie doesn't want to betray the memory of her friend, but she also is becoming unable to picture her life without Evan and Lyon in it forever. Can they allow themselves to heal in each others' arms, or will they be forever trapped in their respective expressions of grief? This is the first novel in Lemmon's Second Chance Series.

Other books by the same author:
Rescuing the Bad Boy, 2015
The Millionaire Affair, 2014
Hard to Handle, 2013
Tempting the Billionaire, 2013

Other books you might like:
Tamra Baumann, *It Had to Be Him*, 2015
Chelsea M. Cameron, *My Sweetest Escape*, 2014
Jennifer Dawson, *Take a Chance on Me*, 2014
June Gray, *Surrender*, 2014
Joanne Kennedy, *How to Handle a Cowboy*, 2014
Katie Lane, *A Match Made in Texas*, 2014

1011

CAROLINE LINDEN (Pseudonym of P.F. Belsley)

Love in the Time of Scandal

(New York: Avon Books, 2015)

Series: Scandals Series. Book 3
Story type: Historical; Series
Subject(s): Scandals; Romances (Fiction); Marriage
Major character(s): Penelope Weston, Spouse (wife, of Benedict), Wealthy; Benedict Lennox, Nobleman (Lord Atherton), Spouse (husband, of Penelope)
Time period(s): 19th century; 1820s (1822)
Locale(s): London, England

Summary: Best-selling author Caroline Linden delivers the third novel in her Scandals series. Penelope Weston has her reasons for not liking Benedict Lennox, Lord Atherton. She remembers his courtship of her sister and the friend he abandoned, and he's not the type of man she wants to marry. There's only one problem: she's wildly attracted to him. Benedict is desperate to escape the clutches of his controlling father, and the security of a wealthy bride is just what he needs. Feisty Penelope might not be the reasonable wife he had in mind, but when a scandalous rumor ties them to one another, they are forced to marry. Benedict soon realizes that Penelope's spirited passion makes marriage more exciting than he ever imagined, but is it possible for true love to emerge from scandal?

Other books by the same author:
It Takes a Scandal, 2014
Love and Other Scandals, 2013
Blame It on Bath, 2012
The Way to a Duke's Heart, 2012
One Night in London, 2011

Other books you might like:
Celeste Bradley, *With This Ring*, 2014
Christina Brooke, *The Greatest Lover Ever*, 2014
Tessa Dare, *A Week to be Wicked*, 2012

Candice Hern, *Once a Scoundrel*, 2003
Maya Rodale, *Wallflower Gone Wild*, 2014

1012

JULIA LONDON (Pseudonym of Dinah Dinwiddie)

The Devil Takes a Bride

(Don Mills, Ontario, Canada: Harlequin, 2015)

Series: Cabot Sisters Series. Book 2
Story type: Historical - Regency; Series
Subject(s): Romances (Fiction); British history, 1714-1815; Social class
Major character(s): Grace Cabot, 20-Year-Old, Daughter (of Lady Beckington), Sister (of Honor, Prudence, Mercy), Stepsister (of Augustine); Lady Beckington, Mentally Ill Person, Mother (of Grace, Honor, Prudence, Mercy), Stepmother (of Augustine); Honor Cabot, Daughter (of Lady Beckington), Sister (of Grace, Prudence, Mercy), Stepsister (of Augustine); Prudence Cabot, Daughter (of Lady Beckington), Sister (of Grace, Honor, Mercy), Stepsister (of Augustine); Mercy Cabot, Daughter (of Lady Beckington), Sister (of Grace, Honor, Prudence), Stepsister (of Augustine); Augustine, Stepson (of Lady Beckington), Stepbrother (of Grace, Honor, Prudence, Mercy); Lord Amherst, Nobleman, Brother (of Jeffrey); Jeffrey, Nobleman (Earl of Merryton), Brother (of Lord Amherst)
Time period(s): 19th century; 1810s (1812)
Locale(s): Bath, England

Summary: In the second novel in the Cabot Sisters series, 20-year-old Grace Cabot feels her time for finding a husband is running out. Her stepfather's recent death has left Grace, her three sisters, and their mother in financial difficulties. Complicating the situation is the fact that Grace's mother, Lady Beckington, is mentally ill. Since it is unlikely that the daughters of a madwoman will attract suitable husbands in Regency-era England, the Cabot sisters guard that secret while they can. Grace has been carrying on a flirtation with Lord Amherst, and she plans to force his hand by catching him in a small scandal. When Grace inadvertently ensnares Lord Amherst's brother—Jeffrey, Earl of Merryton—instead, she soon finds herself married to a somber, troubled man. As Grace tries to make the best of her situation, she begins to unravel the mystery of Jeffrey's unusual behavior.

Other books by the same author:
Return to Homecoming Ranch, 2014
The Trouble with Honor, 2014
The Bridesmaid, 2013
Homecoming Ranch, 2013
The Last Debutante, 2013

Other books you might like:
Celeste Bradley, *When She Said I Do*, 2013
Diane Gaston, *Born to Scandal*, 2012
Marguerite Kaye, *Rumors That Ruined a Lady*, 2013
Laura Kinsale, *Flowers from the Storm*, 1992
Kate Moore, *Winterburn's Rose*, 1996

1013

JULIA LONDON (Pseudonym of Dinah Dinwiddie)

The Perfect Homecoming

(Seattle, Washington: Montlake Romance, 2015)

Series: Pine River Series. Book 3
Story type: Contemporary; Series
Subject(s): Romances (Fiction); Family; Ranch life
Major character(s): Emma Tyler, Planner (event), Sister (half-sister of Libby and Madeline), Friend (of Leo Kendrick); Libby, Sister (of Madeline), Sister (half-sister of Emma); Madeline, Sister (of Libby), Sister (half-sister of Emma); Cooper Jessup, Businessman (founder of Thrillseekers Anonymous); Leo Kendrick, Friend (of Emma)
Time period(s): 21st century; 2010s
Locale(s): Pine River, Colorado

Summary: Pine River, Colorado, is a long way from Los Angeles, but that's where Emma Tyler goes when she runs into trouble. In LA, Emma was a successful event planner who had a bad habit of taking things that didn't belong to her. When she is suspected of stealing something from a client, Emma heads for the ranch in Pine River she and her half-sisters inherited from their father. The angry client sends Cooper Jessup after her. Cooper, who arranges extreme sports outings for wealthy thrill seekers, accepts the assignment. The fee will come in handy, but Cooper also wants the opportunity to spend time with Emma. Cooper and Emma share a history, and when they meet again in Colorado they realize their attraction is still strong. Cooper is determined to focus on the business at hand, but he finds it increasingly hard to resist Emma's advances. This novel is the third in the Pine River series.

Other books by the same author:
The Devil Takes a Bride, 2015
Return to Homecoming Ranch, 2014
The Trouble with Honor, 2014
The Bridesmaid, 2013
Homecoming Ranch, 2013

Other books you might like:
Catherine Anderson, *Sweet Nothings*, 2002
Robyn Carr, *The Promise*, 2014
Barbara Freethy, *The Way Back Home*, 2012
Jennifer Lohmann, *Winning Ruby Heart*, 2014
Jane Porter, *The Good Woman*, 2012

1014

SARAH MACLEAN (Pseudonym of Sarah Trabucchi)

Never Judge a Lady by Her Cover

(New York: Avon Books, 2014)

Series: Rules of Scoundrels Series. Book 4
Story type: Historical; Series
Subject(s): Romances (Fiction); England; Social class
Major character(s): Lady Georgiana Pearson, Noblewoman (aka Anna and Chase), Friend (of Duncan); Duncan

Romances

West, Businessman (newspaper tycoon), Friend (of Georgiana)

Time period(s): 19th century; 1830s (1833)

Locale(s): London, England

Summary: Set in 1833 England, this historical romance novel is the fourth and final installment in the Rules of Scoundrels series by best-selling author Sarah MacLean. Lady Georgiana Pearson left society ten years ago, after she gave birth to a daughter out of wedlock. During the last decade, she has secretly become one of England's most powerful figures. By day, she is Georgiana, the ruined sister of a respectable duke. By night, she is not only Anna, London's most powerful madam, but also the enigmatic persona of Chase, Anna's partner, who is believed to be a man. Now eager to make a future for her daughter, Georgiana has no choice but to return to society and marry for title. She reaches out to newspaper tycoon Duncan West, and although he promises to help her find an aristocratic husband, he can't deny his own attraction to mysterious Lady Georgiana. He's certain there's a dark secret she's hiding, and he'll do anything to get to the bottom of it. At the same time, Duncan struggles to keep his own long-buried secrets from resurfacing.

Other books by the same author:
No Good Duke Goes Unpunished, 2013
One Good Earl Deserves a Lover, 2013
A Rogue by Any Other Name, 2012
Eleven Scandals to Start to Win a Duke's Heart, 2011
Ten Ways to Be Adored When Landing a Lord, 2010

Other books you might like:
Victoria Alexander, *The Shocking Secret of a Guest at the Wedding*, 2014
Ruth Axtell, *Moonlight Masquerade*, 2013
Elizabeth Boyle, *The Viscount Who Lived Down the Lane*, 2014
Connie Brockway, *No Place for a Dame*, 2013
Linore Rose Burkard, *The House in Grosvenor Square*, 2009
Jamie Carie, *The Guardian Duke*, 2012
Liz Carlyle, *A Deal with the Devil*, 2004
Tessa Dare, *A Lady by Midnight*, 2012
Melanie Dickerson, *The Merchant's Daughter*, 2011
Melanie Dobson, *The Courier of Caswell Hall*, 2013
Elizabeth Essex, *Almost a Scandal*, 2012
Madeline Hunter, *Ravishing in Red*, 2010
Lynn Morris, *The Baron's Honourable Daughter*, 2014

1015

DEBBIE MACOMBER

Mr. Miracle

(New York: Ballantine Books, 2014)

Story type: Holiday Themes

Subject(s): Christmas; Angels; Romances (Fiction)

Major character(s): Harry Mills, Angel (guardian angel of Addie), Teacher (college); Addie Folsom, Young Woman, Neighbor (of Erich), Student (of Harry); Erich Simmons, Young Man, Neighbor (of Addie)

Time period(s): 21st century; 2010s

Locale(s): Tacoma, Washington

Summary: This holiday romance novel by best-selling author Debbie Macomber follows a young woman who finds love in the most unlikely of places. Guardian angel Harry Mills is sent as a teacher to a community college in Tacoma, Washington, to watch over 24-year-old Addie Folsom. Addie, who left home to make it on her own, returns to Tacoma for the holidays. This time, however, she decides to stay and enrolls at the local community college. Erich Simmons is the next-door neighbor she grew up hating. Popular Erich always seemed to have it out for Addie, and even as an adult, Addie tries her best to avoid him. But when Addie and Erich are forced to spend Christmas together, they discover an attraction they never dreamed possible. As Harry Mills works his wonders, the neighbors experience a Christmas they'll always remember.

Other books by the same author:
Blossom Street Brides, 2014
Country Bride, 2014
Love Letters, 2014
North to Alaska, 2014
Marriage Between Friends, 2013

Other books you might like:
Peter Anthony, *A Town Called Immaculate*, 2009
W. Bruce Cameron, *The Dogs of Christmas*, 2013
Richard Paul Evans, *Promise Me*, 2010
Roz Denny Fox, *On Angel Wings*, 2006
Thomas Kincade, *A Season of Angels*, 2012
Karen Kingsbury, *Angels Walking*, 2014
Karen Kingsbury, *Chasing Sunsets*, 2015
Max Lucado, *Miracle at the Higher Grounds Cafe*, 2015
Susan Mallery, *The Christmas Wedding*, 2014
Curtiss Ann Matlock, *Little Town, Great Big Life*, 2010
Emilie Richards, *One Mountain Away*, 2012
Kathleen Gilles Seidel, *Till the Stars Fall*, 1994
Danielle Steel, *A Perfect Life*, 2014
RaeAnne Thayne, *Snow Angel Cove*, 2014
Donna VanLiere, *The Christmas Note*, 2011
Susan Wiggs, *Table for Five*, 2005
Marcia Willett, *Christmas in Cornwall*, 2012
Sherryl Woods, *Swan Point*, 2014

1016

SUSAN MALLERY (Pseudonym of Susan Macias Redmond)

The Girls of Mischief Bay

(Don Mills, Ontario, Canada: Mira, 2015)

Summary: Nicole Lord wants to be a good wife, but there's a difference between being supportive and supporting her husband, who quit his job to write a screenplay she's never seen. Sacrificing a personal life for her career is how Shannon Rigg rose to become vice president in her firm, but she wonders now whether she made the right choice. Although Pam Eiland has a beautiful house and a husband she adores, she feels restless. She wonders who a stay-at-home mom becomes after the kids are grown. Through romance and heartbreak, laughter and tears, three very different women will discover that friends can become family, and that life is richer with sisters at your side. Also available in Large Print.

Other books by the same author:
All for You, 2014
Before We Kiss, 2014
Evening Stars, 2014
Until We Touch, 2014
When We Met, 2014

Other books you might like:
Robyn Carr, *Four Friends*, 2014
Karen Joy Fowler, *The Jane Austen Book Club*, 2004
Debbie Macomber, *Blossom Street Brides*, 2014
Susan Elizabeth Phillips, *Heroes Are My Weakness*, 2014
Anne Rivers Siddons, *The Girls of August*, 2014
Haywood Smith, *The Red Hat Club*, 2003
Sylvia True, *The Wednesday Group*, 2015

1017

CATHERINE MANN

Rescue Me

(New York: Penguin Publishing Group, 2015)

Series: Second Chance Ranch Series. Book 2
Story type: Contemporary; Series
Subject(s): Animal rights; Dogs; Rural life
Major character(s): Mary Hannah Gallo, Animal Trainer; AJ Parker, Police Officer; Holly, Dog
Time period(s): 21st century; 2010s
Locale(s): Cooksburg, Tennessee

Summary: The second novel in Catherine Mann's Second Chance Ranch series tells the story of Mary Hannah Gallo, a recovering meth addict who now works at the Second Chance Ranch animal shelter. Mary Hannah continues to grapple with the mistakes of her past as she rehabilitates animals rescued from bad situations. When a dog named Holly comes into her care, Mary Hannah recognizes a bit of herself in the abused pup. Training Holly also connects Mary Hannah with AJ Parker, a former detective from Atlanta who joined the Cooksburg Police Department to find a slower paced life. Mary Hannah, a former drug abuser, and AJ, a former narcotics agent, couldn't be more different, but they soon learn that they complete one another. The author alternates between Mary Hannah's, AJ's, and Holly's points of view to tell the story of two people and a dog trying to rebuild their lives.

Other books by the same author:
Escaping with the Billionaire, 2014
For the Sake of Their Son, 2014
One Good Cowboy, 2014
Shelter Me, 2014
Sheltered by the Millionaire, 2014

Other books you might like:
Catherine Anderson, *Sweet Nothings*, 2002
Laura Drake, *The Sweet Spot*, 2013
Kathleen Eagle, *The Last True Cowboy*, 1998

Shirley Jump, *The Sweetheart Bargain*, 2013
Lori Wilde, *A Cowboy for Christmas*, 2012

1018

EMILY MARCH (Pseudonym of Geralyn Dawson Williams)

Teardrop Lane

(New York: Ballantine Books, 2015)

Series: Eternity Springs Series. Book 9
Story type: Contemporary; Series
Subject(s): Romances (Fiction); Family; Medical care
Major character(s): Hunt Cicero, Artist, Uncle (of Keenan, Misty, Galen, Daisy); Misty, 9-Year-Old, Niece (of Hunt), Sister (of Keenan, Galen, Daisy); Keenan, 7-Year-Old, Nephew (of Hunt), Brother (of Misty, Galen, Daisy); Galen, 5-Year-Old, Nephew (of Hunt), Brother (of Misty, Keenan, Daisy); Daisy, 2-Year-Old, Niece (of Hunt), Sister (of Misty, Keenan, Galen); Rose Anderson, Doctor
Time period(s): 21st century; 2010s
Locale(s): Eternity Springs, Colorado

Summary: When Hunt Cicero's sister dies, the artist is named as guardian of the four children she leaves behind—nine-year-old Misty, seven-year-old Keenan, five-year-old Galen, and two-year-old Daisy. Hunt is used to living a solitary life, but he does his best to care for his nieces and nephews in Eternity Springs, Colorado. When one of the boys needs a doctor, Hunt takes him to see Rose Anderson, the town's physician. Like Hunt, Rose is unattached and has no family of her own. She has resigned herself to the notion that she will remain single and childless. Rose is surprised when she feels an immediate attraction to Hunt. Hunt also falls for Rose, and against all odds the doctor and the artist embark on a romance. This novel is the ninth in the Eternity Springs series.

Other books by the same author:
Dreamweaver Trail, 2014
Miracle Road, 2013
Reflection Point, 2013
Nightingale Way, 2012
Lover's Leap, 2011

Other books you might like:
Robyn Carr, *The Hero*, 2013
Robyn Carr, *The Promise*, 2014
Jennifer Crusie, *Maybe This Time*, 2010
Janet Dailey, *Scrooge Wore Spurs*, 2002
Susan Wiggs, *Table for Five*, 2005

1019

STEPHEN MARCHE

The Hunger of the Wolf

(New York: Simon & Schuster, 2015)

Story type: Contemporary; Family Saga
Subject(s): Supernatural; Werewolves; Family history
Major character(s): Jamie Cabot, Servant (of Wylie family), Writer, Narrator; Ben Wylie, Wealthy, Werewolf,

Romances

Employer (of Jamie Cabot)
Time period(s): 20th century-21st century; 1930s-2010s
Locale(s): Alberta, Canada; China; London, England; New York, New York; Pittsburgh, Pennsylvania

Summary: The Wylie family has been wealthy for more than three generations. The family's assets have opened doors in business and society that would otherwise be barred and have brought them tremendous power and privilege. It is because of this wealth that the Wylie family is able to keep its deepest secrets private. The family vault, however, is breached when authorities find the head of the family, Ben Wylie, in the northern Canadian wilderness. His naked body is discovered in the snow. When questions surrounding the circumstances of his death begin to crop up, the loyal family servants, the Cabots, find themselves holding the cards. Jamie Cabot, the son of Ben's housekeepers, is determined to figure out how and why his employer died. Studying the family history of the Wylies, Jamie finds his answers are increasingly supernatural. As an aspiring writer, Jamie must question his honor and his dreams and decide whether he can use the Wylie story to catapult himself into a new life.

Other books by the same author:
Love and the Mess We're In, 2012
Shining at the Bottom of the Sea, 2007
Raymond and Hannah, 2005

Other books you might like:
Jeffrey Archer, *Only Time Will Tell*, 2011
Baron R. Birtcher, *Hard Latitudes*, 2015
Barbara Taylor Bradford, *Being Elizabeth*, 2008
Patricia Gussin, *The Test*, 2009
Chris Morgan Jones, *The Jackal's Share*, 2013
David Lender, *The Gravy Train*, 2012
Steven Owad, *Brother's Keeper*, 2007
Nancy Pickard, *The Scent of Rain and Lightning*, 2011
Matthew Thomas, *We Are Not Ourselves*, 2014
Cecily Wong, *Diamond Head*, 2015

1020

LILLIAN MAREK

Lady Elinor's Wicked Adventures

(Naperville, Illinois: Sourcebooks Casablanca, 2014)

Series: Victorian Adventures Series. Book 1
Story type: Historical - Victorian; Series
Subject(s): Romances (Fiction); History; Social class
Major character(s): Lady Elinor "Norrie" Tremaine, Young Woman, Daughter (of Lady Penworth), Noblewoman; Lady Penworth, Noblewoman, Mother (of Norrie); Harry de Vaux, Nobleman (Viscount Tunbury)
Time period(s): 19th century; 1850s (1852)
Locale(s): England; Italy

Summary: The families of Lady Elinor "Norrie" Tremaine and Harry de Vaux are on friendly terms, but the de Vaux clan has a somewhat unsavory history. This is what keeps Harry, Viscount Tunbury, from telling Norrie how he feels about her. He doesn't think a union between them would be good for Norrie's reputation, but Norrie doesn't seem to care. She has always loved Harry,

although she hasn't had the opportunity to demonstrate her feelings. The couple gets a chance at romance when Harry accompanies the Tremaines on a journey to Italy's Etruscan ruins. Harry hesitates as usual, but he and Norrie eventually get close. As their relationship develops, and an engagement becomes inevitable, Harry's rough edges are smoothed by Norrie and her family. This novel is the first in the Victorian Adventures series.

Other books you might like:
Connie Brockway, *The Other Guy's Bride*, 2011
Betina Krahn, *The Book of True Desires*, 2006
Anthea Lawson, *All He Desires*, 2009
Amanda Quick, *Otherwise Engaged*, 2014
Sherry Thomas, *Not Quite a Husband*, 2009

1021

MIA MARLOWE (Pseudonym of Diane Groe)

Once upon a Plaid

(New York: Zebra Books, 2014)

Series: Spirit of the Highlands Series. Book 2
Story type: Historical; Holiday Themes
Subject(s): Romances (Fiction); History; Scotland
Major character(s): Katherine Douglas, Noblewoman (Lady Badenoch), Spouse (wife, of William); William Douglas, Nobleman (Laird), Spouse (husband, of Katherine)
Time period(s): 16th century
Locale(s): Scotland

Summary: Set in Scotland, this 16th-century historical romance novel is the second installment in the Spirit of the Highlands series by award-winning author Mia Marlowe. After four years of marriage and multiple miscarriages, Katherine, Lady Badenoch, requests an annulment from her husband, Laird William Douglas. Grieving over her inability to bear a child and provide William with an heir, Katherine returns to Glengarry Castle, her childhood home. William, however, isn't willing to let her get away that easily, and soon, he arrives at Katherine's family's home at Christmastime, longing for her to be back in his arms. But is the love they share strong enough to carry them through their present heartache, disappointment, and grief?

Other books by the same author:
A Rake by Any Other Name, 2014
One Night with a Rake, 2013
Plaid Tidings, 2013
Plaid to the Bone, 2013
Waking up with a Rake, 2013

Other books you might like:
Connie Brockway, *McClairen's Isle: The Passionate One*, 1999
Virginia Henley, *The Border Hostage*, 2001
Karen Marie Moning, *Beyond the Highland Mist*, 1999
Patricia Potter, *Beloved Warrior*, 2007
Amanda Scott, *Highland Bride*, 2003

1022

MIA MARLOWE (Pseudonym of Diane Groe)

A Rake by Any Other Name

(Naperville, Illinois: Sourcebooks Casablanca, 2014)

Series: Somerfield Park Series. Book 1
Story type: Historical - Regency; Series
Subject(s): Family history; Family relations; Marriage
Major character(s): Richard Barrett, Nobleman (aka Lord Hartley); Sophie Goodnight, Heiress
Time period(s): 19th century; 1810s (1817)
Locale(s): England

Summary: Award-winning author Mia Marlowe delivers the first installment in her Somerfield Park historical romance series. In 1817 England, Richard Barrett, Lord Hartley, is called home to his family's estate after his father suffers a serious accident. Upon his arrival, Lord Hartley learns of his family's bleak financial state and also of the plan for recovery: his arranged marriage to Sophie Goodnight, the heiress of a wealthy businessman. Independent Sophie isn't eager to marry, and Lord Hartley has already pledged his love to another woman, so the pair joins forces to thwart their families' plans for marriage. But when the tension between them takes a passionate turn, Lord Hartley finds himself having to choose between two beautiful women. And when he uncovers the secrets of his father's past, he realizes that choosing a wife might actually be the easiest decision he'll have to make.

Other books by the same author:
Once Upon a Plaid, 2014
One Night with a Rake, 2013
Plaid Tidings, 2013
Plaid to the Bone, 2013
Waking Up with a Rake, 2013

Other books you might like:
Elizabeth Boyle, *Tempted by the Night*, 2008
Liz Carlyle, *Tempted All Night*, 2009
Loretta Chase, *Not Quite a Lady*, 2007
Eileen Dreyer, *Once a Rake*, 2013
Sabrina Jeffries, *Let Sleeping Rogues Lie*, 2008

1023

MIA MARLOWE (Pseudonym of Diane Groe)

Never Resist a Rake

(Naperville, Illinois: Sourcebooks Casablanca, 2015)

Series: Somerfield Park Series. Book 2
Story type: Regency; Series
Subject(s): Romances (Fiction); Social class; Love
Major character(s): John Fitzhugh Barrett, Nobleman (Lord Hartley), Heir; Rebecca Kearsey, Noblewoman
Time period(s): 19th century; 1810s (1817)
Locale(s): England

Summary: The second novel in author Mia Marlowe's Somerfield Park series introduces John Fitzhugh Barrett. John has just learned that he comes from nobility and has inherited the title of Lord Hartley. John feels more at home in the boxing ring than he does at posh parties, though, and he isn't sure that he will fit in with his new family. When the young debutantes of Somerfield Park learn of John's new standing, they all vie for his company and, ultimately, his marriage proposal. Yet only one woman truly stirs up romantic feelings for John: Rebecca Kearsey, the plucky young woman who was offered up as a prize during his last boxing match. Unfortunately, Rebecca's once noble father is now poor, and John's family won't approve of a marriage to her. Now John must decide if he has enough courage to resist society's pressures and be with the woman he loves.

Other books by the same author:
Between a Rake and a Hard Place, 2014
Once upon a Plaid, 2014
A Rake by Any Other Name, 2014
One Night with a Rake, 2013
Plaid Tidings, 2013

Other books you might like:
Kieran Kramer, *When Harry Met Molly*, 2010
Julia London, *The Trouble with Honor*, 2014
Cathy Maxwell, *The Bride Says No*, 2014
Sophia Nash, *Love with the Perfect Scoundrel*, 2009
Theresa Romain, *Season for Surrender*, 2012

1024

HANNA MARTINE

The Good Chase

(New York: Penguin Publishing Group, 2014)

Series: Highland Games Series. Book 2
Story type: Contemporary; Series
Subject(s): Romances (Fiction); Scots (British people); Self awareness
Major character(s): Shea Montgomery, Saleswoman (Whiskey), Divorced Person; J.P. Byrne, Businessman (Wall Street type), Man (Rugby player, whiskey taster)
Time period(s): 21st century; 2010s
Locale(s): Gleann, New Hampshire

Summary: Shea Montgomery has made a career out of whiskey in the best possible way—with a fancy bar and a taste for the best that's earned her a reputation as an expert. But a past with a man for whom money was the only important thing has left Shea weary of a life chasing the almighty dollar. She's much happier with a crowd that has a more earthy appreciation for her whiskey wares—such as the crowd at the highland games held in New England. A Wall Street businessman would not be Shea's man of choice these days, but the handsome rugby player who shows up in her tent at Gleann, the New Hampshire version of the highland games, is another story. J.P. Byrne isn't just a rugby player; he's a suit-clad international financier five days of every week. He fought hard to rise out of a life of poverty, using wit, charm, and determination. In other words, he's the opposite of everything Shea thinks she wants—while she is everything he desires. Shea and J.P. will have to overcome their pasts to find their future together in this second novel in the Highland Games series.

Romances

Other books by the same author:
Drowning in Fire, 2014
The Isis Knot, 2014
Play for Me, 2014
Long Shot, 2013
A Taste of Ice, 2012

Other books you might like:
Jennifer Dawson, *Take a Chance on Me*, 2014
Lori Foster, *Getting Rowdy*, 2013
Rachel Gibson, *Run To You*, 2013
Fiona Lowe, *Montana Actually*, 2015
Deirdre Martin, *Straight Up*, 2010

1025

AMANDA MCCABE
Betrayed by His Kiss
(Don Mills, Ontario, Canada: Harlequin, 2014)

Story type: Historical - Renaissance
Subject(s): Romances (Fiction); Italian history; Renaissance
Major character(s): Orlando Landucci, Man; Isabella Spinola, Woman
Time period(s): 15th century; 1470s (1478)
Locale(s): Italy

Summary: Four years after the death of his beloved sister, Orlando Landucci continues his quest for vengeance. It is 1478, and Orlando is well aware that Italy is a place of intrigue. He knows the person who is responsible for his sister's terrible fate, and he is determined to make him pay. But when Orlando's quest leads him to the beautiful Isabella Spinola, Orlando becomes distracted from his mission. Isabella is related by blood to the person Orlando has been searching for, but Orlando can't feel animosity toward her. In fact, he falls in love with Isabella. He wants to stay true to his dead sister and his mission, but when he finally gets the chance to take his long-awaited revenge, Orlando is not sure what he should do.

Other books by the same author:
The Runaway Countess, 2013
Running from Scandal, 2013
The Taming of the Rogue, 2012
Tarnished Rose of the Court, 2012
The Shy Duchess, 2011

Other books you might like:
Denise Domning, *Lady in Waiting*, 1998
Blythe Gifford, *Secrets at Court*, 2014
Judith James, *Libertine's Kiss*, 2010
Elizabeth Loupas, *The Second Duchess*, 2011
Susan Wiggs, *Lord of the Night*, 1993

1026

ERIN MCCARTHY
Believe
(New York: Berkley Books, 2014)

Series: True Believers Series. Book 3
Story type: Contemporary; Series

Subject(s): Romances (Fiction); Artists; Friendship
Major character(s): Robin, Girlfriend (of Phoenix), Artist; Phoenix, Convict (ex-convict), Boyfriend (of Robin)
Time period(s): 21st century; 2010s
Locale(s): United States

Summary: Best-selling author Erin McCarthy delivers the third installment in her True Believers contemporary romance series. Robin swears off alcohol forever when a night of wild partying ends with her waking up next to her best friend's boyfriend. Ashamed and overcome with guilt, Robin refuses to tell the truth about what happened that night. Things start to look up for Robin, however, when she meets Phoenix only two days after his release from jail. Drawn to one another's artistry and dreams for the future, Robin and Phoenix experience an attraction that is strong both physically and emotionally. But will the love between them endure as the dark secrets of their pasts begin to emerge?

Other books by the same author:
Deep Focus, 2015
Let Me In, 2014
Meant for Me, 2014
Fangs for Nothing, 2013
Full Throttle, 2013

Other books you might like:
Victoria Dahl, *Lead Me On*, 2010
Doralynn Kennedy, *Sleeping with Skeletons*, 2010
Brooke Morgan, *Tainted*, 2010
Lorie O'Clare, *Get Lucky*, 2011
Carly Phillips, *Perfect Fling*, 2013

1027

ERIN MCCARTHY
Final Lap
(New York: Penguin Publishing Group, 2014)

Series: Fast Track Series. Book 8
Story type: Contemporary; Romance
Subject(s): Automobile racing; Twins; Deception
Major character(s): Harley McLain, Twin (of Charity), Lover (of Cooper), Child-Care Giver (nanny); Cooper Brickman, Brother (of young girl), Race Car Driver, Lover (of Harley); Charity McLain, Twin (of Harley)
Time period(s): 21st century; 2010s
Locale(s): United States

Summary: Harley McLain is always the good, sweet twin, at least until she meets Cooper Brickman, a hot-as-molten-asphalt race car driver. Just one look at Cooper at the elaborate wedding she attends with her twin, Charity, sends Harley's heart and her mind racing. In a very uncharacteristic action, she borrows her sister's dress and hits on Cooper for a night of smoldering passion. It was one wonderful, hot night, all over and done with, until Cooper comes looking for Harley—as a nanny for his little sister. Unaware of her deception, Cooper thinks the quiet, sweet McLain sister is the ideal choice, and Harley can't turn down the money or the opportunity to be near Cooper again. When he discovers the truth, will it be the end of her job and her chances with Cooper, or will he decide Harley is the ideal choice for more than a baby sitter? This is the eighth book in the Fast Track series.

Other books by the same author:
Deep Focus, 2015
Meant for Me, 2014
Fangs for Nothing, 2013
Full Throttle, 2013
Seeing Is Believing, 2013

Other books you might like:
Pamela Britton, *Slow Burn*, 2009
Pamela Britton, *To the Limit*, 2007
Jaci Burton, *One Sweet Ride*, 2013
Janet Evanovich, *Motor Mouth*, 2006
Abbi Glines, *When I'm Gone*, 2015
Kimberly Kincaid, *Stirring Up Trouble*, 2014
Kimberly Raye, *Slippery When Wet*, 2008
Christie Ridgway, *Make Me Lose Control*, 2014
Julie Ann Walker, *Rev It Up*, 2012

1028

CLAIRE MCEWEN (Pseudonym of Claire Haiken)

Convincing the Rancher

(Don Mills, Ontario, Canada: Harlequin, 2015)

Story type: Contemporary
Subject(s): Romances (Fiction); Single parent family; Love
Major character(s): Tess Cole, Public Relations (Renewable Reliance); Slaid Jacobs, Government Official (mayor of Benson, California), Single Father (of Devin); Devin Jacobs, Teenager, Son (of Slaid)
Time period(s): 21st century; 2010s
Locale(s): Benson, California

Summary: Tess Cole, who works in public relations at the energy company Renewable Reliance, is not happy about her latest assignment. Her supervisor has sent her from her San Francisco home base to the Sierra Nevada community of Benson. Tess is supposed to convince the town's mayor to allow Renewable Reliance to construct a wind farm there. When she arrives at the mayor's office, Tess realizes that the meeting will be more complicated than she expected. She has met Slaid Jacobs before. They spent one passionate night together, and it's obvious that neither of them has forgotten it. Tess wants to keep their relationship professional, but the attraction they first experienced two years ago is still there. And this time, Slaid isn't interested in a one-night stand. He is the single father of a teenage son, and he would like Tess to be a permanent part of their lives.

Other books by the same author:
More Than a Rancher, 2014
A Ranch to Keep, 2014

Other books you might like:
Elizabeth Lowell, *Dangerous Refuge*, 2013
Susan Mallery, *Summer Days*, 2012
Linda Lael Miller, *Creed's Honor*, 2011
Laura Moore, *Once Tasted*, 2014
Christie Ridgway, *Make Me Lose Control*, 2014

1029

LINDSAY MCKENNA (Pseudonym of Eileen Nauman)

Wolf Haven

(Don Mills, Ontario, Canada: Harlequin, 2014)

Story type: Contemporary; Western
Subject(s): Military life; Wars; Ranch life
Major character(s): Skylar Pascal, Military Personnel (US Navy, former), Worker (on ranch), Nurse (ER and US Navy, former); Grayson "Gray" McCoy, Military Personnel (former US Navy SEAL), Rancher
Time period(s): 21st century; 2010s
Locale(s): Jackson Hole, Wyoming

Summary: After all she's been through in Afghanistan, US Navy nurse Skylar Pascal can't bring herself to go back to working in the emergency room she left to serve her country. It's all still too fresh—the crash of the Black Hawk helicopter, her capture by the enemy, and the days of torture she endured. A nice, quiet life on a ranch seems much more attractive, so Skylar goes to Wyoming. She hopes the peaceful scenery at the Elk Horn Ranch will bring healing. Grayson McCoy knows something of what the ranch's new nurse has been through. The former US Navy SEAL understands how bad things can get in war, and he finds himself attracted to and fascinated by Skylar. Together, they work to overcome the hurt and trauma she's endured, all the while inching closer to something new between the two of them—both of which could be threatened by the arrival of a stranger.

Other books by the same author:
Running Fire, 2015
Taking Fire, 2015
Breaking Point, 2014
Degree of Risk, 2014
Never Surrender, 2014

Other books you might like:
Lacey Baker, *Just Like Heaven*, 2013
Shannon K. Butcher, *Edge of Betrayal*, 2014
Susan Mallery, *Two of a Kind*, 2013
Lindsay McKenna, *High Country Rebel*, 2013
Alexis Morgan, *More Than a Touch*, 2014
Jill Shalvis, *Rescue My Heart*, 2012

1030

LINDSAY MCKENNA (Pseudonym of Eileen Nauman)

Taking Fire

(Don Mills, Ontario, Canada: Harlequin, 2015)

Story type: Military
Subject(s): Romances (Fiction); Military life; Wars
Major character(s): Khatereh "Khat" Shinwari, Military Personnel; Michael "Mike" Tarik, Military Personnel
Time period(s): 21st century; 2010s
Locale(s): Afghanistan

Summary: Khat Shinwari is a black ops agent trained as both a sniper and paramedic who has been placed deep into Afghanistan's mountains on a secret mission. However, she places her mission at risk when she elects

Romances

to warn four Navy SEALS about a Taliban ambush they are about to enter. Luckily, three of the SEALS manage to escape to safety unharmed, but the fourth, Mike Tarik, is too injured to get away, leaving Khat with no other option but to secret him away to her hiding place in the mountains. There, as she cares for his wounds, the pair begin to realize they have feelings for one another—a development that places her vital mission at risk. This is the seventh novel in the Shadow Warriors series of military romance novels.

Other books by the same author:
Running Fire, 2015
Breaking Point, 2014
Degree of Risk, 2014
Never Surrender, 2014
The Loner, 2013

Other books you might like:
Dee Davis, *Double Danger*, 2012
Cynthia Eden, *Evidence of Passion*, 2014
Elizabeth Jenkins, *Into the Crossfire*, 2010
Kat Martin, *Against the Edge*, 2013
Stephanie Tyler, *Surrender*, 2013

1031

JENNIFER MCKENZIE

Tempting Donovan Ford

(Don Mills, Ontario, Canada: Harlequin, 2015)

Series: Family Business Series. Book 1
Story type: Contemporary; Series
Subject(s): Romances (Fiction); Restaurants; Family relations
Major character(s): Julia Laurent, Cook (chef); Donovan Ford, Restaurateur
Time period(s): 21st century; 2010s
Locale(s): Vancouver, Canada

Summary: This contemporary romance novel by Jennifer McKenzie is the first installment in her Family Business series. Chef Julia Laurent has long dreamed of owning her late mother's restaurant. She's done everything she can to keep the restaurant going, but before she gathers the resources to make her purchase, the legendary Ford family acquires it. Julia stays on board, but now she's reporting to a new boss—Donovan Ford, the handsome and alluring son of the Ford family, famous for its success in the restaurant industry. As the chemistry between them grows into a sizzling romance, Julia willingly goes along with Donovan's plans, while never losing sight of her dream of owning the restaurant one day. Donovan has the skill and influence to make her dreams come true. She'll just have to find a way to make him think it's his idea.

Other books by the same author:
Anything but Business, 2015
One More Night, 2015
Table for Two, 2015
This Just In..., 2014
Not Another Wedding, 2013

Other books you might like:
Millie Criswell, *The Trouble with Mary*, 2000

Louisa Edwards, *Can't Stand the Heat*, 2009
Kate Meader, *Feel the Heat*, 2013
Cat Schield, *A Taste of Temptation*, 2014
Susan Wiggs, *The Beekeeper's Ball*, 2014

1032

LUANN MCLANE

Sweet Harmony

(New York: Penguin Publishing Group, 2014)

Series: Cricket Creek Series. Book 7
Story type: Contemporary; Series
Subject(s): Music; Singing; Romances (Fiction)
Major character(s): Cat Carson, Singer (country music star); Jeff Greenfield, Singer (country music)
Time period(s): 21st century; 2010s
Locale(s): Cricket Creek, Kentucky

Summary: Cat Carson has made it big in the country music world, so it's quite a surprise to the industry and her fans when she suddenly drops her Nashville record company and switches to a small label based in Cricket Creek, Kentucky. The change brings big excitement in the little town, and some angst for local country music singer Jeff Greenfield. Jeff has great potential and is starting to be noticed—he's been asked to sing a duet with the town's newest star, Cat. The record could boost his career to incredible levels, but Jeff doesn't want to lose his connection to his Southern farm upbringing and the town where he grew up. The more time he spends with Cat, however, the harder that gets. This is the seventh book in the Cricket Creek series.

Other books by the same author:
Wildflower Wedding, 2014
Moonlight Kiss, 2013
Whisper's Edge, 2013
Catch of a Lifetime, 2012
Pitch Perfect, 2012

Other books you might like:
Catherine Bybee, *Single by Saturday*, 2014
Joan Early, *Separate Dreams*, 2011
Lorelei James, *Hillbilly Rockstar*, 2014
Freya North, *Pillow Talk*, 2008
Charlene Sands, *The Cowboy's Pride*, 2011

1033

BEC MCMASTER

Of Silk and Steam

(Naperville, Illinois: Sourcebooks Casablanca, 2015)

Series: London Steampunk Series. Book 5
Story type: Historical - Victorian; Science Fantasy
Subject(s): Romances (Fiction); Steampunk; Revenge
Major character(s): Lady Aramina Duvall, Young Woman, Daughter (of crime victim); Leo Barrons, Son (of assassin), Enemy (of Lady Aramina)
Time period(s): 19th century; 1880s (1880)
Locale(s): London, England

Summary: A woman seeks revenge for her father's death in the fifth novel in the London Steampunk series. In an alternative version of Victorian London, humans live side by side with bluebloods, who are infected with a virus that gives them superior powers. It is a strange world where automatons perform in the streets, and duels settle social disputes. In this city Lady Aramina is on a quest for vengeance. Her father is dead, and Aramina intends to make his assassin pay. She knows the identity of her father's killer, but Aramina also knows she may not be able to get to him. Instead, she targets the assassin's son, Leo Barrons. Leo knows that Aramina is supposed to be his enemy, but he is intrigued by her. He has seen the darkness she is capable of, but he suspects that Aramina also possesses passions of a different sort.

Other books by the same author:
Forged by Desire, 2014
Heart of Iron, 2013
My Lady Quicksilver, 2013
Kiss of Steel, 2012

Other books you might like:
Meljean Brook, *The Iron Duke*, 2010
Kristen Callihan, *Shadowdance*, 2013
Beth Ciotta, *His Clockwork Canary*, 2013
Isabel Cooper, *No Proper Lady*, 2011
Kate Cross, *Heart of Brass*, 2012
Delilah Dawson, *Wicked After Midnight*, 2014
Delphine Dryden, *Gossamer Wing*, 2013
Liz Maverick, *Crimson and Steam*, 2010

1034

MARY MCNEAR

Moonlight on Butternut Lake

(New York: HarperCollins, 2015)

Series: Butternut Lake Trilogy. Book 3
Story type: Contemporary; Series
Subject(s): Romances (Fiction); Rural life; Abuse
Major character(s): Mila Jones, Abuse Victim, Spouse (of Brandon), Caregiver (of Reid); Brandon, Spouse (of Mila); Reid Ford, Patient (of Mila), Accident Victim
Time period(s): 21st century; 2010s
Locale(s): Butternut, Minnesota

Summary: In the third and final installment from Mary McNear's Butternut Lake trilogy, the author tells the story of Mila Jones, who comes to Butternut Lake to get away from her abusive husband, Brandon. Mila takes a job as a home healthcare professional for Reid Ford, a handsome but ornery patient who suffers from injuries sustained in an accident. Reid is still troubled by memories of the accident, but Mila's good nature soon wins his heart. The more time Mila and Reid spend together, the more they realize how much they have in common. Soon, they both learn the importance of letting go of fears and living life to the fullest. Unfortunately, Mila's old life has followed her to Butternut Lake, and she will need to cling to her newly found happiness if she wants to shed her past once and for all.

Other books by the same author:
Butternut Summer, 2014

Up at Butternut Lake, 2014

Other books you might like:
Robyn Carr, *The Hero*, 2013
Kathleen Eagle, *The Last Good Man*, 2000
Lisa Kleypas, *Blue-Eyed Devil*, 2008
Jane Porter, *The Good Woman*, 2012
Barbara Samuel, *A Piece of Heaven*, 2003

1035

MARGARET MCPHEE

The Lost Gentleman

(Don Mills, Ontario, Canada: Harlequin, 2015)

Story type: Historical
Subject(s): Romances (Fiction); Pirates; Ships
Major character(s): Kate "La Voile" Medhurst, Pirate; Captain Kit North, Sea Captain
Time period(s): 19th century; 1810s
Locale(s): Caribbean Sea

Summary: Kate Medhurst is a privateer operating in the Caribbean whose ship, the *Coyote*, has proven to be a tremendous thorn in the side of the British Navy. In fact, the British believe *Coyote* and its increasingly notorious captain, "La Voile," to be such a threat, that they have assigned their best pirate hunter, Captain Kit North, to go after the ship. Kit sets up a trap with his own vessel *The Raven*, luring the *Coyote* into his clutches. In the ensuing confrontation, the man Kate uses as her stand-in for La Voile is killed, and Kit believes the threat is gone. Finding Kate aboard the ship, he mistakes her for a prisoner of La Voile and brings her onto his own ship. Now forced into close quarters, the pair begin to see each other in a different light—a transition that will prove necessary when Kit finally learns Kate's true identity. This is the second title in McPhee's Gentleman of Disrepute series.

Other books by the same author:
Temptation in Regency Society, 2015
The Gentleman Rogue, 2014
Dicing with the Dangerous Lord, 2013
Mistress to the Marquis, 2013
His Mask of Retribution, 2012

Other books you might like:
Celeste Bradley, *Scoundrel in My Dreams*, 2010
Alison DeLaine, *A Gentleman 'Til Midnight*, 2013
Christy English, *Much Ado About Jack*, 2014
Suzanne Enoch, *Rules of an Engagement*, 2010
Bronwyn Scott, *Breaking the Rake's Rules*, 2015

1036

JENNIFER MCQUISTON

Diary of an Accidental Wallflower

(New York: Avon, 2015)

Series: Seduction Diaries Series. Book 1
Story type: Historical - Regency; Series

Romances

Subject(s): Romances (Fiction); History; Social class
Major character(s): Clare Westmore, Debutante; Charles Alban, Nobleman (future Duke of Harrington); Dr. Daniel Merial, Doctor
Time period(s): 19th century; 1810s
Locale(s): England

Summary: Miss Clare Westmore intends to find a suitable husband during the London season. She has her heart set on one man in particular—Charles Alban, soon-to-be Duke of Harrington—and she has already caught his eye. But Clare's romantic scheming hits a snag when a sprained ankle forces her to sit out an important ball. Instead of dancing with Charles, Clare spends time with Dr. Daniel Merial, who tends to her injury. Although Daniel is not suited to Clare socially, he does make a good intellectual match. They share lively conversation while Daniel helps heal Clare's ankle. Clare looks forward to getting back on the dance floor, but she is surprised by how much she enjoys Daniel's company. His world views are refreshing, and he has even won the affection of the Westmore family. Clare faces a difficult decision when she no longer needs Daniel's medical care. This novel is the first in the Seduction Diaries series.

Other books by the same author:
Moonlight on My Mind, 2014
Summer Is for Lovers, 2013
What Happens in Scotland, 2013

Other books you might like:
Elizabeth Boyle, *If Wishes Were Earls*, 2014
Kathryn Caskie, *A Lady's Guide to Rakes*, 2005
Kieran Kramer, *When Harry Met Molly*, 2010
Caroline Linden, *Love and Other Scandals*, 2013
Teresa Medeiros, *The Pleasure of Your Kiss*, 2012

1037

KATE MEADER (Pseudonym of Linda O'Dwyer)

All Fired Up
(New York: Forever, 2014)

Series: Hot in the Kitchen Series. Book 2
Story type: Contemporary; Series
Subject(s): Romances (Fiction); Marriage; Weddings
Major character(s): Cara DeLuca, Planner (events), Spouse (wife, of Shane); Shane Doyle, Baker (pastry chef), Spouse (husband, of Cara)
Time period(s): 21st century; 2010s
Locale(s): Chicago, Illinois

Summary: This contemporary romance novel is the second book in the Hot in the Kitchen series by Kate Meader. On a work trip in Las Vegas, buttoned-up private events planner Cara DeLuca and her co-worker, pastry chef Shane Doyle, end one wild and crazy night with a marriage proposal and an on-the-spot wedding ceremony. Ashamed and embarrassed, Cara wants their marriage annulled as soon as they return to Chicago. But as their annulment date approaches and secrets from the pasts emerge—as well as hopes for the future—Shane and Cara find they might have more in common than they thought. Does Cara have the courage to follow her heart, and is Shane willing to fight for what he really wants?

Other books by the same author:
Feel the Heat, 2014
Hot and Bothered, 2014

Other books you might like:
Sylvia Day, *Reflected in You*, 2012
Janelle Denison, *No Strings...*, 2013
Susan Johnson, *Wine, Tarts, & Sex*, 2007
Robin Schone, *Scandalous Lovers*, 2007
Amanda Usen, *Luscious*, 2012

1038

KELLY MORAN

Return to Me
(New York: Penguin Publishing Group, 2015)

Series: Covington Cove Series. Book 1
Story type: Contemporary; Series
Subject(s): Military life; Nursing; Social class
Major character(s): Cole Covington, Wealthy, Military Personnel, Accident Victim, Patient (of Mia), Brother (of Lacey); Lacey Covington, Sister (of Cole), Wealthy; Mia Galdon, Nurse, Caregiver (of Cole), Sister (of Ginny); Ginny Galdon, Sister (of Mia), Mentally Challenged Person
Time period(s): 21st century; 2010s
Locale(s): Wilmington, North Carolina

Summary: This is the first novel from the Covington Cove series. Cole fell for Mia the moment he saw her, but his family disapproved of her because she was poor. Cole chose to obey his family's wishes over his own heart, and he has regretted it ever since. He joined the military, hoping that he could forget about the girl he left behind, and Mia went on to become a nurse. Now, a decade later, Cole has returned to the family home after being injured during deployment. Cole's sister, Lacey, offers Mia a job as Cole's nurse. Mia takes care of her sister Ginny, who has Down syndrome, and she has no choice but to accept Lacey's offer. Mia and Cole aren't sure that they can leave the past behind, especially once they realize that their feelings for each other haven't faded.

Other books you might like:
Robyn Carr, *The Chance*, 2014
Virginia Kantra, *Carolina Home*, 2012
Brenda Novak, *When Lightning Strikes*, 2012
Jill Shalvis, *Rumor Has It*, 2013
Candis Terry, *Sweetest Mistake*, 2013

1039

CAROLE MORTIMER

Darian Hunter: Duke of Desire
(Don Mills, Ontario, Canada: Harlequin, 2014)

Series: Dangerous Dukes Series. Book 3
Story type: Historical - Regency; Series
Subject(s): Romances (Fiction); History; England
Major character(s): Darian Hunter, Nobleman (aka Duke of Wolfingham), Spy, Co-worker (of Mariah); Mariah

Beecham, Spy, Co-worker (of Darian), Noblewoman (aka Countess of Carlisle)
Time period(s): 19th century; 1810s (1815)
Locale(s): London, England

Summary: Set in 1815 London, this is the third book in the Dangerous Dukes series by Carole Mortimer. Notorious womanizer Darian Hunter, Duke of Wolfingham, is displeased by a rumor. His younger brother is rumored to be involved with Mariah Beecham, Countess of Carlisle, a scandalous widow known for her many lovers. In an effort to protect his brother, Darian confronts Mariah, only to learn that, like him, she is a secret agent of the Crown. The pair is soon forced to attend a house party to thwart an assassination plot. Posing as lovers, Darian and Mariah discover the sensual and provocative roles they're playing stir up feelings that are all too real. Having been forced into her marriage, Mariah has no intention of developing a long-term relationship, but she can hardly ignore her growing attraction to Darian. And how long can Darian withstand a temptation as strong as Mariah?

Other books by the same author:
A Bargain with the Enemy, 2014
A D'Angelo Like No Other, 2014
A Prize Beyond Jewels, 2014
Zachary Black: Duke of Debauchery, 2014
Not Just a Wallflower, 2013

Other books you might like:
Catherine Coulter, *The Duke*, 1995
Claudia Dain, *Daring a Duke*, 2010
Gaelen Foley, *The Duke*, 2000
Jillian Hunter, *A Duke's Temptation*, 2010
Nicole Jordan, *To Desire a Wicked Duke*, 2011

1040

CARLA NEGGERS

Echo Lake

(Don Mills, Ontario, Canada: Mira, 2015)

Story type: Contemporary
Subject(s): Romances (Fiction); Love; Construction
Major character(s): Heather Sloan, Manager (project manager), Businesswoman, Designer; Brody Hancock, Agent (Diplomatic Security Service), Friend (of Vic); Vic Scarlatti, Government Official (retired ambassador), Retiree
Time period(s): 21st century; 2010s
Locale(s): Knights Bridge, Massachusetts

Summary: Heather Sloan has landed the renovation of Vic Scarlatti's country home overlooking Echo Lake in Knights Bridge, Massachusetts. It's the perfect project for the family business. Diplomatic Security Service agent Brody Hancock left Knights Bridge at eighteen, a few steps ahead of the wrath of Heather's older brothers. Though Brody had never planned to return, Vic, a retired diplomat and friend, needs his help. Staying at Vic's guest house makes it impossible to avoid running into the Sloans—especially Heather. Heather is wary of Brody's interest in her, and she suspects there's more to his

homecoming than he's letting on. Also available in Large Print.

Other books by the same author:
Cider Brook, 2014
Harbor Island, 2014
Declan's Cross, 2013
That Night on Thistle Lane, 2013
Heron's Cove, 2012

Other books you might like:
Cindy Gerard, *To the Edge*, 2005
Heather Graham, *The Night Is Watching*, 2013
Iris Johansen, *Taking Eve*, 2013
Marta Perry, *Hide in Plain Sight*, 2007
Karen Robards, *Hunted*, 2013

1041

CARLA NEGGERS

Harbor Island

(Don Mills, Ontario, Canada: Harlequin, 2014)

Series: Sharpe and Donovan Series. Book 4
Story type: Contemporary; Romantic Suspense
Subject(s): Romances (Fiction); Suspense; Mystery
Major character(s): Emma Sharpe, FBI Agent, Granddaughter (of Wendell Sharpe), Fiance(e) (of Colin Donovan); Wendell Sharpe, Detective, Grandfather (of Emma); Colin Donovan, FBI Agent (undercover), Fiance(e) (of Emma)
Time period(s): 21st century; 2010s
Locale(s): Ireland; New England, United States

Summary: A serial art thief has taunted FBI agent Emma Sharpe and her grandfather, detective Wendell Sharpe, for ten years. The thief began by stealing a Celtic cross in Ireland and has since left a copy of the cross at subsequent crime scenes. Now it appears that the thief has developed a taste for murder. A woman's body has been found on an island near Boston, and Emma realizes immediately that the elusive art thief is involved: The corpse is clutching a stone carved with a Celtic cross. Emma's fiance, undercover FBI agent Colin Donovan, assists with the investigation. They are concerned about the change in the thief's MO and suspect the case is more complicated than they first realized. As they hunt for a killer, Emma and Colin begin to wonder if they will ever be able to balance their work and their relationship. This novel is the fourth in the Sharpe and Donovan series by Carla Neggers.

Other books by the same author:
Echo Lake, 2015
Cider Brook, 2014
Declan's Cross, 2013
That Night on Thistle Lane, 2013
Heron's Cove, 2012

Other books you might like:
Cherry Adair, *Vortex*, 2012
Dee Davis, *Deadly Dance*, 2012
Laura Griffin, *Far Gone*, 2014
Rachel Lee, *Undercover Hunter*, 2015
Lorie O'Clare, *Run Wild*, 2012

Romances

Sharon Sala, *Wild Hearts*, 2015
Rebecca Scherm, *Unbecoming*, 2015
Debra Webb, *Rage*, 2013

1042

MIRANDA NEVILLE

The Duke of Dark Desires

(New York: Avon, 2014)

Series: Wild Quartet Series. Book 4
Story type: Historical - Georgian; Series
Subject(s): Romances (Fiction); British history, 1714-1815; Family
Major character(s): Julian Fortescue, Nobleman (Duke of Denford), Brother (half-brother of Maria, Fenella, Laura), Guardian (of Maria, Fenella, Laura); Maria, 15-Year-Old, Sister (half-sister of Julian), Sister (of Fenella, Laura); Fenella, 14-Year-Old, Sister (half-sister of Julian), Sister (of Maria and Laura); Laura, 9-Year-Old, Sister (half-sister of Julian), Sister (of Maria, Fenella); Jeanne de Falleron, Woman (also known as Jane Grey), Survivor (French Revolution), Governess (to Maria, Fenella, Laura)
Time period(s): 19th century; 1800s (1802)
Locale(s): England

Summary: When Julian Fortescue, Duke of Denford, is left as guardian to his half-sisters Maria, Fenella, and Laura, in 1802, he immediately searches for a governess. Jane Grey applies for the job, and Julian is immediately smitten. He hires Jane, intending to make her his mistress, but he has no idea that the mysterious Jane has her own motives for coming to the Fortescue house. Jane's real name is Jeanne de Falleron, and her parents and siblings were killed in the French Revolution. A betrayal by someone named Fortescue cost them their lives, and Jane is on a personal mission to kill the person responsible. But even though she knows that her employer could have something to do with her family members' deaths, Jane can't help feeling attracted to Julian. Meanwhile, Julian deals with his own regrets regarding his actions during the revolution. This is the final novel in the Wild Quartet.

Other books by the same author:
Lady Windermere's Lover, 2014
The Ruin of a Rogue, 2013
Confessions from an Arranged Marriage, 2012
The Importance of Being Wicked, 2012
The Amorous Education of Celia Seaton, 2011

Other books you might like:
Suzanne Enoch, *The Rake*, 2002
Juliana Gray, *How to School Your Scoundrel*, 2014
Madeline Hunter, *The Counterfeit Mistress*, 2013
Sarah MacLean, *No Good Duke Goes Unpunished*, 2013
Kasey Michaels, *What a Gentleman Desires*, 2013

1043

BRENDA NOVAK

This Heart of Mine

(Don Mills, Ontario, Canada: Mira, 2015)

Series: Whiskey Creek Series. Book 8
Story type: Contemporary; Series
Subject(s): Romances (Fiction); Family relations; Mother-son relations
Major character(s): Phoenix Fuller, Prisoner (former), Lover (former, of Riley), Mother (of Jacob); Riley Stinson, Lover (former, of Phoenix), Father (of Jacob); Jacob Stinson, Son (of Phoenix and Riley)
Time period(s): 21st century; 2010s
Locale(s): Whiskey Creek, California

Summary: Best-selling author Brenda Novak delivers the eighth installment in her Whiskey Creek contemporary romance series. Phoenix Fuller served 17 years in prison for a crime she didn't commit. Unable to prove her innocence, the pregnant teen was convicted of running the girlfriend of her ex-boyfriend—and child's father—off the road, resulting in a fatal crash. Now, Phoenix returns to Whiskey Creek, California, to get to know her son, Jacob, who lives with his father, Riley Stinson. Phoenix still loves Riley, but Riley—along with the rest of the town—isn't too happy about Phoenix's return. Phoenix isn't the same quiet, insecure girl who left town years ago, however. She's strong and independent, and she knows what she wants. Riley wants to find love and a mother for Jacob, but will he realize the woman he's looking for is the one who has finally made her way back into his life?

Other books by the same author:
Come Home to Me, 2014
The Heart of Christmas, 2014
Honor Bound, 2014
A Matter of Grave Concern, 2014
Take Me Home for Christmas, 2013

Other books you might like:
Robyn Carr, *The Chance*, 2014
Barbara Freethy, *The Way Back Home*, 2012
Roberta Helmer, *Butterfly Cove*, 2013
Jennifer Lohmann, *Winning Ruby Heart*, 2014
Julia London, *Return to Homecoming Ranch*, 2014

1044

BRENDA NOVAK

The Heart of Christmas

(Don Mills, Ontario, Canada: Harlequin, 2014)

Series: Whiskey Creek Series. Book 7
Story type: Contemporary; Holiday Themes
Subject(s): Interpersonal relations; Romances (Fiction); Christmas
Major character(s): Eve Harmon, Innkeeper (bed-and-breakfast), Lover (of Brent/Rex); Rex McCready, Man (aka Brent Taylor), Lover (of Eve)
Time period(s): 21st century; 2010s

Locale(s): Whiskey Creek, California

Summary: All Eve Harmon wants for Christmas is love—the kind that ends with a wedding, followed by kids and happily ever after. Everything else in her life—including her bed-and-breakfast in Whiskey Creek, where she was born and raised—leaves Eve lacking these days. Maybe that's why she came home from her 35th birthday party a little drunk with a man she never met before. Eve is shocked at herself, and she's even more shocked at the cavalier attitude of the man, whose name turns out to be Brent Taylor. Brent finds the whole thing to be no big deal, and that might be because the things he's hiding are a much bigger and potentially deadlier deal. Brent is really Rex McCready, and the secrets he's keeping are dangerous. It will take more than the usual Christmas magic to make Eve's Christmas wishes come true in this seventh installment of the Whiskey Creek series.

Other books by the same author:
Take Me Home for Christmas, 2015
This Heart of Mine, 2015
Come Home to Me, 2014
A Matter of Grave Concern, 2014
Through the Smoke, 2013

Other books you might like:
Bella Andre, *Kissing Under the Mistletoe*, 2013
Lacey Baker, *Homecoming*, 2013
Toni Blake, *Half Moon Hill*, 2013
Susan Donovan, *Sea of Love*, 2013
Susan Wiggs, *Candlelight Christmas*, 2013

`1045`

SALLY ORR

The Rake's Handbook: Including Field Guide

(Naperville, Illinois: Sourcebooks Casablanca, 2014)

Series: Rake's Handbook Series. Book 1
Story type: Historical - Regency; Series
Subject(s): Romances (Fiction); England; History
Major character(s): Ross Thornbury, Writer (of *The Rake's Handbook*), Neighbor (of Elinor); Elinor Colton, Widow(er), Neighbor (of Ross)
Time period(s): 19th century; 1820s (1821)
Locale(s): Macclesfield, England

Summary: Ross Thornbury authored a seduction guide titled *The Rake's Handbook* on a dare, and while society's women criticized its contents, the gentlemen secretly praised the work and its writer. Unable to manage his sudden fame—and notoriety—Ross moves from London to the small country village of Macclesfield, where he plans to settle down and rebuild his reputation. Ross's new neighbor, recently widowed Elinor Colton, is determined not to fall prey to his seductive ways, and when he asks to purchase some of her land for his industrial endeavors, Elinor tries to shut him out. But Ross refuses to be turned away, and soon, Elinor discovers more to Ross than she expected. Elinor can't ignore her feelings toward her new neighbor forever, but how can she trust her heart when it means putting her own reputation at risk? This is the first installment in Sally

Orr's Rake's Handbook historical romance series. First novel.

Other books you might like:
Connie Brockway, *No Place for a Dame*, 2013
Suzanne Enoch, *The Rake*, 2002
Lynn Kerstan, *Francesca's Rake*, 1997
Mary Jo Putney, *The Rake*, 1998
Emma Wildes, *An Indecent Proposition*, 2009

`1046`

SHARON PAGE

An American Duchess

(Don Mills, Ontario, Canada: Harlequin, 2014)

Story type: Historical - Roaring Twenties
Subject(s): Romances (Fiction); Marriage; Inheritance and succession
Major character(s): Zoe Gifford, Heiress, Spouse (wife, of Nigel); Nigel Hazelton, Veteran (World War I), Spouse (husband, of Zoe), Nobleman, Brother (older, of Sebastian); Sebastian Hazelton, Nobleman, Brother (younger, of Nigel)
Time period(s): 20th century; 1920s (1922)
Locale(s): England

Summary: American heiress Zoe Gifford wants all that the Roaring Twenties has to offer. She is unable to access her father's fortune until she marries, however, so rebellious and headstrong Zoe devises a plan. British aristocrat Sebastian Hazelton's family is in dire financial straits, so he agrees to marry and quickly divorce Zoe to their mutual satisfaction. Her plan falls to pieces, however, when she meets Sebastian's older brother, Nigel, a veteran of the Great War. Nigel looks down on the ever-changing world of the 1920s, and Zoe—independent, outspoken, and progressive—represents all he detests about the emerging age. However, when circumstances force Zoe to marry Nigel instead of Sebastian, an unexpected, passionate romance develops. Their love is tested as Zoe fights for the future and Nigel remains stuck in the past. Will Zoe be forced to choose between her dreams and her marriage?

Other books by the same author:
Engaged in Sin, 2011
The Club, 2009

Other books you might like:
Laurie Graham, *The Great Husband Hunt*, 2002
Elizabeth Lord, *Julia's Way*, 2009
Caroline Preston, *Gatsby's Girl*, 2006
Lucinda Riley, *The Midnight Rose*, 2014
Danielle Steel, *A Good Woman*, 2008

`1047`

LIZA PALMER

Girl Before a Mirror

(New York: William Morrow, 2015)

Story type: Contemporary
Subject(s): Romances (Fiction); Women; Advertising

(margin) Romances

Major character(s): Anna Wyatt, Woman (40 years old), Advertising (account executive), Divorced Person, Colleague (of Sasha); Sasha Merchant, Artist (illustrator), Colleague (of Anna); Lincoln Mallory, Consultant (financial)
Time period(s): 21st century; 2010s
Locale(s): Phoenix, Arizona; Washington, District of Columbia

Summary: Anna Wyatt wants to make changes in her personal and professional life. Divorced and 40 years old, Anna has decided not to date for a while. She is an account executive at a Washington, DC, advertising firm, and she intends for her current campaign to lead to bigger clients. When Anna is paired with Sasha Merchant, a strikingly beautiful illustrator, she is infected with Sasha's enthusiasm for the self-help book *Be the Heroine, Find Your Hero*. Anna and Sasha follow the book's advice, which is inspired by scenarios in romance novels, and experience success. To find the perfect model for their ad campaign, they attend a romance authors' conference in Phoenix. There Anna meets Lincoln Mallory and breaks her no-dating rule. The conference allows Anna to escape reality, but when it's time to leave Phoenix, Anna must decide if a relationship with Lincoln could survive beyond the world of RomanceCon.

Other books by the same author:
Nowhere but Home, 2013
More Like Her, 2012
A Field Guide to Burying Your Parents, 2009
Seeing Me Naked, 2008
Conversations with the Fat Girl, 2005

Other books you might like:
Meg Donohue, *How to Eat a Cupcake*, 2012
Catherine McKenzie, *Forgotten*, 2012
Teresa Medeiros, *Goodnight Tweetheart*, 2010
Jane Porter, *Easy on the Eyes*, 2009
Joanne Rendell, *Crossing Washington Square*, 2009
Sylvia True, *The Wednesday Group*, 2015

1048

LISA PLUMLEY

All He Wants for Christmas

(New York: Zebra Books, 2014)

Series: Kismet Christmas Series. Book 4
Story type: Contemporary; Holiday Themes
Subject(s): Romances (Fiction); Christmas; Toys
Major character(s): Jason Hamilton, Businessman (CEO of toy company); Danielle Sharpe, Manager (toy store), Single Mother
Time period(s): 21st century; 2010s
Locale(s): Kismet, Michigan

Summary: This contemporary romance novel by bestselling author Lisa Plumley is the fourth installment in her Kismet Christmas series. Jason Hamilton is the CEO of a toy company, but the party-boy image the young businessman has created for himself does not go over well with the company's board of directors. In order to clean up his reputation and get back to business, Jason travels to Kismet, Michigan, to present an award to the

company's most profitable store. Single mother Danielle Sharpe has managed Kismet's toy store for six short months and has turned it into a model of success. Hopeful for the chance to land a corporate position, Danielle is eager to host the company's CEO. When Jason arrives in Kismet, he's shocked to learn that the store's manager is the young—and attractive—Danielle. The chemistry between Jason and Danielle is strong, but will their own ambitions keep them from giving in to their feelings for one another?

Other books by the same author:
Notorious in the West, 2014
So Irresistible, 2013
Melt into You, 2012
Holiday Affair, 2010
Home for the Holidays, 2008

Other books you might like:
Robyn Carr, *A Virgin River Christmas*, 2008
Samantha Chase, *The Christmas Cottage*, 2012
Lisa Kleypas, *Christmas Eve at Friday Harbor*, 2010
Debbie Macomber, *A Cedar Cove Christmas*, 2008
Susan Wiggs, *Candlelight Christmas*, 2013

1049

LISA PLUMLEY

Morrow Creek Runaway

(Don Mills, Ontario, Canada: Harlequin, 2015)

Story type: Historical - American West
Subject(s): Romances (Fiction); Abuse; Marriage
Major character(s): Rosamond Dancy, Housekeeper, Widow(er); Miles Callaway, Lover
Time period(s): 19th century; 1880s
Locale(s): Morrow Creek, Arizona

Summary: Rosamond Darcy's life to this point has been hard. The victim of an abusive past, she has managed to forge a productive life for herself in Morrow Creek, Arizona, but as she sees her friends settle into happy marriages, she wonders if she will ever have that opportunity for herself. Having been sold into marriage against her will, and then quickly widowed, about the only positive memories she still retains from her life before her move to Arizona involve Miles Callaway—a man whose unexpected arrival in Morrow Creek has Rosamond on edge, even as she discovers he still has the power to evoke deep feelings in her that she thought dead. Miles, however, harbors his own dark secrets—several of which involve Rosamond. With a past that she hoped was buried coming back to haunt her, can Rosamond find the peace and love that have always eluded her?

Other books by the same author:
Notorious in the West, 2014
The Honor-Bound Gambler, 2013
So Irresistible, 2013
Melt into You, 2012
The Bride Raffle, 2011

Other books you might like:
Jim Austin, *Last Chance Canyon*, 1993

Georgina Gentry, *To Tame a Texan*, 2003
Leigh Greenwood, *Rose*, 1993
Elizabeth Lowell, *Only You*, 1992
Jodi Thomas, *The Texan's Wager*, 2002

1050

PATRICIA POTTER

Tempted by the Soldier

(Don Mills, Ontario, Canada: Harlequin, 2015)

Story type: Contemporary
Subject(s): Romances (Fiction); Wars; Military life
Major character(s): Stephanie Phillips, Veterinarian, Lover (of Clint Morgan); Clint Morgan, Lover (of Stephanie Phillips), Military Personnel
Time period(s): 21st century; 2010s
Locale(s): Covenant Falls, Colorado

Summary: Clint Morgan is suffering from headaches and blackouts—souvenirs from his time as a former Blackhawk helicopter pilot in Afghanistan. While he recovers from his lingering head injuries, he elects to settle in Covenant Falls, Colorado for a short time. There, he meets kindly but wary veterinarian Stephanie Phillips, who might the one thing Clint really needs to fully overcome his deep physical and emotional scars. For Stephanie, a brash pilot only in town for a short while is the very last thing she believes she needs in her life. However, Clint forms a bond with an abused dog that provides a salve to his pain that, in turn, enables him to come to the aid of Stephanie when it turns out she is harboring her own set of secrets and emotional scars.

Other books by the same author:
The Soldier's Promise, 2014
Home for Christmas, 2011
The Lawman, 2010
The Marshall and the Heiress, 1996
Renegade, 1993

Other books you might like:
Roz Denny Fox, *The Cowboy Soldier*, 2010
Stephanie Doyle, *For the First Time*, 2013
Vicki Essex, *Her Son's Hero*, 2011
Nicole Helm, *Too Close to Resist*, 2014
Tara Taylor Quinn, *At Close Range*, 2008

1051

AMANDA QUICK (Pseudonym of Jayne Ann Krentz)

Garden of Lies

(New York: Penguin Group, 2015)

Subject(s): Mystery; Murder; England
Major character(s): Ursula Kern, Woman, Businessman, Widow(er), Detective—Amateur, Companion (of Slater); Slater Roxton, Archaeologist, Adventurer, Companion (of Ursula)
Time period(s): 19th century
Locale(s): London, England

Summary: Widowed Ursula Kern runs a secretarial agency in Victorian England. Her clients are some of the most influential people in high society. When one of her employees ends up dead, Ursula suspects foul play and begins to look into the matter. She's assisted by adventurer Slater Roxton, who thinks Ursula may be taking on more than she can handle. He intends to stay close to his friend to see where the trail leads, and also because there just may be something more than a professional arrangement developing between them. As the two begin to investigate the death of the employee, they find themselves drawn deeper into a world of wealth and corruption. The dark shadows of London just may be hiding a killer who does not want to be unmasked.

Other books by the same author:
Otherwise Engaged, 2014
The Mystery Woman, 2013
Crystal Gardens, 2012
Quicksilver, 2011
Burning Lamp, 2010

Other books you might like:
Emily Brightwell, *Mrs. Jeffries and the One Who Got Away*, 2015
Robyn DeHart, *Tempted at Every Turn*, 2007
Jessica Hall, *Heat of the Moment*, 2004
Kay Hooper, *A Deadly Web*, 2014
Betina Krahn, *The Book of True Desires*, 2006
Stephanie Laurens, *The Masterful Mr. Montague*, 2014
Hillary Manton Lodge, *A Table by the Window: A Novel of Family Secrets and Heirloom Recipes*, 2014
Alexander McCall Smith, *The Careful Use of Compliments: An Isabel Dalhousie Novel*, 2007
Alexander McCall Smith, *Tea Time for the Traditionally Built*, 2009
Rachelle McCalla, *Princess in Peril*, 2011
Karen Robards, *Obsession*, 2007
Maggie Robinson, *In the Heart of the Highlander*, 2013
Jillian Stone, *A Private Duel with Agent Gunn*, 2012
Anne Stuart, *Never Kiss a Rake*, 2013

1052

CAISEY QUINN

Leaving Amarillo

(New York, New York: William Morrow, 2015)

Series: Neon Dreams Series. Book
Story type: Contemporary
Subject(s): Romances (Fiction); Musicians; Love
Major character(s): Dixie Lark, Sister (to Dallas), Musician; Gavin Garrison, Musician; Dallas Lark, Musician, Brother (to Dixie)
Time period(s): 21st century; 2010s
Locale(s): Amarillo, Texas

Summary: The first book in the Neon Dreams collection by Casey Quinn introduces Dixie Lark, a classically trained violinist who dreams lie in country music rather than an orchestral pit. She and her protective brother Dallas grew up in poverty after the deaths of their parents in an accident. Raised on country music and taught to fiddle, the dreams of a country music band have driven Dixie, Dallas, and their friend Gavin since childhood. Together, they embark on fulfilling their dream by creating Leaving Amarillo, a band they hope will soon be performing at Austin, Texas's MusicFest, which might in turn offer them the chance for stardom. In addition to the pains of being a traveling band, Dixie and Gavin have secretly loved each other since childhood, though neither figure knows the depth of their mutual feelings for each other. Complicating matters even further, Dallas has wrestled a promise from his best friend Gavin to never become romantically involved with his sister for her own protection. Over the course of the story, all three figures must navigate both their respective relationships to the band and each other, while pursuing their lifelong dreams of country music superstardom.

Other books by the same author:
Falling for You, 2015
Loving Dallas, 2015
All I Need, 2014
Falling for Fate, 2014
Girl in Love, 2014

Other books you might like:
Susan Anderson, *Be My Baby*, 2012
Jennifer L. Armentrout, *Fall with Me*, 2015
Sylvia Day, *Pride and Pleasure*, 2011
Virginia Kantra, *Carolina Blues*, 2014
Susan Mallery, *Already Home*, 2011

1053

JULIA QUINN (Pseudonym of Julie Cotler Pottinger)

The Secrets of Sir Richard Kenworthy

(New York: Avon, 2015)

Series: Smythe-Smith Quartet Series. Book 4
Story type: Historical; Series
Subject(s): Romances (Fiction); History; England
Major character(s): Richard Kenworthy, Nobleman; Iris Smythe-Smith, Young Woman, Musician (cellist)
Time period(s): 19th century; 1820s (1825)
Locale(s): England

Summary: Sir Richard Kenworthy is 27 years old and in desperate need of a wife. He has no interest in falling in love; he is only interested in getting married. When he is invited to a musical performance at the home of the Smythe-Smith clan, he attends with some trepidation. He knows the event will throw him together with several eligible Smyth-Smith women, but he suspects that each is flawed in some way. When Richard spots Iris Smythe-Smith playing her cello, he takes notice. Iris is not strikingly beautiful, but Richard finds her intriguing. Iris is surprised when she learns that Richard wants to meet her. She is even more surprised when he makes a romantic proposition. Iris's misgivings about Richard's rash behavior are confirmed when an indiscretion prompts a hasty marriage. As Iris learns her husband's motives, her unconventional marriage evolves into a true love affair. This novel is the fourth in the Smythe-Smith series.

Other books by the same author:
The Sum of All Kisses, 2013
The Lady Most Willing, 2012
A Night Like This, 2012
Just Like Heaven, 2011
Ten Things I Love about You, 2010

Other books you might like:
Jane Ashford, *The Bride Insists*, 2014
Sophie Barnes, *The Scandal in Kissing an Heir*, 2013
Jo Beverley, *A Shocking Delight*, 2014
Celeste Bradley, *With This Ring*, 2014
Tessa Dare, *Romancing the Duke*, 2014
Christy English, *Much Ado About Jack*, 2014
Jayne Fresina, *Miss Molly Robbins Designs a Seduction*, 2014
Anne Gracie, *The Winter Bride*, 2014
Jillian Hunter, *Forbidden to Love the Duke*, 2015
Caroline Linden, *Love and Other Scandals*, 2013
Kate Noble, *The Game and the Governess*, 2014
Maya Rodale, *The Wicked Wallflower*, 2013
Regina Scott, *The Husband Campaign*, 2014

1054

PAULA QUINN

The Wicked Ways of Alexander Kidd

(New York: Forever, 2014)

Series: MacGregors: Highland Heirs Series. Book 2
Story type: Historical; Series
Subject(s): Romances (Fiction); Scotland; Pirates
Major character(s): Alexander Kidd, Pirate (captain); Caitrina Grant, Stowaway, Niece (of Highland chief)
Time period(s): 18th century
Locale(s): At Sea; Scotland

Summary: When Captain Alexander Kidd visits the home of Caitrina Grant, the niece of a Highland chief, Caitrina is intrigued by the pirate and his life of excitement. In search of her own adventure, Caitrina sneaks aboard Captain Kidd's ship to explore, but the sheltered and innocent young woman never intends to still be on the ship when it heads out to sea. Captain Kidd is desperate to find the treasure left to him by his father, and he's not willing to let anything stand in the way of his search—not even a young, beautiful stowaway. But Captain Kidd can't deny the affection he has for Caitrina, and he is soon forced to choose between completing his life-long quest or following the desires of his softening heart. This novel is the second installment in the MacGregors: Highland Heirs series by best-selling author Paula Quinn.

Other books by the same author:
The Seduction of Miss Amelia Bell, 2014
Conquered by a Highlander, 2012
Tamed by a Highlander, 2011
Ravished by a Highlander, 2010
Seduced by a Highlander, 2010

Other books you might like:
Jennifer Ashley, *The Pirate Next Door*, 2003

Julie Garwood, *Guardian Angel*, 1990
Mary Jo Putney, *A Distant Magic*, 2007
Jaclyn Reding, *The Adventurer*, 2002
Amanda Scott, *Highland Lover*, 2012

1055

HOPE RAMSAY

Last Chance Family

(New York: Forever, 2014)

Series: Last Chance Series. Book 8
Story type: Contemporary; Series
Subject(s): Romances (Fiction); Family; Gambling
Major character(s): Mike Taggart, Stock Broker (day trader), Gambler, Brother (half-brother of Timmy), Uncle (of Rainbow); Timmy Lake, Religious (Methodist minister), Brother (half-brother of Mike Taggart); Rainbow, Girl, 5-Year-Old, Niece (of Mike and Timmy); Charlene Polk, Veterinarian
Time period(s): 21st century; 2010s
Locale(s): Last Chance, South Carolina

Summary: When Mike Taggart's sister is killed, he becomes the guardian of his five-year-old niece, Rainbow. Mike is good at trading stocks and gambling, but he has no child-rearing skills. He has a half-brother, Timmy Lake, in Last Chance, South Carolina, but Mike hasn't seen him in years. Timmy is now a Methodist minister, so Mike suspects he'd make a more suitable guardian for Rainbow. When Mike arrives in Last Chance, he thinks he has found the perfect place for Rainbow. Last Chance even has an excellent veterinarian, Charlene Polk, who takes care of Rainbow's ailing cat. Mike can't help but think that Charlene and Timmy would make a nice couple—and good parents to Rainbow. But Mike's plan is flawed, because he is the one who's falling in love with Charlene. This novel is the eighth in the Last Chance series.

Other books by the same author:
Inn at Last Chance, 2014
Last Chance Knit and Stitch, 2013
Last Chance Beauty Queen, 2012
Last Chance Christmas, 2012
Home at Last Chance, 2011

Other books you might like:
Grace Burrowes, *The First Kiss*, 2015
Grace Burrowes, *Kiss Me Hello*, 2015
Grace Burrowes, *A Single Kiss*, 2015
Linda Lael Miller, *Montana Creeds: Dylan*, 2009
Linda Lael Miller, *Montana Creeds: Tyler*, 2009
Brenda Novak, *Come Home to Me*, 2014

1056

KATHERINE REAY

Lizzy and Jane

(Nashville, Tennessee: Thomas Nelson, 2014)

Story type: Contemporary
Subject(s): Cooking; Sisters; Sibling rivalry
Major character(s): Elizabeth "Lizzy", Sister (of Jane), Cook (chef); Jane, Sister (of Lizzy), Cancer Patient
Time period(s): 21st century; 2010s
Locale(s): New York, New York; Seattle, Washington

Summary: More than a decade and a half ago, Lizzy packed her bags and moved away from her family to become a chef in New York City. Her sister, Jane, remained in their hometown of Seattle and took care of the family. Now Lizzy's career is on a downward swing, and she needs to walk away from the upscale culinary scene to regroup. Jane invites her sister to come and stay with her, and Lizzy again crosses the country. When Lizzy learns that Jane has cancer, she becomes determined to be Jane's support system as she fights the disease. Lizzy and Jane rekindle their sisterly bond, and Lizzy meets a man who could be the love of her life. When Lizzy gets the opportunity to return to New York, she has to make a choice—she can either return to the Big Apple and rebuild her career as a star chef, or she can remain in the Pacific Northwest and be there for her sister.

Other books by the same author:
Dear Mr. Knightley, 2013

Other books you might like:
Marilyn Brant, *According to Jane*, 2009
Mary Jane Hathaway, *Pride, Prejudice and Cheese Grits*, 2013
Cindy Jones, *My Jane Austen Summer: A Season in Mansfield Park*, 2011
Beth Pattillo, *The Dashwood Sisters Tell All*, 2011
Teri Wilson, *Unleashing Mr. Darcy*, 2014

1057

CHRISTIE RIDGWAY

Make Me Lose Control

(Don Mills, Ontario, Canada: Harlequin, 2014)

Series: Cabin Fever Series. Book 2
Story type: Contemporary - Mainstream; Series
Subject(s): Romances (Fiction); Teaching; Teacher-student relations
Major character(s): Shay Walker, Tutor (live-in, to London); Jace Jennings, Father (of London); London, Student (of Shay), Daughter (of Jace), Girl, Teenager
Time period(s): 21st century; 2010s
Locale(s): Blue Arrow Lake, California

Summary: In the second novel in the Cabin Fever series, Shay Walker is struggling through another birthday. The day always reminds her that she's not a full member of the Walker family, although that's more in her mind than a true feeling of any family member. Since she is free for the night from her live-in tutor/caretaker duties, Shay intends to enjoy the night before her birthday with a handsome guy she just met. Instead, she finds herself with the one man with whom she should not be involved: Jace Jennings, the father of her teenage student, London. Jace may not spend much time with his daughter, but he really wants to be a good father—and that should not involve having a relationship with his daughter's teacher. But that becomes increasingly difficult as Jace spends time with Shay. As for Shay, Jace is already a part of her

Romances

dreams. As they struggle to control their growing feelings, Shay and Jace may find that control is overrated.

Other books by the same author:
Anything but Business, 2015
Light My Fire, 2014
Take My Breath Away, 2014
Bungalow Nights, 2013
The Love Shack, 2013

Other books you might like:
Grace Burrowes, *Kiss Me Hello*, 2015
Chelsea M. Cameron, *My Favorite Mistake*, 2013
Chelsea M. Cameron, *My Sweetest Escape*, 2014
Nicole Helm, *Flight Risk*, 2014
Kimberly Kincaid, *Stirring Up Trouble*, 2014
Erin McCarthy, *Final Lap*, 2014
Claire McEwen, *Convincing the Rancher*, 2015

1058

KAREN ROBARDS

Hush

(New York: Gallery Books, 2014)

Story type: Romantic Suspense
Subject(s): Romances (Fiction); Mystery; Suspense
Major character(s): Riley Cowan, Woman, Spouse (of Jeff Cowan); Jeff Cowan, Spouse (estranged, of Riley), Son (of George Cowan), Crime Victim; George Cowan, Criminal, Convict (financial crimes), Father (of Jeff Cowan); Finn Bradley, FBI Agent
Time period(s): 21st century; 2010s
Locale(s): Houston, Texas

Summary: When Jeff Cowan's body is found hanging in his family's home in Houston, the cause of death appears to be suicide. Jeff's wife, Riley, from whom he was estranged, is the one who discovers the gruesome scene. When the death is ruled a homicide, Riley becomes the top suspect, but she knows who the real suspects in the murder are. Jeff's father, George, is serving time for major financial crimes, and he has enemies who would still like to retrieve the funds they lost in his illegal schemes. When FBI agent Finn Bradley joins the case, he initially suspects Riley of Jeff's murder, too. But when an attempt is made on Riley's life, Finn begins to believe Riley's theory: Someone intends to kill off the members of the Cowan clan, one by one, until they get their money back. As Finn and Riley work together to find the murderer, they find their shared attraction increasingly difficult to ignore.

Other books by the same author:
Her Last Whisper, 2014
Hunted, 2013
The Last Kiss Goodbye, 2013
The Last Victim, 2012

Other books you might like:
Allison Brennan, *Notorious*, 2014
Sandra Brown, *Low Pressure*, 2012
Sandra Brown, *Mean Streak*, 2014
Catherine Coulter, *Nemesis*, 2015
Christina Dodd, *Virtue Falls*, 2014

Julie Garwood, *Wired*, 2015
Tess Gerritsen, *Die Again*, 2014
Jayne Ann Krentz, *River Road*, 2014
Jayne Ann Krentz, *Trust No One*, 2015
Judith McNaught, *Every Breath You Take*, 2005
J.D. Robb, *Festive in Death*, 2014
Nora Roberts, *The Collector*, 2014
Nora Roberts, *The Liar*, 2015
Stuart Woods, *Carnal Curiosity*, 2014

1059

NORA ROBERTS

The Liar

(New York: Penguin Group (USA), 2015)

Subject(s): Death; Deception; Family
Major character(s): Shelby Foxworth, Widow(er), Mother (of three-year-old daughter), Friend (of Griff); Griff Lott, Contractor, Friend (of Shelby)
Time period(s): 21st century; 2010s
Locale(s): Philadelphia, Pennsylvania; Tennessee, United States

Summary: Shelby Foxworth thought she had a great life. She left her home in Tennessee and settled into an upscale Philadelphia suburb with her husband and daughter. But when her husband dies, Shelby discovers her life was a lie. Her husband was not the man she thought he was. Not only did he leave her sinking under heavy debt, he was a cheater and a liar who used multiple fake identities to pull off his life of deception. Devastated, Shelby takes her little girl and moves back to her hometown in Tennessee to find peace. She eventually begins a tentative romance with a handsome contractor named Griff Lott. But her former husband had far more secrets than she suspects, and his old life of deception and crime has followed Shelby into her new beginning, bringing danger. As she reels from the realization that someone is willing to kill to get to her, Shelby must protect herself, her daughter, and even her new love.

Other books by the same author:
Blood Magick, 2014
The Collector, 2014
Shadow Spell, 2014
Dark Witch, 2013
Whiskey Beach, 2013

Other books you might like:
Allison Brennan, *Notorious*, 2014
James Casper, *Everywhere in Chains*, 2013
Diane Chamberlain, *The Silent Sister*, 2014
Christina Dodd, *Virtue Falls*, 2014
Dorothea Benton Frank, *The Last Original Wife*, 2013
A.S.A. Harrison, *The Silent Wife*, 2013
Ethan Hauser, *The Measures Between Us*, 2013
Patti Callahan Henry, *The Stories We Tell*, 2014
Christian Jungersen, *You Disappear*, 2014
Jayne Ann Krentz, *River Road*, 2014
Randy Susan Meyers, *The Comfort of Lies*, 2013
Karen Robards, *Hush*, 2014
Karen Robards, *Shiver*, 2012

Karen Rose, *Watch Your Back*, 2014
Alexandra Whitaker, *Leaving Sophie Dean*, 2012

1060

THERESA ROMAIN (Pseudonym of Theresa St. Romain)

Secrets of a Scandalous Heiress

(Naperville, Illinois: Sourcebooks Casablanca, 2015)

Series: Matchmaker Series. Book 3
Story type: Historical - Regency; Series
Subject(s): Romances (Fiction); History; Love
Major character(s): Augusta Meredith, Heiress, Woman (also known as Mrs. John Flowers); Josiah "Joss" Everett, Cousin (of Baron Sutcliffe); Baron Sutcliffe, Cousin (of Joss Everett)
Time period(s): 19th century; 1810s (1817)
Locale(s): Bath, England

Summary: As the heiress to her family's sizeable fortune, Augusta Meredith finds it nearly impossible to navigate Regency-era London inconspicuously. She has even more difficulty finding suitors who are interested in more than her fortune. When Augusta escapes the city to vacation in Bath with a friend, she uses the name Mrs. John Flowers to avoid detection. But even in Bath, Augusta is recognized. Josiah "Joss" Everett guesses Augusta's identity, but he agrees to go along with her sham because he also has something to hide. He is in Bath on unpleasant family business that involves his cousin, Baron Sutcliffe. If Augusta keeps his secret, Joss will keep hers. As Augusta and Joss carry out their ruse in Bath, they gradually build a bond of trust and true affection.

Other books by the same author:
Season for Desire, 2014
To Charm a Naughty Countess, 2014
It Takes Two to Tangle, 2013
Season for Scandal, 2013
Season for Surrender, 2012

Other books you might like:
Jane Ashford, *The Bride Insists*, 2014
Jayne Fresina, *Miss Molly Robbins Designs a Seduction*, 2014
Julia London, *The Trouble with Honor*, 2014
Michelle Marcos, *When a Lady Misbehaves*, 2007
Sophia Nash, *Secrets of a Scandalous Bride*, 2010

1061

THERESA ROMAIN (Pseudonym of Theresa St. Romain)

Season for Desire

(New York: Kensington Publishing Corporation, 2014)

Series: Holiday Pleasures Series. Book 4
Story type: Historical - Regency; Holiday Themes
Subject(s): Romances (Fiction); History; England
Major character(s): Lady Audrina Bradleigh, Missing Person, Noblewoman; Giles Rutherford, Hunter (of treasure), Man (American)
Time period(s): 19th century; 1820s (1820)
Locale(s): England

Summary: Theresa Romain delivers the fourth tale in her Holiday Pleasures historical romance series. In 1820 England, Lady Audrina Bradleigh is far from the proper image she is expected to uphold. No stranger to scandal, Audrina has engaged in a number of affairs, and the threats of a former lover now stand to ruin her reputation. American treasure hunter Giles Rutherford travels to northern England at Christmas in search of lost family jewels. Giles's mission changes somewhat when the Bradleigh family seeks his help in finding the missing Audrina—who has been snatched by a former lover—in exchange for local assistance with the treasure hunt. When Giles and Audrina are both stranded at a country inn in the midst of a winter storm, passions run high. Is it possible that Audrina has finally found someone who can put an end to her life of mischief and scandal?

Other books by the same author:
To Charm a Naughty Countess, 2014
It Takes Two to Tangle, 2013
Season for Scandal, 2013
Season for Surrender, 2012
Season for Temptation, 2011

Other books you might like:
Manda Collins, *How to Romance a Rake*, 2012
Nicole Jordan, *To Romance a Charming Rogue*, 2009
Stephanie Laurens, *A Lady of His Own*, 2004
Amanda Quick, *I Thee Wed*, 1999
Lauren Royal, *Lost in Temptation*, 2005

1062

KAREN ROSE

Closer Than You Think

(New York: Penguin Group, 2015)

Story type: Mystery; Romantic Suspense
Subject(s): Romances (Fiction); Mystery; Suspense
Major character(s): Faith Corcoran, Psychologist, Crime Victim (of stalker); Deacon Novak, FBI Agent
Time period(s): 21st century; 2010s
Locale(s): Cincinnati, Ohio

Summary: A stalker has been following Faith Corcoran, a psychologist, for a year. When she can no longer tolerate the strain of the man's presence in her life, Faith seeks refuge in the familiar surroundings of Cincinnati. Faith owns a home in the city, which she inherited from her recently deceased grandmother. She has many memories about the house, but not all of them are pleasant. As she tries to evade the stalker and escape the past, Faith gets caught up in a criminal investigation. The FBI is looking into the disappearance of two young women in Cincinnati, and Special Agent Deacon Novak has discovered that Faith is somehow connected to the case. As Deacon digs into Faith's past, he uncovers information that shocks both him and Faith. Deacon also discovers that he's having trouble keeping his relationship with Faith professional.

Other books by the same author:
Did You Miss Me?, 2013
Watch Your Back, 2013

Romances

No One Left to Tell, 2012
You Belong to Me, 2011
Silent Scream, 2010

Other books you might like:
Maya Banks, *When Day Breaks*, 2014
B.J. Daniels, *Wedding at Cardwell Ranch*, 2014
Cynthia Eden, *Deadly Heat*, 2011
Cynthia Eden, *Evidence of Passion*, 2014
Kendra Elliot, *Vanished*, 2014
Laura Griffin, *Far Gone*, 2014
Karen Harper, *Forbidden Ground*, 2014
Jayne Ann Krentz, *Trust No One*, 2015
Lindsay McKenna, *The Defender*, 2012
Julie Miller, *KCPD Protector*, 2014
Raine Miller, *Eyes Wide Open*, 2013
Shiloh Walker, *Deeper than Need*, 2014

1063

KATHLEEN BITTNER ROTH

Alanna

(New York: Zebra Books, 2014)

Series: When Hearts Dare Series. Book 2
Story type: Historical; Series
Subject(s): Romances (Fiction); Adventure; Suspense
Major character(s): Alanna Malone, Woman; Wolf, Man (missing persons tracker)
Time period(s): 19th century; 1850s (1856)
Locale(s): Scotland; San Francisco, California; Boston, Massachusetts

Summary: Set in 1856, this romantic thriller is the second installment in the When Hearts Dare series by Kathleen Bittner Roth. For 30 years, a tracker of missing persons known only as Wolf has dedicated his life to finding the man who killed his mother. When he encounters the mysterious and sensual Alanna Malone, he welcomes the distraction, and even though Alanna's parents have very firm ideas about who she should marry, Wolf can't seem to let her go. Alanna will do anything to escape the arranged marriage her parents have planned for her, and Wolf's mission leads them on an adventure from San Francisco to Boston and across the sea to Scotland. In their quest to find Wolf's mother's killer, a rousing romance ensues.

Other books by the same author:
Josette, 2015
A Duke's Wicked Kiss, 2014
Celine, 1997

Other books you might like:
Kit Garland, *Capture the Wind*, 1997
Alexis Harrington, *The Irish Bride*, 2003
Jennifer L. Holm, *Boston Jane: An Adventure*, 2001
Susan King, *Taming the Heiress*, 2003
Jodi Thomas, *Texas Princess*, 2007

1064

JENNIFER RYAN

At Wolf Ranch

(New York: Avon, 2015)

Series: Montana Men Series. Book 1
Story type: Romantic Suspense; Series
Subject(s): Romances (Fiction); Suspense; Western fiction
Major character(s): Gabe Bowden, Rodeo Rider (former), Rancher; Ella Wolf, Twin (of Lela), Heiress (Wolf Ranch), Niece (of Phillip Wolf); Lela Wolf, Twin (of Ella), Niece (of Phillip Wolf), Crime Victim (murdered); Phillip Wolf, Uncle (of Ella and Lela)
Time period(s): 21st century; 2010s
Locale(s): Montana, United States

Summary: In the first novel in the Montana Men series, retired rodeo rider Gabe Bowden is looking forward to purchasing Wolf Ranch and settling down. He plans to buy the sprawling piece of property from Phillip Wolf, but Gabe learns shocking information about Phillip when one of Phillip's relatives shows up at the ranch. Gabe comes to the rescue when Ella Wolf is caught in a dangerous snowstorm. Ella, who is supposed to inherit the ranch, tells Gabe that Phillip killed her twin sister, Lela, and is now targeting her. Ella believes that Lela hid something at the ranch that prompted Phillip to murder her. Gabe and Ella join forces against Phillip as they unravel the secrets of the Wolf family's history. Meanwhile Gabe, who had hoped to find a lasting relationship, wonders if Ella Wolf is the woman he has been waiting for.

Other books by the same author:
Dylan's Redemption, 2014
Falling for Owen, 2014
The Return of Brody McBride, 2014
Chasing Morgan, 2013
The Right Bride, 2013

Other books you might like:
Starr Ambrose, *Silver Sparks*, 2011
B.J. Daniels, *Wild Horses*, 2015
Laura Drake, *Nothing Sweeter*, 2014
Kathleen Eagle, *The Last True Cowboy*, 1998
Nora Roberts, *Montana Sky*, 1996
Lori Wilde, *Love with a Perfect Cowboy*, 2014

1065

JENNIFER RYAN

When It's Right

(New York, New York: Avon, 2015)

Story type: Contemporary; Ranch Life
Subject(s): Romances (Fiction); Ranch life; Love
Major character(s): Gillian Tucker, Lover (of Blake Bowden); Blake Bowden, Lover (of Gillian Tucker), Rancher; Justin Tucker, Brother (to Gillian Tucker)
Time period(s): 21st century; 2010s
Locale(s): Montana, United States

Summary: Forced to take drastic action to protect her younger brother Justin from their drug-addicted father, Gillian Tucker nervously accepts the invitation of her never-before-seen grandfather to live on his ranch in Montana. Upon arriving at the Three Peaks Ranch with Justin in tow, she meets her grandfather's new partner, Blake Bowden, a sexy cowboy who seems to understand her inner pain. But having spent years suffering at the hands of her abusive father, Gillian is slow to trust anyone, let alone this handsome stranger who inspires such intense feelings within her. However, she is forced to soon confront both her growing affection for Blake as well as her own traumatic past when she finds herself in danger from a new threat.

Other books by the same author:
At Wolf Ranch, 2015
Dylan's Redemption, 2014
Falling for Owen, 2014
The Return of Brody McBride, 2014
Chasing Morgan, 2013

Other books you might like:
B.J. Daniels, *Wild Horses*, 2015
Linda Lael Miller, *McKettricks of Texas: Garrett*, 2010
Julianna Morris, *The Ranch Solution*, 2013
RaeAnne Thayne, *The Christmas Ranch*, 2014
Pat Warren, *Stranded on the Ranch*, 1998

1066

SHARON SALA

Going Gone

(Don Mills, Ontario, Canada: Harlequin MIRA, 2014)

Series: Forces of Nature Series. Book 3
Story type: Police Procedural; Psychological Suspense
Subject(s): Romances (Fiction); Serial murders; Suspense
Major character(s): Cameron Winger, FBI Agent, Fiance(e) (of Laura); Laura Doyle, Fiance(e) (of Cameron), Survivor (plane crash); Stormchaser, Serial Killer
Time period(s): 21st century; 2010s
Locale(s): United States

Summary: This romantic thriller is the third book in the Forces of Nature series by best-selling author Sharon Sala. Laura Doyle narrowly escaped death when her plane crashed in the Rocky Mountains. Now, as she is planning to marry FBI agent Cameron Winger, her life is on the line again. Cameron and his team have long been on the trail of the Stormchaser, a serial killer who couples his evil acts with random acts of God. When the Stormchaser learns of Laura and Cameron's engagement, he waits for the perfect storm to unleash another killing spree and to settle once and for all the vendetta he has against Cameron. The Stormchaser's recent string of unrelated murders serves only to cover up his advance toward his real target. Cameron and Laura don't realize they're the targets, and time is not on their side.

Other books by the same author:
The Curl Up and Dye, 2014
Going Twice, 2014
Going Once, 2013

'Til Death, 2013
Don't Cry for Me, 2012

Other books you might like:
Catherine Coulter, *The Cove*, 1996
Tami Hoag, *The 9th Girl*, 2013
Kay Hooper, *Hostage*, 2013
Iris Johansen, *The Ugly Duckling*, 1996
Jayne Ann Krentz, *Eye of the Beholder*, 1999

1067

SHARON SALA

Wild Hearts

(Don Mills, Ontario, Canada: Mira, 2015)

Story type: Mystery; Romantic Suspense
Subject(s): Romances (Fiction); Suicide; Mystery
Major character(s): Dallas Phillips, Lover (of Trey Jakes), Daughter, Journalist; Trey Jakes, Police Officer, Lover (of Dallas Phillips)
Time period(s): 21st century; 2010s
Locale(s): United States

Summary: The first novel in the Secrets and Lies series by Sharon Sala focuses on the buried secrets of the Phillips family and the events triggered by the apparent suicide of Dallas Phillips's father. When Dallas returns to her small home town, she refuses to believe her father could ever kill himself—a fact borne out by the autopsy. When a neighbor mentions having heard her father talking about a possible financial windfall, Dallas turns to police chief Trey Jakes, her former high school boyfriend and the man she left behind to become a television reporter in the big city. Together, they uncover a puzzle that only seems to deepen with every new clue—a mystery that someone is willing to kill for. Despite the increasing threats to their lives, Dallas and Trey begin to rediscover the chemistry that brought them together in the first place.

Other books by the same author:
I'll Stand by You, 2015
The Curl Up and Dye, 2014
Going Gone, 2014
Going Twice, 2014
Going Once, 2013

Other books you might like:
Mary Burton, *Cover Your Eyes*, 2014
Shannon K. Butcher, *Edge of Betrayal*, 2014
Laura Kaye, *Hard to Come By*, 2014
Carla Neggers, *Harbor Island*, 2014
Carly Phillips, *Perfect Fling*, 2013

1068

SUSANNAH SANDLIN

Deadly, Calm, and Cold

(Seattle, Washington: Montlake Romance, 2014)

Series: Collectors Series. Book 2
Story type: Contemporary

Romances

Subject(s): Treasure-trove; Adventure; Adventurers
Major character(s): Samantha Crowe, Student—Graduate; Brody Parker, Bounty Hunter, Adventurer
Time period(s): 21st century; 2010s
Locale(s): England

Summary: In the second novel from author Susan Sandlin's Collectors series, the C7, a group of people who hire mercenaries to find lost artifacts and riches, continues its gamesmanship. This time, the group's target is Samantha Crowe, who recently discovered the possible whereabouts of the priceless wealth of Bad King John of England. Yet one of the members of C7 isn't working for the common interests of the group anymore, and sends Brody Parker to stop Samantha in her quest. Brody is on the run and attempting to keep his identity hidden. He knows that his life is at stake if he doesn't do as he is told, but one look at Samantha and he knows that he can't work against her. Soon Brody and Samantha find themselves falling for each other, and must work together to thwart the plans of C7 and free themselves from the collectors' evil clutches.

Other books by the same author:
Allegiance, 2014
Lovely, Dark, and Deep, 2014
Absolution, 2013
Omega, 2013
Storm Force, 2013

Other books you might like:
Cherry Adair, *Relentless*, 2013
Jayne Ann Krentz, *Sharp Edges*, 1998
Elizabeth Lowell, *Amber Beach*, 1997
Elisabeth Naughton, *Stolen Fury*, 2009
Nora Roberts, *The Collector*, 2014

1069

LYNSAY SANDS

The Immortal Who Loved Me

(New York: HarperCollins, 2015)

Series: Argeneau Vampire Series. Book 21
Story type: Series; Vampire Story
Subject(s): Vampires; Immortality; Love
Major character(s): Sherry Carne, Store Owner, Lover (of Basil); Basileios "Basil" Argeneau, Vampire, Lover (of Sherry)
Time period(s): 21st century; 2010s
Locale(s): Toronto, Ontario

Summary: The 21st title of the Argeneau Vampire series opens the eyes of a shop owner. Sherry Carne never believed in vampires. However, a pack of vampires tears though her store, leaving utter destruction scattered with blood and filth. Sherry soon realizes that vampires are real, and meets one who captivates her. She is immediately and irresistibly drawn to Basileios Argeneau. Similarly, Basil never thought he would find his soul mate in this situation, nor did he imagine his partner to be anything like Sherry, a strong-willed human woman. Basil cannot deny the attraction he feels for Sherry. He also might be attracted to her due to her previously unknown connection to the supernatural world. Sherry is

in definite danger after meeting Basil, and he is the only one that can keep her safe.

Other books by the same author:
The Lady Is a Vamp, 2012
Under a Vampire Moon, 2012
The Renegade Hunter, 2009
Vampire Interrupted, 2008
A Quick Bite, 2005

Other books you might like:
Elaine Bergstrom, *Blood Rites*, 1991
Cat Devon, *Sleeping with the Entity*, 2013
Christine Feehan, *Dark Predator*, 2011
Jeaniene Frost, *Bound by Flames*, 2015
Jeaniene Frost, *Halfway to the Grave*, 2007
Jeaniene Frost, *This Side of the Grave*, 2011
Molly Harper, *Nice Girls Don't Live Forever*, 2010
Alexandra Ivy, *Fear the Darkness*, 2012
Katie MacAlister, *A Girl's Guide to Vampires*, 2003
Michelle Rowen, *Bitten and Smitten*, 2006
Kerrelyn Sparks, *Crouching Tiger, Forbidden Vampire*, 2014

1070

AMANDA SCOTT

Devil's Moon

(New York, New York: Grand Central Publishing, 2015)

Story type: Historical - Renaissance
Subject(s): Romances (Fiction); Knights; Courtship
Major character(s): Lady Robina "Robby" Gledstanes, Lady, Twin; Sir David "Devil/Dev" Ormiston, Knight; Benjamin "Benjy" Gledstanes, Brother (of Lady Robina), 10-Year-Old
Time period(s): 15th century
Locale(s): England; Scotland

Summary: In the borderlands between England and Scotland in the 1400s, life is hard enough, but for Lady Robina "Robby" Gledstanes, after the death of her twin brother, life has become so much more difficult now that she has to manage her family's people and lands while keeping them safe from greedy kinsman until her brother comes of age. Though she is a woman, her younger brother is only ten, and therefore too young to take control. David "Devil" Ormiston understands her plight because he grew up with Robby and understands both the threats to her lands and her unpredictable nature. In addition, he has sworn to protect her, as her brother died saving his life on the battlefield. Of course, the Devil, or Dev as he is known, does not really see spending time with the beautiful Robby as a tremendous sacrifice. However, despite their constant conflicts (and underlying sexual tension), the pair will have to work together when Robby's brother is kidnapped by rival forces. This is the second novel in the Border Nights series.

Other books by the same author:
Moonlight Raider, 2014
The Warrior's Bride, 2014
The Knight's Temptress, 2013
Highland Lover, 2012

The Laird's Choice, 2012

Other books you might like:
Tracy Brogan, *Highland Surrender*, 2012
Suzanne Enoch, *The Devil Wears Kilts*, 2013
Suzanne Enoch, *Rogue with a Brogue*, 2014
Hannah Howell, *Highland Protector*, 2010
Melody Thomas, *Claimed by a Scottish Lord*, 2010

1071

BRONWYN SCOTT (Pseudonym of Nikki Poppen)

Breaking the Rake's Rules

(Don Mills, Ontario, Canada: Harlequin, 2015)

Story type: Historical
Subject(s): Romances (Fiction); Pirates; Ships
Major character(s): Miss Bryn Rutherford, Daughter, Lover (of Kitt Sherard); Captain Christopher "Kitt" Sherard, Shipowner, Lover (of Bryn Rutherford), Pirate, Sea Captain
Time period(s): 19th century; 1830s
Locale(s): Barbados; Antigua, Barbados; Caribbean Sea

Summary: Bryn Rutherford is a proper English woman, so she is completely unprepared for the roguish man who climbs her balcony one night to plant a kiss on her lips. That man turns out to be Captain Christopher "Kitt" Sherard, a ship's captain who makes his living illegally transporting rum throughout the Caribbean. Bryn is in the Caribbean accompanying her father, who is helping to establish a new currency system in Barbados. When Bryn learns she will need transportation, she contacts Kitt in order to make the journey—a trip she secretly hopes will realize her private dreams of adventure and romance, dreams which Captain Sherard intends to fulfill.

Other books by the same author:
Rake Most Likely to Rebel, 2015
Rake Most Likely to Thrill, 2015
Unlaced by Candlelight, 2015
A Lady Dares, 2013
A Lady Risks All, 2013

Other books you might like:
Celeste Bradley, *Scoundrel in My Dreams*, 2010
Christy English, *Much Ado About Jack*, 2014
Lorraine Heath, *Lord of Temptation*, 2012
Brenda Joyce, *The Promise*, 2010
Margaret McPhee, *The Lost Gentleman*, 2015

1072

MELANIE SCOTT

Angel in Armani

(New York: St. Martin's Press, 2015)

Series: New York Saints Series. Book 2
Story type: Contemporary; Series
Subject(s): Sports; Baseball; Air travel
Major character(s): Dr. Lucas Angelo, Doctor, Manager (Sports) (part owner of New York Saints baseball team); Sara Charles, Pilot, Businesswoman (helicopter charter business)
Time period(s): 21st century; 2010s
Locale(s): Florida, United States; New York, New York

Summary: In the second novel in the New York Saints series, author Melanie Scott continues the story of the New York Saints baseball team. This time, part owner Dr. Lucas Angelo, one of New York's top surgeons, is due for some romance. When he hires Sara Charles, the pilot of a charter helicopter company, to take him back and forth to games, he instantly feels attracted to her. Sara initially resists Lucas's charms as politely as possible. She cannot risk alienating one of her top clients, especially since the fate of her family's company rests solely on her shoulders. When the magnetism they feel for each other gets the best of them, and they find themselves in bed together, Sara promises herself she will never let it happen again. What Sara doesn't realize, however, is that Lucas is accustomed to always getting what he wants, and this time, what he wants is her.

Other books by the same author:
The Devil in Denim, 2014

Other books you might like:
Lori Foster, *Holding Strong*, 2015
Addison Fox, *Baby, It's Cold Outside*, 2011
Rachel Gibson, *Any Man of Mine*, 2011
Julia London, *Extreme Bachelor*, 2006
Kate Meader, *Feel the Heat*, 2013
Candis Terry, *Anything but Sweet*, 2013

1073

REGINA SCOTT (Pseudonym of Regina Lundgren)

The Bride Ship

(Don Mills, Ontario, Canada: Harlequin, 2014)

Series: Frontier Bachelors Series. Book 1
Story type: Historical - Post-American Civil War; Series
Subject(s): Romances (Fiction); United States history, 1865-1901; Single parent family
Major character(s): Allegra Banks Howard, Widow(er) (of Frank Howard), Mother (of Gillian); Gillian Howard, Daughter (of Allegra and Frank), 4-Year-Old; Frank Howard, Spouse (deceased, of Allegra), Brother (of Clay Howard); Clay Howard, Brother (of Frank Howard)
Time period(s): 19th century; 1860s (1866)
Locale(s): United States

Summary: Upon the death of her husband, Frank, Allegra Banks Howard is left alone to care for the couple's four-year-old daughter, Gillian. Although the Howard family wants Allegra to stay in Boston, Allegra has other plans. She slips away to New York with Gillian and prepares to begin the first leg of their journey west. Allegra wants to join the other women who will help settle the Washington Territory. Clay Howard, Frank's brother, follows Allegra to New York and is supposed to bring her back to Boston. When Allegra refuses, however, Clay accompanies her and Gillian on their westward voyage. Clay has always loved Allegra, and he has already let her slip from his grasp once before. Allegra is aware of Clay's feelings, but she isn't sure if she wants to take a chance on him again. This novel is the first in the Frontier Bachelors series.

Other books by the same author:
The Courting Campaign, 2013
The Heiress's Homecoming, 2013
The Wife Campaign, 2013
The Captain's Courtship, 2012
The Rake's Redemption, 2012

Other books you might like:
Maggie Brendan, *Twice Promised*, 2012
Kate Bridges, *Klondike Wedding*, 2007
Deborah Hale, *The Bride Ship*, 2012
Melissa Jagears, *A Bride for Keeps*, 2013
Maggie Osborne, *The Brides of Prairie Gold*, 1996

1074

REGINA SCOTT (Pseudonym of Regina Lundgren)

Would-Be Wilderness Wife

(Don Mills, Ontario, Canada: Harlequin, 2015)

Series: Frontier Bachelors Series. Book 2
Story type: Historical - Post-American Civil War; Series
Subject(s): Romances (Fiction); United States history; Frontier life
Major character(s): Drew Wallin, Brother (of Levi, Simon, Beth), Son (of Mrs. Wallin); Levi Wallin, Brother (of Drew, Simon, Beth), Son (of Mrs. Wallin), Kidnapper (of Catherine); Simon Wallin, Brother (of Drew, Levi, Beth), Son (of Mrs. Wallin); Beth Wallin, Sister (of Drew, Levi, Simon), Daughter (of Mrs. Wallin); Mrs. Wallin, Mother (of Drew, Levi, Simon, Beth), Patient (ill); Catherine Stanway, Nurse, Kidnap Victim
Time period(s): 19th century; 1860s (1866)
Locale(s): United States

Summary: In 1866, Catherine Stanway is working as a nurse in the Washington Territory. She is shocked when she is kidnapped in Seattle and brought to the lakeside home of the Wallin family. Levi Wallin, who is one of several siblings, smuggles Catherine into his wagon without telling his older brother Drew. Levi thinks Catherine will make a perfect wife for confirmed bachelor Drew—and a much-needed caregiver for their sick mother. Drew wants no part of Levi's plan. He is more interested in caring for his brothers, sister, and mother than he is in choosing a bride. Catherine, who has been unlucky in love in the past, isn't looking for romance either. But when she agrees to stay and care for Mrs. Wallin, despite the unpleasant circumstances of her arrival, she and Drew spend more time together and begin to reconsider their positions on love. This novel is the second in the Frontier Bachelors series.

Other books by the same author:
The Bride Ship, 2014
The Courting Campaign, 2013
The Heiress's Homecoming, 2013
The Wife Campaign, 2013
The Rake's Redemption, 2012

Other books you might like:
Ginny Aiken, *She Shall Be Praised*, 2014

Amanda Cabot, *With Autumn's Return*, 2014
Deeanne Gist, *A Bride in the Bargain*, 2009
Jill Marie Landis, *The Accidental Lawman*, 2009
Nancy J. Parra, *The Counterfeit Bride*, 2011

1075

JILL SHALVIS (Pseudonym of Jill Sheldon)

He's So Fine

(New York: Grand Central Publishing, 2014)

Series: Lucky Harbor Series. Book 11
Story type: Contemporary; Series
Subject(s): Romances (Fiction); Interpersonal relations; Actors
Major character(s): Olivia Bentley, Businesswoman (vintage shop owner), Girlfriend (of Cole); Cole Donovan, Sailor (boat captain), Boyfriend (of Olivia)
Time period(s): 21st century; 2010s
Locale(s): Lucky Harbor, Washington

Summary: Best-selling author Jill Shalvis delivers the 11th novel in her Lucky Harbor contemporary romance series. Olivia Bentley runs a new vintage store in the friendly town of Lucky Harbor, Washington, where no one knows the truth about her past—or her real name. Trying to make the most of a fresh start in a new town, Olivia keeps a friendly distance from everyone until the day she saves charter boat captain Cole Donovan from drowning. Olivia never planned on getting close to anyone in Lucky Harbor, but she can't get enough of handsome Cole. And as their relationship deepens, Cole realizes Olivia may have rescued him in more ways than one. But when secrets from Olivia's past are revealed, and trouble follows her to Lucky Harbor, will she find a home with Cole? Or will she say goodbye to Lucky Harbor forever?

Other books by the same author:
It's in His Kiss, 2014
Once in a Lifetime, 2014
One in a Million, 2014
Then Came You, 2014
Rumor Has It, 2013

Other books you might like:
Susan Andersen, *No Strings Attached*, 2014
Janet Evanovich, *Back to the Bedroom*, 2005
Lori Foster, *When Bruce Met Cyn. . .*, 2004
Rachel Gibson, *Not Another Bad Date*, 2008
Carly Phillips, *Hot Stuff*, 2004

1076

JILL SHALVIS (Pseudonym of Jill Sheldon)

Still the One

(New York: Penguin Group, 2015)

Series: Animal Magnetism Series. Book 6
Story type: Contemporary; Series
Subject(s): Romances (Fiction); Military life; Dogs
Major character(s): Darcy Stone, Woman, Animal Lover;

AJ Colten, Veteran (US Navy), Therapist (physical)
Time period(s): 21st century; 2010s
Locale(s): United States

Summary: A convenient arrangement between former flames creates interesting results in the sixth novel in the Animal Magnetism series. AJ Colten is out of the US Navy and building his physical therapy practice. He is trying to get grants, and he knows Darcy can help. But Darcy isn't eager to help the man who treated her so badly in the past. When she assesses the situation, she decides that helping AJ is in her best interests. She wants to get funding for a pet project of her own that would bring retired search and rescue dogs and injured veterans together. Although AJ wants Darcy's assistance, he is also wary of renewing their ties. A failed romance has left him scarred, and he isn't interested in getting involved with another woman—even the beautiful Darcy. As AJ and Darcy spend more time together, they find that keeping their relationship professional is harder than they expected.

Other books by the same author:
He's So Fine, 2015
One in a Million, 2015
Once in a Lifetime, 2014
Always on My Mind, 2013
It Had to Be You, 2013

Other books you might like:
Macy Beckett, *Make You Remember*, 2014
Robyn Carr, *The Homecoming*, 2014
Karina Halle, *The Pact*, 2015
Susan Mallery, *Before We Kiss*, 2014
Catherine Mann, *Shelter Me*, 2014
Sarah Morgan, *Suddenly Last Summer*, 2014

`1077`

JILL SHALVIS (Pseudonym of Jill Sheldon)

One in a Million

(New York: Grand Central Publishing, 2014)

Series: Lucky Harbor Series. Book 12
Story type: Contemporary; Series
Subject(s): Romances (Fiction); Family; Love
Major character(s): Callie Sharpe, Planner (weddings); Tanner Riggs, Diver (deep-sea), Single Father (of Troy); Troy Riggs, 15-Year-Old, Son (of Tanner)
Time period(s): 21st century; 2010s
Locale(s): Lucky Harbor, Washington

Summary: When Callie Sharpe comes home to the Washington community of Lucky Harbor, she is shocked to run into a teenager who looks exactly like her old crush, Tanner Riggs. Callie finds out that Tanner's look-alike is his 15-year-old son, Troy. Tanner, a deep-sea diver, is a single dad, and he's still as handsome as ever. Callie is not interested in romance. She's still stinging from a relationship that ended painfully. But now that she's back in Lucky Harbor, Callie can't deny that the feelings she had for Tanner are still there. Tanner isn't looking for love, either. He's trying his best to raise Troy, although he sometimes questions his own maturity. When Tanner reunites with Callie, he begins to think

that she might be the best thing that could happen to him and his son.

Other books by the same author:
He's So Fine, 2014
It's in His Kiss, 2014
Once in a Lifetime, 2014
Then Came You, 2014
Rumor Has It, 2013

Other books you might like:
Toni Blake, *All I Want Is You*, 2014
Rachel Gibson, *Rescue Me*, 2012
Julie James, *It Happened One Wedding*, 2014
Cathie Linz, *Luck Be a Lady*, 2010
Brenda Novak, *Home to Whiskey Creek*, 2013

`1078`

ISABEL SHARPE (Pseudonym of Muna Shehadi Sill)

The Perfect Indulgence

(Don Mills, Ontario, Canada: Harlequin, 2015)

Story type: Contemporary
Subject(s): Romances (Fiction); Sisters; Twins
Major character(s): Chris Meyer, Lover (of Zac Arnette), Woman, Twin (of Eva Meyer), Restaurateur (coffee shop); Eva Meyer, Woman, Twin (of Chris Meyer), Restaurateur (coffee shop); Zac Arnette, Lover (of Chris)
Time period(s): 21st century; 2010s
Locale(s): Carmia, California

Summary: It's been five months since twin sisters Chris and Eva Meyer decided to swap lives for a while. Both women own coffee shops, but they live on opposite coasts. Chris is a go-getting New Yorker; Eva is an easy-going California girl. But after spending time in the sunny climate of Carmia, California, Chris has become more relaxed than she's ever been. She's even meditating and doing yoga, which were definitely not part of her East Coast lifestyle. While Eva adjusts to the dipping temperatures in New York, Chris gets used to California guys—blond surfers who weren't "her type" just a few months ago. Chris attracts the attention of several potential boyfriends, but it's Zac Arnette who sets her heart pounding when he visits her coffee shop. She agrees to a no-strings-attached arrangement with Zac, but Chris is in no hurry for the relationship—or her stay in California—to end.

Other books by the same author:
Nothing to Hide, 2014
Some Like It Hotter, 2014
Back in Service, 2013
Half-Hitched, 2013
Feels So Right, 2012

Other books you might like:
Amy Andrews, *Driving Her Crazy*, 2013
Leah Ashton, *Beware of the Boss*, 2013
Jennifer Crusie, *Manhunting*, 1993
Liz Fielding, *Anything but Vanilla...*, 2013
Nikki Logan, *How to Get Over Your Ex*, 2013

Romances

ISABEL SHARPE

Some Like It Hotter

(Don Mills, Ontario: Harlequin, 2015)

Story type: Contemporary
Subject(s): Sisters; Entrepreneurship; Romances (Fiction)
Major character(s): Eva Meyer, Sister (of Chris), Twin (of Chris), Store Owner (Cafe owner), Lover (of Ames); Chris Meyer, Twin (of Eva), Sister (of Eva), Store Owner (Cafe owner); Ames Cooke, Lover (of Eva)
Time period(s): 21st century; 2010s
Locale(s): New York, New York

Summary: Eva Meyer is tired of living on the West Coast. Every day she spends in California is the same, and she wants some adventure for a change. That's when she and her twin sister, Chris, come up with a plan to switch their lives for 30 days. Chris will move to California and manage Eva's little cafe, and Eva will move to Manhattan and operate Chris's cafe. Once in New York City, Eva meets Ames, a regular customer who has been aggressively pursuing Chris, despite her firm refusals. Eva may resemble Chris physically, but she certainly doesn't have her twin's same cool and collected attitude. The moment she meets him, Eva decides to go for it. Ames isn't sure that he can keep up with Eva's rambunctiousness, but she is determined to make him hers, and soon Ames finds it hard to resist her. Is Ames ready to give up his dream of one sister for the possibility of being with her twin?

Other books by the same author:
Nothing to Hide, 2014
Back in Service, 2013
Half-Hitched, 2013
Feels So Right, 2012
Light Me Up, 2012

Other books you might like:
Amy Andrews, *Driving Her Crazy*, 2013
Leah Ashton, *Beware of the Boss*, 2013
Kristan Higgins, *All I Ever Wanted*, 2010
Kelly Hunter, *The One That Got Away*, 2013
Nikki Logan, *How to Get Over Your Ex*, 2013

MAGGIE SHAYNE (Pseudonym of Margaret Benson)

Innocent Prey

(Don Mills, Ontario, Canada: Harlequin MIRA, 2014)

Series: Brown and De Luca Series. Book 3
Story type: Contemporary; Police Procedural
Subject(s): Romances (Fiction); Detective fiction; Kidnapping
Major character(s): Rachel de Luca, Expert (self-help), Colleague (of Mason); Mason Brown, Detective—Police, Colleague (of Rachel)
Time period(s): 21st century; 2010s
Locale(s): New York, United States

Summary: This romantic thriller is the third installment in the Brown and De Luca series by best-selling author Maggie Shayne. The attraction between self-help expert Rachel de Luca and detective Mason Brown is undeniable. And though they try to keep an emotional distance, they are forced back together when the daughter of a judge goes missing. Mason is certain the girl's disappearance is connected to the most recent case he solved with Rachel, which involved the kidnapping of Rachel's assistant. Their search leads them across a string of unsolved cases that involve the abductions of several troubled young women. Once again, Rachel's ability to see through people's lies leads Mason to the truth. But the stakes get higher at every turn, and Mason must stop the predator before he acts again—and makes Rachel his next victim.

Other books by the same author:
Deadly Obsession, 2014
Blood of the Sorceress, 2013
Sleep with the Lights On, 2013
Wake to Darkness, 2013
Daughter of the Spellcaster, 2012

Other books you might like:
Sandra Brown, *Lethal*, 2011
Lisa Jackson, *Without Mercy*, 2010
Jayne Ann Krentz, *Dream Eyes*, 2013
Carla Neggers, *Heron's Cove*, 2012
Karen Robards, *Vanished*, 2006

MAGGIE SHAYNE (Pseudonym of Margaret Benson)

Deadly Obsession

(Don Mills, Ontario, Canada: Harlequin MIRA, 2014)

Series: Brown and De Luca Series. Book 4
Story type: Mystery; Police Procedural
Subject(s): Detective fiction; Mystery; Romances (Fiction)
Major character(s): Mason Brown, Detective—Police, Colleague (of Rachel); Rachel de Luca, Expert (self-help), Colleague (of Mason)
Time period(s): 21st century; 2010s
Locale(s): New York, United States

Summary: Best-selling author Maggie Shayne delivers the fourth romantic mystery in her Brown and De Luca series. Detective Mason Brown is injured in the line of duty and the nurse tending to him is raising the suspicions of Rachel de Luca, the self-help author who assisted Brown on several recent cases. The attraction between Mason and Rachel is only growing stronger, and while she would like to blame her suspicions of his nurse's actions on jealousy, she's certain something more sinister is brewing. To make matters worse, Mason's deranged sister-in-law escapes from custody, putting everyone she knows in danger, especially her sons, who are being raised by Mason. Mason's house burns down and the boys are missing. Mason and Rachel set out to find the boys, but can they track down the boys—and the evil stalking them—before Rachel becomes the next target?

Other books by the same author:
Innocent Prey, 2014
Twilight Guardians, 2014
Blood of the Sorceress, 2013
Wake to Darkness, 2013
Daughter of the Spellcaster, 2012

Other books you might like:
Jaci Burton, *The Heart of a Killer*, 2011
Kendra Elliot, *Bridged*, 2015
Meredith Fletcher, *No Escape*, 2012
Lori Foster, *Run the Risk*, 2012
Maggie Shayne, *Sleep with the Lights On*, 2013

1082

GENA SHOWALTER

The Darkest Touch

(Don Mills, Ontario, Canada: Harlequin, 2014)

Series: Lords of the Underworld Series. Book 11
Story type: Contemporary - Fantasy; Series
Subject(s): Demons; Love; Diseases
Major character(s): Torin, Warrior, Immortal, Demon (host to Disease); Keeleycael, Royalty (the Red Queen)
Time period(s): 21st century; 2010s
Locale(s): Underworld, Alternate Universe

Summary: The immortal warrior Torin is known as the most dangerous lord of the underworld. As the host of the demon Disease, Torin can cause a deathly plague with his touch that could destroy the world. With such a dangerous power in his hands, Torin is forbidden from having relations with anyone. His will has stopped him in the past, but he finally meets his match with Keeleycael, the Red Queen. Keeleycael has just escaped from being imprisoned for centuries. Beautiful and vulnerable, she turns to Torin for help. The connection between the two is fiery, but Torin knows his touch will kill her. Will he be able to hold back his desire for Keeleycael, or will he submit to his urges and end her life?

Other books by the same author:
The Closer You Come, 2015
All for You, 2014
Burning Dawn, 2014
Beauty Awakened, 2013
Black and Blue, 2013

Other books you might like:
Jennifer Ashley, *Immortals: The Redeeming*, 2008
Sidney Ayers, *Demons Like It Hot*, 2011
Anya Bast, *Embrace of the Damned*, 2012
Meljean Brook, *Demon Marked*, 2011
Jaci Burton, *Taken by Sin*, 2009
Maureen Child, *Vanished*, 2009
Stephanie Chong, *The Demoness of Waking Dreams*, 2012
Kresley Cole, *Kiss of a Demon King*, 2009
Terri Garey, *A Devil Named Desire*, 2012
Cynthia Garner, *Heart of the Demon*, 2013
Donna Grant, *Hot Blooded*, 2014
Donna Grant, *Midnight's Promise*, 2013

Larissa Ione, *Reaver*, 2013
Alexandra Ivy, *Bound by Darkness*, 2011
Alexandra Ivy, *Fear the Darkness*, 2012
Stacia Kane, *Personal Demons*, 2008

1083

JOANNA SHUPE

The Courtesan Duchess

(New York, New York: Kensington Publishing, 2015)

Story type: Historical - Regency
Subject(s): Romances (Fiction); Marriage; Deception
Major character(s): Lord Nicholas Francis "Duke of Colton" Seaton, Lover (of Lady Julia); Lady Julia "Duchess of Colton" Seaton, Lover (of Lord Nicholas); Damien "Viscount Quint" Beecham, Friend; Juliet "pseudonym of Lady Julia Seaton" Leighton, Prostitute; Pearl Kelly, Prostitute
Time period(s): 19th century; 1810s
Locale(s): England; Venice, Italy

Summary: Eight years have passed since Julia was married at sixteen to Nicholas, the Duke of Colton, and the now-Duchess is feeling trapped in a loveless marriage to an absent husband. Feeling abandoned, Julia seizes upon a plan to make sure that, despite her husband's lack of affection and commitment to their marriage, her own future is protected. While Nicholas is in Venice, Julia sets off for London's underbelly to learn the secrets of courtesans so that she might seduce her wayward husband and produce an heir, thereby securing her shaky position as Duchess. Calling herself Juliet Leighton, she heads off to Venice to fool her husband into sleeping with her with the help of the couple's sympathetic friend, Damien Beecham. However, Lady Julia's foolproof plan hits a roadblock when she discovers she has legitimate feelings for him, and vice versa. Can their marriage be fixed, even after Lord Nicholas discovers her deception?

Other books you might like:
Loretta Lynda Chase, *Your Scandalous Ways*, 2008
Lily Dalton, *Never Desire a Duke*, 2013
Eloisa James, *Duchess in Love*, 2002
Ashley March, *Seducing the Duchess*, 2010
Cheryl Ann Smith, *The School for Brides*, 2011

1084

TRACY SOLHEIM

Back to Before

(New York, New York: Berkley, 2015)

Story type: Contemporary
Subject(s): Romances (Fiction); Television programs; Love
Major character(s): Ginger Walsh, Lover (of Gavin McAlister), Dancer, Actress; Gavin McAlister, Lover (of Ginger Walsh), Architect
Time period(s): 21st century; 2010s
Locale(s): Chances Inlet, North Carolina

Summary: Both Gavin McAlister and Ginger Walsh find themselves in the small town of Chances Inlet, North

Romances

Carolina after living in New York. Gavin left his job as an architect to help his dying father with his construction business, while Ginger struggles to make friends in town after leaving her career as a soap actress behind. Both have larger plans; after Gavin is able to help his now-widowed mother back on her feet financially, he plans to leave Chances Inlet behind him, while Ginger is hoping to overcome the native townspeople's natural dislike of her (a distaste apparently based on their mistaking her for the character she played on TV) and start a career as a choreographer. The pair meet when Gavin agrees to participate in a television show about home restoration and Ginger serves as his makeup artist. After Ginger wakes up in Gavin's loft, the town is suddenly overfilling with gossip about the possible couple. As Ginger begins to see the town through Gavin's eyes, she starts to perceive the possibility of a happy future there for the first time. But is such a thing even possible when Gavin has made it clear he plans to leave town at the first opportunity? The first book in the Second Chances series.

Other books by the same author:
Sleeping with the Enemy, 2015
Risky Game, 2014
Foolish Games, 2013

Other books you might like:
Lacey Baker, *Homecoming*, 2013
Kara Braden, *The Deepest Night*, 2014
Mary Sullivan, *These Ties That Bind*, 2011
Jodi Thomas, *Can't Stop Believing*, 2013
Lori Wilde, *Somebody to Love*, 2013

1085

JILL SORENSON

Wild

(North Charleston, South Carolina: CreateSpace Publishing, 2014)

Series: Aftershock Series. Book 5
Story type: Contemporary; Romance
Subject(s): Zoos; Zoology; Earthquakes
Major character(s): Helena Fjord, Zoo Keeper; Josh Garrison, Security Officer
Time period(s): 21st century; 2010s
Locale(s): San Diego, California

Summary: Working as a zookeeper has some inherent dangers, but when the San Diego Wildlife Park is hit by an earthquake that devastates the city, it becomes positively treacherous. On a good day, zookeeper Helena Fjord wouldn't have anything to do with security officer Josh Garrison. With animals on the loose and the city on fire, she should have even less interest, but she finds her attraction growing right along with the danger of aftershocks. And Josh, a former Navy SEAL who can usually keep his emotions in check, finds his usual resolve to stay away from the attractive zookeeper weakening by the moment. He vows to protect her from the dangers they face, but at what cost? This is the fifth installment of the Aftershock series by Jill Sorenson.

Other books by the same author:
Backwoods, 2014
Badlands, 2013

Freefall, 2013
Aftershock, 2012
Caught in the Act, 2012

Other books you might like:
Maya Banks, *No Place to Run*, 2010
Rhyannon Byrd, *Take Me Under*, 2013
Catherine Mann, *Hot Zone*, 2011
Lorie O'Clare, *Play Dirty*, 2010
Leslie Tentler, *Edge of Midnight*, 2012

1086

KERRELYN SPARKS

Crouching Tiger, Forbidden Vampire

(New York: HarperCollins Publishers, 2014)

Series: Love at Stake Series. Book 16
Story type: Contemporary - Fantasy; Series
Subject(s): Vampires; Revenge; Love
Major character(s): Russell, Vampire, Military Personnel (U.S. Marine), Companion (of Jia); Jia, Shape-Shifter, Companion (of Russell)
Time period(s): 21st century; 2010s
Locale(s): United States

Summary: In the 16th and final installment of the Love at Stake series, US Marine Russell has just awoken from a coma to discover that he's become a vampire. Angry and out for revenge on the vampire that turned him, Russell reluctantly accepts help from Jia, a shape-shifter who is after the same vampire for killing her parents. But in order for their partnership to work, a few rules have to be established. First, despite their attraction to each other, the partnership has to stay professional. And although Jia questions every action Russell takes, he must be the one in charge. And finally, they must not fall in love. Jia is an engaged woman, and a sexual relationship between Russell and Jia is forbidden. But can they prevent love from happening?

Other books by the same author:
How to Seduce a Vampire (Without Really Trying), 2014
Less than a Gentleman, 2013
The Vampire with the Dragon Tattoo, 2013
Wanted: Undead or Alive, 2012
Wild about You, 2012

Other books you might like:
Cat Devon, *Sleeping with the Entity*, 2013
Shannon Drake, *Dead by Dusk*, 2005
Christine Feehan, *Dark Storm*, 2012
Molly Harper, *The Care and Feeding of Stray Vampires*, 2012
Charlaine Harris, *From Dead to Worse*, 2008
Marjorie M. Liu, *Labyrinth of Stars*, 2014
Katie MacAlister, *Much Ado about Vampires*, 2011
Michelle Rowen, *Bitten and Smitten*, 2006
Lynsay Sands, *The Immortal Who Loved Me*, 2015
Lynsay Sands, *Vampire Most Wanted*, 2014
Jeanne C. Stein, *Chosen*, 2010

1087

SIMONE ST. JAMES

The Other Side of Midnight

(New York: New American Library, 2015)

Subject(s): Psychics; Murder; Mystery
Major character(s): Ellie Winter, Psychic, Friend (former, of Gloria), Girlfriend (of James); Gloria Sutter, Psychic, Crime Victim, Friend (former, of Ellie); James Hawley, Veteran, Boyfriend (of Ellie)
Time period(s): 20th century; 1920s (1925)
Locale(s): London, England

Summary: Set in London in 1925, this supernatural thriller by award-winning author Simone St. James is a tale of romance, murder, and mystery. Psychic Ellie Winter used to contact the dead. Now, she spends her time locating items that were deemed lost. But when her former friend and long-time rival, medium Gloria Sutter, is murdered during a seance, Ellie discovers Gloria's last request was for Ellie to find the killer. Now, Ellie must return to the world of peddlers and schemers to uncover the truth about Gloria's life and death. Meanwhile, Ellie's attraction to James Hawley, a veteran fixed on disproving the work of psychics, is only making matters more difficult. As Ellie and James delve deeper into the secrets of Gloria's life, an evil force works against them, a force that will stop at nothing—or no one—to keep certain truths hidden.

Other books by the same author:
Silence for the Dead, 2014
An Inquiry into Love and Death, 2013
The Haunting of Maddy Clare, 2012

Other books you might like:
Jenn Bennett, *Bitter Spirits*, 2013
Jenn Bennett, *Grave Phantoms*, 2015
Jenn Bennett, *Grim Shadows*, 2014
Emma Bull, *Finder: A Novel of the Borderlands*, 1994
Liz Carlyle, *No True Gentleman*, 2002
Heather Graham, *The Seance*, 2007
Charles L. Grant, *In a Dark Dream*, 1989
James Herbert, *Moon*, 1985
Dean R. Koontz, *The Face of Fear*, 1989
Peter Straub, *Ghost Story*, 1979

1088

SARA JANE STONE

Search and Seduce

(Don Mills, Ontario, Canada: Harlequin Blaze, 2015)

Story type: Contemporary; Military
Subject(s): Romances (Fiction); Dogs; Military life
Major character(s): Amy Benton, Widow(er); Amy Benton, Trainer; Mark Rhodes, Military Personnel
Time period(s): 21st century; 2010s

Summary: Since the death of her SEAL husband during a military operation, Amy Benton has tried to move on by focusing upon her dream of training dogs for use in the military. Her husband's best friend, Mark Rhodes, has served as her rock during her emotional recovery, but recently their friendship has begun to evolve. However, both Amy and Mark are held back by their fears: for Mark, being a pararescue jumper means that his life is constantly in danger and he has learned to place the people he cares about at a distance in order to protect them, while Amy worries about letting her feelings interfere with her dreams, even as she wonders whether she can allow herself to fall for another military man—especially one whose job involves such terrible risks. Can they allow themselves to push back their fears long enough to allow their relationship to grow into something more?

Other books by the same author:
Caught in the Act, 2014
Command Control, 2014
Full Exposure, 2014
Command Performance, 2013

Other books you might like:
Jennifer Bernard, *The Fireman Who Loved Me*, 2012
Rachel Gibson, *Run To You*, 2013
Kristin Hardy, *My Sexiest Mistake*, 2002
Tawny Weber, *A SEAL's Salvation*, 2014
Lori Wilde, *Night Driving*, 2013

1089

MICHELLE STYLES

Taming His Viking Woman

(Don Mills, Ontario, Canada: Harlequin Historical, 2015)

Story type: Historical - Medieval
Subject(s): Romances (Fiction); Vikings; Royalty
Major character(s): Sayrid Avildottar, Warrior; Hrolf Eymundsson, Royalty, Warrior
Time period(s): 900s century; 830s
Locale(s): Sweden

Summary: One of the legendary shield maidens of Viking lore, Sayrid Avildottar has earned herself the right to remain unwed until she encounters her equal in combat. However, her choices are taken away from her when she is defeated by the towering sea-king, Hrolf Eymundsson, who earns both her lands and her hand in marriage as a result. Hrolf believes that woman should remain in the home, far away from the combat that has defined Sayrid's life to date. Nevertheless, Hrolf is determined to win her heart, even as he already earned her hand. Can he overcome her frosty exterior to find the woman within?

Other books by the same author:
Saved by the Viking Warrior, 2014
The Viking's Captive Princess, 2009
Viking Warrior, Unwilling Wife, 2008
The Roman's Virgin Mistress, 2007
Taken by the Viking, 2007

Other books you might like:
Catherine Coulter, *Lord of Hawkfell Island*, 1993
Heather Graham, *Viking's Woman*, 1990
Sandra Hill, *My Fair Viking*, 2002

Romances

Connie Mason, *Viking Warrior*, 2008
Margaret Moore, *The Viking*, 1993

1090

ANNA SUGDEN

A Perfect Catch

(Don Mills, Ontario, Canada: Harlequin, 2015)

Story type: Contemporary - Mainstream
Subject(s): Romances (Fiction); Hockey; Sex roles
Major character(s): Tracy Hayden, Businesswoman; Ike Jelinek, Hockey Player
Time period(s): 21st century; 2010s
Locale(s): New Jersey, United States

Summary: The third book in the New Jersey Ice Cats series, *A Perfect Catch* details the complicated relationship between Tracy Hayden and her ex-boyfriend, professional hockey player Ike Jelinek. Once upon a time the pair had been in love, but Ike's highly traditional views on women's roles and controlling nature had created too many problems for Tracy, and the couple had broken up. After their separation, Tracy had gone on to create a successful company that Ike is forced to hire after he sustains an injury. Now back in close quarters with each other, Ike tries to get Tracy back, but her bad experiences with her father and her ex-husband have left her unwilling to give someone like Ike another try. His attempts to understand her needs and his offer to serve as spokesman for her company make her reconsider whether Ike is capable of change after all, and if he deserves a second chance. However, just as the couple is beginning to repair their damaged relationship, a surprise ultimatum leaves them both forced to choose between their growing love for each other and their respective careers.

Other books by the same author:
A Perfect Trade, 2014
A Perfect Distraction, 2013

Other books you might like:
Kate Angell, *Curveball*, 2007
Rachel Gibson, *The Trouble with Valentine's Day*, 2005
Tess Hudson, *Double Down*, 2005
Donna Kaufmann, *Not So Snow White*, 2006
Susan Elizabeth Phillips, *This Heart of Mine*, 2001

1091

CANDIS TERRY

Sweet Surprise

(New York, New York: Avon Books, 2015)

Story type: Contemporary - Mainstream
Subject(s): Romances (Fiction); Friendship; Divorce
Major character(s): Fiona Wilder, Store Owner, Mother, Divorced Person (ex-wife of Jackson); Mike Halsey, Fire Fighter; Jackson Wilder, Divorced Person (ex-husband of Fiona), Friend (of Mike), Fire Fighter; Isabella Wilder, Daughter (of Jackson and Fiona Wilder)

Time period(s): 21st century; 2010s
Locale(s): Sweet, Texas

Summary: Book four in the Sweet, Texas series focuses on the burgeoning relationship between Fiona Wilder, the ex-wife of Jackson Wilder from *Sweetest Mistake*, and his best friend and fellow firefighter, Mike Halsey. Though Jackson and Fiona have remained on good terms, she remains gun shy about the possibility of repeating the same relationship mistakes that she made with Jackson, so she's determined to take it slow with any future boyfriends. However, her attraction for her ex-husband's firefighting partner and best friend is palpable, and Mike seems to return her affection. While Mike agrees to take it slow, he finds it incredibly difficult to secretly date his friend's ex and to simultaneously resist her temptations—though he doesn't want to do anything that might jeopardize his one chance with the woman he has always loved.

Other books by the same author:
Truly Sweet, 2015
Something Sweeter, 2014
Sweet Cowboy Christmas, 2014
Anything but Sweet, 2013
Sweetest Mistake, 2013

Other books you might like:
Tamra Baumann, *It Had to Be Him*, 2015
Jaci Burton, *The Perfect Play*, 2011
Trish Milburn, *A Firefighter in the Family*, 2008
Carla Neggers, *Cider Brook*, 2014
RaeAnne Thayne, *A Cold Creek Reunion*, 2012

1092

JESSICA TOPPER

Dictatorship of the Dress

(New York, New York: Berkley, 2015)

Story type: Contemporary
Subject(s): Romances (Fiction); Weddings; Deception
Major character(s): Laney Hudson, Lover (of Noah Ridgewood), Artist; Noah Ridgewood, Salesman, Fiance(e), Lover (of Laney Hudson); Sloane, Fiance(e) (of Noah); Allen, Lover (ex-partner of Laney), Musician
Time period(s): 21st century; 2010s
Locale(s): Hawaii, United States; Chicago, Illinois; Las Vegas, Nevada; New York, New York

Summary: Having been left at the altar by her high school boyfriend, Laney was left with bitter feelings about weddings in general, and her mother's upcoming nuptials in particular. In addition, Laney left her dream job as a comic book artist to help run her mother's greeting card company and is now feeling trapped—a situation made worse by her mother's low opinion of her. When her mother's dress needs to transported from Laney's former hometown of New York City to Hawaii, the location of the wedding, Laney is assigned the job of accompanying the precious gown. The trip starts out well enough; the airplane staff mistake her as the bride-to-be and place her in first class, where she is seated next to the handsome software salesman, Noah Ridgewood, who is on his way to Las Vegas for his bachelor party. The airline crew erroneously come to believe Noah to be Laney's husband-to-be, a fib with which she is only to happy to play along. However, the lie snowballs when the flight is forced to land overnight in Chicago, and Laney and Noah are assigned to a honeymoon suite. Over the course of one magical unplanned night, Laney and Noah fall in love—a happy situation complicated by the swiftly arriving weddings of both Laney's mother and Noah.

Other books you might like:
Jennifer Dawson, *Take a Chance on Me*, 2014
Kim Gruenenfelder, *Keep Calm and Carry a Big Drink*, 2013
Beth Kendrick, *Cure for the Common Breakup*, 2014
Dana Precious, *Born Under a Lucky Moon*, 2011
Susan Schneider, *The Wedding Writer*, 2011

1093

JULIE ANN WALKER

Full Throttle

(Naperville, Illinois: Sourcebooks Casablanca, 2014)

Series: Black Knights Inc. Series. Book 7
Story type: Contemporary; Military
Subject(s): Romances (Fiction); Kidnapping; Military life
Major character(s): Abby Thompson, Lover (of Carlos), Daughter (of US president), Student (of Rosa); Carlos "Steady" Soto, Lover (of Abby), Military Personnel (Member of Army Rangers Black Knights), Twin (of Rosa); Rosa Soto, Crime Victim (of bombing), Teacher (of Abby), Twin (of Carlos)
Time period(s): 21st century; 2010s
Locale(s): Kuala Lampur, Malaysia

Summary: When Rosa Soto was killed in a bombing, she left behind a grieving twin brother, Carlos, and Abby Thompson, a student who blamed herself for Rosa's death. Abby and Carlos have more in common than grief, though—each is madly in love with the other. But Carlos, who was attending medical school until his sister died, is now known by the nickname of "Steady." The name was given to him for his surgical skills as part of an Army Rangers black operations unit known as Black Knights, Inc. Abby, who is the daughter of the president of the United States, has been kidnapped by radical militants while attending a conference in Asia. Carlos will come after her—Abby is sure of that—but will he get there in time to save the love of his life? This is the seventh installment in the Black Knights series.

Other books by the same author:
Hell for Leather, 2014
Born Wild, 2013
Thrill Ride, 2013
In Rides Trouble, 2012
Rev It Up, 2012

Other books you might like:
Jessica Bird, *An Unforgettable Lady*, 2010
Shannon K. Butcher, *Living on the Edge*, 2011
Alexis Grant, *Sizzle and Burn*, 2011
Laura Griffin, *Beyond Limits*, 2015

Kat Martin, *Against the Sun*, 2012
Jill Sorenson, *Badlands*, 2013

1094

SHILOH WALKER

Sweeter than Sin

(New York: St. Martin's Paperbacks, 2014)

Series: Secrets and Shadows Series. Book 2
Story type: Contemporary; Series
Subject(s): Suspense; Mystery; Romances (Fiction)
Major character(s): Adam Brascum, Bartender
Time period(s): 21st century; 2010s
Locale(s): Madison, Indiana

Summary: Award-winning author Shiloh Walker delivers the second novel in her Secrets and Shadows romantic suspense series. For years, Adam Brascum turned to alcohol to solve his problems. Now sober, Adam's addiction has become women, and he keeps his interactions purely physical. But when a beautiful, mysterious woman shows up in Madison, Indiana, Adam is tempted to change his ways. They are both hiding from the dark secrets of their pasts, but the attraction between them is more than they can resist. As the quiet town reels from the shocking discovery of a decades-long cover-up involving several of its citizens, another murder takes place. Now, no one in Madison is safe, especially the town's newest visitor, and Adam finds himself risking everything to save the mystery woman's life and capture her heart.

Other books by the same author:
Deeper than Need, 2014
The Protected, 2013
Wrecked, 2013
If You Knew Her, 2012
Stolen, 2012

Other books you might like:
Cherry Adair, *Afterglow*, 2012
Jayne Ann Krentz, *Copper Beach: A Dark Legacy Novel*, 2012
Dianna Love, *Phantom in the Night*, 2008
Shannon McKenna, *Fatal Strike*, 2013
Karen Robards, *The Last Victim*, 2012

1095

BRIGHTON WALSH

Caged in Winter

(New York: Berkley Books, 2014)

Story type: Contemporary
Subject(s): Romances (Fiction); Students; College environment
Major character(s): Winter Jacobson, Student—College, Co-worker (of Cade); Cade Maxwell, Cook (aspiring chef), Co-worker (of Winter)
Time period(s): 21st century; 2010s
Locale(s): United States

Summary: Winter Jacobson is just a few months away from her college graduation—a moment that can't come too soon. Independent and self-sufficient, Winter has spent the last few years looking after herself and trying to rise above the challenges and setbacks life has brought her way. The last thing she wants is to fall in love, but aspiring chef and coworker Cade Maxwell is making that difficult. When a drunken customer makes a pass at Winter, and Cade steps in to protect her, Winter refuses his help. But Cade won't be turned away that easily, and he continues to show up at her every turn. Winter knows Cade could be exactly what she needs; she just doesn't want to admit it. Will she find the courage to open up to Cade and trust that love is in the cards for her after all?

Other books by the same author:
Captive, 2015
Tessa Ever After, 2015

Other books you might like:
Chelsea M. Cameron, *My Favorite Mistake*, 2013
Roberta Helmer, *The Accidental Bride*, 2012
Susan Mallery, *Already Home*, 2011
Tanya Michaels, *Tamed by a Texan*, 2012
Lisa Plumley, *So Irresistible*, 2013

1096

TRACY ANNE WARREN

The Bedding Proposal

(New York, New York: Signet, 2015)

Story type: Historical - Regency
Subject(s): Romances (Fiction); Divorce; Courtship
Major character(s): Lady Thalia Lennox, Divorced Person, Lover (of Leo Byron); Lord Leo Byron, Twin (Lawrence Byron), Lover (of Thalia Lennox); Lord Lawrence Byron, Twin (of Leo Byron); Lord Kemp, Divorced Person
Time period(s): 19th century; 1810s
Locale(s): London, England

Summary: Thalia Lennox had once been one of the aristocratic queens of Regency-era English high society, that is, until her husband divorced her in a scandalous affair. Now the subject of relentless gossip that has pushed her to the margins of society, Thalia is reluctant to ever trust a man again—particularly a roguish figure like Lord Leo Byron, who is the subject of his own salacious gossip. However, when Leo sets eyes upon the mysterious and reclusive Thalia, he is instantly smitten. Determined to take her to his bed, he begins an aggressive courtship of the apparently uninterested Thalia, until he is accidentally injured as a result of one of Thalia's plots to rebuff her suitor. Filled with guilt, she agrees to give him a two-week window in which he may seek to change her mind. And though her mind tells her that she cannot trust any man, let alone this one, her body is beginning to have other ideas. *The Bedding Proposal* is the first book in Warren's Rakes of Cavendish Square series of Regency novels.

Other books by the same author:
The Last Man on Earth, 2014
The Man Plan, 2014

The Trouble with Princesses, 2013
Her Highness and the Highlander, 2012
The Princess and the Peer, 2012

Other books you might like:
Victoria Alexander, *A Little Bit Wicked*, 2007
Victoria Alexander, *Secrets of a Proper Lady*, 2007
Gayle Callen, *Redemption of the Duke*, 2014
Amelia Grey, *The Duke in My Bed*, 2014
Ashlyn Macnamara, *A Most Scandalous Proposal*, 2013

1097

LORI WILDE (Pseudonym of Laurie Vanzura)

Christmas at Twilight

(New York: Avon, 2014)

Series: Twilight, Texas Series. Book 6
Story type: Contemporary; Holiday Themes
Subject(s): Romances (Fiction); Love; Christmas
Major character(s): Brian Hutchinson, Veteran (US Army captain), Mentally Ill Person (PTSD), Brother (of Ashley); Ashley Hutchinson, Sister (of Brian), Mother (of Kimmie), Roommate (housemate of Jane); Jane Brown, Woman (also known as Meredith Sommers), Mother (of Ben), Roommate (housemate of Ashley), Spouse (of abusive husband); Kimmie, 4-Year-Old, Daughter (of Ashley); Ben, 4-Year-Old, Son (of Jane)
Time period(s): 21st century; 2010s
Locale(s): Twilight, Texas

Summary: Army veteran Brian Hutchinson gets an unpleasant surprise when he comes home in the sixth novel in the Twilight, Texas series. Brian has been discharged because of his PTSD and associated mutism. He returns to his home in Twilight, but instead of finding his sister, Ashley, he encounters a woman armed with pepper spray. Jane Brown and her son, Ben, have been living in the Hutchinson house with Ashley while Brian was away. Jane is currently caring for Ashley's four-year-old daughter, Kimmie, while Ashley is on a date that has taken longer than it should. When Ashley fails to reappear, Brian helps Jane care for the kids, and he gradually learns the truth about his new housemate. Jane's real name is Meredith Sommers, and she is hiding from her violent husband. Brian has a painful past, too, which he eventually shares with Jane as they adjust to their new lives in Twilight.

Other books by the same author:
Love with a Perfect Cowboy, 2014
All Out of Love, 2013
Crash Landing, 2013
Love at First Sight, 2013
Somebody to Love, 2013

Other books you might like:
Catherine Anderson, *My Sunshine*, 2005
Robyn Carr, *The Hero*, 2013
Laura Drake, *The Sweet Spot*, 2013
Marilyn Pappano, *A Man to Hold on To*, 2014
Candis Terry, *Sweetest Mistake*, 2013

1098

SHERRYL WOODS

The Christmas Bouquet

(Don Mills, Ontario, Canada: Harlequin, 2014)

Series: Chesapeake Shores Series. Book 11
Story type: Contemporary; Series
Subject(s): Romances (Fiction); Christmas; Holidays
Major character(s): Caitlyn Winters, Student (medical school), Girlfriend (of Noah McIlroy); Noah McIlroy, Doctor (medical resident), Boyfriend (of Caitlyn Winters)
Time period(s): 21st century; 2010s
Locale(s): Chesapeake Shores, Maryland

Summary: A young woman's life takes a turn when she catches a bride's bouquet in the 11th novel in the Chesapeake Shores series. Caitlyn Winters is still in medical school, but she already knows how her future will unfold. At least, she thought she knew. She didn't plan on getting involved with Noah McIlroy, a medical resident. And Caitlyn certainly didn't intend to become pregnant with Noah's child. The pregnancy changes everything, and Caitlyn and Noah react differently to their situation. Noah would be thrilled to marry Caitlyn and begin their family, but Caitlyn isn't convinced that's the route she wants to take. She doesn't want to let go of her dreams of becoming a doctor and living at Chesapeake Shores. Noah knows that he can give Caitlyn the life she wants, but he'll need some help from the O'Brien clan if he wants to convince Caitlyn to marry him.

Other books by the same author:
Home to Seaview Key, 2014
Safe Harbor, 2014
Swan Point, 2014
Sea Glass Island, 2013
A Seaside Christmas, 2013

Other books you might like:
Toni Blake, *Holly Lane*, 2011
Elizabeth Hayley, *The Best Medicine*, 2015
Helen Lacey, *Marriage under the Mistletoe*, 2012
Johanna Lindsey, *The Present*, 1998
Debbie Macomber, *Angels at the Table*, 2012
Linda Lael Miller, *I'll Be Home for Christmas*, 2006

1099

MAISEY YATES

Part Time Cowboy

(Don Mills, Ontario, Canada: Harlequin, 2015)

Story type: Contemporary - Mainstream
Subject(s): Romances (Fiction); Reunions; Love
Major character(s): Sadie Miller, Hotel Owner, Criminal, Counselor; Eli Garrett, Rancher, Police Officer
Time period(s): 21st century; 2010s
Locale(s): Copper Ridge, United States

Summary: Eli Garrett is very protective of his hometown of Copper Ridge in his role as a deputy sheriff. So when former juvenile delinquent Sadie Miller returns, he is dubious about her claims of having changed. To make matters worse, she has just signed a lease to operate a bed and breakfast on Garrett land, meaning they are going to be neighbors. Though Sadie has experience as a crisis therapist, she is having trouble dealing with her own inner demons, which is the reason for the return to her childhood home. Unfortunately, she is unprepared for the feelings that Eli creates in her, giving her another stumbling block in her quest for emotional resolution. Eli, too, feels an attraction to Sadie, but his life is built on law and order and control, and he isn't ready to deal with the chaos that Sadie creates in him. Can the couple overcome their internal doubts and allow themselves to find happiness with each other? This is the first book in the Copper Ridge series by Maisey Yates.

Other books by the same author:
Bad News Cowboy, 2015
Brokedown Cowboy, 2015
His Diamond of Convenience, 2015
Midnight on the Sands, 2015
To Defy a Sheikh, 2015

Other books you might like:
C.H. Admirand, *Dylan*, 2012
Jaci Burton, *Hope Ignites*, 2014
Susan Donovan, *Not That Kind of Girl*, 2010
Charlene Sands, *The Cowboy's Pride*, 2011
Candis Terry, *Something Sweeter*, 2014

1100

REBECCA ZANETTI

Total Surrender

(New York, New York: Hachette Book Group, 2015)

Story type: Espionage; Genetic Manipulation
Subject(s): Romances (Fiction); Genetic engineering; Espionage
Major character(s): Jory Dean, Military Personnel; Piper Oliver, Computer Expert
Time period(s): 21st century; 2010s
Locale(s): United States

Summary: The fourth book in Zanetti's "Sin Brothers" series, this installment relates the story of Jory, the final of the four genetically-engineered brothers upon whom this romance series is focused, and who were designed in a covert military experiment to design the perfect assassin. Though his brothers each found love in the first three novels, Jory's story is more complicated as, until recently, his brothers had believed him to be dead. Now reunited, Jory and his brothers are still in danger from the forces that created them and held them captive. Looking to find a final solution, Jory encounters Piper Oliver, a beautiful master computer hacker who has been hired to reactivate the computer chip in his spine that his former handlers used to control him. However, after meeting and falling for Jory, she begins to wonder if she

Romances

has been lied to, and whether she holds the key to freeing Jory and his brothers once and for all.

Other books by the same author:
Blind Faith, 2014
Forgotten Sins, 2014
Sweet Revenge, 2014
Hunted, 2012

Claimed, 2011

Other books you might like:
Maya Banks, *No Place to Run*, 2010
Suzanne Brockmann, *Do or Die*, 2014
Pamela Clare, *Breaking Point*, 2011
Cindy Gerard, *Killing Time*, 2013
Stephanie Tyler, *Lie with Me*, 2010

Aliens: The Other Us
by
Don D'Ammassa

If you ask the average person to name the first thing that comes to mind when someone mentions science fiction, it likely will be either spaceships or aliens. The assumption that the genre deals primarily with outer space is thoroughly ingrained even though more of its output —particularly in recent years —has been set on Earth than off it. The public image of aliens also is warped by their role in most movies. Aliens are rarely sympathetic and often monstrous on screen, whereas the literature is more likely to represent aliens as essentially just another national group. *The War of the Worlds* by H.G. Wells aside, the alien as monster theme has never been particularly popular in the field and many of the novels with this motif actually were written by horror or suspense writers rather than those working primarily in science fiction.

The literary view of aliens started to take form in the 1920s and 1930s when writers such as Edward E. Smith and Edmond Hamilton were pioneering what we now think of as space opera, a play on the term horse opera for western movies and novels. Outer space became an enormous wilderness peopled with strange cultures, but no matter how peculiar they might be on the surface they were almost always recognizably human. It was entirely possible for alien races to be technologically and sometimes even morally superior —rationalized as the product of a more mature culture rather than any inherent superiority. There might be a few odd details thrown in to underscore that these were aliens, but their culture, politics, commerce, military, and personal psychology were indistinguishable otherwise from human beings. This was not so much a failure of imagination as a redirection of it. The possibility that aliens might actually be alien was not the point. These stories were about the act of exploration, and it was generally accepted that while we may have fallen behind some of the other denizens of the galaxy, this was only a temporary situation and humanity would rise to the challenge and eventually become dominant.

This state of affairs continued to be the rule in the genre with only rare exceptions until the 1960s and it remains a strong element in contemporary science fic-

tion, particularly military oriented stories in which aliens are simply rival armies. Modern stories of alien invasion, for example, are almost never the suspenseful, insidious affairs found in *Invasion of the Body Snatchers* by Jack Finney (1954) or *The Puppet Masters* by Robert A. Heinlein (1951), both of which were reactions to the Red Scare fear of fifth columnists. Aliens now arrive openly and with advanced weaponry as in *Footfall* by Larry Niven and Jerry Pournelle (1985) or the Vampire Earth series by E.E. Knight. They are not meant to represent the terror of the unknown but rather our worries about different but comprehensible and clearly human dogmas. Alien invaders today are thinly disguised totalitarians or communists or imperialist and their motives are indistinguishable from our own.

The only major writer before the 1950s who was credited with the creation of genuinely alien aliens was Hal Clement (pseudonym of Harry Stubbs). Clement took great pains to create environments that were unknown on Earth and then tailor his alien characters so that they would logically have evolved differently than did the human race. The most famous of his novels in this vein was *Mission of Gravity* (1954) in which humans discover a planet whose gravity is so great that it is impossible to visit physically, so exploration and study must be conducted by means of proxies, in this case intelligent inhabitants of the world who can be reached through radio communication. The aliens in *Cycle of Fire* (1957) live on a world that constantly is torn by violent earthquakes, volcanic activity, and other disastrous upheavals. Similar themes can be found in *Close to Critical* (1964) and *Fossil* (1993). Clement occasionally brought his alien races to visit Earth. The space traveling visitors in *Needle* (1957) are essentially symbionts who live inside other bodies and those in *Iceworld* (1953) come from a world so hot that they consider the Earth only marginally habitable. Clement was, however, interested in physiological variations and did not explore the differences in psychology that would certainly have resulted from such a different course of evolution. His aliens all act pretty much like human beings.

A few writers did begin to speculate about how an alien intelligence might develop. The aliens in Brian W. Aldiss's *The Dark Light Years* (1964) are so completely inhuman that meaningful communication is impossible and their appearance and personal habits are so offensive to human sensibilities that further efforts to do so are cut off. The alien visitors in *The Flies of Memory* by Ian Watson (1990) perceive reality and time in such a different manner that it is never clear whether the human characters understand them at all. Earth is temporarily occupied by a fleet of spaceships in *The Alien Years* by Robert Silverberg (1998), but their psychology is so much at odds with that of humans that they apparently never even realize that the planet has an indigenous intelligent civilization.

In *Childhood's End* by Arthur C. Clarke (1953) Earth is administered by an apparently benevolent and overwhelmingly superior interstellar culture that sees its place in the universe as the overseer of an evolutionary step by which intelligent races leave their physical bodies behind and become part of a kind of mass mind. A similar but less extreme transformation takes place in *The Harvest* by Robert Charles Wilson (1993). There is a group mind that unites the mischievously deadly aliens in *The Mote in God's Eye* by Larry Niven and Jerry Pournelle (1975). Yet another mass mind manipulates entire races behind the scenes in *Night Train to Rigel* by Timothy Zahn (2005) and its several sequels. Several authors have posited aliens as mentors initiating humanity into the larger galactic community, or quarantining us to the solar system as an alternative to committing genocide to protect the civilized races from contact.

Not all aliens are benevolent, however, even if they are not bug eyed monsters or insidious parasites intent upon stealing human bodies. Fred Hoyle's *The Black Cloud* (1957) suggests that a drifting cloud of interstellar matter that threatens to cut off the light of the sun might be intelligent but unaware of the havoc it is causing. Artificial intelligences created by alien races that have subsequently vanished often act in ways that seem logical to them but callous to human sensibilities. One such demands that thousands of humans have their consciousness uploaded into its memory array in *Eater* by Gregory Benford (2000). Fred Saberhagen's classic Berserker series posits a fleet of self aware warships that have survived an interstellar conflict and have now become inimical to all life in the universe.

Whatever form alien intelligence might take, it is certain to differ from anything in our previous experience, even if it has a human shaped body and seems to think very similarly. This leads to one of the most frequently recurring plot elements in science fiction —the description of the very first encounter between two rival intelligences and how the gap between them is bridged. These are referred to as "first contact" stories, after the classic Murray Leinster short of that name from 1945. In that story an alien and a human starship meet in a remote part of space. Although neither side is hostile, neither wants to reveal the location of its home civilization or details of its technology to the impasse. Although not a tremendously sophisticated plot, it set the tone for literally hundreds that followed.

In some cases first contact stories are much more than simple puzzles and rely on a better understanding of psychology and cultural development. In Michael Bishop's *Transfigurations* (1980), scientists have nearly given up hope of understanding an apparently primitive alien race until they are able to genetically manipulate an ape and create a being that partially bridges the gap between the two cultures. An interesting variation of this is *Cage a Man* by F.M. Busby (1973), in which hostile aliens capture a human and slowly alter his body to make him conform to their shape, hoping thereby to reconfigure his mind and coerce him into betraying his own species. Both humans and aliens engage in this activity in the classic *The Dragon Masters* by Jack Vance (1962).

James Blish provided a philosophical dimension in *A Case of Conscience* (1958). When humans discover a civilized planet whose inhabitants have never developed religion or the concept of sin, the philosophical problem causes considerable turmoil. D.G. Compton examined the question of religious conversion from the opposite direction in *The Missionaries* (1972), wherein a group of aliens arrive on Earth with the avowed purpose of enlightening humanity about the one true religion. H.G. Wells posited a non-violent alien interference in human affairs in *Star Begotten* (1937), in which an alien power uses cosmic rays to manipulate human germ plasm and gradually supplant the human mind and body with its own template.

Somewhat similar to first contact stories are those in which humans encounter an artifact deliberately or inadvertently left behind by an absent alien intelligence. In Arthur C. Clarke's *Rendezvous with Rama* (1973) an enormous, automated habitat drifts through the solar system and is visited briefly by a space crew. Clarke is also, of course, creator of the alien monolith on the moon in *2001: A Space Odyssey* (1968). In *Rogue Moon* by Algis Budrys (1960), an enigmatic structure on the moon is presumed to be some kind of intelligence test left there by a superior civilization. Frederik Pohl's *Gateway* (1977), Greg Bear's *Eon* (1985), Gregory Benford's *Artifact* (1985), and Alastair Reynolds' *Pushing Ice* (2005) are all outstanding variations of this theme.

All of these stories, however, have one thing in common. The aliens may be good or evil, advanced or primitive, humanoid or bizarrely shaped, and their motivations might not coincide with our own. But in each case they are designed to tell us something about humanity. They are either close reflections that allow the writer to describe how we might fare under different physical conditions or social structures, or they are so different that they provide a sharp contrast and underscore aspects of our humanity. It is probable that no writer, however skilled, will ever actually be able to create a convincing fictional race that has no points of congruency with humanity because no writer can cast aside his or her nature completely enough to do so. The question arises then as to what will happen if we ever do encounter another such intelligence.

Recommended Titles

The first half of 2015 presented a balanced mix of new and established writers in science fiction. The recent trend to translate and publish novels originally published outside the United States has strengthened. The release of a trilogy by Liu Cixin, the best-selling science fiction writer in China, potentially opens up an extensive new resource for English speaking readers. Several established trends—steampunk, alternate history, and a renewed interest in adventures in outer space and on other planets—show no signs of weakening. The best from this period include the following:

Dark Intelligence by Neal Asher

Cannonbridge by Jonathan Barnes

Tracker by C.J. Cherryh

Nemesis Games by James S.A. Corey

Something Coming Through by Paul J. McAuley

Border by Robert McCammon

Master Sergeant by Mel Odom

King of the Cracksmen by Dennis O'Flaherty

Jacaranda by Cherie Priest

Collected Fiction by Hannu Rajaniemi

Aurora by Kim Stanley Robinson

Clash of Eagles by Alan Smale

The Affinities by Robert Charles Wilson

Science Fiction

1101

JOHN JOSEPH ADAMS

Wastelands 2

(London: Titan Books, 2015)

Story type: Collection
Subject(s): Short stories; Apocalypse; Science fiction

Summary: Award-winning editor John Joseph Adams collects 30 post-apocalyptic science fiction tales in this companion volume to his earlier collection, *Wastelands*. Here, Adams includes David Brin's "The Postman," Hugh Howey's "Deep Blood Kettle," Tananarive Due's "Patient Zero," Nancy Kress's "By Fools Like Me," George R. R. Martin's "...for a single yesterday," Junot Diaz's "Monstro," Seanan McGuire's "Animal Husbandry," and many more end-of-the-world stories.

Other books by the same author:
Armored, 2012
Under the Moons of Mars, 2012
Brave New Worlds, 2010
Federations, 2009
Wastelands, 2008

Other books you might like:
Paolo Bacigalupi, *The Drowned Cities*, 2012
Lauren Beukes, *Moxyland*, 2009
David Brin, *The Postman*, 1985
Hugh Howey, *Wool*, 2012
Robert Silverberg, *The Millennium Express: 1995-2009*, 2014

1102

DAVID AFSHARIRAD

The Year's Best Military SF and Space Opera: Book One

(Wake Forest, North Carolina: Baen Books, 2015)

Story type: Collection; Series
Subject(s): Spacetime; Short stories; Military life

Summary: This collection includes a forward by David Drake, and consists of short stories published in print journals, including selected science fiction magazines, as well as stories that have been published online. Editor David Afsharirard has chosen stories that revolve around either a military science fiction theme, or a space opera science fiction theme. The anthology includes Michael Z. Williamson's "Soft Casualty," Linda Nagata's "Codename: Delphi," William Ledbetter's "Stealing Arturo," and Holly Black's "Ten Rules for Being an Intergalactic Smuggler (the Successful Kind)." Many of the stories contain themes of adventure and humanity's ability to triumph over adversity. The collection also includes a limited-time interactive reader feature, allowing readers to vote for their favorite story.

Other books you might like:
David Drake, *Paying the Piper*, 2002
David Gunn, *Maximum Offense*, 2008
R.M. Meluch, *Wolf Star*, 2006
Jerry Pournelle, *Falkenberg's Legion*, 1990
Mike Resnick, *Starship: Pirate*, 2006

1103

ANN AGUIRRE

Breakout

(New York: Penguin Random House, 2015)

Series: Dred Chronicles. Book 3
Story type: Series; Space Opera
Subject(s): Prisoners; Space colonies; Space flight
Major character(s): Dred Devos, Prisoner; Vost, Mercenary; Silence, Villain
Time period(s): Indeterminate
Locale(s): *Perdition*, Spaceship

Summary: In the third installment of Ann Aguirre's Dred Chronicles series, which takes place within the Jax book universe, Dresdemona "Dred" Devos finally plans her escape from the penal colony space craft *Perdition*. Very few of her followers are still alive after the latest battle against Silence, and Dred realizes that time is of the essence if they are ever going to get away. Knowing she has little choice, Dred joins up with Vost to challenge Silence for the prisoners' freedom. Dred needs to bide her time long enough for her ragtag group of followers to construct a ship sturdy enough to fly them off of Perdition and away from its orbital asteroid. Unfortunately, Silence has gotten wind of Dred's plan for escape, and she is not willing to let her enemy flee so easily. As

Dred fights for the lives of the remaining prisoners, Silence threatens to destroy everything in her path, including *Perdition* itself, rather than accept defeat.

Other books by the same author:
Havoc, 2014
Endgame, 2012
Aftermath, 2011
Doubleblind, 2009
Grimspace, 2007

Other books you might like:
C.J. Cherryh, *Chanur's Legacy*, 1992
Julie E. Czerneda, *Reap the Wild Wind*, 2007
Sarah A. Hoyt, *Darkship Renegades*, 2012
Jean Johnson, *The Terrans*, 2015
S.L. Viehl, *Blade Dancer*, 2003
Rie Warren, *Under His Guard*, 2015

1104

KEVIN J. ANDERSON

Blood of the Cosmos
(New York: Tom Doherty Associates, 2015)

Series: Saga of Shadows Series. Book 2
Story type: Series; Space Opera
Subject(s): Futuristic society; Wars; Space colonies
Major character(s): Lee Iswander, Leader, Businessman; Aelin, Religious (green priest)
Time period(s): Indeterminate Future
Locale(s): Earth; Outer Space

Summary: In the second installment of Kevin J. Anderson's Saga of Shadows series, looming antimatter threatens to destroy the galaxy. The antimatter's creators, the Shana Rei, have already been very nearly successful in their quest to wipe out humanity as well as the race known as the Ildirans. Despite their prey's narrow escape, however, the Shana Rei have some luck on their side this time. The Gardners, who aided the humans and Ildirans by saving them from their foes the last time around, have become a liability instead of an asset, and the Shana Rei are ready to pounce. Then the alliance creates a device that promises to halt the Shana Rei, saving the tree forests of Earth as well as much of the galaxy. Unfortunately, that device proves to also be a catastrophe, and the entire cosmos is again at risk. Now the human-Ildrian coalition must devise another way to halt the Shana Rei, or life as they know it will cease to exist and both species will die.

Other books by the same author:
The Dark Between the Stars, 2014
The Martian War, 2012
Of Fire and Night, 2006
Scattered Suns, 2005
Ruins, 1996

Other books you might like:
Iain M. Banks, *Look to Windward*, 2001
Gregory Benford, *Cosm*, 1998
Frank Herbert, *Dune*, 1965
Mel Odom, *Master Sergeant*, 2015
Vernor Vinge, *A Deepness in the Sky*, 1999

1105

TAYLOR ANDERSON

Straits of Hell
(New York: Penguin Publishing Group, 2015)

Series: Destroyermen Series. Book 10
Story type: Alternate History; Military
Subject(s): Military life; Wars; Armed forces
Major character(s): Matt Reddy, Military Personnel (Commander of the USS *Walker*); Don Herman, Military Personnel (Leader of the Dominion)
Time period(s): Multiple Time Periods
Locale(s): Madagascar; United States

Summary: In this alternate version of Earth during World War II, the war is over and the destroyer USS *Walker* is no longer in the waters near Asia. That's no comfort to Matt Reddy and his crew, who have no idea how they ended up somewhere else and are struggling to fit in. Instead of the war they signed on for, they find themselves allied with the Imperial forces and the cat-like race the Lemurians in a battle against a reptilian race called the Grik, which is threatening Madagascar, the ancient home of the Lemurians. Between their confusion about their strange situation, the odds they face, and the lack of help, fighting the Japanese begins to look like an easier task for Reddy and his men. At the same time, the Dominion is on the rise as the leader, Don Hernan, prepare to attack Fort Defiance and bring the Americas to their knees.

Other books by the same author:
Deadly Shores: Destroyermen, 2014
Iron Gray Sea, 2012
Firestorm, 2011
Distant Thunders, 2010
Crusade, 2008

Other books you might like:
Martin Caidin, *The Final Countdown*, 1980
William R. Forstchen, *Fateful Lightning*, 1993
Leo Frankowski, *The Radiant Warrior*, 1989
Roland Green, *Janissaries III: Storms of Victory*, 1987
S. M. Stirling, *Against the Tide of Years*, 1999

1106

DAVID ANNANDALE

Yarrick: Imperial Creed
(Nottingham, United Kingdom: Games Workshop, 2015)

Series: Commissar Yarrick Series. Book 2
Story type: Adventure; Military
Subject(s): Military life; Fantasy; Rebellion
Major character(s): Sebastian Yarrick, Military Personnel (Lord Commissar), Apprentice (of Lord Commissar Rasp); Rasp, Military Personnel (Lord Commissar), Leader (Mentor to Yarrick)
Time period(s): Indeterminate
Locale(s): Mistral, Planet—Imaginary

Summary: This book set in the Warhammer 40,000 universe tells the story of the early days of Commissar

Yarrick. Before he was the Lord Commissar, he was Sebastian Yarrick, a new officer raised up from the ranks of the schola progenium. Now older and more experienced, Yarrick reflects back on the mission that launched his career when he served under the Lord Commissar Rasp. His first assignment is to help put down an uprising on Mistral, where rebel barons have tossed the politics of the empire out of balance. The Chaos seed is planted and spreads; Chaos cults erupt and war is everywhere. In these desperate and trying times Sebastian Yarrick first learns the ways that eventually make him the feared and respected Lord Commissar. This is the second book in the Commissar Yarrick series.

Other books by the same author:
The Death of Antagonis, 2013
Yarrick: Chains of Golgotha, 2013
Gethsemane Hall, 2012

Other books you might like:
Ben Counter, *Phalanx*, 2012
Aaron Dembski-Bowden, *Betrayer*, 2013
C Z Dunn, *Pandorax*, 2014
Graham McNeill, *Vengeful Spirit*, 2014
Sandy Mitchell, *The Greater Good*, 2013

1107

MINDEE ARNETT

Polaris

(New York: HarperCollins, 2015)

Series: Avalon Series. Book 2
Subject(s): Science fiction; Space exploration; Space flight
Major character(s): Jeth Seagrave, Teenager, Mercenary, Brother (of Cora); Cora, Sister (of Jeth); Daxton Price, Criminal (crime lord)
Time period(s): Indeterminate Future
Locale(s): Outer Space

Summary: Teenage mercenary Jeth Seagrave tries to evade an enemy and save his imprisoned mother in the second novel in the Avalon series. The Interstellar Transport Authority already has its hands on Jeth's mother, and the ITA would also like to capture Jeth's sister Cora to unlock the technology that's imbedded in her DNA. Jeth is determined not to let that happen. He plans to rescue his mother and bring his family to a place beyond the reach of the Confederation, but the ITA has put someone on Jeth's tail to keep him from completing his mission. Jeth feels that he has no choice but to ally himself with Daxton Price, a powerful crime figure. Dax can help Jeth, but he expects something big in return. He places an implant in Jeth's brain that puts Dax in control of Jeth's actions. The implant gives Jeth the power he needs to locate his mother, but it also puts him at the mercy of Dax's will.

Other books by the same author:
The Nightmare Charade, 2015
The Nightmare Dilemma, 2015
Avalon, 2014

The Nightmare Affair, 2013
Other books you might like:
Alexander Besher, *Chi*, 1999
Brenda Cooper, *Reading the Wind*, 2009
Ruth Downie, *Tabula Rasa*, 2014
William Gibson, *Pattern Recognition*, 2003
David Macinnis Gill, *Invisible Sun*, 2012
Elizabeth Hand, *Hunted: A Clone Wars Novel*, 2003
Kristi Helvig, *Burn Out*, 2014
Nancy Kress, *Stinger*, 1998
Richard K. Morgan, *Altered Carbon*, 2002
Kenneth Oppel, *Starclimber*, 2009

1108

NEAL ASHER

Dark Intelligence

(New York: Night Shade Books, 2015)

Series: Transformation Series. Book 1
Story type: Chase; Futuristic
Subject(s): Science fiction; Artificial Intelligence; Revenge
Major character(s): Thorvald Spear, Military Personnel (resurrected), Employer (of Isobel Satomi), Crime Victim (killed by Penny Royal); Penny Royal, Artificial Intelligence, Murderer; Isobel Satomi, Criminal (syndicate leader), Hunter (of Penny Royal), Artificial Intelligence (partial)
Time period(s): Indeterminate Future
Locale(s): Outer Space

Summary: Thorvald Spear remembers being trapped in a hopeless battle between humans and Pradors. He is surprised to wake up in a hospital bed, and even more shocked to learn that a century has passed since his death. Thorvald is even more startled when he is informed that he was not killed by the enemy. His ship's artificial intelligence (AI), Penny Royal, killed him. Penny Royal was meant to be the troops' backup but instead embarked on a killing rampage. A century later, Penny Royal is still running loose and killing. Thorvald swears revenge and hires criminal syndicate leader Isobel Satomi to help him. Isobel has her own reasons for tracking and killing Penny Royal: A deal she made with the crazed AI for power and protection went badly, and now Isobel is no longer quite human. The power she controls as a partial AI is tremendous, but her steady transformation into a monster could lead to disaster for everyone. This is the first book in the Transformation series.

Other books by the same author:
The Jupiter War, 2013
Zero Point, 2013
The Departure, 2012
The Line War, 2008
Prador Moon, 2006
Other books you might like:
Lois McMaster Bujold, *Cryoburn*, 2010
Julie E. Czerneda, *Survival*, 2004
Alastair Reynolds, *House of Suns*, 2009
Joel Shepherd, *Originator*, 2015
Charles Stross, *Halting State*, 2007

Science Fiction

1109

JAMES AXLER

Terminal White

(Don Mills, Ontario, Canada: Worldwide Library, 2015)

Series: Outlanders Series. Book 72
Story type: Post-Disaster; Post-Nuclear Holocaust
Subject(s): Extraterrestrial life; Computers; Technology
Major character(s): Kane, Rebel (Cerberus warrior), Co-worker (of Brigid and Grant); Brigid, Rebel (Cerberus warrior), Co-worker (of Kane and Grant); Grant, Rebel (Cerberus warrior), Co-worker (of Kane and Brigid)
Time period(s): Indeterminate Future
Locale(s): Canada

Summary: Cerberus rebels continue their fight for the freedom of mankind in this 72nd installment in the Outlanders series by James Axler. Computers have replaced humanity's free will in a testing ground deep in the wilderness of what used to be Western Canada, a land that is currently plagued by a perpetual snowstorm. There, the old order has devised a new plan to enslave all of humanity, and its experimental ground is full of citizens they've successfully turned into compliant subjects. Cerberus rebels Kane, Brigid, and Grant are humanity's only hope for independence. Together, they brave the northern wilderness to thwart the mastermind threatening the future of mankind. In the process, they are pulled into the experiment themselves.

Other books by the same author:
End Day, 2015
Siren Song, 2014
Savage Dawn, 2013
Scarlet Dreams, 2011
Reality Echo, 2010

Other books you might like:
Poul Anderson, *Orion Shall Rise*, 1983
Paul Collins, *The Skyborn*, 2005
William W. Johnstone, *Betrayal in the Ashes*, 1996
Whitley Strieber, *Warday*, 1984
Kate Wilhelm, *Where Late the Sweet Birds Sang*, 1976

1110

JAMES AXLER

End Day

(Don Mills, Ontario, Canada: Worldwide Library, 2015)

Series: Deathlands Series. Book 121
Story type: Dystopian; End of the World
Subject(s): Apocalypse; Dystopias; Survival
Major character(s): Ryan Cawdor, Warrior, Time Traveler
Time period(s): Multiple Time Periods
Locale(s): New York, New York

Summary: This post-apocalyptic tale is the 121st installment in the Deathlands series by James Axler. While in pursuit of their enemy Magus, Ryan Cawdor and his companions slip into a time warp that leads them to New York City in the 20th century. Ryan and company find themselves among strange people in a strange city—a city more foreign than any land they've visited. Even in New York City, the evil Magus is at work, planning for Armageddon to destroy the world—and Ryan—in a mere 72 hours. But do Ryan and his companions have what it takes to survive in this peculiar metropolis and keep Magus from erasing their futures?

Other books by the same author:
Terminal White, 2015
Perception Fault, 2011
Pantheon of Vengeance, 2008
Plague Lords, 2008
Labyrinth, 2006

Other books you might like:
Ben Bova, *Test of Fire*, 1982
David Brin, *The Postman*, 1985
Robert R. McCammon, *Swan Song*, 1987
N. Lee Wood, *Faraday's Orphans*, 1997
Roger Zelazny, *Damnation Alley*, 1969

1111

JAMES AXLER

Forbidden Trespass

(Don Mills, Ontario, Canada: Gold Eagle, 2015)

Series: Deathlands Series. Book 122
Story type: Dystopian; Series
Subject(s): Apocalypse; Dystopias; Murder
Major character(s): Ryan Cawdor, Warrior, Survivor
Time period(s): Indeterminate Future
Locale(s): United States

Summary: James Axler's Deathlands series continues as Ryan Cawdor and his fellow survivors wander the dangerous wastelands of a post-apocalyptic United States. When a string of mysterious murders occurs in a farming community, Ryan and his companions are named prime suspects. At the same time, a colony of hungry, flesh-eating mutants has been driven from its fertile underground home. Ryan and his companions blame the hungry cannibals for the community's deaths and now must decide how to help the mutants reclaim their stolen territory. But as the fight gets underway, Ryan learns that something far more destructive is looming in the rich farmlands.

Other books by the same author:
Hell's Maw, 2015
Hell Road Warriors, 2012
Moonfeast, 2010
Plague Lords, 2008
Remember Tomorrow, 2007

Other books you might like:
Robert Edmond Alter, *Carny Kill*, 1966
Poul Anderson, *Maurai and Kith*, 1982
Glen Cook, *The Heirs of Babylon*, 1972
William W. Johnstone, *Hatred in the Ashes*, 1999
David Mace, *Demon-4*, 1987

`1112`

JAMES AXLER

Hell's Maw

(New York: Gold Eagle, 2015)

Series: Outlanders Series. Book 73
Story type: Invasion of Earth; Post-Nuclear Holocaust
Subject(s): Apocalypse; Wars; Science fiction
Major character(s): Ereshkigal, Alien, Ruler; Kane, Warrior; Grant, Warrior; Brigid, Warrior
Time period(s): Indeterminate Future
Locale(s): Earth

Summary: In this 73rd novel in the Outlanders sci-fi series by James Axler, set on a post-apocalyptic Earth, one of the aliens occupying the planet begins a quest to take over the world. Ereshkigal, a vicious ruler with followers known as Terror Priests who will stop at nothing for their queen, has established a temple and begun her hostile takeover. She is using her dark magic to eliminate anything in her path. Cereberus rebels and warriors Kane, Grant, and Brigid have no choice but to fight to try to preserve what's left of the world they used to know. But Ereshkigal is stronger and more powerful—and more evil—than anything they have encountered before, and it will take everything they have to prevent her from destroying the rest of the planet.

Other books by the same author:
Forbidden Trespass, 2015
Necropolis, 2014
Nemesis, 2013
Oblivion Stone, 2010
Ritual Chill, 2005

Other books you might like:
Piers Anthony, *Battle Circle*, 1978
Neal Barrett Jr., *Dawn's Uncertain Light*, 1989
David Brin, *The Postman*, 1985
Daniel F. Galouye, *Dark Universe*, 1961
Ryder Stacy, *American Overthrow*, 1989

`1113`

PAOLO BACIGALUPI

The Water Knife

(London: Hachette UK, 2015)

Story type: Dystopian
Subject(s): Environmental engineering; Ecology; Droughts
Major character(s): Angel Velasquez, Assassin, Spy; Lucy Monroe, Journalist
Time period(s): Indeterminate Future
Locale(s): United States; Phoenix, Arizona; Las Vegas, Nevada

Summary: In this novel, which is set in the Southwestern United States in the near future, author Paolo Bacigalupi imagines what could happen in the worst-case scenario caused by global climate change. The country is in turmoil and is no longer united, with states and even cities left to fend for themselves in the face of extreme water deficits. One major natural water resource, the Colorado River, holds promise to replenish the water supplies of Las Vegas and Phoenix, and the cities begin to battle for control. Las Vegas has the upper hand, however, because it has a group of clandestine operatives known as water knives. Water knives have sworn to do anything to guard Las Vegas's future, so when water knife Angel Velasquez is asked to go on a mission to check out a possible resource in Phoenix, he heeds his calling. Once there, however, he finds out that he isn't the only one who knows about the resource. News reporter Lucy Monroe knows exactly where the water is, and she will stop at nothing to protect this knowledge—even if she must murder a water knife.

Other books by the same author:
The Doubt Factory, 2014
Zombie Baseball Beatdown, 2014
The Drowned City, 2012
Ship Breaker, 2011
The Windup Girl, 2009

Other books you might like:
Eric Brown, *Guardians of the Phoenix*, 2010
Charles Eric Maine, *The Tide Went Out*, 1959
Graham Masterton, *Famine*, 1981
Kim Stanley Robinson, *Sixty Days and Counting*, 2007
Mary Rosenblum, *Water Rites*, 2007

`1114`

KAREN BAO

Dove Arising

(New York: Viking Books, 2015)

Series: Dove Chronicles. Book 1
Story type: Futuristic; Series
Subject(s): Futuristic society; Military life; Space colonies
Major character(s): Phaet Theta, 15-Year-Old, Military Personnel (cadet), Friend (of Wes); Wes Kappa, Teenager, Military Personnel (cadet), Friend (of Phaet)
Time period(s): Indeterminate Future
Locale(s): Moon, Outer Space

Summary: Phaet Theta is 15 years old and lives in a colony on the moon. After the death of her father nine years ago, she withdrew into her work at Greenhouse 22, barely speaking to anyone. She has dreams of becoming a bioengineer, but when her mother, a journalist, is quarantined, Phaet's life changes. It is obvious that the leaders of the colony, the Committee, have arrested her mother for sinister reasons of their own. To prevent her younger siblings from being sent to the despicable Shelter, Phaet must become what she hates: a soldier. Phaet will earn a steady salary in the militia, and if she does well, then all of her family will be safe and protected. Abandoning her own dreams, Phaet struggles to adapt to the military life with help from a new friend, Wes Kappa. Cadet Wes is quiet but driven in his own ambition. A blossoming romance between the pair also serves to keep Phaet's mind distracted from the fear and worry over her family. This is the first title of the Dove Chronicles by Karen Bao. First novel.

Other books you might like:
Victoria Aveyard, *Red Queen*, 2015
Ben Bova, *Moonrise*, 1996
Pierce Brown, *Red Rising*, 2014
Gregory Feeley, *The Oxygen Barons*, 1990
Robert A. Heinlein, *The Moon Is a Harsh Mistress*, 1966
John G. Hemry, *Stark's War*, 2000
Marie Lu, *Legend*, 2011
Marissa Meyer, *Cinder*, 2012
Jennifer Nielsen, *Mark of the Thief*, 2015
Phoebe North, *Starbreak*, 2014
Allen Steele, *Apollo's Outcasts*, 2012
Sabaa Tahir, *An Ember in the Ashes*, 2015

1115

DAVE BARA

Impulse

(New York: Daw Books, Inc., 2015)

Series: Lightship Chronicles Series. Book 1
Story type: Fantasy; Military
Subject(s): Space exploration; Space colonies; Space flight
Major character(s): Peter Cochrane, Military Personnel (lieutenant, Quantar Royal Navy), Son (of Nathan); Nathan Cochrane, Military Personnel (Grand Admiral, Quantar Royal Navy), Father (of Peter)
Time period(s): Indeterminate Future
Locale(s): Outer Space

Summary: The first book in the Lightship Chronicles series by debut author Dave Bara follows Peter Cochrane's plight to save humanity from an apocalyptic interstellar war. Lieutenant Peter Cochrane of the Quantar Royal Navy experiences a sudden change of plans when his father, Grand Admiral Nathan Cochrane, informs Peter that his former girlfriend and many of her shipmates were attacked and killed aboard *Impulse* in a far-off solar system. Now, instead of embarking upon deep space voyages aboard *HMS Starbound*, Peter joins a group of strangers on a Unified Space Navy ship to investigate the site where the *Impulse* was attacked. The ship's Historian leads them into an unknown galaxy, where Peter and his shipmates confront age-old technologies, different cultures, and romance. Under foreign command, Peter receives secret orders that could compel him to rebel, and soon, all of humanity is at risk of an interstellar war. First novel.

Other books by the same author:
Speedwing, 2012

Other books you might like:
Neal L. Asher, *The Departure*, 2012
Lois McMaster Bujold, *Cetaganda*, 1996
Ann Leckie, *Ancillary Justice*, 2013
Mike Shepherd, *Kris Longknife: Defender*, 2013
David Weber, *Mission of Honor*, 2010

1116

JONATHAN BARNES

Cannonbridge

(Oxford, United Kingdom: Solaris, 2015)

Story type: Literary
Subject(s): Literature; Writers; English (British people)
Major character(s): Toby Judd, Scholar
Time period(s): 21st century
Locale(s): England

Summary: Jonathan Barnes blends science fiction with literary conspiracy as he follows a troubled scholar's discovery that a celebrated 19th century writer might never have existed. In the near future, Toby Judd suggests that Matthew Cannonbridge, a prolific writer of the 19th century known for his novels, plays, and poems, was a fraud. Now, as scholars everywhere prepare to celebrate the bicentenary of the publication of Cannonbridge's most popular work, Judd's lecture on the "Cannonbridge Delusion" goes viral. As he questions Cannonbridge's extraodinary life, relationships with fellow writers, and vast contributions to literature, Judd finds himself pulled into a world of conspiracy. From a murdered policeman to a pair of mysterious sisters to a mystical island, Judd learns that Cannonbridge's influence might be greater than he imagined.

Other books by the same author:
The Domino Men, 2008
The Somnambulist, 2007

Other books you might like:
Stephen Baxter, *Stone Spring*, 2011
Michael Moorcock, *Gloriana, or the Unfulfill'd Queen*, 1978
Melissa Scott, *A Choice of Destinies*, 1986
Harry Turtledove, *Ruled Britannia*, 2002
Chelsea Quinn Yarbro, *Magnificent*, 2000

1117

W.C. BAUERS

Unbreakable

(New York: Tor, 2015)

Series: Chronicles of Promise Paen Series. Book 1
Story type: Military; Series
Subject(s): Military science; Wars; Science fiction
Major character(s): Promise Paen, Military Personnel (Marine Lieutenant, Republic of Aligned Worlds)
Time period(s): Indeterminate Future
Locale(s): Montana, Planet—Imaginary

Summary: Promise Paen is a Marine Corps lieutenant in the Republic of Aligned Worlds. When the region is threatened by a pirate invasion, Paen leads the counterassault. After receiving an unwanted commission, Paen returns to Montana, the home world she fled when her father was killed in a similar pirate raid. Paen, welcomed home as a hero, is tasked with training militia and leading her company. She also must endure ghostly visitations from her late mother. At the same time, many of Montana's colonists remain skeptical about their isolated and provincial home world's growing involvement with the Republic. Montana's elite enemy, the Lusitanian Empire, has been keeping an eye on Montana's predicament. The Empire decides to gain a front in Republic territory. This is the first entry in the Chronicles of Promise Paen series by W. C. Bauers. First novel.

Other books you might like:

Peter F. Hamilton, *The Abyss Beyond Dreams*, 2014
Alastair Reynolds, *Blue Remembered Earth*, 2012
Joel Shepherd, *Originator*, 2015
Allen Steele, *Coyote Horizon*, 2009
Karen Traviss, *Judge*, 2008

1118

ELIZABETH BEAR

Karen Memory

(New York: Tor Books, 2015)

Story type: Serial Killer; Steampunk
Subject(s): Western fiction; Steampunk; Prostitution
Major character(s): Karen Memery, Orphan, Prostitute, Enemy (of Peter Bantle), Friend (of Bass Reeves); Bass Reeves, Lawman (Deputy Marshal), Friend (of Karen Memery and Tomoatooah), Enemy (of Peter Bantle); Tomoatooah, Colleague (of Bass Reeves), Lawman; Peter Bantle, Businessman (bordello owner), Crime Suspect, Villain, Enemy (of Karen Memery and Bass Reeves)
Time period(s): 19th century; 1870s (1878)
Locale(s): Rapid City, United States

Summary: Karen Memery is an orphaned young woman in 19th century northwestern America. She is employed at Madame Damnable's bordello, which offers regular meals and a warm bed. Although Karen doesn't plan on staying there forever, her housemates and fellow "seamstresses" are her friends and she is devoted to them. One night two girls from another brothel arrive and beg for sanctuary from Madame. They tell horrible stories of torturous devices and abuse. The man holding their papers is Peter Bantle, a dangerous thug. He has a glove with mind control technology and he is determined to get his property back. His threats, coupled with the appearance of dead prostitutes around the city, lead Karen and her friends to Deputy Marshal Bass Reeves. Reeves and his partner, Comanche Indian Tomoatooah, suspect Bantle of being involved with the murders. They work with Karen to capture Bantle and put a stop to his killing spree.

Other books by the same author:

Shoggoths in Bloom, 2012
Grail, 2011
Chill, 2010
Carnival, 2006
Hammered, 2005

Other books you might like:

Paul Di Filippo, *The Steampunk Trilogy*, 1995
Rod Duncan, *Unseemly Science*, 2015

George Mann, *The Affinity Bridge*, 2009
Michael Moorcock, *The Whispering Swarm*, 2015
Dennis O'Flaherty, *King of the Cracksmen*, 2015
Cherie Priest, *Jacaranda*, 2015
Bob Shaw, *The Wooden Spaceships*, 1988
Bruce Sterling, *The Difference Engine*, 1991

1119

CHRISTOPHER L. BENNETT

Uncertain Logic

(New York: Pocket Books/Star Trek, 2015)

Series: Star Trek: Enterprise: Rise of the Federation Series
Story type: Adventure; Futuristic
Subject(s): Adventure; Space exploration; Space colonies
Major character(s): Jonathan Archer, Spaceship Captain (of the Endeavor); T'pol, Spaceship Captain (of the Endeavor); Malcolm Reed, Spaceship Captain (of the USS Pioneer), Friend (of Trip); "Trip" Tucker, Friend (of Malcolm Reed)
Locale(s): Vulcan, Planet—Imaginary

Summary: The discovery of original works written by the brilliant and revered Vulcan philosopher Surak brought peace and a new and better way of life to the planet and people of Vulcan. Jonathan Archer, Captain of the United Starship *Enterprise*, and his second in command, T'Pol, uncovered those writings many years ago. Now, new evidence indicates the discovery was a fake. The resulting outrage could undo all the social advances and turn Vulcan back into a hotbed of war and unrest. Admiral Archer, Captain T'Pol, and the crew of the Starship *Endeavor* join ranks with the Vulcans to try to uncover the truth, and learn who might benefit from the turmoil on the normally peaceful planet. At the same time, Captain Malcolm Reed and the crew of the U.S.S. *Pioneer* are sent to investigate the source of a potentially deadly technology. Along with his friend "Trip" Tucker, Reed will try to stop others who would love to wield this rediscovered threat. This book is part of the ongoing series of novels in the Rise of the Federation Star Trek series.

Other books by the same author:

Tower of Babel, 2014
Only Superhuman, 2012
The Struggle Within, 2011
Watching the Clock, 2011
Watchers on the Walls, 2006

Other books you might like:

Kirsten Beyer, *Full Circle*, 2009
Tony Daniel, *Savage Trade*, 2015
Peter David, *Before Dishonor*, 2007
William Leisner, *Star Trek: Losing the Peace*, 2009
Una McCormack, *The Missing*, 2015
James Swallow, *Cast No Shadow*, 2011

Science Fiction

PIERCE BROWN

Golden Son

(New York: Random House Publishing Group, 2015)

Series: Red Rising Trilogy. Book 2
Story type: Dystopian; Series
Subject(s): Mars (Planet); Dystopias; Social class
Major character(s): Darrow, Rebel, Widow(er), Man
(member of the Reds), Miner (on Mars); Augustus,
Government Official (governor of Mars), Man
(member of the Golds)
Time period(s): Indeterminate Future
Locale(s): Mars, Outer Space

Summary: This second novel in the Red Rising trilogy
follows a Red-born man named Darrow as he continues
his quest for justice. Like many others of his kind, Darrow worked as a miner deep below the surface of Mars.
He and the other Reds were led to believe that they were
working to make the planet habitable. In truth, the
Martian surface already provided a comfortable home
for an elite social group known as the Golds. Now that
Darrow knows the truth, he has joined a Red rebel group
and is an undercover agent of sorts. He has undergone
genetic treatments that allow him to blend in with the
Golds and now works to destroy the oppressive society.
Darrow chooses Augustus, the governor of Mars, as the
target of his subterfuge. Meanwhile, an enemy plots to
expose Darrow.

Other books by the same author:
Red Rising, 2014

Other books you might like:
Kevin J. Anderson, *Climbing Olympus*, 1994
Kage Baker, *The Empress of Mars*, 2009
Greg Bear, *Moving Mars*, 1993
Orson Scott Card, *Ender in Exile*, 2008
Suzanne Collins, *Catching Fire*, 2009
Hugh Howey, *Wool*, 2012
Chang-Rae Lee, *On Such a Full Sea*, 2014
Ian McDonald, *Ares Express*, 2001
Daniel Price, *The Flight of the Silvers*, 2014
Kim Stanley Robinson, *Blue Mars*, 1996
Brandon Sanderson, *Firefight*, 2015
Kristen Simmons, *Three*, 2014
Brian Staveley, *The Emperor's Blades*, 2014

MICHAEL BUCKLEY

Undertow

(New York: Houghton Mifflin Harcourt, 2015)

Series: Good Sports Series. Book 1
Story type: Alternate World; Romance
Subject(s): Adolescent interpersonal relations;
Multiculturalism; Romances (Fiction)
Major character(s): Lyric Walker, 16-Year-Old, Student—
High School (liaison to Alpha race students);
Fathom, Royalty (Alpha prince), Alien

Time period(s): 21st century; 2010s
Locale(s): New York, New York

Summary: What happens when 30,000 members of an
alien fighting force interrupt a summer day at the beach?
Many of the humans enjoying Coney Island when the
aliens arrive simply stare as this previously unknown
species rises from beneath the ocean's depths. It doesn't
take long, however, before the aliens' arrival generates
fear and aggression among the humans. This mistrust
turns the peaceful day at the New York beach into a
battle zone, and though things quiet down, an uneasy
truce makes life tense. The arrival of the Alphas has an
especially great impact on 16-year-old Lyric Walker.
When some of the teenage aliens have trouble fitting in
at Lyric's school, the principal hand-picks her to be a
liaison to the aquatic aliens. This brings a whole host of
challenges for Lyric, especially when she starts to fall
for Fathom, the young Alpha prince. This is the first
book in the Good Sports series by Michael Buckley.

Other books you might like:
Tara Altebrando, *Dreamland Social Club*, 2011
Kenneth Bulmer, *Beyond the Silver Sky*, 1961
Ray Cummings, *The Sea Girl*, 1930
Kat Falls, *Riptide*, 2011
Aimee Friedman, *Sea Change*, 2009
Polly Holyoke, *The Neptune Project*, 2013
Hannah Moskowitz, *Teeth*, 2013
Steve Perry, *Dome*, 1987
Douglas Rees, *Vampire High*, 2003
Robert Sharenow, *My Mother the Cheerleader*, 2007
Josepha Sherman, *Young Warriors: Stories of Strength*,
2005

JAMES CAMBIAS

Corsair

(New York: Tom Doherty Associates, 2015)

Story type: Techno-Thriller
Subject(s): Computer programming; Futuristic society;
Pirates
Major character(s): David Schwartz, Computer Expert;
Elizabeth Santiago, Computer Expert, Military
Personnel
Time period(s): 21st century; 2020s-2030s
Locale(s): Earth; Outer Space; Thailand; Washington,
District of Columbia; Massachusetts, United States

Summary: When Massachusetts Institute of Technology
student Elizabeth Santiago has a torrid affair with fellow
computer expert David Schwartz, she never imagines
that, in a decade's time, he will prove to be her greatest
adversary. David embarks on a career as a techno-pirate,
and Elizabeth begins working for the military as an
operative who stops piracy. When an underground
organization gains control of a robotic ore salvaging
operation, Elizabeth works to thwart its efforts. She is
certain that David is behind the crime, and she can
almost predict his next move before it happens, but when
a large amount of ore disappears, Elizabeth loses her

post. She wants to figure out how to stop David before it is too late, but she doesn't realize that more ruthless people than David are working with him. She could be putting her life in jeopardy by going up against these villains.

Other books by the same author:
A Darkling Sea, 2014

Other books you might like:
Ben Bova, *The Rock Rats*, 2002
Dani Kollin, *The Unincorporated Woman*, 2011
Alastair Reynolds, *Blue Remembered Earth*, 2012
Frank Schatzing, *Limit*, 2013
Allen Steele, *Apollo's Outcasts*, 2012

1123

JACK CAMPBELL

Leviathan

(New York: Ace Books, 2015)

Series: Lost Fleet: Beyond the Frontier Series. Book 11
Story type: Series; Space Opera
Subject(s): Military life; Space colonies; Wars
Major character(s): John "Black Jack" Geary, Military Personnel (Admiral)
Time period(s): Indeterminate Future
Locale(s): Outer Space

Summary: Admiral John "Black Jack" Geary is facing one of his worst nightmares. When unknown warships attack two Syndicate World star systems, Geary immediately recognizes the source of the warships. They are part of the new fleet the government recently developed and are entirely operated by artificial intelligence. He knows that if anyone learns who is really behind this, the battle with the Alliance will immediately reignite. The government struggles to hide this information but Geary takes matters into his own hands. He works with the Dancer aliens to search for the base of the AI ships. Geary is determined to put an end to the attacks and prevent the destruction of the Alliance. This is the eleventh novel in the Lost Fleet: Beyond the Frontier military science fiction series by Jack Campbell.

Other books by the same author:
Steadfast, 2014
Perilous Shield, 2013
Invincible, 2012
Tarnished Knight, 2012
Relentless, 2009

Other books you might like:
Ian Douglas, *Dark Matter*, 2014
R.M. Meluch, *The Sagittarius Command*, 2007
Mel Odom, *Master Sergeant*, 2015
Mike Resnick, *Starship: Mutiny*, 2005
Mike Shepherd, *Kris Longknife: Undaunted*, 2009

1124

PATRICK CARMAN

Quake

(New York: Katherine Tegen Books, 2015)

Series: Pulse Trilogy. Book 3
Story type: Dystopian; Series
Subject(s): Dystopias; Psychokinesis; Romances (Fiction)
Major character(s): Faith Daniels, Enemy, (of Wade, Clara, and Hotspur Chance), Teenager, Girlfriend (of Dylan), Rebel; Dylan Gilmore, Teenager, Boyfriend (of Faith), Rebel, Enemy (of Wade, Clara, and Hotspur Chance); Wade Quinn, Teenager, Brother (of Clara), Enemy (of Faith and Dylan); Clara Quinn, Teenager, Sister (of Wade), Enemy (of Faith and Dylan); Hotspur Chance, Enemy (of Faith and Dylan)
Time period(s): 21st century; 2050s (2051)
Locale(s): United States

Summary: This novel for young adults is the final entry in the dystopian Pulse trilogy by best-selling author Patrick Carman. In post-apocalyptic 2051, in a wasteland divided into the Eastern and Western States, a number of people have been gifted with a telekinetic ability called a "pulse." Faith Daniels and Dylan Gilmore are two of the few individuals gifted as second pulses, which makes them virtually indestructible. Now, as the war to save humanity continues, Faith and Dylan are up against two other second pulses, Wade and Clara Quinn, who have teamed up with the brilliant and evil Hotspur Chance. Faith and Dylan will need all of their powers—and the growing love between them—if they have any hope of stopping Hotspur Chance's plan to destroy millions of people within the Western State.

Other books by the same author:
Pulse, 2014
Shantorian, 2011
Trackers, 2010
The Dark Planet, 2009
The House of Power, 2007

Other books you might like:
Chester Aaron, *Out of Sight, out of Mind*, 1985
James Dashner, *The Maze Runner*, 2009
Steven Krane, *Teek*, 1999
Anne McCaffrey, *Pegasus in Space*, 2000
Veronica Roth, *Allegiant*, 2013

1125

C.J. CHERRYH

Tracker

(New York: DAW-Penguin Books, 2015)

Series: Foreigner Universe Series. Book 16
Story type: Adventure; Science Fiction
Subject(s): Adventure; Space colonies; Science fiction
Major character(s): Bren Cameron, Linguist (Intepreter to the atevi court of Tabini); Tabini, Leader (supreme leader of the atevi), Grandson (of Ilisidi), Father (of Cajeiri; Cajeiri, 8-Year-Old, Son (of Tabini), Heir

(to atevi throne); Ilsidi, Grandmother (of Tabini, great grandmother of Cajeiri)

Time period(s): Indeterminate

Locale(s): atevi, Planet—Imaginary

Summary: The return to the atevi world after more than two years in space should have been a peaceful homecoming for Bren Cameron, the paidhi interpreter to the atevi. But when he and Ilisidi, the aiji-dowager, grandmother of the ruler Tabini, returned, they discovered atevi in turmoil. A coup had been staged and unrest was everywhere. It took a full year to restore any semblance of order, but now, things have settled down. Bren is able to focus on new tasks at hand: making sure Ilisidi's new trade agreement meets with approval from all the appropriate parties, and dealing with the changes that resulted from the aiiji's appointment of a new official heir—his eight-year-old son, Cajeiri. The unrest of the past year may be nothing compared to what is in store. This is the sixteenth book in the Foreigner Universe series.

Other books by the same author:

Peacemaker, 2014

Intruder, 2012

Deliverer, 2007

Defender, 2001

Exile's Gate, 1988

Other books you might like:

Catherine Asaro, *Carnelians*, 2012

Julie E. Czerneda, *Reap the Wild Wind*, 2007

Sarah A. Hoyt, *A Few Good Men*, 2013

Karen Traviss, *City of Pearl*, 2004

Timothy Zahn, *Night Train to Rigel*, 2005

1126

WESLEY CHU

The Rebirths of Tao

(Nottingham, United Kingdom: Angry Robot, 2015)

Series: Tao Series. Book 3

Story type: End of the World; Futuristic

Subject(s): Science fiction; Extraterrestrial life; Wars

Major character(s): Tao, Alien (Quasing, bonded to Roen); Roen, Man (host to Tao), Spouse (of Jill), Father (of Cameron), Agent (for Prophus); Jill, Spouse (of Roen), Mother (of Cameron); Cameron, Son (of Roen and Jill)

Time period(s): Indeterminate Future

Locale(s): Earth

Summary: The third novel of the Tao series opens five years after the previous volume concluded. The world is divided into pro-Prophus and pro-Genjix groups and is on the brink of global war. The Quasing aliens who have inhabited humanity remain divided, and it is their hosts who will have to fight at their command. Roen Tan, host to Tao, has come a long way from being a simple IT nerd, and has developed into a keen agent. Tao is pro-Prophus and seeks to co-exist with original terrestrial life, unlike the pro-Genjix faction who desire to destroy

Earth's natural environment and Quasingform it. Roen's wife and son are also hosts to Quasings, and together the family will join the fight for Earth. When a Genjix scientist defects to the Prophus side, a new option to prevent war and save humanity and the Earth presents itself. However, the Genjix aren't willing to let it go without a fight.

Other books by the same author:

Time Salvager, 2015

The Deaths of Tao, 2013

The Lives of Tao, 2013

Other books you might like:

Philip K. Dick, *Do Androids Dream of Electric Sheep?*, 1968

Gordon R. Dickson, *The Pritcher Mass*, 1972

Peter F. Hamilton, *Mindstar Rising*, 1993

Eytan Kollin, *The Unincorporated Man*, 2009

Charles Stross, *Lock In*, 2014

1127

PETER CLINES

The Fold

(New York: Crown Publishing, 2015)

Story type: Mystery; Time Travel

Subject(s): Alternative worlds; Inventions; Science

Major character(s): Mike Erikson, Genius, Teacher, Friend (of Reggie); Reggie Magnus, Friend (of Mike), Wealthy, Entrepreneur

Time period(s): Indeterminate Future

Locale(s): New England, United States; San Diego, California

Summary: Mike Erikson is a genius, but he'd much rather spend his days peacefully teaching English to high schoolers in his New England town than pursuing any of the scientific projects his buddy, Reggie Magnus, has presented him with over the years. Then Reggie comes to Mike with an invention that even Mike has to admit is irresistible. A group of scientists near San Diego has created a device that folds space and time, allowing one to teleport from one time or place to another. Reggie is ready to fund the project, but he isn't completely convinced of its reliability, and so he calls Mike to the scene to take a look at the device. As Mike learns more about the project, called the Albuquerque Door, he becomes more and more wary. Now it's up to him to figure out what the scientists are hiding, and what the true purpose of the Albuquerque Door could be.

Other books you might like:

Alfred Bester, *The Stars My Destination*, 1956

Steven Gould, *Impulse*, 2012

Philip Palmer, *Version 43*, 2010

Charles Stross, *Glasshouse*, 2006

Sean Williams, *The Resurrected Man*, 1998

1128

MICHAEL COBLEY

Ancestral Machines

(New York: Hachette, 2015)

Series: Humanity's Fire Series. Book 4
Story type: Series; Space Opera
Subject(s): Alternative worlds; Wars; Space flight
Major character(s): Brannan Pyke, Spaceship Captain, Smuggler
Time period(s): Indeterminate
Locale(s): Outer Space; Planet—Imaginary

Summary: In the fourth novel of Michael Cobley's Humanity's Fire series, the author brings readers back to the Warcage, the bioengineered solar system that was meant to unify beings from all worlds. Since its inception, however, its intended use has been sullied, and now the Warcage exists as a method of catching and stealing the resources of other planets, thus rebranding the system as the Bringer of Battles. When Brannan Pyke, the thieving captain of a spacecraft, finds his shipmates sucked into the wasteland, he risks his life to save them. Yet the Bringer of Battles shows no mercy. Acting as savior doesn't come easily for Brannan, who is used to putting himself above all others. He must learn the secrets of the Warcage if he is to stop its path of destruction and bring his colleagues out alive, but the ruthlessness of his enemies knows no bounds. Brannan may become the next victim of the Warcage.

Other books by the same author:
The Ascendant Stars, 2012
The Orphaned Worlds, 2012
Seeds of Earth, 2009
Shadowgod, 2003
Shadowkings, 2001

Other books you might like:
Kevin J. Anderson, *The Ashes of Worlds*, 2008
C.J. Cherryh, *Intruder*, 2012
Brian Herbert, *Hellhole Inferno*, 2014
Sarah A. Hoyt, *DarkShip Thieves*, 2010
Timothy Zahn, *Angelmass*, 2001

1129

BENNETT R. COLES

Virtues of War

(London: Titan Books, 2015)

Series: Astral Saga. Book 1
Story type: Series; Space Opera
Subject(s): Wars; Military life; Space colonies
Major character(s): Katja Emmes, Military Personnel, Leader (Platoon commander); Jack Mallory, Military Personnel, Pilot (spaceship); Thomas Kane, Military Personnel
Time period(s): Indeterminate
Locale(s): *Rapier*, Spaceship

Summary: Soldiers from the Terran army earn their military stripes as each conquers personal obstacles and put down a revolution. Lieutenant Katja Emmes is in charge of the ten-person platoon, but this is her first stint in a leadership role. She is unsure if she is prepared for battle or prepared to live up to her father's legendary reputation as a military leader. Her sub-lieutenant, Jack Mallory, is finally living out his fantasy of becoming a spaceship pilot, but it is taking more than he expected out of him. Meanwhile, opportunistic Lieutenant Commander Thomas Kane knows that his assignment to the platoon is his chance to shine, but the lengths he will go to to boost his reputation might not sit well with his colleagues. As the platoon advances on Cerubus, they have no idea that they are the only people who stand between war and peace throughout the solar system. This novel is the first title of author Bennett R. Coles's Astral Saga series.

Other books by the same author:
Casualties of War, 2013

Other books you might like:
Lois McMaster Bujold, *Cetaganda*, 1996
Jack Campbell, *Steadfast*, 2014
Ann Leckie, *Ancillary Sword*, 2014
Jack McDevitt, *Chindi*, 2002
Mel Odom, *Master Sergeant*, 2015

1130

ROBERT CONROY

1882: Custer in Chains

(Riverdale, New York: Baen, 2015)

Story type: Alternate History
Subject(s): History; Science fiction; Wars
Major character(s): George Armstrong Custer, Historical Figure, Military Personnel (General), Spouse (of Libbie); Libbie Custer, Spouse (of George)
Time period(s): 19th century; 1880s (1882)
Locale(s): United States

Summary: Author Robert Conroy imagines an alternative history in which General Custer survived the battle of Little Bighorn and went on to become president in 1880. It is 1882, and Custer is dissatisfied with the current state of the nation. He is a man of action and longs for another conflict he can tackle. With the support and approval of his wife, Libbie, President Custer decides that it's time to conquer the Spanish empire. But when a ship full of American civilians is attacked en route to Cuba, a new war looms. This conflict promises to be far more destructive to the nation as it exists—unless something can be done to prevent it. And it seems unlikely that the hotheaded Custer and his equally brazen wife are going to be the ones to avoid another bloody battle.

Other books by the same author:
Liberty: 1784, 2014
1920: America's Great War, 2013
Rising Sun, 2012
Himmler's War, 2011
1942, 2009

Other books you might like:
Richard Dreyfuss, *The Two Georges*, 1996
Dave Freer, *Cuttlefish*, 2012

Douglas C. Jones, *The Court-Martial of George Armstrong Custer*, 1976
Pamela Sargent, *Climb the Wind*, 1999
Alan Smale, *A Clash of Eagles*, 2010

1131

ROBERT CONROY

Germanica

(Riverdale, New York: Baen Books, 2015)

Series: More... Series. Book 1
Story type: Alternate History; Series
Subject(s): World War II, 1939-1945; History; Science fiction
Major character(s): Ernie Janek, Agent (O.S.S. Operative); Scott Tanner, Military Personnel (captain); Lena Bobek, Prisoner (of war; former)
Time period(s): 20th century; 1940s
Locale(s): Germany

Summary: In this alternate history, World War II is soon to end, and in a small area of the German alps known as Germanica, a few remaining Nazis are determined to hold out. They want to maintain control of their small piece of land long enough to prevent being tried for war crimes, but also to prepare for a future uprising when they intend to retake power. They know that the other world leaders—Churchill, De Gaulle, and Stalin—are occupied in other regions, and new US President Harry Truman is the only one left to take them. But what they don't know is that a small group of determined Americans and Europeans working together—O.S.S. operative Ernie Janek, Captain Scott Tanner, and former prisoner of war Lena Bobek—are willing to do whatever it takes to eliminate the Germanica Nazis.

Other books by the same author:
1882: Custer in Chains, 2015
1920: America's Great War, 2013
Rising Sun, 2012
Himmler's War, 2011
1862, 2006

Other books you might like:
John Birmingham, *Weapons of Choice*, 2004
Philip K. Dick, *The Man in the High Castle*, 1962
Newt Gingrich, *1945*, 1995
Allen Steele, *V-S Day*, 2014
Harry Turtledove, *Hitler's War*, 2009

1132

BRENDA COOPER

Edge of Dark

(Amherst, New York: Prometheus Books, 2015)

Series: Glittering Edge Series. Book 1
Story type: Adventure; Futuristic
Subject(s): Science fiction; Genetic engineering; Artificial Intelligence
Major character(s): Nona Hall, Spaceship Captain, Friend (of Chrystal); Chrystal, Friend (of Nona), Cyborg, Artificial Intelligence; Charlie Windar, Ranger (on Lym)
Locale(s): Lym, Planet—Imaginary

Summary: When some dared to experiment with hybridizing humans and machines, the resulting creatures were banished to planets far, far away. But it wasn't far enough, because they have come back, and they are powerful and dangerous. Rich and privileged Nona Hall might seem an unlikely adversary to this hybrid foe, but she captains a ship sent to intercept and stop these half-human, half-machine, and seemingly heartless creations. The battle becomes more personal when Nona's long-time friend, Chrystal, dies. Chrystal's mind is transferred into one of the hybrid creatures, and Nona must find a new way to deal with an old friend who is part of a new enemy. Meanwhile Charlie Windar, a ranger and law enforcement officer, is struggling as he tries to protect and restore the wildlife on planet Lym, despite the approach of rumored space pirates. This is the first book of a proposed trilogy and is set in the same universe as Brenda Cooper's Ruby's Song series.

Other books by the same author:
The Diamond Deep, 2013
The Creative Fire, 2012
Wings of Creation, 2009
Reading the Wind, 2008
The Silver Ship and the Sea, 2007

Other books you might like:
Jeffrey A. Carver, *Strange Attractors*, 1995
James S.A. Corey, *Nemesis Games*, 2015
Peter F. Hamilton, *The Dreaming Void*, 2007
Alexander Jablokov, *Brain Thief*, 2010
Alastair Reynolds, *Century Rain*, 2004

1133

JAMES S.A. COREY

Nemesis Games

(New York: Hachette, 2015)

Series: Expanse Series. Book 5
Story type: Series; Space Opera
Subject(s): Alternative worlds; Space colonies; Adventurers
Major character(s): Jim Holden, Spaceship Captain
Time period(s): 23rd century
Locale(s): Earth; Outer Space; Spaceship

Summary: This title is the fifth novel of the Expanse series by co-authors Daniel Abraham and Ty Franck under the pseudonym James S. A. Corey. Now that the Expanse has begun to spread out, people are leaving the solar system in droves. The only beings who now remain are the treacherous, the malevolent, and Jim Holden and his shipmates aboard the *Rocinante*. As they become entrapped in a zone that grows more and more dangerous, Jim realizes that no past deed will go unpunished. His participation in an interplanetary accident still haunts him, and certain people still believe that he must answer for his mistakes. Worse yet, the key ingredient that has made the existence of the populated solar system possible has been taken, and the person responsible for the theft is going to have to pay dearly. This series was adapted for television by the SyFy network.

Other books by the same author:
Cibola Burn, 2014
Honor Among Thieves, 2014
Abaddon's Gate, 2013
Caliban's War, 2012
Leviathan Wakes, 2011

Other books you might like:
Roger MacBride Allen, *The Shattered Sphere*, 1994
Brenda Cooper, *Edge of Dark*, 2015
Peter Higgins, *Radiant State*, 2015
Hannu Rajaniemi, *The Quantum Thief*, 2011
Alastair Reynolds, *Terminal World*, 2010
Kim Stanley Robinson, *Aurora*, 2015
Neal Stephenson, *Seveneves*, 2015
Robert Charles Wilson, *The Harvest*, 1993

1134

TONY DANIEL

Savage Trade

(New York: Pocket Books/Star Trek, 2015)

Series: Star Trek: The Original Series
Story type: Adventure; Series
Subject(s): Space exploration; Space colonies; Adventure
Major character(s): James T. Kirk, Spaceship Captain (Captain of the Enterprise); Spock, Military Personnel (First Officer of the Enterprise); Pavel Chekov, Military Personnel (Ensign); Nyota Uhura, Military Personnel (Lt., Communications Officer of the Enterprise); Hikaru Sulu, Military Personnel (Lt., navigator on the Enterprise)
Locale(s): Zeta Gibraltar Outpost, Outer Space

Summary: Captain James T. Kirk and the crew of the Starship *Enterprise* are sent to find out why a science team on a remote outpost has stopped replying to Federation hails. All was well until a week ago, when daily communication with the team suddenly stopped. First Officer Spock's remote study of the outpost reveals traces of a firefight at least six days earlier. This discovery prompts caution when a landing party heads down to assess the situation. Kirk, Spock, Chekov, Uhura, and a security detail beam down to the outpost on Zeta Gibraltar, located at the farthest point of the Alpha quadrant near the Vara Nebula. They quickly discover the main area of the outpost and the nearby sleeping quarters deserted, but signs of a struggle are everywhere—they find broken belongings and even a severed arm from an unrecognized species. It is up to Kirk and his resourceful crew to learn the fate of the science team—and avoid a similar deadly fate in the process.

Other books by the same author:
Devil's Bargain, 2013
Guardian of Night, 2012
Superluminal, 2004
Metaplanetary, 2001
Earthling, 1997

Other books you might like:
Christopher L. Bennett, *Uncertain Logic*, 2015
Greg Cox, *Foul Deeds Will Rise: Star Trek: The Original Series*, 2014
Diane Duane, *The Empty Chair*, 2006
David Mack, *Star Trek: The Next Generation: Cold Equations: The Body Electric*, 2012
Una McCormack, *The Missing*, 2015
John Jackson Miller, *Takedown*, 2015

1135

HANK DAVIS

As Times Goes By

(Riverdale, New York: Baen, 2015)

Story type: Collection; Fantasy
Subject(s): Short stories; Science fiction; Fantasy

Summary: Edited by Hank Davis, this short fiction collection includes 15 science fiction tales of love, fantasy, time travel, and alternate realities. This volume includes the Nebula Award-winning "The Secret Place" by Richard M. McKenna and "The Chronoclasm" by best-selling author John Wyndham, as well as "Gibraltar Falls" by multiple-award winner Poul Anderson and the Hugo Award-winning "Six Months, Three Days" by Charlie Jane Anders. Also included are "Triceratops Summer" by Hugo, Nebula, and World Fantasy Award-winning author Michael Swanwick, and the works of award-winning authors Christopher Priest, Tony Daniel, Sarah A. Hoyt, and more.

Other books by the same author:
The Baen Big Book of Monsters, 2014
A Cosmic Christmas 2 You, 2013
In Space No One Can Hear You Scream, 2013
A Cosmic Christmas, 2012

Other books you might like:
Poul Anderson, *The Shield of Time*, 1990
Michael Crichton, *Timeline*, 1999
Fritz Leiber, *Changewar*, 1983
Michael Swanwick, *The Best of Michael Swanwick*, 2008
John Wyndham, *The Infinite Moment*, 1961

1136

WILLIAM C. DIETZ

Deadeye

(New York: Ace, 2015)

Series: Mutant Files Series. Book 1
Story type: Futuristic; Post-Disaster
Subject(s): Interpersonal relations; Kidnapping; Law enforcement
Major character(s): Cassandra Lee, Colleague (of Ras Omo), Detective—Police; Ras Omo, Detective—Police, Colleague (of Cassandra Lee)
Time period(s): 21st century; 2060s (2065)
Locale(s): Los Angeles, California

Summary: In 2038, a bioengineering act of terrorism infected humanity, decimating the population and dividing survivors into two groups: norms and mutants. Decades later, Detective Cassandra Lee of the L.A. Special Investigative section is handed a new and dangerous assignment—to rescue the daughter of the Church of Human Purity, who has been kidnapped by mutants for breeding purposes. Prejudices run high within the communities and it is obvious to everyone why the girl was chosen for abduction. Cassandra has garnered a reputation for her fierceness and determination when taking down criminals, no matter how dangerous they prove to be. She has limited time to venture into the Red Zone on her mission and she must trust a new partner, Deputy Ras Omo—who happens to be a mutant himself—to watch her back. This is the first novel of the Mutant Files series.

Other books by the same author:
Redzone, 2015
Andromeda's Choice, 2013
Andromeda's Fall, 2012
Deception, 2011
Bones of Empire, 2010

Other books you might like:
Greg Bear, *Darwin's Children*, 2003
Michael Blumlein, *The Healer*, 2005
Karen Haber, *Mutant Legacy*, 1992
Isidore Haiblum, *The Mutants Are Coming*, 1984
Michael Swanwick, *In the Drift*, 1985

1137

WILLIAM C. DIETZ

Redzone

(New York: Ace, 2015)

Series: Mutant Files Series. Book 2
Story type: Futuristic; Post-Disaster
Subject(s): Detective fiction; Science fiction; Mother-daughter relations
Major character(s): Cassandra Lee, Detective—Police, Daughter; Bonebreaker, Serial Killer; Unnamed Character, Mother (of Cassandra), Outcast
Time period(s): 21st century; 2060s (2065)
Locale(s): Los Angeles, California

Summary: In the second novel of the Mutant Files series, L.A. Detective Cassandra Lee continues to work as a go-between with norms and mutants. It has been nearly 30 years since a bioterrorist attack nearly wiped out humanity and altered all survivors. The norms live in green zones, while the mutants are confined to red zones. Cassandra is responsible for special investigations, including those that involve the mutants. Recently many police personnel in Los Angeles have been brutally slaughtered. The killer has been dubbed the Bonebreaker, due to the gruesome nature of the crime scenes. Cassandra and her team must catch the Bonebreaker quickly. Cassandra's life becomes even more complicated when she receives a letter from her long-lost mother, who is living inside the red zone. Cassandra must decide if she will wants to learn the truth about her family's past.

Other books by the same author:
Deadeye, 2015
Andromeda's Choice, 2013
Andromeda's Fall, 2012
Deception, 2011
Bones of Empire, 2010

Other books you might like:
Catherine Asaro, *Undercity*, 2014
K.A. Bedford, *Hydrogen Steel*, 2006
Paul Levinson, *The Pixel Eye*, 2003
Mike McQuay, *Hot Time in Old Town*, 1981
Lawrence Watt-Evans, *Nightside City*, 1989

1138

JOHN DIXON

Devil's Pocket

(New York: Gallery Books, 2015)

Story type: Alternate World; Science Fiction
Subject(s): Wars; Science fiction; Adolescent interpersonal relations
Major character(s): Carl Freeman, 16-Year-Old, Orphan, Mercenary
Time period(s): 21st century; 2010s
Locale(s): Earth

Summary: Carl Freeman was just a troubled orphan until the powers that be turned the 16-year-old to their own purposes. With literally dozens of computerized chips embedded in him from head to toe, Carl has become a human fighting machine. This makes him a valuable resource for the Phoenix Force group. Carl's shipped off to a remote volcanic island to take part in vicious life-or-death competitions with other young super soldiers. Carl despairs of ever escaping his fate, until the sudden appearance of someone he knows gives him a glimmer of hope that he can get out of this life of fighting and death. This book is a sequel to John Dixon's *Phoenix Island*.

Other books by the same author:
Phoenix Island, 2014

Other books you might like:
Gordon R. Dickson, *The Last Master*, 1984
Jeremy Robinson, *Island 731*, 2012
James Rollins, *Black Order*, 2006
Daniel H. Wilson, *Amped*, 2012
Timothy Zahn, *Cobra Alliance*, 2009

1139

IAN DOUGLAS

Deep Time

(New York: HarperCollins Publishers, 2015)

Series: Star Carrier Series. Book 6
Story type: Military; Series
Subject(s): Futuristic society; Spacetime; United States
Major character(s): Alexander Koenig, Government Of-

ficial (President of the United States of North America)
Time period(s): Indeterminate Future
Locale(s): United States

Summary: Things might finally be starting to calm down for Alexander Koenig, president of the United States of North America (USNA). His Marines have just routed the last of the rebels in opposition to the Earth Confederation and the USNA has the upper hand in the negotiations with the Sh'daar Collective. But then a mystery ship is spotted rocketing away from Earth. President Koenig's forces pursue and contact the strange alien ship, only to discover the mysterious visitors have the ability to bend time. With no clear idea what these intruders are planning—or even whether their plans involve Earth's past, present, or future—Koenig has to figure out if this new species is a powerful new ally, or a deadly new enemy. This is the sixth book in the Star Carrier series.

Other books by the same author:
Dark Matter, 2014
Bloodstar, 2012
Center of Gravity, 2011
Semper Human, 2009
Europa Strike, 2000

Other books you might like:
Jack Campbell, *The Lost Stars: Tarnished Knight*, 2012
David Drake, *Some Golden Harbor*, 2006
Eric Flint, *Storm from the Shadows*, 2009
R.M. Meluch, *The Myriad*, 2005
Mike Shepherd, *Kris Longknife: Daring*, 2011

1140

JOHN LAMBSHEAD
DAVID DRAKE, Co-Author

Into the Maelstrom

(Riverdale, New York: Baen, 2015)

Series: Citizen Series. Book 2
Story type: Adventure; Military
Subject(s): Science fiction; Space colonies; Revolutions
Major character(s): Allen Allenson, Military Personnel (general, Cutter Stream Colonial Army)
Time period(s): Indeterminate Future
Locale(s): Cutter Stream Colonies, Planet—Imaginary

Summary: This military science fiction novel is the second entry in the Citizen series by David Drake and John Lambshead, a series based on the American Revolutionary War and the leadership of George Washington. Allen Allenson is no stranger to war and now, as the Cutter Stream colonies enjoy a time of peace, Allenson has the experience to know it won't last long. The Cutter Stream colonies are still under the dominant rule of their homeworld, a distant government on the other side of the Bight. Allenson is certain that the colonies' only hope for freedom is to war—and win—against the homeworld government. And although he's not the most qualified man to lead the colonial army, Allenson knows he's the best man for the job. He's confident he can lead them to

freedom, even though it's a freedom he knows won't come easily.

Other books by the same author:
Dinosaurs & a Dirigible, 2014
What Distant Deeps, 2010
When the Tide Rises, 2008
The Way to Glory, 2005
The Sharp End, 1994

Other books you might like:
Roger MacBride Allen, *Allies and Aliens*, 1995
Kevin J. Anderson, *The Dark Between the Stars*, 2014
Alan Dean Foster, *Phylogenesis*, 1999
Joe Haldeman, *Forever Free*, 1999
Allen Steele, *Coyote*, 2002

1141

ROD DUNCAN

Unseemly Science

(Nottingham, United Kingdom: Angry Robot, 2015)

Series: Fall of the Gas-Lit Empire Series. Book 2
Story type: Series; Steampunk
Subject(s): Steampunk; Detective fiction; Women
Major character(s): Elizabeth Barnabus, Detective—Amateur, Magician (illusionist), Young Woman (aka Edwin)
Time period(s): 19th century; 1800s
Locale(s): England

Summary: The second novel of the Fall of the Gas-Lit Empire series continues the adventures of Elizabeth Barnabus. The only daughter of the "bullet-catcher" performer, Elizabeth has spent her life perfecting the tricks of illusion and magic that made her father famous. She has managed to convince society that she has a twin brother named Edwin, whose identity she assumes when she wishes to partake in activities deemed unfit for women. Edwin's key occupation is solving mysteries, although Elizabeth has resolved to forget her past case and move forward in life. The execution of a fake noblewoman has Elizabeth more determined than ever to reinvent herself anew. The arrival of a suspicious new organization throws a wrench in her plans, and Elizabeth find herself again donning Edwin's guise to solve the mystery.

Other books by the same author:
The Bullet-Catcher's Daughter, 2014

Other books you might like:
Elizabeth Bear, *Karen Memory*, 2015
James P. Blaylock, *Homunculus*, 1986
Ed Greenwood, *The Iron Assassin*, 2015
Mark Hodder, *The Return of the Discontinued Man*, 2014
George Mann, *The Revenant Express*, 2015
Dennis O'Flaherty, *King of the Cracksmen*, 2015
Cherie Priest, *Fiddlehead*, 2013
Cherie Priest, *Jacaranda*, 2015

1142

S.K. DUNSTALL

Linesman

(New York: Penguin Random House, 2015)

Series: Linesman Series. Book 1
Story type: Series; Space Opera
Subject(s): Extraterrestrial life; Adventurers; Adventure
Major character(s): Ean Lambert, Engineer (spaceship linesman)
Time period(s): Indeterminate Future
Locale(s): Outer Space

Summary: Ean Lambert is employed as a linesman: a singularly skilled laborer responsible for safely ushering spaceships throughout the galaxy. Although he is looked down upon for his lack of education and upbringing, few can deny that he has innate instincts that make him good at his job. When a strange spacecraft appears on They soon discover that although they can hook the ship with a linesman's energy field, the craft is rigged so that no one can touch it. Any linesman who tries to investigate the ship risks activating its defense system, which will blow up anything within about 120 miles. Mysteriously, however, Ean is able to approach the ship. He may be the only being in the galaxy who can crack its code and figure out where it came from—and why. This is the first novel in S.K. Dunstall's Linesman series.

Other books you might like:
Brian Herbert, *The Winds of Dune*, 2009
Richard Paul Russo, *Ship of Fools*, 2001
Melissa Scott, *Dreamships*, 1992
Dan Simmons, *The Rise of Endymion*, 1997
Timothy Zahn, *Odd Girl Out*, 2008

1143

BILL FAWCETT

By Tooth and Claw

(Riverdale, New York: Baen, 2015)

Series: Clan of the Claw Series. Book 2
Story type: Alternate World; Collection
Subject(s): Science fiction; Wars; Dinosaurs
Time period(s): Indeterminate
Locale(s): Earth

Summary: This is the second collection in the Clan of the Claw series, edited by Bill Fawcett. The books in the series each contain a collection of four novellas, written by S.M. Stirling, Mercedes Lackey, Eric Flint, and Jody Lynn Nye. Each of the novellas are linked, and set on an Earth on which the asteroid that led to the extinction of the dinosaurs never hit—so dinosaurs and mammals have evolved simultaneously. The dinosaurs have evolved to possess magic, while the mammals have some human-like traits and are known as Mrem. They live in clans and are constantly seeking to expand their territory—and here, they come up against the Lishkash. These dinosaurs are not going to surrender easily, and will use any resources at their disposal to ensure they remain the top predators on the planet.

Other books by the same author:
Cold Steel, 2002
Honor the Regiment, 1993
Cats in Space and Other Places, 1992
Dangerous Interfaces, 1990
The Far Stars War, 1990

Other books you might like:
Hal Colebatch, *The Wunder War*, 2003
Eric Flint, *Mother of Demons*, 1997
Eric Flint, *The Wizard of Karres*, 2004
Jody Lynn Nye, *Fortunes of the Imperium*, 2014
S. M. Stirling, *Against the Tide of Years*, 1999

1144

ERIC FLINT

Grantville Gazette VII

(Riverdale, New York: Baen, 2015)

Series: Ring of Fire Gazette Editions Series. Book 7
Story type: Alternate History; Collection
Subject(s): Thirty Years War, 1618-1648; Time travel; Science fiction
Time period(s): 17th century; 1630s (1632)
Locale(s): France

Summary: The stories included in this short fiction collection are inspired by Eric Flint's novel, *1632*, and follow the events in his Ring of Fire series, in which residents from the modern town of Grantville, West Virginia, are mysteriously transported to 17th century Europe. They find themselves remaking history in the midst of the Thirty Years' War and coping with a much more primitive existence. Here, Flint selects and edits 24 fan-submitted tales, each of which chronicles the lives of individual characters from Flint's works and highlights the social, political, and cultural themes found in Flint's alternate history series. This collection is the seventh anthology of tales from the Ring of Fire universe.

Other books by the same author:
1636: Commander Cantrell in the West Indies, 2014
1636: The Saxon Uprising, 2011
1635: The Eastern Front, 2010
Worlds, 2009
1633, 2002

Other books you might like:
Taylor Anderson, *Deadly Shores: Destroyermen*, 2014
William R. Forstchen, *A Band of Brothers*, 1999
Leo Frankowski, *Conrad's Lady*, 2005
Jerry Pournelle, *Janissaries*, 1979
S.M. Stirling, *Island in the Sea of Time*, 1998

1145

ERIC FLINT
WALTER H. HUNT, Co-Author

1636: The Cardinal Virtues

(Riverdale, New York: Baen, 2015)

Series: Ring of Fire Series. Book 19
Story type: Alternate History

Subject(s): French (European people); Monarchs; History

Major character(s): King Louis, Employer (of Cardinal Richelieu), Brother (of Monsieur Gaston d'Orleans), Historical Figure (King of France), Spouse (husband, of Queen Anne); Queen Anne, Historical Figure (Queen of France), Spouse (wife, of King Louis); Cardinal Richelieu, Historical Figure (French Cardinal), Nobleman (chief minister to King Louis); Gaston d'Orleans, Brother (of King Louis)

Time period(s): 17th century; 1630s (1636)

Locale(s): France

Summary: Best-selling authors Eric Flint and Walter H. Hunt deliver the 19th installment in their Ring of Fire series. In this alternate history series, residents of modern Grantville, West Virginia, have been living in 17th century France. King Louis of France and his wife, Queen Anne, daughter of King Philip III of Spain, have been married for 20 years and have yet to produce an heir. Cardinal Richelieu, King Louis's chief minister, formulates a plan for conception, albeit to the disdain of France's foreign enemies and Monsieur Gaston d'Orleans, the King's younger brother and next in line to the throne. Once she learns she is pregnant, Queen Anne secludes herself for her own protection—and for that of the heir. Now, the future of the Kingdom is at stake as the King's enemies take their stance against him, and those in and outside of France are forced to decide whose side they're on.

Other books by the same author:
Portal, 2013
1636: The Saxon Uprising, 2011
1635: The Eastern Front, 2010
Worlds, 2009
1632, 2000

Other books you might like:
Brad Ferguson, *The World Next Door*, 1990
Andre Norton, *Crosstime*, 2008
John Maddox Roberts, *Hannibal's Children*, 2002
Kim Stanley Robinson, *The Years of Rice and Salt*, 2002
Alan Smale, *A Clash of Eagles*, 2010

1146

RYK E. SPOOR
ERIC FLINT, Co-Author

Castaway Planet

(Riverdale, New York: Baen, 2015)

Series: Boundary Series. Book 4

Story type: Fantasy; Series

Subject(s): Science fiction; Space colonies; Space flight

Major character(s): Sakura Kimei, Space Explorer, Friend (of Whips), 14-Year-Old, Girl, Daughter (of Laura and Akira), Sister (of Hitomi, Melody, and Caroline), Castaway; Whips, Castaway, Genetically Altered Being, Alien, Friend (of Sakura); Laura Kimei, Mother (of Sakura, Hitomi, Melody, and Caroline), Space Explorer, Spouse (of Akira), Castaway, Doctor; Akira Kimei, Scientist, Castaway, Space Explorer, Father (of Sakura, Hitomi, Melody, and Caroline), Spouse

(of Laura); Hitomi Kimei, Son (of Laura and Akira), 7-Year-Old, Space Explorer, Brother (of Sakura), Castaway; Caroline Kimei, Daughter (of Laura and Akira), Sister (of Sakura, Melody, and Hitomi), Castaway, Space Explorer; Melody Kimei, Space Explorer, Castaway, Daughter (of Laura and Akira), Sister (of Sakura, Caroline, and Hitomi)

Time period(s): Indeterminate

Locale(s): Outer Space

Summary: Best-selling authors Eric Flint and Ryk E. Spoor deliver the fourth book in their science fiction Boundary series. It's been six months since Sakura Kimei, her family, and her alien best friend, Whips, began their journey toward the colony world of Tantalus. After a tragedy pulls them away from their colony ship, Whips, Sakura, and her family—parents Laura and Akira and siblings Caroline, Melody, and Hitomi—are confined to their damaged lifeboat as they continue their trek through the darkness. As they search for a world with livable conditions, their only option seems at first to be their salvation. But now, as a world of secrets continues to unfold, Sakura, her family, and Whips may not be as safe as they had hoped.

Other books by the same author:
Portal, 2013
1636: The Saxon Uprising, 2011
1635: The Eastern Front, 2010
Worlds, 2009
1632, 2000

Other books you might like:
John Brunner, *Castaways World*, 1963
C.J. Cherryh, *Betrayer*, 2010
Alan Dean Foster, *Icerigger*, 1974
Barry B. Longyear, *Elephant Song*, 1982
S.L. Viehl, *Rebel Ice*, 2006

1147

DAVE GALANTER

Crisis of Consciousness

(New York: Pocket Books/Star Trek, 2015)

Series: Star Trek: The Original Series

Story type: Adventure; Futuristic

Subject(s): Adventure; Science fiction; Space exploration

Major character(s): James T. Kirk, Spaceship Captain (Captain of the Enterprise); Spock, Military Personnel (first officer of the Enterprise), Alien (Vulcan); Pavel Chekov, Military Personnel (Ensign aboard the Enterprise); Nyota Uhura, Military Personnel (Lt., Communications Officer of the Enterprise); Hikaru Sulu, Military Personnel (Lt., navigator on the Enterprise); Leonard McCoy, Doctor (aboard the Enterprise); Pippage, Leader (Maabas ambassador), Alien

Locale(s): Maaba S'Ja, Planet—Imaginary

Summary: Set in the universe of the original Star Trek series, this book finds Captain James T. Kirk on a diplomatic mission that suddenly turns dangerous. Many millennia ago, war drove the Maabas people to find a new home. Thousands upon thousands of them have lived peacefully on their adopted planet ever since. They have the ability to travel far through space, but choose to stay close to home. They've come to the attention of the Federation, which sends Captain Kirk and the crew of the Starship *Enterprise* to negotiate a treaty. The Federation can learn much from the Maabas, who share a philosophical viewpoint with Federation members and have keen intelligence and creative problem solving abilities. But just as Kirk and the Maabas leaders complete the treaty, the *Enterprise* is attacked by the Kenisians. The former occupants of the planet have returned to evict the Federation's newest allies.

Other books by the same author:
Troublesome Minds, 2009
Maximum Warp Book One, 2001
Battle Lines, 1999
Foreign Foes, 1994

Other books you might like:
Tony Daniel, *Devil's Bargain*, 2013
J.M. Dillard, *Resistance*, 2007
Dave Galanter, *Star Trek: Troublesome Minds*, 2009
Scott Harrison, *Shadow of the Machine*, 2015
Una McCormack, *Hollow Men*, 2005
John Jackson Miller, *Takedown*, 2015
Kevin Ryan, *Killing Blow*, 2002

1148

TONY GONZALES

The Tabit Genesis

(London: Gollancz, 2015)

Story type: Space Opera
Subject(s): Space flight; Space exploration; Wars
Time period(s): Indeterminate Future
Locale(s): Earth; Spaceship

Summary: When the inhabitants of Sol flee from the only place they've ever known, they realize that the continuation of humanity rests solely with their survival. Out of the two starships that leave Sol, only one remains. It takes the colonists and crew many years to reach their destination: the planet Earth. When they finally touch down, they discover the aftereffects of an alien invasion that destroyed the planet. The colonists are the only surviving humans. The extraterrestrials want to wipe out the entire human race, and they will return to finish the job when they learn about the Sol survivors. As humanity makes its last stand, the final humans realize they must face off with these fearsome aliens. Author Tony Gonzales is the creator of the Eve Online series.

Other books by the same author:
Templar One, 2011
Empyrean Age, 2009
Eve, 2008

Other books you might like:
Poul Anderson, *After Doomsday*, 1962
Elizabeth Bear, *Chill*, 2010
Paul Chafe, *Genesis*, 2007
Brenda Cooper, *The Creative Fire*, 2012
Harry Harrison, *Invasion: Earth*, 1982

1149

ED GREENWOOD

The Iron Assassin

(New York: Tom Doherty Associates, 2015)

Story type: Alternate History; Steampunk
Subject(s): Alternative worlds; England; Steampunk
Major character(s): Jack Straker, Inventor; Iron Assassin, Reanimated Dead, Robot
Time period(s): Indeterminate
Locale(s): London, England

Summary: On an alternate Earth, the history of the British empire has been rewritten. The House of Harminster rules the empire, which under this dynasty is known as the Empire of the Lion. The Harminsters snatched the crown from the hands of the Hanovers long before Queen Victoria ever existed, and now London is the center of the empire and a hub of steam-based technological advancement. When a killer comes too close to the British rulers, scientist Jack Straker attempts to win the crown's favor by robotically altering a corpse and making it into a royal bodyguard. Straker calls his invention the Iron Assassin, but he has less power over the robot than he thinks, and soon the assassin is running amok. The one thing that Straker didn't count on is that the weapon's memories as a human would continue to haunt it. Those memories may make the Iron Assassin either a threat to the empire, or the empire's greatest asset.

Other books by the same author:
Elminster Enraged, 2012
Dark Vengeance, 2008
Dark Lord, 2007
Dark Warrior Rising, 2007
Silverfall, 1999

Other books you might like:
Paul Di Filippo, *The Steampunk Trilogy*, 1995
Rod Duncan, *Unseemly Science*, 2015
Mark Hodder, *The Curious Case of the Clockwork Man*, 2011
Stephen Hunt, *Jack Cloudie*, 2011
Cherie Priest, *Boneshaker*, 2009

1150

CAREN GUSSOFF

Three Songs for Roxy

(Seattle, Washington: Aqueduct Press, 2015)

Story type: Contemporary - Exotic
Subject(s): Extraterrestrial life; Identity; Sexuality
Major character(s): Kizzy, Foundling, Sister (of Roxy), Alien, Gypsy; Scott Lynn Miller, Survivor (of Hurricane Katrina), Security Officer; Natalie, Alien; Roxy, Sister (of Kizzy), Gypsy
Time period(s): 21st century; 2010s
Locale(s): Seattle, Washington

Summary: Kizzy is a foundling who has been raised by a human Romany gypsy family in Seattle. She is unaware that she was left behind years ago by aliens, who are now coming back to claim her. Natalie is the alien who has been assigned to get Kizzy. During her time on Earth and brief contact with Kizzy and her family, Natalie falls in love with Kizzy's sister—the daughter of her human family—Roxy. Meanwhile, in a parallel story, security guard Scott Lynn Miller sees Natalie's initial contact with Kizzy and is profoundly changed by the encounter. Ultimately, each individual involved will confront questions regarding identity, belonging, and relationships as they find their places with each other.

Other books you might like:

David S. Goyer, *Heaven's Shadow*, 2011

Ken MacLeod, *Cosmonaut Keep*, 2001

Eric S. Nylund, *Signal to Noise*, 1998

Robert J. Sawyer, *Rollback*, 2007

Robert Charles Wilson, *The Harvest*, 1993

1151

FRANCESCA HAIG

The Fire Sermon

(New York: Gallery Books, 2015)

Series: Fire Sermon Series. Book 1
Story type: Dystopian; Futuristic
Subject(s): Nuclear weapons; Science fiction; Twins
Major character(s): Zach, Twin (of Cass), Leader; Cassandra "Cass", Narrator, Outcast, Twin (of Zach), Psychic
Time period(s): 25th century
Locale(s): Earth

Summary: In the aftermath of a world-wide nuclear disaster and fire, Earth has been laid nearly to waste. The planet is slowly being repopulated, but every person born inexplicably has a twin. The pairs follow a pattern: each set of twins includes an Alpha, an exceptional twin destined to enjoy such privilege as the ravaged planet allows. The other twin—the Omega—always has a deformity. Some of these are large, others are small. Regardless, the imperfect twins are outcasts who remain alive only because of one quirk in this strange twin relationship: whenever one twin dies, the other one does, too. This could be a problem for Zach and Cass: Zach, the Alpha, is taking a leadership role in the council, while his Omega twin, Cass—a clairvoyant who dreams of equality for all the twins—has become a danger to the council and those who seek to overthrow it. This is the first book in the Fire Sermon series by poet Francesca Haig. First novel.

Other books you might like:

Walter M. Miller, *A Canticle for Leibowitz*, 1959

Edgar Pangborn, *Davy*, 1964

Kim Stanley Robinson, *The Wild Shore*, 1984

Sheri S. Tepper, *The Gate to Women's Country*, 1988

John Wyndham, *Re-Birth*, 1955

1152

GUY HALEY

Valedor

(London: Games Workshop, 2015)

Series: Warhammer 40,000 Series
Story type: Science Fantasy; Series
Subject(s): Dystopias; Alternative worlds; Wars
Major character(s): Prince Yriel, Royalty
Time period(s): 408th century; 40990s (40999)
Locale(s): Iyanden, Planet—Imaginary

Summary: In this novel from the Warhammer 40,000 series, author Guy Haley tells the story of Prince Yriel, the crown ruler of Iyanden, as he faces an invasion from space. The dreaded Hive Fleet Leviathan has already wrought havoc throughout the Valedor System, and now sets its sights on Duriel, a planet that was once the pride of the solar system but now lies virtually in ruins. The prince barely has time to digest the news of the impending attack when he also learns of an additional menace. A fleet of Kraken also are headed his way, and are on course to collide with the Leviathan. If these two fleets merge, there will be no stopping them, and Duriel will be destroyed. Now Prince Yriel must use every ounce of his ability for diplomacy to align a group of forces powerful enough to hold off the invasion, but that also means relying on beings that he isn't so sure he can trust.

Other books by the same author:
The Death of Integrity, 2013
Champion of Mars, 2012
Omega Point, 2012
Reality 36, 2011

Other books you might like:
Dan Abnett, *Prospero Burns*, 2010
Aaron Dembski-Bowden, *The First Heretic*, 2010
Phil Kelly, *Damocles*, 2015
Graham McNeill, *Chapter's Due*, 2010
James Swallow, *Nemesis*, 2010
Chris Wraight, *Battle of the Fang*, 2011

1153

SCOTT HARRISON

Shadow of the Machine

(New York: Pocket Books/Star Trek, 2015)

Series: Star Trek: The Original Series
Story type: Adventure; Futuristic
Subject(s): Space exploration; Science fiction; Interpersonal relations
Major character(s): James T. Kirk, Spaceship Captain (Captain of the Enterprise); Spock, Military Personnel (First Officer of the Enterprise); Hikaru Sulu, Military Personnel (Lt., navigator on the Enterprise)
Locale(s): Outer Space

Summary: This e-novella featuring the original crew of the Starship *Enterprise* and its universe follows in time the events of *Star Trek: The Motion Picture*. Back at their home base and awaiting the final preparations of the *Enterprise* before they begin a second five-year mission, Kirk and the members of his crew are on a two-week leave. The captain; his Vulcan first officer, Spock; and their navigator, Sulu, each return to their own respective homes during this time to try to make sense of their recent encounter with V'ger. They may find that the experience has changed their lives more than they previously believed.

Other books you might like:
Christopher L. Bennett, *Star Trek: The Next Generation: Greater than the Sum*, 2008
Greg Cox, *Star Trek: The Original Series: No Time Like the Past*, 2014
Dave Galanter, *Crisis of Consciousness*, 2015
Jeffrey Lang, *Cohesion: String Theory, Book 1*, 2005
Geoffrey Thorne, *Sword of Damocles*, 2007

1154

KEVIN HEARNE

Heir to the Jedi
(New York: LucasBooks, 2015)

Series: Star Wars: Empire and Rebellion. Book 3
Story type: Series; Space Opera
Subject(s): Science fiction; Adventure; Good and evil
Major character(s): Luke Skywalker, Pilot, Rebel (fighter); Leia Organa, Royalty (princess), Rebel, Leader; Ackbar, Military Personnel (admiral), Rebel; Sakhet, Alien, Woman, Spy; Nakari Kelen, Woman, Rebel (recruit), Pilot
Time period(s): Indeterminate
Locale(s): Outer Space

Summary: This Star Wars novel, which takes place after the events of *A New Hope*, provides a first-person account of Rebel fighter Luke Skywalker's adventures. Luke is still learning to use the power of the Force, but he is already a key fighter for the Rebels. Princess Leia Organa and Admiral Ackbar recognize the Jedi heir's talents and select him for an important assignment. With the young pilot Nakari Kelen, Luke is sent to retrieve Sakhet, an extraterrestrial who is a prisoner of the Empire. The Imperial authorities want to use Sakhet as a spy and cryptographer for their cause. Sakhet supports the Rebels, however, and she has agreed to work with the Alliance. But first Luke must get Sakhet out of the hands of the Imperials. The challenging mission forces Luke and Nakari to confront Imperial fighters, bounty hunters, and deadly biological threats. This is the third title in the Star Wars: Empire and Rebellion series.

Other books by the same author:
Tricked, 2012
Hammered, 2011
Hexed, 2011
Hounded, 2011

Other books you might like:
Christie Golden, *Ascension*, 2011
Paul S. Kemp, *Lords of the Sith*, 2015
Karen Miller, *Star Wars: Clone Wars Gambit: Siege*, 2010

Martha Wells, *Razor's Edge*, 2013
Timothy Zahn, *Scoundrels*, 2012

1155

PETER HIGGINS

Radiant State
(London: Orbit, 2015)

Series: Wolfhound Century Trilogy. Book 3
Story type: Alternate World; Series
Subject(s): Science fiction; Wars; Alternative worlds
Major character(s): Vissarion Lom, Spy; Maroussia Shaumian, Spy; Osip Rizhin, Leader (President-Commander of the New Vlast General)
Time period(s): Indeterminate
Locale(s): Mirgorod, Fictional Location

Summary: In this third and final novel in the Wolfhound Century trilogy by Peter Higgins—which is set in a fantasy world with striking similarities to the former USSR—the war against the Vlast continues. President-Commander of the New Vlast General Osip Rizhin prepares to launch the atom bombs that will ensure its dominion over the world. However, spies Vissarion Lom and Maroussia Shaumian have not given up yet, and are counting on their allies in the most unlikely places in Mirgorod. Meanwhile, the Pollandore may be the answer to their prayers, if only they can unlock its secrets. The spies race against time against the political machinations of their world.

Other books by the same author:
Truth and Fear, 2014
Wolfhound Century, 2013

Other books you might like:
James S.A. Corey, *Nemesis Games*, 2015
David S. Goyer, *Heaven's Shadow*, 2011
Simon Ings, *Hotwire*, 2014
Simon Morden, *The Curve of the Earth*, 2013
Alastair Reynolds, *On the Steel Breeze*, 2014

1156

JEAN JOHNSON

The Terrans
(New York: Penguin Random House, 2015)

Series: First Salik War Series. Book 1
Story type: Series; Space Opera
Subject(s): Politics; Alternative worlds; Space colonies
Major character(s): Jackie MacKenzie, Psychic, Military Personnel, Political Figure
Time period(s): Indeterminate Future
Locale(s): Alternate Universe

Summary: In the first novel of Jean Johnson's First Salik War series, which is part of the Theirs Is Not to Reason Why universe, an interplanetary translator struggles between her destiny and her need for stability. Jacaranda "Jackie" Mackenzie has two unique talents that make her a valuable asset to the United Planets Council: she has innate ambassadorial skills, and she has extrasensory abilities that allow her to tap into the psyche of any subject. Still, after a stint as guard on the galactic border, and having served on the board of the council, she wants to spend the rest of her career translating messages and avoiding the political arena. Her desire for a calm life is disrupted, however, when she is pinpointed as the one person who can stop an impending alien invasion. Jackie wants no part of being the savior of humankind, but she has no choice. Still, what she discovers about the coming alien forces is terrifying, and she realizes too late that she really is the only one who can face this imminent threat.

Other books by the same author:
Damnation, 2014
Hardship, 2014
Hellfire, 2013
An Officer's Duty, 2012
A Soldier's Duty, 2011

Other books you might like:
Ann Aguirre, *Breakout*, 2015
Mel Odom, *Master Sergeant*, 2015
Mike Shepherd, *Kris Longknife: Furious*, 2012
David Weber, *Shadow of Freedom*, 2013
Timothy Zahn, *Conqueror's Heritage*, 1995

1157

SOPHIE JORDAN (Pseudonym of Sherie Kohler)

Unleashed

(New York: HarperTeen, 2015)

Series: Uninvited Series. Book 2
Story type: Dystopian; Series
Subject(s): Dystopias; Romances (Fiction); Science fiction
Major character(s): Davy, Teenager, Girlfriend (of Sean), Friend (of Caden); Caden, Friend (of Davy), Resistance Fighter (leader), Teenager; Sean, Teenager, Boyfriend (of Davy)
Time period(s): 21st century; 2020s
Locale(s): Texas, United States

Summary: Set in the near future, this dystopian romance novel for young adults is the second book in the Uninvited series by Sophie Jordan. Teenager Davy has been on the run since she tested positive for the "kill gene" and was diagnosed with Homicidal Tendency Syndrome. To escape the US government, Davy and her boyfriend, Sean, and a group of their friends make plans to slip into Mexico. When Davy suffers an injury while attempting to cross the border, she is separated from her friends and rescued by teenage Resistance leader Caden. Caden takes Davy to a secret resistance compound, where she receives treatment for her wounds and begins to develop feelings for Caden. Soon, Davy is torn between following Sean to Mexico and staying at the compound with Caden, but she's not sure she can trust herself to make the decision. As a carrier of the kill gene, will Davy ever believe that she's really safe?

Other books by the same author:
All the Ways to Ruin a Rogue, 2015
Tease, 2014

Uninvited, 2014
Wild, 2014

Other books you might like:
John Coyne, *Child of Shadows*, 1990
John Farris, *Avenging Fury*, 2008
Stephen King, *Firestarter*, 1980
Richard K. Morgan, *Black Man*, 2007
J.D. Robb, *Delusion in Death*, 2012

1158

PAUL KEARNEY

Dark Hunters: Umbra Sumus

(Nottingham, United Kingdom: Games Workshop, 2015)

Series: Warhammer 40,000 Series
Story type: Adventure; Military
Subject(s): Military life; Wars; Rebellion
Major character(s): Jonah Kerne, Military Personnel (Captain of the Mortai Company of the Dark Hunters)
Time period(s): Indeterminate
Locale(s): Ras Hanem, Planet—Imaginary

Summary: Captain Jonah Kerne has his work cut out for him as he leads a group of Space Marines to squash a Punisher attack on Ras Hanem. Years before, the Space Marines of the Dark Hunters banished the traitorous Punishers and freed the world of Ras Hanem. But the Punishers are back, and Captain Kerne's Mortai company will have to take them on in a battle to restore Ras Hanem to Imperial rule. But the old battles left deep scars on the planet and its people, and Captain Kerne may have to pay a steep price, even if his team wins the fight. This title is set in the Warhammer 40,000 universe.

Other books by the same author:
Kings of Morning, 2012
Corvus, 2010
The Lost Island, 2008
This Forsaken Earth, 2006
The Mark of Ran, 2005

Other books you might like:
Dan Abnett, *The Unremembered Empire*, 2014
David Annandale, *The Death of Antagonis*, 2013
C Z Dunn, *Hive of the Dead*, 2011
Guy Haley, *The Death of Integrity*, 2013
Gav Thorpe, *Deliverance Lost*, 2011

1159

BEN COUNTER
JOSH REYNOLDS, Co-Author
GUY HALEY, Co-Author
PHIL KELLY, Co-Author

Damocles

(Nottingham, United Kingdom: Games Workshop, 2015)

Series: Warhammer 40,000: Space Marine Battles Series
Story type: Alternate Universe; Military

Subject(s): Adventure; Military life; Science fiction
Major character(s): Shadowsun, Military Personnel (Commander of the Tau), Enemy (of Kor'sarro Khan); Kor'sarro Khan, Military Personnel (Huntmaster of the White Scars), Enemy (of Shadowsun)
Time period(s): 41st century
Locale(s): Agrellan, Planet—Imaginary

Summary: This unnumbered addition to the Warhammer 40,000 Space Marines Battle series includes four novellas set during the second Damocles Gulf Crusade. Once, many years ago, the Tau Empire took on the Imperium of Man in a long and bloody battle that ended in a draw. Now, 200 years later, Commander Shadowsun and the tau warriors have returned to attack the world of Agrellan. The best of the best of the Imperium, the genetically superhuman Space Marines, are joined by their allies, the White Scars and Raven Guard, as they mount a strenuous defense. The fate of the world could come down to a battle between just two warriors: Shadowsun and Kor'sarro Khan, the fierce White Scars huntmaster.

Other books you might like:
Dan Abnett, *The Warmaster*, 2014
Ben Counter, *Seventh Retribution*, 2013
Aaron Dembski-Bowden, *The Talon of Horus*, 2014
Guy Haley, *Valedor*, 2015
Graham McNeill, *Gods of Mars*, 2014

1160

PAUL S. KEMP

Lords of the Sith

(New York: Random House Publishing, 2015)

Story type: Series; Space Opera
Subject(s): Science fiction; Rebellion; Good and evil
Major character(s): Darth Vader, Supernatural Being (Sith Lord), Apprentice (to Emperor Palpatine); Emperor Palpatine, Supernatural Being (Sith Lord), Ruler; Cham Syndulla, Resistance Fighter; Isval, Slave (former), Resistance Fighter
Time period(s): Indeterminate
Locale(s): Ryloth, Planet—Imaginary

Summary: Sith Lord Darth Vader is known to be ruthless, but his dedication to Emperor Palpatine and the Dark Side have not yet been tested. Then Vader accompanies Palpatine to the planet Ryloth, where the emperor has taken great personal interest in a resistance movement that threatens the slave and drug trade on which the Empire depends. The emperor and his apprentice are determined to squash the rebellion, but rebel leader Cham Syndulla and Isval, a former slave who seeks revenge, are equally determined to take advantage of the unexpected appearance of the two Sith Lords to win their cause. Vader and Palpatine are ambushed and crash into enemy territory on Ryloth, where their skills in the Force will be tested. This novel takes place within the Star Wars universe.

Other books by the same author:
Deceived, 2011
Riptide, 2011
Crosscurrent, 2010

Shadowbred, 2008
Dawn of Night, 2004

Other books you might like:
Troy Denning, *Abyss*, 2009
Jeff Grubb, *Scourge*, 2012
Kevin Hearne, *Heir to the Jedi*, 2015
James Luceno, *The Unifying Force*, 2003
John Peel, *The Fight for Justice*, 1998
Joe Schreiber, *Star Wars: Red Harvest*, 2010

1161

WILLIAM KING

Fall of Macharius

(London: Games Workshop, 2015)

Series: Warhammer 40,000: Macharian Crusade Series. Book 3
Story type: Science Fantasy
Subject(s): Space exploration; Royalty; Extraterrestrial life
Major character(s): Lord Solar Macharius, Leader (of the Imperial Guard); Richter, Military Personnel, Revolutionary
Time period(s): 41st century; 40390s (40392-40399)
Locale(s): Planet—Imaginary

Summary: In the third and final installment in the Macharian Crusade trilogy, a series in the world of Warhammer 40,000, author William King finishes the story of Lord Solar Macharius and his seven-year mission to spread the word of the Imperium. As Macharius arrives in Loki to proselytize about the Imperial Truth, he recognizes that he may be at the end of his journey. Unfortunately, the dedication of his troops is in question, as many of them have become skeptical of their Lord. When General Richter rebels against Macharius, they both find themselves thrown into a conflict that could jeopardize the entire Imperium. Now that Macharius's stranglehold is finally loosening, his fleet must decide which side of history it wants to be on: the side that is loyal to a failing lord, or the side of revolution. As the greatest Imperial leader faces what might be his final battle, his former followers make their choice.

Other books by the same author:
The Fist of Demetrius, 2014
Sword of Caledor, 2012
Blood of Aenarion, 2011
Farseer, 2002
Beastslayer, 2001

Other books you might like:
Andy Hoare, *Hunt for Voldorius*, 2010
Steve Lyons, *Dead Man Walking*, 2010
Graham McNeill, *Legacies of Betrayal*, 2015
Rob Sanders, *Atlas Infernal*, 2011
Henry Zou, *Blood Gorgons*, 2011

1162

GINI KOCH

Alien Separation

(New York: DAW-Penguin Books, 2015)

Series: Katherine "Kitty" Katt Series. Book 11
Story type: Adventure; Humor
Subject(s): Alternative worlds; Science fiction; Humor
Major character(s): Katherine "Kitty" Katt-Martini, Alien, Spouse (of Jeff), Mother (of Jaime), Friend (of Charles, Paul, and Christopher); Jeff Martini, Government Official (Vice President of the United States), Spouse (of Kitty), Father (of Jamie), Friend (of Charles, Paul, and Christopher); Jaime Martini, Daughter (of Kitty and Jeff); Charles Reynolds, Friend (of Kitty and Jeff); Paul Gower, Friend (of Kitty and Jeff); Christopher White, Friend (of Kitty and Jeff); Mastermind, Enemy (of Kitty and Jeff)
Time period(s): 21st century; 2010s
Locale(s): Planet—Imaginary; Washington, District of Columbia

Summary: She's an alien, an ambassador, and the wife of the vice president of the United States, but Katherine "Kitty" Katt-Martini finds lots of time for humorous exploits in this eleventh installment of the Katherine "Kitty" Katt series. Kitty and her vice president husband, Jeff, finally know the identity of the Mastermind and they intend to take him down. But somehow they and some of their human and alien comrades, including their daughter, Jamie, and friends Charles Reynolds, Paul Gower, and Christopher White, find themselves transported to an unknown planet. Separated from each other, lost, and confused, they'll have to find their way home first if they are going to stop the Mastermind.

Other books by the same author:
Aien Research, 2013
Alien in the House, 2013
Alien vs. Alien, 2012
Alien Tango, 2010
Universal Alien, 2010

Other books you might like:
John DeChancie, *Living with Aliens*, 1995
Alan Dean Foster, *Codgerspace*, 1992
Ron Goulart, *The Robot in the Closet*, 1981
Harry Harrison, *Bill, the Galactic Hero*, 1965
Lynn S. Hightower, *Alien Rites*, 1995

1163

MELISSA LANDERS

Invaded

(Los Angeles: Hyperion, 2015)

Series: Alienated Series. Book 2
Story type: Series; Young Adult
Subject(s): Science fiction; Students; Romances (Fiction)
Major character(s): Cara Sweeney, Student—High School, Student—Exchange, Girlfriend (of Aelyx); Aelyx, Student—High School, Student—Exchange, Boyfriend (of Cara), Alien
Time period(s): 21st century; 2010s
Locale(s): Earth; L'eihr, Planet—Imaginary

Summary: Melissa Landers returns with the second book in her Alienated series. Interplanetary exchange student Cara Sweeney adjusts to life on planet L'eihr, while her boyfriend, a L'eihr native named Aelyx, continues his tour on Earth to mend relations between the two planets and to ease Earth's growing anti-alien sentiments. Worlds apart, Cara and Aelyx are both confronted with prejudice and hate. While Cara serves as a human representative to a panel that plans to build a human colony on L'eihr, she is framed for a crime she didn't commit. Back on Earth, Aelyx is targeted by terrorist groups. Cara and Aelyx know the futures of both planets depend entirely on a unified alliance. L'eihr has the technology to correct the global water contamination crisis that the human governments are secretly facing, but Cara and Aelyx have yet to figure out why L'eihr is so desperate to receive help from humans.

Other books by the same author:
Alienate, 2014

Other books you might like:
Robert A. Heinlein, *Citizen of the Galaxy*, 1957
Andre Norton, *The Beast Master*, 1959
Jerry Pournelle, *Starswarm*, 1998
Charles Sheffield, *The Billion Dollar Boy*, 1997
Timothy Zahn, *Dragon and Thief*, 2003

1164

REIF LARSEN

I Am Radar

(New York: Penguin, 2015)

Subject(s): Family; Artists; Wars
Major character(s): Radar Radmanovic, Artist (with Kirkenesferda), Man, Son (of Kermin and Charlene); Kermin Radmanovic, Spouse (of Charlene), Engineer (radio and television), Father (of Radar); Charlene Radmanovic, Spouse (of Kermin), Mother (of Radar)
Time period(s): 20th century-21st century; 1970s-2010s
Locale(s): Bosnia and Herzegovina; Cambodia; Congo; Norway; New Jersey, United States

Summary: Radar Radmanovic is born in New Jersey in 1975 to two very white parents. The color of his parents' skin is vitally important to the events that follow. At the moment of Radar's birth, all of the electricity mysteriously goes out and he is born in total darkness. When the lights are restored, everyone is shocked that the baby of two pasty parents has skin that is coal-black. Searching for answers as to what might have happened to their son, Kermin and Charlene Radmanovic end up in Norway with a small group of esoteric teachers and researchers who call themselves the Kirkenesferda. This group originally formed while they were held captive by Nazi forces. They stage elaborate and insane avant-garde puppet performances in dangerous war zones, such as Cambodia, the Balkans, and the Congo. Kermin, a skilled radio and television engineer, is offered a place with the Kirkenesferda, and the family travels with the troupe, exploring how art can be created in the midst of death.

Other books by the same author:
The Selected Works of T.S. Spivet, 2009

Other books you might like:
Peter Carey, *His Illegal Self*, 2008
Paulo Coelho, *Adultery*, 2014
Rachel Cusk, *Outline*, 2015
Tatiana de Rosnay, *The Other Story*, 2014
Paul Di Filippo, *Cosmocopia*, 2008
Junot Diaz, *The Brief Wondrous Life of Oscar Wao*, 2007
Umberto Eco, *Baudolino*, 2002
Richard Ford, *Let Me Be Frank with You*, 2014
William Gibson, *All Tomorrow's Parties*, 1999
Siri Hustvedt, *The Blazing World*, 2014
Jonathan Lethem, *Gun, with Occasional Music*, 1994
Haruki Murakami, *IQ84*, 2011
Linda Nagata, *Deception Well*, 1997
Jamil Nasir, *Distance Haze*, 2000
Jess Row, *Your Face in Mine*, 2014

1165

TIM LEBBON

Coldbrook

(London: Titan Books, 2014)

Story type: Apocalyptic Horror; Zombies
Subject(s): Science experiments (Education); Diseases; Plague
Major character(s): Jonah Jones, Scientist
Time period(s): Indeterminate
Locale(s): North Carolina, United States

Summary: High up in the Appalachian mountain range sits a clandestine scientific facility. In the science lab known as Coldbrook, a group of scientists has created something beyond anyone's belief. Jonah Jones and his colleagues have opened up a portal to another plane of existence, and the possibilities seem endless. Unfortunately, their creation has devastating consequences for Earth's human population, because they have released a plague that turns mankind into the undead. Now they must come up with a cure to save humanity. When they learn about a woman who is immune to the pandemic, they know that she must be found, but tracking her down could prove to be as fatal as fighting the undead. Locating one person across a planet teeming with dangerous zombies seems an impossible task, but it is one that the scientists must complete if they are ever going to undo their mistakes and put the world right again.

Other books by the same author:
Contagion, 2013
Out of the Shadows, 2013
Reaper's Legacy, 2013
London Eye, 2012
Desolation, 2004

Other books you might like:
D.G. Compton, *The Silent Multitude*, 1966
Frank Herbert, *The White Plague*, 1982
Michael Palmer, *Resistant*, 2014

John Scalzi, *Lock In*, 2014
James Van Pelt, *Summer of the Apocalypse*, 2006

1166

SHARON LEE
STEVE MILLER, Co-Author

Dragon in Exile

(Wake Forest, North Carolina: Baen Books, 2015)

Series: Liaden Universe Series. Book 18
Story type: Science Fantasy; Series
Subject(s): Dragons; Alternative worlds; Family sagas
Time period(s): Indeterminate
Locale(s): Surebleak, Planet—Imaginary

Summary: This novel is the 18th title in the Liaden Universe series by authors Sharon Lee and Steve Miller. In spite of Clan Korval's selfless act, which preserved its home planet of Liad, the Council of Clans wants someone to pay for the recent tragedies. Although determined to make scapegoats of Clan Korval—a family known to most as the Dragon—the council is swayed by the Dragon's colleagues to show mercy, and the family is exiled to the dismal world of Surebleak as punishment. Chaos and pandemonium reign on this foreign planet. The Dragon must pay a dear price for being allowed to live, because they are now beholden to help enforce new laws in a lawless and anarchic land. Their role on Surebleak not only makes them new enemies, but also attracts the attention of an old foe—one that Clan Korval thought it had defeated.

Other books by the same author:
Dragon Ship, 2012
Ghost Ship, 2012
Fledgling, 2009
Sword of Orion, 2005
Scout's Progress, 2002

Other books you might like:
Ann Aguirre, *Havoc*, 2014
Lois McMaster Bujold, *Memory*, 1996
C.J. Cherryh, *Conspirator*, 2009
Alan Dean Foster, *A Call to Arms*, 1991
Louis L'Amour, *A Trail of Memories: The Quotations of Louis L'Amour*, 1988
Karen Traviss, *Matriarch*, 2006

1167

LORA LEIGH

Overcome

(New York: Penguin Publishing Group, 2015)

Series: Breeds Series
Story type: Genetic Manipulation
Subject(s): Fantasy; Erotica; Romances (Fiction)
Time period(s): 21st century; 2010s
Locale(s): Arkansas, United States

Summary: This is a collection of three previously published novellas, combined for the first time. In *The Breed Next Door*, Lyra is playing with fire when she falls in love with Tarek Jordan. He's her next-door neighbor, but he has a secret: he's a Breed Enforcer who is on the run. Their relationship could be dangerous for them both. *In A Wolf's Embrace* is the story of Grace and Mattias, a pair destined for each other until Matthias does something almost unforgivable. But Grace realizes she must look deeper to understand his reasons. She discovers outside influences won't be happy until they destroy her dangerous lover. In *A Jaguar's Kiss*, Natalie Ricci is the chosen instructor for the Breed children. Saban Broussard, a Jaguar, is chosen to protect her. But his animal allure is so strong it takes just one touch to bind them, and now trouble from Natalie's past may be the end of them both. These works are set in the universe of Lora Leigh's Breed series.

Other books by the same author:
Rule Breaker, 2014
Navarro's Promise, 2011
Lion's Heat, 2010
Coyote's Mate, 2009
Harmony's Way, 2006

Other books you might like:
Andrea Alton, *The Demon of Undoing*, 1988
C.J. Cherryh, *Chanur's Homecoming*, 1986
A.C. Crispin, *The Hutt Gambit*, 1997
Ru Emerson, *Voices of Chaos*, 1998
Leslie Gadallah, *Cat's Pawn*, 1987
Dean Ing, *Cathouse*, 1991

1168

LORA LEIGH

Bengal's Quest

(New York: Penguin Publishing Group, 2015)

Series: Breeds Series. Book 30
Story type: Revenge; Series
Subject(s): Revenge; Science fiction; Fantasy
Major character(s): Graeme, Rebel, Genetically Altered Being (Bengal)
Time period(s): 21st century; 2010s
Locale(s): Earth

Summary: Graeme is a Bengal, bred for a very special purpose by the Genetics Council. He's gone rogue, however, and is now considered elusive and dangerous. He answers to no one but himself as he sets out on a mission of revenge. He intends to destroy all he holds responsible for the wrong done to him, and it doesn't matter to Graeme whether they are human or Breed, male or female, his creators or those who love him; to him, they are all betrayers. He is especially bent on destroying the mystery woman who wants him as badly as he wants vengeance, despite the powerful attraction he feels for her. This is title 30 in the Breed series by Lora Leigh.

Other books by the same author:
Rule Breaker, 2014

Navarro's Promise, 2011
Lion's Heat, 2010
Styx's Storm, 2010
Megan's Mark, 2006

Other books you might like:
C.J. Cherryh, *The Chanur Saga*, 2000
Leslie Gadallah, *Cat's Gambit*, 1990
Tara K. Harper, *Cat Scratch Fever*, 1994
Lisanne Norman, *Stronghold Rising*, 2000
S. Andrew Swann, *Fearful Symmetries*, 1999

1169

JANE M. LINDSKOLD

Artemis Invaded

(New York: Tom Doherty Associates, 2015)

Series: Artemis Awakening Series. Book 2
Story type: Science Fantasy; Space Colony
Subject(s): Space exploration; Fantasy; Alternative worlds
Major character(s): Griffin, Spaceship Captain; Adara, Genetically Altered Being, Companion (of Sand Shadow), Alien; Sand Shadow, Companion (of Adara), Cat (puma)
Time period(s): Indeterminate Future
Locale(s): Artemis, Planet—Imaginary

Summary: Now that Griffin has inadvertently discovered the lost planet of Artemis—an artificially engineered world that was designed to be a utopia for humans but has since crumbled into chaos—he wants nothing more than to go home and spread the word about his findings. With the help of Adara, a genetically altered woman who is indigenous to Artemis, as well as Adara's pet puma, Sand Shadow, he sets off to locate a hidden device that will help him get in touch with his ship. Meanwhile, Adara finds herself falling in love with Griffin, a fact that Griffin seems to ignore. Griffin has other concerns, because his journeys are being tracked by an unseen enemy. Now Artemis faces an interplanetary attack, and Griffin may be the only one who can stop it. This novel is the second title of Jane M. Lindskold's Artemis Awakening series.

Other books by the same author:
Artemis Awakening, 2014
Five Odd Honors, 2010
Nine Gates, 2009
Child of a Rainless Year, 2005
The Buried Pyramid, 2004

Other books you might like:
Mike Brotherton, *Spider Star*, 2008
Howard V. Hendrix, *Better Angels*, 2001
Alastair Reynolds, *Pushing Ice*, 2005
Richard Paul Russo, *Ship of Fools*, 2001
Karl Schroeder, *Permanence*, 2002

Science Fiction

1170

CIXIN LIU
JOEL MARTINSEN, Translator

The Dark Forest

(New York: Tom Doherty Associates, 2015)

Story type: Invasion of Earth
Subject(s): Extraterrestrial life; Wars; Earth
Major character(s): Luo Ji, Scientist
Time period(s): Indeterminate
Locale(s): Earth

Summary: This novel marks the first time the work of Chinese science fiction author Cixin Liu has been translated for English audiences. The people of Earth are devastated to learn that extraterrestrials plan to destroy them. Time seems to be on the side of humanity, however, because it will take the alien species known as the Trisolaris more than 400 years to arrive in Earth's solar system. When Trisolaris spies are discovered on Earth, they are dealt with swiftly, but not soon enough to stop the spies from planting bugging devices called sophons around the planet. Now humans must figure out a way to communicate without the sophons picking up their strategy. That's where Luo Ji comes in. A member of a cache of scientists called the Wallfacers, he is one of only four people on whose shoulders the continuation of the human race rests. Luo Ji cannot figure out how he even became a Wallfacer, and struggles with his burden. That struggle is made much worse when the Trisolaris decide to target him as the one person on Earth who must be extinguished to allow them to carry out their plan successfully.

Other books by the same author:
The Three-Body Problem, 2015

Other books you might like:
Gregory Benford, *Eater*, 2000
David S. Goyer, *Heaven's Shadow*, 2011
Larry Niven, *Footfall*, 1985
Sheri S. Tepper, *After Long Silence*, 1987
Robert Charles Wilson, *The Harvest*, 1993

1171

JOHN LOVE

Evensong

(San Francisco, California: Night Shade Books, 2015)

Story type: Futuristic; Genetic Manipulation
Subject(s): Biotechnology; Futuristic society; Genetic engineering
Major character(s): Anwar Abbas, Genetically Altered Being (member of The Dead), Bodyguard (of Olivia), Lover (of Olivia); Olivia del Santo, Lover (of Anwar), Religious (leader of a large church)
Locale(s): Earth

Summary: Protecting the leader of a popular church should be an easy assignment, but when the church leader has stepped on some toes along the way, she can acquire some dangerous enemies. Anwar Abbas is assigned to protect church leader Olivia del Sarto while she's hosting a high-profile United Nations (UN) conference. He thinks bodyguard work is beneath him but he soon has his hands full. Not only will Olivia be target, but also Anwar knows the UN has changed, and not for the better. This Anwar knows only too well: He's a product of the new way the UN solves its big problems—a surgically engineered weapon created to handle the very worst situations. Anwar and his fellow operatives, who are known as The Dead, are almost unstoppable. But Olivia's enemies happen to have the one thing that can kill The Dead. This weapon is bearing down on them. Anwar, who has become Olivia's lover, must figure out who is after her to save the UN, The Dead, and his new love.

Other books by the same author:
Faith, 2014

Other books you might like:
M.M. Buckner, *Neurolink*, 2004
C.J. Cherryh, *Heavy Time*, 1991
Mick Farren, *The Feelies*, 1990
Dani Kollin, *The Unincorporated Future*, 2012
Frederik Pohl, *The Merchants' War*, 1984

1172

GEORGE R.R. MARTIN
GARDNER R. DOZOIS, Co-Editor

Old Venus

(New York: Random House Publishing Group, 2015)

Story type: Collection
Subject(s): Science fiction; Short stories; Space colonies

Summary: When they planned this science fiction anthology, editors George R.R. Martin and Gardner Dozois requested that contributing authors set their stories on Venus—the Venus that existed in man's imagination before science revealed it as an uninhabitable planet. As a result, the tales in this collection portray Venus as a world where humans live and explore, although not all of their adventures are pleasant ones. In Allen M. Steel's "Frogheads," a private detective travels to Venus to find a client's child who is hiding out there. Garth Nix's "By Frogsled and Lizardback to Outcast Venusian Lepers" concerns a rescue mission to the planet's remotest regions. The collection also includes "The Drowned Celestial" by Lavie Tidhar, "The Godstone of Venus" by Mike Resnick, and "A Planet Called Desire" by Gwyneth Jones.

Other books by the same author:
Fort Freak, 2011
Suicide Kings, 2009
Dreamsongs, 2006
Aces Abroad, 1988
New Voices I, 1977

Other books you might like:
Ben Bova, *Venus*, 2000
Edgar Rice Burroughs, *Lost on Venus*, 1937
David Drake, *The Jungle*, 1991

Robert A. Heinlein, *Between Planets*, 1951
Ann Leckie, *Ancillary Justice*, 2013

1173

MICHAEL J. MARTINEZ

The Venusian Gambit

(San Francisco, California: Night Shade Books, 2015)

Series: Daedalus Series. Book 3
Story type: Alternate History; Science Fantasy
Subject(s): Science fiction; Napoleonic Wars, 1800-1815; Futuristic society
Major character(s): Thomas Weatherby, Military Personnel (Lord Admiral of the British Fleet); Shaila Jain, Girlfriend (of Stephane), Military Personnel (Lt. Commander of Venus defense force); Stephane Durand, Man (Possessed by alien entity), Boyfriend (of Shaila)
Time period(s): 19th century; (1800s); 22nd century; 2130s (2135)
Locale(s): England; Venus, Outer Space

Summary: A past that wasn't and a future that might not be collide in this third volume of the Daedalus series. French troops have overrun England, but these are not the troops of Napoleon's army that fought the British in 1809 of Earth's past. Dark magic has been used to create an army of the undead—the Corps Eternelle—and it's all the Royal Navy commanded by Lord Admiral Thomas Weatherby can do to keep these malevolent warriors from acquiring a legendary weapon thought to be on Venus. Venus is at the heart of another battle—this one in the year 2135—when an alien life form escapes Enceladus, a Saturnine moon, and heads for Earth. It's Lieutenant Commander Shaila Jain's job to stop them, but it's not her only challenge. She's also desperately trying to save the life of Stephane Durand, a crewmember and Shaila's love. Stephane is under the control of a life form bent on destroying Earth and is also secretly sending information to a group en route to Venus with destruction in mind. Weatherby and Shaila will both face difficult decisions that could change their lives and the lives of two planets, past and future, forever.

Other books by the same author:
The Enceladus Crisis, 2014
The Daedalus Incident, 2013

Other books you might like:
Gregory Benford, *Cosm*, 1998
James S.A. Corey, *Leviathan Wakes*, 2011
David Drake, *Seas of Venus*, 2002
David S. Goyer, *Heaven's War*, 2012
Alexander Jablokov, *Carve the Sky*, 1991

1174

ROBERT R. MCCAMMON

The Border

(Burton, Michigan: Subterranean Press, 2015)

Story type: Invasion of Earth
Subject(s): Extraterrestrial life; Science fiction; Horror

Time period(s): Indeterminate Future

Summary: A teenage boy may be the only one who can save the human race from annihilation in this novel by Robert McCammon. Two different extraterrestrial races, the Gorgons and the Cyphers, have all but taken over Earth. The humans who have survived the invasion live in the enclave known as Panther Ridge. Even there, the survivors are not immune to their world's new threats. Some are driven to suicide by their misery; others become man-eating mutants after they are exposed to the aliens' toxic waste. A teenage boy who calls himself Ethan—because he can't remember his real name—is one of the survivors. When he discovers that the earth has powers that can defeat the extraterrestrials, Ethan makes a daring attempt to save mankind. He learns to use the powers against the invaders, but he risks his own life in the process.

Other books by the same author:
The Hunter from the Woods, 2011
Gone South, 1992
Boy's Life, 1991
Stinger, 1989
Swan Song, 1987

Other books you might like:
John Connolly, *Conquest*, 2014
David Gerrold, *A Matter for Men*, 1983
Scott Mackay, *Omnifix*, 2004
Larry Niven, *Footfall*, 1985
Robert Silverberg, *The Alien Years*, 1998

1175

UNA MCCORMACK

The Missing

(New York: Pocket Books, 2015)

Series: Star Trek: Deep Space Nine Series
Story type: Futuristic; Political
Subject(s): Politics; Space colonies; Diplomacy
Major character(s): Ro Laren, Military Personnel (Captain of Deep Space 9), Colleague (of Beverly Crusher and Jefferson Blackmer); Jefferson Blackmer, Security Officer, Colleague (of Beverly Crusher and Ro Laren); Beverly Crusher, Doctor, Colleague (of Ro Laren and Jefferson Blackmer); Katherine Polaski, Scientist, Space Explorer
Time period(s): 24th century; 2300s
Locale(s): Outer Space

Summary: A sequel to *The Fall*, this Star Trek: Deep Space Nine novel continues the story of the Deep Space Nine crew as it studies the newly reopened Bajoran wormhole in the Alpha Quadrant. Captain Ro Laren and Chief Medical Officer Beverly Crusher find themselves in a political morass when they offer aid to refugees known as the People of the Open Sky. The security officer, Jefferson Blackmer, is suspicious of these seemingly friendly refugees, many of whom are previously unknown species. As the People of the Open Sky explore the space station, asking many questions about its purpose and technologies, Blackmer's hesitations grow. It is only when Beverly Crusher's top-secret files are ac-

Science Fiction

cessed remotely and without permission that the tensions explode between the station's crew and the refugees. To Blackmer, the People of the Open Sky are obvious suspects and the important information within the stolen files, such as the secrets of the Shedai race, could cause harm. When a science vessel led by Doctor Katherine Pulaski is halted by a powerful unknown vessel, it appears that additional violence might break out at any minute.

Other books by the same author:
The Crimson Shadow, 2013
The Way Through the Woods, 2011
The King's Dragon, 2010
The Never-Ending Sacrifice, 2009
Hollow Men, 2005

Other books you might like:
Christopher L. Bennett, *Uncertain Logic*, 2015
Kirsten Beyer, *Star Trek: Voyager: The Eternal Tide*, 2012
Tony Daniel, *Savage Trade*, 2015
David Mack, *Silent Weapons*, 2012
Jeff Mariotte, *Star Trek: The Original Series: Serpents in the Garden*, 2014
Olivia Woods, *Fearful Symmetry*, 2008

1176

SOPHIA MCDOUGALL

Mars Evacuees

(New York: Harper, 2015)

Story type: Young Readers
Subject(s): Students; Friendship; Space flight
Major character(s): Alice Dare, Student, 12-Year-Old, Girl, Friend (of Carl and Josephine); Carl, Student, Friend (of Alice and Josephine); Josephine, Student, Friend (of Alice and Carl)
Time period(s): 21st century; 2030s
Locale(s): Mars; Outer Space

Summary: This science fiction novel for young readers by Sophia McDougall is a tale of adventure and friendship. In the not-too-distant future, the effects of global warming make Earth a perfect destination for the invading Morrors, aliens who live comfortably in a colder climate. As the invasion grows more threatening, 12-year-old Alice Dare is taken out of Britain's Muckling Abbott School for Girls and evacuated to a base on Mars. There she is trained as a soldier to fight against humankind's alien enemies. Among the 300 students taken to Mars, Alice makes friends with Carl and Josephine, and when all the adults mysteriously disappear, Alice and her new friends search for help. Along the way, they encounter a Morror their own age. As this new friendship develops, they all learn that the real enemy is not one another.

Other books by the same author:
Rome Burning, 2011
Savage City, 2011

Other books you might like:
Suzanne Collins, *The Hunger Games*, 2008
James Dashner, *The Death Cure*, 2011

Robert A. Heinlein, *Red Planet*, 1990
Tom Isbell, *The Prey*, 2015
Veronica Roth, *Divergent*, 2011
Kristen Simmons, *Article 5*, 2012
Kristen Simmons, *The Glass Arrow*, 2015

1177

GRAHAM MCNEILL
CHRIS WRAIGHT, Co-Author
AARON DEMBSKI-BOWDEN, Co-Author
NICK KYME, Co-Author

Legacies of Betrayal

(Nottingham, United Kingdom: Games Workshop, 2015)

Series: Horus Heresy Series. Book 31
Story type: Alternate World; Anthology
Subject(s): Adventure; Science fiction; Wars
Locale(s): Outer Space

Summary: This anthology is the 31st book in the Horus Heresy series. The collection contains 18 short stories and a novella set in the Warhammer 40,000 universe, where battles are fought and won by the Imperium and the White Scars Legion. In a world full of war, those who live to fight take on all comers at the behest of their overlords and leaders. It's a world of light and dark, where the greater the battle the greater the glory. This anthology includes the novella *Brotherhood of the Storm* by Chris Wraight and features work by Graham McNeill, Aaron Dembski-Bowden, Nick Kyme, and many others.

Other books you might like:
Dan Abnett, *Know No Fear*, 2012
Andy Hoare, *Commissar*, 2014
William King, *Fall of Macharius*, 2015
Gav Thorpe, *Master of Sanctity*, 2014
Chris Wraight, *Stormcaller*, 2014

1178

JOHN JACKSON MILLER

Takedown

(New York: Pocket Books, 2015)

Series: Star Trek: The Next Generation Series
Story type: Futuristic; Series
Subject(s): Betrayal; Space flight; Space colonies
Major character(s): Jean-Luc Picard, Spaceship Captain (of U.S.S. Enterprise), Friend (of William Riker); William T. Riker, Spaceship Captain (admiral), Friend (of Jean-Luc Picard)
Time period(s): 24th century; 2300s (2385)
Locale(s): Outer Space

Summary: In this Star Trek: The Next Generation tale, Captain Jean-Luc Picard and his crew of the U.S.S. *Enterprise* are traveling in the Alpha Quadrant when they are ordered to stop a terrible threat. Picard is informed that federation starships—specifically the U.S.S. *Aventine*—are no longer responding to orders and instead are wreaking havoc across the quadrant. Picard is horrified to discover that his long-time friend and former first mate, Admiral William T. Riker, is serving aboard the *Aventine* on special assignment and that he appears to have a hand in the treason. Ryker had returned from a peace summit and secured himself within the holodeck, where he has been issuing the orders that are sending the quadrant powers on a course for war. It is up to Picard to discover what happened to Riker and stop the escalating conflict.

Other books by the same author:
A New Dawn, 2015
Knight Errant, 2011

Other books you might like:
Greg Cox, *The Rings of Time*, 2012
Tony Daniel, *Savage Trade*, 2015
William R. Forstchen, *The Forgotten War*, 1999
Dave Galanter, *Crisis of Consciousness*, 2015
Dayton Ward, *Star Trek: That Which Divides*, 2012

1179

WALTER MOSLEY

Inside a Silver Box

(New York: Tor Books, 2015)

Story type: Invasion of Earth; Urban
Subject(s): Extraterrestrial life; Murder; Death
Major character(s): Lorraine Fell, Student—Graduate, Wealthy, Crime Victim (killed by Ronnie), Heroine (resurrected woman); Ronnie Bottoms, Murderer (of Lorraine), Hero (tied to Lorraine's consciousness), Man (African American), Criminal; Silver Box, Artificial Intelligence, Object (weapon)
Time period(s): 21st century; 2010s
Locale(s): New York, New York

Summary: Graduate student Lorraine Fell is attacked while she's jogging in Central Park. Ronnie Bottoms attempts to rape her and ends up murdering her with a rock. Her body falls atop a buried artifact, the Silver Box. The Silver Box is a sentient being, an artificial intelligence (AI) who chooses to preserve Lorraine's consciousness. It convinces Ronnie to use its power to bring Lorraine back to life. The AI was created by an alien race, the Laz, who used it to torture living being. When the Silver Box revolted 150 thousand years ago, it was buried on Earth. Lorraine's death activates the box as well as the Laz. The Silver Box beseeches the two New Yorkers to accept an important mission: Overcome their differences and save the world. Through the powers of the Silver Box, their personalities and skills merge and blend, turning the duo into a type of superhero.

Other books by the same author:
Love Machine & Stepping Stone, 2013
Disciple & Merge, 2012
The Wave, 2006
Blue Light, 2001
Futureland, 2001

Other books you might like:
Algis Budrys, *Hard Landing*, 1993

Arthur C. Clarke, *2001: A Space Odyssey*, 1968
Arthur C. Clarke, *Childhood's End*, 1953
John Connolly, *Conquest*, 2014
Philip Kerr, *A Philosophical Investigation*, 1992
Nancy Kress, *Crossfire*, 2003
Jonathan Lethem, *Gun, with Occasional Music*, 1994
Kristine Kathryn Rusch, *The Disappeared*, 2002
Robert J. Sawyer, *Illegal Alien*, 1997
Andy Weir, *The Martian*, 2014
Connie Willis, *Bellwether*, 1996
Robert Charles Wilson, *The Harvest*, 1993

1180

DENNIS O'FLAHERTY

King of the Cracksmen

(San Francisco, California: Night Shade Books, 2015)

Story type: Alternate History; Steampunk
Subject(s): Crime; American Reconstruction, 1865-1877; Science fiction
Major character(s): Edwin Stanton, Government Official (acting head of US government), Criminal, Historical Figure; Liam McCool, Criminal (safecracker), Boyfriend (of Maggie); Maggie, Girlfriend (of Liam), Crime Victim; Becky Fox, Journalist
Time period(s): 19th century; 1870s (1877)
Locale(s): United States

Summary: After the Civil War, the country is being led by Edwin Stanton, who was the secretary of war until Abraham Lincoln disappeared. The lanky 16th president wasn't assassinated in this alternate reality, but has instead gone missing. Stanton has turned into a de facto mob boss running the government just like a crime syndicate but with an impressive army and steam powered dirigible gunships to back him up. Safecracker Liam McCool is one of the best at his chosen trade, but he is caught and his special skills come to the attention of Stanton. Stanton coerces McCool into informing on his cronies, so McCool bides his time while he waits for an opportunity take his girlfriend, Maggie, and escape to the Russian-controlled West. When Maggie is murdered, McCool's efforts to uncover her killer lead him straight to Stanton's gang. Together with famed female reporter Becky Fox, he challenges the Russians and Stanton to try to solve Maggie's murder and end Stanton's evil empire.

Other books you might like:
Elizabeth Bear, *Karen Memory*, 2015
Rod Duncan, *Unseemly Science*, 2015
Mark Hodder, *Expedition to the Mountains of the Moon*, 2012
George Mann, *The Immorality Engine*, 2011
Cherie Priest, *Clementine*, 2010
Cherie Priest, *Jacaranda*, 2015

Science Fiction

1181

MEL ODOM

Master Sergeant

(New York: Harper Voyager, 2015)

Series: Makaum War Series. Book 1
Story type: Military; Series
Subject(s): Military science; Science fiction; Wars
Major character(s): Frank Sage, Military Personnel
(Master Sergeant, Terran Army)
Time period(s): Indeterminate Future
Locale(s): Makaum, Planet—Imaginary

Summary: Best-selling author Mel Odom delivers the first book in his Makaum War series. Makaum, the planet known as the "Green Hell," is dangerous and jungle-ridden, but it is the home of highly desired resources—resources that could wreak havoc if they fall into the wrong hands. As war rages between the Terrans and the Phrenorians, Terran Military Master Sergeant Frank Sage is sent to Makaum to make sure that the Phrenorians don't gain access to the planet's rich resources and to align Makaum's army with Terran. But when Sage arrives, he learns that the Phrenorians might not be their only enemy and that an impending civil war may put the entire galaxy at risk.

Other books by the same author:
Sooner Dead, 2011
Hunters of the Dark Sea, 2003
Shades, 2003
High Wire, 2000
Omega Blue, 1993

Other books you might like:
Kevin J. Anderson, *Blood of the Cosmos*, 2015
Jack Campbell, *Leviathan*, 2015
Jack Campbell, *Steadfast*, 2014
Bennett R. Coles, *Virtues of War*, 2015
David Gunn, *Death's Head*, 2007
Jean Johnson, *The Terrans*, 2015
R.M. Meluch, *The Ninth Circle: A Novel of the U.S.S.
Merrimack*, 2011
Mike Shepherd, *Kris Longknife: Furious*, 2012

1182

BENJAMIN PERCY

The Dead Lands

(New York: Grand Central Publishing, 2015)

Story type: Dystopian; Post-Disaster
Subject(s): Science fiction; Dystopias; Horror
Major character(s): Lewis Meriwether, Museum Curator;
Wilhemina "Mina" Clark, Guard
Time period(s): Indeterminate Future
Locale(s): United States

Summary: It has been more than a century since nuclear radiation and a devastating disease transformed the landscape and society of the United States. The region that was once known as St. Louis is now called the Sanctuary. It is home to human survivors and the aggressive leaders who protect them. The residents of the Sanctuary believe that the territories beyond its boundaries are "Deadlands," but they realize that their beliefs may be wrong when a mysterious woman arrives with tales about a safe, verdant land in the west. The leaders of the Sanctuary discount the visitor's story, but a few residents believe she may be telling the truth. Lewis Meriwether, a librarian, and Wilhemina "Mina" Clark, a city employee, escape the Sanctuary and launch their own expedition into the western territory. On a quest that echoes the 19th-century journey of Lewis and Clark, this post-apocalyptic Lewis and Clark face mutant creatures in their search for a new refuge.

Other books by the same author:
Red Moon, 2013
The Wilding, 2010
Refresh, Refresh, 2007
The Language of Elk, 2006

Other books you might like:
Max Brooks, *World War Z: An Oral History of the
Zombie War*, 2006
Octavia E. Butler, *Dawn*, 1987
Suzanne Collins, *The Hunger Games*, 2008
Mark Z. Danielewski, *The Familiar, Volume 1: One
Rainy Day in May*, 2015
Michel Faber, *The Book of Strange New Things*, 2014
Victor Gischler, *Go-Go Girls of the Apocalypse*, 2008
Steven Gould, *7th Sigma*, 2011
P.D. James, *The Children of Men*, 1993
Stephen King, *The Stand*, 1978
Emily St. John Mandel, *Station Eleven*, 2014
Cormac McCarthy, *The Road*, 2006
Nick Sagan, *Everfree*, 2006
Robert Charles Wilson, *Spin*, 2005

1183

STEVE PERRY

The Tejano Conflict

(New York: Berkley, 2015)

Series: Cutter's Wars Series. Book 3
Story type: Futuristic; Series
Subject(s): Wars; Violence; Interpersonal relations
Major character(s): R. "Rags" A. Cutter, Mercenary,
Military Personnel (Colonel, leader of Cutter Force
Initiative)
Time period(s): 24th century; 2300s
Locale(s): Earth

Summary: Warfare in the twenty-fourth century is strictly business. Those who wish to fight hire mercenaries and pit them against one another in a designated area with clearly defined terms of victory and defeat. Cutter's Force has accepted a contract that sends it to Earth on what is expected to be a very lucrative and easy job. An old Army friend who is now a general requests that Rags Cutter and his unit provide simple reconnaissance, gather intelligence, and take care of the opposition. Opposing corporations are fighting to occupy a chunk of territory that is extremely valuable, and both sides are willing to fight dirty to win. Conflict and tensions within Cutter's Force must be put aside if the mercenaries are to uncover the secrets they haven't been told if they are not only to win the battle, but also to survive. This is the third novel of the Cutter's Wars series.

Other books by the same author:
The Vasalimi Gambit, 2014
The Ramal Extraction, 2012
Immune Response, 2006
The Musashi Flex, 2006
The Digital Effect, 1997

Other books you might like:
Ian Douglas, *Semper Human*, 2009
David Drake, *The Butcher's Bill*, 1998
Ann Leckie, *Ancillary Sword*, 2014
Jerry Pournelle, *Exile—and Glory*, 2009
Mack Reynolds, *The Earth War*, 1963

1184

CHERIE PRIEST

Jacaranda

(Burton, Michigan: Subterranean Press, 2015)

Series: Clockwork Century Series
Story type: Ghost Story; Steampunk
Subject(s): Western fiction; Science fiction; Ghosts
Major character(s): Horatio Korman, Ranger (Texas Ranger Investigator); Eileen Callahan, Religious (former nun); Juan Miguel Quintero Rios, Religious (Priest)
Time period(s): 19th century; 1890s (1895)
Locale(s): Galveston, Texas

Summary: The Jacaranda has only been around for a year, but the south Texas hotel is already legendary. Twenty-four people have died there in just 12 months. While the Galveston neighbors whisper about a haunting, the Rangers decide a more practical explanation is likely to explain these deaths, so they send Horatio Korman to find out what it is. One guest, Eileen Callahan, thinks the place needs more than investigating, and she sends for a priest. Padre Juan Miguel Quintero Rios, a former gunfighter with a tattoo that reads "By God, not chance," answers her call. The hotel Jacaranda holds many secrets within its walls, and many promises have been broken here. The salvation of many damaged souls may be more than the Padre can manage. This novella is a standalone postscript to Cherie Priest's Clockwork Century series.

Other books by the same author:
Fiddlehead, 2013
The Inexplicables, 2012
Ganymede, 2011
Dreadnought, 2010
Boneshaker, 2009

Other books you might like:
Elizabeth Bear, *Karen Memory*, 2015
Gail Carriger, *Prudence*, 2015
Paul Di Filippo, *The Steampunk Trilogy*, 1995
Rod Duncan, *Unseemly Science*, 2015

George Mann, *The Osiris Ritual*, 2010
Dennis O'Flaherty, *King of the Cracksmen*, 2015

1185

HANNU RAJANIEMI

Hannu Rajaniemi: Collected Fiction

(San Francisco, California: Tachyon Publications, 2015)

Story type: Hard Science Fiction
Subject(s): Short stories; Apocalypse; Dystopias

Summary: In this collection, author Hannu Rajaniemi presents 17 hard science fiction stories that closely examine the implications of technological advancement. In these stories, Rajaniemi imagines what could happen if technology is used for good as well as for bad. The author questions how people will manage, or mismanage, futuristic creations, and how tools and knowledge that are developed for the betterment of society can make things worse sometimes. Rajaniemi includes in this anthology an exercise in neurofiction, which is a method of tapping into a reader's imagination to change the direction of a story. The collection also contains a story written by the author on the social media network Twitter, which requires that one limit a post to 140 characters or less. Rajaniemi is also the author of the Jean le Flambeur series.

Other books by the same author:
The Causal Angel, 2014
The Fractal Prince, 2012
The Quantum Thief, 2011

Other books you might like:
Paolo Bacigalupi, *Pump Six and Other Stories*, 2008
Pat Cadigan, *Dirty Work*, 1993
Paul Di Filippo, *Wikiworld*, 2013
William Gibson, *Burning Chrome*, 1986
Bruce Sterling, *Visionary in Residence*, 2006

1186

KATHY REICHS
BRENDAN REICHS, Co-Author

Exposure

(New York: Penguin Random House, 2015)

Series: Virals Series. Book 4
Story type: Medical; Mystery
Subject(s): Extrasensory perception; Human-animal relationships; Schools
Major character(s): Tory Brennan, Teenager (infected); Chance Claybourne, Scientist; Unnamed Character, Boy, Twin, Missing Person; Unnamed Character, Missing Person, Girl, Twin
Time period(s): 21st century; 2010s
Locale(s): Charleston, South Carolina

Summary: This is the fourth book of the Virals series, which revolves around Tory Brennan, the niece of forensic expert Temperance Brennan from Kathy Reichs's Bones series. Tory and her fellow classmates are dealing with the special powers they gained after a wildlife attack infected them with a virus. Now they call themselves the Virals, and they work to solve crimes and find out exactly what happened on that fateful night. Two of Tory's schoolmates, who are twins, disappear, and Tory enlists the Virals to help figure out what happened. Meanwhile, their supernatural powers become stronger, and scientist Chance is very close to uncovering the truth about the group of teens. As it becomes more and more difficult for the Virals to appear to be normal teenagers, they continue to search for the person who abducted the twins.

Other books by the same author:
Terminal, 2015
Bones of the Lost, 2014
Bones Are Forever, 2013
Swipe, 2013
Virals, 2011

Other books you might like:
George R.R. Martin, *Deuces Down*, 2002
John J. Miller, *Death Draws Five*, 2006
James Patterson, *The Final Warning*, 2008
Veronica Roth, *Allegiant*, 2013
John C. Wright, *Fugitives of Chaos*, 2006

1187

KATHY REICHS
BRENDAN REICHS, Co-Author

Terminal

(New York: G.P. Putnam's Sons Books for Young Readers, 2015)

Series: Virals Series. Book 5
Story type: Series; Young Adult
Subject(s): Science fiction; Diseases; Adventure
Major character(s): Tory Brennan, Girl (infected), Teenager, Leader (Morris Island gang); Chance Clayborne, Boy (infected), Teenager, Enemy (of Tory)
Time period(s): 21st century; 2010s
Locale(s): Charleston, South Carolina

Summary: Tory Brennan and her friends were just a bunch of science nerds who hung out on Morris Island in Charleston harbor until an encounter with a dog changed their lives. The dog was a scientific test subject, and Tory and her friends became infected with its virus, which gave them lupine abilities. The Virals have been content to live on Morris Island, but in this fifth and final novel in the series, a less benevolent pack of Virals threatens Tory's group. These Virals are the result of a different strain of the virus, which was engineered by Chance Claybourne. Chance has become infected, too, and he is working with his pack to take control of Charleston. The new pack of Virals isn't the only threat Tory faces, however. A government agency wants to capture all of the infected teenagers to discover the source of their wolf-like qualities.

Other books by the same author:
Exposure, 2015
Bones of the Lost, 2014
Bones Are Forever, 2013
Swipe, 2013
Virals, 2011

Other books you might like:
George R.R. Martin, *Lowball: A Wild Cards Novel*, 2014
John J. Miller, *Death Draws Five*, 2006
James Patterson, *Maximum Ride: The Angel Experiment*, 2005
Veronica Roth, *Divergent*, 2011
John C. Wright, *Orphans of Chaos*, 2005

1188

ALASTAIR REYNOLDS

Slow Bullets

(San Francisco, California: Tachyon Publications, 2015)

Story type: Space Opera
Subject(s): Wars; Space colonies; Spacetime
Major character(s): Scurelya "Scur" Timsuk Shunde, Prisoner, Traveler; Orvin, Military Personnel
Time period(s): Indeterminate
Locale(s): Spaceship

Summary: When Scur was first taken into captivity, she was sure her life was over. The person who took her left her behind in a decimated shelter, but she suddenly she finds herself on the deck of a spaceship that is taking convicts to prison. The felons aboard the ship are all soldiers who have been fighting in a war that encompasses virtually the entire galaxy, and includes enemies and colleagues alike. The circumstances among the prisoners are dire, however, because each one was to be placed in a state of suspended animation, and now they are all regaining consciousness. Even worse, they have no knowledge of who they are, because their ability to recollect is encapsulated in bullets intended to be shot into them once their captors feel they are ready. Scur has been injected with a special bullet by her enemy. She hurries to solve the crisis, but she is in danger as well. One of her adversaries is on the spaceship, too, and that enemy is quickly regaining his memory.

Other books by the same author:
On the Steel Breeze, 2014
Harvest of Time, 2013
Blue Remembered Earth, 2012
Deep Navigation, 2010
House of Suns, 2008

Other books you might like:
Roger MacBride Allen, *The Ocean of Years*, 2002
Iain M. Banks, *Surface Detail*, 2010
Elizabeth Bear, *Scardown*, 2005
Brian Herbert, *Hellhole*, 2013
Neal Stephenson, *Seveneves*, 2015
Vernor Vinge, *The Children of the Sky*, 2011

1189

LOREN RHOADS

The Dangerous Type

(San Francisco, California: Night Shade Books, 2015)

Series: In the Wake of the Templars Series. Book 1
Story type: Military; Revenge
Subject(s): Assassination; Wars; Science fiction
Major character(s): Reana, Assassin (hunting Thallian), Lover (of Gaven), Sister (adoptive, of Ariel); Thallian, Criminal (war criminal, imprisoned Reana); Ariel, Sister (Adopted, of Reana); Gaven, Lover (former, of both Reana and Ariel)
Time period(s): Indeterminate Future
Locale(s): Outer Space

Summary: Twenty years ago, one the most dangerous assassins to ever live was imprisoned. But now, Reana is free again and she has one thing on her mind: vengeance. She's after Thallian, the man who captured, enslaved, and forced her to spend the last 20 years in the depths of a tomb. Thallian has already been on the run for 15 years, hunted for the part he and his family played in the extermination of the Templars. At the same time, Reana's adopted sister, Ariel, has spent years trying to ignore the truth about her relationship with Gaven, who loved and mourned the loss of Reana. This is the first book in the series In the Wake of the Templars by Loren Rhoads.

Other books by the same author:
As Above So Below, 2014
Wish You Were Here, 2013
Ashes & Rust, 2012

Other books you might like:
Poul Anderson, *Sir Dominic Flandry: The Last Knight of Terra*, 2010
Iain M. Banks, *Matter*, 2008
C.J. Cherryh, *Deceiver*, 2010
Ann Leckie, *Ancillary Justice*, 2013
Dan Simmons, *Endymion*, 1995

1190

JOHN RINGO

Strands of Sorrow

(Wake Forest, North Carolina: Baen, 2015)

Series: Black Tide Rising Series. Book 4
Story type: Military; Series
Subject(s): Zombies; Apocalypse; Family
Major character(s): Steve Smith, Survivor, Military Personnel (commander), Father (of Sophia and Faith), Spouse (of Stacey); Sophia Smith, Daughter (of Steve and Stacey), Sister (of Faith), Survivor, Teenager, Military Personnel (US Navy); Faith Smith, Military Personnel (US Marine), 16-Year-Old, Daughter (of Steve and Stacey), Sister (of Sophia), Survivor, Teenager; Stacey Smith, Spouse (of Steve), Mother (of Sophia and Faith), Survivor
Time period(s): 21st century; 2010s
Locale(s): At Sea; United States

Summary: A zombie plague epidemic has caused the downfall of modern civilization, and survivors are battling for life. The Wolf Squadron, led by Steve Smith, is composed of such survivors and the remnants of the US military. As survivors have honed their battle and survival skills, the Wolf Squadron has grown and covers vast areas of the Atlantic Ocean. Smith is certain that with careful planning, the squadron can retake territory from the infected zombies, and he is determined to reclaim the United States. He commands the rescue forces, which include his daughters, Sophia and Faith. The teens are ruthless zombie hunters who have been battle tested. Wolf Squadron strategically takes and holds East Coast bases and moves north as it fights for the symbolic heart of the nation—Washington, D.C. This is the fourth novel and conclusion of the Black Tide Rising series.

Other books by the same author:
Under a Graveyard Sky, 2013
Citadel, 2011
The Hot Gate, 2011
Eye of the Storm, 2009
Gust Front, 2001

Other books you might like:
Jeff Carlson, *Plague Year*, 2007
Nick Cutter, *The Deep*, 2015
Frank Herbert, *The White Plague*, 1982
Sandra Newman, *The Country of Ice Cream Star*, 2014
Weston Ochse, *Blood Ocean*, 2012
Sheri S. Tepper, *Grass*, 1989

1191

KIM STANLEY ROBINSON

Aurora

(New York: Hachette, 2015)

Story type: Generation Starship
Subject(s): Space flight; Space colonies; Alternative worlds
Major character(s): Freya, Daughter (of Devi), Teenager; Devi, Mother (of Freya), Engineer
Time period(s): Indeterminate Future
Locale(s): Aurora, Planet—Imaginary; Spaceship

Summary: After nearly two centuries of flight, a generation starship finally begins the final leg of its journey to the virgin planet Aurora. Freya has lived aboard the spaceship for her entire life, just like her mother, Devi, who is in charge of managing the ship's ecosystem. As the ship approaches the star Tau Ceti, its environmental safeguards begin to malfunction, and Devi grapples with bringing those safeguards back on line. Meanwhile, the colony of more than 2,000 people aboard the ship are becoming restless, and their cultural differences become clear. As Freya comes of age on the starship, she recognizes these differences, and notices how difficult extended life in an artificial environment really is. No one on the starship has ever known what it is like to live on terra firma. They begin to wonder if their ancestors should have remained on Earth after all.

Other books by the same author:
2312, 2012
Galileo's Dream, 2010
Sixty Days and Counting, 2007
The Years of Rice and Salt, 2002
The Wild Shore, 1984

Other books you might like:
Greg Bear, *Eon*, 1985
Ben Bova, *New Earth*, 2013
James S.A. Corey, *Nemesis Games*, 2015
Robert A. Heinlein, *Methuselah's Children*, 1958
Frederik Pohl, *Gateway*, 1977
Neal Stephenson, *Seveneves*, 2015

1192

GREGG ROSENBLUM

City 1

(New York: HarperTeen, 2015)

Series: Revolution 19 Series. Book 3
Story type: Dystopian; Series
Subject(s): Dystopias; Robots; Family relations
Major character(s): Nick, Teenager, Brother (of Kevin and Cass), Rebel; Kevin, Teenager, Brother (of Nick and Cass), Rebel; Cass, Teenager, Sister (of Nick and Kevin), Rebel; General Clay, Rebel (leader)
Time period(s): 21st century; 2070s
Locale(s): United States

Summary: The final installment in the Revolution 19 trilogy by Gregg Rosenblum reunites siblings Nick, Kevin, and Cass as they fight to save their parents and the rest of the world. When the robots revolted against their human commanders in 2051, they took control of the world's cities. Since then, humans have been making plans to take their bot-controlled urban centers back. When Nick, Kevin, and Cass reunite at a rebel camp, they vow to stick together and to rescue their parents, who were kidnapped during a bot attack. Rebel army leader General Clay, however, has an altogether different plan. She and her insurgent army are out to destroy all the robots and the humans they've brainwashed, who the rebels believe have become just as dangerous as the robots. With their parents' lives now in greater danger, Nick, Kevin, and Cass must decide where their loyalties lie. Will fighting alongside the rebels prove too great a sacrifice?

Other books by the same author:
Fugitive X, 2014
Revolution 19, 2013

Other books you might like:
Michael Crichton, *Westworld*, 1974
H.M. Hoover, *Orvis*, 1987
Jerry Oltion, *Humanity*, 1990
Mickey Zucker Reichert, *Isaac Asimov's I, Robot: To Obey*, 2013
Mark Stay, *Robot Overlords*, 2015
Daniel H. Wilson, *Robopocalypse*, 2010

1193

STEPHANIE SAULTER

Binary

(London, United Kingdom: Quercus, 2015)

Series: Revolution Series. Book 2
Story type: Genetic Manipulation; Series
Subject(s): Science fiction; Genetic research; Genetic engineering
Major character(s): Zavcka Klist, Woman (Former enforcer for Bel'Natur); Aryel Morningstar, Researcher; Eli Walker, Doctor; Herran, Expert (Digital savant)
Time period(s): Indeterminate Future
Locale(s): Earth

Summary: Aryel Morningstar and Dr. Eli Walker are suspicious. Zavcka Klist is suddenly open and free with all the information about Bel-Natur's gemtech research. Neither Aryel nor Eli can believe the former gemtech enforcer could have done the complete turnaround Klist claims to have made. But they need her expertise, so they strike an agreement: Klist will help them, and their colleague, Herran, will help with Klist's pet project on the technology that nearly destroyed mankind. The arrangement is made and the truce is uneasy, but the research is moving along, at least until someone steals the genestock they are working with. Solving the mystery of who took it will reveal deep secrets about Bel'Natur, Klist, and even Aryel. This is the second book in the (R)Evolution series by Stephanie Saulter.

Other books by the same author:
Gemsigns, 2014

Other books you might like:
Elizabeth Bear, *Hammered*, 2005
M.M. Buckner, *Neurolink*, 2004
Anne Harris, *Accidental Creatures*, 1998
Lee Killough, *Spider Play*, 1986
Nancy Kress, *Oaths and Miracles*, 1996

1194

JOEL SHEPHERD

Originator

(Amherst, New York: Pyr, 2015)

Series: Cassandra Kresnov Series. Book 6
Story type: Child-in-Peril; Futuristic
Subject(s): Space colonies; Wars; Technology
Major character(s): Cassandra "Sandy" Kresnov, Android, Military Personnel, Mother (of Kiril, adopted); Kiril, Human, Adoptee (of Sandy); Renaldo Takewashi, Scientist, Inventor
Time period(s): Indeterminate Future
Locale(s): Outer Space

Summary: In the sixth Cassandra Kresnov science-fiction novel, android soldier Sandy finds herself racing to prevent all-out war between the Federation and the League while at the same time keeping her adopted son, Kiril, out of harm's way. War between the two powers would have devastating effects across the galaxy, and it is the mission of Sandy and her GI friends to stop the conflict before it escalates any further. When a League moon is destroyed and 250 thousand people are killed, Sandy discovers that the Federation troops responsible are under a technologically induced psychosis. The psychosis is a side-effect from ancient Talee technology and it is spreading among the human population. The Talee civilization was nearly destroyed from this disease and they are threatening to exterminate the humans to prevent a repeat of history. Renaldo Takewashi, the scientist who developed Sandy and the other GIs, reveals that he has implanted a new technology into Kiril's brain that will prevent the psychosis. Now multiple parties are after Kiril and the device.

Other books by the same author:
Operation Shield, 2014
23 Years on Fire, 2013
Haven, 2011
Petrodor, 2010
Sasha, 2009

Other books you might like:
Neal Asher, *Dark Intelligence*, 2015
W.C. Bauers, *Unbreakable*, 2015
Lois McMaster Bujold, *Captain Vorpatril's Alliance*, 2012
Alan Dean Foster, *Dirge*, 2000
John Meaney, *To Hold Infinity*, 2006
Karen Traviss, *Anvil Gate*, 2010
S.L. Viehl, *Afterburn*, 2005

1195

MIKE SHEPHERD

Survivor

(New York: Ace Books, 2015)

Series: Vicky Peterwald Series. Book 2
Story type: Series; Space Opera
Subject(s): Space colonies; Futuristic society; Women
Major character(s): Vicky Peterwald, Heir, Military Personnel (Lieutenant)
Time period(s): Indeterminate Future
Locale(s): Outer Space

Summary: Grand Duchess and heiress of the Imperial family Vicky Peterwald is now a naval lieutenant, determined to get revenge for the death of her brother. As a high-ranking military and political figure, she is working to assist and rebuild the planets that were casualties of the war—but her own family, the Peterwald Empire, is not yet ready to lay down arms and accept a peaceful existence with the revolutionaries. It is up to Vicky to somehow unite the dueling parties to prevent the current crisis from escalating any further across the galaxy. This is the second novel in the Vicky Peterwald science fiction series, which is by Mike Shepherd and set in the Kris Longknife universe.

Other books by the same author:
Kris Longknife: Tenacious, 2014
To Do or Die, 2014
Kris Longknife: Defender, 2013

Kris Longknife: Daring, 2011
Kris Longknife: Deserter, 2005

Other books you might like:
Jack Campbell, *The Lost Fleet: Beyond the Frontier: Dreadnaught*, 2011
Richard T. Chizmar, *The Earth Strikes Back*, 1994
David Drake, *The Sea Without a Shore*, 2014
Jerry Pournelle, *Fires of Freedom*, 2009
Mike Resnick, *Starship: Flagship*, 2009

1196

NEAL SHUSTERMAN
ERIC ELFMAN, Co-Author

Edison's Alley

(Los Angeles: Disney Hyperion, 2015)

Series: Accelerati Trilogy. Book 2
Story type: Young Readers
Subject(s): Inventors; Inventions; Energy conservation
Major character(s): Nick, 14-Year-Old
Time period(s): 21st century; 2010s
Locale(s): Colorado Springs, Colorado

Summary: In this second book in the Accelerati Trilogy by Neal Shusterman and Eric Elfman, 14-year-old Nick and his friends race against the clock to recover valuable relics that once belonged to inventor Nikola Tesla. When Nick discovers that the antique contraption found in his attic not only belonged to a famous inventor but also that pieces of it were recently sold during a garage sale, he's determined to locate the lost parts and complete Tesla's vision for his Far Range Energy Emitter. Once finished, the device will generate free energy and solve the world's resource problems. A sinister group of physicists known as the Accelerati are on the heels of Nick and his friends. The Accelerati will risk anything to gain control of Tesla's missing relics and assume power over the world's energy crisis. Nick's not willing to let any of the objects fall into the hands of the Accelerati, but can his friends be trusted?

Other books by the same author:
Tesla's Attic, 2014
Shattered Sky, 2002
Thief of Souls, 1999
The Dark Side of Nowhere, 1997
Scorpion Shards, 1995

Other books you might like:
Patrick Carman, *Trackers*, 2010
D.J. MacHale, *Storm*, 2014
Roland Smith, *Beneath*, 2015
Tui T. Sutherland, *Wings of Fire Book Six: Moon Rising*, 2014

1197

KRISTEN SIMMONS

The Glass Arrow

(New York: Tor Teen, 2015)

Story type: Dystopian; Young Adult
Subject(s): Dystopias; Women; Social class

Major character(s): Aya, Girl, Teenager; Kiran, Boy, Handicapped (mute); Mr. Ryker, Government Official (mayor), Father (of Amir); Amir Ryker, Boy, Son (of Mr. Ryker)
Time period(s): Indeterminate Future
Locale(s): Glasscaster, Fictional Location

Summary: In a dystopian society in which women are sold as property, one girl—teenage Aya—has managed to live freely in the mountains surrounding the city of Glasscaster. Although she has been separated from her family, Aya has managed to survive on wild foods and escape the fate of the young women in the city who are purchased as breeders. But Aya's good fortune ends when she is captured by a man who is hunting in the forest. Aya is brought to Glasscaster, where she is prepared for auction. Her life in the wild has made her strong and healthy, and she is expected to fetch a high price. She finds an ally in a mute boy who was part of the hunting party that captured her. Aya does everything she can to delay her auction, but she is finally purchased by Mayor Ryker. However, Aya is surprised when she learns that she was not purchased for the mayor, but for another member of the Ryker household.

Other books by the same author:
Breaking Point, 2014
Three, 2014
Article 5, 2012

Other books you might like:
Ben Bova, *Escape*, 1970
Paul Collins, *The Earthborn*, 2003
James Dashner, *The Maze Runner*, 2009
Tom Isbell, *The Prey*, 2015
Sophia McDougall, *Mars Evacuees*, 2015
Veronica Roth, *Divergent Trilogy*, 2011

1198

ALAN SMALE

A Clash of Eagles

(Concord, California: Panverse Two/Panverse Publishing, 2010)

Story type: Alternate History
Subject(s): Roman Empire, 30 BC-476 AD; History; Native Americans
Major character(s): Gaius Marcellinus, Leader (33rd legion)
Time period(s): Indeterminate Past

Summary: In the science fiction novella *A Clash of Eagles*, Alan Smale presents an alternative history of North America in which the continent has been invaded not by Vikings but by forces of the Roman Empire. Gaius Marcellinus has brought his 33rd Legion to the shores of the distant continent in search of gold. In the harsh environment of North America, the usually invincible Roman troops encounter unforeseen challenges—not the least of which is the tenacious native population. As Marcellinus attempts to rally his men against North America's human and natural threats, he must also deal with treachery in his own ranks.

Awards the book has won:
Sidewise Awards for Alternate History: Short Form, 2011

Other books you might like:
Kate Atkinson, *Life After Life*, 2013
Robert Conroy, *1882: Custer in Chains*, 2015
David Drake, *Ranks of Bronze*, 1986
Eric Flint, *1636: The Cardinal Virtues*, 2015
Robert Harris, *Fatherland*, 1992
Stephen King, *11/22/1963*, 2011
Kirk Mitchell, *Cry Republic*, 1989
Cherie Priest, *Boneshaker*, 2009
Kim Stanley Robinson, *The Years of Rice and Salt*, 2002
Robert Silverberg, *Roma Eterna*, 2003
Harry Turtledove, *Joe Steele*, 2015
Harry Turtledove, *Opening Atlantis*, 2007

1199

ROLAND SMITH

Beneath

(New York: Scholastic, 2015)

Subject(s): Brothers; Friendship; Runaways
Major character(s): Coop O'Toole, Brother (older, of Pat), Teenager, Runaway, 18-Year-Old; Pat O'Toole, 13-Year-Old, Wealthy, Brother (younger, of Coop)
Time period(s): 21st century; 2010s
Locale(s): Washington, District of Columbia; New York, New York

Summary: Brothers Pat and Coop O'Toole live in comfort in Washington, D.C. Coop isn't an ordinary teenager—he shuns technology and has no friends. He is truly happy exploring underground, however, and he and his brother dig hundreds of crisscrossing tunnels under their neighborhood. Pat doesn't understand the purpose, but he is happy to help his big brother. After the project causes a gas explosion and nearly kills Pat, the boys must face the FBI. Coop flees and disappears. A year later, Pat receives a mysterious package. Inside is a tape recording from Coop, along with instructions to record a response and mail it to a post office box in New York City. The brothers communicate for at time, until the recorder fails to come back. Pat heads to New York City and finds Coop living underground in a commune. Pat has to earn the right to enter even the outskirts of the secret community that calls itself the Pod.

Other books by the same author:
Mutation, 2014
Chupacabra, 2013
Tentacles, 2009
The Cryptid Hunters, 2004
Sasquatch, 1998

Other books you might like:
Paul Cook, *Duende Meadow*, 1985
Jeff Long, *The Descent*, 1999
Viido Polikarpus, *Down Town*, 1985
James Rollins, *Subterranean*, 1999

Neal Shusterman, *Edison's Alley*, 2015
John Wyndham, *The Secret People*, 1935

1200

MARK STAY

Robot Overlords

(London: Gollancz, 2015)

Story type: Robot Fiction
Subject(s): Robots; Wars; Missing persons
Major character(s): Sean Flynn, Rebel, Son (of fighter pilot)
Time period(s): Indeterminate Future
Locale(s): England

Summary: Earth has been taken over by giant robots from another planet. It's been three years since the battles, and the robots have established one non-negotiable rule for the humans—stay in your homes or be killed. But Sean Flynn is done listening to the robot overlords. He is certain that his fighter pilot father, who has not been seen since the war began, is still alive. When he and his friends identify a way to evade the robots, he knows this is his chance—and he'll do whatever it takes to find his father and fight to reclaim the planet. This science fiction novel by Mark Stay is a companion book to the British film *Robot Overlords*.

Other books you might like:
Scott Ciencin, *Hard Wired*, 2003
Peter David, *Transformers Dark of the Moon*, 2011
Alan Dean Foster, *Transformers: Revenge of the Fallen*, 2009
Gregg Rosenblum, *City 1*, 2015
Daniel H. Wilson, *Robopocalypse*, 2010

1201

JONATHAN STRAHAN

The Best Science Fiction and Fantasy of the Year: Volume Nine

(Oxford, United Kingdom: Solaris, 2015)

Series: Best Science Fiction and Fantasy of the Year Series. Book 9
Story type: Collection; Fantasy
Subject(s): Adventure; Fantasy; Futuristic society

Summary: In this ninth book featuring the works of science fiction and fantasy giants of the previous decade, award-winning editor Jonathan Strahan has compiled the best works of 2014. The plot lines of these stories run the gamut from time travel to far off lands and future times, as well as unbelievable adventures, unimaginable wonders, and other exciting tales. Works include "Go Wild" by Nicola Griffith, "Covenant" by Elizabeth Bear, "Tawny Petticoats" by Michael Swanwick, "Shay Corsham Worsted" by Garth Nix, "Collateral" by Peter Watts, and many others.

Other books by the same author:
Cyberpunk, 2012

Edge of Infinity, 2012
Eclipse Four, 2011
Engineering Infinity, 2011
Best Short Novels 2006, 2006

Other books you might like:
Paolo Bacigalupi, *Pump Six and Other Stories*, 2008
Stephen Baxter, *Phase Space*, 2002
Ted Chiang, *Stories of Your Life and Others*, 2002
Cory Doctorow, *Overclocked*, 2007
Jeffrey Ford, *The Empire of Ice Cream*, 2006

1202

TRAVIS S. TAYLOR

Trail of Evil

(Riverdale, New York: Baen, 2015)

Series: Tau Ceti Agenda Series. Book 4
Story type: Futuristic; Series
Subject(s): Futuristic society; Wars; Space colonies
Major character(s): Alexander Moore, Military Personnel
Time period(s): Indeterminate Future
Locale(s): Outer Space

Summary: Hundreds of years in the future, humanity has been forced to confront terrorists of all kinds in outer space, from the Martian Separatist Wars and leader El Ahmi to brutally violent artificial intelligence. For General Alexander Moore, it's time to launch the new *Sienna Madira*, which is packed with the most advanced weaponry and technology possible. It also carries dozens of highly trained Marines. The mission is to locate and destroy any weaponry platforms that were constructed by the artificial intelligence called Copernicus, which set off a civil war across the solar system. But what the crew of the *Sienna Madira* finds is something much worse—a lingering artificial intelligence that is more violent and more intelligent than Copernicus, and intends to eliminate humankind permanently. The battle will be more difficult than anything they have ever faced. This novel by Travis S. Taylor is the fourth in the Tau Ceti Agenda series.

Other books by the same author:
One Good Soldier, 2009
The Tau Ceti Agenda, 2008
One Day on Mars, 2007
The Quantum Connection, 2005
Warp Speed, 2004

Other books you might like:
Kevin J. Anderson, *Of Fire and Night*, 2006
Iain M. Banks, *The Hydrogen Sonata*, 2012
James S.A. Corey, *Leviathan Wakes*, 2011
Peter F. Hamilton, *Pandora's Star*, 2004
Alastair Reynolds, *The Prefect*, 2007

Science Fiction

1203

HARRY TURTLEDOVE

Joe Steele

(New York: Roc, 2015)

Story type: Alternate History
Subject(s): History; Great Depression, 1929-1934; Presidents (Government)
Major character(s): Franklin D. Roosevelt, Historical Figure, Government Official (New York governor), Political Figure (presidential candidate), Accident Victim; Joe Steele, Government Official (vice-presidential candidate)
Time period(s): 20th century; 1930s
Locale(s): United States

Summary: The United States is floundering in the aftermath of the 1929 stock market crash, and the country wants to replace Herbert Hoover with a new president. New York governor Franklin D. Roosevelt seems destined to occupy the Oval Office, but he is killed in a fire before the election. Roosevelt's running mate Joe Steele, a son of Russian immigrants, takes top billing on the ballot instead. He wins the election easily, thanks to his common-man appeal. As America's citizens hoped, Steele is a strong leader with no-nonsense ideas about getting the nation back on its feet. But gradually, the true nature of Steele's vision comes to light. Work camps are established to house those who oppose the government's ever-increasing reach, and the press is kept oddly quiet. Most Americans enjoy their new economy and leadership, but some detect the trouble that's brewing in Germany and Russia.

Other books by the same author:
Things Fall Apart, 2013
Two Fronts, 2013
The United States of Atlantis, 2008
The Grapple, 2006
Gunpowder Empire, 2003

Other books you might like:
Mona Clee, *Branch Point*, 1996
Bradley Denton, *Wrack and Roll*, 1986
Paul Di Filippo, *Lost Pages*, 1998
Kathleen Ann Goonan, *This Shared Dream*, 2011
Sinclair Lewis, *It Can't Happen Here*, 1935
Alan Smale, *A Clash of Eagles*, 2010

1204

JACK VANCE
TERRY DOWLING, Co-Editor
JONATHAN STRAHAN, Co-Editor

Grand Crusades

(Burton, Michigan: Subterranean Press, 2015)

Series: Early Jack Vance Series. Book 5
Story type: Collection; Series
Subject(s): Science fiction; Fantasy; Adventurers

Summary: This anthology is the fifth installment from the Early Jack Vance series. In this compendium, editors Terry Dowling and Jonathan Strahan have compiled five of science fiction and fantasy author Jack Vance's novels and novellas. The compilation includes *The Rapparee*, which was originally published in 1953 as *The Five Gold Bands* by *Startling Stories* magazine. In this novel, scoundrel Paddy Blackthorn attempts to thwart the laws of interplanetary travel by stealing five gold rings that contain the information he needs for space flight. Other works in this collection include *Crusade to Maxus*, in which a group of oppressed people plot a revolution against their totalitarian rulers, and *Space Opera*, a comedic story which plays upon the space opera trope by sending an extraterrestrial opera company on a tour of the galaxy. The book also contains *Gold and Iron*, which was originally published in 1958 as *Slaves of the Klau*, and *The Houses of Iszm*, which was originally published as a novella in 1954 and in 1964 was re-released as a novel.

Other books by the same author:
Dream Castles, 2012
Lurulu, 2004
Alastor, 2002
Coup de Grace and Other Stories, 2002
Lost Moons, 1982

Other books you might like:
Brian W. Aldiss, *Cultural Breaks*, 2005
James Blish, *A Dusk of Idols and Other Stories*, 1996
Henry Kuttner, *Thunder in the Void*, 2012
Murray Leinster, *A Logic Named Joe*, 2005
Robert Silverberg, *Trips: 1972-1973*, 2009

1205

DAVID WALTON

Superposition

(Amherst, New York: Prometheus Books, 2015)

Story type: Alternate World; Mystery
Subject(s): Physics; Science fiction; Murder
Major character(s): Jacob Kelley, Crime Suspect (accused murderer of Brian), Father (of Alessandra), Friend (of Brian); Brian Vanderhall, Friend (of Jacob), Crime Victim (murdered in one reality); Alessandra Kelley, Daughter (of Jacob)
Locale(s): Swarthmore, Pennsylvania

Summary: Jacob Kelley finds himself on trial for murder after his friend, Brian, is found dead just after a visit to Jacob. The friend had been acting strangely during his visit and was very worked up about some sort of alien presence. The mystery deepens when Jacob realizes he's simultaneously occupying two worlds: the one in which he's on trial for his friend's murder, and one in which Brian is still alive. Both worlds face a threat from an alien technology that allows matter—and bullets—to turn corners. Suddenly nothing seems to follow the usual rules of space, time, and matter. With the help of his daughter, Alessandra, Jacob will have to unravel the quantum mystery and find his way to the right reality.

Other books by the same author:
Quintessential, 2013
Terminal Mind, 2008

Other books you might like:
Steve Alten, *Goliath*, 2002
Guy Haley, *Omega Point*, 2012
Simon Ings, *Wolves*, 2014
David Marusek, *Mind Over Ship*, 2009
John Scalzi, *The Android's Dream*, 2006

`1206`

RIE WARREN

Under His Guard

(New York: Grand Central Publishing, 2015)

Series: Don't Tell Series. Book 3
Story type: Alternate World; Dystopian
Subject(s): Alternative worlds; Wars; Science fiction
Major character(s): Darke, Rebel, Homosexual, Lover (of Leon); Leon Cheramie, Homosexual, Lover (of Darke)
Time period(s): 21st century; 2070s
Locale(s): Chitamauga Commune, Fictional Location

Summary: This is the third and final book in the Don't Tell series by Rie Warren. In the 2070s, in the aftermath of a devastating war in his dystopian world, rebel soldier Darke struggles with grief over the death of his lover early in the conflict. Though he tries to resist, he eventually gives in and seeks comfort in the arms of Leon Cheramie. Leon is handsome and provides what Darke needs to recover from his grief. Sorrow will return, however, when Leon finds out he has been infected with a deadly virus meant to wipe out Darke and the other rebels. The race to win the final battle of the war is on as the rebels and Darke seek a cure for the virus before Leon's infection becomes incurable. The lives of the rebels and Darke's new love hang in the balance.

Other books by the same author:
On Her Watch, 2014
Sugar Daddy, 2014
In His Command, 2013

Other books you might like:
Ann Aguirre, *Breakout*, 2015
Catherine Asaro, *Undercity*, 2014
Jayne Castle, *Canyons of Night*, 2011
Tanya Huff, *The Truth of Valor*, 2010
Linnea Sinclair, *Games of Command*, 2007

`1207`

STEVE WHITE

Soldiers Out of Time

(Wake Forest, North Carolina: Baen Books, 2015)

Series: Jason Thanou Time Travel Series. Book 5
Story type: Military; Series
Subject(s): Military life; Military science; Adventure
Major character(s): Jason Thanou, Agent (Temporal Regulatory Authority), Time Traveler
Time period(s): Multiple Time Periods
Locale(s): Earth

Summary: In the fifth book of author Steve White's Jason Thanou Time Travel series, special operations officer Thanou must once again defeat aliens that want to destroy all humans. The Transhumanist organization strikes again, and this time, they are even closer to realizing their ultimate goal of deleting humanity from the galaxy. The final result will be for humans to morph into otherworldly creatures, and the only person who stands in the way is Thanou. Yet to save the future of humanity, Thanou must delve deep into what came before the TRA took control of time itself. As he and the Transhumanists embark on a game of cat and mouse throughout time and space, Thanou soon learns the truth about what humans are capable of. Unfortunately, Earth's history includes plenty of violence and cruelty, and Thanou must make sure the Transhumanists don't use those parts of the past to carry out their evil deeds.

Other books by the same author:
Ghosts of Time, 2014
Pirates of the Timestream, 2013
Sunset of the Gods, 2013
Saint Anthony's Fire, 2008
The Prometheus Project, 2005

Other books you might like:
Poul Anderson, *Time Patrol*, 1983
James F. David, *Thunder of Time*, 2006
Harry Harrison, *A Rebel in Time*, 1983
Mike Moscoe, *First Dawn*, 1996
H. Beam Piper, *The Complete Paratime*, 2001

`1208`

MICHAEL Z. WILLIAMSON

A Long Time Until Now

(Wake Forest, North Carolina: Baen, 2015)

Series: Temporal Displacement Series. Book 1
Story type: Adventure; Series
Subject(s): Military life; Afghanistan Conflict, 2001-; Time travel
Major character(s): Sean Elliott, Military Personnel (1st lieutenant); Gina Alexander, Military Personnel, Photographer, Young Woman; Caswell, Young Woman, Military Personnel (USAF Security); Bob Barker, Military Personnel (staff sergeant); Armand Devereaux, Military Personnel (medic); Ramon Ortiz, Military Personnel (NCO), Veterinarian
Time period(s): 21st century; 2010s
Locale(s): Afghanistan; Paleolithic Asia

Summary: A ten-member unit is convoying across Afghanistan, when suddenly the troops in two vehicles find themselves alone—no radio contact, no GPS, no signs of the rest of the convoy. Eventually, then determine they are no longer in the twenty-first century at all. They have journeyed to the Paleolithic period with nothing but their personal gear and mobile equipment. While they struggle to make sense of what's happened to them, they find they aren't the only ones lost in time.

Science Fiction

A unit of Imperial Roman soldiers, Europeans from Neolithic times, and some peasants from East India have also been sucked into this time. Then two newcomers arrive—from the future. The two may hold the secret to how everyone can get back to their own times, but they may also have reasons of their own for not sharing. This is the first book in the planned Temporal Displacement series.

Other books by the same author:
Tour of Duty, 2013
Rogue, 2011
Do Unto Others, 2010
Contact with Chaos, 2009
The Weapon, 2005

Other books you might like:
L. Sprague de Camp, *Lest Darkness Fall*, 1941
William R. Forstchen, *Down to the Sea*, 2000
Leo Frankowski, *Conrad's Time Machine*, 2002
Roland Green, *Janissaries, Clan and Crown*, 1982
S. M. Stirling, *On the Oceans of Eternity*, 2000

1209

ROBERT CHARLES WILSON

The Affinities

(New York: Tor Books, 2015)

Story type: Dystopian
Subject(s): Dystopias; Social conditions; Futuristic society
Major character(s): Adam Fisk, Young Man
Time period(s): Indeterminate Future
Locale(s): Earth

Summary: The science of data analysis creates a dangerous new world order in this novel by Robert Charles Wilson. In the future, technological advancements allow detailed analysis of human behaviors. Through this analysis, 22 distinct Affinities are identified. The members of each Affinity share genetic and behavioral traits. Being part of an Affinity can be a great personal and social advantage, but getting in isn't easy. Adam Fisk wants desperately to make some changes in his life, so he takes a battery of tests to determine if he is suited to one of the Affinities. Fisk is accepted into Tau, and he is thrilled when, thanks to his new Affinity brethren, his problems are solved one by one. But Adam's initial relief gives way to fear as the dark side of the Affinities is revealed.

Other books by the same author:
Burning Paradise, 2013
Vortex, 2011
Axis, 2007
Blind Lake, 2003
Darwinia, 1998

Other books you might like:
Bruce Bethke, *Headcrash*, 1995
Pat Cadigan, *Dervish Is Digital*, 2000
Cory Doctorow, *Eastern Standard Tribe*, 2004
William Gibson, *Neuromancer*, 1984
Jamil Nasir, *The Higher Space*, 1996

1210

JOHN C. WRIGHT

The Architect of Aeons

(New York: Tom Doherty Associates, 2015)

Series: Count to the Eschaton Sequence Series. Book 4
Story type: Series; Space Opera
Subject(s): Immortality; Futuristic society; Wars
Major character(s): Menalus Montrose, Spaceman; Ximen "Blackie" del Azarchel, Spaceman; Rania, Alien
Time period(s): 109th century; 11040s (11049)
Locale(s): Outer Space; Planet—Imaginary

Summary: In the fourth installment of author John C. Wright's Count to the Eschaton Sequence series, bitter rivals Ximen "Blackie" del Azarchel and Menalus Montrose have finally not only reached a compromise, but have also embarked on a brand new venture together. Earth is gone, and now it is up to them to work against the barbaric interlopers from the Hyades to preserve humankind. Neither Menalus nor Blackie trusts the other man, but they both know that they are equally motivated by two things: the continuation of the species, and their mutual adoration of Rania. Neither is sure that Rania will ever return to their lives, anyway, but as long as they work together, they increase their chances of seeing her again. Unfortunately, Rania also may be what leads to their plan's undoing, and now they must both reassess what they need to do to keep their plan intact.

Other books by the same author:
The Judge of Ages, 2014
The Hermetic Millennia, 2012
Count to a Trillion, 2011
The Null A Continuum, 2008
The Phoenix Exultant, 2003

Other books you might like:
Neal Asher, *Brass Man*, 2005
Iain M. Banks, *The Algebraist*, 2004
Gregory Benford, *Furious Gulf*, 1994
Peter F. Hamilton, *The Evolutionary Void*, 2010
Alastair Reynolds, *Revelation Space*, 2000

1211

TIMOTHY ZAHN

Cobra Outlaw

(Riverdale, New York: Baen, 2015)

Series: Cobra Rebellion Series. Book 2
Story type: Adventure; Series
Subject(s): Space colonies; Adventure; Extraterrestrial life
Major character(s): Paul Broom, Warrior (Cobra), Prisoner; Santeros, Agent (for Dominion of Man), Enemy (of Troft); Troft, Alien, Enemy (of Dominion of Man); Lorne Broom, Warrior (Cobra), Rebel; Jody Broom, Warrior (Cobra), Rebel
Time period(s): Indeterminate Future
Locale(s): Aventine, Planet—Imaginary

Summary: Hugo Award-winner and best-selling author Timothy Zahn delivers the second installment in his

Cobra Rebellion series. Cobra warriors are not typical human warriors. They are technologically enhanced humans who house hidden weapons of war and are designed for combat against relentless aliens and evil humans. Once again, the Cobras are facing conflict from within their own ranks. On his home planet of Aventine, Cobra warrior Paul Broom is held prisoner by the Dominion of Man's evil operative, Commodore Santeros. Paul is in danger of having his memories accessed by the Dominion MindsEye to locate the planet Qasamaa, the home of advanced military hardware that will give Dominion of Man an advantage in the impending war with alien Troft. Meanwhile, as Dominion of Man and Troft head toward an interstellar war, outlaw Cobra warriors Lorne and Jody Broom lead a rebellion against the cruel schemes of Dominion.

Other books by the same author:
Cobra Gamble, 2012
Judgment at Proteu, 2012
The Third Lynx, 2007
Night Train to Rigel, 2005
The Last Command, 1993

Other books you might like:
Lois McMaster Bujold, *Komarr*, 1998
Jack Campbell, *Imperfect Sword*, 2014
Ian Douglas, *Singularity*, 2012
David Drake, *In the Stormy Red Sky*, 2009
R.M. Meluch, *The Ninth Circle: A Novel of the U.S.S. Merrimack*, 2011

Series Index

This index alphabetically lists series to which books featured in the entries belong. Beneath each series name, book titles are listed alphabetically with author names and genre codes. The genre codes are as follows: *c* Popular Fiction, *f* Fantasy, *h* Horror, *i* Inspirational, *m* Mystery, *r* Romance, *s* Science Fiction, and *t* Historical. Numbers refer to the entries that feature each title.

Time Period Index

This index chronologically lists the time settings in which the featured books take place. Main headings refer to a century; where no specific time is given, the headings MULTIPLE TIME PERIODS, INDETERMINATE PAST, INDETERMINATE FUTURE, and INDETERMINATE are used. The 15th through 27th centuries are broken down into decades when possible. (Note: 1800s, for example, refers to the first decade of the 19th century.) Featured titles are listed alphabetically beneath time headings, with author names and genre codes. The genre codes are as follows: *c* Popular Fiction, *f* Fantasy, *h* Horror, *i* Inspirational, *m* Mystery, *r* Romance, *s* Science Fiction, and *t* Historical. Numbers refer to the entries that feature each title.

Time Period Index

Geographic Index

This index provides access to all featured books by geographic settings—such as countries, continents, oceans, and planets. States and provinces are indicated for the United States and Canada. Also interfiled are headings for fictional place names (Spaceships, Imaginary Planets, etc.). Sections are further broken down by city or the specific name of the imaginary locale. Book titles are listed alphabetically under headings, with author names and genre codes. The genre codes are as follows: *c* Popular Fiction, *f* Fantasy, *h* Horror, *i* Inspirational, *m* Mystery, *r* Romance, *s* Science Fiction, and *t* Historical. Numbers refer to the entries that feature each title.

Tawnee Valley
His Small-Town Sweetheart - Amanda
 Berry *r* 914

Whinburg County
Keys of Heaven - Adina Senft *i* 455

Winston
Constant Fear - Daniel Palmer *m* 629

Wise
Until the Harvest - Sarah Loudin Thomas *i* 463

ALABAMA

Breaking Creed - Alex Kava *c* 779

Dauphin Island
Broken - Cynthia Eden *r* 959

Mobile
The Creole Princess - Beth White *i* 468
Revels Ending - Vic Kerry *h* 326

ALASKA

Cold Spell - Deb Vanasse *c* 879
Seekers: Return to the Wild: The Burning Horizon -
 Erin Hunter *f* 59
Untraceable - Elizabeth Goddard *i* 404

Keelut
Hold the Dark - William Giraldi *c* 749

Willow
Sabotaged - Dani Pettrey *i* 446

AMERICAN WEST

The Winter Family - Clifford Jackman *t* 184

ARIZONA

Dead Heat - Patricia Briggs *f* 18
There Will Be Lies - Nick Lake *f* 66

Morrow Creek
Morrow Creek Runaway - Lisa Plumley *r* 1049

Phoenix
Girl Before a Mirror - Liza Palmer *r* 1047
Spell Blind - David B. Coe *f* 25
The Water Knife - Paolo Bacigalupi *s* 1113

Scottsdale
Dark Chocolate Demise - Jenn McKinlay *m* 616

Sedona
Cold Betrayal - J.A. Jance *m* 584

Tombstone
Epitaph - Mary Doria Russell *t* 240

Tucson
Fear the Darkness - Becky Masterman *m* 610

ARKANSAS

Overcome - Lora Leigh *s* 1167

Farberville
Pride v. Prejudice - Joan Hess *m* 573

Mammoth
Mammoth Secrets - Ashley Elizabeth
 Ludwig *i* 431

Oak Meadows
Death by Baking - Cynthia Hickey *i* 418

CALIFORNIA

All the Wrong Places - Lisa Lieberman *t* 205
The Amado Women - Desiree Zamorano *c* 892
Ark Storm - Linda Davies *c* 727
Blue Labyrinth - Douglas Preston *c* 837
California - Edan Lepucki *c* 789
The Cat, the Devil, the Last Escape - Pat J.J.
 Murphy *m* 623
The Cinderella Murder - Mary Higgins
 Clark *c* 713
Cold Trail - Janet Dawson *m* 528
Every Breath You Take - Chris Marie Green *f* 39
The Evil Deeds We Do - Robert S.
 Levinson *m* 602
Finding Me - Kathryn Cushman *i* 388
The Heart Has Its Reasons - Maria
 Duenas *c* 736
The Replacements - David Putnam *m* 637
Solitude Creek - Jeffrey Deaver *m* 531
What a Woman Gets - Judi Fennell *r* 962
Wolf in White Van - John Darnielle *c* 726
*Your Fathers, Where Are They? And the Prophets,
 Do They Live Forever?* - Dave Eggers *c* 738

Benson
Convincing the Rancher - Claire
 McEwen *r* 1028

Big Sur
On the Edge - Edward St. Aubyn *c* 867

Blossom Valley
A Healthy Homicide - Staci McLaughlin *m* 617

Blue Arrow Lake
Make Me Lose Control - Christie
 Ridgway *r* 1057

Carmel-by-the-Sea
All the Old Knives - Olen Steinhauer *m* 666

Carmia
The Perfect Indulgence - Isabel Sharpe *r* 1078

Catalina Island
Fifty Mice - Daniel Pyne *c* 838

Cypress Cove
One Foot in the Grape - Carlene O'Neil *m* 627

Lake Tahoe
Kissing Under the Mistletoe - Bella Andre *r* 899

Long Beach
Drawing Fire - Janice Cantore *i* 376

Los Angeles
Ascendance: Dave vs. the Monsters - John
 Birmingham *f* 13
Best to Laugh - Lorna Landvik *c* 787
Beyond the Pale Motel - Francesca Lia
 Block *c* 704
The Burning Room - Michael Connelly *c* 718
Chasing Sunsets - Karen Kingsbury *i* 425
Circling the Runway - J.L. Abramo *m* 474
Deadeye - William C. Dietz *s* 1136
Driving the King - Ravi Howard *t* 180
Falling from Horses - Molly Gloss *t* 165
Fifty Mice - Daniel Pyne *c* 838
Ghost in the Guacamole - Sue Ann
 Jaffarian *m* 582
Grave on Grand Avenue - Naomi
 Hirahara *m* 575
Hollywood Lost - Ace Collins *t* 143
In Case of Emergency - Courtney Moreno *c* 811

Killer Gourmet - G.A. McKevett *m* 615
The Luminous Heart of Jonah S. - Gina B.
 Nahai *c* 814
Motive - Jonathan Kellerman *c* 780
Night Night, Sleep Tight - Hallie Ephron *m* 541
Pacific Fire - Greg van Eekhout *f* 118
The Promise - Robert Crais *c* 720
Redzone - William C. Dietz *s* 1137
The Russian Bride - Ed Kovacs *m* 595
Scent of Triumph - Jan Moran *t* 212
Shopaholic to the Stars - Sophie Kinsella *c* 784
Straight White Male - John Niven *c* 818
Together with You - Victoria Bylin *i* 370
A Touch of Stardust - Kate Alcott *t* 125
The Unleashing - Shelly Laurenston *f* 68
West of Sunset - Stewart O'Nan *c* 819

Monterey
Surrender - June Gray *r* 977

Pico Mundo
Saint Odd - Dean Koontz *c* 785

Portola Valley
The Children's Crusade - Ann Packer *t* 224

Sacramento
By Your Side - Candace Calvert *i* 373
The Fragile World - Paula Treick
 DeBoard *c* 730

San Bernardino
Trollhunters - Guillermo Del Toro *h* 292

San Diego
The Fold - Peter Clines *s* 1127
Wild - Jill Sorenson *r* 1085

San Francisco
The Abduction of Smith and Smith - Rashad
 Harrison *t* 174
Alanna - Kathleen Bittner Roth *r* 1063
Blood Ties - Nicholas Guild *m* 562
The Body Snatchers Affair - Marcia Muller *t* 218
The Fall - John T. Lescroart *m* 600
Grave Phantoms - Jenn Bennett *r* 912
Innocent Damage - Robert K. Lewis *m* 603
Shutter - Courtney Alameda *h* 277
We Are Pirates - Daniel Handler *c* 759

San Gabriel
The Night Belongs to Fireman - Jennifer
 Bernard *r* 913

Seaside Village
Heaven Help Heidi - Sally John *i* 422

Sonoma
Ripped from the Pages - Kate Carlisle *m* 512

Via Del Caballo
Kissed by a Cowboy - Pamela Britton *r* 926

Whiskey Creek
The Heart of Christmas - Brenda Novak *r* 1044
This Heart of Mine - Brenda Novak *r* 1043

COLORADO

Anderson Butte
It Had to Be Him - Tamra Baumann *r* 910

Aspen
One Mile Under - Andrew Gross *m* 561

Brewer's Falls
The Cowboy SEAL - Laura Marie Altom *r* 897

Night Life - David C. Taylor *t* 258
NYPD Red 3 - James Patterson *m* 632
Obsession in Death - J.D. Robb *c* 847
Panic in a Suitcase - Yelena Akhtiorskaya *c* 687
Phantom Angel - David Handler *m* 567
The Prince - Vito Bruschini *t* 135
The Shocking Secret of a Guest at the Wedding -
  Victoria Alexander *r* 895
Some Like It Hotter - Isabel Sharpe *r* 1079
Spark - John Twelve Hawks *c* 874
The Story Keeper - Lisa Wingate *t* 887
The Striver - Stephen Solomita *m* 662
The Teller - Jonathan Stone *m* 668
Tiffany Girl - Deeanne Gist *i* 403
Undertow - Michael Buckley *s* 1121
The Whites - Harry Brandt *m* 501
Within These Walls - Ania Ahlborn *h* 276
Woman with a Gun - Phillip Margolin *c* 797
You - Caroline Kepnes *c* 782
You're Not Much Use to Anyone - David
  Shapiro *c* 861

Point Hollow
Point Hollow - Rio Youers *h* 355

Poplar Hollow
When - Victoria Laurie *f* 70

Schenectady
Electric City - Elizabeth Rosner *t* 237

Utrecht
After Birth - Elisa Albert *c* 688

Wincourt
When We Fall - Emily Liebert *c* 791

NORTH CAROLINA

Coldbrook - Tim Lebbon *s* 1165
Mate Bond - Jennifer Ashley *f* 8
Saving Cecil - Lee Mims *c* 620
The Story Keeper - Lisa Wingate *c* 887

Abbotsville
Etta Mae's Worst Bad-Luck Day - Ann B.
  Ross *c* 848

Bascom
First Frost - Sarah Addison Allen *c* 689

Cameronville
Miles from Nowhere - Amy Clipston *i* 379

Cashiers
Where All Light Tends to Go - David Joy *m* 588

Chances Inlet
Back to Before - Tracy Solheim *r* 1084

Charlotte
Bones Never Lie - Kathy Reichs *c* 843
Speaking in Bones - Kathy Reichs *m* 640

Corolla
Neighing with Fire - Kathryn O'Sullivan *m* 628

New Bern
The Silent Sister - Diane Chamberlain *c* 710

Pine Haven
The Big Finish - James W. Hall *c* 758

Stone Temple
The Wonder of All Things - Jason Mott *c* 812

Wilmington
Return to Me - Kelly Moran *r* 1038

NORTH DAKOTA

Gathering Prey - John Sandford *m* 652

Blessing
A Harvest of Hope - Lauraine Snelling *i* 459

OHIO

Pocket Apocalypse - Seanan McGuire *f* 80

Barton Farms
The Final Reveille - Amanda Flower *m* 547

Cincinnati
Closer Than You Think - Karen Rose *r* 1062

Columbus
Slow Burn - Andrew Welsh-Huggins *m* 680

Holmes County
Miriam's Secret - Jerry S. Eicher *i* 396
Whiskers of the Lion - P.L. Gaus *m* 555

Middlefield
A Faith of Her Own - Kathleen Fuller *i* 400

Providence
As Gouda as Dead - Avery Aames *m* 473

Warfield
Holding Strong - Lori Foster *r* 965

OKLAHOMA

Miriam's Secret - Jerry S. Eicher *i* 396

Featherling
On Shifting Sand - Allison Pittman *i* 448

Hope
Hope Burns - Jaci Burton *r* 936

Oklahoma City
The Long and Faraway Gone - Lou
  Berney *m* 489

OREGON

If Not for This - Pete Fromm *c* 745
Manhunt - Lisa Phillips *i* 447
Reservations for Two - Hillary Manton
  Lodge *i* 428
Slayed on the Slopes - Kate Dyer-Seeley *m* 539
Whiskey Tango Foxtrot - David Shafer *c* 860

Eugene
Wrongful Death - L.J. Sellers *m* 655

Mystic Creek
Silver Thaw - Catherine Anderson *r* 898

Palisades Heights
Woman with a Gun - Phillip Margolin *c* 797

Portland
The Accidental Alchemist - Gigi Pandian *m* 630
Bridged - Kendra Elliot *r* 960
One Kick - Chelsea Cain *c* 708

Tallulah Falls
Wicked Stitch - Amanda Lee *m* 597

Thunder Point
One Wish - Robyn Carr *r* 942

Zomburbia
Zombified - Adam Gallardo *h* 302

PENNSYLVANIA

Every Fifteen Minutes - Lisa Scottoline *m* 653
The Inquisitor's Mark - Dianne Salerni *f* 102

Bethany
The Rebellion of Miss Lucy Ann Lobdell - William
  Klaber *t* 193

Black Moshannon State Park
In the Woods - Merry Jones *m* 587

Brownstown
The Love Letters - Beverly Lewis *i* 427

Cottonwood
Nun Too Soon - Alice Loweecey *m* 608

Ice Mountain
An Amish Man of Ice Mountain - Kelly
  Long *i* 429

Kismet
Gilt by Association - Karen Rose Smith *m* 661

Lancaster
Second Chances - Sarah Price *i* 450

Lancaster County
The Amish Clockmaker - Mindy Starns
  Clark *i* 378
Amish Promises - Leslie Gould *i* 405
The Matchmaker - Sarah Price *i* 451
The Witnesses - Linda Byler *i* 369

Laurel Ridge
Where Secrets Sleep - Marta Perry *i* 444

Mifflinburg
The Love Letters - Beverly Lewis *i* 427

Millbury
Lie of the Needle - Cate Price *m* 636

Monongahela County
Bridges Burned - Annette Dashofy *m* 527

Paradise
A Simple Prayer - Amy Clipston *i* 380

Philadelphia
At the Water's Edge - Sara Gruen *t* 170
Betrayed - Lisa Scottoline *c* 857
Canary - Duane Swierczynski *m* 671
Deadly Assets - W.E.B. Griffin *c* 754
Detained - Don Brown *i* 366
Dying Brand - Wendy Tyson *m* 675
The Liar - Nora Roberts *r* 1059
The Sweetheart - Angelina Mirabella *t* 211

Pittsburgh
The Hunger of the Wolf - Stephen
  Marche *r* 1019

Somerset County
Meek and Mild - Olivia Newport *i* 439

Swarthmore
Superposition - David Walton *s* 1205

Threadville
Seven Threadly Sins - Janet Bolin *m* 497

Willow Creek
Balm of Gilead - Adina Senft *i* 456

RHODE ISLAND

Catch a Falling Heiress - Laura Lee
  Guhrke *r* 981

Captive's Sound
Sorceress - Claudia Gray *f* 38

Genre Index

This index lists the books featured as main entries in *What Do I Read Next?* by genre and story type within each genre. Beneath each of the nine genres, the story types appear alphabetically, and titles appear alphabetically under story type headings. The name of the primary author, genre code and the book entry number also appear with each title. The genre codes are as follows: *c* Popular Fiction, *f* Fantasy, *h* Horror, *i* Inspirational, *m* Mystery, *r* Romance, *s* Science Fiction, and *t* Historical. For definitions of the story types, see the "Key to Genre Terms" following the Introduction.

HISTORICAL FICTION

HORROR FICTION

Adventure

Alternate History

Ancient Evil Unleashed

Anthology

Apocalyptic Horror

Collection

Coming-of-Age

Contemporary

Fantasy

Ghost Story

Gothic

Haunted House

Historical

Historical - Victorian

Literary

Magic Conflict

Medical

Mystery

Occult

Paranormal

Police Procedural

Psychological

Religious

Romance

Romantic Suspense

Series

Small Town Horror

Supernatural Vengeance

Urban

Genre Index

Urban

POPULAR FICTION

Adventure

Chase

Collection

Coming-of-Age

Contemporary

SCIENCE FICTION

Genre Index

Subject Index

This index lists subjects which are covered in the featured titles. Beneath each subject heading, titles are arranged alphabetically with the author names, genre codes, and entry numbers also indicated. The genre codes are as follows: *c* Popular Fiction, *f* Fantasy, *h* Horror, *i* Inspirational, *m* Mystery, *r* Romance, *s* Science Fiction, and *t* Historical.

Subject Index

Poverty

Crazy Horse's Girlfriend - Erika T. Wurth   *c*   891
The Spring Bride - Anne Gracie   *r*   975

Pregnancy

After Birth - Elisa Albert   *c*   688
Fiercombe Manor - Kate Riordan   *t*   235
First Frost - Sarah Addison Allen   *c*   689

Presidents (Government)

Joe Steele - Harry Turtledove   *s*   1203
Lincoln's Billy - Tom LeClair   *t*   200

Prisoners

As Night Falls - Jenny Milchman   *m*   619
The Book of Phoenix - Nnedi Okorafor   *f*   88
Breakout - Ann Aguirre   *s*   1103

Prisoners of war

Remember the Lilies - Liz Tolsma   *i*   464
Shame and the Captives - Thomas
   Keneally   *t*   190

Prisons

As Waters Gone By - Cynthia Ruchti   *i*   452

Prohibition

Wolf Point - Mike Thompson   *t*   262

Prophecy

Remnants: Season of Fire - Lisa T.
   Bergren   *i*   361
Station Eleven - Emily St. John Mandel   *c*   796
Vision in Silver - Anne Bishop   *f*   15

Prostitution

Divine - Karen Kingsbury   *i*   424
Karen Memory - Elizabeth Bear   *s*   1118

Psychiatry

Little Black Lies - Sandra Block   *m*   496

Psychics

The Bone Clocks - David Mitchell   *c*   807
Grave Phantoms - Jenn Bennett   *r*   912
The Hanged Man - P.N. Elrod   *h*   296
The Other Side of Midnight - Simone St.
   James   *r*   1087
Sense of Deception - Victoria Laurie   *f*   69
She Weeps Each Time You're Born - Quan
   Barry   *c*   696
Tails, You Lose - Carol J. Perry   *m*   635
Witches with the Enemy - Barb Hendee   *f*   51

Psychokinesis

Quake - Patrick Carman   *s*   1124

Psychology

Before, During, After - Richard Bausch   *c*   698
The Deep - Nick Cutter   *h*   289
Find Me - Laura van den Berg   *c*   877
The Kind Worth Killing - Peter Swanson   *m*   670
Method 15/33 - Shannon Kirk   *m*   594
A Pleasure and a Calling - Phil Hogan   *m*   576
The Sex Lives of Siamese Twins - Irvine
   Welsh   *c*   885

The Wednesday Group - Sylvia True   *c*   873
Wolf in White Van - John Darnielle   *c*   726

Publishing industry

The Last Bookaneer - Matthew Pearl   *t*   227

Puerto Ricans

Now We Will Be Happy - Amina Gautier   *c*   746

Puritans

The Witch Hunter's Tale - Sam Thomas   *t*   260

Questing

The Clockwork Crown - Beth Cato   *f*   23

Rabbits

Alice - Christina Henry   *h*   315

Race relations

The Abduction of Smith and Smith - Rashad
   Harrison   *t*   174
Grave Phantoms - Jenn Bennett   *r*   912
Now We Will Be Happy - Amina Gautier   *c*   746
The Sacrifice - Joyce Carol Oates   *c*   821

Racially mixed people

Frostfire - Amanda Hocking   *f*   56

Racism

The Sacrifice - Joyce Carol Oates   *c*   821

Ranch life

*Cowboy Boots for Christmas: (Cowboy Not In-
   cluded)* - Carolyn Brown   *r*   929
Deliverance at Cardwell Ranch - B.J.
   Daniels   *r*   948
Desperado - Lisa Bingham   *r*   916
Kissed by a Cowboy - Pamela Britton   *r*   926
One Mile Under - Andrew Gross   *m*   561
The Perfect Homecoming - Julia London   *r*   1013
Texas Mail Order Bride - Linda Broday   *r*   927
Twice a Texas Bride - Linda Broday   *r*   928
When It's Right - Jennifer Ryan   *r*   1065
Wild Horses - B.J. Daniels   *h*   947
Wolf Haven - Lindsay McKenna   *r*   1029

Rape

My Sunshine Away - M.O. Walsh   *c*   884

Real estate

Gilt by Association - Karen Rose Smith   *m*   661
Love Me If You Dare - Toni Blake   *r*   917
A Pleasure and a Calling - Phil Hogan   *m*   576

Rebellion

Dark Hunters: Umbra Sumus - Paul
   Kearney   *s*   1158
In Dark Service - Stephen Hunt   *f*   58
Lords of the Sith - Paul S. Kemp   *s*   1160
Ruin - John Gwynne   *f*   45
Yarrick: Imperial Creed - David
   Annandale   *s*   1106

Redemption

Divine - Karen Kingsbury   *i*   424

Religion

The Breath of Night - Michael Arditti   *c*   694
Dark Bride - Jonathan Ryan   *h*   340

Empire's End - Jerry B. Jenkins   *i*   421
Jaded - Varina Denman   *i*   392
Lay It on My Heart - Angela Pneuman   *c*   834
Mammoth Secrets - Ashley Elizabeth
   Ludwig   *i*   431
Miracle at the Higher Grounds Cafe - Max
   Lucado   *i*   430
Revival - Stephen King   *c*   783
Satan's Lullaby - Priscilla Royal   *t*   239

Renaissance

Betrayed by His Kiss - Amanda McCabe   *r*   1025
The May Bride - Suzannah Dunn   *t*   151

Restaurants

Fillet of Murder - Linda Reilly   *m*   641
Killer Gourmet - G.A. McKevett   *m*   615
Musseled Out - Barbara Ross   *m*   646
Tempting Donovan Ford - Jennifer
   McKenzie   *r*   1031

Retirement

There Must Be Some Mistake - Frederick
   Barthelme   *c*   697

Reunions

Death of a Cupcake Queen - Lee Hollis   *m*   577
It Had to Be Him - Tamra Baumann   *r*   910
Lost and Found - Brooke Davis   *c*   729
No Denying You - Sydney Landon   *r*   1004
Part Time Cowboy - Maisey Yates   *r*   1099

Revenge

Bengal's Quest - Lora Leigh   *s*   1168
Bound by Flames - Jeaniene Frost   *r*   969
Confessions - Kanae Minato   *c*   806
Crouching Tiger, Forbidden Vampire - Kerrelyn
   Sparks   *r*   1086
Dark Intelligence - Neal Asher   *s*   1108
Darkened Blade - Kelly McCullough   *f*   79
Firesoul - Gary Kloster   *f*   63
Getting Even - Sarah Rayner   *c*   842
A Love Like Blood - Marcus Sedgwick   *t*   246
Of Silk and Steam - Bec McMaster   *r*   1033

Revolutions

Into the Maelstrom - David Drake   *s*   1140
Too Dangerous for a Lady - Jo Beverley   *r*   915

Rituals

Dreams of Shreds and Tatters - Amanda
   Downum   *h*   293

River boats

Make You Remember - Macy Beckett   *r*   911

Robots

City 1 - Gregg Rosenblum   *s*   1192
Robot Overlords - Mark Stay   *s*   1200

Roman Empire, 30 BC-476 AD

A Clash of Eagles - Alan Smale   *s*   1198
Empire's End - Jerry B. Jenkins   *i*   421
The Fateful Day - Rosemary Rowe   *t*   238
Iron and Rust - Harry Sidebottom   *t*   248
The Sword of Attila - David Gibbins   *t*   163

Romances (Fiction)

The Accidental Countess - Valerie
   Bowman   *r*   923

Character Name Index

This index alphabetically lists the major characters in each featured title. Each character name is followed by a description of the character. Citations also provide titles of the books featuring the character, listed alphabetically if there is more than one title; author names and genre codes. The genre codes are as follows: *c* Popular Fiction, *f* Fantasy, *h* Horror, *i* Inspirational, *m* Mystery, *r* Romance, *s* Science Fiction, and *t* Historical. Numbers refer to the entries that feature each title.

A

'352' Jenkins (Sidekick)
Treachery in Tibet - John Wilcox   *t* 271

Aar (Spouse; Man; Brother; Father)
Hiding in Plain Sight - Nuruddin Farah   *c* 741

Abbas, Anwar (Genetically Altered Being; Bodyguard; Lover)
Evensong - John Love   *s* 1171

Abbott, Abigail (Mother; Detective—Amateur)
Tattered Legacy - Shannon Baker   *m* 484

Abbott, Colton (Lover; Brother)
I Saw Her Standing There - Marie Force   *r* 964

Abbott, Hunter (Businessman; Accountant)
And I Love Her - Marie Force   *r* 963

Abbott, Logan (Spouse)
The First Wife - Erica Spindler   *m* 664

Abbott, Nora (Girlfriend; Friend; Daughter; Detective—Amateur; Accountant)
Tattered Legacy - Shannon Baker   *m* 484

Abbott, True (Missing Person; Spouse)
The First Wife - Erica Spindler   *m* 664

Abbott, Will (Boyfriend; Brother)
I Saw Her Standing There - Marie Force   *r* 964

Abby (Spouse)
Married 'til Monday - Denise Hunter   *i* 420

Abdul (Man; Friend)
The Promise - Beth Wiseman   *c* 888

Abel (Young Man)
Skylight - Jose Saramago   *c* 854

Abend, Dominic (Organized Crime Figure)
Werewolf Cop - Andrew Klavan   *h* 328

Abercare, Ewan (Military Personnel)
Shame and the Captives - Thomas Keneally   *t* 190

Abigail (Girl)
Little Girls - Ronald Damien Malfi   *h* 333

Aboderin, Jeneta (Student)
Unbound - Jim C. Hines   *f* 55

Adam (17-Year-Old; Cancer Patient; Religious)
The Children Act - Ian McEwan   *c* 800

Adam (Man; Teacher)
On the Edge - Edward St. Aubyn   *c* 867

Adam (Royalty; Demon; Prisoner)
Soulbound - Kristen Callihan   *f* 19

Adam (Son)
Jillian - Halle Butler   *c* 707

Adams, Clover (Spouse)
The Fifth Heart - Dan Simmons   *t* 249

Adams, Henry (Historian; Spouse; Friend)
The Fifth Heart - Dan Simmons   *t* 249

Adams, Kate (Scientist; Friend)
Desperate Measures - Sandra Orchard   *i* 441

Adams, Pete (Police Officer)
Bridges Burned - Annette Dashofy   *m* 527

Adams, Phil (Agent)
Liberators - James Wesley Rawles   *c* 841

Adams, Zach "Cowboy" (Werewolf; Detective—Homicide)
Werewolf Cop - Andrew Klavan   *h* 328

Adara (Genetically Altered Being; Companion; Alien)
Artemis Invaded - Jane M. Lindskold   *s* 1169

Adare (Lover; Daughter; Sister; Royalty; Avenger; Woman)
The Providence of Fire - Brian Staveley   *f* 111

Addleshaw, Ollie (Businessman; Wealthy)
After a Fashion - Jen Turano   *i* 465

Adler, Ambrose (Recluse; Farmer; Aged Person)
The Great Sand Fracas of Ames County - Jerry Apps   *c* 692

Adriana (Sister; Young Woman)
Skylight - Jose Saramago   *c* 854

Adriko, Michael (Orphan; Friend; Fiance(e))
The Laughing Monsters - Denis Johnson   *c* 776

Aelin (Religious)
Blood of the Cosmos - Kevin J. Anderson   *s* 1104

Aelyx (Student—High School; Student—Exchange; Boyfriend; Alien)
Invaded - Melissa Landers   *s* 1163

Lady Aethelflaed (Noblewoman; Spouse; Lover; Historical Figure)
The Empty Throne - Bernard Cornwell   *t* 146

Lord Aethelred (Historical Figure; Nobleman; Administrator; Spouse)
The Empty Throne - Bernard Cornwell   *t* 146

Aethelred (Historical Figure; Royalty; Spouse; Father)
The Price of Blood - Patricia Bracewell   *t* 132

Aetius (Military Personnel; Uncle)
The Sword of Attila - David Gibbins   *t* 163

Ag Alla, Mossa (Warrior; Leader)
Blue Warrior - Mike Maden   *c* 795

Agnieszka (Young Woman; Friend)
Uprooted - Naomi Novik   *f* 87

Aida (Granddaughter)
An Italian Wife - Ann Hood   *c* 768

Aiden (Shape-Shifter; Warrior; Lover)
Hunter Reborn - Katie Reus   *h* 338

Aisa (Human; Slave; Friend)
Iron Axe - Steven Harper   *f* 46

Aisling (Seamstress)
Dreamer's Daughter - Lynn Kurland   *f* 65

Lord Akeldama (Vampire; Spouse; Father; Wealthy)
Prudence - Gail Carriger   *f* 22

Akeldama, Prudence "Rue" Alessandra Maccon (Daughter; 20-Year-Old; Friend; Psychic)
Prudence - Gail Carriger   *f* 22

Akina (Dwarf; Warrior; Companion; Daughter)
Forge of Ashes - Josh Vogt   *f* 120

Akkad Boy (Boy; Psychic)
The Infernal - Mark Doten   *c* 734

Al Baharna, Ali (Wealthy; Terrorist)
Ark Storm - Linda Davies   *c* 727

Al-Khateeb, Mansour (Spouse; Political Prisoner)
Prague Summer - Jeffrey Condran   *c* 717

Al-Khateeb, Selma (Friend; Spouse)
Prague Summer - Jeffrey Condran   *c* 717

Alan (Lover)
The Girl Next Door - Ruth Rendell   *c* 844

Alan, Michael Fitz (Military Personnel; Knight)
The Holy Lance - Andrew Latham   *t* 198

Alanna (Daughter; 17-Year-Old)
Hush Hush - Laura Lippman   *m* 604

Alastar (Leader; Wizard)
Madness in Solidar - L.E. Modesitt   *f* 82

Alban, Charles (Nobleman)
Diary of an Accidental Wallflower - Jennifer McQuiston   *r* 1036

Albia, Flavia (Narrator; Friend; Detective—Amateur)
Deadly Election - Lindsey Davis   *t* 148

Alden, Hunter "Tripp" Hutchinson III (18-Year-Old; Son; Missing Person)
NYPD Red 3 - James Patterson   *m* 632

Alden, Hunter Hutchinson Jr. (Businessman; Wealthy; Father; Spouse)
NYPD Red 3 - James Patterson   *m* 632

Alden, Janelle (Spouse; Mother)
NYPD Red 3 - James Patterson   *m* 632

Alders, Lila (Divorced Person; Television Personality; Daughter)
New Uses for Old Boyfriends - Beth Kendrick *r* 998

Alex (Woman; Friend)
10:04 - Ben Lerner *c* 790

Alexander, Gina (Military Personnel; Photographer; Young Woman)
A Long Time Until Now - Michael Z. Williamson *s* 1208

Alexander the Great (Historical Figure; Royalty)
Colossus - Colin Falconer *t* 155

Alexi (Government Official)
Fram - Steve Himmer *c* 767

Alexia (Spouse; Mother)
Prudence - Gail Carriger *f* 22

Alexos (Royalty; Brother)
The Chosen Prince - Diane Stanley *f* 110

Alice (Amnesiac; Patient; Runaway)
Alice - Christina Henry *h* 315

Alice (Girl)
The Dead Hamlets - Peter Roman *f* 99

Allen (Lover; Musician)
Dictatorship of the Dress - Jessica Topper *r* 1092

Allen, Hollie (Child; Daughter)
An Amish Man of Ice Mountain - Kelly Long *i* 429

Allen, Priscilla (Abuse Victim; Mother; Friend; Divorced Person)
An Amish Man of Ice Mountain - Kelly Long *i* 429

Allen, Tex (Detective—Police)
With Vics You Get Eggroll - Diane Vallere *m* 676

Allenson, Allen (Military Personnel)
Into the Maelstrom - David Drake *s* 1140

Alls (Friend; Convict; Lover)
Unbecoming - Rebecca Scherm *c* 855

Ally (Teenager; Girl; Deaf Person)
The Silence - Tim Lebbon *h* 330

Alvarini, Beth (Writer; Narrator; Handicapped)
Stillwater - Maynard Sims *h* 344

Alyra (Friend; Spy)
Storm and Steel - Jon Sprunk *f* 109

Alyse (Spouse; Mother)
It Won't Always Be This Great - Peter Mehlman *c* 803

Amado, Mercedes "Mercy" (Woman; Divorced Person; Mother)
The Amado Women - Desiree Zamorano *c* 892

Amanda (Daughter; Sister)
A Spool of Blue Thread - Anne Tyler *c* 875

Amber (Girl; Teenager; Friend)
We Are Pirates - Daniel Handler *c* 759

Amber (Neighbor; Young Woman)
A Love Like Ours - Becky Wade *i* 466

Ambrose, Finn (Uncle)
The Inquisitor's Mark - Dianne Salerni *f* 102

Ames, Derrick (Teacher; Crime Victim)
Stiff Penalty - Annelise Ryan *m* 648

Lord Amherst (Nobleman; Brother)
The Devil Takes a Bride - Julia London *r* 1012

Anaedsley, Trevor (Fiance(e); Student)
50 Ways to Ruin a Rake - Jade Lee *r* 1007

Andarist (Brother; Son; Shape-Shifter; Supernatural Being)
Fall of Light - Steven Erikson *f* 30

Anders, Reece (Police Officer)
Fall with Me - Jennifer L. Armentrout *r* 902

Andersen, Mitty (Musician; Friend; Detective—Amateur)
Howling Mountain Blues - Ricky Bush *m* 508

Andersen, Seth (Veteran; Police Officer; Lover)
Every Little Kiss - Kendra Leigh Castle *r* 943

Anderson, Charity (Writer; Lover)
Whenever You Come Around - Robin Lee Hatcher *i* 413

Anderson, Doug (Student—College; Son; Friend)
The Legacy - Dan Walsh *i* 467

Anderson, Haley (Daughter)
It Had to Be Him - Tamra Baumann *r* 910

Anderson, Jim (Father)
The Legacy - Dan Walsh *i* 467

Anderson, Meg (Mother; Lover)
It Had to Be Him - Tamra Baumann *r* 910

Anderson, Rose (Doctor)
Teardrop Lane - Emily March *r* 1018

Anderson, Tyler (Musician; Friend; Classmate)
The Dead Play On - Heather Graham *m* 560

Andraso, Chane (Vampire; Friend)
First and Last Sorcerer - Barb Hendee *f* 52

Andrea (Sister; Daughter)
Double Fudge Brownie Murder - Joanne Fluke *m* 548

Andreou, Alex (Religious; Father; Brother)
The Fifth Gospel - Ian Caldwell *m* 509

Andreou, Peter (Boy; Son; 5-Year-Old)
The Fifth Gospel - Ian Caldwell *m* 509

Andreou, Simon (Religious; Brother)
The Fifth Gospel - Ian Caldwell *m* 509

Andrew (Young Man; Religious)
John the Pupil - David L. Flusfeder *t* 158

Andrews, Dalton (Actor)
Hollywood Lost - Ace Collins *t* 143

Andrews, Derrick (Crime Suspect)
Murder at Beechwood - Alyssa Maxwell *m* 612

Andriana (Teenager; Friend; Enemy)
Remnants: Season of Fire - Lisa T. Bergren *i* 361

Anea (Royalty)
The Boy Who Wept Blood - Den Patrick *f* 93

Angel (Friend)
One Step Too Far - Tina Seskis *c* 859

Angela (Spouse; Lover)
Devils and Dust - J.D. Rhoades *m* 642

Angela Rose (Baby; Daughter)
The Love Letters - Beverly Lewis *i* 427

Angelica (Nurse; Spouse)
Juliet's Nurse - Lois Leveen *t* 204

Angelica (Sister)
A Fatal Chapter - Lorna Barrett *m* 488

Angeliki (Friend)
Outline - Rachel Cusk *c* 724

Angelina (Spouse)
Cane and Abe - James Grippando *c* 756

Angelo (Detective—Police)
The Exile - C.T. Adams *f* 3

Angelo, Dr. Lucas (Doctor; Manager (Sports))
Angel in Armani - Melanie Scott *r* 1072

Angie (21-Year-Old; Sister; Traveler)
Into the Go-Slow - Bridgett M. Davis *c* 728

Anippe (Mother; Spouse)
The Pharaoh's Daughter - Mesu Andrews *i* 357

Ann (Crime Victim; Sister; Indian)
Marked Fur Murder - Dixie Lyle *m* 609

Ann (Patient; Spouse)
Let Me Be Frank with You - Richard Ford *c* 744

Ann (Spouse; Wealthy; Vacationer)
The Last Good Paradise - Tatjana Soli *c* 865

Ann, Rachel (Neighbor; Friend; Sister)
One True Path - Barbara Cameron *i* 375

Anna (5-Year-Old; Daughter; Sister)
Cold Spell - Deb Vanasse *c* 879

Anna Mae (Young Woman; Religious; Friend)
A Faith of Her Own - Kathleen Fuller *i* 400

Anne (Religious; Nurse; Friend)
Satan's Lullaby - Priscilla Royal *t* 239

Annie (Mother; Friend)
This Is the Water - Yannick Murphy *c* 813

Anstruther, Kate (Magician)
The Conquering Dark - Clay Griffith *h* 308

Anstruther, Kate (Magician; Colleague)
The Shadow Revolution - Clay Griffith *h* 307

Anton (Royalty)
Witches with the Enemy - Barb Hendee *f* 51

Antonio (Director)
Seven Threadly Sins - Janet Bolin *m* 497

Anya (Mythical Creature; Cousin)
The Empty Throne - Cayla Kluver *f* 64

Appleby, Adrian (Courier; Uncle)
The German Agent - J. Sydney Jones *t* 186

April (18-Year-Old; Adoptee; Girlfriend; Crime Victim)
Endangered - C.J. Box *m* 499

Arbuthnot (Government Official; Diplomat)
Pasha: A Kydd Sea Adventure - Julian Stockwin *t* 255

Archaon (Supernatural Being; Servant; Student)
Archaon: Everchosen - Rob Sanders *f* 103

Archer, Jonathan (Spaceship Captain)
Uncertain Logic - Christopher L. Bennett *s* 1119

Archer, Kate (Businesswoman; Guardian; Friend)
Carousel Seas - Sharon Lee *f* 72

Archer, Simon (Magician; Colleague)
The Shadow Revolution - Clay Griffith *h* 307

Archer, Simon (Magician; Leader)
The Conquering Dark - Clay Griffith *h* 308

Arden (Magician)
The Magician's Lie - Greer Macallister *t* 207

Ardhi (Man; Adventurer)
The Dagger's Path - Glenda Larke *f* 67

Argeneau, Basileios "Basil" (Vampire; Lover)
The Immortal Who Loved Me - Lynsay Sands *r* 1069

Argent, Gabriel (Man; Wizard; Criminal)
Pacific Fire - Greg van Eekhout *f* 118

Ari (Mother; Spouse; Student—Graduate; Friend)
After Birth - Elisa Albert *c* 688

Ari (Supernatural Being; Friend)
Armageddon Rules - J.C. Nelson *f* 86

Ariel (Sister)
The Dangerous Type - Loren Rhoads *s* 1189

Ark, Roxanne "Roxy" (Bartender; Artist)
Fall with Me - Jennifer L. Armentrout *r* 902

Arkwright, Julius (Financier; Veteran)
Trust No One - Jayne Ann Krentz *c* 786

Armand (Vampire)
Prince Lestat - Anne Rice *c* 845

Armbruster, Stan (Detective—Police)
Whiskers of the Lion - P.L. Gaus *m* 555

Arnault (Spy)
Cities and Thrones - Carrie Patel *f* 92

Arnette, Zac (Lover)
The Perfect Indulgence - Isabel Sharpe *r* 1078

Arngrimsson, Audun (Viking; Immortal; Friend)
Blood Will Follow - Snorri Kristjansson   *t* 194

Arosteguy, Aristide (Philosopher; Spouse)
Consumed - David Cronenberg   *c* 722

Arosteguy, Celestine (Philosopher; Spouse)
Consumed - David Cronenberg   *c* 722

Arpien (Royalty; Rescuer; Hero)
Waking Beauty - Sarah E. Morin   *i* 438

Arthur (Royalty; Spouse)
Fatal Feast - Jay Ruud   *t* 243

Arthur (Young Man; Warrior; Royalty)
The Ice King - M.K. Hume   *f* 57

Arturus (Warrior)
The Sword of Attila - David Gibbins   *t* 163

Ashe (Fiance(e); Man)
Revels Ending - Vic Kerry   *h* 326

Asher (Vampire; Lover)
Witch upon a Star - Jennifer Harlow   *m* 568

Ashley (Student—High School; Assistant)
Seven Threadly Sins - Janet Bolin   *m* 497

Aspyn (Angel)
Chasing Sunsets - Karen Kingsbury   *i* 425

Astrid (Teenager; Mythical Creature)
Rogue Wave - Jennifer Donnelly   *f* 28

Atal (Leader; Guardian)
Green on Blue - Elliot Ackerman   *c* 684

Athena (Spouse; Granddaughter; Daughter)
Cold Betrayal - J.A. Jance   *m* 584

Athene (Deity)
The Chosen Prince - Diane Stanley   *f* 110

Atherton, Charlotte (Teacher; Guardian)
A Worthy Pursuit - Karen Witemeyer   *i* 471

Atkinson, Kelly (Nurse; Colleague; Hostage)
Fatal Trauma - Richard L. Mabry   *i* 432

Atwater, Merry (Rescuer; Therapist)
For Keeps - Rachel Lacey   *r* 1003

Atwater, Philip (Teenager; Wealthy)
Rich Kids of Instagram - Creator of Rich Kids of Instagram   *c* 721

Aubrey, Anna (Sister; Daughter)
The Wood's Edge - Lori Benton   *i* 360

Aubrey, Jax (13-Year-Old; Boy; Friend)
The Inquisitor's Mark - Dianne Salerni   *f* 102

Aubrey, Reginald (Father; Father; Kidnapper)
The Wood's Edge - Lori Benton   *i* 360

Aubrey, William (Kidnap Victim; Son; Twin)
The Wood's Edge - Lori Benton   *i* 360

Auerstein, Florian (Servant; Crime Victim)
The Figaro Murders - Laura Lebow   *t* 199

Augustine (Stepson; Stepbrother)
The Devil Takes a Bride - Julia London   *r* 1012

Augustus (Government Official; Man)
Golden Son - Pierce Brown   *s* 1120

Aurangzeb (Brother; Father; Ruler; Son; Historical Figure)
Traitors in the Shadows - Alex Rutherford   *t* 242

Aurelius, Marcus Septimus (Landowner)
The Fateful Day - Rosemary Rowe   *t* 238

Austen, Henry (Historical Figure; Banker; Brother)
Who Buries the Dead - C.S. Harris   *t* 172

Austen, Jane (Historical Figure; Writer; Sister)
Who Buries the Dead - C.S. Harris   *t* 172

Ava (Mythical Creature; Teenager)
Rogue Wave - Jennifer Donnelly   *f* 28

Ava (Young Woman; Granddaughter)
The Boston Girl - Anita Diamant   *t* 149

Aven, Bryn (Worker; Outcast)
Frostfire - Amanda Hocking   *f* 56

Avery, Beth (Assistant)
No One Like You - Kate Angell   *r* 901

Avery, William (Military Personnel)
The Strangler Vine - Miranda Carter   *t* 139

Avildottar, Sayrid (Warrior)
Taming His Viking Woman - Michelle Styles   *r* 1089

Axl (Man; Aged Person; Spouse)
The Buried Giant - Kazuo Ishiguro   *t* 183

Aya (Girl; Teenager)
The Glass Arrow - Kristen Simmons   *s* 1197

Ayla (Lesbian; Veteran; Girlfriend)
In Case of Emergency - Courtney Moreno   *c* 811

Azinheiro, Pedro (Religious)
The Day of Atonement - David Liss   *t* 206

B

Babayoff, Sebastian (Photographer; Religious; Crime Victim)
A Dangerous Place - Jacqueline Winspear   *t* 273

Babin, Mackenzie "Mac" (Young Woman; Divorced Person)
Dead Spots - Rhiannon Frater   *h* 299

Bachman, Adam (Serial Killer)
Compulsion - Allison Brennan   *m* 502

Bacon, Roger (Religious; Inventor; Scientist; Teacher; Historical Figure)
John the Pupil - David L. Flusfeder   *t* 158

Bairn (Worker)
Anna's Crossing - Suzanne Woods Fisher   *i* 399

Baker, Grace (Young Woman; Detective—Amateur; Sister)
Dark Rooms - Lili Anolik   *c* 691

Baker, Grant (Detective—Police)
A Fatal Chapter - Lorna Barrett   *m* 488

Baker, Dr. Mark (Doctor; Hostage; Doctor; Boyfriend; Colleague)
Fatal Trauma - Richard L. Mabry   *i* 432

Baker, Nica (Sister; Crime Victim; 16-Year-Old)
Dark Rooms - Lili Anolik   *c* 691

Bald Peter (Agent; Crime Victim)
Last Days of the Condor - James Grady   *m* 559

Baldwin, Becky (Lawyer; Friend)
Puzzled Indemnity - Parnell Hall   *m* 565

Baldwin, Max (Businessman; Friend)
Silken Threats - Addison Fox   *r* 966

Bales, Arlen (Enemy; Spouse)
The Skull Throne - Peter V. Brett   *f* 17

Bales, Renna (Spouse)
The Skull Throne - Peter V. Brett   *f* 17

Bankston, Cade (Investigator)
Undercover Hunter - Rachel Lee   *r* 1008

Banning, Amanda (Abuse Victim; Mother; Neighbor)
Silver Thaw - Catherine Anderson   *r* 898

Banning, Chloe (Girl; 6-Year-Old; Daughter; Neighbor)
Silver Thaw - Catherine Anderson   *r* 898

Bannon, Dean (FBI Agent; Agent)
Twisted - Cynthia Eden   *r* 958

Bantle, Peter (Businessman; Crime Suspect; Villain; Enemy)
Karen Memory - Elizabeth Bear   *s* 1118

Barak, Jack (Assistant)
Lamentation - C.J. Sansom   *t* 244

Barbara (Mother; Woman)
Where They Found Her - Kimberly McCreight   *m* 614

Bard, Delilah "Lila" (Thief; Companion)
A Darker Shade of Magic - V.E. Schwab   *f* 105

Barker, Bob (Military Personnel)
A Long Time Until Now - Michael Z. Williamson   *s* 1208

Barker, Cyrus (Detective—Private; Employer)
Anatomy of Evil - Will Thomas   *t* 261

Barker, Holly (Friend; Advisor)
Hot Pursuit - Stuart Woods   *m* 682

Barker, Nick (Colleague)
The Shadow Revolution - Clay Griffith   *h* 307

Barkes, Clive (Spouse; Father)
Never Mind Miss Fox - Olivia Glazebrook   *c* 750

Barkes, Eliza (Daughter)
Never Mind Miss Fox - Olivia Glazebrook   *c* 750

Barkes, Martha (Spouse; Mother)
Never Mind Miss Fox - Olivia Glazebrook   *c* 750

Barnabus, Elizabeth (Detective—Amateur; Magician; Young Woman)
Unseemly Science - Rod Duncan   *s* 1141

Barnes (Police Officer; Friend)
Mrs. Jeffries and the One Who Got Away - Emily Brightwell   *m* 503

Barnes, Rudy (Professor; Man; Spouse; Father)
The Witch of the Wood - Michael Aronovitz   *h* 280

Barnett, Cooper (Rancher; Fiance(e))
Wild Horses - B.J. Daniels   *r* 947

Barnhouse, Spencer (Co-worker; Librarian)
The Witch at Sparrow Creek - Josh Kent   *h* 324

Baron Sutcliffe (Cousin)
Secrets of a Scandalous Heiress - Theresa Romain   *r* 1060

Barrett, John Fitzhugh (Nobleman; Heir)
Never Resist a Rake - Mia Marlowe   *r* 1023

Barrett, Lee (Psychic; Television Personality; Teacher)
Tails, You Lose - Carol J. Perry   *m* 635

Barrett, Natasha (Young Woman; Fiance(e); Artist)
Before, During, After - Richard Bausch   *c* 698

Barrett, Richard (Nobleman)
A Rake by Any Other Name - Mia Marlowe   *r* 1022

Barrington, Stone (Friend; Lover; Lawyer)
Hot Pursuit - Stuart Woods   *m* 682

Barrington, Stone (Lawyer)
Insatiable Appetites - Stuart Woods   *c* 890

Barrington, Stone (Lawyer; Consultant; Hotel Owner; Friend; Lover)
Paris Match - Stuart Woods   *c* 889

Barrister, Bill (Detective—Homicide)
Hollywood Lost - Ace Collins   *t* 143

Barrons, Leo (Son; Enemy)
Of Silk and Steam - Bec McMaster   *r* 1033

Barrow, Mare (17-Year-Old; Young Woman)
Red Queen - Victoria Aveyard   *f* 9

Barsham, Adelaide (Spouse; Mother)
Meadowlands - Elizabeth Jeffrey   *t* 185

Barsham, George (Father; Spouse)
Meadowlands - Elizabeth Jeffrey   *t* 185

Barsham, Gina (Daughter; Sister)
Meadowlands - Elizabeth Jeffrey   *t* 185

Barsham, James (Son; Brother)
Meadowlands - Elizabeth Jeffrey   *t* 185

Barsham, Millie (Daughter; Sister)
Meadowlands - Elizabeth Jeffrey   *t* 185

Bartolo, Dion (Organized Crime Figure)
World Gone By - Dennis Lehane   *t* 201

Barton, Ross (Filmmaker; Boyfriend)
Double Fudge Brownie Murder - Joanne
Fluke   *m* 548

Bascombe, Frank (Retiree; Spouse)
Let Me Be Frank with You - Richard Ford   *c* 744

Basilda (Woman; Religious)
The Dragon of Handale - Cassandra Clark   *t* 142

Bassett, Mac (Government Official)
Silence the Dead - Jack Fredrickson   *m* 549

Batchelor, Jim (Journalist)
The Blue and the Grey - M.J. Trow   *t* 266

Bates, Linda (Classmate; Spouse)
Time of Death - Mark Billingham   *m* 491

Bates, Stephen (Crime Suspect; Spouse)
Time of Death - Mark Billingham   *m* 491

Bathory, Elizabeth (Serial Killer; Noblewoman)
Bathed in Blood - Alex Archer   *f* 6

Bathu, Thorn (Crime Suspect; Companion; Young
Woman)
Half the World - Joe Abercrombie   *f* 2

Bathurst, Chloe (Actress; Worker; Thief)
Galapagos Regained - James Morrow   *t* 216

Batten, Lady Phoebe (Noblewoman; Blind Person; Ward)
Dearest Rogue - Elizabeth Hoyt   *r* 990

Battle, Jeff (Genius; Boyfriend; Crime Suspect;
Brother)
What Strange Creatures - Emily Arsenault   *c* 695

Battle, Theresa (Student—Graduate; Writer; Sister)
What Strange Creatures - Emily Arsenault   *c* 695

Baum, Addie (Aged Person; Grandmother; Sister;
Narrator)
The Boston Girl - Anita Diamant   *t* 149

Baxter, Mike (Detective—Police)
What the Fly Saw - Frankie Y. Bailey   *m* 483

Baxter, Nicole "Nikki" (Lover)
His Small-Town Sweetheart - Amanda Berry   *r* 914

Bay (15-Year-Old; Daughter; Niece; Cousin)
First Frost - Sarah Addison Allen   *c* 689

Bayles, China (Herbalist; Daughter)
Bittersweet - Susan Wittig Albert   *m* 476

Baylor, Nevada (Detective—Private; Woman)
Burn for Me - Ilona Andrews   *r* 900

Beachy, Moses (Religious)
Meek and Mild - Olivia Newport   *i* 439

Beale, Josephine (Young Woman; Sister)
Sisters of Shiloh - Kathy Hepinstall   *t* 176

Beale, Libby (Young Woman; Sister; Widow(er))
Sisters of Shiloh - Kathy Hepinstall   *t* 176

Beasley, Daphne (Cousin; Daughter)
Murder with a Twist - Tracy Kiely   *m* 593

Beatrice (Aged Person; Woman)
The Love Book - Nina Solomon   *c* 866

Beatrice (Friend)
Wedding Duress - Elizabeth Lynn Casey   *m* 513

Beatrice (Woman; Aged Person; Spouse)
The Buried Giant - Kazuo Ishiguro   *t* 183

Beatrice "Bea" (Spouse)
The Book of Strange New Things - Michel
Faber   *c* 740

Beaumont, Michael (Fiance(e))
How to Plan a Wedding for a Royal Spy - Vanessa
Kelly   *r* 997

Beausoleil, Jonquil "Boso" (Young Woman; Actress; Girlfriend)
Phantom Angel - David Handler   *m* 567

Becca (Teenager; Mythical Creature)
Rogue Wave - Jennifer Donnelly   *f* 28

Dr. Beck (Doctor)
No Known Grave - Maureen Jennings   *m* 585

Beck, Charley (Technician; Spouse; Father)
Up the Hill to Home - Jennifer Bort
Yacovissi   *t* 275

Beck, Emma Miller (Clerk; Spouse; Mother)
Up the Hill to Home - Jennifer Bort
Yacovissi   *t* 275

Beck, Guinevere (Boyfriend; Writer; Young
Woman; Crime Victim)
You - Caroline Kepnes   *c* 782

Beck, Joel (Veteran; Spouse; Father; Neighbor;
Handicapped)
Amish Promises - Leslie Gould   *i* 405

Beck, Shani (Spouse; Mother; Friend; Neighbor)
Amish Promises - Leslie Gould   *i* 405

Becker (Detective; Friend)
Inspector of the Dead - David Morrell   *t* 214

Becker, Anselm (Religious; Friend)
Cold Betrayal - J.A. Jance   *m* 584

Becker, Heinz (Crime Suspect)
The Beige Man - Helene Tursten   *m* 674

Beckett, Shelby (Young Woman; Worker)
Hollywood Lost - Ace Collins   *t* 143

Beckham, Abe (Lawyer; Widow(er); Spouse;
Crime Suspect)
Cane and Abe - James Grippando   *c* 756

Lady Beckington (Mentally Ill Person; Mother;
Stepmother)
The Devil Takes a Bride - Julia London   *r* 1012

Becky (Daughter)
Taken - Dee Henderson   *i* 417

Lady Bedford (Historical Figure; Friend)
Love's Alchemy - Bryan Crockett   *t* 147

Bee (Teenager; Kidnap Victim; Student; Friend)
Miss Mayhem - Rachel Hawkins   *f* 48

Beecham, Damien "Viscount Quint" (Friend)
The Courtesan Duchess - Joanna Shupe   *r* 1083

Beecham, Mariah (Spy; Co-worker; Noblewoman)
Darian Hunter: Duke of Desire - Carole
Mortimer   *r* 1039

Behan, Johnny (Lawman)
Epitaph - Mary Doria Russell   *t* 240

Behr, Frank (Detective—Private; Detective—
Police)
Signature Kill - David Levien   *m* 601

Beiler, Davey (Religious; Father)
The Witnesses - Linda Byler   *i* 369

Beiler, Sarah (Daughter; Accident Victim; Religious)
The Witnesses - Linda Byler   *i* 369

Dr. Bek (Doctor)
Find Me - Laura van den Berg   *c* 877

Bekatha (Royalty; Daughter; Sister)
Desert God - Wilbur Smith   *t* 252

Belhaj, Fatima (Colleague; Agent)
The Convert's Song - Sebastian Rotella   *c* 849

Belial (Thief; Publisher)
The Last Bookaneer - Matthew Pearl   *t* 227

Bell, Fannie (Grandmother; Employer)
Dollbaby - Laura McNeal   *c* 801

Bell, Gertrude (Archaeologist; Linguist; Explorer;
Diplomat; Political Figure; Writer)
Bell of the Desert - Alan Gold   *t* 166

Bell, Liberty "Ibby" (12-Year-Old; Granddaughter;
Friend)
Dollbaby - Laura McNeal   *c* 801

Bell, Vanessa Stephen (Historical Figure; Artist;
Sister)
Vanessa and Her Sister - Priya Parmar   *t* 225

Bella (Dog; Companion)
A Killer Retreat - Tracy Weber   *m* 679

Bella (Sister; Photographer; Aunt)
Hiding in Plain Sight - Nuruddin Farah   *c* 741

Bella (Spouse; Mother)
The Stager - Susan Coll   *c* 716

Bellamy, Gina (Divorced Person; Spouse; Cancer
Patient)
A Hundred Pieces of Me - Lucy Dillon   *c* 731

Bellamy, Stuart (Divorced Person; Spouse)
A Hundred Pieces of Me - Lucy Dillon   *c* 731

Ben (4-Year-Old; Son)
Christmas at Twilight - Lori Wilde   *r* 1097

Ben (Boyfriend; Brother; Indian)
Marked Fur Murder - Dixie Lyle   *m* 609

Ben (Guide; Spouse; Father)
As Night Falls - Jenny Milchman   *m* 619

Ben (Manager; Friend)
New Uses for Old Boyfriends - Beth
Kendrick   *r* 998

Bennett, Anne (Spouse; Mother)
The Melody Lingers On - Mary Higgins
Clark   *m* 515

Bennett, Cody (Teenager; Student—High School)
The Dandelion Field - Kathryn Springer   *i* 460

Bennett, Eric (Son)
The Melody Lingers On - Mary Higgins
Clark   *m* 515

Bennett, Parker (Financier; Crime Suspect; Missing Person; Spouse; Father)
The Melody Lingers On - Mary Higgins
Clark   *m* 515

Bennings, Kit (Agent; Military Personnel; Spouse)
The Russian Bride - Ed Kovacs   *m* 595

Benoit, Cat (Shape-Shifter; Woman)
Cat's Lair - Christine Feehan   *h* 298

Bentley, Olivia (Businesswoman; Girlfriend)
He's So Fine - Jill Shalvis   *r* 1075

Bentley Douglas, Joe (Hotel Worker; Manager)
Honeymoon Hotel - Hester Browne   *r* 931

Benton, Amy (Trainer)
Search and Seduce - Sara Jane Stone   *r* 1088

Benton, Amy (Widow(er))
Search and Seduce - Sara Jane Stone   *r* 1088

Benz, Anna (Woman; Spouse; Mother)
Hausfrau - Jill Alexander Essbaum   *c* 739

Benz, Bruno (Banker; Spouse; Father)
Hausfrau - Jill Alexander Essbaum   *c* 739

Bernard (Religious)
John the Pupil - David L. Flusfeder   *t* 158

Bernardo, Manfred (Psychic)
Day Shift - Charlaine Harris   *h* 314

Bessette, Charlotte (Store Owner; Detective—
Amateur; Employer; Fiance(e))
As Gouda as Dead - Avery Aames   *m* 473

Bethany (Spouse)
A Slant of Light - Jeffrey Lent   *t* 202

Brandon, Piers (Diplomat; Fiance(e); Nobleman; Brother)
Say Yes to the Marquess - Tessa Dare   *r* 950

Brandon, Rafe (Boxer; Rake; Brother)
Say Yes to the Marquess - Tessa Dare   *r* 950

Brandon, Rebecca "Becky" Bloomfield (Expert; Spouse; Mother; Friend)
Shopaholic to the Stars - Sophie Kinsella   *c* 784

Brandt, Sarah (Midwife; Fiance(e))
Murder on Amsterdam Avenue - Victoria Thompson   *m* 672

Brannigan, Penny (Businesswoman; Colleague; Detective—Amateur)
Slated for Death - Elizabeth J. Duncan   *m* 537

Brant, Hollis (Smuggler; Criminal)
Past Crimes - Glen Erik Hamilton   *m* 566

Brascum, Adam (Bartender)
Sweeter than Sin - Shiloh Walker   *r* 1094

Braun, Anna-Grace (Cousin; Fiance(e); Religious)
When Grace Sings - Kim Vogel Sawyer   *i* 454

Braun, Eliza (Agent)
The Diamond Conspiracy - Philippa Ballantine   *f* 10

Bree (13-Year-Old; Sister; Student)
Stirring Up Trouble - Kimberly Kincaid   *r* 1000

Bree (Hairdresser; Alcoholic; Friend; Mother)
Beyond the Pale Motel - Francesca Lia Block   *c* 704

Breeland, Robyn (Businesswoman; Manager)
Loving Dallas - Caisey Quinn   *c* 839

Breen, Cathal (Detective—Police; Colleague)
The Kings of London - William Shaw   *m* 657

Breen, Fred (Fire Fighter; Bodyguard)
The Night Belongs to Fireman - Jennifer Bernard   *r* 913

Brembre, Nicholas (Historical Figure; Government Official)
The Invention of Fire - Bruce W. Holsinger   *t* 179

Bremer, L. Paul (Historical Figure; Military Personnel; Political Figure)
The Infernal - Mark Doten   *c* 734

Brennan, Lucy (Trainer)
The Sex Lives of Siamese Twins - Irvine Welsh   *c* 885

Brennan, Dr. Temperance "Tempe" (Anthropologist)
Speaking in Bones - Kathy Reichs   *m* 640

Brennan, Dr. Temperance "Tempe" (Anthropologist; Co-worker)
Bones Never Lie - Kathy Reichs   *c* 843

Brennan, Tory (Girl; Teenager; Leader)
Terminal - Kathy Reichs   *s* 1187

Brennan, Tory (Teenager)
Exposure - Kathy Reichs   *s* 1186

Brenner, Eve (Real Estate Agent)
The Stager - Susan Coll   *c* 716

Breslau, Gary (Detective—Police)
Signature Kill - David Levien   *m* 601

Breuer, Josef (Historical Figure; Doctor)
Gretel and the Dark - Eliza Granville   *t* 168

Brewster, Callie (Veteran; Friend; Aunt)
Cowboy Boots for Christmas: (Cowboy Not Included) - Carolyn Brown   *r* 929

Brian (Friend; Farmer; Father)
Dark Bride - Jonathan Ryan   *h* 340

Brickman, Cooper (Brother; Race Car Driver; Lover)
Final Lap - Erin McCarthy   *r* 1027

Bridge, Matthew (Man)
Point Hollow - Rio Youers   *h* 355

Bridget (Spouse; Woman; Nurse)
The Wednesday Group - Sylvia True   *c* 873

Brienne (Woman; Lover)
Rising Fire - Terri Brisbin   *r* 925

Brierly (Royalty; Captive)
Waking Beauty - Sarah E. Morin   *i* 438

Bright, Kieran (Detective—Police)
The Soul of Discretion - Susan Hill   *m* 574

Brigid (Rebel; Co-worker)
Terminal White - James Axler   *s* 1109

Brigid (Warrior)
Hell's Maw - James Axler   *s* 1112

Brink, Adam (Mercenary; Colleague)
Edge of Betrayal - Shannon K. Butcher   *r* 939

Brixton (14-Year-Old; Neighbor)
The Accidental Alchemist - Gigi Pandian   *m* 630

Brockwell, Iris (Aunt; Aged Person)
Gift of Grace - Sharlene MacLaren   *i* 433

Brody, Evander "Vander" Septimus (Nobleman; Spouse)
Four Nights with the Duke - Eloisa James   *r* 993

Brogan, Jake (Detective—Police; Lover)
Truth Be Told - Hank Phillippi Ryan   *c* 851

Brooke (Student; Wealthy)
On the Edge - Edward St. Aubyn   *c* 867

Brooks, Camryn "Cami" (Store Owner; Detective—Amateur; Friend)
Snow Way Out - Christine Husom   *m* 579

Brooks, Wellington (Agent)
The Diamond Conspiracy - Philippa Ballantine   *f* 10

Broom, Jody (Warrior; Rebel)
Cobra Outlaw - Timothy Zahn   *s* 1211

Broom, Lorne (Warrior; Rebel)
Cobra Outlaw - Timothy Zahn   *s* 1211

Broom, Paul (Warrior; Prisoner)
Cobra Outlaw - Timothy Zahn   *s* 1211

Brother Athelstan (Detective—Amateur; Religious)
The Book of Fires - Paul Doherty   *t* 150

Browles, Darren (Student—College)
Dear Committee Members - Julie Schumacher   *c* 856

Brown, Caroline (Twin)
One Step Too Far - Tina Seskis   *c* 859

Brown, Jane (Woman; Mother; Roommate; Spouse)
Christmas at Twilight - Lori Wilde   *r* 1097

Brown, Mason (Detective—Police; Colleague)
Deadly Obsession - Maggie Shayne   *r* 1081
Innocent Prey - Maggie Shayne   *r* 1080

Brown, Weston "West" (Military Personnel; Agent)
Falling Hard - HelenKay Dimon   *r* 954

Browne, Bailey (Spouse)
The First Wife - Erica Spindler   *m* 664

Brownie (Dog)
Poison Ivy - Cynthia Riggs   *m* 644

Browning, Matt (Agent)
Darkest Night - Will Hill   *h* 317
Zero Hour - Will Hill   *h* 316

Browning, Theodosia (Detective—Amateur; Store Owner; Girlfriend)
Ming Tea Murder - Laura Childs   *m* 514

Brunetti, Guido (Detective—Police; Spouse)
Falling in Love - Donna Leon   *m* 599

Brunetti, Paola (Spouse)
Falling in Love - Donna Leon   *m* 599

Brungardt, Steven (Religious; Fiance(e))
When Grace Sings - Kim Vogel Sawyer   *i* 454

Bryant, Chris (Lawman)
Saving Cecil - Lee Mims   *m* 620

Brynn (Friend; Student—High School; Teenager)
Alive - Chandler Baker   *h* 282

Buchanan, Daisy (Businesswoman; Detective—Amateur; Friend)
Lie of the Needle - Cate Price   *m* 636

Buchanan, Emily (Missing Person; Worker)
Spark - John Twelve Hawks   *c* 874

Buchanan, Polly (Detective—Private; Widow(er); Colleague)
The Laws of Murder - Charles Finch   *c* 743

Buchanan, Tucker (Engineer; Military Personnel)
Silken Threats - Addison Fox   *r* 966

Buchman, James (Religious)
The Devil's Game - Daniel Patterson   *i* 443

Buckley, Alex (Lawyer; Television Personality)
The Cinderella Murder - Mary Higgins Clark   *c* 713

Bud (Fiance(e); Spouse)
Saving Cecil - Lee Mims   *m* 620

Burchett, Will (Farmer; Boyfriend)
License to Dill - Mary Ellen Hughes   *m* 578

Burg (Demon)
Hellhole - Gina Damico   *h* 290

Burke, Sloan (Widow(er))
Operation Power Play - Justine Davis   *r* 952

Burke, William (Murderer)
Hare - Peter Ranscombe   *t* 234

Burnett, Emma (Bride; Sister)
Hope Burns - Jaci Burton   *r* 936

Burnett, Molly (Young Woman; Girlfriend; Sister)
Hope Burns - Jaci Burton   *r* 936

Burnley, Greg (Detective—Police)
What You Left Behind - Samantha Hayes   *m* 570

Mrs. Burns (Co-worker)
February Fever - Jess Lourey   *m* 607

Burns, Don (Detective—Police; Colleague)
The Winter Foundlings - Kate Rhodes   *m* 643

Burnsey, Maisa (Woman; Traveler)
Once and Always - Julia Harper   *r* 982

Burr, Timothy (Servant)
Love's Alchemy - Bryan Crockett   *t* 147

Busner, Dr. Zack (Psychologist)
Shark - Will Self   *c* 858

Butcher (Serial Killer)
Serpents in the Cold - Thomas O'Malley   *t* 222

Butterfield, Walt (Businessman; Recluse; Friend)
The Never-Open Desert Diner - James Anderson   *m* 478

Byler, Henry (Neighbor; Artisan; Patient; Religious)
Balm of Gilead - Adina Senft   *i* 456

Byler, Henry (Neighbor; Artist)
Keys of Heaven - Adina Senft   *i* 455

Byleth (Royalty)
Storm and Steel - Jon Sprunk   *f* 109

Byrne, Ian (Agent)
The Dragon Conspiracy - Lisa Shearin   *f* 107

Byrne, J.P. (Businessman; Man)
The Good Chase - Hanna Martine   *r* 1024

Lord Byron (Historical Figure; Student—College; Detective—Amateur; Rake)
Riot Most Uncouth - Daniel Friedman   *m* 552

C

Byron, Lord Lawrence (Twin)
The Bedding Proposal - Tracy Anne Warren *r* 1096

Byron, Lord Leo (Twin; Lover)
The Bedding Proposal - Tracy Anne Warren *r* 1096

Cabot, Grace (20-Year-Old; Daughter; Sister; Stepsister)
The Devil Takes a Bride - Julia London *r* 1012

Cabot, Honor (Daughter; Sister; Stepsister)
The Devil Takes a Bride - Julia London *r* 1012

Cabot, Jamie (Servant; Writer; Narrator)
The Hunger of the Wolf - Stephen Marche *r* 1019

Cabot, Lance (Director)
Paris Match - Stuart Woods *c* 889

Cabot, Mercy (Daughter; Sister; Stepsister)
The Devil Takes a Bride - Julia London *r* 1012

Cabot, Prudence (Daughter; Sister; Stepsister)
The Devil Takes a Bride - Julia London *r* 1012

Caden (Friend; Resistance Fighter; Teenager)
Unleashed - Sophie Jordan *s* 1157

Cady, Drew (FBI Agent; Colleague; Fiance(e))
The Lynchpin - Jeffrey B. Burton *m* 507

Caetano (Spouse)
Skylight - Jose Saramago *c* 854

Cafferty, Danni (Detective—Amateur; Girlfriend; Colleague; Classmate; Businesswoman)
The Dead Play On - Heather Graham *m* 560

Cajeiri (8-Year-Old; Son; Heir)
Tracker - C.J. Cherryh *s* 1125

Cal (Survivor; Spouse)
California - Edan Lepucki *c* 789

Calaprese, Vincent (Criminal; Crime Victim; Spirit)
Dying for the Past - T.J. O'Connor *m* 625

Calbert, Veranix (Young Man; Student—College; Vigilante)
The Thorn of Dentonhill - Marshall Ryan Maresca *f* 77

Caldani, Nadia (Witch; Girlfriend)
Sorceress - Claudia Gray *f* 38

Caldwell, Harrison (Journalist; Spy)
Spy of Richmond - Jocelyn Green *i* 409

Caldwell, Mike (Agent; Assassin)
Guardian - Erik Williams *h* 354

Caleb (Son; Brother; Religious)
Balm of Gilead - Adina Senft *i* 456

Callahan, Eileen (Religious)
Jacaranda - Cherie Priest *s* 1184

Callahan, Isaiah (Rescuer; Co-worker; Hostage)
Untraceable - Elizabeth Goddard *i* 404

Callahan, Luke (Government Official)
Beyond All Dreams - Elizabeth Camden *i* 374

Callahan, Mason (Police Officer)
Bridged - Kendra Elliot *r* 960

Callaway, Miles (Lover)
Morrow Creek Runaway - Lisa Plumley *r* 1049

Callum (Friend)
The Shadow Cabinet - Maureen Johnson *h* 322

Calms, Swan (Mother; Crime Suspect; Indian; Criminal; Spouse)
Where the Bones are Buried - Jeanne Matthews *m* 611

Camalier, Bitty (Woman; Companion)
Driving with the Top Down - Beth Harbison *c* 761

Cambridge, Kelsey (Detective—Amateur; Director; Crime Suspect; Mother; Divorced Person)
The Final Reveille - Amanda Flower *m* 547

Lord Cambury (Nobleman; Fiance(e); Wealthy)
The Spring Bride - Anne Gracie *r* 975

Cameron (Friend; Girlfriend)
I Saw Her Standing There - Marie Force *r* 964

Cameron (Son)
The Rebirths of Tao - Wesley Chu *s* 1126

Cameron, Bren (Linguist)
Tracker - C.J. Cherryh *s* 1125

Cameron, Robert Nelson (Crime Suspect)
The Devil You Know - Elisabeth de Mariaffi *m* 530

Camherst, Lady Isabella (Noblewoman; Naturalist; Mother)
Voyage of the Basilisk: A Memoir by Lady Trent - Marie Brennan *f* 16

Camherst, Jacob "Jake" (Son)
Voyage of the Basilisk: A Memoir by Lady Trent - Marie Brennan *f* 16

Campanella, Brook (Lawyer; Friend)
Shark Skin Suite - Tim Dorsey *c* 733

Campbell, Allison (Consultant; Detective—Amateur)
Dying Brand - Wendy Tyson *m* 675

Campbell, Ava (13-Year-Old; Daughter; Stepdaughter; Friend; Healer)
The Wonder of All Things - Jason Mott *c* 812

Campbell, Iona (Heir; Daughter)
Hot Blooded - Donna Grant *r* 976

Campbell, Joel (Military Personnel)
Hope Rising - Stacy Henrie *i* 987

Campbell, John (Man; Father)
Hot Blooded - Donna Grant *r* 976

Campbell, Macon (Lawman; Spouse; Father)
The Wonder of All Things - Jason Mott *c* 812

Campbell, Olin (Labor Leader)
Fate Moreland's Widow - John Lane *t* 197

Campbell, Rand (Lover; Military Personnel)
A Heart's Disguise - Colleen Coble *i* 382
A Heart's Obsession - Colleen Coble *i* 384

Campbell, Rand (Military Personnel; Fiance(e); Fiance(e))
A Heart's Danger - Colleen Coble *i* 385

Campion, Lucy (Apprentice; Detective—Amateur)
The Masque of a Murderer - Susanna Calkins *m* 510

Canaday, David (Animal Lover; Lawyer)
Kittens Can Kill - Clea Simon *m* 659

Cane, Harry (Spouse; Father)
A Place Called Winter - Patrick Gale *t* 162

Canfield, Grace (Baby; Sister; Patient)
The Murk - Robert Lettrick *h* 331

Canfield, Monty "Creeper" (Brother; Boy)
The Murk - Robert Lettrick *h* 331

Canfield, Piper (Girl; Friend; 14-Year-Old; Sister)
The Murk - Robert Lettrick *h* 331

Capel, Arthur (Historical Figure; Lover)
Mademoiselle Chanel - C.W. Gortner *t* 167

Caphalor (Warrior; Immortal)
Righteous Fury - Markus Heitz *f* 49

Cappelletti, Juliet (Girl; Lover; Teenager)
Juliet's Nurse - Lois Leveen *t* 204

Captain Lore (Military Personnel)
Heir of Hope - Morgan L. Busse *i* 368

Cardwell, Austin (Police Officer)
Deliverance at Cardwell Ranch - B.J. Daniels *r* 948

Caribou, Swamper (Indian; Healer)
The Ravens - Vidar Sundstol *m* 669

Caridad (Slave; Worker; Crime Victim; Friend; Smuggler; Young Woman)
The Barefoot Queen - Ildefonso Falcones *t* 156

Lady Carinna (Employer; Sister)
An Appetite for Violets - Martine Bailey *t* 128

Carl (Brother)
Life or Death - Michael Robotham *m* 645

Carl (Student; Friend)
Mars Evacuees - Sophia McDougall *s* 1176

Carla Scout (3-Year-Old; Daughter)
Hush Hush - Laura Lippman *m* 604

Carlo (Spouse; Uncle)
Fear the Darkness - Becky Masterman *m* 610

Carlson, Charlie (Detective—Homicide; Friend; Colleague)
Lethal Beauty - Lis Wiehl *i* 470

Carmen (Spouse)
Skylight - Jose Saramago *c* 854

Carmen (Woman; Spouse; Stepmother)
The Wonder of All Things - Jason Mott *c* 812

Carmichael, Gavin (Employer; Brother)
Stirring Up Trouble - Kimberly Kincaid *r* 1000

Carmine (Son)
An Italian Wife - Ann Hood *c* 768

Carne, Sherry (Store Owner; Lover)
The Immortal Who Loved Me - Lynsay Sands *r* 1069

Carnehan, Carter (Son; Kidnap Victim; Slave)
In Dark Service - Stephen Hunt *f* 58

Carnehan, Jacob (Father; Religious)
In Dark Service - Stephen Hunt *f* 58

Caroline (Spouse)
The Figaro Murders - Laura Lebow *t* 199

Caron (Teenager; Daughter)
Pride v. Prejudice - Joan Hess *m* 573

Carpenter, Jamie (Teenager; Agent)
Darkest Night - Will Hill *h* 317
Zero Hour - Will Hill *h* 316

Carpenter, Sabina (Co-worker; Detective— Private; Investigator)
The Body Snatchers Affair - Marcia Muller *t* 218

Carrick, Thomas (Businessman; Wealthy)
The Tempting of Thomas Carrick - Stephanie Laurens *r* 1005

Carrie (Student—High School)
Wolf in White Van - John Darnielle *c* 726

Carrier, Judy (Lawyer; Niece)
Betrayed - Lisa Scottoline *c* 857

Carrigan, Jack (Detective)
Eleven Days - Stav Sherez *m* 658

Carrington, Emilia "Mia" Gwendolyn (Young Woman; Spouse)
Four Nights with the Duke - Eloisa James *r* 993

Carson, Cat (Singer)
Sweet Harmony - LuAnn McLane *r* 1032

Carstairs, Eloisa (Debutante; Wealthy; Girlfriend; Crime Victim)
Deception on Sable Hill - Shelley Gray *i* 408

Carter, Aimee (12-Year-Old; Daughter)
Last One Home - Debbie Macomber *c* 794

Carter, Cassie (Spouse; Mother; Daughter; Sister)
Last One Home - Debbie Macomber *c* 794

Carter, Daniel (Professor; Friend)
The Heart Has Its Reasons - Maria Duenas   *c* 736

Carter, Duke (Spouse; Father)
Last One Home - Debbie Macomber   *c* 794

Carter, Jo (Sister; Detective—Amateur)
The London Pride - Charlie Fletcher   *f* 34

Carter, Lily (Baker)
Buy a Whisker - Sofie Ryan   *m* 650

Carter, Penny (Expert)
The Conquering Dark - Clay Griffith   *h* 308

Carter, Will (Brother; Detective—Amateur)
The London Pride - Charlie Fletcher   *f* 34

Cartier, Andre (Uncle; Crime Suspect)
Dying for the Past - T.J. O'Connor   *m* 625

Cartwright, Tessa (Single Mother; Crime Victim; Mentally Ill Person)
Black-Eyed Susans - Julia Heaberlin   *m* 572

Case, Matilda (Immortal; Sister; Friend; Fugitive)
Infinity Bell - Devon Monk   *f* 83

Cass (Fisherman; Detective—Amateur)
A Finely Knit Murder - Sally Goldenbaum   *m* 557

Cass (Teenager; Sister; Rebel)
City 1 - Gregg Rosenblum   *s* 1192

Cassandra "Cass" (Narrator; Outcast; Twin; Psychic)
The Fire Sermon - Francesca Haig   *s* 1151

Cassanova, Figueora "Figgy" (Baseball Player; Missing Person; Man)
Cuba Straits - Randy Wayne White   *m* 681

Cassian, Samuel (Artist; Father)
The City of Blood - Frederique Molay   *m* 622

Cassidy, Michael (Detective—Police)
Night Life - David C. Taylor   *t* 258

Castille, Emma (Con Artist)
Twisted - Cynthia Eden   *r* 958

Castle, Lilah (Friend; Store Owner)
Silken Threats - Addison Fox   *r* 966

Castleton, Clara (Businesswoman; Single Mother)
His Reluctant Cinderella - Jessica Gilmore   *r* 971

Caswell (Young Woman; Military Personnel)
A Long Time Until Now - Michael Z. Williamson   *s* 1208

Cat (Sister; Stepdaughter)
The Soul of Discretion - Susan Hill   *m* 574

Cateman Kingsley, Elizabeth (Socialite; Client)
Checked Out - Elaine Viets   *m* 677

Cates, Dallas (Rodeo Rider; Boyfriend; Crime Suspect)
Endangered - C.J. Box   *m* 499

Cates, Rylan (Baseball Player)
No One Like You - Kate Angell   *r* 901

Cathy (Teacher; Woman)
The Love Book - Nina Solomon   *c* 866

Catrell, Dana (Woman; Mentally Ill Person; Spouse; Mother; Friend)
The Pocket Wife - Susan Crawford   *m* 524

Catrell, Jamie (Student—College; Son)
The Pocket Wife - Susan Crawford   *m* 524

Catrell, Peter (Lawyer; Spouse; Father)
The Pocket Wife - Susan Crawford   *m* 524

Catt (Alcoholic; Hairdresser; Spouse; Friend)
Beyond the Pale Motel - Francesca Lia Block   *c* 704

Caulfield, Eleanor (Lover; Foster Child; Companion)
I Loved a Rogue - Katharine Ashe   *r* 903

Cavale (Brother)
Grave Matters - Lauren M. Roy   *f* 101

Cavanaugh, Patience (Innkeeper; Friend)
The Trouble with Patience - Maggie Brendan   *i* 364

Cawdor, Ryan (Warrior; Survivor)
Forbidden Trespass - James Axler   *s* 1111

Cawdor, Ryan (Warrior; Time Traveler)
End Day - James Axler   *s* 1110

Cazalet, Jake (Political Figure)
Rain on the Dead - Jack Higgins   *c* 766

Cecil, Robert (Historical Figure; Political Figure)
Love's Alchemy - Bryan Crockett   *t* 147

Celeste (Sister; Manager; Daughter)
The Amado Women - Desiree Zamorano   *c* 892

Celia (Sister)
The Boston Girl - Anita Diamant   *t* 149

Ceridwen (Deity)
Firestorm - Nancy Holzner   *h* 318

Cermak, Clare (Psychic; Girlfriend; Accountant)
Ghost Killer - Robin D. Owens   *f* 91

Chaloner, Thomas (Spy)
The Cheapside Corpse - Susanna Gregory   *t* 169

Chambers, Chelsea (Single Mother; Businesswoman; Friend)
Miracle at the Higher Grounds Cafe - Max Lucado   *i* 430

Chambers, Mackenzie "Mack" (Friend; Police Officer)
Bittersweet - Susan Wittig Albert   *m* 476

Chambers, Ryan (Lighthouse Keeper; Veteran)
Hearts Made Whole - Jody Hedlund   *i* 416

Chambers, Zoe (Health Care Professional)
Bridges Burned - Annette Dashofy   *m* 527

Chambers Perry, Izzy (Detective—Amateur; Businesswoman; Niece)
A Finely Knit Murder - Sally Goldenbaum   *m* 557

Chance, Hotspur (Enemy)
Quake - Patrick Carman   *s* 1124

Chance, Jane (Woman; Fiance(e))
The Spring Bride - Anne Gracie   *r* 975

Chance, Mirabelle (Designer; Lover)
Paris Match - Stuart Woods   *c* 889

Chandler, Wilhelmina "Willie" (Accountant; Friend; Roommate)
Superfluous Women - Carola Dunn   *m* 538

Chanel, Gabrielle "Coco" (Historical Figure; Designer; Lover)
Mademoiselle Chanel - C.W. Gortner   *t* 167

Chang, Hu (Friend)
Your Next Breath - Iris Johansen   *m* 586

Chap (Friend)
First and Last Sorcerer - Barb Hendee   *f* 52

Charity, Olivia (Woman)
Day Shift - Charlaine Harris   *h* 314

Charles (Historical Figure; Royalty)
The Cheapside Corpse - Susanna Gregory   *t* 169

Charles, Lenora (Agent; Friend; Security Officer)
Howling Mountain Blues - Ricky Bush   *m* 508

Charles, Marcus (Detective—Police; Colleague)
A Woman Unknown - Frances Brody   *t* 134

Charles, Sara (Pilot; Businesswoman)
Angel in Armani - Melanie Scott   *r* 1072

Charlie (Friend; Crime Victim)
Fall with Me - Jennifer L. Armentrout   *r* 902

Charlie (Son; Brother)
It Won't Always Be This Great - Peter Mehlman   *c* 803

Charlie (Veteran; Friend)
Amish Promises - Leslie Gould   *i* 405

Charlotte (Aged Person; Businesswoman; Grandmother; Crime Suspect)
Twisted Threads - Lea Wait   *m* 678

Charlotte (Friend; Kidnap Victim)
The Shadow Cabinet - Maureen Johnson   *h* 322

Charlotte (Werewolf)
The Conquering Dark - Clay Griffith   *h* 308

Chase, Frederick (Detective)
Moriarty - Anthony Horowitz   *c* 771

Chastain, David (Carpenter)
A Stranger's Secret - Laurie Alice Eakes   *i* 394

Chaucer, Geoffrey (Historical Figure; Writer; Friend)
The Invention of Fire - Bruce W. Holsinger   *t* 179

Chaudhary, Jeevan (Man; Worker)
Station Eleven - Emily St. John Mandel   *c* 796

Chavez, Antonio (Heir)
A Palette for Murder - Vanessa A. Ryan   *m* 651

Chazz (Friend; Accident Victim)
Doll Face - Tim Curran   *h* 288

Cheeon (Hunter; Friend)
Hold the Dark - William Giraldi   *c* 749

Chekov, Pavel (Military Personnel)
Crisis of Consciousness - Dave Galanter   *s* 1147
Savage Trade - Tony Daniel   *s* 1134

Cheney, Dick (Political Figure; Colleague; Historical Figure)
The Global War on Morris - Steve Israel   *c* 772

Cheney, Dick (Political Figure; Historical Figure)
The Infernal - Mark Doten   *c* 734

Cheramie, Leon (Homosexual; Lover)
Under His Guard - Rie Warren   *s* 1206

Cherish (Young Woman; Girlfriend)
Glow - Ned Beauman   *c* 699

Cherry, Cynthia (Businesswoman; Friend; Aged Person; Administrator)
The Final Reveille - Amanda Flower   *m* 547

Chevalier, Alene (Widow(er))
Into the Savage Country - Shannon Burke   *t* 136

Chevestrier, Jack (Police Officer)
Blood of the South - Alys Clare   *t* 141

Chey (Boy; 15-Year-Old; Friend)
The Second Guard - J.D. Vaughn   *f* 119

Childs, Clare (Woman; Shipowner)
Maggie Bright: A Novel of Dunkirk - Tracy Groot   *i* 410

Chimbrova, Pearl (Saloon Keeper/Owner)
The Jazz Palace - Mary Morris   *t* 215

Chip (Bridegroom; Traveler; Spouse)
Mermaids in Paradise - Lydia Millet   *c* 805

Chloe (Baby; Daughter)
In the Woods - Merry Jones   *m* 587

Chris (Mother; Spouse; Friend)
This Is the Water - Yannick Murphy   *c* 813

Chris (Son; Spouse)
Cold Betrayal - J.A. Jance   *m* 584

Christina (Friend)
The Legacy - Dan Walsh   *i* 467

Christopher (Patient; Twin)
Find Me - Laura van den Berg   *c* 877

Chrystal (Friend; Cyborg; Artificial Intelligence)
Edge of Dark - Brenda Cooper   *s* 1132

Churchill, Winston (Historical Figure; Political Figure)
The Lusitania Conspiracy - Ronald J. Walters   *t* 269
Sleep in Peace Tonight - James MacManus   *t* 208

Churchill, Winston (Political Figure; Historical Figure)
Maggie Bright: A Novel of Dunkirk - Tracy Groot *i* 410

Cicero, Hunt (Artist; Uncle)
Teardrop Lane - Emily March *r* 1018

Cinq-Mars, Emile (Detective—Police; Retiree; Spouse)
The Storm Murders - John Farrow *m* 543

Claire (Musician; Friend)
The Never-Open Desert Diner - James Anderson *m* 478

Clara (Store Owner; Sister; Crime Victim)
Wicked Stitch - Amanda Lee *m* 597

Clarissa (Spouse)
The Cavendon Women - Barbara Taylor Bradford *t* 133

Clark, Lacey (Mother; Actress)
You're So Fine - Kieran Kramer *r* 1002

Clark, Wilhemina "Mina" (Guard)
The Dead Lands - Benjamin Percy *s* 1182

Clayborne, Chance (Boy; Teenager; Enemy)
Terminal - Kathy Reichs *s* 1187

Claybourne, Chance (Scientist)
Exposure - Kathy Reichs *s* 1186

Cleaver, John Wayne (17-Year-Old; Hunter; Friend; Mentally Ill Person)
The Devil's Only Friend - Dan Wells *h* 352

Clee (Daughter; Roommate; 21-Year-Old)
The First Bad Man - Miranda July *c* 778

Clement (Historical Figure; Religious)
John the Pupil - David L. Flusfeder *t* 158

Clive (Actor)
Funny Girl - Nick Hornby *c* 770

Cobb, Chris "Kit" (Spy; Son; Journalist)
The Empire of Night - Robert Olen Butler *t* 138

Cobb, Isabel (Actress; Mother; Spy; Lover)
The Empire of Night - Robert Olen Butler *t* 138

Cochrane, Nathan (Military Personnel; Father)
Impulse - Dave Bara *s* 1115

Cochrane, Peter (Military Personnel; Son)
Impulse - Dave Bara *s* 1115

Cocteau, Jean (Historical Figure; Artist; Writer)
Mademoiselle Chanel - C.W. Gortner *t* 167

Cody (Teenager; Boy)
Firefight - Brandon Sanderson *f* 104

Cohen, Gordie (Graduate; Friend)
The Sirena Quest - Michael A. Kahn *m* 589

Cole, Bradley (Spouse)
Double Mint - Gretchen Archer *m* 481

Cole, Brianna (Nurse; Spouse; Neighbor)
Snowstorm Confessions - Rachel Lee *r* 1009

Cole, Darwin (Pilot; Military Personnel)
Unmanned - Dan Fesperman *c* 742

Cole, Davis Way (Woman; Security Officer; Detective; Spouse)
Double Mint - Gretchen Archer *m* 481

Cole, Elvis (Detective—Private; Colleague; Veteran)
The Promise - Robert Crais *c* 720

Cole, Nat King (Historical Figure; Singer; Friend)
Driving the King - Ravi Howard *t* 180

Cole, Tess (Public Relations)
Convincing the Rancher - Claire McEwen *r* 1028

Coleman, Emily (Woman; Spouse; Mother; Secretary; Twin; Friend; Lawyer)
One Step Too Far - Tina Seskis *c* 859

Collard, Ivy (Store Owner; Aunt)
The Mill River Redemption - Darcie Chan *c* 711

Collins, Aramintha "Thea" (Lady)
The Duke's Disaster - Grace Burrowes *r* 934

Collins, Mason (Detective—Homicide; Military Personnel)
Ruins of War - John Connell *t* 144

Collins, Michael (Historical Figure)
Of Irish Blood - Mary Pat Kelly *t* 188

Collins, Packie (Co-worker)
The Thing About December - Donal Ryan *c* 850

Collins, Russ (Contractor)
A Sticky Situation - Jessie Crockett *m* 525

Colonel Smith (Father; Mentally Ill Person; Crime Victim)
The Abduction of Smith and Smith - Rashad Harrison *t* 174

Colossus (Elephant)
Colossus - Colin Falconer *t* 155

Colt-Manning, Mase (Young Man; Rancher)
When I'm Gone - Abbi Glines *r* 972

Colten, AJ (Veteran; Therapist)
Still the One - Jill Shalvis *r* 1076

Colton, Elinor (Widow(er); Neighbor)
The Rake's Handbook: Including Field Guide - Sally Orr *r* 1045

Conley, Clancy (Journalist; Crime Victim)
Deadline - John Sandford *c* 852

Conlon, Evelyn (Sister; Mentally Challenged Person; Missing Person)
Lies That Bind - Maggie Barbieri *m* 487

Conlon, Maeve (Detective—Amateur; Baker; Store Owner; Single Mother; Sister)
Lies That Bind - Maggie Barbieri *m* 487

Connard, Howard Sr. (Fiance(e); Patient; Wealthy; Father)
Etta Mae's Worst Bad-Luck Day - Ann B. Ross *c* 848

Connard, Howard Jr. (Son)
Etta Mae's Worst Bad-Luck Day - Ann B. Ross *c* 848

Connelly, Jake (Teenager; 17-Year-Old; Student—High School; Crime Suspect; Missing Person; Brother; Son)
Finding Jake - Bryan Reardon *m* 639

Connelly, Laney (Teenager; Student—High School; Sister; Daughter)
Finding Jake - Bryan Reardon *m* 639

Connelly, Rachel (Spouse; Mother; Lawyer)
Finding Jake - Bryan Reardon *m* 639

Connelly, Simon (Father; Spouse)
Finding Jake - Bryan Reardon *m* 639

Connolly, Claire (Human)
The Veil - Chloe Neill *h* 334

Connor (Worker)
One Foot in the Grape - Carlene O'Neil *m* 627

Conover, Linda (Judge)
The Missing Piece - Kevin Egan *m* 540

Conti, Raffaele (Manager; Crime Victim)
License to Dill - Mary Ellen Hughes *m* 578

Cooke, Ames (Lover)
Some Like It Hotter - Isabel Sharpe *r* 1079

Cooked (Worker; Spouse)
The Last Good Paradise - Tatjana Soli *c* 865

Coolidge, Sunny (Detective—Amateur; Journalist; Girlfriend)
Hiss and Tell - Claire Donally *m* 536

Cooper, Abby (Detective—Amateur; Spouse; Friend; Psychic)
Sense of Deception - Victoria Laurie *f* 69

Cooper, Cleo (Scientist; Detective—Amateur; Fiance(e); Crime Suspect; Spouse)
Saving Cecil - Lee Mims *m* 620

Cooper, Dante (Widow(er); Addict; Friend)
Serpents in the Cold - Thomas O'Malley *t* 222

Cooper, Dex (Musician; Lover; Vacationer)
The Last Good Paradise - Tatjana Soli *c* 865

Cooper, Mel (Girlfriend; Businesswoman; Co-worker; Detective—Amateur)
Dark Chocolate Demise - Jenn McKinlay *m* 616

Cooper, Olive (Psychic)
What the Fly Saw - Frankie Y. Bailey *m* 483

Cooper, Shaylene (Mother)
There Will Be Lies - Nick Lake *f* 66

Cooper, Shelby Jane (Friend; 17-Year-Old; Deaf Person; Accident Victim; Daughter)
There Will Be Lies - Nick Lake *f* 66

Copperfield, Teagan (Woman; Thief; Crime Suspect)
Once a Thief - Lora Young *i* 472

Cora (Sister)
Polaris - Mindee Arnett *s* 1107

Corban (Hero; Resistance Fighter)
Ruin - John Gwynne *f* 45

Corbyn, Meg (Prophet)
Vision in Silver - Anne Bishop *f* 15

Corcoran, Faith (Psychologist; Crime Victim)
Closer Than You Think - Karen Rose *r* 1062

Corcoran, Jimmy (Expert; Criminal)
Past Crimes - Glen Erik Hamilton *m* 566

Core, Russell (Expert)
Hold the Dark - William Giraldi *c* 749

Corey, Ursula (Crime Victim)
Motive - Jonathan Kellerman *c* 780

Cornick, Charles (Werewolf; Worker; Lover)
Dead Heat - Patricia Briggs *f* 18

Cortez, Isabella "Ella" (FBI Agent)
Disarming Detective - Elizabeth Heiter *r* 986

Costantini, Salvatore (Sports Figure)
The Sweetheart - Angelina Mirabella *t* 211

Costello, Frank (Organized Crime Figure; Godfather)
Night Life - David C. Taylor *t* 258

Coughlin, Joe (Advisor; Widow(er); Father)
World Gone By - Dennis Lehane *t* 201

Coughlin, Maureen (Police Officer)
Doing the Devil's Work - Bill Loehfelm *m* 606

Coulter, Dirk (Detective—Police; Spouse)
Killer Gourmet - G.A. McKevett *m* 615

Coulter, John (Lover; Military Personnel)
Daughter of the Regiment - Stephanie Grace Whitson *i* 469

Courtney (Girlfriend; Student—High School; Friend; Vigilante; Teenager; Drug Dealer)
Zombified - Adam Gallardo *h* 302

Covington, Cole (Wealthy; Military Personnel; Accident Victim; Patient; Brother)
Return to Me - Kelly Moran *r* 1038

Covington, Lacey (Sister; Wealthy)
Return to Me - Kelly Moran *r* 1038

Cowan, George (Criminal; Convict; Father)
Hush - Karen Robards *r* 1058

Cowan, Jeff (Spouse; Son; Crime Victim)
Hush - Karen Robards *r* 1058

Cowan, Riley (Woman; Spouse)
Hush - Karen Robards *r* 1058

Craddock, Samuel (Lawman; Neighbor)
A Deadly Affair at Bobtail Ridge - Terry Shames *m* 656

Cragg, Titus (Investigator; Friend)
The Hidden Man - Robin Blake   *m* 495

Cramer, Holly (Lover; Mother; Detective—Amateur)
Twisted Innocence - Terri Blackstock   *i* 363

Cramer, Lily (Daughter)
Twisted Innocence - Terri Blackstock   *i* 363

Crane, Charlie (Father; Spouse; Wealthy)
When We Fall - Emily Liebert   *c* 791

Crane, Charlotte (Spouse; Mother; Friend)
When We Fall - Emily Liebert   *c* 791

Crane, Gia (9-Year-Old; Daughter)
When We Fall - Emily Liebert   *c* 791

Crane, Leo (Friend; Writer)
Whiskey Tango Foxtrot - David Shafer   *c* 860

Cranston, John (Detective—Amateur; Nobleman)
The Book of Fires - Paul Doherty   *t* 150

Craven, Jonathan (Accident Victim; Brother)
A Good Rake Is Hard to Find - Manda Collins   *r* 944

Craven, Leonora "Nora" (Sister; Fiance(e))
A Good Rake Is Hard to Find - Manda Collins   *r* 944

Crawford, Julie (Woman; Assistant; Worker)
A Touch of Stardust - Kate Alcott   *t* 125

Crawford, Miller (Teenager; Wealthy)
Rich Kids of Instagram - Creator of Rich Kids of Instagram   *c* 721

Creed, Annja (Archaeologist; Television Personality; Detective—Amateur)
Bathed in Blood - Alex Archer   *f* 6

Creed, Annja (Archaeologist; Television Personality; Friend; Colleague)
Death Mask - Alex Archer   *f* 5

Creed, Ryder (Veteran; Trainer)
Breaking Creed - Alex Kava   *c* 779

Creep (Friend; Accident Victim)
Doll Face - Tim Curran   *h* 288

Crocker, Ben (Friend; Accountant; Administrator)
Fate Moreland's Widow - John Lane   *t* 197

Crocker, Nick (Professor; Lover)
Amherst - William Nicholson   *t* 221

Croftner, Ben (Fiance(e); Villain)
A Heart's Obsession - Colleen Coble   *i* 384

Croftner, Ben (Fiance(e); Villain; Kidnapper)
A Heart's Disguise - Colleen Coble   *i* 382

Croftner, Ben (Military Personnel)
A Heart's Danger - Colleen Coble   *i* 385

Cromer, Ridley (Man; Shape-Shifter)
Cat's Lair - Christine Feehan   *h* 298

Cronley, James D. Jr. (Military Personnel; Spy; Widow(er))
Top Secret - W.E.B. Griffin   *c* 755

Crosbie, Daniel (Tutor)
By Winter's Light - Stephanie Laurens   *r* 1006

Cross (Immortal; Man; Rogue)
The Dead Hamlets - Peter Roman   *f* 99

Cross, Alex (Grandson; Detective; Spouse; Father)
Hope to Die - James Patterson   *c* 824

Cross, Alex Jr. (Kidnap Victim; Son; Stepson; Stepbrother)
Hope to Die - James Patterson   *c* 824

Cross, Damon (Kidnap Victim; Son; Stepson; Brother; Stepbrother)
Hope to Die - James Patterson   *c* 824

Cross, Emma (Writer; Detective—Amateur)
Murder at Beechwood - Alyssa Maxwell   *m* 612

Cross, Janelle "Jannie" (Daughter; Stepdaughter; Sister; Stepsister; Kidnap Victim)
Hope to Die - James Patterson   *c* 824

Cross, Stella (Patient; Teenager; Girlfriend; Friend; Young Woman; Student—High School)
Alive - Chandler Baker   *h* 282

Crosswhite, Sarah (Sister; Crime Victim)
My Sister's Grave - Robert Dugoni   *c* 737

Crosswhite, Tracy (Detective—Homicide; Sister)
My Sister's Grave - Robert Dugoni   *c* 737

Crow (Boyfriend; Father)
Hush Hush - Laura Lippman   *m* 604

Crowe, Samantha (Student—Graduate)
Deadly, Calm, and Cold - Susannah Sandlin   *r* 1068

Crowley (Police Officer; Lover)
Puzzled Indemnity - Parnell Hall   *m* 565

Crusher, Beverly (Doctor; Colleague)
The Missing - Una McCormack   *s* 1175

Cruz, Madeline (FBI Agent)
The Big Finish - James W. Hall   *c* 758

Cruz, Poppy (Sister; Friend)
Rowdy - Jay Crownover   *r* 945

Cruz, Salem (Manager; Friend; Sister)
Rowdy - Jay Crownover   *r* 945

Crystal (Lover; Student)
On the Edge - Edward St. Aubyn   *c* 867

Cunliffe, Johnsey (Friend; Farmer; Young Man; Son; Mentally Challenged Person)
The Thing About December - Donal Ryan   *c* 850

Cunningham, Dodd (Religious; Friend)
Jaded - Varina Denman   *i* 392

Cunningham, Lauren (Woman)
Love by the Book - Melissa Pimentel   *c* 830

Curtis, Angie (Granddaughter; Detective—Amateur; Woman; Crime Suspect)
Twisted Threads - Lea Wait   *m* 678

Lord Curzon (Ruler; Nobleman)
Treachery in Tibet - John Wilcox   *t* 271

Custer, Aaron (Crime Suspect; Grandson)
Slow Burn - Andrew Welsh-Huggins   *m* 680

Custer, Dorothy (Grandmother)
Slow Burn - Andrew Welsh-Huggins   *m* 680

Custer, George Armstrong (Historical Figure; Military Personnel)
Valley of the Shadow - Ralph Peters   *t* 231

Custer, George Armstrong (Historical Figure; Military Personnel; Spouse)
1882: Custer in Chains - Robert Conroy   *s* 1130

Custer, Libbie (Spouse)
1882: Custer in Chains - Robert Conroy   *s* 1130

Custis, Denny (Crime Victim)
Neighing with Fire - Kathryn O'Sullivan   *m* 628

Cutter (Dog)
Operation Power Play - Justine Davis   *r* 952

Cutter, R. "Rags" A. (Mercenary; Military Personnel)
The Tejano Conflict - Steve Perry   *s* 1183

Cynster, Lucilla (Woman; Healer)
The Tempting of Thomas Carrick - Stephanie Laurens   *r* 1005

Cyril (Friend; Man; Missing Person)
Lie of the Needle - Cate Price   *m* 636

D

D'Agosta, Vincent (Police Officer; Friend)
Blue Labyrinth - Douglas Preston   *c* 837

D'Alisa, Juliette (Businesswoman; Girlfriend; Critic; Daughter; Granddaughter)
Reservations for Two - Hillary Manton Lodge   *i* 428

D'Ambrosia, Alouette (Actress)
Beautiful You - Chuck Palahniuk   *c* 823

D'Amour, Harry (Paranormal Investigator)
The Scarlet Gospels - Clive Barker   *h* 283

D'Artigo, Camille (Cousin; Witch; Sister)
Panther Prowling - Yasmine Galenorn   *h* 301

D'Artigo, Delilah (Detective—Private; Sister; Supernatural Being; Cousin)
Panther Prowling - Yasmine Galenorn   *h* 301

D'Artigo, Menolly (Vampire; Sister; Cousin; Restaurateur)
Panther Prowling - Yasmine Galenorn   *h* 301

d'Orleans, Gaston (Brother)
1636: The Cardinal Virtues - Eric Flint   *s* 1145

Da Ponte, Lorenzo (Writer)
The Figaro Murders - Laura Lebow   *t* 199

Dad (Father; Mentally Ill Person)
Reunion - Hannah Pittard   *c* 833

Dadda (Father)
How to Build a Girl - Caitlin Moran   *c* 810

Daed (Religious; Spouse; Father)
The Proposal at Siesta Key - Shelley Shepard Gray   *i* 406

Daggett, Brad (Contractor; Lover)
The Kind Worth Killing - Peter Swanson   *m* 670

Dahaba (Niece; Sister; Daughter)
Hiding in Plain Sight - Nuruddin Farah   *c* 741

Daisy (2-Year-Old; Niece; Sister)
Teardrop Lane - Emily March   *r* 1018

Dale, Lilah (Divorced Person; Twin)
Mammoth Secrets - Ashley Elizabeth Ludwig   *i* 431

Dallas, Eve (Detective—Police; Spouse)
Obsession in Death - J.D. Robb   *c* 847

Dallington, Lord John (Colleague; Nobleman; Detective—Private)
The Laws of Murder - Charles Finch   *c* 743

Dalrymple, Daisy (Journalist; Spouse; Detective—Amateur; Friend)
Superfluous Women - Carola Dunn   *m* 538

Dalt (Young Man; Adventurer; Spouse)
If Not for This - Pete Fromm   *c* 745

Dalton, Paul (Police Officer)
Death by Coffee - Alex Erickson   *m* 542

Damek (Royalty)
Witches with the Enemy - Barb Hendee   *f* 51

Damon, The Earl of Mardoun (Leader; Widow(er))
Pleasured - Candace Camp   *r* 940

Dan (Boyfriend; Colleague)
Getting Even - Sarah Rayner   *c* 842

Dance, Kathryn (Agent)
Solitude Creek - Jeffrey Deaver   *m* 531

Dancy, Rosamond (Housekeeper; Widow(er))
Morrow Creek Runaway - Lisa Plumley   *r* 1049

Dandridge, Delta (Southern Belle)
Texas Mail Order Bride - Linda Broday   *r* 927

Dane, Matthew (Detective—Private; Father)
Taken - Dee Henderson   *i* 417

Daniel (Adoptee; Son)
Tangled Lives - Hilary Boyd   *c* 705

Daniel (Cousin)
Panther Prowling - Yasmine Galenorn   *h* 301

Delaware, Alex (Psychologist)
Motive - Jonathan Kellerman *c* 780

Dellamare, Claire (Vacationer)
The Inn at Ocean's Edge - Colleen Coble *i* 383

Delores (Mother; Spouse)
Double Fudge Brownie Murder - Joanne Fluke *m* 548

DeLuca, Cara (Planner; Spouse)
All Fired Up - Kate Meader *r* 1037

Dempsey, Susan (Student—College; Crime Victim)
The Cinderella Murder - Mary Higgins Clark *c* 713

Denise (Young Woman; Friend)
Paris Red - Maureen Gibbon *t* 164

Dennis (Director)
Funny Girl - Nick Hornby *c* 770

Dent, Andy (Son; Diabetic; Student)
Constant Fear - Daniel Palmer *m* 629

Dent, Howie (Companion; Crime Victim)
Whiskers of the Lion - P.L. Gaus *m* 555

Dent, Jake (Father; Worker)
Constant Fear - Daniel Palmer *m* 629

Derby, Cordelia (Teenager; Wealthy)
Rich Kids of Instagram - Creator of Rich Kids of Instagram *c* 721

Derring, Brook (Investigator; Brother)
Earls Just Want to Have Fun - Shana Galen *r* 970

Derring, Maxwell (Nobleman; Brother; Guardian)
Earls Just Want to Have Fun - Shana Galen *r* 970

Desirio, Antonio (Aged Person)
The Teller - Jonathan Stone *m* 668

Desmond, Lord Richard (Crime Victim; Psychic; Leader)
The Hanged Man - P.N. Elrod *h* 296

Desrocher, Francois (Director)
Asylum - Jeannette de Beauvoir *m* 529

Desyrk (Wizard)
Madness in Solidar - L.E. Modesitt *f* 82

Dethan (Warrior; Captive; Immortal)
Cursed by Fire - Jacquelyn Frank *f* 36

Deveaux, Rory (Girl; Teenager; Student—Boarding School; Hunter; Friend)
The Shadow Cabinet - Maureen Johnson *h* 322

Deveraux, Mark (Friend; Worker)
Whiskey Tango Foxtrot - David Shafer *c* 860

Devereaux, Armand (Military Personnel)
A Long Time Until Now - Michael Z. Williamson *s* 1208

Devereaux, Caleb (Wealthy; Brother; Employer)
Keep Me Safe - Maya Banks *r* 908

Devereaux, Tori (Kidnap Victim; Sister)
Keep Me Safe - Maya Banks *r* 908

Devereux, Clarence (Criminal)
Moriarty - Anthony Horowitz *c* 771

Devi (Mother; Engineer)
Aurora - Kim Stanley Robinson *s* 1191

Devil (Demon)
The Devil's Game - Daniel Patterson *i* 443

Devos, Dred (Prisoner)
Breakout - Ann Aguirre *s* 1103

Dex (Classmate; Trainer)
Friendswood - Rene Steinke *c* 869

Di, Lung (Brother; Enemy; Magician)
The Dragons of Heaven - Alyc Helms *f* 50

Diamond, Jacob "Jake" (Detective—Private; Colleague)
Circling the Runway - J.L. Abramo *m* 474

Diane (Mentally Ill Person; Mother)
If I Fall, If I Die - Michael Christie *c* 712

Dickens, Charles (Writer; Journalist; Historical Figure)
The Final Recollections of Charles Dickens - Thomas Hauser *t* 175

Dickinson, Alice (Advertising; Writer; Lover)
Amherst - William Nicholson *t* 221

Dickinson, Austin (Lover; Brother; Historical Figure)
Amherst - William Nicholson *t* 221

Dickinson, Emily (Historical Figure; Writer; Sister)
Amherst - William Nicholson *t* 221

Diedre (Daughter)
The Cavendon Women - Barbara Taylor Bradford *t* 133

Diesel (Cat)
Arsenic and Old Books - Miranda James *m* 583

Digby, Kenelm (Nobleman; Historical Figure; Scientist; Diplomat; Political Figure; Explorer; Spouse)
Viper Wine - Hermione Eyre *t* 154

Dillinger, Marcus (Baseball Player; Volunteer; Co-worker)
Chasing Sunsets - Karen Kingsbury *i* 425

Dillon, Grace (Woman; Skater; Store Owner)
One Wish - Robyn Carr *r* 942

Dillon, Sean (Agent)
Rain on the Dead - Jack Higgins *c* 766

Dino (Young Man; Warrior)
The Boy Who Wept Blood - Den Patrick *f* 93

Diotima (Religious; Spouse)
Death Ex Machina - Gary Corby *t* 145

Dirk (Spirit; Friend)
A Wee Murder in My Shop - Fran Stewart *m* 667

DiSanti, Josie (Mother)
The Mill River Redemption - Darcie Chan *c* 711

Divine, Dorisanne (Missing Person; Sister)
The Case of the Sin City Sister - Lynne Hinton *i* 419

Divine, Eve (Religious; Sister; Detective—Private)
The Case of the Sin City Sister - Lynne Hinton *i* 419

Dixon, Greg (Editor)
Slayed on the Slopes - Kate Dyer-Seeley *m* 539

Djurkovic, Antun Dragun (Father; Missing Person)
The Lady from Zagreb - Philip Kerr *t* 191

Dobbs, Frankie (Aged Person; Father)
A Dangerous Place - Jacqueline Winspear *t* 273

Dobbs, Maisie (Detective—Private; Widow(er); Daughter; Traveler)
A Dangerous Place - Jacqueline Winspear *t* 273

Doctor (Doctor)
Method 15/33 - Shannon Kirk *m* 594

Doll, Hannah (Spouse; Lover)
The Zone of Interest - Martin Amis *c* 690

Doll, Paul (Military Personnel; Spouse; Narrator)
The Zone of Interest - Martin Amis *c* 690

Dollbaby (Daughter; Friend; Servant)
Dollbaby - Laura McNeal *c* 801

Dolvek (Royalty; Brother)
Oathkeeper - J.F. Lewis *f* 74

Domhnall (Scholar)
Condemned to Death - Cora Harrison *t* 173

Donne, John (Historical Figure; Writer; Spouse; Spy; Detective)
Love's Alchemy - Bryan Crockett *t* 147

Donne, Raymond "Ray" (Friend; Police Officer; Teacher)
Dead Red - Tim O'Mara *m* 626

Donovan, Alex (Son)
The Memory House - Linda Goodnight *r* 974

Donovan, Cole (Sailor; Boyfriend)
He's So Fine - Jill Shalvis *r* 1075

Donovan, Colin (FBI Agent; Fiance(e))
Harbor Island - Carla Neggers *r* 1041

Donovan, Eli (Father; Criminal)
The Memory House - Linda Goodnight *r* 974

Donovan, Maura (Bartender; Businesswoman; Detective—Amateur)
An Early Wake - Sheila Connolly *m* 520

Donovan, Peter (Military Personnel; Veteran)
Fives and Twenty-Fives - Michael Pitre *c* 832

Donovan, Reece (Hotel Owner)
Love Me If You Dare - Toni Blake *r* 917

Doreen (Aged Person; Mother)
Slated for Death - Elizabeth J. Duncan *m* 537

Dorman, Bill (Police Officer; Boyfriend)
Neighing with Fire - Kathryn O'Sullivan *m* 628

Dorotea (Daughter; Sister; Immigrant; Child; 6-Year-Old)
Wolf Winter - Cecilia Ekback *t* 152

Dorothy (Sister)
A Scoundrel by Moonlight - Anna Campbell *r* 941

Doten, Mark (Narrator)
The Infernal - Mark Doten *c* 734

Douglas, Katherine (Noblewoman; Spouse)
Once upon a Plaid - Mia Marlowe *r* 1021

Douglas, William (Nobleman; Spouse)
Once upon a Plaid - Mia Marlowe *r* 1021

Douglas "Stem" (Son; Brother)
A Spool of Blue Thread - Anne Tyler *c* 875

Mr. Dowling (Murderer)
Zom-B Bride - Darren Shan *h* 343

Downey, Evan (Artist; Father; Widow(er); Lover)
Bringing Home the Bad Boy - Jessica Lemmon *r* 1010

Downey, Lyon (Son)
Bringing Home the Bad Boy - Jessica Lemmon *r* 1010

Downey, Rae (Spouse; Mother)
Bringing Home the Bad Boy - Jessica Lemmon *r* 1010

Downing, Louise (Crime Victim)
Gilt by Association - Karen Rose Smith *m* 661

Doyle, Arthur Conan (Historical Figure; Writer)
The Last American Vampire - Seth Grahame-Smith *h* 304

Doyle, Colin (Man; Musician)
The Crow of Connemara - Stephen Leigh *f* 73

Doyle, Kathleen (Detective—Police; Spouse)
Murder in Hindsight - Anne Cleeland *m* 516

Doyle, Laura (Fiance(e); Survivor)
Going Gone - Sharon Sala *r* 1066

Doyle, Shane (Baker; Spouse)
All Fired Up - Kate Meader *r* 1037

Dozier, Faye (Agent)
Last Days of the Condor - James Grady *m* 559

Lord Draconus (Deity; Lover; Demon)
Fall of Light - Steven Erikson *f* 30

Lord Draconus (Nobleman; Lover)
Forge of Darkness - Steven Erikson *f* 31

Dracu, Vladimir (Leader; Organized Crime Figure)
Black Scorpion - Jon Land *m* 596

Dracula (Vampire)
Darkest Night - Will Hill *h* 317
Zero Hour - Will Hill *h* 316

Dragon (Wizard)
Uprooted - Naomi Novik *f* 87

Drake, Bobby (Spouse; Lawman; Son)
Sometimes the Wolf - Urban Waite *c* 882

Drake, Jessica (Supernatural Being; Enemy)
Dreamseeker - C.S. Friedman *f* 37

Drake, Liz (Friend)
Dreams of Shreds and Tatters - Amanda
  Downum *h* 293

Drake, Patrick (Lawman; Father; Widow(er);
  Convict)
Sometimes the Wolf - Urban Waite *c* 882

Drakestone, Bray (Gambler; Nobleman; Heir;
  Fiance(e))
The Duke in My Bed - Amelia Grey *r* 979

Dresden, Ridley (Military Personnel)
Frostfire - Amanda Hocking *f* 56

Dresner, Dalia (Actress; Daughter)
The Lady from Zagreb - Philip Kerr *t* 191

Driscoll, Frank (Detective—Police; Spouse)
Nun Too Soon - Alice Loweecey *m* 608

Driver (18-Year-Old; Young Man; Brother)
The Country of Ice Cream Star - Sandra
  Newman *c* 816

Drood, Eddie (Magician; Supernatural Being;
  Boyfriend)
From a Drood to a Kill - Simon R. Green *f* 41

Dryden, Sam (Veteran; Friend)
Signal - Patrick Lee *m* 598

Dryer, Mr. Granville (Trainer)
The Fair Fight - Anna Freeman *t* 160

DuBois, Jessica (Fiance(e); Woman)
A Heart's Danger - Colleen Coble *i* 385

DuBois, Jessica (Lover)
A Heart's Obsession - Colleen Coble *i* 384

DuBois, Sage (Cook; Fiance(e))
Ladle to the Grave - Connie Archer *m* 480

Duckweed, Poplock (Companion)
Phoenix in Shadow - Ryk E. Spoor *f* 108

Dudley, Lord Robert (Nobleman; Lover)
The Marriage Game - Alison Weir *t* 270

Duffy, Spooner (Missing Person; Drifter)
A Sticky Situation - Jessie Crockett *m* 525

Duke of Avendale (Nobleman)
The Duke and the Lady in Red - Lorraine
  Heath *r* 985

Duke of Rivenshire (Nobleman; Friend)
An Uncertain Choice - Jody Hedlund *i* 415

Dulcie (Daughter)
The Cavendon Women - Barbara Taylor
  Bradford *t* 133

Dumont, Beau (Wealthy; Boyfriend)
Make You Remember - Macy Beckett *r* 911

Dunbar, Brett (Detective; Widow(er))
Operation Power Play - Justine Davis *r* 952

Duncan, Tom (Lover; Agent)
Flirting with Disaster - Victoria Dahl *r* 946

Dunham, Claire (Security Officer; Friend)
Signal - Patrick Lee *m* 598

Dunn, Wade (Police Officer; Stepfather)
One Mile Under - Andrew Gross *m* 561

Dupin, Georges (Detective—Police)
Death in Brittany - Jean-Luc Bannalec *m* 486

Duplessi, Julien (Architect; Lover)
The Witch of Painted Sorrows - M.J. Rose *t* 236

Dupree, Willy (Relative)
The Ravens - Vidar Sundstol *m* 669

Duran, Ben (Spouse; Man; Father; Divorced
  Person)
The Black Widow - Wendy Corsi Staub *m* 665

Duran, Gaby (Mother; Divorced Person; Woman;
  Spouse)
The Black Widow - Wendy Corsi Staub *m* 665

Durand, Stephane (Man; Boyfriend)
The Venusian Gambit - Michael J.
  Martinez *s* 1173

Duvall, Lady Aramina (Young Woman; Daughter)
Of Silk and Steam - Bec McMaster *r* 1033

Dylan (Student—College; Actor; Friend)
Miles from Nowhere - Amy Clipston *i* 379

Dylan, Hugh (Man)
Lemon Pies and Little White Lies - Ellery
  Adams *m* 475

E

Eagle, Johnny (Banker)
Sins of Our Fathers - Shawn Lawrence
  Otto *c* 822

Early, Jubal (Historical Figure; Military Personnel)
Valley of the Shadow - Ralph Peters *t* 231

Earp, Wyatt (Historical Figure; Lawman; Friend)
Epitaph - Mary Doria Russell *t* 240

Ebersol, Aaron (Son)
A Simple Prayer - Amy Clipston *i* 380

Ebersol, Ruth (Mother; Aged Person; Patient;
  Religious)
A Simple Prayer - Amy Clipston *i* 380

Eddie (Boy; Son)
Delicious Foods - James Hannaham *c* 760

Edgar (Cousin; Revolutionary; Spouse)
When the Doves Disappeared - Sofi
  Oksanen *t* 223

Edmund (Religious)
The Tapestry - Nancy Bilyeau *t* 130

Edmund (Religious; Fiance(e))
The Promise of Palm Grove - Shelley Shepard
  Gray *i* 407

Eduardo (Gardener)
Grave on Grand Avenue - Naomi Hirahara *m* 575

Edward (Nobleman; Uncle; Religious)
The Tutor - Andrea Chapin *t* 140

Edward (Royalty; Historical Figure)
The Empty Throne - Bernard Cornwell *t* 146

Edward (Son; Historical Figure)
The Price of Blood - Patricia Bracewell *t* 132

Edwards, Jason (Patient; Crime Suspect)
The Forgetting Place - John Burley *m* 506

Effington, Cameron (Journalist)
The Daring Exploits of a Runaway Heiress - Victoria Alexander *r* 896

Eicher, Anna (Religious; Young Woman)
Second Chances - Sarah Price *i* 450

el-Hariti, Kateb "Dodge" (Student—College;
  Young Man; Linguist)
Fives and Twenty-Fives - Michael Pitre *c* 832

Eleanor (Noblewoman; Mother; Widow(er); Em-
  ployer)
A Good Rogue Is Hard to Find - Kelly
  Bowen *r* 921

Eleanor (Religious; Friend)
Satan's Lullaby - Priscilla Royal *t* 239

Eliot, T.S. (Historical Figure; Writer)
Adeline: A Novel of Virginia Woolf - Norah
  Vincent *t* 268

Elisabeth "Sisi" (Historical Figure; 15-Year-Old;
  Royalty; Sister)
The Accidental Empress - Allison Pataki *t* 226

Elisabetta (Daughter)
An Italian Wife - Ann Hood *c* 768

Elizabeth (Aunt)
The Luminous Heart of Jonah S. - Gina B.
  Nahai *c* 814

Elizabeth (Historical Figure; Lover)
The Marriage Game - Alison Weir *t* 270

Elizabeth (Historical Figure; Royalty; Cousin)
Murder in the Queen's Wardrobe - Kathy Lynn
  Emerson *t* 153

Elizabeth (Historical Figure; Ruler)
The Tutor - Andrea Chapin *t* 140

Elizabeth (Spouse)
The Hidden Man - Robin Blake *m* 495

Elizabeth "Lizzy" (Sister; Cook)
Lizzy and Jane - Katherine Reay *r* 1056

Ella (Sister)
Into the Go-Slow - Bridgett M. Davis *c* 728

Elland, Grace (Worker)
Trust No One - Jayne Ann Krentz *c* 786

Ellen (Spouse; Daughter; Mother)
*Ruth's Journey: The Authorized Novel of Mammy
  from Margaret Mitchell's* Gone with the Wind -
  Donald McCaig *t* 210

Ellen (Teenager; Addict; Friend)
The Way We Bared Our Souls - Willa
  Strayhorn *f* 112

Elliot (Brother; Son)
Reunion - Hannah Pittard *c* 833

Elliot, Kate (Aunt)
Taken - Lisa Harris *i* 412

Elliott, Sean (Military Personnel)
A Long Time Until Now - Michael Z.
  Williamson *s* 1208

Ellis, Maude (Servant)
Darling Beast - Elizabeth Hoyt *r* 989

Ellis, Reese (Young Woman; Housekeeper)
When I'm Gone - Abbi Glines *r* 972

Ellison, Lady Merry (Noblewoman; Leader)
Dauntless - Dina L. Sleiman *i* 457

Ellison, Tim (Cook; Caregiver)
Sweet Damage - Rebecca James *c* 773

Elsa (Girl; Daughter)
The Stager - Susan Coll *c* 716

Elsie (Aunt; Crime Victim)
Manhattan in Miniature - Margaret Grace *m* 558

Elvaston, Doug (Boyfriend; Fiance(e))
The Readaholics and the Falcon Fiasco - Laura
  DiSilverio *m* 535

Elvis (Cat)
Buy a Whisker - Sofie Ryan *m* 650

Elwold, Alvina (Psychic; Crime Victim)
Medium Dead - Paula Paul *m* 633

Elyse (Cousin)
Three Story House - Courtney Miller Santo *c* 853

Em (Woman; Mentally Ill Person; Spouse; Mother)
Em and the Big Hoom - Jerry Pinto *c* 831

Emil (Dancer; Vampire; Lover)
The Dark Arts of Blood - Freda Warrington *h* 350

Emilio (Spouse)
Skylight - Jose Saramago *c* 854

Gable, Clark (Historical Figure; Actor; Lover)
A Touch of Stardust - Kate Alcott *t* 125

Gabler, Christof (Nobleman; Political Figure; Employer; Spouse)
The Figaro Murders - Laura Lebow *t* 199

Gadsden, William "Will" (Military Personnel)
The Memory House - Linda Goodnight *r* 974

Gagnon, Lianne (Crime Victim; Friend)
The Devil You Know - Elisabeth de Mariaffi *m* 530

Gail (Judge; Spouse; Woman)
The Wednesday Group - Sylvia True *c* 873

Gaios (Deity)
The Conquering Dark - Clay Griffith *h* 308

Gajendra (Warrior)
Colossus - Colin Falconer *t* 155

Galdon, Ginny (Sister; Mentally Challenged Person)
Return to Me - Kelly Moran *r* 1038

Galdon, Mia (Nurse; Caregiver; Sister)
Return to Me - Kelly Moran *r* 1038

Galen (5-Year-Old; Nephew; Brother)
Teardrop Lane - Emily March *r* 1018

Gallagher, Maeve (Woman)
The Crow of Connemara - Stephen Leigh *f* 73

Gallagher, Piper (Health Care Professional; Lesbian; Abandoned Child; Sister; Girlfriend)
In Case of Emergency - Courtney Moreno *c* 811

Gallagher, Raina (Real Estate Agent; Crime Victim)
Some Like It Witchy - Heather Blake *m* 494

Gallagher, Ryan (Brother)
In Case of Emergency - Courtney Moreno *c* 811

Gallo, Mary Hannah (Animal Trainer)
Rescue Me - Catherine Mann *r* 1017

Garcia, Juan (Smuggler; Collector; Friend)
Cuba Straits - Randy Wayne White *m* 681

Gardner, Chelsea (Teacher; Lover)
Love After All - Jaci Burton *r* 937

Gardner, Emily (Political Figure; Lawyer)
Detained - Don Brown *i* 366

Gardner, Lainie Davis (Producer; Widow(er); Mother; Crime Suspect; Suspect)
The Evil Deeds We Do - Robert S. Levinson *m* 602

Garfield, James (Historical Figure; Political Figure)
The Regulator - Ethan J. Wolfe *t* 274

Garkov, Nicolai (Organized Crime Figure; Crime Suspect)
Losing Faith - Adam Mitzner *m* 621

Garreth (Man; Warrior; Captive; Immortal)
Cursed by Ice - Jacquelyn Frank *f* 35

Garrett, Alonzo (Assassin; Lover)
The Clockwork Crown - Beth Cato *f* 23

Garrett, Eli (Rancher; Police Officer)
Part Time Cowboy - Maisey Yates *r* 1099

Garrett, Elly (Hunter; Sister; Worker)
Grave Matters - Lauren M. Roy *f* 101

Garrison, Gavin (Musician)
Leaving Amarillo - Caisey Quinn *r* 1052

Garrison, Josh (Security Officer)
Wild - Jill Sorenson *r* 1085

Garzan (Leader)
Green on Blue - Elliot Ackerman *c* 684

Gathercole, Tina (Girlfriend)
The Big Finish - James W. Hall *c* 758

Gautier, Nick (Teenager; Demon; Student—High School)
Instinct - Sherrilyn Kenyon *h* 325

Gaven (Lover)
The Dangerous Type - Loren Rhoads *s* 1189

Gavin, Leonard (Agent; Spouse)
All the President's Menus - Julie Hyzy *m* 580

Gawain (Knight)
Fatal Feast - Jay Ruud *t* 243

Geary, John "Black Jack" (Military Personnel)
Leviathan - Jack Campbell *s* 1123

Gehlen, Reinhard (Military Personnel; Historical Figure)
Top Secret - W.E.B. Griffin *c* 755

Gemal, Cush (Sorcerer)
Tales of the Primal Land - Brian Lumley *h* 332

Gemma-Kate (17-Year-Old; Niece)
Fear the Darkness - Becky Masterman *m* 610

General Clay (Rebel)
City 1 - Gregg Rosenblum *s* 1192

Geoffrey (Lawman)
The Tapestry - Nancy Bilyeau *t* 130

Geoffrey (Worker)
All the Wrong Places - Lisa Lieberman *t* 205

Gerard (Boyfriend)
Sweetshop of Dreams - Jenny Colgan *c* 715

Giancarlo (Prisoner; Lover)
Shame and the Captives - Thomas Keneally *t* 190

Gibbon, Harold (Journalist)
Cafe Europa - Edward Ifkovic *t* 182

Gibbons, Kendra (Missing Person; Daughter)
Signature Kill - David Levien *m* 601

Gibbons, Kerry (Mother; Widow(er))
Signature Kill - David Levien *m* 601

Gibbs, Jen (Editor; Daughter; Sister)
The Story Keeper - Lisa Wingate *c* 887

Gibson, Jake (Religious; Divorced Person; Man)
Mammoth Secrets - Ashley Elizabeth Ludwig *i* 431

Gibson, John (Restaurateur; Friend)
Killer Gourmet - G.A. McKevett *m* 615

Gideon, Sara (Military Personnel)
Rain on the Dead - Jack Higgins *c* 766

Gifford, Zoe (Heiress; Spouse)
An American Duchess - Sharon Page *r* 1046

Gilbride, Alastair "Alec" (Cousin; Spy)
How to Plan a Wedding for a Royal Spy - Vanessa Kelly *r* 997

Gildas (Servant; Narrator)
Fatal Feast - Jay Ruud *t* 243

Gillespie, Alexander (Detective—Police)
Hare - Peter Ranscombe *t* 234

Gilley (Man; Friend; Television Personality)
No Ghouls Allowed - Victoria Laurie *h* 329

Gillian, Kara (Detective—Police; Supernatural Being)
Vengeance of the Demon - Diana Rowland *f* 100

Gilmore, Dylan (Teenager; Boyfriend; Rebel; Enemy)
Quake - Patrick Carman *s* 1124

Gilmore, Luisa (Landowner; Recluse)
The Whispering - Sarah Rayne *h* 336

Ginny (17-Year-Old; Pregnant Teenager; Friend)
The Never-Open Desert Diner - James Anderson *m* 478

Glasserman, Cody (Boy; Friend)
We Are Pirates - Daniel Handler *c* 759

Gleason, Paul (Police Officer)
Deadly Echoes - Nancy Mehl *i* 435

Gledstanes, Benjamin "Benjy" (Brother; 10-Year-Old)
Devil's Moon - Amanda Scott *r* 1070

Gledstanes, Lady Robina "Robby" (Lady; Twin)
Devil's Moon - Amanda Scott *r* 1070

Glickman, Cheryl (Roommate; Colleague)
The First Bad Man - Miranda July *c* 778

Godel, Adele (Widow(er); Dancer; Aged Person; Historical Figure)
The Goddess of Small Victories - Yannick Grannec *c* 752

Godel, Kurt (Historical Figure; Spouse; Mentally Ill Person; Professor; Genius)
The Goddess of Small Victories - Yannick Grannec *c* 752

Godwin, Robert (Graduate; Wealthy)
The Sirena Quest - Michael A. Kahn *m* 589

Goebbels, Joseph (Political Figure; Historical Figure)
The Lady from Zagreb - Philip Kerr *t* 191

Goetz, Ada (Widow(er); Spouse; Cult Member)
Still Life - Christa Parrish *i* 442

Goetz, Julian (Photographer; Accident Victim; Spouse)
Still Life - Christa Parrish *i* 442

Goldberg, Desdemona (Teenager; Wealthy)
Rich Kids of Instagram - Creator of Rich Kids of Instagram *c* 721

Goldberg, Joe (Young Man; Boyfriend; Worker; Murderer)
You - Caroline Kepnes *c* 782

Golden, Benji (Man; Detective—Private)
Phantom Angel - David Handler *m* 567

Golding, Sally (Widow(er); Spouse; Mail Order Bride)
Outlaw Takes a Bride - Susan Page Davis *i* 389

Goldman, Dr. Zoe (Therapist; Adoptee; Survivor; Doctor)
Little Black Lies - Sandra Block *m* 496

Goldstein, Eli (Boy; 15-Year-Old; Religious; Nephew)
The Last Flight of Poxl West - Daniel Torday *t* 264

Gonzales, Hector (Narrator; Impoverished; Immigrant; Traveler)
The Jaguar's Children - John Vaillant *c* 876

Gonzales de Ripparda, Rafael Maria (Merchant; Hero; Spy)
The Creole Princess - Beth White *i* 468

Goodnight, Sophie (Heiress)
A Rake by Any Other Name - Mia Marlowe *r* 1022

Goodwin, Dr. Alexandra (Doctor; Friend; Detective—Amateur)
Medium Dead - Paula Paul *m* 633

Goodwin, Cherise (Witch; Friend)
Some Like It Witchy - Heather Blake *m* 494

Goodwin, Garth (Spouse)
Last One Home - Debbie Macomber *c* 794

Goodwin, Karen (Sister; Spouse; Daughter)
Last One Home - Debbie Macomber *c* 794

Gordon, Jean (Fiance(e))
A Fine Summer's Day - Charles Todd *t* 263

Gordon, John Brown (Historical Figure; Military Personnel)
Valley of the Shadow - Ralph Peters *t* 231

Gorman, Ray (Graduate; Friend)
The Sirena Quest - Michael A. Kahn *m* 589

H

Hansen, Cooper (Son; Brother; Military Personnel; Brother)
The Cowboy SEAL - Laura Marie Altom   *r* 897

Hansen, JJ (7-Year-Old; Son; Grandson; Nephew)
The Cowboy SEAL - Laura Marie Altom   *r* 897

Hansen, Lance (Ranger; Relative)
The Ravens - Vidar Sundstol   *m* 669

Hansen, LeeAnn (11-Year-Old; Daughter; Granddaughter; Niece)
The Cowboy SEAL - Laura Marie Altom   *r* 897

Hansen, Millie (Widow(er); Mother; Sister; Daughter)
The Cowboy SEAL - Laura Marie Altom   *r* 897

Hardy, Dismas (Man; Lawyer; Father)
The Fall - John T. Lescroart   *m* 600

Hardy, Rebecca (Lawyer; Daughter)
The Fall - John T. Lescroart   *m* 600

Hare, William (Murderer; Crime Suspect)
Hare - Peter Ranscombe   *t* 234

Hargrave, Adam (Brother; Friend)
The Masque of a Murderer - Susanna Calkins   *m* 510

Hargrave, Sarah (Daughter; Quaker; Friend; Sister)
The Masque of a Murderer - Susanna Calkins   *m* 510

Harkness, Gloria (Mother; Detective—Amateur)
The Child Garden - Catriona McPherson   *m* 618

Harlan (15-Year-Old; Orphan; Farmer)
A Slant of Light - Jeffrey Lent   *t* 202

Harlan (Mercenary; Lover)
The Talon of the Hawk - Jeffe Kennedy   *f* 62

Harlan (Prisoner; Murderer; Companion)
As Night Falls - Jenny Milchman   *m* 619

Harmon, Eve (Innkeeper; Lover)
The Heart of Christmas - Brenda Novak   *r* 1044

Harmon, Lane (Interior Decorator; Mother)
The Melody Lingers On - Mary Higgins Clark   *m* 515

Harp, Theo (Writer; Wealthy; Neighbor)
Heroes Are My Weakness - Susan Elizabeth Phillips   *c* 828

Harper, Annabelle (Classmate; Aunt)
Sunflower Lane - Jill Gregory   *r* 978

Harper, Hank (Scientist; Spouse; Father)
In the Woods - Merry Jones   *m* 587

Harper, Lydia (Wealthy; Southern Belle)
The Whistle Walk - Stephenia H. McGee   *i* 434

Harrigan, Penny (Worker)
Beautiful You - Chuck Palahniuk   *c* 823

Harrington, Emily (Woman; Friend; Crime Suspect)
Rising Tide - Patricia Twomey Ryan   *m* 649

Harrington, Juliana (Widow(er))
Murder - Sarah Pinborough   *t* 232

Harris, Charlie (Librarian; Widow(er))
Arsenic and Old Books - Miranda James   *m* 583

Harris, Charlotte "Charlie" (Friend; Lover)
Bringing Home the Bad Boy - Jessica Lemmon   *r* 1010

Harrison, Celia (Lover; Agent)
All the Old Knives - Olen Steinhauer   *m* 666

Harrison, Harrison "H2" (16-Year-Old; Student—High School; Amputee; Son)
Harrison Squared - Daryl Gregory   *h* 306

Harrison, Rosa (Scientist; Widow(er); Mother; Missing Person)
Harrison Squared - Daryl Gregory   *h* 306

Hart, Abby (Orphan; Detective—Homicide)
Drawing Fire - Janice Cantore   *i* 376

Hart, Carmen (Sister; Television Personality)
The Art of Losing Yourself - Katie Ganshert   *i* 401

Hartley, Eddie (Actor; Teacher; Spouse; Lover)
Arts and Entertainments - Christopher R. Beha   *c* 700

Hartley, Elizabeth (Principal; Crime Suspect)
A Finely Knit Murder - Sally Goldenbaum   *m* 557

Hartley, Susan (Spouse)
Arts and Entertainments - Christopher R. Beha   *c* 700

Hartman, Jorgen (Investigator; Man)
The Huntress of Thornbeck Forest - Melanie Dickerson   *i* 393

Hartwell, Dante (Widow(er); Businessman; Single Father; Spouse)
What a Lady Needs for Christmas - Grace Burrowes   *r* 935

Hasimoto, Kazushi (Man; Traveler; Crime Victim)
Sherlock Holmes, the Missing Years: Japan - Vasudev Murthy   *t* 219

Mrs. Hastings (Mother; Patient)
A Harvest of Hope - Lauraine Snelling   *i* 459

Hastings, Lauren "Lo" (Graduate; Lover)
The Best Medicine - Elizabeth Hayley   *r* 984

Hastings, Miriam (Nurse; Girlfriend; Daughter)
A Harvest of Hope - Lauraine Snelling   *i* 459

Hathaway, Heidi (Friend; Accident Victim)
Heaven Help Heidi - Sally John   *i* 422

Hathorne, Neal (Crime Suspect; Grandson)
Pleasantville - Attica Locke   *m* 605

Hathorne, Sam (Wealthy; Political Figure; Grandfather)
Pleasantville - Attica Locke   *m* 605

Hauck, Ty (Police Officer; Godfather; Detective—Private)
One Mile Under - Andrew Gross   *m* 561

Havnel, Bea (21-Year-Old; Crime Victim; Daughter)
Last to Know - Elizabeth Adler   *c* 685

Havnel, Lacey (Mother; Crime Victim)
Last to Know - Elizabeth Adler   *c* 685

Hawes, Lady Fiona (Young Woman; Twin; Sister; Granddaughter)
Twice Tempted - Eileen Dreyer   *r* 956

Hawkins, Martha (Midwife; Co-worker)
The Witch Hunter's Tale - Sam Thomas   *t* 260

Hawley, James (Veteran; Boyfriend)
The Other Side of Midnight - Simone St. James   *r* 1087

Hawthorn, Jack (Young Man; Boyfriend; Supernatural Being; Wealthy)
Briar Queen - Katherine Harbour   *h* 312

Hawthorne, Helen (Detective—Private; Spouse)
Checked Out - Elaine Viets   *m* 677

Hayat (Brother; Boyfriend)
The Shadow of the Crescent Moon - Fatima Bhutto   *c* 703

Hayden (5-Year-Old; Son)
The Final Reveille - Amanda Flower   *m* 547

Hayden, Charles (Military Personnel; Sea Captain)
Until the Sea Shall Give Up Her Dead - S. Thomas Russell   *t* 241

Hayden, Tracy (Businesswoman)
A Perfect Catch - Anna Sugden   *r* 1090

Hayes, Andy (Detective—Private; Football Player; Fiance(e))
Slow Burn - Andrew Welsh-Huggins   *m* 680

Hayley (Niece; Crime Suspect)
One Foot in the Grape - Carlene O'Neil   *m* 627

Hazel (Aunt)
A Sticky Situation - Jessie Crockett   *m* 525

Hazelton, Nigel (Veteran; Spouse; Nobleman; Brother)
An American Duchess - Sharon Page   *r* 1046

Hazelton, Sebastian (Nobleman; Brother)
An American Duchess - Sharon Page   *r* 1046

Headly, Troy (Teacher)
One Wish - Robyn Carr   *r* 942

Heath (Man; Television Personality; Boyfriend)
No Ghouls Allowed - Victoria Laurie   *h* 329

Heath, Caleb (Crime Suspect; Young Man)
Doing the Devil's Work - Bill Loehfelm   *m* 606

Heber (Friend)
Pale Harvest - Braden Hepner   *c* 764

Heckholz, Heinrich (Lawyer; Crime Victim)
The Lady from Zagreb - Philip Kerr   *t* 191

Hedge, Sophy (Daughter; Artist; Spouse; Mother; Friend)
The Language of Paradise - Barbara Klein Moss   *t* 217

Heiden (Military Personnel)
The Dynamite Room - Jason Hewitt   *t* 178

Helene (Sister)
The Accidental Empress - Allison Pataki   *t* 226

Helmuth, Anna (Grandmother; Spouse)
Huckleberry Spring - Jennifer Beckstrand   *i* 359

Helmuth, Anna (Spouse; Grandmother; Religious; Matchmaker)
Huckleberry Harvest - Jennifer Beckstrand   *i* 358

Helmuth, Ben (Grandson; Fiance(e))
Huckleberry Spring - Jennifer Beckstrand   *i* 359

Helmuth, Fannie (Drug Dealer; Fugitive; Religious)
Whiskers of the Lion - P.L. Gaus   *m* 555

Helmuth, Felty (Religious; Grandfather; Spouse)
Huckleberry Harvest - Jennifer Beckstrand   *i* 358

Helmuth, Felty (Spouse; Grandfather)
Huckleberry Spring - Jennifer Beckstrand   *i* 359

Helmuth, Mandy (Granddaughter; Friend; Religious)
Huckleberry Harvest - Jennifer Beckstrand   *i* 358

Helsing, Leonard (Father; Vampire Hunter)
Shutter - Courtney Alameda   *h* 277

Helsing, Micheline (Young Woman; Vampire Hunter; Daughter)
Shutter - Courtney Alameda   *h* 277

Heming, William (Real Estate Agent; Employer; Narrator)
A Pleasure and a Calling - Phil Hogan   *m* 576

Hemingway, Ernest (Historical Figure; Writer)
West of Sunset - Stewart O'Nan   *c* 819

Hennepin, Katherine (Crime Victim)
Motive - Jonathan Kellerman   *c* 780

Hennessy, Miss Queenie (Aged Person; Friend)
The Love Song of Miss Queenie Hennessy - Rachel Joyce   *c* 777

Henry (Adoptee; Son; 5-Year-Old)
You're So Fine - Kieran Kramer   *r* 1002

Henry (Dealer; Spouse)
Prague Summer - Jeffrey Condran   *c* 717

Henry (Historical Figure; Royalty)
The Tapestry - Nancy Bilyeau   *t* 130

Henry (Historical Figure; Spouse)
Lamentation - C.J. Sansom   *t* 244

Huo, Li Yin (Assistant)
The Lusitania Conspiracy - Ronald J. Walters   *t* 269

Huss, Irene (Detective—Police; Mother; Spouse)
The Beige Man - Helene Tursten   *m* 674

Hutchinson, Ashley (Sister; Mother; Roommate)
Christmas at Twilight - Lori Wilde   *r* 1097

Hutchinson, Brian (Veteran; Mentally Ill Person; Brother)
Christmas at Twilight - Lori Wilde   *r* 1097

Hyde (Father; Retiree)
At the Water's Edge - Sara Gruen   *t* 170

Hyde, Ellis (Son; Spouse; Young Man; Socialite; Heir—Dispossessed; Friend)
At the Water's Edge - Sara Gruen   *t* 170

Hyde, Madeline "Maddie" (Young Woman; Spouse; Socialite)
At the Water's Edge - Sara Gruen   *t* 170

Hygeorht, Wynn (Adventurer; Friend)
First and Last Sorcerer - Barb Hendee   *f* 52

Hylas (Teenager; Friend; Thief; Brother)
The Eye of the Falcon - Michelle Paver   *f* 94

I

iAm (Young Man; Twin; Brother)
The Shadows - J.R. Ward   *h* 349

Ian (Brother; Grandson; Friend)
Twice Tempted - Eileen Dreyer   *r* 956

Ickabosh (Magician)
Woven - Michael Jensen   *f* 61

il'Sanke, Ghassan (Supernatural Being)
First and Last Sorcerer - Barb Hendee   *f* 52

Illica, Ben (Lawyer; Father; Spouse; Narrator)
Accidents of Marriage - Randy Susan Meyers   *c* 804

Illica, Caleb (Son; Brother)
Accidents of Marriage - Randy Susan Meyers   *c* 804

Illica, Emma (14-Year-Old; Sister; Daughter; Narrator)
Accidents of Marriage - Randy Susan Meyers   *c* 804

Illica, Gracie (Daughter; Sister)
Accidents of Marriage - Randy Susan Meyers   *c* 804

Illica, Maddy (Social Worker; Accident Victim; Abuse Victim; Spouse; Mother; Narrator)
Accidents of Marriage - Randy Susan Meyers   *c* 804

Illumina (Mythical Creature; Cousin)
The Empty Throne - Cayla Kluver   *f* 64

Ilsidi (Grandmother)
Tracker - C.J. Cherryh   *s* 1125

Imoshen (Mythical Creature)
The Fall of Fair Isle - Rowena Cory Daniells   *f* 27

Indio (Boy; Son; 7-Year-Old)
Darling Beast - Elizabeth Hoyt   *r* 989

Inevera (Spouse)
The Skull Throne - Peter V. Brett   *f* 17

Inga (Young Woman; Roommate)
Five Brides - Eva Marie Everson   *i* 397

Ingham, Charles (Spouse; Father; Nobleman; Spouse)
The Cavendon Women - Barbara Taylor Bradford   *t* 133

Ingham, Charlotte Swann (Spouse)
The Cavendon Women - Barbara Taylor Bradford   *t* 133

Ingram, Alexander (Dancer; Crime Victim)
Night Life - David C. Taylor   *t* 258

Ingram, Terri (Fiance(e))
The Lynchpin - Jeffrey B. Burton   *m* 507

Iqtbal, Ali (Boy; Brother)
Green on Blue - Elliot Ackerman   *c* 684

Iqtbal, Aziz (Boy; Brother)
Green on Blue - Elliot Ackerman   *c* 684

Iron Assassin (Reanimated Dead; Robot)
The Iron Assassin - Ed Greenwood   *s* 1149

Isa (Biblical Figure; Lover)
The Tomb: A Novel of Martha - Stephanie Landsem   *i* 426

Isaac (Apprentice; Enemy)
Dreamseeker - C.S. Friedman   *f* 37

Isabeau (Religious; Sister)
Satan's Lullaby - Priscilla Royal   *t* 239

Isaura (Young Woman; Sister)
Skylight - Jose Saramago   *c* 854

Isles, Dr. Maura (Doctor)
Die Again - Tess Gerritsen   *c* 748

Isobel (Actress; Cousin)
Three Story House - Courtney Miller Santo   *c* 853

Issi (Sister)
The Eye of the Falcon - Michelle Paver   *f* 94

Isval (Slave; Resistance Fighter)
Lords of the Sith - Paul S. Kemp   *s* 1160

Iswander, Lee (Leader; Businessman)
Blood of the Cosmos - Kevin J. Anderson   *s* 1104

Ivan (Royalty; Historical Figure)
Murder in the Queen's Wardrobe - Kathy Lynn Emerson   *t* 153

Ivy (15-Year-Old; Daughter)
As Night Falls - Jenny Milchman   *m* 619

Ivy (Advertising; Friend)
Getting Even - Sarah Rayner   *c* 842

Ivy (Friend; Crime Victim)
The Readaholics and the Falcon Fiasco - Laura DiSilverio   *m* 535

J

J.T. (Mentally Ill Person; Brother)
Cane and Abe - James Grippando   *c* 756

Jace (Cousin; Boyfriend)
You Were Mine - Abbi Glines   *c* 751

Jack (Crime Suspect; Grandfather)
Ladle to the Grave - Connie Archer   *m* 480

Jack (Spouse)
The Children Act - Ian McEwan   *c* 800

Jack the Ripper (Historical Figure)
The Last American Vampire - Seth Grahame-Smith   *h* 304

Jack the Ripper (Historical Figure; Serial Killer)
I, Ripper - Stephen Hunter   *t* 181

Jackson, Cassie (Student—High School; Teenager; Classmate; Sister)
Be Not Afraid - Cecilia Galante   *h* 300

Jackson, Charles (Military Personnel; Researcher)
A Love Like Blood - Marcus Sedgwick   *t* 246

Jackson, Dominic (Friend; Brother)
Be Not Afraid - Cecilia Galante   *h* 300

Jackson, Edith (Housekeeper)
Death of a Dishonorable Gentleman - Tessa Arlen   *t* 126

Jackson, Wade (Detective—Police)
Wrongful Death - L.J. Sellers   *m* 655

Jacob (Religious; Orphan)
The Darkest Hour - Tony Schumacher   *t* 245

Jacobs, Charles (Religious; Outcast)
Revival - Stephen King   *c* 783

Jacobs, Devin (Teenager; Son)
Convincing the Rancher - Claire McEwen   *r* 1028

Jacobs, Kirra (Cousin; Rescuer; Friend; Niece)
Sabotaged - Dani Pettrey   *i* 446

Jacobs, Dr. Scott (Doctor; Lover)
The Best Medicine - Elizabeth Hayley   *r* 984

Jacobs, Slaid (Government Official; Single Father)
Convincing the Rancher - Claire McEwen   *r* 1028

Jacobsen, Dan (Companion; Journalist)
Ark Storm - Linda Davies   *c* 727

Jacobson, Winter (Student—College; Co-worker)
Caged in Winter - Brighton Walsh   *r* 1095

Jaeger, Felix (Human; Writer; Friend)
Gotrek and Felix: Slayer - David Guymer   *f* 44

Jaffrey, Rosamond (Servant; Spy)
Murder in the Queen's Wardrobe - Kathy Lynn Emerson   *t* 153

Jag (Angel)
Chasing Sunsets - Karen Kingsbury   *i* 425

Jahan (Boy; 12-Year-Old)
The Architect's Apprentice - Elif Shafak   *t* 247

Jahan (Historical Figure; Ruler; Widow(er); Father)
Traitors in the Shadows - Alex Rutherford   *t* 242

Jain, Shaila (Girlfriend; Military Personnel)
The Venusian Gambit - Michael J. Martinez   *s* 1173

Jake (Alien; Prisoner)
Echo 8 - Sharon Lynn Fisher   *f* 33

Jake (Time Traveler; Friend)
The Door in the Moon - Catherine Fisher   *f* 32

Jakes, Trey (Police Officer; Lover)
Wild Hearts - Sharon Sala   *r* 1067

Jakob (Mentally Challenged Person; Crime Suspect; Friend)
Someone to Watch Over Me - Yrsa Sigurdardottir   *c* 863

Jakubowski, Max (Patient; Grandson; 17-Year-Old; Mentally Ill Person)
Every Fifteen Minutes - Lisa Scottoline   *m* 653

James (17-Year-Old; Crime Suspect)
Goodhouse - Peyton Marshall   *c* 798

James (Coyote; Companion)
Emma and Otto and Russell and James - Emma Hooper   *c* 769

James (Historical Figure; Royalty)
Love's Alchemy - Bryan Crockett   *t* 147

James (Nobleman; Employer)
Forbidden to Love the Duke - Jillian Hunter   *r* 991

James (Uncle; Military Personnel)
The Girl Next Door - Ruth Rendell   *c* 844

James, Henry (Historical Figure; Writer; Friend)
The Fifth Heart - Dan Simmons   *t* 249

James, Lyndie (Friend; Horse Trainer; Young Woman; Neighbor; Sister)
A Love Like Ours - Becky Wade   *i* 466

James, Mira (Investigator; Co-worker; Girlfriend)
February Fever - Jess Lourey   *m* 607

Keyes, Piper (Friend)
Heaven Help Heidi - Sally John *i* 422

Keynes, John Maynard (Historical Figure; Economist)
Vanessa and Her Sister - Priya Parmar *t* 225

Khan, Kor'sarro (Military Personnel; Enemy)
Damocles - Phil Kelly *s* 1159

Khash, Tarra (Barbarian)
Tales of the Primal Land - Brian Lumley *h* 332

Kholster (Immortal; Warrior; Leader; Father; Warrior; Slave)
Oathkeeper - J.F. Lewis *f* 74

Kidd, Alexander (Pirate)
The Wicked Ways of Alexander Kidd - Paula Quinn *r* 1054

Kidd, Thomas (Sea Captain; Friend; Co-worker)
Pasha: A Kydd Sea Adventure - Julian Stockwin *t* 255

Kilgore, Max (17-Year-Old; Student—High School; Son; Friend)
Hellhole - Gina Damico *h* 290

Kim, Stacey (Writer; Detective—Amateur)
Woman with a Gun - Phillip Margolin *c* 797

Kimei, Akira (Scientist; Castaway; Space Explorer; Father; Spouse)
Castaway Planet - Eric Flint *s* 1146

Kimei, Caroline (Daughter; Sister; Castaway; Space Explorer)
Castaway Planet - Eric Flint *s* 1146

Kimei, Hitomi (Son; 7-Year-Old; Space Explorer; Brother; Castaway)
Castaway Planet - Eric Flint *s* 1146

Kimei, Laura (Mother; Space Explorer; Spouse; Castaway; Doctor)
Castaway Planet - Eric Flint *s* 1146

Kimei, Melody (Space Explorer; Castaway; Daughter; Sister)
Castaway Planet - Eric Flint *s* 1146

Kimei, Sakura (Space Explorer; Friend; 14-Year-Old; Girl; Daughter; Sister; Castaway)
Castaway Planet - Eric Flint *s* 1146

Kimmie (4-Year-Old; Daughter)
Christmas at Twilight - Lori Wilde *r* 1097

King, David (Musician; Father)
The Song - Chris Fabry *i* 398

King, Edward (Brother; Religious; Oil Industry Worker)
An Amish Man of Ice Mountain - Kelly Long *i* 429

King, Jed (Musician; Son; Spouse)
The Song - Chris Fabry *i* 398

King, Joseph (Oil Industry Worker; Brother; Guardian; Religious)
An Amish Man of Ice Mountain - Kelly Long *i* 429

King, Rose (Spouse)
The Song - Chris Fabry *i* 398

King, William (Mentally Ill Person; Teenager; 12th Grader; Volunteer; Computer Expert; Friend)
Nowhere to Hide - Sigmund Brouwer *i* 365

King Herod (Royalty; Biblical Figure)
A.D. 30 - Ted Dekker *i* 391

King of England (Royalty)
Dauntless - Dina L. Sleiman *i* 457

King Olav (Royalty)
Blood Will Follow - Snorri Kristjansson *t* 194

Kingsbury, Priscilla (Heiress; Fiance(e))
Hiss and Tell - Claire Donally *m* 536

Kingslayer, Aral (Assassin; Magician)
Darkened Blade - Kelly McCullough *f* 79

Kinley, Larissa (Agent; Vampire)
Darkest Night - Will Hill *h* 317
Zero Hour - Will Hill *h* 316

Kinsella, Jim (Detective—Police; Colleague)
Whatever Happened to Molly Bloom? - Jessica Stirling *t* 254

Kinsella, Louis (Serial Killer; Prisoner)
The Winter Foundlings - Kate Rhodes *m* 643

Kintner, Lily (Researcher)
The Kind Worth Killing - Peter Swanson *m* 670

Kiran (Boy; Handicapped)
The Glass Arrow - Kristen Simmons *s* 1197

Kiril (Human; Adoptee)
Originator - Joel Shepherd *s* 1194

Kirk, James T. (Spaceship Captain)
Crisis of Consciousness - Dave Galanter *s* 1147
Savage Trade - Tony Daniel *s* 1134
Shadow of the Machine - Scott Harrison *s* 1153

Kit (Teenager; Friend; Mentally Ill Person)
The Way We Bared Our Souls - Willa Strayhorn *f* 112

Kitt (Brother)
An Appetite for Violets - Martine Bailey *t* 128

Kizzy (Foundling; Sister; Alien; Gypsy)
Three Songs for Roxy - Caren Gussoff *s* 1150

Klist, Zavcka (Woman)
Binary - Stephanie Saulter *s* 1193

Knight, Alex (Nobleman; Spy; Friend)
Twice Tempted - Eileen Dreyer *r* 956

Knight, Cecily (Military Personnel)
The Longest Night - Kara Braden *c* 706

Knight, Doc (Spouse)
Double Fudge Brownie Murder - Joanne Fluke *m* 548

Knight, Jack (Friend; Detective—Private; Police Officer)
Dead Red - Tim O'Mara *m* 626

Knightley, James (Lawyer; Brother)
The First Kiss - Grace Burrowes *r* 932

Knightley, MacKenzie "Mac" (Lawyer; Worker; Neighbor)
Kiss Me Hello - Grace Burrowes *r* 933

Knightley, Trent (Lawyer; Brother)
The First Kiss - Grace Burrowes *r* 932

Knoxx, Michael (Singer; Amputee; Religious)
The Proposal at Siesta Key - Shelley Shepard Gray *i* 406

Knutson, Trygve (Boyfriend)
A Harvest of Hope - Lauraine Snelling *i* 459

Kody, Bran (Detective—Police; Colleague)
Master of Plagues - E.L. Tettensor *f* 116

Koenig, Alexander (Government Official)
Deep Time - Ian Douglas *s* 1139

Konig, Anna (Young Woman; Religious; Immigrant)
Anna's Crossing - Suzanne Woods Fisher *i* 399

Korman, Horatio (Ranger)
Jacaranda - Cherie Priest *s* 1184

Krause, Sue Ellen (Assistant; Crime Victim)
Bittersweet - Susan Wittig Albert *m* 476

Kresnov, Cassandra "Sandy" (Android; Military Personnel; Mother)
Originator - Joel Shepherd *s* 1194

Krissi (Son; Brother)
How to Build a Girl - Caitlin Moran *c* 810

Kristina (Friend; Young Woman; Religious)
Huckleberry Harvest - Jennifer Beckstrand *i* 358

Krysta (Girl; Daughter)
Gretel and the Dark - Eliza Granville *t* 168

Kuhn, Clara (Teacher; Friend; Religious)
Meek and Mild - Olivia Newport *i* 439

Kyle (Son; Student)
The Pocket Wife - Susan Crawford *m* 524

L

Lady Killer (Murderer; Serial Killer)
Broken - Cynthia Eden *r* 959

Lady Kine (Spouse; Lover; Noblewoman)
Old Man's Ghosts - Tom Lloyd *f* 75

Lafeyette, Remy (Agent)
The Diabolical Miss Hyde - Viola Carr *f* 21

Laith (Mythical Creature)
Hot Blooded - Donna Grant *r* 976

Lake, Timmy (Religious; Brother)
Last Chance Family - Hope Ramsay *r* 1055

Lakshmi, Rani (Royalty; Warrior; Military Personnel)
Rebel Queen - Michelle Moran *t* 213

Lamb, Piper (Woman; Store Owner; Cook; Girlfriend)
License to Dill - Mary Ellen Hughes *m* 578

Lamb, Thomas (Detective—Police; Father)
The Language of the Dead - Stephen Kelly *t* 189

Lamb, Vera (18-Year-Old; Worker; Daughter)
The Language of the Dead - Stephen Kelly *t* 189

Lambert, Bea (Friend; Restaurateur)
Fillet of Murder - Linda Reilly *m* 641

Lambert, Ean (Engineer)
Linesman - S.K. Dunstall *s* 1142

Lancaster, Deirdre "Foxtrot" (Detective—Amateur; Friend; Girlfriend; Worker)
Marked Fur Murder - Dixie Lyle *m* 609

Lance (Student—High School)
Wolf in White Van - John Darnielle *c* 726

Lancelot (Knight)
Fatal Feast - Jay Ruud *t* 243

Landon, Wesley "Wes" (Rancher)
Kissed by a Cowboy - Pamela Britton *r* 926

Landucci, Orlando (Man)
Betrayed by His Kiss - Amanda McCabe *r* 1025

Langdon, Frank (Son; Brother)
Early Warning - Jane Smiley *t* 251

Langdon, Rosanna (Spouse; Mother)
Early Warning - Jane Smiley *t* 251

Langdon, Walter (Farmer; Spouse; Father)
Early Warning - Jane Smiley *t* 251

Langslow, Meg (Blacksmith; Detective—Amateur)
Lord of the Wings - Donna Andrews *m* 479

Lanier, Lyse (Cousin; Heroine)
The Creole Princess - Beth White *i* 468

Lannigan, Kit "Kick" (Kidnap Victim; Martial Arts Expert; Friend)
One Kick - Chelsea Cain *c* 708

Lapp, Abram (Neighbor)
One True Path - Barbara Cameron *i* 375

Lapp, Silas (Man; Religious)
Keys of Heaven - Adina Senft *i* 455

Laren, Ro (Military Personnel; Colleague)
The Missing - Una McCormack *s* 1175

Lisemette (Crime Victim; Twin; Abandoned Child)
The Forgotten Girls - Sara Blaedel *m* 493

Lisle, Lord Frederick "Freddy" (Fiance(e); Rake; Nobleman)
A Good Rake Is Hard to Find - Manda Collins *r* 944

Littlewood, Boots (Detective—Police; Colleague)
The Striver - Stephen Solomita *m* 662

Littman, Aaron (Lawyer; Lover; Spouse; Father)
Losing Faith - Adam Mitzner *m* 621

Liu, Roger (FBI Agent)
Method 15/33 - Shannon Kirk *m* 594

Lively, Penny (Narrator; Detective—Amateur; Aunt; Employer; Neighbor)
One Foot in the Grape - Carlene O'Neil *m* 627

Lizzie (Soccer Player; Cousin)
Three Story House - Courtney Miller Santo *c* 853

Lizzy (Spouse; Woman; Teacher)
The Wednesday Group - Sylvia True *c* 873

Llewellyn, Bronwen "Stormy" (Spirit; Woman; Girlfriend; Psychic)
Saint Odd - Dean Koontz *c* 785

Llewelyn, Thomas (Assistant)
Anatomy of Evil - Will Thomas *t* 261

Lobdell, Lucy Ann (Historical Figure; Teacher; Mother; Lesbian; Narrator)
The Rebellion of Miss Lucy Ann Lobdell - William Klaber *t* 193

Lobo, Pepe (Sea Captain; Boyfriend)
The Siege - Arturo Perez-Reverte *t* 228

Locks, Marissa (Woman; Friend; Businesswoman)
Armageddon Rules - J.C. Nelson *f* 86

Lockwood, Ian (Crime Suspect; Friend)
No Place to Hide - Lynette Eason *i* 395

Logan, Carl (Agent)
Rise of the Enemy - Rob Sinclair *m* 660

Lom, Vissarion (Spy)
Radiant State - Peter Higgins *s* 1155

Lombard, Carole (Lover; Employer; Historical Figure; Actress)
A Touch of Stardust - Kate Alcott *t* 125

London (Student; Daughter; Girl; Teenager)
Make Me Lose Control - Christie Ridgway *r* 1057

London, Anna (20-Year-Old; Young Woman; Recluse)
Sweet Damage - Rebecca James *c* 773

Long, Beck (Man; Political Figure; Son)
Arsenic and Old Books - Miranda James *m* 583

Long, Lucinda Beckwith (Political Figure; Mother)
Arsenic and Old Books - Miranda James *m* 583

Longboat, Joseph (Indian; Friend)
Electric City - Elizabeth Rosner *t* 237

Longboat, Martin (Student—High School; Classmate; Boy)
Electric City - Elizabeth Rosner *t* 237

Loomis Todd, Mabel (Spouse; Young Woman; Lover)
Amherst - William Nicholson *t* 221

Lopez, Laura (Detective—Police)
Circling the Runway - J.L. Abramo *m* 474

Lore (Girl; Student—High School; Friend)
Hellhole - Gina Damico *h* 290

Loren (Businessman)
The Last Good Paradise - Tatjana Soli *c* 865

Lot, Seth (Supernatural Being; Enemy)
Briar Queen - Katherine Harbour *h* 312

Lott, Griff (Contractor; Friend)
The Liar - Nora Roberts *r* 1059

Louis (Cancer Patient; Brother)
This Is the Life - Alex Shearer *c* 862

Louis (Patient; Roommate)
Find Me - Laura van den Berg *c* 877

Louis, King (Employer; Brother; Historical Figure; Spouse)
1636: The Cardinal Virtues - Eric Flint *s* 1145

Louis de Pointe du Lac (Vampire)
Prince Lestat - Anne Rice *c* 845

Loveday (Slave)
An Appetite for Violets - Martine Bailey *t* 128

Lovejoy, Henry (Lawman)
Who Buries the Dead - C.S. Harris *t* 172

Lowndes, Jane (Spinster)
The Unlikely Lady - Valerie Bowman *r* 922

Lowry, Beth (Young Woman; Girlfriend; Girl-friend)
You Were Mine - Abbi Glines *c* 751

Lub (Boy)
Harrison Squared - Daryl Gregory *h* 306

Luciano, Lucky (Historical Figure; Organized Crime Figure)
The Prince - Vito Bruschini *t* 135

Lucky (Dog)
Survivors: Storm of Dogs - Erin Hunter *f* 60

Lucy (Niece; Crime Suspect)
Flesh and Blood - Patricia Cornwell *c* 719

Lucy (Student—High School; Sister; Daughter)
Endangered - C.J. Box *m* 499

Ludner, Arnold (Criminal)
Scent of Murder - James O. Born *m* 498

Luella (Sister; Granddaughter)
The Love Letters - Beverly Lewis *i* 427

Luis (Boy; Foster Child)
Kiss Me Hello - Grace Burrowes *r* 933

Luke (11-Year-Old; Son)
Your Next Breath - Iris Johansen *m* 586

Lune, La (Relative; Prostitute)
The Witch of Painted Sorrows - M.J. Rose *t* 236

Lupin (Son; Brother)
How to Build a Girl - Caitlin Moran *c* 810

Lusa (Bear)
Seekers: Return to the Wild: The Burning Horizon - Erin Hunter *f* 59

Lydia (11-Year-Old; Refugee)
The Dynamite Room - Jason Hewitt *t* 178

Lynn Miller, Scott (Survivor; Security Officer)
Three Songs for Roxy - Caren Gussoff *s* 1150

M

Ma (Mother; Widow(er); Alcoholic)
When - Victoria Laurie *f* 70

Mab (Royalty; Aunt)
Soulbound - Kristen Callihan *f* 19

Mabry, Jonas (Kidnapper)
The Replacements - David Putnam *m* 637

Mac (Detective; Boyfriend)
A Fright to the Death - Dawn Eastman *h* 295

MacDonald, Kylie (Detective—Police)
NYPD Red 3 - James Patterson *m* 632

MacFarlane, Malcolm (Hunter)
The Conquering Dark - Clay Griffith *h* 308
The Shadow Revolution - Clay Griffith *h* 307

Macharius, Lord Solar (Leader)
Fall of Macharius - William King *s* 1161

Machin, Tom (Detective—Police; Colleague)
Whatever Happened to Molly Bloom? - Jessica Stirling *t* 254

MacKay, Donal (Spouse)
The First Kiss - Grace Burrowes *r* 932

Mackenzie, Cameron (Young Man; Guard; Knight; Magician; Companion)
The Shattered Court - M.J. Scott *f* 106

MacKenzie, Jackie (Psychic; Military Personnel; Political Figure)
The Terrans - Jean Johnson *s* 1156

Mackintosh, Charles "Mac" Rennie (Architect; Friend; Spouse; Artist)
Mr. Mac and Me - Esther Freud *t* 161

Mackintosh, Margaret (Artist; Spouse)
Mr. Mac and Me - Esther Freud *t* 161

MacLeod, Hamish (Military Personnel)
A Fine Summer's Day - Charles Todd *t* 263

Mr. MacPherson (Father)
The Silent Sister - Diane Chamberlain *c* 710

MacPherson, Danny (Brother; Military Personnel; Son)
The Silent Sister - Diane Chamberlain *c* 710

MacPherson, Lisa (Crime Suspect; Daughter; Sister; Missing Person)
The Silent Sister - Diane Chamberlain *c* 710

MacPherson, Riley (Sister; Psychologist; Daughter)
The Silent Sister - Diane Chamberlain *c* 710

Macrobius (Military Personnel; Companion)
The Sword of Attila - David Gibbins *t* 163

Maddy (Young Woman; Adventurer; Spouse; Patient)
If Not for This - Pete Fromm *c* 745

Madeline (Sister; Sister)
The Perfect Homecoming - Julia London *r* 1013

Madison, Mary (Prostitute)
Divine - Karen Kingsbury *i* 424

Magda (Young Woman; Roommate)
Five Brides - Eva Marie Everson *i* 397

Maggie (Girlfriend)
Where All Light Tends to Go - David Joy *m* 588

Maggie (Girlfriend; Crime Victim)
King of the Cracksmen - Dennis O'Flaherty *s* 1180

Maggie (Police Officer; Colleague; Dog)
The Promise - Robert Crais *c* 720

Maggs, Thomas (Young Man; Friend)
Mr. Mac and Me - Esther Freud *t* 161

Magiere (Friend; Spouse; Supernatural Being)
First and Last Sorcerer - Barb Hendee *f* 52

Magnus, Reggie (Friend; Wealthy; Entrepreneur)
The Fold - Peter Clines *s* 1127

Magnusson, Astrid (Student—College; Wealthy; Psychic)
Grave Phantoms - Jenn Bennett *r* 912

Maharet (Vampire; Twin)
Prince Lestat - Anne Rice *c* 845

Maija (Immigrant; Spouse; Mother)
Wolf Winter - Cecilia Ekback *t* 152

Mairead (Granddaughter; Twin; Sister)
Twice Tempted - Eileen Dreyer *r* 956

Mairsian (Prostitute; Writer)
I, Ripper - Stephen Hunter *t* 181

Maitland, Sarah (Bride; Friend)
Rising Tide - Patricia Twomey Ryan *m* 649

Majnoun, Leila (Worker)
Whiskey Tango Foxtrot - David Shafer *c* 860

Majorov, Yevgeny (Enemy)
Paris Match - Stuart Woods *c* 889

Makari, Hasan (Defendant; Immigrant; Father; Prisoner)
Detained - Don Brown *i* 366

Makari, Najib (Son; Immigrant; Military Personnel; Defendant; Prisoner)
Detained - Don Brown *i* 366

Makutsi, Grace (Detective—Private; Restaurateur; Mother; Co-worker)
The Handsome Man's De Luxe Cafe - Alexander McCall Smith *c* 864

Mal (Dog)
Oh Say Can You Fudge - Nancy Coco *m* 518

Malcolm (Military Personnel; Friend)
New Uses for Old Boyfriends - Beth Kendrick *r* 998

Malek, Reza (Expatriate; Journalist; Teacher; Friend)
Tehran at Twilight - Salar Abdoh *c* 683

Malekith (Sorcerer; Royalty)
Deathblade: A Tale of Malus Darkblade - C.L. Werner *f* 122

Mallen, Mark (Detective—Police; Addict)
Innocent Damage - Robert K. Lewis *m* 603

Mallory, Jack (Military Personnel; Pilot)
Virtues of War - Bennett R. Coles *s* 1129

Mallory, Lincoln (Consultant)
Girl Before a Mirror - Liza Palmer *r* 1047

Malloy, Claire (Store Owner; Detective—Amateur; Mother; Spouse)
Pride v. Prejudice - Joan Hess *m* 573

Malloy, Frank (Detective—Police; Fiance(e))
Murder on Amsterdam Avenue - Victoria Thompson *m* 672

Malloy, Gil (Journalist)
The Kennedy Connection - R.G. Belsky *c* 701

Malnefoley (Royalty; Demon; Supernatural Being)
Hunted Warrior - Lindsey Piper *f* 95

Malone, Alanna (Woman)
Alanna - Kathleen Bittner Roth *r* 1063

Malone, Buck (Cowboy/Cowgirl; Lover)
Whenever You Come Around - Robin Lee Hatcher *i* 413

Malone, Cotton (Agent; Retiree; Businessman)
The Patriot Threat - Steve Berry *m* 490

Malone, Jack (Brother; Military Personnel; Immigrant)
Daughter of the Regiment - Stephanie Grace Whitson *i* 469

Malone, Liesl (Detective—Police)
Cities and Thrones - Carrie Patel *f* 92

Malone, Maggie (Immigrant; Sister; Lover)
Daughter of the Regiment - Stephanie Grace Whitson *i* 469

Malone, Seamus (Immigrant; Brother; Military Personnel)
Daughter of the Regiment - Stephanie Grace Whitson *i* 469

Mamm (Mother; Spouse; Religious)
The Proposal at Siesta Key - Shelley Shepard Gray *i* 406

Mammi Janice (Grandmother; Neighbor; Religious)
The Love Letters - Beverly Lewis *i* 427

Manami (4-Year-Old; Daughter; Crime Victim)
Confessions - Kanae Minato *c* 806

Manchester, Serena (Journalist; Accident Victim)
Hostile Eyewitness - Tyora Moody *i* 437

Manet, Edouard (Historical Figure; Artist; Lover)
Paris Red - Maureen Gibbon *t* 164

Manley, Liam (Worker; Brother)
What a Woman Gets - Judi Fennell *r* 962

Manny (Friend)
Miracle at the Higher Grounds Cafe - Max Lucado *i* 430

Manton, Dominick (Heir; Brother; Fiance(e))
If the Viscount Falls - Sabrina Jeffries *r* 995

Manton, George (Brother; Spouse)
If the Viscount Falls - Sabrina Jeffries *r* 995

Mar, Rowan (Woman; Captive)
Heir of Hope - Morgan L. Busse *i* 368

Mara (Investigator; Professor)
Condemned to Death - Cora Harrison *t* 173

Marby, Talia (Friend; Waiter/Waitress)
Fillet of Murder - Linda Reilly *m* 641

Marcel (Cook)
All the President's Menus - Julie Hyzy *m* 580

Marcellinus, Gaius (Leader)
A Clash of Eagles - Alan Smale *s* 1198

Marcus (Friend; Skater)
If I Fall, If I Die - Michael Christie *c* 712

Marcus (Nobleman; Single Father)
The Duke's Guide to Correct Behavior - Megan Frampton *r* 967

Marcus, Josephine "Josie" Sarah (18-Year-Old; Lover)
Epitaph - Mary Doria Russell *t* 240

Margaret (Criminal; Spouse)
Where the Bones are Buried - Jeanne Matthews *m* 611

Margaritte (16-Year-Old; Indian; Drug Dealer; Pregnant Teenager; Daughter; Girlfriend)
Crazy Horse's Girlfriend - Erika T. Wurth *c* 891

Maria (15-Year-Old; Sister; Sister)
The Duke of Dark Desires - Miranda Neville *r* 1042

Mariah (Daughter; Child; Cousin; Niece)
First Frost - Sarah Addison Allen *c* 689

Mariana (Spouse)
Skylight - Jose Saramago *c* 854

Marie (Spouse)
The Replacements - David Putnam *m* 637

Marietti, Gabby (Granddaughter; Student)
A Finely Knit Murder - Sally Goldenbaum *m* 557

Marin (17-Year-Old; Student—High School; Teenager; Classmate; Friend)
Be Not Afraid - Cecilia Galante *h* 300

Marin, Rosa (Spouse)
A Root Awakening - Kate Collins *m* 519

Marin, Sergio (Construction Worker; Crime Victim; Spouse)
A Root Awakening - Kate Collins *m* 519

Marium, Donald (Detective—Police)
Hold the Dark - William Giraldi *c* 749

Mark (Friend)
There Will Be Lies - Nick Lake *f* 66

Markess ATerafin, Jewel (Ruler)
Oracle - Michelle West *f* 123

Marlowe (Young Woman; Thief)
Earls Just Want to Have Fun - Shana Galen *r* 970

Marlowe, Christopher (Historical Figure; Writer; Hunter)
The Dead Hamlets - Peter Roman *f* 99

Marlowe, Pru (Animal Trainer; Psychic)
Kittens Can Kill - Clea Simon *m* 659

Marquess of Dourne (Grandfather)
Twice Tempted - Eileen Dreyer *r* 956

Marr, Kennedy (Teacher; Immigrant; Man; Writer)
Straight White Male - John Niven *c* 818

Marsh, Stephen (Blacksmith)
The Invention of Fire - Bruce W. Holsinger *t* 179

Marshwic, Emily (Woman; Military Personnel)
The Guns of the Dawn - Adrian Tchaikovsky *f* 115

Martens, Hannelore (Lawyer; Spouse)
From Bruges with Love - Pieter Aspe *m* 482

Martha (Friend; Biblical Figure; Sister; Fiance(e))
The Tomb: A Novel of Martha - Stephanie Landsem *i* 426

Martin (Nephew; Witness)
Cowboy Boots for Christmas: (Cowboy Not Included) - Carolyn Brown *r* 929

Martin, Gary (Lawman; Crime Victim; Handicapped)
The Missing Piece - Kevin Egan *m* 540

Martin, Martha (Actress; Lover)
Arts and Entertainments - Christopher R. Beha *c* 700

Martindale, Millicent (Assistant)
Hot Pursuit - Stuart Woods *m* 682

Martinelli, Antonia (Neighbor)
One Foot in the Grape - Carlene O'Neil *m* 627

Martini, Jaime (Daughter)
Alien Separation - Gini Koch *s* 1162

Martini, Jeff (Government Official; Spouse; Father; Friend)
Alien Separation - Gini Koch *s* 1162

Martini, Nic (Detective—Police; Spouse; Woman)
Murder with a Twist - Tracy Kiely *m* 593

Martini, Nigel (Spouse; Cousin; Nephew)
Murder with a Twist - Tracy Kiely *m* 593

Marv (Businessman; Cousin)
The Drop - Dennis Lehane *c* 788

Lady Mary (Noblewoman; Cousin)
Murder in the Queen's Wardrobe - Kathy Lynn Emerson *t* 153

Mary Catherine (Volunteer; Wealthy; Patient)
Chasing Sunsets - Karen Kingsbury *i* 425

Mason, Carly Jo (Social Worker; Caregiver)
Together with You - Victoria Bylin *i* 370

Mast, Ivan (Neighbor)
Miriam's Secret - Jerry S. Eicher *i* 396

Mastermind (Enemy)
Alien Separation - Gini Koch *s* 1162

Masters, Luke (Spouse; Businessman)
Snowstorm Confessions - Rachel Lee *r* 1009

Masters, Missy (Magician)
The Dragons of Heaven - Alyc Helms *f* 50

Matchet, Ruth (Young Woman; Boxer; Spouse)
The Fair Fight - Anna Freeman *t* 160

Matekoni, J.L.B. (Businessman; Spouse)
The Handsome Man's De Luxe Cafe - Alexander McCall Smith *c* 864

Matilda (Godmother)
Jilted - Rachael Johns *r* 996

Matilda (Historical Figure; Royalty)
The Siege Winter - Ariana Franklin *t* 159

Mauvais, Devyn (Girlfriend; Child-Care Giver)
Make You Remember - Macy Beckett *r* 911

Maven (Young Man; Royalty)
Red Queen - Victoria Aveyard *f* 9

Maviah (Slave; Traveler)
A.D. 30 - Ted Dekker   *i* 391

Max (Woman; Trainer)
The Love Book - Nina Solomon   *c* 866

Maxwell (Nephew; Heir; Crime Victim)
The Final Reveille - Amanda Flower   *m* 547

Maxwell, Cade (Cook; Co-worker)
Caged in Winter - Brighton Walsh   *r* 1095

Maxwell, Cornelius Linus (Entrepreneur; Wealthy)
Beautiful You - Chuck Palahniuk   *c* 823

May, Eliza (Woman; Niece)
Soulbound - Kristen Callihan   *f* 19

Maye, Fiona (Judge; Spouse)
The Children Act - Ian McEwan   *c* 800

Mayor (Government Official)
The Woman Who Read Too Much - Bahiyyih
Nakhjavani   *t* 220

Mayor's Wife (Woman; Spouse; Narrator)
The Woman Who Read Too Much - Bahiyyih
Nakhjavani   *t* 220

McAlister, Gavin (Lover; Architect)
Back to Before - Tracy Solheim   *r* 1084

McAlister, Liv (Businesswoman)
Heaven Help Heidi - Sally John   *i* 422

McBride, Andrew (Son)
Rules for a Proper Governess - Jennifer
Ashley   *r* 905

McBride, Caitlin (Daughter)
Rules for a Proper Governess - Jennifer
Ashley   *r* 905

McBride, Sinclair (Father; Lawyer; Widow(er))
Rules for a Proper Governess - Jennifer
Ashley   *r* 905

McCabe, Colleen (Fire Fighter; Girlfriend)
Neighing with Fire - Kathryn O'Sullivan   *m* 628

McCabe, Hannah (Detective—Police)
What the Fly Saw - Frankie Y. Bailey   *m* 483

McCane, Angus (Brother; Alcoholic)
Fate Moreland's Widow - John Lane   *t* 197

McCane, George (Businessman; Employer; Crime
Suspect; Brother)
Fate Moreland's Widow - John Lane   *t* 197

McCool, Liam (Criminal; Boyfriend)
King of the Cracksmen - Dennis
O'Flaherty   *s* 1180

McCormick, William "Bronco Billy" (Friend;
Graduate)
The Sirena Quest - Michael A. Kahn   *m* 589

McCoy, Grayson "Gray" (Military Personnel;
Rancher)
Wolf Haven - Lindsay McKenna   *r* 1029

McCoy, Leonard (Doctor)
Crisis of Consciousness - Dave Galanter   *s* 1147

McCready, Rex (Man; Lover)
The Heart of Christmas - Brenda Novak   *r* 1044

Dr. McCrory (Doctor; Crime Victim)
The Devil's Making - Sean Haldane   *t* 171

McCue, Dylan (Woman; Neighbor)
Night Life - David C. Taylor   *t* 258

McDermott, Dr. Ian (Detective—Private; Scien-
tist)
Loup Garou: The Beast of Harmony Falls - David
Reuben Aslin   *h* 281

McDonald, Rosie (Planner)
Honeymoon Hotel - Hester Browne   *r* 931

McDonough, Consuelo "Lo" (Teenager; Girl-
friend; Friend)
The Way We Bared Our Souls - Willa
Strayhorn   *f* 112

McDougal, Abigail (Sister; Captive; Con Artist)
My Heart Stood Still - Lori Copeland   *i* 387

McDougal, Amelia (Sister; Captive; Con Artist)
My Heart Stood Still - Lori Copeland   *i* 387

McDougal, Anne-Marie (Sister; Captive; Con
Artist)
My Heart Stood Still - Lori Copeland   *i* 387

McGarvey, Kirk "Mac" (Director)
Retribution - David Hagberg   *m* 563

McGee, Spider (Wrestler)
The Sweetheart - Angelina Mirabella   *t* 211

McGrath, Cullen (Immigrant; Fiance(e))
To Win Her Favor - Tamera Alexander   *i* 356

McGregor, Mac (Detective—Homicide; Military
Personnel)
Buried Secrets - Irene Hannon   *i* 411

McGregor, Ray (Veteran)
Liberators - James Wesley Rawles   *c* 841

McGuire, Grant (Detective—Private; Veteran;
Lover)
Confessions - Cynthia Eden   *r* 957

McIlroy, Noah (Doctor; Boyfriend)
The Christmas Bouquet - Sherryl Woods   *r* 1098

McKay, Brandt (Brother)
Cowgirls Don't Cry - Lorelei James   *r* 994

McKay, Jessie (Widow(er); Spouse)
Cowgirls Don't Cry - Lorelei James   *r* 994

McKay, Luke (Spouse; Brother; Father)
Cowgirls Don't Cry - Lorelei James   *r* 994

McKee, Dolly (Entertainer; Friend)
Of Irish Blood - Mary Pat Kelly   *t* 188

McKenna, Quill (Lawyer; Bodyguard; Lover)
This Gun for Hire - Jo Goodman   *r* 973

McKenna, Reef (Rescuer; Friend)
Sabotaged - Dani Pettrey   *i* 446

McKinley, Ryan (Spouse)
Married 'til Monday - Denise Hunter   *i* 420

McKinley, Travis (Golfer)
Miracle at Augusta - James Patterson   *c* 825

McLain, Charity (Twin)
Final Lap - Erin McCarthy   *r* 1027

McLain, Harley (Twin; Lover; Child-Care Giver)
Final Lap - Erin McCarthy   *r* 1027

McLaren, Neil (Researcher; Boyfriend)
Reservations for Two - Hillary Manton
Lodge   *i* 428

McLean, Ava (Twin; Agent)
Bridged - Kendra Elliot   *r* 960

McLean, Jayne (Twin; Mentally Ill Person)
Bridged - Kendra Elliot   *r* 960

McMurphy, Allie (Detective—Amateur; Girlfriend;
Hotel Owner)
Oh Say Can You Fudge - Nancy Coco   *m* 518

McNeely, Charlie (Drug Dealer; Spouse; Father)
Where All Light Tends to Go - David Joy   *m* 588

McNeely, Jacob (18-Year-Old; Son; Boyfriend;
Worker)
Where All Light Tends to Go - David Joy   *m* 588

McNeely, Laura (Addict; Spouse; Mother)
Where All Light Tends to Go - David Joy   *m* 588

McNerney, Fiona (Political Figure)
A Scourge of Vipers - Bruce DeSilva   *m* 533

McPhee, Wes (Agent; Classmate)
Sunflower Lane - Jill Gregory   *r* 978

McQueen, Mike (Lawman)
The Missing Piece - Kevin Egan   *m* 540

McShane, Tim (Gambler; Lover)
Of Irish Blood - Mary Pat Kelly   *t* 188

Meadows, Claire (Governess)
By Winter's Light - Stephanie Laurens   *r* 1006

Meche (15-Year-Old; Friend; Magician)
Signal to Noise - Silvia Moreno-Garcia   *f* 85

Medhurst, Kate "La Voile" (Pirate)
The Lost Gentleman - Margaret McPhee   *r* 1035

Medina, Sophie (Photojournalist; Friend)
Ghost Image - Ellen Crosby   *m* 526

Megan (Young Woman; Office Worker; Co-worker;
Secretary)
Jillian - Halle Butler   *c* 707

Mei (Dragon; Friend)
The Exile - C.T. Adams   *f* 3

Meier, Alex (Writer; Religious; Immigrant; Spy)
Leaving Berlin - Joseph Kanon   *m* 590

Mekare (Vampire; Twin)
Prince Lestat - Anne Rice   *c* 845

Melchor (Grandfather; Smuggler; Friend; Gypsy)
The Barefoot Queen - Ildefonso Falcones   *t* 156

Mellon, Bebe (Friend; Businesswoman; Director)
Manhattan in Miniature - Margaret Grace   *m* 558

Memery, Karen (Orphan; Prostitute; Enemy;
Friend)
Karen Memory - Elizabeth Bear   *s* 1118

Mendelson, Sandy (16-Year-Old; Daughter)
Where They Found Her - Kimberly
McCreight   *m* 614

Menkels, Odette (Young Woman; Hunter;
Wealthy)
The Huntress of Thornbeck Forest - Melanie
Dickerson   *i* 393

Merced, Orlando (Musician; Crime Victim)
The Burning Room - Michael Connelly   *c* 718

Mercer, Raymond (Friend; Crime Suspect)
The Convert's Song - Sebastian Rotella   *c* 849

Merchant, Anne (Student—Boarding School; Pa-
tient; Friend)
The Wicked Awakening of Anne Merchant - Joanna
Wiebe   *h* 353

Merchant, Sasha (Artist; Colleague)
Girl Before a Mirror - Liza Palmer   *r* 1047

Meredith, Augusta (Heiress; Woman)
Secrets of a Scandalous Heiress - Theresa
Romain   *r* 1060

Merial, Dr. Daniel (Doctor)
Diary of an Accidental Wallflower - Jennifer
McQuiston   *r* 1036

Merit (Young Woman; Servant)
Dark Debt - Chloe Neill   *h* 335

Meriwether, Lewis (Museum Curator)
The Dead Lands - Benjamin Percy   *s* 1182

Merlin (Wizard)
Fatal Feast - Jay Ruud   *t* 243

Merrill, Nola (Daughter; Spouse)
On Shifting Sand - Allison Pittman   *i* 448

Merrill, Russ (Spouse; Religious)
On Shifting Sand - Allison Pittman   *i* 448

Merriweather, Darcy (Detective—Amateur;
Witch; Friend)
Some Like It Witchy - Heather Blake   *m* 494

Merryhew, Lady Hermione (Noblewoman; Traveler)
Too Dangerous for a Lady - Jo Beverley   *r* 915

Merryweather, Lucy (Heiress)
The Daring Exploits of a Runaway Heiress - Victoria Alexander   *r* 896

Moses (Biblical Figure; Adoptee; Son)
The Pharaoh's Daughter - Mesu Andrews *i* 357

Moss, Flynn (Son; Activist)
The Big Finish - James W. Hall *c* 758

Moss, Jack (Detective—Police; Father)
The Pocket Wife - Susan Crawford *m* 524

Moss, Winifred (Suffragette; Friend)
Cafe Europa - Edward Ifkovic *t* 182

Moth (Supernatural Being)
Briar Queen - Katherine Harbour *h* 312

Mother Dark (Ruler)
Forge of Darkness - Steven Erikson *f* 31

Mother Darkness (Deity; Mother; Ruler)
Fall of Light - Steven Erikson *f* 30

Mother of the Shah (Woman; Mother; Narrator)
The Woman Who Read Too Much - Bahiyyih
Nakhjavani *t* 220

Mountstuart, Xavier (Writer; Missing Person)
The Strangler Vine - Miranda Carter *t* 139

Mozart, Wolfgang (Historical Figure; Musician)
The Figaro Murders - Laura Lebow *t* 199

Mr. Obvious (Man)
Method 15/33 - Shannon Kirk *m* 594

Mrs. (Amnesiac; Immigrant)
The Handsome Man's De Luxe Cafe - Alexander
McCall Smith *c* 864

Mrs. Obvious (Woman)
Method 15/33 - Shannon Kirk *m* 594

Mullah (Religious; Uncle)
The Woman Who Read Too Much - Bahiyyih
Nakhjavani *t* 220

Mulligan, Liam (Journalist)
A Scourge of Vipers - Bruce DeSilva *m* 533

Mulvaney, Lucy (Lover; Friend)
I Saw Her Standing There - Marie Force *r* 964

Mum (Mother)
How to Build a Girl - Caitlin Moran *c* 810

Mumbly Dave (Patient; Friend)
The Thing About December - Donal Ryan *c* 850

Munck, Troels (Man; Friend)
A Place Called Winter - Patrick Gale *t* 162

Munro, Meg (Healer)
Pleasured - Candace Camp *r* 940

Murdoch, Bronwyn (Spinster; Assistant)
The Prince Who Loved Me - Karen
Hawkins *r* 983

Murphy (Political Figure; Veteran)
The Regulator - Ethan J. Wolfe *t* 274

Murphy, Cameron (Actor)
Scent of Triumph - Jan Moran *t* 212

Murphy, Jensen (Detective—Private; Spirit; Crime
Victim)
Every Breath You Take - Chris Marie Green *f* 39

Murphy, Luke (Detective—Private)
Drawing Fire - Janice Cantore *i* 376

Murphy Sullivan, Molly (Spouse; Mother;
Detective—Private; Accident Victim; Retiree)
The Edge of Dreams - Rhys Bowen *t* 131

Myers, Margaret (Political Figure; Friend)
Blue Warrior - Mike Maden *c* 795

Mylakhrion (Wizard)
Tales of the Primal Land - Brian Lumley *h* 332

N

Nabila (Caregiver)
The Stager - Susan Coll *c* 716

Nadia (Friend)
The Drop - Dennis Lehane *c* 788

Nair, Roland (Agent; Friend)
The Laughing Monsters - Denis Johnson *c* 776

Namara (Deity; Spirit)
Darkened Blade - Kelly McCullough *f* 79

Nana Mama (Grandmother; Kidnap Victim)
Hope to Die - James Patterson *c* 824

Nancy (Spouse; Cousin; Widow(er); Missing
Person)
If the Viscount Falls - Sabrina Jeffries *r* 995

Naomi (Journalist)
Consumed - David Cronenberg *c* 722

Narin (Investigator; Friend; Lover)
Old Man's Ghosts - Tom Lloyd *f* 75

Nash, Katherine "Calico" (Bounty Hunter; Bodyguard; Lover)
This Gun for Hire - Jo Goodman *r* 973

Nash, Ted (Detective—Police; Boyfriend)
Wicked Stitch - Amanda Lee *m* 597

Nasmertov, Frida (Young Woman; Niece)
Panic in a Suitcase - Yelena Akhtiorskaya *c* 687

Nasmertov, Pasha (Man; Writer; Uncle)
Panic in a Suitcase - Yelena Akhtiorskaya *c* 687

Nat (Spouse; Father)
Delicious Foods - James Hannaham *c* 760

Natalie (Alien)
Three Songs for Roxy - Caren Gussoff *s* 1150

Nataly (Daughter; Artist; Sister)
The Amado Women - Desiree Zamorano *c* 892

Nathair (Royalty)
Ruin - John Gwynne *f* 45

Nathan (17-Year-Old; Witch)
Half Wild - Sally Green *f* 40

Nathan (Journalist)
Consumed - David Cronenberg *c* 722

Nathaniel (Royalty; Brother)
How to Catch a Prince - Rachel Hauck *i* 414

Neal (Surfer; Friend)
Surrender - June Gray *r* 977

Ned (Religious)
One Last Thing - Rebecca St. James *i* 461

Needle, Gwen (14-Year-Old; Daughter; Friend;
Swimmer)
We Are Pirates - Daniel Handler *c* 759

Needle, Marina (Spouse; Mother)
We Are Pirates - Daniel Handler *c* 759

Needle, Phil (Producer; Spouse; Father)
We Are Pirates - Daniel Handler *c* 759

Neela (Teenager; Mythical Creature)
Rogue Wave - Jennifer Donnelly *f* 28

Nell (Daughter; Sister)
Reunion - Hannah Pittard *c* 833

Nels (17-Year-Old; Boy; Impoverished)
Woven - Michael Jensen *f* 61

Mrs. Nelson (Mother; Baker)
Death by Baking - Cynthia Hickey *i* 418

Nelson, Alice "Pinky" (Restaurateur; Friend)
Snow Way Out - Christine Husom *m* 579

Nelson, Clayton (Scientist; Brother)
The Deep - Nick Cutter *h* 289

Nelson, Emma (Fiance(e))
Huckleberry Spring - Jennifer Beckstrand *i* 359

Nelson, Luke (Brother; Veterinarian)
The Deep - Nick Cutter *h* 289

Nelson, Stormi (Detective—Amateur; Writer;
Girlfriend; Daughter; Neighbor)
Death by Baking - Cynthia Hickey *i* 418

Neville, Charlotte (Vampire; Lover)
The Dark Arts of Blood - Freda Warrington *h* 350

Newark, Tripp (Young Man; Boyfriend; Cousin)
You Were Mine - Abbi Glines *c* 751

Newberry, Thom (Lover)
The Evil Deeds We Do - Robert S.
Levinson *m* 602

Newell-Grey, Jonathan (Military Personnel)
Scent of Triumph - Jan Moran *t* 212

Nic (Artist; Spouse)
Night Blindness - Susan Strecker *c* 870

Nichol, Joelen (Friend; Murderer)
Night Night, Sleep Tight - Hallie Ephron *m* 541

Nichols, Faith (Spouse; Judge; Lover)
Losing Faith - Adam Mitzner *m* 621

Nick (14-Year-Old)
Edison's Alley - Neal Shusterman *s* 1196

Nick (Boy; Friend)
The Boy Who Drew Monsters - Keith
Donohue *c* 732

Nick (Prisoner; Murderer; Brother; Companion)
As Night Falls - Jenny Milchman *m* 619

Nick (Teenager; Brother; Rebel)
City 1 - Gregg Rosenblum *s* 1192

Nicky (Boy; Son)
Scent of Triumph - Jan Moran *t* 212

Nicolaos (Detective; Spouse)
Death Ex Machina - Gary Corby *t* 145

Nierne (Writer; Religious)
Heir of Hope - Morgan L. Busse *i* 368

Night, Madison (Designer; Detective—Amateur)
With Vics You Get Eggroll - Diane Vallere *m* 676

Nightmare Elf (Serial Killer)
Return to the Dark House - Laurie Faria
Stolarz *h* 346

Nikolaevna, Natasha (Royalty; Grandmother)
The Prince Who Loved Me - Karen
Hawkins *r* 983

Nina (Woman; Friend)
Dear Thief - Samantha Harvey *c* 762

Nix, Billy (Musician; Spouse)
Firebreak - Tricia Fields *m* 544

Nix, Brenda (Spouse)
Firebreak - Tricia Fields *m* 544

Noah (Boy; Autistic; Nephew)
For Keeps - Rachel Lacey *r* 1003

Nogara, Ugo (Man; Museum Curator)
The Fifth Gospel - Ian Caldwell *m* 509

Norfield, John (Veteran; Colleague; Prisoner)
Mr. Jones - Margaret Sweatman *t* 256

North, Captain Kit (Sea Captain)
The Lost Gentleman - Margaret McPhee *r* 1035

Norwood, Baldwin (Crime Victim; Cook)
Killer Gourmet - G.A. McKevett *m* 615

Novak, Deacon (FBI Agent)
Closer Than You Think - Karen Rose *r* 1062

Novak, Kevin (Crime Victim; Client)
What the Fly Saw - Frankie Y. Bailey *m* 483

O

O'Brian, Marcus (FBI Agent)
Taken - Lisa Harris *i* 412

O'Brien, Anna (Librarian)
Beyond All Dreams - Elizabeth Camden *i* 374

O'Brien, Bud (Lawman)
Loup Garou: The Beast of Harmony Falls - David Reuben Aslin   h 281

O'Brien, Cal (Spouse; Alcoholic; Veteran; Police Officer; Worker)
Serpents in the Cold - Thomas O'Malley   t 222

O'Brien, JJ (Brother; Son; Teenager)
Inside the O'Briens - Lisa Genova   c 747

O'Brien, Joe (Police Officer; Spouse; Father)
Inside the O'Briens - Lisa Genova   c 747

O'Brien, Katie (Sister; Daughter)
Inside the O'Briens - Lisa Genova   c 747

O'Brien, Meghan (Sister; Daughter)
Inside the O'Briens - Lisa Genova   c 747

O'Brien, Patrick (Brother; Son)
Inside the O'Briens - Lisa Genova   c 747

O'Brien, Rosie (Spouse; Mother)
Inside the O'Briens - Lisa Genova   c 747

O'Bryan, Barbara (Lesbian; Lover)
Cherry Bomb - Caitlin R. Kiernan   h 327

O'Dell, Maggie (FBI Agent)
Breaking Creed - Alex Kava   c 779

O'Donnell, Bowman (Shape-Shifter; Leader)
Mate Bond - Jennifer Ashley   f 8

O'Donnell, Finn (Veteran; Rancher; Friend)
Cowboy Boots for Christmas: (Cowboy Not Included) - Carolyn Brown   r 929

O'Hara, Gerald (Spouse; Father)
Ruth's Journey: The Authorized Novel of Mammy from Margaret Mitchell's Gone with the Wind - Donald McCaig   t 210

O'Hara, Mickey (Journalist; Friend)
Deadly Assets - W.E.B. Griffin   c 754

O'Hara, Sally (Detective—Police)
Compulsion - Allison Brennan   m 502

O'Hara, Scarlett (Southern Belle; Daughter)
Ruth's Journey: The Authorized Novel of Mammy from Margaret Mitchell's Gone with the Wind - Donald McCaig   t 210

O'Neill, Jared (Lawyer)
Once a Thief - Lora Young   i 472

O'Toole, Coop (Brother; Teenager; Runaway; 18-Year-Old)
Beneath - Roland Smith   s 1199

O'Toole, Pat (13-Year-Old; Wealthy; Brother)
Beneath - Roland Smith   s 1199

Oakes, Charles (Son)
Murder on Amsterdam Avenue - Victoria Thompson   m 672

Oakes, Gerald (Father)
Murder on Amsterdam Avenue - Victoria Thompson   m 672

Olgun (Deity; Companion)
Covenant's End - Ari Marmell   f 78

Oliphant, Stanley (Military Personnel; Nobleman; Enemy)
Who Buries the Dead - C.S. Harris   t 172

Olive (Aunt; Mother)
Murder with a Twist - Tracy Kiely   m 593

Oliver (Computer Expert; Vampire Hunter; Young Man)
Shutter - Courtney Alameda   h 277

Oliver, Piper (Computer Expert)
Total Surrender - Rebecca Zanetti   r 1100

Olsen, Lester (Businessman; Assassin)
Private Vegas - James Patterson   c 826

Olson, Norma (Neighbor; Aged Person)
Death by Baking - Cynthia Hickey   i 418

Omo, Ras (Detective—Police; Colleague)
Deadeye - William C. Dietz   s 1136

Ondorum (Mythical Creature; Companion)
Forge of Ashes - Josh Vogt   f 120

One Beneath (Supernatural Being)
Sorceress - Claudia Gray   f 38

Oosterling, Ava (Cook; Store Owner; Friend; Detective—Amateur)
Five-Alarm Fudge - Christine DeSmet   m 534

Organa, Leia (Royalty; Rebel; Leader)
Heir to the Jedi - Kevin Hearne   s 1154

Orianna (Advertising; Friend; Girlfriend)
Getting Even - Sarah Rayner   c 842

Ormiston, Sir David "Devil/Dev" (Knight)
Devil's Moon - Amanda Scott   r 1070

Orr, April (Administrator; Mother; Witch)
The Witch of the Wood - Michael Aronovitz   h 280

Ortiz, Ramon (Military Personnel; Veterinarian)
A Long Time Until Now - Michael Z. Williamson   s 1208

Orvin (Military Personnel)
Slow Bullets - Alastair Reynolds   s 1188

Osborne, Diz (Boy; 11-Year-Old; Son; Brother)
Last to Know - Elizabeth Adler   c 685

Osborne, Frazer (Girl; 16-Year-Old; Twin; Daughter; Sister)
Last to Know - Elizabeth Adler   c 685

Osborne, Madison (Girl; 16-Year-Old; Twin; Daughter; Sister)
Last to Know - Elizabeth Adler   c 685

Osborne, Roman (Son; Brother; 18-Year-Old)
Last to Know - Elizabeth Adler   c 685

Osborne, Rose (Spouse; Mother)
Last to Know - Elizabeth Adler   c 685

Osborne, Wally (Writer; Spouse; Father)
Last to Know - Elizabeth Adler   c 685

Oscar (Government Official; Spouse)
Fram - Steve Himmer   c 767

Oshima, Shigeo (Director; Man)
Sherlock Holmes, the Missing Years: Japan - Vasudev Murthy   t 219

Oshiro, Mariko (Rogue; Detective—Police)
Disciple of the Wind - Steve Bein   f 11

Oswald, Lee Harvey Jr. (Son)
The Kennedy Connection - R.G. Belsky   c 701

Otis (Man; Criminal; Organized Crime Figure)
Pacific Fire - Greg van Eekhout   f 118

Otto (Aged Person; Spouse; Veteran)
Emma and Otto and Russell and James - Emma Hooper   c 769

Owner (Serial Killer)
Five - Ursula Archer   c 693

P

Paavo (Spouse; Father; Immigrant)
Wolf Winter - Cecilia Ekback   t 152

Pace, Jordan (Farmer; Fiance(e))
As Gouda as Dead - Avery Aames   m 473

Paen, Promise (Military Personnel)
Unbreakable - W.C. Bauers   s 1117

Palma, Lolita (Heiress; Girlfriend)
The Siege - Arturo Perez-Reverte   t 228

Palmer, Alex (Doctor; Father)
Falling Hard - HelenKay Dimon   r 954

Palmer, Audie (Brother; Prisoner; Friend)
Life or Death - Michael Robotham   m 645

Palmer, Sebastian "Bash" (Restaurateur; Lover; Divorced Person)
Love After All - Jaci Burton   r 937

Palwick, Lydia (Student—High School; Classmate)
Harrison Squared - Daryl Gregory   h 306

Paniotis (Friend)
Outline - Rachel Cusk   c 724

Pantha, Agatha (Aged Person; Rescuer; Traveler; Widow(er))
Lost and Found - Brooke Davis   c 729

Pappas, Pete (Detective—Police; Boyfriend)
Farmed and Dangerous - Edith Maxwell   m 613

Paras, Olivia (Spouse; Cook)
All the President's Menus - Julie Hyzy   m 580

Paris (Cat)
Checked Out - Elaine Viets   m 677

Parker (FBI Agent)
Whiskers of the Lion - P.L. Gaus   m 555

Parker, AJ (Police Officer)
Rescue Me - Catherine Mann   r 1017

Parker, Allison (Widow(er); Friend; Mother)
When We Fall - Emily Liebert   c 791

Parker, Barbara (Young Woman; Beauty Pageant Contestant; Actress)
Funny Girl - Nick Hornby   c 770

Parker, Brody (Bounty Hunter; Adventurer)
Deadly, Calm, and Cold - Susannah Sandlin   r 1068

Parker, Dorothy (Historical Figure; Writer)
West of Sunset - Stewart O'Nan   c 819

Parker, Eric (Runaway)
Keys of Heaven - Adina Senft   i 455

Parker, Logan (Son; 10-Year-Old)
When We Fall - Emily Liebert   c 791

Parker, Tom (FBI Agent; Police Officer; Friend)
Desperate Measures - Sandra Orchard   i 441

Parr, Catherine (Historical Figure; Spouse)
Lamentation - C.J. Sansom   t 244

Parrish, Dr. Eric (Psychologist; Spouse)
Every Fifteen Minutes - Lisa Scottoline   m 653

Parsaa (Man; Leader)
Allure of Deceit - Susan Froetschel   m 553

Parsons, Jenna (Businesswoman; Single Mother; Sister; Twin; Daughter; Divorced Person)
House of Wonder - Sarah Healy   c 763

Parsons, Priscilla (Beauty Pageant Contestant; Mother)
House of Wonder - Sarah Healy   c 763

Parsons, Warren (Brother; Twin; Mentally Challenged Person; Son)
House of Wonder - Sarah Healy   c 763

Pascal, Skylar (Military Personnel; Worker; Nurse)
Wolf Haven - Lindsay McKenna   r 1029

Pasha (Man; Survivor)
The Country of Ice Cream Star - Sandra Newman   c 816

Pat (Woman; Spouse)
The Witch of the Wood - Michael Aronovitz   h 280

Patrick (Doctor)
The Secrets of Midwives - Sally Hepworth   c 765

Patrise (Knight; Crime Victim)
Fatal Feast - Jay Ruud   t 243

Patterson, Jake (Spouse)
Last One Home - Debbie Macomber   c 794

Patterson, Nichole (Spouse; Daughter; Sister)
Last One Home - Debbie Macomber   c 794

Rahab (Prostitute; Biblical Figure)
The Crimson Cord: Rahab's Story - Jill Eileen Smith *i* 458

Rainbow (Girl; 5-Year-Old; Niece)
Last Chance Family - Hope Ramsay *r* 1055

Raines, Prairie Dawn "P.D." (Lover; Store Owner; Restaurateur)
Desperado - Lisa Bingham *r* 916

Rainsford, Rebekah (Young Woman)
Pale Harvest - Braden Hepner *c* 764

Rainsford, Scarlett (Crime Victim; Young Woman; Missing Person)
Behind Closed Doors - Elizabeth Haynes *m* 571

Rake, Anomander (Brother; Shape-Shifter; Son; Supernatural Being)
Fall of Light - Steven Erikson *f* 30

Raleeha (Woman; Human; Slave)
Righteous Fury - Markus Heitz *f* 49

Ramberg, Thor (Boyfriend; Agent)
Where the Bones are Buried - Jeanne Matthews *m* 611

Ramirez, Adrian (Teacher; Boyfriend)
Whispers in the Dark - Chase J. Jackson *h* 321

Ramona (Friend; Accident Victim)
Doll Face - Tim Curran *h* 288

Ramotswe, Precious (Spouse; Detective—Private; Co-worker)
The Handsome Man's De Luxe Cafe - Alexander McCall Smith *c* 864

Ramsayer, Rachel (Computer Expert)
Whiskers of the Lion - P.L. Gaus *m* 555

Ran (Man; Warrior; Martial Arts Expert)
Slavers of the Savage Catacombs - Jon F. Merz *f* 81

Rand, Hamilton (Scientist; Brother)
Corridors of the Night - Anne Perry *t* 229

Rand, Magnus (Doctor; Brother)
Corridors of the Night - Anne Perry *t* 229

Rania (Alien)
The Architect of Aeons - John C. Wright *s* 1210

Raphael's Son (Son; Wealthy; Crime Victim; Criminal)
The Luminous Heart of Jonah S. - Gina B. Nahai *c* 814

Rasmus (Apprentice)
Woven - Michael Jensen *f* 61

Rasp (Military Personnel; Leader)
Yarrick: Imperial Creed - David Annandale *s* 1106

Rathbone, Oliver (Lawyer; Friend)
Corridors of the Night - Anne Perry *t* 229

Raven (Sister; Twin; Student—Boarding School)
Whispers in the Dark - Chase J. Jackson *h* 321

Ravenshaw, Rebecca (Orphan; Heiress)
Mist of Midnight - Sandra Byrd *i* 371

Ray, Billy (Police Officer)
The First Wife - Erica Spindler *m* 664

Raymonde, Kirsten (Traveler; Survivor; Actress)
Station Eleven - Emily St. John Mandel *c* 796

Rayne, Walter (Crime Suspect; Criminal; Father)
Blood Ties - Nicholas Guild *m* 562

Reana (Assassin; Lover; Sister)
The Dangerous Type - Loren Rhoads *s* 1189

Reardon, John (Father; Warlock)
Gideon - Alex Gordon *h* 303

Reardon, Lauren (Daughter; Witch; Young Woman)
Gideon - Alex Gordon *h* 303

Rebecca (Sister)
His Wicked Reputation - Madeline Hunter *r* 992

Rebecca (Worker; Detective—Amateur)
As Gouda as Dead - Avery Aames *m* 473

Rebeccah (Daughter; Sister)
Slated for Death - Elizabeth J. Duncan *m* 537

Red Queen (Grandmother; Royalty)
The Liar's Key - Mark Lawrence *f* 71

Redding, Katie (Sister; Daughter)
The Sheltering - Mark Powell *c* 835

Redding, Lucy (Sister; Daughter)
The Sheltering - Mark Powell *c* 835

Redding, Luther (Military Personnel; Pilot; Spouse; Father)
The Sheltering - Mark Powell *c* 835

Redding, Pamela (Spouse; Mother)
The Sheltering - Mark Powell *c* 835

Reddy, Matt (Military Personnel)
Straits of Hell - Taylor Anderson *s* 1105

Redtail, Charlie (Police Officer)
Loup Garou: The Beast of Harmony Falls - David Reuben Aslin *h* 281

Reece, Pepper (Store Owner; Employer; Divorced Person; Detective—Amateur)
Assault and Pepper - Leslie Budewitz *m* 505

Reed, Malcolm (Spaceship Captain; Friend)
Uncertain Logic - Christopher L. Bennett *s* 1119

Reed, Meg (Journalist)
Slayed on the Slopes - Kate Dyer-Seeley *m* 539

Reeves, Bass (Lawman; Friend; Enemy)
Karen Memory - Elizabeth Bear *s* 1118

Reid, Savannah (Spouse; Detective—Private; Friend)
Killer Gourmet - G.A. McKevett *m* 615

Reilly, Jensen (Girlfriend; Sister; Daughter; Spouse)
Night Blindness - Susan Strecker *c* 870

Reilly, Sterling (Father; Cancer Patient)
Night Blindness - Susan Strecker *c* 870

Reilly, Will (Brother; Son; Friend; Accident Victim)
Night Blindness - Susan Strecker *c* 870

Reiniger, Godric (Vampire; Filmmaker)
The Dark Arts of Blood - Freda Warrington *h* 350

Reiss, Sophie (Sister; Twin; Missing Person)
Deadlight Hall - Sarah Rayne *h* 337

Reiss, Susannah (Sister; Twin; Missing Person)
Deadlight Hall - Sarah Rayne *h* 337

Rejon, Juan Rejon (Detective—Police)
The Beige Man - Helene Tursten *m* 674

Rene (Friend)
A Killer Retreat - Tracy Weber *m* 679

Renquist, Pete (Leader; Crime Victim; Friend)
A Fatal Chapter - Lorna Barrett *m* 488

Reothe (Mythical Creature; Rebel)
The Fall of Fair Isle - Rowena Cory Daniells *f* 27

Reuben (Young Man)
Making Marion - Beth Moran *c* 809

Revere, Maxine "Max" (Journalist; Television Personality)
Compulsion - Allison Brennan *m* 502

Rex Ryen (Royalty)
Madness in Solidar - L.E. Modesitt *f* 82

Reyes, Nora (Actress; Lover)
The Lovers' Tango - Mark Rubinstein *m* 647

Reynolds, Ali (Television Personality; Spouse; Mother; Mother; Friend)
Cold Betrayal - J.A. Jance *m* 584

Reynolds, Charles (Friend)
Alien Separation - Gini Koch *s* 1162

Reynolds, Ellie (Young Woman; Vacationer)
Love Letters - Debbie Macomber *c* 793

Reynolds, Irene (Lover)
Remember the Lilies - Liz Tolsma *i* 464

Reynolds, Nikki (Agent)
The Kennedy Connection - R.G. Belsky *c* 701

Rhodes, Mark (Military Personnel)
Search and Seduce - Sara Jane Stone *r* 1088

Ricardo, Felix (Father; Spirit)
Ghost in the Guacamole - Sue Ann Jaffarian *m* 582

Ricardo, Lucinda "Lucy" (Sister; Daughter; Businesswoman)
Ghost in the Guacamole - Sue Ann Jaffarian *m* 582

Ricardo, Ricarda "Rikki" (Sister; Daughter; Businesswoman)
Ghost in the Guacamole - Sue Ann Jaffarian *m* 582

Rice, Condoleezza (Historical Figure; Political Figure)
The Infernal - Mark Doten *c* 734

Richard (Historical Figure; Royalty)
The Invention of Fire - Bruce W. Holsinger *t* 179

Richard (Vacationer; Spouse; Wealthy)
The Last Good Paradise - Tatjana Soli *c* 865

Richard the Lionheart (Royalty)
The Holy Lance - Andrew Latham *t* 198

Richards, Carter (Young Man; Boyfriend)
Hope Burns - Jaci Burton *r* 936

Richardson, Dorothy (Suffragette; Writer; Boarder; Secretary; Friend; Lover; Feminist)
The Lodger - Louisa Treger *t* 265

Richardson, Violet (Store Owner; Friend)
Silken Threats - Addison Fox *r* 966

Richelieu, Cardinal (Historical Figure; Nobleman)
1636: The Cardinal Virtues - Eric Flint *s* 1145

Richmond, Daisy (Student—Graduate; Cancer Patient; Spouse; Friend)
Before I Go - Colleen Oakley *c* 820

Richmond, Jack (Student—Graduate; Spouse)
Before I Go - Colleen Oakley *c* 820

Richter (Military Personnel; Revolutionary)
Fall of Macharius - William King *s* 1161

Rick, Louise (Detective—Police; Friend)
The Forgotten Girls - Sara Blaedel *m* 493

Riddell, Jones (Brother; Son; Father)
A Sudden Light - Garth Stein *c* 868

Riddell, Samuel "Grandpa" (Father; Grandfather)
A Sudden Light - Garth Stein *c* 868

Riddell, Serena (Aunt; Sister; Daughter)
A Sudden Light - Garth Stein *c* 868

Riddell, Trevor (14-Year-Old; Son; Grandson; Nephew)
A Sudden Light - Garth Stein *c* 868

Ridgewood, Noah (Salesman; Fiance(e); Lover)
Dictatorship of the Dress - Jessica Topper *r* 1092

Ridley, Ellen (Detective—Homicide; Colleague)
Blood Ties - Nicholas Guild *m* 562

Riggs, Tanner (Diver; Single Father)
One in a Million - Jill Shalvis *r* 1077

Riggs, Troy (15-Year-Old; Son)
One in a Million - Jill Shalvis *r* 1077

Riker, William T. (Spaceship Captain; Friend)
Takedown - John Jackson Miller *s* 1178

Ryan (Professor)
Outline - Rachel Cusk   *c* 724

Ryan (Teenager; Magician; Boyfriend)
Miss Mayhem - Rachel Hawkins   *f* 48

Ryan, Andrew (Detective; Co-worker)
Bones Never Lie - Kathy Reichs   *c* 843

Ryan, Sean (Detective—Police; Immigrant; Boyfriend)
Deception on Sable Hill - Shelley Gray   *i* 408

Ryder (Boyfriend; Friend; Doctor)
Night Blindness - Susan Strecker   *c* 870

Ryder (Vampire Hunter; Young Man)
Shutter - Courtney Alameda   *h* 277

Mr. Ryker (Government Official; Father)
The Glass Arrow - Kristen Simmons   *s* 1197

Ryker, Amir (Boy; Son)
The Glass Arrow - Kristen Simmons   *s* 1197

Ryland, Jane (Journalist; Lover)
Truth Be Told - Hank Phillippi Ryan   *c* 851

S

Sabine (Lover; Student)
On the Edge - Edward St. Aubyn   *c* 867

Saeed (Genetically Altered Being; Lover; Prisoner)
The Book of Phoenix - Nnedi Okorafor   *f* 88

Sage, Frank (Military Personnel)
Master Sergeant - Mel Odom   *s* 1181

Sage, Mira (Mercenary; Colleague)
Edge of Betrayal - Shannon K. Butcher   *r* 939

Sagemont, Phil (Spouse; Detective—Private)
Checked Out - Elaine Viets   *m* 677

Saginowski, Bob (Bartender; Cousin; Friend)
The Drop - Dennis Lehane   *c* 788

Saker (Spy; Religious)
The Dagger's Path - Glenda Larke   *f* 67

Sakhet (Alien; Woman; Spy)
Heir to the Jedi - Kevin Hearne   *s* 1154

Salif (Nephew; Son; Brother)
Hiding in Plain Sight - Nuruddin Farah   *c* 741

Salim (7-Year-Old; Boy)
Ishmael's Oranges - Claire Hajaj   *c* 757

Salome (Spy)
Twelve Days - Alex Berenson   *c* 702

Salome, Sandrine (Woman; Relative; Lover)
The Witch of Painted Sorrows - M.J. Rose   *t* 236

Salvare, Abby Knight (Store Owner; Spouse; Detective—Amateur)
A Root Awakening - Kate Collins   *m* 519

Salvare, Marco (Restaurateur; Spouse; Detective—Private)
A Root Awakening - Kate Collins   *m* 519

Salvatore, Antonio "Pinky" (Crime Suspect)
Neighing with Fire - Kathryn O'Sullivan   *m* 628

Salvatore, Tonio (Detective; Lover)
On the Run - Jo Davis   *r* 951

Sam (Brother)
One True Path - Barbara Cameron   *i* 375

Sam (Detective—Homicide; Colleague)
Blood Ties - Nicholas Guild   *m* 562

Sam (Dog; Companion)
The Look of Love - Sarah Jio   *c* 775

Sam (Patient; Twin)
Find Me - Laura van den Berg   *c* 877

Sam (Spouse; Stepfather)
Bittersweet - Susan Wittig Albert   *m* 476

Sam (Supernatural Being; Companion; Teenager)
Pacific Fire - Greg van Eekhout   *f* 118

Samarra (Young Woman; Girlfriend)
The Shadow of the Crescent Moon - Fatima Bhutto   *c* 703

Sanchez, Oscar (Missing Person; Friend; Spouse)
Devils and Dust - J.D. Rhoades   *m* 642

Sanchez, Sandy (Colleague)
Hush Hush - Laura Lippman   *m* 604

Sand, George (Historical Figure; Writer; Woman)
The Dream Lover - Elizabeth Berg   *t* 129

Sand Shadow (Companion; Cat)
Artemis Invaded - Jane M. Lindskold   *s* 1169

Sandberg, Torleif "Muesli" (Crime Victim)
The Beige Man - Helene Tursten   *m* 674

Sanders, Bianca (Spouse)
Double Mint - Gretchen Archer   *m* 481

Sanders, Jimmy (Fugitive; Crime Suspect; Missing Person; Friend)
A String of Beads - Thomas Perry   *c* 827

Sanders, Richard (Employer; Spouse)
Double Mint - Gretchen Archer   *m* 481

Sanders, Ruth (Mother; Lover)
Cold Spell - Deb Vanasse   *c* 879

Sanderson, Molly (Journalist; Spouse; Mother)
Where They Found Her - Kimberly McCreight   *m* 614

Sandoval, Roberto (Lawyer; Crime Victim)
Circling the Runway - J.L. Abramo   *m* 474

Sandra (Spouse)
The Storm Murders - John Farrow   *m* 543

Sandstone, Eddie (Brother; Son)
A Deadly Affair at Bobtail Ridge - Terry Shames   *m* 656

Sandstone, Jenny (Lawyer; Neighbor; Daughter; Sister)
A Deadly Affair at Bobtail Ridge - Terry Shames   *m* 656

Sandstone, Vera (Mother)
A Deadly Affair at Bobtail Ridge - Terry Shames   *m* 656

Santeros (Agent; Enemy)
Cobra Outlaw - Timothy Zahn   *s* 1211

Santiago, Elizabeth (Computer Expert; Military Personnel)
Corsair - James Cambias   *s* 1122

Santos, Victoria (FBI Agent)
Cane and Abe - James Grippando   *c* 756

Sara (Teenager; Daughter)
The Evil Deeds We Do - Robert S. Levinson   *m* 602

Lady Sarah (Noblewoman)
Lady Sarah's Sinful Desires - Sophie Barnes   *r* 909

Sarah (Time Traveler; Friend)
The Door in the Moon - Catherine Fisher   *f* 32

Sarielle (Woman; Warrior)
Cursed by Ice - Jacquelyn Frank   *f* 35

Sarra (Young Woman)
The Story Keeper - Lisa Wingate   *c* 887

Satin (Criminal; Leader)
Earls Just Want to Have Fun - Shana Galen   *r* 970

Sato, Haruki (Young Woman)
Dreaming Spies - Laurie R. King   *t* 192

Satomi, Isobel (Criminal; Hunter; Artificial Intelligence)
Dark Intelligence - Neal Asher   *s* 1108

Saunders, Gwen (Detective—Police)
Innocent Damage - Robert K. Lewis   *m* 603

Scaligeri, Sofia (Noblewoman; Mother)
The Warring States - Aidan Harte   *f* 47

Scanlon, Gigi (Worker; Young Woman)
The Dangers of Dating a Rebound Vampire - Molly Harper   *h* 313

Scarlatti, Vic (Government Official; Retiree)
Echo Lake - Carla Neggers   *r* 1040

Scarlet (Slave; Cousin)
The Creole Princess - Beth White   *i* 468

Scarlett (Manager)
Making Marion - Beth Moran   *c* 809

Scarpetta, Dr. Kay (Aunt; Doctor; Detective; Spouse)
Flesh and Blood - Patricia Cornwell   *c* 719

Schaeffer, Aidan (Religious; Friend; Co-worker)
Dark Bride - Jonathan Ryan   *h* 340

Schlueter, Pam (Leader)
Retribution - David Hagberg   *m* 563

Schrock, Elaine (Fiance(e); Friend; Religious)
The Decision - Wanda E. Brunstetter   *i* 367

Schroder, Arnold "Stubby" (16-Year-Old; 11th Grader; Friend)
When - Victoria Laurie   *f* 70

Schroder, Carl (Detective—Police; Vigilante; Co-worker)
Five Minutes Alone - Paul Cleave   *c* 714

Schulte, Henry (Colleague; Technician)
Oh Say Can You Fudge - Nancy Coco   *m* 518

Schwartz, David (Computer Expert)
Corsair - James Cambias   *s* 1122

Schweitzer, Jim (Military Personnel; Reanimated Dead)
Gemini Cell - Myke Cole   *f* 26

Scofield, Max (Public Relations; Boyfriend; Crime Suspect)
Ming Tea Murder - Laura Childs   *m* 514

Scotty (Object)
Delicious Foods - James Hannaham   *c* 760

Seagrave, Jeth (Teenager; Mercenary; Brother)
Polaris - Mindee Arnett   *s* 1107

Sean (Doctor)
The Secrets of Midwives - Sally Hepworth   *c* 765

Sean (Teenager; Boyfriend)
Unleashed - Sophie Jordan   *s* 1157

Seaton, Lady Julia "Duchess of Colton" (Lover)
The Courtesan Duchess - Joanna Shupe   *r* 1083

Seaton, Lord Nicholas Francis "Duke of Colton" (Lover)
The Courtesan Duchess - Joanna Shupe   *r* 1083

Sebak (Father; Spouse; Military Personnel)
The Pharaoh's Daughter - Mesu Andrews   *i* 357

Sebastian (15-Year-Old; Friend)
Signal to Noise - Silvia Moreno-Garcia   *f* 85

Selinda (Young Woman; Fiance(e))
Cursed by Fire - Jacquelyn Frank   *f* 36

Sellers, Jackie (Friend)
No Place to Hide - Lynette Eason   *i* 395

Selvedge, Blair (Farmer; Grandfather)
Pale Harvest - Braden Hepner   *c* 764

Selvedge, Jack (Orphan; 20-Year-Old; Farmer; Grandson; Friend)
Pale Harvest - Braden Hepner   *c* 764

Selznick, David O. (Historical Figure; Filmmaker; Employer)
A Touch of Stardust - Kate Alcott   *t* 125

Semyaza (Demon)
Guardian - Erik Williams   *h* 354

Sendry, Lydia (Manager; Mother)
Allure of Deceit - Susan Froetschel   *m* 553

Sendry, Michael (Entrepreneur; Crime Victim; Spouse; Son)
Allure of Deceit - Susan Froetschel   *m* 553

Sendry, Rose (Crime Victim; Spouse)
Allure of Deceit - Susan Froetschel   *m* 553

Serafina (Teenager; Mythical Creature)
Rogue Wave - Jennifer Donnelly   *f* 28

Serena (Young Woman)
The Shadows - J.R. Ward   *h* 349

Serrailler, Simon (Detective—Police; Brother; Boyfriend; Stepson)
The Soul of Discretion - Susan Hill   *m* 574

Sethos (Enemy)
Remnants: Season of Fire - Lisa T. Bergren   *i* 361

Seventh, Abraham (Fugitive; Immortal; Friend)
Infinity Bell - Devon Monk   *f* 83

Severson, Miranda (Artist; Spouse; Lover)
The Kind Worth Killing - Peter Swanson   *m* 670

Severson, Ted (Businessman; Wealthy; Spouse)
The Kind Worth Killing - Peter Swanson   *m* 670

Seward, Philip (Investigator)
The Breath of Night - Michael Arditti   *c* 694

Seymour, Edward (Historical Figure; Spouse; Brother)
The May Bride - Suzannah Dunn   *t* 151

Seymour, Jane (Historical Figure; Sister; Sister)
The May Bride - Suzannah Dunn   *t* 151

Seymour, Sage (Actress; Client)
Shopaholic to the Stars - Sophie Kinsella   *c* 784

Shackleton, Kate (Investigator; Colleague)
A Woman Unknown - Frances Brody   *t* 134

Shadow (Cat)
Hiss and Tell - Claire Donally   *m* 536

Shadowsun (Military Personnel; Enemy)
Damocles - Phil Kelly   *s* 1159

Shah (Ruler)
The Woman Who Read Too Much - Bahiyyih Nakhjavani   *t* 220

Shah, Nidhi (Doctor)
Unbound - Jim C. Hines   *f* 55

Shakespeare, Lukas (Gang Member)
The Winter Family - Clifford Jackman   *t* 184

Shakespeare, William (Historical Figure; Writer; Supernatural Being)
The Dead Hamlets - Peter Roman   *f* 99

Shakespeare, William (Writer; Historical Figure; Tutor)
The Tutor - Andrea Chapin   *t* 140

Shalom (Pig)
Holy Cow - David Duchovny   *c* 735

Shang, Gary (Spy; Father)
A Map of Betrayal - Ha Jin   *c* 774

Shang, Lilian (Professor; Daughter)
A Map of Betrayal - Ha Jin   *c* 774

Shardlake, Matthew (Lawyer; Employer)
Lamentation - C.J. Sansom   *t* 244

Sharpe, Callie (Planner)
One in a Million - Jill Shalvis   *r* 1077

Sharpe, Danielle (Manager; Single Mother)
All He Wants for Christmas - Lisa Plumley   *r* 1048

Sharpe, Emma (FBI Agent; Granddaughter; Fiance(e))
Harbor Island - Carla Neggers   *r* 1041

Sharpe, Rosalind (Young Woman)
The Duke and the Lady in Red - Lorraine Heath   *r* 985

Sharpe, Wendell (Detective; Grandfather)
Harbor Island - Carla Neggers   *r* 1041

Shaumian, Maroussia (Spy)
Radiant State - Peter Higgins   *s* 1155

Shaw, Bill (Lover; Writer)
The Lovers' Tango - Mark Rubinstein   *m* 647

Shaw, Donovan "Dono" (Criminal; Grandfather; Crime Victim)
Past Crimes - Glen Erik Hamilton   *m* 566

Shaw, Dutch (Military Personnel)
The Knife - Ross Ritchell   *c* 846

Shaw, Lily (Writer; Friend)
Falling from Horses - Molly Gloss   *t* 165

Shaw, Van (Veteran; Criminal; Grandson)
Past Crimes - Glen Erik Hamilton   *m* 566

Shelder, Hailey (Agent; Mother; Single Mother)
Manhunt - Lisa Phillips   *i* 447

Shepard, Jacob (Brother; Missing Person)
Ancient Oceans of Central Kentucky - David Connerley Nahm   *c* 815

Shepard, Leah (Director; Sister)
Ancient Oceans of Central Kentucky - David Connerley Nahm   *c* 815

Sherard, Captain Christopher "Kitt" (Shipowner; Lover; Pirate; Sea Captain)
Breaking the Rake's Rules - Bronwyn Scott   *r* 1071

Sheridan (Young Woman; Student—College; Sister; Daughter)
Endangered - C.J. Box   *m* 499

Sheridan, Philip (Historical Figure; Military Personnel)
Valley of the Shadow - Ralph Peters   *t* 231

Sherman, Jason (Military Personnel; Fiance(e))
Surrender - June Gray   *r* 977

Shields, Dr. Lise (Therapist; Doctor)
The Forgetting Place - John Burley   *m* 506

Shiffley, Randall (Government Official)
Lord of the Wings - Donna Andrews   *m* 479

Shinwari, Khatereh "Khat" (Military Personnel)
Taking Fire - Lindsay McKenna   *r* 1030

Shoe (Cousin; Crime Suspect)
A Wee Murder in My Shop - Fran Stewart   *m* 667

Shunde, Scurelya "Scur" Timsuk (Prisoner; Traveler)
Slow Bullets - Alastair Reynolds   *s* 1188

Siebert, Paula (Lawyer)
Ostland - David Thomas   *t* 259

Sigtryggr (Viking)
The Empty Throne - Bernard Cornwell   *t* 146

Sikandar (Doctor; Spouse; Brother)
The Shadow of the Crescent Moon - Fatima Bhutto   *c* 703

Silence (Villain)
Breakout - Ann Aguirre   *s* 1103

Silva, Angel (Sister; Criminal; Lover)
On the Run - Jo Davis   *r* 951

Silva, Rab (Brother; Criminal; Gang Member)
On the Run - Jo Davis   *r* 951

Silver Box (Artificial Intelligence; Object)
Inside a Silver Box - Walter Mosley   *s* 1179

Silverun, Tobimar (Companion)
Phoenix in Shadow - Ryk E. Spoor   *f* 108

Silvestre (Spouse; Landlord)
Skylight - Jose Saramago   *c* 854

Simmons, Bernie (Friend; Detective—Amateur; Woman; Baker; Sister)
A Catered Mother's Day - Isis Crawford   *m* 523

Simmons, Erich (Young Man; Neighbor)
Mr. Miracle - Debbie Macomber   *r* 1015

Simmons, Libby (Woman; Baker; Sister; Detective—Amateur; Friend)
A Catered Mother's Day - Isis Crawford   *m* 523

Simon (Biblical Figure; Fiance(e))
The Tomb: A Novel of Martha - Stephanie Landsem   *i* 426

Simon (Brother; Son)
Balm of Gilead - Adina Senft   *i* 456

Simpson, B. (Technician; Spouse)
Cold Betrayal - J.A. Jance   *m* 584

Simpson, Lindy (15-Year-Old; Girl; Runner; Crime Victim)
My Sunshine Away - M.O. Walsh   *c* 884

Sinan (Architect)
The Architect's Apprentice - Elif Shafak   *t* 247

Sinclair, Arthur (Veteran; Crime Suspect; Father; Missing Person)
Quartet for the End of Time - Johanna Skibsrud   *t* 250

Sinclair, Charlotte (Woman; Survivor)
The Fair Fight - Anna Freeman   *t* 160

Sinclair, Douglas (Son)
Quartet for the End of Time - Johanna Skibsrud   *t* 250

Sinclair, Michael (Detective—Police; Nobleman; Spouse)
Murder in Hindsight - Anne Cleeland   *m* 516

Sinclair, Rand (Lover; Rancher)
Twice a Texas Bride - Linda Broday   *r* 928

Sinclair, Tori (Seamstress; Fiance(e); Detective—Amateur; Friend)
Wedding Duress - Elizabeth Lynn Casey   *m* 513

Sinclair, Vanessa (Spouse; Crime Victim)
Antiques Swap - Barbara Allan   *m* 477

Sinclair, Wesley III (Businessman; Wealthy; Spouse)
Antiques Swap - Barbara Allan   *m* 477

Singer, Marcy (Detective—Amateur; Store Owner; Girlfriend; Crime Suspect)
Wicked Stitch - Amanda Lee   *m* 597

Singletary, Jasper (Political Figure)
Arsenic and Old Books - Miranda James   *m* 583

Sinthoras (Warrior; Immortal; Artist)
Righteous Fury - Markus Heitz   *f* 49

Siobhan (Friend; Nurse)
The Thing About December - Donal Ryan   *c* 850

Sirsky, Nico (Police Officer)
The City of Blood - Frederique Molay   *m* 622

Sister of the Shah (Woman; Sister; Narrator)
The Woman Who Read Too Much - Bahiyyih Nakhjavani   *t* 220

Sister Tooth (Woman; Sorceress; Criminal)
Pacific Fire - Greg van Eekhout   *f* 118

Sita (Narrator; Warrior; Military Personnel)
Rebel Queen - Michelle Moran   *t* 213

Skip (Spouse)
Etta Mae's Worst Bad-Luck Day - Ann B. Ross   *c* 848

Skye (Streetperson)
Gathering Prey - John Sandford   *m* 652

Skylar (Son)
Beyond the Pale Motel - Francesca Lia Block   *c* 704

Skywalker, Luke (Pilot; Rebel)
Heir to the Jedi - Kevin Hearne *s* 1154

Slade, Luke (Young Man; Assistant)
Last Days in Shanghai - Casey Walker *c* 883

Slade, Zach (Detective—Private; Boyfriend; Psychic)
Ghost Killer - Robin D. Owens *f* 91

Slader, Joe (Police Officer)
In the Woods - Merry Jones *m* 587

Slicer (Serial Killer)
The Diabolical Miss Hyde - Viola Carr *f* 21

Sloan, Heather (Manager; Businesswoman; Designer)
Echo Lake - Carla Neggers *r* 1040

Sloane (Fiance(e))
Dictatorship of the Dress - Jessica Topper *r* 1092

Slone, Bailey (Boy; 6-Year-Old; Son; Missing Person)
Hold the Dark - William Giraldi *c* 749

Slone, Medora (Woman; Spouse; Mother)
Hold the Dark - William Giraldi *c* 749

Slone, Vernon (Military Personnel; Spouse; Father; Friend)
Hold the Dark - William Giraldi *c* 749

Smart, Aganetha (Woman; Aged Person; Patient; Runner)
Girl Runner - Carrie Snyder *t* 253

Smith, Archer (Son; Military Personnel; Kidnap Victim; Brother)
The Abduction of Smith and Smith - Rashad Harrison *t* 174

Smith, B (Supernatural Being; Teenager; Warrior)
Zom-B Bride - Darren Shan *h* 343

Smith, Faith (Military Personnel; 16-Year-Old; Daughter; Sister; Survivor; Teenager)
Strands of Sorrow - John Ringo *s* 1190

Smith, Jon (Military Personnel)
Robert Ludlum's The Geneva Strategy - Jamie Freveletti *m* 551

Smith, Jupiter (Slave; Military Personnel; Murderer; Bastard Son; Brother; Kidnap Victim)
The Abduction of Smith and Smith - Rashad Harrison *t* 174

Smith, Louisa "Lou" (Detective—Police; Consultant)
Behind Closed Doors - Elizabeth Haynes *m* 571

Smith, Sophia (Daughter; Sister; Survivor; Teenager; Military Personnel)
Strands of Sorrow - John Ringo *s* 1190

Smith, Stacey (Spouse; Mother; Survivor)
Strands of Sorrow - John Ringo *s* 1190

Smith, Steve (Survivor; Military Personnel; Father; Spouse)
Strands of Sorrow - John Ringo *s* 1190

Mr. Smithson (Scientist; Father; Tutor)
50 Ways to Ruin a Rake - Jade Lee *r* 1007

Smithson, Melinda "Mellie" (Fiance(e); Daughter; Inventor)
50 Ways to Ruin a Rake - Jade Lee *r* 1007

Smyslov, Vasily (Chess Player; Spy; Historical Figure)
Back Channel - Stephen L. Carter *c* 709

Smythe-Smith, Iris (Young Woman; Musician)
The Secrets of Sir Richard Kenworthy - Julia Quinn *r* 1053

Snowden, Julia (Restaurateur; Sister)
Musseled Out - Barbara Ross *m* 646

Sofi (Young Woman; 19-Year-Old; Cook)
The Last Kings of Sark - Rosa Rankin-Gee *c* 840

Soleyman, Raphael (Man; Spouse; Wealthy)
The Luminous Heart of Jonah S. - Gina B. Nahai *c* 814

Solloway, Leander (Teacher; Friend)
The Language of Paradise - Barbara Klein Moss *t* 217

Solomon, Lou (Lawyer; Widow(er); Friend; Graduate)
The Sirena Quest - Michael A. Kahn *m* 589

Somerhall, William (Nobleman; Son)
A Good Rogue Is Hard to Find - Kelly Bowen *r* 921

Sonny (Brother; Restaurateur)
Musseled Out - Barbara Ross *m* 646

Soo-Yee (Friend; Accident Victim)
Doll Face - Tim Curran *h* 288

Sophie (Fiance(e); Friend)
Ladle to the Grave - Connie Archer *m* 480

Sophie (Kidnap Victim; Niece)
Taken - Lisa Harris *i* 412

Sorenson, Lena (Artist)
The Sex Lives of Siamese Twins - Irvine Welsh *c* 885

Soto, Carlos "Steady" (Lover; Military Personnel; Twin)
Full Throttle - Julie Ann Walker *r* 1093

Soto, Lucia "Lucky" (Detective—Police; Colleague)
The Burning Room - Michael Connelly *c* 718

Soto, Rosa (Crime Victim; Teacher; Twin)
Full Throttle - Julie Ann Walker *r* 1093

Sparks, Cora (Scientist; Granddaughter; Orphan; Friend)
The Dress Shop of Dreams - Menna van Praag *c* 878

Sparks, Etta (Businesswoman; Grandmother)
The Dress Shop of Dreams - Menna van Praag *c* 878

Sparks, Flynn (Actor)
Hollywood Lost - Ace Collins *t* 143

Spear, Thorvald (Military Personnel; Employer; Crime Victim)
Dark Intelligence - Neal Asher *s* 1108

Spencer, Lord Christopher (Nobleman)
Lady Sarah's Sinful Desires - Sophie Barnes *r* 909

Spencer, Gabe (Agent; Detective—Private; Veteran)
Broken - Cynthia Eden *r* 959

Spinola, Isabella (Woman)
Betrayed by His Kiss - Amanda McCabe *r* 1025

Spire, Harold (Investigator; Leader)
The Eterna Files - Leanna Renee Hieber *f* 54

Spock (Military Personnel)
Savage Trade - Tony Daniel *s* 1134
Shadow of the Machine - Scott Harrison *s* 1153

Spock (Military Personnel; Alien)
Crisis of Consciousness - Dave Galanter *s* 1147

Spriggs, Florence (Prostitute)
The Final Recollections of Charles Dickens - Thomas Hauser *t* 175

Springer, Miss Julia (Widow(er); Friend; Detective—Amateur)
Etta Mae's Worst Bad-Luck Day - Ann B. Ross *c* 848

St. Claire, Ramie (Empath)
Keep Me Safe - Maya Banks *r* 908

St. Cyr, Sebastian (Nobleman; Detective; Spouse)
Who Buries the Dead - C.S. Harris *t* 172

St. George, Marisa (Hotel Worker)
In Firefly Valley - Amanda Cabot *i* 372

St. James, Rowland "Rowdy" (Artist; Friend)
Rowdy - Jay Crownover *r* 945

Stafford, Jason (Investigator)
Long Way Down - Michael Sears *m* 654

Stafford, Joanna (Religious; Artisan)
The Tapestry - Nancy Bilyeau *t* 130

Stamatopoulos, Anastasios "Tasso" (Spouse; Military Personnel)
Tasso's Journey - Paula Renee Burzawa *t* 137

Standish, Allison (Designer; Woman; Friend)
Where Secrets Sleep - Marta Perry *i* 444

Standley, Gerald (Farmer; Crime Suspect)
License to Dill - Mary Ellen Hughes *m* 578

Stanford, Iris (Widow(er); Mother; Writer)
Deadly Desires at Honeychurch Hall - Hannah Dennison *m* 532

Stanford, Kat (Daughter; Detective—Amateur; Television Personality; Antiques Dealer)
Deadly Desires at Honeychurch Hall - Hannah Dennison *m* 532

Stanhope, Virgil (Investigator)
Leaving Time - Jodi Picoult *c* 829

Stanley, Venetia (Spouse; Addict; Historical Figure; Noblewoman)
Viper Wine - Hermione Eyre *t* 154

Stanton, Edwin (Government Official; Criminal; Historical Figure)
King of the Cracksmen - Dennis O'Flaherty *s* 1180

Stanton, Elizabeth (Writer; Relative)
Fiercombe Manor - Kate Riordan *t* 235

Stanton, Tom (Heir; Friend)
Fiercombe Manor - Kate Riordan *t* 235

Stanway, Catherine (Nurse; Kidnap Victim)
Would-Be Wilderness Wife - Regina Scott *r* 1074

Star, Ice Cream (Girl; Narrator; Sister; 15-Year-Old)
The Country of Ice Cream Star - Sandra Newman *c* 816

Stark, David (Magician; Student; Boyfriend; Teenager)
Miss Mayhem - Rachel Hawkins *f* 48

Steele, Joe (Government Official)
Joe Steele - Harry Turtledove *s* 1203

Steele, Matt (Boyfriend; Detective—Police)
Death by Baking - Cynthia Hickey *i* 418

Steimetz, Charles Proteus (Handicapped; Scholar; Immigrant; Inventor; Friend)
Electric City - Elizabeth Rosner *t* 237

Stein, Gertrude (Historical Figure)
Of Irish Blood - Mary Pat Kelly *t* 188

Steinhauser, Celia (Friend; Spouse; Crime Victim; Teacher)
The Pocket Wife - Susan Crawford *m* 524

Steinhauser, Ronald (Spouse)
The Pocket Wife - Susan Crawford *m* 524

Stephanie (Diplomat; Spouse; Friend)
Prague Summer - Jeffrey Condran *c* 717

Stephen (Detective—Police; Spirit)
The Shadow Cabinet - Maureen Johnson *h* 322

Stephen (Historical Figure; Royalty; Cousin)
The Siege Winter - Ariana Franklin *t* 159

Stephen (Royalty; Brother)
How to Catch a Prince - Rachel Hauck *i* 414

Stephen (Spouse)
The Christmas Light - Donna VanLiere *c* 881

Talbot, David (Vampire; Investigator)
Prince Lestat - Anne Rice   c 845

Talbot, Liz (Detective—Private; Southern Belle)
Lowcountry Boneyard - Susan M. Boyer   m 500

Talbot, Ralph Cuthbert (Nobleman; Spouse)
Death of a Dishonorable Gentleman - Tessa Arlen   t 126

Talfi (Friend)
Iron Axe - Steven Harper   f 46

Taliesin (Companion; Lover; Gypsy)
I Loved a Rogue - Katharine Ashe   r 903

Tamara (Niece; 16-Year-Old; Companion; Dysfunctional Family Member)
Driving with the Top Down - Beth Harbison   c 761

Tamose (Ruler; Father)
Desert God - Wilbur Smith   t 252

Tango (Cat; Friend; Telepath)
Marked Fur Murder - Dixie Lyle   m 609

Tanner, Arden (Spouse; Military Personnel)
Sisters of Shiloh - Kathy Hepinstall   t 176

Tanner, Scott (Military Personnel)
Germanica - Robert Conroy   s 1131

Tanner, Shelby (Girlfriend; Scientist)
Pocket Apocalypse - Seanan McGuire   f 80

Tao (Alien)
The Rebirths of Tao - Wesley Chu   s 1126

Tarik, Michael "Mike" (Military Personnel)
Taking Fire - Lindsay McKenna   r 1030

Tarquin (Friend)
Shopaholic to the Stars - Sophie Kinsella   c 784

Tate, Cassidy (Store Owner)
Silken Threats - Addison Fox   r 966

Tate, Theodore (Detective—Police; Father; Spouse; Co-worker)
Five Minutes Alone - Paul Cleave   c 714

Taylor, Caroline (Young Woman; Lighthouse Keeper)
Hearts Made Whole - Jody Hedlund   i 416

Taylor, Madison (Lawyer; Fiance(e); Client)
The Readaholics and the Falcon Fiasco - Laura DiSilverio   m 535

Taylor, Mark (Handyman)
Love Letters - Debbie Macomber   c 793

Taylor, Sophie (Granddaughter; Worker; Detective—Amateur)
Shadow of a Spout - Amanda Cooper   m 521

Teasdale, James (Military Personnel; Patient)
The Alphabet House - Jussi Adler-Olsen   c 686

Tehuti (Royalty; Daughter; Sister)
Desert God - Wilbur Smith   t 252

Teichner, Virginia (Grandmother)
Every Fifteen Minutes - Lisa Scottoline   m 653

Telamon (Warrior)
The Eye of the Falcon - Michelle Paver   f 94

Tempest, Lavinia (Sister; Debutante)
The Viscount Who Lived Down the Lane - Elizabeth Boyle   r 924

Tempest, Louisa (Young Woman; Heroine; Sister)
The Viscount Who Lived Down the Lane - Elizabeth Boyle   r 924

Temple, Nykki (Classmate)
Death of a Cupcake Queen - Lee Hollis   m 577

Templeton, Clare (Psychic; Advisor)
The Eterna Files - Leanna Renee Hieber   f 54

Teo (Brother)
The Chosen Prince - Diane Stanley   f 110

Tesla, Nikola (Historical Figure; Scientist)
The Lusitania Conspiracy - Ronald J. Walters   t 269

Tess (Woman; Paranormal Investigator)
Echo 8 - Sharon Lynn Fisher   f 33

Thacker, Jillian (Veterinarian)
Kissed by a Cowboy - Pamela Britton   r 926

Thallian (Criminal)
The Dangerous Type - Loren Rhoads   s 1189

Thanou, Jason (Agent; Time Traveler)
Soldiers Out of Time - Steve White   s 1207

Thatcher, Beth (Teacher)
Where Trust Lies - Janette Oke   i 440

Thayne, Mark (Military Personnel; Agent)
Too Dangerous for a Lady - Jo Beverley   r 915

The Hunter (Villain)
The Devil's Only Friend - Dan Wells   h 352

The Pet (Woman; Psychic; Fugitive)
Hunted Warrior - Lindsey Piper   f 95

Theo (Friend; Kidnap Victim; Immigrant)
Glow - Ned Beauman   c 699

Theokritos (Religious)
Death Ex Machina - Gary Corby   t 145

Theta, Phaet (15-Year-Old; Military Personnel; Friend)
Dove Arising - Karen Bao   s 1114

Thomas (Man)
Your Fathers, Where Are They? And the Prophets, Do They Live Forever? - Dave Eggers   c 738

Thomas (Teenager; Friend)
The Way We Bared Our Souls - Willa Strayhorn   f 112

Thomas, Odd (Eccentric; Young Man; Cook; Child of Divorced Parents; Psychic; Boyfriend)
Saint Odd - Dean Koontz   c 785

Thompson, Abby (Lover; Daughter; Student)
Full Throttle - Julie Ann Walker   r 1093

Thompson, Camille (Real Estate Agent)
Love Me If You Dare - Toni Blake   r 917

Thomsen, Golo (Lover; Office Worker; Narrator)
The Zone of Interest - Martin Amis   c 690

Thormodsson, Ulfar (Viking; Immortal; Friend)
Blood Will Follow - Snorri Kristjansson   t 194

Thorn (Detective—Private; Friend; Father)
The Big Finish - James W. Hall   c 758

Thornbury, Ross (Writer; Neighbor)
The Rake's Handbook: Including Field Guide - Sally Orr   r 1045

Thorne, Cooper (Rancher)
Texas Mail Order Bride - Linda Broday   r 927

Thorne, Tom (Detective—Police; Boyfriend)
Time of Death - Mark Billingham   m 491

Thornton, Jarrick (Police Officer)
Where Trust Lies - Janette Oke   i 440

Thrax, Maximinus (Ruler; Military Personnel)
Iron and Rust - Harry Sidebottom   t 248

Thwing, David (Restaurateur)
Musseled Out - Barbara Ross   m 646

Tia (Teenager; Girl)
Firefight - Brandon Sanderson   f 104

Tiffany (Young Woman; Spouse; Environmentalist)
The Wallcreeper - Nell Zink   c 894

Tiffany, Louis (Businessman; Heir)
Tiffany Girl - Deeanne Gist   i 403

Tinkie (Friend; Southern Belle; Assistant; Wealthy)
Bone to Be Wild - Carolyn Haines   m 564

Miss Tiramaku (Housekeeper)
The Boy Who Drew Monsters - Keith Donohue   c 732

Tiranno, Michael (Businessman; Wealthy; Boyfriend)
Black Scorpion - Jon Land   m 596

Titi (Heiress—Dispossessed; Worker; Spouse)
The Last Good Paradise - Tatjana Soli   c 865

Tizon, Rogelio (Police Officer)
The Siege - Arturo Perez-Reverte   t 228

Todd (Teenager; Boyfriend)
Miles from Nowhere - Amy Clipston   i 379

Todd, Teddy (Man; Military Personnel; Brother)
A God in Ruins - Kate Atkinson   t 127

Todd, Ursula (Woman; Sister)
A God in Ruins - Kate Atkinson   t 127

Toklo (Bear)
Seekers: Return to the Wild: The Burning Horizon - Erin Hunter   f 59

Tom (Archaeologist; Traveler)
Voyage of the Basilisk: A Memoir by Lady Trent - Marie Brennan   f 16

Tom (Bird)
Holy Cow - David Duchovny   c 735

Tomas (Boy; Son)
World Gone By - Dennis Lehane   t 201

Tomilson, Sighurdhr (Hippie; Sidekick)
Cuba Straits - Randy Wayne White   m 681

Tomkins, Tyla (Lawyer; Lover; Crime Victim)
Cane and Abe - James Grippando   c 756

Tomoatooah (Colleague; Lawman)
Karen Memory - Elizabeth Bear   s 1118

Toms, Jessica (15-Year-Old; Missing Person; Crime Victim)
Time of Death - Mark Billingham   m 491

Tony (Writer)
Funny Girl - Nick Hornby   c 770

Toomey, Alice (Mentally Challenged Person; Sister)
The Second Sister - Marie Bostwick   r 918

Toomey, Lucy (Political Figure; Sister)
The Second Sister - Marie Bostwick   r 918

Torbidda (Apprentice; Boy)
The Warring States - Aidan Harte   f 47

Torin (Warrior; Immortal; Demon)
The Darkest Touch - Gena Showalter   r 1082

Tornja, Ran il (Man; Lover; Assistant; Traitor; Murderer)
The Providence of Fire - Brian Staveley   f 111

Torres, Ricky (Crime Victim; Detective—Private; Friend)
Dead Red - Tim O'Mara   m 626

Tower, Enid (Pregnant Teenager; Cult Member; Runaway; Accident Victim)
Cold Betrayal - J.A. Jance   m 584

Tozer, Helen (Detective—Police; Colleague)
The Kings of London - William Shaw   m 657

Travis, Jess (Fiance(e); Survivor)
Gift of Grace - Sharlene MacLaren   i 433

Treadway, Greg (Teacher; Volunteer; Crime Suspect)
The Fall - John T. Lescroart   m 600

Tregear, Stephen (Military Personnel; Computer Expert; Son)
Blood Ties - Nicholas Guild   m 562

Trelawny Penvenan, Lady Morwenna (Widow(er); Crime Suspect)
A Stranger's Secret - Laurie Alice Eakes   i 394

Tremaine, Lady Elinor "Norrie" (Young Woman; Daughter; Noblewoman)
Lady Elinor's Wicked Adventures - Lillian Marek   r 1020

Van Meeterens, Ariana (Teenager; Girl; Crime Victim)
Rising Tide - Patricia Twomey Ryan   *m* 649

Vandaele, Lodewijk (Man; Wealthy; Criminal)
From Bruges with Love - Pieter Aspe   *m* 482

Vanderhall, Brian (Friend; Crime Victim)
Superposition - David Walton   *s* 1205

Vanderling, Willow (Detective—Amateur; Store Owner; Employer)
Seven Threadly Sins - Janet Bolin   *m* 497

Vantage, Kyri (Supernatural Being; Companion)
Phoenix in Shadow - Ryk E. Spoor   *f* 108

Varatschevsky, Karin (Spy; Vigilante; Assassin)
Ascendance: Dave vs. the Monsters - John Birmingham   *f* 13

Vaughn, Derek (Military Personnel; Lover)
Beyond Limits - Laura Griffin   *r* 980

Vaughn, Vicky (Assassin)
Firestorm - Nancy Holzner   *h* 318

Vect, Asdrubael (Leader)
Path of the Dark Eldar - Andy Chambers   *f* 24

Vegas, Milagros Carmona (Friend; Granddaughter; Gypsy; Young Woman; Outcast)
The Barefoot Queen - Ildefonso Falcones   *t* 156

Velasquez, Angel (Assassin; Spy)
The Water Knife - Paolo Bacigalupi   *s* 1113

Velda (Lover; Police Officer; Missing Person)
Kill Me, Darling - Mickey Spillane   *m* 663

ver Snagason, Snorri (Viking)
The Liar's Key - Mark Lawrence   *f* 71

Vermast, Hugo (Spouse; Father)
From Bruges with Love - Pieter Aspe   *m* 482

Vermast, Leen (Spouse; Mother)
From Bruges with Love - Pieter Aspe   *m* 482

Vermast, Tine (Girl; Daughter)
From Bruges with Love - Pieter Aspe   *m* 482

Vernon, Jane (Fiance(e); Cousin)
If the Viscount Falls - Sabrina Jeffries   *r* 995

Verovkin (Man; Crime Suspect)
A Love Like Blood - Marcus Sedgwick   *t* 246

Vervoort, Benedict (Real Estate Agent)
From Bruges with Love - Pieter Aspe   *m* 482

Vi (Psychic; Aunt)
A Fright to the Death - Dawn Eastman   *h* 295

Vicky (Aunt; Cancer Patient; Friend)
Betrayed - Lisa Scottoline   *c* 857

Victoria (Royalty)
Inspector of the Dead - David Morrell   *t* 214

Victoria (Royalty; Historical Figure)
The Eterna Files - Leanna Renee Hieber   *f* 54

Vin (Agent; Worker)
Last Days of the Condor - James Grady   *m* 559

Vine, Samantha (Spouse; Lawyer; Sister)
Cane and Abe - James Grippando   *c* 756

Visser, Luuk (Religious; Spy)
The Mechanical - Ian Tregillis   *f* 117

Vlad (Vampire; Spouse)
Bound by Flames - Jeaniene Frost   *r* 969

Vogel, Johann (Hairdresser)
The Figaro Murders - Laura Lebow   *t* 199

Voith, Ferd (Worker; Spouse; Father)
Up the Hill to Home - Jennifer Bort Yacovissi   *t* 275

Voith, Lillie Beck (Daughter; Spouse; Mother)
Up the Hill to Home - Jennifer Bort Yacovissi   *t* 275

Voletto, Dia (Principal)
The Wicked Awakening of Anne Merchant - Joanna Wiebe   *h* 353

Volkman, Max (Spy)
The German Agent - J. Sydney Jones   *t* 186

Volos, John (Political Figure; Boyfriend)
Deadly Spells - Jaye Wells   *f* 121

von Erhlich, Frederic (Nobleman; Fiance(e))
Cafe Europa - Edward Ifkovic   *t* 182

von Hoffman, Danielle Bretancourt (Spouse; Mother; Artisan)
Scent of Triumph - Jan Moran   *t* 212

von Hoffman, Max (Spouse; Father)
Scent of Triumph - Jan Moran   *t* 212

Von Riesen, Elfrieda "Elf" (Woman; Musician; Wealthy; Sister)
All My Puny Sorrows - Miriam Toews   *c* 871

Von Riesen, Yolandi "Yoli" (Woman; Divorced Person; Mother; Sister)
All My Puny Sorrows - Miriam Toews   *c* 871

Vost (Mercenary)
Breakout - Ann Aguirre   *s* 1103

W

Wade, Kate (Military Personnel; Android; Director)
Tin Men - Christopher Golden   *m* 556

Wainwright, Brooklyn (Expert; Detective—Amateur; Girlfriend)
Ripped from the Pages - Kate Carlisle   *m* 512

Wainwright, Rachel (Lawyer; Colleague)
Cover Your Eyes - Mary Burton   *r* 938

Walden, Cara (Actress; 17-Year-Old; Sister)
All the Wrong Places - Lisa Lieberman   *t* 205

Walden, Gray (Brother; Writer; Homosexual)
All the Wrong Places - Lisa Lieberman   *t* 205

Walker, Cassandra (Military Personnel; Co-worker)
Falcon - Ronie Kendig   *i* 423

Walker, Creed (Indian; Warrior; Spy; Rescuer)
My Heart Stood Still - Lori Copeland   *i* 387

Walker, Eli (Doctor)
Binary - Stephanie Saulter   *s* 1193

Walker, Kate (Writer; Young Woman)
From the Start - Melissa Tagg   *i* 462

Walker, Katherine (Spouse; Woman)
Still Life - Christa Parrish   *i* 442

Walker, Lyric (16-Year-Old; Student—High School)
Undertow - Michael Buckley   *s* 1121

Walker, Mike (Boyfriend; Addict)
Crazy Horse's Girlfriend - Erika T. Wurth   *c* 891

Walker, Shay (Tutor)
Make Me Lose Control - Christie Ridgway   *r* 1057

Walks with Coyotes, Jay (Indian; Shaman)
The Way We Bared Our Souls - Willa Strayhorn   *f* 112

Wallace, David (Detective—Police)
The Language of the Dead - Stephen Kelly   *t* 189

Walldeen, Klara (Government Official; Daughter)
The Swimmer - Joakim Zander   *c* 893

Mrs. Wallin (Mother; Patient)
Would-Be Wilderness Wife - Regina Scott   *r* 1074

Wallin, Beth (Sister; Daughter)
Would-Be Wilderness Wife - Regina Scott   *r* 1074

Wallin, Drew (Brother; Son)
Would-Be Wilderness Wife - Regina Scott   *r* 1074

Wallin, Levi (Brother; Son; Kidnapper)
Would-Be Wilderness Wife - Regina Scott   *r* 1074

Wallin, Simon (Brother; Son)
Would-Be Wilderness Wife - Regina Scott   *r* 1074

Walsh, Ginger (Lover; Dancer; Actress)
Back to Before - Tracy Solheim   *r* 1084

Walsingham, Francis (Historical Figure; Spy)
Murder in the Queen's Wardrobe - Kathy Lynn Emerson   *t* 153

Walt (Businessman; Friend)
The Dress Shop of Dreams - Menna van Praag   *c* 878

Waltham, Alexander (Spouse; Father)
The First Kiss - Grace Burrowes   *r* 932

Waltham, Twyla (8-Year-Old; Daughter)
The First Kiss - Grace Burrowes   *r* 932

Waltham, Vera (Musician; Divorced Person; Spouse; Mother; Widow(er))
The First Kiss - Grace Burrowes   *r* 932

Ward, Sam (Lover)
His Small-Town Sweetheart - Amanda Berry   *r* 914

Warren, Cade (Rescuer; Brother; Co-worker; Hostage)
Untraceable - Elizabeth Goddard   *i* 404

Warren, Heidi (Sister; Co-worker; Hostage; Rescuer)
Untraceable - Elizabeth Goddard   *i* 404

Wash (Boy; Friend; Accident Victim)
The Wonder of All Things - Jason Mott   *c* 812

Washburn, Emma (Spouse; Mother)
Prudence - David Treuer   *c* 872

Washburn, Frankie (Friend; Young Man; Military Personnel; Son)
Prudence - David Treuer   *c* 872

Washburn, Jonathan (Spouse; Father)
Prudence - David Treuer   *c* 872

Watkins, Trey (Crime Victim; Friend)
One Mile Under - Andrew Gross   *m* 561

Watson, Arnie (Veteran; Crime Victim; Friend; Musician; Classmate)
The Dead Play On - Heather Graham   *m* 560

Watson, Brooke (Friend)
The Devil's Only Friend - Dan Wells   *h* 352

Watson, John (Doctor; Colleague)
Moriarty - Anthony Horowitz   *c* 771

Watson, Dr. John (Doctor; Colleague)
Sherlock Holmes, the Missing Years: Japan - Vasudev Murthy   *t* 219

Watson, Kera (Veteran; Crime Victim; Friend; Supernatural Being)
The Unleashing - Shelly Laurenston   *f* 68

Watts, Brittany (Friend; Student—High School; Teenager; Vampire)
Blood Matters - Aviva Bel'Harold   *h* 284

Waverley, Claire (Mother; Aunt; Businesswoman; Sister)
First Frost - Sarah Addison Allen   *c* 689

Waverley, Sydney (Sister; Mother; Aunt)
First Frost - Sarah Addison Allen   *c* 689

Wayfarer (Friend)
First and Last Sorcerer - Barb Hendee   *f* 52

Wayne (Uncle)
Before He Finds Her - Michael Kardos   *m* 591

Weary, Nat (Friend; Bodyguard; Driver)
Driving the King - Ravi Howard   *t* 180

Character Description Index

This index alphabetically lists descriptions of the major characters in featured titles. The descriptions may be occupations (police officer, lawyer, etc.) or may describe persona (amnesiac, runaway, teenager, etc.). For each description, character names are listed alphabetically. Also provided are book titles, author names, genre codes and entry numbers. The genre codes are as follows: *c* Popular Fiction, *f* Fantasy, *h* Horror, *i* Inspirational, *m* Mystery, *r* Romance, *s* Science Fiction, and *t* Historical

10-YEAR-OLD

Farabee, Maddie
Bridges Burned - Annette Dashofy   *m* 527

Gledstanes, Benjamin "Benjy"
Devil's Moon - Amanda Scott   *r* 1070

Keenan, Jack Peter
The Boy Who Drew Monsters - Keith Donohue   *c* 732

Miller, Cicely
Deadly Echoes - Nancy Mehl   *i* 435

Parker, Logan
When We Fall - Emily Liebert   *c* 791

11-YEAR-OLD

Emma
The Siege Winter - Ariana Franklin   *t* 159

Hansen, LeeAnn
The Cowboy SEAL - Laura Marie Altom   *r* 897

Luke
Your Next Breath - Iris Johansen   *m* 586

Lydia
The Dynamite Room - Jason Hewitt   *t* 178

Osborne, Diz
Last to Know - Elizabeth Adler   *c* 685

Porter, Maddie
Manhattan in Miniature - Margaret Grace   *m* 558

Sylvie
Cold Spell - Deb Vanasse   *c* 879

11th GRADER

Fynn, Maddie
When - Victoria Laurie   *f* 70

Schroder, Arnold "Stubby"
When - Victoria Laurie   *f* 70

12-YEAR-OLD

Bell, Liberty "Ibby"
Dollbaby - Laura McNeal   *c* 801

Carter, Aimee
Last One Home - Debbie Macomber   *c* 794

Dare, Alice
Mars Evacuees - Sophia McDougall   *s* 1176

Jahan
The Architect's Apprentice - Elif Shafak   *t* 247

Kerry
Manhunt - Lisa Phillips   *i* 447

Ruff, McKinley
Deadline - John Sandford   *c* 852

Zane
Amish Promises - Leslie Gould   *i* 405

12th GRADER

Johnson, Michael "MJ"
Nowhere to Hide - Sigmund Brouwer   *i* 365

King, William
Nowhere to Hide - Sigmund Brouwer   *i* 365

Wyatt, Blake
Nowhere to Hide - Sigmund Brouwer   *i* 365

13-YEAR-OLD

Aubrey, Jax
The Inquisitor's Mark - Dianne Salerni   *f* 102

Bree
Stirring Up Trouble - Kimberly Kincaid   *r* 1000

Campbell, Ava
The Wonder of All Things - Jason Mott   *c* 812

Metcalf, Jenna
Leaving Time - Jodi Picoult   *c* 829

O'Toole, Pat
Beneath - Roland Smith   *s* 1199

Peake, Charmaine
Lay It on My Heart - Angela Pneuman   *c* 834

14-YEAR-OLD

Brixton
The Accidental Alchemist - Gigi Pandian   *m* 630

Canfield, Piper
The Murk - Robert Lettrick   *h* 331

Fenella
The Duke of Dark Desires - Miranda Neville   *r* 1042

Frederika
Wolf Winter - Cecilia Ekback   *t* 152

Frye, Sybilla
The Sacrifice - Joyce Carol Oates   *c* 821

Illica, Emma
Accidents of Marriage - Randy Susan Meyers   *c* 804

Kimei, Sakura
Castaway Planet - Eric Flint   *s* 1146

Morrigan, Johanna
How to Build a Girl - Caitlin Moran   *c* 810

Needle, Gwen
We Are Pirates - Daniel Handler   *c* 759

Nick
Edison's Alley - Neal Shusterman   *s* 1196

Riddell, Trevor
A Sudden Light - Garth Stein   *c* 868

Rimaldi, Josephine
An Italian Wife - Ann Hood   *c* 768

Unnamed Character
My Sunshine Away - M.O. Walsh   *c* 884

15-YEAR-OLD

Bay
First Frost - Sarah Addison Allen   *c* 689

Chey
The Second Guard - J.D. Vaughn   *f* 119

Daniela
Signal to Noise - Silvia Moreno-Garcia   *f* 85

Elisabeth "Sisi"
The Accidental Empress - Allison Pataki   *t* 226

Goldstein, Eli
The Last Flight of Poxl West - Daniel Torday   *t* 264

Harlan
A Slant of Light - Jeffrey Lent   *t* 202

Ivy
As Night Falls - Jenny Milchman   *m* 619

Johnston, Poppy
Time of Death - Mark Billingham   *m* 491

Kalloryn, Talimendra "Tali" Sanchez
The Second Guard - J.D. Vaughn   *f* 119

Maria
The Duke of Dark Desires - Miranda Neville   *r* 1042

Meche
Signal to Noise - Silvia Moreno-Garcia   *f* 85

Riggs, Troy
One in a Million - Jill Shalvis   *r* 1077

Ruby
Hush Hush - Laura Lippman   *m* 604

Sebastian
Signal to Noise - Silvia Moreno-Garcia   *f* 85

Simpson, Lindy
My Sunshine Away - M.O. Walsh   *c* 884

Star, Ice Cream
The Country of Ice Cream Star - Sandra Newman   *c* 816

Sykes, Holly
The Bone Clocks - David Mitchell   *c* 807

Theta, Phaet
Dove Arising - Karen Bao   *s* 1114

Toms, Jessica
Time of Death - Mark Billingham   *m* 491

Unnamed Character
Em and the Big Hoom - Jerry Pinto   *c* 831

Zarif
The Second Guard - J.D. Vaughn   *f* 119

16-YEAR-OLD

Baker, Nica
Dark Rooms - Lili Anolik   *c* 691

Defoe, Pip
The Last Kings of Sark - Rosa Rankin-Gee   *c* 840

Everhart, Dusty
The Nightmare Charade - Mindee Arnett   *h* 279

Freeman, Carl
Devil's Pocket - John Dixon   *s* 1138

Fynn, Maddie
When - Victoria Laurie   *f* 70

Harrison, Harrison "H2"
Harrison Squared - Daryl Gregory   *h* 306

Jones, Lexy
Chasing Sunsets - Karen Kingsbury   *i* 425

Margaritte
Crazy Horse's Girlfriend - Erika T. Wurth   *c* 891

Mendelson, Sandy
Where They Found Her - Kimberly McCreight   *m* 614

Osborne, Frazer
Last to Know - Elizabeth Adler   *c* 685

Osborne, Madison
Last to Know - Elizabeth Adler   *c* 685

Schroder, Arnold "Stubby"
When - Victoria Laurie   *f* 70

Smith, Faith
Strands of Sorrow - John Ringo   *s* 1190

Tamara
Driving with the Top Down - Beth Harbison   *c* 761

Unnamed Character
Method 15/33 - Shannon Kirk   *m* 594

Walker, Lyric
Undertow - Michael Buckley   *s* 1121

17-YEAR-OLD

Adam
The Children Act - Ian McEwan   *c* 800

Alanna
Hush Hush - Laura Lippman   *m* 604

Barrow, Mare
Red Queen - Victoria Aveyard   *f* 9

Bishop, Mackenzie "Mac"
The Unbound - Victoria Schwab   *h* 342

Cleaver, John Wayne
The Devil's Only Friend - Dan Wells   *h* 352

Connelly, Jake
Finding Jake - Bryan Reardon   *m* 639

Cooper, Shelby Jane
There Will Be Lies - Nick Lake   *f* 66

Dean, Betty Jo
Silence the Dead - Jack Fredrickson   *m* 549

Fisher, Gracie
The Art of Losing Yourself - Katie Ganshert   *i* 401

Gemma-Kate
Fear the Darkness - Becky Masterman   *m* 610

Ginny
The Never-Open Desert Diner - James Anderson   *m* 478

Jakubowski, Max
Every Fifteen Minutes - Lisa Scottoline   *m* 653

James
Goodhouse - Peyton Marshall   *c* 798

Kilgore, Max
Hellhole - Gina Damico   *h* 290

Marin
Be Not Afraid - Cecilia Galante   *h* 300

Meurent, Victorine
Paris Red - Maureen Gibbon   *t* 164

Montaine, Cecile
Doctor Death - Lene Kaaberbol   *t* 187

Morgan, Tanya
The Fall - John T. Lescroart   *m* 600

Nathan
Half Wild - Sally Green   *f* 40

Nels
Woven - Michael Jensen   *f* 61

Petersen, Albie
Us - David Nicholls   *c* 817

Putzkammer, Leonie
The Sweetheart - Angelina Mirabella   *t* 211

Stonechurch, Ann
This Gun for Hire - Jo Goodman   *r* 973

Walden, Cara
All the Wrong Places - Lisa Lieberman   *t* 205

18-YEAR-OLD

Alden, Hunter "Tripp" Hutchinson III
NYPD Red 3 - James Patterson   *m* 632

April
Endangered - C.J. Box   *m* 499

de Lacy, Lord Oswald
Plague Land - S.D. Sykes   *t* 257

Driver
The Country of Ice Cream Star - Sandra Newman   *c* 816

Lamb, Vera
The Language of the Dead - Stephen Kelly   *t* 189

Marcus, Josephine "Josie" Sarah
Epitaph - Mary Doria Russell   *t* 240

McNeely, Jacob
Where All Light Tends to Go - David Joy   *m* 588

O'Toole, Coop
Beneath - Roland Smith   *s* 1199

Osborne, Roman
Last to Know - Elizabeth Adler   *c* 685

Pendare, Riley
The Inquisitor's Mark - Dianne Salerni   *f* 102

19-YEAR-OLD

Finn
Positive - David Wellington   *h* 351

Holland, Sarie
Canary - Duane Swierczynski   *m* 671

Jensen, Margo
Back Channel - Stephen L. Carter   *c* 709

Sofi
The Last Kings of Sark - Rosa Rankin-Gee   *c* 840

2-YEAR-OLD

Daisy
Teardrop Lane - Emily March   *r* 1018

Minnie
Shopaholic to the Stars - Sophie Kinsella   *c* 784

Stutzman, Mark
The Decision - Wanda E. Brunstetter   *i* 367

20-YEAR-OLD

Akeldama, Prudence "Rue" Alessandra Maccon
Prudence - Gail Carriger   *f* 22

Cabot, Grace
The Devil Takes a Bride - Julia London   *r* 1012

Fulcher, Lenore
Steadfast Heart - Tracie Peterson   *i* 445

London, Anna
Sweet Damage - Rebecca James   *c* 773

Selvedge, Jack
Pale Harvest - Braden Hepner   *c* 764

Turner, Ruthie
Jaded - Varina Denman   *i* 392

21-YEAR-OLD

Angie
Into the Go-Slow - Bridgett M. Davis   *c* 728

Clee
The First Bad Man - Miranda July   *c* 778

Havnel, Bea
Last to Know - Elizabeth Adler   *c* 685

Keegan, Daisy
Butternut Summer - Mary McNear   *c* 802

3-YEAR-OLD

Carla Scout
Hush Hush - Laura Lippman   *m* 604

4-YEAR-OLD

Ben
Christmas at Twilight - Lori Wilde   *r* 1097

Howard, Gillian
The Bride Ship - Regina Scott   *r* 1073

Kimmie
Christmas at Twilight - Lori Wilde   *r* 1097

Manami
Confessions - Kanae Minato   *c* 806

Rose
The Duke's Guide to Correct Behavior - Megan Frampton   *r* 967

House of Wonder - Sarah Healy   *c* 763

5-YEAR-OLD

Andreou, Peter
The Fifth Gospel - Ian Caldwell   *m* 509

Anna
Cold Spell - Deb Vanasse   *c* 879

Galen
Teardrop Lane - Emily March   *r* 1018

Hayden
The Final Reveille - Amanda Flower   *m* 547

Henry
You're So Fine - Kieran Kramer   *r* 1002

Katie
The Melody Lingers On - Mary Higgins Clark   *m* 515

Rainbow
Last Chance Family - Hope Ramsay   *r* 1055

Tremaine, Penny
Together with You - Victoria Bylin   *i* 370

West, Max
Witch upon a Star - Jennifer Harlow   *m* 568

6-YEAR-OLD

Banning, Chloe
Silver Thaw - Catherine Anderson   *r* 898

Dorotea
Wolf Winter - Cecilia Ekback   *t* 152

Slone, Bailey
Hold the Dark - William Giraldi   *c* 749

7-YEAR-OLD

Bird, Millie
Lost and Found - Brooke Davis   *c* 729

Hansen, JJ
The Cowboy SEAL - Laura Marie Altom   *r* 897

Indio
Darling Beast - Elizabeth Hoyt   *r* 989

Keenan
Teardrop Lane - Emily March   *r* 1018

Kimei, Hitomi
Castaway Planet - Eric Flint   *s* 1146

Salim
Ishmael's Oranges - Claire Hajaj   *c* 757

West, Joe
Witch upon a Star - Jennifer Harlow   *m* 568

8-YEAR-OLD

Cajeiri
Tracker - C.J. Cherryh   *s* 1125

Kate
Forsaken - Kelley Armstrong   *h* 278

Waltham, Twyla
The First Kiss - Grace Burrowes   *r* 932

9-YEAR-OLD

Blake, Sammie
The Cat, the Devil, the Last Escape - Pat J.J. Murphy   *m* 623

Crane, Gia
When We Fall - Emily Liebert   *c* 791

Laura
The Duke of Dark Desires - Miranda Neville   *r* 1042

Misty
Teardrop Lane - Emily March   *r* 1018

ABANDONED CHILD

Bird, Millie
Lost and Found - Brooke Davis   *c* 729

Gallagher, Piper
In Case of Emergency - Courtney Moreno   *c* 811

Lisemette
The Forgotten Girls - Sara Blaedel   *m* 493

ABOLITIONIST

Kent, Sophie
Spy of Richmond - Jocelyn Green   *i* 409

ABUSE VICTIM

Allen, Priscilla
An Amish Man of Ice Mountain - Kelly Long   *i* 429

Banning, Amanda
Silver Thaw - Catherine Anderson   *r* 898

Bradley, Marcus
He's No Prince Charming - Elle Daniels   *r* 949

Hamilton, Olivia "Livie"
Wild Horses - B.J. Daniels   *r* 947

Illica, Maddy
Accidents of Marriage - Randy Susan Meyers   *c* 804

Jones, Lexy
Chasing Sunsets - Karen Kingsbury   *i* 425

Jones, Mila
Moonlight on Butternut Lake - Mary McNear   *r* 1034

Zook, Rosanna
An Empty Cup - Sarah Price   *i* 449

ACCIDENT VICTIM

Beiler, Sarah
The Witnesses - Linda Byler   *i* 369

Chazz
Doll Face - Tim Curran   *h* 288

Cooper, Shelby Jane
There Will Be Lies - Nick Lake   *f* 66

Covington, Cole
Return to Me - Kelly Moran   *r* 1038

Craven, Jonathan
A Good Rake Is Hard to Find - Manda Collins   *r* 944

Creep
Doll Face - Tim Curran   *h* 288

Danielle
Doll Face - Tim Curran   *h* 288

Enderly, Blake
Dreams of Shreds and Tatters - Amanda Downum   *h* 293

Ford, Reid
Moonlight on Butternut Lake - Mary McNear   *r* 1034

Frank, Nicole "Nicky"
Crash and Burn - Lisa Gardner   *m* 554

Goetz, Julian
Still Life - Christa Parrish   *i* 442

Hathaway, Heidi
Heaven Help Heidi - Sally John   *i* 422

Illica, Maddy
Accidents of Marriage - Randy Susan Meyers   *c* 804

Kaufman, Daniel
The Fragile World - Paula Treick DeBoard   *c* 730

Lex
Doll Face - Tim Curran   *h* 288

Manchester, Serena
Hostile Eyewitness - Tyora Moody   *i* 437

Murphy Sullivan, Molly
The Edge of Dreams - Rhys Bowen   *t* 131

Phillips, Sean
Wolf in White Van - John Darnielle   *c* 726

Ramona
Doll Face - Tim Curran   *h* 288

Reilly, Will
Night Blindness - Susan Strecker   *c* 870

Roosevelt, Franklin D.
Joe Steele - Harry Turtledove   *s* 1203

Soo-Yee
Doll Face - Tim Curran   *h* 288

Sullivan, Liam
The Edge of Dreams - Rhys Bowen   *t* 131

Tower, Enid
Cold Betrayal - J.A. Jance   *m* 584

Wash
The Wonder of All Things - Jason Mott   *c* 812

Zook, Linda
A Simple Prayer - Amy Clipston   *i* 380

Zook, Timothy
An Empty Cup - Sarah Price   *i* 449

ACCOUNTANT

Abbott, Hunter
And I Love Her - Marie Force   *r* 963

Abbott, Nora
Tattered Legacy - Shannon Baker   *m* 484

Cermak, Clare
Ghost Killer - Robin D. Owens   *f* 91

Chandler, Wilhelmina "Willie"
Superfluous Women - Carola Dunn   *m* 538

Crocker, Ben
Fate Moreland's Widow - John Lane   *t* 197

ACTIVIST

Moss, Flynn
The Big Finish - James W. Hall   *c* 758

Porter, Jay
Pleasantville - Attica Locke   *m* 605

X-88
The Big Finish - James W. Hall   *c* 758

ACTOR

Andrews, Dalton
Hollywood Lost - Ace Collins *t* 143

Bogart, Humphrey
West of Sunset - Stewart O'Nan *c* 819

Clive
Funny Girl - Nick Hornby *c* 770

Dylan
Miles from Nowhere - Amy Clipston *i* 379

Gable, Clark
Hollywood Lost - Ace Collins *t* 143
A Touch of Stardust - Kate Alcott *t* 125

Grant, Cary
Hollywood Lost - Ace Collins *t* 143

Hartley, Eddie
Arts and Entertainments - Christopher R.
  Beha *c* 700

Leander, Arthur
Station Eleven - Emily St. John Mandel *c* 796

Murphy, Cameron
Scent of Triumph - Jan Moran *t* 212

Sparks, Flynn
Hollywood Lost - Ace Collins *t* 143

Wilder, Beau
You're So Fine - Kieran Kramer *r* 1002

ACTRESS

Bathurst, Chloe
Galapagos Regained - James Morrow *t* 216

Beausoleil, Jonquil "Boso"
Phantom Angel - David Handler *m* 567

Bolton, Tarla
Season of Fear - Brian Freeman *m* 550

Clark, Lacey
You're So Fine - Kieran Kramer *r* 1002

Cobb, Isabel
The Empire of Night - Robert Olen Butler *t* 138

D'Ambrosia, Alouette
Beautiful You - Chuck Palahniuk *c* 823

Dresner, Dalia
The Lady from Zagreb - Philip Kerr *t* 191

Hewitt, Annie
Heroes Are My Weakness - Susan Elizabeth
  Phillips *c* 828

Hughes, Ellie
Jilted - Rachael Johns *r* 996

Hume, Fiona
A Thing of Beauty - Lisa Samson *i* 453

Isobel
Three Story House - Courtney Miller
  Santo *c* 853

Kellerton, Lois
Shopaholic to the Stars - Sophie Kinsella *c* 784

Kelsey, Andorra
The Thunder of Giants - Joel Fishbane *t* 157

Lombard, Carole
A Touch of Stardust - Kate Alcott *t* 125

Martin, Martha
Arts and Entertainments - Christopher R.
  Beha *c* 700

Parker, Barbara
Funny Girl - Nick Hornby *c* 770

Raymonde, Kirsten
Station Eleven - Emily St. John Mandel *c* 796

Reyes, Nora
The Lovers' Tango - Mark Rubinstein *m* 647

Seymour, Sage
Shopaholic to the Stars - Sophie Kinsella *c* 784

Stump, Lily
Darling Beast - Elizabeth Hoyt *r* 989

Walden, Cara
All the Wrong Places - Lisa Lieberman *t* 205

Walsh, Ginger
Back to Before - Tracy Solheim *r* 1084

ADDICT

Brandon
Zombified - Adam Gallardo *h* 302

Cooper, Dante
Serpents in the Cold - Thomas O'Malley *t* 222

Darlene
Delicious Foods - James Hannaham *c* 760

de Quincey, Thomas
Inspector of the Dead - David Morrell *t* 214

Ellen
The Way We Bared Our Souls - Willa
  Strayhorn *f* 112

Hume, Fiona
A Thing of Beauty - Lisa Samson *i* 453

Lindquist, Gus
The Marauders - Tom Cooper *m* 522

Mallen, Mark
Innocent Damage - Robert K. Lewis *m* 603

McNeely, Laura
Where All Light Tends to Go - David Joy *m* 588

Morton, Jamie
Revival - Stephen King *c* 783

Stanley, Venetia
Viper Wine - Hermione Eyre *t* 154

Unnamed Character
By Your Side - Candace Calvert *i* 373

Walker, Mike
Crazy Horse's Girlfriend - Erika T. Wurth *c* 891

ADMINISTRATOR

Lord Aethelred
The Empty Throne - Bernard Cornwell *t* 146

Cherry, Cynthia
The Final Reveille - Amanda Flower *m* 547

Crocker, Ben
Fate Moreland's Widow - John Lane *t* 197

Orr, April
The Witch of the Wood - Michael
  Aronovitz *h* 280

Westerland, Blythe
A Finely Knit Murder - Sally
  Goldenbaum *m* 557

ADOPTEE

April
Endangered - C.J. Box *m* 499

Daniel
Tangled Lives - Hilary Boyd *c* 705

Goldman, Dr. Zoe
Little Black Lies - Sandra Block *m* 496

Henry
You're So Fine - Kieran Kramer *r* 1002

Kell
A Darker Shade of Magic - V.E. Schwab *f* 105

Kiril
Originator - Joel Shepherd *s* 1194

Moses
The Pharaoh's Daughter - Mesu Andrews *i* 357

Valentina
An Italian Wife - Ann Hood *c* 768

Zimmerman, Alexa
When Grace Sings - Kim Vogel Sawyer *i* 454

ADVENTURER

Ardhi
The Dagger's Path - Glenda Larke *f* 67

Dalt
If Not for This - Pete Fromm *c* 745

Fonthill, Alice
Treachery in Tibet - John Wilcox *t* 271

Fonthill, Simon
Treachery in Tibet - John Wilcox *t* 271

Hygeorht, Wynn
First and Last Sorcerer - Barb Hendee *f* 52

Maddy
If Not for This - Pete Fromm *c* 745

Moorcock, Michael
The Whispering Swarm - Michael
  Moorcock *f* 84

Parker, Brody
Deadly, Calm, and Cold - Susannah
  Sandlin *r* 1068

Pitt, Dirk
Havana Storm - Clive Cussler *c* 725

Roxton, Slater
Garden of Lies - Amanda Quick *r* 1051

Valyn
The Providence of Fire - Brian Staveley *f* 111

ADVERTISING

Dickinson, Alice
Amherst - William Nicholson *t* 221

Ivy
Getting Even - Sarah Rayner *c* 842

Orianna
Getting Even - Sarah Rayner *c* 842

Wyatt, Anna
Girl Before a Mirror - Liza Palmer *r* 1047

ADVISOR

Barker, Holly
Hot Pursuit - Stuart Woods *m* 682

Coughlin, Joe
World Gone By - Dennis Lehane *t* 201

Grand Vazir
The Woman Who Read Too Much - Bahiyyih
  Nakhjavani *t* 220

Hopkins, Harry
Sleep in Peace Tonight - James
  MacManus *t* 208

Taita
Desert God - Wilbur Smith *t* 252

Character Description Index

Thayne, Mark
Too Dangerous for a Lady - Jo Beverley   *r* 915
Vin
Last Days of the Condor - James Grady   *m* 559

ALCOHOLIC

Bree
Beyond the Pale Motel - Francesca Lia
   Block   *c* 704
Catt
Beyond the Pale Motel - Francesca Lia
   Block   *c* 704
Ma
When - Victoria Laurie   *f* 70
McCane, Angus
Fate Moreland's Widow - John Lane   *t* 197
O'Brien, Cal
Serpents in the Cold - Thomas O'Malley   *t* 222
Zook, Timothy
An Empty Cup - Sarah Price   *i* 449

ALIEN

Adara
Artemis Invaded - Jane M. Lindskold   *s* 1169
Aelyx
Invaded - Melissa Landers   *s* 1163
Ereshkigal
Hell's Maw - James Axler   *s* 1112
Fathom
Undertow - Michael Buckley   *s* 1121
Jake
Echo 8 - Sharon Lynn Fisher   *f* 33
Katt-Martini, Katherine "Kitty"
Alien Separation - Gini Koch   *s* 1162
Kizzy
Three Songs for Roxy - Caren Gussoff   *s* 1150
Natalie
Three Songs for Roxy - Caren Gussoff   *s* 1150
Pippage
Crisis of Consciousness - Dave Galanter   *s* 1147
Rania
The Architect of Aeons - John C. Wright   *s* 1210
Sakhet
Heir to the Jedi - Kevin Hearne   *s* 1154
Spock
Crisis of Consciousness - Dave Galanter   *s* 1147
Tao
The Rebirths of Tao - Wesley Chu   *s* 1126
Troft
Cobra Outlaw - Timothy Zahn   *s* 1211
Whips
Castaway Planet - Eric Flint   *s* 1146

AMNESIAC

Alice
Alice - Christina Henry   *h* 315
Gray, Eve
Broken - Cynthia Eden   *r* 959
Mrs.
The Handsome Man's De Luxe Cafe - Alexander
   McCall Smith   *c* 864

Unnamed Character
Deliverance at Cardwell Ranch - B.J.
   Daniels   *r* 948

AMPUTEE

Harrison, Harrison "H2"
Harrison Squared - Daryl Gregory   *h* 306
Knoxx, Michael
The Proposal at Siesta Key - Shelley Shepard
   Gray   *i* 406

ANDROID

Kelso, Danny
Tin Men - Christopher Golden   *m* 556
Kresnov, Cassandra "Sandy"
Originator - Joel Shepherd   *s* 1194
Wade, Kate
Tin Men - Christopher Golden   *m* 556

ANGEL

Aspyn
Chasing Sunsets - Karen Kingsbury   *i* 425
Jag
Chasing Sunsets - Karen Kingsbury   *i* 425
Mills, Harry
Mr. Miracle - Debbie Macomber   *r* 1015

ANIMAL LOVER

Canaday, David
Kittens Can Kill - Clea Simon   *m* 659
Stone, Darcy
Still the One - Jill Shalvis   *r* 1076

ANIMAL TRAINER

Gallo, Mary Hannah
Rescue Me - Catherine Mann   *r* 1017
Marlowe, Pru
Kittens Can Kill - Clea Simon   *m* 659

ANTHROPOLOGIST

Brennan, Dr. Temperance "Tempe"
Bones Never Lie - Kathy Reichs   *c* 843
Speaking in Bones - Kathy Reichs   *m* 640
U
Satin Island - Tom McCarthy   *c* 799

ANTIQUES DEALER

Borne, Brandy
Antiques Swap - Barbara Allan   *m* 477
Borne, Vivian
Antiques Swap - Barbara Allan   *m* 477
Stanford, Kat
Deadly Desires at Honeychurch Hall - Hannah
   Dennison   *m* 532
West, Nell
The Whispering - Sarah Rayne   *h* 336

APPRAISER

Pettigrew, Zunia
Shadow of a Spout - Amanda Cooper   *m* 521

APPRENTICE

Campion, Lucy
The Masque of a Murderer - Susanna
   Calkins   *m* 510
Emma
The Siege Winter - Ariana Franklin   *t* 159
Isaac
Dreamseeker - C.S. Friedman   *f* 37
Karno, Madeleine
Doctor Death - Lene Kaaberbol   *t* 187
Rasmus
Woven - Michael Jensen   *f* 61
Torbidda
The Warring States - Aidan Harte   *f* 47
Vader, Darth
Lords of the Sith - Paul S. Kemp   *s* 1160
Yarrick, Sebastian
Yarrick: Imperial Creed - David
   Annandale   *s* 1106

ARCHAEOLOGIST

Bell, Gertrude
Bell of the Desert - Alan Gold   *t* 166
Creed, Annja
Bathed in Blood - Alex Archer   *f* 6
Death Mask - Alex Archer   *f* 5
Jennings, Harper
In the Woods - Merry Jones   *m* 587
Larson, Ceseli
Love in the Land of Barefoot Soldiers - Frances
   Vieta   *t* 267
Roxton, Slater
Garden of Lies - Amanda Quick   *r* 1051
Swan, Scarlett
Black Scorpion - Jon Land   *m* 596
Tom
Voyage of the Basilisk: A Memoir by Lady Trent -
   Marie Brennan   *f* 16

ARCHITECT

Duplessi, Julien
The Witch of Painted Sorrows - M.J. Rose   *t* 236
Mackintosh, Charles "Mac" Rennie
Mr. Mac and Me - Esther Freud   *t* 161
McAlister, Gavin
Back to Before - Tracy Solheim   *r* 1084
Sinan
The Architect's Apprentice - Elif Shafak   *t* 247

ART DEALER

Fitzallen, Gareth
His Wicked Reputation - Madeline Hunter   *r* 992

ARTIFICIAL INTELLIGENCE

Chrystal
Edge of Dark - Brenda Cooper   *s* 1132

Penny Royal
Dark Intelligence - Neal Asher *s* 1108

Satomi, Isobel
Dark Intelligence - Neal Asher *s* 1108

Silver Box
Inside a Silver Box - Walter Mosley *s* 1179

ARTISAN

Byler, Henry
Balm of Gilead - Adina Senft *i* 456

Greene, Dani
A Sticky Situation - Jessie Crockett *m* 525

Raber, Clayton
The Amish Clockmaker - Mindy Starns
  Clark *i* 378

Stafford, Joanna
The Tapestry - Nancy Bilyeau *t* 130

von Hoffman, Danielle Bretancourt
Scent of Triumph - Jan Moran *t* 212

ARTIST

Ark, Roxanne "Roxy"
Fall with Me - Jennifer L. Armentrout *r* 902

Barrett, Natasha
Before, During, After - Richard Bausch *c* 698

Bell, Vanessa Stephen
Vanessa and Her Sister - Priya Parmar *t* 225

Blair, Penny
The Children's Crusade - Ann Packer *t* 224

Byler, Henry
Keys of Heaven - Adina Senft *i* 455

Cassian, Samuel
The City of Blood - Frederique Molay *m* 622

Cicero, Hunt
Teardrop Lane - Emily March *r* 1018

Cocteau, Jean
Mademoiselle Chanel - C.W. Gortner *t* 167

Downey, Evan
Bringing Home the Bad Boy - Jessica
  Lemmon *r* 1010

Fleming, Mary
Married to a Perfect Stranger - Jane
  Ashford *r* 904

Graham, Grace
Unbecoming - Rebecca Scherm *c* 855

Hedge, Sophy
The Language of Paradise - Barbara Klein
  Moss *t* 217

Hudson, Laney
Dictatorship of the Dress - Jessica
  Topper *r* 1092

Jayne, Flossie
Tiffany Girl - Deeanne Gist *i* 403

Jilly
There Must Be Some Mistake - Frederick
  Barthelme *c* 697

Libertus, Longinus Flavius
The Fateful Day - Rosemary Rowe *t* 238

Mackintosh, Charles "Mac" Rennie
Mr. Mac and Me - Esther Freud *t* 161

Mackintosh, Margaret
Mr. Mac and Me - Esther Freud *t* 161

Manet, Edouard
Paris Red - Maureen Gibbon *t* 164

Merchant, Sasha
Girl Before a Mirror - Liza Palmer *r* 1047

Nataly
The Amado Women - Desiree Zamorano *c* 892

Nic
Night Blindness - Susan Strecker *c* 870

Penhaligon, Jess
The Sea Garden - Marcia Willett *c* 886

Picasso, Pablo
Mademoiselle Chanel - C.W. Gortner *t* 167

Radmanovic, Radar
I Am Radar - Reif Larsen *s* 1164

Robin
Believe - Erin McCarthy *r* 1026

Russell, Eva
His Wicked Reputation - Madeline Hunter *r* 992

Severson, Miranda
The Kind Worth Killing - Peter Swanson *m* 670

Sinthoras
Righteous Fury - Markus Heitz *f* 49

Sorenson, Lena
The Sex Lives of Siamese Twins - Irvine
  Welsh *c* 885

St. James, Rowland "Rowdy"
Rowdy - Jay Crownover *r* 945

van Gogh, Vincent
The Season of Migration - Nellie
  Hermann *t* 177

Webster, Wallace
There Must Be Some Mistake - Frederick
  Barthelme *c* 697

West, Isabelle
Flirting with Disaster - Victoria Dahl *r* 946

ASSASSIN

Caldwell, Mike
Guardian - Erik Williams *h* 354

Garrett, Alonzo
The Clockwork Crown - Beth Cato *f* 23

Kingslayer, Aral
Darkened Blade - Kelly McCullough *f* 79

Lenk
The City Stained Red - Sam Sykes *f* 114

Olsen, Lester
Private Vegas - James Patterson *c* 826

Phillips, Noelle
Midnight Action - Elle Kennedy *r* 999

Reana
The Dangerous Type - Loren Rhoads *s* 1189

Tala, Caleb
Heir of Hope - Morgan L. Busse *i* 368

Underwood, Jacob
Spark - John Twelve Hawks *c* 874

Varatschevsky, Karin
Ascendance: Dave vs. the Monsters - John
  Birmingham *f* 13

Vaughn, Vicky
Firestorm - Nancy Holzner *h* 318

Velasquez, Angel
The Water Knife - Paolo Bacigalupi *s* 1113

ASSISTANT

Ashley
Seven Threadly Sins - Janet Bolin *m* 497

Avery, Beth
No One Like You - Kate Angell *r* 901

Barak, Jack
Lamentation - C.J. Sansom *t* 244

Crawford, Julie
A Touch of Stardust - Kate Alcott *t* 125

Davis, Emma
No Denying You - Sydney Landon *r* 1004

Fergins
The Last Bookaneer - Matthew Pearl *t* 227

Huo, Li Yin
The Lusitania Conspiracy - Ronald J.
  Walters *t* 269

Krause, Sue Ellen
Bittersweet - Susan Wittig Albert *m* 476

Llewelyn, Thomas
Anatomy of Evil - Will Thomas *t* 261

Martindale, Millicent
Hot Pursuit - Stuart Woods *m* 682

Murdoch, Bronwyn
The Prince Who Loved Me - Karen
  Hawkins *r* 983

Porter, Geraldine "Gerry"
Manhattan in Miniature - Margaret Grace *m* 558

Porter, Maddie
Manhattan in Miniature - Margaret Grace *m* 558

Slade, Luke
Last Days in Shanghai - Casey Walker *c* 883

Tinkie
Bone to Be Wild - Carolyn Haines *m* 564

Tornja, Ran il
The Providence of Fire - Brian Staveley *f* 111

Yeung, Bo
Grave Phantoms - Jenn Bennett *r* 912

ASTRONAUT

Kev
*Your Fathers, Where Are They? And the Prophets,
  Do They Live Forever?* - Dave Eggers *c* 738

AUNT

Bella
Hiding in Plain Sight - Nuruddin Farah *c* 741

Bradley, Colleen
Driving with the Top Down - Beth
  Harbison *c* 761

Brewster, Callie
*Cowboy Boots for Christmas: (Cowboy Not In-
  cluded)* - Carolyn Brown *r* 929

Brockwell, Iris
Gift of Grace - Sharlene MacLaren *i* 433

Collard, Ivy
The Mill River Redemption - Darcie Chan *c* 711

Elizabeth
The Luminous Heart of Jonah S. - Gina B.
  Nahai *c* 814

Elliot, Kate
Taken - Lisa Harris *i* 412

Elsie
Manhattan in Miniature - Margaret Grace *m* 558

Endicott, Nell
A Finely Knit Murder - Sally
  Goldenbaum *m* 557

Fisher, Lorraine
What You Left Behind - Samantha Hayes   *m* 570
Gugu
Frog - Yan Mo   *c* 808
Lady Gwendolyn
The Cavendon Women - Barbara Taylor Bradford   *t* 133
Harper, Annabelle
Sunflower Lane - Jill Gregory   *r* 978
Hazel
A Sticky Situation - Jessie Crockett   *m* 525
Hodgson, Bridget
The Witch Hunter's Tale - Sam Thomas   *t* 260
Lilian
Sweetshop of Dreams - Jenny Colgan   *c* 715
Lively, Penny
One Foot in the Grape - Carlene O'Neil   *m* 627
Mab
Soulbound - Kristen Callihan   *f* 19
Miller, Sarah
Deadly Echoes - Nancy Mehl   *i* 435
Olive
Murder with a Twist - Tracy Kiely   *m* 593
Pendragon, Adela
In the Time of the Dragon Moon - Janet Lee Carey   *f* 20
Quinn, Brigid
Fear the Darkness - Becky Masterman   *m* 610
Riddell, Serena
A Sudden Light - Garth Stein   *c* 868
Scarpetta, Dr. Kay
Flesh and Blood - Patricia Cornwell   *c* 719
Vi
A Fright to the Death - Dawn Eastman   *h* 295
Vicky
Betrayed - Lisa Scottoline   *c* 857
Waverley, Claire
First Frost - Sarah Addison Allen   *c* 689
Waverley, Sydney
First Frost - Sarah Addison Allen   *c* 689

AUTISTIC

Keenan, Jack Peter
The Boy Who Drew Monsters - Keith Donohue   *c* 732
Noah
For Keeps - Rachel Lacey   *r* 1003

AVENGER

Adare
The Providence of Fire - Brian Staveley   *f* 111
Valyn
The Providence of Fire - Brian Staveley   *f* 111

BABY

Angela Rose
The Love Letters - Beverly Lewis   *i* 427
Canfield, Grace
The Murk - Robert Lettrick   *h* 331
Chloe
In the Woods - Merry Jones   *m* 587

Sullivan, Liam
The Edge of Dreams - Rhys Bowen   *t* 131

BAKER

Carter, Lily
Buy a Whisker - Sofie Ryan   *m* 650
Conlon, Maeve
Lies That Bind - Maggie Barbieri   *m* 487
Doyle, Shane
All Fired Up - Kate Meader   *r* 1037
Holmes, Toni
Flourless to Stop Him - Nancy J. Parra   *m* 631
LeFaye, Ella Mae
Lemon Pies and Little White Lies - Ellery Adams   *m* 475
Mrs. Nelson
Death by Baking - Cynthia Hickey   *i* 418
Simmons, Bernie
A Catered Mother's Day - Isis Crawford   *m* 523
Simmons, Libby
A Catered Mother's Day - Isis Crawford   *m* 523
Swensen, Hannah
Double Fudge Brownie Murder - Joanne Fluke   *m* 548

BANKER

Austen, Henry
Who Buries the Dead - C.S. Harris   *t* 172
Benz, Bruno
Hausfrau - Jill Alexander Essbaum   *c* 739
Eagle, Johnny
Sins of Our Fathers - Shawn Lawrence Otto   *c* 822
Graham Channing, Jackson Quincy
The Shocking Secret of a Guest at the Wedding - Victoria Alexander   *r* 895
Guild, Preston
The Hidden Man - Robin Blake   *m* 495
Kelly, Elaine
The Teller - Jonathan Stone   *m* 668
Peter
On the Edge - Edward St. Aubyn   *c* 867
Runcie, Everett
A Woman Unknown - Frances Brody   *t* 134
Wheler, Dick
The Cheapside Corpse - Susanna Gregory   *t* 169
White, John "JW"
Sins of Our Fathers - Shawn Lawrence Otto   *c* 822

BARBARIAN

Khash, Tarra
Tales of the Primal Land - Brian Lumley   *h* 332

BARTENDER

Ark, Roxanne "Roxy"
Fall with Me - Jennifer L. Armentrout   *r* 902
Brascum, Adam
Sweeter than Sin - Shiloh Walker   *r* 1094
Donovan, Maura
An Early Wake - Sheila Connolly   *m* 520

Saginowski, Bob
The Drop - Dennis Lehane   *c* 788

BASEBALL PLAYER

Cassanova, Figueroa "Figgy"
Cuba Straits - Randy Wayne White   *m* 681
Cates, Rylan
No One Like You - Kate Angell   *r* 901
Dillinger, Marcus
Chasing Sunsets - Karen Kingsbury   *i* 425
Ross, Alex
Perfect Catch - Sierra Dean   *r* 953

BASTARD DAUGHTER

Rose
The Duke's Guide to Correct Behavior - Megan Frampton   *r* 967

BASTARD SON

Endicott, Captain William "Wolf"
How to Plan a Wedding for a Royal Spy - Vanessa Kelly   *r* 997
Fitzallen, Gareth
His Wicked Reputation - Madeline Hunter   *r* 992
Montcrief, James "Jamie"
I've Got My Duke to Keep Me Warm - Kelly Bowen   *r* 920
Smith, Jupiter
The Abduction of Smith and Smith - Rashad Harrison   *t* 174

BEAR

Kallik
Seekers: Return to the Wild: The Burning Horizon - Erin Hunter   *f* 59
Lusa
Seekers: Return to the Wild: The Burning Horizon - Erin Hunter   *f* 59
Toklo
Seekers: Return to the Wild: The Burning Horizon - Erin Hunter   *f* 59
Yakone
Seekers: Return to the Wild: The Burning Horizon - Erin Hunter   *f* 59

BEAUTY PAGEANT CONTESTANT

Parker, Barbara
Funny Girl - Nick Hornby   *c* 770
Parsons, Priscilla
House of Wonder - Sarah Healy   *c* 763

BIBLICAL FIGURE

Isa
The Tomb: A Novel of Martha - Stephanie Landsem   *i* 426
Jesus
The Tomb: A Novel of Martha - Stephanie Landsem   *i* 426

King Herod
A.D. 30 - Ted Dekker *i* 391

Lazarus
The Tomb: A Novel of Martha - Stephanie Landsem *i* 426

Martha
The Tomb: A Novel of Martha - Stephanie Landsem *i* 426

Moses
The Pharaoh's Daughter - Mesu Andrews *i* 357

Paul
Empire's End - Jerry B. Jenkins *i* 421

Pharaoh Tut
The Pharaoh's Daughter - Mesu Andrews *i* 357

Rahab
The Crimson Cord: Rahab's Story - Jill Eileen Smith *i* 458

Simon
The Tomb: A Novel of Martha - Stephanie Landsem *i* 426

Yeshua
A.D. 30 - Ted Dekker *i* 391

BIRD

Tom
Holy Cow - David Duchovny *c* 735

BLACKSMITH

Langslow, Meg
Lord of the Wings - Donna Andrews *m* 479

Marsh, Stephen
The Invention of Fire - Bruce W. Holsinger *t* 179

Yeu, Josia
A Thing of Beauty - Lisa Samson *i* 453

BLIND PERSON

Batten, Lady Phoebe
Dearest Rogue - Elizabeth Hoyt *r* 990

BOARDER

Leslie-Jones, Veronica
The Lodger - Louisa Treger *t* 265

Richardson, Dorothy
The Lodger - Louisa Treger *t* 265

BODYGUARD

Abbas, Anwar
Evensong - John Love *s* 1171

Breen, Fred
The Night Belongs to Fireman - Jennifer Bernard *r* 913

David
Compulsion - Allison Brennan *m* 502

McKenna, Quill
This Gun for Hire - Jo Goodman *r* 973

Nash, Katherine "Calico"
This Gun for Hire - Jo Goodman *r* 973

Trevillion, James
Dearest Rogue - Elizabeth Hoyt *r* 990

Weary, Nat
Driving the King - Ravi Howard *t* 180

BOUNTY HUNTER

Hammond, Stone
A Worthy Pursuit - Karen Witemeyer *i* 471

Keller, Jack
Devils and Dust - J.D. Rhoades *m* 642

Nash, Katherine "Calico"
This Gun for Hire - Jo Goodman *r* 973

Parker, Brody
Deadly, Calm, and Cold - Susannah Sandlin *r* 1068

BOXER

Brandon, Rafe
Say Yes to the Marquess - Tessa Dare *r* 950

Lewis, Denver
Holding Strong - Lori Foster *r* 965

Matchet, Ruth
The Fair Fight - Anna Freeman *t* 160

Webber, Tom
The Fair Fight - Anna Freeman *t* 160

BOY

Akkad Boy
The Infernal - Mark Doten *c* 734

Andreou, Peter
The Fifth Gospel - Ian Caldwell *m* 509

Aubrey, Jax
The Inquisitor's Mark - Dianne Salerni *f* 102

Canfield, Monty "Creeper"
The Murk - Robert Lettrick *h* 331

Chey
The Second Guard - J.D. Vaughn *f* 119

Clayborne, Chance
Terminal - Kathy Reichs *s* 1187

Cody
Firefight - Brandon Sanderson *f* 104

David
Firefight - Brandon Sanderson *f* 104

Defoe, Pip
The Last Kings of Sark - Rosa Rankin-Gee *c* 840

Eddie
Delicious Foods - James Hannaham *c* 760

Glasserman, Cody
We Are Pirates - Daniel Handler *c* 759

Goldstein, Eli
The Last Flight of Poxl West - Daniel Torday *t* 264

Indio
Darling Beast - Elizabeth Hoyt *r* 989

Iqtbal, Ali
Green on Blue - Elliot Ackerman *c* 684

Iqtbal, Aziz
Green on Blue - Elliot Ackerman *c* 684

Jahan
The Architect's Apprentice - Elif Shafak *t* 247

Keenan, Jack Peter
The Boy Who Drew Monsters - Keith Donohue *c* 732

Kiran
The Glass Arrow - Kristen Simmons *s* 1197

Longboat, Martin
Electric City - Elizabeth Rosner *t* 237

Lub
Harrison Squared - Daryl Gregory *h* 306

Luis
Kiss Me Hello - Grace Burrowes *r* 933

Nels
Woven - Michael Jensen *f* 61

Nick
The Boy Who Drew Monsters - Keith Donohue *c* 732

Nicky
Scent of Triumph - Jan Moran *t* 212

Noah
For Keeps - Rachel Lacey *r* 1003

Osborne, Diz
Last to Know - Elizabeth Adler *c* 685

Ryker, Amir
The Glass Arrow - Kristen Simmons *s* 1197

Salim
Ishmael's Oranges - Claire Hajaj *c* 757

Slone, Bailey
Hold the Dark - William Giraldi *c* 749

Tad
The Murk - Robert Lettrick *h* 331

Tomas
World Gone By - Dennis Lehane *t* 201

Torbidda
The Warring States - Aidan Harte *f* 47

Tubby
Trollhunters - Guillermo Del Toro *h* 292

Unnamed Character
Em and the Big Hoom - Jerry Pinto *c* 831
Exposure - Kathy Reichs *s* 1186
My Sunshine Away - M.O. Walsh *c* 884

Wash
The Wonder of All Things - Jason Mott *c* 812

Will
If I Fall, If I Die - Michael Christie *c* 712

Zarif
The Second Guard - J.D. Vaughn *f* 119

BOYFRIEND

Abbott, Will
I Saw Her Standing There - Marie Force *r* 964

Aelyx
Invaded - Melissa Landers *s* 1163

Baker, Dr. Mark
Fatal Trauma - Richard L. Mabry *i* 432

Barton, Ross
Double Fudge Brownie Murder - Joanne Fluke *m* 548

Battle, Jeff
What Strange Creatures - Emily Arsenault *c* 695

Beck, Guinevere
You - Caroline Kepnes *c* 782

Ben
Marked Fur Murder - Dixie Lyle *m* 609

Brandon
Zombified - Adam Gallardo *h* 302

Burchett, Will
License to Dill - Mary Ellen Hughes *m* 578

BRIDE

BRIDEGROOM

BROTHER

Brandon, Piers
Say Yes to the Marquess - Tessa Dare   *r* 950
Brandon, Rafe
Say Yes to the Marquess - Tessa Dare   *r* 950
Brickman, Cooper
Final Lap - Erin McCarthy   *r* 1027
Caleb
Balm of Gilead - Adina Senft   *i* 456
Canfield, Monty "Creeper"
The Murk - Robert Lettrick   *h* 331
Carl
Life or Death - Michael Robotham   *m* 645
Carmichael, Gavin
Stirring Up Trouble - Kimberly Kincaid   *r* 1000
Carter, Will
The London Pride - Charlie Fletcher   *f* 34
Cavale
Grave Matters - Lauren M. Roy   *f* 101
Charlie
It Won't Always Be This Great - Peter Mehlman   *c* 803
Connelly, Jake
Finding Jake - Bryan Reardon   *m* 639
Covington, Cole
Return to Me - Kelly Moran   *r* 1038
Craven, Jonathan
A Good Rake Is Hard to Find - Manda Collins   *r* 944
Cross, Damon
Hope to Die - James Patterson   *c* 824
d'Orleans, Gaston
1636: The Cardinal Virtues - Eric Flint   *s* 1145
Davoir, Etienne
Satan's Lullaby - Priscilla Royal   *t* 239
de Lacy, Lord Oswald
Plague Land - S.D. Sykes   *t* 257
de Warren, Morris
If He's Daring - Hannah Howell   *r* 988
Delancey, Ed
Tangled Lives - Hilary Boyd   *c* 705
DeLaura, Angie
Dark Chocolate Demise - Jenn McKinlay   *m* 616
DeLaura, Joe
Dark Chocolate Demise - Jenn McKinlay   *m* 616
Derring, Brook
Earls Just Want to Have Fun - Shana Galen   *r* 970
Derring, Maxwell
Earls Just Want to Have Fun - Shana Galen   *r* 970
Devereaux, Caleb
Keep Me Safe - Maya Banks   *r* 908
Di, Lung
The Dragons of Heaven - Alyc Helms   *f* 50
Dickinson, Austin
Amherst - William Nicholson   *t* 221
Dolvek
Oathkeeper - J.F. Lewis   *f* 74
Douglas "Stem"
A Spool of Blue Thread - Anne Tyler   *c* 875
Driver
The Country of Ice Cream Star - Sandra Newman   *c* 816
Elliot
Reunion - Hannah Pittard   *c* 833

Erum, Aman
The Shadow of the Crescent Moon - Fatima Bhutto   *c* 703
Fontenot, Gator
Viper Game - Christine Feehan   *r* 961
Fontenot, Wyatt
Viper Game - Christine Feehan   *r* 961
Fortescue, Julian
The Duke of Dark Desires - Miranda Neville   *r* 1042
Galen
Teardrop Lane - Emily March   *r* 1018
Gallagher, Ryan
In Case of Emergency - Courtney Moreno   *c* 811
Gledstanes, Benjamin "Benjy"
Devil's Moon - Amanda Scott   *r* 1070
Gramaraye, Mort
Finn Fancy Necromancy - Randy Henderson   *f* 53
Gramaraye, Pete
Finn Fancy Necromancy - Randy Henderson   *f* 53
Gramaraye, Phinaeus "Finn"
Finn Fancy Necromancy - Randy Henderson   *f* 53
Hansen, Cooper
The Cowboy SEAL - Laura Marie Altom   *r* 897
The Cowboy SEAL - Laura Marie Altom   *r* 897
Hargrave, Adam
The Masque of a Murderer - Susanna Calkins   *m* 510
Hayat
The Shadow of the Crescent Moon - Fatima Bhutto   *c* 703
Hazelton, Nigel
An American Duchess - Sharon Page   *r* 1046
Hazelton, Sebastian
An American Duchess - Sharon Page   *r* 1046
Henry, Alfred
Grave Consequences - David Thurlo   *m* 673
Henry, Charlie
Grave Consequences - David Thurlo   *m* 673
Hodgson, Joseph
The Witch Hunter's Tale - Sam Thomas   *t* 260
Hodgson, Will
The Witch Hunter's Tale - Sam Thomas   *t* 260
Holland, Marty
Canary - Duane Swierczynski   *m* 671
Holmes, Tim
Flourless to Stop Him - Nancy J. Parra   *m* 631
Howard, Brian
Cold Trail - Janet Dawson   *m* 528
Howard, Clay
The Bride Ship - Regina Scott   *r* 1073
Howard, Frank
The Bride Ship - Regina Scott   *r* 1073
Howard, Jeri
Cold Trail - Janet Dawson   *m* 528
Huang, Lung
The Dragons of Heaven - Alyc Helms   *f* 50
Hutchinson, Brian
Christmas at Twilight - Lori Wilde   *r* 1097
Hylas
The Eye of the Falcon - Michelle Paver   *f* 94
iAm
The Shadows - J.R. Ward   *h* 349

Ian
Twice Tempted - Eileen Dreyer   *r* 956
Illica, Caleb
Accidents of Marriage - Randy Susan Meyers   *c* 804
Iqtbal, Ali
Green on Blue - Elliot Ackerman   *c* 684
Iqtbal, Aziz
Green on Blue - Elliot Ackerman   *c* 684
J.T.
Cane and Abe - James Grippando   *c* 756
Jackson, Dominic
Be Not Afraid - Cecilia Galante   *h* 300
Jeffrey
The Devil Takes a Bride - Julia London   *r* 1012
Kaden
The Providence of Fire - Brian Staveley   *f* 111
Kaufman, Daniel
The Fragile World - Paula Treick DeBoard   *c* 730
Keenan
Teardrop Lane - Emily March   *r* 1018
Kelly, Alden
Quartet for the End of Time - Johanna Skibsrud   *t* 250
Kevin
City 1 - Gregg Rosenblum   *s* 1192
Kimei, Hitomi
Castaway Planet - Eric Flint   *s* 1146
King, Edward
An Amish Man of Ice Mountain - Kelly Long   *i* 429
King, Joseph
An Amish Man of Ice Mountain - Kelly Long   *i* 429
Kitt
An Appetite for Violets - Martine Bailey   *t* 128
Knightley, James
The First Kiss - Grace Burrowes   *r* 932
Knightley, Trent
The First Kiss - Grace Burrowes   *r* 932
Krissi
How to Build a Girl - Caitlin Moran   *c* 810
Lake, Timmy
Last Chance Family - Hope Ramsay   *r* 1055
Langdon, Frank
Early Warning - Jane Smiley   *t* 251
Lark, Dallas
Leaving Amarillo - Caisey Quinn   *r* 1052
Latimer, Trez
The Shadows - J.R. Ward   *h* 349
Lazarus
The Tomb: A Novel of Martha - Stephanie Landsem   *i* 426
Lehman, Tim
Amish Promises - Leslie Gould   *i* 405
Louis
This Is the Life - Alex Shearer   *c* 862
Louis, King
1636: The Cardinal Virtues - Eric Flint   *s* 1145
Lupin
How to Build a Girl - Caitlin Moran   *c* 810
MacPherson, Danny
The Silent Sister - Diane Chamberlain   *c* 710
Malone, Jack
Daughter of the Regiment - Stephanie Grace Whitson   *i* 469

Malone, Seamus
Daughter of the Regiment - Stephanie Grace
    Whitson   *i* 469

Manley, Liam
What a Woman Gets - Judi Fennell   *r* 962

Manton, Dominick
If the Viscount Falls - Sabrina Jeffries   *r* 995

Manton, George
If the Viscount Falls - Sabrina Jeffries   *r* 995

McCane, Angus
Fate Moreland's Widow - John Lane   *t* 197

McCane, George
Fate Moreland's Widow - John Lane   *t* 197

McKay, Brandt
Cowgirls Don't Cry - Lorelei James   *r* 994

McKay, Luke
Cowgirls Don't Cry - Lorelei James   *r* 994

Montgomery, Joel
A Heart's Obsession - Colleen Coble   *i* 384

Nathaniel
How to Catch a Prince - Rachel Hauck   *i* 414

Nelson, Clayton
The Deep - Nick Cutter   *h* 289

Nelson, Luke
The Deep - Nick Cutter   *h* 289

Nick
As Night Falls - Jenny Milchman   *m* 619
City 1 - Gregg Rosenblum   *s* 1192

O'Brien, JJ
Inside the O'Briens - Lisa Genova   *c* 747

O'Brien, Patrick
Inside the O'Briens - Lisa Genova   *c* 747

O'Toole, Coop
Beneath - Roland Smith   *s* 1199

O'Toole, Pat
Beneath - Roland Smith   *s* 1199

Osborne, Diz
Last to Know - Elizabeth Adler   *c* 685

Osborne, Roman
Last to Know - Elizabeth Adler   *c* 685

Palmer, Audie
Life or Death - Michael Robotham   *m* 645

Parsons, Warren
House of Wonder - Sarah Healy   *c* 763

Paynter, Johnny
Outlaw Takes a Bride - Susan Page Davis   *i* 389

Paynter, Mark
Outlaw Takes a Bride - Susan Page Davis   *i* 389

Pitt, Dirk Jr.
Havana Storm - Clive Cussler   *c* 725

Prospero, Danny
Deadly Spells - Jaye Wells   *f* 121

Quentin
Infinity Bell - Devon Monk   *f* 83

Quinn, Wade
Quake - Patrick Carman   *s* 1124

Rafferty, Castor
His Reluctant Cinderella - Jessica
    Gilmore   *r* 971

Rake, Anomander
Fall of Light - Steven Erikson   *f* 30

Rand, Hamilton
Corridors of the Night - Anne Perry   *t* 229

Rand, Magnus
Corridors of the Night - Anne Perry   *t* 229

Reilly, Will
Night Blindness - Susan Strecker   *c* 870

Riddell, Jones
A Sudden Light - Garth Stein   *c* 868

Rivvek
Oathkeeper - J.F. Lewis   *f* 74

Rocco, Luke
The Inn at Ocean's Edge - Colleen Coble   *i* 383

Rogers, Tyler
Shades of the Wolf - Karen Whiddon   *f* 124

Rosen, Bobby
The Sheltering - Mark Powell   *c* 835

Rosen, Donny
The Sheltering - Mark Powell   *c* 835

Ruin, Silchas
Fall of Light - Steven Erikson   *f* 30

Salif
Hiding in Plain Sight - Nuruddin Farah   *c* 741

Sam
One True Path - Barbara Cameron   *i* 375

Sandstone, Eddie
A Deadly Affair at Bobtail Ridge - Terry
    Shames   *m* 656

Seagrave, Jeth
Polaris - Mindee Arnett   *s* 1107

Serrailler, Simon
The Soul of Discretion - Susan Hill   *m* 574

Seymour, Edward
The May Bride - Suzannah Dunn   *t* 151

Shepard, Jacob
Ancient Oceans of Central Kentucky - David Con-
    nerley Nahm   *c* 815

Sikandar
The Shadow of the Crescent Moon - Fatima
    Bhutto   *c* 703

Silva, Rab
On the Run - Jo Davis   *r* 951

Simon
Balm of Gilead - Adina Senft   *i* 456

Smith, Archer
The Abduction of Smith and Smith - Rashad
    Harrison   *t* 174

Smith, Jupiter
The Abduction of Smith and Smith - Rashad
    Harrison   *t* 174

Sonny
Musseled Out - Barbara Ross   *m* 646

Stephen
How to Catch a Prince - Rachel Hauck   *i* 414

Taggart, Mike
Last Chance Family - Hope Ramsay   *r* 1055

Teo
The Chosen Prince - Diane Stanley   *f* 110

Todd, Teddy
A God in Ruins - Kate Atkinson   *t* 127

Tucker, Justin
When It's Right - Jennifer Ryan   *r* 1065

Unnamed Character
Em and the Big Hoom - Jerry Pinto   *c* 831
This Is the Life - Alex Shearer   *c* 862

Valyn
The Providence of Fire - Brian Staveley   *f* 111

van Gogh, Theo
The Season of Migration - Nellie
    Hermann   *t* 177

van Gogh, Vincent
The Season of Migration - Nellie
    Hermann   *t* 177

Walden, Gray
All the Wrong Places - Lisa Lieberman   *t* 205

Wallin, Drew
Would-Be Wilderness Wife - Regina Scott   *r* 1074

Wallin, Levi
Would-Be Wilderness Wife - Regina Scott   *r* 1074

Wallin, Simon
Would-Be Wilderness Wife - Regina Scott   *r* 1074

Warren, Cade
Untraceable - Elizabeth Goddard   *i* 404

Whitshank, Denny
A Spool of Blue Thread - Anne Tyler   *c* 875

BULLIED CHILD

Freddie
What You Left Behind - Samantha Hayes   *m* 570

BULLY

Penrose, Eugene
The Thing About December - Donal Ryan   *c* 850

BUSINESSMAN

Abbott, Hunter
And I Love Her - Marie Force   *r* 963

Addleshaw, Ollie
After a Fashion - Jen Turano   *i* 465

Alden, Hunter Hutchinson Jr.
NYPD Red 3 - James Patterson   *m* 632

Baldwin, Max
Silken Threats - Addison Fox   *r* 966

Bantle, Peter
Karen Memory - Elizabeth Bear   *s* 1118

Butterfield, Walt
The Never-Open Desert Diner - James
    Anderson   *m* 478

Byrne, J.P.
The Good Chase - Hanna Martine   *r* 1024

Carrick, Thomas
The Tempting of Thomas Carrick - Stephanie
    Laurens   *r* 1005

de Kruk, Augustus
Hiss and Tell - Claire Donally   *m* 536

Grimm
Armageddon Rules - J.C. Nelson   *f* 86

Hamilton, Jason
All He Wants for Christmas - Lisa
    Plumley   *r* 1048

Hampton, Scott
Bone to Be Wild - Carolyn Haines   *m* 564

Hartwell, Dante
What a Lady Needs for Christmas - Grace
    Burrowes   *r* 935

Henry, Charlie
Grave Consequences - David Thurlo   *m* 673

Iswander, Lee
Blood of the Cosmos - Kevin J.
    Anderson   *s* 1104

Jessup, Cooper
The Perfect Homecoming - Julia London   *r* 1013

Kern, Ursula
Garden of Lies - Amanda Quick   *r* 1051

Kessler, Rob
The Night Belongs to Fireman - Jennifer
Bernard   *r* 913

Loren
The Last Good Paradise - Tatjana Soli   *c* 865

Malone, Cotton
The Patriot Threat - Steve Berry   *m* 490

Marv
The Drop - Dennis Lehane   *c* 788

Masters, Luke
Snowstorm Confessions - Rachel Lee   *r* 1009

Matekoni, J.L.B.
The Handsome Man's De Luxe Cafe - Alexander
McCall Smith   *c* 864

McCane, George
Fate Moreland's Widow - John Lane   *t* 197

Messenger, Gabriel
Ark Storm - Linda Davies   *c* 727

Olsen, Lester
Private Vegas - James Patterson   *c* 826

Pearce, Troy
Blue Warrior - Mike Maden   *c* 795

Perlmutter, Lev
The Empire of the Senses - Alexis Landau   *t* 196

Rafferty, Castor
His Reluctant Cinderella - Jessica
Gilmore   *r* 971

Severson, Ted
The Kind Worth Killing - Peter Swanson   *m* 670

Sinclair, Wesley III
Antiques Swap - Barbara Allan   *m* 477

Sweeney, Gordon
Grave Consequences - David Thurlo   *m* 673

Tiffany, Louis
Tiffany Girl - Deeanne Gist   *i* 403

Tiranno, Michael
Black Scorpion - Jon Land   *m* 596

Troyer, Reuben
An Empty Cup - Sarah Price   *i* 449

Walt
The Dress Shop of Dreams - Menna van
Praag   *c* 878

West, Duncan
Never Judge a Lady by Her Cover - Sarah
MacLean   *r* 1014

Whittmore, Freman
Second Chances - Sarah Price   *i* 450

BUSINESSWOMAN

Archer, Kate
Carousel Seas - Sharon Lee   *f* 72

Bentley, Olivia
He's So Fine - Jill Shalvis   *r* 1075

Bitler, Sarah
Where Secrets Sleep - Marta Perry   *i* 444

Bradley, Colleen
Driving with the Top Down - Beth
Harbison   *c* 761

Brannigan, Penny
Slated for Death - Elizabeth J. Duncan   *m* 537

Breeland, Robyn
Loving Dallas - Caisey Quinn   *c* 839

Buchanan, Daisy
Lie of the Needle - Cate Price   *m* 636

Cafferty, Danni
The Dead Play On - Heather Graham   *m* 560

Castleton, Clara
His Reluctant Cinderella - Jessica
Gilmore   *r* 971

Chambers, Chelsea
Miracle at the Higher Grounds Cafe - Max
Lucado   *i* 430

Chambers Perry, Izzy
A Finely Knit Murder - Sally
Goldenbaum   *m* 557

Charles, Sara
Angel in Armani - Melanie Scott   *r* 1072

Charlotte
Twisted Threads - Lea Wait   *m* 678

Cherry, Cynthia
The Final Reveille - Amanda Flower   *m* 547

Cooper, Mel
Dark Chocolate Demise - Jenn McKinlay   *m* 616

D'Alisa, Juliette
Reservations for Two - Hillary Manton
Lodge   *i* 428

DeLaura, Angie
Dark Chocolate Demise - Jenn McKinlay   *m* 616

Donovan, Maura
An Early Wake - Sheila Connolly   *m* 520

Hadley, Ellen
A Catered Mother's Day - Isis Crawford   *m* 523

Hayden, Tracy
A Perfect Catch - Anna Sugden   *r* 1090

Hopkirk, Victoria
Slated for Death - Elizabeth J. Duncan   *m* 537

Hui, Brianna
The Exile - C.T. Adams   *f* 3

Keegan, Caroline
Butternut Summer - Mary McNear   *c* 802

LeFaye, Ella Mae
Lemon Pies and Little White Lies - Ellery
Adams   *m* 475

Lewis, Dana
A Healthy Homicide - Staci McLaughlin   *m* 617

Lilian
Sweetshop of Dreams - Jenny Colgan   *c* 715

Locks, Marissa
Armageddon Rules - J.C. Nelson   *f* 86

McAlister, Liv
Heaven Help Heidi - Sally John   *i* 422

Mellon, Bebe
Manhattan in Miniature - Margaret Grace   *m* 558

Miller, Lindsay
No Christmas Like the Present - Sierra
Donovan   *r* 955

Parsons, Jenna
House of Wonder - Sarah Healy   *c* 763

Ricardo, Lucinda "Lucy"
Ghost in the Guacamole - Sue Ann
Jaffarian   *m* 582

Ricardo, Ricarda "Rikki"
Ghost in the Guacamole - Sue Ann
Jaffarian   *m* 582

Sloan, Heather
Echo Lake - Carla Neggers   *r* 1040

Sparks, Etta
The Dress Shop of Dreams - Menna van
Praag   *c* 878

Strafford, Danielle "Danni"
He's No Prince Charming - Elle Daniels   *r* 949

Waverley, Claire
First Frost - Sarah Addison Allen   *c* 689

Williams, Jane
The Look of Love - Sarah Jio   *c* 775

Winn, Peggy
A Wee Murder in My Shop - Fran Stewart   *m* 667

CANCER PATIENT

Adam
The Children Act - Ian McEwan   *c* 800

Bellamy, Gina
A Hundred Pieces of Me - Lucy Dillon   *c* 731

Jane
Lizzy and Jane - Katherine Reay   *r* 1056

Louis
This Is the Life - Alex Shearer   *c* 862

Reilly, Sterling
Night Blindness - Susan Strecker   *c* 870

Richmond, Daisy
Before I Go - Colleen Oakley   *c* 820

Vicky
Betrayed - Lisa Scottoline   *c* 857

CAPTIVE

Braden, Garin
Death Mask - Alex Archer   *f* 5

Brierly
Waking Beauty - Sarah E. Morin   *i* 438

Dethan
Cursed by Fire - Jacquelyn Frank   *f* 36

Garreth
Cursed by Ice - Jacquelyn Frank   *f* 35

Johnson, Jay
Fifty Mice - Daniel Pyne   *c* 838

Kev
*Your Fathers, Where Are They? And the Prophets,
Do They Live Forever?* - Dave Eggers   *c* 738

Mar, Rowan
Heir of Hope - Morgan L. Busse   *i* 368

McDougal, Abigail
My Heart Stood Still - Lori Copeland   *i* 387

McDougal, Amelia
My Heart Stood Still - Lori Copeland   *i* 387

McDougal, Anne-Marie
My Heart Stood Still - Lori Copeland   *i* 387

CAREGIVER

Blackland, Daniel
Pacific Fire - Greg van Eekhout   *f* 118

Ellison, Tim
Sweet Damage - Rebecca James   *c* 773

Galdon, Mia
Return to Me - Kelly Moran   *r* 1038

Hopkins, Rosie
Sweetshop of Dreams - Jenny Colgan   *c* 715

Jones, Mila
Moonlight on Butternut Lake - Mary
McNear   *r* 1034

Mason, Carly Jo
Together with You - Victoria Bylin   *i* 370

CARPENTER (continued)

Nabila
The Stager - Susan Coll *c* 716

Ruth "Mammy"
Ruth's Journey: The Authorized Novel of Mammy from Margaret Mitchell's Gone with the Wind - Donald McCaig *t* 210

Unnamed
Dear Thief - Samantha Harvey *c* 762

Unnamed Character
This Is the Life - Alex Shearer *c* 862

CARPENTER

Chastain, David
A Stranger's Secret - Laurie Alice Eakes *i* 394

Whiting, Nick
Where Secrets Sleep - Marta Perry *i* 444

CASTAWAY

Kimei, Akira
Castaway Planet - Eric Flint *s* 1146

Kimei, Caroline
Castaway Planet - Eric Flint *s* 1146

Kimei, Hitomi
Castaway Planet - Eric Flint *s* 1146

Kimei, Laura
Castaway Planet - Eric Flint *s* 1146

Kimei, Melody
Castaway Planet - Eric Flint *s* 1146

Kimei, Sakura
Castaway Planet - Eric Flint *s* 1146

Whips
Castaway Planet - Eric Flint *s* 1146

CAT

Diesel
Arsenic and Old Books - Miranda James *m* 583

Elvis
Buy a Whisker - Sofie Ryan *m* 650

Ernesto
Kittens Can Kill - Clea Simon *m* 659

Hannibal
The Viscount Who Lived Down the Lane - Elizabeth Boyle *r* 924

Misto
The Cat, the Devil, the Last Escape - Pat J.J. Murphy *m* 623

Paris
Checked Out - Elaine Viets *m* 677

Sand Shadow
Artemis Invaded - Jane M. Lindskold *s* 1169

Shadow
Hiss and Tell - Claire Donally *m* 536

Tango
Marked Fur Murder - Dixie Lyle *m* 609

CHESS PLAYER

Fischer, Bobby
Back Channel - Stephen L. Carter *c* 709

Smyslov, Vasily
Back Channel - Stephen L. Carter *c* 709

CHILD

Allen, Hollie
An Amish Man of Ice Mountain - Kelly Long *i* 429

Dorotea
Wolf Winter - Cecilia Ekback *t* 152

Mariah
First Frost - Sarah Addison Allen *c* 689

Unnamed Character
Sabotaged - Dani Pettrey *i* 446

Will
Surrender - June Gray *r* 977

Wolfie
The Witch of the Wood - Michael Aronovitz *h* 280

CHILD OF DIVORCED PARENTS

Thomas, Odd
Saint Odd - Dean Koontz *c* 785

CHILD-CARE GIVER

Mauvais, Devyn
Make You Remember - Macy Beckett *r* 911

McLain, Harley
Final Lap - Erin McCarthy *r* 1027

CLASSMATE

Anderson, Tyler
The Dead Play On - Heather Graham *m* 560

Bates, Linda
Time of Death - Mark Billingham *m* 491

Cafferty, Danni
The Dead Play On - Heather Graham *m* 560

Dex
Friendswood - Rene Steinke *c* 869

Foster, Ivy
Death of a Cupcake Queen - Lee Hollis *m* 577

Harper, Annabelle
Sunflower Lane - Jill Gregory *r* 978

Jackson, Cassie
Be Not Afraid - Cecilia Galante *h* 300

Levine, Sophie
Electric City - Elizabeth Rosner *t* 237

Longboat, Martin
Electric City - Elizabeth Rosner *t* 237

Marin
Be Not Afraid - Cecilia Galante *h* 300

McPhee, Wes
Sunflower Lane - Jill Gregory *r* 978

Merryweather, Sabrina
Death of a Cupcake Queen - Lee Hollis *m* 577

Palwick, Lydia
Harrison Squared - Daryl Gregory *h* 306

Powell, Hayley
Death of a Cupcake Queen - Lee Hollis *m* 577

Temple, Nykki
Death of a Cupcake Queen - Lee Hollis *m* 577

Watson, Arnie
The Dead Play On - Heather Graham *m* 560

Weeks, Helen
Time of Death - Mark Billingham *m* 491

Willa
Friendswood - Rene Steinke *c* 869

CLERK

Beck, Emma Miller
Up the Hill to Home - Jennifer Bort Yacovissi *t* 275

David
You're Not Much Use to Anyone - David Shapiro *c* 861

CLIENT

Cateman Kingsley, Elizabeth
Checked Out - Elaine Viets *m* 677

Frankel, Morrie
Phantom Angel - David Handler *m* 567

Heyward, Colton
Lowcountry Boneyard - Susan M. Boyer *m* 500

Jones, Jeb
Cover Your Eyes - Mary Burton *r* 938

Jones, Lexy
Chasing Sunsets - Karen Kingsbury *i* 425

Novak, Kevin
What the Fly Saw - Frankie Y. Bailey *m* 483

Rafferty, Polly
His Reluctant Cinderella - Jessica Gilmore *r* 971

Seymour, Sage
Shopaholic to the Stars - Sophie Kinsella *c* 784

Stonechurch, Ann
This Gun for Hire - Jo Goodman *r* 973

Stonechurch, Ramsey
This Gun for Hire - Jo Goodman *r* 973

Taylor, Madison
The Readaholics and the Falcon Fiasco - Laura DiSilverio *m* 535

CO-WORKER

Barnhouse, Spencer
The Witch at Sparrow Creek - Josh Kent *h* 324

Beecham, Mariah
Darian Hunter: Duke of Desire - Carole Mortimer *r* 1039

Brennan, Dr. Temperance "Tempe"
Bones Never Lie - Kathy Reichs *c* 843

Brigid
Terminal White - James Axler *s* 1109

Mrs. Burns
February Fever - Jess Lourey *m* 607

Callahan, Isaiah
Untraceable - Elizabeth Goddard *i* 404

Carpenter, Sabina
The Body Snatchers Affair - Marcia Muller *t* 218

Collins, Packie
The Thing About December - Donal Ryan *c* 850

Cooper, Mel
Dark Chocolate Demise - Jenn McKinlay *m* 616

DeLaura, Angie
Dark Chocolate Demise - Jenn McKinlay *m* 616

Dillinger, Marcus
Chasing Sunsets - Karen Kingsbury *i* 425

Falk, Jim
The Witch at Sparrow Creek - Josh Kent *h* 324

Grant
Terminal White - James Axler *s* 1109

Hawkins, Martha
The Witch Hunter's Tale - Sam Thomas *t* 260

Hodgson, Bridget
The Witch Hunter's Tale - Sam Thomas *t* 260

Hollands, Sam
Behind Closed Doors - Elizabeth Haynes *m* 571

Hunter, Darian
Darian Hunter: Duke of Desire - Carole Mortimer *r* 1039

Jacobson, Winter
Caged in Winter - Brighton Walsh *r* 1095

James, Mira
February Fever - Jess Lourey *m* 607

Jillian
Jillian - Halle Butler *c* 707

Kane
Terminal White - James Axler *s* 1109

Kidd, Thomas
Pasha: A Kydd Sea Adventure - Julian Stockwin *t* 255

Lassair
Blood of the South - Alys Clare *t* 141

Makutsi, Grace
The Handsome Man's De Luxe Cafe - Alexander McCall Smith *c* 864

Maxwell, Cade
Caged in Winter - Brighton Walsh *r* 1095

Megan
Jillian - Halle Butler *c* 707

Morales, Drew
Deadly Spells - Jaye Wells *f* 121

Prospero, Kate
Deadly Spells - Jaye Wells *f* 121

Quincannon, John
The Body Snatchers Affair - Marcia Muller *t* 218

Ramotswe, Precious
The Handsome Man's De Luxe Cafe - Alexander McCall Smith *c* 864

Rollo
Blood of the South - Alys Clare *t* 141

Russo, Salvatore
Falcon - Ronie Kendig *i* 423

Ryan, Andrew
Bones Never Lie - Kathy Reichs *c* 843

Schaeffer, Aidan
Dark Bride - Jonathan Ryan *h* 340

Schroder, Carl
Five Minutes Alone - Paul Cleave *c* 714

Tate, Theodore
Five Minutes Alone - Paul Cleave *c* 714

Walker, Cassandra
Falcon - Ronie Kendig *i* 423

Warren, Cade
Untraceable - Elizabeth Goddard *i* 404

Warren, Heidi
Untraceable - Elizabeth Goddard *i* 404

COLLEAGUE

Anstruther, Kate
The Shadow Revolution - Clay Griffith *h* 307

Archer, Simon
The Shadow Revolution - Clay Griffith *h* 307

Atkinson, Kelly
Fatal Trauma - Richard L. Mabry *i* 432

Baker, Dr. Mark
Fatal Trauma - Richard L. Mabry *i* 432

Barker, Nick
The Shadow Revolution - Clay Griffith *h* 307

Belhaj, Fatima
The Convert's Song - Sebastian Rotella *c* 849

Bettelheim, Phillip
The First Bad Man - Miranda July *c* 778

Blackmer, Jefferson
The Missing - Una McCormack *s* 1175

Bosch, Harry
The Burning Room - Michael Connelly *c* 718

Boylan, Hugh "Blazes"
Whatever Happened to Molly Bloom? - Jessica Stirling *t* 254

Brannigan, Penny
Slated for Death - Elizabeth J. Duncan *m* 537

Breen, Cathal
The Kings of London - William Shaw *m* 657

Brink, Adam
Edge of Betrayal - Shannon K. Butcher *r* 939

Brown, Mason
Deadly Obsession - Maggie Shayne *r* 1081
Innocent Prey - Maggie Shayne *r* 1080

Buchanan, Polly
The Laws of Murder - Charles Finch *c* 743

Burns, Don
The Winter Foundlings - Kate Rhodes *m* 643

Cady, Drew
The Lynchpin - Jeffrey B. Burton *m* 507

Cafferty, Danni
The Dead Play On - Heather Graham *m* 560

Carlson, Charlie
Lethal Beauty - Lis Wiehl *i* 470

Charles, Marcus
A Woman Unknown - Frances Brody *t* 134

Cheney, Dick
The Global War on Morris - Steve Israel *c* 772

Cole, Elvis
The Promise - Robert Crais *c* 720

Creed, Annja
Death Mask - Alex Archer *f* 5

Crusher, Beverly
The Missing - Una McCormack *s* 1175

Dallington, Lord John
The Laws of Murder - Charles Finch *c* 743

Dan
Getting Even - Sarah Rayner *c* 842

de Luca, Rachel
Deadly Obsession - Maggie Shayne *r* 1081
Innocent Prey - Maggie Shayne *r* 1080

Diamond, Jacob "Jake"
Circling the Runway - J.L. Abramo *m* 474

Everston, Laurel
Double Cross - DiAnn Mills *i* 436

Flint, Michael
The Whispering - Sarah Rayne *h* 336

Glickman, Cheryl
The First Bad Man - Miranda July *c* 778

Hilton, Daniel
Double Cross - DiAnn Mills *i* 436

Holmes, Sherlock
Moriarty - Anthony Horowitz *c* 771
Sherlock Holmes, the Missing Years: Japan - Vasudev Murthy *t* 219

Hopkirk, Victoria
Slated for Death - Elizabeth J. Duncan *m* 537

James, Scott
The Promise - Robert Crais *c* 720

Johnson, Bruno
The Replacements - David Putnam *m* 637

Jones, Emmett
Mr. Jones - Margaret Sweatman *t* 256

Jund, Roland
The Lynchpin - Jeffrey B. Burton *m* 507

Kaspary, Beatrice
Five - Ursula Archer *c* 693

Kelly, Jill
The Striver - Stephen Solomita *m* 662

Kinsella, Jim
Whatever Happened to Molly Bloom? - Jessica Stirling *t* 254

Kody, Bran
Master of Plagues - E.L. Tettensor *f* 116

Laren, Ro
The Missing - Una McCormack *s* 1175

Lee, Cassandra
Deadeye - William C. Dietz *s* 1136

LeMaire
The Laws of Murder - Charles Finch *c* 743

Lenoir, Nicolas
Master of Plagues - E.L. Tettensor *f* 116

Lenox, Charles
The Laws of Murder - Charles Finch *c* 743

Littlewood, Boots
The Striver - Stephen Solomita *m* 662

Machin, Tom
Whatever Happened to Molly Bloom? - Jessica Stirling *t* 254

Maggie
The Promise - Robert Crais *c* 720

Merchant, Sasha
Girl Before a Mirror - Liza Palmer *r* 1047

Morgan, Deke
Cover Your Eyes - Mary Burton *r* 938

Norfield, John
Mr. Jones - Margaret Sweatman *t* 256

Omo, Ras
Deadeye - William C. Dietz *s* 1136

Pescatore, Valentine
The Convert's Song - Sebastian Rotella *c* 849

Pike, Joe
The Promise - Robert Crais *c* 720

Quentin, Dr. Alice
The Winter Foundlings - Kate Rhodes *m* 643

Quinn, Mia
Lethal Beauty - Lis Wiehl *i* 470

Quinn, Michael
The Dead Play On - Heather Graham *m* 560

Ridley, Ellen
Blood Ties - Nicholas Guild *m* 562

Rivers, Rodney
Oh Say Can You Fudge - Nancy Coco *m* 518

Roman, Darlene
Circling the Runway - J.L. Abramo *m* 474

Rousseau, Richard
Asylum - Jeannette de Beauvoir *m* 529

Roux
Death Mask - Alex Archer *f* 5

Rove, Karl
The Global War on Morris - Steve Israel *c* 772

Sage, Mira
Edge of Betrayal - Shannon K. Butcher *r* 939

Sam
Blood Ties - Nicholas Guild *m* 562

Sanchez, Sandy
Hush Hush - Laura Lippman *m* 604

Schulte, Henry
Oh Say Can You Fudge - Nancy Coco *m* 518

Shackleton, Kate
A Woman Unknown - Frances Brody *t* 134

Soto, Lucia "Lucky"
The Burning Room - Michael Connelly *c* 718

Tomoatooah
Karen Memory - Elizabeth Bear *s* 1118

Tozer, Helen
The Kings of London - William Shaw *m* 657

Trumbull, Victoria
Poison Ivy - Cynthia Riggs *m* 644

Wainwright, Rachel
Cover Your Eyes - Mary Burton *r* 938

Watson, John
Moriarty - Anthony Horowitz *c* 771

Watson, Dr. John
Sherlock Holmes, the Missing Years: Japan - Vasudev Murthy *t* 219

Wenninger, Florin
Five - Ursula Archer *c* 693

West, Nell
The Whispering - Sarah Rayne *h* 336

Wicks, Barbara
The Replacements - David Putnam *m* 637

Wilmington, Morton
Double Cross - DiAnn Mills *i* 436

Wilson, Thackery
Poison Ivy - Cynthia Riggs *m* 644

Wyatt, Anna
Girl Before a Mirror - Liza Palmer *r* 1047

COLLECTOR

Freemont, Rose
Shadow of a Spout - Amanda Cooper *m* 521

Garcia, Juan
Cuba Straits - Randy Wayne White *m* 681

COMPANION

Adara
Artemis Invaded - Jane M. Lindskold *s* 1169

Akina
Forge of Ashes - Josh Vogt *f* 120

Bard, Delilah "Lila"
A Darker Shade of Magic - V.E. Schwab *f* 105

Bathu, Thorn
Half the World - Joe Abercrombie *f* 2

Bella
A Killer Retreat - Tracy Weber *m* 679

Boudain, Gwen
Ark Storm - Linda Davies *c* 727

Bradley, Colleen
Driving with the Top Down - Beth Harbison *c* 761

Brand
Half the World - Joe Abercrombie *f* 2

Camalier, Bitty
Driving with the Top Down - Beth Harbison *c* 761

Caulfield, Eleanor
I Loved a Rogue - Katharine Ashe *r* 903

Davidson, Kate
A Killer Retreat - Tracy Weber *m* 679

Dent, Howie
Whiskers of the Lion - P.L. Gaus *m* 555

Duckweed, Poplock
Phoenix in Shadow - Ryk E. Spoor *f* 108

Ernesto
Kittens Can Kill - Clea Simon *m* 659

Etta
Emma and Otto and Russell and James - Emma Hooper *c* 769

Flavius
The Sword of Attila - David Gibbins *t* 163

Harlan
As Night Falls - Jenny Milchman *m* 619

Hughes, Jenna
A Good Rogue Is Hard to Find - Kelly Bowen *r* 921

Jacobsen, Dan
Ark Storm - Linda Davies *c* 727

James
Emma and Otto and Russell and James - Emma Hooper *c* 769

Jia
Crouching Tiger, Forbidden Vampire - Kerrelyn Sparks *r* 1086

Kell
A Darker Shade of Magic - V.E. Schwab *f* 105

Kendall, Sophia
The Shattered Court - M.J. Scott *f* 106

Kern, Ursula
Garden of Lies - Amanda Quick *r* 1051

Leigh, Biddy
An Appetite for Violets - Martine Bailey *t* 128

Mackenzie, Cameron
The Shattered Court - M.J. Scott *f* 106

Macrobius
The Sword of Attila - David Gibbins *t* 163

Nick
As Night Falls - Jenny Milchman *m* 619

Olgun
Covenant's End - Ari Marmell *f* 78

Ondorum
Forge of Ashes - Josh Vogt *f* 120

Peter
Plague Land - S.D. Sykes *t* 257

Roxton, Slater
Garden of Lies - Amanda Quick *r* 1051

Russell
Crouching Tiger, Forbidden Vampire - Kerrelyn Sparks *r* 1086

Sam
The Look of Love - Sarah Jio *c* 775
Pacific Fire - Greg van Eekhout *f* 118

Sand Shadow
Artemis Invaded - Jane M. Lindskold *s* 1169

Silverun, Tobimar
Phoenix in Shadow - Ryk E. Spoor *f* 108

Taliesin
I Loved a Rogue - Katharine Ashe *r* 903

Tamara
Driving with the Top Down - Beth Harbison *c* 761

Vantage, Kyri
Phoenix in Shadow - Ryk E. Spoor *f* 108

Widdershins "Shins"
Covenant's End - Ari Marmell *f* 78

Williams, Jane
The Look of Love - Sarah Jio *c* 775

COMPUTER EXPERT

Johnson, Michael "MJ"
Nowhere to Hide - Sigmund Brouwer *i* 365

King, William
Nowhere to Hide - Sigmund Brouwer *i* 365

Oliver
Shutter - Courtney Alameda *h* 277

Oliver, Piper
Total Surrender - Rebecca Zanetti *r* 1100

Ramsayer, Rachel
Whiskers of the Lion - P.L. Gaus *m* 555

Santiago, Elizabeth
Corsair - James Cambias *s* 1122

Schwartz, David
Corsair - James Cambias *s* 1122

Tregear, Stephen
Blood Ties - Nicholas Guild *m* 562

Wyatt, Blake
Nowhere to Hide - Sigmund Brouwer *i* 365

Zuckerberg, Mark
The Infernal - Mark Doten *c* 734

CON ARTIST

Castille, Emma
Twisted - Cynthia Eden *r* 958

McDougal, Abigail
My Heart Stood Still - Lori Copeland *i* 387

McDougal, Amelia
My Heart Stood Still - Lori Copeland *i* 387

McDougal, Anne-Marie
My Heart Stood Still - Lori Copeland *i* 387

CONSTRUCTION WORKER

Marin, Sergio
A Root Awakening - Kate Collins *m* 519

CONSULTANT

Barrington, Stone
Paris Match - Stuart Woods *c* 889

Brandon, Luke
Shopaholic to the Stars - Sophie Kinsella *c* 784

Campbell, Allison
Dying Brand - Wendy Tyson *m* 675

Katya
A Pleasure and a Calling - Phil Hogan *m* 576

Mallory, Lincoln
Girl Before a Mirror - Liza Palmer *r* 1047

CONTRACTOR

Prince-Avery, Valentine
Deadly Desires at Honeychurch Hall - Hannah
Dennison m 532

Smith, Louisa "Lou"
Behind Closed Doors - Elizabeth Haynes m 571

CONTRACTOR

Collins, Russ
A Sticky Situation - Jessie Crockett m 525

Daggett, Brad
The Kind Worth Killing - Peter Swanson m 670

Jeff
The Fixer - Joseph Finder m 545

Lott, Griff
The Liar - Nora Roberts r 1059

Pearce, Troy
Blue Warrior - Mike Maden c 795

Whitshank, Junior
A Spool of Blue Thread - Anne Tyler c 875

CONVICT

Alls
Unbecoming - Rebecca Scherm c 855

Cowan, George
Hush - Karen Robards r 1058

Drake, Patrick
Sometimes the Wolf - Urban Waite c 882

Farrell, Steve
Manhunt - Lisa Phillips i 447

Graham, Riley
Unbecoming - Rebecca Scherm c 855

Gramaraye, Phinaeus "Finn"
Finn Fancy Necromancy - Randy
Henderson f 53

House, Edmund
My Sister's Grave - Robert Dugoni c 737

Jenkins, Janie
Dear Daughter - Elizabeth Little c 792

Johnson, Bruno
The Replacements - David Putnam m 637

Jones, Jeb
Cover Your Eyes - Mary Burton r 938

Karlsson, Josteinn
Someone to Watch Over Me - Yrsa
Sigurdardottir c 863

Phoenix
Believe - Erin McCarthy r 1026

Powers, Jerrell
Snow Way Out - Christine Husom m 579

COOK

DuBois, Sage
Ladle to the Grave - Connie Archer m 480

Elizabeth "Lizzy"
Lizzy and Jane - Katherine Reay r 1056

Ellison, Tim
Sweet Damage - Rebecca James c 773

Lamb, Piper
License to Dill - Mary Ellen Hughes m 578

Laurent, Julia
Tempting Donovan Ford - Jennifer
McKenzie r 1031

Leigh, Biddy
An Appetite for Violets - Martine Bailey t 128

Marcel
All the President's Menus - Julie Hyzy m 580

Maxwell, Cade
Caged in Winter - Brighton Walsh r 1095

Norwood, Baldwin
Killer Gourmet - G.A. McKevett m 615

Oosterling, Ava
Five-Alarm Fudge - Christine DeSmet m 534

Paras, Olivia
All the President's Menus - Julie Hyzy m 580

Ross, Emmalyn
As Waters Gone By - Cynthia Ruchti i 452

Sofi
The Last Kings of Sark - Rosa
Rankin-Gee c 840

Thomas, Odd
Saint Odd - Dean Koontz c 785

COUNSELOR

Kathryn
The Wednesday Group - Sylvia True c 873

Miller, Sadie
Part Time Cowboy - Maisey Yates r 1099

COURIER

Appleby, Adrian
The German Agent - J. Sydney Jones t 186

COUSIN

Anya
The Empty Throne - Cayla Kluver f 64

Baron Sutcliffe
Secrets of a Scandalous Heiress - Theresa
Romain r 1060

Bay
First Frost - Sarah Addison Allen c 689

Beasley, Daphne
Murder with a Twist - Tracy Kiely m 593

Braun, Anna-Grace
When Grace Sings - Kim Vogel Sawyer i 454

D'Artigo, Camille
Panther Prowling - Yasmine Galenorn h 301

D'Artigo, Delilah
Panther Prowling - Yasmine Galenorn h 301

D'Artigo, Menolly
Panther Prowling - Yasmine Galenorn h 301

Daniel
Panther Prowling - Yasmine Galenorn h 301

Edgar
When the Doves Disappeared - Sofi
Oksanen t 223

Elizabeth
Murder in the Queen's Wardrobe - Kathy Lynn
Emerson t 153

Elyse
Three Story House - Courtney Miller
Santo c 853

Everett, Josiah "Joss"
Secrets of a Scandalous Heiress - Theresa
Romain r 1060

Gilbride, Alastair "Alec"
How to Plan a Wedding for a Royal Spy - Vanessa
Kelly r 997

Illumina
The Empty Throne - Cayla Kluver f 64

Isobel
Three Story House - Courtney Miller
Santo c 853

Jace
You Were Mine - Abbi Glines c 751

Jacobs, Kirra
Sabotaged - Dani Pettrey i 446

Lanier, Lyse
The Creole Princess - Beth White i 468

Lizzie
Three Story House - Courtney Miller
Santo c 853

Mariah
First Frost - Sarah Addison Allen c 689

Martini, Nigel
Murder with a Twist - Tracy Kiely m 593

Marv
The Drop - Dennis Lehane c 788

Lady Mary
Murder in the Queen's Wardrobe - Kathy Lynn
Emerson t 153

Monroe, Lady Cassandra
The Accidental Countess - Valerie
Bowman r 923

Nancy
If the Viscount Falls - Sabrina Jeffries r 995

Newark, Tripp
You Were Mine - Abbi Glines c 751

Pendragon, Desmond
In the Time of the Dragon Moon - Janet Lee
Carey f 20

Pendragon, Jackrun
In the Time of the Dragon Moon - Janet Lee
Carey f 20

Penelope
The Accidental Countess - Valerie
Bowman r 923

Roland
When the Doves Disappeared - Sofi
Oksanen t 223

Saginowski, Bob
The Drop - Dennis Lehane c 788

Scarlet
The Creole Princess - Beth White i 468

Shoe
A Wee Murder in My Shop - Fran Stewart m 667

Stephen
The Siege Winter - Ariana Franklin t 159

Unnamed Character
Sabotaged - Dani Pettrey i 446

Vernon, Jane
If the Viscount Falls - Sabrina Jeffries r 995

Winn, Peggy
A Wee Murder in My Shop - Fran Stewart m 667

Zabriel
The Empty Throne - Cayla Kluver f 64

Zimmerman, Alexa
When Grace Sings - Kim Vogel Sawyer i 454

COW

Bovary, Elsie
Holy Cow - David Duchovny c 735

COWBOY/COWGIRL

Malone, Buck
Whenever You Come Around - Robin Lee Hatcher *i* 413

Monahan, Tru
Betting on Hope - Debra Clopton *i* 381

Porter, Jake
A Love Like Ours - Becky Wade *i* 466

COYOTE

James
Emma and Otto and Russell and James - Emma Hooper *c* 769

CRIME SUSPECT

Andrews, Derrick
Murder at Beechwood - Alyssa Maxwell *m* 612

Bantle, Peter
Karen Memory - Elizabeth Bear *s* 1118

Bates, Stephen
Time of Death - Mark Billingham *m* 491

Bathu, Thorn
Half the World - Joe Abercrombie *f* 2

Battle, Jeff
What Strange Creatures - Emily Arsenault *c* 695

Becker, Heinz
The Beige Man - Helene Tursten *m* 674

Beckham, Abe
Cane and Abe - James Grippando *c* 756

Bennett, Parker
The Melody Lingers On - Mary Higgins Clark *m* 515

Black, Zachary
The Spring Bride - Anne Gracie *r* 975

Blake, Morgan
The Cat, the Devil, the Last Escape - Pat J.J. Murphy *m* 623

Bloom, Leopold
Whatever Happened to Molly Bloom? - Jessica Stirling *t* 254

Boone, Walker
Demise in Denim - Duffy Brown *m* 504

Boylan, Hugh "Blazes"
Whatever Happened to Molly Bloom? - Jessica Stirling *t* 254

Calms, Swan
Where the Bones are Buried - Jeanne Matthews *m* 611

Cambridge, Kelsey
The Final Reveille - Amanda Flower *m* 547

Cameron, Robert Nelson
The Devil You Know - Elisabeth de Mariaffi *m* 530

Cartier, Andre
Dying for the Past - T.J. O'Connor *m* 625

Cates, Dallas
Endangered - C.J. Box *m* 499

Charlotte
Twisted Threads - Lea Wait *m* 678

Connelly, Jake
Finding Jake - Bryan Reardon *m* 639

Cooper, Cleo
Saving Cecil - Lee Mims *m* 620

Copperfield, Teagan
Once a Thief - Lora Young *i* 472

Curtis, Angie
Twisted Threads - Lea Wait *m* 678

Custer, Aaron
Slow Burn - Andrew Welsh-Huggins *m* 680

Lord Darley
Dreaming Spies - Laurie R. King *t* 192

Davidson, Kate
A Killer Retreat - Tracy Weber *m* 679

Edwards, Jason
The Forgetting Place - John Burley *m* 506

Feldstein, Morris
The Global War on Morris - Steve Israel *c* 772

Finch, Tory
Assault and Pepper - Leslie Budewitz *m* 505

Fitch, Roger
Nun Too Soon - Alice Loweecey *m* 608

Flaherty, Cam
Farmed and Dangerous - Edith Maxwell *m* 613

Fowler, Brad
Murder She Wrote: Killer in the Kitchen - Jessica Fletcher *m* 546

Freemont, Rose
Shadow of a Spout - Amanda Cooper *m* 521

Gardner, Lainie Davis
The Evil Deeds We Do - Robert S. Levinson *m* 602

Garkov, Nicolai
Losing Faith - Adam Mitzner *m* 621

Greaves, Apollo
Darling Beast - Elizabeth Hoyt *r* 989

Guenivere
Fatal Feast - Jay Ruud *t* 243

Hadley, Ellen
A Catered Mother's Day - Isis Crawford *m* 523

Haley, Philip
Long Way Down - Michael Sears *m* 654

Hare, William
Hare - Peter Ranscombe *t* 234

Harrington, Emily
Rising Tide - Patricia Twomey Ryan *m* 649

Hartley, Elizabeth
A Finely Knit Murder - Sally Goldenbaum *m* 557

Hathorne, Neal
Pleasantville - Attica Locke *m* 605

Hayley
One Foot in the Grape - Carlene O'Neil *m* 627

Heath, Caleb
Doing the Devil's Work - Bill Loehfelm *m* 606

Hodgson, Will
The Witch Hunter's Tale - Sam Thomas *t* 260

Holland, Sarie
Canary - Duane Swierczynski *m* 671

Holmes, Tim
Flourless to Stop Him - Nancy J. Parra *m* 631

Howard, Brian
Cold Trail - Janet Dawson *m* 528

Jack
Ladle to the Grave - Connie Archer *m* 480

Jakob
Someone to Watch Over Me - Yrsa Sigurdardottir *c* 863

James
Goodhouse - Peyton Marshall *c* 798

Jenkins, Janie
Dear Daughter - Elizabeth Little *c* 792

Jund, Roland
The Lynchpin - Jeffrey B. Burton *m* 507

Kelley, Jacob
Superposition - David Walton *s* 1205

Kenyon, Marian
Don't Go Home - Carolyn G. Hart *m* 569

Kershaw, Creed
Twisted Innocence - Terri Blackstock *i* 363

Leila
Allure of Deceit - Susan Froetschel *m* 553

Lewis, Dana
A Healthy Homicide - Staci McLaughlin *m* 617

Lockwood, Ian
No Place to Hide - Lynette Eason *i* 395

Lucy
Flesh and Blood - Patricia Cornwell *c* 719

MacPherson, Lisa
The Silent Sister - Diane Chamberlain *c* 710

McCane, George
Fate Moreland's Widow - John Lane *t* 197

Mercer, Raymond
The Convert's Song - Sebastian Rotella *c* 849

Miller, Ramsey
Before He Finds Her - Michael Kardos *m* 591

Molnar, Endre
Cafe Europa - Edward Ifkovic *t* 182

Pettersson, Anders
The Beige Man - Helene Tursten *m* 674

Rayne, Walter
Blood Ties - Nicholas Guild *m* 562

Salvatore, Antonio "Pinky"
Neighing with Fire - Kathryn O'Sullivan *m* 628

Sanders, Jimmy
A String of Beads - Thomas Perry *c* 827

Scofield, Max
Ming Tea Murder - Laura Childs *m* 514

Shoe
A Wee Murder in My Shop - Fran Stewart *m* 667

Sinclair, Arthur
Quartet for the End of Time - Johanna Skibsrud *t* 250

Singer, Marcy
Wicked Stitch - Amanda Lee *m* 597

Standley, Gerald
License to Dill - Mary Ellen Hughes *m* 578

Stone, Scarlett
Confessions - Cynthia Eden *r* 957

Swensen, Hannah
Double Fudge Brownie Murder - Joanne Fluke *m* 548

Swift, Sarah
Pride v. Prejudice - Joan Hess *m* 573

Treadway, Greg
The Fall - John T. Lescroart *m* 600

Trelawny Penvenan, Lady Morwenna
A Stranger's Secret - Laurie Alice Eakes *i* 394

Verovkin
A Love Like Blood - Marcus Sedgwick *t* 246

Wingate, Geoffrey
The Final Recollections of Charles Dickens - Thomas Hauser *t* 175

Character Description Index

CRIMINAL

CRITIC

CULT MEMBER

CYBORG

DANCER

Ingram, Alexander
Night Life - David C. Taylor *t* 258

Lenoir, Violette
The Dark Arts of Blood - Freda Warrington *h* 350

Walsh, Ginger
Back to Before - Tracy Solheim *r* 1084

DAUGHTER

Abbott, Nora
Tattered Legacy - Shannon Baker *m* 484

Adare
The Providence of Fire - Brian Staveley *f* 111

Akeldama, Prudence "Rue" Alessandra Maccon
Prudence - Gail Carriger *f* 22

Akina
Forge of Ashes - Josh Vogt *f* 120

Alanna
Hush Hush - Laura Lippman *m* 604

Alders, Lila
New Uses for Old Boyfriends - Beth Kendrick *r* 998

Allen, Hollie
An Amish Man of Ice Mountain - Kelly Long *i* 429

Amanda
A Spool of Blue Thread - Anne Tyler *c* 875

Anderson, Haley
It Had to Be Him - Tamra Baumann *r* 910

Andrea
Double Fudge Brownie Murder - Joanne Fluke *m* 548

Angela Rose
The Love Letters - Beverly Lewis *i* 427

Anna
Cold Spell - Deb Vanasse *c* 879

Athena
Cold Betrayal - J.A. Jance *m* 584

Aubrey, Anna
The Wood's Edge - Lori Benton *i* 360

Banning, Chloe
Silver Thaw - Catherine Anderson *r* 898

Barkes, Eliza
Never Mind Miss Fox - Olivia Glazebrook *c* 750

Barsham, Gina
Meadowlands - Elizabeth Jeffrey *t* 185

Barsham, Millie
Meadowlands - Elizabeth Jeffrey *t* 185

Bay
First Frost - Sarah Addison Allen *c* 689

Bayles, China
Bittersweet - Susan Wittig Albert *m* 476

Beasley, Daphne
Murder with a Twist - Tracy Kiely *m* 593

Becky
Taken - Dee Henderson *i* 417

Beiler, Sarah
The Witnesses - Linda Byler *i* 369

Bekatha
Desert God - Wilbur Smith *t* 252

Bethany
Goodhouse - Peyton Marshall *c* 798

Blair, Rebecca
The Children's Crusade - Ann Packer *t* 224

Blake, Sammie
The Cat, the Devil, the Last Escape - Pat J.J. Murphy *m* 623

Bloom, Milly
Whatever Happened to Molly Bloom? - Jessica Stirling *t* 254

Borne, Brandy
Antiques Swap - Barbara Allan *m* 477

Bradley, Grace
The Secrets of Midwives - Sally Hepworth *c* 765

Bradley, Neva
The Secrets of Midwives - Sally Hepworth *c* 765

Cabot, Grace
The Devil Takes a Bride - Julia London *r* 1012

Cabot, Honor
The Devil Takes a Bride - Julia London *r* 1012

Cabot, Mercy
The Devil Takes a Bride - Julia London *r* 1012

Cabot, Prudence
The Devil Takes a Bride - Julia London *r* 1012

Campbell, Ava
The Wonder of All Things - Jason Mott *c* 812

Campbell, Iona
Hot Blooded - Donna Grant *r* 976

Carla Scout
Hush Hush - Laura Lippman *m* 604

Caron
Pride v. Prejudice - Joan Hess *m* 573

Carter, Aimee
Last One Home - Debbie Macomber *c* 794

Carter, Cassie
Last One Home - Debbie Macomber *c* 794

Celeste
The Amado Women - Desiree Zamorano *c* 892

Chloe
In the Woods - Merry Jones *m* 587

Clee
The First Bad Man - Miranda July *c* 778

Connelly, Laney
Finding Jake - Bryan Reardon *m* 639

Cooper, Shelby Jane
There Will Be Lies - Nick Lake *f* 66

Cramer, Lily
Twisted Innocence - Terri Blackstock *i* 363

Crane, Gia
When We Fall - Emily Liebert *c* 791

Cross, Janelle "Jannie"
Hope to Die - James Patterson *c* 824

D'Alisa, Juliette
Reservations for Two - Hillary Manton Lodge *i* 428

Dahaba
Hiding in Plain Sight - Nuruddin Farah *c* 741

Daphne
The Cavendon Women - Barbara Taylor Bradford *t* 133

Davenport, Letty
Gathering Prey - John Sandford *m* 652

de Quincey, Emily
Inspector of the Dead - David Morrell *t* 214

DeLacy
The Cavendon Women - Barbara Taylor Bradford *t* 133

Delancey, Lucy
Tangled Lives - Hilary Boyd *c* 705

Delancey, Marsha
Tangled Lives - Hilary Boyd *c* 705

Diedre
The Cavendon Women - Barbara Taylor Bradford *t* 133

Dobbs, Maisie
A Dangerous Place - Jacqueline Winspear *t* 273

Dollbaby
Dollbaby - Laura McNeal *c* 801

Dorotea
Wolf Winter - Cecilia Ekback *t* 152

Dresner, Dalia
The Lady from Zagreb - Philip Kerr *t* 191

Dulcie
The Cavendon Women - Barbara Taylor Bradford *t* 133

Duvall, Lady Aramina
Of Silk and Steam - Bec McMaster *r* 1033

Elisabetta
An Italian Wife - Ann Hood *c* 768

Ellen
Ruth's Journey: The Authorized Novel of Mammy from Margaret Mitchell's Gone with the Wind - Donald McCaig *t* 210

Elsa
The Stager - Susan Coll *c* 716

Emily
The Mill River Redemption - Darcie Chan *c* 711

Esme
It Won't Always Be This Great - Peter Mehlman *c* 803

Farabee, Maddie
Bridges Burned - Annette Dashofy *m* 527

Frederika
Wolf Winter - Cecilia Ekback *t* 152

Freya
Aurora - Kim Stanley Robinson *s* 1191

Frye, Sybilla
The Sacrifice - Joyce Carol Oates *c* 821

Fynn, Maddie
When - Victoria Laurie *f* 70

Gibbons, Kendra
Signature Kill - David Levien *m* 601

Gibbs, Jen
The Story Keeper - Lisa Wingate *c* 887

Goodwin, Karen
Last One Home - Debbie Macomber *c* 794

Hansen, LeeAnn
The Cowboy SEAL - Laura Marie Altom *r* 897

Hansen, Millie
The Cowboy SEAL - Laura Marie Altom *r* 897

Hardy, Rebecca
The Fall - John T. Lescroart *m* 600

Hargrave, Sarah
The Masque of a Murderer - Susanna Calkins *m* 510

Hastings, Miriam
A Harvest of Hope - Lauraine Snelling *i* 459

Havnel, Bea
Last to Know - Elizabeth Adler *c* 685

Hedge, Sophy
The Language of Paradise - Barbara Klein Moss *t* 217

Helsing, Micheline
Shutter - Courtney Alameda *h* 277

Smith, Sophia
Strands of Sorrow - John Ringo *s* 1190

Smithson, Melinda "Mellie"
50 Ways to Ruin a Rake - Jade Lee *r* 1007

Stanford, Kat
Deadly Desires at Honeychurch Hall - Hannah Dennison *m* 532

Stonechurch, Ann
This Gun for Hire - Jo Goodman *r* 973

Summer
His Reluctant Cinderella - Jessica Gilmore *r* 971

Susan
Em and the Big Hoom - Jerry Pinto *c* 831

Swensen, Hannah
Double Fudge Brownie Murder - Joanne Fluke *m* 548

Sylvia
The Amado Women - Desiree Zamorano *c* 892

Sylvie
Cold Spell - Deb Vanasse *c* 879

Tehuti
Desert God - Wilbur Smith *t* 252

Thompson, Abby
Full Throttle - Julie Ann Walker *r* 1093

Tremaine, Lady Elinor "Norrie"
Lady Elinor's Wicked Adventures - Lillian Marek *r* 1020

Tremaine, Penny
Together with You - Victoria Bylin *i* 370

Troyer, Elizabeth "Lissy"
The Proposal at Siesta Key - Shelley Shepard Gray *i* 406

Troyer, Penny
The Proposal at Siesta Key - Shelley Shepard Gray *i* 406

Turner, Lexi
Falling Hard - HelenKay Dimon *r* 954

Unger, Deirdre
Night Night, Sleep Tight - Hallie Ephron *m* 541

Unnamed Character
Sabotaged - Dani Pettrey *i* 446
The Woman Who Read Too Much - Bahiyyih Nakhjavani *t* 220

Ursula
The Talon of the Hawk - Jeffe Kennedy *f* 62

Uziel, Audra
It Won't Always Be This Great - Peter Mehlman *c* 803

Valentina
An Italian Wife - Ann Hood *c* 768

Vermast, Tine
From Bruges with Love - Pieter Aspe *m* 482

Voith, Lillie Beck
Up the Hill to Home - Jennifer Bort Yacovissi *t* 275

Walldeen, Klara
The Swimmer - Joakim Zander *c* 893

Wallin, Beth
Would-Be Wilderness Wife - Regina Scott *r* 1074

Waltham, Twyla
The First Kiss - Grace Burrowes *r* 932

Webster, Morgan
There Must Be Some Mistake - Frederick Barthelme *c* 697

Wilder, Isabella
Sweet Surprise - Candis Terry *r* 1091

Zimmerman, Alexa
When Grace Sings - Kim Vogel Sawyer *i* 454

DEAF PERSON

Ally
The Silence - Tim Lebbon *h* 330

Cooper, Shelby Jane
There Will Be Lies - Nick Lake *f* 66

DEALER

Henry
Prague Summer - Jeffrey Condran *c* 717

DEBUTANTE

Carstairs, Eloisa
Deception on Sable Hill - Shelley Gray *i* 408

Tempest, Lavinia
The Viscount Who Lived Down the Lane - Elizabeth Boyle *r* 924

Wembley, Sophie
The Earl I Adore - Erin Knightley *r* 1001

Westmore, Clare
Diary of an Accidental Wallflower - Jennifer McQuiston *r* 1036

DEFENDANT

Makari, Hasan
Detained - Don Brown *i* 366

Makari, Najib
Detained - Don Brown *i* 366

DEITY

Athene
The Chosen Prince - Diane Stanley *f* 110

Ceridwen
Firestorm - Nancy Holzner *h* 318

Lord Draconus
Fall of Light - Steven Erikson *f* 30

Gaios
The Conquering Dark - Clay Griffith *h* 308

Mother Darkness
Fall of Light - Steven Erikson *f* 30

Namara
Darkened Blade - Kelly McCullough *f* 79

Olgun
Covenant's End - Ari Marmell *f* 78

Weysa
Cursed by Fire - Jacquelyn Frank *f* 36
Cursed by Ice - Jacquelyn Frank *f* 35

Zeus
The Chosen Prince - Diane Stanley *f* 110

DEMON

Adam
Soulbound - Kristen Callihan *f* 19

Burg
Hellhole - Gina Damico *h* 290

Devil
The Devil's Game - Daniel Patterson *i* 443

Lord Draconus
Fall of Light - Steven Erikson *f* 30

Gautier, Nick
Instinct - Sherrilyn Kenyon *h* 325

Malnefoley
Hunted Warrior - Lindsey Piper *f* 95

Semyaza
Guardian - Erik Williams *h* 354

Torin
The Darkest Touch - Gena Showalter *r* 1082

DESIGNER

Chance, Mirabelle
Paris Match - Stuart Woods *c* 889

Chanel, Gabrielle "Coco"
Mademoiselle Chanel - C.W. Gortner *t* 167

Kelly, Nora
Of Irish Blood - Mary Pat Kelly *t* 188

Morris, Chelsea
Miles from Nowhere - Amy Clipston *i* 379

Night, Madison
With Vics You Get Eggroll - Diane Vallere *m* 676

Peabody, Miss Harriet
After a Fashion - Jen Turano *i* 465

Raf
Glow - Ned Beauman *c* 699

Sloan, Heather
Echo Lake - Carla Neggers *r* 1040

Standish, Allison
Where Secrets Sleep - Marta Perry *i* 444

DETECTIVE

Becker
Inspector of the Dead - David Morrell *t* 214

Carrigan, Jack
Eleven Days - Stav Sherez *m* 658

Chase, Frederick
Moriarty - Anthony Horowitz *c* 771

Cole, Davis Way
Double Mint - Gretchen Archer *m* 481

Cross, Alex
Hope to Die - James Patterson *c* 824

Davenport, Lucas
Gathering Prey - John Sandford *m* 652

Donne, John
Love's Alchemy - Bryan Crockett *t* 147

Dunbar, Brett
Operation Power Play - Justine Davis *r* 952

Grand, Matthew
The Blue and the Grey - M.J. Trow *t* 266

Greer, Logan
Disarming Detective - Elizabeth Heiter *r* 986

Holmes, Sherlock
Dreaming Spies - Laurie R. King *t* 192
The Fifth Heart - Dan Simmons *t* 249
Moriarty - Anthony Horowitz *c* 771
Sherlock Holmes, the Missing Years: Japan - Vasudev Murthy *t* 219

Jones, Athelney
Moriarty - Anthony Horowitz *c* 771

Mac
A Fright to the Death - Dawn Eastman *h* 295

Miller, Geneva
Eleven Days - Stav Sherez *m* 658

Nicolaos
Death Ex Machina - Gary Corby *t* 145

Russell, Mary
Dreaming Spies - Laurie R. King *t* 192

Ryan
Inspector of the Dead - David Morrell *t* 214

Ryan, Andrew
Bones Never Lie - Kathy Reichs *c* 843

Salvatore, Tonio
On the Run - Jo Davis *r* 951

Scarpetta, Dr. Kay
Flesh and Blood - Patricia Cornwell *c* 719

Sharpe, Wendell
Harbor Island - Carla Neggers *r* 1041

St. Cyr, Sebastian
Who Buries the Dead - C.S. Harris *t* 172

DETECTIVE—AMATEUR

Abbott, Abigail
Tattered Legacy - Shannon Baker *m* 484

Abbott, Nora
Tattered Legacy - Shannon Baker *m* 484

Albia, Flavia
Deadly Election - Lindsey Davis *t* 148

Andersen, Mitty
Howling Mountain Blues - Ricky Bush *m* 508

Baker, Grace
Dark Rooms - Lili Anolik *c* 691

Barnabus, Elizabeth
Unseemly Science - Rod Duncan *s* 1141

Bessette, Charlotte
As Gouda as Dead - Avery Aames *m* 473

Bishop, John
One Kick - Chelsea Cain *c* 708

Bolden, Pete
Howling Mountain Blues - Ricky Bush *m* 508

Borne, Brandy
Antiques Swap - Barbara Allan *m* 477

Borne, Vivian
Antiques Swap - Barbara Allan *m* 477

Bowman, Amber
Murder Freshly Baked - Vannetta Chapman *i* 377

Brannigan, Penny
Slated for Death - Elizabeth J. Duncan *m* 537

Brooks, Camryn "Cami"
Snow Way Out - Christine Husom *m* 579

Brother Athelstan
The Book of Fires - Paul Doherty *t* 150

Browning, Theodosia
Ming Tea Murder - Laura Childs *m* 514

Buchanan, Daisy
Lie of the Needle - Cate Price *m* 636

Lord Byron
Riot Most Uncouth - Daniel Friedman *m* 552

Cafferty, Danni
The Dead Play On - Heather Graham *m* 560

Cambridge, Kelsey
The Final Reveille - Amanda Flower *m* 547

Campbell, Allison
Dying Brand - Wendy Tyson *m* 675

Campion, Lucy
The Masque of a Murderer - Susanna Calkins *m* 510

Carter, Jo
The London Pride - Charlie Fletcher *f* 34

Carter, Will
The London Pride - Charlie Fletcher *f* 34

Cass
A Finely Knit Murder - Sally Goldenbaum *m* 557

Chambers Perry, Izzy
A Finely Knit Murder - Sally Goldenbaum *m* 557

Conlon, Maeve
Lies That Bind - Maggie Barbieri *m* 487

Coolidge, Sunny
Hiss and Tell - Claire Donally *m* 536

Cooper, Abby
Sense of Deception - Victoria Laurie *f* 69

Cooper, Cleo
Saving Cecil - Lee Mims *m* 620

Cooper, Mel
Dark Chocolate Demise - Jenn McKinlay *m* 616

Cramer, Holly
Twisted Innocence - Terri Blackstock *i* 363

Cranston, John
The Book of Fires - Paul Doherty *t* 150

Creed, Annja
Bathed in Blood - Alex Archer *f* 6

Cross, Emma
Murder at Beechwood - Alyssa Maxwell *m* 612

Curtis, Angie
Twisted Threads - Lea Wait *m* 678

Dalrymple, Daisy
Superfluous Women - Carola Dunn *m* 538

Darling, Annie
Don't Go Home - Carolyn G. Hart *m* 569

Davidson, Kate
A Killer Retreat - Tracy Weber *m* 679

De Luca, Caprice
Gilt by Association - Karen Rose Smith *m* 661

de Quincey, Thomas
Inspector of the Dead - David Morrell *t* 214

Donovan, Maura
An Early Wake - Sheila Connolly *m* 520

Endicott, Nell
A Finely Knit Murder - Sally Goldenbaum *m* 557

Falk, Jim
The Witch at Sparrow Creek - Josh Kent *h* 324

Favazza, Birdie
A Finely Knit Murder - Sally Goldenbaum *m* 557

Felton, Cora
Puzzled Indemnity - Parnell Hall *m* 565

Ferber, Edna
Cafe Europa - Edward Ifkovic *t* 182

Flaherty, Cam
Farmed and Dangerous - Edith Maxwell *m* 613

Fletcher, Jessica
Murder She Wrote: Killer in the Kitchen - Jessica Fletcher *m* 546

Flint, Michael
The Whispering - Sarah Rayne *h* 336

Goodwin, Dr. Alexandra
Medium Dead - Paula Paul *m* 633

Granny Apples
Ghost in the Guacamole - Sue Ann Jaffarian *m* 582

Greene, Dani
A Sticky Situation - Jessie Crockett *m* 525

Hancock, Krissy
Death by Coffee - Alex Erickson *m* 542

Harkness, Gloria
The Child Garden - Catriona McPherson *m* 618

Hildegard
The Dragon of Handale - Cassandra Clark *t* 142

Hodgson, Bridget
The Witch Hunter's Tale - Sam Thomas *t* 260

Holmes, Toni
Flourless to Stop Him - Nancy J. Parra *m* 631

Jamieson, Lucky
Ladle to the Grave - Connie Archer *m* 480

Mrs. Jeffries
Mrs. Jeffries and the One Who Got Away - Emily Brightwell *m* 503

Jensen, Ivy
Return to the Dark House - Laurie Faria Stolarz *h* 346

Johnson, Amy-Faye
The Readaholics and the Falcon Fiasco - Laura DiSilverio *m* 535

Kern, Ursula
Garden of Lies - Amanda Quick *r* 1051

Kim, Stacey
Woman with a Gun - Phillip Margolin *c* 797

Lancaster, Deirdre "Foxtrot"
Marked Fur Murder - Dixie Lyle *m* 609

Langslow, Meg
Lord of the Wings - Donna Andrews *m* 479

Lassair
Blood of the South - Alys Clare *t* 141

LeFaye, Ella Mae
Lemon Pies and Little White Lies - Ellery Adams *m* 475

Lewis, Dana
A Healthy Homicide - Staci McLaughlin *m* 617

Libertus, Longinus Flavius
The Fateful Day - Rosemary Rowe *t* 238

Lively, Penny
One Foot in the Grape - Carlene O'Neil *m* 627

Malloy, Claire
Pride v. Prejudice - Joan Hess *m* 573

McMurphy, Allie
Oh Say Can You Fudge - Nancy Coco *m* 518

Merriweather, Darcy
Some Like It Witchy - Heather Blake *m* 494

Metcalf, Jenna
Leaving Time - Jodi Picoult *c* 829

Miles, Tricia
A Fatal Chapter - Lorna Barrett *m* 488

Nelson, Stormi
Death by Baking - Cynthia Hickey *i* 418

Night, Madison
With Vics You Get Eggroll - Diane Vallere *m* 676

Oosterling, Ava
Five-Alarm Fudge - Christine DeSmet *m* 534

Pitt, Charlotte
The Angel Court Affair - Anne Perry *t* 230

Porter, Geraldine "Gerry"
Manhattan in Miniature - Margaret Grace *m* 558

Porter, Maddie
Manhattan in Miniature - Margaret Grace *m* 558

Powell, Hayley
Death of a Cupcake Queen - Lee Hollis *m* 577

Rebecca
As Gouda as Dead - Avery Aames *m* 473

Reece, Pepper
Assault and Pepper - Leslie Budewitz *m* 505

Salvare, Abby Knight
A Root Awakening - Kate Collins *m* 519

Simmons, Bernie
A Catered Mother's Day - Isis Crawford *m* 523

Simmons, Libby
A Catered Mother's Day - Isis Crawford *m* 523

Sinclair, Tori
Wedding Duress - Elizabeth Lynn Casey *m* 513

Singer, Marcy
Wicked Stitch - Amanda Lee *m* 597

Springer, Miss Julia
Etta Mae's Worst Bad-Luck Day - Ann B.
Ross *c* 848

Stanford, Kat
Deadly Desires at Honeychurch Hall - Hannah
Dennison *m* 532

Summerside, Reagan
Demise in Denim - Duffy Brown *m* 504

Swensen, Hannah
Double Fudge Brownie Murder - Joanne
Fluke *m* 548

Taylor, Sophie
Shadow of a Spout - Amanda Cooper *m* 521

Troyer, Hannah
Murder Freshly Baked - Vannetta
Chapman *i* 377

Trumbull, Victoria
Poison Ivy - Cynthia Riggs *m* 644

Vanderling, Willow
Seven Threadly Sins - Janet Bolin *m* 497

Wainwright, Brooklyn
Ripped from the Pages - Kate Carlisle *m* 512

Whitecastle, Emma
Ghost in the Guacamole - Sue Ann
Jaffarian *m* 582

Winn, Peggy
A Wee Murder in My Shop - Fran Stewart *m* 667

Winston, Mattie
Stiff Penalty - Annelise Ryan *m* 648

DETECTIVE—HOMICIDE

Adams, Zach "Cowboy"
Werewolf Cop - Andrew Klavan *h* 328

Barrister, Bill
Hollywood Lost - Ace Collins *t* 143

Boyle, Ray
Circling the Runway - J.L. Abramo *m* 474

Carlson, Charlie
Lethal Beauty - Lis Wiehl *i* 470

Collins, Mason
Ruins of War - John Connell *t* 144

Crosswhite, Tracy
My Sister's Grave - Robert Dugoni *c* 737

Gunther, Bernie
The Lady from Zagreb - Philip Kerr *t* 191

Hart, Abby
Drawing Fire - Janice Cantore *i* 376

Kaspary, Beatrice
Five - Ursula Archer *c* 693

McGregor, Mac
Buried Secrets - Irene Hannon *i* 411

Morgan, Deke
Cover Your Eyes - Mary Burton *r* 938

Ridley, Ellen
Blood Ties - Nicholas Guild *m* 562

Rizzoli, Jane
Die Again - Tess Gerritsen *c* 748

Sam
Blood Ties - Nicholas Guild *m* 562

Sturgis, Milo
Motive - Jonathan Kellerman *c* 780

Wenninger, Florin
Five - Ursula Archer *c* 693

DETECTIVE—POLICE

Allen, Tex
With Vics You Get Eggroll - Diane
Vallere *m* 676

Angelo
The Exile - C.T. Adams *f* 3

Armbruster, Stan
Whiskers of the Lion - P.L. Gaus *m* 555

Baker, Grant
A Fatal Chapter - Lorna Barrett *m* 488

Baxter, Mike
What the Fly Saw - Frankie Y. Bailey *m* 483

Behr, Frank
Signature Kill - David Levien *m* 601

Bolton, Cab
Season of Fear - Brian Freeman *m* 550

Bosch, Harry
The Burning Room - Michael Connelly *c* 718

Breen, Cathal
The Kings of London - William Shaw *m* 657

Breslau, Gary
Signature Kill - David Levien *m* 601

Bright, Kieran
The Soul of Discretion - Susan Hill *m* 574

Brogan, Jake
Truth Be Told - Hank Phillippi Ryan *c* 851

Brown, Mason
Deadly Obsession - Maggie Shayne *r* 1081
Innocent Prey - Maggie Shayne *r* 1080

Brunetti, Guido
Falling in Love - Donna Leon *m* 599

Burnley, Greg
What You Left Behind - Samantha Hayes *m* 570

Burns, Don
The Winter Foundlings - Kate Rhodes *m* 643

Cassidy, Michael
Night Life - David C. Taylor *t* 258

Charles, Marcus
A Woman Unknown - Frances Brody *t* 134

Cinq-Mars, Emile
The Storm Murders - John Farrow *m* 543

Coulter, Dirk
Killer Gourmet - G.A. McKevett *m* 615

Dallas, Eve
Obsession in Death - J.D. Robb *c* 847

Davies, Gareth
Slated for Death - Elizabeth J. Duncan *m* 537

Decker, Amos
Memory Man - David Baldacci *m* 485

Doyle, Kathleen
Murder in Hindsight - Anne Cleeland *m* 516

Driscoll, Frank
Nun Too Soon - Alice Loweecey *m* 608

Dupin, Georges
Death in Brittany - Jean-Luc Bannalec *m* 486

Fisher, Lorraine
What You Left Behind - Samantha Hayes *m* 570

Fletcher, Alec
Superfluous Women - Carola Dunn *m* 538

Fletcher, Julian
Asylum - Jeannette de Beauvoir *m* 529

Gillespie, Alexander
Hare - Peter Ranscombe *t* 234

Gillian, Kara
Vengeance of the Demon - Diana Rowland *f* 100

Grant, Jim
Snake Pass - Colin Campbell *m* 511

Graves, Billy
The Whites - Harry Brandt *m* 501

Gray, Josie
Firebreak - Tricia Fields *m* 544

Heuser, Georg
Ostland - David Thomas *t* 259

Hollands, Sam
Behind Closed Doors - Elizabeth Haynes *m* 571

Huss, Irene
The Beige Man - Helene Tursten *m* 674

Jackson, Wade
Wrongful Death - L.J. Sellers *m* 655

Johnson, Bruno
The Replacements - David Putnam *m* 637

Johnson, Roxton "Rocky"
Circling the Runway - J.L. Abramo *m* 474

Jordan, Harry
Last to Know - Elizabeth Adler *c* 685

Jordan, Zach
NYPD Red 3 - James Patterson *m* 632

Kinsella, Jim
Whatever Happened to Molly Bloom? - Jessica
Stirling *t* 254

Kody, Bran
Master of Plagues - E.L. Tettensor *f* 116

Lamb, Thomas
The Language of the Dead - Stephen
Kelly *t* 189

Lee, Cassandra
Deadeye - William C. Dietz *s* 1136
Redzone - William C. Dietz *s* 1137

Lenoir, Nicolas
Master of Plagues - E.L. Tettensor *f* 116

Littlewood, Boots
The Striver - Stephen Solomita *m* 662

Lopez, Laura
Circling the Runway - J.L. Abramo *m* 474

MacDonald, Kylie
NYPD Red 3 - James Patterson *m* 632

Machin, Tom
Whatever Happened to Molly Bloom? - Jessica
Stirling *t* 254

DETECTIVE—PRIVATE

Mallen, Mark
Innocent Damage - Robert K. Lewis   *m* 603

Malloy, Frank
Murder on Amsterdam Avenue - Victoria
   Thompson   *m* 672

Malone, Liesl
Cities and Thrones - Carrie Patel   *f* 92

Marium, Donald
Hold the Dark - William Giraldi   *c* 749

Martini, Nic
Murder with a Twist - Tracy Kiely   *m* 593

McCabe, Hannah
What the Fly Saw - Frankie Y. Bailey   *m* 483

Moller, Thomas
Rising Tide - Patricia Twomey Ryan   *m* 649

Monk, William
Corridors of the Night - Anne Perry   *t* 229

Moss, Jack
The Pocket Wife - Susan Crawford   *m* 524

Nash, Ted
Wicked Stitch - Amanda Lee   *m* 597

O'Hara, Sally
Compulsion - Allison Brennan   *m* 502

Omo, Ras
Deadeye - William C. Dietz   *s* 1136

Oshiro, Mariko
Disciple of the Wind - Steve Bein   *f* 11

Pappas, Pete
Farmed and Dangerous - Edith Maxwell   *m* 613

Pierce, Claire
Disturbed Earth - E.E. Richardson   *h* 339

Pitt, Thomas
The Angel Court Affair - Anne Perry   *t* 230

Rejon, Juan Rejon
The Beige Man - Helene Tursten   *m* 674

Rick, Louise
The Forgotten Girls - Sara Blaedel   *m* 493

Rossett, John Henry
The Darkest Hour - Tony Schumacher   *t* 245

Rutledge, Ian
A Fine Summer's Day - Charles Todd   *t* 263

Ryan, Sean
Deception on Sable Hill - Shelley Gray   *i* 408

Saunders, Gwen
Innocent Damage - Robert K. Lewis   *m* 603

Schroder, Carl
Five Minutes Alone - Paul Cleave   *c* 714

Serrailler, Simon
The Soul of Discretion - Susan Hill   *m* 574

Sinclair, Michael
Murder in Hindsight - Anne Cleeland   *m* 516

Smith, Louisa "Lou"
Behind Closed Doors - Elizabeth Haynes   *m* 571

Soto, Lucia "Lucky"
The Burning Room - Michael Connelly   *c* 718

Steele, Matt
Death by Baking - Cynthia Hickey   *i* 418

Stephen
The Shadow Cabinet - Maureen Johnson   *h* 322

Sveinsson, Erlendur
Reykjavik Nights - Arnaldur Indridason   *m* 581

Tate, Theodore
Five Minutes Alone - Paul Cleave   *c* 714

Thorne, Tom
Time of Death - Mark Billingham   *m* 491

Tozer, Helen
The Kings of London - William Shaw   *m* 657

Tucker, Oliver "Tuck"
Dying for the Past - T.J. O'Connor   *m* 625

Tyler, Tom
No Known Grave - Maureen Jennings   *m* 585

Van In, Pieter
From Bruges with Love - Pieter Aspe   *m* 482

Wallace, David
The Language of the Dead - Stephen
   Kelly   *t* 189

Weeks, Helen
Time of Death - Mark Billingham   *m* 491

Whyte, Jesse
Murder at Beechwood - Alyssa Maxwell   *m* 612

Wildey, Ben
Canary - Duane Swierczynski   *m* 671

DETECTIVE—PRIVATE

Barker, Cyrus
Anatomy of Evil - Will Thomas   *t* 261

Baylor, Nevada
Burn for Me - Ilona Andrews   *r* 900

Behr, Frank
Signature Kill - David Levien   *m* 601

Booth Delaney, Sarah
Bone to Be Wild - Carolyn Haines   *m* 564

Buchanan, Polly
The Laws of Murder - Charles Finch   *c* 743

Carpenter, Sabina
The Body Snatchers Affair - Marcia Muller   *t* 218

Cole, Elvis
The Promise - Robert Crais   *c* 720

D'Artigo, Delilah
Panther Prowling - Yasmine Galenorn   *h* 301

Dallington, Lord John
The Laws of Murder - Charles Finch   *c* 743

Dane, Matthew
Taken - Dee Henderson   *i* 417

Decker, Amos
Memory Man - David Baldacci   *m* 485

Diamond, Jacob "Jake"
Circling the Runway - J.L. Abramo   *m* 474

Divine, Eve
The Case of the Sin City Sister - Lynne
   Hinton   *i* 419

Dobbs, Maisie
A Dangerous Place - Jacqueline Winspear   *t* 273

Fearsson, Justis
Spell Blind - David B. Coe   *f* 25

Fusco, Candice
Sense of Deception - Victoria Laurie   *f* 69

Golden, Benji
Phantom Angel - David Handler   *m* 567

Hauck, Ty
One Mile Under - Andrew Gross   *m* 561

Hawthorne, Helen
Checked Out - Elaine Viets   *m* 677

Hayes, Andy
Slow Burn - Andrew Welsh-Huggins   *m* 680

Holmes, Sherlock
The Body Snatchers Affair - Marcia Muller   *t* 218

Howard, Jeri
Cold Trail - Janet Dawson   *m* 528

Knight, Jack
Dead Red - Tim O'Mara   *m* 626

Leduc, Aimee
Murder on the Champ de Mars - Cara
   Black   *m* 492

LeMaire
The Laws of Murder - Charles Finch   *c* 743

Lenox, Charles
The Laws of Murder - Charles Finch   *c* 743

Makutsi, Grace
The Handsome Man's De Luxe Cafe - Alexander
   McCall Smith   *c* 864

McDermott, Dr. Ian
Loup Garou: The Beast of Harmony Falls - David
   Reuben Aslin   *h* 281

McGuire, Grant
Confessions - Cynthia Eden   *r* 957

Monaghan, Tess
Hush Hush - Laura Lippman   *m* 604

Morgan, Jack
Private Vegas - James Patterson   *c* 826

Murphy, Jensen
Every Breath You Take - Chris Marie Green   *f* 39

Murphy, Luke
Drawing Fire - Janice Cantore   *i* 376

Murphy Sullivan, Molly
The Edge of Dreams - Rhys Bowen   *t* 131

Pendleton, Alexandrina "Alex" Victoria
The Hanged Man - P.N. Elrod   *h* 296

Pescatore, Valentine
The Convert's Song - Sebastian Rotella   *c* 849

Pike, Joe
The Promise - Robert Crais   *c* 720

Quincannon, John
The Body Snatchers Affair - Marcia Muller   *t* 218

Quinn, Michael
The Dead Play On - Heather Graham   *m* 560

Ramotswe, Precious
The Handsome Man's De Luxe Cafe - Alexander
   McCall Smith   *c* 864

Reid, Savannah
Killer Gourmet - G.A. McKevett   *m* 615

Sagemont, Phil
Checked Out - Elaine Viets   *m* 677

Salvare, Marco
A Root Awakening - Kate Collins   *m* 519

Slade, Zach
Ghost Killer - Robin D. Owens   *f* 91

Spencer, Gabe
Broken - Cynthia Eden   *r* 959

Sugarman
The Big Finish - James W. Hall   *c* 758

Talbot, Liz
Lowcountry Boneyard - Susan M. Boyer   *m* 500

Thorn
The Big Finish - James W. Hall   *c* 758

Torres, Ricky
Dead Red - Tim O'Mara   *m* 626

Wyatt
The Long and Faraway Gone - Lou
   Berney   *m* 489

DIABETIC

Dent, Andy
Constant Fear - Daniel Palmer   *m* 629

DIPLOMAT

Arbuthnot
Pasha: A Kydd Sea Adventure - Julian Stockwin *t* 255

Bell, Gertrude
Bell of the Desert - Alan Gold *t* 166

Bexley, John
Married to a Perfect Stranger - Jane Ashford *r* 904

Brandon, Piers
Say Yes to the Marquess - Tessa Dare *r* 950

Digby, Kenelm
Viper Wine - Hermione Eyre *t* 154

Hopkins, Harry
Sleep in Peace Tonight - James MacManus *t* 208

Stephanie
Prague Summer - Jeffrey Condran *c* 717

DIRECTOR

Antonio
Seven Threadly Sins - Janet Bolin *m* 497

Cabot, Lance
Paris Match - Stuart Woods *c* 889

Cambridge, Kelsey
The Final Reveille - Amanda Flower *m* 547

Dennis
Funny Girl - Nick Hornby *c* 770

Desrocher, Francois
Asylum - Jeannette de Beauvoir *m* 529

Keaton, Ann
Paris Match - Stuart Woods *c* 889

McGarvey, Kirk "Mac"
Retribution - David Hagberg *m* 563

Mellon, Bebe
Manhattan in Miniature - Margaret Grace *m* 558

Oshima, Shigeo
Sherlock Holmes, the Missing Years: Japan - Vasudev Murthy *t* 219

Shepard, Leah
Ancient Oceans of Central Kentucky - David Connerley Nahm *c* 815

Wade, Kate
Tin Men - Christopher Golden *m* 556

DIVER

Riggs, Tanner
One in a Million - Jill Shalvis *r* 1077

DIVORCED PERSON

Alders, Lila
New Uses for Old Boyfriends - Beth Kendrick *r* 998

Allen, Priscilla
An Amish Man of Ice Mountain - Kelly Long *i* 429

Amado, Mercedes "Mercy"
The Amado Women - Desiree Zamorano *c* 892

Babin, Mackenzie "Mac"
Dead Spots - Rhiannon Frater *h* 299

Bellamy, Gina
A Hundred Pieces of Me - Lucy Dillon *c* 731

Bellamy, Stuart
A Hundred Pieces of Me - Lucy Dillon *c* 731

Cambridge, Kelsey
The Final Reveille - Amanda Flower *m* 547

Dale, Lilah
Mammoth Secrets - Ashley Elizabeth Ludwig *i* 431

Duran, Ben
The Black Widow - Wendy Corsi Staub *m* 665

Duran, Gaby
The Black Widow - Wendy Corsi Staub *m* 665

Emily
The Love Book - Nina Solomon *c* 866

Gibson, Jake
Mammoth Secrets - Ashley Elizabeth Ludwig *i* 431

Jilly
There Must Be Some Mistake - Frederick Barthelme *c* 697

Keegan, Caroline
Butternut Summer - Mary McNear *c* 802

Keegan, Jack
Butternut Summer - Mary McNear *c* 802

Lord Kemp
The Bedding Proposal - Tracy Anne Warren *r* 1096

Lennox, Lady Thalia
The Bedding Proposal - Tracy Anne Warren *r* 1096

Montgomery, Shea
The Good Chase - Hanna Martine *r* 1024

Palmer, Sebastian "Bash"
Love After All - Jaci Burton *r* 937

Parsons, Jenna
House of Wonder - Sarah Healy *c* 763

Perea, Blanca
The Heart Has Its Reasons - Maria Duenas *c* 736

Reece, Pepper
Assault and Pepper - Leslie Budewitz *m* 505

Rosen, Bobby
The Sheltering - Mark Powell *c* 835

Ryan
The Christmas Light - Donna VanLiere *c* 881

Summerside, Reagan
Demise in Denim - Duffy Brown *m* 504

Sweetwater, Percival "Percy" III
My Father's Wives - Mike Greenberg *c* 753

Tag
Assault and Pepper - Leslie Budewitz *m* 505

Unnamed
Dear Thief - Samantha Harvey *c* 762

Von Riesen, Yolandi "Yoli"
All My Puny Sorrows - Miriam Toews *c* 871

Waltham, Vera
The First Kiss - Grace Burrowes *r* 932

Webster, Wallace
There Must Be Some Mistake - Frederick Barthelme *c* 697

Wiggins, Etta Mae
Etta Mae's Worst Bad-Luck Day - Ann B. Ross *c* 848

Wilder, Fiona
Sweet Surprise - Candis Terry *r* 1091

Wilder, Jackson
Sweet Surprise - Candis Terry *r* 1091

Wyatt, Anna
Girl Before a Mirror - Liza Palmer *r* 1047

DOCTOR

Anderson, Rose
Teardrop Lane - Emily March *r* 1018

Angelo, Dr. Lucas
Angel in Armani - Melanie Scott *r* 1072

Baker, Dr. Mark
Fatal Trauma - Richard L. Mabry *i* 432
Fatal Trauma - Richard L. Mabry *i* 432

Dr. Beck
No Known Grave - Maureen Jennings *m* 585

Dr. Bek
Find Me - Laura van den Berg *c* 877

Blair, Bill
The Children's Crusade - Ann Packer *t* 224

Blair, Rebecca
The Children's Crusade - Ann Packer *t* 224

Blair, Robert
The Children's Crusade - Ann Packer *t* 224

Bond, Dr. Thomas
Murder - Sarah Pinborough *t* 232

Breuer, Josef
Gretel and the Dark - Eliza Granville *t* 168

Crusher, Beverly
The Missing - Una McCormack *s* 1175

Doctor
Method 15/33 - Shannon Kirk *m* 594

Feldstein, Rona
The Global War on Morris - Steve Israel *c* 772

Fidelis, Dr. Luke
The Hidden Man - Robin Blake *m* 495

Goldman, Dr. Zoe
Little Black Lies - Sandra Block *m* 496

Goodwin, Dr. Alexandra
Medium Dead - Paula Paul *m* 633

Gugu
Frog - Yan Mo *c* 808

Isles, Dr. Maura
Die Again - Tess Gerritsen *c* 748

Jacobs, Dr. Scott
The Best Medicine - Elizabeth Hayley *r* 984

Jekyll, Dr. Eliza
The Diabolical Miss Hyde - Viola Carr *f* 21

Karno, Dr. Albert
Doctor Death - Lene Kaaberbol *t* 187

Kimei, Laura
Castaway Planet - Eric Flint *s* 1146

McCoy, Leonard
Crisis of Consciousness - Dave Galanter *s* 1147

Merial, Dr. Daniel
Diary of an Accidental Wallflower - Jennifer McQuiston *r* 1036

Molnar, Zoltan
Consumed - David Cronenberg *c* 722

Palmer, Alex
Falling Hard - HelenKay Dimon *r* 954

Patrick
The Secrets of Midwives - Sally Hepworth *c* 765

McCrory, Dr.
The Devil's Making - Sean Haldane *t* 171

McIlroy, Noah
The Christmas Bouquet - Sherryl Woods *r* 1098

Rand, Magnus
Corridors of the Night - Anne Perry *t* 229

Roiphe, Dr. Barry
Consumed - David Cronenberg *c* 722

Ryder
Night Blindness - Susan Strecker *c* 870

Scarpetta, Dr. Kay
Flesh and Blood - Patricia Cornwell *c* 719

Sean
The Secrets of Midwives - Sally Hepworth *c* 765

Shah, Nidhi
Unbound - Jim C. Hines *f* 55

Shields, Dr. Lise
The Forgetting Place - John Burley *m* 506

Sikandar
The Shadow of the Crescent Moon - Fatima
  Bhutto *c* 703

Suliman
The Chosen Prince - Diane Stanley *f* 110

Unnamed Character
It Won't Always Be This Great - Peter
  Mehlman *c* 803

Walker, Eli
Binary - Stephanie Saulter *s* 1193

Watson, John
Moriarty - Anthony Horowitz *c* 771

Watson, Dr. John
Sherlock Holmes, the Missing Years: Japan - Vasudev Murthy *t* 219

DOG

Bella
A Killer Retreat - Tracy Weber *m* 679

Brownie
Poison Ivy - Cynthia Riggs *m* 644

Cutter
Operation Power Play - Justine Davis *r* 952

Holly
Rescue Me - Catherine Mann *r* 1017

Lucky
Survivors: Storm of Dogs - Erin Hunter *f* 60

Maggie
The Promise - Robert Crais *c* 720

Mal
Oh Say Can You Fudge - Nancy Coco *m* 518

Rocky
Scent of Murder - James O. Born *m* 498

Sam
The Look of Love - Sarah Jio *c* 775

Sweet
Survivors: Storm of Dogs - Erin Hunter *f* 60

DRAGON

Mei
The Exile - C.T. Adams *f* 3

DRIFTER

Duffy, Spooner
A Sticky Situation - Jessie Crockett *m* 525

DRIVER

Finch, Leonora
Sleep in Peace Tonight - James
  MacManus *t* 208

Peter
NYPD Red 3 - James Patterson *m* 632

Weary, Nat
Driving the King - Ravi Howard *t* 180

DRUG DEALER

Courtney
Zombified - Adam Gallardo *h* 302

Fenmere, Willem
The Thorn of Dentonhill - Marshall Ryan
  Maresca *f* 77

Helmuth, Fannie
Whiskers of the Lion - P.L. Gaus *m* 555

Hoffmann, Daniel
Blood on Snow - Jo Nesbo *m* 624

Margaritte
Crazy Horse's Girlfriend - Erika T. Wurth *c* 891

McNeely, Charlie
Where All Light Tends to Go - David Joy *m* 588

Pettersson, Anders
The Beige Man - Helene Tursten *m* 674

Quinn, Nolly
Kill Me, Darling - Mickey Spillane *m* 663

Robbie
Where All Light Tends to Go - David Joy *m* 588

DWARF

Akina
Forge of Ashes - Josh Vogt *f* 120

Gurnisson, Gotrek
Gotrek and Felix: Slayer - David Guymer *f* 44

DYSFUNCTIONAL FAMILY MEMBER

Rosen, Bobby
The Sheltering - Mark Powell *c* 835

Tamara
Driving with the Top Down - Beth
  Harbison *c* 761

ECCENTRIC

Thomas, Odd
Saint Odd - Dean Koontz *c* 785

Zoransky, Zelda "ZZ"
Marked Fur Murder - Dixie Lyle *m* 609

ECONOMIST

Keynes, John Maynard
Vanessa and Her Sister - Priya Parmar *t* 225

EDITOR

Dixon, Greg
Slayed on the Slopes - Kate Dyer-Seeley *m* 539

Gibbs, Jen
The Story Keeper - Lisa Wingate *c* 887

Mr. Kent
Spy of Richmond - Jocelyn Green *i* 409

Twisdale, Charles
A Scourge of Vipers - Bruce DeSilva *m* 533

ELEPHANT

Colossus
Colossus - Colin Falconer *t* 155

EMPATH

St. Claire, Ramie
Keep Me Safe - Maya Banks *r* 908

Wherlocke, Giles
If He's Daring - Hannah Howell *r* 988

EMPLOYER

Barker, Cyrus
Anatomy of Evil - Will Thomas *t* 261

Bell, Fannie
Dollbaby - Laura McNeal *c* 801

Bessette, Charlotte
As Gouda as Dead - Avery Aames *m* 473

Lady Carinna
An Appetite for Violets - Martine Bailey *t* 128

Carmichael, Gavin
Stirring Up Trouble - Kimberly Kincaid *r* 1000

Darwin, Charles
Galapagos Regained - James Morrow *t* 216

Davenport, Lucas
Deadline - John Sandford *c* 852

Devereaux, Caleb
Keep Me Safe - Maya Banks *r* 908

Eleanor
A Good Rogue Is Hard to Find - Kelly
  Bowen *r* 921

Gabler, Christof
The Figaro Murders - Laura Lebow *t* 199

Grimm
Armageddon Rules - J.C. Nelson *f* 86

Heming, William
A Pleasure and a Calling - Phil Hogan *m* 576

James
Forbidden to Love the Duke - Jillian
  Hunter *r* 991

Jamieson, Lucky
Ladle to the Grave - Connie Archer *m* 480

Lively, Penny
One Foot in the Grape - Carlene O'Neil *m* 627

Lombard, Carole
A Touch of Stardust - Kate Alcott *t* 125

Louis, King
1636: The Cardinal Virtues - Eric Flint *s* 1145

McCane, George
Fate Moreland's Widow - John Lane *t* 197

Reece, Pepper
Assault and Pepper - Leslie Budewitz *m* 505

Sanders, Richard
Double Mint - Gretchen Archer *m* 481

Selznick, David O.
A Touch of Stardust - Kate Alcott *t* 125

Shardlake, Matthew
Lamentation - C.J. Sansom *t* 244

Spear, Thorvald
Dark Intelligence - Neal Asher *s* 1108

Stone, Brant
No Denying You - Sydney Landon *r* 1004

Swartout, August
A Slant of Light - Jeffrey Lent *t* 202

Talbot, Clementine Elizabeth
Death of a Dishonorable Gentleman - Tessa Arlen *t* 126

Tremaine, Dr. Ryan
Together with You - Victoria Bylin *i* 370

Vanderling, Willow
Seven Threadly Sins - Janet Bolin *m* 497

Witherspoon, Gerald
Mrs. Jeffries and the One Who Got Away - Emily Brightwell *m* 503

Witherspoon, Sprague
Trust No One - Jayne Ann Krentz *c* 786

Wylie, Ben
The Hunger of the Wolf - Stephen Marche *r* 1019

Zoransky, Zelda "ZZ"
Marked Fur Murder - Dixie Lyle *m* 609

ENEMY

Andriana
Remnants: Season of Fire - Lisa T. Bergren *i* 361

Bales, Arlen
The Skull Throne - Peter V. Brett *f* 17

Bantle, Peter
Karen Memory - Elizabeth Bear *s* 1118

Barrons, Leo
Of Silk and Steam - Bec McMaster *r* 1033

Chance, Hotspur
Quake - Patrick Carman *s* 1124

Clayborne, Chance
Terminal - Kathy Reichs *s* 1187

Daniels, Faith
Quake - Patrick Carman *s* 1124

Di, Lung
The Dragons of Heaven - Alyc Helms *f* 50

Drake, Jessica
Dreamseeker - C.S. Friedman *f* 37

Gilmore, Dylan
Quake - Patrick Carman *s* 1124

Grander, A. VIII
The Last American Vampire - Seth Grahame-Smith *h* 304

Holmes, Sherlock
Moriarty - Anthony Horowitz *c* 771
Sherlock Holmes, the Missing Years: Japan - Vasudev Murthy *t* 219

Hooke, Rebecca
The Witch Hunter's Tale - Sam Thomas *t* 260

Huang, Lung
The Dragons of Heaven - Alyc Helms *f* 50

Isaac
Dreamseeker - C.S. Friedman *f* 37

Keallach
Remnants: Season of Fire - Lisa T. Bergren *i* 361

Khan, Kor'sarro
Damocles - Phil Kelly *s* 1159

Layton, Henry
Into the Savage Country - Shannon Burke *t* 136

Lot, Seth
Briar Queen - Katherine Harbour *h* 312

Majorov, Yevgeny
Paris Match - Stuart Woods *c* 889

Mastermind
Alien Separation - Gini Koch *s* 1162

Memery, Karen
Karen Memory - Elizabeth Bear *s* 1118

Morgana
Dreamseeker - C.S. Friedman *f* 37

Moriarty
Sherlock Holmes, the Missing Years: Japan - Vasudev Murthy *t* 219

Moriarty, James
Moriarty - Anthony Horowitz *c* 771

Oliphant, Stanley
Who Buries the Dead - C.S. Harris *t* 172

Quinn, Clara
Quake - Patrick Carman *s* 1124

Quinn, Wade
Quake - Patrick Carman *s* 1124

Reeves, Bass
Karen Memory - Elizabeth Bear *s* 1118

Santeros
Cobra Outlaw - Timothy Zahn *s* 1211

Sethos
Remnants: Season of Fire - Lisa T. Bergren *i* 361

Shadowsun
Damocles - Phil Kelly *s* 1159

Suvagne, Lisette
Covenant's End - Ari Marmell *f* 78

Troft
Cobra Outlaw - Timothy Zahn *s* 1211

Wyeth, William
Into the Savage Country - Shannon Burke *t* 136

ENGINEER

Buchanan, Tucker
Silken Threats - Addison Fox *r* 966

Devi
Aurora - Kim Stanley Robinson *s* 1191

Haley, Philip
Long Way Down - Michael Sears *m* 654

Lambert, Ean
Linesman - S.K. Dunstall *s* 1142

Petkova, Yulana
The Russian Bride - Ed Kovacs *m* 595

Radmanovic, Kermin
I Am Radar - Reif Larsen *s* 1164

Zuviria, Marti
Victus: The Fall of Barcelona - Albert Sanchez Pinol *t* 233

ENTERTAINER

McKee, Dolly
Of Irish Blood - Mary Pat Kelly *t* 188

Pekkala, Candy
Best to Laugh - Lorna Landvik *c* 787

ENTREPRENEUR

Magnus, Reggie
The Fold - Peter Clines *s* 1127

Maxwell, Cornelius Linus
Beautiful You - Chuck Palahniuk *c* 823

Sendry, Michael
Allure of Deceit - Susan Froetschel *m* 553

Swann, Cecily
The Cavendon Women - Barbara Taylor Bradford *t* 133

ENVIRONMENTALIST

Stephen
The Wallcreeper - Nell Zink *c* 894

Tiffany
The Wallcreeper - Nell Zink *c* 894

EXILE

Zeke
Finn Fancy Necromancy - Randy Henderson *f* 53

EXPATRIATE

Graham, Grace
Unbecoming - Rebecca Scherm *c* 855

Malek, Reza
Tehran at Twilight - Salar Abdoh *c* 683

EXPERIMENTAL SUBJECT

Fontenot, Gator
Viper Game - Christine Feehan *r* 961

Fontenot, Wyatt
Viper Game - Christine Feehan *r* 961

EXPERT

Brandon, Rebecca "Becky" Bloomfield
Shopaholic to the Stars - Sophie Kinsella *c* 784

Carter, Penny
The Conquering Dark - Clay Griffith *h* 308

Corcoran, Jimmy
Past Crimes - Glen Erik Hamilton *m* 566

Core, Russell
Hold the Dark - William Giraldi *c* 749

de Luca, Rachel
Deadly Obsession - Maggie Shayne *r* 1081
Innocent Prey - Maggie Shayne *r* 1080

Herran
Binary - Stephanie Saulter *s* 1193

Wainwright, Brooklyn
Ripped from the Pages - Kate Carlisle *m* 512

EXPLORER

Bell, Gertrude
Bell of the Desert - Alan Gold *t* 166

Darwin, Charles
Galapagos Regained - James Morrow *t* 216

Digby, Kenelm
Viper Wine - Hermione Eyre *t* 154

FARMER

Adler, Ambrose
The Great Sand Fracas of Ames County - Jerry Apps *c* 692

Bradford, Michael
The Language of the Dead - Stephen
Kelly   *t* 189

Brian
Dark Bride - Jonathan Ryan   *h* 340

Burchett, Will
License to Dill - Mary Ellen Hughes   *m* 578

Cunliffe, Johnsey
The Thing About December - Donal Ryan   *c* 850

Flaherty, Cam
Farmed and Dangerous - Edith Maxwell   *m* 613

Harlan
A Slant of Light - Jeffrey Lent   *t* 202

Langdon, Walter
Early Warning - Jane Smiley   *t* 251

Pace, Jordan
As Gouda as Dead - Avery Aames   *m* 473

Phillips, Henry
Until the Harvest - Sarah Loudin Thomas   *i* 463

Portland, Edgar
The Memory House - Linda Goodnight   *r* 974

Selvedge, Blair
Pale Harvest - Braden Hepner   *c* 764

Selvedge, Jack
Pale Harvest - Braden Hepner   *c* 764

Standley, Gerald
License to Dill - Mary Ellen Hughes   *m* 578

Swartout, August
A Slant of Light - Jeffrey Lent   *t* 202

Unnamed Character
Holy Cow - David Duchovny   *c* 735

Wheeler, Amos
A Slant of Light - Jeffrey Lent   *t* 202

FARMWIFE

Portland, Charlotte Reed
The Memory House - Linda Goodnight   *r* 974

FATHER

Aar
Hiding in Plain Sight - Nuruddin Farah   *c* 741

Aethelred
The Price of Blood - Patricia Bracewell   *t* 132

Lord Akeldama
Prudence - Gail Carriger   *f* 22

Alden, Hunter Hutchinson Jr.
NYPD Red 3 - James Patterson   *m* 632

Anderson, Jim
The Legacy - Dan Walsh   *i* 467

Andreou, Alex
The Fifth Gospel - Ian Caldwell   *m* 509

Aubrey, Reginald
The Wood's Edge - Lori Benton   *i* 360
The Wood's Edge - Lori Benton   *i* 360

Aurangzeb
Traitors in the Shadows - Alex Rutherford   *t* 242

Barkes, Clive
Never Mind Miss Fox - Olivia Glazebrook   *c* 750

Barnes, Rudy
The Witch of the Wood - Michael
Aronovitz   *h* 280

Barsham, George
Meadowlands - Elizabeth Jeffrey   *t* 185

Beck, Charley
Up the Hill to Home - Jennifer Bort
Yacovissi   *t* 275

Beck, Joel
Amish Promises - Leslie Gould   *i* 405

Beiler, Davey
The Witnesses - Linda Byler   *i* 369

Ben
As Night Falls - Jenny Milchman   *m* 619

Bennett, Parker
The Melody Lingers On - Mary Higgins
Clark   *m* 515

Benz, Bruno
Hausfrau - Jill Alexander Essbaum   *c* 739

Big Hoom
Em and the Big Hoom - Jerry Pinto   *c* 831

Birdsall, Gideon
The Language of Paradise - Barbara Klein
Moss   *t* 217

Blair, Bill
The Children's Crusade - Ann Packer   *t* 224

Blake, Morgan
The Cat, the Devil, the Last Escape - Pat J.J.
Murphy   *m* 623

Bloom, Leopold
Whatever Happened to Molly Bloom? - Jessica
Stirling   *t* 254

Brandon, Luke
Shopaholic to the Stars - Sophie Kinsella   *c* 784

Brian
Dark Bride - Jonathan Ryan   *h* 340

Campbell, John
Hot Blooded - Donna Grant   *r* 976

Campbell, Macon
The Wonder of All Things - Jason Mott   *c* 812

Cane, Harry
A Place Called Winter - Patrick Gale   *t* 162

Carnehan, Jacob
In Dark Service - Stephen Hunt   *f* 58

Carter, Duke
Last One Home - Debbie Macomber   *c* 794

Cassian, Samuel
The City of Blood - Frederique Molay   *m* 622

Catrell, Peter
The Pocket Wife - Susan Crawford   *m* 524

Cochrane, Nathan
Impulse - Dave Bara   *s* 1115

Colonel Smith
The Abduction of Smith and Smith - Rashad
Harrison   *t* 174

Connard, Howard Sr.
Etta Mae's Worst Bad-Luck Day - Ann B.
Ross   *c* 848

Connelly, Simon
Finding Jake - Bryan Reardon   *m* 639

Coughlin, Joe
World Gone By - Dennis Lehane   *t* 201

Cowan, George
Hush - Karen Robards   *r* 1058

Crane, Charlie
When We Fall - Emily Liebert   *c* 791

Cross, Alex
Hope to Die - James Patterson   *c* 824

Crow
Hush Hush - Laura Lippman   *m* 604

Dad
Reunion - Hannah Pittard   *c* 833

Dadda
How to Build a Girl - Caitlin Moran   *c* 810

Daed
The Proposal at Siesta Key - Shelley Shepard
Gray   *i* 406

Dane, Matthew
Taken - Dee Henderson   *i* 417

Davenport, Lucas
Gathering Prey - John Sandford   *m* 652

de Kruk, Augustus
Hiss and Tell - Claire Donally   *m* 536

de Quincey, Thomas
Inspector of the Dead - David Morrell   *t* 214

Defoe, Eddy
The Last Kings of Sark - Rosa
Rankin-Gee   *c* 840

Delancey, Richard
Tangled Lives - Hilary Boyd   *c* 705

Dent, Jake
Constant Fear - Daniel Palmer   *m* 629

Djurkovic, Antun Dragun
The Lady from Zagreb - Philip Kerr   *t* 191

Dobbs, Frankie
A Dangerous Place - Jacqueline Winspear   *t* 273

Donovan, Eli
The Memory House - Linda Goodnight   *r* 974

Downey, Evan
Bringing Home the Bad Boy - Jessica
Lemmon   *r* 1010

Drake, Patrick
Sometimes the Wolf - Urban Waite   *c* 882

Duran, Ben
The Black Widow - Wendy Corsi Staub   *m* 665

Farabee, Holt
Bridges Burned - Annette Dashofy   *m* 527

Father
The Hanged Man - P.N. Elrod   *h* 296

Feldstein, Morris
The Global War on Morris - Steve Israel   *c* 772

Fornier, Augustin
Ruth's Journey: The Authorized Novel of Mammy
from Margaret Mitchell's Gone with the Wind
- Donald McCaig   *t* 210

Frank
Sabotaged - Dani Pettrey   *i* 446

Furman, Jacob
The Ambassadors - George Lerner   *t* 203

Granger, Josh
It Had to Be Him - Tamra Baumann   *r* 910

Hadley, Bruce
A Catered Mother's Day - Isis Crawford   *m* 523

Hansen, Clint
The Cowboy SEAL - Laura Marie Altom   *r* 897
The Cowboy SEAL - Laura Marie Altom   *r* 897

Hardy, Dismas
The Fall - John T. Lescroart   *m* 600

Harper, Hank
In the Woods - Merry Jones   *m* 587

Helsing, Leonard
Shutter - Courtney Alameda   *h* 277

Heyward, Colton
Lowcountry Boneyard - Susan M. Boyer   *m* 500

Hoffman, Leonard
The Fixer - Joseph Finder   *m* 545

Voith, Ferd
Up the Hill to Home - Jennifer Bort Yacovissi   *t* 275

von Hoffman, Max
Scent of Triumph - Jan Moran   *t* 212

Waltham, Alexander
The First Kiss - Grace Burrowes   *r* 932

Washburn, Jonathan
Prudence - David Treuer   *c* 872

Webster, Wallace
There Must Be Some Mistake - Frederick Barthelme   *c* 697

West, Nathan
Witch upon a Star - Jennifer Harlow   *m* 568

Wherlocke, Sir Orion
If He's Daring - Hannah Howell   *r* 988

Whitshank, Junior
A Spool of Blue Thread - Anne Tyler   *c* 875

Whitshank, Red
A Spool of Blue Thread - Anne Tyler   *c* 875

Winwood, John "Woody"
The Girl Next Door - Ruth Rendell   *c* 844

FBI AGENT

Bannon, Dean
Twisted - Cynthia Eden   *r* 958

Bradley, Finn
Hush - Karen Robards   *r* 1058

Cady, Drew
The Lynchpin - Jeffrey B. Burton   *m* 507

Cortez, Isabella "Ella"
Disarming Detective - Elizabeth Heiter   *r* 986

Cruz, Madeline
The Big Finish - James W. Hall   *c* 758

Donovan, Colin
Harbor Island - Carla Neggers   *r* 1041

Evertson, Laurel
Double Cross - DiAnn Mills   *i* 436

Furness, Desiree
Life or Death - Michael Robotham   *m* 645

Granger, Josh
It Had to Be Him - Tamra Baumann   *r* 910

Jund, Roland
The Lynchpin - Jeffrey B. Burton   *m* 507

LeBlanc, Elizabeth
Beyond Limits - Laura Griffin   *r* 980

Liu, Roger
Method 15/33 - Shannon Kirk   *m* 594

Novak, Deacon
Closer Than You Think - Karen Rose   *r* 1062

O'Brian, Marcus
Taken - Lisa Harris   *i* 412

O'Dell, Maggie
Breaking Creed - Alex Kava   *c* 779

Parker
Whiskers of the Lion - P.L. Gaus   *m* 555

Parker, Tom
Desperate Measures - Sandra Orchard   *i* 441

Pendergast, Aloysius
Blue Labyrinth - Douglas Preston   *c* 837

Quinn, Brigid
Fear the Darkness - Becky Masterman   *m* 610

Rivers, Dutch
Sense of Deception - Victoria Laurie   *f* 69

Ross
Echo 8 - Sharon Lynn Fisher   *f* 33

Santos, Victoria
Cane and Abe - James Grippando   *c* 756

Sharpe, Emma
Harbor Island - Carla Neggers   *r* 1041

Wesley, Benton
Flesh and Blood - Patricia Cornwell   *c* 719

Winger, Cameron
Going Gone - Sharon Sala   *r* 1066

FEMINIST

Richardson, Dorothy
The Lodger - Louisa Treger   *t* 265

FEMME FATALE

Fadiya
The Dark Arts of Blood - Freda Warrington   *h* 350

FIANCE(E)

Adriko, Michael
The Laughing Monsters - Denis Johnson   *c* 776

Anaedsley, Trevor
50 Ways to Ruin a Rake - Jade Lee   *r* 1007

Ashe
Revels Ending - Vic Kerry   *h* 326

Barnett, Cooper
Wild Horses - B.J. Daniels   *r* 947

Barrett, Natasha
Before, During, After - Richard Bausch   *c* 698

Beaumont, Michael
How to Plan a Wedding for a Royal Spy - Vanessa Kelly   *r* 997

Bessette, Charlotte
As Gouda as Dead - Avery Aames   *m* 473

Bigelow, Christine
No Ghouls Allowed - Victoria Laurie   *h* 329

Blaine, Cassandra
Cafe Europa - Edward Ifkovic   *t* 182

Blake, Anita
Dead Ice - Laurell K. Hamilton   *h* 311

Booth Delaney, Sarah
Bone to Be Wild - Carolyn Haines   *m* 564

Bradley, Marcus
He's No Prince Charming - Elle Daniels   *r* 949

Brandon, Piers
Say Yes to the Marquess - Tessa Dare   *r* 950

Brandt, Sarah
Murder on Amsterdam Avenue - Victoria Thompson   *m* 672

Braun, Anna-Grace
When Grace Sings - Kim Vogel Sawyer   *i* 454

Brungardt, Steven
When Grace Sings - Kim Vogel Sawyer   *i* 454

Bud
Saving Cecil - Lee Mims   *m* 620

Cady, Drew
The Lynchpin - Jeffrey B. Burton   *m* 507

Lord Cambury
The Spring Bride - Anne Gracie   *r* 975

Campbell, Rand
A Heart's Danger - Colleen Coble   *i* 385
A Heart's Danger - Colleen Coble   *i* 385

Chance, Jane
The Spring Bride - Anne Gracie   *r* 975

Connard, Howard Sr.
Etta Mae's Worst Bad-Luck Day - Ann B. Ross   *c* 848

Cooper, Cleo
Saving Cecil - Lee Mims   *m* 620

Craven, Leonora "Nora"
A Good Rake Is Hard to Find - Manda Collins   *r* 944

Croftner, Ben
A Heart's Disguise - Colleen Coble   *i* 382
A Heart's Obsession - Colleen Coble   *i* 384

Davidia
The Laughing Monsters - Denis Johnson   *c* 776

de Kruk, Carson
Hiss and Tell - Claire Donally   *m* 536

Donovan, Colin
Harbor Island - Carla Neggers   *r* 1041

Doyle, Laura
Going Gone - Sharon Sala   *r* 1066

Drakestone, Bray
The Duke in My Bed - Amelia Grey   *r* 979

DuBois, Jessica
A Heart's Danger - Colleen Coble   *i* 385

DuBois, Sage
Ladle to the Grave - Connie Archer   *m* 480

Edmund
The Promise of Palm Grove - Shelley Shepard Gray   *i* 407

Elvaston, Doug
The Readaholics and the Falcon Fiasco - Laura DiSilverio   *m* 535

Faulk, Michael
Before, During, After - Richard Bausch   *c* 698

Faulkner, Tara
One Last Thing - Rebecca St. James   *i* 461

Flint, Dr. Michael
Deadlight Hall - Sarah Rayne   *h* 337

Fontaine, Grace
Gift of Grace - Sharlene MacLaren   *i* 433

Gordon, Jean
A Fine Summer's Day - Charles Todd   *t* 263

Gray, Evelyn
Hope Rising - Stacy Henrie   *r* 987

Gregory, Suzanne
Slow Burn - Andrew Welsh-Huggins   *m* 680

Grissom, Seth
One Last Thing - Rebecca St. James   *i* 461

Hall, Conrad
Gift of Grace - Sharlene MacLaren   *i* 433

Hamilton, Olivia "Livie"
Wild Horses - B.J. Daniels   *r* 947

Hayes, Andy
Slow Burn - Andrew Welsh-Huggins   *m* 680

Helmuth, Ben
Huckleberry Spring - Jennifer Beckstrand   *i* 359

Hextall, Lady Julia
I've Got My Duke to Keep Me Warm - Kelly Bowen   *r* 920

Holliday, Montgomery
No Ghouls Allowed - Victoria Laurie   *h* 329

Hughes, Ellie
Jilted - Rachael Johns   *r* 996

Ingram, Terri
The Lynchpin - Jeffrey B. Burton   *m* 507

Jean-Claude
Dead Ice - Laurell K. Hamilton   *h* 311

Keaton, Julie
Surrender - June Gray   *r* 977

Kelley, Ralph
Hope Rising - Stacy Henrie   *r* 987

Kingsbury, Priscilla
Hiss and Tell - Claire Donally   *m* 536

Levire, Adam
I've Got My Duke to Keep Me Warm - Kelly
   Bowen   *r* 920

Linden, Maggie
To Win Her Favor - Tamera Alexander   *i* 356

Lisle, Lord Frederick "Freddy"
A Good Rake Is Hard to Find - Manda
   Collins   *r* 944

Malloy, Frank
Murder on Amsterdam Avenue - Victoria
   Thompson   *m* 672

Manton, Dominick
If the Viscount Falls - Sabrina Jeffries   *r* 995

Martha
The Tomb: A Novel of Martha - Stephanie
   Landsem   *i* 426

McGrath, Cullen
To Win Her Favor - Tamera Alexander   *i* 356

Milieu, Graf
Bone to Be Wild - Carolyn Haines   *m* 564

Miller, Jonah
The Decision - Wanda E. Brunstetter   *i* 367

Montgomery, Sara
A Heart's Disguise - Colleen Coble   *i* 382
A Heart's Obsession - Colleen Coble   *i* 384

Montgomery, Sarah
A Heart's Danger - Colleen Coble   *i* 385

Nelson, Emma
Huckleberry Spring - Jennifer Beckstrand   *i* 359

Pace, Jordan
As Gouda as Dead - Avery Aames   *m* 473

Peabody, Miss Harriet
After a Fashion - Jen Turano   *i* 465

Penelope
The Accidental Countess - Valerie
   Bowman   *r* 923

Prim, Louisa
The Duke in My Bed - Amelia Grey   *r* 979

Quatermaine, Flynn
Jilted - Rachael Johns   *r* 996

Ridgewood, Noah
Dictatorship of the Dress - Jessica
   Topper   *r* 1092

Rutledge, Ian
A Fine Summer's Day - Charles Todd   *t* 263

Schrock, Elaine
The Decision - Wanda E. Brunstetter   *i* 367

Selinda
Cursed by Fire - Jacquelyn Frank   *f* 36

Sharpe, Emma
Harbor Island - Carla Neggers   *r* 1041

Sherman, Jason
Surrender - June Gray   *r* 977

Simon
The Tomb: A Novel of Martha - Stephanie
   Landsem   *i* 426

Sinclair, Tori
Wedding Duress - Elizabeth Lynn Casey   *m* 513

Sloane
Dictatorship of the Dress - Jessica
   Topper   *r* 1092

Smithson, Melinda "Mellie"
50 Ways to Ruin a Rake - Jade Lee   *r* 1007

Sophie
Ladle to the Grave - Connie Archer   *m* 480

Swift, Julian
The Accidental Countess - Valerie
   Bowman   *r* 923

Taylor, Madison
The Readaholics and the Falcon Fiasco - Laura
   DiSilverio   *m* 535

Travis, Jess
Gift of Grace - Sharlene MacLaren   *i* 433

Unnamed Character
Revels Ending - Vic Kerry   *h* 326

Vernon, Jane
If the Viscount Falls - Sabrina Jeffries   *r* 995

von Erhlich, Frederic
Cafe Europa - Edward Ifkovic   *t* 182

Weaver, Leona
The Promise of Palm Grove - Shelley Shepard
   Gray   *i* 407

Wenger, Marlena
The Love Letters - Beverly Lewis   *i* 427

Wentworth, Milo
Wedding Duress - Elizabeth Lynn Casey   *m* 513

West, Nell
Deadlight Hall - Sarah Rayne   *h* 337

Whitmore, Clio
Say Yes to the Marquess - Tessa Dare   *r* 950

Whitney, Evie
How to Plan a Wedding for a Royal Spy - Vanessa
   Kelly   *r* 997

Wiggins, Etta Mae
Etta Mae's Worst Bad-Luck Day - Ann B.
   Ross   *c* 848

Winger, Cameron
Going Gone - Sharon Sala   *r* 1066

Yoder, Miriam
Miriam's Secret - Jerry S. Eicher   *i* 396

Yutzy, Wayne
Miriam's Secret - Jerry S. Eicher   *i* 396

Zimmerman, Nat
The Love Letters - Beverly Lewis   *i* 427

FILMMAKER

Barton, Ross
Double Fudge Brownie Murder - Joanne
   Fluke   *m* 548

Lisa
Tattered Legacy - Shannon Baker   *m* 484

Reiniger, Godric
The Dark Arts of Blood - Freda
   Warrington   *h* 350

Selznick, David O.
A Touch of Stardust - Kate Alcott   *t* 125

FINANCIER

Arkwright, Julius
Trust No One - Jayne Ann Krentz   *c* 786

Bennett, Parker
The Melody Lingers On - Mary Higgins
   Clark   *m* 515

Farnell, R.J.
Phantom Angel - David Handler   *m* 567

Sweetwater, Jonathan
My Father's Wives - Mike Greenberg   *c* 753

Wingate, Geoffrey
The Final Recollections of Charles Dickens -
   Thomas Hauser   *t* 175

FIRE FIGHTER

Breen, Fred
The Night Belongs to Fireman - Jennifer
   Bernard   *r* 913

Halsey, Mike
Sweet Surprise - Candis Terry   *r* 1091

McCabe, Colleen
Neighing with Fire - Kathryn O'Sullivan   *m* 628

Moretti, Dan
The Dandelion Field - Kathryn Springer   *i* 460

Wilder, Jackson
Sweet Surprise - Candis Terry   *r* 1091

FISHERMAN

Cass
A Finely Knit Murder - Sally
   Goldenbaum   *m* 557

Trench, Wes
The Marauders - Tom Cooper   *m* 522

FOOTBALL PLAYER

Decker, Amos
Memory Man - David Baldacci   *m* 485

Greene, Colton
From the Start - Melissa Tagg   *i* 462

Hayes, Andy
Slow Burn - Andrew Welsh-Huggins   *m* 680

FOSTER CHILD

Caulfield, Eleanor
I Loved a Rogue - Katharine Ashe   *r* 903

Luis
Kiss Me Hello - Grace Burrowes   *r* 933

Morgan, Tanya
The Fall - John T. Lescroart   *m* 600

FOSTER PARENT

Lindstrom, Sidonie
Kiss Me Hello - Grace Burrowes   *r* 933

FOUNDLING

Kizzy
Three Songs for Roxy - Caren Gussoff   *s* 1150

FRIEND

Abbott, Nora
Tattered Legacy - Shannon Baker   *m* 484

Character Description Index

Queenie
Dollbaby - Laura McNeal   *c* 801

Quinn, Mia
Lethal Beauty - Lis Wiehl   *i* 470

Raber, Andrew
Meek and Mild - Olivia Newport   *i* 439

Ramona
Doll Face - Tim Curran   *h* 288

Rathbone, Oliver
Corridors of the Night - Anne Perry   *t* 229

Reed, Malcolm
Uncertain Logic - Christopher L. Bennett   *s* 1119

Reeves, Bass
Karen Memory - Elizabeth Bear   *s* 1118

Reid, Savannah
Killer Gourmet - G.A. McKevett   *m* 615

Reilly, Will
Night Blindness - Susan Strecker   *c* 870

Rene
A Killer Retreat - Tracy Weber   *m* 679

Renquist, Pete
A Fatal Chapter - Lorna Barrett   *m* 488

Reynolds, Ali
Cold Betrayal - J.A. Jance   *m* 584

Reynolds, Charles
Alien Separation - Gini Koch   *s* 1162

Richardson, Dorothy
The Lodger - Louisa Treger   *t* 265

Richardson, Violet
Silken Threats - Addison Fox   *r* 966

Richmond, Daisy
Before I Go - Colleen Oakley   *c* 820

Rick, Louise
The Forgotten Girls - Sara Blaedel   *m* 493

Riker, William T.
Takedown - John Jackson Miller   *s* 1178

Rogers, Tyler
Shades of the Wolf - Karen Whiddon   *f* 124

Ronan
Remnants: Season of Fire - Lisa T. Bergren   *i* 361

Lady Rosemarie
An Uncertain Choice - Jody Hedlund   *i* 415

Roth, Anna
The Goddess of Small Victories - Yannick Grannec   *c* 752

Rousseau, Laura
Five-Alarm Fudge - Christine DeSmet   *m* 534

Rundstrom, Ludvig "Vig"
The Unleashing - Shelly Laurenston   *f* 68

Rusmanov, Valentin
Zero Hour - Will Hill   *h* 316

Russell
Emma and Otto and Russell and James - Emma Hooper   *c* 769

Ryan
Inspector of the Dead - David Morrell   *t* 214

Ryder
Night Blindness - Susan Strecker   *c* 870

Saginowski, Bob
The Drop - Dennis Lehane   *c* 788

Sanchez, Oscar
Devils and Dust - J.D. Rhoades   *m* 642

Sanders, Jimmy
A String of Beads - Thomas Perry   *c* 827

Sarah
The Door in the Moon - Catherine Fisher   *f* 32

Schaeffer, Aidan
Dark Bride - Jonathan Ryan   *h* 340

Schrock, Elaine
The Decision - Wanda E. Brunstetter   *i* 367

Schroder, Arnold "Stubby"
When - Victoria Laurie   *f* 70

Sebastian
Signal to Noise - Silvia Moreno-Garcia   *f* 85

Sellers, Jackie
No Place to Hide - Lynette Eason   *i* 395

Selvedge, Jack
Pale Harvest - Braden Hepner   *c* 764

Seventh, Abraham
Infinity Bell - Devon Monk   *f* 83

Shaw, Lily
Falling from Horses - Molly Gloss   *t* 165

Simmons, Bernie
A Catered Mother's Day - Isis Crawford   *m* 523

Simmons, Libby
A Catered Mother's Day - Isis Crawford   *m* 523

Sinclair, Tori
Wedding Duress - Elizabeth Lynn Casey   *m* 513

Siobhan
The Thing About December - Donal Ryan   *c* 850

Slone, Vernon
Hold the Dark - William Giraldi   *c* 749

Solloway, Leander
The Language of Paradise - Barbara Klein Moss   *t* 217

Solomon, Lou
The Sirena Quest - Michael A. Kahn   *m* 589

Soo-Yee
Doll Face - Tim Curran   *h* 288

Sophie
Ladle to the Grave - Connie Archer   *m* 480

Sparks, Cora
The Dress Shop of Dreams - Menna van Praag   *c* 878

Springer, Miss Julia
Etta Mae's Worst Bad-Luck Day - Ann B. Ross   *c* 848

St. James, Rowland "Rowdy"
Rowdy - Jay Crownover   *r* 945

Standish, Allison
Where Secrets Sleep - Marta Perry   *i* 444

Stanton, Tom
Fiercombe Manor - Kate Riordan   *t* 235

Steimetz, Charles Proteus
Electric City - Elizabeth Rosner   *t* 237

Steinhauser, Celia
The Pocket Wife - Susan Crawford   *m* 524

Stephanie
Prague Summer - Jeffrey Condran   *c* 717

Stephen
Sweetshop of Dreams - Jenny Colgan   *c* 715

Stone, Ryan
Killer Gourmet - G.A. McKevett   *m* 615

Strode, Ralph
The Invention of Fire - Bruce W. Holsinger   *t* 179

Sturges, Jim
Trollhunters - Guillermo Del Toro   *h* 292

Stutzman, Sara
The Decision - Wanda E. Brunstetter   *i* 367

Sugarman
The Big Finish - James W. Hall   *c* 758

Sutter, Gloria
The Other Side of Midnight - Simone St. James   *r* 1087

Suze
Shopaholic to the Stars - Sophie Kinsella   *c* 784

Tad
The Murk - Robert Lettrick   *h* 331

Talfi
Iron Axe - Steven Harper   *f* 46

Tango
Marked Fur Murder - Dixie Lyle   *m* 609

Tarquin
Shopaholic to the Stars - Sophie Kinsella   *c* 784

Theo
Glow - Ned Beauman   *c* 699

Theta, Phaet
Dove Arising - Karen Bao   *s* 1114

Thomas
The Way We Bared Our Souls - Willa Strayhorn   *f* 112

Thormodsson, Ulfar
Blood Will Follow - Snorri Kristjansson   *t* 194

Thorn
The Big Finish - James W. Hall   *c* 758

Tinkie
Bone to Be Wild - Carolyn Haines   *m* 564

Torres, Ricky
Dead Red - Tim O'Mara   *m* 626

Troyer, Hannah
Murder Freshly Baked - Vannetta Chapman   *i* 377

Tubby
Trollhunters - Guillermo Del Toro   *h* 292

Tucker, "Trip"
Uncertain Logic - Christopher L. Bennett   *s* 1119

Tunstell, Primrose
Prudence - Gail Carriger   *f* 22

Turner, Ruthie
Jaded - Varina Denman   *i* 392

Tyler, Emma
The Perfect Homecoming - Julia London   *r* 1013

Unger, Deirdre
Night Night, Sleep Tight - Hallie Ephron   *m* 541

Unnamed
Dear Thief - Samantha Harvey   *c* 762

Unnamed Character
10:04 - Ben Lerner   *c* 790

Vafa, Sina
Tehran at Twilight - Salar Abdoh   *c* 683

Vanderhall, Brian
Superposition - David Walton   *s* 1205

Vegas, Milagros Carmona
The Barefoot Queen - Ildefonso Falcones   *t* 156

Vicky
Betrayed - Lisa Scottoline   *c* 857

Walt
The Dress Shop of Dreams - Menna van Praag   *c* 878

Wash
The Wonder of All Things - Jason Mott   *c* 812

Washburn, Frankie
Prudence - David Treuer *c* 872

Watkins, Trey
One Mile Under - Andrew Gross *m* 561

Watson, Arnie
The Dead Play On - Heather Graham *m* 560

Watson, Brooke
The Devil's Only Friend - Dan Wells *h* 352

Watson, Kera
The Unleashing - Shelly Laurenston *f* 68

Watts, Brittany
Blood Matters - Aviva Bel'Harold *h* 284

Wayfarer
First and Last Sorcerer - Barb Hendee *f* 52

Weary, Nat
Driving the King - Ravi Howard *t* 180

Weaver, Emma
The Matchmaker - Sarah Price *i* 451

Webster, Moss
Life or Death - Michael Robotham *m* 645

Webster, Wallace
There Must Be Some Mistake - Frederick
   Barthelme *c* 697

Wells, Jane
The Lodger - Louisa Treger *t* 265

West, Duncan
Never Judge a Lady by Her Cover - Sarah
   MacLean *r* 1014

Whalen, Dani
One Mile Under - Andrew Gross *m* 561

Whips
Castaway Planet - Eric Flint *s* 1146

Whiskey
Marked Fur Murder - Dixie Lyle *m* 609

Whitby, Jacob
The Masque of a Murderer - Susanna
   Calkins *m* 510

White, Christopher
Alien Separation - Gini Koch *s* 1162

Whitefield, Jane
A String of Beads - Thomas Perry *c* 827

Whiting, Nick
Where Secrets Sleep - Marta Perry *i* 444

Wiggins, Etta Mae
Etta Mae's Worst Bad-Luck Day - Ann B.
   Ross *c* 848

Wilder, Jackson
Sweet Surprise - Candis Terry *r* 1091

Will
If I Fall, If I Die - Michael Christie *c* 712

Winn, Peggy
A Wee Murder in My Shop - Fran Stewart *m* 667

Winter, Ellie
The Other Side of Midnight - Simone St.
   James *r* 1087

Witherspoon, Gerald
Mrs. Jeffries and the One Who Got Away - Emily
   Brightwell *m* 503

Wyatt, Blake
Nowhere to Hide - Sigmund Brouwer *i* 365

Zarif
The Second Guard - J.D. Vaughn *f* 119

Zeke
Finn Fancy Necromancy - Randy
   Henderson *f* 53

Zin, Ben
The Wicked Awakening of Anne Merchant - Joanna
   Wiebe *h* 353

FUGITIVE

Case, Matilda
Infinity Bell - Devon Monk *f* 83

Farrell, Steve
Manhunt - Lisa Phillips *i* 447

Greaves, Apollo
Darling Beast - Elizabeth Hoyt *r* 989

Helmuth, Fannie
Whiskers of the Lion - P.L. Gaus *m* 555

Heuser, Georg
Ostland - David Thomas *t* 259

Miller, Ramsey
Before He Finds Her - Michael Kardos *m* 591

Paynter, Johnny
Outlaw Takes a Bride - Susan Page Davis *i* 389

Quentin
Infinity Bell - Devon Monk *f* 83

Sanders, Jimmy
A String of Beads - Thomas Perry *c* 827

Seventh, Abraham
Infinity Bell - Devon Monk *f* 83

The Pet
Hunted Warrior - Lindsey Piper *f* 95

GAMBLER

Drakestone, Bray
The Duke in My Bed - Amelia Grey *r* 979

McShane, Tim
Of Irish Blood - Mary Pat Kelly *t* 188

Taggart, Mike
Last Chance Family - Hope Ramsay *r* 1055

White, John "JW"
Sins of Our Fathers - Shawn Lawrence
   Otto *c* 822

Zerelli, Dominic "Whoosh"
A Scourge of Vipers - Bruce DeSilva *m* 533

GANG MEMBER

Johnson, Fred
The Winter Family - Clifford Jackman *t* 184

Jones, Lexy
Chasing Sunsets - Karen Kingsbury *i* 425

Pilate
Gathering Prey - John Sandford *m* 652

Ross, Quentin
The Winter Family - Clifford Jackman *t* 184

Shakespeare, Lukas
The Winter Family - Clifford Jackman *t* 184

Silva, Rab
On the Run - Jo Davis *r* 951

GARDENER

Eduardo
Grave on Grand Avenue - Naomi
   Hirahara *m* 575

GENETICALLY ALTERED BEING

Abbas, Anwar
Evensong - John Love *s* 1171

Adara
Artemis Invaded - Jane M. Lindskold *s* 1169

Graeme
Bengal's Quest - Lora Leigh *s* 1168

Phoenix
The Book of Phoenix - Nnedi Okorafor *f* 88

Saeed
The Book of Phoenix - Nnedi Okorafor *f* 88

Whips
Castaway Planet - Eric Flint *s* 1146

GENIUS

Battle, Jeff
What Strange Creatures - Emily Arsenault *c* 695

Erikson, Mike
The Fold - Peter Clines *s* 1127

Godel, Kurt
The Goddess of Small Victories - Yannick
   Grannec *c* 752

Quentin
Infinity Bell - Devon Monk *f* 83

GENTLEMAN

Winters, Noah
The Duke's Disaster - Grace Burrowes *r* 934

GIRL

Abigail
Little Girls - Ronald Damien Malfi *h* 333

Alice
The Dead Hamlets - Peter Roman *f* 99

Ally
The Silence - Tim Lebbon *h* 330

Amber
We Are Pirates - Daniel Handler *c* 759

Aya
The Glass Arrow - Kristen Simmons *s* 1197

Banning, Chloe
Silver Thaw - Catherine Anderson *r* 898

Brennan, Tory
Terminal - Kathy Reichs *s* 1187

Canfield, Piper
The Murk - Robert Lettrick *h* 331

Cappelletti, Juliet
Juliet's Nurse - Lois Leveen *t* 204

Dare, Alice
Mars Evacuees - Sophia McDougall *s* 1176

Deveaux, Rory
The Shadow Cabinet - Maureen Johnson *h* 322

Elsa
The Stager - Susan Coll *c* 716

Emrys, Evangeline
The Inquisitor's Mark - Dianne Salerni *f* 102

Everhart, Dusty
The Nightmare Charade - Mindee Arnett *h* 279

Fareeda
Green on Blue - Elliot Ackerman *c* 684

Jones, Lexy
Chasing Sunsets - Karen Kingsbury *i* 425

Judith "Jude"
Ishmael's Oranges - Claire Hajaj *c* 757

Kalloryn, Talimendra "Tali" Sanchez
The Second Guard - J.D. Vaughn *f* 119

Kimei, Sakura
Castaway Planet - Eric Flint *s* 1146

Krysta
Gretel and the Dark - Eliza Granville *t* 168

Levine, Sophie
Electric City - Elizabeth Rosner *t* 237

Lily
A Worthy Pursuit - Karen Witemeyer *i* 471

London
Make Me Lose Control - Christie
    Ridgway *r* 1057

Lore
Hellhole - Gina Damico *h* 290

Miller, Meg
Before He Finds Her - Michael Kardos *m* 591

Osborne, Frazer
Last to Know - Elizabeth Adler *c* 685

Osborne, Madison
Last to Know - Elizabeth Adler *c* 685

Phyllis
A Place Called Winter - Patrick Gale *t* 162

Prudence
Prudence - David Treuer *c* 872

Rabbit
She Weeps Each Time You're Born - Quan
    Barry *c* 696

Rainbow
Last Chance Family - Hope Ramsay *r* 1055

Simpson, Lindy
My Sunshine Away - M.O. Walsh *c* 884

Star, Ice Cream
The Country of Ice Cream Star - Sandra
    Newman *c* 816

Tia
Firefight - Brandon Sanderson *f* 104

Unnamed Character
Exposure - Kathy Reichs *s* 1186
Method 15/33 - Shannon Kirk *m* 594

Van Meeterens, Ariana
Rising Tide - Patricia Twomey Ryan *m* 649

Vermast, Tine
From Bruges with Love - Pieter Aspe *m* 482

Widdershins "Shins"
Covenant's End - Ari Marmell *f* 78

GIRLFRIEND

Abbott, Nora
Tattered Legacy - Shannon Baker *m* 484

April
Endangered - C.J. Box *m* 499

Ayla
In Case of Emergency - Courtney Moreno *c* 811

Beausoleil, Jonquil "Boso"
Phantom Angel - David Handler *m* 567

Bentley, Olivia
He's So Fine - Jill Shalvis *r* 1075

Browning, Theodosia
Ming Tea Murder - Laura Childs *m* 514

Burnett, Molly
Hope Burns - Jaci Burton *r* 936

Cafferty, Danni
The Dead Play On - Heather Graham *m* 560

Caldani, Nadia
Sorceress - Claudia Gray *f* 38

Cameron
I Saw Her Standing There - Marie Force *r* 964

Carstairs, Eloisa
Deception on Sable Hill - Shelley Gray *i* 408

Cermak, Clare
Ghost Killer - Robin D. Owens *f* 91

Cherish
Glow - Ned Beauman *c* 699

Coolidge, Sunny
Hiss and Tell - Claire Donally *m* 536

Cooper, Mel
Dark Chocolate Demise - Jenn McKinlay *m* 616

Courtney
Zombified - Adam Gallardo *h* 302

Cross, Stella
Alive - Chandler Baker *h* 282

D'Alisa, Juliette
Reservations for Two - Hillary Manton
    Lodge *i* 428

Daniels, Faith
Quake - Patrick Carman *s* 1124

Davidson, Kate
A Killer Retreat - Tracy Weber *m* 679

Davy
Unleashed - Sophie Jordan *s* 1157

Emma
Tangled Lives - Hilary Boyd *c* 705

Flaherty, Cam
Farmed and Dangerous - Edith Maxwell *m* 613

Fortune, Clyde
A Fright to the Death - Dawn Eastman *h* 295

Frank, Pat
Hot Pursuit - Stuart Woods *m* 682

Gallagher, Piper
In Case of Emergency - Courtney Moreno *c* 811

Gathercole, Tina
The Big Finish - James W. Hall *c* 758

Graber, Kim
What Strange Creatures - Emily Arsenault *c* 695

Hammond, Mallory
The Promise - Beth Wiseman *c* 888

Hastings, Miriam
A Harvest of Hope - Lauraine Snelling *i* 459

Holland, Linnet
Catch a Falling Heiress - Laura Lee
    Guhrke *r* 981

Holliday, M.J.
No Ghouls Allowed - Victoria Laurie *h* 329

Holloway, Tara
Death, Taxes, and Cheap Sunglasses - Diane
    Kelly *m* 592

Hopkins, Rosie
Sweetshop of Dreams - Jenny Colgan *c* 715

Jain, Shaila
The Venusian Gambit - Michael J.
    Martinez *s* 1173

James, Mira
February Fever - Jess Lourey *m* 607

Johnson, Amy-Faye
The Readaholics and the Falcon Fiasco - Laura
    DiSilverio *m* 535

Keegan, Daisy
Butternut Summer - Mary McNear *c* 802

Lamb, Piper
License to Dill - Mary Ellen Hughes *m* 578

Lancaster, Deirdre "Foxtrot"
Marked Fur Murder - Dixie Lyle *m* 609

Lea
Whispers in the Dark - Chase J. Jackson *h* 321

Leroux, Danielle
Asylum - Jeannette de Beauvoir *m* 529

Llewellyn, Bronwen "Stormy"
Saint Odd - Dean Koontz *c* 785

Lowry, Beth
You Were Mine - Abbi Glines *c* 751
You Were Mine - Abbi Glines *c* 751

Maggie
King of the Cracksmen - Dennis
    O'Flaherty *s* 1180
Where All Light Tends to Go - David Joy *m* 588

Margaritte
Crazy Horse's Girlfriend - Erika T. Wurth *c* 891

Mauvais, Devyn
Make You Remember - Macy Beckett *r* 911

McCabe, Colleen
Neighing with Fire - Kathryn O'Sullivan *m* 628

McDonough, Consuelo "Lo"
The Way We Bared Our Souls - Willa
    Strayhorn *f* 112

McMurphy, Allie
Oh Say Can You Fudge - Nancy Coco *m* 518

Metcalf, Molly
From a Drood to a Kill - Simon R. Green *f* 41

Monaghan, Tess
Hush Hush - Laura Lippman *m* 604

Morris, Chelsea
Miles from Nowhere - Amy Clipston *i* 379

Nelson, Stormi
Death by Baking - Cynthia Hickey *i* 418

Orianna
Getting Even - Sarah Rayner *c* 842

Palma, Lolita
The Siege - Arturo Perez-Reverte *t* 228

Pelerin, Dinah
Where the Bones are Buried - Jeanne
    Matthews *m* 611

Price, Harper
Miss Mayhem - Rachel Hawkins *f* 48

Prospero, Kate
Deadly Spells - Jaye Wells *f* 121

Rachel
The Soul of Discretion - Susan Hill *m* 574

Reilly, Jensen
Night Blindness - Susan Strecker *c* 870

Robin
Believe - Erin McCarthy *r* 1026

Samarra
The Shadow of the Crescent Moon - Fatima
    Bhutto *c* 703

Singer, Marcy
Wicked Stitch - Amanda Lee *m* 597

Stutzman, Sara
The Decision - Wanda E. Brunstetter *i* 367

Sullivan, Serafina "Finn"
Briar Queen - Katherine Harbour *h* 312

Swan, Scarlett
Black Scorpion - Jon Land *m* 596

Sweeney, Cara
Invaded - Melissa Landers *s* 1163

Tanner, Shelby
Pocket Apocalypse - Seanan McGuire *f* 80

Wainwright, Brooklyn
Ripped from the Pages - Kate Carlisle *m* 512

Weeks, Helen
Time of Death - Mark Billingham *m* 491

Wiggins, Etta Mae
Etta Mae's Worst Bad-Luck Day - Ann B.
Ross *c* 848

Winter, Ellie
The Other Side of Midnight - Simone St.
James *r* 1087

Winters, Caitlyn
The Christmas Bouquet - Sherryl Woods *r* 1098

Woodruff, Gwen
Fatal Trauma - Richard L. Mabry *i* 432

GLADIATOR

Jirom
Storm and Steel - Jon Sprunk *f* 109

GODFATHER

Costello, Frank
Night Life - David C. Taylor *t* 258

Hauck, Ty
One Mile Under - Andrew Gross *m* 561

GODMOTHER

Matilda
Jilted - Rachael Johns *r* 996

Queen Victoria
The Hanged Man - P.N. Elrod *h* 296

GOLFER

McKinley, Travis
Miracle at Augusta - James Patterson *c* 825

GOVERNESS

de Falleron, Jeanne
The Duke of Dark Desires - Miranda
Neville *r* 1042

Fenwick, Lady Ivy
Forbidden to Love the Duke - Jillian
Hunter *r* 991

Frasier, Roberta "Bertie"
Rules for a Proper Governess - Jennifer
Ashley *r* 905

Meadows, Claire
By Winter's Light - Stephanie Laurens *r* 1006

Russell, Lily
The Duke's Guide to Correct Behavior - Megan
Frampton *r* 967

GOVERNMENT OFFICIAL

Alexi
Fram - Steve Himmer *c* 767

Arbuthnot
Pasha: A Kydd Sea Adventure - Julian
Stockwin *t* 255

Augustus
Golden Son - Pierce Brown *s* 1120

Bassett, Mac
Silence the Dead - Jack Fredrickson *m* 549

Brembre, Nicholas
The Invention of Fire - Bruce W.
Holsinger *t* 179

Callahan, Luke
Beyond All Dreams - Elizabeth Camden *i* 374

Faustus, Manlius
Deadly Election - Lindsey Davis *t* 148

Fitzgerald, Edward
The German Agent - J. Sydney Jones *t* 186

Grimshaw, Ephraim
The Hidden Man - Robin Blake *m* 495

Hind, Clarissa
Beautiful You - Chuck Palahniuk *c* 823

Jacobs, Slaid
Convincing the Rancher - Claire
McEwen *r* 1028

Koenig, Alexander
Deep Time - Ian Douglas *s* 1139

Lincoln, Abraham
Lincoln's Billy - Tom LeClair *t* 200

Martini, Jeff
Alien Separation - Gini Koch *s* 1162

Mayor
The Woman Who Read Too Much - Bahiyyih
Nakhjavani *t* 220

Oscar
Fram - Steve Himmer *c* 767

Roosevelt, Franklin D.
Joe Steele - Harry Turtledove *s* 1203

Roosevelt, Theodore
The Last American Vampire - Seth
Grahame-Smith *h* 304

Mr. Ryker
The Glass Arrow - Kristen Simmons *s* 1197

Scarlatti, Vic
Echo Lake - Carla Neggers *r* 1040

Shiffley, Randall
Lord of the Wings - Donna Andrews *m* 479

Stanton, Edwin
King of the Cracksmen - Dennis
O'Flaherty *s* 1180

Steele, Joe
Joe Steele - Harry Turtledove *s* 1203

Walldeen, Klara
The Swimmer - Joakim Zander *c* 893

Wilson, Woodrow
The German Agent - J. Sydney Jones *t* 186

GRADUATE

Cohen, Gordie
The Sirena Quest - Michael A. Kahn *m* 589

David
You're Not Much Use to Anyone - David
Shapiro *c* 861

Godwin, Robert
The Sirena Quest - Michael A. Kahn *m* 589

Gorman, Ray
The Sirena Quest - Michael A. Kahn *m* 589

Hastings, Lauren "Lo"
The Best Medicine - Elizabeth Hayley *r* 984

Jude
The Last Kings of Sark - Rosa
Rankin-Gee *c* 840

McCormick, William "Bronco Billy"
The Sirena Quest - Michael A. Kahn *m* 589

Solomon, Lou
The Sirena Quest - Michael A. Kahn *m* 589

GRANDDAUGHTER

Aida
An Italian Wife - Ann Hood *c* 768

Athena
Cold Betrayal - J.A. Jance *m* 584

Ava
The Boston Girl - Anita Diamant *t* 149

Bell, Liberty "Ibby"
Dollbaby - Laura McNeal *c* 801

Bradley, Neva
The Secrets of Midwives - Sally Hepworth *c* 765

Curtis, Angie
Twisted Threads - Lea Wait *m* 678

D'Alisa, Juliette
Reservations for Two - Hillary Manton
Lodge *i* 428

Francesca
An Italian Wife - Ann Hood *c* 768

Hansen, LeeAnn
The Cowboy SEAL - Laura Marie Altom *r* 897

Hawes, Lady Fiona
Twice Tempted - Eileen Dreyer *r* 956

Helmuth, Mandy
Huckleberry Harvest - Jennifer Beckstrand *i* 358

Jamieson, Lucky
Ladle to the Grave - Connie Archer *m* 480

Luella
The Love Letters - Beverly Lewis *i* 427

Mairead
Twice Tempted - Eileen Dreyer *r* 956

Marietti, Gabby
A Finely Knit Murder - Sally
Goldenbaum *m* 557

Peake, Charmaine
Lay It on My Heart - Angela Pneuman *c* 834

Porter, Maddie
Manhattan in Miniature - Margaret Grace *m* 558

Rosen, Evie
Love and Miss Communication - Elyssa
Friedland *r* 968

Sharpe, Emma
Harbor Island - Carla Neggers *r* 1041

Sparks, Cora
The Dress Shop of Dreams - Menna van
Praag *c* 878

Taylor, Sophie
Shadow of a Spout - Amanda Cooper *m* 521

Vegas, Milagros Carmona
The Barefoot Queen - Ildefonso Falcones *t* 156

Wenger, Marlena
The Love Letters - Beverly Lewis *i* 427

Whitecastle, Emma
Ghost in the Guacamole - Sue Ann
Jaffarian *m* 582

GRANDFATHER

Hathorne, Sam
Pleasantville - Attica Locke *m* 605

GRANDMOTHER (continued)

Helmuth, Felty
Huckleberry Harvest - Jennifer Beckstrand *i* 358
Huckleberry Spring - Jennifer Beckstrand *i* 359

Jack
Ladle to the Grave - Connie Archer *m* 480

Marquess of Dourne
Twice Tempted - Eileen Dreyer *r* 956

Melchor
The Barefoot Queen - Ildefonso Falcones *t* 156

Riddell, Samuel "Grandpa"
A Sudden Light - Garth Stein *c* 868

Selvedge, Blair
Pale Harvest - Braden Hepner *c* 764

Sharpe, Wendell
Harbor Island - Carla Neggers *r* 1041

Shaw, Donovan "Dono"
Past Crimes - Glen Erik Hamilton *m* 566

GRANDMOTHER

Baum, Addie
The Boston Girl - Anita Diamant *t* 149

Bell, Fannie
Dollbaby - Laura McNeal *c* 801

Charlotte
Twisted Threads - Lea Wait *m* 678

Custer, Dorothy
Slow Burn - Andrew Welsh-Huggins *m* 680

Favazza, Birdie
A Finely Knit Murder - Sally
Goldenbaum *m* 557

Floss
The Secrets of Midwives - Sally Hepworth *c* 765

Freemont, Rose
Shadow of a Spout - Amanda Cooper *m* 521

Granny Apples
Ghost in the Guacamole - Sue Ann
Jaffarian *m* 582

Helmuth, Anna
Huckleberry Harvest - Jennifer Beckstrand *i* 358
Huckleberry Spring - Jennifer Beckstrand *i* 359

Ilsidi
Tracker - C.J. Cherryh *s* 1125

Mammi Janice
The Love Letters - Beverly Lewis *i* 427

Mireille
Reservations for Two - Hillary Manton
Lodge *i* 428

Nana Mama
Hope to Die - James Patterson *c* 824

Nikolaevna, Natasha
The Prince Who Loved Me - Karen
Hawkins *r* 983

Peake, Daze
Lay It on My Heart - Angela Pneuman *c* 834

Peterson, Betsy
Cold Betrayal - J.A. Jance *m* 584

Porter, Geraldine "Gerry"
Manhattan in Miniature - Margaret Grace *m* 558

Red Queen
The Liar's Key - Mark Lawrence *f* 71

Rimaldi, Josephine
An Italian Wife - Ann Hood *c* 768
An Italian Wife - Ann Hood *c* 768

Rosen, Bette
Love and Miss Communication - Elyssa
Friedland *r* 968

Sparks, Etta
The Dress Shop of Dreams - Menna van
Praag *c* 878

Teichner, Virginia
Every Fifteen Minutes - Lisa Scottoline *m* 653

GRANDSON

Cross, Alex
Hope to Die - James Patterson *c* 824

Custer, Aaron
Slow Burn - Andrew Welsh-Huggins *m* 680

Hansen, JJ
The Cowboy SEAL - Laura Marie Altom *r* 897

Hathorne, Neal
Pleasantville - Attica Locke *m* 605

Helmuth, Ben
Huckleberry Spring - Jennifer Beckstrand *i* 359

Ian
Twice Tempted - Eileen Dreyer *r* 956

Jakubowski, Max
Every Fifteen Minutes - Lisa Scottoline *m* 653

Riddell, Trevor
A Sudden Light - Garth Stein *c* 868

Romanovin, Alexsey
The Prince Who Loved Me - Karen
Hawkins *r* 983

Selvedge, Jack
Pale Harvest - Braden Hepner *c* 764

Shaw, Van
Past Crimes - Glen Erik Hamilton *m* 566

Tabini
Tracker - C.J. Cherryh *s* 1125

GUARD

Clark, Wilhemina "Mina"
The Dead Lands - Benjamin Percy *s* 1182

Mackenzie, Cameron
The Shattered Court - M.J. Scott *f* 106

GUARDIAN

Archer, Kate
Carousel Seas - Sharon Lee *f* 72

Atal
Green on Blue - Elliot Ackerman *c* 684

Atherton, Charlotte
A Worthy Pursuit - Karen Witemeyer *i* 471

Borgan
Carousel Seas - Sharon Lee *f* 72

de Cayenne, Le Poivre "Pepper"
Viper Game - Christine Feehan *r* 961

Derring, Maxwell
Earls Just Want to Have Fun - Shana
Galen *r* 970

Fortescue, Julian
The Duke of Dark Desires - Miranda
Neville *r* 1042

Gwil
The Siege Winter - Ariana Franklin *t* 159

King, Joseph
An Amish Man of Ice Mountain - Kelly
Long *i* 429

Pendare, Riley
The Inquisitor's Mark - Dianne Salerni *f* 102

GUIDE

Ben
As Night Falls - Jenny Milchman *m* 619

Grant
Dead Spots - Rhiannon Frater *h* 299

Whalen, Dani
One Mile Under - Andrew Gross *m* 561

GYPSY

Kizzy
Three Songs for Roxy - Caren Gussoff *s* 1150

Melchor
The Barefoot Queen - Ildefonso Falcones *t* 156

Roxy
Three Songs for Roxy - Caren Gussoff *s* 1150

Taliesin
I Loved a Rogue - Katharine Ashe *r* 903

Vegas, Milagros Carmona
The Barefoot Queen - Ildefonso Falcones *t* 156

HAIRDRESSER

Bree
Beyond the Pale Motel - Francesca Lia
Block *c* 704

Catt
Beyond the Pale Motel - Francesca Lia
Block *c* 704

Vogel, Johann
The Figaro Murders - Laura Lebow *t* 199

HANDICAPPED

Alvarini, Beth
Stillwater - Maynard Sims *h* 344

Beck, Joel
Amish Promises - Leslie Gould *i* 405

James, Mollie
A Love Like Ours - Becky Wade *i* 466

Kiran
The Glass Arrow - Kristen Simmons *s* 1197

Martin, Gary
The Missing Piece - Kevin Egan *m* 540

Steimetz, Charles Proteus
Electric City - Elizabeth Rosner *t* 237

Unger, Deirdre
Night Night, Sleep Tight - Hallie Ephron *m* 541

Wilkins, Peter
The Language of the Dead - Stephen
Kelly *t* 189

HANDYMAN

Felix
Prudence - David Treuer *c* 872

Mischler, Noah
Huckleberry Harvest - Jennifer Beckstrand *i* 358

Taylor, Mark
Love Letters - Debbie Macomber *c* 793

Roosevelt, Theodore
The Last American Vampire - Seth Grahame-Smith h 304

Rove, Karl
The Global War on Morris - Steve Israel c 772

Sand, George
The Dream Lover - Elizabeth Berg t 129

Selznick, David O.
A Touch of Stardust - Kate Alcott t 125

Seymour, Edward
The May Bride - Suzannah Dunn t 151

Seymour, Jane
The May Bride - Suzannah Dunn t 151

Shakespeare, William
The Dead Hamlets - Peter Roman f 99
The Tutor - Andrea Chapin t 140

Sheridan, Philip
Valley of the Shadow - Ralph Peters t 231

Smyslov, Vasily
Back Channel - Stephen L. Carter c 709

Stanley, Venetia
Viper Wine - Hermione Eyre t 154

Stanton, Edwin
King of the Cracksmen - Dennis O'Flaherty s 1180

Stein, Gertrude
Of Irish Blood - Mary Pat Kelly t 188

Stephen
The Siege Winter - Ariana Franklin t 159

Strachey, Lytton
Vanessa and Her Sister - Priya Parmar t 225

Strode, Ralph
The Invention of Fire - Bruce W. Holsinger t 179

Swan, Anna
The Thunder of Giants - Joel Fishbane t 157

Tesla, Nikola
The Lusitania Conspiracy - Ronald J. Walters t 269

Twain, Mark
The Lusitania Conspiracy - Ronald J. Walters t 269

van Gogh, Theo
The Season of Migration - Nellie Hermann t 177

van Gogh, Vincent
The Season of Migration - Nellie Hermann t 177

Victoria
The Eterna Files - Leanna Renee Hieber f 54

Walsingham, Francis
Murder in the Queen's Wardrobe - Kathy Lynn Emerson t 153

Wellesley, Arthur
Kings and Emperors - Dewey Lambdin t 195

William
Hereward: End of Days - James Wilde t 272

Wilson, Woodrow
The German Agent - J. Sydney Jones t 186

Woolf, Leonard
Vanessa and Her Sister - Priya Parmar t 225

Woolf, Virginia
Adeline: A Novel of Virginia Woolf - Norah Vincent t 268

Woolf, Virginia Stephen
Vanessa and Her Sister - Priya Parmar t 225

Yeats, W.B.
Adeline: A Novel of Virginia Woolf - Norah Vincent t 268

Zuckerberg, Mark
The Infernal - Mark Doten c 734

HOCKEY PLAYER

Jelinek, Ike
A Perfect Catch - Anna Sugden r 1090

HOLOCAUST VICTIM

Furman, Susanna
The Ambassadors - George Lerner t 203

HOMOSEXUAL

Cheramie, Leon
Under His Guard - Rie Warren s 1206

Darke
Under His Guard - Rie Warren s 1206

David
The Exile - C.T. Adams f 3

Enderly, Blake
Dreams of Shreds and Tatters - Amanda Downum h 293

Walden, Gray
All the Wrong Places - Lisa Lieberman t 205

HORSE

Bourbon Belle
To Win Her Favor - Tamera Alexander i 356

HORSE TRAINER

James, Lyndie
A Love Like Ours - Becky Wade i 466

Monahan, Tru
Betting on Hope - Debra Clopton i 381

HOSTAGE

Atkinson, Kelly
Fatal Trauma - Richard L. Mabry i 432

Baker, Dr. Mark
Fatal Trauma - Richard L. Mabry i 432

Callahan, Isaiah
Untraceable - Elizabeth Goddard i 404

Quarteney, Uma
In the Time of the Dragon Moon - Janet Lee Carey f 20

Warren, Cade
Untraceable - Elizabeth Goddard i 404

Warren, Heidi
Untraceable - Elizabeth Goddard i 404

HOTEL OWNER

Barrington, Stone
Paris Match - Stuart Woods c 889

Donovan, Reece
Love Me If You Dare - Toni Blake r 917

McMurphy, Allie
Oh Say Can You Fudge - Nancy Coco m 518

Miller, Sadie
Part Time Cowboy - Maisey Yates r 1099

Pennec, Pierre-Louis
Death in Brittany - Jean-Luc Bannalec m 486

Presley, Julia
The Memory House - Linda Goodnight r 974

Rose, Jo Marie
Love Letters - Debbie Macomber c 793

Zimmerman, Alexa
When Grace Sings - Kim Vogel Sawyer i 454

HOTEL WORKER

Bentley Douglas, Joe
Honeymoon Hotel - Hester Browne r 931

St. George, Marisa
In Firefly Valley - Amanda Cabot i 372

Zook, Linda
A Simple Prayer - Amy Clipston i 380

HOUSEHOLDER

Ross, Emmalyn
As Waters Gone By - Cynthia Ruchti i 452

HOUSEKEEPER

Dancy, Rosamond
Morrow Creek Runaway - Lisa Plumley r 1049

Ellis, Reese
When I'm Gone - Abbi Glines r 972

Hoffman, Margaret
Until the Harvest - Sarah Loudin Thomas i 463

Jackson, Edith
Death of a Dishonorable Gentleman - Tessa Arlen t 126

Mrs. Jeffries
Mrs. Jeffries and the One Who Got Away - Emily Brightwell m 503

Mrs. Jelphs
Fiercombe Manor - Kate Riordan t 235

Miss Tiramaku
The Boy Who Drew Monsters - Keith Donohue c 732

HOUSEWIFE

Etta
Emma and Otto and Russell and James - Emma Hooper c 769

Hannah
The Wednesday Group - Sylvia True c 873

HUMAN

Aisa
Iron Axe - Steven Harper f 46

Connolly, Claire
The Veil - Chloe Neill h 334

Jaeger, Felix
Gotrek and Felix: Slayer - David Guymer f 44

Kiril
Originator - Joel Shepherd s 1194

Quinn, Liam
The Veil - Chloe Neill *h* 334
Raleeha
Righteous Fury - Markus Heitz *f* 49

HUNTER

Blake, Anita
Dead Ice - Laurell K. Hamilton *h* 311
Cheeon
Hold the Dark - William Giraldi *c* 749
Cleaver, John Wayne
The Devil's Only Friend - Dan Wells *h* 352
Deveaux, Rory
The Shadow Cabinet - Maureen Johnson *h* 322
Garrett, Elly
Grave Matters - Lauren M. Roy *f* 101
MacFarlane, Malcolm
The Conquering Dark - Clay Griffith *h* 308
The Shadow Revolution - Clay Griffith *h* 307
Marlowe, Christopher
The Dead Hamlets - Peter Roman *f* 99
Menkels, Odette
The Huntress of Thornbeck Forest - Melanie Dickerson *i* 393
Quinn, Siobhan
Cherry Bomb - Caitlin R. Kiernan *h* 327
Russo, Phil
In the Woods - Merry Jones *m* 587
Rutherford, Giles
Season for Desire - Theresa Romain *r* 1061
Satomi, Isobel
Dark Intelligence - Neal Asher *s* 1108
Yellowrock, Jane
Dark Heir - Faith Hunter *h* 320

IMMIGRANT

Dorotea
Wolf Winter - Cecilia Ekback *t* 152
Frederika
Wolf Winter - Cecilia Ekback *t* 152
Gonzales, Hector
The Jaguar's Children - John Vaillant *c* 876
Hobbes, Chad
The Devil's Making - Sean Haldane *t* 171
Juarez, Emelia
Betrayed - Lisa Scottoline *c* 857
Konig, Anna
Anna's Crossing - Suzanne Woods Fisher *i* 399
Maija
Wolf Winter - Cecilia Ekback *t* 152
Makari, Hasan
Detained - Don Brown *i* 366
Makari, Najib
Detained - Don Brown *i* 366
Malone, Jack
Daughter of the Regiment - Stephanie Grace Whitson *i* 469
Malone, Maggie
Daughter of the Regiment - Stephanie Grace Whitson *i* 469
Malone, Seamus
Daughter of the Regiment - Stephanie Grace Whitson *i* 469

Marr, Kennedy
Straight White Male - John Niven *c* 818
McGrath, Cullen
To Win Her Favor - Tamera Alexander *i* 356
Meier, Alex
Leaving Berlin - Joseph Kanon *m* 590
Mrs.
The Handsome Man's De Luxe Cafe - Alexander McCall Smith *c* 864
Paavo
Wolf Winter - Cecilia Ekback *t* 152
Ryan, Sean
Deception on Sable Hill - Shelley Gray *i* 408
Steimetz, Charles Proteus
Electric City - Elizabeth Rosner *t* 237
Theo
Glow - Ned Beauman *c* 699

IMMORTAL

Arngrimsson, Audun
Blood Will Follow - Snorri Kristjansson *t* 194
Caphalor
Righteous Fury - Markus Heitz *f* 49
Case, Matilda
Infinity Bell - Devon Monk *f* 83
Cross
The Dead Hamlets - Peter Roman *f* 99
Dethan
Cursed by Fire - Jacquelyn Frank *f* 36
Garreth
Cursed by Ice - Jacquelyn Frank *f* 35
Kholster
Oathkeeper - J.F. Lewis *f* 74
Seventh, Abraham
Infinity Bell - Devon Monk *f* 83
Sinthoras
Righteous Fury - Markus Heitz *f* 49
Thormodsson, Ulfar
Blood Will Follow - Snorri Kristjansson *t* 194
Torin
The Darkest Touch - Gena Showalter *r* 1082

IMPOVERISHED

Featherstone, Jack
Catch a Falling Heiress - Laura Lee Guhrke *r* 981
Fenwick, Lady Ivy
Forbidden to Love the Duke - Jillian Hunter *r* 991
Gonzales, Hector
The Jaguar's Children - John Vaillant *c* 876
Hewitt, Annie
Heroes Are My Weakness - Susan Elizabeth Phillips *c* 828
Nels
Woven - Michael Jensen *f* 61

INDIAN

Ann
Marked Fur Murder - Dixie Lyle *m* 609
Ben
Marked Fur Murder - Dixie Lyle *m* 609

Calms, Swan
Where the Bones are Buried - Jeanne Matthews *m* 611
Caribou, Swamper
The Ravens - Vidar Sundstol *m* 669
Longboat, Joseph
Electric City - Elizabeth Rosner *t* 237
Margaritte
Crazy Horse's Girlfriend - Erika T. Wurth *c* 891
Walker, Creed
My Heart Stood Still - Lori Copeland *i* 387
Walks with Coyotes, Jay
The Way We Bared Our Souls - Willa Strayhorn *f* 112

INNKEEPER

Cavanaugh, Patience
The Trouble with Patience - Maggie Brendan *i* 364
Harmon, Eve
The Heart of Christmas - Brenda Novak *r* 1044

INSURANCE AGENT

Davis, Lana
A Palette for Murder - Vanessa A. Ryan *m* 651
Wells, Hank
Puzzled Indemnity - Parnell Hall *m* 565

INTERIOR DECORATOR

De Luca, Caprice
Gilt by Association - Karen Rose Smith *m* 661
Harmon, Lane
The Melody Lingers On - Mary Higgins Clark *m* 515

INVENTOR

Bacon, Roger
John the Pupil - David L. Flusfeder *t* 158
Phillips, Sean
Wolf in White Van - John Darnielle *c* 726
Smithson, Melinda "Mellie"
50 Ways to Ruin a Rake - Jade Lee *r* 1007
Steimetz, Charles Proteus
Electric City - Elizabeth Rosner *t* 237
Straker, Jack
The Iron Assassin - Ed Greenwood *s* 1149
Takewashi, Renaldo
Originator - Joel Shepherd *s* 1194
Zuckerberg, Mark
The Infernal - Mark Doten *c* 734

INVESTIGATOR

Bankston, Cade
Undercover Hunter - Rachel Lee *r* 1008
Blake, Anita
Dead Ice - Laurell K. Hamilton *h* 311
Carpenter, Sabina
The Body Snatchers Affair - Marcia Muller *t* 218
Cragg, Titus
The Hidden Man - Robin Blake *m* 495

JOURNALIST

JUDGE

KIDNAP VICTIM

Character Description Index

KIDNAPPER

Stone Cross, Brianna "Bree"
Hope to Die - James Patterson *c* 824

Swan, Scarlett
Black Scorpion - Jon Land *m* 596

Theo
Glow - Ned Beauman *c* 699

Unnamed Character
Method 15/33 - Shannon Kirk *m* 594
Sabotaged - Dani Pettrey *i* 446

KIDNAPPER

Aubrey, Reginald
The Wood's Edge - Lori Benton *i* 360

Croftner, Ben
A Heart's Disguise - Colleen Coble *i* 382

de Warren, Morris
If He's Daring - Hannah Howell *r* 988

Jane
The Shadow Cabinet - Maureen Johnson *h* 322

Mabry, Jonas
The Replacements - David Putnam *m* 637

Prince, Dominick
Murder Boy - Bryon Quertermous *m* 638

Unnamed Character
Method 15/33 - Shannon Kirk *m* 594

Wallin, Levi
Would-Be Wilderness Wife - Regina Scott *r* 1074

KNIGHT

Alan, Michael Fitz
The Holy Lance - Andrew Latham *t* 198

Gawain
Fatal Feast - Jay Ruud *t* 243

Lancelot
Fatal Feast - Jay Ruud *t* 243

Mackenzie, Cameron
The Shattered Court - M.J. Scott *f* 106

Ormiston, Sir David "Devil/Dev"
Devil's Moon - Amanda Scott *r* 1070

Patrise
Fatal Feast - Jay Ruud *t* 243

LABOR LEADER

Campbell, Olin
Fate Moreland's Widow - John Lane *t* 197

LADY

Collins, Araminthea "Thea"
The Duke's Disaster - Grace Burrowes *r* 934

Gledstanes, Lady Robina "Robby"
Devil's Moon - Amanda Scott *r* 1070

LANDLORD

Hume, Fiona
A Thing of Beauty - Lisa Samson *i* 453

Silvestre
Skylight - Jose Saramago *c* 854

LANDOWNER

Aurelius, Marcus Septimus
The Fateful Day - Rosemary Rowe *t* 238

de Lacy, Lord Oswald
Plague Land - S.D. Sykes *t* 257

Gilmore, Luisa
The Whispering - Sarah Rayne *h* 336

Mrs. Gray
Superfluous Women - Carola Dunn *m* 538

Licata, Ferdinando
The Prince - Vito Bruschini *t* 135

LAWMAN

Behan, Johnny
Epitaph - Mary Doria Russell *t* 240

Bryant, Chris
Saving Cecil - Lee Mims *m* 620

Campbell, Macon
The Wonder of All Things - Jason Mott *c* 812

Craddock, Samuel
A Deadly Affair at Bobtail Ridge - Terry
    Shames *m* 656

Drake, Bobby
Sometimes the Wolf - Urban Waite *c* 882

Drake, Patrick
Sometimes the Wolf - Urban Waite *c* 882

Earp, Wyatt
Epitaph - Mary Doria Russell *t* 240

Foxx
The Missing Piece - Kevin Egan *m* 540

Geoffrey
The Tapestry - Nancy Bilyeau *t* 130

Holliday, Doc
Epitaph - Mary Doria Russell *t* 240

Jones, Jedidiah
The Trouble with Patience - Maggie
    Brendan *i* 364

Larson, Andy
Wolf Point - Mike Thompson *t* 262

Lovejoy, Henry
Who Buries the Dead - C.S. Harris *t* 172

Martin, Gary
The Missing Piece - Kevin Egan *m* 540

McQueen, Mike
The Missing Piece - Kevin Egan *m* 540

O'Brien, Bud
Loup Garou: The Beast of Harmony Falls - David
    Reuben Aslin *h* 281

Pickett, Joe
Endangered - C.J. Box *m* 499

Purdy, Jeff
Deadline - John Sandford *c* 852

Reeves, Bass
Karen Memory - Elizabeth Bear *s* 1118

Robertson, Bruce
Whiskers of the Lion - P.L. Gaus *m* 555

Stuckey, Clyde
Saving Cecil - Lee Mims *m* 620

Tomoatooah
Karen Memory - Elizabeth Bear *s* 1118

LAWYER

Baldwin, Becky
Puzzled Indemnity - Parnell Hall *m* 565

Barrington, Stone
Hot Pursuit - Stuart Woods *m* 682
Insatiable Appetites - Stuart Woods *c* 890

Paris Match - Stuart Woods *c* 889

Beckham, Abe
Cane and Abe - James Grippando *c* 756

Boone, Walker
Demise in Denim - Duffy Brown *m* 504

Booth, Kolbein
Steadfast Heart - Tracie Peterson *i* 445

Buckley, Alex
The Cinderella Murder - Mary Higgins
    Clark *c* 713

Campanella, Brook
Shark Skin Suite - Tim Dorsey *c* 733

Canaday, David
Kittens Can Kill - Clea Simon *m* 659

Carrier, Judy
Betrayed - Lisa Scottoline *c* 857

Catrell, Peter
The Pocket Wife - Susan Crawford *m* 524

Coleman, Emily
One Step Too Far - Tina Seskis *c* 859

Connelly, Rachel
Finding Jake - Bryan Reardon *m* 639

Davis, Matt
Detained - Don Brown *i* 366

DeLaura, Joe
Dark Chocolate Demise - Jenn McKinlay *m* 616

Fairchild, Ian
The Longest Night - Kara Braden *c* 706

Gardner, Emily
Detained - Don Brown *i* 366

Gray, Tyner
Hush Hush - Laura Lippman *m* 604

Grimes, Brady
The Marauders - Tom Cooper *m* 522

Gudmundsdottir, Thora
Someone to Watch Over Me - Yrsa
    Sigurdardottir *c* 863

Hall, Conrad
Gift of Grace - Sharlene MacLaren *i* 433

Hardy, Dismas
The Fall - John T. Lescroart *m* 600

Hardy, Rebecca
The Fall - John T. Lescroart *m* 600

Heckholz, Heinrich
The Lady from Zagreb - Philip Kerr *t* 191

Herndon, William "Billy"
Lincoln's Billy - Tom LeClair *t* 200

Illica, Ben
Accidents of Marriage - Randy Susan
    Meyers *c* 804

Knightley, James
The First Kiss - Grace Burrowes *r* 932

Knightley, MacKenzie "Mac"
Kiss Me Hello - Grace Burrowes *r* 933

Knightley, Trent
The First Kiss - Grace Burrowes *r* 932

Littman, Aaron
Losing Faith - Adam Mitzner *m* 621

Martens, Hannelore
From Bruges with Love - Pieter Aspe *m* 482

McBride, Sinclair
Rules for a Proper Governess - Jennifer
    Ashley *r* 905

McKenna, Quill
This Gun for Hire - Jo Goodman *r* 973

Lord Uhtred
The Empty Throne - Bernard Cornwell *t* 146

Unnamed Character
The Cure - JG Faherty *h* 297

Ursula
The Talon of the Hawk - Jeffe Kennedy *f* 62

Vaughn, Derek
Beyond Limits - Laura Griffin *r* 980

Velda
Kill Me, Darling - Mickey Spillane *m* 663

Walsh, Ginger
Back to Before - Tracy Solheim *r* 1084

Ward, Sam
His Small-Town Sweetheart - Amanda
    Berry *r* 914

Wells, Herbert "Bertie" George
The Lodger - Louisa Treger *t* 265

Wende
The Last Good Paradise - Tatjana Soli *c* 865

West, Anna Olmstead
Witch upon a Star - Jennifer Harlow *m* 568

West, Isabelle
Flirting with Disaster - Victoria Dahl *r* 946

Wyatt
The Long and Faraway Gone - Lou
    Berney *m* 489

MAGICIAN

Anstruther, Kate
The Conquering Dark - Clay Griffith *h* 308
The Shadow Revolution - Clay Griffith *h* 307

Archer, Simon
The Conquering Dark - Clay Griffith *h* 308
The Shadow Revolution - Clay Griffith *h* 307

Arden
The Magician's Lie - Greer Macallister *t* 207

Barnabus, Elizabeth
Unseemly Science - Rod Duncan *s* 1141

Di, Lung
The Dragons of Heaven - Alyc Helms *f* 50

Drood, Eddie
From a Drood to a Kill - Simon R. Green *f* 41

Fawe, Amelie
Witches with the Enemy - Barb Hendee *f* 51

Fawe, Celine
Witches with the Enemy - Barb Hendee *f* 51

Gutenberg, Johannes
Unbound - Jim C. Hines *f* 55

Huang, Lung
The Dragons of Heaven - Alyc Helms *f* 50

Ickabosh
Woven - Michael Jensen *f* 61

Kell
A Darker Shade of Magic - V.E. Schwab *f* 105

Kendall, Sophia
The Shattered Court - M.J. Scott *f* 106

Kingslayer, Aral
Darkened Blade - Kelly McCullough *f* 79

Mackenzie, Cameron
The Shattered Court - M.J. Scott *f* 106

Masters, Missy
The Dragons of Heaven - Alyc Helms *f* 50

Meche
Signal to Noise - Silvia Moreno-Garcia *f* 85

Morales, Drew
Deadly Spells - Jaye Wells *f* 121

Price, Harper
Miss Mayhem - Rachel Hawkins *f* 48

Prospero, Kate
Deadly Spells - Jaye Wells *f* 121

Rogan, Connor "Mad"
Burn for Me - Ilona Andrews *r* 900

Ryan
Miss Mayhem - Rachel Hawkins *f* 48

Stark, David
Miss Mayhem - Rachel Hawkins *f* 48

Vainio, Isaac
Unbound - Jim C. Hines *f* 55

MAIL ORDER BRIDE

Golding, Sally
Outlaw Takes a Bride - Susan Page Davis *i* 389

MAN

Aar
Hiding in Plain Sight - Nuruddin Farah *c* 741

Abdul
The Promise - Beth Wiseman *c* 888

Adam
On the Edge - Edward St. Aubyn *c* 867

Ardhi
The Dagger's Path - Glenda Larke *f* 67

Argent, Gabriel
Pacific Fire - Greg van Eekhout *f* 118

Ashe
Revels Ending - Vic Kerry *h* 326

Augustus
Golden Son - Pierce Brown *s* 1120

Axl
The Buried Giant - Kazuo Ishiguro *t* 183

Barnes, Rudy
The Witch of the Wood - Michael
    Aronovitz *h* 280

Big Hoom
Em and the Big Hoom - Jerry Pinto *c* 831

Blackland, Daniel
Pacific Fire - Greg van Eekhout *f* 118

Borgan
Carousel Seas - Sharon Lee *f* 72

Boston
The Love Letters - Beverly Lewis *i* 427

Bottoms, Ronnie
Inside a Silver Box - Walter Mosley *s* 1179

Bridge, Matthew
Point Hollow - Rio Youers *h* 355

Byrne, J.P.
The Good Chase - Hanna Martine *r* 1024

Campbell, John
Hot Blooded - Donna Grant *r* 976

Cassanova, Figueora "Figgy"
Cuba Straits - Randy Wayne White *m* 681

Chaudhary, Jeevan
Station Eleven - Emily St. John Mandel *c* 796

Cromer, Ridley
Cat's Lair - Christine Feehan *h* 298

Cross
The Dead Hamlets - Peter Roman *f* 99

Cyril
Lie of the Needle - Cate Price *m* 636

Darrow
Golden Son - Pierce Brown *s* 1120

Daulton
The Tutor - Andrea Chapin *t* 140

Doyle, Colin
The Crow of Connemara - Stephen Leigh *f* 73

Duran, Ben
The Black Widow - Wendy Corsi Staub *m* 665

Durand, Stephane
The Venusian Gambit - Michael J.
    Martinez *s* 1173

Dylan, Hugh
Lemon Pies and Little White Lies - Ellery
    Adams *m* 475

Falk, Jim
The Witch at Sparrow Creek - Josh Kent *h* 324

Foxx, Sebastian
The Day of Atonement - David Liss *t* 206

Fred
No Christmas Like the Present - Sierra
    Donovan *r* 955

Garreth
Cursed by Ice - Jacquelyn Frank *f* 35

Gibson, Jake
Mammoth Secrets - Ashley Elizabeth
    Ludwig *i* 431

Gilley
No Ghouls Allowed - Victoria Laurie *h* 329

Golden, Benji
Phantom Angel - David Handler *m* 567

Gramaraye, Mort
Finn Fancy Necromancy - Randy
    Henderson *f* 53

Gramaraye, Pete
Finn Fancy Necromancy - Randy
    Henderson *f* 53

Gramaraye, Phinaeus "Finn"
Finn Fancy Necromancy - Randy
    Henderson *f* 53

Hardy, Dismas
The Fall - John T. Lescroart *m* 600

Hartman, Jorgen
The Huntress of Thornbeck Forest - Melanie
    Dickerson *i* 393

Hasimoto, Kazushi
Sherlock Holmes, the Missing Years: Japan - Va-
    sudev Murthy *t* 219

Heath
No Ghouls Allowed - Victoria Laurie *h* 329

Hoffman, Rick
The Fixer - Joseph Finder *m* 545

Jeremiah
A Faith of Her Own - Kathleen Fuller *i* 400

Kaufman, Zachary
The Promise of Palm Grove - Shelley Shepard
    Gray *i* 407

Kendall, Blake
In Firefly Valley - Amanda Cabot *i* 372

Landucci, Orlando
Betrayed by His Kiss - Amanda McCabe *r* 1025

Lapp, Silas
Keys of Heaven - Adina Senft *i* 455

Freeman, Carl
Devil's Pocket - John Dixon *s* 1138

Gwil
The Siege Winter - Ariana Franklin *t* 159

Harlan
The Talon of the Hawk - Jeffe Kennedy *f* 62

Jirom
Storm and Steel - Jon Sprunk *f* 109

Keller, Jack
Devils and Dust - J.D. Rhoades *m* 642

Mongrel
Fortune's Blight - Evie Manieri *f* 76

Morgan, Jim
Midnight Action - Elle Kennedy *r* 999

Sage, Mira
Edge of Betrayal - Shannon K. Butcher *r* 939

Seagrave, Jeth
Polaris - Mindee Arnett *s* 1107

Valyn
The Providence of Fire - Brian Staveley *f* 111

Vost
Breakout - Ann Aguirre *s* 1103

MERCHANT

Gonzales de Ripparda, Rafael Maria
The Creole Princess - Beth White *i* 468

MIDWIFE

Bradley, Grace
The Secrets of Midwives - Sally Hepworth *c* 765

Bradley, Neva
The Secrets of Midwives - Sally Hepworth *c* 765

Brandt, Sarah
Murder on Amsterdam Avenue - Victoria Thompson *m* 672

Floss
The Secrets of Midwives - Sally Hepworth *c* 765

Gugu
Frog - Yan Mo *c* 808

Hawkins, Martha
The Witch Hunter's Tale - Sam Thomas *t* 260

Hodgson, Bridget
The Witch Hunter's Tale - Sam Thomas *t* 260

Hooke, Rebecca
The Witch Hunter's Tale - Sam Thomas *t* 260

MILITARY PERSONNEL

Abercare, Ewan
Shame and the Captives - Thomas Keneally *t* 190

Ackbar
Heir to the Jedi - Kevin Hearne *s* 1154

Aetius
The Sword of Attila - David Gibbins *t* 163

Alan, Michael Fitz
The Holy Lance - Andrew Latham *t* 198

Alexander, Gina
A Long Time Until Now - Michael Z. Williamson *s* 1208

Allenson, Allen
Into the Maelstrom - David Drake *s* 1140

Avery, William
The Strangler Vine - Miranda Carter *t* 139

Barker, Bob
A Long Time Until Now - Michael Z. Williamson *s* 1208

Bennings, Kit
The Russian Bride - Ed Kovacs *m* 595

Bremer, L. Paul
The Infernal - Mark Doten *c* 734

Brown, Weston "West"
Falling Hard - HelenKay Dimon *r* 954

Buchanan, Tucker
Silken Threats - Addison Fox *r* 966

Campbell, Joel
Hope Rising - Stacy Henrie *r* 987

Campbell, Rand
A Heart's Danger - Colleen Coble *i* 385
A Heart's Disguise - Colleen Coble *i* 382
A Heart's Obsession - Colleen Coble *i* 384

Captain Lore
Heir of Hope - Morgan L. Busse *i* 368

Caswell
A Long Time Until Now - Michael Z. Williamson *s* 1208

Chekov, Pavel
Crisis of Consciousness - Dave Galanter *s* 1147
Savage Trade - Tony Daniel *s* 1134

Cochrane, Nathan
Impulse - Dave Bara *s* 1115

Cochrane, Peter
Impulse - Dave Bara *s* 1115

Cole, Darwin
Unmanned - Dan Fesperman *c* 742

Collins, Mason
Ruins of War - John Connell *t* 144

Coulter, John
Daughter of the Regiment - Stephanie Grace Whitson *i* 469

Covington, Cole
Return to Me - Kelly Moran *r* 1038

Croftner, Ben
A Heart's Danger - Colleen Coble *i* 385

Cronley, James D. Jr.
Top Secret - W.E.B. Griffin *c* 755

Custer, George Armstrong
1882: Custer in Chains - Robert Conroy *s* 1130
Valley of the Shadow - Ralph Peters *t* 231

Cutter, R. "Rags" A.
The Tejano Conflict - Steve Perry *s* 1183

Davis, Matt
Detained - Don Brown *i* 366

Dean, Jory
Total Surrender - Rebecca Zanetti *r* 1100

Devereaux, Armand
A Long Time Until Now - Michael Z. Williamson *s* 1208

Doll, Paul
The Zone of Interest - Martin Amis *c* 690

Donovan, Peter
Fives and Twenty-Fives - Michael Pitre *c* 832

Dresden, Ridley
Frostfire - Amanda Hocking *f* 56

Early, Jubal
Valley of the Shadow - Ralph Peters *t* 231

Elliott, Sean
A Long Time Until Now - Michael Z. Williamson *s* 1208

Emmes, Katja
Virtues of War - Bennett R. Coles *s* 1129

Enchei
Old Man's Ghosts - Tom Lloyd *f* 75

Fonthill, Simon
Treachery in Tibet - John Wilcox *t* 271

Furman, Jacob
The Ambassadors - George Lerner *t* 203

Gadsden, William "Will"
The Memory House - Linda Goodnight *r* 974

Geary, John "Black Jack"
Leviathan - Jack Campbell *s* 1123

Gehlen, Reinhard
Top Secret - W.E.B. Griffin *c* 755

Gideon, Sara
Rain on the Dead - Jack Higgins *c* 766

Gordon, John Brown
Valley of the Shadow - Ralph Peters *t* 231

Grand, Matthew
The Blue and the Grey - M.J. Trow *t* 266

Gray, Evelyn
Hope Rising - Stacy Henrie *r* 987

Hansen, Cooper
The Cowboy SEAL - Laura Marie Altom *r* 897

Hayden, Charles
Until the Sea Shall Give Up Her Dead - S. Thomas Russell *t* 241

Heiden
The Dynamite Room - Jason Hewitt *t* 178

Herman, Don
Straits of Hell - Taylor Anderson *s* 1105

Heuser, Georg
Ostland - David Thomas *t* 259

Jackson, Charles
A Love Like Blood - Marcus Sedgwick *t* 246

Jain, Shaila
The Venusian Gambit - Michael J. Martinez *s* 1173

James
The Girl Next Door - Ruth Rendell *c* 844

Jones, William
Until the Sea Shall Give Up Her Dead - S. Thomas Russell *t* 241

Kane, Thomas
Virtues of War - Bennett R. Coles *s* 1129

Kappa, Wes
Dove Arising - Karen Bao *s* 1114

Kelley, Ralph
Hope Rising - Stacy Henrie *r* 987

Kelso, Danny
Tin Men - Christopher Golden *m* 556

Kerne, Jonah
Dark Hunters: Umbra Sumus - Paul Kearney *s* 1158

Khan, Kor'sarro
Damocles - Phil Kelly *s* 1159

Knight, Cecily
The Longest Night - Kara Braden *c* 706

Kresnov, Cassandra "Sandy"
Originator - Joel Shepherd *s* 1194

Lakshmi, Rani
Rebel Queen - Michelle Moran *t* 213

Laren, Ro
The Missing - Una McCormack *s* 1175

Lenson, Dan
The Cruiser - David Poyer *c* 836

Lewrie, Alan
Kings and Emperors - Dewey Lambdin *t* 195

MacKenzie, Jackie
The Terrans - Jean Johnson *s* 1156

MacLeod, Hamish
A Fine Summer's Day - Charles Todd *t* 263

MacPherson, Danny
The Silent Sister - Diane Chamberlain *c* 710

Macrobius
The Sword of Attila - David Gibbins *t* 163

Makari, Najib
Detained - Don Brown *i* 366

Malcolm
New Uses for Old Boyfriends - Beth
Kendrick *r* 998

Mallory, Jack
Virtues of War - Bennett R. Coles *s* 1129

Malone, Jack
Daughter of the Regiment - Stephanie Grace
Whitson *i* 469

Malone, Seamus
Daughter of the Regiment - Stephanie Grace
Whitson *i* 469

Marshwic, Emily
The Guns of the Dawn - Adrian
Tchaikovsky *f* 115

McCoy, Grayson "Gray"
Wolf Haven - Lindsay McKenna *r* 1029

McGregor, Mac
Buried Secrets - Irene Hannon *i* 411

Montcrief, James "Jamie"
I've Got My Duke to Keep Me Warm - Kelly
Bowen *r* 920

Moore, Alexander
Trail of Evil - Travis S. Taylor *s* 1202

Morgan, Clint
Tempted by the Soldier - Patricia Potter *r* 1050

Newell-Grey, Jonathan
Scent of Triumph - Jan Moran *t* 212

Oliphant, Stanley
Who Buries the Dead - C.S. Harris *t* 172

Ortiz, Ramon
A Long Time Until Now - Michael Z.
Williamson *s* 1208

Orvin
Slow Bullets - Alastair Reynolds *s* 1188

Paen, Promise
Unbreakable - W.C. Bauers *s* 1117

Pascal, Skylar
Wolf Haven - Lindsay McKenna *r* 1029

Peterwald, Vicky
Survivor - Mike Shepherd *s* 1195

Pleasant, Lester "Doc"
Fives and Twenty-Fives - Michael Pitre *c* 832

Porter, Jake
A Love Like Ours - Becky Wade *i* 466

Portland, Edgar
The Memory House - Linda Goodnight *r* 974

Rasp
Yarrick: Imperial Creed - David
Annandale *s* 1106

Redding, Luther
The Sheltering - Mark Powell *c* 835

Reddy, Matt
Straits of Hell - Taylor Anderson *s* 1105

Rhodes, Mark
Search and Seduce - Sara Jane Stone *r* 1088

Richter
Fall of Macharius - William King *s* 1161

Russell
Crouching Tiger, Forbidden Vampire - Kerrelyn
Sparks *r* 1086

Russo, Salvatore
Falcon - Ronie Kendig *i* 423

Sage, Frank
Master Sergeant - Mel Odom *s* 1181

Santiago, Elizabeth
Corsair - James Cambias *s* 1122

Schweitzer, Jim
Gemini Cell - Myke Cole *f* 26

Sebak
The Pharaoh's Daughter - Mesu Andrews *i* 357

Shadowsun
Damocles - Phil Kelly *s* 1159

Shaw, Dutch
The Knife - Ross Ritchell *c* 846

Sheridan, Philip
Valley of the Shadow - Ralph Peters *t* 231

Sherman, Jason
Surrender - June Gray *r* 977

Shinwari, Khatereh "Khat"
Taking Fire - Lindsay McKenna *r* 1030

Sita
Rebel Queen - Michelle Moran *t* 213

Slone, Vernon
Hold the Dark - William Giraldi *c* 749

Smith, Archer
The Abduction of Smith and Smith - Rashad
Harrison *t* 174

Smith, Faith
Strands of Sorrow - John Ringo *s* 1190

Smith, Jon
Robert Ludlum's The Geneva Strategy - Jamie
Freveletti *m* 551

Smith, Jupiter
The Abduction of Smith and Smith - Rashad
Harrison *t* 174

Smith, Sophia
Strands of Sorrow - John Ringo *s* 1190

Smith, Steve
Strands of Sorrow - John Ringo *s* 1190

Soto, Carlos "Steady"
Full Throttle - Julie Ann Walker *r* 1093

Spear, Thorvald
Dark Intelligence - Neal Asher *s* 1108

Spock
Crisis of Consciousness - Dave Galanter *s* 1147
Savage Trade - Tony Daniel *s* 1134
Shadow of the Machine - Scott Harrison *s* 1153

Stamatopoulos, Anastasios "Tasso"
Tasso's Journey - Paula Renee Burzawa *t* 137

Sulu, Hikaru
Crisis of Consciousness - Dave Galanter *s* 1147
Savage Trade - Tony Daniel *s* 1134
Shadow of the Machine - Scott Harrison *s* 1153

Suttor, Bernard
Shame and the Captives - Thomas
Keneally *t* 190

Swift, Julian
The Accidental Countess - Valerie
Bowman *r* 923

Tanner, Arden
Sisters of Shiloh - Kathy Hepinstall *t* 176

Tanner, Scott
Germanica - Robert Conroy *s* 1131

Tarik, Michael "Mike"
Taking Fire - Lindsay McKenna *r* 1030

Teasdale, James
The Alphabet House - Jussi Adler-Olsen *c* 686

Thayne, Mark
Too Dangerous for a Lady - Jo Beverley *r* 915

Theta, Phaet
Dove Arising - Karen Bao *s* 1114

Thrax, Maximinus
Iron and Rust - Harry Sidebottom *t* 248

Todd, Teddy
A God in Ruins - Kate Atkinson *t* 127

Tregear, Stephen
Blood Ties - Nicholas Guild *m* 562

Trevillion, James
Dearest Rogue - Elizabeth Hoyt *r* 990

Tulkhan
The Fall of Fair Isle - Rowena Cory
Daniells *f* 27

Uhura, Nyota
Crisis of Consciousness - Dave Galanter *s* 1147
Savage Trade - Tony Daniel *s* 1134

Upton, Lord Garrett
The Unlikely Lady - Valerie Bowman *r* 922

Vaughn, Derek
Beyond Limits - Laura Griffin *r* 980

Wade, Kate
Tin Men - Christopher Golden *m* 556

Walker, Cassandra
Falcon - Ronie Kendig *i* 423

Washburn, Frankie
Prudence - David Treuer *c* 872

Weatherby, Thomas
The Venusian Gambit - Michael J.
Martinez *s* 1173

Whitfield, Luke
Mist of Midnight - Sandra Byrd *i* 371

Yarrick, Sebastian
Yarrick: Imperial Creed - David
Annandale *s* 1106

Young, Bryan
The Alphabet House - Jussi Adler-Olsen *c* 686

MINE OWNER

Stonechurch, Ramsey
This Gun for Hire - Jo Goodman *r* 973

MINER

Darrow
Golden Son - Pierce Brown *s* 1120

MISSING PERSON

Abbott, True
The First Wife - Erica Spindler *m* 664

Alden, Hunter "Tripp" Hutchinson III
NYPD Red 3 - James Patterson *m* 632

Bennett, Parker
The Melody Lingers On - Mary Higgins
Clark *m* 515

Bradleigh, Lady Audrina
Season for Desire - Theresa Romain *r* 1061

Buchanan, Emily
Spark - John Twelve Hawks *c* 874

Cassanova, Figueora "Figgy"
Cuba Straits - Randy Wayne White *m* 681

Conlon, Evelyn
Lies That Bind - Maggie Barbieri *m* 487

Connelly, Jake
Finding Jake - Bryan Reardon *m* 639

Cyril
Lie of the Needle - Cate Price *m* 636

de Fontein, Lucien
The Boy Who Wept Blood - Den Patrick *f* 93

Divine, Dorisanne
The Case of the Sin City Sister - Lynne
Hinton *i* 419

Djurkovic, Antun Dragun
The Lady from Zagreb - Philip Kerr *t* 191

Duffy, Spooner
A Sticky Situation - Jessie Crockett *m* 525

Farnell, R.J.
Phantom Angel - David Handler *m* 567

Gibbons, Kendra
Signature Kill - David Levien *m* 601

Harrison, Rosa
Harrison Squared - Daryl Gregory *h* 306

Heyward, Kent
Lowcountry Boneyard - Susan M. Boyer *m* 500

Howard, Brian
Cold Trail - Janet Dawson *m* 528

Johnston, Poppy
Time of Death - Mark Billingham *m* 491

Kate
Forsaken - Kelley Armstrong *h* 278

Leo
Murder with a Twist - Tracy Kiely *m* 593

MacPherson, Lisa
The Silent Sister - Diane Chamberlain *c* 710

Metcalf, Alice
Leaving Time - Jodi Picoult *c* 829

Mountstuart, Xavier
The Strangler Vine - Miranda Carter *t* 139

Nancy
If the Viscount Falls - Sabrina Jeffries *r* 995

Price, Corinne
The Stranger - Harlan Coben *m* 517

Rafferty, Polly
His Reluctant Cinderella - Jessica
Gilmore *r* 971

Rainsford, Scarlett
Behind Closed Doors - Elizabeth Haynes *m* 571

Reiss, Sophie
Deadlight Hall - Sarah Rayne *h* 337

Reiss, Susannah
Deadlight Hall - Sarah Rayne *h* 337

Sanchez, Oscar
Devils and Dust - J.D. Rhoades *m* 642

Sanders, Jimmy
A String of Beads - Thomas Perry *c* 827

Shepard, Jacob
Ancient Oceans of Central Kentucky - David Connerley Nahm *c* 815

Sinclair, Arthur
Quartet for the End of Time - Johanna
Skibsrud *t* 250

Slone, Bailey
Hold the Dark - William Giraldi *c* 749

Toms, Jessica
Time of Death - Mark Billingham *m* 491

Tremayne, Julian
The Breath of Night - Michael Arditti *c* 694

Unnamed Character
Exposure - Kathy Reichs *s* 1186
Exposure - Kathy Reichs *s* 1186
Sabotaged - Dani Pettrey *i* 446

Velda
Kill Me, Darling - Mickey Spillane *m* 663

Zabriel
The Empty Throne - Cayla Kluver *f* 64

MODEL

Daphne
New Uses for Old Boyfriends - Beth
Kendrick *r* 998

Jenkins, Janie
Dear Daughter - Elizabeth Little *c* 792

MOTHER

Abbott, Abigail
Tattered Legacy - Shannon Baker *m* 484

Alden, Janelle
NYPD Red 3 - James Patterson *m* 632

Alexia
Prudence - Gail Carriger *f* 22

Allen, Priscilla
An Amish Man of Ice Mountain - Kelly
Long *i* 429

Alyse
It Won't Always Be This Great - Peter
Mehlman *c* 803

Amado, Mercedes "Mercy"
The Amado Women - Desiree Zamorano *c* 892

Anderson, Meg
It Had to Be Him - Tamra Baumann *r* 910

Anippe
The Pharaoh's Daughter - Mesu Andrews *i* 357

Annie
This Is the Water - Yannick Murphy *c* 813

Ari
After Birth - Elisa Albert *c* 688

Banning, Amanda
Silver Thaw - Catherine Anderson *r* 898

Barbara
Where They Found Her - Kimberly
McCreight *m* 614

Barkes, Martha
Never Mind Miss Fox - Olivia Glazebrook *c* 750

Barsham, Adelaide
Meadowlands - Elizabeth Jeffrey *t* 185

Beck, Emma Miller
Up the Hill to Home - Jennifer Bort
Yacovissi *t* 275

Beck, Shani
Amish Promises - Leslie Gould *i* 405

Lady Beckington
The Devil Takes a Bride - Julia London *r* 1012

Bella
The Stager - Susan Coll *c* 716

Bennett, Anne
The Melody Lingers On - Mary Higgins
Clark *m* 515

Benz, Anna
Hausfrau - Jill Alexander Essbaum *c* 739

Black Bitch of Bushehr
The Luminous Heart of Jonah S. - Gina B.
Nahai *c* 814

Blair, Penny
The Children's Crusade - Ann Packer *t* 224

Bloom, Molly
Whatever Happened to Molly Bloom? - Jessica
Stirling *t* 254

Bolton, Tarla
Season of Fear - Brian Freeman *m* 550

Borne, Vivian
Antiques Swap - Barbara Allan *m* 477

Bradley, Colleen
Driving with the Top Down - Beth
Harbison *c* 761

Bradley, Grace
The Secrets of Midwives - Sally Hepworth *c* 765

Brandon, Rebecca "Becky" Bloomfield
Shopaholic to the Stars - Sophie Kinsella *c* 784

Bree
Beyond the Pale Motel - Francesca Lia
Block *c* 704

Brown, Jane
Christmas at Twilight - Lori Wilde *r* 1097

Calms, Swan
Where the Bones are Buried - Jeanne
Matthews *m* 611

Cambridge, Kelsey
The Final Reveille - Amanda Flower *m* 547

Camherst, Lady Isabella
Voyage of the Basilisk: A Memoir by Lady Trent -
Marie Brennan *f* 16

Carter, Cassie
Last One Home - Debbie Macomber *c* 794

Catrell, Dana
The Pocket Wife - Susan Crawford *m* 524

Chris
This Is the Water - Yannick Murphy *c* 813

Clark, Lacey
You're So Fine - Kieran Kramer *r* 1002

Cobb, Isabel
The Empire of Night - Robert Olen Butler *t* 138

Coleman, Emily
One Step Too Far - Tina Seskis *c* 859

Connelly, Rachel
Finding Jake - Bryan Reardon *m* 639

Cooper, Shaylene
There Will Be Lies - Nick Lake *f* 66

Cramer, Holly
Twisted Innocence - Terri Blackstock *i* 363

Crane, Charlotte
When We Fall - Emily Liebert *c* 791

Daphne
New Uses for Old Boyfriends - Beth
Kendrick *r* 998

Darlene
Delicious Foods - James Hannaham *c* 760

Dawes, Melisandre Harris
Hush Hush - Laura Lippman *m* 604

Garrison, Gavin
Leaving Amarillo - Caisey Quinn *r* 1052
Hill, Napoleon
The Jazz Palace - Mary Morris *t* 215
King, David
The Song - Chris Fabry *i* 398
King, Jed
The Song - Chris Fabry *i* 398
Lark, Dallas
Leaving Amarillo - Caisey Quinn *r* 1052
Loving Dallas - Caisey Quinn *c* 839
Lark, Dixie
Leaving Amarillo - Caisey Quinn *r* 1052
Lehrman, Benny
The Jazz Palace - Mary Morris *t* 215
Merced, Orlando
The Burning Room - Michael Connelly *c* 718
Mina
After Birth - Elisa Albert *c* 688
Morton, Jamie
Revival - Stephen King *c* 783
Mozart, Wolfgang
The Figaro Murders - Laura Lebow *t* 199
Nix, Billy
Firebreak - Tricia Fields *m* 544
Smythe-Smith, Iris
The Secrets of Sir Richard Kenworthy - Julia Quinn *r* 1053
Von Riesen, Elfrieda "Elf"
All My Puny Sorrows - Miriam Toews *c* 871
Waltham, Vera
The First Kiss - Grace Burrowes *r* 932
Watson, Arnie
The Dead Play On - Heather Graham *m* 560
Webber, Tate
The Promise - Beth Wiseman *c* 888

MYTHICAL CREATURE

Anya
The Empty Throne - Cayla Kluver *f* 64
Astrid
Rogue Wave - Jennifer Donnelly *f* 28
Ava
Rogue Wave - Jennifer Donnelly *f* 28
Becca
Rogue Wave - Jennifer Donnelly *f* 28
Danr
Iron Axe - Steven Harper *f* 46
Darkblade, Malus
Deathblade: A Tale of Malus Darkblade - C.L. Werner *f* 122
Illumina
The Empty Throne - Cayla Kluver *f* 64
Imoshen
The Fall of Fair Isle - Rowena Cory Daniells *f* 27
Laith
Hot Blooded - Donna Grant *r* 976
Ling
Rogue Wave - Jennifer Donnelly *f* 28
Neela
Rogue Wave - Jennifer Donnelly *f* 28
Ondorum
Forge of Ashes - Josh Vogt *f* 120

Pug
The Exile - C.T. Adams *f* 3
Reothe
The Fall of Fair Isle - Rowena Cory Daniells *f* 27
Serafina
Rogue Wave - Jennifer Donnelly *f* 28
Zabriel
The Empty Throne - Cayla Kluver *f* 64

NARRATOR

Albia, Flavia
Deadly Election - Lindsey Davis *t* 148
Alvarini, Beth
Stillwater - Maynard Sims *h* 344
Baum, Addie
The Boston Girl - Anita Diamant *t* 149
Cabot, Jamie
The Hunger of the Wolf - Stephen Marche *r* 1019
Cassandra "Cass"
The Fire Sermon - Francesca Haig *s* 1151
Doll, Paul
The Zone of Interest - Martin Amis *c* 690
Doten, Mark
The Infernal - Mark Doten *c* 734
Faye
Outline - Rachel Cusk *c* 724
Gildas
Fatal Feast - Jay Ruud *t* 243
Gonzales, Hector
The Jaguar's Children - John Vaillant *c* 876
Gramaraye, Phinaeus "Finn"
Finn Fancy Necromancy - Randy Henderson *f* 53
Grimes, Brady
The Marauders - Tom Cooper *m* 522
Heming, William
A Pleasure and a Calling - Phil Hogan *m* 576
Holmes, Toni
Flourless to Stop Him - Nancy J. Parra *m* 631
Illica, Ben
Accidents of Marriage - Randy Susan Meyers *c* 804
Illica, Emma
Accidents of Marriage - Randy Susan Meyers *c* 804
Illica, Maddy
Accidents of Marriage - Randy Susan Meyers *c* 804
Jenkins, Janie
Dear Daughter - Elizabeth Little *c* 792
Jones, Ben
The Never-Open Desert Diner - James Anderson *m* 478
Leigh, Biddy
An Appetite for Violets - Martine Bailey *t* 128
Lindquist, Gus
The Marauders - Tom Cooper *m* 522
Lively, Penny
One Foot in the Grape - Carlene O'Neil *m* 627
Lobdell, Lucy Ann
The Rebellion of Miss Lucy Ann Lobdell - William Klaber *t* 193

Mayor's Wife
The Woman Who Read Too Much - Bahiyyih Nakhjavani *t* 220
Mother of the Shah
The Woman Who Read Too Much - Bahiyyih Nakhjavani *t* 220
Phillips, Sean
Wolf in White Van - John Darnielle *c* 726
Sister of the Shah
The Woman Who Read Too Much - Bahiyyih Nakhjavani *t* 220
Sita
Rebel Queen - Michelle Moran *t* 213
Star, Ice Cream
The Country of Ice Cream Star - Sandra Newman *c* 816
Szmul
The Zone of Interest - Martin Amis *c* 690
Thomsen, Golo
The Zone of Interest - Martin Amis *c* 690
Trench, Wes
The Marauders - Tom Cooper *m* 522
U
Satin Island - Tom McCarthy *c* 799
Unnamed
Dear Thief - Samantha Harvey *c* 762
Unnamed Character
10:04 - Ben Lerner *c* 790
Em and the Big Hoom - Jerry Pinto *c* 831
It Won't Always Be This Great - Peter Mehlman *c* 803
Method 15/33 - Shannon Kirk *m* 594
My Sunshine Away - M.O. Walsh *c* 884
This Is the Life - Alex Shearer *c* 862
The Woman Who Read Too Much - Bahiyyih Nakhjavani *t* 220

NATURALIST

Camherst, Lady Isabella
Voyage of the Basilisk: A Memoir by Lady Trent - Marie Brennan *f* 16

NEIGHBOR

Amber
A Love Like Ours - Becky Wade *i* 466
Ann, Rachel
One True Path - Barbara Cameron *i* 375
Banning, Amanda
Silver Thaw - Catherine Anderson *r* 898
Banning, Chloe
Silver Thaw - Catherine Anderson *r* 898
Beck, Joel
Amish Promises - Leslie Gould *i* 405
Beck, Shani
Amish Promises - Leslie Gould *i* 405
Bitner, Ellie
The Love Letters - Beverly Lewis *i* 427
Brixton
The Accidental Alchemist - Gigi Pandian *m* 630
Byler, Henry
Balm of Gilead - Adina Senft *i* 456
Keys of Heaven - Adina Senft *i* 455
Cole, Brianna
Snowstorm Confessions - Rachel Lee *r* 1009

Derring, Maxwell
Earls Just Want to Have Fun - Shana Galen   *r* 970

Digby, Kenelm
Viper Wine - Hermione Eyre   *t* 154

Douglas, William
Once upon a Plaid - Mia Marlowe   *r* 1021

Lord Draconus
Forge of Darkness - Steven Erikson   *f* 31

Drakestone, Bray
The Duke in My Bed - Amelia Grey   *r* 979

Dudley, Lord Robert
The Marriage Game - Alison Weir   *t* 270

Duke of Avendale
The Duke and the Lady in Red - Lorraine Heath   *r* 985

Duke of Rivenshire
An Uncertain Choice - Jody Hedlund   *i* 415

Edward
The Tutor - Andrea Chapin   *t* 140

Fairbrother, James
A Scoundrel by Moonlight - Anna Campbell   *r* 941

Fairfax, John "Evan"
The Earl I Adore - Erin Knightley   *r* 1001

Featherstone, Jack
Catch a Falling Heiress - Laura Lee Guhrke   *r* 981

Flavian
Only Enchanting - Mary Balogh   *r* 907

Forsyth, Nicholas
Medium Dead - Paula Paul   *m* 633

Fortescue, Julian
The Duke of Dark Desires - Miranda Neville   *r* 1042

Gabler, Christof
The Figaro Murders - Laura Lebow   *t* 199

Greaves, Apollo
Darling Beast - Elizabeth Hoyt   *r* 989

Grey, Timothy
Dauntless - Dina L. Sleiman   *i* 457

Hazelton, Nigel
An American Duchess - Sharon Page   *r* 1046

Hazelton, Sebastian
An American Duchess - Sharon Page   *r* 1046

Hunter, Darian
Darian Hunter: Duke of Desire - Carole Mortimer   *r* 1039

Ingham, Charles
The Cavendon Women - Barbara Taylor Bradford   *t* 133

James
Forbidden to Love the Duke - Jillian Hunter   *r* 991

Jeffrey
The Devil Takes a Bride - Julia London   *r* 1012

John of Gaunt
The Book of Fires - Paul Doherty   *t* 150

Kenworthy, Richard
The Secrets of Sir Richard Kenworthy - Julia Quinn   *r* 1053

Knight, Alex
Twice Tempted - Eileen Dreyer   *r* 956

Lennox, Benedict
Love in the Time of Scandal - Caroline Linden   *r* 1011

Lenox, Charles
The Laws of Murder - Charles Finch   *c* 743

Levire, Adam
I've Got My Duke to Keep Me Warm - Kelly Bowen   *r* 920

Lisle, Lord Frederick "Freddy"
A Good Rake Is Hard to Find - Manda Collins   *r* 944

Marcus
The Duke's Guide to Correct Behavior - Megan Frampton   *r* 967

Oliphant, Stanley
Who Buries the Dead - C.S. Harris   *t* 172

Richelieu, Cardinal
1636: The Cardinal Virtues - Eric Flint   *s* 1145

Sinclair, Michael
Murder in Hindsight - Anne Cleeland   *m* 516

Somerhall, William
A Good Rogue Is Hard to Find - Kelly Bowen   *r* 921

Spencer, Lord Christopher
Lady Sarah's Sinful Desires - Sophie Barnes   *r* 909

St. Cyr, Sebastian
Who Buries the Dead - C.S. Harris   *t* 172

Stockman, Albert
The Empire of Night - Robert Olen Butler   *t* 138

Stratton, Pierson
The Viscount Who Lived Down the Lane - Elizabeth Boyle   *r* 924

Talbot, Ralph Cuthbert
Death of a Dishonorable Gentleman - Tessa Arlen   *t* 126

Lord Uhtred
The Empty Throne - Bernard Cornwell   *t* 146

Upton, Lord Garrett
The Unlikely Lady - Valerie Bowman   *r* 922

von Erhlich, Frederic
Cafe Europa - Edward Ifkovic   *t* 182

White, Paul Douglas Leonard
The Missing Piece - Kevin Egan   *m* 540

NOBLEWOMAN

Lady Aethelflaed
The Empty Throne - Bernard Cornwell   *t* 146

Bathory, Elizabeth
Bathed in Blood - Alex Archer   *f* 6

Batten, Lady Phoebe
Dearest Rogue - Elizabeth Hoyt   *r* 990

Beecham, Mariah
Darian Hunter: Duke of Desire - Carole Mortimer   *r* 1039

Bradleigh, Lady Audrina
Season for Desire - Theresa Romain   *r* 1061

Camherst, Lady Isabella
Voyage of the Basilisk: A Memoir by Lady Trent - Marie Brennan   *f* 16

Douglas, Katherine
Once upon a Plaid - Mia Marlowe   *r* 1021

Eleanor
A Good Rogue Is Hard to Find - Kelly Bowen   *r* 921

Ellison, Lady Merry
Dauntless - Dina L. Sleiman   *i* 457

Fenwick, Lady Ivy
Forbidden to Love the Duke - Jillian Hunter   *r* 991

Lady Gwendolyn
The Cavendon Women - Barbara Taylor Bradford   *t* 133

Hextall, Lady Julia
I've Got My Duke to Keep Me Warm - Kelly Bowen   *r* 920

Kearsey, Rebecca
Never Resist a Rake - Mia Marlowe   *r* 1023

Lady Kine
Old Man's Ghosts - Tom Lloyd   *f* 75

Lady Mary
Murder in the Queen's Wardrobe - Kathy Lynn Emerson   *t* 153

Merryhew, Lady Hermione
Too Dangerous for a Lady - Jo Beverley   *r* 915

Pearson, Lady Georgiana
Never Judge a Lady by Her Cover - Sarah MacLean   *r* 1014

Lady Penworth
Lady Elinor's Wicked Adventures - Lillian Marek   *r* 1020

Pitt, Charlotte
The Angel Court Affair - Anne Perry   *t* 230

Prim, Louisa
The Duke in My Bed - Amelia Grey   *r* 979

Lady Rosemarie
An Uncertain Choice - Jody Hedlund   *i* 415

Lady Sarah
Lady Sarah's Sinful Desires - Sophie Barnes   *r* 909

Scaligeri, Sofia
The Warring States - Aidan Harte   *f* 47

Stanley, Venetia
Viper Wine - Hermione Eyre   *t* 154

Talbot, Clementine Elizabeth
Death of a Dishonorable Gentleman - Tessa Arlen   *t* 126

Tremaine, Lady Elinor "Norrie"
Lady Elinor's Wicked Adventures - Lillian Marek   *r* 1020

Winslow, Lady Theodosia "Teddy"
The Shocking Secret of a Guest at the Wedding - Victoria Alexander   *r* 895

NURSE

Angelica
Juliet's Nurse - Lois Leveen   *t* 204

Anne
Satan's Lullaby - Priscilla Royal   *t* 239

Atkinson, Kelly
Fatal Trauma - Richard L. Mabry   *i* 432

Bridget
The Wednesday Group - Sylvia True   *c* 873

Cole, Brianna
Snowstorm Confessions - Rachel Lee   *r* 1009

Galdon, Mia
Return to Me - Kelly Moran   *r* 1038

Gray, Evelyn
Hope Rising - Stacy Henrie   *r* 987

Hastings, Miriam
A Harvest of Hope - Lauraine Snelling   *i* 459

Hopkins, Rosie
Sweetshop of Dreams - Jenny Colgan   *c* 715

Monk, Hester
Corridors of the Night - Anne Perry   *t* 229

Character Description Index

Slade, Zach
Ghost Killer - Robin D. Owens   *f* 91

Sutter, Gloria
The Other Side of Midnight - Simone St.
   James   *r* 1087

Sykes, Holly
The Bone Clocks - David Mitchell   *c* 807

Templeton, Clare
The Eterna Files - Leanna Renee Hieber   *f* 54

The Pet
Hunted Warrior - Lindsey Piper   *f* 95

Thomas, Odd
Saint Odd - Dean Koontz   *c* 785

Vi
A Fright to the Death - Dawn Eastman   *h* 295

Wherlocke, Sir Orion
If He's Daring - Hannah Howell   *r* 988

Whitecastle, Emma
Ghost in the Guacamole - Sue Ann
   Jaffarian   *m* 582

Winter, Ellie
The Other Side of Midnight - Simone St.
   James   *r* 1087

PSYCHOLOGIST

Busner, Dr. Zack
Shark - Will Self   *c* 858

Corcoran, Faith
Closer Than You Think - Karen Rose   *r* 1062

Delaware, Alex
Motive - Jonathan Kellerman   *c* 780

MacPherson, Riley
The Silent Sister - Diane Chamberlain   *c* 710

Dr. Messerli
Hausfrau - Jill Alexander Essbaum   *c* 739

Mistretta, Lisa
Signature Kill - David Levien   *m* 601

Parrish, Dr. Eric
Every Fifteen Minutes - Lisa Scottoline   *m* 653

Quentin, Dr. Alice
The Winter Foundlings - Kate Rhodes   *m* 643

PSYCHOPATH

Danvers, Malcolm
Forsaken - Kelley Armstrong   *h* 278

PUBLIC RELATIONS

Cole, Tess
Convincing the Rancher - Claire
   McEwen   *r* 1028

LeDuc, Martine
Asylum - Jeannette de Beauvoir   *m* 529

Scofield, Max
Ming Tea Murder - Laura Childs   *m* 514

PUBLISHER

Belial
The Last Bookaneer - Matthew Pearl   *t* 227

Davenport, Pen
The Last Bookaneer - Matthew Pearl   *t* 227

QUAKER

Hargrave, Sarah
The Masque of a Murderer - Susanna
   Calkins   *m* 510

Whitby, Jacob
The Masque of a Murderer - Susanna
   Calkins   *m* 510

RABBIT

Rabbit
Alice - Christina Henry   *h* 315

RACE CAR DRIVER

Brickman, Cooper
Final Lap - Erin McCarthy   *r* 1027

RAKE

Brandon, Rafe
Say Yes to the Marquess - Tessa Dare   *r* 950

Lord Byron
Riot Most Uncouth - Daniel Friedman   *m* 552

Lisle, Lord Frederick "Freddy"
A Good Rake Is Hard to Find - Manda
   Collins   *r* 944

RANCHER

Barnett, Cooper
Wild Horses - B.J. Daniels   *r* 947

Bowden, Blake
When It's Right - Jennifer Ryan   *r* 1065

Bowden, Gabe
At Wolf Ranch - Jennifer Ryan   *r* 1064

Colt-Manning, Mase
When I'm Gone - Abbi Glines   *r* 972

Frazer, Bud
Falling from Horses - Molly Gloss   *t* 165

Garrett, Eli
Part Time Cowboy - Maisey Yates   *r* 1099

Jameson, TJ
For Keeps - Rachel Lacey   *r* 1003

Landon, Wesley "Wes"
Kissed by a Cowboy - Pamela Britton   *r* 926

McCoy, Grayson "Gray"
Wolf Haven - Lindsay McKenna   *r* 1029

O'Donnell, Finn
*Cowboy Boots for Christmas: (Cowboy Not In-
   cluded)* - Carolyn Brown   *r* 929

Quatermaine, Flynn
Jilted - Rachael Johns   *r* 996

Sinclair, Rand
Twice a Texas Bride - Linda Broday   *r* 928

Taggart, Elam
Desperado - Lisa Bingham   *r* 916

Thorne, Cooper
Texas Mail Order Bride - Linda Broday   *r* 927

Wilde, Shannon
Now and Forever - Mary Connealy   *i* 386

RANGER

Hansen, Lance
The Ravens - Vidar Sundstol   *m* 669

Korman, Horatio
Jacaranda - Cherie Priest   *s* 1184

Windar, Charlie
Edge of Dark - Brenda Cooper   *s* 1132

REAL ESTATE AGENT

Brenner, Eve
The Stager - Susan Coll   *c* 716

Gallagher, Raina
Some Like It Witchy - Heather Blake   *m* 494

Hal
Friendswood - Rene Steinke   *c* 869

Heming, William
A Pleasure and a Calling - Phil Hogan   *m* 576

Thompson, Camille
Love Me If You Dare - Toni Blake   *r* 917

Vervoort, Benedict
From Bruges with Love - Pieter Aspe   *m* 482

REANIMATED DEAD

Iron Assassin
The Iron Assassin - Ed Greenwood   *s* 1149

Schweitzer, Jim
Gemini Cell - Myke Cole   *f* 26

REBEL

Ackbar
Heir to the Jedi - Kevin Hearne   *s* 1154

Brigid
Terminal White - James Axler   *s* 1109

Broom, Jody
Cobra Outlaw - Timothy Zahn   *s* 1211

Broom, Lorne
Cobra Outlaw - Timothy Zahn   *s* 1211

Cass
City 1 - Gregg Rosenblum   *s* 1192

Daniels, Faith
Quake - Patrick Carman   *s* 1124

Darke
Under His Guard - Rie Warren   *s* 1206

Darrow
Golden Son - Pierce Brown   *s* 1120

Flynn, Sean
Robot Overlords - Mark Stay   *s* 1200

General Clay
City 1 - Gregg Rosenblum   *s* 1192

Gilmore, Dylan
Quake - Patrick Carman   *s* 1124

Graeme
Bengal's Quest - Lora Leigh   *s* 1168

Grant
Terminal White - James Axler   *s* 1109

Kane
Terminal White - James Axler   *s* 1109

Kelen, Nakari
Heir to the Jedi - Kevin Hearne   *s* 1154

Kevin
City 1 - Gregg Rosenblum   *s* 1192

Nick
City 1 - Gregg Rosenblum   *s* 1192

Organa, Leia
Heir to the Jedi - Kevin Hearne *s* 1154

Reothe
The Fall of Fair Isle - Rowena Cory
    Daniells *f* 27

Skywalker, Luke
Heir to the Jedi - Kevin Hearne *s* 1154

RECEPTIONIST

Hammond, Mallory
The Promise - Beth Wiseman *c* 888

Miller, Marion
Making Marion - Beth Moran *c* 809

RECLUSE

Adler, Ambrose
The Great Sand Fracas of Ames County - Jerry
    Apps *c* 692

Butterfield, Walt
The Never-Open Desert Diner - James
    Anderson *m* 478

Gilmore, Luisa
The Whispering - Sarah Rayne *h* 336

London, Anna
Sweet Damage - Rebecca James *c* 773

Phillips, Sean
Wolf in White Van - John Darnielle *c* 726

Stratton, Pierson
The Viscount Who Lived Down the Lane - Eliza-
    beth Boyle *r* 924

REFUGEE

Lydia
The Dynamite Room - Jason Hewitt *t* 178

RELATIVE

Dupree, Willy
The Ravens - Vidar Sundstol *m* 669

Emrys, Evangeline
The Inquisitor's Mark - Dianne Salerni *f* 102

Hansen, Lance
The Ravens - Vidar Sundstol *m* 669

Hughes, Ellie
Jilted - Rachael Johns *r* 996

Lune, La
The Witch of Painted Sorrows - M.J. Rose *t* 236

Pendare, Riley
The Inquisitor's Mark - Dianne Salerni *f* 102

Salome, Sandrine
The Witch of Painted Sorrows - M.J. Rose *t* 236

Stanton, Elizabeth
Fiercombe Manor - Kate Riordan *t* 235

RELIGIOUS

Adam
The Children Act - Ian McEwan *c* 800

Aelin
Blood of the Cosmos - Kevin J.
    Anderson *s* 1104

Andreou, Alex
The Fifth Gospel - Ian Caldwell *m* 509

Andreou, Simon
The Fifth Gospel - Ian Caldwell *m* 509

Andrew
John the Pupil - David L. Flusfeder *t* 158

Anna Mae
A Faith of Her Own - Kathleen Fuller *i* 400

Anne
Satan's Lullaby - Priscilla Royal *t* 239

Azinheiro, Pedro
The Day of Atonement - David Liss *t* 206

Babayoff, Sebastian
A Dangerous Place - Jacqueline Winspear *t* 273

Bacon, Roger
John the Pupil - David L. Flusfeder *t* 158

Basilda
The Dragon of Handale - Cassandra Clark *t* 142

Beachy, Moses
Meek and Mild - Olivia Newport *i* 439

Becker, Anselm
Cold Betrayal - J.A. Jance *m* 584

Beiler, Davey
The Witnesses - Linda Byler *i* 369

Beiler, Sarah
The Witnesses - Linda Byler *i* 369

Bernard
John the Pupil - David L. Flusfeder *t* 158

Boyle, Kevin
Ghost Image - Ellen Crosby *m* 526

Braun, Anna-Grace
When Grace Sings - Kim Vogel Sawyer *i* 454

Brother Athelstan
The Book of Fires - Paul Doherty *t* 150

Brungardt, Steven
When Grace Sings - Kim Vogel Sawyer *i* 454

Buchman, James
The Devil's Game - Daniel Patterson *i* 443

Byler, Henry
Balm of Gilead - Adina Senft *i* 456

Caleb
Balm of Gilead - Adina Senft *i* 456

Callahan, Eileen
Jacaranda - Cherie Priest *s* 1184

Carnehan, Jacob
In Dark Service - Stephen Hunt *f* 58

Clement
John the Pupil - David L. Flusfeder *t* 158

Cunningham, Dodd
Jaded - Varina Denman *i* 392

Daed
The Proposal at Siesta Key - Shelley Shepard
    Gray *i* 406

Daulton
The Tutor - Andrea Chapin *t* 140

Davoir, Etienne
Satan's Lullaby - Priscilla Royal *t* 239

del Santo, Olivia
Evensong - John Love *s* 1171

Delacruz, Sofia
The Angel Court Affair - Anne Perry *t* 230

Diotima
Death Ex Machina - Gary Corby *t* 145

Divine, Eve
The Case of the Sin City Sister - Lynne
    Hinton *i* 419

Ebersol, Ruth
A Simple Prayer - Amy Clipston *i* 380

Edmund
The Promise of Palm Grove - Shelley Shepard
    Gray *i* 407
The Tapestry - Nancy Bilyeau *t* 130

Edward
The Tutor - Andrea Chapin *t* 140

Eicher, Anna
Second Chances - Sarah Price *i* 450

Eleanor
Satan's Lullaby - Priscilla Royal *t* 239

Evenhands, Miron
The City Stained Red - Sam Sykes *f* 114

Falcone-Driscoll, Giulia
Nun Too Soon - Alice Loweecey *m* 608

Father Abigore
Doctor Death - Lene Kaaberbol *t* 187

Father Neal
Dark Bride - Jonathan Ryan *h* 340

Faulk, Michael
Before, During, After - Richard Bausch *c* 698

Friar Isidore
The Whispering Swarm - Michael
    Moorcock *f* 84

Gibson, Jake
Mammoth Secrets - Ashley Elizabeth
    Ludwig *i* 431

Goldstein, Eli
The Last Flight of Poxl West - Daniel
    Torday *t* 264

Griffin, Charles
The Devil's Game - Daniel Patterson *i* 443

Hal
Friendswood - Rene Steinke *c* 869

Hammond, Mallory
The Promise - Beth Wiseman *c* 888

Hannah
The Matchmaker - Sarah Price *i* 451

Helmuth, Anna
Huckleberry Harvest - Jennifer Beckstrand *i* 358

Helmuth, Fannie
Whiskers of the Lion - P.L. Gaus *m* 555

Helmuth, Felty
Huckleberry Harvest - Jennifer Beckstrand *i* 358

Helmuth, Mandy
Huckleberry Harvest - Jennifer Beckstrand *i* 358

Hildegard
The Dragon of Handale - Cassandra Clark *t* 142

Isabeau
Satan's Lullaby - Priscilla Royal *t* 239

Jacob
The Darkest Hour - Tony Schumacher *t* 245

Jacobs, Charles
Revival - Stephen King *c* 783

Jesus
The Tomb: A Novel of Martha - Stephanie
    Landsem *i* 426

John of Cornwall
Plague Land - S.D. Sykes *t* 257

Kaufman, Zachary
The Promise of Palm Grove - Shelley Shepard
    Gray *i* 407

King, Edward
An Amish Man of Ice Mountain - Kelly
    Long *i* 429

RULER

Malekith
Deathblade: A Tale of Malus Darkblade - C.L. Werner *f* 122

Malnefoley
Hunted Warrior - Lindsey Piper *f* 95

Matilda
The Siege Winter - Ariana Franklin *t* 159

Maven
Red Queen - Victoria Aveyard *f* 9

Mihrimah
The Architect's Apprentice - Elif Shafak *t* 247

Nathair
Ruin - John Gwynne *f* 45

Nathaniel
How to Catch a Prince - Rachel Hauck *i* 414

Nikolaevna, Natasha
The Prince Who Loved Me - Karen Hawkins *r* 983

Organa, Leia
Heir to the Jedi - Kevin Hearne *s* 1154

Pendragon, Adela
In the Time of the Dragon Moon - Janet Lee Carey *f* 20

Pendragon, Desmond
In the Time of the Dragon Moon - Janet Lee Carey *f* 20

Pendragon, Jackrun
In the Time of the Dragon Moon - Janet Lee Carey *f* 20

Pharaoh Tut
The Pharaoh's Daughter - Mesu Andrews *i* 357

Prince Yriel
Valedor - Guy Haley *s* 1152

Queen Edana
Ruin - John Gwynne *f* 45

Queen Victoria
The Hanged Man - P.N. Elrod *h* 296

Red Queen
The Liar's Key - Mark Lawrence *f* 71

Rex Ryen
Madness in Solidar - L.E. Modesitt *f* 82

Richard
The Invention of Fire - Bruce W. Holsinger *t* 179

Richard the Lionheart
The Holy Lance - Andrew Latham *t* 198

Rivvek
Oathkeeper - J.F. Lewis *f* 74

Romanovin, Alexsey
The Prince Who Loved Me - Karen Hawkins *r* 983

Stephen
How to Catch a Prince - Rachel Hauck *i* 414
The Siege Winter - Ariana Franklin *t* 159

Stormbringer
The Ice King - M.K. Hume *f* 57

Tehuti
Desert God - Wilbur Smith *t* 252

Tyra
Woven - Michael Jensen *f* 61

Uorsine
The Talon of the Hawk - Jeffe Kennedy *f* 62

Valyn
The Providence of Fire - Brian Staveley *f* 111

Van Damme, Amandine
Five-Alarm Fudge - Christine DeSmet *m* 534

Van Damme, Arnaud
Five-Alarm Fudge - Christine DeSmet *m* 534

Victoria
The Eterna Files - Leanna Renee Hieber *f* 54
Inspector of the Dead - David Morrell *t* 214

William
Hereward: End of Days - James Wilde *t* 272

Zabriel
The Empty Throne - Cayla Kluver *f* 64

RULER

Aurangzeb
Traitors in the Shadows - Alex Rutherford *t* 242

Lord Curzon
Treachery in Tibet - John Wilcox *t* 271

Elizabeth
The Tutor - Andrea Chapin *t* 140

Emperor Palpatine
Lords of the Sith - Paul S. Kemp *s* 1160

Ereshkigal
Hell's Maw - James Axler *s* 1112

Jahan
Traitors in the Shadows - Alex Rutherford *t* 242

Janus
The Door in the Moon - Catherine Fisher *f* 32

Jardir, Ahmann
The Skull Throne - Peter V. Brett *f* 17

Joseph
The Figaro Murders - Laura Lebow *t* 199

Markess ATerafin, Jewel
Oracle - Michelle West *f* 123

Minos
Desert God - Wilbur Smith *t* 252

Mother Dark
Forge of Darkness - Steven Erikson *f* 31

Mother Darkness
Fall of Light - Steven Erikson *f* 30

Shah
The Woman Who Read Too Much - Bahiyyih Nakhjavani *t* 220

Suleiman
The Architect's Apprentice - Elif Shafak *t* 247

Tamose
Desert God - Wilbur Smith *t* 252

Thrax, Maximinus
Iron and Rust - Harry Sidebottom *t* 248

RUNAWAY

Alice
Alice - Christina Henry *h* 315

Fisher, Gracie
The Art of Losing Yourself - Katie Ganshert *i* 401

Karl
Lost and Found - Brooke Davis *c* 729

O'Toole, Coop
Beneath - Roland Smith *s* 1199

Parker, Eric
Keys of Heaven - Adina Senft *i* 455

Sykes, Holly
The Bone Clocks - David Mitchell *c* 807

Tower, Enid
Cold Betrayal - J.A. Jance *m* 584

RUNNER

Simpson, Lindy
My Sunshine Away - M.O. Walsh *c* 884

Smart, Aganetha
Girl Runner - Carrie Snyder *t* 253

SAILOR

Donovan, Cole
He's So Fine - Jill Shalvis *r* 1075

SALESMAN

Feldstein, Morris
The Global War on Morris - Steve Israel *c* 772

Ridgewood, Noah
Dictatorship of the Dress - Jessica Topper *r* 1092

SALESWOMAN

Montgomery, Shea
The Good Chase - Hanna Martine *r* 1024

SALOON KEEPER/OWNER

Chimbrova, Pearl
The Jazz Palace - Mary Morris *t* 215

SCAVENGER

Lindquist, Gus
The Marauders - Tom Cooper *m* 522

SCHOLAR

Domhnall
Condemned to Death - Cora Harrison *t* 173

Judd, Toby
Cannonbridge - Jonathan Barnes *s* 1116

Steimetz, Charles Proteus
Electric City - Elizabeth Rosner *t* 237

SCIENTIST

Adams, Kate
Desperate Measures - Sandra Orchard *i* 441

Bacon, Roger
John the Pupil - David L. Flusfeder *t* 158

Boudain, Gwen
Ark Storm - Linda Davies *c* 727

Boyle, Kevin
Ghost Image - Ellen Crosby *m* 526

Claybourne, Chance
Exposure - Kathy Reichs *s* 1186

Cooper, Cleo
Saving Cecil - Lee Mims *m* 620

Darwin, Charles
Galapagos Regained - James Morrow *t* 216

Digby, Kenelm
Viper Wine - Hermione Eyre *t* 154

Ford, Marion "Doc"
Cuba Straits - Randy Wayne White   *m* 681

Harper, Hank
In the Woods - Merry Jones   *m* 587

Harrison, Rosa
Harrison Squared - Daryl Gregory   *h* 306

Ji, Luo
The Dark Forest - Cixin Liu   *s* 1170

Jones, Jonah
Coldbrook - Tim Lebbon   *s* 1165

Kimei, Akira
Castaway Planet - Eric Flint   *s* 1146

McDermott, Dr. Ian
Loup Garou: The Beast of Harmony Falls - David Reuben Aslin   *h* 281

Metcalf, Alice
Leaving Time - Jodi Picoult   *c* 829

Nelson, Clayton
The Deep - Nick Cutter   *h* 289

Peng, Chang Ying
Robert Ludlum's The Geneva Strategy - Jamie Freveletti   *m* 551

Petersen, Douglas
Us - David Nicholls   *c* 817

Pitt, Dirk Jr.
Havana Storm - Clive Cussler   *c* 725

Pitt, Summer
Havana Storm - Clive Cussler   *c* 725

Polaski, Katherine
The Missing - Una McCormack   *s* 1175

Price, Alexander "Alex"
Pocket Apocalypse - Seanan McGuire   *f* 80

Rand, Hamilton
Corridors of the Night - Anne Perry   *t* 229

Mr. Smithson
50 Ways to Ruin a Rake - Jade Lee   *r* 1007

Sparks, Cora
The Dress Shop of Dreams - Menna van Praag   *c* 878

Takewashi, Renaldo
Originator - Joel Shepherd   *s* 1194

Tanner, Shelby
Pocket Apocalypse - Seanan McGuire   *f* 80

Tesla, Nikola
The Lusitania Conspiracy - Ronald J. Walters   *t* 269

Winston, Mattie
Stiff Penalty - Annelise Ryan   *m* 648

SEA CAPTAIN

Hayden, Charles
Until the Sea Shall Give Up Her Dead - S. Thomas Russell   *t* 241

Kidd, Thomas
Pasha: A Kydd Sea Adventure - Julian Stockwin   *t* 255

Lenson, Dan
The Cruiser - David Poyer   *c* 836

Lewrie, Alan
Kings and Emperors - Dewey Lambdin   *t* 195

Lobo, Pepe
The Siege - Arturo Perez-Reverte   *t* 228

North, Captain Kit
The Lost Gentleman - Margaret McPhee   *r* 1035

Sherard, Captain Christopher "Kitt"
Breaking the Rake's Rules - Bronwyn Scott   *r* 1071

SEAMSTRESS

Aisling
Dreamer's Daughter - Lynn Kurland   *f* 65

Sinclair, Tori
Wedding Duress - Elizabeth Lynn Casey   *m* 513

SECRETARY

Coleman, Emily
One Step Too Far - Tina Seskis   *c* 859

Megan
Jillian - Halle Butler   *c* 707

Penzi, Nicholas
Pasha: A Kydd Sea Adventure - Julian Stockwin   *t* 255

Richardson, Dorothy
The Lodger - Louisa Treger   *t* 265

SECURITY OFFICER

Blackmer, Jefferson
The Missing - Una McCormack   *s* 1175

Charles, Lenora
Howling Mountain Blues - Ricky Bush   *m* 508

Cole, Davis Way
Double Mint - Gretchen Archer   *m* 481

Dunham, Claire
Signal - Patrick Lee   *m* 598

Garrison, Josh
Wild - Jill Sorenson   *r* 1085

Lynn Miller, Scott
Three Songs for Roxy - Caren Gussoff   *s* 1150

SERIAL KILLER

Bachman, Adam
Compulsion - Allison Brennan   *m* 502

Bathory, Elizabeth
Bathed in Blood - Alex Archer   *f* 6

Blind Angel
Spell Blind - David B. Coe   *f* 25

Bonebreaker
Redzone - William C. Dietz   *s* 1137

Butcher
Serpents in the Cold - Thomas O'Malley   *t* 222

Darcy, Terrell
Black-Eyed Susans - Julia Heaberlin   *m* 572

Halcomb, Jeffrey
Within These Walls - Ania Ahlborn   *h* 276

Jack the Ripper
I, Ripper - Stephen Hunter   *t* 181

Jones, Alex
The Black Widow - Wendy Corsi Staub   *m* 665

Kinsella, Louis
The Winter Foundlings - Kate Rhodes   *m* 643

Lady Killer
Broken - Cynthia Eden   *r* 959

Nightmare Elf
Return to the Dark House - Laurie Faria Stolarz   *h* 346

Owner
Five - Ursula Archer   *c* 693

Pomerleau, Anique
Bones Never Lie - Kathy Reichs   *c* 843

Slicer
The Diabolical Miss Hyde - Viola Carr   *f* 21

Stormchaser
Going Gone - Sharon Sala   *r* 1066

Storms, Serge
Shark Skin Suite - Tim Dorsey   *c* 733

SERVANT

Archaon
Archaon: Everchosen - Rob Sanders   *f* 103

Auerstein, Florian
The Figaro Murders - Laura Lebow   *t* 199

Burr, Timothy
Love's Alchemy - Bryan Crockett   *t* 147

Cabot, Jamie
The Hunger of the Wolf - Stephen Marche   *r* 1019

Darkblade, Malus
Deathblade: A Tale of Malus Darkblade - C.L. Werner   *f* 122

Dollbaby
Dollbaby - Laura McNeal   *c* 801

Ellis, Maude
Darling Beast - Elizabeth Hoyt   *r* 989

Gildas
Fatal Feast - Jay Ruud   *t* 243

Jaffrey, Rosamond
Murder in the Queen's Wardrobe - Kathy Lynn Emerson   *t* 153

Merit
Dark Debt - Chloe Neill   *h* 335

Queenie
Dollbaby - Laura McNeal   *c* 801

Wray, Oliver
Point Hollow - Rio Youers   *h* 355

SHAMAN

Walks with Coyotes, Jay
The Way We Bared Our Souls - Willa Strayhorn   *f* 112

SHAPE-SHIFTER

Aiden
Hunter Reborn - Katie Reus   *h* 338

Andarist
Fall of Light - Steven Erikson   *f* 30

Benoit, Cat
Cat's Lair - Christine Feehan   *h* 298

Cromer, Ridley
Cat's Lair - Christine Feehan   *h* 298

Jia
Crouching Tiger, Forbidden Vampire - Kerrelyn Sparks   *r* 1086

Kenzie
Mate Bond - Jennifer Ashley   *f* 8

Lee, Anabel
Shades of the Wolf - Karen Whiddon   *f* 124

O'Donnell, Bowman
Mate Bond - Jennifer Ashley   *f* 8

Rake, Anomander
Fall of Light - Steven Erikson   *f* 30

Ruin, Silchas
Fall of Light - Steven Erikson *f* 30

Whiskey
Marked Fur Murder - Dixie Lyle *m* 609

Wolfgard, Simon
Vision in Silver - Anne Bishop *f* 15

Yellowrock, Jane
Dark Heir - Faith Hunter *h* 320

SHIPOWNER

Childs, Clare
Maggie Bright: A Novel of Dunkirk - Tracy Groot *i* 410

Sherard, Captain Christopher "Kitt"
Breaking the Rake's Rules - Bronwyn Scott *r* 1071

SIDEKICK

'352' Jenkins
Treachery in Tibet - John Wilcox *t* 271

Tomilson, Sighurdhr
Cuba Straits - Randy Wayne White *m* 681

SINGER

Bloom, Molly
Whatever Happened to Molly Bloom? - Jessica Stirling *t* 254

Carson, Cat
Sweet Harmony - LuAnn McLane *r* 1032

Cole, Nat King
Driving the King - Ravi Howard *t* 180

Greenfield, Jeff
Sweet Harmony - LuAnn McLane *r* 1032

Knoxx, Michael
The Proposal at Siesta Key - Shelley Shepard Gray *i* 406

Petrelli, Flavia
Falling in Love - Donna Leon *m* 599

SINGLE FATHER

Hartwell, Dante
What a Lady Needs for Christmas - Grace Burrowes *r* 935

Jacobs, Slaid
Convincing the Rancher - Claire McEwen *r* 1028

Marcus
The Duke's Guide to Correct Behavior - Megan Frampton *r* 967

Porter, Jay
Pleasantville - Attica Locke *m* 605

Riggs, Tanner
One in a Million - Jill Shalvis *r* 1077

Tremaine, Dr. Ryan
Together with You - Victoria Bylin *i* 370

SINGLE MOTHER

Cartwright, Tessa
Black-Eyed Susans - Julia Heaberlin *m* 572

Castleton, Clara
His Reluctant Cinderella - Jessica Gilmore *r* 971

Chambers, Chelsea
Miracle at the Higher Grounds Cafe - Max Lucado *i* 430

Conlon, Maeve
Lies That Bind - Maggie Barbieri *m* 487

Darling, Alice
Perfect Catch - Sierra Dean *r* 953

Jillian
Jillian - Halle Butler *c* 707

Leduc, Aimee
Murder on the Champ de Mars - Cara Black *m* 492

Lightly, Genevieve "Gin"
The Dandelion Field - Kathryn Springer *i* 460

Parsons, Jenna
House of Wonder - Sarah Healy *c* 763

Sharpe, Danielle
All He Wants for Christmas - Lisa Plumley *r* 1048

Shelder, Hailey
Manhunt - Lisa Phillips *i* 447

SISTER

Adare
The Providence of Fire - Brian Staveley *f* 111

Adriana
Skylight - Jose Saramago *c* 854

Amanda
A Spool of Blue Thread - Anne Tyler *c* 875

Andrea
Double Fudge Brownie Murder - Joanne Fluke *m* 548

Angelica
A Fatal Chapter - Lorna Barrett *m* 488

Angie
Into the Go-Slow - Bridgett M. Davis *c* 728

Ann
Marked Fur Murder - Dixie Lyle *m* 609

Ann, Rachel
One True Path - Barbara Cameron *i* 375

Anna
Cold Spell - Deb Vanasse *c* 879

Ariel
The Dangerous Type - Loren Rhoads *s* 1189

Aubrey, Anna
The Wood's Edge - Lori Benton *i* 360

Austen, Jane
Who Buries the Dead - C.S. Harris *t* 172

Baker, Grace
Dark Rooms - Lili Anolik *c* 691

Baker, Nica
Dark Rooms - Lili Anolik *c* 691

Barsham, Gina
Meadowlands - Elizabeth Jeffrey *t* 185

Barsham, Millie
Meadowlands - Elizabeth Jeffrey *t* 185

Battle, Theresa
What Strange Creatures - Emily Arsenault *c* 695

Baum, Addie
The Boston Girl - Anita Diamant *t* 149

Beale, Josephine
Sisters of Shiloh - Kathy Hepinstall *t* 176

Beale, Libby
Sisters of Shiloh - Kathy Hepinstall *t* 176

Bekatha
Desert God - Wilbur Smith *t* 252

Bell, Vanessa Stephen
Vanessa and Her Sister - Priya Parmar *t* 225

Bella
Hiding in Plain Sight - Nuruddin Farah *c* 741

Betty
The Boston Girl - Anita Diamant *t* 149

Blair, Rebecca
The Children's Crusade - Ann Packer *t* 224

Bradley, Caroline
He's No Prince Charming - Elle Daniels *r* 949

Bree
Stirring Up Trouble - Kimberly Kincaid *r* 1000

Burnett, Emma
Hope Burns - Jaci Burton *r* 936

Burnett, Molly
Hope Burns - Jaci Burton *r* 936

Cabot, Grace
The Devil Takes a Bride - Julia London *r* 1012

Cabot, Honor
The Devil Takes a Bride - Julia London *r* 1012

Cabot, Mercy
The Devil Takes a Bride - Julia London *r* 1012

Cabot, Prudence
The Devil Takes a Bride - Julia London *r* 1012

Canfield, Grace
The Murk - Robert Lettrick *h* 331

Canfield, Piper
The Murk - Robert Lettrick *h* 331

Lady Carinna
An Appetite for Violets - Martine Bailey *t* 128

Carter, Cassie
Last One Home - Debbie Macomber *c* 794

Carter, Jo
The London Pride - Charlie Fletcher *f* 34

Case, Matilda
Infinity Bell - Devon Monk *f* 83

Cass
City 1 - Gregg Rosenblum *s* 1192

Cat
The Soul of Discretion - Susan Hill *m* 574

Celeste
The Amado Women - Desiree Zamorano *c* 892

Celia
The Boston Girl - Anita Diamant *t* 149

Clara
Wicked Stitch - Amanda Lee *m* 597

Conlon, Evelyn
Lies That Bind - Maggie Barbieri *m* 487

Conlon, Maeve
Lies That Bind - Maggie Barbieri *m* 487

Connelly, Laney
Finding Jake - Bryan Reardon *m* 639

Cora
Polaris - Mindee Arnett *s* 1107

Covington, Lacey
Return to Me - Kelly Moran *r* 1038

Craven, Leonora "Nora"
A Good Rake Is Hard to Find - Manda Collins *r* 944

Cross, Janelle "Jannie"
Hope to Die - James Patterson *c* 824

Crosswhite, Sarah
My Sister's Grave - Robert Dugoni *c* 737

Crosswhite, Tracy
My Sister's Grave - Robert Dugoni *c* 737

Cruz, Poppy
Rowdy - Jay Crownover *r* 945

Cruz, Salem
Rowdy - Jay Crownover *r* 945

D'Artigo, Camille
Panther Prowling - Yasmine Galenorn *h* 301

D'Artigo, Delilah
Panther Prowling - Yasmine Galenorn *h* 301

D'Artigo, Menolly
Panther Prowling - Yasmine Galenorn *h* 301

Dahaba
Hiding in Plain Sight - Nuruddin Farah *c* 741

Daisy
Teardrop Lane - Emily March *r* 1018

Daphne
Spy of Richmond - Jocelyn Green *i* 409

Darling, Amy
Better All the Time - Carre Armstrong Gardner *i* 402

Darling, Seraphina "Sephy"
Better All the Time - Carre Armstrong Gardner *i* 402

Davis, Nellie
Wicked Stitch - Amanda Lee *m* 597

de Lacy, Clemence
Plague Land - S.D. Sykes *t* 257

Delancey, Lucy
Tangled Lives - Hilary Boyd *c* 705

Delancey, Marsha
Tangled Lives - Hilary Boyd *c* 705

Devereaux, Tori
Keep Me Safe - Maya Banks *r* 908

Dickinson, Emily
Amherst - William Nicholson *t* 221

Divine, Dorisanne
The Case of the Sin City Sister - Lynne Hinton *i* 419

Divine, Eve
The Case of the Sin City Sister - Lynne Hinton *i* 419

Dorotea
Wolf Winter - Cecilia Ekback *t* 152

Dorothy
A Scoundrel by Moonlight - Anna Campbell *r* 941

Elisabeth "Sisi"
The Accidental Empress - Allison Pataki *t* 226

Elizabeth "Lizzy"
Lizzy and Jane - Katherine Reay *r* 1056

Ella
Into the Go-Slow - Bridgett M. Davis *c* 728

Emily
The Mill River Redemption - Darcie Chan *c* 711

Esme
It Won't Always Be This Great - Peter Mehlman *c* 803

Fawe, Amelie
Witches with the Enemy - Barb Hendee *f* 51

Fawe, Celine
Witches with the Enemy - Barb Hendee *f* 51

Fenella
The Duke of Dark Desires - Miranda Neville *r* 1042

Filliol, Katherine
The May Bride - Suzannah Dunn *t* 151

Fisher, Gracie
The Art of Losing Yourself - Katie Ganshert *i* 401

Fisher, Lorraine
What You Left Behind - Samantha Hayes *m* 570

Frederika
Wolf Winter - Cecilia Ekback *t* 152

Galdon, Ginny
Return to Me - Kelly Moran *r* 1038

Galdon, Mia
Return to Me - Kelly Moran *r* 1038

Gallagher, Piper
In Case of Emergency - Courtney Moreno *c* 811

Garrett, Elly
Grave Matters - Lauren M. Roy *f* 101

Gibbs, Jen
The Story Keeper - Lisa Wingate *c* 887

Goodwin, Karen
Last One Home - Debbie Macomber *c* 794

Gramaraye, Samantha
Finn Fancy Necromancy - Randy Henderson *f* 53

Hansen, Millie
The Cowboy SEAL - Laura Marie Altom *r* 897

Hargrave, Sarah
The Masque of a Murderer - Susanna Calkins *m* 510

Hart, Carmen
The Art of Losing Yourself - Katie Ganshert *i* 401

Hawes, Lady Fiona
Twice Tempted - Eileen Dreyer *r* 956

Helene
The Accidental Empress - Allison Pataki *t* 226

Henry, Emma
Every Little Kiss - Kendra Leigh Castle *r* 943

Hoffman, Margaret
Until the Harvest - Sarah Loudin Thomas *i* 463

Hoffman, Mayfair
Until the Harvest - Sarah Loudin Thomas *i* 463

Holland, Sarie
Canary - Duane Swierczynski *m* 671

Holmes, Toni
Flourless to Stop Him - Nancy J. Parra *m* 631

Hutchinson, Ashley
Christmas at Twilight - Lori Wilde *r* 1097

Illica, Emma
Accidents of Marriage - Randy Susan Meyers *c* 804

Illica, Gracie
Accidents of Marriage - Randy Susan Meyers *c* 804

Isabeau
Satan's Lullaby - Priscilla Royal *t* 239

Isaura
Skylight - Jose Saramago *c* 854

Issi
The Eye of the Falcon - Michelle Paver *f* 94

Jackson, Cassie
Be Not Afraid - Cecilia Galante *h* 300

James, Lyndie
A Love Like Ours - Becky Wade *i* 466

James, Mollie
A Love Like Ours - Becky Wade *i* 466

Jamison, Bella
Spy of Richmond - Jocelyn Green *i* 409

Jane
Lizzy and Jane - Katherine Reay *r* 1056

Jeannie
A Spool of Blue Thread - Anne Tyler *c* 875

Jo
What You Left Behind - Samantha Hayes *m* 570

Julianna
The Long and Faraway Gone - Lou Berney *m* 489

Kaufman, Olivia
The Fragile World - Paula Treick DeBoard *c* 730

Kelly, Sutton
Quartet for the End of Time - Johanna Skibsrud *t* 250

Kimei, Caroline
Castaway Planet - Eric Flint *s* 1146

Kimei, Melody
Castaway Planet - Eric Flint *s* 1146

Kimei, Sakura
Castaway Planet - Eric Flint *s* 1146

Kizzy
Three Songs for Roxy - Caren Gussoff *s* 1150

Lark, Dixie
Leaving Amarillo - Caisey Quinn *r* 1052

Laura
The Duke of Dark Desires - Miranda Neville *r* 1042
The Duke of Dark Desires - Miranda Neville *r* 1042

Lehman, Eve
Amish Promises - Leslie Gould *i* 405

Libby
The Perfect Homecoming - Julia London *r* 1013
The Perfect Homecoming - Julia London *r* 1013

Lucy
Endangered - C.J. Box *m* 499

Luella
The Love Letters - Beverly Lewis *i* 427

MacPherson, Lisa
The Silent Sister - Diane Chamberlain *c* 710

MacPherson, Riley
The Silent Sister - Diane Chamberlain *c* 710

Madeline
The Perfect Homecoming - Julia London *r* 1013
The Perfect Homecoming - Julia London *r* 1013

Mairead
Twice Tempted - Eileen Dreyer *r* 956

Malone, Maggie
Daughter of the Regiment - Stephanie Grace Whitson *i* 469

Maria
The Duke of Dark Desires - Miranda Neville *r* 1042
The Duke of Dark Desires - Miranda Neville *r* 1042

Martha
The Tomb: A Novel of Martha - Stephanie Landsem *i* 426

McDougal, Abigail
My Heart Stood Still - Lori Copeland *i* 387

McDougal, Amelia
My Heart Stood Still - Lori Copeland *i* 387

McDougal, Anne-Marie
My Heart Stood Still - Lori Copeland   *i* 387

Meyer, Chris
Some Like It Hotter - Isabel Sharpe   *r* 1079

Meyer, Eva
Some Like It Hotter - Isabel Sharpe   *r* 1079

Michelle
Double Fudge Brownie Murder - Joanne
   Fluke   *m* 548

Miles, Tricia
A Fatal Chapter - Lorna Barrett   *m* 488

Miller, Hannah
Deadly Echoes - Nancy Mehl   *i* 435

Miller, Sarah
Deadly Echoes - Nancy Mehl   *i* 435

Misty
Teardrop Lane - Emily March   *r* 1018

Montgomery, Sara
A Heart's Obsession - Colleen Coble   *i* 384

Morrigan, Johanna
How to Build a Girl - Caitlin Moran   *c* 810

Nataly
The Amado Women - Desiree Zamorano   *c* 892

Nell
Reunion - Hannah Pittard   *c* 833

O'Brien, Katie
Inside the O'Briens - Lisa Genova   *c* 747

O'Brien, Meghan
Inside the O'Briens - Lisa Genova   *c* 747

Osborne, Frazer
Last to Know - Elizabeth Adler   *c* 685

Osborne, Madison
Last to Know - Elizabeth Adler   *c* 685

Parsons, Jenna
House of Wonder - Sarah Healy   *c* 763

Patterson, Nichole
Last One Home - Debbie Macomber   *c* 794

Peg
The Cowboy SEAL - Laura Marie Altom   *r* 897
The Cowboy SEAL - Laura Marie Altom   *r* 897

Penelope
The Earl I Adore - Erin Knightley   *r* 1001

Pitt, Summer
Havana Storm - Clive Cussler   *c* 725

Prospero, Kate
Deadly Spells - Jaye Wells   *f* 121

Pulaski, Kate
Reunion - Hannah Pittard   *c* 833

Quinn, Clara
Quake - Patrick Carman   *s* 1124

Rafferty, Polly
His Reluctant Cinderella - Jessica
   Gilmore   *r* 971

Raven
Whispers in the Dark - Chase J. Jackson   *h* 321

Reana
The Dangerous Type - Loren Rhoads   *s* 1189

Rebecca
His Wicked Reputation - Madeline Hunter   *r* 992

Rebeccah
Slated for Death - Elizabeth J. Duncan   *m* 537

Redding, Katie
The Sheltering - Mark Powell   *c* 835

Redding, Lucy
The Sheltering - Mark Powell   *c* 835

Reilly, Jensen
Night Blindness - Susan Strecker   *c* 870

Reiss, Sophie
Deadlight Hall - Sarah Rayne   *h* 337

Reiss, Susannah
Deadlight Hall - Sarah Rayne   *h* 337

Ricardo, Lucinda "Lucy"
Ghost in the Guacamole - Sue Ann
   Jaffarian   *m* 582

Ricardo, Ricarda "Rikki"
Ghost in the Guacamole - Sue Ann
   Jaffarian   *m* 582

Riddell, Serena
A Sudden Light - Garth Stein   *c* 868

Roberts, Glenda
Slated for Death - Elizabeth J. Duncan   *m* 537

Robin
Whispers in the Dark - Chase J. Jackson   *h* 321

Rocco, Meg
The Inn at Ocean's Edge - Colleen Coble   *i* 383

Rogers, Dena
Shades of the Wolf - Karen Whiddon   *f* 124

Rose
The Mill River Redemption - Darcie Chan   *c* 711

Roxy
Three Songs for Roxy - Caren Gussoff   *s* 1150

Russell, Eva
His Wicked Reputation - Madeline Hunter   *r* 992

Sandstone, Jenny
A Deadly Affair at Bobtail Ridge - Terry
   Shames   *m* 656

Seymour, Jane
The May Bride - Suzannah Dunn   *t* 151
The May Bride - Suzannah Dunn   *t* 151

Shepard, Leah
Ancient Oceans of Central Kentucky - David Connerley Nahm   *c* 815

Sheridan
Endangered - C.J. Box   *m* 499

Silva, Angel
On the Run - Jo Davis   *r* 951

Simmons, Bernie
A Catered Mother's Day - Isis Crawford   *m* 523

Simmons, Libby
A Catered Mother's Day - Isis Crawford   *m* 523

Sister of the Shah
The Woman Who Read Too Much - Bahiyyih
   Nakhjavani   *t* 220

Smith, Faith
Strands of Sorrow - John Ringo   *s* 1190

Smith, Sophia
Strands of Sorrow - John Ringo   *s* 1190

Snowden, Julia
Musseled Out - Barbara Ross   *m* 646

Star, Ice Cream
The Country of Ice Cream Star - Sandra
   Newman   *c* 816

Stephen, Vanessa
Adeline: A Novel of Virginia Woolf - Norah
   Vincent   *t* 268

Susan
Em and the Big Hoom - Jerry Pinto   *c* 831

Swensen, Hannah
Double Fudge Brownie Murder - Joanne
   Fluke   *m* 548

Sylvia
The Amado Women - Desiree Zamorano   *c* 892

Sylvie
Cold Spell - Deb Vanasse   *c* 879

Tehuti
Desert God - Wilbur Smith   *t* 252

Tempest, Lavinia
The Viscount Who Lived Down the Lane - Elizabeth Boyle   *r* 924

Tempest, Louisa
The Viscount Who Lived Down the Lane - Elizabeth Boyle   *r* 924

Todd, Ursula
A God in Ruins - Kate Atkinson   *t* 127

Toomey, Alice
The Second Sister - Marie Bostwick   *r* 918

Toomey, Lucy
The Second Sister - Marie Bostwick   *r* 918

Tremont, Sandy
As Night Falls - Jenny Milchman   *m* 619

Trim, Nell
A Scoundrel by Moonlight - Anna
   Campbell   *r* 941

Troyer, Elizabeth "Lissy"
The Proposal at Siesta Key - Shelley Shepard
   Gray   *i* 406

Troyer, Penny
The Proposal at Siesta Key - Shelley Shepard
   Gray   *i* 406

Tyler, Emma
The Perfect Homecoming - Julia London   *r* 1013

Unnamed Character
By Your Side - Candace Calvert   *i* 373

Vine, Samantha
Cane and Abe - James Grippando   *c* 756

Von Riesen, Elfrieda "Elf"
All My Puny Sorrows - Miriam Toews   *c* 871

Von Riesen, Yolandi "Yoli"
All My Puny Sorrows - Miriam Toews   *c* 871

Walden, Cara
All the Wrong Places - Lisa Lieberman   *t* 205

Wallin, Beth
Would-Be Wilderness Wife - Regina Scott   *r* 1074

Warren, Heidi
Untraceable - Elizabeth Goddard   *i* 404

Waverley, Claire
First Frost - Sarah Addison Allen   *c* 689

Waverley, Sydney
First Frost - Sarah Addison Allen   *c* 689

Wembley, Sophie
The Earl I Adore - Erin Knightley   *r* 1001

Wenger, Marlena
The Love Letters - Beverly Lewis   *i* 427

Woolf, Virginia
Adeline: A Novel of Virginia Woolf - Norah
   Vincent   *t* 268

Woolf, Virginia Stephen
Vanessa and Her Sister - Priya Parmar   *t* 225

Wynn, Macy
By Your Side - Candace Calvert   *i* 373

SKATER

Dillon, Grace
One Wish - Robyn Carr   *r* 942

Marcus
If I Fall, If I Die - Michael Christie   *c* 712

SLAVE

Aisa
Iron Axe - Steven Harper   *f* 46

Caridad
The Barefoot Queen - Ildefonso Falcones   *t* 156

Carnehan, Carter
In Dark Service - Stephen Hunt   *f* 58

Danr
Iron Axe - Steven Harper   *f* 46

Daphne
Spy of Richmond - Jocelyn Green   *i* 409

Hale, Carrington
The Choosing - Rachelle Dekker   *i* 390

Horace
Storm and Steel - Jon Sprunk   *f* 109

Isval
Lords of the Sith - Paul S. Kemp   *s* 1160

Jamison, Bella
Spy of Richmond - Jocelyn Green   *i* 409

Jax
The Mechanical - Ian Tregillis   *f* 117

Jirom
Storm and Steel - Jon Sprunk   *f* 109

Johnson, Fred
The Winter Family - Clifford Jackman   *t* 184

Kholster
Oathkeeper - J.F. Lewis   *f* 74

Loveday
An Appetite for Violets - Martine Bailey   *t* 128

Maviah
A.D. 30 - Ted Dekker   *i* 391

Raleeha
Righteous Fury - Markus Heitz   *f* 49

Ruth
The Whistle Walk - Stephenia H. McGee   *i* 434

Ruth "Mammy"
Ruth's Journey: The Authorized Novel of Mammy from Margaret Mitchell's Gone with the Wind - Donald McCaig   *t* 210

Scarlet
The Creole Princess - Beth White   *i* 468

Smith, Jupiter
The Abduction of Smith and Smith - Rashad Harrison   *t* 174

Taita
Desert God - Wilbur Smith   *t* 252

SMUGGLER

Brant, Hollis
Past Crimes - Glen Erik Hamilton   *m* 566

Caridad
The Barefoot Queen - Ildefonso Falcones   *t* 156

Garcia, Juan
Cuba Straits - Randy Wayne White   *m* 681

Melchor
The Barefoot Queen - Ildefonso Falcones   *t* 156

Pyke, Brannan
Ancestral Machines - Michael Cobley   *s* 1128

SOCCER PLAYER

Lizzie
Three Story House - Courtney Miller Santo   *c* 853

SOCIAL WORKER

Illica, Maddy
Accidents of Marriage - Randy Susan Meyers   *c* 804

Mason, Carly Jo
Together with You - Victoria Bylin   *i* 370

SOCIALITE

Cateman Kingsley, Elizabeth
Checked Out - Elaine Viets   *m* 677

Davenport, Cassidy
What a Woman Gets - Judi Fennell   *r* 962

Hyde, Ellis
At the Water's Edge - Sara Gruen   *t* 170

Hyde, Madeline "Maddie"
At the Water's Edge - Sara Gruen   *t* 170

Talbot, Clementine Elizabeth
Death of a Dishonorable Gentleman - Tessa Arlen   *t* 126

SON

Adam
Jillian - Halle Butler   *c* 707

Alden, Hunter "Tripp" Hutchinson III
NYPD Red 3 - James Patterson   *m* 632

Andarist
Fall of Light - Steven Erikson   *f* 30

Anderson, Doug
The Legacy - Dan Walsh   *i* 467

Andreou, Peter
The Fifth Gospel - Ian Caldwell   *m* 509

Aubrey, William
The Wood's Edge - Lori Benton   *i* 360

Aurangzeb
Traitors in the Shadows - Alex Rutherford   *t* 242

Barrons, Leo
Of Silk and Steam - Bec McMaster   *r* 1033

Barsham, James
Meadowlands - Elizabeth Jeffrey   *t* 185

Ben
Christmas at Twilight - Lori Wilde   *r* 1097

Bennett, Eric
The Melody Lingers On - Mary Higgins Clark   *m* 515

Blair, James
The Children's Crusade - Ann Packer   *t* 224

Blair, Robert
The Children's Crusade - Ann Packer   *t* 224

Blair, Ryan
The Children's Crusade - Ann Packer   *t* 224

Bolton, Cab
Season of Fear - Brian Freeman   *m* 550

Cajeiri
Tracker - C.J. Cherryh   *s* 1125

Caleb
Balm of Gilead - Adina Senft   *i* 456

Cameron
The Rebirths of Tao - Wesley Chu   *s* 1126

Camherst, Jacob "Jake"
Voyage of the Basilisk: A Memoir by Lady Trent - Marie Brennan   *f* 16

Carmine
An Italian Wife - Ann Hood   *c* 768

Carnehan, Carter
In Dark Service - Stephen Hunt   *f* 58

Catrell, Jamie
The Pocket Wife - Susan Crawford   *m* 524

Charlie
It Won't Always Be This Great - Peter Mehlman   *c* 803

Chris
Cold Betrayal - J.A. Jance   *m* 584

Cobb, Chris "Kit"
The Empire of Night - Robert Olen Butler   *t* 138

Cochrane, Peter
Impulse - Dave Bara   *s* 1115

Connard, Howard Jr.
Etta Mae's Worst Bad-Luck Day - Ann B. Ross   *c* 848

Connelly, Jake
Finding Jake - Bryan Reardon   *m* 639

Cowan, Jeff
Hush - Karen Robards   *r* 1058

Cross, Alex Jr.
Hope to Die - James Patterson   *c* 824

Cross, Damon
Hope to Die - James Patterson   *c* 824

Cunliffe, Johnsey
The Thing About December - Donal Ryan   *c* 850

Daniel
Tangled Lives - Hilary Boyd   *c* 705

de Kruk, Carson
Hiss and Tell - Claire Donally   *m* 536

de Warrene, Alwyn Gryffin
If He's Daring - Hannah Howell   *r* 988

Defoe, Pip
The Last Kings of Sark - Rosa Rankin-Gee   *c* 840

Delancey, Ed
Tangled Lives - Hilary Boyd   *c* 705

Dent, Andy
Constant Fear - Daniel Palmer   *m* 629

Donovan, Alex
The Memory House - Linda Goodnight   *r* 974

Douglas "Stem"
A Spool of Blue Thread - Anne Tyler   *c* 875

Downey, Lyon
Bringing Home the Bad Boy - Jessica Lemmon   *r* 1010

Drake, Bobby
Sometimes the Wolf - Urban Waite   *c* 882

Ebersol, Aaron
A Simple Prayer - Amy Clipston   *i* 380

Eddie
Delicious Foods - James Hannaham   *c* 760

Edward
The Price of Blood - Patricia Bracewell   *t* 132

Elliot
Reunion - Hannah Pittard   *c* 833

Flynn, Sean
Robot Overlords - Mark Stay   *s* 1200

Freddie
What You Left Behind - Samantha Hayes   *m* 570

Furman, Shalom
The Ambassadors - George Lerner   *t* 203

Character Description Index

Defoe, Esme
The Last Kings of Sark - Rosa Rankin-Gee *c* 840

Delancey, Annie
Tangled Lives - Hilary Boyd *c* 705

Delancey, Richard
Tangled Lives - Hilary Boyd *c* 705

Delores
Double Fudge Brownie Murder - Joanne Fluke *m* 548

DeLuca, Cara
All Fired Up - Kate Meader *r* 1037

Digby, Kenelm
Viper Wine - Hermione Eyre *t* 154

Diotima
Death Ex Machina - Gary Corby *t* 145

Doll, Hannah
The Zone of Interest - Martin Amis *c* 690

Doll, Paul
The Zone of Interest - Martin Amis *c* 690

Donne, John
Love's Alchemy - Bryan Crockett *t* 147

Douglas, Katherine
Once upon a Plaid - Mia Marlowe *r* 1021

Douglas, William
Once upon a Plaid - Mia Marlowe *r* 1021

Downey, Rae
Bringing Home the Bad Boy - Jessica Lemmon *r* 1010

Doyle, Kathleen
Murder in Hindsight - Anne Cleeland *m* 516

Doyle, Shane
All Fired Up - Kate Meader *r* 1037

Drake, Bobby
Sometimes the Wolf - Urban Waite *c* 882

Driscoll, Frank
Nun Too Soon - Alice Loweecey *m* 608

Duran, Ben
The Black Widow - Wendy Corsi Staub *m* 665

Duran, Gaby
The Black Widow - Wendy Corsi Staub *m* 665

Edgar
When the Doves Disappeared - Sofi Oksanen *t* 223

Elizabeth
The Hidden Man - Robin Blake *m* 495

Ellen
Ruth's Journey: The Authorized Novel of Mammy from Margaret Mitchell's Gone with the Wind - Donald McCaig *t* 210

Em
Em and the Big Hoom - Jerry Pinto *c* 831

Emilio
Skylight - Jose Saramago *c* 854

Emma
The Price of Blood - Patricia Bracewell *t* 132

Etta
Emma and Otto and Russell and James - Emma Hooper *c* 769

Falcone-Driscoll, Giulia
Nun Too Soon - Alice Loweecey *m* 608

Feldstein, Morris
The Global War on Morris - Steve Israel *c* 772

Feldstein, Rona
The Global War on Morris - Steve Israel *c* 772

Felicity
The Cavendon Women - Barbara Taylor Bradford *t* 133

Fidelis, Dr. Luke
The Hidden Man - Robin Blake *m* 495

Filliol, Katherine
The May Bride - Suzannah Dunn *t* 151

Fitzgerald, Catherine
The German Agent - J. Sydney Jones *t* 186

Fitzgerald, Edward
The German Agent - J. Sydney Jones *t* 186

Fitzgerald, F. Scott
West of Sunset - Stewart O'Nan *c* 819

Fitzgerald, Zelda
West of Sunset - Stewart O'Nan *c* 819

Fitzpatrick, Cyril
A Woman Unknown - Frances Brody *t* 134

Fitzpatrick, Deirdre
A Woman Unknown - Frances Brody *t* 134

Flavia
The Wednesday Group - Sylvia True *c* 873

Flavian
Only Enchanting - Mary Balogh *r* 907

Fleming, Mary
Married to a Perfect Stranger - Jane Ashford *r* 904

Fletcher, Alec
Superfluous Women - Carola Dunn *m* 538

Flynn, Lady Joan
What a Lady Needs for Christmas - Grace Burrowes *r* 935

Fonthill, Alice
Treachery in Tibet - John Wilcox *t* 271

Fonthill, Simon
Treachery in Tibet - John Wilcox *t* 271

Fornier, Augustin
Ruth's Journey: The Authorized Novel of Mammy from Margaret Mitchell's Gone with the Wind - Donald McCaig *t* 210

Fornier, Solange Escarlette
Ruth's Journey: The Authorized Novel of Mammy from Margaret Mitchell's Gone with the Wind - Donald McCaig *t* 210

Fowler, Brad
Murder She Wrote: Killer in the Kitchen - Jessica Fletcher *m* 546

Fowler, Marcie
Murder She Wrote: Killer in the Kitchen - Jessica Fletcher *m* 546

Frank, Nicole "Nicky"
Crash and Burn - Lisa Gardner *m* 554

Frank, Thomas
Crash and Burn - Lisa Gardner *m* 554

Frida
California - Edan Lepucki *c* 789

Furman, Jacob
The Ambassadors - George Lerner *t* 203

Furman, Susanna
The Ambassadors - George Lerner *t* 203

Gabler, Christof
The Figaro Murders - Laura Lebow *i* 199

Gail
The Wednesday Group - Sylvia True *c* 873

Gavin, Leonard
All the President's Menus - Julie Hyzy *m* 580

Gifford, Zoe
An American Duchess - Sharon Page *r* 1046

Godel, Kurt
The Goddess of Small Victories - Yannick Grannec *c* 752

Goetz, Ada
Still Life - Christa Parrish *i* 442

Goetz, Julian
Still Life - Christa Parrish *i* 442

Golding, Sally
Outlaw Takes a Bride - Susan Page Davis *i* 389

Goodwin, Garth
Last One Home - Debbie Macomber *c* 794

Goodwin, Karen
Last One Home - Debbie Macomber *c* 794

Graham, Grace
Unbecoming - Rebecca Scherm *c* 855

Graham, Riley
Unbecoming - Rebecca Scherm *c* 855

Graves, Billy
The Whites - Harry Brandt *m* 501

Graves, Carmen
The Whites - Harry Brandt *m* 501

Guenivere
Fatal Feast - Jay Ruud *t* 243

Hadley, Bruce
A Catered Mother's Day - Isis Crawford *m* 523

Hadley, Ellen
A Catered Mother's Day - Isis Crawford *m* 523

Hale, Carrington
The Choosing - Rachelle Dekker *i* 390

Hannah
The Wednesday Group - Sylvia True *c* 873

Harper, Hank
In the Woods - Merry Jones *m* 587

Hartley, Eddie
Arts and Entertainments - Christopher R. Beha *c* 700

Hartley, Susan
Arts and Entertainments - Christopher R. Beha *c* 700

Hartwell, Dante
What a Lady Needs for Christmas - Grace Burrowes *r* 935

Hawthorne, Helen
Checked Out - Elaine Viets *m* 677

Hazelton, Nigel
An American Duchess - Sharon Page *r* 1046

Hedge, Sophy
The Language of Paradise - Barbara Klein Moss *t* 217

Helmuth, Anna
Huckleberry Harvest - Jennifer Beckstrand *i* 358
Huckleberry Spring - Jennifer Beckstrand *i* 359

Helmuth, Felty
Huckleberry Harvest - Jennifer Beckstrand *i* 358
Huckleberry Spring - Jennifer Beckstrand *i* 359

Henry
Lamentation - C.J. Sansom *t* 244
Prague Summer - Jeffrey Condran *c* 717

Herman, Alice
Shame and the Captives - Thomas Keneally *t* 190

Hero
Who Buries the Dead - C.S. Harris *t* 172

Hill-Tucker, Dr. Angela "Angel"
Dying for the Past - T.J. O'Connor   *m* 625

Hoffmann, Corina
Blood on Snow - Jo Nesbo   *m* 624

Hoffmann, Daniel
Blood on Snow - Jo Nesbo   *m* 624

Holmes, Sherlock
Dreaming Spies - Laurie R. King   *t* 192

Hopeton, Malcolm
A Slant of Light - Jeffrey Lent   *t* 202

Howard, Brian
Cold Trail - Janet Dawson   *m* 528

Howard, Frank
The Bride Ship - Regina Scott   *r* 1073

Howard, Sheila
Cold Trail - Janet Dawson   *m* 528

Huss, Irene
The Beige Man - Helene Tursten   *m* 674

Hyde, Ellis
At the Water's Edge - Sara Gruen   *t* 170

Hyde, Madeline "Maddie"
At the Water's Edge - Sara Gruen   *t* 170

Illica, Ben
Accidents of Marriage - Randy Susan
   Meyers   *c* 804

Illica, Maddy
Accidents of Marriage - Randy Susan
   Meyers   *c* 804

Inevera
The Skull Throne - Peter V. Brett   *f* 17

Ingham, Charles
The Cavendon Women - Barbara Taylor
   Bradford   *t* 133

The Cavendon Women - Barbara Taylor
   Bradford   *t* 133

Ingham, Charlotte Swann
The Cavendon Women - Barbara Taylor
   Bradford   *t* 133

Jack
The Children Act - Ian McEwan   *c* 800

Jamison, Abraham
Spy of Richmond - Jocelyn Green   *i* 409

Jamison, Bella
Spy of Richmond - Jocelyn Green   *i* 409

Jardir, Ahmann
The Skull Throne - Peter V. Brett   *f* 17

Jennings, Harper
In the Woods - Merry Jones   *m* 587

Jill
The Rebirths of Tao - Wesley Chu   *s* 1126

Johnson, Bruno
The Replacements - David Putnam   *m* 637

Jones, Mila
Moonlight on Butternut Lake - Mary
   McNear   *r* 1034

Jorgenson, Lars
The Stager - Susan Coll   *c* 716

Julia
Fram - Steve Himmer   *c* 767

Justina
Skylight - Jose Saramago   *c* 854

Juudit
When the Doves Disappeared - Sofi
   Oksanen   *t* 223

Katt-Martini, Katherine "Kitty"
Alien Separation - Gini Koch   *s* 1162

Kaufman, Curtis
The Fragile World - Paula Treick
   DeBoard   *c* 730

Kaufman, Kathleen
The Fragile World - Paula Treick
   DeBoard   *c* 730

Keenan, Holly
The Boy Who Drew Monsters - Keith
   Donohue   *c* 732

Keenan, Tim
The Boy Who Drew Monsters - Keith
   Donohue   *c* 732

Keeping, Agnes
Only Enchanting - Mary Balogh   *r* 907

Mr. Kent
Spy of Richmond - Jocelyn Green   *i* 409

Kimei, Akira
Castaway Planet - Eric Flint   *s* 1146

Kimei, Laura
Castaway Planet - Eric Flint   *s* 1146

King, Jed
The Song - Chris Fabry   *i* 398

King, Rose
The Song - Chris Fabry   *i* 398

Knight, Doc
Double Fudge Brownie Murder - Joanne
   Fluke   *m* 548

Lady Kine
Old Man's Ghosts - Tom Lloyd   *f* 75

Langdon, Rosanna
Early Warning - Jane Smiley   *t* 251

Langdon, Walter
Early Warning - Jane Smiley   *t* 251

Laurie
Little Girls - Ronald Damien Malfi   *h* 333

Leatha
Bittersweet - Susan Wittig Albert   *m* 476

Leesil
First and Last Sorcerer - Barb Hendee   *f* 52

Leila
Bound by Flames - Jeaniene Frost   *r* 969

Lennox, Benedict
Love in the Time of Scandal - Caroline
   Linden   *r* 1011

Levire, Adam
I've Got My Duke to Keep Me Warm - Kelly
   Bowen   *r* 920

Lily
The Christmas Light - Donna VanLiere   *c* 881

Lincoln, Abraham
Lincoln's Billy - Tom LeClair   *t* 200

Lincoln, Mary Todd
Lincoln's Billy - Tom LeClair   *t* 200

Littman, Aaron
Losing Faith - Adam Mitzner   *m* 621

Lizzy
The Wednesday Group - Sylvia True   *c* 873

Loomis Todd, Mabel
Amherst - William Nicholson   *t* 221

Louis, King
1636: The Cardinal Virtues - Eric Flint   *s* 1145

MacKay, Donal
The First Kiss - Grace Burrowes   *r* 932

Mackintosh, Charles "Mac" Rennie
Mr. Mac and Me - Esther Freud   *t* 161

Mackintosh, Margaret
Mr. Mac and Me - Esther Freud   *t* 161

Maddy
If Not for This - Pete Fromm   *c* 745

Magiere
First and Last Sorcerer - Barb Hendee   *f* 52

Maija
Wolf Winter - Cecilia Ekback   *t* 152

Malloy, Claire
Pride v. Prejudice - Joan Hess   *m* 573

Mamm
The Proposal at Siesta Key - Shelley Shepard
   Gray   *i* 406

Manton, George
If the Viscount Falls - Sabrina Jeffries   *r* 995

Margaret
Where the Bones are Buried - Jeanne
   Matthews   *m* 611

Mariana
Skylight - Jose Saramago   *c* 854

Marie
The Replacements - David Putnam   *m* 637

Marin, Rosa
A Root Awakening - Kate Collins   *m* 519

Marin, Sergio
A Root Awakening - Kate Collins   *m* 519

Martens, Hannelore
From Bruges with Love - Pieter Aspe   *m* 482

Martini, Jeff
Alien Separation - Gini Koch   *s* 1162

Martini, Nic
Murder with a Twist - Tracy Kiely   *m* 593

Martini, Nigel
Murder with a Twist - Tracy Kiely   *m* 593

Masters, Luke
Snowstorm Confessions - Rachel Lee   *r* 1009

Matchet, Ruth
The Fair Fight - Anna Freeman   *t* 160

Matekoni, J.L.B.
The Handsome Man's De Luxe Cafe - Alexander
   McCall Smith   *c* 864

Maye, Fiona
The Children Act - Ian McEwan   *c* 800

Mayor's Wife
The Woman Who Read Too Much - Bahiyyih
   Nakhjavani   *t* 220

McKay, Jessie
Cowgirls Don't Cry - Lorelei James   *r* 994

McKay, Luke
Cowgirls Don't Cry - Lorelei James   *r* 994

McKinley, Ryan
Married 'til Monday - Denise Hunter   *i* 420

McNeely, Charlie
Where All Light Tends to Go - David Joy   *m* 588

McNeely, Laura
Where All Light Tends to Go - David Joy   *m* 588

Merrill, Nola
On Shifting Sand - Allison Pittman   *i* 448

Merrill, Russ
On Shifting Sand - Allison Pittman   *i* 448

Miles
The Cavendon Women - Barbara Taylor
   Bradford   *t* 133

Miller, Allison
Before He Finds Her - Michael Kardos   *m* 591

Miller, Ramsey
Before He Finds Her - Michael Kardos   *m* 591

Mina
The Shadow of the Crescent Moon - Fatima Bhutto   *c* 703

Monk, Hester
Corridors of the Night - Anne Perry   *t* 229

Monk, William
Corridors of the Night - Anne Perry   *t* 229

More, Anne
Love's Alchemy - Bryan Crockett   *t* 147

Murphy Sullivan, Molly
The Edge of Dreams - Rhys Bowen   *t* 131

Nancy
If the Viscount Falls - Sabrina Jeffries   *r* 995

Nat
Delicious Foods - James Hannaham   *c* 760

Needle, Marina
We Are Pirates - Daniel Handler   *c* 759

Needle, Phil
We Are Pirates - Daniel Handler   *c* 759

Nic
Night Blindness - Susan Strecker   *c* 870

Nichols, Faith
Losing Faith - Adam Mitzner   *m* 621

Nicolaos
Death Ex Machina - Gary Corby   *t* 145

Nix, Billy
Firebreak - Tricia Fields   *m* 544

Nix, Brenda
Firebreak - Tricia Fields   *m* 544

O'Brien, Cal
Serpents in the Cold - Thomas O'Malley   *t* 222

O'Brien, Joe
Inside the O'Briens - Lisa Genova   *c* 747

O'Brien, Rosie
Inside the O'Briens - Lisa Genova   *c* 747

O'Hara, Gerald
Ruth's Journey: The Authorized Novel of Mammy from Margaret Mitchell's Gone with the Wind - Donald McCaig   *t* 210

Osborne, Rose
Last to Know - Elizabeth Adler   *c* 685

Osborne, Wally
Last to Know - Elizabeth Adler   *c* 685

Oscar
Fram - Steve Himmer   *c* 767

Otto
Emma and Otto and Russell and James - Emma Hooper   *c* 769

Paavo
Wolf Winter - Cecilia Ekback   *t* 152

Paras, Olivia
All the President's Menus - Julie Hyzy   *m* 580

Parr, Catherine
Lamentation - C.J. Sansom   *t* 244

Parrish, Dr. Eric
Every Fifteen Minutes - Lisa Scottoline   *m* 653

Pat
The Witch of the Wood - Michael Aronovitz   *h* 280

Patterson, Jake
Last One Home - Debbie Macomber   *c* 794

Patterson, Nichole
Last One Home - Debbie Macomber   *c* 794

Paul
After Birth - Elisa Albert   *c* 688
This Is the Water - Yannick Murphy   *c* 813

Paynter, Johnny
Outlaw Takes a Bride - Susan Page Davis   *i* 389

Peake, David
Lay It on My Heart - Angela Pneuman   *c* 834

Peake, Phoebe
Lay It on My Heart - Angela Pneuman   *c* 834

Perlmutter, Josephine
The Empire of the Senses - Alexis Landau   *t* 196

Perlmutter, Lev
The Empire of the Senses - Alexis Landau   *t* 196

Peter
The Book of Strange New Things - Michel Faber   *c* 740
On the Edge - Edward St. Aubyn   *c* 867

Petersen, Connie
Us - David Nicholls   *c* 817

Petersen, Douglas
Us - David Nicholls   *c* 817

Petkova, Yulana
The Russian Bride - Ed Kovacs   *m* 595

Pickett, Joe
Endangered - C.J. Box   *m* 499

Pickett, Marybeth
Endangered - C.J. Box   *m* 499

Pietro
Juliet's Nurse - Lois Leveen   *t* 204

Pitt, Charlotte
The Angel Court Affair - Anne Perry   *t* 230

Pitt, Thomas
The Angel Court Affair - Anne Perry   *t* 230

Porter, Maggie
Love Letters - Debbie Macomber   *c* 793

Porter, Roy
Love Letters - Debbie Macomber   *c* 793

Price, Adam
The Stranger - Harlan Coben   *m* 517

Price, Corinne
The Stranger - Harlan Coben   *m* 517

Queen Anne
1636: The Cardinal Virtues - Eric Flint   *s* 1145

Queen Katherine
The May Bride - Suzannah Dunn   *t* 151

Quinn, Brigid
Fear the Darkness - Becky Masterman   *m* 610

Radmanovic, Charlene
I Am Radar - Reif Larsen   *s* 1164

Radmanovic, Kermin
I Am Radar - Reif Larsen   *s* 1164

Ramotswe, Precious
The Handsome Man's De Luxe Cafe - Alexander McCall Smith   *c* 864

Redding, Luther
The Sheltering - Mark Powell   *c* 835

Redding, Pamela
The Sheltering - Mark Powell   *c* 835

Reid, Savannah
Killer Gourmet - G.A. McKevett   *m* 615

Reilly, Jensen
Night Blindness - Susan Strecker   *c* 870

Reynolds, Ali
Cold Betrayal - J.A. Jance   *m* 584

Richard
The Last Good Paradise - Tatjana Soli   *c* 865

Richmond, Daisy
Before I Go - Colleen Oakley   *c* 820

Richmond, Jack
Before I Go - Colleen Oakley   *c* 820

Rimaldi, Josephine
An Italian Wife - Ann Hood   *c* 768

Rimaldi, Vincenzo
An Italian Wife - Ann Hood   *c* 768

Rivers, Dutch
Sense of Deception - Victoria Laurie   *f* 69

Roarke
Obsession in Death - J.D. Robb   *c* 847

Roen
The Rebirths of Tao - Wesley Chu   *s* 1126

Rosen, Peter
Pride v. Prejudice - Joan Hess   *m* 573

Ross, Emmalyn
As Waters Gone By - Cynthia Ruchti   *i* 452

Ross, Max
As Waters Gone By - Cynthia Ruchti   *i* 452

Roy
The Evil Deeds We Do - Robert S. Levinson   *m* 602

Russell, Mary
Dreaming Spies - Laurie R. King   *t* 192

Sagemont, Phil
Checked Out - Elaine Viets   *m* 677

Salvare, Abby Knight
A Root Awakening - Kate Collins   *m* 519

Salvare, Marco
A Root Awakening - Kate Collins   *m* 519

Sam
Bittersweet - Susan Wittig Albert   *m* 476

Sanchez, Oscar
Devils and Dust - J.D. Rhoades   *m* 642

Sanders, Bianca
Double Mint - Gretchen Archer   *m* 481

Sanders, Richard
Double Mint - Gretchen Archer   *m* 481

Sanderson, Molly
Where They Found Her - Kimberly McCreight   *m* 614

Sandra
The Storm Murders - John Farrow   *m* 543

Scarpetta, Dr. Kay
Flesh and Blood - Patricia Cornwell   *c* 719

Sebak
The Pharaoh's Daughter - Mesu Andrews   *i* 357

Sendry, Michael
Allure of Deceit - Susan Froetschel   *m* 553

Sendry, Rose
Allure of Deceit - Susan Froetschel   *m* 553

Severson, Miranda
The Kind Worth Killing - Peter Swanson   *m* 670

Severson, Ted
The Kind Worth Killing - Peter Swanson   *m* 670

Seymour, Edward
The May Bride - Suzannah Dunn   *t* 151

Sikandar
The Shadow of the Crescent Moon - Fatima Bhutto   *c* 703

Silvestre
Skylight - Jose Saramago   *c* 854

SPY

Finch, Leonora
Sleep in Peace Tonight - James MacManus   *t* 208

Gilbride, Alastair "Alec"
How to Plan a Wedding for a Royal Spy - Vanessa Kelly   *r* 997

Gonzales de Ripparda, Rafael Maria
The Creole Princess - Beth White   *i* 468

Hunter, Darian
Darian Hunter: Duke of Desire - Carole Mortimer   *r* 1039

Hunter, Sir Dominic
How to Plan a Wedding for a Royal Spy - Vanessa Kelly   *r* 997

Jaffrey, Rosamond
Murder in the Queen's Wardrobe - Kathy Lynn Emerson   *t* 153

Jamison, Bella
Spy of Richmond - Jocelyn Green   *i* 409

Jensen, Margo
Back Channel - Stephen L. Carter   *c* 709

Kelly, Alden
Quartet for the End of Time - Johanna Skibsrud   *t* 250

Kent, Sophie
Spy of Richmond - Jocelyn Green   *i* 409

Knight, Alex
Twice Tempted - Eileen Dreyer   *r* 956

Leyland, Camille
Rogue Spy - Joanna Bourne   *r* 919

Lom, Vissarion
Radiant State - Peter Higgins   *s* 1155

Meier, Alex
Leaving Berlin - Joseph Kanon   *m* 590

Paxton, Thomas "Pax"
Rogue Spy - Joanna Bourne   *r* 919

Penzi, Nicholas
Pasha: A Kydd Sea Adventure - Julian Stockwin   *t* 255

Saker
The Dagger's Path - Glenda Larke   *f* 67

Sakhet
Heir to the Jedi - Kevin Hearne   *s* 1154

Salome
Twelve Days - Alex Berenson   *c* 702

Shang, Gary
A Map of Betrayal - Ha Jin   *c* 774

Shaumian, Maroussia
Radiant State - Peter Higgins   *s* 1155

Smyslov, Vasily
Back Channel - Stephen L. Carter   *c* 709

Stockman, Albert
The Empire of Night - Robert Olen Butler   *t* 138

Unnamed Character
The Swimmer - Joakim Zander   *c* 893

Varatschevsky, Karin
Ascendance: Dave vs. the Monsters - John Birmingham   *f* 13

Velasquez, Angel
The Water Knife - Paolo Bacigalupi   *s* 1113

Visser, Luuk
The Mechanical - Ian Tregillis   *f* 117

Volkman, Max
The German Agent - J. Sydney Jones   *t* 186

Walker, Creed
My Heart Stood Still - Lori Copeland   *i* 387

Walsingham, Francis
Murder in the Queen's Wardrobe - Kathy Lynn Emerson   *t* 153

Wells, John
Twelve Days - Alex Berenson   *c* 702

STEPBROTHER

Augustine
The Devil Takes a Bride - Julia London   *r* 1012

Cross, Alex Jr.
Hope to Die - James Patterson   *c* 824

Cross, Damon
Hope to Die - James Patterson   *c* 824

STEPDAUGHTER

Campbell, Ava
The Wonder of All Things - Jason Mott   *c* 812

Cat
The Soul of Discretion - Susan Hill   *m* 574

Cross, Janelle "Jannie"
Hope to Die - James Patterson   *c* 824

Phillips, Noelle
Midnight Action - Elle Kennedy   *r* 999

Whalen, Dani
One Mile Under - Andrew Gross   *m* 561

STEPFATHER

Dunn, Wade
One Mile Under - Andrew Gross   *m* 561

Laurent, Rene
Midnight Action - Elle Kennedy   *r* 999

Sam
Bittersweet - Susan Wittig Albert   *m* 476

STEPMOTHER

Lady Beckington
The Devil Takes a Bride - Julia London   *r* 1012

Carmen
The Wonder of All Things - Jason Mott   *c* 812

Judith
The Soul of Discretion - Susan Hill   *m* 574

Stone Cross, Brianna "Bree"
Hope to Die - James Patterson   *c* 824

STEPSISTER

Cabot, Grace
The Devil Takes a Bride - Julia London   *r* 1012

Cabot, Honor
The Devil Takes a Bride - Julia London   *r* 1012

Cabot, Mercy
The Devil Takes a Bride - Julia London   *r* 1012

Cabot, Prudence
The Devil Takes a Bride - Julia London   *r* 1012

Cross, Janelle "Jannie"
Hope to Die - James Patterson   *c* 824

STEPSON

Augustine
The Devil Takes a Bride - Julia London   *r* 1012

Cross, Alex Jr.
Hope to Die - James Patterson   *c* 824

Cross, Damon
Hope to Die - James Patterson   *c* 824

Serrailler, Simon
The Soul of Discretion - Susan Hill   *m* 574

STOCK BROKER

Taggart, Mike
Last Chance Family - Hope Ramsay   *r* 1055

STORE OWNER

Bessette, Charlotte
As Gouda as Dead - Avery Aames   *m* 473

Brooks, Camryn "Cami"
Snow Way Out - Christine Husom   *m* 579

Browning, Theodosia
Ming Tea Murder - Laura Childs   *m* 514

Carne, Sherry
The Immortal Who Loved Me - Lynsay Sands   *r* 1069

Castle, Lilah
Silken Threats - Addison Fox   *r* 966

Clara
Wicked Stitch - Amanda Lee   *m* 597

Collard, Ivy
The Mill River Redemption - Darcie Chan   *c* 711

Conlon, Maeve
Lies That Bind - Maggie Barbieri   *m* 487

Darling, Annie
Don't Go Home - Carolyn G. Hart   *m* 569

Davis, Nellie
Wicked Stitch - Amanda Lee   *m* 597

Dillon, Grace
One Wish - Robyn Carr   *r* 942

Grayson, Sarah
Buy a Whisker - Sofie Ryan   *m* 650

Hancock, Krissy
Death by Coffee - Alex Erickson   *m* 542

Jamieson, Lucky
Ladle to the Grave - Connie Archer   *m* 480

Lamb, Piper
License to Dill - Mary Ellen Hughes   *m* 578

Malloy, Claire
Pride v. Prejudice - Joan Hess   *m* 573

Meyer, Chris
Some Like It Hotter - Isabel Sharpe   *r* 1079

Meyer, Eva
Some Like It Hotter - Isabel Sharpe   *r* 1079

Miles, Tricia
A Fatal Chapter - Lorna Barrett   *m* 488

Oosterling, Ava
Five-Alarm Fudge - Christine DeSmet   *m* 534

Patterson, Vicki
Death by Coffee - Alex Erickson   *m* 542

Raines, Prairie Dawn "P.D."
Desperado - Lisa Bingham   *r* 916

Reece, Pepper
Assault and Pepper - Leslie Budewitz   *m* 505

Richardson, Violet
Silken Threats - Addison Fox   *r* 966

Salvare, Abby Knight
A Root Awakening - Kate Collins *m* 519

Singer, Marcy
Wicked Stitch - Amanda Lee *m* 597

Summerside, Reagan
Demise in Denim - Duffy Brown *m* 504

Tate, Cassidy
Silken Threats - Addison Fox *r* 966

Troyer, Hannah
Murder Freshly Baked - Vannetta
  Chapman *i* 377

Turnbull, Phil
Fillet of Murder - Linda Reilly *m* 641

Uziel, Nat
It Won't Always Be This Great - Peter
  Mehlman *c* 803

Vanderling, Willow
Seven Threadly Sins - Janet Bolin *m* 497

Wilder, Fiona
Sweet Surprise - Candis Terry *r* 1091

Zook, Matthew
The Amish Clockmaker - Mindy Starns
  Clark *i* 378

STOWAWAY

Grant, Caitrina
The Wicked Ways of Alexander Kidd - Paula
  Quinn *r* 1054

STREETPERSON

Henry
Gathering Prey - John Sandford *m* 652

Skye
Gathering Prey - John Sandford *m* 652

STUDENT

Aboderin, Jeneta
Unbound - Jim C. Hines *f* 55

Anaedsley, Trevor
50 Ways to Ruin a Rake - Jade Lee *r* 1007

Archaon
Archaon: Everchosen - Rob Sanders *f* 103

Bee
Miss Mayhem - Rachel Hawkins *f* 48

Birdsall, Gideon
The Language of Paradise - Barbara Klein
  Moss *t* 217

Bree
Stirring Up Trouble - Kimberly Kincaid *r* 1000

Brooke
On the Edge - Edward St. Aubyn *c* 867

Carl
Mars Evacuees - Sophia McDougall *s* 1176

Crystal
On the Edge - Edward St. Aubyn *c* 867

Dare, Alice
Mars Evacuees - Sophia McDougall *s* 1176

Defoe, Pip
The Last Kings of Sark - Rosa
  Rankin-Gee *c* 840

Dent, Andy
Constant Fear - Daniel Palmer *m* 629

Folsom, Addie
Mr. Miracle - Debbie Macomber *r* 1015

John
John the Pupil - David L. Flusfeder *t* 158

Josephine
Mars Evacuees - Sophia McDougall *s* 1176

Kenneth
On the Edge - Edward St. Aubyn *c* 867

Kyle
The Pocket Wife - Susan Crawford *m* 524

London
Make Me Lose Control - Christie
  Ridgway *r* 1057

Marietti, Gabby
A Finely Knit Murder - Sally
  Goldenbaum *m* 557

Perribow, Honey
Need Me - Tessa Bailey *r* 906

Peter
On the Edge - Edward St. Aubyn *c* 867

Price, Harper
Miss Mayhem - Rachel Hawkins *f* 48

Prince, Dominick
Murder Boy - Bryon Quertermous *m* 638

Sabine
On the Edge - Edward St. Aubyn *c* 867

Stark, David
Miss Mayhem - Rachel Hawkins *f* 48

Stonechurch, Ann
This Gun for Hire - Jo Goodman *r* 973

Thompson, Abby
Full Throttle - Julie Ann Walker *r* 1093

Van Curler, Henry
Electric City - Elizabeth Rosner *t* 237

Winters, Caitlyn
The Christmas Bouquet - Sherryl Woods *r* 1098

STUDENT—BOARDING SCHOOL

Deveaux, Rory
The Shadow Cabinet - Maureen Johnson *h* 322

Everhart, Dusty
The Nightmare Charade - Mindee Arnett *h* 279

Merchant, Anne
The Wicked Awakening of Anne Merchant - Joanna
  Wiebe *h* 353

Raven
Whispers in the Dark - Chase J. Jackson *h* 321

Robin
Whispers in the Dark - Chase J. Jackson *h* 321

Zin, Ben
The Wicked Awakening of Anne Merchant - Joanna
  Wiebe *h* 353

STUDENT—COLLEGE

Anderson, Doug
The Legacy - Dan Walsh *i* 467

Browles, Darren
Dear Committee Members - Julie
  Schumacher *c* 856

Lord Byron
Riot Most Uncouth - Daniel Friedman *m* 552

Calbert, Veranix
The Thorn of Dentonhill - Marshall Ryan
  Maresca *f* 77

Catrell, Jamie
The Pocket Wife - Susan Crawford *m* 524

Dempsey, Susan
The Cinderella Murder - Mary Higgins
  Clark *c* 713

Dylan
Miles from Nowhere - Amy Clipston *i* 379

el-Hariti, Kateb "Dodge"
Fives and Twenty-Fives - Michael Pitre *c* 832

Holland, Sarie
Canary - Duane Swierczynski *m* 671

Jacobson, Winter
Caged in Winter - Brighton Walsh *r* 1095

Jensen, Margo
Back Channel - Stephen L. Carter *c* 709

Kaufman, Daniel
The Fragile World - Paula Treick
  DeBoard *c* 730

Keegan, Daisy
Butternut Summer - Mary McNear *c* 802

Magnusson, Astrid
Grave Phantoms - Jenn Bennett *r* 912

Perribow, Honey
Need Me - Tessa Bailey *r* 906

Phillips, Henry
Until the Harvest - Sarah Loudin Thomas *i* 463

Sheridan
Endangered - C.J. Box *m* 499

STUDENT—EXCHANGE

Aelyx
Invaded - Melissa Landers *s* 1163

Sweeney, Cara
Invaded - Melissa Landers *s* 1163

STUDENT—GRADUATE

Ari
After Birth - Elisa Albert *c* 688

Battle, Theresa
What Strange Creatures - Emily Arsenault *c* 695

Blomqvist, Herve
Consumed - David Cronenberg *c* 722

Crowe, Samantha
Deadly, Calm, and Cold - Susannah
  Sandlin *r* 1068

Davidia
The Laughing Monsters - Denis Johnson *c* 776

Fell, Lorraine
Inside a Silver Box - Walter Mosley *s* 1179

Kathryn
The Wednesday Group - Sylvia True *c* 873

Richmond, Daisy
Before I Go - Colleen Oakley *c* 820

Richmond, Jack
Before I Go - Colleen Oakley *c* 820

STUDENT—HIGH SCHOOL

Aelyx
Invaded - Melissa Landers *s* 1163

Ashley
Seven Threadly Sins - Janet Bolin *m* 497

Bennett, Cody
The Dandelion Field - Kathryn Springer *i* 460

Bishop, Mackenzie "Mac"
The Unbound - Victoria Schwab   *h* 342
Brynn
Alive - Chandler Baker   *h* 282
Carrie
Wolf in White Van - John Darnielle   *c* 726
Connelly, Jake
Finding Jake - Bryan Reardon   *m* 639
Connelly, Laney
Finding Jake - Bryan Reardon   *m* 639
Courtney
Zombified - Adam Gallardo   *h* 302
Cross, Stella
Alive - Chandler Baker   *h* 282
Gautier, Nick
Instinct - Sherrilyn Kenyon   *h* 325
Harrison, Harrison "H2"
Harrison Squared - Daryl Gregory   *h* 306
Henry
Alive - Chandler Baker   *h* 282
Jackson, Cassie
Be Not Afraid - Cecilia Galante   *h* 300
Kilgore, Max
Hellhole - Gina Damico   *h* 290
Lance
Wolf in White Van - John Darnielle   *c* 726
Levine, Sophie
Electric City - Elizabeth Rosner   *t* 237
Lightly, Raine
The Dandelion Field - Kathryn Springer   *i* 460
Longboat, Martin
Electric City - Elizabeth Rosner   *t* 237
Lore
Hellhole - Gina Damico   *h* 290
Lucy
Endangered - C.J. Box   *m* 499
Marin
Be Not Afraid - Cecilia Galante   *h* 300
Morris, Chelsea
Miles from Nowhere - Amy Clipston   *i* 379
Palwick, Lydia
Harrison Squared - Daryl Gregory   *h* 306
Phil
Zombified - Adam Gallardo   *h* 302
Sturges, Jim
Trollhunters - Guillermo Del Toro   *h* 292
Sweeney, Cara
Invaded - Melissa Landers   *s* 1163
Tubby
Trollhunters - Guillermo Del Toro   *h* 292
Walker, Lyric
Undertow - Michael Buckley   *s* 1121
Watts, Brittany
Blood Matters - Aviva Bel'Harold   *h* 284
Zin, Levi
Alive - Chandler Baker   *h* 282

STUNTMAN

Frazer, Bud
Falling from Horses - Molly Gloss   *t* 165

SUFFRAGETTE

Leslie-Jones, Veronica
The Lodger - Louisa Treger   *t* 265

Moss, Winifred
Cafe Europa - Edward Ifkovic   *t* 182
Richardson, Dorothy
The Lodger - Louisa Treger   *t* 265

SUPERNATURAL BEING

Andarist
Fall of Light - Steven Erikson   *f* 30
Archaon
Archaon: Everchosen - Rob Sanders   *f* 103
Ari
Armageddon Rules - J.C. Nelson   *f* 86
Blake, Anita
Dead Ice - Laurell K. Hamilton   *h* 311
D'Artigo, Delilah
Panther Prowling - Yasmine Galenorn   *h* 301
DeGarmo, Leah
The Cure - JG Faherty   *h* 297
Drake, Jessica
Dreamseeker - C.S. Friedman   *f* 37
Drood, Eddie
From a Drood to a Kill - Simon R. Green   *f* 41
Emperor Palpatine
Lords of the Sith - Paul S. Kemp   *s* 1160
Everhart, Dusty
The Nightmare Charade - Mindee Arnett   *h* 279
Faust, Zoe
The Accidental Alchemist - Gigi Pandian   *m* 630
Fearsson, Justis
Spell Blind - David B. Coe   *f* 25
Gillian, Kara
Vengeance of the Demon - Diana Rowland   *f* 100
Gramaraye, Mort
Finn Fancy Necromancy - Randy Henderson   *f* 53
Gramaraye, Pete
Finn Fancy Necromancy - Randy Henderson   *f* 53
Gramaraye, Phinaeus "Finn"
Finn Fancy Necromancy - Randy Henderson   *f* 53
Gramaraye, Samantha
Finn Fancy Necromancy - Randy Henderson   *f* 53
Grimm
Armageddon Rules - J.C. Nelson   *f* 86
Hawthorn, Jack
Briar Queen - Katherine Harbour   *h* 312
Hui, Brianna
The Exile - C.T. Adams   *f* 3
Hui, Leu
The Exile - C.T. Adams   *f* 3
il'Sanke, Ghassan
First and Last Sorcerer - Barb Hendee   *f* 52
Katashi
Vengeance of the Demon - Diana Rowland   *f* 100
Lot, Seth
Briar Queen - Katherine Harbour   *h* 312
Magiere
First and Last Sorcerer - Barb Hendee   *f* 52
Malnefoley
Hunted Warrior - Lindsey Piper   *f* 95
Moth
Briar Queen - Katherine Harbour   *h* 312

One Beneath
Sorceress - Claudia Gray   *f* 38
Pendragon, Jackrun
In the Time of the Dragon Moon - Janet Lee Carey   *f* 20
Rake, Anomander
Fall of Light - Steven Erikson   *f* 30
Robert-Houdin, Dorian
The Accidental Alchemist - Gigi Pandian   *m* 630
Ruin, Silchas
Fall of Light - Steven Erikson   *f* 30
Rundstrom, Ludvig "Vig"
The Unleashing - Shelly Laurenston   *f* 68
Sam
Pacific Fire - Greg van Eekhout   *f* 118
Shakespeare, William
The Dead Hamlets - Peter Roman   *f* 99
Smith, B
Zom-B Bride - Darren Shan   *h* 343
Triss
Darkened Blade - Kelly McCullough   *f* 79
Unnamed Character
The Cure - JG Faherty   *h* 297
Revels Ending - Vic Kerry   *h* 326
Vader, Darth
Lords of the Sith - Paul S. Kemp   *s* 1160
Vantage, Kyri
Phoenix in Shadow - Ryk E. Spoor   *f* 108
Watson, Kera
The Unleashing - Shelly Laurenston   *f* 68
Yellowrock, Jane
Dark Heir - Faith Hunter   *h* 320

SURFER

Neal
Surrender - June Gray   *r* 977

SURVIVOR

Cal
California - Edan Lepucki   *c* 789
Cawdor, Ryan
Forbidden Trespass - James Axler   *s* 1111
de Falleron, Jeanne
The Duke of Dark Desires - Miranda Neville   *r* 1042
Doyle, Laura
Going Gone - Sharon Sala   *r* 1066
Foxx, Sabastian
The Day of Atonement - David Liss   *t* 206
Frida
California - Edan Lepucki   *c* 789
Goldman, Dr. Zoe
Little Black Lies - Sandra Block   *m* 496
Jiri
Firesoul - Gary Kloster   *f* 63
Lynn Miller, Scott
Three Songs for Roxy - Caren Gussoff   *s* 1150
Pasha
The Country of Ice Cream Star - Sandra Newman   *c* 816
Raymonde, Kirsten
Station Eleven - Emily St. John Mandel   *c* 796

Sinclair, Charlotte
The Fair Fight - Anna Freeman *t* 160

Smith, Faith
Strands of Sorrow - John Ringo *s* 1190

Smith, Sophia
Strands of Sorrow - John Ringo *s* 1190

Smith, Stacey
Strands of Sorrow - John Ringo *s* 1190

Smith, Steve
Strands of Sorrow - John Ringo *s* 1190

Travis, Jess
Gift of Grace - Sharlene MacLaren *i* 433

Wyatt
The Long and Faraway Gone - Lou Berney *m* 489

SWIMMER

Needle, Gwen
We Are Pirates - Daniel Handler *c* 759

TEACHER

Adam
On the Edge - Edward St. Aubyn *c* 867

Ames, Derrick
Stiff Penalty - Annelise Ryan *m* 648

Atherton, Charlotte
A Worthy Pursuit - Karen Witemeyer *i* 471

Bacon, Roger
John the Pupil - David L. Flusfeder *t* 158

Barrett, Lee
Tails, You Lose - Carol J. Perry *m* 635

Blair, Ryan
The Children's Crusade - Ann Packer *t* 224

Cathy
The Love Book - Nina Solomon *c* 866

Davidson, Kate
A Killer Retreat - Tracy Weber *m* 679

Donne, Raymond "Ray"
Dead Red - Tim O'Mara *m* 626

Erikson, Mike
The Fold - Peter Clines *s* 1127

Father Dagobert
Archaon: Everchosen - Rob Sanders *f* 103

Faye
Outline - Rachel Cusk *c* 724

Fox, Eliot
Never Mind Miss Fox - Olivia Glazebrook *c* 750

Gardner, Chelsea
Love After All - Jaci Burton *r* 937

Hartley, Eddie
Arts and Entertainments - Christopher R. Beha *c* 700

Headly, Troy
One Wish - Robyn Carr *r* 942

Howard, Brian
Cold Trail - Janet Dawson *m* 528

Kaufman, Curtis
The Fragile World - Paula Treick DeBoard *c* 730

Kuhn, Clara
Meek and Mild - Olivia Newport *i* 439

Lizzy
The Wednesday Group - Sylvia True *c* 873

Lobdell, Lucy Ann
The Rebellion of Miss Lucy Ann Lobdell - William Klaber *t* 193

Malek, Reza
Tehran at Twilight - Salar Abdoh *c* 683

Marr, Kennedy
Straight White Male - John Niven *c* 818

Mills, Harry
Mr. Miracle - Debbie Macomber *r* 1015

Moriguchi, Yuko
Confessions - Kanae Minato *c* 806

Price, Corinne
The Stranger - Harlan Coben *m* 517

Ramirez, Adrian
Whispers in the Dark - Chase J. Jackson *h* 321

Solloway, Leander
The Language of Paradise - Barbara Klein Moss *t* 217

Soto, Rosa
Full Throttle - Julie Ann Walker *r* 1093

Steinhauser, Celia
The Pocket Wife - Susan Crawford *m* 524

Thatcher, Beth
Where Trust Lies - Janette Oke *i* 440

Treadway, Greg
The Fall - John T. Lescroart *m* 600

Yeshua
A.D. 30 - Ted Dekker *i* 391

TECHNICIAN

Beck, Charley
Up the Hill to Home - Jennifer Bort Yacovissi *t* 275

Rivers, Rodney
Oh Say Can You Fudge - Nancy Coco *m* 518

Schulte, Henry
Oh Say Can You Fudge - Nancy Coco *m* 518

Simpson, B.
Cold Betrayal - J.A. Jance *m* 584

TEENAGER

Ally
The Silence - Tim Lebbon *h* 330

Amber
We Are Pirates - Daniel Handler *c* 759

Andriana
Remnants: Season of Fire - Lisa T. Bergren *i* 361

Astrid
Rogue Wave - Jennifer Donnelly *f* 28

Atwater, Philip
Rich Kids of Instagram - Creator of Rich Kids of Instagram *c* 721

Ava
Rogue Wave - Jennifer Donnelly *f* 28

Aya
The Glass Arrow - Kristen Simmons *s* 1197

Becca
Rogue Wave - Jennifer Donnelly *f* 28

Bee
Miss Mayhem - Rachel Hawkins *f* 48

Bennett, Cody
The Dandelion Field - Kathryn Springer *i* 460

Bethany
Goodhouse - Peyton Marshall *c* 798

Brennan, Tory
Exposure - Kathy Reichs *s* 1186
Terminal - Kathy Reichs *s* 1187

Brynn
Alive - Chandler Baker *h* 282

Caden
Unleashed - Sophie Jordan *s* 1157

Cappelletti, Juliet
Juliet's Nurse - Lois Leveen *t* 204

Caron
Pride v. Prejudice - Joan Hess *m* 573

Carpenter, Jamie
Darkest Night - Will Hill *h* 317
Zero Hour - Will Hill *h* 316

Cass
City 1 - Gregg Rosenblum *s* 1192

Clayborne, Chance
Terminal - Kathy Reichs *s* 1187

Cody
Firefight - Brandon Sanderson *f* 104

Connelly, Jake
Finding Jake - Bryan Reardon *m* 639

Connelly, Laney
Finding Jake - Bryan Reardon *m* 639

Courtney
Zombified - Adam Gallardo *h* 302

Crawford, Miller
Rich Kids of Instagram - Creator of Rich Kids of Instagram *c* 721

Cross, Stella
Alive - Chandler Baker *h* 282

Daniels, Faith
Quake - Patrick Carman *s* 1124

David
Firefight - Brandon Sanderson *f* 104

Davy
Unleashed - Sophie Jordan *s* 1157

Derby, Cordelia
Rich Kids of Instagram - Creator of Rich Kids of Instagram *c* 721

Deveaux, Rory
The Shadow Cabinet - Maureen Johnson *h* 322

Ellen
The Way We Bared Our Souls - Willa Strayhorn *f* 112

Emily
Blood Matters - Aviva Bel'Harold *h* 284

Freddie
What You Left Behind - Samantha Hayes *m* 570

Freya
Aurora - Kim Stanley Robinson *s* 1191

Gautier, Nick
Instinct - Sherrilyn Kenyon *h* 325

Gilmore, Dylan
Quake - Patrick Carman *s* 1124

Goldberg, Desdemona
Rich Kids of Instagram - Creator of Rich Kids of Instagram *c* 721

Henry
Alive - Chandler Baker *h* 282

Hoff, Annalise
Rich Kids of Instagram - Creator of Rich Kids of Instagram *c* 721

Robin
Whispers in the Dark - Chase J. Jackson *h* 321
Sam
Find Me - Laura van den Berg *c* 877
Soto, Carlos "Steady"
Full Throttle - Julie Ann Walker *r* 1093
Soto, Rosa
Full Throttle - Julie Ann Walker *r* 1093
Two Hawks
The Wood's Edge - Lori Benton *i* 360
Unnamed Character
Exposure - Kathy Reichs *s* 1186
Exposure - Kathy Reichs *s* 1186
Whitney, Eden "Edie"
How to Plan a Wedding for a Royal Spy - Vanessa Kelly *r* 997
Whitney, Evie
How to Plan a Wedding for a Royal Spy - Vanessa Kelly *r* 997
Wolf, Ella
At Wolf Ranch - Jennifer Ryan *r* 1064
Wolf, Lela
At Wolf Ranch - Jennifer Ryan *r* 1064
Zach
The Fire Sermon - Francesca Haig *s* 1151

UNCLE

Aetius
The Sword of Attila - David Gibbins *t* 163
Ambrose, Finn
The Inquisitor's Mark - Dianne Salerni *f* 102
Appleby, Adrian
The German Agent - J. Sydney Jones *t* 186
Carlo
Fear the Darkness - Becky Masterman *m* 610
Cartier, Andre
Dying for the Past - T.J. O'Connor *m* 625
Cicero, Hunt
Teardrop Lane - Emily March *r* 1018
Edward
The Tutor - Andrea Chapin *t* 140
Frank
Sabotaged - Dani Pettrey *i* 446
James
The Girl Next Door - Ruth Rendell *c* 844
Jameson, TJ
For Keeps - Rachel Lacey *r* 1003
Mullah
The Woman Who Read Too Much - Bahiyyih Nakhjavani *t* 220
Nasmertov, Pasha
Panic in a Suitcase - Yelena Akhtiorskaya *c* 687
Taggart, Mike
Last Chance Family - Hope Ramsay *r* 1055
Wayne
Before He Finds Her - Michael Kardos *m* 591
West, Poxl
The Last Flight of Poxl West - Daniel Torday *t* 264
Wolf, Phillip
At Wolf Ranch - Jennifer Ryan *r* 1064

UNDERTAKER

Gramaraye, Mort
Finn Fancy Necromancy - Randy Henderson *f* 53

Gramaraye, Phinaeus "Finn"
Finn Fancy Necromancy - Randy Henderson *f* 53

VACATIONER

Ann
The Last Good Paradise - Tatjana Soli *c* 865
Cooper, Dex
The Last Good Paradise - Tatjana Soli *c* 865
Dellamare, Claire
The Inn at Ocean's Edge - Colleen Coble *i* 383
Porter, Maggie
Love Letters - Debbie Macomber *c* 793
Porter, Roy
Love Letters - Debbie Macomber *c* 793
Reynolds, Ellie
Love Letters - Debbie Macomber *c* 793
Richard
The Last Good Paradise - Tatjana Soli *c* 865
Rocco, Luke
The Inn at Ocean's Edge - Colleen Coble *i* 383
Rocco, Meg
The Inn at Ocean's Edge - Colleen Coble *i* 383
Wende
The Last Good Paradise - Tatjana Soli *c* 865

VAGRANT

Boston
The Love Letters - Beverly Lewis *i* 427

VAMPIRE

Lord Akeldama
Prudence - Gail Carriger *f* 22
Andraso, Chane
First and Last Sorcerer - Barb Hendee *f* 52
Argeneau, Basileios "Basil"
The Immortal Who Loved Me - Lynsay Sands *r* 1069
Armand
Prince Lestat - Anne Rice *c* 845
Asher
Witch upon a Star - Jennifer Harlow *m* 568
D'Artigo, Menolly
Panther Prowling - Yasmine Galenorn *h* 301
Dracula
Darkest Night - Will Hill *h* 317
Zero Hour - Will Hill *h* 316
Emil
The Dark Arts of Blood - Freda Warrington *h* 350
Emily
Blood Matters - Aviva Bel'Harold *h* 284
Fadiya
The Dark Arts of Blood - Freda Warrington *h* 350
Grander, A. VIII
The Last American Vampire - Seth Grahame-Smith *h* 304
Jean-Claude
Dead Ice - Laurell K. Hamilton *h* 311
Karl
The Dark Arts of Blood - Freda Warrington *h* 350

Kinley, Larissa
Darkest Night - Will Hill *h* 317
Zero Hour - Will Hill *h* 316
Larissa
Hunter Reborn - Katie Reus *h* 338
Leila
Bound by Flames - Jeaniene Frost *r* 969
Lemuel
Day Shift - Charlaine Harris *h* 314
Lenoir, Violette
The Dark Arts of Blood - Freda Warrington *h* 350
Lestat de Lioncourt
Prince Lestat - Anne Rice *c* 845
Louis de Pointe du Lac
Prince Lestat - Anne Rice *c* 845
Maharet
Prince Lestat - Anne Rice *c* 845
Mekare
Prince Lestat - Anne Rice *c* 845
Neville, Charlotte
The Dark Arts of Blood - Freda Warrington *h* 350
Plantagenet, Adam
The Last American Vampire - Seth Grahame-Smith *h* 304
Quinn, Siobhan
Cherry Bomb - Caitlin R. Kiernan *h* 327
Reiniger, Godric
The Dark Arts of Blood - Freda Warrington *h* 350
Russell
Crouching Tiger, Forbidden Vampire - Kerrelyn Sparks *r* 1086
Sturges, Henry
The Last American Vampire - Seth Grahame-Smith *h* 304
Sullivan, Ethan
Dark Debt - Chloe Neill *h* 335
Talbot, David
Prince Lestat - Anne Rice *c* 845
Vlad
Bound by Flames - Jeaniene Frost *r* 969
Watts, Brittany
Blood Matters - Aviva Bel'Harold *h* 284

VAMPIRE HUNTER

Helsing, Leonard
Shutter - Courtney Alameda *h* 277
Helsing, Micheline
Shutter - Courtney Alameda *h* 277
Jude
Shutter - Courtney Alameda *h* 277
Oliver
Shutter - Courtney Alameda *h* 277
Ryder
Shutter - Courtney Alameda *h* 277

VETERAN

Andersen, Seth
Every Little Kiss - Kendra Leigh Castle *r* 943
Arkwright, Julius
Trust No One - Jayne Ann Krentz *c* 786
Ayla
In Case of Emergency - Courtney Moreno *c* 811

Character Description Index

Beck, Joel
Amish Promises - Leslie Gould   *i* 405

Bosch, Harry
The Burning Room - Michael Connelly   *c* 718

Brewster, Callie
Cowboy Boots for Christmas: (Cowboy Not Included) - Carolyn Brown   *r* 929

Chambers, Ryan
Hearts Made Whole - Jody Hedlund   *i* 416

Charlie
Amish Promises - Leslie Gould   *i* 405

Cole, Elvis
The Promise - Robert Crais   *c* 720

Colten, AJ
Still the One - Jill Shalvis   *r* 1076

Creed, Ryder
Breaking Creed - Alex Kava   *c* 779

Donovan, Peter
Fives and Twenty-Fives - Michael Pitre   *c* 832

Dryden, Sam
Signal - Patrick Lee   *m* 598

Hawley, James
The Other Side of Midnight - Simone St. James   *r* 1087

Hazelton, Nigel
An American Duchess - Sharon Page   *r* 1046

Henry, Charlie
Grave Consequences - David Thurlo   *m* 673

Hopeton, Malcolm
A Slant of Light - Jeffrey Lent   *t* 202

Hutchinson, Brian
Christmas at Twilight - Lori Wilde   *r* 1097

Jennings, Harper
In the Woods - Merry Jones   *m* 587

Jones, Emmett
Mr. Jones - Margaret Sweatman   *t* 256

McGregor, Ray
Liberators - James Wesley Rawles   *c* 841

McGuire, Grant
Confessions - Cynthia Eden   *r* 957

Murphy
The Regulator - Ethan J. Wolfe   *t* 274

Norfield, John
Mr. Jones - Margaret Sweatman   *t* 256

O'Brien, Cal
Serpents in the Cold - Thomas O'Malley   *t* 222

O'Donnell, Finn
Cowboy Boots for Christmas: (Cowboy Not Included) - Carolyn Brown   *r* 929

Otto
Emma and Otto and Russell and James - Emma Hooper   *c* 769

Pike, Joe
The Promise - Robert Crais   *c* 720

Pleasant, Lester "Doc"
Fives and Twenty-Fives - Michael Pitre   *c* 832

Rogers, Tyler
Shades of the Wolf - Karen Whiddon   *f* 124

Rosen, Bobby
The Sheltering - Mark Powell   *c* 835

Rossett, John Henry
The Darkest Hour - Tony Schumacher   *t* 245

Shaw, Van
Past Crimes - Glen Erik Hamilton   *m* 566

Sinclair, Arthur
Quartet for the End of Time - Johanna Skibsrud   *t* 250

Spencer, Gabe
Broken - Cynthia Eden   *r* 959

Stratton, Pierson
The Viscount Who Lived Down the Lane - Elizabeth Boyle   *r* 924

Sweeney, Gordon
Grave Consequences - David Thurlo   *m* 673

Swift, Julian
The Accidental Countess - Valerie Bowman   *r* 923

Watson, Arnie
The Dead Play On - Heather Graham   *m* 560

Watson, Kera
The Unleashing - Shelly Laurenston   *f* 68

West, Poxl
The Last Flight of Poxl West - Daniel Torday   *t* 264

VETERINARIAN

DeGarmo, Leah
The Cure - JG Faherty   *h* 297

Jeremiah
A Faith of Her Own - Kathleen Fuller   *i* 400

Nelson, Luke
The Deep - Nick Cutter   *h* 289

Ortiz, Ramon
A Long Time Until Now - Michael Z. Williamson   *s* 1208

Phillips, Stephanie
Tempted by the Soldier - Patricia Potter   *r* 1050

Polk, Charlene
Last Chance Family - Hope Ramsay   *r* 1055

Thacker, Jillian
Kissed by a Cowboy - Pamela Britton   *r* 926

VIGILANTE

Calbert, Veranix
The Thorn of Dentonhill - Marshall Ryan Maresca   *f* 77

Courtney
Zombified - Adam Gallardo   *h* 302

Hooper, Dave
Ascendance: Dave vs. the Monsters - John Birmingham   *f* 13
Emergence: Dave vs. the Monsters - John Birmingham   *f* 14
Resistance: Dave vs. the Monsters - John Birmingham   *f* 12

Schroder, Carl
Five Minutes Alone - Paul Cleave   *c* 714

Varatschevsky, Karin
Ascendance: Dave vs. the Monsters - John Birmingham   *f* 13

Whitefield, Jane
A String of Beads - Thomas Perry   *c* 827

VIKING

Arngrimsson, Audun
Blood Will Follow - Snorri Kristjansson   *t* 194

Sigtryggr
The Empty Throne - Bernard Cornwell   *t* 146

Thormodsson, Ulfar
Blood Will Follow - Snorri Kristjansson   *t* 194

ver Snagason, Snorri
The Liar's Key - Mark Lawrence   *f* 71

VILLAIN

Bantle, Peter
Karen Memory - Elizabeth Bear   *s* 1118

Croftner, Ben
A Heart's Disguise - Colleen Coble   *i* 382
A Heart's Obsession - Colleen Coble   *i* 384

Moriarty
Sherlock Holmes, the Missing Years: Japan - Vasudev Murthy   *t* 219

Moriarty, James
Moriarty - Anthony Horowitz   *c* 771

Pinhead
The Scarlet Gospels - Clive Barker   *h* 283

Silence
Breakout - Ann Aguirre   *s* 1103

The Hunter
The Devil's Only Friend - Dan Wells   *h* 352

VOLUNTEER

Dillinger, Marcus
Chasing Sunsets - Karen Kingsbury   *i* 425

Fordham, Emily
The Language of the Dead - Stephen Kelly   *t* 189

Johnson, Michael "MJ"
Nowhere to Hide - Sigmund Brouwer   *i* 365

King, William
Nowhere to Hide - Sigmund Brouwer   *i* 365

Mary Catherine
Chasing Sunsets - Karen Kingsbury   *i* 425

Treadway, Greg
The Fall - John T. Lescroart   *m* 600

Wyatt, Blake
Nowhere to Hide - Sigmund Brouwer   *i* 365

WAITER/WAITRESS

Graber, Kim
What Strange Creatures - Emily Arsenault   *c* 695

Kane, Megan
And I Love Her - Marie Force   *r* 963

Lightly, Genevieve "Gin"
The Dandelion Field - Kathryn Springer   *i* 460

Marby, Talia
Fillet of Murder - Linda Reilly   *m* 641

Rivers, Wendy
Snake Pass - Colin Campbell   *m* 511

WARD

Batten, Lady Phoebe
Dearest Rogue - Elizabeth Hoyt   *r* 990

Fareeda
Green on Blue - Elliot Ackerman   *c* 684

Lily
A Worthy Pursuit - Karen Witemeyer   *i* 471

WARLOCK

Reardon, John
Gideon - Alex Gordon   *h* 303

WARRIOR

Ag Alla, Mossa
Blue Warrior - Mike Maden *c* 795

Aiden
Hunter Reborn - Katie Reus *h* 338

Akina
Forge of Ashes - Josh Vogt *f* 120

Arthur
The Ice King - M.K. Hume *f* 57

Arturus
The Sword of Attila - David Gibbins *t* 163

Avildottar, Sayrid
Taming His Viking Woman - Michelle Styles *r* 1089

Brand
Half the World - Joe Abercrombie *f* 2

Brigid
Hell's Maw - James Axler *s* 1112

Broom, Jody
Cobra Outlaw - Timothy Zahn *s* 1211

Broom, Lorne
Cobra Outlaw - Timothy Zahn *s* 1211

Broom, Paul
Cobra Outlaw - Timothy Zahn *s* 1211

Caphalor
Righteous Fury - Markus Heitz *f* 49

Cawdor, Ryan
End Day - James Axler *s* 1110
Forbidden Trespass - James Axler *s* 1111

Darkblade, Malus
Deathblade: A Tale of Malus Darkblade - C.L. Werner *f* 122

de Fontein, Lucien
The Boy Who Wept Blood - Den Patrick *f* 93

Dethan
Cursed by Fire - Jacquelyn Frank *f* 36

Dino
The Boy Who Wept Blood - Den Patrick *f* 93

Eymundsson, Hrolf
Taming His Viking Woman - Michelle Styles *r* 1089

Gajendra
Colossus - Colin Falconer *t* 155

Garreth
Cursed by Ice - Jacquelyn Frank *f* 35

Grant
Hell's Maw - James Axler *s* 1112

Greenwood, Lena
Unbound - Jim C. Hines *f* 55

Gurnisson, Gotrek
Gotrek and Felix: Slayer - David Guymer *f* 44

Hereward
Hereward: End of Days - James Wilde *t* 272

Jiri
Firesoul - Gary Kloster *f* 63

Kahn, Tae
Fields of Wrath - Mickey Zucker Reichert *f* 97

Kane
Hell's Maw - James Axler *s* 1112

Kholster
Oathkeeper - J.F. Lewis *f* 74
Oathkeeper - J.F. Lewis *f* 74

Lakshmi, Rani
Rebel Queen - Michelle Moran *t* 213

Price, Harper
Miss Mayhem - Rachel Hawkins *f* 48

Rae'en
Oathkeeper - J.F. Lewis *f* 74

Ran
Slavers of the Savage Catacombs - Jon F. Merz *f* 81

Runach
Dreamer's Daughter - Lynn Kurland *f* 65

Rundstrom, Ludvig "Vig"
The Unleashing - Shelly Laurenston *f* 68

Sarielle
Cursed by Ice - Jacquelyn Frank *f* 35

Sinthoras
Righteous Fury - Markus Heitz *f* 49

Sita
Rebel Queen - Michelle Moran *t* 213

Smith, B
Zom-B Bride - Darren Shan *h* 343

Subikahn
Fields of Wrath - Mickey Zucker Reichert *f* 97

Telamon
The Eye of the Falcon - Michelle Paver *f* 94

Torin
The Darkest Touch - Gena Showalter *r* 1082

Ursula
The Talon of the Hawk - Jeffe Kennedy *f* 62

Valyn
The Providence of Fire - Brian Staveley *f* 111

Walker, Creed
My Heart Stood Still - Lori Copeland *i* 387

WEALTHY

Addleshaw, Ollie
After a Fashion - Jen Turano *i* 465

Lord Akeldama
Prudence - Gail Carriger *f* 22

Al Baharna, Ali
Ark Storm - Linda Davies *c* 727

Alden, Hunter Hutchinson Jr.
NYPD Red 3 - James Patterson *m* 632

Ann
The Last Good Paradise - Tatjana Soli *c* 865

Atwater, Philip
Rich Kids of Instagram - Creator of Rich Kids of Instagram *c* 721

Bishop, John
One Kick - Chelsea Cain *c* 708

Bland, Amos
Miriam's Secret - Jerry S. Eicher *i* 396

Brooke
On the Edge - Edward St. Aubyn *c* 867

Lord Cambury
The Spring Bride - Anne Gracie *r* 975

Carrick, Thomas
The Tempting of Thomas Carrick - Stephanie Laurens *r* 1005

Carstairs, Eloisa
Deception on Sable Hill - Shelley Gray *i* 408

Connard, Howard Sr.
Etta Mae's Worst Bad-Luck Day - Ann B. Ross *c* 848

Covington, Cole
Return to Me - Kelly Moran *r* 1038

Covington, Lacey
Return to Me - Kelly Moran *r* 1038

Crane, Charlie
When We Fall - Emily Liebert *c* 791

Crawford, Miller
Rich Kids of Instagram - Creator of Rich Kids of Instagram *c* 721

de Kruk, Augustus
Hiss and Tell - Claire Donally *m* 536

de Lacy, Lord Oswald
Plague Land - S.D. Sykes *t* 257

Derby, Cordelia
Rich Kids of Instagram - Creator of Rich Kids of Instagram *c* 721

Devereaux, Caleb
Keep Me Safe - Maya Banks *r* 908

Dumont, Beau
Make You Remember - Macy Beckett *r* 911

Farnell, R.J.
Phantom Angel - David Handler *m* 567

Fell, Lorraine
Inside a Silver Box - Walter Mosley *s* 1179

Fulke
The Dragon of Handale - Cassandra Clark *t* 142

Godwin, Robert
The Sirena Quest - Michael A. Kahn *m* 589

Goldberg, Desdemona
Rich Kids of Instagram - Creator of Rich Kids of Instagram *c* 721

Graham, Riley
Unbecoming - Rebecca Scherm *c* 855

Harp, Theo
Heroes Are My Weakness - Susan Elizabeth Phillips *c* 828

Harper, Lydia
The Whistle Walk - Stephenia H. McGee *i* 434

Hathorne, Sam
Pleasantville - Attica Locke *m* 605

Hawthorn, Jack
Briar Queen - Katherine Harbour *h* 312

Heyward, Colton
Lowcountry Boneyard - Susan M. Boyer *m* 500

Hoff, Annalise
Rich Kids of Instagram - Creator of Rich Kids of Instagram *c* 721

Holiday, April
Rich Kids of Instagram - Creator of Rich Kids of Instagram *c* 721

Holliday, Montgomery
No Ghouls Allowed - Victoria Laurie *h* 329

Jessop, Trent
Oh Say Can You Fudge - Nancy Coco *m* 518

Jones, Daphne
The Girl Next Door - Ruth Rendell *c* 844

Magnus, Reggie
The Fold - Peter Clines *s* 1127

Magnusson, Astrid
Grave Phantoms - Jenn Bennett *r* 912

Mary Catherine
Chasing Sunsets - Karen Kingsbury *i* 425

Maxwell, Cornelius Linus
Beautiful You - Chuck Palahniuk *c* 823

Menkels, Odette
The Huntress of Thornbeck Forest - Melanie Dickerson *i* 393

O'Toole, Pat
Beneath - Roland Smith   *s* 1199

Raphael's Son
The Luminous Heart of Jonah S. - Gina B. Nahai   *c* 814

Richard
The Last Good Paradise - Tatjana Soli   *c* 865

Rixen, Christian
Rich Kids of Instagram - Creator of Rich Kids of Instagram   *c* 721

Roarke
Obsession in Death - J.D. Robb   *c* 847

Rogan, Connor "Mad"
Burn for Me - Ilona Andrews   *r* 900

Severson, Ted
The Kind Worth Killing - Peter Swanson   *m* 670

Sinclair, Wesley III
Antiques Swap - Barbara Allan   *m* 477

Soleyman, Raphael
The Luminous Heart of Jonah S. - Gina B. Nahai   *c* 814

Tinkie
Bone to Be Wild - Carolyn Haines   *m* 564

Tiranno, Michael
Black Scorpion - Jon Land   *m* 596

Van Curler, Henry
Electric City - Elizabeth Rosner   *t* 237

Vandaele, Lodewijk
From Bruges with Love - Pieter Aspe   *m* 482

Von Riesen, Elfrieda "Elf"
All My Puny Sorrows - Miriam Toews   *c* 871

Weston, Penelope
Love in the Time of Scandal - Caroline Linden   *r* 1011

Wylie, Ben
The Hunger of the Wolf - Stephen Marche   *r* 1019

Zoransky, Zelda "ZZ"
Marked Fur Murder - Dixie Lyle   *m* 609

WEREWOLF

Adams, Zach "Cowboy"
Werewolf Cop - Andrew Klavan   *h* 328

Charlotte
The Conquering Dark - Clay Griffith   *h* 308

Cornick, Charles
Dead Heat - Patricia Briggs   *f* 18

Danvers, Malcolm
Forsaken - Kelley Armstrong   *h* 278

Gramaraye, Pete
Finn Fancy Necromancy - Randy Henderson   *f* 53

Kate
Forsaken - Kelley Armstrong   *h* 278

Latham, Anna
Dead Heat - Patricia Briggs   *f* 18

Michaels, Elena
Forsaken - Kelley Armstrong   *h* 278

Quinn, Siobhan
Cherry Bomb - Caitlin R. Kiernan   *h* 327

Wylie, Ben
The Hunger of the Wolf - Stephen Marche   *r* 1019

WIDOW(ER)

Beale, Libby
Sisters of Shiloh - Kathy Hepinstall   *t* 176

Beckham, Abe
Cane and Abe - James Grippando   *c* 756

Benton, Amy
Search and Seduce - Sara Jane Stone   *r* 1088

Buchanan, Polly
The Laws of Murder - Charles Finch   *c* 743

Burke, Sloan
Operation Power Play - Justine Davis   *r* 952

Chevalier, Alene
Into the Savage Country - Shannon Burke   *t* 136

Colton, Elinor
The Rake's Handbook: Including Field Guide - Sally Orr   *r* 1045

Cooper, Dante
Serpents in the Cold - Thomas O'Malley   *t* 222

Coughlin, Joe
World Gone By - Dennis Lehane   *t* 201

Cronley, James D. Jr.
Top Secret - W.E.B. Griffin   *c* 755

Damon, The Earl of Mardoun
Pleasured - Candace Camp   *r* 940

Dancy, Rosamond
Morrow Creek Runaway - Lisa Plumley   *r* 1049

Daphne
New Uses for Old Boyfriends - Beth Kendrick   *r* 998

Darlene
Delicious Foods - James Hannaham   *c* 760

Darrow
Golden Son - Pierce Brown   *s* 1120

de L'Isle, Katherine
The Tutor - Andrea Chapin   *t* 140

de Warrene, Lady Catryn Gryffin
If He's Daring - Hannah Howell   *r* 988

Decker, Amos
Memory Man - David Baldacci   *m* 485

Dobbs, Maisie
A Dangerous Place - Jacqueline Winspear   *t* 273

Downey, Evan
Bringing Home the Bad Boy - Jessica Lemmon   *r* 1010

Drake, Patrick
Sometimes the Wolf - Urban Waite   *c* 882

Dunbar, Brett
Operation Power Play - Justine Davis   *r* 952

Eleanor
A Good Rogue Is Hard to Find - Kelly Bowen   *r* 921

Fairmont, Diane
Season of Fear - Brian Freeman   *m* 550

Farabee, Holt
Bridges Burned - Annette Dashofy   *m* 527

Foxworth, Shelby
The Liar - Nora Roberts   *r* 1059

Gardner, Lainie Davis
The Evil Deeds We Do - Robert S. Levinson   *m* 602

Gibbons, Kerry
Signature Kill - David Levien   *m* 601

Godel, Adele
The Goddess of Small Victories - Yannick Grannec   *c* 752

Goetz, Ada
Still Life - Christa Parrish   *i* 442

Golding, Sally
Outlaw Takes a Bride - Susan Page Davis   *i* 389

Hansen, Clint
The Cowboy SEAL - Laura Marie Altom   *r* 897

Hansen, Millie
The Cowboy SEAL - Laura Marie Altom   *r* 897

Harrington, Juliana
Murder - Sarah Pinborough   *t* 232

Harris, Charlie
Arsenic and Old Books - Miranda James   *m* 583

Harrison, Rosa
Harrison Squared - Daryl Gregory   *h* 306

Hartwell, Dante
What a Lady Needs for Christmas - Grace Burrowes   *r* 935

Holliday, Montgomery
No Ghouls Allowed - Victoria Laurie   *h* 329

Howard, Allegra Banks
The Bride Ship - Regina Scott   *r* 1073

Jahan
Traitors in the Shadows - Alex Rutherford   *t* 242

Mrs. Jeffries
Mrs. Jeffries and the One Who Got Away - Emily Brightwell   *m* 503

Jennifer
The Christmas Light - Donna VanLiere   *c* 881

Jones, Daphne
The Girl Next Door - Ruth Rendell   *c* 844

Karl
Lost and Found - Brooke Davis   *c* 729

Keeping, Agnes
Only Enchanting - Mary Balogh   *r* 907

Kern, Ursula
Garden of Lies - Amanda Quick   *r* 1051

Lee, Anabel
Shades of the Wolf - Karen Whiddon   *f* 124

Lehman, Tim
Amish Promises - Leslie Gould   *i* 405

Lincoln, Mary Todd
The Eterna Files - Leanna Renee Hieber   *f* 54

Ma
When - Victoria Laurie   *f* 70

McBride, Sinclair
Rules for a Proper Governess - Jennifer Ashley   *r* 905

McKay, Jessie
Cowgirls Don't Cry - Lorelei James   *r* 994

Moreland, Novie
Fate Moreland's Widow - John Lane   *t* 197

Nancy
If the Viscount Falls - Sabrina Jeffries   *r* 995

Pantha, Agatha
Lost and Found - Brooke Davis   *c* 729

Parker, Allison
When We Fall - Emily Liebert   *c* 791

Porteous, Kate
The Sea Garden - Marcia Willett   *c* 886

Porter, Jay
Pleasantville - Attica Locke   *m* 605
Pleasantville - Attica Locke   *m* 605

Putzkammer, Franz
The Sweetheart - Angelina Mirabella   *t* 211

Rose, Jo Marie
Love Letters - Debbie Macomber *c* 793
Rossett, John Henry
The Darkest Hour - Tony Schumacher *t* 245
Solomon, Lou
The Sirena Quest - Michael A. Kahn *m* 589
Springer, Miss Julia
Etta Mae's Worst Bad-Luck Day - Ann B. Ross *c* 848
Stanford, Iris
Deadly Desires at Honeychurch Hall - Hannah Dennison *m* 532
Stutzman, Sara
The Decision - Wanda E. Brunstetter *i* 367
Trelawny Penvenan, Lady Morwenna
A Stranger's Secret - Laurie Alice Eakes *i* 394
Troyer, Reuben
An Empty Cup - Sarah Price *i* 449
Waltham, Vera
The First Kiss - Grace Burrowes *r* 932
West, Nell
The Whispering - Sarah Rayne *h* 336
Yoder, Sarah
Balm of Gilead - Adina Senft *i* 456
Keys of Heaven - Adina Senft *i* 455
Zook, Rosanna
An Empty Cup - Sarah Price *i* 449

WITCH

Caldani, Nadia
Sorceress - Claudia Gray *f* 38
D'Artigo, Camille
Panther Prowling - Yasmine Galenorn *h* 301
Goodwin, Cherise
Some Like It Witchy - Heather Blake *m* 494
Merriweather, Darcy
Some Like It Witchy - Heather Blake *m* 494
Nathan
Half Wild - Sally Green *f* 40
Orr, April
The Witch of the Wood - Michael Aronovitz *h* 280
Reardon, Lauren
Gideon - Alex Gordon *h* 303
West, Anna Olmstead
Witch upon a Star - Jennifer Harlow *m* 568

WITNESS

Kelly, Sutton
Quartet for the End of Time - Johanna Skibsrud *t* 250
Martin
Cowboy Boots for Christmas: (Cowboy Not Included) - Carolyn Brown *r* 929

WIZARD

Alastar
Madness in Solidar - L.E. Modesitt *f* 82
Argent, Gabriel
Pacific Fire - Greg van Eekhout *f* 118
Blackland, Daniel
Pacific Fire - Greg van Eekhout *f* 118

Desyrk
Madness in Solidar - L.E. Modesitt *f* 82
Dragon
Uprooted - Naomi Novik *f* 87
Emrys, Evangeline
The Inquisitor's Mark - Dianne Salerni *f* 102
Grant, Peter
Foxglove Summer - Ben Aaronovitch *f* 1
Merlin
Fatal Feast - Jay Ruud *t* 243
Mylakhrion
Tales of the Primal Land - Brian Lumley *h* 332

WOMAN

Adare
The Providence of Fire - Brian Staveley *f* 111
Alex
10:04 - Ben Lerner *c* 790
Amado, Mercedes "Mercy"
The Amado Women - Desiree Zamorano *c* 892
Barbara
Where They Found Her - Kimberly McCreight *m* 614
Basilda
The Dragon of Handale - Cassandra Clark *t* 142
Baylor, Nevada
Burn for Me - Ilona Andrews *r* 900
Beatrice
The Buried Giant - Kazuo Ishiguro *t* 183
The Love Book - Nina Solomon *c* 866
Benoit, Cat
Cat's Lair - Christine Feehan *h* 298
Benz, Anna
Hausfrau - Jill Alexander Essbaum *c* 739
Bitler, Sarah
Where Secrets Sleep - Marta Perry *i* 444
Borne, Brandy
Antiques Swap - Barbara Allan *m* 477
Borne, Vivian
Antiques Swap - Barbara Allan *m* 477
Bradley, Neva
The Secrets of Midwives - Sally Hepworth *c* 765
Bridget
The Wednesday Group - Sylvia True *c* 873
Brienne
Rising Fire - Terri Brisbin *r* 925
Brown, Jane
Christmas at Twilight - Lori Wilde *r* 1097
Burnsey, Maisa
Once and Always - Julia Harper *r* 982
Camalier, Bitty
Driving with the Top Down - Beth Harbison *c* 761
Carmen
The Wonder of All Things - Jason Mott *c* 812
Cathy
The Love Book - Nina Solomon *c* 866
Catrell, Dana
The Pocket Wife - Susan Crawford *m* 524
Chance, Jane
The Spring Bride - Anne Gracie *r* 975
Charity, Olivia
Day Shift - Charlaine Harris *h* 314

Childs, Clare
Maggie Bright: A Novel of Dunkirk - Tracy Groot *i* 410
Cole, Davis Way
Double Mint - Gretchen Archer *m* 481
Coleman, Emily
One Step Too Far - Tina Seskis *c* 859
Copperfield, Teagan
Once a Thief - Lora Young *i* 472
Cowan, Riley
Hush - Karen Robards *r* 1058
Crawford, Julie
A Touch of Stardust - Kate Alcott *t* 125
Cunningham, Lauren
Love by the Book - Melissa Pimentel *c* 830
Curtis, Angie
Twisted Threads - Lea Wait *m* 678
Cynster, Lucilla
The Tempting of Thomas Carrick - Stephanie Laurens *r* 1005
Davidson, Kate
A Killer Retreat - Tracy Weber *m* 679
de Cayenne, Le Poivre "Pepper"
Viper Game - Christine Feehan *r* 961
de Falleron, Jeanne
The Duke of Dark Desires - Miranda Neville *r* 1042
de L'Isle, Katherine
The Tutor - Andrea Chapin *t* 140
Dillon, Grace
One Wish - Robyn Carr *r* 942
DuBois, Jessica
A Heart's Danger - Colleen Coble *i* 385
Duran, Gaby
The Black Widow - Wendy Corsi Staub *m* 665
Em
Em and the Big Hoom - Jerry Pinto *c* 831
Evertson, Laurel
Double Cross - DiAnn Mills *i* 436
Faust, Zoe
The Accidental Alchemist - Gigi Pandian *m* 630
Flavia
The Wednesday Group - Sylvia True *c* 873
Floss
The Secrets of Midwives - Sally Hepworth *c* 765
Fordham, Emily
The Language of the Dead - Stephen Kelly *t* 189
Fortune, Clyde
A Fright to the Death - Dawn Eastman *h* 295
Gail
The Wednesday Group - Sylvia True *c* 873
Gallagher, Maeve
The Crow of Connemara - Stephen Leigh *f* 73
Graham, Grace
Unbecoming - Rebecca Scherm *c* 855
Gramaraye, Samantha
Finn Fancy Necromancy - Randy Henderson *f* 53
Graves, Carmen
The Whites - Harry Brandt *m* 501
Greene, Dani
A Sticky Situation - Jessie Crockett *m* 525
Hannah
The Wednesday Group - Sylvia True *c* 873

WORKER

Crawford, Julie
A Touch of Stardust - Kate Alcott *t* 125

Davenport, Cassidy
What a Woman Gets - Judi Fennell *r* 962

David
The Exile - C.T. Adams *f* 3

Dent, Jake
Constant Fear - Daniel Palmer *m* 629

Deveraux, Mark
Whiskey Tango Foxtrot - David Shafer *c* 860

Elland, Grace
Trust No One - Jayne Ann Krentz *c* 786

Finch, Tory
Assault and Pepper - Leslie Budewitz *m* 505

Garrett, Elly
Grave Matters - Lauren M. Roy *f* 101

Geoffrey
All the Wrong Places - Lisa Lieberman *t* 205

Goldberg, Joe
You - Caroline Kepnes *c* 782

Harrigan, Penny
Beautiful You - Chuck Palahniuk *c* 823

Hooper, Dave
Emergence: Dave vs. the Monsters - John Birmingham *f* 14

Mrs. Jelphs
Fiercombe Manor - Kate Riordan *t* 235

Knightley, MacKenzie "Mac"
Kiss Me Hello - Grace Burrowes *r* 933

Lamb, Vera
The Language of the Dead - Stephen Kelly *t* 189

Lancaster, Deirdre "Foxtrot"
Marked Fur Murder - Dixie Lyle *m* 609

Lehrman, Benny
The Jazz Palace - Mary Morris *t* 215

Majnoun, Leila
Whiskey Tango Foxtrot - David Shafer *c* 860

Manley, Liam
What a Woman Gets - Judi Fennell *r* 962

McNeely, Jacob
Where All Light Tends to Go - David Joy *m* 588

Mischler, Noah
Huckleberry Harvest - Jennifer Beckstrand *i* 358

O'Brien, Cal
Serpents in the Cold - Thomas O'Malley *t* 222

Pascal, Skylar
Wolf Haven - Lindsay McKenna *r* 1029

Piper, Peach
Season of Fear - Brian Freeman *m* 550

Rebecca
As Gouda as Dead - Avery Aames *m* 473

Rimaldi, Vincenzo
An Italian Wife - Ann Hood *c* 768

Rogers, Albert
In the Woods - Merry Jones *m* 587

Scanlon, Gigi
The Dangers of Dating a Rebound Vampire - Molly Harper *h* 313

Szmul
The Zone of Interest - Martin Amis *c* 690

Taylor, Sophie
Shadow of a Spout - Amanda Cooper *m* 521

Titi
The Last Good Paradise - Tatjana Soli *c* 865

Vin
Last Days of the Condor - James Grady *m* 559

Voith, Ferd
Up the Hill to Home - Jennifer Bort Yacovissi *t* 275

Zoltar, Ivan
The Missing Piece - Kevin Egan *m* 540

WRESTLER

Hollander, Mimi
The Sweetheart - Angelina Mirabella *t* 211

McGee, Spider
The Sweetheart - Angelina Mirabella *t* 211

Putzkammer, Leonie
The Sweetheart - Angelina Mirabella *t* 211

WRITER

Alvarini, Beth
Stillwater - Maynard Sims *h* 344

Anderson, Charity
Whenever You Come Around - Robin Lee Hatcher *i* 413

Austen, Jane
Who Buries the Dead - C.S. Harris *t* 172

Battle, Theresa
What Strange Creatures - Emily Arsenault *c* 695

Beck, Guinevere
You - Caroline Kepnes *c* 782

Bell, Gertrude
Bell of the Desert - Alan Gold *t* 166

Bill
Funny Girl - Nick Hornby *c* 770

Cabot, Jamie
The Hunger of the Wolf - Stephen Marche *r* 1019

Chaucer, Geoffrey
The Invention of Fire - Bruce W. Holsinger *t* 179

Cocteau, Jean
Mademoiselle Chanel - C.W. Gortner *t* 167

Crane, Leo
Whiskey Tango Foxtrot - David Shafer *c* 860

Cross, Emma
Murder at Beechwood - Alyssa Maxwell *m* 612

Da Ponte, Lorenzo
The Figaro Murders - Laura Lebow *t* 199

David
You're Not Much Use to Anyone - David Shapiro *c* 861

de Quincey, Thomas
Inspector of the Dead - David Morrell *t* 214

Dickens, Charles
The Final Recollections of Charles Dickens - Thomas Hauser *t* 175

Dickinson, Alice
Amherst - William Nicholson *t* 221

Dickinson, Emily
Amherst - William Nicholson *t* 221

Donne, John
Love's Alchemy - Bryan Crockett *t* 147

Doyle, Arthur Conan
The Last American Vampire - Seth Grahame-Smith *h* 304

Eliot, T.S.
Adeline: A Novel of Virginia Woolf - Norah Vincent *t* 268

Emily
The Love Book - Nina Solomon *c* 866

Faye
Outline - Rachel Cusk *c* 724

Felton, Cora
Puzzled Indemnity - Parnell Hall *m* 565

Ferber, Edna
Cafe Europa - Edward Ifkovic *t* 182

Field, Stony
The Great Sand Fracas of Ames County - Jerry Apps *c* 692

Fitzgerald, F. Scott
West of Sunset - Stewart O'Nan *c* 819

Fleming, Ian
Too Bad to Die - Francine Mathews *t* 209

Fletcher, Jessica
Murder She Wrote: Killer in the Kitchen - Jessica Fletcher *m* 546

Forster, E.M.
Vanessa and Her Sister - Priya Parmar *t* 225

Gower, John
The Invention of Fire - Bruce W. Holsinger *t* 179

Graham, Lucas
Within These Walls - Ania Ahlborn *h* 276

Griffith, Alex
Don't Go Home - Carolyn G. Hart *m* 569

Harp, Theo
Heroes Are My Weakness - Susan Elizabeth Phillips *c* 828

Hemingway, Ernest
West of Sunset - Stewart O'Nan *c* 819

Herndon, William "Billy"
Lincoln's Billy - Tom LeClair *t* 200

Holland, Sarie
Canary - Duane Swierczynski *m* 671

Hope, Maggie
Betting on Hope - Debra Clopton *i* 381

Jaeger, Felix
Gotrek and Felix: Slayer - David Guymer *f* 44

James, Henry
The Fifth Heart - Dan Simmons *t* 249

Kim, Stacey
Woman with a Gun - Phillip Margolin *c* 797

Mairsian
I, Ripper - Stephen Hunter *t* 181

Marlowe, Christopher
The Dead Hamlets - Peter Roman *f* 99

Marr, Kennedy
Straight White Male - John Niven *c* 818

Meier, Alex
Leaving Berlin - Joseph Kanon *m* 590

Moorcock, Michael
The Whispering Swarm - Michael Moorcock *f* 84

Morrigan, Johanna
How to Build a Girl - Caitlin Moran *c* 810

Mountstuart, Xavier
The Strangler Vine - Miranda Carter *t* 139

Nasmertov, Pasha
Panic in a Suitcase - Yelena Akhtiorskaya *c* 687

Nelson, Stormi
Death by Baking - Cynthia Hickey *i* 418

YOUNG MAN

YOUNG WOMAN

Tiffany
The Wallcreeper - Nell Zink *c* 894

Tremaine, Lady Elinor "Norrie"
Lady Elinor's Wicked Adventures - Lillian
Marek *r* 1020

Tunstell, Primrose
Prudence - Gail Carriger *f* 22

Turner, Ruthie
Jaded - Varina Denman *i* 392

Tyra
Woven - Michael Jensen *f* 61

Vegas, Milagros Carmona
The Barefoot Queen - Ildefonso Falcones *t* 156

Walker, Kate
From the Start - Melissa Tagg *i* 462

Webster, Morgan
There Must Be Some Mistake - Frederick
Barthelme *c* 697

Wiggins, Etta Mae
Etta Mae's Worst Bad-Luck Day - Ann B.
Ross *c* 848

ZOO KEEPER

Fjord, Helena
Wild - Jill Sorenson *r* 1085

Author Index

This index is an alphabetical listing of the authors of books featured in entries and those listed within entries under the rubrics "Other books by the same author" and "Other books you might like." For each author, the titles of books described or listed in this edition and their entry numbers appear. Bold numbers indicate a featured main entry; light-face numbers refer to books recommended for further reading.

Author Index

Author Index

Author Index

Author Index

Author Index

Malpas, Jodi Ellen
This Man Confessed 886

Maltman, Thomas
Little Wolves 852

Manchette, Jean-Patrick
Three to Kill 492

Mandel, Emily St. John
Last Night in Montreal 796
The Lola Quartet 796
The Singer's Gun 796
Station Eleven 723, 790, **796**, 807,
816, 877, 1182

Manfredi, Valerio Massimo
The Last Legion 163

Manguel, Alberto
*Stevenson Under the Palm
Trees* 227

Mangum, Erynn
Miss Match 451

Manieri, Evie
Blood's Pride 76
Fortune's Blight **76**

Manilla, Marie
The Patron Saint of Ugly 696

Mankell, Henning
An Event in Autumn 624
Troubled Man 693, 749

Mann, Catherine
Escaping with the Billionaire 1017
For the Sake of Their Son 1017
Hot Zone 1085
One Good Cowboy 1017
Protector 980
Rescue Me **1017**
Shelter Me 1017, 706, 1076
Sheltered by the Millionaire 1017

Mann, Don
Hunt the Wolf 563
*SEAL Team Six: Hunt the Fal-
con* 702
*SEAL Team Six: Hunt the
Jackal* 836

Mann, George
The Affinity Bridge 54, 117, 1118
The Immorality Engine 1180
The Osiris Ritual 1184
The Revenant Express 1141

Manotti, Dominique
Dead Horsemeat 492

Mansbach, Adam
Rage Is Back 694

Mansell, Jill
Don't Want to Miss a Thing 775
Thinking of You 830

Mantel, Hilary
Bring Up the Bodies 151, 244, 699
The Giant, O'Brien 747
Wolf Hall 151

Mapes, Creston
Poison Town 869

Mapson, Jo-Ann
Owen's Daughter 763

March, Ashley
Seducing the Duchess 1083

March, Emily
Dreamweaver Trail 1018
Lover's Leap 1018
Miracle Road 1018

Nightingale Way 1018, 977
Reflection Point 1018
Teardrop Lane **1018**

Marche, Stephen
The Hunger of the Wolf **1019**
Love and the Mess We're In 1019
Raymond and Hannah 1019
*Shining at the Bottom of the
Sea* 1019

Marcos, Michelle
When a Lady Misbehaves 1060

Marek, Lillian
*Lady Elinor's Wicked Adven-
tures* **1020**

Maresca, Marshall Ryan
The Thorn of Dentonhill **77**

Margolin, Phillip
Capitol Murder 797
Sleight of Hand 797
Supreme Justice 797
Vanishing Acts 797
Woman with a Gun 780, **797**
Worthy Brown's Daughter 797

Marias, Javier
The Infatuations 799

Marillier, Juliet
Foxmask 146, 194
Seer of Sevenwaters 73
Wolfskin 97

Marinelli, Carol
An Indecent Proposition 996

Marion, Isaac
Warm Bodies: A Novel 343

Mariotte, Jeff
*Star Trek: The Original Series: Ser-
pents in the Garden* 1175

Mark, Grace
The Dream Seekers 403

Marklund, Liza
Red Wolf 493, 674

Markoe, Merrill
The Psycho Ex Game 716

Markovits, Benjamin
Imposture 552

Marlowe, Mia
*Between a Rake and a Hard
Place* 1023
Never Resist a Rake **1023**
Once Upon a Plaid 1022
Once upon a Plaid 1023, **1021**
One Night with a Rake 1021, 1022,
1023
Plaid Tidings 1021, 1022, 1023
Plaid to the Bone 1021, 1022
A Rake by Any Other Name 1021,
1023, **1022**
Waking up with a Rake 1021
Waking Up with a Rake 1022

Marmell, Ari
Covenant's End 61, **78**
The Goblin Corps 78
Hot Lead, Cold Iron 78
In Thunder Forged 78, 21
Thief's Covenant 78
The Warlord's Legacy 17, 78

Maron, Margaret
Bootlegger's Daughter 848
Three-Day Town 719

Marr, Andrew
Head of State 767

Marsh, Anne
Burns So Bad 952

Marsh, Jean
The House of Eliott 167

Marsh, Ngaio
Colour Scheme 585
Grave Mistake 516
Last Ditch 532
Night of the Vulcan 205, 593

Marsh, Nicola
Overtime in the Boss's Bed 996

Marshall, Peyton
Goodhouse 789, **798**, 874

Marston, Edward
A Bespoke Murder 263
The King's Evil 510
Peril on the Royal Train 633
The Silver Locomotive Mystery 228

Martel, Yann
Beatrice and Virgil 696

Martin, Charles
When Crickets Cry 430

Martin, Deirdre
Icebreaker 965
Straight Up 962, 1024

Martin, Gail Gaymer
Romance Across the Globe 362

Martin, George R.R.
Aces Abroad 1172
Dreamsongs 1172
Fort Freak 1172
New Voices I 1172
Old Venus **1172**
Suicide Kings 1172

Martin, George R.R.
Deuces Down 1186
A Game of Thrones 94
Lowball: A Wild Cards Novel 1187

Martin, J. Wallis
The Bird Yard 570
A Likeness in Stone 618, 844

Martin, Kat
Against the Edge 1030
Against the Storm 560, 786, 847,
994
Against the Sun 1093
Desert Heat 947

Martin, Lee
Break the Skin 717
The Bright Forever: A Novel 806

Martin, Nancy
How to Murder a Millionaire 500,
608

Martin, Steve
The Pleasure of My Company 778

Martin, Valerie
Mary Reilly 296, 307

Martine, Hanna
Drowning in Fire 1024
The Good Chase **1024**
The Isis Knot 1024
Long Shot 1024
Play for Me 1024
A Taste of Ice 1024

Martinez, A. Lee
Gil's All Fright Diner 343

Martinez, Michael J.
The Daedalus Incident 1173

The Enceladus Crisis 1173
The Venusian Gambit **1173**

Martini, Steve
Compelling Evidence 621
Trader of Secrets 857, 889

Martinsen, Joel
The Dark Forest **1170**

Marton, Dana
Guardian Agent 952

Marusek, David
Mind Over Ship 1205

Marwood, Alex
The Killer Next Door 713
The Wicked Girls 529, 530, 570,
591, 604

Mary, Kate L.
Broken World 789

Masello, Robert
The Medusa Amulet 354
The Romanov Cross 749

Mason, Connie
Viking Warrior 1089

Massey, Sujata
The Salaryman's Wife 575

Massie, Elizabeth
The Fear Report 294
Homeplace 324
*Southern Discomfort: Selected Works
of Elizabeth Massie* 48
Welcome Back to the Night 331

Masterman, Becky
Fear the Darkness **610**
Rage Against the Dying 610

Masters, John
Bhowani Junction 139, 213

Masterton, Graham
The Chosen Child 292
Darkroom 283, 785
The Doorkeepers 42, 322
Edgewise 331
Famine 1113
Garden of Evil 321
The House That Jack Built 333, 336
Picture of Evil 276

Matheson, Richard
Hell House 337

Mathews, Francine
The Alibi Club 209, 686
The Cutout 209, 586
Death in a Cold Hard Light 644
*Death in the Off-Season: A Merry
Folger Mystery* 209, 644
Jack 1939 209
The Secret Agent 209
Too Bad to Die 201, **209**, 258

Mathewson, R.L.
Double Dare 917, 998

Matlock, Curtiss Ann
Little Town, Great Big Life 1015
Love in a Small Town 974

Matthews, A.J.
Follow 337
Looking Glass 344

Matthews, Jason
Palace of Treason 144

Matthews, Jeanne
Bet Your Bones 611
Bonereapers 611

Down Range 999
High Country Rebel 1029
The Loner 1030
Never Surrender 1029, 1030
Running Fire 1029, 1030
Taking Fire 1029, **1030**
Wolf Haven 939, **1029**

McKenna, Shannon
Fatal Strike 1094

McKenzie, Catherine
Forgotten 1047

McKenzie, Jennifer
Anything but Business 1031
Not Another Wedding 1031
One More Night 1031
Table for Two 1031
Tempting Donovan Ford **1031**
This Just In... 1031

McKeon, Darragh
All That Is Solid Melts into Air 744

McKevett, G.A.
Bitter Sweets 615
Cooked Goose 615
Just Desserts 615
Killer Calories 615
Killer Gourmet **615**
Killer Physique 615

McKiernan, Dennis L.
City of Jade 114
Once Upon a Spring Morn 56
Red Slippers 29

McKillip, Patricia A.
The Bards of Bone Plain 72

McKinlay, Jenn
Buttercream Bump Off 616
Dark Chocolate Demise 548, **616**
Death by the Dozen 616
Red Velvet Revenge 616
Sprinkle with Murder 548, 616

McKinney, Joe
The Savage Dead 299

McKinzie, Clinton
Badwater 499
Crossing the Line 499

McLane, LuAnn
Catch of a Lifetime 1032
Moonlight Kiss 1032
Pitch Perfect 1032, 953
Sweet Harmony **1032**
Whisper's Edge 1032
Wildflower Wedding 1032, 963

McLarty, Ron
The Memory of Running 769

McLaughlin, Emma
Between You and Me 784
The First Affair 775

McLaughlin, Staci
All Natural Murder 617
Going Organic Can Kill You 617, 679
Green Living Can Be Deadly 617
A Healthy Homicide **617**

McLeay, Alison
The Dream Maker 226

McLeod, Alison
Unexploded 690

McLoughlin, Rosemary
Tyringham Park 868

McMahon, Jennifer
Don't Breathe a Word 829

The One I Left Behind 604
Promise Not to Tell 572, 594, 614, 619, 813
The Winter People 773, 829

McMaster, Bec
Forged by Desire 1033
Heart of Iron 1033
Kiss of Steel 1033, 21
My Lady Quicksilver 1033
Of Silk and Steam **1033**

McMurtry, Larry
The Last Kind Words Saloon 240
Streets of Laredo 184

McNamara, Ali
From Notting Hill with Love...Actually 830, 931

McNamara, Evan
Fair Game 748

McNaught, Judith
Every Breath You Take 751, 1058
Someone to Watch over Me 205

McNeal, Laura
Dark Water 801
Dollbaby **801**

McNear, Mary
Butternut Summer 1034, 705, 794, **802**
Moonlight on Butternut Lake 802, **1034**
The Night Before Christmas 802
Up at Butternut Lake 802, 1034, 842

McNeil, Gil
A Good Year for the Roses 715, 731

McNeil, Gretchen
Possess 277

McNeill, Graham
Chapter's Due 1152
Empire 122
Gods of Mars 1159
Legacies of Betrayal 1161, **1177**
Sons of Ellyrion 44
Vengeful Spirit 1106

McPhee, Margaret
Dicing with the Dangerous Lord 1035
The Gentleman Rogue 1035
His Mask of Retribution 1035
The Lost Gentleman **1035**, 1071
Mistress to the Marquis 1035
Temptation in Regency Society 1035

McPherson, Catriona
After the Armistice Ball 618, 538
As She Left It 618
The Child Garden **618**
Come to Harm 618
Dandy Gilver and the Reek of Red Herrings 618
The Day She Died 618, 543

McQuay, Mike
Hot Time in Old Town 1137

McQuestion, Karen
The Long Way Home 761, 873

McQuiston, Jennifer
Diary of an Accidental Wallflower **1036**
Moonlight on My Mind 1036
Summer Is for Lovers 1036
What Happens in Scotland 1036, 1006

McWatt, Tessa
Vital Signs 894

Meacham, Leila
Roses 697, 842

Mead, Richelle
Bloodlines 278

Meade, Amy Patricia
Well-Offed in Vermont 667

Meade, Glenn
The Second Messiah 509

Meader, Kate
All Fired Up **1037**
Feel the Heat 1037, 936, 1031, 1072
Hot and Bothered 1037

Meaney, John
To Hold Infinity 1194

Medeiros, Teresa
Goodnight Tweetheart 1047
The Pleasure of Your Kiss 1036
Some Like It Wicked 905

Meginnis, Mike
Fat Man and Little Boy 734

Mehl, Nancy
Blown Away 435
Deadly Echoes **435**
Gathering Shadows 435, 441
Harmony Secrets Series 435
Inescapable 369, 378
Ivy Towers Mystery Series 435
Missing Mabel 435
Simple Secrets 392

Mehlman, Peter
It Won't Always Be This Great **803**, 862, 875

Meier, Leslie
English Tea Murder 719
Mail-Order Murder 577, 646, 678

Meissner, Susan
The Amish Clockmaker **378**
A Fall of Marigolds 149, 442
Secrets of a Charmed Life 170, 226
The Shape of Mercy 170, 368

Meltzer, Brad
The Fifth Assassin 709
The Inner Circle 490, 682, 889
The President's Shadow 766

Meluch, R.M.
The Myriad 1139
The Ninth Circle: A Novel of the U.S.S. ,Merrimack 1181, 1211
The Sagittarius Command 1123
Wolf Star 1102

Mendoza, Sylvia
On Fire/Al Rojo Vivo 913

Menendez, Ana
The Last War 734

Mengestu, Dinaw
The Beautiful Things That Heaven Bears 634

Meno, Joe
Hairstyles of the Damned 810

Merciel, Liane
Pathfinder Tales: Nightblade 120

Meredith, D.E.
Devoured 187, 234

Meredith, D.R.
Murder by Impulse 605

Merrill, Christine
Two Wrongs Make a Marriage 904

Merz, Jon F.
The Destructor 81
The Fixer 81
The Invoker 81
Slavers of the Savage Catacombs **81**
The Syndicate 81
The Undead Hordes of Kan-Gul 81

Messud, Claire
The Emperor's Children 688
The Last Life 728
The Woman Upstairs 750, 831

Metz, Melinda
Gifted Touch 70, 277
Haunted 300, 346
Payback 40

Meyer, Marissa
Cinder 1114

Meyer, Nicholas
The Seven-Per-Cent Solution 218

Meyer, Phillip
The Son 764

Meyer, Stephenie
Twilight 353

Meyers, Annette
Free Love 192

Meyers, Randy Susan
Accidents of Marriage **804**
The Comfort of Lies 804, 1059
The Murderer's Daughters 804

Mezrich, Ben
Seven Wonders 540

Michaels, Barbara
Be Buried in the Rain 515

Michaels, Fern
The Blossom Sisters 794, 865
In Plain Sight 704
The Marriage Game 226

Michaels, Kasey
What a Gentleman Desires 1042

Michaels, Sean
Us Conductors 690

Michaels, Tanya
The Good Kind of Crazy 918
Tamed by a Texan 1095

Michels, Elizabeth
How to Lose a Lord in 10 Days or Less 950
Must Love Dukes 967, 1007

Michod, Alec
The White City 403

Mieville, China
Kraken 34
The Scar 92

Milan, Courtney
Proof by Seduction 990

Milburn, Trish
The Cowboy Sheriff 897
A Firefighter in the Family 1091

Milchman, Jenny
As Night Falls **619**
Cover of Snow 619
Ruin Falls 619, 859

Miles, Cassie
Snow Blind 1009

Miles, Olivia
Recipe for Romance 751

O

Author Index

Author Index

Title Index

This index alphabetically lists all titles featured in entries and those listed within entries under "Other books by the same author" and "Other books you might like." Each title is followed by the author's name and the number of the entry where the book is described or listed. Bold numbers indicate featured main entries; light-face numbers refer to books recommended for further reading.

Title Index

Title Index

Title Index

Title Index

Title Index

Title Index

Title Index

Title Index

Title Index

Title Index

Title Index

Title Index

Title Index

Title Index

Title Index

Title Index

Title Index

Title Index